Numerical Methods, Software, and Analysis

Numerical Methods, Software, and Analysis

JOHN R. RICE
Purdue University

McGRAW-HILL BOOK COMPANY

New York St. Louis San Francisco Auckland Bogotá Hamburg
Johannesburg London Madrid Mexico Montreal New Delhi
Panama Paris São Paulo Singapore Sydney Tokyo Toronto

Numerical Methods, Software, and Analysis

1234567890KGPKGP898765432

ISBN 0-07-052208-1

This book was set in Times Roman by Composition Resources. The editors were Charles E. Stewart and Jonathan Palace; the production supervisor was Joe Campanella. The drawings were done by Larry Miller. The cover was designed by Anne Canevari Green.
Kingsport Press, Inc., was printer and binder.

Library of Congress Cataloging in Publication Data

Rice, John Rischard.

Numerical methods, software, and analysis.

Includes index.
1. Numerical analysis — Data processing. I. Title.
QA297.R49 1983 519.4 82-20810
ISBN 0-07-052208-1

CONTENTS

**Advanced or peripheral material

* Other material skipped in one-semester course

PREFACE

Objectives

Modern science depends on our capability to carry out substantial computations to explore the consequence of the laws of nature. These laws are expressed as mathematical models, and numerical methods are used throughout the computation. The **objective** of this text is to introduce science and engineering students to the **methods, tools, and ideas of numerical computation.** These students are assumed to have taken the standard introductory calculus sequence, plus an elementary introduction to matrix theory, ordinary differential equations, and Fortran programming.

An introductory course in numerical methods faces a fundamental problem: students who want to do realistic computations need to know more than they can learn in one course. This text has about twice as much material as can be covered in a typical one-term course, and yet most topics are not covered in depth. The use of **high-quality mathematical software** is the leading way out of the dilemma of too little time to learn too much knowledge and know-how. The mathematical software approach is based on the premise that experts in numerical computation can incorporate enough of their experience and know-how into a computer program so that it performs better than the program a typical scientist can create with a reasonable effort. The validity of this approach has been established in many areas of numerical computation; the objective of this text may be restated as to present **scientific problem solving using standard mathematical software.**

Organization and Content

This book is organized into three parts, as shown in the diagram on the top of the next page. Part I is background and preliminary material. Few instructors will cover this thoroughly; in a one-term course it is feasible to summarize the main ideas in a few lectures. Part II is the core of the course, presenting the principal methods and ideas of numerical computation. Part III contains very relevent, but somewhat independent, material about software engineering and performance evaluation. There is rarely time in a one-term course to cover this material in detail, yet it is important that young scientists gain some appreciation for this material.

A fairly uniform approach is used in each area of numerical computation. First, an intuitive development is made of the problems and the basic methods for their solution. Then, relevent mathematical software is reviewed and its use outlined. In many areas rather extensive examples and case studies are given. Finally, a deeper analysis of the methods is presented as in traditional numerical analysis texts.

The use of mathematical software tools may resolve the dilemma facing the practicing scientist, but it still leaves a dilemma for the instructor using this text: **should one emphasize how to use the software or understanding how it works?** This is not an easy choice to make; ample material is presented so that an instructor may choose whatever balance seems appropriate for the students' needs and the instructor's taste. Some sections and chapters are "starred" to help organize the material. The **double-starred items** contain material that is either more advanced (for example, osculatory interpolation and adaptive quadrature) or somewhat peripheral to the main topics (for example, sources of matrix problems and

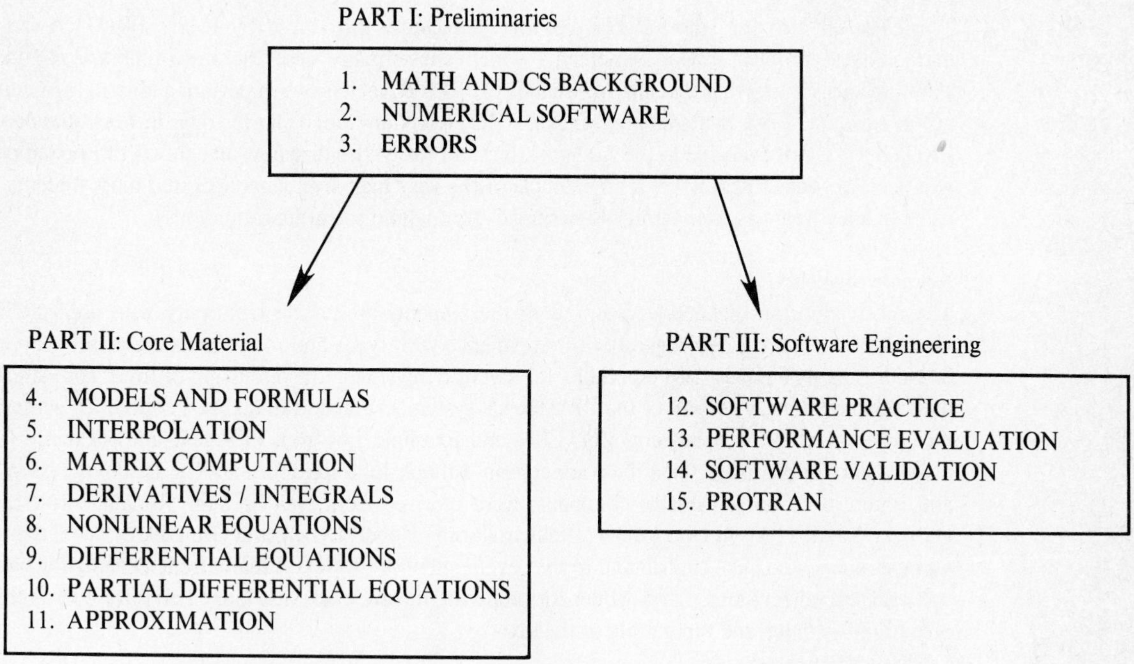

reporting computational experiments). Since the remaining material is still more than can be covered in a one-term course, the **single-starred items** are suggested as candidates to be skipped. Some single-starred chapters also have single-starred sections; this provides suggested topics for an instructor who wants to cover these chapters briefly. The dependence of the chapters is shown in the following diagram.

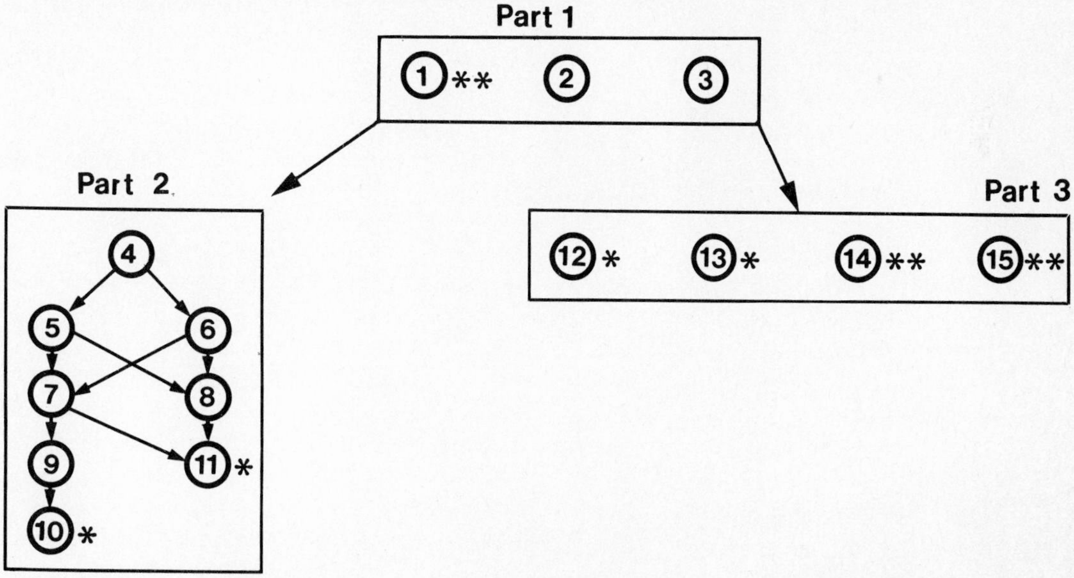

Software

This text discusses numerous programs and software packages, but it is not intended to be a user's guide for this software. The **IMSL library** and **ACM Algorithms** are discussed systematically as they are the most widely available general collections of high-quality mathematical software. It is **not** essential to have this particular software; any reasonably complete program library will have programs similar to those used in most examples and problems. We note (see Chapter 12) that the cost of developing just one good program is more than the cost of acquiring several hundred good programs from IMSL, ACM, and similar sources. These sources should be viewed as providing the initial step toward a **software parts technology** which might dramatically reduce the present heavy burden of software development costs.

This text also uses the PROTRAN system recently introduced by IMSL. PROTRAN provides mathematical problem-solving statements which substantially ease the use of library routines and simultaneously improve programming reliability. PROTRAN has two important additional attractions for use in this text. First, example programs in PROTRAN are much shorter than in Fortran, and even if PROTRAN is not available to the students, they can easily visualize how an equivalent Fortran program would be. Second, PROTRAN is an example of the very high level languages that most students will be using in a few years as this methodology spreads throughout scientific computation.

Acknowledgments

The most important acknowledgment is to the students at Purdue University who used preliminary versions of this text. Their suggestions and patience with typos and rough spots are greatly appreciated. Second, I thank Thomas Aird especially, for carefully reviewing the discussion of IMSL software and for making a preliminary version of the PROTRAN system available. I thank Carl deBoor for permission to include the text of two programs (INTERV and Example 5.6) from PPPACK and for many valuable insights into the nature of scientific computation. I thank John Reid for material used in the cover design and Figure 6.3. Many valuable comments were received from Neil Berman, Ronald Boisvert, Henry Darilek, Wayne Dyksen, Don Kainer, Iftekhar Karimi, Robert Lynch, and Granville Sewell. I thank them and the others who have contributed to the development of this text. I thank Irene Bellamy for typing the text and several revisions, Larry Miller for preparing the art work, and Gary Lelvis for coordinating the preparation, typing, and typesetting of the text.

John R. Rice

**1 MATHEMATICS AND COMPUTER SCIENCE BACKGROUND

The background assumed in this text is a basic sequence in calculus, an introduction to differential equations and linear algebra (or matrices), and a working knowledge of Fortran programming. The purpose of this chapter is to give a highly condensed review of this background. The material provides references for the rest of the text, and the problems allow instructors or students to check their knowledge against the assumed background in calculus and linear algebra. Many instructors will choose to spend little, if any, time presenting this material in lectures.

Some material in this book requires more background and experience than presented here, for example, the chapter on partial differential equations. An instructor must judge whether the students have the necessary experience and maturity for such material; some instructors might choose to use the material here as a first introduction to the topic. The sections marked by ** contain material which is more advanced or peripheral and which can be skipped; all the material requiring more background is in such sections.

CALCULUS 1.1

The principal topics in calculus are the real and complex number systems, the concept of limits and convergence, and the properties of functions. **Convergence of a sequence** of numbers x_i is defined as follows: *The sequence x_i converges to the limit x^* if, given any tolerance $\epsilon > 0$, there is an index $N = N(\epsilon)$ so that for all $i \geq N$ we have $|x_i - x^*| \leq \epsilon$.* The notation for this is

$$\lim_{i \to \infty} x_i = x^*$$

Convergence is also a principal topic of numerical computation, but with a different emphasis. In calculus one studies limits and convergence with analytic tools; one tries to obtain the limit or to show that convergence takes place. In computations, one has the same problem but little or no theoretical knowledge about the sequence. One is frequently reduced to using empirical or intuitive tests for convergence; often the principal task is to actually estimate the value of the tolerance ϵ for a given x_i.

The study of functions in calculus revolves about continuity, derivatives, and integrals. A function $f(x)$ is **continuous** if

$$\lim_{x_i \to x^*} f(x_i) = f(x^*)$$

holds for all x^* and all ways for the x_i to converge to x^*. We list six theorems from calculus which are useful for estimating values that appear in numerical computation.

Theorem 1.1 (Mean value theorem for continuous functions) *Let $f(x)$ be continuous on the interval $[a, b]$. Consider points XHI and XLOW in $[a, b]$ and a value y so that $f(XLOW) \le y \le f(XHI)$. Then there is a point ξ in $[a, b]$ so that*

$$f(\xi) = y$$

Theorem 1.2 (Mean value theorem for sums) *Let $f(x)$ be continuous on the interval $[a, b]$, let $x_1, x_2, \ldots, x_n$ be points in $[a, b]$, and let $w_1, w_2, \ldots, w_n$ be positive numbers. Then there is a point ξ in $[a, b]$ so that*

$$\sum_{i=1}^{n} w_i f(x_i) = f(\xi) \sum_{i=1}^{n} w_i$$

Theorem 1.3 (Mean value theorem for integrals) *Let $f(x)$ be continuous on the interval $[a, b]$ and let $w(x)$ be a nonnegative function $[w(x) \ge 0]$ on $[a, b]$. Then there is a point ξ in $[a, b]$ so that*

$$\int_a^b w(x)f(x)dx = f(\xi) \int_a^b w(x)dx$$

Theorems 1.2 and 1.3 show the analogy that exists between sums and integrals. This fact derives from the definition of the **integral** as

$$\int_a^b f(x)dx = \lim_{\max|x_{i+1} - x_i| \to 0} \sum_i f(x_i)(x_{i+1} - x_i)$$

where the points x_i, with $x_i < x_{i+1}$, are a partition of $[a, b]$. This analogy shows up for many numerical methods where one variation applies to sums and another applies to integrals. Theorem 1.2 is proved from Theorem 1.1, and then Theorem 1.3 is proved by a similar method. The assumption that $w(x) \ge 0$ ($w_i > 0$) may be replaced by $w(x) \le 0$ ($w_i < 0$) in these theorems; it is *essential* that $w(x)$ be on one sign shown by the example $w(x) = f(x) = x$ and $[a, b] = [-1, 1]$.

Theorem 1.4 (Continuous functions assume max/min values) *Let $f(x)$ be continuous on $[a, b]$ with $|a|, |b| < \infty$. Then there are points XHI and XLOW in $[a, b]$ so that for all x in $[a, b]$*

$$f(XHI) \le f(x) \le f(XLOW)$$

The **derivative** of $f(x)$ is defined by

$$\frac{df}{dx} = f'(x) = \lim_{h \to 0} \frac{f(x+h) - f(x)}{h}$$

As an illustration of the difference between theory and practice, the quantity $[f(x+h) - f(x)]/h$ can be replaced by $[f(x+h) - f(x-h)]/(2h)$ with no change in the theory but with a dramatic improvement in the rate of convergence; that is, much more accurate estimates of $f'(x)$ are obtained for a given value of h. The kth derivative is the derivative of the $(k-1)$th derivative; they are denoted by d^kf/dx^k or $f''(x)$, $f'''(x)$, $f^{(4)}(x)$, $f^{(5)}(x)$, . . .

Theorem 1.5 (Mean value theorem for derivatives) *Let $f(x)$ be continuous and differentiable in $[a, b]$ with $|a|, |b| < \infty$. Then there is a point ξ in $[a, b]$ so that*

$$\frac{f(b) - f(a)}{b - a} = f'(\xi)$$

Equivalently, given c and x in [a, b] there is a point ξ between x and c so that

$$f(x) = f(c) + f'(\xi)(x-c)$$

The special case of Theorem 1.5 with $f(a) = f(b) = 0$ *is known as* **Rolle's theorem**. It states that *if $f(a) = f(b) = 0$, then there is a point ξ between a and b so that $f'(\xi) = 0$.* This is derived from Theorem 1.5 by multiplying through by b − a, renaming a, b as x, c, and then applying the first form to the smaller interval [x, c] or [c, x], depending on the relation between x and c.

A very important tool in numerical analysis is the extension of the second part of Theorem 1.5 to use higher derivatives.

Theorem 1.6 (Taylor's series with remainder) *Let f(x) have n+1 continuous derivatives in [a, b]. Given points x and c in [a, b] we have*

$$f(x) = f(c) + f'(c)(x-c) + f''(c)\frac{(x-c)^2}{2!} + f'''(c)\frac{(x-c)^3}{3!} + \ldots + f^{(n)}(c)\frac{(x-c)^n}{n!} + R_{n+1}(x)$$

where R_{n+1} has either one of the following forms (ξ is a point between x and c):

$$R_{n+1}(x) = f^{(n+1)}(\xi)\frac{(x-c)^{n+1}}{(n+1)!}$$

$$R_{n+1}(x) = \frac{1}{n!}\int_c^x (x-t)^n f^{(n+1)}(t)dt$$

If a function f depends on several variables, one can differentiate it with respect to one variable, say x, while keeping all the rest fixed. This is the **partial derivative** of f and is denoted by $\partial f/\partial x$ or f_x. Higher-order and mixed derivatives are defined by successive differentiation. Taylor's series for functions of several variables is a direct extension of the formula in Theorem 1.6, although the number of terms in it grows rapidly. For two variables it is

$$f(x,y) = f(c,d) + f_x(x-c) + f_y(y-d) + \frac{1}{2}[f_{xx}(x-c)^2 + 2f_{xy}(x-c)(y-d) + f_{yy}(y-d)^2] + \ldots$$

where all the partial derivatives are evaluated at the point (c, d).

Theorem 1.7 (Chain rule for derivatives) *Let $f(x, y, \ldots, z)$ have continuous first partial derivatives with respect to all its variables. Let $x = x(t)$, $y = y(t)$, …, $z = z(t)$ be continuously differentiable functions of t. Then $g(t) = f(x(t), y(t), \ldots, z(t))$ is continuously differentiable and*

$$g'(t) = f_x x'(t) + f_y y'(t) + \ldots + f_z z'(t)$$

Finally we state

Theorem 1.8 (Fundamental theorem of algebra) *Let p(x) be a polynomial of degree $n \geq 1$, that is,*

$$p(x) = a_0 + a_1x + a_2x^2 + \ldots + a_nx^n$$

where the a_i are real or complex numbers and $a_n \neq 0$. Then there is a complex number ξ so that $p(\xi) = 0$.

PROBLEMS 1.1

1.1.1 Determine the following limits:

(A) $\lim_{x\to 1} \frac{x^{10}-1}{x^9-1}$

(B) $\lim_{x\to 0} \frac{x-\sin x}{x^3}$

(C) $\lim_{x\to \pi/2} \frac{1-\sin x}{\pi-2x}$

(D) $\lim_{n\to\infty} \frac{n}{n+\sqrt{n}}$

(E) $\lim_{x\to 0} \frac{\tan x}{x}$

(F) $\lim_{n\to\infty} [\log(n+1)-\log(n)]$

1.1.2 Find the mean value ξ of Theorem 1.3 for the following integrals:

(A) $\int_0^1 x^2 dx$, with $f(x) = x^2$

(B) $\int_0^1 x^2 dx$, with $f(x) = x$

(C) $\int_0^2 \sqrt{x}\,(x^2+1)dx$ with $f(x) = \sqrt{x}$

(D) $\int_0^2 \sqrt{x}\,(x^2+1)dx$ with $f(x) = x^2+1$

1.1.3 Find the mean value ξ of Theorem 1.5 for the following:

(A) $f(x) = x^2-4x+3,\quad a=1, b=4$

(B) $f(x) = x^{3/2},\quad a=0, b=9$

(C) $f(x) = x+1/x,\quad a=1, b=9$

1.1.4 Find f′ and f″ for each of the following:

(A) $f(x) = \sqrt{2x+3}$

(B) $f(x) = \sin 2x$

(C) $f^2(x) - x^2 = 1$

(D) $x = \cos\theta$, $f(x) = \sin\theta$

1.1.5 Give the first four terms of the Taylor's series at c for the following functions:

(A) $f(x) = (1+x)^k, c=0$

(B) $f(x) = \log x, c=1$

(C) $f(x) = e^x, c=0$

(D) $f(x) = 1/x, c=-1$

(E) $f(x) = \sin x, c=\pi/6$

(F) $f(x) = \sqrt{1-x^3}$, $c=-2$

1.1.6 Obtain the Taylor's series for sin x and cos x with $c = 0$. Square each of them, add the results, and verify that $\sin^2 x + \cos^2 x = 1$.

1.1.7 Find f_x and f_y for each of the following:

(A) $f(x, y) = x^2-2xy + 4y^2$

(B) $f(x, y) = (x+y)/(x-y)$

(C) $f(x, y) = x \log(y^2/x)$

(D) $f(x, y) = \ln(y+z)$ where $z(x, y) = ye^{x-y}$

1.1.8 Find df/dt for each of the following:

(A) $f(x, y) = x^2+xy,\quad x=3t,\quad y=t^3$

(B) $f(x, y) = \sqrt{x^2+y^2}$, $x=t^2,\quad y=e^t-e^{-t}$

1.1.9 Give the first six terms of the Taylor's series for the following:

(A) $f(x, y) = (x+y)^3,\quad c=0, d=0$

(B) $f(x, y) = e^{x+1/y},\quad c=0, d=1$

(C) $f(x, y) = \log(x^2-y^2),\quad c=1, d=1$

VECTORS, MATRICES, AND LINEAR EQUATIONS 1.2

Vectors are *directed line segments* (they have length, direction, and position) in N-dimensional space. They are considered to be **column vectors** unless otherwise stated, and thus

$$\mathbf{y} = \begin{pmatrix} y_1 \\ y_2 \\ \vdots \\ y_N \end{pmatrix}$$

The **transpose** is indicated by the superscript T, which changes columns into rows and vice versa. Vectors are usually expressed in terms of a **basis**; a standard set $\mathbf{b}_1, \mathbf{b}_2, \ldots, \mathbf{b}_N$ of vectors is chosen, and all other vectors are expressed in terms of the basis $\mathbf{b}_i$, $i = 1, 2, \ldots, N$:

$$\mathbf{y} = y_1\mathbf{b}_1 + y_2\mathbf{b}_2 + \ldots + y_N\mathbf{b}_N$$

The coefficients y_i of this representation are the **components of y**, and the representation is commonly written in the compact form

$$\mathbf{y} = (y_1, y_2, \ldots, y_N)^T$$

The basis vectors define a **coordinate system**, and the components y_i are the coordinates of the point at the end of the vector. The usual basis vectors are of the form (0, 0, . . ., 0, 1, 0, . . . 0, 0). The standard **arithmetic** operations are (for vectors **x**, **y**, **z**, and scalar a) as follows:

Addition: $\mathbf{x} + \mathbf{y} = \mathbf{y} + \mathbf{x} = (x_1 + y_1, x_2 + y_2, \ldots x_N + y_N)^T$

$$\mathbf{x} - \mathbf{y} = -(\mathbf{y} - \mathbf{x}) \qquad (\mathbf{x} + \mathbf{y}) + \mathbf{z} = \mathbf{x} + (\mathbf{y} + \mathbf{z})$$

Multiplication by scalar: $a\mathbf{x} = (ax_1, ax_2, \ldots, ax_N)$

$$a(\mathbf{x} + \mathbf{y}) = a\mathbf{x} + a\mathbf{y}$$

A set $\mathbf{x}_1, \mathbf{x}_2, \ldots, \mathbf{x}_N$ of vectors is **linearly independent** if no *linear combination* $\sum_{i=1}^{N} \alpha_i \mathbf{x}_i$ of them is zero except for the zero combination; that is,

$$\sum_{i=1}^{N} \alpha_i \mathbf{x}_i = 0 \qquad \text{implies} \qquad \alpha_i = 0 \text{ for all i}$$

A set of vectors $\mathbf{x}_1, \ldots, \mathbf{x}_N$ **spans** a space if every vector in that space can be written as a linear combination of the set $\mathbf{x}_1, \ldots, \mathbf{x}_N$. A set of basis vectors must be linearly independent. The **dimension** of a vector space is the minimal number of vectors required to span the space; each basis of an N-dimensional space must have N vectors in it.

The **dot product** or *inner product* of two vectors **x** and **y** is

$$\mathbf{x}^T\mathbf{y} = \mathbf{x}\cdot\mathbf{y} = (\mathbf{x}, \mathbf{y}) = \sum_{i=1}^{N} x_i y_i$$

where the x_i, y_i are the components of **x** and **y**. Two vectors are **orthogonal** vectors (perpendicular) if $\mathbf{x}^T\mathbf{y} = 0$. The size of a vector may be measured by the **Euclidean norm** $||\mathbf{x}||_2$ where

$$||\mathbf{x}||_2^2 = \mathbf{x}^T\mathbf{x} = \sum_i x_i^2$$

This is the usual Euclidean length in the case of two or three dimensions. The double bar denotes a **norm**, and another norm frequently convenient is

$$||\mathbf{x}||_\infty = \max_i |x_i|$$

The angle θ between two vectors is defined from

$$\cos\theta = \frac{\mathbf{x}^T\mathbf{y}}{||\mathbf{x}||_2||\mathbf{y}||_2}$$

The format for vectors must match that of matrices, and so vectors are normally considered to be **column vectors**. To write a vector as

$$\mathbf{x} = \begin{pmatrix} 2 \\ 1 \\ 4 \\ -2 \end{pmatrix}$$

complicates the format of the text, and so we write **x** as $(2, 1, 4, -2)^T$ and, in general, write vectors horizontally with the transpose **T** unless the column format is necessary for clarity. At times we also use **row vectors**, which are vectors whose matrix format is actually horizontal, e.g., a row from a matrix.

Once coordinates are introduced for the vectors, then linear functions of vectors can be concretely represented by a two-dimensional array of numbers, a **matrix**:

$$A = \begin{pmatrix} 1 & 6 & -2 \\ 4 & 17 & -12 \\ 0 & 42 & 6.1 \end{pmatrix} = (a_{ij})$$

If **y** is a linear function of **x**, then each component y_k of **y** is a linear function of the components x_j of **x**, and we have for each k that

$$y_k = a_{k1}x_1 + a_{k2}x_2 + \ldots + a_{kN}x_N$$

The coefficients are collected into the matrix A, and the linear function is denoted by A**x**.

The rules for manipulating matrices are those required by the linear mappings. Thus A + B is to be the representation of the sum of the two linear functions represented by A and B. One has A + B = C where

$c_{ij} = a_{ij} + b_{ij}$. The **matrix product** AB represents the effect of applying the function B, then applying the function A. The following calculation shows that

$$AB = C$$

where $c_{ij} = \Sigma_k a_{ik} b_{kj}$. We have $\mathbf{y} = B\mathbf{x}$ and $\mathbf{z} = A\mathbf{y}$ and want to determine C so that $\mathbf{z} = C\mathbf{x}$. We express the relationship in terms of components:

$$y_k = \sum_{j=1}^{N} b_{kj} x_j \qquad z_i = \sum_{k=1}^{N} a_{ik} y_k$$

Thus

$$z_i = \sum_{k=1}^{N} a_{ik} \left(\sum_{j=1}^{N} b_{kj} x_j \right) = \sum_{j=1}^{N} \left(\sum_{k=1}^{N} a_{ik} b_{kj} \right) x_j$$

$$= \sum_{j=1}^{N} c_{ij} x_j$$

and so c_{ij} is given by the above formula. The i, jth element of C is the dot product of the ith row of A with the jth column of B. We have the *arithmetic* rules

$$A + B = B + A$$
$$AB \neq BA \qquad \text{except in special cases}$$

The transpose A^T of A is obtained by reflecting A about its **diagonal** (the a_{ii} elements). That is, $a^T_{ij} = a_{ji}$. The **identity** matrix is all zeros except for 1s on the diagonal:

$$I = \begin{pmatrix} 1 & 0 & 0 \\ 0 & 1 & 0 \\ 0 & 0 & 1 \end{pmatrix}$$

An identity matrix is necessarily *square* (has the same number of rows and columns). One sees that $IA = AI = A$. The **inverse** A^{-1} of A is a matrix so that $A^{-1}A = I$. Not all matrices have an inverse and, indeed, one can have $AB = 0$ without either A or B being the zero matrix:

$$\begin{pmatrix} 1 & 1 \\ 1 & 1 \end{pmatrix} \begin{pmatrix} 1 & 1 \\ -1 & -1 \end{pmatrix} = \begin{pmatrix} 0 & 0 \\ 0 & 0 \end{pmatrix}$$

If A has an inverse, then we say A is **nonsingular**. We have the following equivalent statements for a square matrix A:

A is nonsingular

A^{-1} exists

The columns of A are linearly independent

The rows of A are linearly independent

$A\mathbf{x} = \mathbf{0}$ implies that $\mathbf{x} = \mathbf{0}$

The **linear equations** problem is this: Given A and **b**, find the vector **x** so that $A\mathbf{x} = \mathbf{b}$. If A is nonsingular (this makes A square), then this problem always has a unique solution for each **b**. If A has more rows than columns (there are more equations than variables), then the problem is usually unsolvable, and if A has more columns than rows, there are usually infinitely many solutions. A system of equations is **homogeneous** if the right side is zero, for example, $A\mathbf{x} = \mathbf{0}$. The oldest and standard method for solving this problem is by *Gauss elimination* (please forget *Cramer's rule*, as it is terribly inefficient).

Gauss elimination is illustrated by an example. The original system

$$\begin{aligned} 2x_1 + 2x_2 + 4x_3 &= 5 \\ 6x_1 - x_2 + x_3 &= 7 \\ 4x_1 - 10x_2 - 12x_3 &= -4 \end{aligned}$$

becomes

$$\begin{aligned} 2x_1 + 2x_2 + 4x_3 &= 5 \\ -7x_2 - 11x_3 &= -8 \qquad \text{Subtract 3 times row 1 from row 2} \\ -14x_2 - 20x_3 &= -14 \qquad \text{Subtract 2 times row 1 from row 3} \end{aligned}$$

which becomes

$$\begin{aligned} 2x_1 + 2x_2 + 4x_3 &= 5 \\ -7x_2 - 11x_3 &= -8 \\ 2x_3 &= 2 \qquad \text{Subtract 2 times row 2 from row 3} \end{aligned}$$

The matrix of this system of equations is **upper triangular**, which means that all elements below the diagonal are zero (*lower triangular* means all elements above the diagonal are zero). This system can be solved quickly by **back substitution**:

$$x_3 = \frac{2}{2} = 1$$

$$-7x_2 = -8 + 11x_3 = 3 \qquad \text{so } x_2 = -\frac{3}{7}$$

$$2x_1 = 5 - 2x_2 - 4x_3 = \frac{13}{7} \qquad \text{so } x_1 = \frac{13}{14}$$

The analogous process applied to a lower-triangular system is called **forward substitution**.

A matrix is a **permutation matrix** if each element is a 0 or 1 and there is exactly one 1 per row or column, for example:

$$\begin{pmatrix} 0 & 1 & 0 & 0 \\ 1 & 0 & 0 & 0 \\ 0 & 0 & 1 & 0 \\ 0 & 0 & 0 & 1 \end{pmatrix} \qquad \begin{pmatrix} 1 & 0 & 0 \\ 0 & 0 & 1 \\ 0 & 1 & 0 \end{pmatrix}$$

Multiplication by a permutation matrix, on the left or right, has the effect of permuting or interchanging the rows or columns of the matrix. This property gives them their name, and they are useful in formulas to indicate interchanges of rows and columns; they are rarely used in actual calculations.

On a few occasions we refer to an **eigenvalue** of the matrix A. This is a number λ such that $A\mathbf{x} = \lambda\mathbf{x}$ for some nonzero vector $\mathbf{x}$; the vector $\mathbf{x}$ is called an **eigenvector**. A linear mapping applied to an eigenvector simply multiplies the eigenvector by the constant λ, the eigenvalue. An N by N matrix has N eigenvalues and normally, but not always, has N eigenvectors. The **spectral radius** $\rho(A)$ of A is the largest of the absolute values of the eigenvalues of A. The spectral radius plays a fundamental role in the convergence of iterations involving matrices.

We measure the size or **norm of a matrix** by

$$||A|| = \max_{||\mathbf{x}||=1} ||A\mathbf{x}||$$

The norm is the maximum amount a vector of length 1 is magnified by applying A. This norm is defined in terms of a vector norm, and different vector norms give different norms for A. The norm can be expressed explicitly for the two vector norms introduced earlier. The results are

$$||A||_2 = \max_{||\mathbf{x}||_2=1} ||A\mathbf{x}||_2 = \sqrt{\text{max eigenvalue of } A^T A}$$

$$||A||_\infty = \max_{||\mathbf{x}||_\infty=1} ||A\mathbf{x}||_\infty = \max_i \sum_{j=1}^{N} |a_{ij}| = \textit{row-sum norm}$$

The row-sum norm is widely used because it is easy to calculate. It is easy to show that $\rho(A) \le ||A||$ for any norm, and so the row-sum norm provides a simple estimate of the spectral radius of a matrix.

PROBLEMS 1.2

1.2.1 Compute $||\mathbf{x}||_2$ and $||\mathbf{x}||_\infty$ for each of the following:

(A) $(1, 2, 3, 4)^T$

(B) $(0, -1, 0, -2, 0, 1)^T$

(C) $(0, 1, -2, 3, -4)^T$

(D) $(4, 1, -3.2, 8.6, -1.5, -2.5)^T$

1.2.2 Compute the angle θ between the following pairs of vectors:

(A) $(1, 1, 1, 1)^T, (-1, 1, -1, 1)^T$

(B) $(1, 0, 2, 0)^T, (0, 1, -1, 2)^T$

(C) $(1, 2, -1, 3)^T, (2, 4, -2, 6)^T$

(D) $(1.1, 2.3, -4.7, 2.0)^T, (3.2, 1.2, -2.3, -4.7)^T$

1.2.3 Find the Euclidean norm of $(2, -2, 4)^T$ and the dot product of the vectors $(2, -3.4, 1)^T$ and $(4, -3, 2)^T$.

1.2.4 Determine if the vector $(6, 1, -6, 2)^T$ is in the space spanned by the vectors $(1, 1, -1, 1)^T$, $(-1, 0, 1, 1)^T$, and $(1, -1, -1, 0)^T$. What is the dimension of the space spanned by these three vectors?

1.2.5 Do the vectors

$$\mathbf{b}_1 = (1, 0, 0, -1)^T \quad \mathbf{b}_2 = (0, -1, 1, 0)^T$$
$$\mathbf{b}_3 = (0, 0, -1, 1)^T \quad \mathbf{b}_4 = (1, 1, 0, 0)^T$$

form a basis for vectors of dimension 4?

1.2.6 Prove that the three vectors

$$\mathbf{b}_1 = (1, 2, 3, 4)^T$$
$$\mathbf{b}_2 = (2, 1, 0, 4)^T$$
$$\mathbf{b}_3 = (0, 1, 1, 4)^T$$

are linearly independent. Do they form a basis of a three-dimensional space?

1.2.7 Suppose that $\mathbf{x}_1, \mathbf{x}_2, \ldots, \mathbf{x}_m$ are linearly independent, but $\mathbf{x}_1, \mathbf{x}_2, \ldots, \mathbf{x}_m, \mathbf{x}_{m+1}$ are not. Show that $\mathbf{x}_{m+1}$ is a linear combination of $\mathbf{x}_1, \mathbf{x}_2, \ldots \mathbf{x}_m$.

1.2.8 Let $\mathbf{x}_1 = (1, 2, 1)^T$, $\mathbf{x}_2 = (1, 2, 3)^T$, and $\mathbf{x}_3 = (3, 6, 5)^T$. Show that these vectors are linearly dependent but that they span a two-dimensional space. Find a basis for this space.

1.2.9 For any two vectors $\mathbf{x}$ and $\mathbf{y}$ show that we have

$$||\mathbf{x}||_\infty - ||\mathbf{y}||_\infty \le ||\mathbf{x}-\mathbf{y}||_\infty$$

This inequality holds for all vectors norms.

1.2.10 For two nonzero vectors $\mathbf{x}$ and $\mathbf{y}$ show that $||\mathbf{x}+\mathbf{y}||_2 = ||\mathbf{x}||_2 + ||\mathbf{y}||_2$ if and only if $\mathbf{y} = a\mathbf{x}$ for some nonnegative constant a.

1.2.11 Show that $A = \begin{pmatrix} 1 & 2 \\ 2 & 4 \end{pmatrix}$ is singular.

1.2.12 Find a nonzero solution to the system

$$x_1 - 2x_2 + x_3 = 0$$
$$x_1 + x_2 - 2x_3 = 0$$

1.2.13 Let

$$A = \begin{pmatrix} 1 & 2 & 3 \\ 0 & -1 & 2 \\ 2 & 0 & 2 \end{pmatrix} \quad B = \begin{pmatrix} 1 & 1 & 2 \\ -1 & 1 & -1 \\ 1 & 0 & 2 \end{pmatrix} \quad C = \begin{pmatrix} 1 & 0 & 1 \\ 0 & 1 & 2 \\ 2 & 0 & 1 \end{pmatrix}$$

(A) Compute AB and BA and show that $AB \neq BA$.

(B) Find $(A + B) + C$ and $A + (B + C)$.

(C) Show that $(AB)C = A(BC)$.

(D) Show that $(AB)^T = B^TA^T$.

1.2.14 Show that the matrix A is singular:

$$A = \begin{pmatrix} 3 & 1 & 0 \\ 2 & -1 & -1 \\ 4 & 3 & 1 \end{pmatrix}$$

1.2.15 Write the following system of linear equations in matrix form $A\mathbf{x} = \mathbf{b}$ and identify the matrix A and right-side vector $\mathbf{b}$:

$$\begin{aligned} 2x_1 + x_2 - 3x_3 + 4x_4 - 2 &= 0 \\ x_1 + x_2 - x_3 &= 1 \\ 2x_2 + x_4 - 7x_3 &= 8 \\ 1 + x_1 + x_2 + x_3 + x_4 &= 5 \end{aligned}$$

1.2.16 Suppose that B is **diagonal** ($b_{ij} = 0$ except if $i = j$). Show that BA is found by multiplying the first row of A by b_{11}, the second row by b_{22}, etc. How is AB found?

1.2.17 Test the following systems of equations for **consistency** (the existence of at least one solution).

(A)
$$\begin{aligned} x + y + 2z + w &= 5 \\ 2x + 3y - z - 2w &= 2 \\ 4x + 5y + 3z &= 7 \end{aligned}$$

(B)
$$\begin{aligned} x + y + z + w &= 0 \\ x + 3y + 2z + 4w &= 0 \\ 2x + z - w &= 0 \end{aligned}$$

1.2.18 Show that

$$A = \begin{pmatrix} 1 & 1 \\ 0 & 2 \end{pmatrix}$$

is nonsingular by finding its inverse.

1.2.19 Compute the inverses of

$$A = \begin{pmatrix} 1 & 1 \\ 0 & 1 \end{pmatrix} \quad B = \begin{pmatrix} 1 & 0 \\ 1 & 1 \end{pmatrix}$$

and AB. Show that $A^{-1}B^{-1}$ is not $(AB)^{-1}$ but $B^{-1}A^{-1}$ is $(AB)^{-1}$.

1.2.20 Calculate the number of additions and multiplications necessary to multiply an N by N matrix by an N vector, and to multiply two N by N matrices.

1.2.21 Compute $||A||_\infty$ for the matrix

$$A = \begin{pmatrix} 1 & 0 & 2 & -1 \\ 6 & -4 & 3 & 0 \\ 4 & 0 & -4 & 2 \\ 1 & 5 & 1 & 6 \end{pmatrix}$$

1.2.22 Find a 3 by 3 matrix $A \neq 0$ and a vector $\mathbf{x} \neq 0$ so that $A\mathbf{x} = 0$.

1.2.23 Let $A = I - 2\mathbf{x}\mathbf{x}^T$, where $\mathbf{x}$ is a column vector with $\mathbf{x}^T\mathbf{x} = 1$. Show that $A^TA = I$ and $A^2 = I$.

1.2.24 Show for a nonsingular matrix A that $\mathbf{x}^TA^TA\mathbf{x} = 0$ if and only if $\mathbf{x}^T\mathbf{x} = 0$.

1.2.25 Let $\mathbf{x}$ be a row vector. Show that $\mathbf{x}\mathbf{x}^T = \mathbf{x}\cdot\mathbf{x} = (||\mathbf{x}||_2)^2$. What is $\mathbf{x}^T\mathbf{x}$?

1.2.26 Suppose for every vector $\mathbf{x}$ we define the function F as follows:

(A) $F(\mathbf{x}) = (x_3, x_1)^T$

(B) $F(\mathbf{x}) = (x_1 + x_2, 0, x_3)^T$

(C) $F(\mathbf{x}) = (x_2, 0, x_1 - x_2, x_3, 0)^T$

Show that each of these definitions makes F a linear function.

1.2.27 Find one solution of

$$x_1 + 2x_2 = 3$$
$$2x_1 + 4x_2 = 6$$

and then find a solution of the corresponding homogeneous system

$$x_1 + 2x_2 = 0$$
$$2x_1 + 4x_2 = 0$$

Show that any multiple of the solution of the homogeneous system can be added to the first solution to obtain yet another solution of the first system.

1.2.28 Write a program which carries out matrix addition and/or multiplication. The input is two square matrices A and B, their order N, and a mode switch MODE with MODE = 1 for addition and MODE = 2 for multiplication. The output is to be the matrix C = A + B or C = AB.

DIFFERENTIAL EQUATIONS 1.3

The simplest differential equation is

$$y'(x) = f(x) \qquad y(a) = y_0$$

which has the solution

$$y(x) = y_0 + \int_a^x f(t)dt$$

The value y_0 is the initial value for this differential equation. More complicated differential equations are

$$y'(x) = 3x - 2y \qquad y(a) = y_0 \qquad \text{Equation 1.3.1}$$

$$y'(x) = x^2e^x + 4y \qquad y(a) = y_0 \qquad \text{Equation 1.3.2}$$

$$y'(x) = 3x - 2y^2 \qquad y(a) = y_0 \qquad \text{Equation 1.3.3}$$

$$y''(x) + 3y'(x) - y(x) = x^2 \cos(x) \qquad y(a) = y_0,\ y'(a) = y_1 \qquad \text{Equation 1.3.4}$$

$$y''(x) + \cos(x)y'(x) - \sin(x)y(x) = x^2 - \cos(x) \qquad y(a) = y_0,\ y(b) = y_1 \qquad \text{Equation 1.3.5}$$

$$y''(x) = x^2y - y'y + 3y^2 \qquad y(a) = y_0,\ y'(a) = y_1 \qquad \text{Equation 1.3.6}$$

$$((x^2+1)y_x)_x = x \sin x \qquad y(a) = y_0,\ y(b) = y_1 \qquad \text{Equation 1.3.7}$$

Differential equations are classified in the following ways: The **order** of the equation is the number of the highest derivative in the equation. Equations 1.3.1 to 1.3.3 are first order, and 1.3.4 to 1.3.7 are second order. The equation is **linear** if all appearances of y and its derivatives appear linearly, otherwise the equation is **nonlinear**. Equations 1.3.3 and 1.3.6 are nonlinear; note that a term like $y'y$ makes an equation nonlinear.

A differential equation problem requires a differential equation plus other conditions to specify the solution completely. The number of conditions is normally the order of the differential equations. If all the conditions are given at one point, then the problem is called an **initial value problem.** Equations 1.3.1 to 1.3.4 and 1.3.6 are initial value problems. Other problems are called **boundary value problems,** and the associated conditions are **boundary conditions.** These conditions may be more complex than suggested by the above equations; for example, 1.3.6 could have any one of the following sets of boundary conditions:

$$y(a) = y_0 \qquad 6y(b) - 3y'(b) = 4$$

$$y(a) = y_0 \qquad \int_a^b y(t) \sin t \, dt = 1$$

$$y'(a) = 0 \qquad \int_a^b [(y(t) + y'(t)]^2 \, dt = 1$$

The general linear differential equation of order n is

$$y^{(n)} + a_1(x)y^{(n-1)}(x) + \ldots + a_{n-1}(x)y'(x) + a_n(x)y(x) = g(x) \qquad \text{Equation 1.3.8}$$

The principal theorem about this equation is:

Theorem 1.9 *Assume that g(x) and all the coefficient functions $a_j(x)$ of 1.3.8 are continuous in [a, b]. Then the solution y(x) of 1.3.8 is continuous in [a, b] and can be written in the form*

$$y(x) = y_p(x) + \sum_{j=1}^{n} c_j u_j(x)$$

The constants c_j are arbitrary, and every solution of 1.3.8 is obtained by choosing them appropriately.

The solution $y_p(x)$ in Theorem 1.9 is the **particular solution** of 1.3.8, and the sum is a **general solution.** If $g(x) = 0$, then $y_p(x) = 0$ and 1.3.8 is said to be **homogeneous.** We see that the general solution is the solution of the homogeneous equation.

If equation 1.3.8 has constant coefficients $[a_j(x) = a_j]$, then the general solution may be expressed in terms of the **characteristic polynomial**

$$p(t) = t^n + a_1t^{n-1} + \ldots + a_{n-1}t + a_n$$

A consequence of Theorem 1.8 is that $p(t)$ has n roots r_j, $j = 1, 2, \ldots, n$. The functions $u_j(x)$ in Theorem 1.9 are e^{r_jx}. Recall that the r_j might be complex numbers; if the a_j are all real, then the complex roots occur in pairs $s+it$ and $s-it$ where $i^2 = -1$ with s and t real. One may manipulate $c_je^{r_jx} + c_{j+1}e^{r_{j+1}x}$ for such a pair into the form

$$e^{sx}(d_j \cos tx + d_{j+1} \sin tx)$$

where d_j and d_{j+1} are real numbers. The general solution of a constant coefficient differential equation is a combination of exponential and trigonometric functions.

Equations which involve partial derivatives are called **partial differential equations.** They are very important in modeling physical problems; a brief background for them is given at the beginning of Chapter 10.

PROGRAMMING 1.4

There are several areas of knowledge about programming that are needed for scientific computation. These include knowledge about:

The programming language
The computer system in which the language runs
How to debug programs and verify the correctness of results
How to organize computations and express them clearly

We assume that the reader has had an introduction to Fortran programming and hence has had some contact with all these areas. A common error is to believe that once one has made a few programs work, one has learned all one needs to know about programming. Consider an analogy with playing golf: One can take 2 or 3 clubs out to the course and, with patience, eventually get the ball in each of the holes (with luck, only one golf ball is needed). One still has a very long way to go before becoming an expert golf player. Most students using this text will be beginners in programming; the purpose of this section is to summarize the knowledge areas in programming so that students can judge those that need their attention and practice.

This book is based on Fortran, the "standard" language for scientific and numerical computations. We do not give a systematic review of Fortran; we assume that the student has a reference manual of some kind. Fortran is the "standard" for three reasons: (1) most scientists and engineers doing computations know it and can use it locally; (2) there is an enormous amount of existing software in Fortran; and (3) Fortran allows one to do most things needed in numerical computation in a fairly direct manner. One thing that Fortran is not is standardized. There are two standard Fortrans: Fortran 66 and Fortran 77. Fortran 66 is what most people think of as Fortran, since Fortran 77 is only gradually becoming widely available.

Fortran 66 has a standard definition, but very few Fortran compilers implement Fortran exactly according to this standard. Most Fortrans have been "enhanced" by adding some nonstandard features. In addition, a few Fortran facilities are frequently implemented in different ways by different compiler writers. The effects of all these variations or **Fortran dialects** are compounded by the fact that different underlying computers can make large differences in the behavior of a given Fortran program. The key point to realize is the following fact: **A substantial Fortran program is unlikely to work correctly when moved to a new system unless careful consideration has been given to this aspect of the program.**

For one-shot programs this point is irrelevant; the program is not going to be moved to another system. The bulk of the effort in programming is not like student homework assignments; it is the creation of programs that have a long life span of use. Even if programs are not moved to another location, it is likely that the local computer system will change its Fortran compiler during the life span of the program. We do not attempt to systematically study this problem — that is the topic for some other course — but some further discussion is given in Chapter 13. Note that having programs that are well-organized and clearly expressed and knowing how to verify the correctness of results are important parts of handling this problem.

There is one aspect of Fortran programming that causes so much trouble in numerical computation that it merits review here. That is the mechanism for **passing arrays to subprograms.** Consider a program that has a one-dimensional array VECT and a two-dimensional array COEF. The programmer decides that these arrays might be used with sizes up to 5 and 5 by 5; he or she specifies that memory space is set aside for them by the Fortran statement

```
DIMENSION VECT(5), COEF(5,5)
```

This is a **storage allocation** request; the program can use sizes less than 5 but not more. Suppose now that in a particular case the program is to be run with

$$\text{VECT} = (\,10,\ 11,\ 12\,)$$

$$\text{COEF} = \begin{pmatrix} 1 & 2 & 3 \\ 4 & 5 & 6 \\ 7 & 8 & 9 \end{pmatrix}$$

The actual or working sizes (called **ranges**) are 3, not 5. These numbers are stored in the computer's memory as follows:

←	VECT	→			←			COEF						→
10	11	12	—	—	1	4	7	—	—	2	5	8	—	—

						COEF								→
3	6	9	—	—	—	—	—	—	—	—	—	—	—	—

The elements of VECT are just listed in order, and the elements of COEF are stored in sequence *by columns.* The dashes indicate storage locations in the computer's memory that are not being used.

Now suppose we want to send VECT and COEF to a subprogram (it might solve a system of linear equations, for example).

```
CALL COMPUT(ANSWER, VECT, COEF, ...)
```

In order for the subroutine COMPUT to obtain the information about VECT and COEF, it must know:

Where VECT starts

Where COEF starts

The length of the columns of COEF as declared for storage allocation

The actual sizes of VECT and COEF to be used

The first two items are passed by Fortran where one puts the names VECT and COEF in the arguments to COMPUT. The second pair of items must be explicitly passed as arguments, and they are different. Thus one would have

```
NSTORE = 5
NACTUL = 3
CALL COMPUT(ANSWER,VECT,COEF,NACTUL,NSTORE)
```

The subroutine COMPUT starts off as

```
SUBROUTINE COMPUT(ANSWER,VECT,COEF,NACTUL,NSTORE)
REAL VECT(NSTORE), COEF(NSTORE,NSTORE)
```

and uses NACTUL to control its computation. Suppose one had REAL COEF(NACTUL,NACTUL) instead of REAL COEF(NSTORE,NSTORE) with NSTORE=5, NACTUL=3 in the subroutine COMPUT. Then the value to COEF(2,3) is 2 because the COEF storage locations would be interpreted as

← COLUMN 1 →			← COLUMN 2 →			← COLUMN 3 →		
1	4	7	—	—	2	5	8	—

This Fortran facility is called **variable dimensions** or **adjustable arrays.**

One sometimes sees the declaration for COMPUT in the simpler form

```
REAL VECT(1),COEF(NSTORE,1)
```

This is sufficient information to retrieve the values of VECT and COEF correctly even though it is illogical (because VECT is longer than 1, for example) and some Fortran compilers say it is an error. In a few Fortran systems this will fail to work properly in certain circumstances. Fortran 77 recognizes the illogic of this simple form and allows the declaration

```
REAL VECT(*), COEF(NSTORE,*)
```

where * explicitly shows that values for these storage dimensions are not given (and not needed).

Debugging programs is an art as well as a science, and it must be learned through practice. There are several effective tactics to use.

Intermediate output: The most important tactic is to print out intermediate results which provide clues to incorrect results. This simple and very effective approach is resisted by students, probably because Fortran usually requires FORMAT statements for output and students do not like to write them. Many newer Fortran compilers and Fortran 77 provide easy, unformatted output, and so there is no excuse for not providing generous intermediate output for a program that is not working properly. Many instructors take the position that they refuse to help a student debug a program until it has ample intermediate output.

Explain program to a friend: Humans have the ability and tendency to read things as they should be rather than as they are. Once a program has been read several times, it is hard to spot small errors because the mind simply corrects them as it reads. If one takes a program and explains it to a friend, one is forced to focus attention on each detail. It is surprising how often one sees the error in the middle of such an explanation. It is often completely "obvious," but it has been passed over every time.

Use compiler and debugging tools: For many years there have been Fortran compilers that produce good **diagnostics.** That is, Fortran errors are detected and informative messages given about the location and kind of error. Alas, there are still many compilers whose diagnostics are poor. Some compilers go further and issue *warning* or *caution* messages for things that are not strictly illegal, but which are unusual or likely to be errors. Examples of this are:

A variable used before a value is assigned to it

Test of equality between floating point variables

GO TO the next statement

Such compilers usually have a switch to set the level of diagnostics, and asking for all possible checking is a good thing to do while developing a program.

Some compilers go further and provide various other facilities to aid in program development, debugging, and checking. Examples of these facilities are:

1. **Cross-reference tables.** These tables list all variables and labels along with information about where they are set and used. A typing error in a variable name, for example, will produce a variable which is either set and never used or used and never set. A perusal of the cross-reference tables shows such errors.

2. **Tracing.** Statements can be inserted specifying that a variable is to be *traced.* Every time its value is changed, the new value is printed and the location given of the change. Tracing can also be done for labels and subprograms.

3. **Subscript checking.** A common error is to have the subscripts on arrays get out of bounds. This can cause the program to write results inside the program code (thereby ruining it) and strange things happen (usually an unexplained stop) when this code is executed. Such errors are hard to find because they show up at a place different from the location of the error. Less dramatic, but even more difficult to locate, are instances where the values of variables are changed. Some compilers have a mode of operation called *subscript range checking* where the actual index of an array is checked against the declared dimensions and a diagnostic is issued if the index is out of bounds. In the earlier terminology, **the ranges are checked against the storage allocation.** A few compilers do this checking for all programs automatically.

4. **Language standards checking.** If a program is expected to have a long life or to be used at several locations, then it is important to develop it without using nonstandard Fortran constructions. Some compilers have switches that signal every nonstandard statement (to either the Fortran 66 or the Fortran 77 standard). These checks greatly facilitate developing portable programs. However, one must keep in mind that using standard Fortran is only one part of creating portable Fortran programs. This is because a few "standard" facilities are, in fact, not implemented according to the standards on some major systems (for example, NAMELIST, test for end-of-file) and because there are many effects of changing systems and machines besides language standards.

Nevertheless, using such standards checking will prevent certain embarrassments. An acquaintance of mine told me of this wonderfully fast program he had. I asked him to send me a copy so I could see how it worked. When I compiled it, there were more lines of diagnostics than Fortran. He had used all the fancy features of his local Fortran; my local Fortran had most of these features but implemented differently. I sent the program back (with the diagnostics) and said I would wait until a portable version was available. He responded that he could not imagine how I could do computing with a system that had so many errors in the Fortran compiler.

Finally, there are programs which perform other important services for program development. Examples of such services are:

1. **Reformatting of programs:** indenting DO-loops, renumbering the statements, and generally polishing the appearance of the program. Such reformatting can greatly increase the readability of a program.

2. **Managing large programs:** allowing one to create versions (to test ideas) without destroying previous versions, allowing one to make certain kinds of changes wholesale (e.g., changing a COMMON statement in all of 50 different programs with one command).

3. **Static language analysis:** performing more detailed analysis of the program to detect things like uninitialized variables, code segments that can never be reached, or certain kinds of infinite loops.

In the future these services will be combined into a **programming environment** for Fortran where they are all integrated and easy to use. This should greatly facilitate the development of programs and improve their reliability.

The last topic on programming we discuss is the need to learn **good programming practices.** These practices have one goal: to make the program as clear and understandable as possible. It is easy to believe that if the logic in a program is confused and contorted, then the programmer was also confused and there are likely to be hidden pitfalls in the program. It is certainly true that it is hard to change such a program — or even get it to work in the first place. There is no magic formula that produces clarity in programming, just as there is no formula for clarity in writing English. It takes practice learning how to follow various guidelines and knowing which principles take precedence in a given situation. The term **structured programming** is often used to refer to the use of a consistent set of principles to aid clarity in programming. Common among these principles are:

1. Use **lots of comments** to explain what the program is doing. Give explicit definitions of the variables and outline the logical structure of the computation.

2. Use **meaningful names for variables** (this can be a challenge in Fortran where one is limited to 6 character names).

3. Make the **types of variables obvious.** One can explicitly declare all variables (this is particularly important for programs with a long life) or perhaps say "all variables in this program are REAL" or develop some other obvious method.

4. Only use **simple logical control structures,** that is,

    if-then-else

    iteration (i.e., DO-loop)

    case statements

    subprograms

    exits

    Even when using a Fortran without these statements as part of the language, one should pretend these are the only ones available and build them from simpler Fortran. Above all, do not intertwine various logical constructions in the program.

5. Use **indentation** to show the logical structure of the program.

2
NUMERICAL SOFTWARE

A basic premise of this text is that most basic numerical computations should be made with standard software that someone else wrote. These programs form a set of tools for practicing scientists and engineers; as with all basic tools, they should be acquired, not handcrafted by each user. Even though one should use "off-the-shelf" programs as tools, one must also understand the principles of the tools. Thus, this text focuses on how numerical methods and software work while introducing some basic numerical software. This chapter presents a brief survey of numerical software.

Numerical software from outside sources comes in four basic forms. **Individual programs** (perhaps with a few subprograms) are the most common; they are designed to carry out one specific computation. A **software package** is a set of programs for a particular problem area and is usually narrowly focused. Examples include packages for linear equations, initial value problems in ordinary differential equations, elementary functions, etc. A **numerical software library** is a much larger set of programs to support general numerical computations. About 500 programs are required for good support, and the library must have well-organized documentation. The programs in the library are selected to provide a maximum of capabilities, user convenience, and reliability. The fourth form is the **software system;** this is a package together with a specialized user interface. Thus, the system user (either with cards or with a terminal) writes in a special language for this system. For example, a statistics system has statements about means, histograms, or correlations; a differential equation system has statements about initial conditions. There are several very widely used statistical systems; perhaps as much as half of all statistical computations in the United States are done with these systems.

Software provides a new and rapid means of dissemination of knowledge through the scientific community. Traditionally, new problem-solving methods are disseminated by a three-stage process of research journal articles, books that survey research results, and finally textbooks. The scientist studies these publications to absorb the knowledge, which is then applied to a particular problem; that is, the scientist writes his or her own program. The typical off-the-shelf program solves a standard problem, and so important new knowledge of techniques and methods, i.e., know-how, can be incorporated into new software. Then this new research know-how can be used (and quickly too!) by scientists without the need to absorb the knowledge themselves. In the long run, this might be the most significant aspect of software.

THE LIBRARY CONCEPT 2.1

It was recognized very early that program libraries are important in computing; one of the first major books on computers (published in 1951) contained an extensive discussion of them. The motivation for using a library program is simple: one avoids writing and debugging a new program. Program development is *very* expensive and, often equally important, *very* time-consuming. The manufacturers of computers in the 1960s supplied a library of programs for their machines. In addition, there were nationwide efforts to develop libraries and set up facilities to exchange programs. In spite of multimillion-dollar efforts, these libraries were poor and the program exchange facilities were failures.

The two basic flaws in the programs were that they were unreliable and hard to use. This, of course, made people wary of using the programs. Behind these flaws was the fact that the people writing the programs were either inexperienced in numerical computation or not motivated to produce easily used programs, or both. The first case often occurred in manufacture's libraries where junior programmers translated simple methods from textbooks into Fortran. The second case often occurred where a good program was developed for a particular problem and was then put into a library or exchange service without making the user interface flexible to handle a variety of similar problems, without testing the program on similar problems, and without good documentation. None of these crucial things was done because it was not important to the programmer or employer that the programs be easily used by other people. Not all the programs of this era were bad, but if 50 percent, or even 30 percent, of the programs in a library are poor, people quickly stop using it.

By the early 1970s, it was generally realized that good libraries require a special effort, and experience had illustrated a large number of problems to avoid. Since that time a number of successful software packages, libraries, and systems have been developed. One should not underestimate the difficulty or importance of this achievement, and like many other good ideas, it took a lot of effort, many failures, and considerable expertise to bring the program library concept to fruition. Even now there are difficulties with libraries in keeping up with all the latest developments. There are still substantial improvements taking place for basic numerical software, and when one has a library of 500 programs, it is inevitable that some do not employ the latest and best methods. But if the group of 10 or 20 programmers that work full time on a library cannot keep abreast of the latest developments, think how much worse off the working scientist is who has only a few days a year for such things.

This text is primarily related to the library from IMSL, Inc. They provide a high-quality, general purpose library for numerical computations; it is the most widely used in the United States. This text is mostly concerned with basic numerical methods, and so other libraries are likely to have programs with capabilities similar to those discussed here. The IMSL library also has a convenient user interface, the PROTRAN system (see Section 2.5 for more details) which greatly facilitates the use of the IMSL programs.

USING A LIBRARY 2.2

A library of programs has a table of contents and an index of some kind. Thus, if one wants to generate random numbers, for example, one locates the name of a program that generates random numbers. Chapter G of the IMSL library is *Generating and Testing Random Numbers.* This chapter has 35 programs, most of which come in two forms: one as a function and the other as a subroutine. The fact that there are 35 programs illustrates that there are many different kinds of random numbers (uniform, normal, binomial, chi-squared, etc.) and many tests for random number types; this is how a subroutine library gets up to 500 programs. One can also use the IMSL KWIC index looking for "random numbers" and locate the line

```
GGUBFS BASIC UNIFORM (0,1)   RANDOM NUMBER GENERATOR - FUNCTION FORM OF GGUBS
```

which shows that GGUBFS is a function to produce uniformly distributed random numbers.

Once the name is known, then one must locate a write-up describing what the program does and how to use it. There are three approaches to **program documentation:**

1. *A library manual:* A set of books gives a write-up of all programs plus other helpful material. This set will have over 1000 pages for a normal-sized library.

2. *Self-documentation:* The first comments of the program provide complete documentation of the program.

3. *A HELP system:* Documentation is made available at a terminal or on printer output in response to something like HELP GGUBFS.

For example, parts of the IMSL documentation of GGUBFS and GGUBS are shown in Figure 2.1. The initial segments are comments that appear in the Fortran code; one can read how to use the program once one obtains a copy of it. This example is particularly simple; it is usual for the comments to take a full page, and some programs require several pages just for this part. The manual also contains a discussion of the algorithm used and references; this is not shown here.

```
IMSL ROUTINE NAME   - GGUBFS
PURPOSE             - BASIC UNIFORM (0,1) RANDOM NUMBER GENERATOR -
                        FUNCTION FORM OF GGUBS
USAGE               - FUNCTION GGUBFS (DSEED)
ARGUMENTS    GGUBFS - RESULTANT DEVIATE.
             DSEED  - INPUT/OUTPUT DOUBLE PRECISION VARIABLE
                        ASSIGNED AN INTEGER VALUE IN THE
                        EXCLUSIVE RANGE (1.D0, 2147483647.D0).
                        DSEED IS REPLACED BY A NEW VALUE TO BE
                        USED IN A SUBSEQUENT CALL.
IMSL ROUTINE NAME   - GGUBS
PURPOSE             - BASIC UNIFORM (0,1) PSEUDO-RANDOM NUMBER
                        GENERATOR
USAGE               - CALL GGUBS (DSEED,NR,R)
ARGUMENTS    DSEED  - INPUT/OUTPUT DOUBLE PRECISION VARIABLE
                        ASSIGNED AN INTEGER VALUE IN THE
                        EXCLUSIVE RANGE (1.D0, 2147483647.D0).
                        DSEED IS REPLACED BY A NEW VALUE TO BE
                        USED IN A SUBSEQUENT CALL.
             NR     - INPUT NUMBER OF DEVIATES TO BE GENERATED.
             R      - OUTPUT VECTOR OF LENGTH NR CONTAINING THE
                        PSEUDO-RANDOM UNIFORM (0,1) DEVIATES
```

Examples

One hundred (100) random numbers in the interval (0,1) are generated in this example by making 100 calls to GGUBFS or one call to GGUBS with input DSEED = 123457.D0.

Input:

```
  REAL                R(100)
  DOUBLE PRECISION  DSEED
  DSEED =  123457.D0
  N    =  100
  DO 5 I = 1,N
5 R(I) = GGUBFS (DSEED)
```

Input:

```
INTEGER              NR
REAL                 R(100)
DOUBLE PRECISION  DSEED
DSEED =  123457.D0
NR    =  100
CALL GGUBS (DSEED,NR,R)
```

Output:

```
DSEED =  801129707.D0
R(1)  = .96622
   .
   .
   .
R(100)= .37306
```

Output:

```
DSEED =  801129707.D0
R(1)  = .96622
   .
   .
   .
R(100)= .37306
```

Figure 2.1 **Typical library documentation.** The first part is from comments in the program, the second part is from the manual.

Using a program library is simple in principle; in practice it is a different story. Assume that the library is reliable, the programs are reasonably well documented, and the programs are reasonably flexible to adapt to typical user requirements. The problems that remain include:

1. *Understanding the program write-up.* Library program documentation tends to be concise; the essential information is given, but the density is so high that the first run or two are bad because of some elementary oversight on the part of the user. It is a very definite art to design a program user interface so that a user naturally jumps to the right conclusions as the write-up is first read. There seems to be little doubt that even the best programs with the best write-ups can be confusing and intimidating; this is why so much software is being put into specialized systems where the user interface is more natural and under better control.

2. *Inscrutable parameters.* Library programs achieve flexibility by having parameters; these are the knobs the user needs to tune the program to a particular problem. A user with a simple problem has to set values for parameters that are irrelevant to the problem and whose purpose is not understood. Thus, the user is not sure whether the parameters are irrelevant or what values to use.

   For example, the IMSL program GGUBFS has the argument (input value) DSEED. This parameter allows one to get the same random numbers in different parts of a run by resetting DSEED to a fixed value. Or it allows one to get different random numbers for different runs of the same program by simply changing the value of DSEED from run to run. But many users have never heard of seeding a random number generator and do not know what value to assign. In not understanding DSEED's purpose, they also might miss the fact that it must be double precision; at least one run is wasted to learn this fact.

   Much more serious are parameters whose values *no one knows how to set.* Some numerical methods need to be tuned for different problems by adjusting parameters for scaling, for convergence tests, for tolerances, etc. The library program writer realizes this, and so these parameters appear in the argument list. Typically, most program users do not understand the details (or even the general principle) of the method; they do not even know what the parameter is supposed to do, never mind what value it should have. Even well-informed users might have no idea what tolerance for "iterate differences" should be used, or how big the first step of a method should be, or how many subdivisions of an interval should be allowed before restarting a scheme. The values of these parameters might be determinable only after experimentations; this is time-consuming for an informed user, mystifying for an uninformed one.

3. *Workspace.* Many programs require some extra memory space for intermediate results in a computation; this is called **workspace.** The amount needed depends on the problem size, and so it cannot be set once and for all inside the library program. The space must be supplied to the library program by the user's program as an argument which is an array. Some users do not understand what workspace is for, and so they make mistakes in passing the right amount, or they pass a simple variable instead of an array which makes the program behave in mysterious ways.

4. *Array and function arguments.* It is easy to forget that a function argument to a subprogram must be declared in an EXTERNAL statement. This means another run wasted. More serious is the fact that many programmers do not understand how variable dimensioned arrays are passed in Fortran, because they do not make a distinction in their minds between the size of the memory needed for an array and the size of the array as used in a particular calculation. The size of the memory is set in a declaration, say

```
REAL A(10,10)
DIMENSION B(10),X(10)
```

   and the size used need only stay within this memory allocation. Thus, one can solve a 5 by 5 linear system A*X = B with these declarations, and only a portion of the allocated memory is used. The memory size and working size of arrays are frequently the same, and this tends to obscure the distinction between the two quantities. See Section 6.5.B for more discussion of storage allocation for Fortran arrays.

   The working size of an array in some languages is a specific variable, the **range,** which is distinct from the declared dimension. Thus, in the PROTRAN system one has declarations like

```
$DECLARATIONS
VECTOR B(N=10), X(N=10)
MATRIX A(NROW=10,NCOL=10)
```

   which state that the working size of B and X is the value of N; the working size of A is an NROW by NCOL matrix. It is possible that range variables will be part of Fortran in the next version of the standard language.

5. *Too many choices.* A library will frequently have several programs that can be applied to the same problem. The basic reason is that different methods are used and no one method works well for all problems. The user must, of course, choose just one program; even though the documentation might give some guidance, it is not always possible to know which program to use. Experimenting with several programs is time-consuming and frustrating.

The problem of too many choices is compounded by the fact that a particular computing installation may have several libraries and packages that cover the same problem area. Even if each one of these has only one program for a particular problem, a user must choose from a set of 8 to 10 programs. For example, the Purdue University Computing Center library has about 100 different programs for solving a linear system of equations. Not all are applicable to the same problem; some programs are single precision, some are double precision, some are complex, some apply to symmetric matrices, some to band matrices, and so forth. Even so, it is confusing when one must make a choice. Most users do not discover all the programs they may use; once they locate one that is applicable, they tend to use it from then on unless it proves unreliable.

STANDARD NUMERICAL SOFTWARE *2.3

Individual Programs 2.3.A

There are several journals that publish individual computer programs: **ACM Transactions on Mathematical Software, Applied Statistics, BIT, The Computer Journal,** and **Numerische Mathematik.** The **ACM Algorithms** series contains over 550 items and is available as the **Collected Algorithms of the Association for Computing Machinery.** This series started in the early 1960s. Only a few of the early algorithms are still important because many of them are very elementary, as, for example, to compute n factorial. The early algorithms were all in Algol 60, but the policy changed about 1970 to allow "the most appropriate language," and now most of the algorithms are in Fortran. All the algorithms published since 1975 are available in machine readable form (cards or tapes) for a nominal charge from the **ACM Algorithms Distribution Service.**

These algorithms cover a wide variety of topics, but the bulk of them are mathematical or numerical in nature. The editorial policy since the early 1970s has been to emphasize usefulness in the selection of algorithms to be published, and the series contains many very useful programs. Some are quite large: Algorithm 524 is a complete, portable multiple-precision package of 8405 lines of Fortran, or about 140 pages, and Algorithm 568 is a "portable directory system" of 16,891 Fortran lines, or almost 300 pages. At the other extreme, Algorithm 515 generates a vector from a lexicographical index and is only 48 lines long. The complete list of algorithms from 1975 to 1981 is given in Table 2.1; these are available from the ACM Algorithms Distribution Service, c/o IMSL, Inc., Sixth Floor, NBC Building, 7500 Bellaire Boulevard, Houston, Texas, 77036. The prices depend on the form and number of the algorithms.

Software Libraries 2.3.B

Three general libraries of programs for numerical computations are widely available in the United States:

IMSL — IMSL, Inc.

NAG — Numerical Algorithms Group, Oxford University

SL/MATH — IBM Corporation

The last is specifically for IBM computers. The characteristics of the IMSL library are surveyed in the next section. There are also several general statistical program libraries; the most widely used is probably

BMD — BioMedical Department, UCLA

The ACM Algorithms **Table 2.1**

Algorithm Number	Lines	Title
493	721	Zeros of a Real Polynominal
494	155	PDEONE, Solution of Systems of Partial Differential Equations
495	298	Solution of an Over Determined System of Linear Equations in the Chebyshev Norm
496	430	The LZ Algorithm to Solve the Generalized Eigenvalue Problem for Complex Matrices
497	607	Automatic Integration of Functional Differential Equations
498	348	Airy Functions Using Chebyshev Series Approximations
499	746	An Efficient Scanning Technique
500	344	Minimization of Unconstrained Multivariate Functions
501	611	Fortran Translation of Algorithm 409, Discrete Chebyshev Curve Fit
502	328	Dependence of Solution of Nonlinear Systems on a Parameter
503	1927	An Automatic Program for Fredholm Integral Equations of the Second Kind
504	555	GERK: Global Error Estimation for Ordinary Differential Equations
505	144	A List Insertion Sort for Keys with Arbitrary Key Distribution
506	563	HQR3 and EXCHNG: Fortran Subroutines for Calculating and Ordering the Eigenvalues of a Real Upper Hessenberg Matrix
507	88	Procedures for Quintic Natural Spline Interpolation
508	565	Matrix Bandwidth and Profile Reduction
509	227	A Hybrid Profile Reduction Algorithm
510	326	Piecewise Linear Approximations to Tabulated Data
511	1512	CDC 6600 Subroutines IBESS and JBESS for Bessel Functions $I_\upsilon(x)$ and $J_\upsilon(x)$, $x \geq 0, \upsilon \geq 0$
512	140	A Normalized Algorithm for the Solution of Positive Definite Symmetric Quindiagonal Systems of Linear Equations
513	108	Analysis of In-Situ Transposition
514	76	A New Method of Cubic Curve Fitting Using Local Data
515	48	Generation of a Vector from the Lexicographical Index
516	415	An Algorithm for Obtaining Confidence Intervals and Point Estimates Based on Ranks in the Two-Sample Location Problem
517	383	A Program for Computing the Condition Numbers of Matrix Eigenvalues without Computing Eigenvectors
518	63	Incomplete Bessel Function I0: The Von Meses Distribution
519	351	Three Algorithms for Computing Kolmogorov-Smirnov Probabilities with Arbitrary Boundaries and Certification of Algorithm 487
520	498	An Automatic Revised Simplex Method for Constrained Resource Network Scheduling
521	237	Repeated Integrals of the Coerror Function
522	1404	ESOLVE, Congruence Techniques for the Exact Solution of Integer Systems of Linear Equations
523	368	CONVEX, A New Convex Hull Algorithm for Planar Sets
524	8405	MP, A Fortran Multiple-Precision Arithmetic Package
525	2251	ADAPT, Adaptive Smooth Curve Fitting
526	1800	Bivariate Interpolation and Smooth Surface Fitting for Irregularly Distributed Data Points
527	2656	A Fortran Implementation of the Generalized Marching Algorithm
528	2844	Framework for a Portable Library
529	280	Permutations to Block Triangular Form
530	612	An Algorithm for Computing the Eigensystem of Skew-Symmetric Matrices and a Class of Symmetric Matrices
531	684	Contour Plotting
532	5760	Software for Roundoff Analysis
533	1548	NSPIV, A Fortran Subroutine for Sparse Gaussian Elimination with Partial Pivoting
534	1142	STINT: STiff (differential equations) INTegrator
535	1097	The QZ Algorithm to Solve the Generalized Eigenvalue Problem for Complex Matrices
536	720	An Efficient One-Way Enciphering Algorithm
537	360	Characteristic Values of Mathieu's Differential Equations
538	1512	Eigenvectors and Eigenvalues of Real Generalized Symmetric Matrices by Simultaneous Iteration
539	14,472	Basic Linear Algebra Subprogram for Fortran Usage
540	3312	PDECOL, General Collocation Software for Partial Differential Equations
541	5472	Efficient Fortran Subprograms for the Solution of Separable Elliptic Partial Differential Equations

The ACM Algorithms *(Cont.)*

542	900	Incomplete Gamma Functions
543	1296	FFT9, Fast Solution of Helmholtz-Type Partial Differential Equations
544	2304	L2A and L2B, Weighted Least Squares Solutions by Modified Gram-Schmidt with Iterative Refinement
545	2592	An Optimized Mass Storage FFT
546	540	SOLVEBLOK
547	612	Fortran Routines for Discrete Cubic Spline Interpolation and Smoothing
548	252	Solution of the Assignment Problem
549	360	Weierstrass' Elliptic Functions
550	648	Solid Polyhedron Measures
551	828	A Fortran Subroutine for the L_1 Solution of Overdetermined Systems of Linear Equations
552	504	Solution of the Constrained l_1 Linear Approximation Problem
553	1404	M3RK, An Explicit Time Integrator for Semidiscrete Parabolic Equations
554	612	BRENTM, A Fortran Subroutine for the Numerical Solution of Systems of Nonlinear Equations
555	1260	Chow-Yoke Algorithm for Fixed Points or Zeros of C^2 Maps
556	864	Exponential Integrals
557	792	PAGP, A Partitioning Algorithm for (Linear) Goal Programming Problems
558	720	A Program for the Multifacility Location Problem with Rectilinear Distance by the Minimum-Cut Approach
559	576	The Stationary Point of a Quadratic Function Subject to Linear Constraints
560	3132	JNF, An Algorithm for Numerical Computation of the Jordan Normal Form of a Complex Matrix
561	396	Fortran Implementation of Heap Programs for Efficient Table Maintenance
562	288	Shortest Path Lengths
563	3610	A Program for Linearly Constrained Discrete l_1 Problems
564	1042	A Test Problem Generator for Discrete Linear l_1 Approximation Problems
565	3159	PDETWO/PSETM/GEARB: Solution of Systems of Two-Dimensional Nonlinear Partial Differential Equations
566	6760	FORTRAN Subroutines for Testing Unconstrained Optimization Software
567	1114	Extended-Range Arithmetic and Normalized Legendre Polynomials
568	16,891	PDS-A Portable Directory System
569	7725	COLSYS: Collocation Software for Boundary Value ODE's
570	1538	LOPSI: A Simultaneous Iteration Algorithm for Real Matrices
571	397	Statistics for von Mises' and Fisher's Distribution of Directions: $I_1(x)/I_0(x)$, $I_{1.5}(x)/I_{0.5}(x)$
572	2024	Solution of the Helmholtz Equation for the Dirichlet Problem on General Bounded Three Dimensional Regions
573	13,080	NL2SOL — An Adaptive Nonlinear Least-Squares Algorithm
574	897	Shape-Preserving Osculatory Quadratic Splines
575	262	Permutations for a Zero-Free Diagonal
576	901	A FORTRAN Program for Solving Ax = b
577	1048	Algorithms for Incomplete Elliptic Integrals
578	515	Solution of Real Linear Equations in a Paged Virtual Store
579	260	CPSC, Complex Power Series Coefficients
580	1558	QRUP: A Set of FORTRAN Routines for Updating R Factorizations

Software Packages 2.3.C

There are a substantial number of important, specialized software packages. We briefly describe some of them here; more details are given in relevant chapters for some of these. The following list is not complete; it illustrates the variety of packages and includes most of those mentioned elsewhere in this book.

In addition to marketing a library, IMSL also provides a software distribution service; they operate the ACM Algorithms Distribution Service as well. Most of the packages listed below are available from IMSL at a nominal charge ($40 to $100). IMSL does not provide any support for these packages. Write to IMSL, Inc., Sixth Floor, NBC Building, 7500 Bellaire Boulevard, Houston, Texas, 77036, for specific prices and ordering information.

BLAS — *Basic Linear Algebra Subroutines*
This is ACM Algorithm 539, which contains 38 Fortran subprograms for the basic operations of numerical linear algebra (e.g., matrix multiply or vector add). The objective is fast execution. The programs are in four versions: Fortran and assembly language for the IBM 360/370, and CDC 6000 series and Univac 1100 series computers.

DEPACK — *Differential Equations Package*
This is a set of Fortran programs for ordinary differential equations available from the National Energy Software Center, Argonne National Laboratory, Argonne, Illinois, 60439.

DSS — *Differential System Simulator*
This system of Fortran programs provides for the integration of initial value problems in ordinary or partial differential equations. It is available from W.E. Schiesser, Department of Chemical Engineering, Lehigh University, Bethlehem, Pennsylvania, 18015, for a cost of about $1,000.

EISPACK — *Matrix Eigensystem Routines*
This is a systematized collection of 51 programs for the calculation of eigenvalues and eigenvectors of matrices. They have been certified on 15 different computer systems and are available from IMSL. See: *Matrix Eigensystems Routines — EISPACK Guide,* B.T. Smith et al., Lecture Notes in Computer Science No. 6, Second Edition, Springer-Verlag, New York (1976), 551 pages.

FISHPAK — *Routines for the Helmholtz Problem in Two or Three Dimensions*
This is a collection for solving the Poisson problem

$$\frac{\partial^2 u}{\partial x^2} + \frac{\partial^2 u}{\partial y^2} = f(x, y)$$

on a rectangle and related problems. Several different coordinate systems are allowed. This is available for a nominal charge from the National Center for Atmospheric Research, Boulder, Colorado 80307. This is ACM Algorithm 541, but some additions have been made since Algorithm 541 was published.

FUNPACK — *Special Function Subroutines*
This is a collection of Fortran and assembly language progams for the more important special functions: exponential integral, elliptic integrals of the first and second kind, Bessel functions, and the Dawson integral. This is available from the National Energy Software Center, Argonne National Laboratory, Argonne, Illinois 60439. See: *The FUNPACK Package of Special Function Subroutines,* W. J. Cody, ACM Trans. Math. Software 1 (1975), pp. 13-25.

ITPACK — *Iterative Methods*
This is a collection of Fortran programs to apply iterative methods to solve linear systems when the coefficient matrix is large and sparse. They are particularly suited for problems that arise from elliptic partial differential equations. This is available from IMSL.

LINPACK — *Linear Algebra Package*
This is a collection of Fortran programs for solving linear systems of equations (not sparse matrix methods). They have been certified and are generally more efficient than similar programs. This is available from IMSL. See: *LINPACK User's Guide,* J. J. Dongarra et al., SIAM Publications (1979).

PPPACK — *Piecewise Polynomial and Spline Routines*
These are the programs in the book *A Practical Guide to Splines* by Carl de Boor. See Lecture Notes in Applied Mathematics No. 27, Springer-Verlag, New York (1979). They form a basic set of tools to manipulate piecewise polynominals and splines and are available from IMSL (*B-SPLINE Package*).

ROSEPACK — *Robust Statistics Package*
This is a set of Fortran programs for robust statistical computations available from IMSL.

Software Systems 2.3.D

We discuss three examples of software systems: PROTRAN is a user interface to the IMSL library and is discussed in more detail in Section 2.5, as it is used from time to time in this book. SPSS (Statistical Package for the Social Sciences) provides a user interface of a somewhat different nature for general statistical computation. ELLPACK (Elliptic Partial Differential Equations) is an example of a specialized problem solving system.

The following is a simple SPSS program.

```
RUN NAME        DEFINE,CROSSTABULATE, THEN SAVE AN SPSS SYSTEM FILE
FILE NAME       PARSTUDY, SURVEY OF PARTY PREFERENCES
VARIABLE LIST   ID,PARTYPRF,AGE,SEX,RELIGION
INPUT FORMAT    FIXED(F4.0,1X,A1,1X,F2.0,1X,A1,1X,F1.0)
N OF CASES      20
INPUT MEDIUM    CARD
VAR LABELS      ID,SURVEY RESPONDENT'S ID/
                PARTYPRF,POLITICAL PARTY PREF/
                AGE,AGE IN YEARS
VALUE LABELS    PARTYPRF ('C')CONSERVATIVE ('L')LIBERAL ('S')SOCIAL CREDIT
                        ('N')NEW DEMOCRAFT  ('R')NO RESPONSE/
                SEX ('M')MALE ('F')FEMALE/
                RELIGION (1)PROTESTANT (2)CATHOLIC (3)JEWISH (4) OTHER
MISSING VALUES  PARTYPRF ('R')/AGE(0)
PRINT FORMAT    PARTYPRF SEX (A)
CROSSTABS       TABLE= SEX BY PARTYPRF
OPTIONS         3,5
STATISTICS      1,3
READ INPUT DATA
3029 C 34 F 2
   *** 19 MORE DATA CARDS ***
SAVE FILE
FINISH
DEFINE,CROSSTABULATE, THEN SAVE AN SPSS SYSTEM FILE
FILE    PRESTUDY (CREATION DATE = 08/29/80)    SURVEY OF PARTY PREFERENCES
```

We do not attempt to explain SPSS in detail; we just note that the first eight statements (RUN NAME through VALUE LABELS) define data, that is, the variables in the set with formats and names. The next two statements (MISSING VALUES and PRINT FORMAT) specify what is to be done for certain things. The key statement is CROSSTABS, followed by its OPTIONS and STATISTICS; it specifies the computation to be made. The user, of course, must know the meanings of options 3 and 5 and of statistics 1 and 3. After that, the data is given and specified to be saved. The word FINISH indicates the program is finished.

The SPSS language is simple; all statement names are in columns 1 to 15, and complex program structure is not usual. The statements are individual statements of fact or requests for action. The power of SPSS is that some of the requests invoke a large program to do extensive calculations. The output from CROSSTABS is shown below. This rather elementary data analysis procedure is accomplished with a minimum of instructions. The output has been reformatted slightly here.

```
* * * * * * * * * * CROSSTABULATION OF * * * * * * * * * * * * * * *
    SEX                     BY PARTYPRF POLITICAL PARTY PREF
* * * * * * * * * * * * * * * * * * * * * * * * * * * * * * * * * * * *
                    PARTYPRF
            COUNT  I
            COL PCT ISOCIAL C NEW DEMO LIBERAL  CONSERVA  ROW
                   IREDIT    CRAT               TIVE      TOTAL
                   I S      I N      I L      I C      I
SEX         --------I--------I--------I--------I--------I
       M           I     2  I     2  I     2  I     4  I    10
  MALE             I  66.7  I  40.0  I  28.6  I 100.0  I  52.6
                  -I--------I--------I--------I--------I
       F           I     1  I     3  I     5  I     0  I     9
FEMALE             I  33.3  I  60.0  I  71.4  I   0.0  I  47.4
                  -I--------I--------I--------I--------I
            COLUMN       3        5        7        4       19
             TOTAL    15.6     26.3     36.8     21.1    100.0
CHI SQUARE =     5.78243 WITH   3 DEGREES OF FREEDOM,SIGNIFICANCE = 0.123
CONTINGENCY COEFFICIENT =    0.48304
NUMBER OF MISSING OBSERVATIONS =  1
```

Someone familiar with statistics can interpret this output easily, and the information is obtained with a minimal effort.

The ELLPACK system is a problem-solving system for elliptic partial differential equations which has a simple, mathematical language to express computations. See Section 10.4.B for more information.

Elliptic partial differential equations are similar to the following example:

$$u_{xx} + u_{yy} + 3u_x - 4u = e^{x+y}\sin(\pi x)$$ **Equation 2.3.1**

We use the common notation $\partial^2 u/\partial x^2 = u_{xx}$, $\partial^2 u/\partial y^2 = u_{yy}$, etc. There is an associated domain and set of boundary conditions, as shown in Figure 2.2. The problem is to determine $u(x, y)$ so that 2.3.1 is satisfied inside the domain and $u(x, y)$ takes on the assigned values on the boundaries of the domain. Partial differential equations are the standard mathematical models for many physical problems, e.g., fluid flow, heat flow, nuclear reactions, plasma physics, stresses and strains in materials, vibrations, and so on.

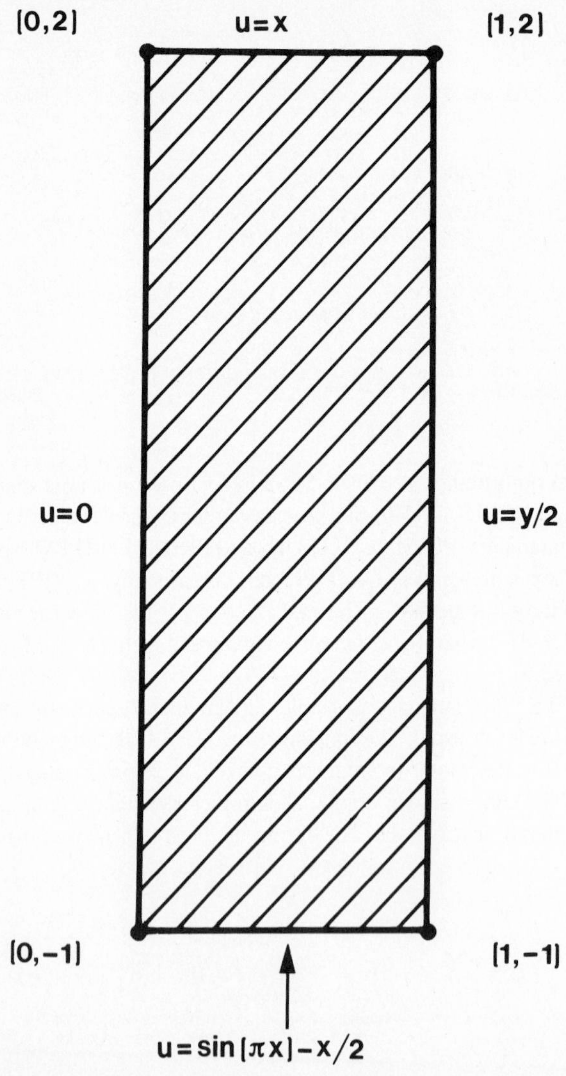

Figure 2.2 **Domain and boundary conditions for an elliptic partial differential equation.** The function u(x, y) is to satisfy the differential equation in the domain and have the specified values on the boundaries.

Figure 2.3 shows the ELLPACK program used to solve this problem. The first segment, EQUATION, gives the equation using the reserved word UXX for u_{xx}, etc. The segment BOUNDARY gives the (x, y) coordinates of the domain along with the boundary conditions to be satisfied. A more complicated statement is used if the domain is not a rectangle. The third segment, GRID, specifies that the domain is

```
EQUATION.   UXX + UYY + 3.*UX -4.*U = EXP(X+Y)*SIN(X)
*
BOUNDARY.   U = 0.0                   ON X =  0.0
            U = SIN(PI*X)-X/2.        ON Y = -1.0
            U = Y/2.                  ON X =  1.0
            U = X                     ON Y =  2.0
GRID.       6 X POINTS   $  16 Y POINTS
*
DISCRETIZATION.       5 POINT STAR
INDEXING.             NATURAL
SOLUTION.             LINPACK BAND
*
OUTPUT.        TABLE(U)     $     PLOT(U)
OPTIONS.       TIME         $     MEMORY
END.
```

SOLUTION CONTOURS

CONTOUR	VALUE
1	-5.00E-01
2	-3.33E-01
3	-1.67E-01
4	-6.80E-12
5	1.67E-01
6	3.33E-01
7	5.00E-01
8	6.67E-01
9	8.33E-01
10	1.00E+00

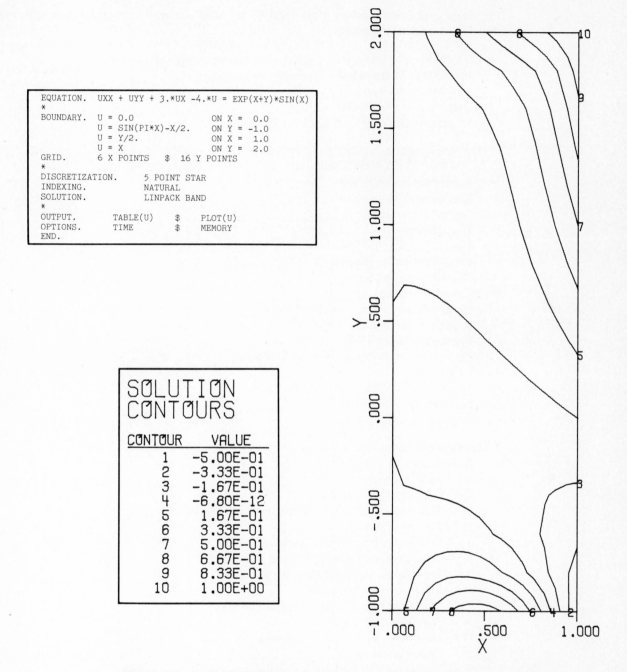

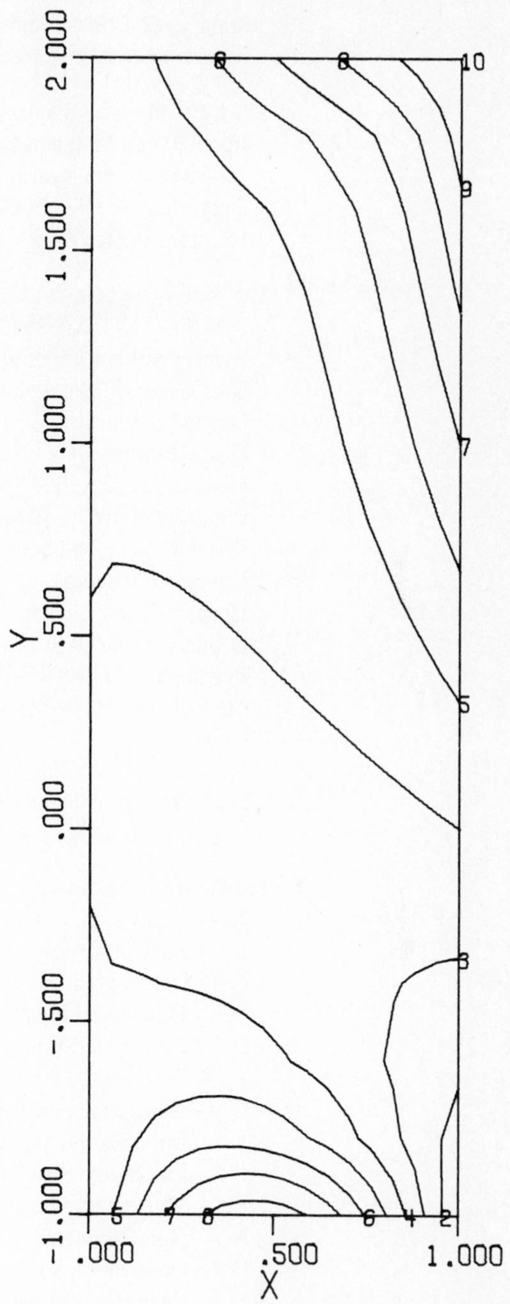

Figure 2.3 **An ELLPACK program and contour plot.** This is an example of a very high level, problem-solving system for a special application area.

covered by a rectangular grid which is to be used by a numerical method. The next three lines specify a common method for solving this problem; see Chapter 10 for more information. The next two lines ask for output (the contour plot from PLOT(U) is shown in Figure 2.3); the other output is not given here. The END. terminates the ELLPACK program.

The ELLPACK system analyzes this problem statement and creates a Fortran program of about 500 lines, which then solves the problem using programs in the ELLPACK library. A program like this example leads to the execution of perhaps 2,000 to 5,000 lines of Fortran, depending on the method chosen to solve it. Special systems of this type are very convenient and very cost-effective. Such systems are appearing throughout science, engineering, and applied mathematics for solving specific kinds of problems.

THE IMSL LIBRARY 2.4

This section gives a brief summary of the IMSL library as an example of a general purpose library of programs for numerical computation.

The IMSL library is available on a yearly rental basis (currently about $1500) from:
International Mathematical & Statistical Libraries, Inc.
7500 Bellaire Boulevard
Sixth Floor — NBC Building
Houston, Texas 77036   Phone (713) 772-1927

The library comes in both source text and compiled form for the following computer systems:
IBM 360/370/43XX/30XX Series and compatible mainframes (Amdahl, etc.)
Siemens System 7.500/7.700
Data General Eclipse/Nova
Digital Equipment PDP-11 Series
Digital Equipment VAX-11 Series
Hewlett Packard 3000 Series
Prime 300/400/500, 50 Series
Perkin-Elmer 32 bit Series
Univac 1100 Series
Honeywell and Cii Honeywell Bull 6000/66/68/DPS8 Series
Digital Equipment System 10/20
Burroughs 6000/7000 Series
Control Data 6000/7000 and Cyber 70/170 Series
Cray-1
Data General MV/8000 and MV/6000
Harris 80/100/300/500/800
Control Data Cyber 200 Series

The library is divided into chapters as follows:
A — Analysis of Variance
B — Basic Statistics
C — Categorized Data Analysis
D — Differential Equations, Quadrature, and Differentiation
E — Eigensystem Analysis
F — Forecasting, Econometrics, Time Series, and Transforms
G — Generation and Testing of Random Numbers
I — Interpolation, Approximation, and Smoothing
L — Linear Algebraic Equations
M — Mathematical and Statistical Special Functions
N — Non-Parametric Statistics
O — Observation Structure and Multivariate Statistics
R — Regression Analysis
S — Sampling
U — Utility Functions
V — Vector and Matrix Arithmetic
Z — Zeros and Extrema, Linear Programming

Programs in Chapters D, E, G, I, L, U, V, and Z are related to the problems and methods discussed in this book; no discussion of the extensive statistical capabilities in the library is given. The names of all programs in a particular chapter start with the letter of the chapter. The length of names is limited to six characters by Fortran; the result is many odd names. There is no way to have 500 programs with nice, mnemonic names when one is limited to six characters.

Versions of the library are targeted for specific machines, and many machine dependencies (e.g., word lengths and number ranges) are incorporated in each specific version. In addition, compiler and system idiosyncracies that affect library programs are also taken care of.

The library has certain conventions which, once learned, aid in using it. Some of the more useful are:

1. Argument lists are usually ordered by:
   Input arguments
   Input and output arguments
   Output arguments
   Working storage arrays
   Error indicators

2. There is no printed output except for utility programs. The program UERTST is referenced by most programs and may print a one-line error message with the value of IER. Output from UERTST may be switched off by using UERSET. IER is a standard variable which indicates the kind of error that occurs. Its value is an integer, and the values fall into three ranges.

$32 < \text{IER} \leq 64$	Warning; certain suspicious conditions detected.
$64 < \text{IER} \leq 128$	Warning with fix. More serious conditions are detected and fixed; results might not be good.
$129 \leq \text{IER}$	Fatal error; conditions arose which prevent the computations from finishing.

3. There are special matrix-vector storage modes which are discussed in detail in Chapter 6. The storage formats (data structures) for matrices are: full, symmetric, band, band symmetric, and hermitian.

The IMSL library has a three-volume manual of documentation which contains general discussions as well as individual program write-ups. The program documentation has four parts:

1. *Usage Information:* purpose and description of the arguments. This is reproduced as the initial comments of the program. Some remarks may also be included.

2. *Algorithm:* brief description of the method along with references (except for very simple programs).

3. *Programming Notes:* remarks about how to use the program or its relation to other programs.

4. *Example:* simple case with problem description, code to use library program, and generated output.

THE PROTRAN SYSTEM 2.5

The PROTRAN system is an extension of Fortran which brings many of the IMSL library programs into the language in a simple, natural way. It is used at many places in this book for two reasons: (1) it provides much shorter programs for various examples, and (2) it is an example of the high-level languages that will spread throughout numerical and scientific computation in the coming years. This section is a very brief introduction, just sufficient to allow one to read the PROTRAN programs. The language is almost self-explanatory, and so not much discussion is needed. For those who have access to the PROTRAN system, there is a more thorough and technical introduction in Chapter 15, which covers PROTRAN for the topics of this text. There are extensive statistical facilities in PROTRAN which we do not discuss at all.

PROTRAN makes three principal additions to Fortran:

1. *Vectors and matrices* are new variable types.

2. *Problem-solving statements* allow direct, easy access to the capabilities of the IMSL library.

3. *Convenience* facilities provide shorter and more readable programs.

The net result is much more productive programming; one more step is made toward having computers understand people, rather than vice-versa.

The PROTRAN system is built on Fortran, and so Fortran and PROTRAN statements may be intermixed. The dollar sign ($) is used to identify PROTRAN statements. A program with PROTRAN statements is translated into Fortran. See Section 6.5.C for a complete example of the over 120 lines of

Fortran that are generated from the simple PROTRAN program segment for solving a system of linear equations.

```
 $DECLARATIONS
  MATRIX A(5,5)
  VECTOR B(N=5),X(N=5)
 $ASSIGN A = (1., 2., 3 )
+            (3., 0., 1.)
+            (4., 5., 6 )
         B = ( -1, 0.0, 6.85 )
 $LINSYS A*X=B
 $PRINT A,X,B
 $END
```

A programmer normally does not need to look at the intermediate Fortran program generated by the PROTRAN system.

Simple Statements 2.5.A

We first summarize the convenience statements, as they are simple and may be used later. They are given by example first, then followed by a few remarks.

```
$ AVERAGE X(I) + 3.2*Y(I)/(1.+T)  ; FOR( I=1,26 ) ; IS XYBAR
$ MAX X(I,J) - A(J)*B(I)  ; FOR(J = K,K+I,2) ;IS XABI
$ MIN 2.3*COS(X) - F4KB(X-2.1) ; FOR( X=1., 5.5, 0.1 ); IS F4MIN
$ PLOT VEC1,VEC2,VEC3 ; VS BVECTR; SYMBOLS = 'A', 'B', '*'
$ PLOT COS(X)-3.2*F44(X,T), SIN(X)-2.3*F95(X,1.5*T)
       FOR( X = 2.5, T+1.2 )
       TITLE = 'VECTORS AND FUNCTIONS CANNOT BE MIXED IN PLOTS'
       XLABEL = 'X-AXIS'  ; YLABEL = ' TRIG DIFFERENCES'
$ PRINT SCALAR, VECTR1, MATRIX, VECTR2, SCALR2, MATRX2
$ PRODUCT 1.+1./N ; FOR( N=1,101) ; IS PON
$ SUM SIN(X)/X ;FOR ( X=A,B,  .001) ; IS SUMSIN
$END
```

All the convenience statements are of the simple form shown except PLOT; it has several other optional phrases (NPOINTS = number of points to plot, COLUMNS = number — 80 or 129 — of columns used by the plot, XRANGE and YRANGE to set the range of the plot). One cannot mix vectors and functions in the same plot. The results from the AVERAGE statement, MAX statement, etc., are assigned to the variable following IS. The PRINT statement applies only to variables; expressions are not allowed.

Declarations, Scalars, Vectors, and Matrices 2.5.B

Declarations are mainly used for vectors and matrices, and so we defer most of the discussion for the moment. In addition, there is an IMPLICIT statement which associates types with the first letters of names, for example,

```
 IMPLICIT INTEGER(I-K), DOUBLE PRECISION (A-H,S-Y)
A         REAL(L-R), COMPLEX(Z)
```

The declaration SCALAR is needed at times so that the PROTRAN system can compute certain quantities correctly. Consider

```
$SUM X(I)*Y(I) ; FOR(I=1,N) ; IS DPSUM
```

where X,Y are real and DPSUM is to be double precision. Because the result DPSUM is to be double precision, it is used in the computation of the sum; all SUM statements, PRODUCT statements, etc., use the type of the answer. The declaration

```
DOUBLE PRECISION SCALAR DPSUM
```

accomplishes this and also declares DPSUM to be double precision as a Fortran variable.

There are three topics to discuss about vectors and matrices:

1. Their types, properties, and declarations

2. Assignment of values and arithmetic

3. Output

The output is covered by the PRINT and PLOT statements in Section 2.5.A.

Vectors and matrices must be declared explicitly, similar in spirit to Fortran arrays. In addition to the usual Fortran dimensions, one may also have **range variables** for vectors and matrices. The Fortran DIMENSION declarations specify the amount of storage set aside (allocated) for arrays; the range variables specify the actual or working size of the vectors and matrices. For example,

```
$ DECLARATIONS
 REAL MATRIX A(N=10, M=10), B(N=10, K=2)
 REAL VECTOR X(M=10)
```

defines the matrices A and B with a_{ij}, $i = 1, 2, \ldots, N$; $j = 1, 2, \ldots, M$, and b_{ik} with $i = 1, 2, \ldots, N$, and $k = 1, \ldots, K$. The storage allocated for these arrays is: $100 = 10 \times 10$ for A, $20 = 10 \times 2$ for B, and 10 for X. The working sizes must not exceed these limits. Changing N changes the working sizes of both A and B. The vector X has the same number M of elements as A has columns. The effect of the range variables is illustrated by the following example.

Effect of Range Variables — Example 2.1

A PROTRAN program for solving linear systems is shown along with its output. The storage allocation allows for a 10 by 10 system to be defined with two right sides. The program actually solves a 5 by 5 system with one right side.

```
   $DECLARATION
    REAL MATRIX A(N=10,M=10), B(N=10,K=2)
    REAL VECTOR X(M=10) $
    N = 5
    K = 1
    READ 15, ((A(I,J),I=1,N), J=1,N), ((B(I,J),I=1,N),J=1,K)
15      FORMAT( 10F7.3 )
    M = N
    $PRINT A,B
    $LINSYS A*X = B
    $PRINT X
    $END

        OUTPUT FROM PROTRAN PROGRAM

A

         1          2          3          4          5
1     1.10000    1.20000   -1.00000     -.10000     0.00000
2     4.40000    2.30000    2.00000    20.00000    10.00000
3     3.30000    3.40000   -3.00000     -.30000   -20.00000
4     2.20000    4.50000    4.00000    40.00000   -30.00000
5     5.50000    5.60000   -5.00000     -.50000    40.00000

B

         1
1     1.00000
2     0.00000
3     5.10000
4     6.60000
5     7.70000

X

      -.72727    -8.62500    -12.39003    2.40025    -.01875
```

An important feature of PROTRAN is that the system is aware of all the dimension and range variables of all vectors and matrices and uses this information to be sure that library routines have arguments that are of legal size. For example, if the statement M = N is replaced by M = 7, then a diagnostic is printed because the linear system is incorrectly formed. Similarly, if K = 2 is assigned, then an error results because the solution variable X cannot contain the problem solution. This extensive checking is one reason the intermediate Fortran is so much longer than an original PROTRAN program.

This example also illustrates how Fortran and PROTRAN are mixed. A $ must precede each new PROTRAN statement and must terminate any PROTRAN statement that is followed by Fortran. The $END statement serves as both a STOP and END (or RETURN and END in a subprogram).

Declarations in PROTRAN follow the word $DECLARATIONS and are of the general form

type — **storage format** — **data structure** — list of variables

The **type** can be INTEGER, REAL, etc., and the **data structure** can be SCALAR, VECTOR, or MATRIX. The **storage format** applies only to matrices, and five types are supported by the IMSL library: FULL, SYMMETRIC, BAND, BAND SYMMETRIC, and HERMITIAN. There are special methods to assign the storage sizes for special matrices. For example, a band matrix declaration is

```
BAND MATRIX BND(100,1,1), B2(100, NLOW = 3, NUP = 5)
```

which declares two matrices of order 100. BND is tridiagonal (it has one upper and one lower diagonal) and B2 has storage for 9 diagonals: the main diagonal plus three lower ones and five upper ones. The range variables NLOW and NUP indicate the actual number of diagonals for B2.

Vector-matrix assignments and arithmetic can be done in Fortran in the usual ways, including reading in values. For matrices in special storage formats, one must take care to make assignments properly. In PROTRAN one may make assignments with constants, with simple vector-matrix expressions, or with formulas for elements, for example,

```
$ASSIGN      A = (0,1,0)
          B(K) = MAXO(K,2)
             C = A+B
             D = C'*B
          E(I) = I**2 + 1
    IDENT(I,J) = MINO(I,J)/J - MINO(I,J+1)/(J+1)
        S(I,J) = 3.2*COS(XBAR-3.2*I) - J/3.7
             T = S*C
            M2 = ( 0.423, 5.804 )
+                ( 2.751, 4.386*XBAR/(1+COS(ZBAR)) )
```

Assignments of constant values to matrices with special storage formats must be done properly. The apostrophe (′) denotes transpose, and so $C' \times B$ is the dot product of the vectors C and B. Note that the Fortran continuation (a character in column 6) is required if the assignment of an item requires more than one line.

Problem-Solving Statements 2.5.C

The PROTRAN problem-solving statements are of the form

$ **Keyword** — **Problem Definition** — **Phrases**

Many of the phrases are optional. The problem-solving statements mentioned in this text are indicated below with one example each:

```
$ APPROXIMATE DATA ; VS XPOINT ; BY SFIT
$ DERIVATIVE COS(X**3.2)/(2.2+X**2*A) ; D(X) ; AT 7.923 ; IS DBX
$ DIFEQU Y' = FUN(T,Y); ON(0.,A+1); INITIAL = YSTART
        ERRTARGET = 0.003 ; DEFINE
        ====
   FUN(1) = 4.2*Y(1) - 2.4*Y(2)**2 + CONST/(A+1)
   FUN(2) = Y(1)*EXP(-Y(2)/(T+ABAR)) - CONST
        ====
$ EIGSYS A*X = LAMBDA*X ; SYMMETRIC ; NOSAVE
$ RANDOM ; ARRAY XRAND ; SEED = 1012075 ; NORMAL(2.5,SIGMA)
$ INTEGRAL COS(PI*X)**2/(1.+A*X**3) ; FOR(X=0,2.5); IS ANS3
           ERRTARGET = 0.00001; ABSOLUTE
$ INTERPOLATE DATA; VS XPTS ; USING COSF(K,T),K,T; NPOINTS = 7
              COEFFICIENTS = ACOS
$ LINSYS A*X = B ; POSDEF
$ NONLIN F(Z) = 0; GUESS = AGUESS; SOLUTION = ABEST ; DEFINE
  ====
  F(1) = Z(1)/Z(2) - 2.4*A(1)*X
  F(2) = COS(Z(1)-Z(2)) + BSTAR/(Z(1)+Z(2))
  ====
$ POLYNOMIAL COEF ; ROOTS = ZEROS
```

The keyword abbreviations are: DIFEQU for SOLVE DIFFERENTIAL EQUATION, RANDOM for GENERATE RANDOM NUMBERS, LINSYS for SOLVE LINEAR SYSTEM and NONLIN for SOLVE NONLINEAR SYSTEM.

REFERENCES

A few books and articles that provide considerable general discussion of numerical software are listed below.

W. J. Cody, *The Construction of Numerical Subroutine Libraries,* SIAM Review, *16* (1974), pp. 36-46.

D. J. Evans (ed.), *Software for Numerical Mathematics,* Academic Press, Inc., New York (1974).

D. Jacobs (ed.), *Numerical Software — Needs and Availability,* Academic Press, Inc., New York (1978).

John R. Rice, "Software for Numerical Computation," in *Research Directions in Software Technology* (P. Wegner, ed.), M.I.T. Press, Cambridge (1979), chap. 16, pp. 688-708.

John R. Rice (ed.), *Mathematical Software,* Academic Press, Inc., New York (1971).

3
ERRORS, ROUND-OFF, AND STABILITY

SOURCES OF UNCERTAINTY 3.1

Even though we always strive to get the "exact" answers to problems, we rarely achieve this. Uncertainty and errors can be introduced at every step of the formulation and solution of problems. The nature of uncertainty in problem solving is discussed in this chapter. Errors introduced in the numerical computation part of problem solving are examined in detail.

The problem-solving process is divided into three phases:

1. Precise formulation of a mathematical model and related numerical model
2. Construction of a method to solve the numerical problem
3. Implementation of the method to compute a solution

This process is illustrated in Figure 3.1 with the sources of uncertainty identified. Blunders and "avoidable" errors (for example, copying the wrong formula or a program bug) are not considered here even though they are a real source of uncertainty in problem solving. The uncertainties introduced contaminate the solution, and it is important to attempt to *balance the uncertainties*. If the uncertainty in the mathematical model is about 1 percent, then it is pointless to implement a method so that 6 digits of accuracy are obtained in that phase of the solution. Balancing the uncertainties is not easy in large problems whose solutions are divided up among a dozen or a hundred people.

Real Problems and Mathematical Models 3.1.A

The formulation of mathematical models is outside the scope of this book, but this phase of problem solving is so important that a few general comments are in order. It is not practical for a mathematical model to represent every aspect of a real problem. The gravity of the moon exerts a force on a bridge, but it is not worthwhile to include it in a model used to design the bridge. The best models are those that include just those features of the real problem needed to reduce the uncertainty at this phase to an acceptable level.

It is natural when having trouble with a problem to adjust or enlarge the mathematical model. Caution should be exercised here, because one can change a model from one easy to analyze to one almost

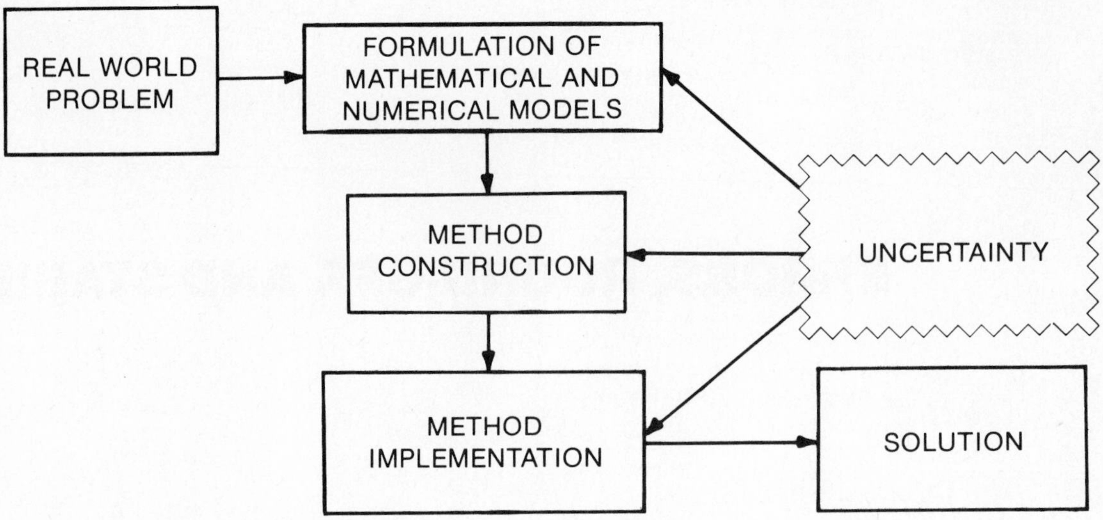

Figure 3.1 Diagram of the problem-solving process showing where uncertainties enter.

impossible to analyze just by adding a few terms here and there. A **common fallacy** in problem solving is the belief that enhancing the model will automatically lead to better results. The model enhancement may make the problem much more difficult mathematically or numerically and result in much larger uncertainties entering at later stages of the solution process. One must always keep the balance of uncertainties in mind when developing a model.

A mathematized model contains more than equations and relationships; it also contains data that must come from the real world. Uncertainties in the data can have the largest effect of all. Thus, variations (uncertainties) in the strengths of steel beams or bolts are more important in bridge design than the gravitational attraction of the moon.

Finally, one wants to keep in mind the possibility of *reformulating the model in a mathematically equivalent way.* If there is a cubic polynomial in the model, it can be written as $a + bx + cx^2 + dx^3$ or as $r(x - z_1)\ (x - z_2)\ (x - z_3)$. A simple change like this can reduce the computational difficulties and uncertainties by an order of magnitude. Part of the art of problem solving is knowing when such changes will help.

Constructing and Implementing Methods 3.1.B

Mathematics is used for model building because it provides a standard language and framework. This book is concerned with taking some of the standard pieces of models (for example, differential equations or matrix expressions) and producing actual numerical results. Some of this can, in principle, be done exactly (for example, solving 12 linear equations) and some cannot [for example, evaluating $\int_1^2 (\sin x)/(x + e^x)dx$]. Most of the methods and software in this book are for the latter situations; they compute things approximately which cannot be computed exactly.

When a standard mathematical problem is first attacked, the goal is just to be able to solve it, period. Later, one wants to solve it more efficiently or more accurately. Most of the problems considered in this book were first attacked a century or two ago, and so the emphasis now is on efficiency and accuracy. One reason there are so many methods is that their efficiency and accuracy vary considerably from example to example.

Problem solving is complicated by the fact that it is usually not practical to do the arithmetic exactly; the number of digits in the numbers gets too big. Thus, problems like solving linear equations, which can be done exactly in principle, are also solved only approximately in practice. This inexact arithmetic also adversely affects many of the approximate methods for problems that cannot be solved exactly.

NUMERICAL APPROXIMATIONS **3.2**

Frequently the first step in analyzing a mathematical model is to replace it by a **numerical model**. A numerical model is one where everything, in principle, can be calculated in a finite number of steps. Most of this is truncating, or stopping early, a mathematical limiting process that defines something. For example,

$$e^x = \sum_{m=0}^{\infty} \frac{x^m}{m!}$$

$$\frac{df}{dx} = \lim_{\delta x \to 0} \frac{f(x+\delta x) - f(x)}{\delta x}$$

must be replaced by finite, computable expressions. The exponential function is included in Fortran, and one just writes EXP(X); a finite scheme is used by the Fortran system to approximate e^x. The derivative can often be calculated analytically, but if not, then some formula to approximate it must be used. Several of these are presented later; the obvious formula

$$\frac{df}{dx} \sim \frac{f(x+\delta x) - f(x)}{\delta x}$$

using a very small value for δx is a poor choice.

Truncation Error **3.2.A**

The error made in truncating an infinite process is the **truncation error**. In many cases, the truncation error is exactly the difference between the mathematical model and the numerical model. One of the principal tasks of numerical analysis is to estimate theoretically the truncation error. One of the principal difficulties in actual computation is to realistically estimate the truncation error.

In most numerical models there is a parameter that governs the truncation error: for example, the number N of terms used in an infinite series or the size δx used in a derivative formula. A common and practical way to estimate the truncation error is to vary this parameter (let N get bigger or δx get smaller) and observe the computed results. If the computed results "settle down" or "converge" sufficiently, then we might decide the truncation error (as well as other computation errors) is small enough to produce an acceptable result. This process is testing for convergence, and many programs have a **convergence test** in them to decide when the results have converged sufficiently. Unfortunately, *testing for convergence is a mathematically unsolvable problem.* On an intuitive level this means that it cannot be done reliably; mathematically speaking, this means that given any test for convergence, there is a problem where this test fails. The following example illustrates this.

The Impossibility of Testing for Convergence in Integration **Example 3.1**

Suppose one is to compute

$$A = \int_1^2 \frac{\sin x}{x}\, dx$$

correct to 5 decimal digits. A numerical method will sum some values of $(\sin x)/x$ in some simple-minded or clever way, then apply a test to decide when to stop. A simple-minded numerical method might estimate A as

$$A \sim 0.1 \times \left[\frac{\sin(1.0)}{1.0} + 2 \times \frac{\sin(1.2)}{1.2} + 2 \times \frac{\sin(1.4)}{1.4} + 2 \times \frac{\sin(1.6)}{1.6} + 2 \times \frac{\sin(1.8)}{1.8} + \frac{\sin(2.0)}{2.0}\right]$$

using the six points 1.0, 1.2, 1.4, 1.6, 1.8, and 2.0.

Suppose the convergence test to compute A is eventually passed using N points x_i. Assume the x_i are numbered so that $x_i < x_{i+1}$ and consider the sawtooth function s(x) defined as follows (see Figure 3.2):

$s(x_i) = 0$ for all i

$s(y_i) = 1$ for $y_i = \dfrac{x_i + x_{i+1}}{2}$ and i = 1 to N − 1

s(x) is linear in between the x_i and y_i

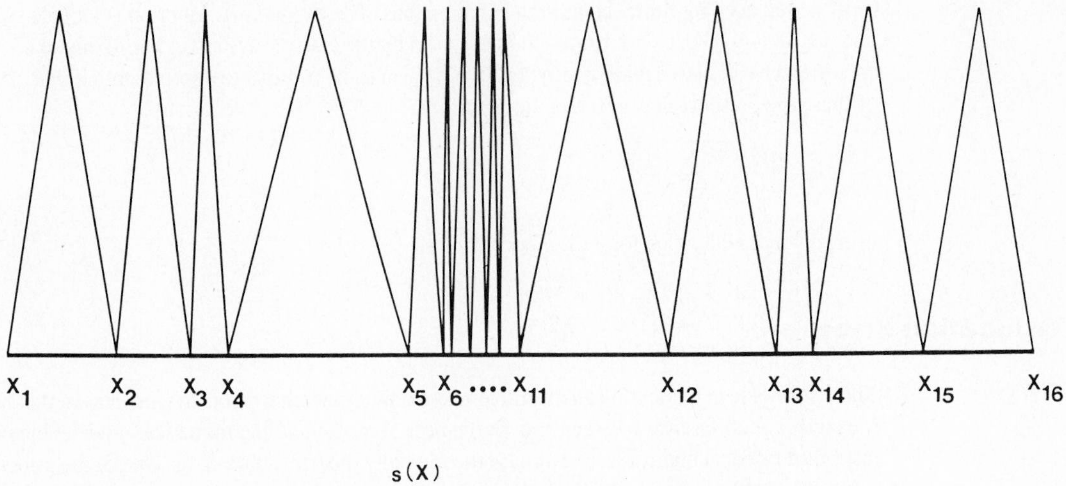

Figure 3.2 **The sawtooth function s(x) used to show that it is impossible to test for convergence.** The sawtooth is zero at all the points x_i used to estimate the integral value and is 1.0 halfway between the x_i.

Now consider using this method to integrate $g(x) = (\sin x)/x + c \times s(x)$; its integral is

$$G = \int_1^2 g(x)dx = \int_1^2 \frac{\sin x}{x} dx + c \int_1^2 s(x)dx = A + c \times B$$

where B is the integral of s(x) and is positive.

The numerical method produces exactly the same approximate value for A as for G because g(x) and (sin x)/x have exactly the same values at all the points x_i that the method uses. Yet by increasing c, the true values of the two integrals can be made as far apart as one pleases. Thus, we see that it is impossible to compute the values A and G of these integrals accurately.

The idea behind the above example can be adapted to any convergence test; this means that methods for numerical computation must always be prepared for problems that are impossible to solve. There are two **protective steps** to take here. The *first* is to *assume the difficulty does not exist.* More explicitly, one states in concrete terms which problems the method applies to and disclaims responsibility for the others. For the method in the example above, one can say that it applies only to functions which, for example,

1. Are monotonic

2. Oscillate at most once in any interval of length .0001 or less

3. Have second derivative less than 10 on [1, 2]

4. Have fourth derivative less than 10,000,000 on [1, 2]

Each of these assumptions rules out the "pathological" sawtooth function and allows one to devise a convergence test which always works (if we ignore the difficulties of round-off discussed in the next section).

It is important that one attempt to specify the assumptions of a numerical method, but one must admit that stating such assumptions is more pleasing in principle than in practice. We examine the very serious shortcomings for each of the four assumptions made above:

1. This one is easy to test, but it restricts the method to too small a set of problems.

2. This is easy to test, and most problems satisfy it, but its use requires the function to be evaluated at least 10,000 times during the computation. This is grossly excessive in almost all cases.

3. This assumption is rather restrictive; more seriously, one *cannot* test to see if it is satisfied. The calculation of a second derivative is itself an unsolvable problem for many functions.

4. This also cannot be tested reliably; it is not very restrictive, but its use requires excessive evaluation of the function in most cases.

The statement of assumptions as a protective step is helpful, but it rarely gives ironclad guarantees that a method will always work in practice. The **second protective step** is not to use a simple convergence test. Unless one is very sure of the situation, convergence should be double- or even triple-checked. It is usually not very expensive to use two or three convergence tests; only one is used until it is passed. Accepting a bad result might be rare, but it can also be costly.

Order of Convergence **3.2.B**

One needs to measure how fast the truncation error goes to zero as the parameters of the method vary. This is used for comparing methods and for obtaining an intuitive feel for the efficiency of a method. This is done by comparing the behavior of the truncation error with standard functions, and we say things such as

1. The method converges like $1/N$

2. The method converges like $1/k^{3.5}$

3. The method converges like h^2

4. The method converges exponentially (the error is, for example, like e^{-N})

5. The truncation error is of order $1/N^5$

6. The order of the error is h^4

7. The rate of convergence is $(\log N)/N$

The term **order of convergence** has a technical meaning as well as the general meaning used here. The phrase *rate of convergence* is also used for order of convergence. In iterative methods the order of convergence is calculated by a specific formula. If this result is 2, then one says the method is second order; a second-order method for differential equations is something completely different. The term *linear convergence* means that the error is reduced (approximately) by a constant factor at each step (the parameter of the method is usually an integer going to infinity). There is a precise mathematical definition and notation for order. The phrases "behaves like $1/N^2$" or "is of order $1/N^2$" are replaced by "$= 0(1/N^2)$." The **big 0** is defined as follows: *A function $f(x)$ is said to be $0(g(x))$ as x tends to L if*

$$\lim_{x \to L} \left| \frac{f(x)}{g(x)} \right| < \infty$$

We see that $5/N^2$, $10/N^2 + 1/N^3$, and $-6.2/N^2 + e^{-N}/N$ are all $0(1/N^2)$ as N tends to L = infinity while $4h$, $3h + h^2/\log h$, and $-h + h^2 - h^3$ are all $0(h)$ as h tends to L = zero.

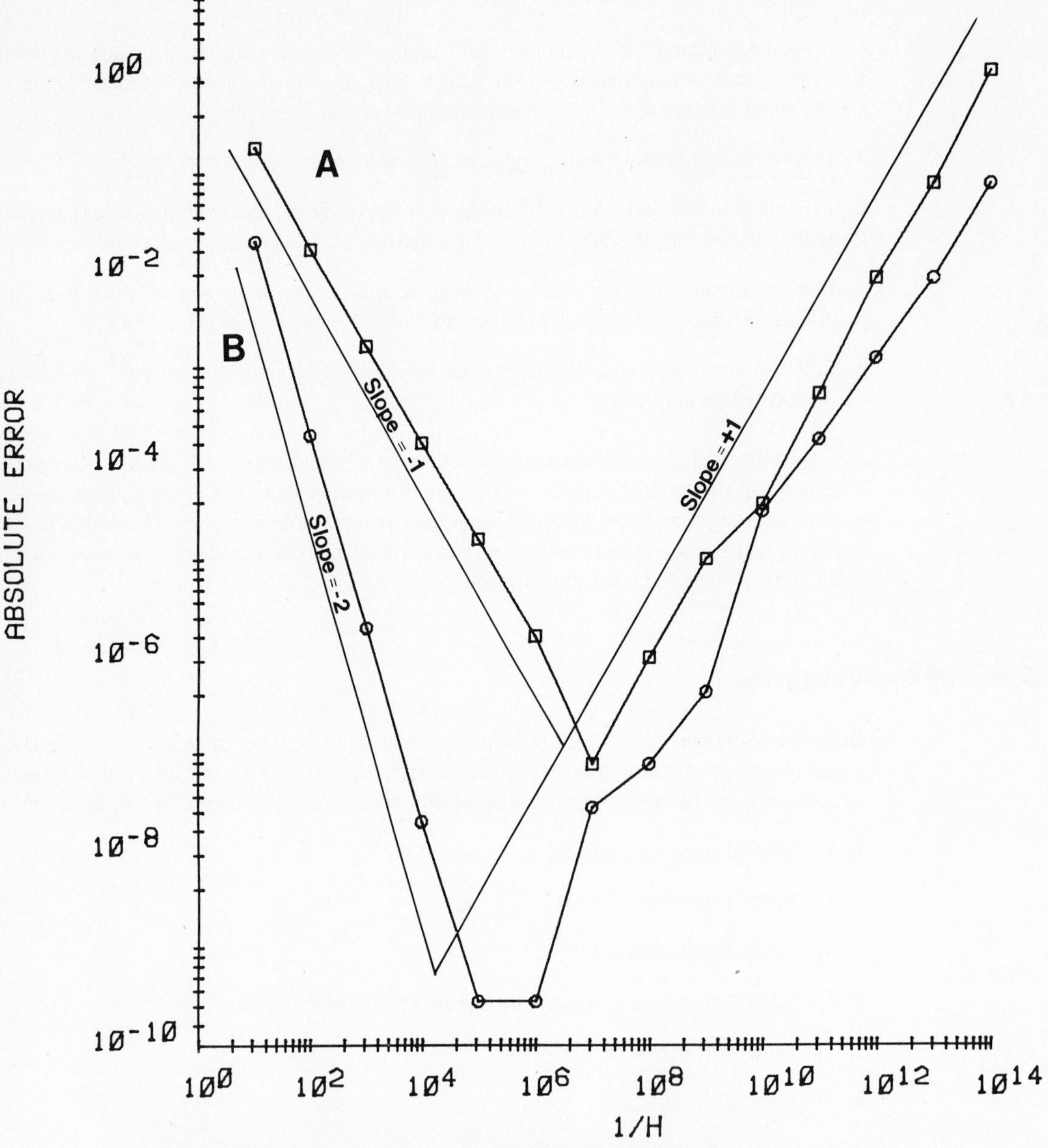

Figure 3.3 **Log-log plots of the error in simple difference formulas.** The orders of convergence are h for A and h^2 for B. Note that round-off effects ruin the formulas well before we obtain the accuracy of the 15 digits used in the computation. The round-off effect is of order h^{-1}.

The order of convergence can be complicated [for example, $h^{1.5}/(\log h)$], but for some simple cases special terms are frequently used. If the order is an integer power (for example, h^2, N^3, x^5), then one says the convergence order is that power (2, 3, or 5) or that the convergence is second, third, or fifth order. Similarly, one speaks of *exponential* or *logarithmic convergence* if the order involves an exponential function (such as e^{-N}) or a logarithm (for example, $1/\log N$ or $-1/\log h$).

Typical Orders of Convergence — Example 3.2

We consider the order of convergence for three computations:

1. Derivative estimation for $f(x) = \sin x^2$ at $x = .5$ by

A. $$\frac{f(x+h) - f(x)}{h}$$

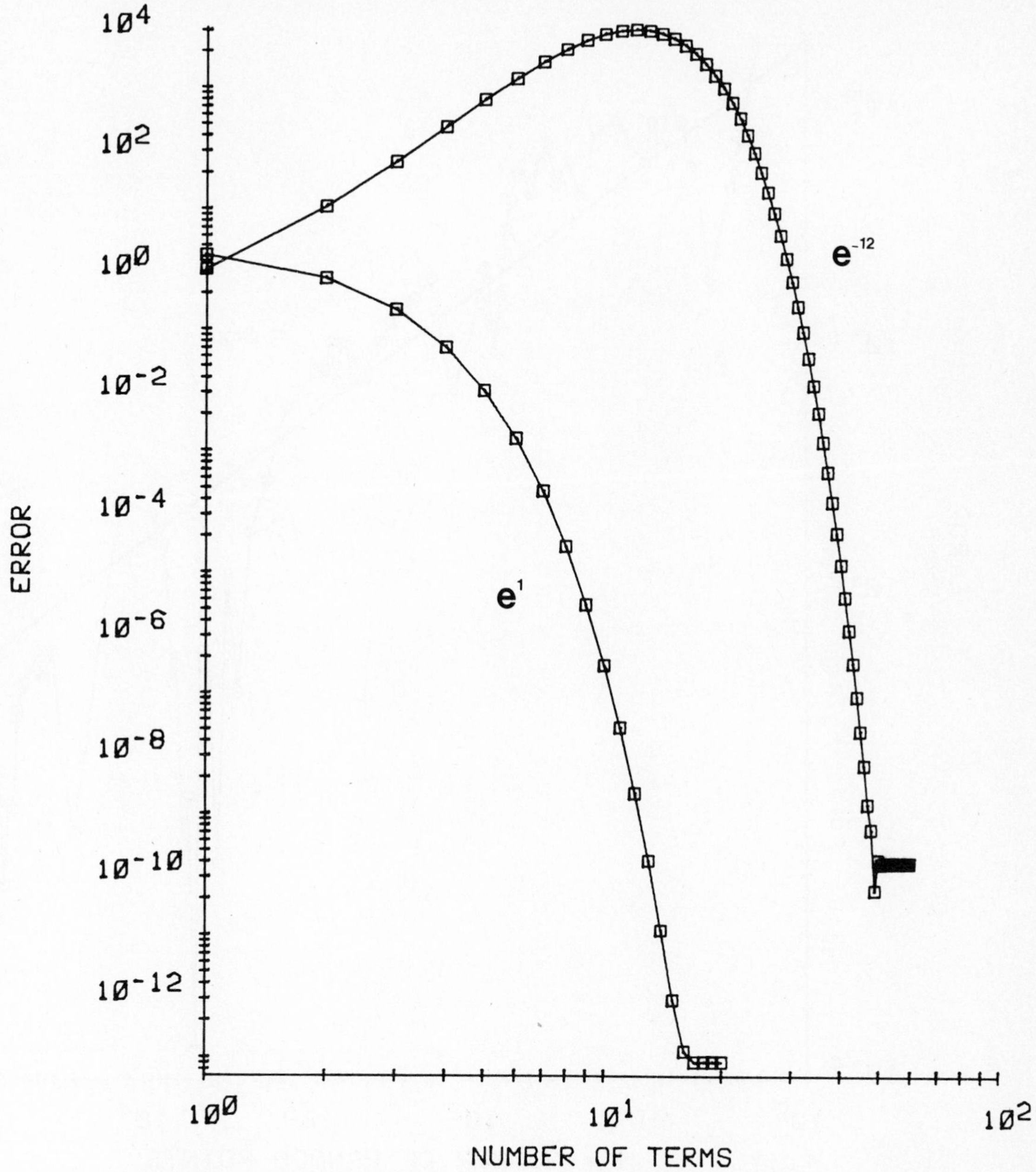

Figure 3.4 **Log-log plot of the error in Taylor's series for e^x.** The convergence is very fast; round-off ruins the accuracy at $x = -12$ before it does at $x = 1$.

B. $\dfrac{f(x+h) - f(x-h)}{2h}$

2. Taylor's series from e and e^{-12} from $e^x = \sum_{N=0}^{\infty} \dfrac{x^N}{N!}$.

3. Monte Carlo integration for $\int_0^2 \frac{2}{1+x}\,dx$. Here we choose a pair (x, y) at random with x, y in [0, 2], and compare y with $2/(1+x)$. If $y \le 2/(1+x)$, then the point (x, y) is under the curve $y = 2/(1+x)$ and 1 is added a variable SUM. After M pairs, the integral is estimated by the fraction SUM/M of points that are under the curve.

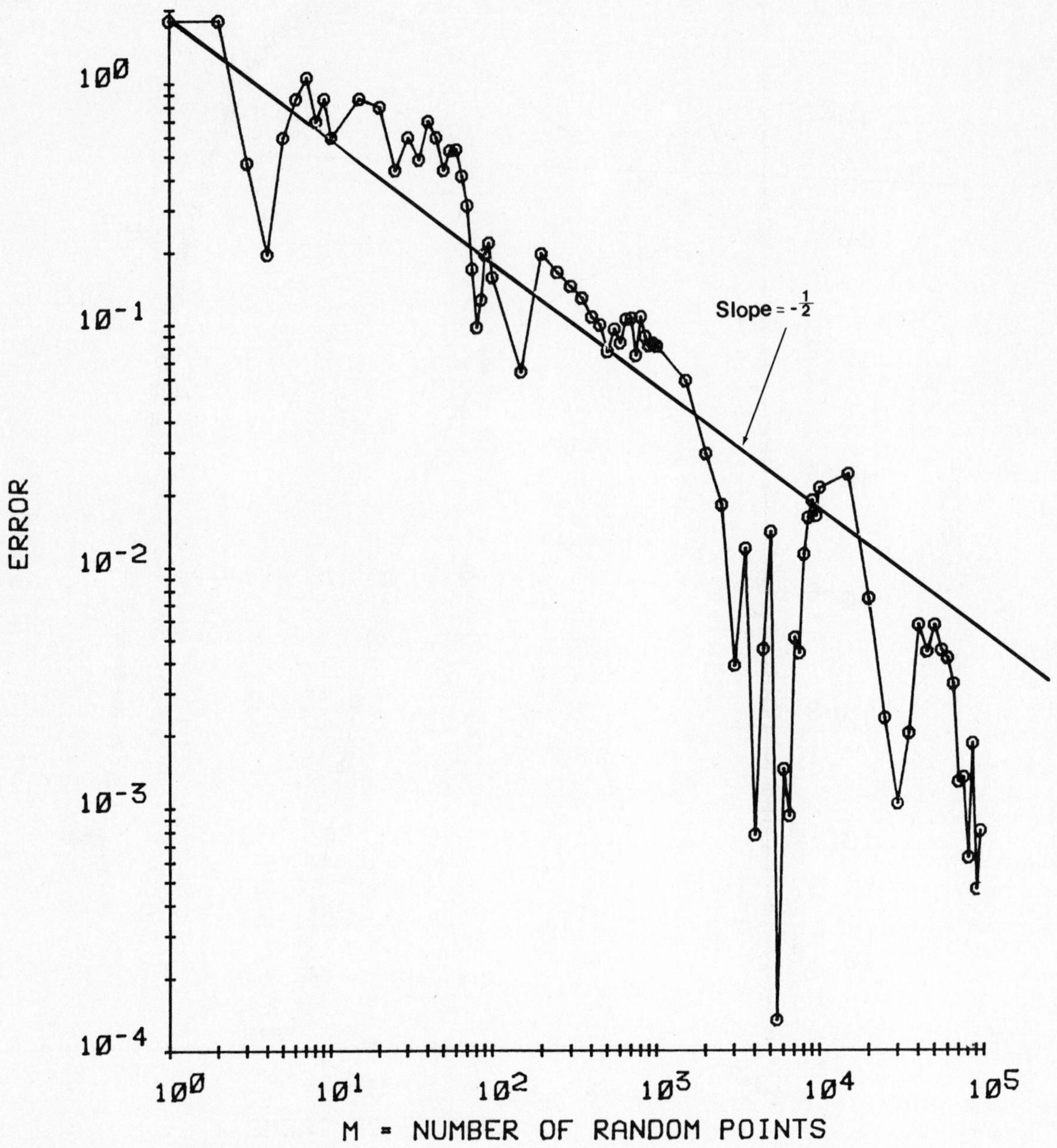

Figure 3.5 **Log-log plot of the error in Monte Carlo integration.** The convergence is $0(1/\sqrt{M})$, and this approach is not practical for accurate results.

The error versus the parameters (h, N = number of terms and M = number of points) are plotted in Figures 3.3, 3.4, and 3.5. The plots are on a log-log scale because this can directly show the exponent in the convergence rate. That is, if error = $(\text{parameter})^k$, then the slope of the plot is k. The theoretical orders of convergence for these three processes are h and h^2 for 1A and 1B, 1/N! for 2, and $1/\sqrt{M}$ for 3. The lines with slopes 1, 2, and $-1/2$ are plotted on Figures 3.3 and 3.5, and the observed error behavior agrees well with theory. The round-off error effect in Figure 3.3 is theoretically of order h^{-1}, and this experiment agrees well with this. The Taylor's series for e^x converges faster than any power of N, and so the error plot in Figure 3.4 is not linear on a log-log plot.

The random nature of the Monte Carlo estimates of the integral is obvious from Figure 3.5. The error does decrease as $1/\sqrt{M}$ in theory, and the observed errors do follow the line with slope $-1/2$ to a certain extent. The error is not a smooth function, and there are many large oscillations between the points plotted in Figure 3.5.

PROBLEMS 3.2

3.2.1 Experimentally determine the order of convergence of the following infinite series.

(A) $\sum_{N=1}^{\infty} \frac{1}{1+N^2}$

(B) $\sum_{N=1}^{\infty} \frac{2.5}{2N + 4N^4}$

(C) $\sum_{N=1}^{\infty} \frac{\cos(1/N)}{2 + 3N^{6.5}}$

Hint: Obtain a "true" value of the sums by taking a number of terms much larger than used in the rest of the experiment.

3.2.2 Examine the results for Problem 3.2.1 and give a rule that relates the order of convergence of such series with the powers that appear in the terms. Check that the rule applies to

(A) $\sum_{N=1}^{\infty} \frac{(-1)^N N + N^2}{1+ N^7}$

(B) $\sum_{N=1}^{\infty} \frac{1 + N^2 e^{-N/5}}{1 + N^6}$

3.2.3 Show both theoretically and experimentally that

$$\frac{\sin x}{x} = 1 + 0(x^2)$$

as x tends to zero.

3.2.4 The mathematical definition of an integral on [0, 1] leads to the **Riemann sum**

$$R_N(f) = \sum_{i=1}^{N} f(x_i)\delta x$$

where $\delta x = 1/N$ and $x_i = (i-1)/N$. Then we have

$$\int_0^1 f(x)dx = \lim_{N\to\infty} R_N(f)$$

Experimentally determine the rate of convergence in this limit as $N\to\infty$ for $f(x) = e^x$.

3.2.5 Replace the Monte Carlo integration of $2/(1 + x)$ in Example 3.2 by Riemann sum integration (see Problem 3.2.4). Experimentally determine the rate of convergence of this new method.

3.2.6 Singularities or near singularities can slow down the rate of convergence of difference formulas. Experimentally determine the rate of convergence of formula 1A of Example 3.2 applied to the following:

(A) $e^{-x^2/100}$ at $x = .1$

(B) $|x-1.23|^{1.23}$ at $x = 1.23$

3.2.7 Use the mean value theorem for derivatives to establish theoretically that formula 1A of Example 3.2 has order of convergence $O(h)$.

3.2.8 Two Taylor's series for logarithms are

$$\log(1+x) = x - \frac{x^2}{2} + \frac{x^3}{3} - \frac{x^4}{4} + \frac{x^5}{5} - \ldots$$

$$\log\left(\frac{1+x}{1-x}\right) = 2\left(x + \frac{x^3}{3} + \frac{x^5}{5} + \frac{x^7}{7} + \ldots\right)$$

(A) Use the first series to compute log 2; experimentally estimate its rate of convergence.

(B) Use the second series to compute log 2 (set $x = 1/3$) and experimentally estimate its rate of convergence.

3.2.9 A fast but not easily derived algorithm for π is the following, initialized with $A = 0$, $B = E = 1$, $D = .25$, and $C = 1/SQRT(2)$:

```
   DO 10 K=1, NLOOP
      A=B
      B=(B+C)/2.
      C=SQRT(A*C)
      D=D-E*(B-A)**2
      E=E+E
      PI1=B*B/D
      PI2=(B+C)**2/(4.*D)
10 CONTINUE
```

Implement this algorithm and compare the rates of convergence of PI1 and PI2 with the algorithms of the case study of Section 3.4.

3.2.10 We have

$$\lim_{x\to 0} \frac{(1-e^x)}{x} = 1$$

(A) Show this is correct by using the Taylor's series for e^x.

(B) Set $x = 1/k$ and let k go to infinity. Experimentally determine the rate of convergence in this limit as k goes to infinity.

ROUND-OFF ERRORS 3.3

Floating Point Arithmetic 3.3.A

It is not practical to do arithmetic exactly in a lengthy calculation. Numbers are represented inside a computer in some form of **scientific notation**; that is, x is represented by $m \times b^e$, where m is the *fractional part* or mantissa, b is the *base* (usually 2), and e is the *exponent*. A limited number of digits is allowed for m and e. For the sake of simplicity in this discussion, we assume that $b = 10$ and the limits on m and e are 6 and 2 digits, respectively, plus a sign. If the true result of a computation (say $.123456 \times 10^{-4}$ times

$.654321 \times 10^2$ or $.123456 \times 10^{-4}$ plus $.654321 \times 10^2$) requires more than 6 digits for m, then the result is rounded off to 6 digits some way. Ideally, one does **perfect rounding**, that is, rounds the true result to the nearest representable number and, in case of ties, rounds to the nearest even last digit. Many computers use much less satisfactory schemes; for example, **chopping** is where any extra digits are just discarded. If the number 1.23456999999 is chopped to six digits, it is represented as $.123456 \times 10^1$. Chopping the similar schemes can greatly increase the inaccuracies due to round-off errors. See Problem 3.3.10 for unexpected round-off errors that occur for computers with base 2 or 16. Table 3.1 gives the characteristics of the numbers for a variety of computers.

Floating Point Characteristics of Computers **Table 3.1**

b = base of the arithmetic
N = number of digits in the fractional part
M = number of digits in the exponent
ulp = one unit in the last place
rel = relative error in representing a number

	SINGLE PRECISION					DOUBLE PRECISION				
Computer	b	N	M	ulp	rel	b	N	M	ulp	rel
Burroughs 7700	8	13	2	2×10^{-12}	1×10^{-11}	8	26	5	3×10^{-24}	3×10^{-23}
CDC — 6000/7000										
Cyber 70/170	2	48	11	4×10^{-15}	7×10^{-15}	2	96	11	1×10^{-29}	3×10^{-29}
Cray	2	48	15	4×10^{-15}	7×10^{-15}	2	96	15	1×10^{-29}	3×10^{-29}
Data General	16	6	7†	6×10^{-8}	1×10^{-7}	16	14	7†	1×10^{-17}	2×10^{-16}
DEC — DEC 10	2	27	8	7×10^{-9}	1×10^{-8}	2	62	8	2×10^{-19}	4×10^{-19}
DEC 11/VAX	2	23	8	1×10^{-7}	2×10^{-7}	2	55	8	3×10^{-17}	6×10^{-17}
Harris	2	23	7	1×10^{-7}	2×10^{-7}	2	38	7	4×10^{-12}	7×10^{-12}
Hewlett Packard 3000	2	22	9	2×10^{-7}	5×10^{-7}	2	54	9	6×10^{-17}	3×10^{-16}
Honeywell 6000	2	27	7	7×10^{-9}	1×10^{-8}	2	63	7	1×10^{-19}	2×10^{-19}
IBM 360/370	16	6	7†	6×10^{-8}	1×10^{-7}	16	14	7†	1×10^{-17}	2×10^{-16}
IEEE standard chip	2	23	8	1×10^{-7}	2×10^{-7}	2	52	11	2×10^{-16}	5×10^{-16}
Perkin-Elmer	16	6	7†	6×10^{-8}	1×10^{-7}	16	14	7†	1×10^{-17}	2×10^{-16}
Prime	2	23	8	1×10^{-7}	2×10^{-7}	2	47	15	7×10^{-15}	1×10^{-14}
Siemens	16	6	7†	6×10^{-8}	1×10^{-7}	16	14	7†	1×10^{-17}	2×10^{-16}
Univac 1100	2	27	8	7×10^{-9}	1×10^{-8}	2	60	11	9×10^{-19}	2×10^{-18}
Xerox Sigma	16	6	7†	6×10^{-8}	1×10^{-7}	16	14	7†	1×10^{-17}	2×10^{-16}

†These are binary digits, not hexadecimal; the largest number is about $16^{128} = 10^{154}$ where $128 = 2^7$.

If the true result requires too many digits for the exponent e (say 1.2×10^{-38} times 2.1×10^{-66} or 1.2×10^{55} times 2.1×10^{51}), then we have **underflow** (e goes off the negative end of the exponent range) or **overflow** (e goes off the positive end of the exponent range). These events are very likely to completely ruin a computation, and most computer systems detect them and stop the computation.

Numbers in scientific notation are called **floating point numbers** or *real* numbers. There are also **fixed point numbers** or *integer* numbers, which are simply integers. Computers normally have separate hardware to process each of these two kinds of numbers. The floating point numbers are usually **normalized**; that is, the fractional part is between 1 and 1/b in size (that is, $b^{-1} \le |m| < 1$). This prevents us from having any leading zeros and maximizes the number of nonzero digits present to represent a number. Zero is a special number and cannot be normalized. Most computers also have special hardware for **double precision** numbers, which are floating point numbers with approximately twice as many digits for the fractional part. The use of double precision numbers and arithmetic greatly reduces the effect of finite precision arithmetic.

It is not easy to know in advance how much precision (number of digits in the fractional part) is needed to obtain satisfactory results from a computation. One always hopes that the precision built into the computer's number system (either single precision or double precision) is enough so that one does not have to worry about round-off errors. Unfortunately, one cannot just assume this is so, and there must be some check made. Chapter 14 is devoted to the validation of numerical computations, and several techniques are discussed there which can be used to check for round-off error effects. Here we just discuss the basic ideas of error propagation and show by examples that round-off errors can ruin a very ordinary computation very quickly.

Figure 3.6 shows how round-off can make a theoretically smooth curve into a jumbled mess. The polynomial $p(x) = (x - 1)^6$ is written out in the powers of x as

$$p(x) = x^6 - 6x^5 + 15x^4 - 20x^3 + 15x^2 - 6x + 1 \qquad \textbf{Equation 3.3.1}$$

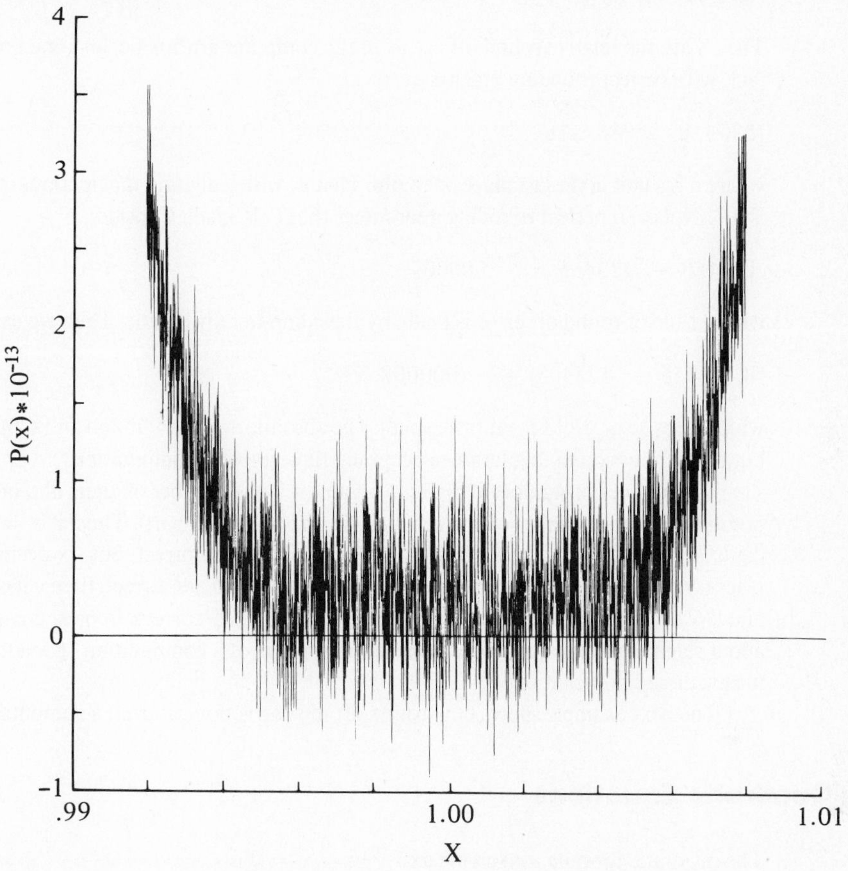

Figure 3.6 **Plot of the values of $x^6 - 6x^5 + 15x^4 - 20x^3 + 15x^2 - 6x + 1$.** It is evaluated in a Fortran statement with 14 decimal digits of accuracy. Theoretically, this polynomial is zero at $x = 1$ and positive everywhere else.

It is plotted near $x = 1$ in Figure 3.6. This example is an extreme case, but such occur more often than one expects. Visualize the difficulty a numerical method would have in solving the equation $p(x) = 0$.

Propagation of Round-Off Errors 3.3.B

Let $fl(op)$ indicate the floating point value obtained from the operation *op*. Here *op* stands for something like $a + b$ or $x \times y$. The error in the arithmetic due to round-off is then $op - fl(op)$. We may be interested in the **absolute error**

$$|fl(op) - op|$$

or the **relative error**

$$\frac{|fl(op) - op|}{|op|}$$

The relative error is usually the more important error measure: one wants to know how many digits in a computed result are correct, which is what the relative error indicates. There are simple formulas for the errors in arithmetic:

$$\begin{aligned} fl(x \times y) &= x \times y(1+\delta_1) \\ fl(x/y) &= x/y(1+\delta_2) \\ fl(x \pm y) &= x \pm y(1+\delta_3) \end{aligned}$$

The δ's are the relative round-off errors in the computer arithmetic, and one hopes that they are small. In fact, with perfect rounding one has

$$|\delta_1| \le u \qquad |\delta_2| \le u$$

where u is a **unit in the last place** or an **ulp.** That is, with k digits in the fractional part and with base b, an ulp is b^{-k}. Not even perfect rounding guarantees that δ_3 is small. Consider

$$.123456 - .123465 = -.000009$$

where 1 ulp of round-off error is made by the computer arithmetic. Then we can have

$$fl(.123456 - .123465) = -.000008$$

which gives $\delta_3 = .11111$, far from small. The absolute error of addition and subtraction is, of course, small, but this is not enough to guarantee accuracy throughout a computation.

The number of **significant digits** in a value x is the number of digits of x in floating point or scientific notation (i.e., the number of correct digits in the fractional part). Thus, if x = .00234976 and only the digits 234 are correct, then x has three significant digits correct, but six decimal digits and five decimal places correct. If y = 4042.693 and only the digits 40426 are correct, then y has both five significant digits and five decimal digits correct, but only one decimal place correct. In most computations one is concerned about significant digits, and when one loosely speaks of a computation "good to three digits," one usually means three significant digits.

The next example shows how round-off in subtraction can ruin a computation.

Solving Quadratic Equations — Example 3.3

The quadratic formula for solving $ax^2 + bx + c = 0$ is

$$x = \frac{-b \pm \sqrt{b^2 - 4ac}}{2a}$$

In a Fortran program to solve such a problem, one would expect to find something like

```
SDISC = SQRT(B*B-4.*A*C)
X1    = (-B+SDISC)/(2.*A)
X2    = (-B-SDISC)/(2.*A)
```

Suppose the Fortran code is run on a machine with 5 decimal digit arithmetic with A = 1, C = 2, and B varying as shown in the table below. We see that the value for X2 becomes 100 percent round-off error where B is as large as 1000.

B	SDISC	X2	True Value	Relative Error, Percent
5.2123	4.3781	−.4171	−.41708	.004
11.111	10.745	−.183	−.18302	.01
12.123	11.789	−.167	−.16728	.16
52.123	52.046	−.0385	−.038399	2.9
121.23	121.20	−.015	−.016500	9.1
521.23	521.22	−.005	−.0038371	30.3
1212.3	1212.3	0	−.0016498	100.0

The loss of accuracy in solving quadratic equations can be avoided in several ways. One of the simplest is to change the method to use the fact that the product $X1 \times X2$ of the roots equals the constant term C.

```
SDISC = SQRT(B*B-4.*A*C)
IF(B.LT.0)      THEN
     X1 = (-B+SDISC)/(2.*A)
  ELSE
     X1 = (-B-SDISC)/(2.*A)
ENDIF
X2 = C/X1
```

This method applied to $x^2 + 1212.3x + 2 = 0$ in 5 decimal digit arithmetic produces $X1 = -1212.3$ and $X2 = -.0016498$. These are the rounded values of the true solutions.

There are two important lessons to be learned from Example 3.3:

1. *Round-off errors can completely ruin a short, simple computation.*

2. *A simple change in the method might eliminate adverse round-off effects.*

The clue to the trouble in Example 3.3 is that two nearly equal numbers are subtracted, which allows the round-off error to become a dominant part of the result. When a computation is suspected of being sensitive to round-off, this is one of the things to look for.

−8.0000000000	−8.000000xxxx
32.0000000000	32.00000xxxxx
−85.3333333333	−85.33333xxxxx
170.6666666666	170.6666xxxxxx
−273.0666666666	−273.0666xxxxxx
364.0888888888	364.0888xxxxxx
−416.1015873015	−416.1015xxxxxx
416.1015873015	416.1015xxxxxx
−369.8680776014	−369.8680xxxxxx
295.8944620811	295.8944xxxxxx
−215.1959724226	−215.1959xxxxxx
143.4639816150	143.4639xxxxxx
−88.2855271477	−88.28552xxxxx
50.4488726558	50.44887xxxxx
−26.9060654164	−26.90606xxxxx
13.4530327082	13.45303xxxxx
−6.3308389215	−6.330838xxxx
2.8137061873	2.813706xxxx
−1.1847183946	−1.184718xxxx
.4738873578	.4738873xxx
−.1805285172	−.1805285xxx
.0656467335	.06564673xx
−.0228336464	−.02283364xx
.0076112154	.007611215x
−.0024355889	−.002435588x
.0007494119	.0007494119
−.0002220479	−.0002220479
.0000634422	.0000634422
−.0000175013	−.0000175013
.0000046670	.0000046670
−.0000012043	−.0000012043
.0000003010	.0000003010
−.0000000729	−.0000000729
.0000000171	.0000000171
−.0000000039	−.0000000039
.0000000008	.0000000008
−.0000000001	−.0000000001
Sum = 0.00033546	Sum = 0.0003xxxx

Another, less obvious instance of this occurs in computation 2 of Example 3.2. Note in Figure 3.4 that the accuracy of the value for e^{-12} is much lower than that of e. The largest term in the Taylor's series for e^{-12} is 9505, while the final result is about .000006. There must be subtractions taking place to cancel out the large terms, and this results in less accuracy in the final result. If the calculation is redone as in single precision on a short word length machine (the DEC VAX, for example), the estimated value for e^{-12} is −.000905, which has a relative error of about 15,000 percent.

The actual computed values of the terms for e^{-8} are listed on page 45 on the left, while on the right all digits past the seventh are replaced by x's. The x's represent unknown digits, and any digit in the sum which involves one of them cannot be accurate. As one sees, the fifth place to the right of the decimal point has numerous x's in it, and so the digit in that place of the sum cannot be correct (except by chance).

Stability and Condition of Problems 3.3.C

Some computations are very sensitive to round-off and others are not. In the example above, sensitivity to round-off was eliminated by changing the formula or method. This is not always possible; there are many problems which are inherently sensitive to round-off errors and any other uncertainties. Thus we must distinguish between sensitivity of *methods* and sensitivity inherent in *problems*.

The word **stability** appears throughout numerical computations and, in general, refers to continuous dependence of a solution on the data of the problem or method. If one says that a method is *numerically unstable*, one means that the round-off error effects are grossly magnified by the method. Stability also has precise technical meanings (not all the same) in different areas as well as this general one.

The large errors that can occur in an unstable computation are illustrated in the following simple example.

An Unstable Recurrence **Table 3.2**

i	COMPUTED VALUES FOR X_i (NUMBER OF DIGITS USED) 4	8	16	True Values of X_i
1	30.00	30.0000	30.0000	30.0000
2	25.00	25.0000	25.0000	25.0000
3	20.83	20.8333	20.8333	20.8333
4	17.36	17.3611	17.3611	17.3611
5	14.46	14.4676	14.4676	14.4676
6	12.07	12.0563	12.0563	12.0563
7	10.00	10.0470	10.0469	10.0469
8	8.518	8.3724	8.3724	8.3742
9	6.541	6.9773	6.9770	6.9770
10	7.121	5.8133	5.8142	5.8142
11	.925	4.8478	4.8452	4.8452
12	15.790	4.0296	4.0376	4.0376
13	−31.920	3.3888	3.3647	3.3647
14	108.700	2.7318	2.8039	2.8039
16	954.600	1.2978	1.9472	1.9472
18	8576.000	−4.4918	1.3522	1.3522
20	77170.000	−51.6565	.9390	.9390
22	6.9×10^5	−472.7080	.6521	.6521
25	-1.8×10^7	12781.1000	.3776	.3774
28	5.0×10^8	−345079.0000	.2134	.2184
30	4.5×10^9	-3.1×10^6	.1071	.1517
35	-1.1×10^{12}	7.5×10^8	10.8822	.0609
40	-1.1×10^{14}	-1.8×10^{11}	−2629.5300	.0245
50	1.5×10^{19}	-1.0×10^{16}	-1.5×10^8	.0039
75	1.3×10^{31}	9.2×10^{27}	1.3×10^{20}	.0000

An Unstable Recurrence Formula

Example 3.4

Solving differential equations usually leads to difference equations; for example,

$$X_{i+2} = -(13/6)X_{i+1} + (5/2)X_i$$

This equation defines a sequence of $X_1, X_2, X_3, X_4, \ldots$ once the first two values, X_1 and X_2, are given. The initial conditions of the differential equation become initial conditions for the difference equations, for example,

$$X_1 = 30 \qquad X_2 = 25$$

It would seem straightforward to solve for all the X_i; one just uses the difference equation itself to compute them in succession. Table 3.2 shows the values one obtains using 4, 8, and 16 decimal digit arithmetic. The true solution $X_i = 36(5/6)^i$ is also shown.

This difference equation is unstable, and the computation quickly "blows up." One nice thing about unstable computations is that they usually produce huge, nonsense numbers that one is not tempted to accept as correct. However, imagine that one wanted only 30 terms of the X_i and was using a computer with 16 decimal digits. How would one know that the last term is in error by 50 percent?

The word **condition** is used to describe the sensitivity of problems to uncertainty. Visualize the solution of a problem being obtained by evaluating a function f(x). Then, if x is changed a little to $x + \delta x$, the value f(x) also changes. The relative *condition number* of this change is

$$\frac{|f(x+\delta x) - f(x)|}{|f(x)|} \bigg/ \left|\frac{\delta x}{x}\right|$$

The expression may be rewritten as

$$\frac{f(x+\delta x) - f(x)}{\delta x} \times \frac{x}{f(x)}$$

and, for δx very small, we have

$$\text{Condition number} \sim \frac{xf'(x)}{f(x)}$$

Equation 3.3.1

This number estimates how much an uncertainty in the data x of a problem is magnified in its solution f(x). If this number is large, then the problem is said to be **ill-conditioned** or poorly conditioned.

This formula is for the simple case of a function of a single variable; it is not so easy to obtain such formulas for more complex problems that depend on many variables of different types. However, we can see three different ways that a problem can have a large condition number:

1. *$f'(x)$ may be large while x and $f(x)$ are not.*

If we evaluate $1 + \sqrt{|x-1|}$ for x very close to 1, then x and f(x) are nearly 1, but $f'(x)$ is large and the computed value is highly sensitive to changes in x.

2. *$f(x)$ may be small while x and $f'(x)$ are not.*

This is the reason for the behavior seen in Figure 3.5. The Taylor's series for sin(x) with x near π or e^{-x} with x large (see Example 3.2, computation 2) also exhibit this form of ill-conditioning.

3. *x may be large while $f'(x)$ and $f(x)$ are not.*

The evaluation of sin(x) for x near $1{,}000{,}000\pi$ is poorly conditioned.

One may also speak of a computation being ill-conditioned, and this is the same as saying it is numerically unstable. The condition number gives more information than just saying something is numerically unstable. The condition number gives more information than just saying something is numerically unstable. It is rarely possible to obtain accurate values for condition numbers but, fortunately, one rarely needs much accuracy; an order of magnitude is often enough to know.

Note that it is almost impossible for a method to be numerically stable for an ill-conditioned problem. The result actually computed can usually be interpreted as being equivalent to the exact result for slightly changed data for the problem. Thus round-off errors effectively change the data of the problem which, in turn, introduces large errors into the solution of an ill-conditioned problem. To see how this works, consider the problem of determining the height of a mountain on the moon by taking the difference between radar measurements of the distances to its top and bottom as measured from the earth. If the mountain is 1,000 meters high, then the exact quantities might be

Distance to top = 379,427,623 meters
Distance to bottom = 379,428,623 meters

If a round-off error of 1 unit in the seventh place is made in the subtraction, that is,

$$fl(379{,}428{,}623 - 379{,}427{,}623) = 900$$

then this 10 percent error in the result is equivalent to changing the distance to the top of the mountain from 379,427,623 to 379,427,723 meters.

An Ill-Conditioned Line Intersection Problem — Example 3.5

Figure 3.7 shows two nearly parallel lines; the problem is to compute the point P of their intersection. It is intuitively clear that a minor change in one line (shown dotted in Figure 3.7) changes the point of intersection to $(P + \delta P)$, which is far from P.

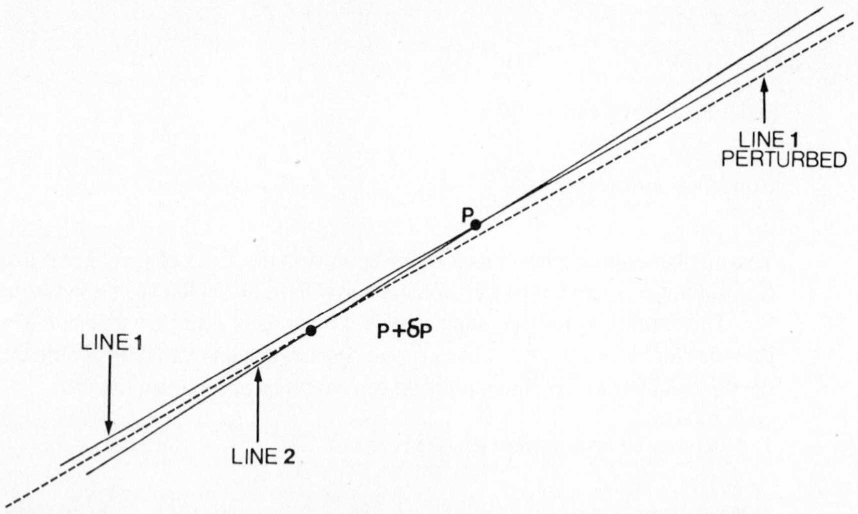

Figure 3.7 Illustration of the ill-conditioned problem of finding the intersection of two nearly parallel lines.

A mathematical model of this problem is obtained by introducing a coordinate system and writing equations for the lines, for example,

$y = a_1x + b_1$ for line 1
$y = a_2x + b_2$ for line 2

Then one would solve the linear system of equations

$$a_1x - y = -b_1$$
$$a_2x - y = -b_2$$

with the a_1 and a_2 nearly equal since the lines are nearly parallel. This numerical problem is unstable or ill-conditioned, as it reflects the ill-conditioning of the original problem.

Example 3.5 illustrates a poorly conditioned problem; there is nothing that can be done to make a method for its solution numerically stable. The next example seems to be the same, but it can be brought into a well-conditioned problem by a simple reformulation of the mathematical model. It is important to be able to recognize ill-conditioned problems and computations. It is even more important to be able to recognize when the ill-conditioning can be removed by a reformulation of the mathematical model or numerical method.

A Line Intersection Problem Made Ill-Conditioned by a Poor Choice of Coordinates

Example 3.6

Figure 3.8 shows two lines; the problem is to compute the point P of intersection. It is intuitively clear that this is a well-conditioned problem, yet a poorly conditioned computation can be obtained for it.

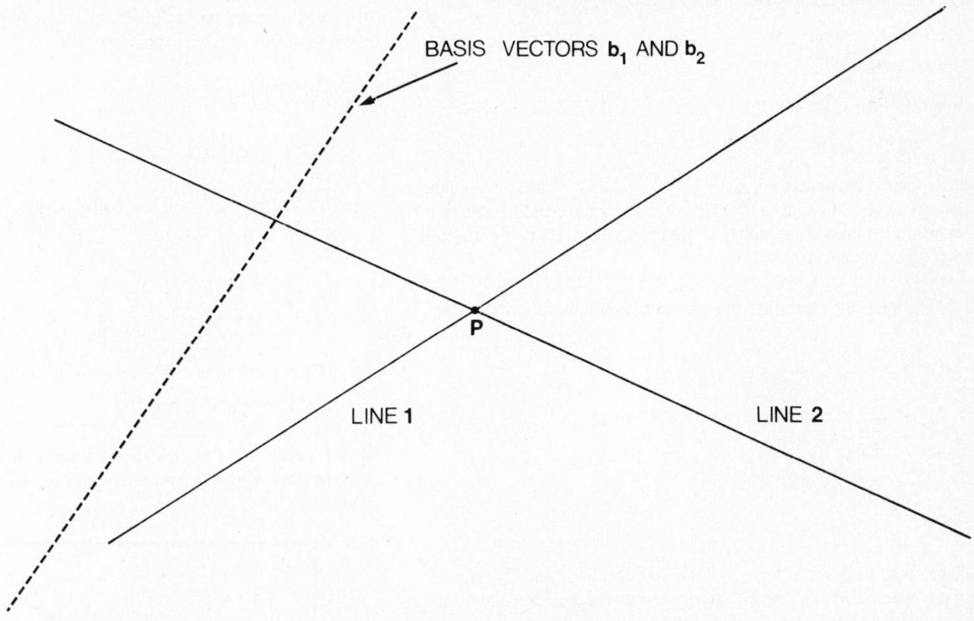

Figure 3.8 The illustration of the problem of finding the intersection of two lines. This problem is made ill-conditioned by choosing basis vector $\mathbf{b}_1$ and $\mathbf{b}_2$, which are nearly parallel and indistinguishable on this plot.

A mathematical model is obtained by introducing a coordinate system. Any two vectors will do for a basis, and we choose to use the unusual basis b_1 and b_2 in Figure 3.8, namely, in the usual coordinate system.

$$\mathbf{b}_1 = (.5703958095, .8213701274)$$
$$\mathbf{b}_2 = (.5703955766, .8213701274)$$

This seems to be silly; we comment on this after the example is finished. Every vector $\mathbf{x}$ can be expressed as

$$\mathbf{x} = x\mathbf{b}_1 + y\mathbf{b}_2$$

and (x, y) are the coordinates of a point in the plane.

The equations of the two lines in this coordinate system are

$$y = -.0000000513 + .9999998843x \qquad \text{for line 1}$$
$$y = -.0000015753 + 1.000001596x \qquad \text{for line 2}$$

and the point P of intersection has coordinates (−.8903429339, .8903427796). Note that the mathematical model (linear equations problem) is very ill-conditioned; a change of .0000017117 in the data (coefficient of x for line 1) makes the two lines parallel, and so there would be no solution.

The poor choice of a basis in the example above made the problem poorly conditioned. In this case it is easy to see that this is a silly choice; in more complex problems it is not so easy to see that a poor choice has been made. In fact, a poor choice is sometimes the most natural thing to do. For example, in problems involving polynominals, one naturally takes vectors based on 1, x, x^2, . . . , x^N as a basis, but these are terribly ill-conditioned even for N moderate in size.

PROBLEMS 3.3

3.3.1 The Taylor's series for cos(x) is

$$1 - x^2 + \frac{x^4}{4!} - \frac{x^6}{6!} + \ldots$$

Estimate the number of decimal digits of accuracy lost using this series to evaluate cos(5), cos(50), and cos(500).

3.3.2 The following expressions are numerically unstable for x near zero.

(A) $\dfrac{1 - \cos x}{\sin^2 x}$

(B) $\sin(100\pi + x) - \sin(x)$

(C) $2 - \sin x - \cos x - e^{-x}$

Evaluate these expressions for $x = 10^{-3}, 10^{-5}$, and 10^{-7}, and estimate the accuracy obtained. Manipulate the expression into a numerically stable form and estimate the accuracy obtained in evaluating them. **Hint**: Use Taylor's series or trigonometric identities.

3.3.3 The following expressions are numerically unstable for x very large.

(A) $x - \sqrt{x^2 - 1}$

(B) $e^{-\frac{2}{x}} - \dfrac{x}{1 + x}$

(C) $\sin\left(\dfrac{100\, x^5 \pi}{3 + x^5}\right)$

Evaluate these expressions for $x = 10^3$, 10^5, and 10^7, and estimate the accuracy obtained. Manipulate the expressions into a numerically stable form and estimate the accuracy obtained in evaluating them.

3.3.4 Compare the accuracy obtained by evaluating e^{-12} as in Example 3.2, using $e^{-12} = 1/e^{12}$ and then using the Taylor's series for e^{12}.

3.3.5 The following infinite series converges rapidly at first, then slows down drastically:

$$\sum_{N=1}^{\infty} \frac{N}{1 + N^5 e^{-N/5} + N^{2.5}}$$

(A) Estimate the rate of convergence based on examining the first 10 terms of the series.

(B) Estimate the rate of convergence based on examining the sum for 200 to 300 terms.

(C) Sum the first 500 terms of the series in 5-digit arithmetic (with chopping) in two orders: first terms from 1 to 500, then from 500 to 1. Explain the difference in the results. **Hint**: To implement 5-digit **chopping arithmetic**, use the following Fortran statements after the

```
SUM = SUM + TERM
```

statement:

```
NPOINT = ALOG10(SUM+1)
FACTOR = 10.**(5-NPOINT)
ISUM = FACTOR*SUM
SUM = FLOAT(ISUM)/FACTOR
```

3.3.6 Write a program to estimate experimentally the stability (condition number) for a given function at a given set of points. Let f(x) denote the function and XTRY(I) for I = 1, 2, . . . NTRY be the given points. Have the program print out its results in a nice format. Run this program for the following functons and point sets.

(A) $f(x) = \prod_{i=1}^{11} (x - i) - 10^{-7} x^9$

XTRY = 0, 1.5, 3, 7, 10, 11

(B) $f(x) = 128x^8 - 256x^6 + 160x^4 - 32x^2 + 1$

XTRY = 0, .5, 1.0, 2.5

(C) f(x) =

$$\frac{(3\sqrt{x - 2.6} + 1.26)\sin[(x+1)e^{.2(x+1)}]\cos[(x+1)e^{-.3(x+1)}]}{[1 + (x-2)^4]\,[(\sqrt{|x|} + 1)/(1 + 3\sqrt{|x|})] + \log[(1 + x^2)/(1 + \sin^2 x)]}$$

XTRY = 1, 0, 1, 2, 2.6, 200

3.3.7 Consider the triangle shown where a, h, and the angle θ are known, and the side b is to be determined by arithmetic and algebra (no trigonometry allowed).

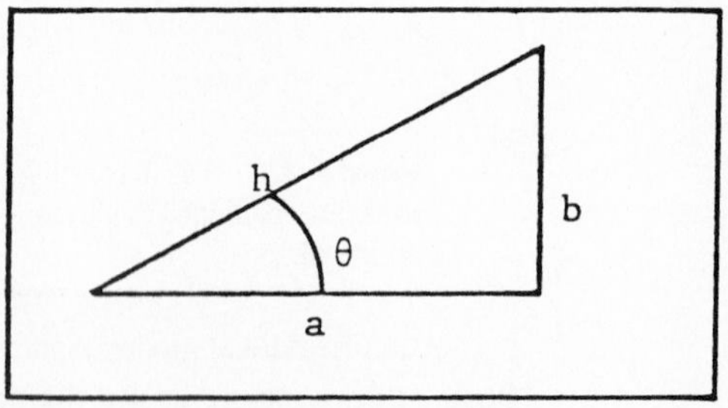

(A) Explain the difficulty with the formula $b = \sqrt{h^2 - a^2}$ that occurs where a and h are almost equal.

(B) Find another way to compute b which is accurate in this case. **Hint**: Try trigonometry and then replace the trig functions by series expansions or use the series expansion $\sqrt{1 - x} = 1 - x/2 - x^2/8 - x^3/16 - 5x^4/128 \ldots$

3.3.8 Consider a computer with precision in the arithmetic of 10 decimal digits. Suppose x and y are two numbers between 100 and 103. Estimate the relative errors in the computed values of xy, x + y, and x − y if the arithmetic in the machine (A) uses proper rounding and (B) chops.

3.3.9 The following Fortran program has different output depending on the computer and compiler used. Run it on your system and then explain how the results could differ. **Hint**: The computer must change the decimal numbers to the internal number system (usually binary). Some compilers are "clever" and precompute constants like 1./3. during the compilation, and they sometimes use different rounding for the arithmetic than during normal execution.

```
   THIRD = 1./3.
   HALF  = 1./2.
   I     = 3.*THIRD
   J     = 2.*HALF
   X     = 1.
   Y     = 3.
   Z     = X/Y
   K     = 3.*Z
   PRINT 10, THIRD, HALF, Z, I, J, K
10 FORMAT(3F15.10, 3I5)
   STOP
   END
```

3.3.10 There can be I/O (input-output) round-off just due to the Fortran input-output operations. The nature of it depends very much on the compiler and local system. The following program should show some of these effects. Run this program (or a slightly modified one) and explain the differences in the numbers read in and printed out.

```
   READ 10, X, Y, Z, W
10 FORMAT(4F15.10)
   PRINT 20, X, X, X, X
   PRINT 20, Y, Y, Y, Y
   PRINT 20, Z, Z, Z, Z
   PRINT 20, W, W, W, W
20 FORMAT(F15.10, F20.5, E15.5, O20)
   STOP
   END
```

Prepare input with X, Y, Z, W = .1, 1.0, 100.0, 10000000.0, 2.0625, 2.125, 2.2; .333333333, .5, .99999999, 1.00000001, 30.03125, 30.03152, 1.25390625, 1.35390625, and 1.37390625.

3.3.11 Consider the sum

$$Y = \sum_{N=K}^{L} 4^{\max(N,-100)} + \frac{1}{|N|+1}$$

Write two programs (or one combined program) that compute Y. One is to evaluate the sum from K to L (the usual way) and the other evaluates the sum backwards (from L to K). Run these programs for the following pairs of values of K and L: (−2000, 10), (−200, 18), (−200, 21). Explain the differences between the results and why one way of evaluating the sum is more accurate than the other.

3.3.12 Consider the following two Fortran programs:

```
   T=1./3.
   SUM=0.0
   DO 10 J=1,300
10    SUM=SUM+T
   PRINT 20,T,SUM
20 FORMAT(25X,2E20.15)
   STOP

   END
```

```
      REAL RANX(300)
C     GET 300 RANDOM NUMBERS
       CALL GGUBS(0.,300,RANX)
      T=1./3.
      SUM=0.0
      DO 10 J=1,300
         X=RANX(J)-.5
         SUM=SUM+(1.+X)*T
10       SUM=SUM-X*T
      PRINT 20,T,SUM
   20 FORMAT(5X,2E20.15)
      STOP
      END
```

(A) Determine the exact value of SUM for each program.

(B) Explain the difference in accuracy, if any, between the two programs and why one is more accurate than the other.

Hint: If the computer uses chopping, then the value from the first program will be low while the second will be more accurate.

3.3.13 Consider the problem of computing checking account balances for a bank. A Fortran program for this is outlined below with the crucial computation missing.

```
C     BAL=ACCOUNT BALANCE DW=DEPOSIT OR WITHDRAWAL
      BAL=0.0
      READ 5,NDW
    5 FORMAT(I6)
      DO 100 N=1, NDW
         READ 10,DW
   10    FORMAT(F10.2)
C        BALANCE CALCULATION GOES HERE
  100 CONTINUE
      IF(BAL.GT.0.) PRINT 200,BAL
      IF(BAL.EQ.0.) PRINT 210
      IF(BAL.LT.0.) PRINT 220,BAL
  200 FORMAT( '  POSITIVE BALANCE='F20.2)
  210 FORMAT( '  ZERO BALANCE')
  220 FORMAT( '  NEGATIVE BALANCE='F20.2/
     A        '  SEND OVERDRAFT LETTER')
      STOP
      END
```

(A) Almost all systems produce incorrect results if the balance calculation is done with the statement

```
BAL = BAL + DW
```

Run the program with NDW = 11, the first ten entries 1.10, and the eleventh −11.00, and see if your system computes the correct balance.

(B) Give a detailed analysis of the execution of the program with the input of part A which shows that a correct result cannot be obtained on a binary, octal, or hexadecimal machine which uses either proper rounding or chopping arithmetic. Assume only 5 digits for simplicity in the fractional part of the numbers.

(C) Give a Fortran code that does the calculation correctly. **Hint**: The calculation must be done in cents and not in dollars.

3.3.14 Consider the evaluation of $x^2 - y^2$ in a Fortran program. Assume that X and Y are computed values for x and y with relative errors ERRX and ERRY. The evaluation can be made as F, G, and H in the following three ways:

$$\begin{aligned}
F &= X\times X - Y\times Y \\
G &= (X+Y)\,(X-Y) \\
H1 &= (X+Y)\times X \\
H2 &= (X+Y)\times Y \\
H &= H1 - H2
\end{aligned}$$

(A) Express the errors of F, G, and H in terms of ERRX and ERRY. Give conditions on X and Y where the relative error in the computed result is much larger than ERRX or ERRY.

(B) Assume now that X and Y are exact values and that each arithmetic operation introduces an error of 1 ulp. Also consider the possibility of overflow or underflow (obtaining numbers whose exponents are too large or too small). Assume the arithmetic is evaluated in left to right order. Describe situations where each of these three methods is best for evaluating $x^2 - y^2$.

3.3.15 Consider the following program (MACHEP is to be provided a value near machine round-off):

```
    MACHEP=
    DO 20 J=1,200,20
       X=-J
       SINX=SIN(X)
       Y   =SINX**2+COS(X)**2
       FACT=X
       SIN2=0.0
       DO 10 L=1,100
          XL=2*L-1
          SIN2=SIN2+FACT
          FACT=-X*X*FACT/((XL+1)*(XL+2.))
          IF( ABS(FACT) .LT. MACHEP) GO TO 15
10     CONTINUE
       PRINT 11
11     FORMAT('  WHOOPS')
15     PRINT 18, X, Y, SINX, SIN2
18     FORMAT(F8.1, 3F20.10)
20  CONTINUE
    STOP
    END
```

(A) Explain what this program does.

(B) Explain the lack of accuracy in the values computed. Run the program to see what happens on your machine. The value of MACHEP and the format statements may need adjustment for your computer system.

3.3.16 The following program is a simple test of the **accuracy of the Fortran SIN/COS routines.** Run it on your system and estimate the accuracy you obtain. Compare that with what you would expect.

```
      REAL RANX(10)
C          GET 10 RANDOM NUMBERS
      CALL GGUBS(0., 10, RANX)
      A = 18.84955592
      DO    200 I = 1,5
            X  = RANX(J)*A
            ZS = SIN(X)+SIN(-X)
            ZC = COS(X)-COS(-X)
            Z3 = SIN(X)-(3.*SIN(X/3.)-4.*SIN(X/3.)**3)
            PRINT 100, X, ZS, ZC, Z3
  100       FORMAT( F15.8, 3F15.12)
  200 CONTINUE
C     NBIT IS NUMBER OF BITS IN FRACTIONAL PART
      NBIT =
      X = 1.
      DO    300 I = 1, NBIT
            X = X/2.
            IF( I .LT. NBIT/2) GO TO 250
            S  = SIN(X)
            DS = X - S
            RS = X/S
            PRINT 220, X, X, S, S, DS, RS
  220       FORMAT('  SIN TEST FOR X  = ' O21, E10.3/
     A             '            SIN(X) = ' O21, E10.3/
     B             '  DIFF,RATIO       = ' 2E10.3)
            GO TO 300
  250       C = COS(X)
            X2 = 1. - X * X
            DC = X2-C
            RC = X2/C
            PRINT 270, X, X2, X2, C, C, DC, RC
  270       FORMAT( '  COS TEST FOR X = ' E10.3/
     A              '  1 - X * X      = ' O21, E10.3/
     B              '  COS(X)         = ' O21, E10.3/
     C              '  DIFF,RATIO     = ' 2E10.3)
  300 CONTINUE
      STOP
      END
```

3.3.17 The program in Problem 3.3.16 uses trigonometric identities to check for accuracy. Comment on the usefulness of the following identities for such checking (the first one is attributed to Euler for this purpose).

(A) $\sin(x) = \sin(x+\pi/5) + \sin(x-\pi/5) - \sin(x+2\pi/5)$

(B) $\sin^3(x) = 1/4(-\sin^3 x + 3\sin x)$

(C) $\sin(5x) = 5\sin(x) - 20\sin^3(x) + 16\sin^5(x)$

Hint: Consider what happens for x very small or very large.

3.3.18 Run the program in Problem 3.2.9 with NLOOP so large that round-off effects affect its accuracy. How stable is this algorithm for π? Compare its stability with the algorithm in Section 3.4.

CASE STUDY: CALCULATION OF π 3.4

Five algorithms are given to calculate π which illustrate the various effects of round-off on somewhat different computations. The five algorithms are

1. *Infinite series*

$$\pi = 4(1 - 1/3 + 1/5 - 1/7 + 1/9 - \ldots)$$

2. *Taylor's series for arcsin(1/2) = $\pi/6$*

$$\pi = 6\left(.5 + \frac{(.5)^2}{2\times3} + \frac{1\times3(.5)^4}{2\times4\times5} + \frac{1\times3\times5(.5)^6}{2\times4\times6\times7} + \frac{1\times3\times5\times7(.5)^8}{2\times4\times6\times8\times9} + \ldots \right)$$

3. *Archimedes' method*

Place 4, 8, 16, ..., 2^P, ... triangles inside a circle as shown in the diagram for 8 triangles. The area of each triangle is 1/2 sin(θ). The values of sin(θ) are computed by the half-angle formula

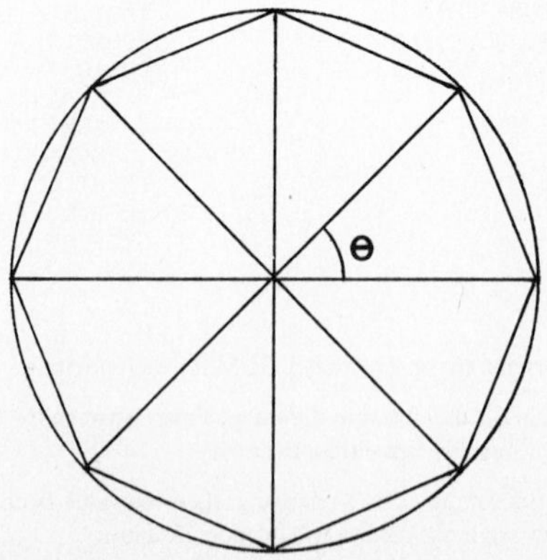

$$\sin(\theta) = \sqrt{[1-\cos(2\theta)]/2}$$

and

$$\cos(\theta) = \sqrt{1-\sin^2\theta}$$

The calculation is initialized by $\sin(\pi/4) = \cos(\pi/4) = 1/\sqrt{2}$. As the number of triangles grows, they fill up the circle and their total area approaches π. Archimedes carried out a similar procedure by hand with 96 triangles and obtained

$$3.1409\ldots = 3\frac{1137}{8069} < \pi < 3\frac{1335}{9347} = 3.1428\ldots$$

4. *Trapezoidal rule for quarter circle*

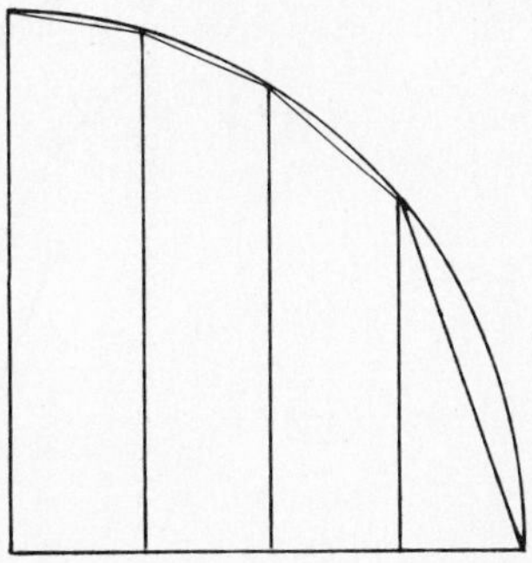

Instead of inscribing triangles in a circle, we inscribe trapezoids in a quarter circle as shown in the diagram. As the number of trapezoids increases, the sum of their areas approaches $\pi/4$.

5. *Monte Carlo integration*

Use the algorithm of Example 3.2, computation 3, to estimate the area of the quarter circle.

These algorithms are implemented in Fortran below. They were run on short word length machine (DEC VAX with about 7 decimal digits), and the results are given in Table 3.3.

Values for π Obtained by Five Methods **Table 3.3**

Computations made with 32-bit binary machine (VAX). Figure 3.9 gives log-log plots from calculations made with a 60-bit machine.

	METHOD				
K	1	2	3	4	5
1			2.828427		
2		3.1250000	3.061467		
3		3.1390624	3.121444		
4		3.1411550	3.136546		
5		3.1415110	3.140333		
6		3.1415765	3.141286		
7		3.1415892	3.141519		
8		3.1415918	3.141208		
9		3.1415923	3.142451		
10		3.1415923	3.142451		
12		3.1415923	3.162278		
15		3.1415923	2.828427		
20		3.1415923			
25		3.1415923			
100				3.140417	
200				3.141176	
500				3.141488	
1000	3.140593			3.141556	3.076000
2000	3.141090			3.141580	3.138000
3000	3.141260			3.141586	3.170667
4000	3.141345			3.141592	3.157000
5000	3.141397			3.141590	3.172000
8000	3.141472				3.161500
10000	3.141498				3.159600
20000	3.141547				3.158000
35000	3.141569				3.151886
50000	3.141573				3.143360

The main points to observe from this case study are that only one of the five methods achieves anything like the 7 decimal digits of accuracy that one would expect. Two of the algorithms are too slow (1 and 5) and, in any case, method 1 would have its result too heavily contaminated by round-off. Method 5 is only marginally affected by round-off, but it would take about 10^{14} pairs of random numbers to achieve

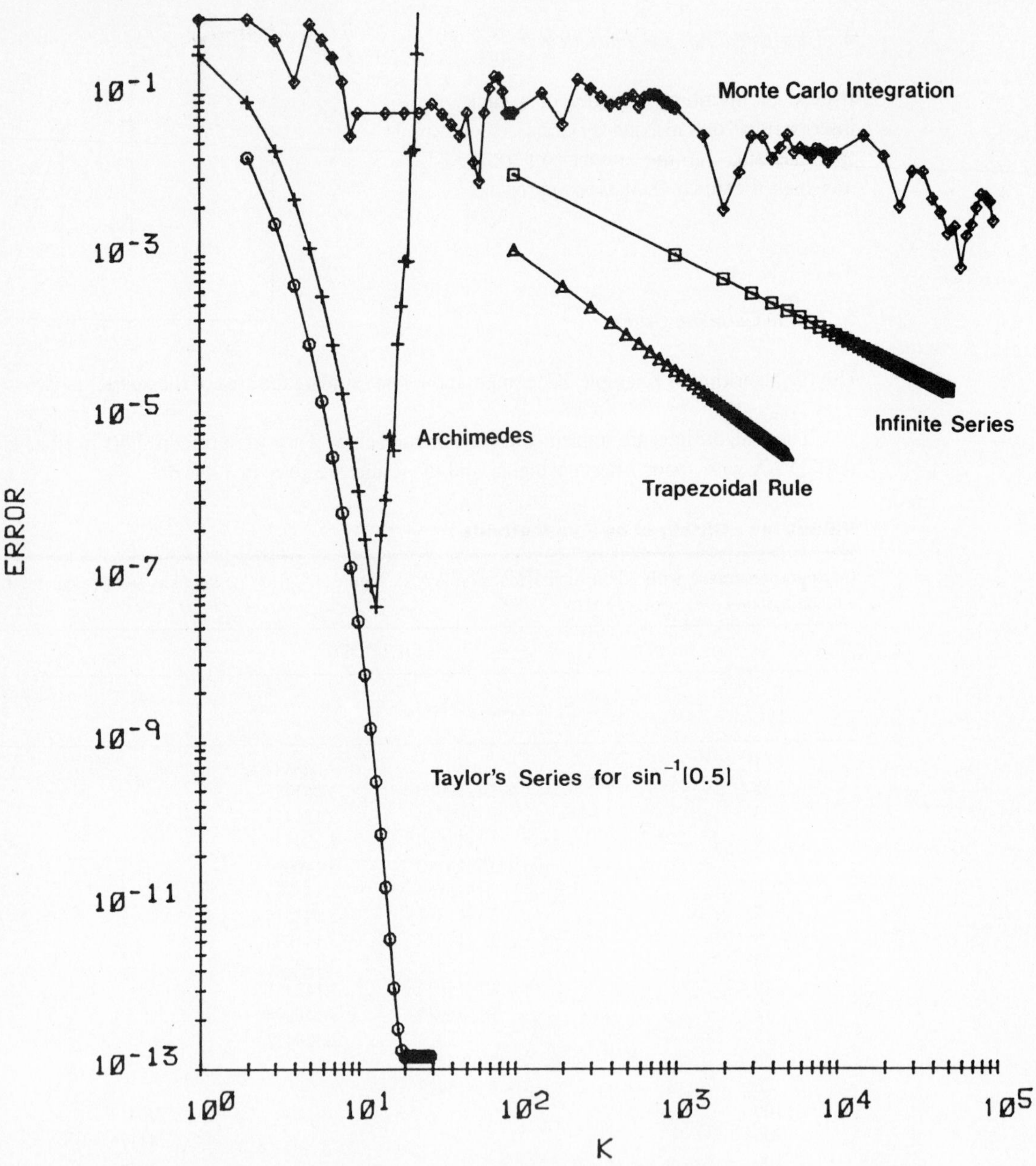

Figure 3.9 Log-log plots of the error for the five methods to estimate π. Computations made with 14.5 decimal digit arithmetic (CDC 6500).

7 digits of accuracy. Archimedes' method is rapidly convergent but also numerically unstable. It starts to blow up before it achieves more than 5 digits correct.

The method using trapezoids is converging; one can slow the error is $O(N^{-3/2})$, but round-off prevents a highly accurate result from being obtained.

The behavior of the methods is seen in Figure 3.9, where the error is plotted against the number of terms. One sees the wide difference in convergence rates and also where round-off starts to affect the accuracy. Methods 1, 2, and 5 have theoretical rates of convergence of $1/N$, $1/N^{1.5}$, and $1/N^{0.5}$, respectively. These rates are observed quite accurately for methods 1 and 2; method 5 shows a general trend compatible with the theory. Note that Archimedes' method is unstable, and that once the instability sets in, the error increases very rapidly.

Fortran Programs for Case Study 3.4

All five methods are combined into one program here. The output control was varied to produce all the data of Table 3.2.

```
C         AN ACCURATE VALUE OF PI
      DATA PI / 3.14159 26535 89793 23846 26433 83280 /
C
C      1.  INFINITE SERIES FOR PI
C     SIGN = PLUS OR MINUS FOUR
      SIGN = 4.0
      SUM  = 4.0
      DO 10 K= 2,50000
          SIGN = -SIGN
          SUM  = SUM  + SIGN/(2*K-1)
          ERR  = SUM -PI
          IF( MOD(K,1000) .EQ. 0 )
     A    WRITE(6,600) K,SUM,ERR, ALOG10(ABS(ERR)),ALOG10(FLOAT(K))
  600         FORMAT(I8,' TERMS,  SUM AND ERROR ='  2F17.12,'  LOGS OF ER
     AR AND K = ' ,2F8.4)
   10 CONTINUE
C
C      2.  TAYLORS SERIES FOR ARCSIN(.5) TIMES 6
C     TERM = NEXT TERM IN SERIES FOR X = .5
      SUM  = 3.0
      TERM = SUM*.25/6
      DO 20 K = 2,30
          SUM  = SUM + TERM
          TERM = TERM*(2*K-1)**2*.25/((2*K)*(2*K+1))
          ERR  = SUM - PI
          WRITE(6,600) K,SUM, ERR, ALOG10(ABS(ERR)),ALOG10(FLOAT(K))
   20 CONTINUE
C
C      3.  ARCHIMEDES METHOD
C
C     SINE   = SIN(THETA)          COSINE = COS(THETA)
      SINE   = 1./SQRT(2.)
      COSINE = SINE
      DO 30 K = 1,25
          SUM    = 2**(K+1)*SINE
          SINE   = SQRT((1.-COSINE)/2.)
          COSINE= SQRT(1.-SINE**2)
          ERR    = SUM - PI
          WRITE(6,600) K,SUM,ERR,ALOG10(ABS(ERR)),ALOG10(FLOAT(K))
   30 CONTINUE
C
C      4.  TRAZPEZOIDS FOR AREA OF QUARTER CIRCLE
C
C     NTRAP = NUMBER OF TRAPEZOIDS
      DO 40 NTRAP = 100,5000,100
          SUM  = 0.
          TRAP = NTRAP
C                    SIMPLE, INEFFICIENT SUMMATION USED HERE
          DO 35 K = 1,NTRAP
   35         SUM = SUM + SQRT(1.-((K-1)/TRAP)**2)
     A                  + SQRT(1.-(K/TRAP)**2)
          SUM = 2.*SUM/TRAP
          ERR = SUM - PI
          WRITE(6,600) NTRAP,SUM,ERR,ALOG10(ABS(ERR)),ALOG10(TRAP)
   40 CONTINUE
C
C      5.  MONTE CARLO INTEGRATION OF QUARTER CIRCLE
C
C     KOUNT = NUMBER OF TIMES RANDOM POINT IS INSIDE QUARTER CIRCLE
C             IT INCLUDES THE FACTOR OF 4
      KOUNT = 0
      DO 50 K = 1,50000
C              GET TWO RANDOM NUMBERS, UNIFORM ON (0,1)
          X = GGUBFS(1,357D0)
          Y = GGUBFS(1.357D0)
          IF( Y .LE. SQRT(1.-X*X)) KOUNT = KOUNT+4
          EST = KOUNT/FLOAT(K)
          ERR = EST- PI
          IF( MOD(K,1000) .EQ. 0 )
     A    WRITE(6,600) K,EST,ERR,ALOG10(ABS(ERR)),ALOG10(FLOAT(K))
   50 CONTINUE
      STOP
      END
```

Method 1 was run some years ago on an IBM 7094 with 8 decimal digit arithmetic (36-bit binary word). The results are shown in the table below. One can show theoretically that π is always strictly between the odd- and even-numbered estimates from this infinite series. From the 10,000th and 10,001st estimates, we have

$$3.14134410 < \pi < 3.14154407$$

and from the 49,999th and 50,000th we have

$$3.14074582 < \pi < 3.14078581$$

This incorrect result arises because round-off effects invalidate the theory. This computer uses chopping arithmetic, which means the result of adding a term to the sum of the series *always* rounds down. This introduced a "drift" in the computation, which caused the contradictory situation to arise.

100	3.13159150
200	3.13658985
500	3.13958517
1000	3.14057764
2000	3.14106262
2400	3.14114031
2600	3.14116955
3000	3.14121476
5000	3.14131844
8000	3.14134881
8001	3.14159879
10000	3.14134410
10001	3.14154407
20000	3.14124539
20001	3.14134538
49999	3.14974582
50000	3.14078581

HOW TO ESTIMATE ERRORS AND UNCERTAINITY 3.5

One almost never knows the error in a computed result unless one already knows the true solution, and so one must settle for estimates of the error. Much of this book is about how to make error estimates. Chapter 14 is devoted to this topic and summarizes the general approaches to this crucial topic. After all, if one is not concerned about the errors in a computation, one can write a program that prints .784279 for the answer and save all the costs of programming and execution.

There are three basic approaches to error estimation. The first is **forward error analysis**, where one uses the theory of the numerical method plus information about the uncertainty in the problem and attempts to predict the error in the computed result. The information one might use includes the size of round-off, the measurement errors in problem data, the truncation errors in obtaining the numerical model from the mathematical model, and the differences between the mathematical model and the original physical model. Often a forward error analysis is very complicated and long, and sometimes this approach is impossible even for crude predictions about the errors in complex computations. Forward error analysis tends to be pessimistic in that the predicted errors are usually larger, sometimes many orders of magnitude larger, than the actual errors.

The second approach is **backward error analysis**, where one takes a computed solution and sees how close it comes to solving the original problem. For example, if one is to solve an equation for X and finds that .7804 satisfies this equation to within .00000002 then one might say .7804 is good enough. This approach gives little or no information about the error in .7804 as a solution, but if the terms in the equation have measurement errors of .000005, there is little point in trying to find a more accurate solution. The backward error is often called the **residual** in equations. This approach requires that the problems involve satisfying some conditions (such as an equation) which can be tested with a trial solution. This prevents it from being applicable to all numerical computations, e.g., numerically estimating the value of π or the value of an integral.

The third approach is **experimental error analysis,** where one experiments with changing the computations, the method, or the data to see the effect they have on the results. If one truly wants certainty about the accuracy of a computed value, then one should give the problem to two (or even more) different groups and ask each to solve it. The groups are not allowed to talk together, preventing a wrong idea from being passed around. Such precautions are actually taken for critical parts of the design of aircraft, military systems, and space vehicles. There are less drastic and cheaper variations of this approach which can be used for more ordinary computations.

The relationship between these three approaches is illustrated in Figure 3.10.

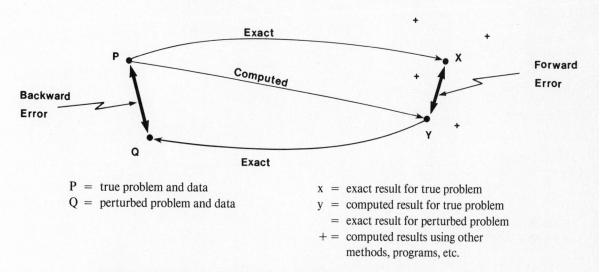

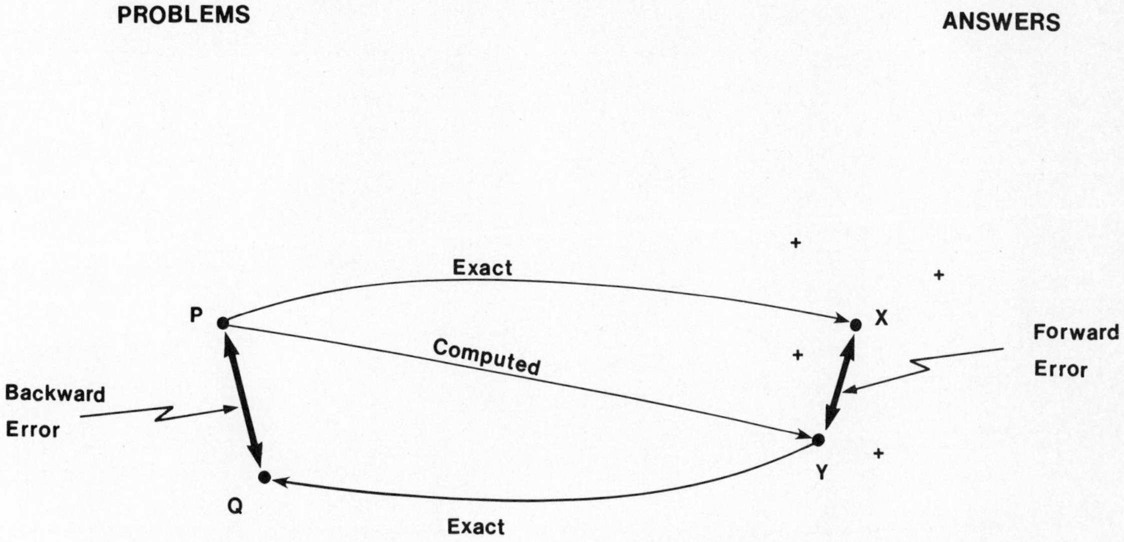

P = true problem and data
Q = perturbed problem and data

x = exact result for true problem
y = computed result for true problem
= exact result for perturbed problem
+ = computed results using other methods, programs, etc.

Figure 3.10 **The three approaches to estimating errors.** The forward error is the actual error in the computed solution y. The backward error is how close y comes to exactly solving the original problem. The four pluses are for other methods, and they, along with y, give an idea of how big the forward error is.

REFERENCES

Most texts in numerical analysis have a general introduction to round-off error and stability. The following book concentrates on the effects of round-off in program performance.

Pat H. Sterbenz, *Floating-Point Computation*, Prentice Hall, Englewood Cliffs, New Jersey (1974).

4

MODELS AND FORMULAS FOR NUMERICAL COMPUTATION

Methods for numerical computation involving functions are based on some assumption or **model** of these functions. There are two different models involved: (1) the numerical model defined in Chapter 3, which relates to modeling the mathematical objects and formulas, and (2) the function model discussed here. A function model should be as realistic as possible, and this is why there are so many numerical methods. Each time one incorporates some new information into a computation — or refines the model for a problem's solution — a new method results. The number of possible models is unlimited, but there are two standard models for functions — **polynomials** and **piecewise polynomials** — which are discussed in detail in this chapter.

Once the numerical and function models are chosen, then there is a standard approach for deriving numerical methods, at least for linear methods. This approach is the second topic in this chapter.

POLYNOMIALS 4.1

In deriving both formulas and approximations, one of the common objectives is to obtain expressions easy to manipulate and evaluate. This often means that polynomials are to be used; this section presents the basic techniques for handling polynomials in numerical computations.

Evaluation and Manipulation of Polynomials 4.1.A

A **polynomial** p(x) of **degree** n is a function of the form

$$p(x) = a_0 + a_1x + a_2x^2 + \ldots + a_nx^n \qquad \textbf{Equation 4.1.1}$$

If $a_n \neq 0$, then p(x) is said to be of *exact degree* n. Equation 4.1.1 is the **power form** of p(x) and is the standard mathematical representation for theoretical discussions. Numerical computations often benefit from using other representations, one of which is the *shifted power form*

$$p(x) = b_0 + b_1(x-c) + b_2(x-c)^2 + \ldots + b_n(x-c)^n \qquad \textbf{Equation 4.1.2}$$

It is easy to see that given the *center* c in this form, one can compute the a_i of Equation 4.1.1 from the b_i of Equation 4.1.2 and vice versa.

The reason for using other representations is that the **power form may be numerically unstable.** Consider a simple parabola centered at x = 5555.5:

$$p(x) = 1 + (x-5555.5)^2$$

Its power form representation is

$$p(x) = 30863581.25 - 11111x + x^2$$

If we now compute p(5555) and p(5554.5) in 6-digit arithmetic directly from the power form, we get

$$\begin{aligned} p(5555) &= .308636 \times 10^8 - .11111 \times 10^5 (.5555 \times 10^4) + (.5555 \times 10^4)^2 \\ &= .308636 \times 10^8 - .617216 \times 10^8 + .308580 \times 10^8 \\ &= 0 \\ p(5554.5) &= .308636 \times 10^8 - .617160 \times 10^8 + .308525 \times 10^8 \\ &= .000001 \times 10^8 = 100 \end{aligned}$$

Using the same arithmetic on the shifted form produces accurate results. Note that shifting can be accomplished by making a change of variable t = x − c and then using the power form. *It is always wise to make a change of variable to shift the center near the middle of the x values being used in a polynomial.*

The **Newton form** is a third representation which uses several different "centers" as follows:

$$\begin{aligned} p(x) = {} & a_0 + a_1 (x-c_1) + a_2 (x-c_1)(x-c_2) \\ & + a_3 (x-c_1)(x-c_2)(x-c_3) + \ldots \\ & + a_n (x-c_1)(x-c_2)(x-c_3) \ldots (x-c_n) \end{aligned}$$

Equation 4.1.3

The representations in Equations 4.1.1 and 4.1.2 are special cases of the Newton form; 4.1.2 has all the c_i equal and 4.1.1 has them all equal to zero. The Newton form is more easily written and evaluated in the **nested form**

$$\begin{aligned} p(x) = {} & a_0 + (x-c_1)[a_1 + (x-c_2)[a_3 + \ldots \\ & + (x-c_{n-1})[a_{n-1}) + a_n(x-c_n)]\ldots]] \end{aligned}$$

Equation 4.1.4

This form is efficiently evaluated starting from the inside and working out as specified by the following algorithm.

Nested Multiplication Algorithm for Evaluation of the Newton Form

Given the coefficients a_i and centers c_i of the Newton form for 4.1.3 and a point z, compute

$d_n = a_n$
For i = n−1, n−2, . . . ,0, do
  $d_i = a_i + (z-c_{i+1})d_{i+1}$
Then $p(z) = d_0$.

Algorithm 4.1.1

If one only wants to evaluate p(z), then one would just use one d value in this algorithm. However, these quantities are of interest in themselves because *the d_i are the coefficients of the Newton form with c_n replaced by z.* That is,

$$\begin{aligned} p(x) &= d_0 + (x-z)[d_1 + (x-c_1)[d_2 + (x-c_2)[d_3 + \ldots + (x-c_{n-2})[d_{n-1} + d_n(x-c_{n-1})]\ldots]]] \\ &= d_0 + (x-z)\, q(x) \end{aligned}$$

where $q(x)$ is a new polynomial of degree $n-1$. This fact may be established by directly substituting values for d_i from the algorithm into this form and then comparing this with Equation 4.1.3. Thus, the nested multiplication algorithm is useful for changing the set of c_i from one Newton form to another. In particular, by repeated application it can be used to change from the power form (where all the c_i are zero) to the Newton form.

Another application of the nested multiplication algorithm is given in Problems 4.1.2 and 4.1.3, where it is applied to produce the derivatives of the Newton form.

PROBLEMS 4.1

4.1.1 Use the nested multiplication algorithm to make the indicated changes in the following polynomials:

(A) $37024181 - 24339x + 4x^2$	Change centers to $x = 3042$
(B) $1 + (x-1)[2 + (x-2)[3 + 4(x-3)]]$	Replace center 3 by -1
(C) $1 - 6x + 18x^2 - 26x^3 + 54x^4$	Put in Newton form with centers $-2, -1, -1, +1$

4.1.2 Consider the following **algorithm for derivatives of Newton polynomial form.** The polynomial $p(x)$ is given in Newton form with coefficients $a_0, a_1, \ldots, a_n$, and centers $c_1, c_2, \ldots, c_n$, and the jth derivative at $x = z$ is required. Then

Step 1. Change the centers by the nested multiplication algorithm to be $z, \ldots, z, c_{j+1}, c_{j+2}, \ldots, c_n$ (the first j centers all z). Let $b_0, b_1, \ldots, b_n$ be the coefficients in the new representation.

Step 2. At $x = z$ we have

$$\frac{d^k p(x)}{dx^k} = k!b_k \qquad \text{for } k = 0, 1, 2, \ldots, j$$

Prove this algorithm is correct. **Hint:** Show that $p(x)$ in the new representation is

$$p(x) = \sum_{k=0}^{j} b_k(x-z)^k + (x-z)^{j+1}q(x)$$

where $q(x)$ is another polynomial.

4.1.3 Apply the algorithm for derivatives of Newton polynomial form (Problem 4.1.2) to compute the indicated derivatives of the following polynomials:

(A) $1 + (x-1)[2+(x-2)[3+4(x-3)]]$	Second derivative at $x = 0$
(B) $3 + (x-3)[1+(x+1)(x-2)[-1+4(x-5)]]$	First derivative at $x = 2.5$
(C) $-1 - (x+2)[-2-(x+3)[16+5(x-6)]]$	Second derivative at $x = 1$

4.1.4 Figure 3.3 shows a substantial round-off effect in evaluating e^{-12} from its Taylor's series. Consider four alternative ways to compute e^x for x near -12:

Method 1. Use the Taylor's series.

Method 2. Obtain the Taylor's series for e^x at $x = -12$. That is,

$$e^x = \sum_{n=0}^{\infty} a_n (x+12)^n$$

where $a_n = e^{-12}/n!$ and e^{-12} is evaluated by dividing 1 by e 12 times.

Method 3. Take the Taylor's series and apply the nested multiplication algorithm successively to generate polynomials centered at $x = -12$, which represent the partial sum of the Taylor's series. Then evaluate these polynomials.

Method 4. Use the Taylor's series for e^x for x near 12 and then take the reciprocal.

(A) Carry out each of these four methods and use them to evaluate $e^{-12.5}$. Make log-log plots of the error similar to Figure 3.3 and discuss the success of each method in reducing round-off effects.

(B) Discuss the applicability of each of these four methods to a more complicated function which is known only from its Taylor's series expansion, for example,

$$f(x) = \sum_{n=0}^{\infty} a_n x^n \qquad a_n = \frac{(1+1/n)}{(n-2/n)n!}$$

4.1.5 Write an efficient Fortran code to evaluate a polynomial and its derivative with coefficients A(I), I = 1 to NDEGRE. Put the code inside the following program, complete the program, and run typical cases.

```
      REAL A(20)
      READ 10, NDEGRE, (A(K), K=1, NDEGRE)
    5 READ 11, X
      IF (  X .EQ. 123456.) STOP
C              EVALUATE POLYNOMIAL P AND DERIVATIVE PPRIME
      PRINT 20, X, P, PPRIME
      GO TO 5
      END
```

PIECEWISE POLYNOMIALS 4.2

Examples given later show that polynomial models have some very severe limitations in practice. Since the 1960s it has been realized that piecewise polynomials do not have these limitations, and yet they are almost as simple to use as ordinary polynomials. They are now used in all areas of numerical computation. A piecewise polynomial $pp(x)$ is a set of k polynomials $p_i(x)$ of degree n and $k+1$ **break points** (or *knots*) t_i so that

$$pp(x) = p_i(x) \qquad \text{for } x \epsilon [t_i, t_{i+1}],\ i = 1, 2, \ldots, k \qquad \textbf{Equation 4.2.1}$$

The information about $pp(x)$ is an array A of polynomial coefficients.

$A = (a_{ij})$ where $p_i(x)$ has coefficients $a_{i0}, a_{i1}, \ldots, a_{in}$

and the set $T = (t_1, t_2, \ldots, t_{k+1})$ of break points.

The evaluation of a piecewise polynomial occurs in two steps. Given x,

Step 1: Locate the index i so that the interval $[t_i, t_{i+1}]$ contains x

Step 2: Evaluate the ith polynomial $p_i(x)$ by nested multiplication

Note that different representations can be used for each piece of pp(x). Stable numerical evaluations usually occur if the polynomial pieces are centered at the break points. That is, one should use the representation

$$p_i(x) = a_{i0} + a_{i1}(x-t_i) + a_{i2}(x-t_i)^2 + \ldots + a_{in}(x-t_i)^n$$ **Equation 4.2.2**

There are many ways to carry out Step 1 of the evaluations of pp(x). A simple linear search of the intervals is not bad if there are only a few break points. If there are many break points, then one should be more clever and use some form of binary search. For nine break points (eight polynomial pieces) one first tests if $x \geq t_5$ (t_5 is the middle point); then, according to the outcome, one next tests if $x \geq t_3$ or if $x \geq t_7$ (t_3 and t_7 are the 1/4 and 3/4 points). One more test serves to locate the interval. In general, a binary search can locate the correct interval out of 2^n intervals with only n tests.

The software collection PPPACK has an extensive set of programs for handling piecewise polynomials and splines. The next example shows one of the programs INTERV of this package; it is designed to carry out Step 1 of piecewise polynomial evaluation. The program is longer than one expects because it makes a number of checks on the search for the interval (a sign of robust software). It is difficult to read the program because it is designed to be very efficient in certain situations. The design of this program involves a model of its use where one is frequently "walking along" pp(x) in the evaluation [for example, in plotting pp(x)]. The program saves the previously located interval and starts the binary search there.

The Program INTERV for Locating the Interval in Evaluating a Piecewise Polynomial

Example 4.1

The comments in this program explain its operation, so this is not repeated here. An interesting sidelight about this program is that many attempts have been made to rewrite the program to make it much more understandable without sacrificing any efficiency. These attempts have not met with much success, and thus the program is a prime example for the debate about how much, if any, efficiency must be sacrificed in order to obtain well-structured, understandable programs.

One should consider INTERV as a low-level building block for piecewise polynomial software, and thus the value placed on efficiency is much higher than for general programming. One can argue that, like programs for Fortran Input/Output or evaluating sin(x), no one wants to read INTERV; they just want to get the result quickly.

```
      SUBROUTINE INTERV ( XT, LXT, X, LEFT, MFLAG )
COMPUTES  LEFT = MAX( I , 1 .LE. I .LE. LXT  .AND.  XT(I) .LE. X )  .
C
C******  I N P U T  ******
C  XT.....A REAL SEQUENCE, OF LENGTH  LXT , ASSUMED TO BE NONDECREASING
C  LXT.....NUMBER OF TERMS IN THE SEQUENCE  XT .
C  X.....THE POINT WHOSE LOCATION WITH RESPECT TO THE SEQUENCE  XT  IS
C        TO BE DETERMINED.
C
C******  O U T P U T  ******
C  LEFT, MFLAG.....BOTH INTEGERS, WHOSE VALUE IS
C
C   1    -1      IF                X .LT.  XT(1)
C   I     0      IF   XT(I)  .LE. X .LT. XT(I+1)
C  LXT    1      IF  XT(LXT) .LE. X
C
C        IN PARTICULAR,  MFLAG = 0 IS THE 'USUAL' CASE.  MFLAG .NE. 0
C        INDICATES THAT  X  LIES OUTSIDE THE HALFOPEN INTERVAL
C        XT(1) .LE. Y .LT. XT(LXT) . THE ASYMMETRIC TREATMENT OF THE
```

```
C          INTERVAL IS DUE TO THE DECISION TO MAKE ALL PP FUNCTIONS CONT-     200
C          INUOUS FROM THE RIGHT.                                             210
C                                                                             220
C****** M E T H O D ******                                                    230
C    THE PROGRAM IS DESIGNED TO BE EFFICIENT IN THE COMMON SITUATION THAT     240
C    IT IS CALLED REPEATEDLY, WITH  X  TAKEN FROM AN INCREASING OR DECREA-    250
C    SING SEQUENCE. THIS WILL HAPPEN, E.G., WHEN A PP FUNCTION IS TO BE       260
C    GRAPHED. THE FIRST GUESS FOR  LEFT  IS THEREFORE TAKEN TO BE THE VAL-    270
C    UE RETURNED AT THE PREVIOUS CALL AND STORED IN THE  L O C A L  VARIA-    280
C    BLE ILO . A FIRST CHECK ASCERTAINS THAT  ILO .LT. LXT (THIS IS NEC-      290
C    ESSARY SINCE THE PRESENT CALL MAY HAVE NOTHING TO DO WITH THE PREVI-     300
C    OUS CALL). THEN, IF  XT(ILO) .LE. X .LT. XT(ILO+1), WE SET  LEFT =       310
C    ILO  AND ARE DONE AFTER JUST THREE COMPARISONS.                          320
C        OTHERWISE, WE REPEATEDLY DOUBLE THE DIFFERENCE  ISTEP = IHI - ILO    330
C    WHILE ALSO MOVING  ILO  AND  IHI  IN THE DIRECTION OF  X , UNTIL         340
C                    XT(ILO) .LE. X .LT. XT(IHI) ,                            350
C    AFTER WHICH WE USE BISECTION TO GET, IN ADDITION, ILO+1 = IHI .          360
C    LEFT = ILO  IS THEN RETURNED.                                            370
C                                                                             380
       INTEGER LEFT,LXT,MFLAG,   IHI,ILO,ISTEP,MIDDLE                         390
       REAL X,XT(LXT)                                                         400
       DATA ILO /1/                                                           410
C      SAVE ILO  (A VALID FORTRAN STATEMENT IN THE NEW 1977 STANDARD)         420
       IHI = ILO + 1                                                          430
       IF (IHI .LT. LXT)                    GO TO 20                          440
          IF (X .GE. XT(LXT))               GO TO 110                         450
          IF (LXT .LE. 1)                   GO TO 90                          460
          ILO = LXT - 1                                                       470
          IHI = LXT                                                           480
C                                                                             490
   20  IF (X .GE. XT(IHI))                  GO TO 40                          500
       IF (X .GE. XT(ILO))                  GO TO 100                         510
C                                                                             520
C              **** NOW X .LT. XT(ILO) . DECREASE  ILO  TO CAPTURE  X .       530
       ISTEP = 1                                                             540
   31     IHI = ILO                                                          550
          ILO = IHI - ISTEP                                                  560
          IF (ILO .LE. 1)                   GO TO 35                          570
          IF (X .GE. XT(ILO))               GO TO 50                          580
          ISTEP = ISTEP*2                                                    590
                                            GO TO 31                          600
   35  ILO = 1                                                               610
       IF (X .LT. XT(1))                    GO TO 90                          620
                                            GO TO 50                          630
C              **** NOW X .GE. XT(IHI) . INCREASE  IHI  TO CAPTURE  X .       640
   40  ISTEP = 1                                                             650
   41     ILO = IHI                                                          660
          IHI = ILO + ISTEP                                                  670
          IF (IHI .GE. LXT)                 GO TO 45                          680
          IF (X .LT. XT(IHI))               GO TO 50                          690
          ISTEP = ISTEP*2                                                    700
                                            GO TO 41                          710
   45  IF (X .GE. XT(LXT))                  GO TO 110                         720
       IHI = LXT                                                             730
C                                                                             740
C              **** NOW XT(ILO) .LE. X .LT. XT(IHI) . NARROW THE INTERVAL.    750
   50  MIDDLE = (ILO + IHI)/2                                                 760
       IF (MIDDLE .EQ. ILO)                 GO TO 100                         770
C      NOTE. IT IS ASSUMED THAT MIDDLE = ILO IN CASE IHI = ILO+1 .           780
       IF (X .LT. XT(MIDDLE))               GO TO 53                          790
          ILO = MIDDLE                                                       800
                                            GO TO 50                          810
   53     IHI = MIDDLE                                                       820
                                            GO TO 50                          830
C**** SET OUTPUT AND RETURN.                                                  840
   90  MFLAG = -1                                                            850
       LEFT = 1                                                              860
                                            RETURN                            870
  100  MFLAG = 0                                                             880
       LEFT = ILO                                                            890
                                            RETURN                            900
  110  MFLAG = 1                                                             910
       LEFT = LXT                                                            920
                                            RETURN                            930
       END                                                                    940
```

PROBLEMS

4.2

4.2.1 Write a program to evaluate a piecewise polynomial pp(x) using INTERV of Example 4.1. Its first line should be

```
REAL FUNCTION PPVALU (BREAK,COEF,K,N,X)
```

where COEF   = array of dimension N by K of polynomial coefficients

BREAK   = list of break points in increasing order

K   = number of break points less one

N   = degree of polynomial pieces plus one

Note that there is no "last" break point, so pp(x) has its last polynomial piece extending to infinity.

4.2.2 Use the program PPVALU from Problem 4.2.1 (or PPPACK) to create a program to plot piecewise polynomials. Run the program on several examples to show that it works. **Hint:** Use the IMSL library routine USPLT for the plotting.

4.2.3 Describe an algorithm that uses simple binary search to locate the knot interval $[t_i, t_{i+1}]$ that contains a given point x. Implement this algorithm in Fortran as INTERB with the same first line as the program INTERV. Develop a set of test data for INTERB that indicates that it is correct. Run this set of data with the input and output nicely labeled to verify that INTERB works.

4.2.4 Repeat Problems 4.2.1 and 4.2.2 with INTERB of Problem 4.2.3 replacing INTERV.

4.2.5 Study the program INTERV and the methods used to provide extra efficiency, and compare them with the program INTERB of Problems 4.2.3. Describe two applications of splines: (A) one where INTERV is much more efficient than INTERB, and (B) one where the two programs are of nearly equal efficiency.

SPLINES 4.3

While piecewise polynomials do not have the flexibility weakness of ordinary polynomials, they are not nice smooth curves that one usually likes to use. **Splines** are piecewise polynomials of degree n joined together at the break points with $n-1$ continuous derivatives. The break points of splines are called **knots,** presumably because this is where the polynomial pieces are tied together. If n is 2 or 3 or more, then the spline is smooth. Most people believe that the eye cannot see a jump in the third derivative of a curve, so that a cubic polynomial spline always appears smooth to the eye.

There are two classical examples of splines, the **step functions** (splines of degree 0) and **broken lines** (splines of degree 1). Examples of them are illustrated in Figure 4.1, and neither of them is smooth. A parabolic spline approximation to a histogram is shown in Figure 4.2 and appears quite smooth. The histogram has height h_i at the knot t_i, and the area under each piece of the parabolic spline is the same as the corresponding step in the histogram. Detailed examination of parabolic splines can reveal jumps in the second derivative (curvature) of the curves.

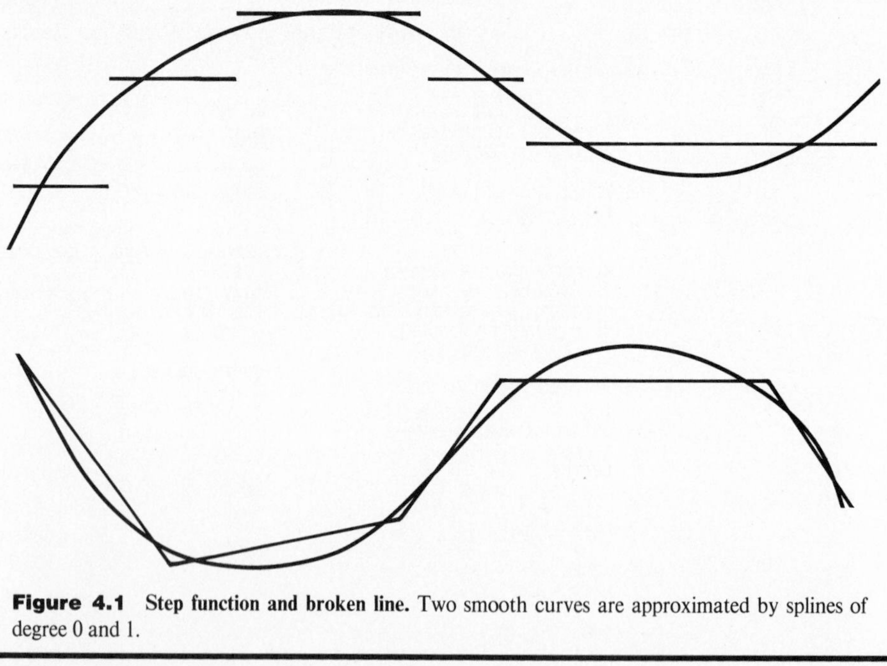

Figure 4.1 **Step function and broken line.** Two smooth curves are approximated by splines of degree 0 and 1.

There are more than aesthetic reasons for having continuous curvature. Suppose the curve is used in a numerically controlled milling machine. The program in the milling machine makes the tool follow the curved path; if there is a jump in the second derivative of the curve, then there must be a jump in the force applied to the tool (recall that force = mass × acceleration and acceleration is the second derivative of position). An attempt to make a jump change in the force may gouge the material being milled and ruin it.

There are more ways to represent splines than piecewise polynomials in general because the smooth joining conditions allow one to eliminate some coefficients. This is most easily seen for the broken lines

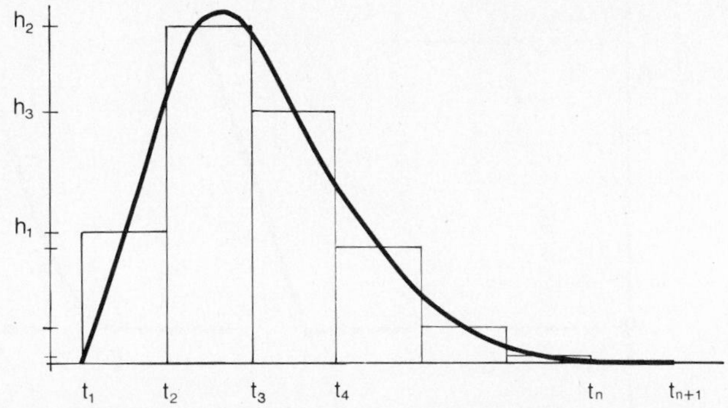

Figure 4.2 **A parabolic spline.** This parabolic spline is computed so that it has the same area in each piece of the histogram shown. Note that a histogram is just a spline of degree 0.

where one only needs to have the knots and values at the knots. This representation uses a_{i0} and t_i, $i = 1, 2, \ldots, k+1$ (note there is one more a_{i0} here than in Equation 4.2.1). It is more compact with only $2k + 2$ numbers, compared with $3k + 1$ for Equation 4.2.1, but it is more work to evaluate. Once the correct ith interval is found, one would use the formula

$$a_{0i} + \left[\frac{a_{0,i+1} - a_{0i}}{t_{i+1} - t_i} \right] (x - t_i)$$

to evaluate pp(x). Thus, we have to calculate a_{1i} [the coefficient of $(x - t_i)$] during the evaluation.

A similar representation exists for higher-degree splines. To derive it, consider going along the spline starting from the left end. In the first interval $[t_1, t_2]$, the spline can be any polynomial, so we need the coefficients $a_{10}, a_{11}, \ldots, a_{1n}$. In the next interval, the first $(n-1)$ derivatives of $p_2(x)$ are determined at t_2 to be equal to those of $p_1(x)$ at t_2; they can be calculated from the a_{1j} for $j = 0$ to n. The nth derivative of $p_2(x)$ at t_2 may be anything; let us call $n!b_2$ the *jump* or change in the nth derivative moving from $p_1(x)$ to $p_2(x)$. Since the $p_i(x)$ are polynomials of degree n, the nth derivative of pp(x) is just a step function and $n!b_2$ is the size of the jump at the first step. This process can now be repeated for the third knot, fourth knot, etc. (we ignore how one would actually evaluate all the derivatives to be matched up because they are not going to be used explicitly). Thus, we get a representation of pp(x) with the coefficients a_{1j} of $p_1(x)$ plus the jumps b_i for $i = 2, 3, \ldots, k$. The number of coefficients is $n+k$ compared to $k(n+1)$ for the usual piecewise polynomial representation.

The representation developed above can be put into a simple mathematical form using the **truncated power basis.** We use the function

$$(x-t)_+^i = \begin{cases} (x-t)^i & \text{if } x \geq t \\ 0 & \text{if } x \leq t \end{cases}$$ **Equation 4.3.1**

which is usually viewed as a function of x with t as a parameter. These functions are plotted for $i = 0, 1, 2$, and 3 in Figure 4.3. The integrals and derivatives of $(x-t)_+^i$ are easily computed; in particular, one sees that similar to the power functions x^i, one has

$$\frac{d^j(x-t)_+^i}{dx^j} = i(i-1) \ldots (i-j+1)\,(x-t)_+^{i-j} \qquad \text{for } j \leq i$$

Thus, the nth derivative of $(x-t)_+^n$ is just a step function, 0 to the left of t and n! to the right. This is exactly the kind of function needed to move from $p_1(x)$ to $p_2(x)$; $p_1(x) + b_2(x-t_2)_+^n$ in the second interval $[t_2, t_3]$ is just $p_1(x)$ with a jump of $n!b_2$ in the nth derivative at t_2. Thus, we have the **truncated power representation of splines.**

$$pp(x) = \sum_{j=0}^{n} a_j(x-t_1)^j + \sum_{i=2}^{k} b_i(x-t_i)_+^n$$ **Equation 4.3.2**

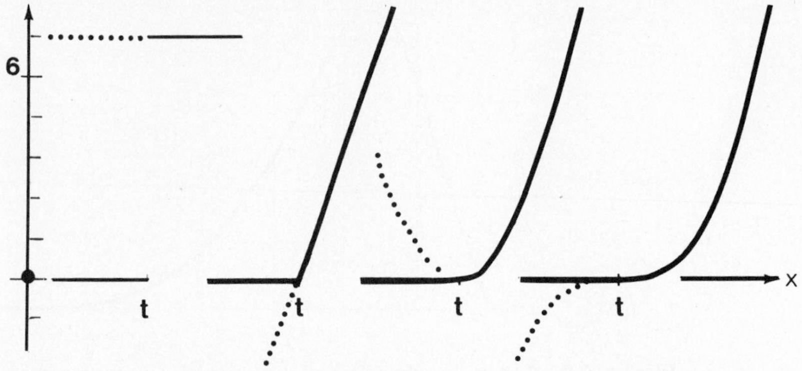

Figure 4.3 **The truncated power basis functions.** The functions $6(x-t)_+^0$, $6(x-t)_+$, $3(x-t)_+^2$, and $(x-t)_+^3$ are plotted for $t-2 \le x \le t+2$. Note how they become smoother and the eye cannot see the break in the cubic one.

The truncated power representation is very useful for analytical and theoretical studies of splines. Unfortunately, it is sometimes *numerically unstable.* For large k, the b_i become rather large with alternating signs, which introduces cancellation errors in the evaluation of 4.3.2. This is analogous to what happens when ordinary polynomials become numerically unstable.

A Broken Line Whose Truncated Power Representation Is Numerically Unstable — Example 4.2

The broken line is shown in Figure 4.4; most of the derivative jumps are chosen to be zero so that this example will be simple. The knots are .01, 1.01, 2.01, 3.01, 4.01, 5−h, 5+h, 6.01, 7.01, 8.01, 9.01, and 10. The .01s are present so that roundoff occurs in a calculation. This broken line f(x) has the representation

$$f(x) = 1.25 + b_4(x-4.01)_+ + b_5(x-5+h)_+ + b_6(x-5-h)_+ + b_7(x-6.01)_+$$

The slope between t_5 and t_6 is large, $-.75/h$, as h becomes small. Thus b_5 is large, negatively. This must be corrected by b_6, so it is large positively. A further correction is needed for the next interval, so b_7 is not zero.

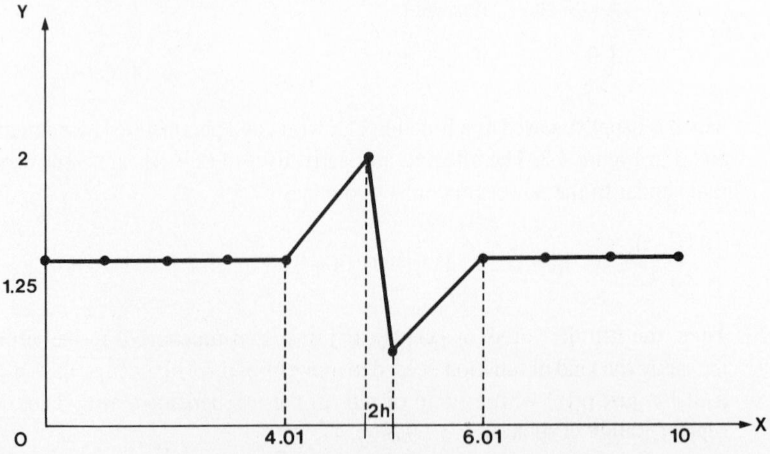

Figure 4.4 **A broken line with unstable truncated power representation.** The knots (break points) are shown as dots; the fifth and sixth are separated by a small amount, 2h.

To be specific, take h = .05. We compute

$$b_4 = .797872 \qquad b_5 = -15.797872$$
$$b_6 = 15.78125 \qquad b_7 = -.78125$$

If f(x) is evaluated in 4-decimal-digit arithmetic at x = 6.62, one finds

$$f(6.62) = 1.25 + .7979(2.61) - 15.80(1.67) + 15.78(1.57) - .7812(.61)$$
$$= 1.236$$

Thus, the value is off by 14 in the third decimal from the correct value 1.25.

If more oscillations are introduced, then the effect in this example is amplified and several oscillations can cause severe round-off problems (see Problem 4.3.2), especially for higher-degree splines.

There is a third representation of splines which uses the **B-splines.** These functions have several mathematical definitions, the most useful of which involves divided differences introduced in the next chapter (see Example 5.2). In the meantime, we give a definition in terms of properties rather than formulas. We assume for the moment that it is possible to satisfy all these properties. *The B-spline B(x) of degree n and knots* $s_1, s_2, \ldots, s_{n+2}$ *satisfies the following:*

1. B(x) is identically zero outside $[s_1, s_{n+2}]$
2. $B(x) > 0$ inside $[s_1, s_{n+2}]$
3. If the knots are in some larger set $t_1, \ldots, t_m$ with $s_1 \geq t_n$ and $s_{n+2} \leq t_{m-n}$, then the sum of all the B-splines with knots t_j is equal to 1 at each point of $[s_1, s_{n+2}]$

The first two properties specify everything about a B-spline except its size; the normalization in the third condition is a little awkward to state but quite useful. The fact that B(x) is nonzero only on n+1 intervals has important consequences in several applications. Figure 4.5 shows plots of B-splines of degree 1, 2, and 3.

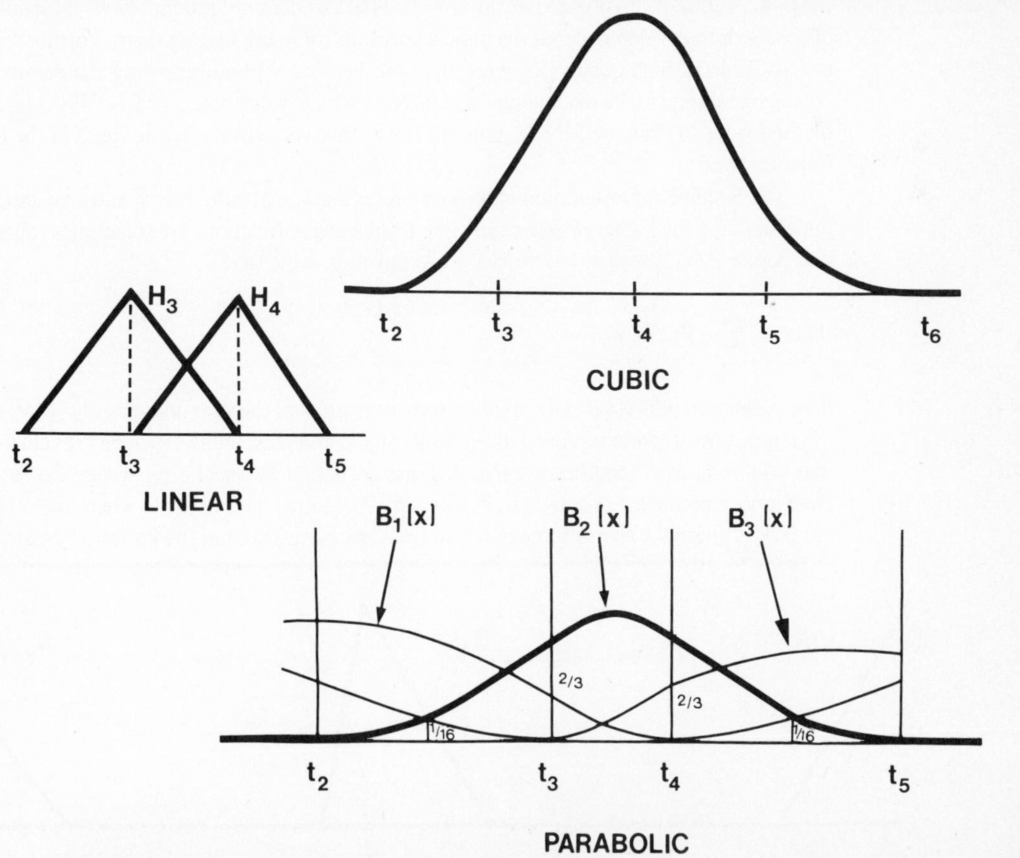

Figure 4.5 **B-spline examples of degree 1, 2, and 3.** Note that the B-splines are positive on 2, 3, and 4 intervals, respectively.

These functions provide the **B-spline representation** of splines. For the knots $t_1, \ldots, t_{k+1}$ define $B_i(x)$ as the B-spline with knots $t_{i-n}, \ldots, t_{i+1}$ (n artificial knots are added to the left of t_1 and to the right of t_{k+1}; their choice is arbitrary and they do not affect the usefulness of the representation). Then every spline s(x) of degree n with knots t_i may be written in a unique way as

$$s(x) = \sum_{i=1}^{n+k} a_i B_i(x)$$ **Equation 4.3.3**

This representation has a number of desirable properties:

1. It is compact; exactly n + k coefficients plus the knots are used.

2. It is numerically stable.

3. The coefficients a_i are closely related to s(x); for example,

(A) The number of sign changes in s(x) are no more than the number of sign changes in the a_i.

(B) The a_i are close to the values of $s(t_i)$.

4. It can be evaluated efficiently.

5. It is easily extended to other piecewise polynomials as discussed in the next subsection.

The B-spline representation has one real drawback; namely, the B-splines are unfamiliar functions. They have a lot of nice properties, but these properties are not trivial to derive. One should view B-splines as new elementary or special functions, analogous to sines or Bessel functions. That is, one learns to use them without knowing the details of how to do everything with them or establish all their properties. Again, by analogy, just try to establish the power series for sin(x) from its geometrical definitions — or, starting from the power series, try to prove that $\sin(\pi) = 0$. This text does not attempt to establish all the nice properties of splines or to develop in detail the basic algorithms for manipulating them. Fortunately, these algorithms are available as high-quality software that can be used without knowing the details of the algorithms. Again, one should make the analogy with SIN(X) which is just used as part of Fortran; a few experts know the best ways to evaluate SIN(X), and one hopes that very good ways are used in the Fortran elementary function library.

The **B-spline representation of broken lines** is mathematically simple and provides a good example for understanding the higher-degree cases. The B-spline basis functions are sometimes called *hat functions*; the first-degree $B_i(x)$ is zero at t_{i-1} and t_{i+1}, and one at t_i. Note that if

$$b(x) = \sum_{i=1}^{k+1} a_i B_i(x)$$

then evaluation of b(x) actually involves only two terms of the sum no matter how large k is. This is one of the reasons this representation is numerically stable and reasonably efficient to evaluate. It is also obvious that $b(t_i) = a_i$, so the coefficients a_i in this case are actual values of b(t). We see that $B_1(x)$ and $B_{k+1}(x)$ are "half a hat functions," as shown in Figure 4.6. The dotted lines indicate where the other halves might be; but it does not make any difference where they are. Note also that the knots can be anything; only a slight

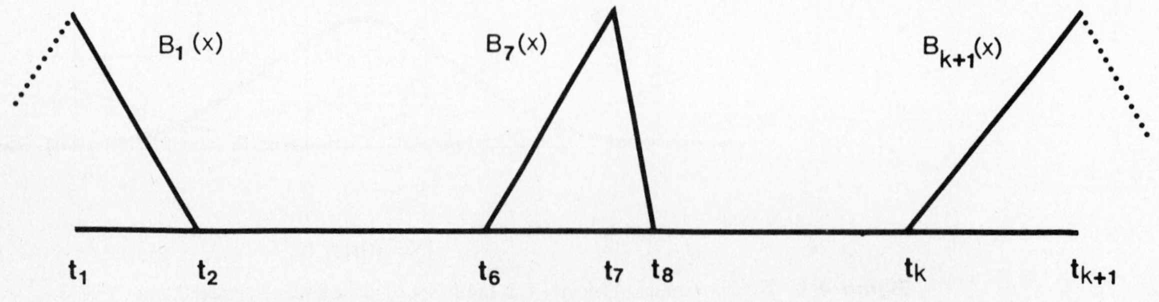

Figure 4.6 The first-degree B-splines

computational advantage is gained from a uniform distribution of the knots. One of the great strengths of splines and piecewise polynomials is the flexibility they acquire from adjusting the break points to accommodate the function being approximated.

PROBLEMS 4.3

4.3.1 Determine the truncated power representation of the broken lines given below with their break points and corresponding values:

(A) Break points (1, 2, 3, 5, 8), values (1, 1, 2, 2, 4)

(B) Break points (1, 20.2, 20.5, 33), values (0, 2.2, 2.3, 1)

(C) Break points (110, 112, 114, 117), values (3000, 3004, 3001, 3002)

4.3.2 Modify the broken line in Example 4.2 with the break points at 6.01 and 7.01 changed to $6.5-h$ and $6.5+h$, and the break points 8.01 and 9.01 changed to $8.5-h$ and $8.5+h$. The values at the new break points are 2, .5, 2, and .5, respectively. Determine the truncated power representation accurately for $h = .02$. Then truncate the coefficients b_i to 4 decimal digits and evaluate f(9.9) in 4-digit arithmetic. Compare this computed result with the exact value.

4.3.3 Give an algorithm to evaluate first-degree B-splines to be used in Equation 4.3.3. Use INTERV of Example 4.1 and implement the algorithm as a Fortran function subprogram with first line

```
REAL FUNCTION BLVALU (A,T,K1,X)
```

where A is the array of coefficients a_i, T is the set of break points, K1 is $k+1$, and X is the point of evaluation. Write a test program to show that BLVALU works properly.

4.3.4 Give an algorithm to evaluate the derivative of a broken line from the B-spline representation of Equation 4.3.3. Write a Fortran function BLDERV similar to BLVALU of Problem 4.3.3 and prepare a program to show it works.

4.3.5 Compare the computational cost of evaluating splines for the three representations (Equations 4.2.1, 4.3.2, and 4.3.3) in the case of broken lines. Use the algorithm of Problem 4.3.3 to evaluate the first-degree B-splines. Use the number of arithmetic operations to measure the cost and obtain expressions for the minimum, average, and maximum number of comparisons, additions, and multiplications as a function of the number $k+1$ of break points. (Assume k is a power of 2 for simplicity.)

4.3.6 Show that the first-degree B-spline is given explicitly by

$$B_i(x) = \begin{cases} \dfrac{x-t_{i-1}}{t_i-t_{i-1}} & t_{i-1} \le x \le t_i \\[2ex] \dfrac{t_{i+1}-x}{t_{i+1}-t_i} & t_i \le x \le t_{i+1} \end{cases}$$

4.3.7 Show that the **parabolic B-spline** with knots x_0, x_0+h, x_0+2h, and x_0+3h is given explicitly by

$$B(x) = \frac{2}{3}(x-x_0)^2/h^2 \qquad \text{if } x_0 \le x \le x_0+h$$

$$B(x) = \frac{2}{3} + \frac{4}{3h}(x-x_0-h) - \frac{4}{3h^2}(x-x_0-h)^2 \qquad \text{if } x_0+h \le x \le x_0+2h$$

$$B(x) = \frac{2}{3}(x-x_0-3h)^2/h^2 \qquad \text{if } x_0+2h \le x \le x_0+3h$$

$$B(x) = 0 \qquad \text{if } x < x_0 \text{ or } x > x_0+3h$$

4.3.8 Consider **first-degree splines with equispaced knots** and the function B(x) defined by

$$B(x) = 0 \qquad \text{if } x < 0 \text{ or } x > 2$$
$$B(x) = x \qquad \text{if } 0 \le x \le 1$$
$$B(x) = 2-x \qquad \text{if } 1 \le x \le 2$$

Given an interval [a, b], partition it into k subintervals of length $H = (b-a)/k$ to produce knots $t_i = a + H(i-1)$ for $i = 1, 2, \ldots, k+1$.

(A) Show that the functions

$$b_i(x) = B\left(\frac{x-a}{H} + 2 - i\right) \qquad i = 1, 2, \ldots, k+1$$

form a basis for the first-degree splines with the knots t_i.

(B) Show that the functions

$$c_1(x) = x-a$$
$$c_2(x) = b-x$$
$$c_i(x) = B\left(\frac{x-a}{H} + 3 - i\right) \qquad i = 3, 4, \ldots, k+1$$

form a basis for the first-degree splines with the knots t_i.

(C) Suppose $s(x) = \sum_{i=1}^{11} a_i b_i(x)$, where the a_i are known and placed in a Fortran array A. Let XLOW and XHI denote the endpoints of the interval [a,b] and $H = (XHI - XLOW)/10$. Write a simple, efficient program to evaluate s(x) which appears as follows:

```
      FUNCTION S(X)
      REAL A(11)
      DATA A/1.2,...,9.8/, XLOW,XHI,H/0.5,4.5,0.4/
C         PUT EVALUATION CODE HERE
      END
```

OTHER PIECEWISE POLYNOMIALS AND SPLINES WITH MULTIPLE KNOTS **4.4

The piecewise polynomials of Section 4.2 consist of completely unconnected polynomials, while the splines of Section 4.3 are connected as smoothly as possible. In between these two extremes there are very useful piecewise polynomials with less than maximum smoothness. These are the **C^r-piecewise polynomials** which are joined together with r continuous derivatives ($r = 0$ means just continuity). General piecewise polynomials are C^{-1} and splines are C^{n-1}-piecewise polynomials. It is common to abbreviate this name by leaving out the word *piecewise* and substituting for *polynomial* the words *linear, quadratic, cubic,* etc., indicating the degree. Thus C^1-cubics are C^1-piecewise polynomials of degree 3. For historical reasons, C^1-cubics are also called **Hermite cubics.**

The most commonly used piecewise polynomials (besides splines) are C^0-quadratics and C^1-cubics; examples of these are shown in Figure 4.7. Note that the C^1-cubics are rather smooth curves; reducing the smoothness requirement on cubic splines to obtain C^1-cubics greatly reduces the work of certain computations (interpolation, for example) and makes C^1-cubics the best choice for some applications. The linear splines and C^1-cubics are the first two members of a sequence of interesting piecewise polynomials, the $C^{(n-1)/2}$-piecewise polynomials of odd degree. The value $(n-1)/2$ is as large as the smoothness can be and still have the reduction of computations effort mentioned for C^1-cubics. The next members of this sequence are the C^2-quintics.

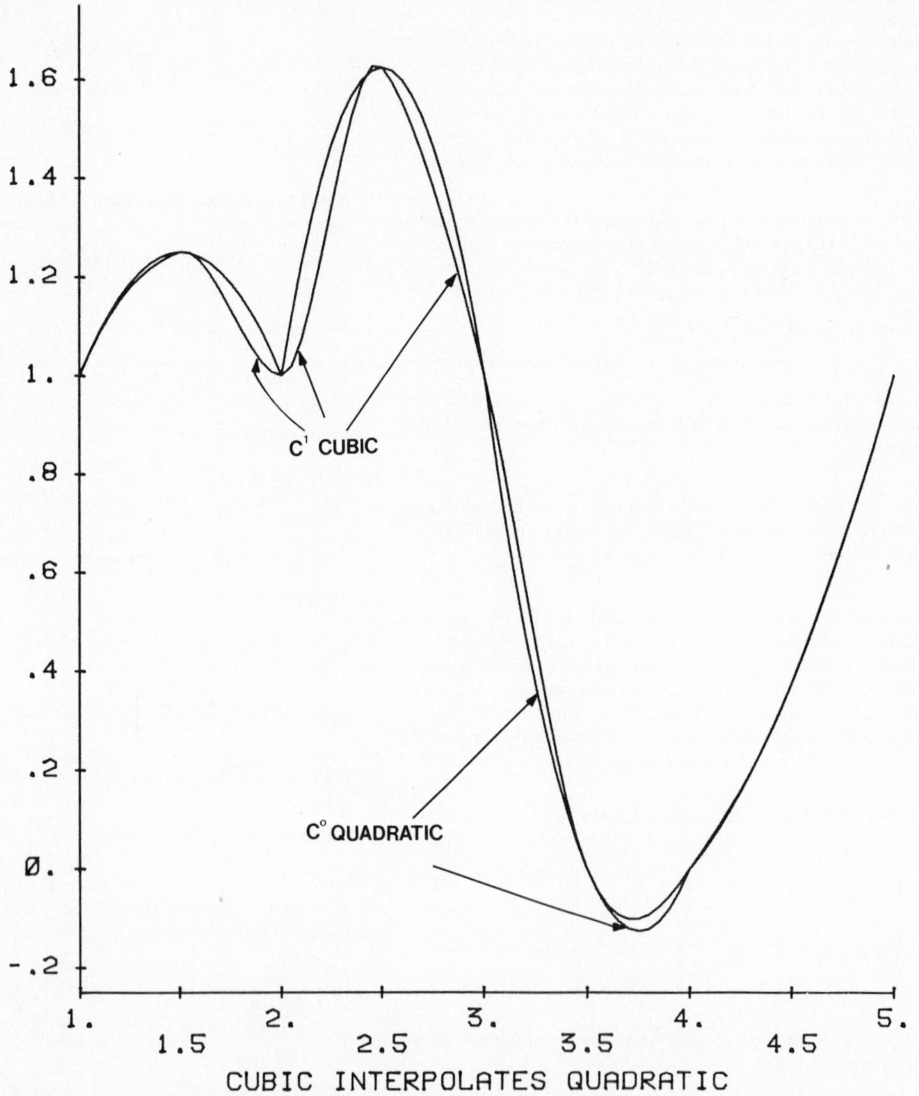

Figure 4.7 **Examples of C^0-quadratics and C^1-cubics.** These two examples have knots at 1, 2, 3, 4, and 5; they interpolate the values 1, 1, 1, 0, and 1 there, respectively.

The piecewise polynomial representation can be used here without change. **The truncated power representation of C^r-piecewise polynomials** is as follows:

$$pp(x) = \sum_{j=0}^{n} a_j(x-t_1)^j + \sum_{\ell=0}^{n-r-1} \sum_{i=2}^{k} b_{i\ell}(x-t_i)_+^{n-\ell} \qquad \textbf{Equation 4.4.1}$$

The terms $(x-t_i)_+^n$, $(x-t_i)_+^{n-1}$, . . . , $(x-t_i)_+^{r+1}$ introduce jumps in the nth and (n − 1)th to (r + 1)th derivatives at the break point t_i. The B-spline representations are also applicable after some extension of the definition of splines.

We define **splines with multiple knots** as follows: Suppose in the knot sequence $t_1, t_2, \ldots, t_{k+1}$ we have $t_i = t_{i+1} = \ldots = t_{i+m}$. Then the spline at t_i may have a jump in its (n − m)th derivative. That this is a natural interpretation of multiple knot is illustrated in Figure 4.8, where broken lines are shown as their two knots coalesce. The limiting case is a step function, and one degree of smoothness is lost.

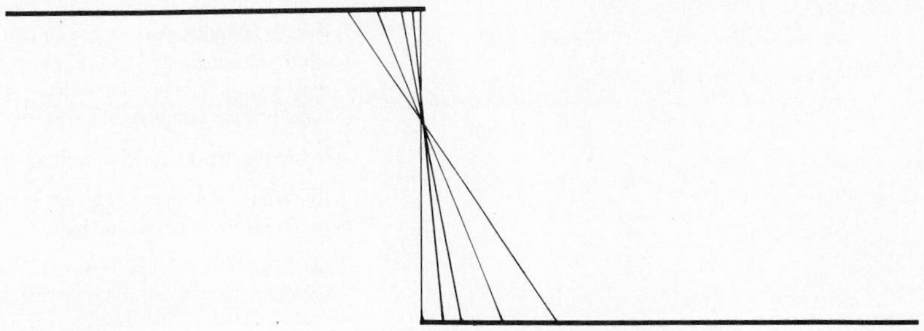

Figure 4.8 **Formation of a jump by coalescing two knots of broken lines.**

With this definition we can define **B-splines with multiple knots** just by repeating the knots in the set of knots. Figure 4.9 shows the five parabolic B-splines for the knots 0, 1, 1, 3, 4, 6, 6, 6. The algorithms using the B-spline representation can all be extended in a numerically stable way to handle multiple knots.

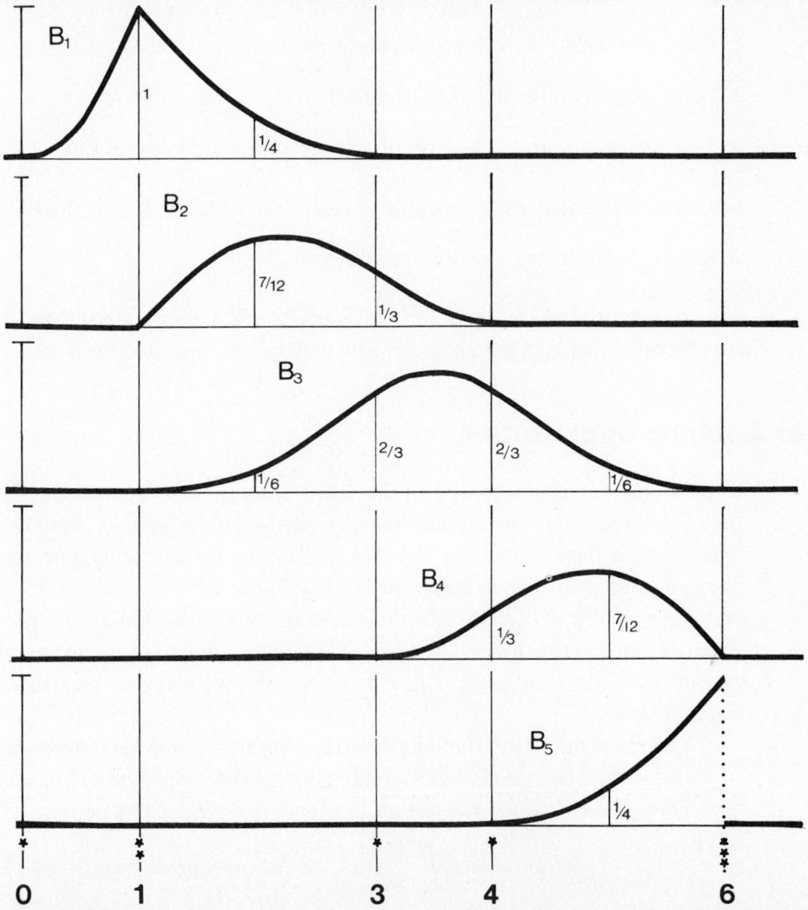

Figure 4.9 **The parabolic B-splines for the knots 0, 1, 1, 3, 4, 6, 6, 6.** Note the connection between smoothness and multiplicity of the knots.

PROBLEMS 4.4

4.4.1 Show that an alternate **Hermite cubic representation** exists of the form

$$f(x) = \sum_{i=1}^{k+1} f(x_i)h_i(x) + f'(x_i)h^1_i(x)$$

where

$$h_i(x) = \begin{cases} -\dfrac{2(x-t_{i-1})^3}{(t_i-t_{i-1})^3} + 3\dfrac{(x-t_{i-1})^2}{(t_i-t_{i-1})^2} & t_{i-1} \le x \le t_i \\[2ex] -\dfrac{2(t_{i+1}-x)^3}{(t_{i+1}-t_i)^3} + 3\dfrac{(t_{i+1}-x)^2}{(t_{i+1}-t_i)^2} & t_i \le x \le t_{i+1} \end{cases}$$

and

$$h^1_i(x) = \begin{cases} \dfrac{(x-t_{i-1})^2(x-t_i)}{(t_i-t_{i-1})^2} & t_{i-1} \le x \le t_i \\[2ex] \dfrac{(x-t_i)(t_{i+1}-x)^2}{(t_{i+1}-t_i)^2} & t_i \le x \le t_{i+1} \end{cases}$$

Give a rough sketch of the basis functions $h_i(x)$ and $h^1_i(x)$.

4.4.2 Hermite quintics are piecewise polynomials of degree 5 with two continuous derivatives (also known as **C^2-quintics**). These functions have a representation analogous to that in Problem 4.4.1 for Hermite cubics. Three types of basis functions are used: $h_i(x)$, $h^1_i(x)$, and $h^2_i(x)$.

(A) What are the conditions that the $h_i(x)$, $h^1_i(x)$, and $h^2_i(x)$ must satisfy?

(B) What is the formula for representing the Hermite quintic in terms of basis functions $h_i(x)$, $h^1_i(x)$, and $h^2_i(x)$?

(C) Sketch these basis functions. Exact formulas are not required for these sketches; just give an argument that shows your sketch is plausible.

GENERAL METHODS FOR DERIVING FORMULAS 4.5

The principal theme of this book is the derivation, use, and analysis of formulas for mathematical problem solving. The majority of formulas or methods are derived by the **method of analytic substitution.** The usual approach to numerical computation has three steps:

1. Choose a model for the functions in the problem
2. Solve the problem exactly for the model
3. Use the result as an estimate of the solution of the original problem

It is in the second step that the method of analytic substitution is used; this step can often be rephrased by

2′. Obtain formulas that are exact for the model

In each problem area there are "best ways" to select models and impose exactness, but we can illustrate the general principle of this approach here and discuss these selections later.

Models for Analytic Substitution 4.5.A

Good choices for models depend on the nature of the problem at hand, but there is one simple rule to note: *the model must allow one to find the exact solution of the problem.* For example, if the problem involves integration, a model involving (sin x)/x is likely to be useless because one cannot integrate (sin x)/x. Similarly, models involving complicated functions like $xe^{x/(1+x)}$ or $\sin(1+x^2)/(1+\log x)$ are likely to lead to very messy mathematical analysis that prevents solving the problem for the model. As in most scientific endeavors, one must consider the tradeoff between a model difficult to analyze but very accurate and one easy to analyze but inaccurate. Sometimes it is very worthwhile to spend more effort in analysis to produce better methods.

A common model for a function is a polynomial; polynomials allow easy solutions for many problems. As noted earlier, polynomials are usually good models only for local behavior so that other models are needed for global behavior. For example, polynomials are good for deriving a formula to estimate $f''(x)$ but poor for deriving a formula for $\int_0^{10} f(x)dx$. Sometimes one can obtain good global models by putting a lot of local models together. This is essentially why piecewise polynomials are so useful as models; in many cases the model is not explicitly given, so one might not even be aware that a piecewise polynomial model is used.

Most formulas for numerical computation are linear, at least at the start. If simple linear formulas are combined in a nonlinear problem, then one usually gets a nonlinear method. An important fact to know is this: **A linear model plus a linear problem must produce a linear formula.** The importance of this is illustrated by considering the following problem in detail:

Given: The values of $f(x)$ at $x = x_1$, x_2, and x_3

To estimate: The value of $f'(x)$ at x_0

We choose polynomials of degree 2 as our model for f(x). Then the method of analytic substitution proceeds as follows:

1. Determine the quadratic polynomial p(x) so that

$$p(x_i) = f(x_i) \qquad \text{for } i = 1, 2, 3$$

2. Compute $p'(x)$ at $x = x_0$ analytically

3. Use this value to estimate $f'(x_0)$

We could carry out this method exactly as described, computing p(x) by interpolation and then differentiating p(x). However, we observe

(A) *Polynomials are a linear model.* The model is linear in the coefficients $a_0, a_1, \ldots$ of the polynomial.

(B) *Differentiations is a linear operation.* We know from calculus that

$$(af(x) + bg(x))' = af'(x) + bg'(x)$$

The rule stated above implies

(C) *There must be a linear formula.* Its form is

$$f'(x_0) \sim c_1f(x_1) + c_2f(x_2) + c_3f(x_3)$$ **Equation 4.5.1**

where c_1, c_2, and c_3 are constants independent of the function f(x).

We can compute these three constants once and for all to avoid having to carry out the computations in steps 1 and 2 above. The rest of this section is concerned with basic techniques used to compute such constants.

The Method of Undetermined Coefficients 4.5.B

We first state the method of analytic substitution in a more specific form for a *linear model and problem.* Let A(f) denote the quantity to be estimated; it depends linearly on the function f(x), so $A(f+g) = A(f) + A(g)$ and $A(af) = aA(f)$ if a is constant. The information about f(x) is linear and denoted by $\lambda_i(f)$, $i = 1, 2, \ldots, k$. The quantities $\lambda_i(f)$ are **linear functionals,** so, like A(f), they depend linearly on f(x). The common examples of linear functionals are (1) values $f(x_i)$ at some point x_i (these are **point functionals**); (2) values of derivatives at some point, for example, $f''(3.1)$; (3) values of integrals, for example,

$$\int_0^{2.6} f(x)dx\,, \quad \int_0^{6.2} x^2f(x)dx$$

and (4) any linear combinations of (1), (2), or (3). An example of a complicated linear functional is

$$\lambda(f) = f(0.1) + f'(1.0) + (x^2+2)f''(.5) + x^2\int_0^1 (t^2+1)f'(t)dt - \cos(x)f'(2)/(1+x)$$

Almost all the information one knows about functions in practice is in the form of linear functionals.

We now express the answer A(f) in terms of the known data $\lambda_i(f)$ as

$$A(f) = \sum_{i=1}^{k} c_i\lambda_i(f) + E(f)$$ **Equation 4.5.2**

where E(f) is the error. The method we use is to replace f by a *linear model,* compute the coefficients c_i so that 4.5.2 is correct for the model with E(f) = 0, and then use the resulting formula for f(x) and hope that the error E(f) is small. A linear model for a function f(x) means that

$$f(x) \sim a_1b_1(x) + a_2b_2(x) + \ldots + a_nb_n(x) \qquad \textbf{Equation 4.5.3}$$

where the $b_i(x)$ are the **modeling functions** or **basis functions.** If we substitute 4.5.3 into 4.5.2, we obtain

$$A\left(\sum_{j=1}^{n} a_jb_j(x)\right) = \sum_{i=1}^{k} c_i\lambda_i\left(\sum_{j=1}^{n} a_jb_j(x)\right) + E \qquad \textbf{Equation 4.5.4}$$

Now disregard E and use the fact that A and the λ_i are linear to obtain

$$\sum_{j=1}^{n} a_jA(b_j) = \sum_{i=1}^{k} c_i \sum_{j=1}^{n} a_j\lambda_i(b_j) \qquad \textbf{Equation 4.5.5}$$

Being able to "solve the problem for the model" means that we can calculate $A(b_j)$ and $\lambda_i(b_j)$ for all i and j. The requirement that the "formula is exact for the model" means that Equation 4.5.5 must hold for any choice of the a_j. The **method of undetermined coefficients** is then to (1) choose various values of the a_j and (2) solve the resulting linear system for the coefficients c_i. Since 4.5.5 is a linear system, there must be as many equations as unknowns; that is, we must have n = k or *there must be as many basis functions as linear functionals.*

Three-Point Differentiation Formulas — Example 4.3

Consider Equation 4.5.1. The model uses the basis functions 1, x, and x^2, that is,

$$f(x) \sim a_1 + a_2x + a_3x^2 = p(x)$$

We have changed the indexes on the coefficients of p(x) to agree with 4.5.2. The λ are just the point functionals $\lambda_1(f) = f(x_1)$, $\lambda_2(f) = f(x_2)$, and $\lambda_3(f) = f(x_3)$, and the answer for the model is $a_2 + 2a_3x_0$. Thus, Equation 4.5.5 in this case is

$$a_2 + 2a_3x_0 = c_1(a_1+a_2x_1+a_3x_1^2) + c_2(a_1+a_2x_2+a_3x_2^2) + c_3(a_1+a_2x_3+a_3x_3^2)$$

Simple choices for the a's are (1, 0, 0), (0, 1, 0), and (0, 0, 1) , which produces the three equations

$$\begin{aligned} 0 &= c_1 + c_2 + c_3 \\ 1 &= c_1x_1 + c_2x_2 + c_3x_3 \\ 2x_0 &= c_1x_13^2 \end{aligned} \qquad \textbf{Equation 4.5.6}$$

One can solve 4.5.6 for the c_i in terms of the x_i to obtain a general three-point differentiation formula; in most cases one has specific values for the x_i to use in 4.5.6.

Equation 4.5.6 is a general system of three equations in three unknowns. A little cleverness in choosing the basis functions can lead to a system which is easy to solve. For example, take $b_1(x) = 1$ as before and

$$b_2(x) = (x-x_1)(x-x_2) \qquad b_3(x) = (x-x_1)$$

Then, with the same choices for the a's, we obtain the three equations

$$\begin{aligned} 0 &= c_1 + c_2 + c_3 \\ 2x_0 - (x_1+x_2) &= 0 + 0 + c_3(x_3-x_1)(x_3-x_2) \\ 1 &= 0 + c_2(x_2-x_1) + c_3(x_3-x_1) \end{aligned} \qquad \textbf{Equation 4.5.7}$$

This system is much easier to solve than the system 4.5.6: one sees immediately that

$$c_3 = \frac{2x_0 - (x_1+x_2)}{(x_3-x_1)(x_3-x_2)}$$

and a simple calculation (or just observing that the formulas for the c_i must be symmetric in the x_i) gives

$$c_2 = \frac{2x_0 - (x_1+x_3)}{(x_2-x_1)(x_2-x_3)} \qquad c_1 = \frac{2x_0 - (x_2+x_3)}{(x_1-x_2)(x_1-x_3)}$$

The technique used to obtain 4.5.7 instead of 4.5.6 can be used in general and can be quite convenient. The trick is to choose the basis functions $b_j(x)$ so that $\lambda_i(b_j) = 0$ for lots of i. It is possible to choose the basis b_j so that

$$\lambda_i(b_j) = 0 \qquad \text{for } i \neq j$$
$$\lambda_i(b_i) = 1$$

Equation 4.5.8

Such a basis $\{b_i\}$ is called a **dual basis** for the linear functionals $\{\lambda_i\}$. The relation 4.5.8 is very useful in analysis; for deriving formulas it is usually easier to choose a partially dual basis — otherwise one spends too much effort finding the dual basis.

The Taylor's Series Method **4.5.C

The Taylor's series is a convenient tool for deriving formulas involving derivatives and point values. It is equivalent to the method of undetermined coefficients in principle, but its mechanics differ. Its main attraction is that it generates formulas for the error E(f) as a by-product. The basic idea is to expand the function f(x) in a Taylor's series at each point where its value is known. One of these points is taken as the origin for the expansion. One then manipulates these expansions to eliminate unknown derivatives or values and to obtain an expression for the desired value in terms of given information.

The method is illustrated by rederiving the three-point differentiation formulas of Example 4.3. The expansions of f(x) are for $x = x_1$, x_2, and x_3, and we choose x_0 as the origin. The expansions are given in terms of $h_1 = (x_1 - x_0)$, $h_2 = (x_2 - x_0)$, and $h_3 = (x_3 - x_0)$. The three expansions to be made are of the values

$$f(x_1) = f(x_0+(x_1-x_0)) = f(x_0+h_1)$$
$$f(x_2) = f(x_0+(x_2-x_0)) = f(x_0+h_2)$$
$$f(x_3) = f(x_0+(x_3-x_0)) = f(x_0+h_3)$$

The expansions are, up to third-order terms in h,

$$f(x_1) = f(x_0) + h_1 f'(x_0) + h_1^2 f''(x_0)/2 + h_1^3 f'''(x_0)/6 + \ldots$$
$$f(x_2) = f(x_0) + h_2 f'(x_0) + h_2^2 f''(x_0)/2 + h_2^3 f'''(x_0)/6 + \ldots$$
$$f(x_3) = f(x_0) + h_3 f'(x_0) + h_3^2 f''(x_0)/2 + h_3^3 f'''(x_0)/6 + \ldots$$

Equation 4.5.9

In Equation 4.5.9 the values of $f(x_1)$, $f(x_2)$, and $f(x_3)$ are given, and the value of $f'(x_0)$ is to be estimated. All other unknown values are to be eliminated — as far as possible. These unknown values are $f(x_0)$, $f''(x_0)$, $f'''(x_0)$, etc. For three linear equations one can eliminate two unknowns; thus, we choose to eliminate $f(x_0)$ and $f''(x_0)$. If one subtracts the first and last pairs of equations in 4.5.9, one obtains

$$f(x_2) - f(x_1) = (h_2-h_1)f'(x_0) + \frac{1}{2}(h_2^2-h_1^2)f''(x_0) + \frac{1}{6}(h_2^3-h_1^3)f'''(x_0) + \ldots$$

Equation 4.5.10

$$f(x_3) - f(x_2) = (h_3-h_2)f'(x_0) + \frac{1}{2}(h_3^2-h_2^2)f''(x_0) + \frac{1}{6}(h_3^3-h_2^3)f'''(x_0) + \ldots$$

To eliminate $f''(x_0)$ from 4.5.10, one multiplies the first equations by $h_3^2 - h_2^2$ and the second by $h_2^2 - h_1^2$ and subtracts. After some simplification ($h_2 - h_1 = x_2 - x_1$, for example), one obtains

$$[f(x_2)-f(x_1)]\,(x_3-x_2)\,(x_2+x_3-2x_0) - [f(x_3)-f(x_2)]\,(x_2-x_1)\,(x_1+x_2-2x_0)$$
$$= (x_2-x_1)\,(x_3-x_2)\,(x_3-x_1)\,f'(x_0) + O(h^5)f'''(x_0) + \ldots$$

One solves this equation for $f'(x_0)$ and rearranges the terms to obtain the following [note that $(x_2-x_1)(x_3-x_2)(x_3-x_1) = O(h^3)$ where $h = \max(h_1, h_2, h_3)$]:

$$f'(x_0) = \frac{2x_0 - (x_2+x_3)}{(x_1-x_2)(x_1-x_3)} f(x_1) + \frac{2x_0 - (x_1+x_3)}{(x_2-x_1)(x_2-x_3)} f(x_2)$$ **Equation 4.5.11**

$$+ \frac{2x_0 - (x_1+x_2)}{(x_3-x_1)(x_3-x_2)} f(x_3) + \frac{O(h^5)f'''(x_0)}{O(h^3)} + \ldots$$

This formula agrees with the one previously obtained, as it must; it also provides an error estimate in the term $O(h^5)f'''(x_0)/O(h^3)$, which is $O(h^2)f'''(x_0)$. If one carries out the details of the algebra, one can find the coefficient of $f'''(x_0)$ exactly.

The Taylor's series method usually turns out to involve more algebra than the method of undetermined coefficients. On the other hand, some people find it easier to understand and like the way that the error estimate is produced along with the numerical formula. There are times when the algebra is greatly simplified. Consider 4.5.10 where $x_0 = x_2$ and $x_2 - x_1 = x_3 - x_2$, which is the most likely case. Then, with $h = h_1 = h_3$ and $h_2 = 0$, we see that $h_2^2 - h_1^2 = -h^2$ and $h_3^2 - h_2^2 = h^2$, so that merely adding the two equations in 4.5.10 eliminates the $f''(x_0)$ term.

Superaccurate Formulas **4.5D

Sometimes formulas for numerical computation are more accurate than they "should be." By this we mean that the formula is exact for basis functions *not included in the model to derive the formulas*. One must be careful in interpreting this statement because every formula is "'accidentally exact" for many functions. For example, the useless formula

$$f'(0) = f(0) + 3f(1) + f(2)$$

is exact for the function $f(x) = \cos(\pi x/2)$. Thus, the basis function for which exactness is obtained must be "interesting"; this usually means they are the next ones in a logical sequence, e.g., the next higher degree polynomial.

Superaccuracy most often comes from some kind of symmetry in the problem and formula. The three-point differentiation formula for Example 4.3 is a case in point; if $x_0 = x_2$, $x_1 = x_0 - h$, and $x_3 = x_0 + h$, then the coefficients of 4.5.2, 4.5.7, or 4.5.11 are

$$c_1 = -1/(2h) \qquad c_2 = 0 \qquad c_3 = 1/(2h)$$

This produces the classical simple formula

$$f'(x_0) \sim \frac{f(x_0+h) - f(x_0-h)}{2h}$$

Note that it involves only *two* pieces of given information (or two linear functionals) and is exact for *three* basis functions: 1, x, and x^2.

Another way to interpret superaccurate formulas is that they have some coefficients equal to zero, so the corresponding information need not be known. Forcing certain coefficients to be zero is one of the ways to discover superaccurate formulas. Superaccurate formulas are, of course, very useful, and most numerical problems have such formulas. The details of the techniques used to derive them vary from problem to problem, so no general method can be presented for deriving them beyond saying that one should look for such formulas. A particularly striking case of superaccurate formulas occurs in numerical integration. The Gauss formulas estimate the integral of f(x) in terms of n function values $f(x_i)$ and n first-derivative values $f'(x_i)$. Yet *all* the coefficients of the first-derivative values are zero, so one actually does not need to know any of them.

PROBLEMS 4.5

4.5.1 Described below are a number of problems for the method of undetermined coefficients. In each case, obtain a formula to estimate the value of a particular linear functional applied to f(x) in terms of given information [other linear functionals applied to f(x)]. A model for the function f(x) is specified in each case, and the formula is to be exact for the model.

	Value to estimate	Given information	Model for function f(x)
(A)	$f'(x_0)$	$f(x_1), f(x_2), f(x_3)$	1, sinx, cosx
(B)	$\int_{x_1}^{x_2} f(x)dx$	$f(x_1), f(x_2)$	1, x
(C)	$\int_{x_1}^{x_3} f(x)dx$	$f(x_1), f(x_2), f(x_3)$	$1, x, x^2$
(D)	$\int_{x_1}^{x_2} f(x)dx$	$f(x_1), f'(x_1), f(x_2)$	$1, x, x^2$
(E)	$f((x_1+x_2)/2)$	$f(x_1), f(x_2), f'(x_2)$	$1, x, x^2$
(F)	$\int_{x_1}^{x_2} \sqrt{x}\, f(x)dx$	$f(x_1), f(x_2)$	1, x
(G)	$\int_{0}^{x_2} \sqrt{x}\, f(x)dx$	$f(0), f(x_2), f'(x_2)$	$1, x, x^2$
(H)	$\int_{0}^{x_2} f(x)dx$	$f\left(\frac{x_2}{2}\right), f(x_2), f'(x_2)$	$\sqrt{x}, x\sqrt{x}, x^2\sqrt{x}$
(I)	$f'(x_0)$	$f(x_1), f(x_2), f'(x_2)$	$1, x, x^2$

4.5.2 For a model with basis 1 and x, find another basis which is dual to the linear functionals given below:

(A) $f(x_1)$, $f(x_2)$

(B) $\int_0^1 f dx$, $f(1/2)$

(C) $f(0)$, $f'(0)$

4.5.3 For a model with basis 1, x, and x^2, find another basis which is dual to the linear functionals $f(x_1)$, $f'(x_1)$, and $f(x_2)$. Use this basis to derive the formulas for Problem 4.5.1, parts (D), (E), (G), (H), and (I). Compare the work (amount of algebra) of finding the dual basis plus deriving the formula with the work of deriving the formulas directly from the basis 1, x, and x^2.

4.5.4 Use the Taylor's series method to derive the formulas for Problem 4.5.1, parts (A), (C), (E), and (I).

4.5.5 Derive a formula to estimate $\int_0^1 f(x)dx$ in terms of $f(x_1)$ and $f(x_2)$ using the model with basis 1 and x for f(x). Show that if $x_1 = 1/2$, then a superaccurate formula is obtained; that is, the value $f(x_2)$ need not be used. This formula is called the **midpoint rule.**

4.5.6 Derive a formula to estimate $\int_0^1 \sqrt{x}\, f(x)dx$ in terms of $f(x_0)$ using the model 1 for f(x). Show that choosing $x_0 = .6$ gives a superaccurate formula, one that is exact for using the model with basis 1 and x for f(x).

4.5.7 Assume the values are known for the following linear functionals of f(x):

$f(0) \quad f(1) \quad f'(.5) \quad \int_0^1 f(x)dx \quad \int_0^1 xf(x)dx$

A formula to estimate f(.5) is to be obtained from these values.

(A) Use the method of undetermined coefficients to derive a system of equations to be solved so that the formula is exact for polynomials of degree 4. Do not solve the system.

(B) Use the Taylor's series method to derive a system of equations for coefficients of the formula which is exact for polynomials of degree 4. Do not solve the system.

4.5.8 Consider the formula for numerical integration

$$\int_0^1 f(x)dx \sim a_0 f(0) + a_1 f(1) + b_0 f'(0) + b_1 f'(1)$$

(A) Use cubic polynomials as a model for f(x) and derive the system of equations for the coefficients a_0, a_1, b_0, and b_1 for each of the methods: undetermined coefficients and Taylor's series.

(B) Compare the difficulty in understanding each method and the effort needed to derive these equations.

4.5.9 Express the cubic polynomial model for Problem 4.5.8 using the basis functions for Hermite cubics of Problem 4.4.1. Show that the coefficients of the formula are integrals of these basis functions.

4.5.10 Show that the basis functions for Hermite cubics of Problem 4.4.1 can be used to obtain the dual basis for the linear functionals $f(x_1)$, $f'(x_1)$, $f(x_2)$, and $f'(x_2)$. Give the dual C^1 cubics that form a dual basis for these four linear functionals. Extract from this basis a set of cubic polynomials that are the dual basis for these functionals..

4.5.11 Derive a formula to estimate the linear functional $\int_0^1 f(x)dx$ in terms of the values of f(0), f(1), and f'(1/4) using quadratic polynomials to model f(x).

4.5.12 **Richardson extrapolation** is based on a model for the error in a numerical process. Let x_k be the kth estimate of solution x^* and *assume* one knows that

$$x_k \sim x^* + ch^n$$

when ch^n is an error term model involving an unknown constant c and n and h are known (from an analysis of the numerical process). Given two estimates x_k and x_{k+1} where x_{k+1} is computed using rh instead of h, show that the Richardson extrapolation estimate

$$x_R = \frac{x_{k+1} - r^n x_k}{1 - r^n}$$

provides a better estimate of x^*. **Hint:** Eliminate the unknown constant c from the equations for x_k and x_{k+1} and solve for x^*.

4.5.13 Extend Richardson extrapolation to a numerical process which has the model

$$x_k \sim x^* + \frac{c}{k^n}$$

Obtain the Richardson extrapolation estimate

$$x_R = \frac{x_{k+1} - r^n x_k}{1 - r^n}$$

where $r = k/(k+1)$.

5
INTERPOLATION

Interpolation is the first numerical problem studied in this book because its methods are used so much in deriving other methods. Making things "exact" in the method of analytic substitution is interpolation. Thus, interpolation is a tool for deriving formulas as well as for solving problems.

Interpolation provides a basic tool for taking some data about a function, curve, process, etc., and extending that information to a wider domain. This extension is, of course, only approximate, and its accuracy depends on many factors. Interpolation as a tool may be viewed as a special case of the *approximation of functions and data,* which is the subject of Chapter 11. In approximation, one does as well as possible within certain limits (e.g., only 10 coefficients and 27 conditions to satisfy); approximation becomes interpolation when the limits allow one to satisfy all the conditions exactly.

Most of this chapter is devoted to special methods for special interpolation problems, for example, polynomials and particular kinds of piecewise polynomials. The first section considers general interpolation using linear equation solvers; this works for any situation, but for the special interpolation problems it is often less efficient and/or less stable than specialized methods.

GENERAL INTERPOLATION USING LINEAR EQUATION SOLVERS — 5.1

The **general interpolation problem** is as follows:

Given: 1. A set of interpolation points x_i, $i = 1, 2, \ldots, N$
2. A set of values y_i, $i = 1, 2, \ldots, N$
3. A set of basis functions $b_j(x)$, $j = 1, 2, \ldots, N$

Find: Coefficients a_j, $j = 1, 2, \ldots, N$, so that

$$y_i = \sum_{j=1}^{N} a_j b_j(x_i) \qquad i = 1, 2, \ldots, N$$

Equation 5.1.1

Equation 5.1.1 is just a linear equation problem; set the matrix $B = \{b_j(x_i)\}$ and the vectors $\mathbf{y} = (y_i)$ and $\mathbf{a} = (a_j)$; then 5.1.1 is written as

$$\mathbf{y} = B\mathbf{a}$$

The number N of unknown coefficients a_j in this problem is also called the number of *(free) parameters* or *degrees of freedom* of the problem. These terms are used in other situations and nonlinear problems where it might not be so easy to determine the number of free parameters.

It is not automatic that the general interpolation problem has a solution. Consider $b_1(x) = 1$, $b_2(x) = x^2$, $x_1 = 1$, $x_2 = -1$, $y_1 = 1$, and $y_2 = 0$. Since the basis functions $b_1(x)$ and $b_2(x)$ are *even* $[b(x) = b(-x)]$, it follows that the value of $a_1b_1(x) + a_2b_2(x)$ is the same at 1 and -1. The coefficient matrix B is

$$\begin{pmatrix} 1 & 1^2 \\ 1 & (-1)^2 \end{pmatrix} \qquad \begin{pmatrix} 1 & 1 \\ 1 & 1 \end{pmatrix}$$

which is singular.

The common mathematical functions x^j, e^{jx}, $\log jx$, etc. are frequently nearly linearly dependent, and thus naturally stated interpolation problems can be terribly ill-conditioned. This is illustrated in the following Example 5.1 and Problems 5.1.2, 5.1.3, and 5.1.4.

An Ill-Conditioned Interpolation Problem — Example 5.1

Suppose one has a sample of material composed of 5 radioactive substances. The jth substance is known to decay (emit radioactivity) at the rate e^{-d_jt}. One can, in principle, determine the proportions of the substances as follows:

1. Measure the radioactivity levels $r_1, \ldots, r_5$ at 5 different times

2. Solve the interpolation problem

$$r_i = \sum_{j=1}^{5} a_j e^{-d_j t_i} \qquad i = 1, 2, \ldots, 5$$

This procedure is carried out for the following specific case:

1. Substance half-lives = 13.5 hours, 37 hours, 63 hours, 4.5 days, and 7 days. The decay rates are computed (with days as the units) from decay rate = $-\ln(.5)$/half-life:

$$\begin{aligned} d_1 &= 1.2322761654 \\ d_2 &= .4496089819 \\ d_3 &= .2640560688 \\ d_4 &= .1540327068 \\ d_5 &= .0990210256 \end{aligned}$$

2. Radioactivity measurements are taken with the values normalized so that the first reading is 100.

Wednesday,	11:00 a.m.	100.000000	$= r_1$
Thursday,	12:15 p.m.	75.6954486	$= r_2$
Friday,	10:30 a.m.	62.25816823	$= r_3$
Monday,	11:15 a.m.	37.24408152	$= r_4$
Tuesday,	noon	31.95247397	$= r_5$

The times are converted to days to give

$$\begin{aligned} t_1 &= 0 \\ t_2 &= 1.052083333 \\ t_3 &= 1.979166667 \\ t_4 &= 5.010416667 \\ t_5 &= 6.041666667 \end{aligned}$$

3. The interpolation problem is solved to obtain the true percentages of the substances:

Substance	1	2	3	4	5
Percentage	9.8624	15.293	21.039	18.736	35.0696

So far this example is completely unrealistic in the accuracy assumed for the physical measurements. Typical levels of uncertainty are listed below:

±2 minutes accuracy in clock
±10 seconds accuracy in clock
±15 minutes in values for half-lives
±10 seconds in values for half-lives
±1% accuracy in radioactivity meters
±.001% in accuracy in radioactivity meter

The effects of these uncertainties are shown in Table 5.1. The computed substance percentages are obtained by first perturbing the problem data by small amounts within the uncertainty limit given and then recomputing the solution of the linear equation (interpolation) problem.

The Effect of Data Uncertainty in an Interpolation Problem **Table 5.1**

UNCERTAINTY		COMPUTED SUBSTANCE PERCENTAGES					
Actual	Percentage	1	2	3	4	5	Maximum Percentage Error
Clock:							
±2 min	0.139	9.39	255.82	−1534.65	3185.54	−1816.11	16902
±10 sec	0.0116	9.85	23.58	−35.42	136.55	−34.57	629
Half-life:							
±15 min	1.85	10.85	−107.43	705.30	−1238.63	729.91	6711
±10 sec	0.0206	9.87	14.14	27.89	5.27	42.82	71
Meter:							
±1%	1.0	9.45	174.83	−848.92	1575.62	−810.09	8310
±.001%	0.001	9.862	15.387	20.552	19.587	34.120	4.5
True values	=	9.8624	15.293	21.039	18.736	35.0696	

The extreme ill-conditioning or numerical instability is obvious from these results; only two cases even produce physically possible values. The uncertainty in the values for the clock, half-life, and meter are multiplied by factors of about 50,000, 3,500, and 5,000, respectively, by this problem-solving process. These factors are approximate condition numbers for solving this problem. Note that some answers (percentage of substance 1) are much more stable than others (percentages of substances 4 and 5).

The problem in this example is so ill-conditioned that there is little hope of obtaining reliable results from the computations. This ill-conditioning is inherent in the original problem; there is nothing wrong with the numerical methods used. The only way to achieve better results is to completely reformulate the problem, something that is not easy to do in this case because the physical situation cannot be changed and its mathematical model (using exponential functions) seems to be determined by the physical situation.

PROBLEMS 5.1

5.1.1 Write a Fortran program using a library linear equation solver to solve the following general interpolation problems.

(A) $\mathbf{x} = (0, 1, 2, \ldots, 7)$
$\mathbf{y} = (0, 1, 0, -1, 0, 1, 0, -1)$
$b_j(x) = \sin(jx),\ j = 1, 2, \ldots, 8$

(B) $\mathbf{x} = (1, 2, 4, 8)$
$\mathbf{y} = (.5, .3, .1, .05)$
$b_j(x) = e^{r_j x}$ for $\mathbf{r} = (0, -1, -2, -3)$

(C) $x_i = [(i-1)/10]^2$ for $i = 1, 2, \ldots, 6$
$y_i = \dfrac{1}{1+i^2}$ for $i = 1, 2, \ldots, 6$

The basis functions are 1, x, x^2, e^x, e^{-x}, and $1/(1+x)$.

Evaluate the resulting interpolant and print output that verifies the program works correctly.

5.1.2 The families of functions given below are ill-conditioned for interpolation. They have a parameter α as well as the number n of functions. Determine experimentally how the ill-conditioning depends on the parameter α (e.g., it becomes better or worse as α gets closer to some values) for small values of n (say n = 3 and 5).

(A) $b_j(x) = e^{-\alpha x/j}$ $\quad j = 1, 2, \ldots, n$

(B) $b_j(x) = e^{-\alpha jx}$ $\quad j = 1, 2, \ldots, n$

(C) $b_j(x) = \dfrac{1}{\alpha + jx}$ $\quad j = 1, 2, \ldots, n$

(D) $b_j(x) = \log(1 + \alpha jx)$ $\quad j = 1, 2, \ldots, n$

5.1.3 Write a program to solve the problem of Example 5.1. Print out the coefficient matrix of the linear system of equations and comment on any unusual properties it has. Estimate the condition numbers for perturbations in the clock, half-life, and meter more accurately by taking several smaller random perturbations in these values. On this basis estimate the accuracy required for the clock, the half-life values, and the meter so that the amounts of the substances can be estimated to within 1/2 percent.

5.1.4 Consider the families (A), (B), (C), and (D) in Problem 5.1.2 for $\alpha = 1$ and determine the value n where the interpolation problem on the set $x_i = (i-1)/n$ for $i = 1, 2, \ldots, n+1$ is ill-conditioned to the extent that 6 decimal digits are expected to be lost in solving the interpolation problem. **Hint:** Generate some coefficients a_i and evaluate y_i values by summing $\sum_{j=1}^{n+1} a_j b_j(x_i)$. Then solve the interpolation problem with these y_i and see how close the computed a_j are to the original ones.

5.1.5 Determine the condition number of the interpolation problems A, B, C, and D in Problem 5.1.4 as n increases. (See Section 3.3.C for the definition of condition number.) How does the condition behave as a function of n? **Hint:** Plot the condition number versus n on log-log paper.

INTERPOLATION METHODS FOR POLYNOMIALS 5.2

The polynomial interpolation problem occurs when the functions $b_j(x)$ of the general interpolation problem are chosen as a basis for polynomials, for example, $b_j(x) = x^{j-1}$ for $j = 1, 2, \ldots, n+1$. The first method considered in this section shows that the polynomial interpolation problem can always be solved provided the interpolation points x_i are distinct. It follows from Theorem 1.8 (the Fundamental Theorem of Algebra) that a nonzero polynomial of degree n has at most n zeros. This means that *the polynomial interpolation problem always has a unique solution.* If there were two solutions, then their difference would be zero at n + 1 points, which implies their difference is identically zero since it is a polynomial of degree n.

Lagrange Polynomial Interpolation 5.2.A

We have already seen that there are several ways to represent a polynomial; now we present another way that makes the interpolation problem completely trivial. One can write down the answer without any calculation at all. As in the general interpolation problem we have the (x_i, y_i) values, and the basis functions to use are x^{j-1}, $j = 1, 2, \ldots, n+1$. The clever trick of this method is to define the **Lagrange polynomials for the points** x_i; they are

$$\ell_i(x) = \prod_{\substack{j=1 \\ j \neq i}}^{n+1} \frac{(x - x_j)}{(x_i - x_j)} \qquad i = 1, 2, \ldots, n+1$$

Equation 5.2.1

Note that there are n + 1 interpolation points because a polynomial of degree n has n + 1 coefficients. There are n terms in the product of the numerator of Equation 5.2.1, and the denominator is a constant. We observe that (see Figure 5.1 for n = 8)

$$\ell_i(x_k) = \begin{cases} 1 & k = i \\ 0 & k \neq i \end{cases}$$

Equation 5.2.2

We see that $\ell_i(x)$ is a polynomial of degree n; these polynomials form a dual basis for the linear functionals of point evaluation. Therefore, we have that

$$p(x) = \sum_{i=1}^{n+1} y_i \ell_i(x)$$

Equation 5.2.3

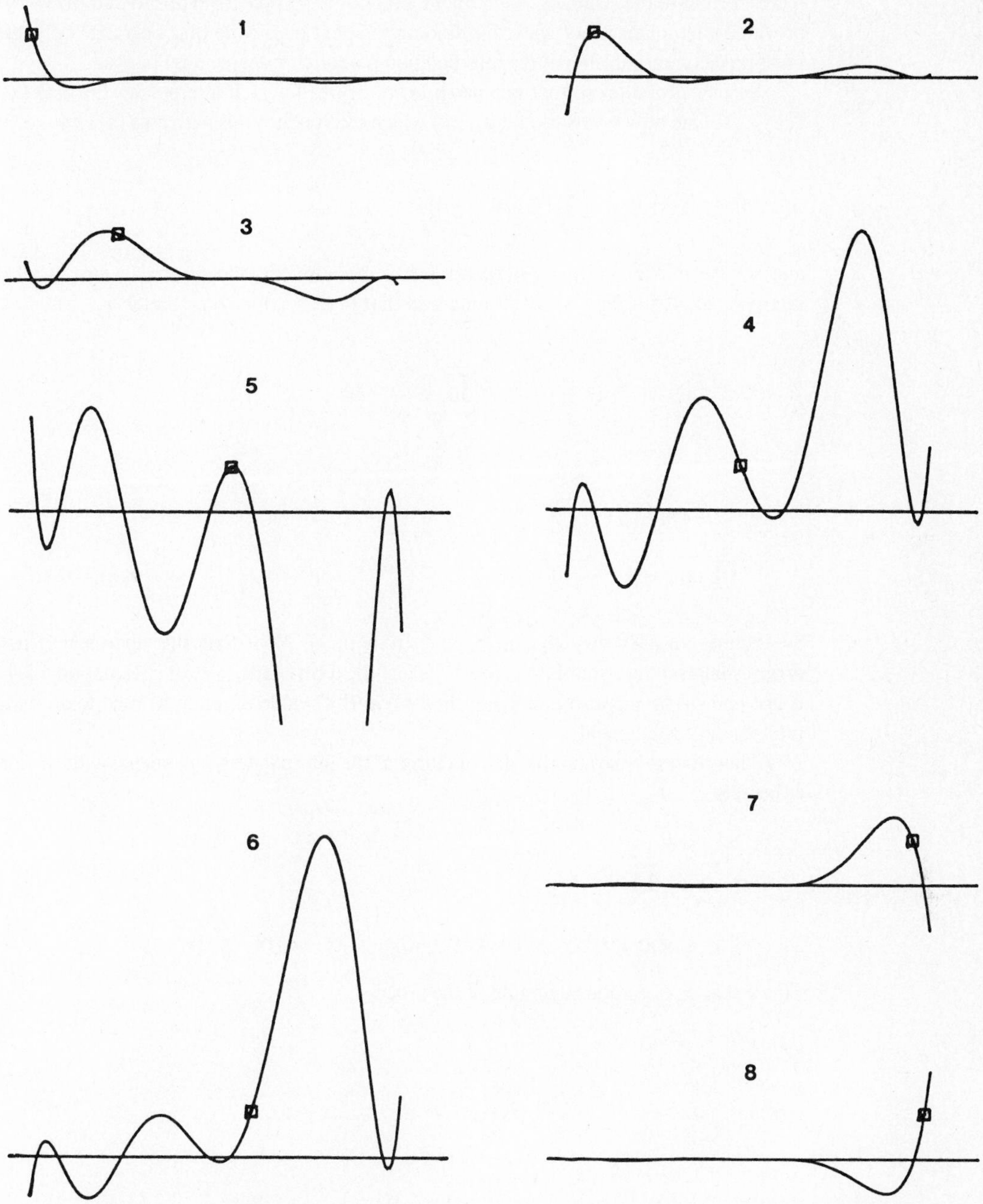

Figure 5.1 **Lagrange polynomials.** The Lagrange polynomials $\ell_i(x)$ are plotted for the 8 points 0.1, 0.2, 0.5, 0.9, 1.0, 1.1, 1.7, and 1.75.

is a polynomial of degree n which satisfies $p(x_i) = y_i$. This construction shows that *polynomials of degree n can interpolate any set of* $n+1$ *data* (provided the x_i are all distinct).

Equation 5.2.3 defines the **Lagrange polynomial form** for representing a polynomial. It has an obvious disadvantage in that the form is awkward to manipulate both analytically and numerically; however, there are times when the ease it gives for solving the interpolation problem more than offsets these disadvantages.

Newton Interpolation and Divided Differences 5.2.B

It is common in applications to want to interpolate a function or some data several times, each time increasing the polynomial degree along with the number of data used. One may need some overall accuracy in the result but not know the required polynomial degree, and so one starts out with the degree low and increases it until the accuracy requirement is met. It is possible to do this so that the work of computing the previous interpolant is not wasted in finding the next one. Note that Lagrange polynomial interpolation must be redone completely if the interpolation points x_i or degree n is changed.

Specifically, suppose that one has $p_k(x)$ of degree k which interpolates the data (x_i, y_i) for $i = 0, 1, 2, \ldots, k$. One now wants to find $p_{k+1}(x)$ which interpolates this data plus (x_{k+1}, y_{k+1}). Write

$$p_{k+1}(x) = p_k(x) + \alpha \prod_{i=0}^{k} (x - x_i)$$

and we see that $p_{k+1}(x_j) = p_k(x_j)$ for $j \leq k$ because the added term is zero at all of the previously interpolated points. Now we determine α so that $p_{k+1}(x_{k+1}) = y_{k+1}$, that is

$$y_{k+1} = p_{k+1}(x_{k+1}) = p_k(x_{k+1}) + \alpha \prod_{i=0}^{k} (x_{k+1} - x_i)$$ **Equation 5.2.4**

or

$$\alpha = \frac{y_{k+1} - p_k(x_{k+1})}{\prod_{i=0}^{k} (x_{k+1} - x_i)}$$

So there is an easy way to find $p_{k+1}(x)$ from $p_k(x)$. Note that this approach is natural for making **error estimates;** the error of $p_k(x)$ at x_{k+1} is just the term $\alpha\Pi(x_{k+1} - x_i)$ in Equation 5.2.4. If the value y_{k+1} is not known, so α is also unknown, then a "nearby" value of α can be used to estimate the error of the interpolation polynomial.

This process builds up the **Newton form of the interpolating polynomial** with the interpolation points as centers:

$$\begin{aligned} p(x) &= \sum_{i=0}^{n} a_i \prod_{j=0}^{i-1} (x - x_j) \\ &= a_0 + a_1(x - x_0) + a_2(x - x_0)(x - x_1) + a_3(x - x_0)(x - x_1)(x - x_2) + \ldots \end{aligned}$$

To see this, consider the beginning of the process:

$$p_0(x) = y_0 = a_0$$

$$p_1(x) = p_0(x) + \frac{y_1 - p_0(x_1)}{x_1 - x_0}(x - x_0) = a_0 + a_1(x - x_0)$$

$$\begin{aligned} p_2(x) &= p_1(x) + \frac{y_2 - p_1(x_2)}{(x_2 - x_0)(x_2 - x_1)}(x - x_0)(x - x_1) \\ &= a_0 + a_1(x - x_0) + a_2(x - x_0)(x - x_1) \end{aligned}$$

$$\begin{aligned} p_3(x) &= p_2(x) + \frac{y_3 - p_2(x_3)}{(x_3 - x_0)(x_3 - x_1)(x_3 - x_2)}(x - x_0)(x - x_1)(x - x_2) \\ &= a_0 + a_1(x - x_0) + a_2(x - x_0)(x - x_1) + a_3(x - x_0)(x - x_1)(x - x_2) \end{aligned}$$

This is exactly the Newton form of Equation 4.1.3.

The process of determining the coefficients of the Newton form could be carried out directly from Equation 5.2.4, but there is a simpler, more efficient way. The coefficient a_k in the Newton form is called the **kth divided difference** of the data (x_i, y_i). We also define the **kth divided difference of the function f(x) at the points x_i** by setting $y_i = f(x_i)$; it is denoted by

$$f[x_0, x_1, \ldots, x_k]$$

With this notation the polynomial interpolating the function $f(x)$ at $x_0, x_1, \ldots, x_n$ is written as

$$p(x) = \sum_{i=0}^{n} f[x_0, \ldots, x_i] \prod_{j=0}^{i-1} (x - x_j) \qquad \textbf{Equation 5.2.5}$$

The divided differences satisfy a simple formula which allows them to be computed efficiently:

$$f[x_0, \ldots, x_n] = \frac{f[x_1, \ldots, x_n] - f[x_0, \ldots, x_{n-1}]}{x_n - x_0} \qquad \textbf{Equation 5.2.6}$$

It is to be established in Problem 5.2.12 that the divided difference of $f(x)$ does not depend on the order of the points in the difference.

Equation 5.2.6 is established as follows. Let $q(x)$ interpolate $f(x)$ at $x_0, x_1, \ldots, x_{n-1}$ and $r(x)$ interpolate $f(x)$ at $x_1, x_2, \ldots, x_n$. Then one can check that

$$p(x) = \frac{x - x_0}{x_n - x_0} r(x) - \frac{x - x_n}{x_n - x_0} q(x) \qquad \textbf{Equation 5.2.7}$$

interpolates $f(x)$ at $x_0, x_1, \ldots, x_n$. The leading coefficient of x^n in $p(x)$ is $f[x_0, \ldots, x_n]$ by definition, and the leading coefficients (for x^{n-1}) of $r(x)$ and $q(x)$ are, again by definition, $f[x_1, \ldots, x_n]$ and $f[x_0, \ldots, x_{n-1}]$. Equating coefficients of x^n in Equation 5.2.7 produces Equation 5.2.6.

The formula for generating divided differences is conveniently implemented in terms of a **divided difference table** shown in Figure 5.2. The first two columns are the data (x_i, y_i) or $(x_i, f(x_i))$, and the remainder of the table is generated from 5.2.6. The divided difference coefficients for the Newton interpolating polynomial are on the top diagonal.

x_i	y_i	First	Second	Third	Fourth
x_0	$f[x_0]$				
		$f[x_0,x_1]$			
x_1	$f[x_1]$		$f[x_0,x_1,x_2]$		
		$f[x_1,x_2]$		$f[x_0,x_1,x_2,x_3]$	
x_2	$f[x_2]$		$f[x_1,x_2,x_3]$		$f[x_0,x_1,x_2,x_3,x_4]$
		$f[x_2,x_3]$		$f[x_1,x_2,x_3,x_4]$	
x_3	$f[x_3]$		$f[x_2,x_3,x_4]$		
		$f[x_3,x_4]$			
x_4	$f[x_4]$				

Figure 5.2 The divided difference table. The first two columns are given data. The dashed line shows how a table value depends on the given data.

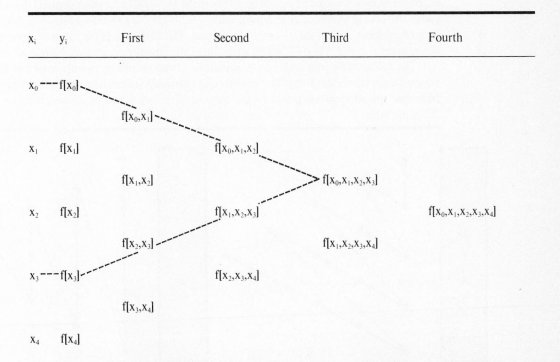

An example of a complete divided difference table is given below.

i	x_i	y_i	First	Second	Third	Fourth	Fifth
1	1.0	0.0					
			0.352				
2	1.5	0.176		−0.102			
			0.250		0.017556		
3	2.0	0.301		−0.049333		−0.002756	
			0.176		0.010667		0.000122
4	3.0	0.477		−0.028		−0.002267	
			0.134		0.005		
5	3.5	0.544		−0.018			
			0.116				
6	4.0	0.602					

The cubic polynomial that interpolates the y_i at 1.0, 1.5, 2.0, and 3.0 is

$$0.0 + .352(x-1) - .102(x-1)(x-1.5) + 0.017556\,(x-1)(x-1.5)(x-2)$$

The one that interpolates the y_i at 1.5, 2.0, 3.0, and 3.5 is read off from the *second* diagonal of the divided difference table as

$$0.176 + .250(x-1.5) - 0.049333(x-1.5)(x-2) + 0.010667(x-1.5)(x-2)(x-3)$$

This polynomial and the one that interpolates at 2.0, 3.0, 3.5, and 4.0 are evaluated at $x = 2.5$ to estimate the value $y(2.5)$ as 0.40400 or 0.39725, respectively. A rough estimate of the error for $y(2.5)$ can be made from the next term in the Newton interpolating polynomial, which is

$$y[1.0, 1.5, 2.0, 3.0, 2.5] \prod_{i=1}^{5} (2.5-x_i) = .375\; y[1.0, 1.5, 2.0, 3.0, 2.5]$$

Of course the divided difference $y[1.0, 1.5, 2.0, 3.0, 2.5]$ is not known, but using the fourth divided difference with 3.5 instead of 2.5 gives $.375 \times (0.003) = .00183$, which suggests the error in $y(2.5)$ is about .002. If a similar calculation is made using -0.002267 as an estimate for $y[1.5, 2.0, 3.0, 3.5, 2.5]$, an error of about $.375 \times .002 \sim .001$ is suggested. The difference in the values of the two interpolating polynomials at $x = 2.5$ is .007, which is consistent with the two rough error estimates.

The divided difference table can be generated in various orders; two are shown in Figure 5.3. The diagonal order has the advantage that another interpolation point can be added easily using the same order. Note that the interpolation points do not have to be in any particular numerical order in the divided difference table.

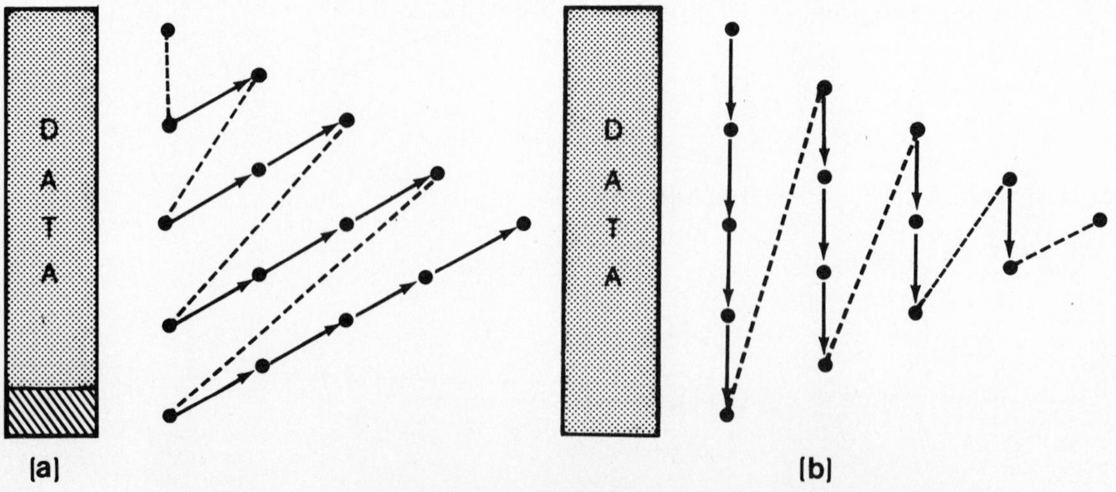

Figure 5.3 Orderings for generating the divided difference table. (a) Allows the addition of a new interpolation point to the table with no change to the algorithm.

Algorithms to Compute Divided Difference Tables

Given the first two columns containing x_i and $f(x_i)$, we have for evaluating the table by columns

For $k = 1, 2, \ldots, n$ do: **Algorithm 5.2.1**
For $i = 0, \ldots, n-k$ do:

$$f[x_i, \ldots, x_{i+k}] = \frac{f[x_{i+1}, \ldots, x_{i+k}] - f[x_i, \ldots, x_{i+k-1}]}{x_{i+k} - x_i}$$

To evaluate the table by diagonals we have

For $k = 1$ to n do: **Algorithm 5.2.2**
For $i = 1$ to k do:

$$f[x_{k-i}, \ldots, x_k] = \frac{f[x_{k-i+1}, \ldots, x_k] - f[x_{k-i}, \ldots, x_{k-1}]}{x_k - x_{k-i}}$$

A computer program for difference tables would, for example, define $d_{ij} = f[x_i, \ldots, x_j]$ and make the table triangular-shaped rather than diamond-shaped as in Figure 5.2. If all one wants is the Newton interpolating polynomial, one can eliminate the two-dimensional array by noting that in either algorithm there are only n "active" numbers at any stage.

Algorithms to Compute the Newton Interpolating Polynomial Coefficients

Given the x_i and $f(x_i)$, initialize the coefficients a_i by $a_i = f(x_i), i=0, 1, 2, \ldots, n$. The coefficients may then be computed by columns as

For $k = 1, 2, \ldots, n$ do: **Algorithm 5.2.3**
For $i = k-1, \ldots, n-1$ do:
$a_{i+1} = (a_{i+1} - a_i)/(x_{i+1} - x_{i+1-k})$

The computation by diagonals is more complicated; define d_i as the diagonal elements with the highest index at the top right. Initialize the computation by $d_i = f(x_{n-i})$ and $a_0 = f(x_0)$, then use

For $k = 1, 2, \ldots, n$ do: **Algorithm 5.2.4**
For $i = 1, 2, \ldots, k$ do:

$$d_{n-k+i} = \frac{d_{n-k+i-1} - d_{n-k+i}}{x_k - x_{k-i}}$$

Algorithm 5.2.4 gives the Newton interpolation polynomial using the x_i in reverse order, that is,

$$p(x) = \sum_{i=0}^{n} d_i \prod_{j=n}^{n-i+1} (x - x_j)$$

B-Spline Definition as a Divided Difference — Example 5.2

Let the sequence $\{t_i\}$ of knots be given and denote the truncated power function by

$$T(x, t) = (t-x)_+^n = \begin{cases} (t-x)^n & \text{if } t \geq x \\ 0 & \text{if } t \leq x \end{cases}$$

Then the ith **B-spline of degree** n is defined to be

$$B_i(x) = (t_{i+n+1} - t_i)T[x; t_i, t_{i+1}, \ldots, t_{i+n+1}]$$ **Equation 5.2.8**

Here, the notation for divided differences of a function of two variables uses a separating semicolon, and then the points of the divided difference are listed on each side of it. In this case the differences are applied only to the t variable; x still varies in the normal fashion.

Consider the case of first degree so that Equation 5.2.8 is

$$B_i(x) = (t_{i+2} - t_i)T[x; t_i, t_{i+1}, t_{i+2}]$$

To compute the value of $B_i(x)$, first consider the case where $t_{i+2} < x$. Then $T(x, t) = 0$, its divided differences are zero, and $B_i(x)$ is zero. Next consider $x < t_i$ and apply the definition of divided differences to obtain

$$T(x; t_i, t_{i+1}) = \frac{(t_{i+1} - x) - (t_i - x)}{t_{i+1} - t_i} = 1$$

$$T(x; t_{i+1}, t_{i+2}) = \frac{(t_{i+2} - x) - (t_i - x)}{t_{i+2} - t_{i+1}} = 1$$

The first divided difference is a constant, and so the second divided difference [and hence $B_i(x)$] is zero. Suppose now that $t_i \le x \le t_{i+1}$; then we have by direct application of the definition of divided differences

$$T[x; t_i, t_{i+1}] = \frac{(t_{i+1} - x) - 0}{t_{i+1} - t_i}$$

$$T[x; t_{i+1}, t_{i+2}] = \frac{(t_{i+2} - x) - (t_{i+1} - x)}{t_{i+2} - t_{i+1}} = 1$$

$$(t_{i+2} - t_i)T[x; t_i, t_{i+1}, t_{i+2}] = (t_{i+2} - t_i)\frac{1 - \dfrac{t_{i+1} - x}{t_{i+1} - t_i}}{t_{i+2} - t_i} = \frac{x - t_i}{t_{i+1} - t_i}$$

Thus, for x in this interval, $B_i(x)$ starts out at zero for $x = t_i$ and rises to one at $x = t_{i+1}$. A similar calculation shows for $t_{i+1} \le x \le t_{i+2}$ that $B_i(x) = (t_{i+2} - x)/(t_{i+1} - t_{i+2})$ which starts out at one for $x = t_{i+1}$ and drops to zero for $x = t_{i+2}$.

It now easily follows, for degree = 1, that for all x we have

$$\sum_{i=1}^{k} B_i(x) = 1$$

For any x there are at most two nonzero terms in the sum; one is $(x - t_i)/(t_{i+1} - t_i)$ for $B_i(x)$ and one is $(t_{i+1} - x)/(t_{i+1} - t_i)$ for $B_{i-1}(x)$; these two terms sum to 1.

Osculatory Interpolation and B-Splines with Multiple Knots **5.2.C

"Osculatory" is derived from the Latin word "to kiss" and means to interpolate with matching of certain derivatives. The ultimate in osculatory interpolation is the *Taylor's series* at x_0:

$$p(x) = \sum_{j=0}^{n} f^{(j)}(x_0)\frac{(x - x_0)^j}{j!}$$

This nth-degree polynomial interpolates f(x) and its first n derivatives at x_0. In Problem 4.4.1 we see **Hermite interpolation**, where one interpolates the value and first derivative at each point.

One may interpret osculatory interpolation as ordinary interpolation with multiple interpolation points. Divided differences and Newton interpolation extend naturally to cover this situation. Consider a small piece of the divided difference table written in triangular rather than diamond-shaped format:

x_1	$f(x_1)$	$f[x_1, x_2]$	$f[x_1, x_2, x_3]$
x_2	$f(x_2)$	$f[x_2, x_3]$	
x_3	$f(x_3)$		

Suppose that x_2 moves to x_1; we see that

$$f[x_1, x_2] = \frac{f(x_2) - f(x_1)}{x_2 - x_1}$$

converges to $f'(x_1)$ by the definition of the derivative. Thus, we may define

$$f[x_1, x_1] = f'(x_1)$$

and expect this to be a consistent definition. The difference table now appears as

x_1	$f(x_1)$	$f'(x_1)$	$f[x_1, x_1, x_3]$
x_1	$f(x_1)$	$f[x_1, x_3]$	
x_3	$f(x_3)$		

where

$$f[x_1, x_1, x_3] = \frac{f[x_1, x_3] - f'(x_1)}{x_3 - x_1}$$

Suppose now that x_3 moves to x_1, and replace $f(x_3)$ by the Taylor's series at x_1, that is, $f(x_3) = f(x_1) + f'(x_1)(x_3 - x_1) + f''(x_1)(x_3 - x_1)^2/2 + \ldots$. Then $f[x_1, x_3]$ is seen to be $f'(x_1)(x_3 - x_1) + f''(x_1)(x_3 - x_1)/2 + \ldots$ so that $f[x_1, x_1, x_3]$ converges to $f''(x_1)/2$. Thus a segment of a divided-difference table with a triple of identical points appears as

x_1	$f(x_1)$		
		$f'(x_1)$	
x_1	$f(x_1)$		$\frac{1}{2} f''(x_1)$
		$f'(x_1)$	
x_1	$f(x_1)$		

The above discussion motivates the general definition of **divided differences with multiple points.** Given the points $x_0, x_1, \ldots, x_n$, assume they are ordered so that identical points are numbered in sequence. Construct the divided difference table as follows:

1. Place the values $f(x_i)$ in the table.

2. For $k = 1, 2, \ldots, n$ and all i do:

If $x_i = x_{i+k}$, set $f[x_i, \ldots, x_{i+k}] = \frac{1}{k!} f^{(k)}(x_i)$

3. Complete the table with the divided difference recurrence relation 5.2.6.

The entries in this table are the divided differences. It is obvious that using divided differences with multiple points requires that $f(x)$ have the appropriate number of derivatives. It is proved later that if $f(x)$ is smooth enough, then this definition is valid. That is, the $f[x_0, \ldots, x_k]$ so defined depend continuously on the points x_i, and the Newton interpolation polynomial does interpolate $f(x)$ in the specified osculatory manner.

Osculatory Interpolation of sin(x) — Example 5.3

A polynomial is to be constructed to interpolate sin(x) once at $x = 0$, twice at $x = \pi/6$, and three times at $x = \pi/3$. Further, so we can distinguish between sin(x) and the interpolating polynomial, we interpolate $.5 + \sin(x)$ at $x = \pi/12$ and $x = \pi/4$ and interpolate $-.5 + \sin(x)$ at $\pi/2$. The divided difference table for this is initialized as follows (only approximate numerical values are given):

x	f(x)	First	Second
0	0		
$\pi/12$	$.5+\sin(\pi/12) = .759$		
$\pi/6$	$.5$	$\cos(\pi/6) = .866$	
$\pi/6$	$.5$		
$\pi/4$	$.5+\sin(\pi/4) = 1.207$		
$\pi/3$	$\sin(\pi/3) = .866$	$\cos(\pi/3) = .5$	
$\pi/3$	$\sin(\pi/3) = .866$	$\cos(\pi/3) = .5$	$-\sin(\pi/3)/2 = -.433$
$\pi/3$	$\sin(\pi/3) = .866$		
$\pi/2$	$.5$		

The resulting polynomial interpolant is plotted in Figure 5.4. There is "accidental" interpolation at x = .22.

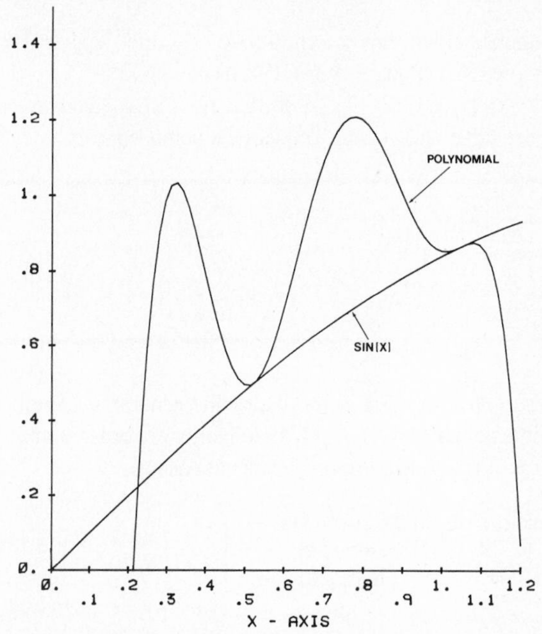

Figure 5.4 **Osculatory interpolation of sin(x).** Sin(x) is plotted with a polynomial that interpolates it once at x = 0, twice at x = $\pi/6$, and three times at x = $\pi/3$. The interpolation seen at x = .22 is accidental.

Once multiple points are allowed in divided differences, we can define B-splines with multiple knots by the same formula as before, Equation 5.2.8. The power of divided differences is that they allow this extension easily while more direct, algebraic approaches become very messy. See Figure 4.9 for examples of parabolic B-splines with knots of multiplicity 2 and 3.

PROBLEMS 5.2

5.2.1 Develop an algorithm for **evaluation of the Lagrange polynomial** form which is efficient. How many multiplications and additions are required as a function of n? **Hint:** Set $b_i = y_i / \prod_{\substack{j=1 \\ i \neq j}}^{n+1} (x_i - x_j)$ and then write Equation 5.2.3 as

$$p(x) = \prod_{i=1}^{n+1} (x - x_i) \sum_{j=1}^{n} \frac{b_j}{(x - x_j)}$$

5.2.2 Show that the direct evaluation of p(x) from Equation 5.2.3 requires $O(n^2)$ additions and multiplications.

5.2.3 Compute the table of divided differences for the following sets of data (use only 5 values from E and F).

(A)

x	sin(x)
0°	.0000
5°	.0872
10°	.1736
15°	.2588

(B)

x	log(cos(x)) + 1
0	1.0000
.0320	.9998
.0844	.9985
.1484	.9954
.2007	.9912

(C)

x	ln(x)
1	.0000
2	.6931
3	1.0986
4	1.3863
5	1.6094
6	1.7918

(D)

x	e^x
−1.5	.223130
0	.000000
1.0	2.718282
1.6	4.953032
2.1	8.166170

(E)

t	Solubility of Chlorine
10	3.148
15	2.680
20	2.299
30	1.799
40	1.438
50	1.225
60	1.023
70	0.862
80	0.683

(F)

t	Vapor Pressure of Cesium
244	0.29
249.5	0.31
272	0.99
278.4	1.01
315	3.18
350	6.72
397	15.88
670	760.0

5.2.4 Use the divided difference tables from Problem 5.2.3 to interpolate for the following values. Use a third-degree polynomial.

(A) sin(6°), sin(17°)

(B) log(cos(.01)), log(cos(.18))

(C) ln(.5), ln(5.1)

(D) $e^{-.5}, e^{1.4}$

(E) Solubility at 22, 46

(F) Vapor pressure at 275, 400

5.2.5 Estimate the error in the interpolated values for Problem 5.2.4 (except part A) using the estimates of the fourth divided differences at appropriate points. For parts B, C, and D, compare the error estimates with the actual errors.

5.2.6 Write a Fortran program that interpolates e^x at the points 0, 1.0, −0.5, 0.6, 1.2, 0.2 by polynomials of degree 2, 3, 4, and 5. Evaluate the result at x = 0.5. Use Algorithms 5.2.4 and 4.1.1; print (with appropriate labels) the Newton coefficients, the value found, and its absolute error. Is the next term in the Newton polynomial a good estimate of the error in the current interpolation?

5.2.7 Modify Algorithms 4.1.1 and 5.2.4 so that the Newton coefficients are indexed in descending order, that is,

$$p(x) = \sum_{i=0}^{n} a_{n-i} \prod_{j=0}^{i-1} (x - x_j)$$

Repeat Problem 5.2.6 to verify that the modified algorithms are correct.

5.2.8 The polynomial that interpolates a polynomial p(x) of the same degree should reproduce p(x). To check the accuracy of the interpolation process, compute the interpolants $p^*(x)$ of the following polynomials at the specified points and then evaluate the difference $[p(x) - p^*(x)]$ at the check points.

Polynomial	Interpolation Points	Check Points
(A) $1+x+x^2+x^3$	1, 2, 3, 4	1.5, 3.5
(B) $1+\frac{x}{2}+\frac{x^2}{6}+\frac{x^3}{24}+\frac{x^4}{120}$	−1, −.5, 1, 2, 3.5	0, 1.5, 5.0
(C) $\prod_{j=1}^{6}(x-j)$	0, 1, 2, 3, 4, 5	6, 7
(D) $\prod_{j=1}^{20}(x-j)$	0, 1, 2, . . . , 19	15.5, 16.5, 20
(E) $\prod_{j=1}^{20}(x-2^{-j})$	0, 2^{-j} for j = 1, 2, . . . , 19	2^{-20}, .3, 1.0
(F) $\sum_{j=1}^{20} x^j/j!$	j×.1 for j = 0, 1, . . . , 19	−1.0, 0, .25, 2.0

Write a Fortran program to do these computations; print the results with appropriate messages.

5.2.9 There is a tremendous difference in the interpolation errors for Problems 5.2.8(D) at x = 20 and 5.2.8(F) at x = 2.0. Explain this in terms of the size of the coefficients of the interpolating polynomials.

5.2.10 In Example 5.2 derive the explicit formula for $(t_{i+2}-t_i)T[x; t_i, t_{i+1}, t_{i+2}]$ for $t_{i+1} \le x \le t_{i+2}$ and degree equal one.

5.2.11 Show that the kth divided difference of a polynomial of degree n is a polynomial of degree n−k. That is, consider $p[x_1, x_2, \ldots, x_k, x]$ as a function of the last point x of the difference. **Hint:** Apply Formula 5.2.6 to the polynomial in power form and use induction on the degree of the polynomial.

5.2.12 Show that **the divided difference is a symmetric function.** That is, $f[x_1, x_2, \ldots, x_k] = f[y_1, y_2, \ldots, y_k]$ if the set $\{y_i\}$ is a permutation of the set $\{x_i\}$. **Hint:** Use the fact that the Newton interpolation polynomial does not depend on any order in the interpolation points.

5.2.13 Verify directly from the definition (Equation 5.2.8) of a parabolic B-spline that it has a jump discontinuity at a triple knot.

INTERPOLATION METHODS FOR PIECEWISE POLYNOMIALS 5.3

No special method is needed for piecewise polynomial interpolation unless the pieces are to be joined up smoothly. One can use the general interpolation approach by adding the smoothness conditions to the system of equations for interpolation. This approach uses the power form with centers at the break points for the polynomials, Equation 4.2.2.

A simple example follows: Interpolate $f(x)$ at $x_j = j$, $j = 1, 2, \ldots, 6$ by a piecewise quadratic with break points $t_1 = 1, t_2 = 2.5, t_3 = 4.5$. The piecewise quadratic is to be C^0 at $x = 2.5$ and C^1 at $x = 4.5$. The system of linear equations to be solved is then:

Interpolation equations

$$a_{i0} + a_{i1}(x_j - t_i) + a_{i2}(x_j - t_i)^2 = f(x_j) \qquad \begin{array}{l} i = 1 \text{ for } j = 1, 2 \\ i = 2 \text{ for } j = 3, 4 \\ i = 3 \text{ for } j = 5, 6 \end{array}$$

Smoothness at t_2

$$a_{10} + a_{11}(1.5) + a_{12}(1.5)^2 = a_{20}$$

Smoothness at t_3 (note $t_3 - t_2 = 2.0$)

$$a_{20} + a_{21}(2.0) + a_{22}(2.0)^2 = a_{30}$$
$$a_{21} + 2a_{22} \times 2.0 = a_{31}$$

Consider a piecewise polynomial pp(x) of degree n with $k+1$ break points t_j which has v_j continuous derivatives at the ith break point. The number of independent coefficients is $M = (n+1)k - \sum_{j=2}^{k} v_j$; if, as usual, v_j is a constant v, then $M = k(n-v) + v + k$. In order for the linear equations to be solvable, the break points must be related to the interpolation points x_j, $j = 1, 2, \ldots, n$ with $x_j < x_{j+1}$. For example, it is obvious that one cannot put 10 interpolation points in an interval where pp(x) is a polynomial of degree 3. In order to know if interpolation is possible, expand the break points to a new set $T = t_1, t_2, \ldots, t_{n+1}$ by repeating each break point (t_j) $n - v_j$ times for $2 \leq j \leq k$. Add n points to the left of t_1 and to the right of t_{k+1}. For example, if $n = 3$ (cubics), $k = 3$ (3 pieces), $v_2 = 0$ (continuity only at t_2), $v_3 = 2$ (continuous second derivative at t_3), then there are 12 points in T ordered as

$$t_0\ t_0\ t_0 \quad t_1 \quad t_2\ t_2\ t_2 \quad t_3 \quad t_4 \quad t_5\ t_5\ t_5$$

These are then renumbered as t_1 through t_{12}. Interpolation is possible if, after renumbering the set T, the interpolation points x_i satisfy the **piecewise polynomial interpolation conditions**

$$t_i < x_i < t_{i+n+1} \qquad \textbf{Equation 5.3.1}$$

This general method of computing the interpolating piecewise polynomial is satisfactory for simple problems or for problems involving a variety of smoothness conditions and/or polynomial degrees for the pieces. It is inefficient when the degrees and smoothness conditions are all the same and the number of smoothness conditions is substantial; this is especially so for splines. The reason for this is that one can choose the basis functions to satisfy the smoothness conditions automatically, and thus the number of equations to be solved is greatly reduced.

Hermite Cubic Interpolation 5.3.A

Hermite interpolation means interpolation to values and derivatives of f(x) at a given set of points. The Hermite cubics (or C^1 cubic piecewise polynomials) have value and first derivative continuous at the knots. **Hermite cubic interpolation** means using Hermite cubics to do Hermite interpolation at the knots. There is a trivial solution of this problem using the Hermite cubic representation of Problem 4.2.13. With this representation the piecewise polynomial pp(x) which does Hermite cubic interpolation of f(x) at the break points $t_1, t_2, \ldots, t_{k+1}$ is

$$pp(x) = \sum_{i=1}^{k+1} f(x_i)h_i(x) + f'(x_i)h_i^{|}(x) \qquad \textbf{Equation 5.3.2}$$

This formula is analogous to Lagrange polynomial interpolation in that the representation makes the solution of the interpolation problem trivial. The Hermite cubic basis polynomials $h_i(x)$ and $h_i^{|}(x)$ are shown in Figure 5.5.

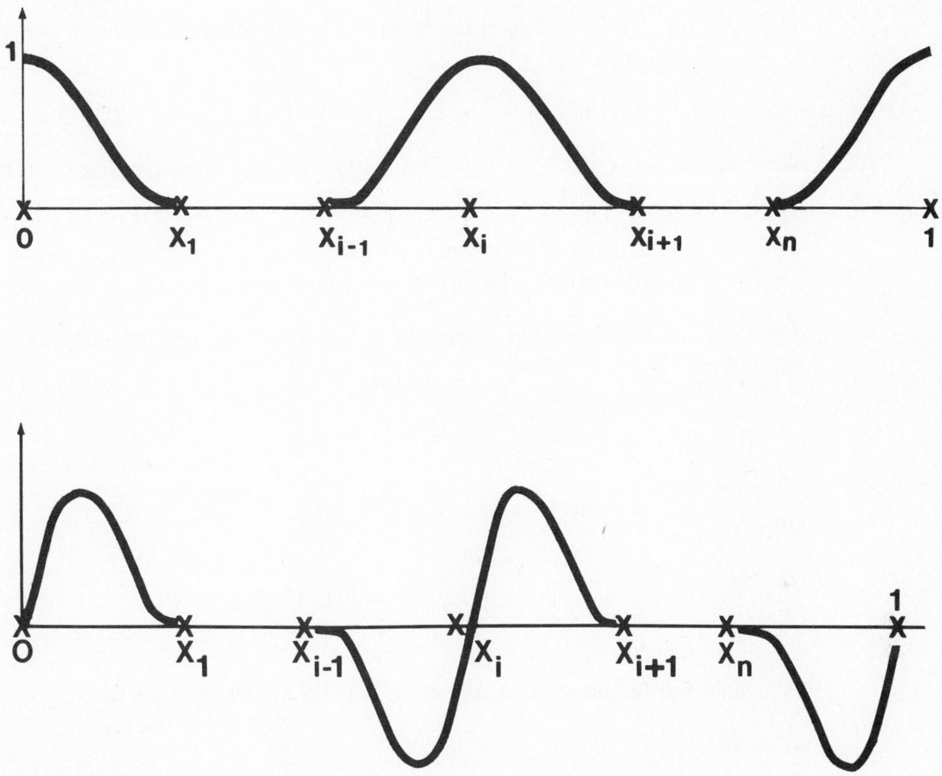

Figure 5.5 The Hermite cubic basis polynomials. These polynomials allow the solution of the Hermite cubic interpolation problem to be written down without any computation.

Hermite cubic interpolation is *local*; the interpolant only depends on the data at two neighboring interpolation points. In other words, a cubic polynomial is determined by its value and derivative at 2 points so that for $x \epsilon [x_i, x_{i+1}]$ there must be a formula involving cubic polynomials $p_1(x), \ldots, p_4(x)$ of the form

$$pp(x) = pp(x_i)p_1(x) + pp'(x_i)p_2(x) + pp(x_{i+1})p_3(x) + pp'(x_{i+1})p_4(x)$$

The polynomials $p_1(x), \ldots, p_4(x)$ can be determined directly from Equation 5.3.2 and the formulas in Problem 4.4.1. If we set $h = (x_{i+1} - x_i)$ and $y = x/h$, these can be simplified to bring the above equation into the form

$$\begin{aligned} pp(x) = {} & pp(x_i) + [pp(x_{i+1}) - pp(x_i)]y^2(3-2y) \\ & + h[pp'(x_i)(1-y) - pp'(x_{i+1})y]y(1-y) \end{aligned} \qquad \textbf{Equation 5.3.3}$$

Cubic Spline Interpolation **5.3.B

A cubic spline with k+1 interior knots $\{t_i\}$ has $4 + (k-1) = k+3$ coefficients or degrees of freedom. One may count these as 4 for the cubic in the first interval $[t_1, t_2]$ plus 1 in each of the remaining intervals. Thus, one can hope to interpolate at $k+3$ points. Clearly there must be some limitation on the location of these points; they could not all be in the first interval. The common approach is to interpolate at the knots and then determine the remaining 2 coefficients in various ways.

We use the shifted power form to represent the spline $s(x)$ so that for x in $[t_i, t_{i+1}]$

$$s(x) = a_{i0} + a_{i1}(x-t_i) + a_{i2}(x-t_i)^2 + a_{i3}(x-t_i)^3 \qquad \textbf{Equation 5.3.4}$$

The values to interpolate are $f_i = f(x_i)$, and we see immediately that $a_{i0} = f_i$. We now proceed to develop a system of linear equations for the slopes a_{i1} at the knots. The continuity of the second derivative of $s(x)$ gives

$$2a_{i2} + 6a_{i3} = 2a_{i+1,2} \qquad \textbf{Equation 5.3.5}$$

The cubic $s(x)$ can be written in the Newton form for interpolation of its own value and derivative at $x = t_i, t_{i+1}$ as follows:

$$s(x) = s(t_i) + s[t_i, t_i](x-t_i) + s[t_i, t_i, t_{i+1}](x-t_i)^2 + s[t_i, t_i, t_{i+1}, t_{i+1}](x-t_i)^2(x-t_{i+1})$$

We replace $x - t_{i+1}$ by $x - t_i - (t_{i+1}-t_i)$, set $h_i = t_{i+1}-t_i$, and combine terms to get

$$\begin{aligned} s(x) = {} & s(t_i) + s[t_i, t_i](x-t_i) \\ & + (s[t_i, t_i, t_{i+1}] - s[t_i, t_i, t_{i+1}, t_{i+1}]h_i)(x-t_i)^2 \\ & + s[t_i, t_i, t_{i+1}, t_{i+1}](x-t_i)^3 \end{aligned} \qquad \textbf{Equation 5.3.6}$$

The third and fourth divided differences in Equation 5.3.6 can be expressed in terms of lower-order differences:

$$s[t_i, t_i, t_{i+1}] = \frac{s[t_i, t_{i+1}] - s[t_i, t_i]}{h_i}$$

$$\begin{aligned} s[t_i, t_i, t_{i+1}, t_{i+1}] &= \frac{s[t_i, t_{i+1}, t_{i+1}] - s[t_i, t_i, t_{i+1}]}{h_i} \\ &= \frac{s[t_i, t_i] + s[t_{i+1}, t_{i+1}] - 2s[t_i, t_{i+1}]}{h_i^2} \end{aligned}$$

Comparing coefficients of $(x-t_i)$ powers in Equations 5.3.4 and 5.3.6 gives

$$a_{i0} = s(t_i)$$

$$a_{i1} = s[t_i, t_i]$$

$$a_{i3} = \frac{a_{i1} + a_{i+1,1} - 2s[t_i, t_{i+1}]}{h_i^2}$$

$$a_{i2} = \frac{s[t_i, t_{i+1}] - a_{i1}}{h_i} - a_{i3}h_i$$

Note that $s[t_i, t_{i+1}] = f[t_i, t_{i+1}]$ by the interpolation requirement. Substitute these into Equation 5.3.5, replace a_{i3} in the expression for a_{i2}, and simplify to obtain

$$h_{i+1}a_{i1} + 2(h_i+h_{i+1})a_{i+1,1} + h_ia_{i+2,1} = 3(f[t_i, t_{i+1}]h_{i+1} + f[t_{i+1}, t_{i+2}]h_i) \qquad \textbf{Equation 5.3.7}$$

These equations for the a_{i1}, $i = 1, 2, \ldots, k+1$, hold for $i = 1, 2, \ldots, k-1$, and so there are 2 fewer equations than unknowns. Two of the a_{i1} can be assigned arbitrarily, and then this linear system of equations is solved for the remaining a_{i1}. Once the a_{i1} are known, the remaining coefficients are obtained from the formulas used to derive Equation 5.3.7. This system is especially simple (it is *tridiagonal*), and it is shown in the next chapter how to solve it efficiently.

Note that **cubic spline interpolation is global**; the spline depends everywhere on its value at each interpolation point.

One common way to assign the 2 unknown slopes is to assume $f'(t_1)$ and $f'(t_{k+1})$ are known (or use estimates for them) and set $a_{11} = f'(t_1)$, $a_{k+1,1} = f'(t_{k+1})$. These are the **endpoint derivative conditions.** A second common way is to use the **natural spline interpolant condition** that $s''(x) = 0$ at t_1 and t_{k+1}. This gives the two extra equations needed by expressing a_{12} and $a_{k+1,2}$ in terms of slopes at knots. This choice is not highly recommended because it is usually an unnatural choice in spite of its name. If no additional information is known about f(x) (for example, if one is interpolating tabulated values), then the best choice for two more equations is the **not-a-knot condition.** One removes t_2 and t_k as knots by making the cubic pieces join up with 3 continuous derivatives. This gives the equations

$$a_{11}h_1 + a_{12}(t_3 - t_1) = \frac{[h_1 + 2(t_3 - t_1)]h_2 f[t_1, t_2] + h_1^2 f[t_2, t_3]}{t_3 - t_1}$$

Equation 5.3.8

$$a_{k,1}(t_{k+1} - t_{k-1}) + a_{k+1,1}h_k = \frac{h_k^2 f[t_k, t_{k+1}] + [h_k + 2(t_{k+1} - t_{k-1})]f[t_{k-1}, t_k]}{t_{k+1} - t_{k-1}}$$

to add to the system 5.3.7. After (or even before) solving 5.3.7, one renumbers the knots and coefficients to eliminate the redundant intervals $[t_2, t_3]$ and $[t_{k-2}, t_{k-1}]$ and their corresponding polynomial pieces.

PROBLEMS 5.3

5.3.1 Interpolate $e^{x/6}$ at the points 1, 2, . . . , 6 by piecewise quadratics joined with one continuous derivative at the break point 2.5 and 2 continuous derivatives at 4.5. Write a Fortran program to carry out the computations and find the maximum error the interpolant makes on the points 1, 1.05, 1.10, . . . , 6. **Hint:** Use the equations given at the beginning of the chapter.

5.3.2 Interpolate $\sqrt{x}$ by a piecewise polynomial pp(x) which is linear in [0,.001], quadratic in [.001, .01], and cubic in [.01, .1], [.1, .5]. Make pp(x) C^0 at .001, C^1 at .01, and C^2 at .1. Interpolate at the break points plus the midpoints of the second, third, and fourth intervals. Write a program to carry out the computations and find the maximum error the interpolant makes on the points 0, 10^{-5}, 10^{-4}, 5×10^{-4}, 10^{-3}, 5×10^{-3}, 10^{-2}, 5×10^{-2}, 10^{-1}, .02, .04, . . . , .5. **Hint:** Use the technique discussed at the beginning of the chapter.

5.3.3 Examine the results from Problem 5.3.2 and adjust the break points to reduce the maximum error. **Hint:** Move the break points to shorten the intervals with the larger errors.

5.3.4 Start with Equation 5.3.3 and express pp(x) in the shifted power form. That is,

$$pp(x) = a_{i0} + a_{i1}(x - x_i) + a_{i2}(x - x_1)^2 + a_{i3}(x - x_i)^3$$

and then obtain formulas for the coefficients a_{ij} in terms of the values and slopes of pp(x) at x_i and x_{i-1}.

5.3.5 Compare doing Hermite cubic interpolation using the general technique at the beginning of the chapter with using the formulas from Problem 5.3.4. Specifically, write a program to interpolate $1/(1+x^2)$ at 0, .2, . . . , 2.0 for each method and then compare (a) the length of the programs and (b) the execution time to compute the interpolants. **Hint:** You might put each program in a DO-loop to execute it many times (with the printing suppressed) so that a more accurate timing is achieved.

5.3.6 Compare doing cubic spline interpolations using the general technique at the beginning of the chapter with solving 5.3.7 and 5.3.8. Use the specific case in Problem 5.3.5 for the comparison.

5.3.7 Find the number of equations to be solved for cubic spline interpolation using (a) Equations 5.3.7 and 5.3.8 and (b) the general method given at the beginning of Section 5.3.

5.3.8 Derive the two equations to be added to the system 5.3.7 for natural spline interpolation.

5.3.9 An alternate system for cubic spline interpolation is obtained by finding a system of equations for the second derivatives of the spline at the knots. With the notation of Section 5.3.B, derive the following system.

$$\frac{h_i a_{i2}}{3} + \frac{2(h_i + h_{i+1})}{3} a_{i+1,2} + \frac{h_{i+2} a_{i+2,2}}{3}$$

$$= -\frac{f[t_i, t_{i+1}]}{h_i} + \frac{f[t_{i+1}, t_{i+2}]}{h_{i+1}}$$

5.3.10 Given that one has obtained the a_{i2} from the system of equations in Problem 5.3.9 plus two others, derive formulas to obtain the a_{i1} and a_{i3}.

5.3.11 Consider a piecewise polynomial pp(x) of degree n with k + 1 break points which has v_i continuous derivatives at the ith break point, $2 \le i \le k$. Show that the number of independent coefficients of pp(x) is

$$(n+1)k - \sum_{i=2}^{k} v_j$$

5.3.12 Show that the first-degree B-spline basis of Problem 4.3.8, part A, is a dual basis for the linear functionals $f(a + H(i-1))$ for i = 1, 2, . . . , k + 1. What are the implications of this for interpolation by linear splines?

5.3.13 Show how to solve the interpolation problem for linear splines using the basis of part B of Problem 4.3.8.

SOFTWARE FOR INTERPOLATION 5.4

In the previous section we noted that general interpolation problems are solved by using linear equation solvers. There is not much software available for general interpolation because it does little beyond calling on linear equation solvers. The PROTRAN system does provide this convenience, as the following example illustrates.

```
        $DECLARATIONS
        VECTOR DATA(10), XPOINT(3), CEXP(3), UNIFRM(10), FX(3)
C                CONSTRUCT DATA, XPOINT, UNIFRM AND FX = F(XPOINT)
        $ASSIGN  DATA(J) =  1./(1.+J**2)
                 UNIFRM(J) = (J-1)
                 XPOINT(J) = 1. + (J-1)*.5
                     FX(K) = F(XPOINT(K))
C                INTERPOLATE DATA BY POLYNOMIALS, RESULT IS PDATA(X)
        $INTERPOLATE, DATA ; VS UNIFRM; USING POLYNOMIALS; BY PDATA
C                INTERPOLATE GIVEN F(X) BY EXP(K,X) FOR K = 1 TO 3
        $INTERP, FX ; USING EBASIS(K,X),K,X ; VS XPOINT ; BY EXPFIT
                     COEFFICIENTS = CEXP
C
C........REMAINDER OF PROGRAM AND DEFINITION OF EBASIS(K,X) AS FORTRAN FUNCTION
```

Here DATA is interpolated by a polynomial (of degree 9 since there are 10 points) at the UNIFRM points. The resulting interpolant is the function PDATA. Then the function F is interpolated by the three functions defined in the EBASIS function (for example, e^x, e^{2x}, and e^{4x}). The interpolation is at 3 equally spaced points in the interval [1.0, 2.0] (that is, 1.0, 1.5, and 2.0); the coefficients of the interpolation are CEXP(I) for I = 1 to 3. EXPFIT is a Fortran function created, which is the resulting interpolant.

Most software for interpolation is for specialized problems where one can take some advantage and also relieve the user of a more significant amount of programming effort.

The ACM Collected Algorithms contains 20 algorithms for interpolation. Several of them are very easy or very specialized. Algorithms 167, 186, and 169 (in Algol) form a set for the computation and evaluation of polynomial interpolants using divided differences with multiple interpolation points. Algorithms 472 and 480 (in Algol) do spline interpolation and smoothing; equivalent programs are in PPPACK. Algorithm 507 is a Fortran implementation of Algorithm 472 for the special case of quintic splines; it executes about 6 times as fast. Algorithm 547 is a variation on Algorithm 480 for "discrete" smoothing using cubic splines.

Algorithms 433, 474, 476, 514, and 526 are all piecewise polynomial interpolation methods with something added to provide better fits. The examples in this and the next section show that piecewise polynomials may do much better than just polynomials, but there are still cases where they (especially for splines) do not do as well as one would like. These algorithms should provide "nice" fits to almost any data. Algorithms 474 and 526 are for two-dimensional data (surface fitting).

Software for Polynomial Interpolation 5.4.A

There are special techniques for polynomial interpolation; the most likely candidate is Newton interpolation. Here one builds the divided difference table and, possibly, converts the result to the shifted power form at the end. There is no widely available software to do this, and so one must use linear equation solvers or write one's own program to implement Newton interpolation. The Fortran code in the next example does this in about a dozen lines.

The Runge Example: Polynomial Interpolation Can Do Very Poorly Example 5.4

Polynomial interpolation might give unexpectedly poor results; the classic Runge example involves interpolating $1/(1+x^2)$ at equally spaced points in an interval like $[-5, 5]$ or $[-8, 8]$. This interpolation is *unstable* in the sense that the maximum error between $1/(1+x^2)$ and its polynomial interpolant grows very rapidly as the degree n of the polynomial increases. Two examples of the interpolants are shown in Figure 5.6; the program to calculate and plot the interpolant is given to illustrate the simplicity of using Newton interpolation. About 15 lines of Fortran are needed to compute the interpolant and its maximum error; another 8 or so are needed for the plotting.

The behavior seen in Figure 5.6 occurs for many other simple, smooth functions. Part of the difficulty is that polynomials are not terribly good for approximating a wide variety of curves; the other part is that uniformly spaced points are not very good choices for polynomial interpolation. The **Chebyshev points** are far superior. The $n+1$ Chebyshev points for the interval [a, b] are given by

$$x_i = \frac{a+b}{2} + \frac{(a-b)}{2} \cos \frac{2i+1}{2n+2} \pi \qquad i = 0, 1, \ldots, n \qquad \textbf{Equation 5.4.1}$$

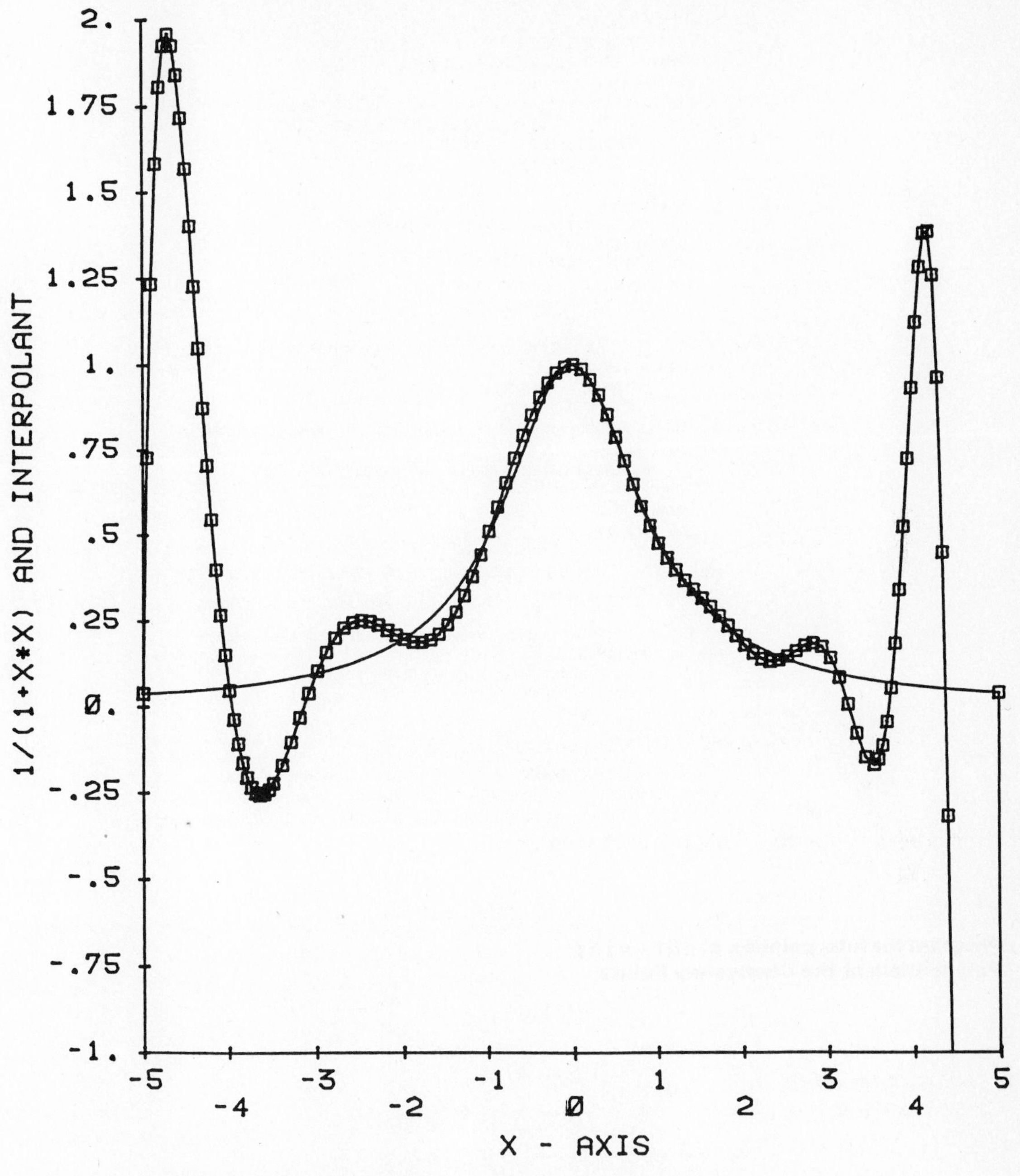

Figure 5.6 **The Runge example.** The function $1/(1+x^2)$ is interpolated at $n+1$ equally spaced points in $[-5, 5]$. The polynomials for $n = 10$ (left half) and $n = 16$ (right half) are shown. The right half goes down to -14 near $x = 1.0$.

These points bunch up near the ends of the interval and thus help prevent large errors there, as seen in Figure 5.6. The effectiveness of this choice of interpolation points is seen from the following example.

Polynomial Interpolation of $1/(1+x^2)$ at the Chebyshev Points — Example 5.5

We interpolate $1/(1+x^2)$ at the Chebyshevs points with the following program. The resulting interpolant is given in Figure 5.7, and it is a dramatic improvement over the results of Example 5.4.

Program for the Runge Example: Interpolation of $1/(1+x^2)$ by Polynomials

```
      REAL DDIF(20),XPTS(20)
      REAL  Y(200),PLOT(200),RANGE(4)
      DATA RANGE / 4*0. /
C     INTERPOLATE 1/(1+X**2) ON (-5,5) BY POLYNOMIALS OF DEGREE N
C                    AT N+1 UNIFORMLY SPACED POINTS
C              ARITHMETIC STATEMENT FUNCTION
      F(X) = 1./(1.+X*X)
      N = 9
      XMAX = 5.
C              INITIALIZE DIVIDED DIFFERENCES
      H = XMAX/N*2.
      DO 10 K = 1,N+1
          XPTS(K) = 5. + (K-1)*H
          DDIF(K) = F(XPTS(K))
   10 CONTINUE
C              CALCULATE DIVIDED DIFFERENCE TABLE BY ALGORITHM 5.2.3
      DO 20 K = 1,N
          DO 20 J = -1,N-K-1
              I = N-J
              DDIF(I) = (DDIF(I)-DDIF(I-1))/(XPTS(I)-XPTS(I-K))
   20 CONTINUE
C         ESTIMATE MAXIMUM ERROR AND PREPARE FOR PLOT
      H = 2.*XMAX/199.
      EMAX = 0.0
      DO 30 J =1,200
          YJ   = (J-1)*H - XMAX
C              COMPUTE POLYNOMIAL VALUE BY NESTED MULTIPLICATION
          POLYV = DDIF(N+1)
          DO 25 K = 1,N
               POLYV = DDIF(N+1-K) + (YJ-XPTS(N+1-K))*POLYV
   25     CONTINUE
          EMAX = AMAX1(EMAX,ABS(F(YJ)-POLYV))
          PLOT(J)= POLYV
          Y(J)   = YJ
   30 CONTINUE
C           USE IMSL ROUTINE USPLO TO PLOT F(X) AND INTERPOLANT
      PRINT 40, N, EMAX
   40   FORMAT('  FOR DEGREE =' I3 ' THE MAX ERROR IS' E13.5 )
      CALL USPLO(Y,PLOT,200,200,1,1,1H ,1,1HX,1,1HY,1,RANGE,1H1,1,IER)
      STOP
      END
```

Program for Interpolation of $1/(1+x^2)$ by Polynomials at the Chebyshev Points

```
$DECLARATIONS
VECTOR CHEBY(11),FX(11) $
PI = 4.*ATAN(1.)
$ASSIGN  CHEBY(I) = -10.*COS((2*I+1)*PI/20)
          FX(I) = F(CHEBY(I))
$INTERPOLATE, FX ; USING POLYNOMIALS; BY POLYV ; VS CHEBY
$MAX ABS(POLYV(X)-1./(1.+X*X))  ; FOR(X=-5.,5.,.05) ; IS ERRMAX
$PRINT ERRMAX
$PLOT, POLYV(X) ; FOR(X= -5,5)
TITLE ='POLYNOMIAL INTERPOLATION AT CHEBYSHEV POINTS FOR 1/(1+X*X)'
   XLABEL = 'X-AXIS' ; YLABEL = 'Y-AXIS'
$END
FUNCTION F(X)
F = 1./(1.+X*X)
$END
```

The same degrees are used for the polynomials in this example as before, but the error now decreases for larger degrees. The error does not, however, decrease very rapidly, and the interpolant has "wiggles" that are not present in the original function $1/(1+x^2)$. In other words, while the difference between $1/(1+x^2)$ and its interpolant is fairly small, the interpolating polynomial does very poorly in approximating the derivatives of $1/(1+x^2)$.

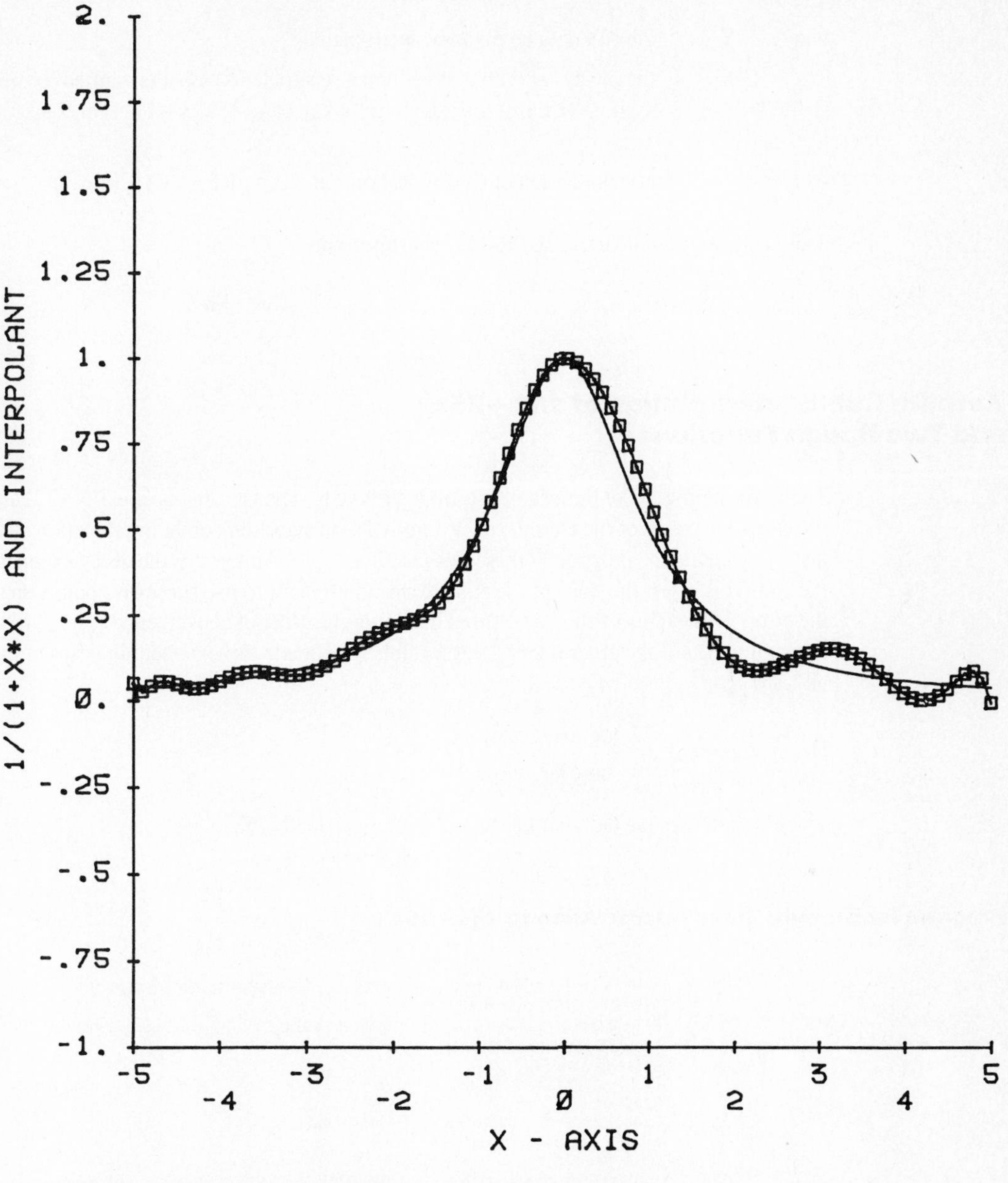

Figure 5.7 Polynomial interpolation of $1/(1+x^2)$ at the Chebyshev points. The polynomials of degree 10 (left half) and 16 (right half) are shown which interpolate at the Chebyshev points.

Software for Hermite Cubic Interpolation 5.4.B

Hermite cubic piecewise polynomial interpolation is also simple to implement, and thus there is little widely available software especially designed for this task. Example 5.6 below presents a program which shows the simple nature of this software.

The IMSL library has a routine IQHSCU which does **quasi-Hermite cubic interpolation**. Given the data points (x_i, y_i), estimated values y_i' of the derivative at the x_i are computed from

$$y_i' \sim \frac{y_{i+1} - y_{i-1}}{x_{i+1} - x_{i-1}}$$

This is just the divided difference using the two neighboring points; special formulas are used for the first and last points. The call to IQHSCU is

```
CALL IQHSCU (X,Y,NX,COEF,IC,IER)
```

where X,Y = the NX data points to be interpolated

COEF = the array of cubic polynomial coefficients for the shifted power form, that is, a_{ij} = COEF(i, j) for j ≥ 1 and $pp(x) = y_i + a_{i1}(x-x_i) + a_{i2}(x-x_i)^2 + a_{i3}(x-x_i)^3$ for $x \epsilon [x_i, x_{i+1}]$

IC = row dimension of COEF declaration, i.e., in REAL COEF(IC,3)

This is the program used by the PROTRAN statement:

```
$INTERPOLATE FDATA; USING HERMITES; VS XPTS ; BY HINTER
```

Hermite Cubic Interpolation of $1/(1+25x^2)$ and Two Rough Functions — Example 5.6

The Fortran program of this example is from PPPACK. The DO 20 loop and PNATX assignment contain the key components of the Hermite cubic interpolation algorithm; other interpolation methods can be used just by changing the program at these two places. Of special interest is the decay exponent computed near the end. This is just the slope of the straight line interpolant to two successive points on the log-log plot of the error. This exponent should be the exponent in the order of convergence as h = 1/N goes to zero. We expect it to be 4 if the order is $0(N^{-4})$. A formula to estimate this exponent in terms of the error err_i for N_i pieces is

$$\text{Decay exponent} = \frac{\log err_i - \log err_{i-1}}{\log N_i - \log N_{i-1}} \qquad \textbf{Equation 5.4.2}$$

The program uses the fact that $\log N_i - \log N_{i-1} = \log(N_i/N_{i-1})$.

Program for Hermite Cubic Interpolation to $1/(1+25x^2)$

```
C     EXAMPLE 5.6. RUNGE EXAMPLE, WITH CUBIC HERMITE INTERPOLATION
      INTEGER I,ISTEP,J,N,NM1
      REAL ALOGER,ALGERP,C(4,20),DECAY,DIVDF1,DIVDF3,DTAU,DX,ERRMAX,G,H
     *    ,PNATX,STEP,TAU(20)
      DATA STEP, ISTEP /20., 20/
      G(X) = 1./(1.+(5.*X)**2)
      PRINT 600
  600 FORMAT(28H  N   MAX.ERROR   DECAY EXP.//)
      DECAY = 0.
      DO 40 N=2,20,2
C        CHOOSE INTERPOLATION POINTS  TAU(1), ..., TAU(N) , EQUALLY
C        SPACED IN (-1,1), AND SET  C(1,I) = G(TAU(I)), C(2,I) =
C        GPRIME(TAU(I)) = -50.*TAU(I)*G(TAU(I))**2, I=1,...,N.
         NM1 = N-1
         H = 2./FLOAT(NM1)
         DO 10 I=1,N
            TAU(I) = FLOAT(I-1)*H - 1.
            C(1,I) = G(TAU(I))
   10       C(2,I) = -50.*TAU(I)*C(1,I)**2
C
C        CALCULATE THE COEFFICIENTS OF THE POLYNOMIAL PIECES
         DO 20 I=1,NM1
            DTAU = TAU(I+1) - TAU(I)
            DIVDF1 = (C(1,I+1) - C(1,I))/DTAU
            DIVDF3 = C(2,I) + C(2,I+1) - 2.*DIVDF1
            C(3,I) = (DIVDF1 - C(2,I) - DIVDF3)/DTAU
   20       C(4,I) = (DIVDF3/DTAU)/DTAU
C
C        ESTIMATE MAX.INTERPOLATION ERROR ON (-1,1).
         ERRMAX = 0.
         DO 30 I=2,N
            DX = (TAU(I)-TAU(I-1))/STEP
            DO 30 J=1,ISTEP
               H = FLOAT(J)*DX
C              EVALUATE (I-1)ST CUBIC PIECE
C
```

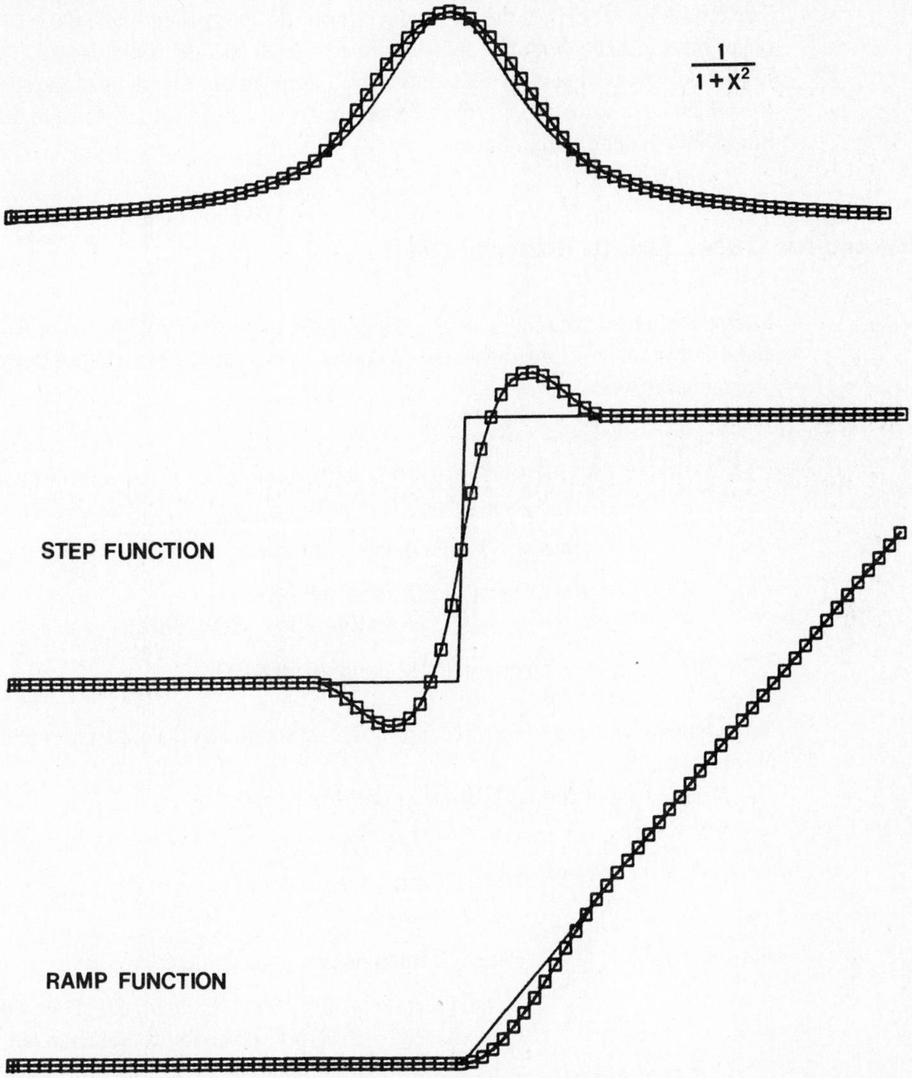

Figure 5.8 **Hermite cubic interpolation of $1/(1+25x^2)$, x_+, and x_+^0.** The interpolants shown have 6 cubic pieces.

```
                PNATX = C(1,I-1)+H*(C(2,I-1)+H*(C(3,I-1)+H*C(4,I-1)))
C
   30           ERRMAX = AMAX1(ERRMAX,ABS(G(TAU(I-1)+H)-PNATX))
            ALOGER = ALOG(ERRMAX)
            IF (N .GT. 2)  DECAY =
     *         (ALOGER - ALGERP)/ALOG(FLOAT(N)/FLOAT(N-2))
            ALGERP = ALOGER
   40       PRINT 640,N,ERRMAX,DECAY
  640  FORMAT(I3,E12.4,F11.2)
       STOP
       END
```

The output from this program is shown in the table to the right. Note that the error of the interpolation is decreasing nicely. The decay exponent is approaching the theoretical value of -4, which corresponds to the error being of order N^{-4}.

The same program has been modified to interpolate x_+^0 and x_+ on the interval $[-2, 2]$ with uniformly spaced interpolation points. The results for all three functions are shown in Figure 5.8.

OUTPUT FROM ABOVE PROGRAM

N	MAX.ERROR	DECAY EXP.
2	.9246+00	.00
4	.5407+00	-.77
6	.2500+00	-1.90
8	.1141+00	-2.73
10	.5562-01	-3.22
12	.2932-01	-3.51
14	.1661-01	-3.69
16	.1000-01	-3.80
18	.6339-02	-3.87
20	.4195-02	-3.92

Hermite cubic interpolation of $1/(1+25x^2)$ on $[-1, 1]$ is the same as interpolation of $1/(1+x^2)$ on $[-5, 5]$. The results are very good; the maximum error of the interpolant is about 0.03. Note how the interpolants have some difficulty with the discontinuity at $x = 0$ (as one would expect). This does not propagate far because of the local nature of Hermite cubic interpolation. The slope of the step function is undefined at $x = 0$, and so a value of 5 is arbitrarily assigned. One can adjust this value to make the "overshoot" in the interpolant larger or disappear.

Software for Cubic Spline Interpolation 5.4.C

Interpolation by cubic splines is more complicated than either polynomial or Hermite cubic interpolation, and a fair number of programs exist to do this interpolation. The IMSL library contains a simple-to-use program as follows:

```
CALL ICSCCU(X,Y,NX,COEF,IC,IER)
```

where X,Y = arrays of NX data points to interpolate

COEF = array of spline coefficients; for $x \epsilon [x_i, x_{i+1}]$

$$s(x) = y_i + \text{COEF}(i,1)(x-x_i) + \text{COEF}(i,2)(x-x_i)^2 + \text{COEF}(i,3)(x-x_i)^3$$

IC = row dimension in the declaration of COEF

No endpoint conditions are required for this program; it uses the not-a-knot condition discussed at the end of Section 5.3.B.

A more flexible routine CUBSPL in PPPACK is used as

```
CALL CUBSPL(XPTS,C,NX,ILEFT,IRIGHT)
```

where XPTS = the NX interpolation points

C = two-dimensional array with, *on input,* C(1, I) = values to interpolate, I = 1 to NX. C(2, 1), C(2, NX) = condition values at left and right ends

ILEFT,IRIGHT = switches to select conditions at left and right ends

= 0 means use not-a-knot condition

= 1 means slopes at end are in C(2, 1), C(2, NX)

= 2 means second derivatives at end are in C(2, 1), C(2, NX)

Upon output the C array is changed to the cubic spline coefficients, and so, for $x \epsilon$[XPTS(i), XPTS(i+1)] = $[x_i, x_{i+1}]$,

$$s(x) = C(1, i) + C(2, i)(x-x_i) + C(3, i)(x-x_i)^2 + C(4, i)(x-x_i)^3$$

The choices of ILEFT = IRIGHT = 0 give the same interpolation as ICSCCU.

The IMSL library has two other cubic spline interpolation programs. ICSICU provides the facilities of CUBSPL with ILEFT and IRIGHT $\neq$ 0; it is used as

```
CALL ICSICU(X,Y,NX,BPAR,COEF,IC,IER)
```

where the additional parameter BPAR = vector of 4 end conditions so that

$$2s''(x_1) + \text{BPAR}(1)\, s''(x_2) = \text{BPAR}(2)$$
$$\text{BPAR}(3)\, s''(x_{NX-1}) + 2s''(x_{NX}) = \text{BPAR}(4)$$

Most cubic spline interpolation routines require end conditions as input; this is very useful if they are known, but frustrating when one only has tabulated data. If the second derivatives of the data are known, one sets BPAR(1) = BPAR(3) = 0 and BPAR(2) and BPAR(4) to twice these known values. If the first derivatives y_1' and y_{NX}' of the data are known, then one can use the formulas ($h_i = x_{i+1} - x_i$)

$$\begin{aligned} \text{BPAR}(1) &= \text{BPAR}(3) = 1 \\ \text{BPAR}(2) &= 6((y_2 - y_1)/h_1 - y_1')/h_1 \\ \text{BPAR}(4) &= 6((y_{NX} - y_{NX-1})/h_{NX-1} - y_{NX}')/h_{NX-1} \end{aligned}$$

The third cubic spline interpolation program in the IMSL library is ICSPLN, which imposes periodic end conditions:

$$\begin{aligned} s(X_1) &= s(X_{NX}) \\ s'(X_1) &= s'(X_{NX}) \\ s''(X_1) &= s''(X_{NX}) \end{aligned}$$

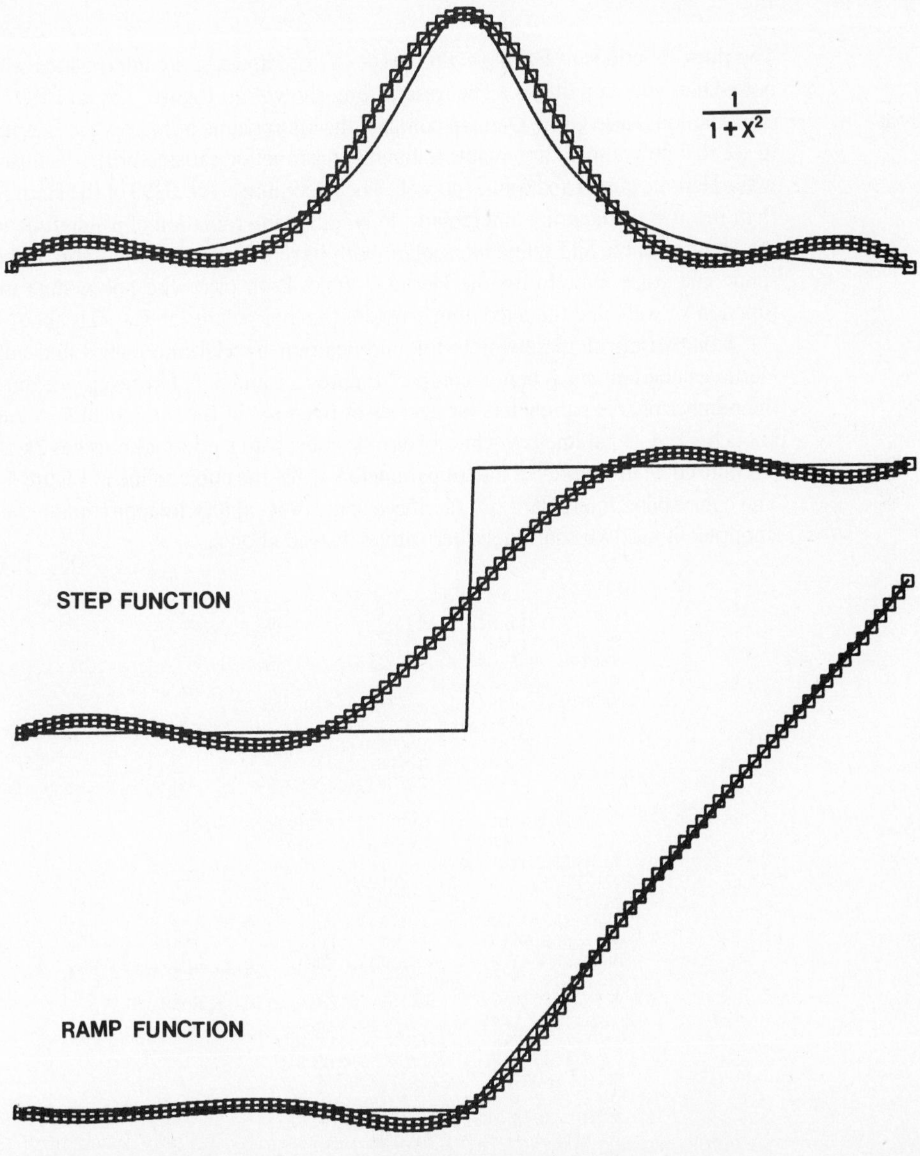

Figure 5.9 Cubic spline interpolation of three functions. The functions $1/(1+x^2)$, x_+^0, and x_+ are interpolated on $[-5, 5]$, $[-2, 2]$, and $[-2, 2]$, respectively, using cubic splines with 6 pieces.

This condition is the one wanted for closed curves in the plane. Thus, let (x_i, y_i), $i = 1$ to $NX-1$, be a point set in the plane, then set $t_i = i$, $X_{NX} = X_1$, and $y_{NX} = y_1$, and interpolate the two data sets (t_i, x_i), (t_i, y_i), $i = 1$ to NX by cubic splines $s_1(x)$ and $s_2(x)$ with periodic boundary conditions. Then the parameterized curve $x = s_1(t)$, $y = s_2(t)$ for $1 \le t \le NX$ is a smooth closed curve in the plane that interpolates the given data.

Both the IMSL library and PPPACK have routines (ICSEVU and PPVALU, respectively) to take the computed coefficients and evaluate the cubic spline at a given set of points.

The PROTRAN system provides cubic spline interpolation as follows:

```
$INTERPOLATE FDATA; USING SPLINES; VS XPTS; BY SINTER
```

The not-a-knot end conditions are used.

Cubic Spline Interpolation of $1/(1+x^2)$ and Two Rough Functions

Example 5.7

The three functions of Example 5.6, $1/(1+x^2)$, x_+^0, and x_+, are interpolated with cubic splines using the not-a-knot end conditions. The results are shown in Figure 5.9; a PROTRAN program for this computation is also given. One can compare the interpolants of $1/(1+x^2)$ in Examples 5.4, 5.5, 5.6, and here to see that polynomials are unable to handle this function satisfactorily (even using the Chebyshev points) while Hermite cubics and splines do well. The maximum error .0293 of the Hermite cubic interpolant is less than the .078 of the spline interpolant. Polynomial interpolation of a step function is not very successful; the Hermite cubic and spline interpolant both have a "hump" at the jump; it then rapidly decays for the spline and stops entirely for the Hermite cubic. Both piecewise polynomial methods handle the ramp function x_+ well, and the maximum errors of the interpolants at $x = 0$ is about the same (.043).

Comparison of these results for interpolation by Hermite cubics and cubic splines suggests that Hermite cubics do much better (compare Figures 5.8 and 5.9). However, one must take into consideration the number of free parameters (or degrees of freedom) in the interpolants. A cubic spline with k interior knots has $k + 4$ parameters, while a Hermite cubic with k interior knots has $2k + 4$ parameters. Thus the Hermite cubic in Figure 5.8 has 14 parameters while the cubic spline in Figure 5.9 only has 9 parameters. The cubic spline interpolant has sacrificed some of its ability to approximate the functions in order to be smoother (it has two continuous derivatives instead of one).

```
C         EXAMPLE 5.7     CUBIC SPLINE INTERPOLATION
C         OF 1/(1+X*X), STEP AND RAMP FUNCTIONS
      $DECLARATIONS
      VECTOR  UNI5(N=20), UNI2(N=20), SMTH5(N=20),X02(N=20),X12(N=20) $
      N = 7
      $ASSIGN  UNI5(I) = -5.+(I-1)*10./(N-1)
               UNI2(I) = -2.+(I-1)* 4./(N-1)
              SMTH5(I) = SMOOTH(UNI5(I))
                X02(I) = X0(UNI2(I))
                X12(I) = X1(UNI2(I))
C
C         THE THREE CUBIC SPLINE INTERPOLANTS ARE
C              CS1(X), CS2(X) AND CS3(X)
      $INTERPOLATE, SMTH5  ; USING SPLINES; BY CS1 ; VS UNI5
      $INTERP     , X02    ; USING SPLINES; BY CS2 ; VS UNI2
      $INTERP,      X12    ; USING SPLINES; BY CS3 ; VS UNI2
      $MAX ABS(SMOOTH(X)-CS1(X)); FOR( X=-5,5.,.02); IS ERR1
      $MAX ABS(XO(X)     -CS2(X)); FOR( X=-2,2.,.01); IS ERR2
      $MAX ABS(X1(X)     -CS3(X)); FOR( X=-2,2.,.01); IS ERR3  $
      PRINT 10, ERR1,ERR2,ERR3
   10 FORMAT(10X,'CUBIC SPLINE INTERPOLATION ERRORS ARE' /
     A 10X,' 1. 1/(1+X*X)      '  F12.8 /
     B 10X,' 2. STEP FUNCTION '  F12.8 /
     C 10X,' 3. RAMP FUNCTION '  F12.8 )
      $PLOT SMOOTH(X),CS1(X); FOR(X= -5.,5.)
         TITLE =  'CUBIC SPLINE INTERPOLATION OF 1/(1+X*X)'
      $PLOT  XO(X),CS2(X)  ; FOR(X= -2,2)
         TITLE = 'CUBIC SPLINE INTERPOLATION OF STEP FUNCTION'
      $PLOT, X1(X),CS3(X)  ; FOR(X= -2.,2.)
         TITLE = 'CUBIC SPLINE INTERPOLATION OF RAMP FUNCTION'
      $END
      FUNCTION SMOOTH(X)
      SMOOTH = 1./(1.+X*X)
```

```
RETURN
END
FUNCTION XO(X)
XO = 0.
IF( X .LT. 0. )         RETURN
XO = 1.
RETURN
END
FUNCTION X1(X)
X1 = 0.
IF( X .LT. 0. )         RETURN
X1 = X
RETURN
END
```

PROBLEMS 5.4

5.4.1 Modify the program of Example 5.4 to interpolate e^x at the same points. Note how the polynomial no longer blows up at the ends. Estimate the order of the error as n increases.

5.4.2 Modify the program of Example 5.4 to produce a subroutine for **polynomial interpolation**. The first lines of the subroutine should be

```
SUBROUTINE POLINT (Y,XPTS,NPTS,DDIF)
REAL Y(NPTS), XPTS(NPTS), DDIF(NPTS)
```

where Y,XPTS = data to be interpolated at NPTS points

DDIF = divided difference coefficients of the Newton interpolation polynomial

NPTS = number of interpolation points = polynomial degree plus one

Apply the subroutine to an example function [for example, $1/(1+x^2)$] and produce output that indicates it is correct.

5.4.3 Modify the program of Example 5.4 to produce a subroutine for **polynomial interpolation of a function at the Chebyshev points**. The first lines of the subroutine should be

```
SUBROUTINE POLCHB(F,A,B,NPTS,DDIF)
REAL XPTS(NPTS), DDIF(NPTS)
```

where F = function to be interpolated

DDIF = divided difference coefficients of the Newton interpolation polynomial

(A,B) = interval of interpolation

NPTS = the number of interpolation points (use Equation 4.5.1)

Apply the subroutine to an example function [for example, $1/(1+x^2)$] and produce output that indicates it is correct.

5.4.4 Use the program of Example 5.6 to create a subroutine to do **Hermite cubic interpolation**. The first lines of the program should be

```
SUBROUTINE HERM(F,FPRIME,XPTS,NPTS,CUBCOE)
REAL XPTS(NPTS), CUBCOE(NPTS,4)
```

where F = function to interpolate

FPRIME = derivative of F

XPTS = interpolation points

NPTS = number of XPTS = number of cubic pieces plus 1

CUBCOE = cubic polynomial coefficients so for $x \in [XPTS(i), XPTS(i+1)]$ we have the following formula for the Hermite cubics

$$pp(x) = CUBCOE(i,1) + CUBCOE(i,2)\,[x - XPTS(i)] + CUBCOE(i,3)\,[x - XPTS(i)]^2 + CUBCOE(i,4)\,[x - XPTS(i)]^3$$

Note that CUBCOE is declared with one row more than needed to simplify the calling sequence of HERM. Apply the program to interpolate $1/(1+x^2)$ and produce output that indicates it is correct.

5.4.5 Compare the effectiveness of interpolation methods for the following functions. Specifically, compute the polynomial interpolant using both uniformly spaced and Chebyshev points in the given intervals and a Hermite cubic interpolant at uniform points. Estimate the order of the error as the degree or number of pieces increase.

(A) e^{-10x} on [0, 3]

(B) $\min(|x|, |x-2|)$ on [−1, 3]

(C) $\cos(1+x^2)$ on [0, 3]

(D) $e^{(x-1)/x}$ on [0, 3]

(E) $\sin(x)$ on [0, 1]

5.4.6 The process of **inverse interpolation** is to interchange the role of the independent and dependent variables. Thus, given the data $(x_i, f(x_i))$ for $f(x)$, one transforms it to $(y_i, g(y_i))$ for $g(y) = f^{-1}(y)$ and $y_i = f(x_i), g(y_i) = x_i$. One then interpolates the data $(y_i, g(y_i))$ instead of the original data.

(A) Explain why this does not work if f(x) is not monotone in the interval.

(B) Use the example $f(x) = \sqrt[3]{x}\,\cos(x)$ for $x \in [-.5, .3]$ to show that inverse interpolation gives a better approximation than ordinary interpolation. **Hint**: Apply the program of Problem 5.4.2 to both the original and inverse interpolation problems and compare the results.

(C) Explain how inverse interpolation is useful for **inverting a function** [i.e., finding a value of x so that f(x) has a specified value]. Consider the specific case of computing x so that $\sin(x) = .25$. **Hint**: Take 5 points $x_i = .22 + i \times .01$, apply inverse polynomial interpolation to the table $(x_i, \sin(x_i))$, and evaluate the result for $y = .25$.

5.4.7 Use the decay exponent formula 5.4.2 to experimentally determine the rate of convergence of cubic spline interpolation for the following functions:

(A) $1/(1+x^2)$ on [−5, 5]

(B) $x^2e^{-x^2}$ on [0, 1]

(C) $\frac{1}{x}$ on [.02, .5]

(D) x_+^k on [−2, 2] for k = 0, 1, 2, 2.5

5.4.8 Investigate the effectiveness of interpolation at the Chebyshev points for Hermite cubic interpolation. Give an argument why this choice of interpolation points should not be as effective as a uniform set for an ordinary, well-behaved function. Provide computational results which support the argument.

5.4.9 The power of piecewise polynomials comes partly from the possibility of selecting the break points to match the behavior of a function. For each of the functions given: (a) determine a scheme for selecting break points which is suitable for the function, and (b) use these break points with either Hermite cubic or cubic spline interpolation and show that they give substantially better approximations than using uniformly distributed break points.

(A) $12(x-1)\sin[\pi/(x^2+.4x+.1)]$ on $[-2, 2]$

(B) $|x|^k \text{sign}(x)$ for $k = .1, .5$ on $[-1, 1]$

(C) $(x^5-x^4+1.2x^3-x^2+.2x)/(x^4-x^3+2.3x^2-2x-.6)$ on $[-5, 5]$

5.4.10 **ACM Algorithm 416** is an Algol program to evaluate a polynomial from either given values (the interpolation problem) or given divided differences. Translate this algorithm to Fortran, and run several test problems to illustrate the use of the algorithm and to verify the correctness of the translation.

5.4.11 The following **titanium data** is well known as physical data which is difficult to represent well by a mathematical model. Compute polynomial interpolants of this data of degrees 5, 10, 15, and 20. Choose the interpolation points more or less equally spaced between 585 and 1065. Have the program produce the maximum error of the interpolating polynomial and graphs of the data and the error. **Hint:** Use the IMSL routine USPLO for the graphs and modify the program of Example 5.4; alternatively use the PROTRAN system.

Titanium data

The abscissas are $x_i = 575 + ih$, for $i = 1$ to 49, $h = 10$. The ordinates are

.644, .622, .638, .649, .652, .639, .646, .657, .652, .655
.644, .663, .663, .668, .676, .676, .686, .679, .678, .683
.694, .699, .710, .730, .763, .812, .907, 1.044, 1.336, 1.881
2.169, 2.075, 1.598, 1.211, .916, .746, .672, .627, .615, .607
.606, .609, .603, .601, .603, .601, .611, .601, .608

5.4.12 Repeat Problem 5.4.11 with Hermite cubics instead of polynomials. Use 2, 5, 8, and 11 pieces. **Hint:** Use IMSL routine IQHSCU or modify the program of Example 5.6. Use ICSEVU to prepare data for the graph; alternatively use the PROTAN system.

5.4.13 Repeat Problem 5.4.12 with cubic splines instead of Hermite cubics. **Hint:** Use the IMSL routine ICSICU or ICSCCU instead of IQHSCU; alternately use PROTRAN.

5.4.14 Use the IMSL routine ICSPLN to interpolate points on a circle. Choose NX points $x_i = \cos\ [2(i-1)\pi/(NX-1)]$, $y_i = \sin\ [2(i-1)\pi/(NX-1)]$ for NX $-$ 5 and 10, then interpolate this data by a periodic cubic spline.

(A) Plot the resulting curve in the plane and comment on how circular it appears.

(B) Modify (x_2, y_2) to be r times the value for a circle and investigate the effect of changing r. Try, for example, $r = .1, .5, .9, 1.1, 1.5$, and 2.

5.4.15 Pretty curves with loops can be obtained as follows: Set $\theta = \pi/(NX-1)$, $x_i^T = r^T\cos[2(i-1)\theta]$, $x_i^B = r^B\cos[2(i-1)\theta + \theta/2]$, $x_i^{M\pm} = \cos[2(i-1)\theta + \theta/2 \pm \theta/6]$, and let y_i have a similar definition with cos replaced by sin. Define the data set of 4NX points as (x_i^T, y_i^T), (x_i^{M+}, y_i^{M+}), (x_i^B, y_i^B), (x_i^{M-}, y_i^{M-}) for $i = 1$ to NX. Various values of r^T and r^B give curves with loops. Create data sets for NX = 4, 8, 12, and $r^T = 1.25$, $r^B = .8$, interpolate the data with ICSPLN, and plot the resulting curves.

CHOICE OF INTERPOLATION FORMS AND POINTS *5.5

The choice of what functions or model to use for interpolation and where to do the interpolation depends heavily on the use to be made of the interpolant. There are three common uses of interpolation:

1. The derivation of formulas
2. Local replacement or manipulation of information
3. Global replacement or manipulation of information

Several examples of the **derivation of formulas** are given in the next section; the formulas themselves also can be divided into the local or global types. A key requirement here is that the model be easy to manipulate mathematically and easy to analyze; polynomials are usually the most convenient.

In the **local use of interpolation** one visualizes a situation where the only thing that counts is information from a small part of a function or subset of the data. In some cases, such as estimating derivatives of functions, one can make the domain for function values as small as one likes. In other cases, such as with a large table of experimental data, there is a limit on how small the domain can be, yet it is small in relation to the size of the table. In these cases, one can — and should — formulate a *model* of how the function or data behaves locally. Low-degree polynomials are usually adequate models of local behavior unless some singularity or contaminated data is present.

The **global use of interpolation** involves a model of the global behavior of the function or data. There is a much wider variety of global behaviors and one must check — and perhaps double check — that the model chosen is adequate. Polynomials are much less successful as global models; there are many ordinary-appearing functions and data sets which cannot be adequately modeled by polynomials. The strength and attraction of splines and piecewise polynomials is their flexibility in global behavior. It is better to use *approximation* instead of interpolation for global representations of data and functions (see Chapter 11).

The choice of the model (polynomials, splines, etc.) is the most crucial step in interpolation, but even after a choice is made, there are two important questions remaining:

1. How does one represent or parameterize the model?
2. Where does one interpolate?

Assessment of Polynomial Representations 5.5.A

Four methods for representing polynomials are discussed in this chapter:

Power form: $$p(x) = \sum_{i=0}^{n} a_i x^i$$

Shifted power form: $$p(x) = \sum_{i=0}^{n} b_i (x-c)^i$$

Newton form: $$p(x) = \sum_{i=0}^{n} d_i \prod_{j=1}^{i} (x-c_j)$$

Lagrange form: $$p(x) = \sum_{i=0}^{n} p_i \ell_i(x) = \prod_{j=0}^{n} (x-x_j) \sum_{i=0}^{n} \frac{q_i}{(x-x_i)}$$

Here new coefficients $q_i = p_i \pi(x_i - x_j)$ are introduced to make $p(x)$ easier to evaluate. There is another elementary representation:

Root-product form: $$p(x) = a \prod_{i=1}^{n} (x-r_i)$$

There is also an important representation which is introduced in Chapter 11:

Orthogonal polynomial form: $$p(x) = \sum_{i=0}^{n} e_i P_i(x)$$

where the $P_i(x)$ are orthogonal polynomials (e.g., Legendre polynomials).

These representations are compared in several respects:

1. Ease of mathematical manipulation and analysis
2. Work to evaluate
3. Numerical stability
4. Ease to solve the interpolation problem

The results are presented in Table 5.2. The assessments given in Table 5.2 are for worst cases. Thus, the power form is not always numerically unstable, but there is a substantial risk that it is. The operation counts given are in terms of the polynomial degree n; those for evaluation use the abbreviations A for addition and M for multiplication. Thus, the evaluation of the Newton form requires 2n additions and n multiplications. See Problems 5.5.1 to 5.5.4 and 5.5.11 for further details about the numerical stability properties of these forms.

Assessment of Polynomial Representations **Table 5.2**

The assessments are typical worst cases; the operation counts for evaluation are given in terms of the polynomial degree n.

Representation	Math Analysis	Evaluation Count	Numerical Stability	Solve for Interpolant
Power	Easy	Low = $n(A+M)$	Bad	Hard = $O(n^3)$
Shifted power	Easy	Low = $n(A+M)$	Poor-bad	Hard = $O(n^3)$
Newton	Moderate	Medium = $n(2A+M)$	Fair-good	Moderate = $O(n^2)$
Lagrange	Hard	Medium = $2n(A+M)$	Good	Easy = $O(1)$
Root product	Hard	Low = $n(A+M)$	Good	Hard = ?
Orthogonal polynomial	Moderate	High = $3n(A+M)$	Good	Hard = $O(n^3)$

Assessment of Piecewise Polynomial Representations 5.5.B

The strengths and weaknesses of the three representations of splines are listed; each includes the set $\{t_i\}$ of knots:

1. *Polynomial Pieces* (Equation 4.2.2). This is usually the most efficient if the coefficients of the spline are already computed and the spline is only being used (such as in plotting) and not manipulated. This representation uses many more coefficients than necessary. Smoothness is hard to preserve in this representation; just adding two splines introduces small jumps at the knots due to round-off, and these can be troublesome.

2. *Truncated Powers* (Equation 4.3.2). This is nice for theoretical analysis; the algebra and calculus of truncated powers are simple. It might be a numerically unstable representation and becomes computationally inefficient as the number of knots increases.

3. *B-splines* (Equation 4.3.3). This is best for numerical computations with splines; it is both numerically stable and efficient to evaluate. It has several nice properties, but the B-splines are algebraically complicated. One needs software support in the form of a set of routines (such as INTERV in Example 4.1) to provide the basic facilities of manipulating B-splines; such as for computing values and derivatives, and for simple interpolation.

Selection of Interpolation Points **5.5.C

The interpolation points are where the interpolant (polynomial or otherwise) obtains the information about the function or data being represented. Obviously, these points must contain sufficient information; that is to say, if one only looks at these values, they give a good picture of the behavior of the function or data. It follows then that one must have many interpolation points in places where rapid changes take place and one can (perhaps) use fewer where nothing much is happening. This simple guide to selecting interpolation points is complicated by the following facts:

1. Polynomials tend to oscillate too much, especially near the ends of the range of interpolation.

2. People may "know" that "nothing much is happening" some place and assume the interpolant "knows" this also. People tend to view a scattering of data points as indication that the behavior is to be "more or less smooth" between the given points. Mathematical models view the same situation as a license to do whatever wild thing they want between the data points.

3. Data are sometimes contaminated by random errors, and the interpolation points must "miss" these errors.

4. Data are often given at specific points, and one has no control over where to interpolate.

These considerations lead to the following rule:

Always check to make sure that an interpolant behaves in the expected way.

If it does not, the usual remedies are:

1. Use approximation instead of interpolation (see Chapter 11).

2. Change the basis functions so that they can better fit the data. If a polynomial interpolant is oscillating too much, it is usually unproductive to raise the polynomial degree.

3. Adjust the interpolation points. One may need more points in places where the interpolant is poor, or one may need more points at the ends of the interval to "pin down" a polynomial interpolant better.

Example 5.5 shows how much better for interpolation the Chebyshev points are than a uniform set of points. Another good set of points is the **Gauss points** or zeros of the Legendre polynomials. There is no simple formula for them; some are given in Table 7.2. These points are also useful for other numerical methods.

A Data Set Difficult for Interpolation — Example 5.8

The data tabulated and plotted in Figure 5.10 are taken from an actual example. It has three important characteristics:

1. The behavior is difficult to model mathematically.
2. There is inadequate data between 12.5 and 14.0. The scientist knew that all the values from 12.5 on are the same, but the scientist was very annoyed when the library programs that were used gave oscillations there.
3. The data are typical of many real-world behaviors. Figure 5.11 shows interpolation of this data using three models: polynomials, Hermite cubics, and cubic splines. Interpolation is made at 6, 9, and 13

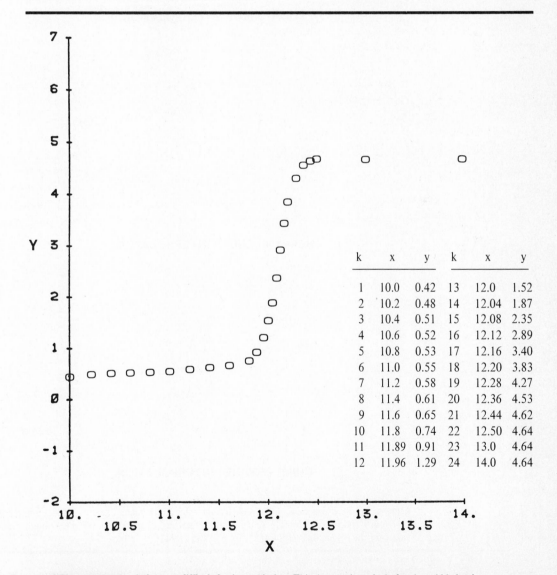

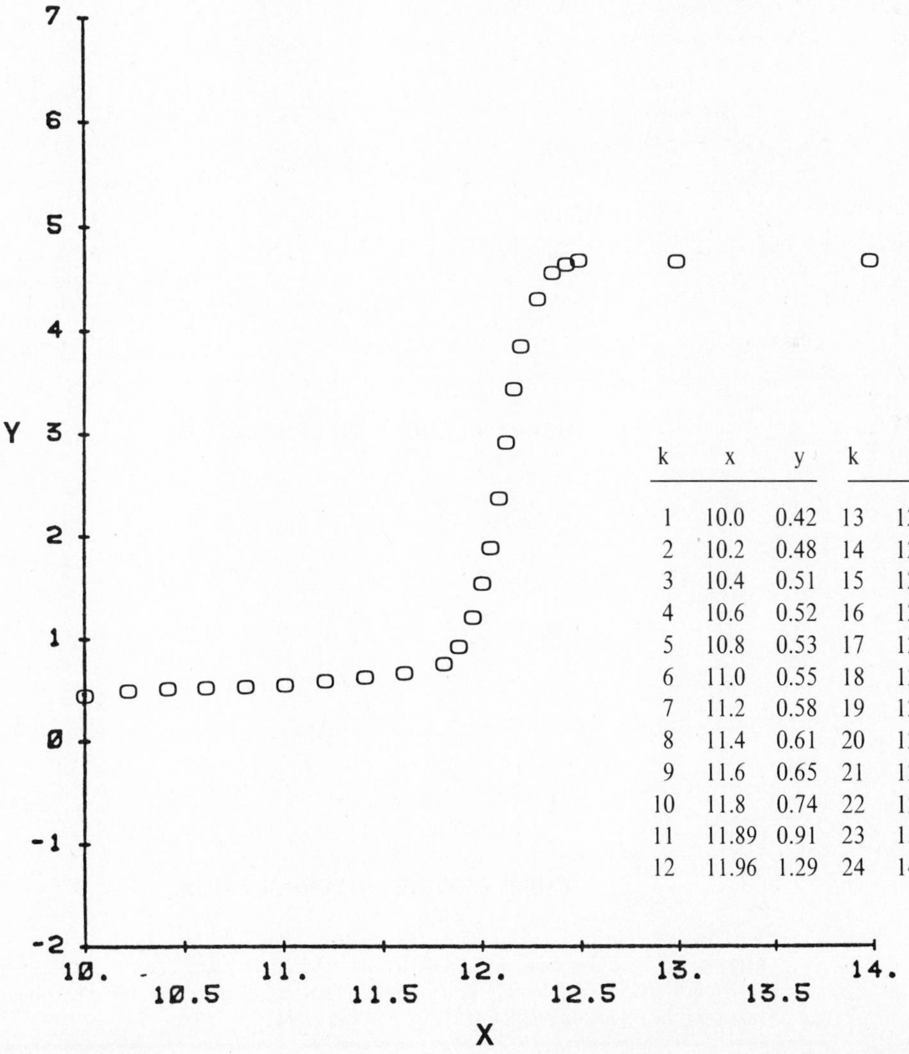

k	x	y	k	x	y
1	10.0	0.42	13	12.0	1.52
2	10.2	0.48	14	12.04	1.87
3	10.4	0.51	15	12.08	2.35
4	10.6	0.52	16	12.12	2.89
5	10.8	0.53	17	12.16	3.40
6	11.0	0.55	18	12.20	3.83
7	11.2	0.58	19	12.28	4.27
8	11.4	0.61	20	12.36	4.53
9	11.6	0.65	21	12.44	4.62
10	11.8	0.74	22	12.50	4.64
11	11.89	0.91	23	13.0	4.64
12	11.96	1.29	24	14.0	4.64

Figure 5.10 **A data set difficult for interpolation.** This data set is typical of real-world behavior, yet it is difficult to model mathematically.

points. Six points are clearly too few, but this case is included to illustrate this fact. Figure 5.12 shows the models obtained when data is filled in between 12.5 and 14.0 to specify explicitly the constant behavior in this interval.

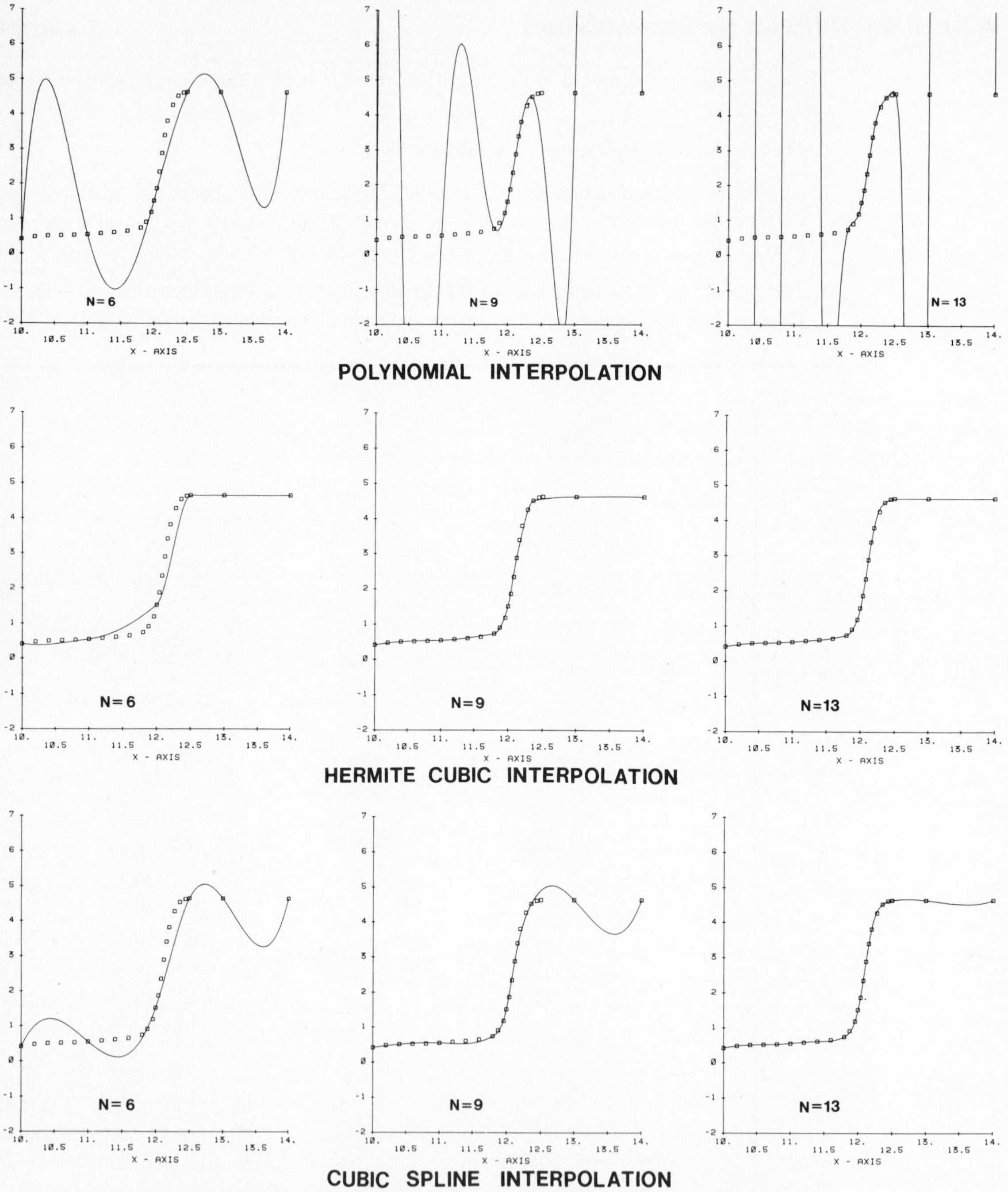

Figure 5.11 **Polynomial, spline, and Hermite cubic interpolants.** The difficult data is interpolated at N = 6, 9, and 13 points by polynomials, cubic splines, and Hermite cubics. The maximum unplotted values for the polynomial cases are 252(N = 9) and 78941(N = 13).

The most obvious conclusion from Figure 5.11 is that polynomial interpolation is terrible for these data. The higher the degree, the worse it is. Changing the location of the interpolation points does not materially improve the quality of the results.

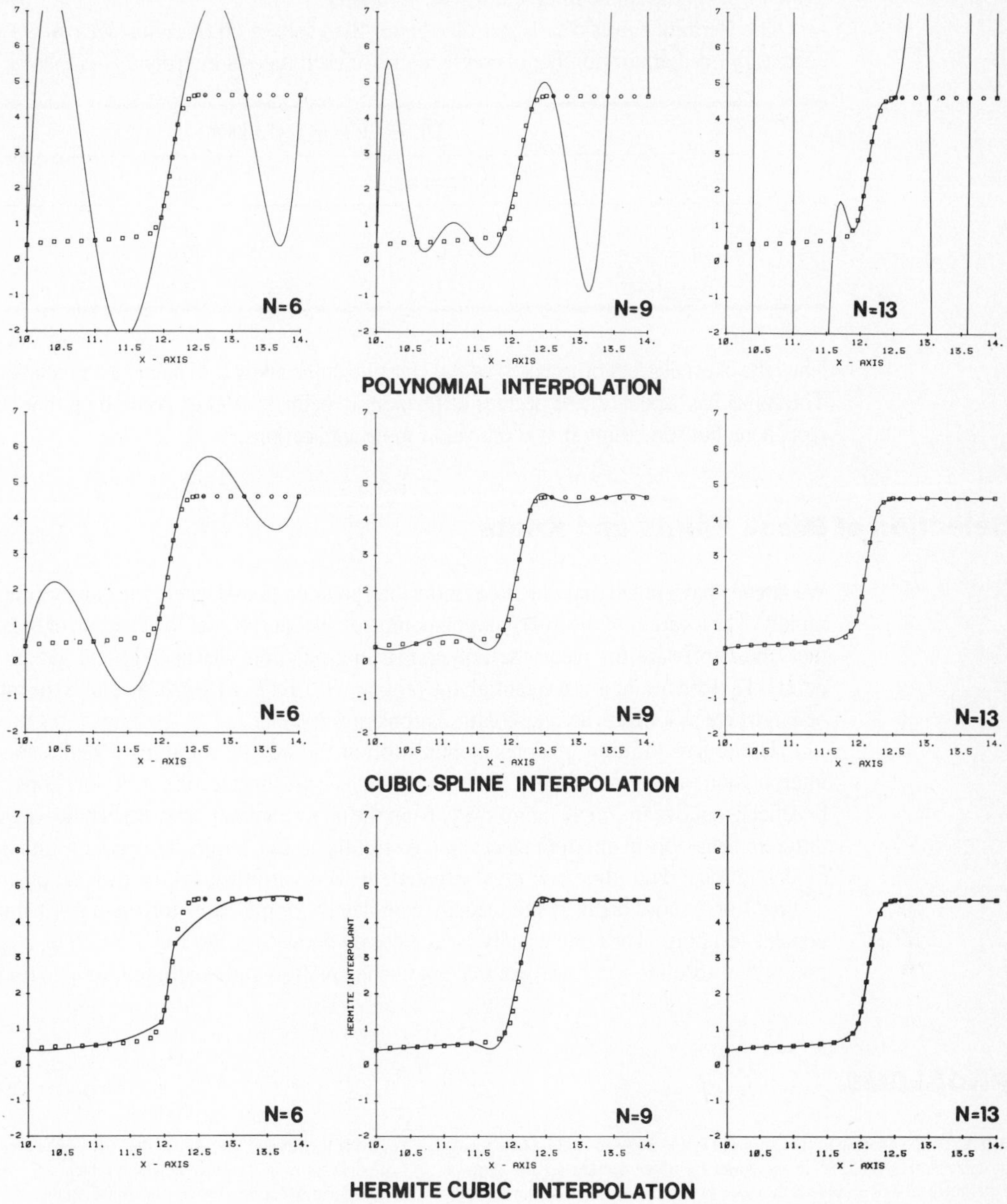

Figure 5.12 **Effect of filling in the missing, but "known" information.** The difficult data has extra points filled into the flat part and the interpolation is done again at 6, 9, and 13 points. The maximum unplotted values for the polynomial case are 25(N = 9) and 1346(N = 13).

The piecewise polynomial interpolants do poorly for 6 points (x = 10, 11, 12, 12.50, 13, and 14); some improvement might occur using different interpolation points. However, 6 points are barely adequate to describe this curve. Hermite cubic interpolation (as implemented in IQHSCU of the IMSL library) does an excellent job with 9 and 13 points. Hermite cubics seem to sense the unspecified fact that the curve is flat along the top right. The cubic spline interpolants for 9 and 13 points show a little extraneous oscillation, especially at the top right where we assume the curve is flat but where the data are missing. Both piecewise polynomial models are tremendous improvements over the polynomial models.

Figure 5.12 shows the interpolants after filling in the data between x = 12.5 and 14. This has little effect for interpolation at 6 points; 6 points is not enough information about this curve with or without the missing data. Filling in the missing data tremendously improves the polynomial interpolant; the maximum error is cut by a factor of 10 for 9 points and by 60 for 13 points. Alas, even this amount of improvement is not enough to make polynomial interpolation useful. In contrast, filling in the missing data eliminates the extra wiggle in the spline interpolant with 13 points.

The Hermite cubics clearly perform better than splines on this data. We can see why if we count the degrees of freedom (or number of coefficients) for each type of interpolant, as follows:

DEGREES OF FREEDOM			
N	Polynomial	Spline	Hermite cubic
6	6	6	12
9	9	9	18
13	13	13	26

Thus the extra degrees of freedom of the Hermite cubic allow it to achieve a much better fit than a spline. The spline has "spent" these degrees of freedom in being smoother, something that cannot be seen in the plots here, but something that is crucial in some applications.

Selection of Break Points and Knots **5.5.D

We already have noted that one needs more interpolation points where the data or function varies the most rapidly. The location of the interpolation points somewhat specifies the location of break points or knots. In fact, most software for piecewise polynomial interpolation selects the break points to be interpolation points. This constraint is not essential; the program SPLINT of PPPACK allows the interpolation points to be anywhere as long as the interpolation problem is solvable.

The proper location of break points is often the key to obtaining a really good model of data by interpolation (or approximation). There is no simple rule for selecting these locations. Sometimes it is very beneficial to move the break points away from the interpolation points, especially when the data have quite different behaviors in different places. If it is essential to use the smallest possible number of break points in modeling some data, then one must experiment with various break point locations. On the other hand, adding 1 or 2 more break points usually completely compensates for them not being placed in the best possible locations. Thus one usually faces a choice between using 1 or 2 (or 10 or 20 percent) more break points than absolutely necessary or making further analysis and experimentation to find the best locations.

PROBLEMS 5.5

5.5.1 The polynomial $p(x) = x^2 - 11111x + 30863681.25$ is numerically unstable near $x = 5555$ in the power form (see Section 4.1.A). Show by experiments that it is numerically stable in the shifted power form with center 5555 and in the Newton form with centers 5555 and 5554.

5.5.2 The root product form with complex roots can be modified to use quadratic factors and real arithmetic. Thus, if $p(x)$ has a complex conjugate pair of roots $r_1 = \alpha + i\beta$ and $r_2 = \alpha - i\beta$, then $p(x)$ has a factor $x^2 - 2\alpha x + \alpha^2 + \beta^2$ or $\beta^2 + (x-\alpha)^2$. Thus, if we number the complex pairs at the end, the root product form becomes

$$a \prod_{i=0}^{k} (x - r_i) \prod_{i=k+1}^{k+(n-k)/2} [\beta_i^2 + (x-\alpha_i)^2]$$

Find the root product form for the polynomial in Problem 5.5.1 and determine its numerical stability near $x = 5555$ by experiments.

5.5.3 The shifted root product form is obtained by choosing a value c near the center of the roots of the polynomial and using the representation (see Problem 5.5.2 for notation)

$$a \prod_{i=0}^{k} [(x-c) - r_i] \prod_{i=k+1}^{n} \{\beta_i^2 + [(x-c) - \alpha_i]^2\}$$

This is the normal way to use the root product form. Find the shifted root product form for the polynomial in Problem 5.5.1 with center 5555. Show by experiments that this form is numerically stable.

5.5.4 Repeat Problems 5.5.1 and 5.5.3 for the following polynomials, shifts, centers, and evaluation points:

(A) $p(x) = x^3 + 3005x^2 + 3010009x + 1005009005$
center for shifted forms = -1000
center for Newton form = $-1000, -990$
evaluation points = $-998.6, -1003$

Hint: $x = -1001$ is a root of $p(x)$

(B) $p(x) = 4x(x-2)(x-4)(x-6)$
center for shifted forms = 3.0
centers for Newton form = 1, 3, 5, 7
evaluation points = 1.01, 3.2

(C) $p(x) = (t^2+1)[(t-2)^2+2][(t-4)^2+4](t^2-1)$ where $t = x-32$
center for shifted forms = 32
centers for Newton form = 25, 26, 28, 30, 30, 32, 32, 35
evaluation points = 25.5, 32.1, 34.2, 36

Hint: The power form of p(x) is

$$x^8 - 268x^7 + 31{,}266x^6 - 2{,}133{,}328x^5 + 90{,}443{,}247x^4$$
$$- 2{,}398{,}244{,}956x^3 + 42{,}002{,}703{,}026x^2 - 410{,}452{,}230{,}448x$$
$$+ 1{,}758{,}233{,}782{,}800$$

5.5.5 Give an algorithm for the evaluation of the root product form analogous to Algorithm 4.1.1

5.5.6 Give an algorithm for the evaluation of the root product form with complex roots analogous to Algorithm 4.1.1. Express the number of additions and multiplications required in terms of the polynomial degree n and the number k of real roots.

5.5.7 Fill in the data of Example 5.8 with the value 4.64 at x = 12.6, 12.8, . . . , 14.0. Use the IMSL routine ICSICU to obtain experimentally the best 5 interpolation points for these data. Compare your results with uniformly spaced interpolation (i.e., at x = 10, 11, 12, 13, and 14). **Hint:** Use the end condition of derivative = 0 at the right end and second derivative equal to second divided difference at the left end. Once the interpolant is computed with ICSICU, use ICSEVU to evaluate the spline at all the data points (including the filled-in ones) and then compute the maximum difference between the interpolant and the data (at all the data points).

5.5.8 Use the program SPLINT of PPPACK experimentally to locate the best knots for interpolation of the data
value 4.64 at 12.6, 12.8, . . . , 13.8, and use 5 knots. Compare the values obtained this way with those using uniform knots and interpolation points and with the results of Problem 5.5.7.

5.5.9 Repeat the study of Example 5.8 using the data below for the viscosity of ethyl alcohol solutions in water as a function of the percent of alcohol.

%	Viscosity	%	Viscosity
10	3.311	60	5.75
15	4.32	65	5.273
20	5.319	70	4.762
25	6.19	75	4.200
30	6.94	80	3.690
35	7.09	85	3.212
40	7.14	90	2.732
45	6.89	95	2.253
50	6.58	100	1.773
55	6.18		

Hint: Use the PROTRAN system to compute the interpolant and plot the results. If PROTRAN is not available, then compute the polynomial interpolant using a linear equation solver (or use any local library software for polynomial interpolation). Use the IMSL routines ICSICU and IQHSCU to compute the spline and cubic Hermite interpolants, and use ICSEVU to evaluate the interpolants and USPLO to obtain rough plots.

5.5.10 Repeat Problem 5.5.9 with the data below for the freezing point of glycerine-water mixtures as a function of the percent of glycerine by weight.

%	Freezing Point
0	32
10	29.1
20	23.4
30	14.9
40	4.3
50	−7.4
60	−28.5
70	−36
80	−2.3
90	29.1
100	62.6

5.5.11 Let the polynomial $p_n(x)$ with coefficients $\mathbf{a} = (a_0, a_1, \ldots, a_n)$ be written as $p(\mathbf{a}, x)$. Different representations have different coefficients. The **condition number of a polynomial's representation** is

$$\text{Cond}(p) = \max_{\|\delta\mathbf{a}\|} \frac{\|p(\mathbf{a}, x) - p(\mathbf{a}+\delta\mathbf{a}, x)\| \; \|\mathbf{a}\|}{\|p(\mathbf{a}, x)\| \; \|\delta\mathbf{a}\|}$$

where $\|p(\mathbf{a}, x)\| = \max_x |p(\mathbf{a}, x)|$, $\|\mathbf{a}\| = \max_i |a_i|$, and $\delta\mathbf{a}$ = (small) perturbation of **a**. The **condition of a representation** is the largest value that the condition number can have for any polynomial of degree n: $C = \max_p \text{Cond}(p)$.

(A) Give an intuitive explanation of what it means for Cond(p) or C to be large. What is its practical effect?

(B) Write a Fortran program to estimate experimentally C for each of the representations in Section 5.5.A except the othogonal polynomial one. Take degrees of 5 and 10 and generate the coefficients at random with $\|\mathbf{a}\| = 1.0$; then make about five random perturbations $\delta\mathbf{a}$ with $\|\delta\mathbf{a}\| = .001$. Take the maximum of p(x) on the interval [0, 1] (say, using 100 points).

(C) Repeat the calculation of part (B) for the polynomials in Problem 5.5.4 using the intervals [−1010, −990], [0,10] and [25, 35] for A, B, and C, respectively.

(D) Estimate numerically [as in part (B)] the condition of the power form representation of the following polynomials defined on the interval [0, 20]:

$$p_1(x) = x(x-10)(x-20)$$

$$p_2(x) = \prod_{i=1}^{6} [x - 4(i-1)]$$

$$p_3(x) = \prod_{i=1}^{11} [x - 2(i-1)]$$

$$p_4(x) = \prod_{i=0}^{20} (x - i)$$

Hint: To compute the power form, use Algorithm 4.1.1 repeatedly to move the centers all to zero.

(E) The **Chebyshev polynomial** $T_{20}(x)$ of degree 20 is

$$524288x^{20} - 2{,}621{,}440x^{18} + 5{,}570{,}560x^{16}$$
$$- 6{,}553{,}600x^{14} + 4{,}659{,}200x^{12} - 2{,}050{,}048x^{10}$$
$$+ 549{,}120x^8 - 84{,}480x^6 + 6{,}600x^4 - 200x^2 + 1$$

The zeros of $T_{20}(x)$ are $\cos((2i+1)\pi/40)$ which are in the interval [−1, 1] for $i = 0, 1, \ldots, 19$; $T_{20}(x)$ varies between plus and minus one in this interval. Numerically estimate the condition of the power and the root product representations of $T_{20}(x)$. This is an orthogonal polynomial, and so its orthogonal polynomial representation has $e_{20} = 1$ and $e_i = 0$ for $i \le 19$.

5.5.12 Do a study of the effect of the choice of polynomial interpolation points in the interval [0, 1]. Use 3 point sets for interpolation: equispaced, Chebyshev (Equation 5.4.1), and the **arc sine points**

$$x_i = \frac{1}{2} + \frac{1}{\pi}\sin^{-1}(2i/n - 1) \qquad i = 0, 1, 2, \ldots, n$$

For each of the functions listed below,

(A) Compute polynomial interpolants on the 3 point sets for polynomial degree n = 1, 2, 3, 5, 8, 10, and 15. Estimate the maximum error the interpolant makes on the entire interval [0, 1].

(B) Graph these errors and estimate the order of convergence of the error as a function of n.

(C) Discuss the effectiveness of these choices for interpolation points.

Function list:

(a) e^x

(b) $\dfrac{1}{1+x^2}$

(c) $\frac{1}{1+40x^2}$

(d) $(x-.5)^2\text{sign}(x-.5)$

(e) $|x-.5|$

(f) $\sqrt{1-x^2}$

(g) $\frac{1}{\pi}\sin^{-1}(2x-1)$

5.5.13 Repeat the study of Problem 5.5.12 for Hermite cubic interpolation, using the point sets as break points.

5.5.14 Repeat the study of Problem 5.5.12 for cubic spline interpolation. Choose the end conditions so that the first or second derivative, as you wish, is matched exactly.

5.5.15 Repeat Problem 5.5.14 using the not-a-knot end conditions. Compare the results with those of Problem 5.5.14.

ERROR ANALYSIS FOR INTERPOLATION 5.6

The principal results in this section are estimates of the errors in polynomial and piecewise polynomial interpolation. This is the first "serious" error analysis in this book, and so some preliminary results and notation are introduced. These will be used for the error analysis of other methods and, perhaps more importantly, they provide a standard framework for understanding and analyzing the errors in formulas from the method of analytic substitution. Connections are also established between divided differences and more common mathematical objects like derivatives and integrals.

Norms and Linear Operators 5.6.A

Every science needs quantitative measures. Numerical analysis needs to measure the size of functions, linear functionals, and any other objects it encounters (for example, vectors and matrices). The process of interpolation is an example of a **linear operator**, a mechanism that *takes one function, produces another function, and is linear.* In interpolation one is given a function f(x) (or, perhaps, just some values from an unknown function), and one obtains another function p(x), the interpolating polynomial. In mathematical terms, we denote the linear operator by L so that interpolation is expressed by

$$p(x) = L(f(x)) \qquad \textbf{Equation 5.6.1}$$

or, more simply, $p = Lf$. Linearity is expressed by $L(f(x) + g(x)) = L(f(x)) + L(g(x))$ and $L(cf(x)) = cL(f(x))$ for any constant c. The difference between a linear operator L and a linear functional λ is that L produces functions while λ produces numbers.

A **norm** is the extension of absolute value to other mathematical objects. One **norm of a function** f(x) on the interval [a, b] is defined by

$$||f||_{[a,b]} = \max_{x\epsilon[a,b]} |f(x)| \qquad \textbf{Equation 5.6.2}$$

The subscript [a, b] usually can be omitted because the context specifies the interval. In Chapter 11 on approximation, other norms of functions are introduced.

The **norm of a linear functional** is defined by

$$||\lambda|| = \max_{||f||=1} |\lambda(f)| \qquad \textbf{Equation 5.6.3}$$

The norm is the largest value that can be produced from a function of size one. A particular interval [a, b] is assumed for the functions in 5.6.3 even though it is not explicitly specified in the definition. Consider the linear functionals $\int_0^1 f\,dx$ and $f'(0)$ for functions defined on [0, 1]. We see that

$$\left|\left|\int_0^1\right|\right| = 1 \qquad \left|\left|\frac{d}{dx}\right|\right| = +\infty$$

because the integral can never be larger than 1 [and $f(x) \equiv 1$ produces this value] while the derivative of $f(x)$ can be as large as one pleases [and $f(x) = \sqrt{x}$ has $f'(0) = +\infty$].

The **norm of a linear operator** L is defined in a similar way by

$$||L|| = \max_{||f||=1} ||L(f)|| \qquad \textbf{Equation 5.6.4}$$

Again a particular interval [a, b] is assumed for f(x) in 5.6.4. Consider three linear operators:

$L_1(f)$ = interpolation of f(x) by a straight line through f(a) and f(b)
$L_2(f)$ = first two terms of the Taylor's series of f(x) at a, that is, $L_2(f) = f(a) + (x-a)f'(a)$. This is osculatory interpolation of f(x) by a straight line at x = a.

$$L_3(f) = \int_0^1 (x-t)^2 f(t)dt$$

It is obvious that $||L_1|| = 1$; the straight line can never be larger in value than $\max(|f(a)|, |f(b)|)$. The example $f(x) = \sqrt{x}$ shows that $||L_2|| = +\infty$. For L_3 we have

$$\left|\int_0^1 (x-t)^2 f(t)\,dt\right| \le \max_{t\in[0,1]} |f(t)| \int_0^1 (x-t)^2 dt$$
$$\le ||f||/3$$

The value $||f||/3$ is assumed for $f(x) = 1$. Thus, Equation 5.6.4 gives $||L_3|| = 1/3$.

It is to be shown in Problem 5.6.1 that norms have the following properties:

1. The norm is not negative.

2. The norm is zero if and only if the object is identically zero.

3. Multiplying the object by a constant c multiplies the norm by |c|, that is,

$$||cf|| = |c|\,||f|| \qquad ||c\lambda|| = |c|\,||\lambda|| \qquad ||cL|| = |c|\,||L||$$

4. The **triangle inequality** holds, that is,

$$||f + g|| \le ||f|| + ||g||$$
$$||\lambda_1 + \lambda_2|| \le ||\lambda_1|| + ||\lambda_2||$$
$$||L_1 + L_2|| \le ||L_1|| + ||L_2||$$

Many numerical methods involve linear combinations of function values, and the following result gives an easy way to calculate norms for such methods.

Theorem 5.1 *Let the linear functional λ and linear operator L be linear combinations of function values:*

$$\lambda(f) = \sum_{i=1}^{n} a_i f(t_i)$$

$$L(f) = \sum_{i=1}^{n} a_i(x) f(t_i)$$

Then

$$|\lambda| = \sum_{i=1}^{n} |a_i| \qquad ||L|| = \sum_{i=1}^{n} ||a_i(x)||$$

Proof: The proofs are the same for both cases; we give that for λ. We have

$$|\lambda(f)| = \left|\sum_{i=1}^{n} a_i f(t_i)\right| \le \sum_{i=1}^{n} |a_i|\,|f(t_i)| \le \max|f(t)| \sum_{i=1}^{n} |a_i|$$

$$= ||f|| \sum_{i=1}^{n} |a_i|$$

which shows that $|\lambda| \le \sum_{i=1}^{n} |a_i|$. Take f(x) so that $f(t_i) = \text{sign } a_i$, and we have $a_i f(t_i) = |a_i|$, which gives

$$|\lambda(f)| = \sum_{i=1}^{n} |a_i|$$

for this particular f(x). This concludes the proof.

Recall the formulas of Example 4.3 (3-point differentiation formula):

$$\lambda(f) = \frac{2x_0 - (x_2+x_3)}{(x_1-x_2)(x_1-x_3)} f(x_1) + \frac{2x_0 - (x_1+x_3)}{(x_2-x_1)(x_2-x_3)} f(x_2) + \frac{2x_0 - (x_1+x_2)}{(x_3 - x_1)(x_3 - x_2)} f(x_3)$$

and Equation 5.2.3 (Lagrange interpolation):

$$L(f) = \sum_{j=1}^{n+1} \ell_j(x) f_j$$

In the first case, we see that the coefficients of λ become infinite as the x_i coalesce, and so the norm of λ can be very large. For the common equally spaced case of Section 4.5.D we have

$$\lambda(f) = \frac{f(x_0+h) - f(x_0-h)}{2h}$$

so $|\lambda| = 1/h$. For polynomial interpolation we have

$$||L|| = \sum_{j=1}^{n+1} ||\ell_j(x)||$$

which depends in a complicated way on the location of the interpolation points.

Divided Differences and Derivatives 5.6.B

We have already used the fact that divided differences are closely related to derivatives; we now state and prove the exact nature of the relationship. This is easily done for divided differences with distinct points; it is a little more complicated for multiple points.

Theorem 5.2 *Let f(x) have m continuous derivatives on the interval (a, b) and let $x_0, x_1, \ldots, x_m$ be $m+1$ distinct points in [a, b]. Then there is a point ξ in (a, b) so that*

$$f[x_0, x_1, \ldots, x_m] = \frac{f^{(m)}(\xi)}{m!} \qquad \textbf{Equation 5.6.5}$$

Proof: For $m = 1$ this is just Theorem 1.5, the mean value theorem for derivatives. For $m > 1$, let p(x) interpolate f(x) at the x_i and introduce the error function $e(x) = f(x) - p(x)$. Since f(x) has m continuous derivatives, so does e(x). The error e(x) has $m+1$ zeros, one at each x_i, and so $e'(x)$ must have m zeros in (a, b) by Rolle's theorem (see Theorem 1.5). Since $e'(x)$ has m zeros, it follows again from Rolle's theorem that $e''(x)$ has $m-1$ zeros in (a, b). We continue in this way until we reach $e^{(m)}(x)$ which has one zero; call it ξ. At this point we have

$$e^{(m)}(\xi) = f^{(m)}(\xi) - p^{(m)}(\xi) = 0 \qquad \textbf{Equation 5.6.6}$$

We can calculate $p^{(m)}(\xi)$ from the fact that $p(x) = f[x_0, x_1, \ldots, x_m]x^m +$ lower-order terms in x which makes $p^{(m)}(x) = f[x_0, x_1, \ldots, x_m]m!$, a constant. Substitution of this into 5.6.6 gives 5.6.5 and concludes the proof.

Note that the point ξ must lie somewhere among the x_i, that is, $\min x_i \le \xi \le \max x_i$.

The next theorem extends Theorem 5.2 to include multiple points. While the proof is somewhat messy, this is nevertheless the simplest approach to osculatory interpolation and related problems.

Theorem 5.3 *Let f(x) have m continuous derivatives on the interval (a, b) and let $x_0, x_1, \ldots, x_m$ be points in [a, b]. Then there is a point ξ in (a, b) so that Equation 5.6.5 holds and the value of $f[x_0, x_1, \ldots, x_m]$ depends continuously on the points x_i.*

Proof: The proof is by induction on m. For m = 0 the theorem is obviously true. Assume then that the theorem is true for n = m − 1 and consider the case n = m. We first state the second part of the conclusion more specifically as:

Given $x_i^{(j)}$ *so that* $\lim_{j\to\infty} x_i^{(j)} = x_i$

then

$$\lim_{j\to\infty} f[x_0^{(j)}, x_1^{(j)}, \ldots, x_m^{(j)}] = f[x_0, x_1, \ldots, x_m] \qquad \textbf{Equation 5.6.7}$$

We now prove 5.6.7 for m = n with the additional assumption that the x_i are not all the same.

Assume the x_i are ordered so that we have $x_0 < x_n$ and thus, for all j sufficiently large, $x_0^{(j)} < x_n^{(j)}$. Consider the definition of divided differences

$$f[x_0^{(j)}, x_i^{(j)}, \ldots, x_n^{(j)}] = \frac{f[x_0^{(j)}, x_1^{(j)}, \ldots, x_{n-1}^{(j)}] - f[x_1^{(j)}, \ldots, x_n^{(j)}]}{x_0^{(j)} - x_n^{(j)}}$$

Take the limit as $j\to\infty$, and the right side becomes the definition of $f[x_0, x_1, \ldots, x_n]$ by the induction hypothesis 5.6.7 with n = m − 1. This established 5.6.7 for n = m.

Next we establish 5.6.5. If the x_i are all the same, 5.6.5 is just the definition of $f[x_0, x_1, \ldots, x_m]$, and so we consider now the case $x_0 < x_n$. We may choose $x_i^{(j)}$ so that the $x_i^{(j)}$ are all distinct and

$$\lim_{j\to\infty} x_i^{(j)} = x_i$$

For each fixed n we apply Theorem 5.2 to show the existence of $\xi^{(j)}$ so that

$$f[x_0^{(j)}, x_1^{(j)}, \ldots, x_n^{(j)}] = f^{(n)}(\xi^{(j)})/n! \qquad \textbf{Equation 5.6.8}$$

Now Equation 5.6.7 is valid for m = n, and so we have

$$\lim_{j\to\infty} f[x_0^{(j)}, x_1^{(j)}, \ldots, x_n^{(j)}] = f[x_0, x_1, \ldots, x_n]$$

while the continuity of $f^{(n)}$ implies there is an ξ so that

$$\lim_{j\to\infty} f^{(n)}(\xi^{(j)}) = f^{(n)}(\xi)$$

This completes the induction step for 5.6.5 and establishes it; we still have left the case of all equal x_i for 5.6.7.

We apply 5.6.5 to conclude that Equation 5.6.8 holds for any set of $x_i^{(j)}$ converging to $x_0 = x_1 = \ldots = x_n$. Since $\min x_i^{(j)} \le \xi^{(j)} \le \max x_i^{(j)}$, we have $\xi^{(j)}$ converging to x_0 also. Thus we have by definition that

$$f[x_0, x_0, \ldots, x_0] = f^{(n)}(x_0)/n!$$

and by 5.6.5 that

$$\lim_{j\to\infty} f[x_0^{(j)}, x_1^{(j)}, \ldots, x_n^{(j)}] = \lim_{j\to\infty} f^{(n)}(\xi^{(j)})/n!$$

The right sides of these two equations are equal because $f^{(n)}(x)$ is continuous, which establishes 5.6.7 in this case and concludes the proof.

Error Analysis for Polynomial Interpolation 5.6.C

Already in the discussion of the method of analytic substitution we used the basic equation for error analysis:

True value = estimate + error

In the case of interpolation the true value is a function, say $f(x)$, the estimate is the interpolant, say $p_n(x)$, and the error is what we want to analyze now. Let $E_n(f, x)$ or $E_n(f)$ denote the error in interpolation by polynomials of degree n. Then we have

$$f(x) = p_n(x) + E_n(f, x) \qquad \textbf{Equation 5.6.9}$$

We already have an exact formula for the **polynomial interpolation** error:

$$E_n(f, x) = f[x_0, x_1, \ldots, x_n, x] \prod_{i=0}^{n} (x - x_i) \qquad \textbf{Equation 5.6.10}$$

which follows from Equation 5.2.4 and the definition of the divided difference. We can express this error in other ways as in the following theorem.

Theorem 5.4 *Let $f(x)$ have $n+1$ continuous derivatives and let $p_n(x)$ be the polynomial of degree n that interpolates $f(x)$ at the points $x_0, x_1, \ldots, x_n$. Then the error $E_n(f, x)$ of the interpolant at the point x is given by any one of the three formulas:*

A. $E_n(f, x) = f[x_0, x_1, \ldots, x_n, x] \prod_{i=0}^{n} (x - x_i)$

B. $E_n(f, x) = f^{(n+1)}(\xi) \prod_{i=0}^{n} (x - x_i)/(n+1)!$ *where ξ is a point so that* $\min(x_i, x) \le \xi \le \max(x_i, x)$

C. $E_n(f, x) = \dfrac{1}{n!}\displaystyle\int_{x_0}^{x} (x_0 - t)^n f^{(n+1)}(t)\, dt$

Proof: Conclusion A just restates Equation 5.6.10, B follows directly from Theorem 5.3, and C comes from the Taylor's series with integral remainder Theorem 1.6.

We apply Theorem 5.4 to obtain an estimate for the Hermite cubic interpolation error. Let $pp(x)$ be the Hermite cubic interpolant to $f(x)$ with the break points $t_1, t_2, \ldots, t_{k+1}$. Then we have

$$f(x) = pp(x) + E_{HC}(f, x)$$

Theorem 5.5 *Let $f(x)$ have 4 continuous derivatives and $pp(x)$ be the Hermite cubic interpolant of $f(x)$ at the break points $t_1, t_2, \ldots, t_{k+1}$. Then the error $E_{HC}(f, x)$ of the interpolant at the point x is given by any one of the following*

A. $E_{HC}(f, x) = f[t_i, t_i, t_{i+1}, t_{i+1}, x]\,(x - t_i)^2(x - t_{i+1})^2$ *where* $t_i \le x \le t_{i+1}$

B. $E_{HC}(f, x) = f^{(4)}(\xi)\,(x - t_i)^2(x - t_{i+1})^2/24$ *where* $t_i \le x \le t_{i+1}$

Set $h = \max(t_{i+1} - t_i)$ then we have the bound

C. $||E_{HC}(f, x)|| \le ||f^{(4)}||h^4/384$

Proof: The error formulas A and B are obtained directly from Theorem 5.4 by specializing to the case of cubic polynomials and noting that $pp(x)$ between x_i and x_{i+1} is determined by interpolation at these 2 points. The estimate C is obtained from B by taking the maximum of both sides and noting that $(x - t_i)^2(x - t_{i+1})^2 \le h^4/16$.

Theorem 5.5.C shows how the error in Hermite cubic interpolation depends on the spacing of the break points. For comparison purposes we state a version of Theorem 5.4 which explicitly shows how the error of polynomial interpolation depends on the length of the interval h in which the interpolation is made.

Theorem 5.6 *In Theorem 5.4 assume that all the x_i are in the interval $[x_0 - h/2, x_0 + h/2]$. Let the distribution of the interpolation points be fixed in this interval as h becomes small. Then we have*

$$||E_n(f)|| \le ||f^{(n+1)}||h^{n+1}/(n+1)!$$

Proof: In Theorem 5.4.B replace each $x - x_i$ by h and use the maximum value of $f^{(n+1)}(x)$.

Given a function f(x), there is a polynomial $p_n^*(x)$ which is a **best polynomial approximation** to f(x) in the sense that $||f-p_n||$ is minimized for polynomials of degree n by $p_n^*(x)$. The idea of best approximation is extended to any model for f(x) by replacing the polynomial $p_n(x)$ by $\sum_{i=1}^{n} a_i b_i(x)$ where the $b_i(x)$ are basis functions for the model. Approximation is discussed in Chapter 11, but it is clear that one hopes that interpolation produces a polynomial close to $p^*(x)$. If we set

$$E_n^*(f) = f - p_n^*$$

then we have by definition that $||E_n^*(f)|| \leq ||E_n(f)||$, and so an interpolating polynomial does provide a bound on the best possible error.

The next theorem shows how to generate error estimates of numerical methods obtained by the method of analytical substitution from knowledge of $||E_n^*(f)||$ or $||E_n(f)||$ and simple estimates from Theorem 5.1 on the norms of linear functionals and operators.

Theorem 5.7 *Given a model for $f(x)$ with basis functions $b_i(x)$ for $i = 0, 1, \ldots, n-1$, let $E^*(f)$ be the error of the best approximation to $f(x)$. Let L be a linear operator or a linear functional so that $L(b_i(x)) = 0$ for each i. Then*

A. $||L(f)|| \leq ||L||\ ||E^*(f)||$

For a polynomial model p_n set $E_n(f) = f - p_n$, and we have

B. $||L(f)|| \leq ||L||\ ||E_n^*(f)|| \leq ||L||\ ||E_n(f)||$

Proof: Let $b^*(x) = \Sigma a_i b_i(x)$ be the best approximation to f(x) from the model. From linearity we have that

$$L(f) = L(f-b^*+b^*) = L(f-b^*) + L(b^*)$$

Recall that $||L(g)|| \leq ||L||\ ||g||$ for any linear operator, and the assumption $L(b_i(x)) = 0$ implies that $L(b^*) = 0$. This gives

$$||L(f)|| = ||L(f-b^*)|| \leq ||L||\ ||f - b^*|| = ||L||\ ||E^*(f)||$$

This establishes part A of the theorem, and B is just the special case of polynomials combined with the observation that $||E_n^*(f)|| \leq E_n(f)||$ is always true.

Applications of Theorem 5.7 to Estimating Errors

Example 5.9

The use of Theorem 5.7 is illustrated here for two common cases (the trapezoidal rule for integration and 3-point differentiation formulas) and one unusual one (obtaining a lower bound on the error of linear interpolation).

A. *The Error in the Trapezoidal Rule:* The trapezoidal rule is a simple method to estimate an integral as follows:

$$\int_0^h f(x)dx \sim h[f(0)+f(h)]/2$$

The error in this method is the linear functional

$$\lambda(f) = h[f(0)+f(h)]/2 - \int_0^h f(x)dx$$

and one calculates from Theorem 5.1 and the properties of norms that $||\lambda|| = 2h$. The trapezoidal rule is exact for straight lines so that $\lambda(p_1) = 0$ for any first-degree polynomial p_1. Now apply Theorem 5.7 to obtain

$$|\lambda(f)| \leq 2h||E_1(f)||$$

and if f(x) has two derivatives, we apply Theorem 5.6 to obtain $|\lambda(f)| \leq h^3||f''||$. If one uses Theorem 5.4.B and the fact that $(x-x_i) \leq h/2$, one obtains $||E_1(f)|| \leq ||f''||h^2/8$ and the better estimate

$$|\lambda(f)| \leq h^3||f''||/4$$

This is not the best possible error estimate; a more detailed analysis shows the constant 1/4 can be replaced by 1/12, but this is a good estimate easily obtained. Note that in practice one rarely knows a quantity like $||f''||$ with accuracy.

B. *The Error in Differentiation.* The formula

$$f'(x) \sim \frac{f(x+h) - f(x-h)}{2h}$$

is derived in Example 4.3 to estimate the derivative for a particular function f(x). The error in this formula is the linear operator

$$L(f) = \frac{f(x+h) - f(x-h)}{2h} - f'(x)$$

whose norm is given by

$$||L(f)|| = 1/h + ||f'||$$

This differentiation formula is superaccurate in that it is exact for any quadratic polynomial $p_2(x)$ so that $L(p_2(x)) = 0$. Assume f(x) has three continuous derivatives; then we apply Theorems 5.6 and 5.7 to obtain

$$||L(f)|| \leq (1/h+||f'||)h^3||f'''||/6$$

As h become small, the term 1/h dominates $||f'||$, and so we have the error estimate

$$||L(f)|| \leq ||f'''||h^2/6$$

This error estimate is the best possible with the given information.

C. *The Error in Straight-Line Interpolation.* It is easy to check that the linear functional

$$\lambda(f) = f(-a) - 2f(0) + f(a)$$

is zero for all linear polynomials. By Theorem 5.1 its norm is 4. Rewrite the equation of Theorem 5.7 as

$$||E_n(f)|| \geq ||L(f)||/||L||$$

Now consider interpolation of $f(x) = e^x$ and $f(x) = \log(x+1)$ by straight lines on the interval $[-1/2, 1/2]$. With $a = 1/2$ we have

$$\lambda(e^x) = .25525$$
$$\lambda(\log(1+x)) = -.12494$$

Thus the errors of linear interpolation on $[-1/2, 1/2]$ (no matter what the interpolation points are) satisfy

$$||E_1(e^x)|| \geq .0638$$
$$||E_1(\log(1+x))|| \geq .0312$$

Error Analysis for Piecewise Polynomial and Spline Interpolation **5.6.D

If the piecewise polynomial interpolant is obtained in a simple, local manner, then it may be possible to obtain error estimates by direct application of polynomial results. This is done in Theorem 5.5 for Hermite cubic interpolation. Global interpolation methods such as splines require more difficult analysis, beyond the scope of this book. We just state the error estimates.

We first consider fixed break point or fixed knot interpolation. That is, the break points or knots t_1, $t_2, \ldots, t_{k+1}$ are fixed independently of the function f(x). The error of the interpolant pp(x) of degree n with these break points is

$E_{n,k}(f, x) = f(x) - pp(x)$

There is a large variety of interpolation processes possible when one considers all the combinations of n, k, location of break points, and location of interpolation points. Let the interpolation points be x_j, $j = 1, 2, \ldots, M$, where M is the total number of coefficients (degrees of freedom) of pp(x). The value of M depends on n, k and the smoothness of pp(x); if pp(x) has m continuous derivatives at each knot, then $M = k(n-m) + m + 1$. See Problem 5.3.11 and the discussion of the interpolation conditions 5.3.1.

For the next theorem we use the $k+1$ breakpoints t_i and the M interpolation points x_j. The *distribution* of the t_i and x_j is the way these points are distributed in [a, b]; that is, with $H = b-a$,

$$t_i = a + \theta(i/k)H$$
$$x_j = a + \sigma(j/n)H$$

where θ and σ are functions with $\theta(0) = \sigma(0) = 0$ and $\theta(1) = \sigma(1) = 1$.

Theorem 5.8 *Let $f(x)$ have $n+1$ continuous derivatives in [a, b]. There is a constant K which depends on n and the distribution of the breakpoints and interpolation points so that*

$$||E_{n,k}(f, x)|| \leq Kh^{n+1}||f^{(n+1)}||$$

where $h = max(t_{i+1} - t_i)$. If k increases and the spacing of the t_i and x_j only changes proportionally in the interval [a, b], then K does not change.

Note that K does not change as the number of break points increases as long as the distribution remains the same. The theorem remains true with much less restrictive assumptions on the distribution of the break points and interpolation points.

This theorem may be paraphrased by saying that piecewise polynomial and spline interpolation give the expected error $O(h^{n+1})$ provided the break point and interpolation point distributions stay reasonable.

The strength of piecewise polynomials lies in the possibility to place the break points to model the behavior of f(x) so that an "unreasonable" distribution of break points does not always give large errors. Indeed, the next theorem shows that if one places the break points properly, then one gets good approximations for a class of functions so large that it contains all functions that might appear in real problems.

To put the next theorem in context, we rephrase the results of Theorems 5.6 and 5.8 in terms of the number of parameters of the interpolant. For polynomials that number is n and, if h is fixed, we get no information about $||E_n(f)||$ as n changes because we do not know how $||f^{(n+1)}||$ changes. Suppose that the smoothness of f(x) is fixed [i.e., we know $f^{(m+1)}$ is continuous] and that the polynomial degree n increases. It is known that the best possible error is given by

$$||E_n^*(f)|| = O\left(\frac{1}{n^{m+1}}\right) \qquad \textbf{Equation 5.6.11}$$

and, if the interpolation is done at the Chebyshev points, then

$$||E_n(f)|| = O\left(\frac{\log n}{n^{m+1}}\right) \qquad \textbf{Equation 5.6.12}$$

which is nearly as good as 5.6.11. The proofs of these two facts are too lengthy to include here.

For piecewise polynomial interpolation, the parameter that increases is k, the number of pieces. In Theorem 5.8 we have h = constant/k for a fixed distribution of the break points and interpolation points in the interval. Thus we have, with the same assumption that $f^{(m+1)}$ is continuous,

$$||E_{n,k}(f)|| = O\left(\frac{1}{k^{m+1}}\right) \qquad \textbf{Equation 5.6.13}$$

Comparing 5.6.11 and 5.6.13, we see almost identical error behaviors; the polynomial degree n and the number k of break points play the same role in the error bounds.

For the final result, let $E_{pp}^*(f, x)$ denote the error of the best possible piecewise polynomial approximation $pp^*(f, x)$ to f(x) using k pieces with polynomial degree m. The polynomial degree m is related to the smoothness of f(x) and, for simplicity, we omit attaching the m and k to E_{pp}^* and pp^*. Here the break points of pp* are adjusted to give the smallest possible error; this is called approximation with **variable break points** or **variable knots.** The approximation pp* depends nonlinearly on m, k and f(x) and is difficult (but not impossible) to compute; it is very difficult to analyze. The following result is known:

Theorem 5.9. *Assume f(x) is continuous in [a, b], has a finite number of singularities of various types in its derivatives, and between these singular points $f^{(m+1)}$ is continuous so that*

$$\sigma(f) = \int_a^b [f^{(m+1)}(x)]^{\frac{1}{m+1}} dx < \infty \qquad \textbf{Equation 5.6.14}$$

Then there is a constant K depending only on m so that

$$||E^*_{pp}(f)|| \le K\sigma(f)/k^{m+1} = O\left(\frac{1}{k^{m+1}}\right)$$

We first note that almost all functions have $\sigma(f)$ finite. For example, if $f(x) = x^\alpha$ on [0, 1], then

$$f^{(m+1)} = \text{const} \times x^{\alpha-m-1}$$

blows up very rapidly near x = 0 if α is small and m is large. Yet

$$\int_0^1 (x^{\alpha-m-1})^{\frac{1}{m+1}} dx = \int_0^1 x^{\frac{\alpha}{m+1}-1} dx = \frac{m+1}{\alpha}$$

is finite if $\alpha > 0$.

The important fact about Theorem 5.9 is that the same error estimate is obtained as for Theorem 5.8 even though the function f(x) is no longer assumed to be smooth. The assumptions on f(x) in Theorem 5.9 can be made even weaker (e.g., an infinite number of singular points is allowed) and the conclusion remains true. It is, of course, not possible to remove the assumption that f(x) be continuous unless one also allows the piecewise polynomials to be discontinuous — which can happen by having enough break points coalesce.

PROBLEMS 5.6

5.6.1 For the norms of functions, linear functionals, and linear operators defined in Section 5.5.A, establish the four properties listed just before Theorem 5.1.

5.6.2 Show that $||L(f)|| \le ||L||\ ||f||$ for any linear operator or linear functional L.

5.6.3 Compute the norm of the following linear functionals

(A) $f(1.5)$

(B) $f(0) + h^2 f''(0)$

(C) $f(0) + \int_0^1 e^{-t} f(t)dt$

(D) $f(0) + 4f(h) + 2f(2h) + 4f(3h) + f(4h)$

(E) $\int_0^{2\pi} \cos(3x)f(x-1)dx$

(F) $\int_0^1 x^2 f'(x+1)dx$

5.6.4 If one applies integration by parts to Problem 5.6.3(F), one obtains another linear functional. Compute its norm and explain why it is not the same value as the norm of the original one.

5.6.5 Identify the following as linear functionals, linear operators, or neither.

(A) $\int_0^1 e^x f(x-t)dx$

(B) $f''(x) + \cos(x)f'(x) - 3\sin(x)f(x)$

(C) $f(x-1) + f'(0)\int_0^1 (x-t)_+^2 f(t)dt$

(D) $\frac{\partial^2 f}{\partial x^2} + \frac{\partial^2 f}{\partial y^2} - e^{x+y}f(x,y)$

(E) $2f(1) + \int_1^\infty f(t)f(x-t)dx$

(F) $f(0) + f'(0)h + f''(0)h^2/2 + f'''(0)h^3/6$

(G) $\max_{0\le x\le 1} f(x)$

5.6.6 The least squares norm of a function is defined by

$$||f||_2 = \sqrt{\int_a^b f(x)^2 dx}$$

Repeat Problem 5.6.1 for this norm of functions, except do not attempt to establish the triangle inequality (it is true, but hard to establish).

5.6.7 Compute the least-squares norms of the following functions on the indicated intervals

(A) $\frac{1}{x}$ on [0, 1]

(B) $\frac{1}{\sqrt{x}}$ on [0, 1]

(C) x on [1, 2]

(D) $\frac{1}{x}$ on [1, ∞]

(E) $\frac{x}{x+1}$ on [1, ∞]

(F) $\frac{1}{\sqrt{|x-1/2|}}$ on [0, 1]

5.6.8 The least-squares norm of a function f(x) is $||f||_2$ defined in Problem 5.6.6. Use it to define the least-squares norms of linear functionals and linear operators. Compute the least-squares norms of the following linear functionals.

(A) $f(0)$

(B) $f'(1)$

(C) $\int_0^\infty f(x)dx$

(D) $\int_0^1 f(x)dx$

Hint for (D): Show that $f(x) = 1$ determines the norm. Consider functions g which vary from 1 slightly over a small interval and which keep the integral equal to 1, then show that $||g||_2$ is increased and hence the value of the linear functional is decreased.

5.6.9 Compute the **norm of linear interpolation** on [a, b] at the points a and b. **Hint**: Use the Lagrange basis functions.

5.6.10 Estimate the order of the norm of **equispaced polynomial interpolation** experimentally. Write a Fortran program that estimates $||\ell_j(x)||$ for the Lagrange basis functions for equispaced interpolation. Sum these norms to estimate the norm of the polynomial interpolation operator for degrees 1, 2, 4, 6, 10, 15, and 20. Plot the results on a log-log graph to show that the norm grows exponentially.

5.6.11 Use the conclusion of Problem 5.6.10 to argue that equispaced polynomial interpolation might fail. Correlate the discussion with the results of Example 5.4.

5.6.12 Estimate the order of the **norm of polynomial interpolation at the Chebyshev points** experimentally. Repeat the procedure of Problem 5.6.10 and plot the results on a semi-log graph to conclude that the norm grows logarithmically.

5.6.13 Use the result of Problem 5.6.12 to establish Equation 5.6.12. Discuss conclusions about interpolation at the Chebyshev points. **Hint**: Use Theorem 5.7.

5.6.14 As the degree increases, the error in polynomial interpolation depends on the value of $||f^{(n+1)}||/(n+1)!$. Estimate the order of magnitude of this factor as n increases for the following functions on [0, 1].

(A) e^x

(B) $x^{3.5}$

(C) $\sin(3x)$

(D) $\frac{1}{1+x^2}$

(E) $e^{\sqrt{x}}$

(F) $\frac{1}{10+x}$

Discuss how effective high-degree polynomial interpolation is for each of these functions.

5.6.15 For each of the functions in Problem 5.6.14, estimate the error for Hermite cubic interpolation on [0, 1] using 5, 10, 50, and 100 pieces. How do these errors compare to the error in equispaced polynomial interpolation with degrees 10, 20, 100, and 200 (which have the same number of unknown coefficients)?

5.6.16 The **Simpson Rule** for numerical integration of f(x) on [0, h] is $h(f(0) + 4f(h/2) + f(h))/6$. It is exact for cubic polynomials. Use Theorem 5.7 to derive an error estimate for this estimate of the integral of f(x), and assume f(x) has five continuous derivatives.

5.6.17 The usual definition of the derivative in the calculus uses the linear functional

$$\frac{f(x+h) - f(x)}{h}$$

Show that this estimate of $f'(x)$ is exact for polynomials of degree 1. Use Theorem 5.7 to derive an error estimate for this approximation to the derivative. Show that as an estimate of $f'(x+h/2)$, it is exact for quadratic polynomials.

5.6.18 Compute straight-line interpolants of e^x and $\log(1+x)$ on [−1/2, 1/2] and estimate the accuracy of the error estimates of Example 5.9.C.

5.6.19 Find a linear functional (not identically zero) involving the four function values $f(-2a)$, $f(-a)$, $f(a)$, and $f(2a)$ which is zero for all quadratic polynomials. Use it to obtain lower bounds on the errors of quadratic interpolation on (−1/2, 1/2) of e^x and $\log(1+x)$.

5.6.20 Repeat Problem 5.6.18 for quadratic interpolation using the estimates of Problem 5.6.19.

5.6.21 Find a linear functional involving $f(-2a)$, $f(-a)$, $f(0)$, $f(a)$, and $f(2a)$ which is zero for all cubic polynomials. Use it to obtain a lower bound on the errors of cubic interpolation on (−.1, .1) of $\cos(x)$ and $1/(1+x^2)$.

5.6.22 Evaluate the advantage of using variable knots by comparing broken line interpolants of $\sqrt{x}$. First use equispaced knots and estimate the maximum error for various numbers k of knots. Plot the error on log-log paper and show that it is $O(1/\sqrt{k})$; the decay exponent is −1/2. Then for k knots use the points

$$t_i = \left(\frac{i-1}{k-1}\right)^4 \quad \text{for } i = 1,2,\ldots,k$$

Plot the error and show that it is $O(1/k^2)$; the decay exponent is −2.

5.6.23 Show how each of the experimental results of Problem 5.6.22 is predicted by a theorem in this chapter.

6
MATRICES AND LINEAR EQUATIONS

The simplest mathematical models are linear, and thus linear models are very common. They are also important because the analysis and study of even the most complicated situations frequently begins with a simplified linear model. The most common problem arising from linear models is the solution of systems of linear equations. These problems are expressed in terms of matrices, and this chapter covers a variety of matrix computation problems in addition to solving linear equations.

TYPES AND SOURCES OF MATRIX COMPUTATION PROBLEMS **6.1

Linear Systems of Equations, Ax = b 6.1.A

There are numerous physical systems which naturally lead to linear equations. Consider, for example, the balance of forces on a structure (such as a bridge, building, or aircraft frame). As illustrated in Figure 6.1, there are forces from the weight of the bridge and truck which are balanced by the forces at the ends of the bridge. These forces are propagated along the iron beams, and at every node they must balance out to zero (otherwise the bridge would begin moving). If we decompose the forces into horizontal (x) and vertical (y) components, then at each node there are two equations:

$$\begin{array}{ll} \text{Sum x forces} = 0 \quad \text{at node i} & \\ & \text{for i} = 1, 2, \ldots \\ \text{Sum y forces} = 0 \quad \text{at node i} & \end{array}$$

These equations are assembled into one large linear system which one can solve to find the unknown forces in the various beams. Some of the forces are known (weights of beams and truck), which give terms to be moved to the right side of the linear equations so that the system is not homogeneous.

Similarly, an electrical network (Figure 6.2) satisfies Kirchhoff's laws for the balance of currents at the nodes and voltages around the loops. These formulas are linear in the values of the resistances and power sources and lead to a system of linear equations for all the unknown values.

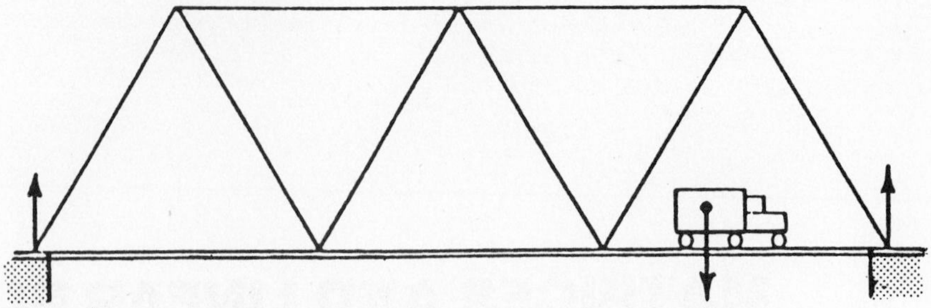

Figure 6.1 The forces on a bridge satisfy a linear system of equations.

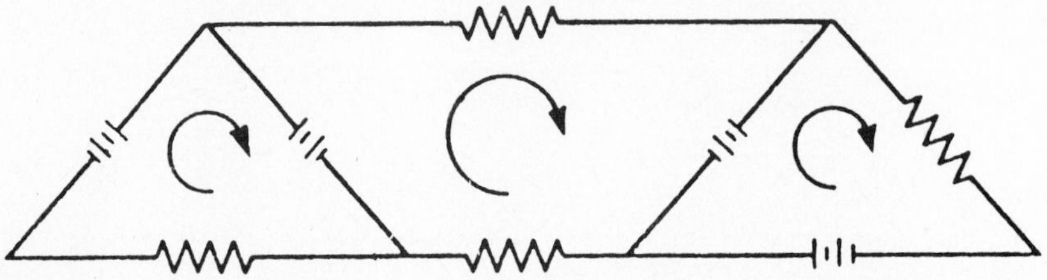

Figure 6.2 The currents and voltages in an electrical circuit satisfy a linear system of equations.

The three steps in solving a problem of this type are:

1. **Formulate a mathematical model** of the system (building structure, electrical network, etc.). One explicitly computes the matrix coefficients a_{ij} based on physical principles of the system.
2. **Compute the forcing function** (external forces on the structure, external loads, inputs to the network, etc.). One explicitly computes the b_i based on an analysis of the particular external circumstances of the problem.
3. **Solve the linear system** $Ax = \mathbf{b}$ to obtain the solution $\mathbf{x}$.

The first two of these steps depend on knowledge of the physical situation (structural engineering, physics, etc.). The third step uses a numerical computation algorithm; one objective of mathematical software is to provide a reliable, efficient tool for this part of the problem solving.

Many physical systems are modeled by differential equations, for example,

$$\frac{d^2y}{dx^2} + \cos(x)y = \log(x+4), \qquad y(0) = 0,\ y(1) = 1$$ **Equation 6.1.1**

which usually cannot be solved by formulas. The finite difference approach is to **discretize** the interval [0, 1] as shown here:

$$x_0 = 0 \quad x_1 \quad x_2 \quad x_3 \quad x_4 \quad 1 = x_5$$

and replace the derivative by a simple divided difference, for example,

$$\left.\frac{d^2y}{dx^2}\right|_{x=x_3} = \frac{y(x_2) - 2y(x_3) + y(x_4)}{(.2)^2} \qquad \left(.2 = \frac{1}{5} = x_4 - x_3\right)$$

The approximating difference equation at x_3 is then

$$\frac{y(x_2) - 2y(x_3) + y(x_4)}{(.2)^2} + \cos(x_3)y(x_3) = \log(x_3+4)$$

There is one such equation at each discretization point $x_j = j*.2$ which leads to a linear system for approximate values of the solution of the differential equation. If one multiplies each equation by $(.2)^2 = .04$, then the linear system of four equations is [with $y_i = y(x_i)$]

$$\begin{bmatrix} -2+.04\cos(x_1) & 1 & 0 & 0 \\ 1 & -2+.04\cos(x_2) & 1 & 0 \\ 0 & 1 & -2+.04\cos(x_3) & 1 \\ 0 & 0 & 1 & -2+.04\cos(x_4) \end{bmatrix} \begin{bmatrix} y_1 \\ y_2 \\ y_3 \\ y_4 \end{bmatrix}$$

$$= \begin{bmatrix} 0+.04\log(x_1+4) \\ .04\log(x_2+4) \\ .04\log(x_3+4) \\ -1+.04\log(x_4+4) \end{bmatrix}$$

The boundary conditions $y_0 = 0$ and $y_5 = 1$ are used to eliminate these variables; they produce terms for the right side of the first and last equations.

As for bridges and electrical circuits, we see there is an analysis stage (deriving the differential equation and then finding good approximating difference equations) which may be quite complicated. Then there is the numerical computation problem to solve $A\mathbf{x} = \mathbf{b}$ which can be solved with standard mathematical software.

If the differential equation is not linear, then a nonlinear system of equations results. Suppose, for example, that the physical situation led to the differential equation model

$$\frac{d^2y}{dx^2} + \cos(x)y = \log(x+y)$$

A simple-minded but sometimes effective strategy for such a problem is as follows:

```
Guess at y(x) and call this y^0(x)
For i = 1, 2, ..., limit, do:
    Solve d^2y/dx^2 = cos(x)y = log (y+y^(i-1)) for y(x) and set y^i(x) = y(x)
    If max|y^i(x)-y^(i-1)(x)| is sufficiently small, exit loop
End loop
```

With this approach the procedure outlined for the linear differential equation becomes the inner loop of the computation. It is clear that certain steps can be taken to make the inner loop solution more efficient than just repeating the linear problem solution over and over. Two points are noteworthy here:

1. A standard tool like "solve $A\mathbf{x} = \mathbf{b}$" can become part of the inner loop of a large calculation, and thus it is essential that it be done efficiently.

2. This standard tool can become "buried" in relation to the total problem solution, and it is essential that this tool be reliable. It could be buried so deep that the programmer is not really aware that the tool is being used and an error in it would be very difficult to diagnose.

Types of Matrices 6.1.B

A matrix A from $A\mathbf{x} = \mathbf{b}$ may have a variety of special characteristics. Some of these arise naturally from the modeling process and reflect "real-world" situations. Others arise during the analysis and solution of equations and are artificial but still important.

Matrices where most of the elements are zero are called **sparse matrices**. The basic source of sparsity is models with a local connection or local influence principle. Thus in a bridge, the equations at a node only involve the beams that meet there. Their number is about the same whether the bridge is 50 feet in length with 10 beams or 5 miles long with 10,000 beams. Thus, for a big bridge, most coefficients in any particular equation are zero.

The sparseness for bridge models follows from the obvious physical fact that no one beam goes the length of a long bridge. Electrical networks may have distant nodes connected, yet in practice the models of these networks are also sparse — and the bigger they are, the more sparse they are. Again, when differential equations are approximated by difference equations, the difference approximations are entirely local; in the difference equations for 6.1.1, there are only three nonzero coefficients in any one equation no matter how many difference equations there are.

Linear systems with 100,000 unknowns have been solved. The matrix for such a system has 10^{10} elements and, if it were full, it could not be stored in existing computer systems (never mind solving the equations). Such a large system can be solved only if it is sparse (or some very special formulas are applicable). Figure 6.3 shows the patterns of nonzero elements for two large sparse matrices from real applications.

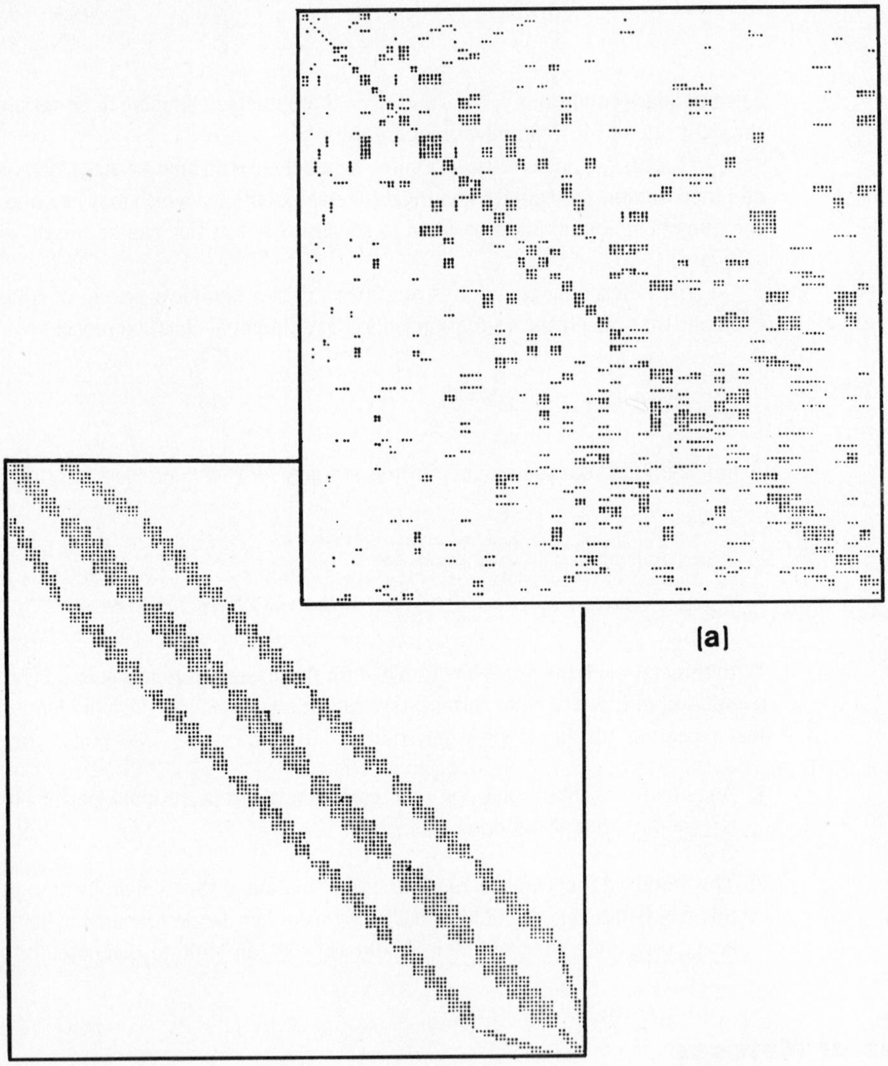

(a)

(b)

Figure 6.3 **Two large sparse matrices.** Each dot indicates a nonzero element. Much larger sparse matrices occur in practice, but one cannot see the dots if the pattern is reduced to this size. (Courtesy of John Reid, A.E.R.E. Harwell.)

Many applications lead to matrices which are not only sparse but also have an organized pattern of nonzero elements. The most common of these is the **band matrix** where $a_{ij} = 0$ if $|i-j| >$ bandwidth (see Figure 6.4). For example, the finite difference matrix for 6.1.1 has a bandwidth of 1. Such a matrix is called **tridiagonal.** Any model where there is a local influence principle will lead to a band matrix if the equations and unknowns are numbered properly. Consider a regular rectangular pattern such as that shown in Figure

6.5, where the equation at each node just involves the variables "attached to" the node (five of them). The pattern of nonzero elements in the matrix is also shown in Figure 6.5. If the underlying physical object being modeled is not quite so regular, then the matrix is still banded but the pattern of nonzero elements is not so regular.

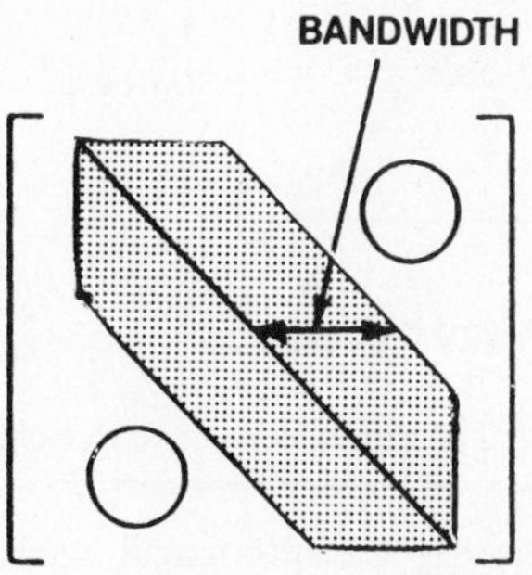

Figure 6.4 The pattern of nonzero elements in a band matrix. The bandwidth is usually much smaller than the size of the matrix.

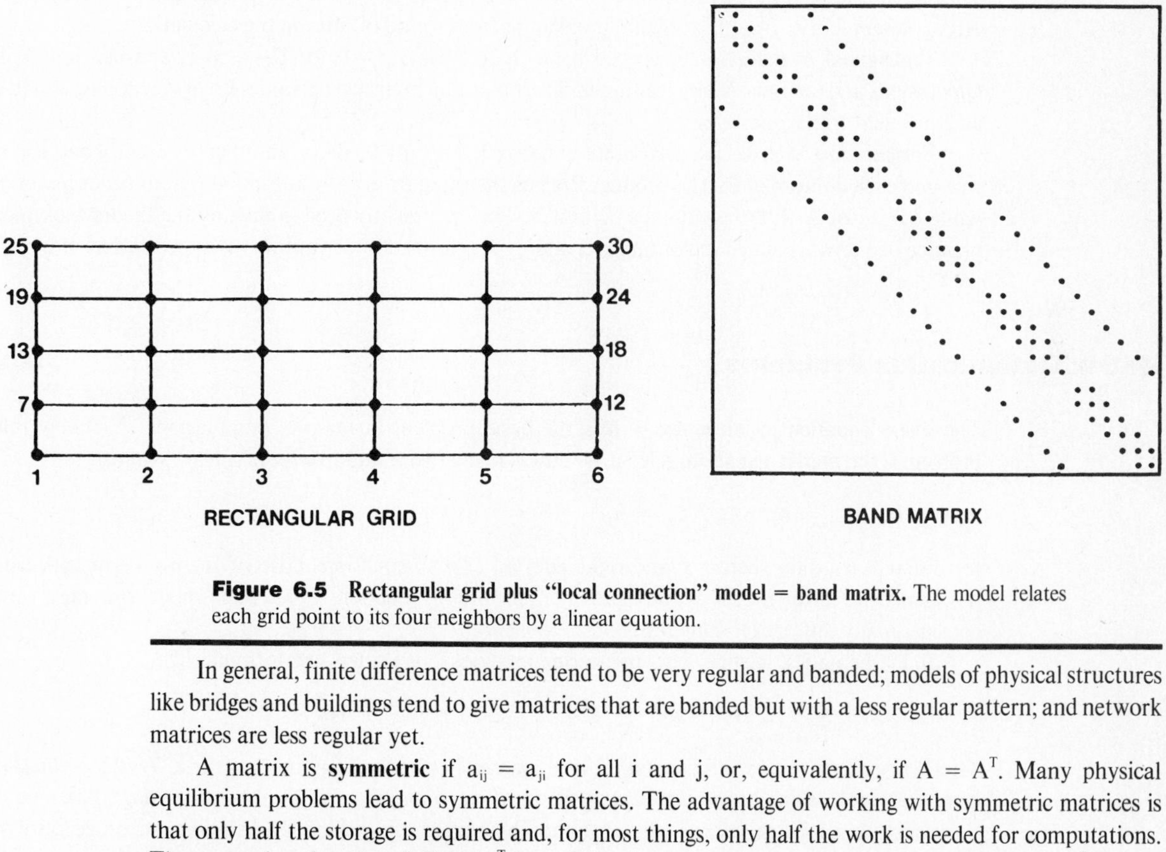

Figure 6.5 Rectangular grid plus "local connection" model = band matrix. The model relates each grid point to its four neighbors by a linear equation.

In general, finite difference matrices tend to be very regular and banded; models of physical structures like bridges and buildings tend to give matrices that are banded but with a less regular pattern; and network matrices are less regular yet.

A matrix is **symmetric** if $a_{ij} = a_{ji}$ for all i and j, or, equivalently, if $A = A^T$. Many physical equilibrium problems lead to symmetric matrices. The advantage of working with symmetric matrices is that only half the storage is required and, for most things, only half the work is needed for computations. The properties of **positive definite** ($\mathbf{x}^T A\mathbf{x} > 0$ for all nonzero vectors **x**) and **positive semidefinite** ($\mathbf{x}^T A\mathbf{x} \geq 0$ for all **x**) are often associated with symmetric matrices.

The analysis of numerical computation focuses on matrices whose special form allows one to do the computation easily. Thus the goal of Gauss elimination is to obtain a simple matrix where the equations can be solved easily. Some of these special matrices are listed here:

Diagonal Matrices: Here $a_{ij} = 0$ except for $i = j$. It is trivial to do calculations with diagonal matrices. The reason that eigenvectors are of interest is that, with them as basis (or coordinate vectors), the representation of the model is a diagonal matrix.

Triangular Matrices: The two types are shown in Figure 6.6, and they are both easy to work with. Linear equations can be solved by forward or backward substitution; the eigenvalues are the diagonal elements.

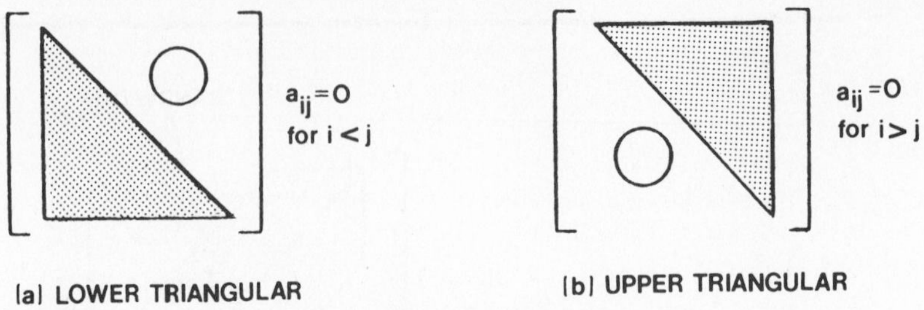

Figure 6.6 The pattern of nonzero elements for triangular matrices.

Orthogonal Matrices: If A is orthogonal, then $A^TA = I$ or $A^T = A^{-1}$, and it is easy to solve the linear system $A\mathbf{x} = \mathbf{b}$ as $\mathbf{x} = A^T\mathbf{b}$. Orthogonal matrices do not change the length ($||x||_2$) of any vector. We see that if $\mathbf{y} = A\mathbf{x}$, then

$$||\mathbf{x}||_2^2 = \mathbf{x}^T\mathbf{x} = \mathbf{x}^TI\mathbf{x} = \mathbf{x}^TA^TA\mathbf{x} = (A\mathbf{x})^TA\mathbf{x} = \mathbf{y}^T\mathbf{y} = ||\mathbf{y}||_2^2$$

This is important in numerical computations where we do not want the manipulations to magnify any errors present (either from the original problem or from round-off during the calculation).

Tridiagonal Matrices: This special band matrix has $a_{ij} = 0$ for $|i-j| > 1$, and it arises both in applications and analysis. Many techniques for computing matrix eigenvalues involve reducing a matrix to an equivalent tridiagonal form.

Permutation Matrices: A permutation matrix P has only 0s or 1s, and there is exactly one 1 in each row and each column of P. The product PA has the same rows as A but in a different order (permuted), while AP is just A with the columns permuted. They are mainly used in making the theory look nice; in practice one uses a pointer vector (indirect addressing) instead of permuting rows or columns of a matrix.

Matrix Computation Problems 6.1.C

The **linear equation problem** $A\mathbf{x} = \mathbf{b}$ is the basic problem in matrix computations. A closely related problem is the **matrix equation**, $AX = B$. This is really just a multiple set of linear systems

$$A\mathbf{x}_1 = \mathbf{b}_1, A\mathbf{x}_2 = \mathbf{b}_2, \ldots, A\mathbf{x}_m = \mathbf{b}_m$$

for different solution vectors $\mathbf{x}_i$ and right sides $\mathbf{b}_1$. Matrix equations arise frequently because A usually represents the linear model and **b** represents the forcing function. For a fixed model one may want to consider many different forcing functions.

In mathematics, science, and engineering textbooks, one often sees formulas like

$$\mathbf{x} = A^{-1}\mathbf{b} \qquad \mathbf{y} = B^{-1}(I+2A)\mathbf{b} \qquad \mathbf{z} = B^{-1}(2A+I)\,(C^{-1}+A)\mathbf{b} + \mathbf{d}$$

These suggest that one would compute some **matrix inverses** to compute **x**, **y**, or **z**. *This is an inefficient computational approach; one almost never needs to invert matrices to compute other things.* Later we show that computing a matrix inverse required about three times the arithmetic and twice the storage as solving a linear system. Any matrix expression applied to a vector can be evaluated efficiently without inverting any matrices. More generally, we show later that A^{-1} is not worthwhile to compute even when one has $\mathbf{x}_i = A^{-1}\mathbf{b}_i$ for many i.

There are some problems in statistics and engineering where one needs to see the inverse matrix and not just use it to find something else. If one is not actually examining the elements of an inverse matrix, then it is likely that one should not be computing it.

Determinants play a central role in introductory linear algebra and matrix theory, yet *determinants serve no useful purpose in matrix computations.* They became a standard part of matrix theory because certain formulas look nice. There are only a very few places where determinants are needed in the theory of matrix computations (none in the basic theory), and it is very rare that one needs the actual value of the determinant. **Cramer's rule** is an incredibly inefficient method for solving linear equations (see Problem 6.2.36). One sometimes hears, "I can't solve the system because the determinant is zero." Using the best method to compute determinants, one discovers whether the system can be solved or not *before* one has the value of the determinant. The size of a determinant has no bearing on the validity of solving $\mathbf{Ax} = \mathbf{b}$; one might be safe with $\det(A) = 10^{-48}$ and in trouble with $\det(A) = 6.8$. To see this, just consider the effect of multiplying all the equations in the m by m system $\mathbf{Ax} = \mathbf{b}$ by 100. The determinant is changed by 100^m, but the computation is essentially unaffected.

The principal technique in matrix computations is manipulating the problem into a simple form where the solution is trivial — or at least easy. For example, the objective of Gauss elimination for $\mathbf{Ax} = \mathbf{b}$ is to obtain $\mathbf{Tx} = \mathbf{c}$ where T is triangular, and hence it is easy to compute $\mathbf{x}$. Similarly, if $\mathbf{Ax} = \mathbf{b}$ can be manipulated into $Rx = c$ where R is orthogonal, then $\mathbf{x} = R^T\mathbf{c}$ is easily found.

The simplest matrices of all are the diagonal matrices; if we could easily transform our problems so that the matrices are diagonal, then matrix computations would be easy. For most matrices A, there is a matrix E so that

$$E^{-1}AE = D \qquad \textbf{Equation 6.1.2}$$

where D is diagonal. The columns of E are the **eigenvectors** of A, and the diagonal elements of D are the **eigenvalues** of A. The **eigenvalue** and **eigenvector problem** is to compute D and E for a given matrix A. Equation 6.1.2 can be rewritten as

$$AE = ED$$

which, in vector form, is

$$A\mathbf{e}_i = d_i\mathbf{e}_i \qquad \textbf{Equation 6.1.3}$$

This is the standard way to define the eigenvector $\mathbf{e}_i$ and associated eigenvalue d_i.

PROBLEMS 6.1

6.1.1 Prove that the sum and product of two lower (upper) triangular matrices are lower (upper) triangular.

6.1.2 Prove that the inverse of a nonsingular lower (upper) triangular matrix is lower (upper) triangular.

6.1.3 Let A be an $N \times N$ band matrix with bandwidth $K < N/2$. Show that A^2 has bandwidth 2K.

6.1.4 Suppose the tridiagonal matrix A is factored so that $A = LU$ where L is lower triangular and U is upper triangular. Show that L and U are also tridiagonal.

6.1.5 Show that a symmetric triangular matrix is diagonal.

6.1.6 Construct an example which shows that the product of two symmetric matrices need not be symmetric.

6.1.7 Let A be symmetric and B be another matrix. Show that B^TAB is symmetric.

6.1.8 Show that the product of two symmetric matrices is symmetric if and only if they commute, that is, $AB = BA$.

6.1.9 Assume A is lower triangular and is orthogonal. Show that A is diagonal. What are the diagonal elements of A?

6.1.10 Show that, if the columns of A are linearly independent, then A^TA is positive definite (that is, $\mathbf{x}^TA^TA\mathbf{x} > 0$ for all $\mathbf{x} \neq 0$). Consider the matrix

$$A = \begin{pmatrix} 1000 & 1020 \\ 1000 & 1000 \\ 1000 & 1000 \end{pmatrix}$$

and compute $B = A^TA$ using four-digit decimal arithmetic. Show that B is *not* positive definite by considering $\mathbf{x} = (1, -1)^T$. Explain this apparent contradiction.

6.1.11 Recall the system of equations obtained by the discretization of the differential equation 6.1.1. Show that the corresponding linear system is tridiagonal for discretizing any differential equation of the form

$$a(x)y'' + b(x)y' + c(x)y = f(x) \qquad y(x_0) = y_0,\ y(x_1) = y_1$$

6.1.12 Give an intuitive argument that the matrix of the models should be sparse for each of the following organizations: (a) electrical power network for a public utility; (b) regional sewage disposal and water treatment system; (c) U.S. Post Office; and (d) assembly-line operation for building cars.

6.1.13 Show how to compute the vector

$$\mathbf{x} = B^{-1}(2A+I)\,(C^{-1}+A)\mathbf{b}$$

without computing any matrix inverses (just use the vector-matrix arithmetic operations and solve linear systems of equations).

6.1.14 Consider the systems of equations

$$\text{(A)} \quad ix_i = b_i \qquad i = 1, 2, \ldots, M$$

$$\text{(B)} \quad \frac{x_i}{i} = c_i \qquad i = 1, 2, \ldots, M$$

$$\text{(C)} \quad \frac{x_i}{10} = d_i \qquad i = 1, 2, \ldots, M$$

Display the coefficient matrix and compute its determinant for $M = 5$, 10, 20, and 50. Do you anticipate any trouble in solving these systems of equations?

GAUSS ELIMINATION, LU-FACTORIZATION, AND PIVOTING — 6.2

The algorithm for eliminating unknowns illustrated in Chapter 1 dates from at least 250 B.C. even though it is called Gauss elimination. We give another example of this algorithm in a more difficult case and express all the steps in terms of matrices. This example contains all the essential elements of the theoretical analysis given later. After the example, some of the many variants of the algorithm are presented along with the crucial technique of pivoting and the important, but not well-understood, problem of scaling.

Gauss Elimination for a Singular but Consistent Linear System — Example 6.1

We consider the system of linear equations

Equation 6.2.1

$$\begin{aligned} x + y + z + w &= 4 \\ 2x + 3y + z + w &= 7 \\ x + y + z + w &= 4 \\ x + 2y + 2z + 2w &= 7 \end{aligned} \qquad \text{or } A\mathbf{x} = \mathbf{b}$$

After the first Gauss elimination step we have

$$\begin{array}{rl} x + y + z + w = 4 & \text{multipliers of row 1} \\ y - z - w = -1 & -2 \\ 0 = 0 & -1 \\ y + z + w = 3 & -1 \end{array}$$

After the next step we have

$$\begin{array}{rl} x + y + z + w = 4 & \\ y - z - w = -1 & \text{multipliers of row 2} \\ 0 = 0 & 0 \\ 2z + 2w = 4 & -1 \end{array}$$

We now interchange the third and fourth equations to obtain

Equation 6.2.2

$$\begin{aligned} x + y + z + w &= 4 \\ y - z - w &= -1 \\ 2z + 2w &= 4 \\ 0 &= 0 \end{aligned}$$

The permutation matrix that interchanges these two rows is

$$P_3 = \begin{pmatrix} 1 & 0 & 0 & 0 \\ 0 & 1 & 0 & 0 \\ 0 & 0 & 0 & 1 \\ 0 & 0 & 1 & 0 \end{pmatrix}$$

The objective here is to transform 6.2.1 into $U\mathbf{x} = \mathbf{c}$ where U is upper triangular. This is accomplished with 6.2.2, and we now consider how to express all these steps in terms of matrix operations and to relate U and **c** to A and **b**. The matrix U is of the form MPA where P is a permutation matrix and M is a lower triangular matrix formed from the multipliers. To see this, recall that a basic Gauss elimination step like "multiply row 1 by m_4 and add to row 4." is accomplished by multiplying on the left by

$$\begin{pmatrix} 1 & 0 & 0 & 0 \\ 0 & 1 & 0 & 0 \\ 0 & 0 & 1 & 0 \\ m_4 & 0 & 0 & 1 \end{pmatrix}$$

which is the identity with one more element m_4 in column 1 (the row 4 position). One may easily verify that such matrices have a simple multiplication rule:

$$\begin{pmatrix} 1 & 0 & 0 & 0 \\ 0 & 1 & 0 & 0 \\ 0 & 0 & 1 & 0 \\ m_4 & 0 & 0 & 1 \end{pmatrix} \begin{pmatrix} 1 & 0 & 0 & 0 \\ m_2 & 1 & 0 & 0 \\ 0 & 0 & 1 & 0 \\ 0 & 0 & 0 & 1 \end{pmatrix} \begin{pmatrix} 1 & 0 & 0 & 0 \\ 0 & 1 & 0 & 0 \\ m_3 & 0 & 1 & 0 \\ 0 & 0 & 0 & 1 \end{pmatrix} = \begin{pmatrix} 1 & 0 & 0 & 0 \\ m_2 & 1 & 0 & 0 \\ m_3 & 0 & 1 & 0 \\ m_4 & 0 & 0 & 1 \end{pmatrix}$$

Thus the effect of all the row manipulations made above can be expressed in matrix terms by the product

$$\underset{\text{Eliminate z}}{\begin{pmatrix} 1 & 0 & 0 & 0 \\ 0 & 1 & 0 & 0 \\ 0 & 0 & 1 & 0 \\ 0 & 0 & 0 & 1 \end{pmatrix}} \underset{\text{Switch rows 3 and 4}}{\begin{pmatrix} 1 & 0 & 0 & 0 \\ 0 & 1 & 0 & 0 \\ 0 & 0 & 0 & 1 \\ 0 & 0 & 1 & 0 \end{pmatrix}} \underset{\text{Eliminate y}}{\begin{pmatrix} 1 & 0 & 0 & 0 \\ 0 & 1 & 0 & 0 \\ 0 & 0 & 1 & 0 \\ 0 & -1 & 0 & 1 \end{pmatrix}} \underset{\text{Eliminate x}}{\begin{pmatrix} 1 & 0 & 0 & 0 \\ -2 & 1 & 0 & 0 \\ -1 & 0 & 1 & 0 \\ -1 & 0 & 0 & 1 \end{pmatrix}}$$

$$= \begin{pmatrix} 1 & 0 & 0 & 0 \\ -2 & 1 & 0 & 0 \\ 1 & -1 & 0 & 1 \\ -1 & 0 & 1 & 0 \end{pmatrix} = \text{Total effect}$$

It is easy to check that the "total effect" matrix is

$$\begin{pmatrix} 1 & 0 & 0 & 0 \\ -2 & 1 & 0 & 0 \\ -1 & -1 & 1 & 0 \\ 1 & 0 & 0 & 1 \end{pmatrix} \begin{pmatrix} 1 & 0 & 0 & 0 \\ 0 & 1 & 0 & 0 \\ 0 & 0 & 0 & 1 \\ 0 & 0 & 1 & 0 \end{pmatrix}$$

This shows what is intuitively clear: we could make all the row interchanges in advance (if we knew them) and then apply Gauss elimination (the multiplier matrices) without row interchanges. The final matrix representation of Gauss elimination for this example is

$$\underset{\substack{\text{M} \\ \text{Total effect} \\ \text{of} \\ \text{multipliers}}}{\begin{pmatrix} 1 & 0 & 0 & 0 \\ -2 & 1 & 0 & 0 \\ -1 & -1 & 1 & 0 \\ 1 & 0 & 0 & 1 \end{pmatrix}} \underset{\substack{\text{P} \\ \text{Total effect} \\ \text{of row} \\ \text{switches}}}{\begin{pmatrix} 1 & 0 & 0 & 0 \\ 0 & 1 & 0 & 0 \\ 0 & 0 & 0 & 1 \\ 0 & 0 & 1 & 0 \end{pmatrix}} \underset{\substack{\text{A} \\ \text{Original} \\ \text{matrix}}}{\begin{pmatrix} 1 & 1 & 1 & 1 \\ 2 & 3 & 1 & 1 \\ 1 & 1 & 1 & 1 \\ 1 & 2 & 2 & 2 \end{pmatrix}} = \underset{\substack{\text{U} \\ \text{Upper} \\ \text{triangular} \\ \text{matrix}}}{\begin{pmatrix} 1 & 1 & 1 & 1 \\ 0 & 1 & -1 & -1 \\ 0 & 0 & 2 & 2 \\ 0 & 0 & 0 & 0 \end{pmatrix}}$$

To continue the solution process, we compute **MPb**, which gives the column vector $(4, -1, 4, 0)^T$. Note that in practice we do *not* compute M, we just keep the multipliers because we can compute **Mb** from them just as fast as we can from M itself. Note also that the multipliers can be saved in the matrix A at the places where zeros are introduced. Thus the multiplier used to zero out a_{jk} is stored in a_{jk} for later use.

We now attempt to back-substitute to find the solution. We cannot solve the last equation $0 = 0$ for anything, but it is automatically satisfied for any value of w. Thus, we can pick w arbitrarily. We show the back substitution for three choices of w:

w = 0 case	w = 1 case	w = 6.7 case
2z = 4 so z = 2	2z = 4 − 2 so z = 1	2z = 4 − 13.4 so z = −4.7
y = −1 + 2 = 1	y = −1 + 2 = 1	y = −1 + 2 = 1
x = 4 − 3 = 1	x = 4 − 3 = 1	x = 4 − 3 = 1

This, of course, illustrates the fact that a singular system A**x** = **b** which is consistent (i.e., has one solution) has infinitely many solutions.

Note that if the third component of **b** is *not* equal to 4, then the final equation becomes "zero = something not zero," which is contradictory, and thus the singular system A**x** = **b** would have no solution at all. A little reflection about Gauss elimination with pivoting shows that:

1. A *is singular if* U *has a zero on the diagonal.*

2. *For singular* A, A**x** = **b** *is consistent if back substitution with diagonal zeros occurs only in equations of the form 0 = 0. The unknowns associated with the diagonal zeros in these equations can be assigned arbitrarily.*

Pivoting in Gauss Elimination 6.2.A

The process of interchanging rows in Gauss elimination so that one has a nonzero diagonal element is called **pivoting**, and the matrix elements used for the elimination are the **pivots**. The use of nonzero pivots is sufficient for the theoretical correctness of Gauss elimination, but more care must be taken in computation if one is to obtain reliable results. This is seen from the following example.

The Effect of Small Pivots in Gauss Elimination — Example 6.2

Consider the simple system

$$.000100\,x + y = 1 \qquad\qquad x = 1.00010$$
$$\text{Solution:}$$
$$x + y = 2 \qquad\qquad y = .99990$$

to be solved using *three-digit arithmetic*. That is, only the three most significant decimal digits of any number are retained as the result of an arithmetic operation. We assume the result is rounded. With Gauss elimination we multiply the first equation by −10,000 and add it to the second equation to obtain

$$.000100\,x + y = 1 \qquad\qquad x = 0.000$$
$$\text{Solution:}$$
$$-10{,}000\,y = -10{,}000 \qquad\qquad y = 1.000$$

A computational disaster has occurred.

If we switch the equations (that is, we *pivot*) to obtain

$$x + y = 2$$
$$.000100\,x + y = 1$$

then Gauss elimination produces the system (again with three-digit arithmetic)

$$x + y = 2 \qquad\qquad x = 1.00$$
$$\text{Solution:}$$
$$y = 1 \qquad\qquad y = 1.00$$

This solution is as good as one could hope for using three-digit arithmetic.

The lesson of this example is this: *It is not enough just to avoid zero pivots; one must also avoid relatively small ones.*

There are two standard pivoting strategies. The first is **partial pivoting**: at the kth step, interchange the rows of the matrix so that the largest remaining element in the kth column is used as pivot. That is, after the pivoting,

$$|a_{kk}| = \max |a_{ik}| \qquad \text{for } i = k, k+1, \ldots, n$$

The second is **complete pivoting**: at the kth step, interchange both the rows and columns of the matrix so that the largest number in the remaining matrix is used as pivot. That is, after the pivoting,

$$|a_{kk}| = \max |a_{ij}| \quad \text{for } i = k, k+1, \ldots, n; \quad j = k, k+1, \ldots, n$$

and the unknowns are renumbered.

Round-off affects numerical computations in two ways: (1) some problems are inherently sensitive to round-off and other uncertainties, and (2) some algorithms enormously magnify any round-off and other uncertainties. There is little one can do about the first difficulty besides hoping to identify such problems. Pivoting is an example of a technique to eliminate the second difficulty in Example 6.2.

It is not easy to answer the general question: *"How well does pivoting control error magnification?"* The following facts are known:

Fact 1 (Proved). Complete pivoting is safe; errors are never magnified unreasonably. The **magnification factor** is no more than

$$f_n = (n \times 2 \times 3^{1/2} \times 4^{1/3} \times 5^{1/4} \times \ldots \times n^{1/(n-1)})^{1/2}$$

for an n by n system of equations. The following table shows that f_n grows rather slowly:

n	5	10	15	20	30	50	80	100
f_n	5.73	18.30	39.09	69.77	155.5	536.17	1915.51	3552.41

Any error (either in the system at the start or made during the calcuation) is transmitted into the solution magnified by at most the magnification factor f_n.

Fact 2 (Experimentally Observed). The probability that trouble occurs using partial pivoting is *very* small. It is unusual for the error magnification with partial pivoting to be more than twice that with complete pivoting. The increase in the magnification factor f_n seen in practice is rarely more than a factor of 8 and is frequently close to 1, especially for ill-conditioned problems.

Fact 3 (By Example). There is an n by n matrix whose magnification factor using partial pivoting is 2^n. We have

n	5	10	15	20	30	50	80	100
2^n	32	1024	32768	10^6	10^9	10^{15}	10^{24}	10^{30}

If the costs of partial and complete pivoting were nearly the same, then one would always use complete pivoting. However, the cost of complete pivoting is comparable to the rest of the whole solution process. A subtraction and test must be made for each matrix element where Gauss elimination uses an add and multiply, and one intuitively concludes that complete pivoting approximately doubles the cost of Gauss elimination. On the other hand, the cost of partial pivoting is almost negligible.

Fact 4 (Conclusion). The price of complete safety is very high, and one can reasonably ask: "Why should I pay twice the cost just to protect myelf from a situation so rare that it took numerical analysts years to find an example of it?" The result is that complete pivoting is rarely used. This is not simply a calculated risk, but, as we discuss in Section 6.6, there are other things one can do for protection from excessive error magnification.

We express the Gauss elimination algorithm in a compact, natural programming language form. We consider a square n by n matrix A = (a_{ij}) and wish to solve A**x** = **b**. This algorithm stores the upper triangular factor U and the matrix of multipliers over the matrix A, thereby destroying it.

Gauss Elimination with Partial Pivoting for Solving Ax = b

Algorithm 6.2.1

```
                              LOOP OVER COLUMNS OF A
For k = 1 to n-1 do
          FIND MAXIMUM ELEMENT IN COLUMN K
    imax = row index so that |a_imax,k| = max|a_i,k| , for i≥k
          TEST FOR ZERO PIVOT (SINGULARITY).  BUFFER IS A
          SMALL MACHINE DEPENDENT NUMBER TO GAUGE ROUND-OFF
    If |a_imax,k| ≤ buffer then go to end of k-loop
          INTERCHANGE ROWS K AND IMAX
    For j = 1 to n interchange a_kj and a_imax,j
          INTERCHANGE CORRESPONDING RIGHT SIDES
    Interchange b_k and b_imax

                              LOOP OVER ROWS OF A
    For i = k+1 to n do
          COMPUTE MULTIPLIER, SAVE IN K-TH COLUMN
          m = a_ik = a_ik/a_kk
                  LOOP OVER ELEMENTS OF ROW I
       For j = k+1 to n do
            a_ij = a_ij - m*a_kj
       end of j-loop
               DO CORRESPONDING RIGHT SIDE
       b_i = b_i - m*b_k
    end of i-loop
end of k-loop
    BACK SUBSTITUTION          LOOP OVER ROWS OF A IN REVERSE ORDER
For i = n to 1 do
       SUBSTITUTE KNOWN VALUES INTO RIGHT SIDE
    r = b_i - sum(a_ij x_j; for j = i+1,n)
       TEST FOR ZERO PIVOT
    If |a_ii| > buffer then x_i = r/a_ii
            TEST FOR RIGHT SIDE ALSO EQUAL TO ZERO,
            ASSIGN ZERO TO SOLUTION AND PRINT MESSAGE
       else if |r| ≤ buffer then x_i = 0, print
            ''A is singular, system is consistent''
                 OR PRINT ERROR MESSAGE
            else print ''A is singular, inconsistent system''
end of i-loop
```

Note how the multipliers and U are both stored in the matrix A. Each multiplier is written in the spot where an element of A has just been zeroed. The diagonal elements of M are 1, and so they need not be saved explicitly. While this strategy is irrelevant when just solving $\mathbf{Ax} = \mathbf{b}$, there are other situations where it is very helpful to save both U and the multipliers.

Scaling and Testing for Floating Point Zero 6.2.B

The explicit algorithm forces us to consider the question of exactly when a computed number is "zero." We would be mathematically correct to set *buffer* = 0 in the algorithm, but this does not make sense in practice. Numbers which would be zero in exact arithmetic are almost sure to be nonzero in floating point arithmetic because of round-off errors. To decide whether a number is zero we must consider the scale of two things: *the scale of the numbers in the problem and the scale of the machine.*

The *machine scale* comes from the precision (number of digits carried) in the computer. Thus in a machine which carries 10 decimal digits, we might consider a pivot of 1.2×10^{-10} to be just residual round-off error and properly taken to be zero. *But,* this would be wrong if all the numbers in the matrix A are of size 10^{-8}. So, we would like to *scale the problem* so that a small number like 1.2×10^{-10} is just round-off noise.

There are two natural ways to scale the problem $\mathbf{Ax} = \mathbf{b}$. We can multiply each equation by a factor (e.g., by 10^8 if all the a_{ij} in the matrix are of size 10^{-8}) to adjust the size of the numbers. We can also multiply the columns of A; this corresponds to a change in units (inches to miles) in measuring the size of the unknowns. Alas, there are some problems where scaling is not so easy, and no satisfactory, completely automatic scaling method has been found. Two examples of troublesome matrices are given below. Neither one of these simple techniques or their combination properly scales the following matrices:

$$\begin{pmatrix} 1 & 10^{10} & 10^{20} \\ 10^{10} & 10^{30} & 10^{50} \\ 10^{20} & 10^{40} & 10^{80} \end{pmatrix} \qquad \begin{pmatrix} 1 & 10^{20} & 10^{10} & 1 \\ 10^{20} & 10^{20} & 1 & 10^{40} \\ 10^{10} & 1 & 10^{40} & 10^{50} \\ 1 & 10^{40} & 10^{50} & 1 \end{pmatrix}$$

Fortunately, most problems can be scaled without difficulty. The crucial point is to choose units (which is what scaling amounts to) which are natural to the problem and that do not distort the relationships between the sizes of things. The examples above show that this cannot always be done, but it usually can be done easily for real problems. It is also prudent to have ordinary-sized numbers, and the most common technique is to multiply each row (equation) so that the largest number in that row is 1. Assuming this is done, we then turn to the choice of a value for *buffer*. If the machine has t digits in base b, then buffer $= c \times b^{-t}$ is appropriate for some small value of c. The coefficient c should be 3 or 4 and should grow gradually as the matrix size increases. There are at most $2n^2$ arithmetic operations performed on any one a_{ij}, and so $c = n^2$ is the largest value one would consider. However, one expects there to be considerable cancellations in the round-off, so $c = n$ should be safe. Most numerical computation is done with relatively high precision (10 to 15 decimal digits), and one can be generous with the choice of c in these cases.

Scaling affects Gauss elimination with partial pivoting in a very direct way. Consider the 2 by 2 system of Example 6.2 with the first equation multiplied by 20,000:

$$\begin{aligned} 2x + 20000y &= 20000 \\ x + \quad\quad y &= \quad 2 \end{aligned}$$

Partial pivoting causes no interchange of rows and the result of Gauss elimination is, using **three-digit arithmetic,**

$$\begin{aligned} 2x + 20000y &= 20000 \\ -10000y &= -10000 \end{aligned} \qquad \text{Solution:} \quad \begin{aligned} x &= 0.000 \\ y &= 1.000 \end{aligned}$$

The computational disaster has occurred once again in spite of using partial pivoting. The remedy is either to scale the equations or to use **Gauss elimination with scaled partial pivoting**, discussed at the end of the next subsection.

We summarize by listing the following facts:

Fact 1. The computations are more robust (less sensitive to uncertainties) if all the elements of A are about the same size.

Fact 2. There is no known way to accomplish this in general, and matrices exist which cannot be scaled well.

Fact 3. The usual practice is to scale the rows (by dividing each equation by the largest coefficient in it). This is rather reliable for the problems that usually occur, and one hopes that the *a posteriori* tests discussed in Section 6.6 and Chapter 14 give a warning if trouble occurs. An alternative and reliable practice is to use Gauss elimination with scaled partial pivoting, Algorithm 6.2.4 below.

Algorithm Variations 6.2.C

There are numerous variations of the basic algorithm 6.2.1. Their selection is one aspect of the software design, and some cases are examined in Sections 6.4 and 6.5. The more common variations are listed here:

1. The matrix A is not destroyed; auxiliary workspace is provided instead of using parts of A as workspace.

2. The rows of A are not explicitly interchanged in pivoting; instead pointers are used to keep track of the order of elimination.

3. The matrix A is just factored, that is, the multipliers and the upper triangular factor U are computed. Both are saved for solving $A\mathbf{x} = \mathbf{b}$ later, possibly for many different **b**'s.

4. An option is available to solve for many different right sides, i.e., for solving the matrix equation $AX = B$.

5. Compute A^{-1} by solving the matrix equation $AX = I$. The right sides are successively the columns of the identity matrix, and the solutions are the columns of A^{-1}. See Problems 6.2.30 and 6.2.31, where it is shown that this can be done with less work than one would expect.

A less obvious and more interesting variation, **Crout reduction**, results from observing that the order of the arithmetic can be changed. Recall that, in the basic Gauss algorithm, each a_{ij} is modified numerous times during the calculation. A little reflection shows that we do not have to do these operations as we go. If all the information is kept (as it usually is), then we can wait and do all the operations on a_{ij} at once. The algorithm is given below, but in simplified form without pivoting, back substitution, or testing for zero pivots.

Crout Algorithm for the Factorization of A

Algorithm 6.2.2

```
                    LOOP OVER THE PIVOTS
For k = 1 to n do
        COMPUTE AND SAVE MULTIPLIERS IN REST OF COLUMN K
           THE PIVOTS (DIAGONALS OF U) ARE ALL ONES
    For i = k to n do
        aik = aik - sum (aij*ajk; for j = 1,k-1)
    end of i-loop
        COMPUTE THE ELEMENTS IN THE REST OF ROW K
    For j = k+1 to n do
        akj = (akj-sum (aki*aij; for i = 1,k-1))/akk
    end of j-loop
end of k-loop
```

Note that this algorithm does not produce the same numbers as the basic Gauss algorithm given earlier. The difference is in the normalization in the factorization MA = U; the Gauss algorithm is normalized by setting the diagonal elements of M to 1, while the Crout algorithm has the diagonal elements of U equal to 1. A minor change can be made to either algorithm to produce the same factorization as the other (modulo the differences in how round-off errors enter). Again U and the multipliers are stored on top of A, destroying it.

Even though the Crout variant seems to be just another way to do the same thing as Gauss elimination, there are two distinct situations where Crout can be advantageous. The first is where intermediate results are "expensive" to record, such as in copying the numbers using a hand-held calculator. With the Crout algorithm, one can carry out the summations in the inner loops without writing down the intermediate partial sums. This can result in a large savings in time. This is also a great improvement in reliability since recording numbers by hand is quite error-prone.

The second advantage is for computers with comparatively fast higher-precision arithmetic or with an especially fast dot product operation. That is, the sums

$$\text{sum } (a_{ij} * a_{jk};\ \text{for } j = 1,k-1)$$
$$\text{sum } (a_{ki} * a_{ij};\ \text{for } i = 1,k-1)$$

are done better (more accurately, faster, or both).

Finally, there are special versions of Gauss elimination for symmetric matrices which cut the work by half. The most important is the **Cholesky algorithm** for symmetric positive-definite matrices. Its operation is seen from the 2 by 2 case. We have

$$A = \begin{pmatrix} a_{11} & a_{12} \\ a_{21} & a_{22} \end{pmatrix} \qquad L = \begin{pmatrix} \ell_{11} & 0 \\ \ell_{21} & \ell_{22} \end{pmatrix}$$

and require that $A = LL^T$ or, in terms of elements,

$$a_{11} = \ell_{11}^2 \qquad a_{12} = \ell_{11}\ell_{21}$$
$$a_{21} = \ell_{21}\ell_{11} \qquad a_{22} = \ell_{21}^2 + \ell_{22}^2$$

Recall that A positive-definite means that $\mathbf{x}^T A\mathbf{x} > 0$ for all $\mathbf{x} \neq 0$, and so $a_{11} > 0$ [just take $\mathbf{x} = (1, 0)^T$]. Thus $\ell_{11} = \sqrt{a_{11}}$ is possible. The element ℓ_{21} is then determined from the equation for a_{21}, and then

$$\ell_{22} = \sqrt{a_{22} - \ell_{21}^2} = \sqrt{a_{22} - a_{12}^2/a_{11}}$$

To show this is possible, take $\mathbf{x} = (a_{12}, -a_{11})^T$ in the relation $\mathbf{x}^T A\mathbf{x} > 0$. This gives $\mathbf{x}^T A\mathbf{x} = a_{11}^2 a_{22} - a_{12}^2 a_{11} = a_{11}^2(a_{22} - a_{12}^2/a_{11}) > 0$, and so the square root in the formula for ℓ_{22} is real.

This approach works in general and is specified in Algorithm 6.2.3. Note that no pivoting is required for positive-definite matrices.

Cholesky Algorithm for Factorization of a Symmetric, Positive-Definite Matrix

Algorithm 6.2.3

```
                            LOOP OVER COLUMNS OF A
For k = 1 to n do
        COMPUTE THE NEXT ROW VECTOR
           EXCEPT FOR THE DIAGONAL ELEMENT
    For i = 1 to k-1 do
        a_ki = (a_ki-sum (a_ij a_kj; for j = 1,i-1))/a_ii
    end of i-loop
        COMPUTE THE DIAGONAL ELEMENT
    t = a_kk - sum (a_kj^2; for j = 1,k-1)
    If t>0 then a_kk = √t else a_kk = 0
end of k-loop
        THE FACTOR L IS NOW THE LOWER TRIANGULAR PART OF A
```

The variable t is used to provide insurance against round-off trouble when a_{kk} is nearly zero. This algorithm actually only requires that A be positive-semidefinite, that is $\mathbf{x}^T A\mathbf{x} \geq 0$ for all $\mathbf{x}$.

The final variation is to do the **scaling** of the equations during the Gauss elimination. This uses no less work than scaling the equations beforehand, but it relieves the programmer from the burden of remembering to do it. This is especially important for library software providing reliability for those users who are unaware of the importance of scaling. The algorithm is a simple variation of ordinary Gauss elimination, and only the differing part is given here.

Gauss Elimination with Scaled Partial Pivoting

Algorithm 6.2.4

```
                 COMPUTE SCALE FACTORS FOR EACH ROW
For i = 1 to n do
    s_i = max |a_i,j|     for 1 ≤ j ≤ n
                        LOOP OVER COLUMNS OF A
For k = 1 to n-1 do
        FIND SCALED MAXIMUM ELEMENT IN COLUMN K
  imax = row index so that |a_imax,k/s_i| = max |a_i,k/s_i|   for i ≥ k
  ..... REMAINDER OF ALGORITHM IS IDENTICAL WITH ALGORITHM 6.2.1 .....
```

Operations Count for Gauss Elimination **6.2.D**

The work of solving $A\mathbf{x} = \mathbf{b}$ by Gauss elimination can be estimated directly by counting the arithmetic operations. This counting goes as follows: The matrix at the kth stage appears as shown in Figure 6.7.

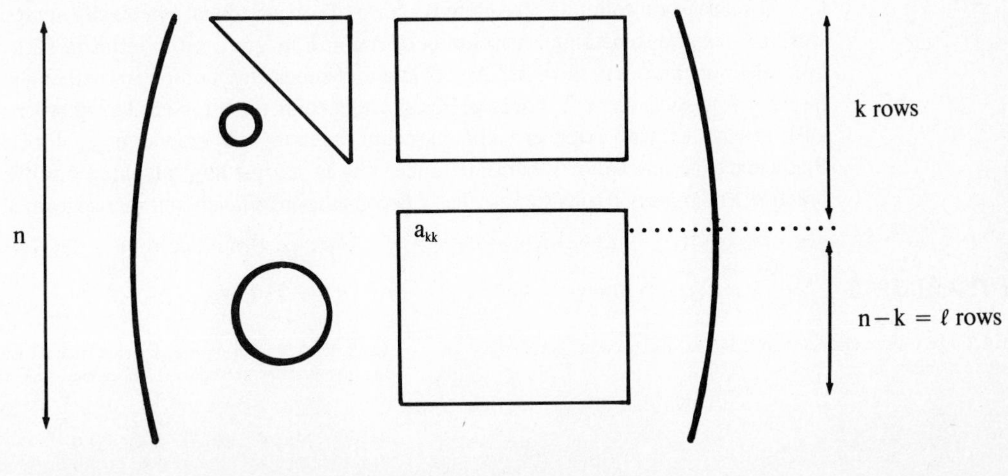

Figure 6.7 The matrix at the stage of eliminating the kth unknown.

The work for the next elimination is in three steps:

1. Multipliers: $m_i = a_{ik}/a_{kk}$, $\quad i = k+1$ to n
2. Elimination: $a_{ij} = a_{ij} - m_i * a_{kj}$, $\quad i = k+1$ to n, $j = k+1$ to n
3. Right side: $b_i = b_i - m_i * b_k$, $\quad i = k+1$ to n

Operations for step 1 are ℓ divides (or 1 divide and ℓ multiplies) where $\ell = n-k$; operations for step 2 are $\ell \times [\ell$ adds $+ \ell$ multiplies]; operations for step 3 are $\ell \times$ [1 add + multiply].

We introduce the abbreviations A = add, M = multiply, D = divide. Now sum these expressions for all values of k to obtain

$$\sum_{k=1}^{n-1} (\text{operations for step 1}) = \left(\sum_{k=1}^{n-1} \ell\right) D = \left(\sum_{k=1}^{n-1} n-k\right) D = \left(\sum_{i=1}^{n-1} i\right) D = \frac{n(n-1)}{2} D$$

By replacing the divisions by multiplies, this is also $(n-1)\,D + n(n-1)\,M/2$.

$$\sum_{k=1}^{n-1} (\text{operations for step 2}) = (A+M) \sum_{k=1}^{n-1} \ell^2 = (A+M) \sum_{i=1}^{n-1} i^2 = \frac{n(n-1)(2n-1)}{6} (A+M)$$

The work for the factorization is the sum of these two counts:

$$\left(\frac{n^3}{3} + \text{lower-order terms}\right) (A+M)$$

The operations count for the right side is

$$(A+M) \sum_{k=1}^{n-1} \ell = \frac{n(n-1)}{2} (A+M)$$

and the work for back substitution is seen to be

$$\sum_{i=n}^{\ell} [i(A+M) + 1D] = \frac{n(n-1)}{2} (A+M) + nD)$$

The total for processing the right side (forward substitution) and back substitution is thus

$$(n^2 + \text{lower-order terms}) (A+M)$$

The primary work of Gauss elimination is the $n^3/3$ operations $(A+M)$ to obtain the factorization.

This operation counting procedure is a form of **computational complexity** analysis. One estimates the work to compute something (the solution of $Ax = \mathbf{b}$ in this case) in terms of basic machine operations (arithmetic operations in this case). An obvious and important question is whether Gauss elimination is the fastest way to solve $Ax = \mathbf{b}$. For large enough values of n, the **Strassen algorithm** for matrix multiplication leads to a method with a smaller arithmetic count. It requires the order of $n^{2.7}$ multiplications and additions. Study and experimentation is currently under way to see just how advantageous this new algorithm is in practice. Preliminary results suggest that it becomes more efficient in practice for n above 250.

PROBLEMS 6.2

6.2.1 Use Gauss elimination to show that the following system does not have a solution:

$$\begin{aligned} 3x_1 + x_2 \quad\quad &= 1.5 \\ 2x_1 - x_2 - x_3 &= 2 \\ 4x_1 + 3x_2 + x_3 &= 0 \end{aligned}$$

6.2.2 Solve the following system with a hand calculator using only three significant decimal digits at each step. Check the answer by substituting back into the equations, and estimate its accuracy. The exact solution is $(1, 1, 1, 1)^T$.

$$\begin{aligned} .31x_1 + .14x_2 + .30x_3 + .27x_4 &= 1.02 \\ .26x_1 + .32x_2 + .18x_3 + .24x_4 &= 1.00 \\ .61x_1 + .22x_2 + .20x_3 + .31x_4 &= 1.34 \\ .40x_1 + .34x_2 + .36x_3 + .17x_4 &= 1.27 \end{aligned}$$

6.2.3 Solve the following system with a hand calculator using only four correctly rounded significant digits at each step. Check the answer by substituting back into the equations, and estimate its accuracy. The exact solution is $(10, 1)^T$.

$$
\begin{aligned}
.0003x_1 + 1.556x_2 &= 1.569 \\
.3454x_1 - 2.346x_2 &= 1.018
\end{aligned}
$$

6.2.4 Solve the following system with a hand calculator using only four correctly rounded significant digits at each step. Do this three times — once with a_{11} as the pivot element, once with a_{21} as the pivot element, and once with complete pivoting. Compare the answers with the exact solution $(1.000, 0.5000)^T$.

$$
\begin{aligned}
.002110x_1 + .08204x_2 &= .04313 \\
.3370x_1 + 12.84x_2 &= 6.757
\end{aligned}
$$

6.2.5 Show that the following matrix A is nonsingular, but that it cannot be written as the LU product of lower and upper triangular matrices. Explain why this does not contradict the conclusion stated at the end of Example 6.1.

$$
A = \begin{pmatrix} 1 & 2 & 3 \\ 2 & 4 & 1 \\ -1 & 0 & 2 \end{pmatrix}
$$

6.2.6 Give an example of a linear system $A\mathbf{x} = \mathbf{b}$ where det(A) is much less than round-off (compared to the size of the elements of A) and yet where there is no numerical difficulty encountered in solving $A\mathbf{x} = \mathbf{b}$.

6.2.7 Carry out Gauss elimination to solve the system

$$
\begin{aligned}
2x + 3y - z + w &= 5 \\
x + 2y + 3z - w &= -6 \\
4x + 5y - 9z + 6w &= 28 \\
x + y - 4z - 2w &= 7
\end{aligned}
$$

and obtain all its solutions.

6.2.8 Implement Algorithm 6.2.1 as a Fortran subroutine. Explain the objectives in designing the calling sequence. Explain the source of the value for the machine-dependent constant "buffer."

6.2.9 Implement Algorithm 6.2.1 as a set of three Fortran subroutines. FACTOR forms the LU factorization without pivoting, replacing A with it. FSUB is to apply the appropriate result from FACTOR to the right side of the system. BSUB is to do the back substitution. Give a complete description of the calling sequence variables. Outline the Fortran program that would use these three subroutines to solve the following problem:
The matrices A and B have dimensions 10 by 10 and 20 by 20.

There are seven systems $A\mathbf{x}_i = \mathbf{b}_i$ to be solved with right-side vectors in the Fortran array B(10, 7).

There are 16 systems $A\mathbf{y}_i = \mathbf{e}_i$ to be solved with new right-side vectors in the Fortran array B(10, 16).

6.2.10 Consider two library routines FACTOR(A) and SOLVE (A,X,B) where, for simplicity, various arguments about the size of A or the problem are omitted. FACTOR(A) replaces the matrix A by its two triangular factors. SOLVE (A,X,B) assumes A is *already* factored and actually solves $A\mathbf{x} = \mathbf{b}$.

Suppose you are to compute the vector $\mathbf{y}$ from the formula

$$\mathbf{y} = B(2C + D^{-1})\mathbf{x} + (I - B^{-1}L)\mathbf{z}$$

Outline a Fortran program to compute $\mathbf{y}$ using FACTOR and SOLVE, but one which does not compute any matrix inverses. For brevity use statements like "add vector V to S" or "multiply matrix M times vector V" in the description to indicate the standard vector-matrix arithmetic operations. Make it clear how you use variables and retain information.

6.2.11 Suppose the matrix A is factored into LU where $L = \ell_{ij}$ is lower triangular and $U = u_{ij}$ is upper triangular. Describe how to use this information to compute

(A) The solution of $A\mathbf{x} = \mathbf{b}$

(B) The determinant of A

(C) The inverse of A

Be specific and give details in terms of matrix elements.

6.2.12 Suppose the matrix A is factored as in Algorithm 6.2.1 with the multipliers saved in M and the upper triangular factor U given. Describe how to use this information to compute

(A) The solution of $A\mathbf{x} = \mathbf{b}$

(B) The inverse of A

(C) The determinant of A

Be specific and give details in terms of matrix elements.

6.2.13 Consider the following linear system of equations:

$$
\begin{aligned}
.9x + 2.7y &= 3.15 \\
.8x - .4y &= .56
\end{aligned}
$$

(A) Scale the matrix to make its rows of equal size as vectors.

(B) Carry out Gauss elimination and give the multipliers matrix M and upper triangular factor U as well as the solution.

6.2.14 Give an efficient algorithm based on Algorithm 6.2.1 for reducing a tridiagonal matrix to upper triangular form. Assume no pivoting is needed.

6.2.15 Outline a Fortran subroutine to implement the algorithm in Problem 6.2.14 so that it is efficient in storage. Describe in detail the data structures used and the calling sequence.

6.2.16 Extend the algorithm and programs of Problems 6.2.14 and 6.2.15 to band matrices with bandwidth K. Assume no pivoting is needed.

6.2.17 Incorporate partial pivoting into the program of Problem 6.2.16. How much more storage does this require?

6.2.18 Give an efficient algorithm without pivoting based on Algorithm 6.2.1 for solving a linear system $A\mathbf{x} = \mathbf{b}$ where A is symmetric and only the upper half of A is actually given.

6.2.19 Incorporate scaling into Algorithm 6.2.1 by making the maximum element in each row equal to 1.0.

(A) Give the modification of Algorithm 6.2.1 that results.

(B) Outline a Fortran program to implement this algorithm.

(C) Write the Fortran program of part B and run it on an example where the scaling makes a large improvement in the accuracy obtained. **Hint**: Choose a matrix which, after scaling, has a very small pivot but where this pivot element is large before scaling.

6.2.20 Make a diagram that shows the sequence in which Algorithm 6.2.2 processes the elements of the matrix A.

6.2.21 Give an efficient algorithm based on Algorithm 6.2.2 for reducing a tridiagonal matrix to upper triangular form. Assume no pivoting is needed.

6.2.22 Outline a Fortran subroutine to implement the algorithm in Problem 6.2.21 so that it is efficient in storage. Describe in detail the data structures used and the calling sequence.

6.2.23 Extend the algorithm and programs of Problems 6.2.21 and 6.2.22 to band matrices with bandwidth K. Assume no pivoting is needed.

6.2.24 Incorporate partial pivoting in Problem 6.2.23. How much more storage does this require?

6.2.25 Give an efficient algorithm based on Algorithm 6.2.3 for reducing a symmetric band matrix to upper triangular form.

6.2.26 Outline a Fortran subroutine to implement the algorithm of Problem 6.2.25 so that it is efficient in storage. Describe in detail the data structures and calling sequence.

6.2.27 Modify Algorithm 6.2.1 for four variations: (A) the matrix A is not destroyed; (B) pointers are used for pivoting rather than explicit interchanges of rows (this is an example of indirect addressing or subscripted subscripts); (C) solve the matrix equation AX = B where B is a n by m matrix; (D) compute A^{-1}.

6.2.28 Explain the relationship between the following three methods for solving $Ax = b$: Gauss elimination (factorization), Crout reduction, and Cholesky decomposition.

6.2.29 An "x-matrix" has a pattern of nonzero elements that forms an "x" as in the following 5 by 5 and 6 by 6 examples:

$$\begin{pmatrix} x & x & x & x & x \\ 0 & x & x & x & 0 \\ 0 & 0 & x & 0 & 0 \\ 0 & x & x & x & 0 \\ x & x & x & x & x \end{pmatrix} \quad \begin{pmatrix} x & x & x & x & x & x \\ 0 & x & x & x & x & 0 \\ 0 & 0 & x & x & 0 & 0 \\ 0 & 0 & x & x & 0 & 0 \\ 0 & x & x & x & x & 0 \\ x & x & x & x & x & x \end{pmatrix}$$

(A) In the spirit of Gauss elimination, describe an algorithm to transform a general matrix into this form by solving a sequence of 2 by 2 problems.

(B) Show how one can back-substitute in an x-matrix by solving a sequence of 2 by 2 problems.

(C) Make operations counts for parts (A) and (B) and compare the work of this scheme with ordinary Gauss elimination. Ignore pivoting.

6.2.30 Develop a special **algorithm for matrix inversion** as follows. Let $e_i = (0, 0, \ldots, 0, 1, 0, \ldots, 0)^T$ with the 1 in the ith position so that e_i is the ith column of the identity. The colums x_i of A^{-1} are calculated by solving $Ax_i = e_i$ for $i = 1, 2, \ldots, N$. Assume that A has been factored using the first part of Algorithm 6.2.1. Give an efficient algorithm (based on the back-substitution part of Algorithm 6.2.1) to compute the x_i. The algorithm is to take into account the special nature of the right sides e_i.

6.2.31 Make an operations count for the algorithm of Problem 6.2.30 to show that it requires n^3 multiplications to invert a matrix. Show that $n^3/3$ multiplications are saved compared with the work to solve $Ax_i = b_i$ for $i = 1, 2, \ldots, n$ where b_i are arbitrary right sides.

6.2.32 Consider a band matrix of order n with bandwidth K. Make an **operations count for band matrices** for the algorithm of Problem 6.2.23 and show that the principal term is nK^2.

6.2.33 The matrix A is diagonally dominant if

$$|a_{ii}| \geq \sum_{j \neq i} |a_{ij}| \qquad \text{for all } i$$

Let A be a symmetric, diagonally dominant matrix. After one step of Gauss elimination the resulting matrix is of the form

$$\begin{pmatrix} a & y^T \\ 0 & A_1 \end{pmatrix}$$

(A) Show that A_1 is diagonally dominant.

(B) Show that Gauss elimination with and without partial pivoting are the same thing for symmetric, diagonally dominant matrices.

6.2.34 Show that (A) Gauss elimination without pivoting cannot fail for a diagonally dominant matrix, (B) if A is diagonally dominant, then A is nonsingular. **Hint:** Use Problem 6.2.33.

6.2.35 Solve the system

$$\begin{aligned} x_1 + 1.001\, x_2 &= 2.001 \\ x_1 + x_2 &= 2 \end{aligned}$$

Compute the residual $r = (Ay\text{-}b)$ for $y = (2, 0)^T$ and compare the relative size $||x-y||/||x||$ of the error in the solution with the size $||r||/||b||$ of the residual relative to the right side. Next solve

$$\begin{aligned} x_1 + 1.001\, x_2 &= 1 \\ x_1 + x_2 &= 0 \end{aligned}$$

Compute the residual for $z = (-1001, 1000)^T$ and compare the relative size of the error in the solution with the size of the residual relative to the right side. What do you conclude about the size of the residual as an indicator of the accuracy of a computed solution?

6.2.36 Cramer's rule for solving $Ax = b$ expresses each unknown x_i as the ratio $\det(A_i)/\det(A)$ where A_i is the matrix A with the ith column replaced by **b**. Suppose that each determinant in this rule is evaluated by the standard scheme (expansion by minors) as the sum of (n-1)! products of n factors each. Estimate how many multiplications are then required to solve $Ax = b$ for n = 10, 25, and 100. Translate this into computer time if each multiplication (and all associated other operations) takes 1 microsecond. **Hint:** For large n, Sterling's formula

$$n! \sim \sqrt{2\pi n}\, e^{-n} n^n$$

can be used. There are about 3×10^{15} microseconds in a century. The sun will have burned out before the computation with n = 100 is complete.

ITERATION METHODS FOR LINEAR SYSTEMS *6.3

The Gauss elimination algorithm for solving $Ax = b$ is a finite or **direct method**. One has, ignoring round-off errors, the exact answer at the end of a finite number of steps. **Iteration methods** for $Ax = b$ are infinite methods and produce only approximate answers. They are easy to define and widely used. However, they should be used only in special circumstances, and therefore here we just outline the basic ideas and provide a guide as to when they might be appropriate. If one thinks iteration methods should be used, then a more thorough study of the problem and particular methods is advised. Iteration methods are attractive for sparse matrices, because then they use much less memory than direct methods, and so they might be used even though they require more execution time. Partial differential equations often lead to large sparse linear systems where iteration methods are attractive.

Jacobi, Gauss-Seidel, and SOR Iteration 6.3.A

We start with two old and simple methods; the first is the **Jacobi method**, illustrated with the following linear system:

$$
\begin{aligned}
3x_1 + 4x_2 - x_3 &= 7 \\
2x_1 + 6x_2 + 3x_3 &= -2 \\
-x_1 + x_2 + 4x_3 &= 4
\end{aligned}
$$

We can rewrite this system $\mathbf{Ax} = \mathbf{b}$ in the form

$$
\begin{aligned}
x_1 &= \frac{1}{3}[\ 7 \qquad\qquad - 4x_2 + x_3] \\
x_2 &= \frac{1}{6}[-2 - 2x_1 \qquad\quad - 3x_3] \\
x_3 &= \frac{1}{4}[\ 4 + x_1 - x_2 \qquad\quad]
\end{aligned}
$$

which is of the form $\mathbf{x} = \mathbf{Bx} + \mathbf{g}$ where

$$
\mathbf{B} = \begin{pmatrix} 0 & -\frac{4}{3} & \frac{1}{3} \\ -\frac{2}{6} & 0 & -\frac{3}{6} \\ \frac{1}{4} & -\frac{1}{4} & 0 \end{pmatrix} \qquad \mathbf{g} = \left(\frac{7}{3}, -\frac{2}{6}, \frac{4}{4}\right)^T
$$

We see that we have solved the jth equation explicitly for the jth unknown and put everything else on the right side. The Jacobi method is to guess at $\mathbf{x}$, say $\mathbf{x}^{(0)}$, and do the iteration

$$\mathbf{x}^{(k+1)} = \mathbf{Bx}^{(k)} + \mathbf{g} \qquad k = 0, 1, 2, \ldots \qquad \textbf{Equation 6.3.1}$$

This method depends on having the right numbering of the equations and unknowns so that one solves the jth equation for the "right" unknown.

The second old method is the **Gauss-Seidel method**. We rewrite the same system used above as

$$
\begin{aligned}
3x_1 \qquad\qquad\quad &= 7 - 4x_2 + x_3 \\
2x_1 + 6x_2 \qquad\ &= -2 - 3x_3 \\
-x_1 + x_2 + 4x_3 &= 4
\end{aligned}
$$

In the jth equation we have moved to the right-hand side all terms involving x_k with $k > j$. This system is of the form $(\mathbf{L}+\mathbf{D})\mathbf{x} = -\mathbf{Ux} + \mathbf{g}$ where

$$
\mathbf{L} + \mathbf{D} = \begin{pmatrix} 3 & 0 & 0 \\ 2 & 6 & 0 \\ -1 & 1 & 4 \end{pmatrix} \qquad \mathbf{U} = \begin{pmatrix} 0 & 4 & -1 \\ 0 & 0 & 3 \\ 0 & 0 & 0 \end{pmatrix} \qquad \mathbf{g} = \mathbf{b}
$$

D denotes the diagonal of A, U the upper triangular part, and L the lower triangular part. We then apply the iteration

$$(\mathbf{L} + \mathbf{D})\mathbf{x}^{(k+1)} = -\mathbf{Ux}^{(k)} + \mathbf{g} \qquad k = 0, 1, 2, \ldots \qquad \textbf{Equation 6.3.2}$$

after making an initial guess $\mathbf{x}^{(0)}$. Note that the calculation here is almost exactly the same as the Jacobi method. The arithmetic steps are the same; the difference is that new values for the x_i are used here as soon as computed, while in the Jacobi method they are not used until the next iteration.

Finally, we consider **systematic overrelaxation** (or **SOR**) iteration. The idea is to take the change produced in a Gauss-Seidel step and extrapolate it by an amount q. One might think of this symbolically as

$$\mathbf{x}^{(k+1)} = \mathbf{x}^{(k)} + \mathbf{Q}[\mathbf{x}_{GS}^{(k+1)} - \mathbf{x}^{(k)}]$$

where Q is a diagonal extrapolation matrix and $\mathbf{x}_{GS}^{(k+1)}$ indicates the Gauss-Seidel result. SOR is slightly different in that new values in $\mathbf{x}$ are used as soon as they are computed; the iteration is

$$\mathbf{x}^{(k+1)} = \mathbf{x}^{(k)} + \mathbf{QD}^{-1}[\mathbf{b} - (\mathbf{D} + \mathbf{U})\mathbf{x}^{(k)} - \mathbf{Lx}^{(k+1)}] \qquad \textbf{Equation 6.3.3}$$

It turns out that the best extrapolation occurs with all the extrapolation parameters the same, and so Q is a constant matrix and can be replaced by a constant in 6.3.3. This constant is usually denoted by ω, and it is called the **relaxation parameter**. The matrix formulation 6.3.3 is just used for analysis; an actual computation uses elements of the equations and not matrices.

The analysis of iteration methods uses one of two standard forms.

$$\begin{aligned} \mathbf{x}^{(k+1)} &= \mathbf{x}^{(k)} + H[\mathbf{b} - A\mathbf{x}^{(k)}] \\ \mathbf{x}^{(k+1)} &= B\mathbf{x}^{(k)} + \mathbf{g} \end{aligned} \qquad \textbf{Equation 6.3.4}$$

Let $\mathbf{x}^\star$ be the true solution of $A\mathbf{x} = \mathbf{b}$, and define the error $\epsilon_k = \mathbf{x}^\star - \mathbf{x}^{(k)}$. It is easy to see that

$$\epsilon_{k+1} = (I-HA)\epsilon_k \qquad \epsilon_{k+1} = B\epsilon_k$$

The *spectral radius* $\rho(A)$ of A is defined as the absolute value of the largest (in absolute value) eigenvalue of A. We state without proof the **basic convergence theorem** for iteration methods.

Theorem 6.1 *A necessary and sufficient condition for the iteration 6.3.4 to converge is*

$$\begin{aligned} \rho(I-HA) &< 1 \\ \rho(B) &< 1 \end{aligned}$$

The order of convergence of 6.3.4 is $\rho(I-HA)$ or $\rho(B)$, that is, $\epsilon_k = o(\rho^k)$.

One can use any means available to estimate $\rho(B)$ and attempt to determine if a particular iteration is convergent. Recall from the end of Section 1.2 that $\rho(B) \le ||B||$ for any norm, and that the simplest norms to try are the row-sum or column-sum norms. For the Jacobi method we have

$$\mathbf{x}^{(k+1)} = -D^{-1}(A-D)\mathbf{x}^{(k)} + D^{-1}\mathbf{b}$$

that is, $B = -D^{-1}(A-D) = I - D^{-1}A$. The row-sum and column-sum norms lead to the convergence criteria of **strict diagonal dominance**:

$$|a_{ii}| > \sum_{\substack{j=1\\ j\ne i}}^{n} |a_{ij}| \quad \text{or} \quad |a_{jj}| > \sum_{\substack{i=1\\ i\ne j}}^{n} |a_{ij}| \qquad \textbf{Equation 6.3.5}$$

If A is strictly diagonally dominant, then $||B|| < 1$, and the Jacobi iteration converges. For the Gauss-Seidel method we have

$$\begin{aligned} \mathbf{x}^{(k+1)} &= -(D + L)^{-1}U\mathbf{x}^{(k)} + (D + L)^{-1}\mathbf{b} \\ &= [I-(D + L)^{-1}A]\mathbf{x}^{(k)} + (D + L)^{-1}\mathbf{b} \end{aligned}$$

that is, $B = I - (D+L)^{-1}A$. In terms of the residual $\mathbf{r} = \mathbf{b} - A\mathbf{x}$ we have

$$\mathbf{x}^{(k+1)} = \mathbf{x}^{(k)} + (D + L)^{-1}[\mathbf{b} - A\mathbf{x}^{(k)}]$$

and so $H = (D + L)^{-1}$. The matrix governing the convergence of the SOR method is

$$B = (I + QD^{-1}L)^{-1}[I - QD^{-1}(D + U)] = (D + QL)^{-1}(D - DQ - QU)$$

Convergence occurs when the matrices B or $I - HA$ are "small." For the Jacobi method this means that $D^{-1}A - I$ is small or that D^{-1} is a fair approximation to A^{-1}. For Gauss-Seidel to converge, $(D+L)^{-1}$ must be a fair approximation to A^{-1}. This may be restated as follows: The Jacobi iteration assumes that A is "nearly diagonal," and the Gauss-Seidel iteration assumes that A is "nearly lower triangular."

There are three widely held errors in belief about iteration. The first two are not particularly serious, but the third is. The three statements below correct these errors.

1. *Diagonal dominance is not required for either the Jacobi or Gauss-Seidel methods to converge.* One merely needs to try the matrix

$$A = \begin{pmatrix} 8 & 2 & 1 \\ 10 & 4 & 1 \\ 50 & 25 & 2 \end{pmatrix} \qquad \textbf{Equation 6.3.6}$$

for Gauss-Seidel iteration.

2. *It is not always true that if the Jacobi method works, then Gauss-Seidel works even better.* The belief that Gauss-Seidel is always better than Jacobi comes from the fact that *if A is symmetric and positive definite and satisfies certain other conditions,* then Gauss-Seidel converges twice as fast as Jacobi.

3. *Iteration methods are not better for ill-conditioned problems than Gauss elimination.* It is often believed that the source of trouble in Gauss elimination for ill-conditioned problems is the steady accumulation of thousands or millions of round-off errors during the computation. This is not so — the inaccuracy often arises almost entirely in one single arithmetic step of elimination. In any case, iteration methods applied to ill-conditioned problems produce the same amount of garbage as direct methods do.

When Iteration Methods Should Be Considered 6.3.B

Iteration methods are used primarily when A (and hence B and H) are large and sparse. If B or H is sparse (say they have p nonzero elements per row), then one iteration requires about pn operations for a matrix of order n. Thus K iterations require about pKn operations and, for comparison with Gauss elimination for full matrices, we have iteration cheaper if the number K of iterations to achieve satisfactory accuracy satisfies

$$K < \frac{n^2}{3p}$$

If A is a band matrix of width d (small compared to n), then the work for Gauss elimination is about d^2n, while K iterations require work of about 2dnK. Thus, for iteration to pay off by reducing arithmetic, the number K of iterations to achieve satisfactory accuracy for a band matrix must satisfy

$$K < \frac{d}{2}$$

For matrices derived from partial differential equations, the bandwidth is usually about $\sqrt{n}$, but the band is itself sparse so that p is 4 or 6 or so. In this situation, the work for Gauss elimination is n^2 while the work for K iterations is perhaps 6Kn. Thus, iteration methods should be considered if they require less than n/6 iterations for satisfactory accuracy. However, the overriding consideration might be the memory required, which is about n^2 for Gauss elimination and pn for an iteration method. For these problems one may have n in the range of 100 to 1,000,000 with 10,000 a not-unusual case.

PROBLEMS 6.3

6.3.1 Write a program to use the Gauss-Seidel iteration to solve the system

$$\begin{aligned} 2x_1 - x_2 &= 1 \\ -x_{i-1} + 2x_i - x_{i+1} &= 0 \quad i = 2, 3, \ldots, n-1 \\ -x_{n-1} + 2x_n &= 1 \end{aligned}$$

for n = 20. Start with $\mathbf{x}^{(0)} = 0$ and terminate the iteration when

$$\frac{||\mathbf{x}^{(k)} - \mathbf{x}^{(k-1)}||_\infty}{||\mathbf{x}^{(k)}||_\infty} < 10^{-6}$$

The exact solution is $x_i = 1$ for all i. What is the accuracy achieved?

6.3.2 Compare the computer time required to solve the system in Problem 6.3.1 by Gauss-Seidel with that required by Gauss elimination. Gauss-Seidel for Problem 6.3.1 converges in about 466 iterations.

6.3.3 Apply the Jacobi method to Problem 6.3.1 for 100 iterations and find the number of Gauss-Seidel iterations that gives the same accuracy.

6.3.4 Let B be N by N and upper triangular with $a_{ii} = 0$ for all i. Show that $B^n = 0$. Use this to show that both Jacobi and Gauss-Seidel converge in a finite number of iterations whenever A is upper triangular (and nonsingular). How many iterations does it take for Gauss-Seidel to converge if A is lower triangular?

6.3.5 Consider a system of linear equations whose coefficient matrix is partitioned into four matrices and the solution and right-side vectors are partitioned into two vectors each, that is, with A and D square:

$$\begin{pmatrix} A & B \\ C & D \end{pmatrix} \begin{pmatrix} \mathbf{x} \\ \mathbf{y} \end{pmatrix} = \begin{pmatrix} \mathbf{c}_1 \\ \mathbf{c}_2 \end{pmatrix}$$

We define a **block-Jacobi iteration** as follows:

Iterate Step 1: Guess at **y** and solve for **x** from the system $A\mathbf{x} = \mathbf{c}_1 - B\mathbf{y}$.

Step 2: Use the resulting **x** and solve for **y** from the system $D\mathbf{y} = \mathbf{c}_2 - C\mathbf{x}$. Use this as the next guess at **y**.

(A) Formulate this iteration in matrix terms.

(B) Give an example of a 5 by 5 system (A is 3 by 3 and D is 2 by 2) where one would expect this method to converge rapidly.

(C) Give the matrix that governs the convergence of this method.

6.3.6 To solve $A\mathbf{x} = \mathbf{b}$ by iteration, partition A into three parts: T is the tridiagonal part, U is the part above T, and L is the part below T. The iteration scheme is to guess at **x**, put this into the L and U parts of A, move these to the right-hand side, solve the resulting tridiagonal system for a better estimate of **x**, and then overrelax this iteration (or extrapolate the change in the estimates) by a factor w. The final result is the next estimate of **x**.

(A) Formulate this iterative method in matrix terms.

(B) Find the matrix which governs the convergence of the iteration.

(C) Give the operation count for one iteration of this method.

6.3.7 Suppose that you are required to solve the following system by Gauss-Seidel iteration:

$$\begin{aligned} 2x + y - \frac{1}{2}z + 8w &= 4 \\ 6x + 2y + 8z + 14w &= 12 \\ x - 6y + 10z + 9w &= 1 \\ 2x + 11y + 3z - 4w &= 4 \end{aligned}$$

(A) Describe what you would do first.

(B) Carry out several iterations (with initial guess = 0) and estimate approximately how many iterations it would take to get six digits correct in the solution.

6.3.8 Apply Jacobi and Gauss-Seidel iteration to the problem $\mathbf{Ax} = (8, 8, 29)^T$ with initial guess $= (-1, 1, 0)^T$ and A the matrix in Equation 6.3.6. How many iterations does it take for these to converge to 10^{-4} accuracy?

6.3.9 Consider a system of equations that "almost" breaks up into two parts:

$$\sum_{j=1}^{n} a_{ij}x_j + \sum_{j=1}^{m} e_{ij}y_j = c_i \qquad i = 1, 2, \ldots, n$$

$$\sum_{j=1}^{n} h_{ij}x_j + \sum_{j=1}^{m} b_{ij}y_j = c_{i+n} \qquad i = 1, 2, \ldots, m$$

The matrices $E = (e_{ij})$ and $H = (h_{ij})$ are "small" compared to A and B. Suppose that A is much smaller than B and that B is heavily diagonally dominant. So one proceeds to apply the following scheme:

Step 1. Guess at **y** and solve for **x** exactly from the first set of equations.

Step 2. Given this **x**, solve for an improved estimate of **y** by one iteration of Gauss-Seidel on the second set of equations.

Then iterate steps 1 and 2 to take a vector pair $(\mathbf{x}^{(k)}, \mathbf{y}^{(k)})$, into $(\mathbf{x}^{(k+1)}, \mathbf{y}^{(k+1)})$.

(A) Express the original linear system in matrix form.

(B) Express each of steps 1 and 2 in matrix form.

(C) Express the iteration scheme in matrix form.

(D) Exhibit the matrix which governs the convergence of this scheme.

SOFTWARE FOR LINEAR EQUATIONS 6.4

There is a large amount of software for linear equations, so much that one can hardly count the number of programs, never mind evaluate them. For example, the library of the Purdue University Computing Center has well over 100 programs for solving $\mathbf{Ax} = \mathbf{b}$. A fair number of programs (but much fewer than 100) is justified when one considers arithmetic types like single precision, double precision, and complex or special matrix data structures like symmetric, band, and positive-definite. However, much of this program pollution is due to duplication. We restrict ourselves here to discussing four general collections of linear equation software (the IMSL library, LINPACK, ITPACK, and the Yale Sparse Matrix Package) and those ACM Algorithms that provide some special facilities. Software for eigensystem computations is discussed at the end of this chapter.

The software for linear equations provides a good example of the value of using library programs. Gauss elimination is a simple algorithm and easily translated into Fortran. Even so, the IMSL and LINPACK routines will probably run 2 to 5 times as fast as the typical translation of Algorithms 6.2.1 or 6.2.4 and will, in addition, supply built-in protection against some subtle difficulties.

The ACM Algorithms 6.4.A

There are over 50 ACM Algorithms for solving $\mathbf{Ax} = \mathbf{b}$ or performing closely related operations (e.g., matrix inversions and determinants). We mention seven of them which provide unusual capabilities in Fortran.

1. *Algorithm 408:* This set of routines provides various facilities for a matrix A which is sparse (most of the elements of A are zero). A corrected and improved version is available through the ACM Algorithms Distribution Service.

2. *Algorithm 432:* Solves the matrix equation $AX + XB = C$.

3. *Algorithm 467: Matrix Transpose.* For a general rectangular matrix A, this produces A^T in the same storage area. Also in the IMSL library as VTRAN.

4. *Algorithm 470:* Solves $\mathbf{Ax} = \mathbf{b}$ where $A = T + R$, T is tridiagonal, and R is of low rank (for example, R is zero except for one column). This algorithm provides high efficiency for these problems.

5. *Algorithm 522: Exact solution.* Multiprecision integer arithmetic plus special techniques are used to obtain the exact solution of $\mathbf{Ax} = \mathbf{b}$.

6. *Algorithm 539: The BLAS (Basic Linear Algebra Subroutines).* This is a collection of 38 Fortran callable subprograms to provide basic support for vector-matrix computations. Implementations in Fortran and assembly language for major computers are given; the objective is to provide high efficiency within Fortran computations. There are versions of each for single precision, double precision, and complex vectors. The facilities provided are listed below; they involve a number of useful operations not defined in this book.

Vector dot product	Swap **x** and **y**
Compute a**x** + **y**	Euclidean norm of **x**
Givens rotations	Sum of $\lvert x_i \rvert$
Modified Givens rotations	Index of $\lvert x_i \rvert$ maximum
Copy **x** to **y**	Compute a**x**

All these subroutines are in the IMSL library as VBLA.

7. *Algorithm 546:* Solves A**x** = **b** where A is "almost block diagonal," a type of matrix that arises naturally from interpolation or finite element methods involving piecewise polynomials. Less arithmetic and storage is used than required by considering A as a band matrix.

Three Software Packages 6.4.B

There are three complementary software packages of note:

LINPACK	A collection of programs for direct methods to solve A**x** = **b** and related computations.
ITPACK	A collection of programs for iteration methods to solve A**x** = **b**.
YALEPACK	A collection of programs for direct, sparse matrix methods to solve A**x** = **b**.

All three of these packages are available from IMSL, Inc., NBC Building, 6th Floor, 7500 Bellaire Blvd., Houston, Texas 77036 for a nominal charge. We consider them in reverse order and in increasing detail.

The **Yale Sparse Matrix Package**, or YALEPACK, is a substantial collection of programs for sparse matrix computations. A technical discussion of these programs and their techniques is beyond the scope of this book.

The **ITPACK** collection is a highly modular set of programs for iterative methods. The package is oriented toward the sparse matrices that arise in solving partial differential equations and in other applications. The programs do apply to full matrices even though this is rarely profitable. The package is organized around four basic iterations and two convergence acceleration schemes. There is the **SOR iteration** method mentioned in Section 6.3; the optimum relaxation parameter is automatically estimated. Then there are **Jacobi, symmetric SOR**, and **reduced system** (red-black ordering) iteration, each with **semi-iterative** and **conjugate gradient acceleration**. Again, all the parameters for these iterations are automatically estimated. The practical and theoretical background for ITPACK is given in the book by L. Hageman and D. Young in the references.

The **LINPACK** collection of programs is concerned with direct methods for general (or full), symmetric, symmetric positive-definite, triangular, and tridiagonal matrices; there are also programs for least-squares problems along with the QR and singular value decompositions of rectangular matrices. The programs are intended to be completely machine independent, fully portable, and run with good efficiency in most computing environments. The basic reference for this collection is the *LINPACK User's Guide* by J. J. Dongarra, J. R. Bunch, C. B. Moler, and G. W. Stewart, Soc. Indust. Appl. Math., 1979.

The scope of the LINPACK collection is seen from the naming scheme and Table 6.1. All LINPACK program names consist of five letters in the form TXXYY. The first letter, T, indicates the matrix data type. Standard Fortran allows the use of three such types:

S REAL (single precision)

D DOUBLE PRECISION

C COMPLEX

Programs in the LINPACK Collection **Table 6.1**

The codes for the matrix data types, matrix form and the computations performed are given in the text. The first set of programs are for solving $A\mathbf{x} = \mathbf{b}$ and related computations; the second set is for solving linear least-squares problems.

Matrix Form	COMPUTATION PERFORMED CO	FA	SL	DI	Matrix Data Types Allowed
GE = General	X	X	X	X	S, D, C, Z
GB = General band	X	X	X	X	S, D, C, Z
PO = Positive definite	X	X	X	X	S, D, C, Z
PP = Positive definite packed	X	X	X	X	S, D, C, Z
PB = Positive definite band	X	X	X	X	S, D, C, Z
SI = Symmetric indefinite	X	X	X	X	S, D, C, Z
SP = Symmetric indefinite packed	X	X	X	X	S, D, C, Z
HI = Hermitian indefinite	X	X	X	X	C, Z
HP = Hermitian indefinite packed	X	X	X	X	C, Z
TR = Triangular	X		X	X	S, D, C, Z
GT = General tridiagonal			X		S, D, C, Z
PT = Positive definite tridiagonal			X		S, D, C, Z

Matrix Decomposition	OPERATION PERFORMED DC	SL	UD	DD	EX	Matrix Data Types Allowed
CH = Cholesky	X		X	X	X	S, D, C, Z
QR = Orthogonal	X	X				S, D, C, Z
SV = Singular value	X					S, D, C, Z

In addition, some Fortran systems allow a double precision complex type:

Z COMPLEX*16

The next two letters, XX, indicate the form of the matrix or its decomposition:

GE General

GB General band

PO Positive definite

PP Positive definite packed

PB Positive definite band

SI Symmetric indefinite

SP Symmetric indefinite packed

HI Hermitian indefinite

HP Hermitian indefinite packed

TR Triangular

GT General tridiagonal

PT Positive definite tridiagonal

CH Cholesky decomposition

QR Orthogonal-triangular decomposition

SV Singular value decomposition

The final two letters, YY, indicate the computation done by a particular subroutine:

FA Factor

CO Factor and estimate condition

SL Solve

DI Determinant and/or inverse and/or inertia

DC Decompose

UD Update

DD Downdate

EX Exchange

The LINPACK programs provide a modular approach to solving A**x** = **b**. We describe the operation for single-precision, general matrices, as it is typical. One first factors the matrix A using SGEFA or SGECO (the latter also provides a condition number estimate). The matrix A is replaced by its factors, and a vector of pivoting indexes is provided for later use. One then uses SGESL to do the forward and backward substitution to solve the system of linear equations. The simplest case for using these programs is shown below.

```
      REAL A(20,20), B(20)
      INTEGER IPVT(20)
C                 OBTAIN A, B FOR A 10 BY 10 A*X=B PROBLEM
      READ 10, ((A(I,J), I=1,10), J=1,10), (B(I),I=1,10)
   10 FORMAT(10F8.3)
C                 FACTOR THE MATRIX A
      CALL SGEFA(A,20,10,IPVT,IFLAG)
      IF (IFLAG .NE. 0) THEN
          PRINT 20, IFLAG
   20     FORMAT(' *** SINGULAR MATRIX, ZERO PIVOT IN COLUMN' I3)
          STOP
      END IF
C                 SOLVE THE LINEAR SYSTEM
      CALL SGESL(A,20,10,IPVT,B,0)
      PRINT 30, (B(I),I=1,10)
   30 FORMAT(' THE SOLUTION IS' /5X,10F12.6)
      STOP
      END
```

The IMSL Library Software 6.4.C

The linear equations software in the IMSL library is for direct methods applied to five matrix forms: general (or full), band, symmetric, symmetric positive-definite, and band symmetric. The basic IMSL programs for solving A**x** = **b** are given below along with their arguments.

```
                  FULL MATRIX
LEQT1F  (A,NSOLS,NEQS,KDIMA,B,ITEST,WORK,IER)
                  FULL COMPLEX MATRIX
LEQT1C  (A,NEQS,KDIMA,B,NSOLS,KDIMB,IJOB,WORK,IER)
                  SYMMETRIC MATRIX
LEQ1S   (A,NEQS,B,NSOLS,KDIMB,IJOB,IWORK,WORK,IER)
                  SYMMETRIC POSITIVE-DEFINITE MATRIX
LEQT1P  (A,NSOLS,NEQS,B,KDIMB,ITEST,DET1,DET2,IER)
                  BAND MATRIX
LEQT1B  (A,NEQS,NLOW,NUP,KDIMA,B,NSOLS,KDIMB,IJOB,WORK,IER)
                  POSITIVE-DEFINITE BAND MATRIX
LEQ1PB  (A,NEQS,NLOW,KDIMA,B,KDIMB,NSOLS,ITEST,DET1,DET2,IER)
```

where the arguments are:

A,B	The matrix and right side. The solution is placed in B and A is replaced by its factors.
NEQS	The number of equations.
NSOLS	The number of solutions (right sides).
KDIMA,KDIMB	The row dimensions declared for the arrays A and B.
WORK,IWORK	Workspace arrays.

IER	Error flag.
ITEST	Accuracy test request. Assuming the elements of A and B are correct to ITEST digits, a check is made if X is the exact solution for a linear equation problem with A and B perturbed by less than $10^{-\text{ITEST}}$.
IJOB	Switch to control program action =0 Factor A and solve $A\mathbf{x} = \mathbf{b}$ =1 Factor A only =2 Solve $A\mathbf{x} = \mathbf{b}$ assuming A is already factored
NLOW,NUP	Number of lower and upper diagonals of a band matrix.
DET1,DET2	Determinant of A returned in the form DET1 * 2^{DET2}.

The IMSL library documentation must be consulted for more detailed definitions, e.g., the required sizes of the workspace arrays.

There is a second, "high-accuracy" version of each of these programs which uses iterative improvement (see Section 6.6.D) to obtain a solution to $A\mathbf{x} = \mathbf{b}$ which is "exact." That is, the solution returned is within an ulp or two of the exact solution of the linear equations *as they exist inside the machine.* This exactness is often illusionary, for example, changing the numbers in A or **b** from decimal to binary can change the solution by much more than an ulp. These programs are named by changing the "1" in the above names to a "2," except for LEQT1C, whose high-accuracy version is named LEQ2C.

Four data structures (or storage schemes) are used. The symmetric and symmetric positive-definite use the same data structure, a single vector of length $n(n+1)/2$ for an n by n symmetric matrix. The element a_{ij} for $i \geq j$ is the kth element of the vector where $k = j + i(i-1)/2$. The band and band symmetric data structures store the diagonals of A in a rectangular array, say B. If A is n by n and has k lower diagonals and j upper diagonals, then the array B is n by $(k+j+1)$. The lower diagonals start with zeros and the upper diagonals end with zeros to make them of length n in the array B. For the band symmetric data structure the lower diagonals are not stored.

The programmer must be careful when using the special matrix data structures to get the matrix defined correctly. There are a number of vector-matrix utilities to perform matrix arithmetic and I/O for these data structures. The PROTRAN ASSIGN statement takes care of these details automatically.

All the programs discussed so far (and later also) are in single precision. The IMSL library does not contain separate double-precision programs. Instead, for short-word-length machines (32-bit words), the library comes in a single-precision version and a double-precision version. A user can select one or the other version to use but cannot mix programs from the two versions (at least not without making some changes). Thus the names of the single-precision and double-precision programs can be — and are — the same. There are many library programs which do not need double precision even for short-word-length machines, and these are in single precision for both versions of the IMSL library. Almost all of the linear equations and vector-matrix programs have two versions.

There is a version LEQOF of LEQT1F for linear systems whose coefficient matrix does not fit in main memory. It appears as

```
LEQOF( IUNITA,IUNITW,NEQS,KOLREC,B,NSOLS,NDIMB,IJOB,WORK,IER)
```

where the arguments are as defined above except for

IUNITA	Fortran READ unit number of the file where the matrix A is stored. A is stored unformatted and by columns with KOLREC columns per record.
IUNITW	Fortran unit number of a workspace file (not used if IJOB=1).

LEQOF uses a "profile" method where two blocks of KOLREC columns are held in main memory at a time.

In addition to these basic linear equation solvers, there are four other groups of programs:

1. *Matrix Inversion.* A set of 8 programs (all names start with LIN) for matrix inversion, determinant calculations, and linear equation solving. Most of the capabilities of this set of programs are also in the basic set discussed above.

2. *Basic Utilities.* A set of 9 programs (all names start with LU) which do (a) factorization, (b) forward and backward substitution, and (c) iterative improvement for each of the full, positive-definite, and positive-definite band matrices. These programs are analogous to the LINPACK programs, and the other IMSL linear equation solvers are built from them.

3. *Related Computations.*

   LLSQF Computes least-squares solution of overdetermined systems

   LLBQF High-accuracy version of LLSQF which uses iterative improvement

   LSVDF Singular value decomposition of a matrix

   LGINF Computes generalized inverse of a full matrix

4. *Support Vector-Matrix Utilities.* Over 100 programs to provide the following facilities:

   The BLAS

   Matrix storage conversions (e.g., band storage to full)

   Matrix arithmetic (for all storage schemes)

   Vector-matrix norms (e.g., maximum element in a vector)

   Transposition, sorting, permutations, etc.

   Other (e.g., Householder transformation, extended precision storage)

All these support utility programs have names starting with V. There are also a number of vector-matrix printing programs in the "Special I/O" category. These programs have names starting with US.

PROTRAN is designed to allow one to simply say "solve $\mathbf{Ax} = \mathbf{b}$." In order to accomplish this, PROTRAN includes vector and matrix variables, and, in fact, one can say

```
$LINSYS A*X = B
```

to solve a linear system. A simple program to use this statement is as follows:

```
      $DECLARATIONS
      MATRIX A(4,4)
      VECTOR B(4),X(4)
C                         DEFINE LINEAR SYSTEM
      $ASSIGN  A =   ( 1, 2, 3, 4 )
     +               ( 0, 2,-1, 6 )
     +               ( 4, 1, 2, 1 )
     +               ( 5, 4, 3,-2 )
               B =   ( 8, 15.5, 10, 8 )
C                         SOLVE LINEAR SYSTEM AND PRINT SOLUTION
      $LINSYS A*X = B
      $PRINT X
      $END
```

The next program illustrates PROTRAN's facilities for solving linear systems; each of the four matrix data structures is used.

```
      $DECLARATIONS
      REAL MATRIX M(4,4), VBS(10,4), XBS(10,4)
      BAND MATRIX B(NEQS=10,NLOW=1,NUP=1)
      SYMMETRIC MATRIX S(8,8)
      BAND SYMMETRIC MATRIX BS(NBS=10,KBAND=3)
      VECTOR  VM(4),VB(10),VS(10),XM(4),XB(10),XS(10) $
C
C                    CHANGE SYMMETRIC BAND SIZE THROUGH RANGE VARIABLES
      NBS = 8
      KBAND = 2
C                    DEFINE THE FOUR MATRICES
C                    M = REAL AND FULL
      $ASSIGN  M(I,J) = I/FLOAT(J)
C                    B = TRIDIAGONAL  OF (1,-2,1) TYPE
               B(I,J) =  -2. + IABS(I-J)*3.
C                    S = SYMMETRIC  HILBERT MATRIX
               S(I,J) =  1./(I+J-1)
```

```
C                BS= SYMMETRIC BAND
            BS(I,J)= EXP(1.-IABS(I-J))
C
C                DEFINE THE FOUR RIGHT SIDE VECTORS
      $ASSIGN  VM =  ( 1, 1.5, -1.5, 3.62)
               VB(I) = COS(.5*I) - I+3.
               VS(I) =  1.
C                FOURTH SYSTEM POSSIBLY HAS FOUR SOLUTIONS
               VBS(I,J) = COS(.5*(I*J)) - I +3./J
C
C                SOLVE THE FOUR LINEAR SYSTEMS
C                SHOWING ALL PROTRAN OPTIONS AT LEAST ONCE
      $LINSYS M*XM = VM ; NOSAVE
      $PRINT M, XM
C
      $LINSYS B*XB = VB   ; EQUATIONS = 6; HIGHACCURACY
      $PRINT  B, XB
C
      $LINSYS S*XS = VS   ; EQUATI = 6    ; HIGHAC
      $PRINT  S, XS
C
      $LINSYS  BS*XBS = VBS ; RHS = 2  ;  POSDEF
      $PRINT  BS, XBS, VBS
      $END
```

The use of the linear equations software from LINPACK, the IMSL library, and PROTRAN is illustrated by two examples. The first example solves a linear system involving the Hilbert matrix, a very ill-conditioned problem. The second example is of the solution of an ordinary differential equation problem.

A Linear System Involving the Hilbert Matrix — Example 6.3

The Hilbert matrix H has elements $h_{ij} = 1/(i+j-1)$, and it is the traditional example of a severely ill-conditioned matrix. The norm of the 10 by 10 Hilbert matrix is 2.93, but the norm of its inverse is 10^{13}. The example calculation is first shown in complete detail by a PROTRAN program. Then we give the linear equations solution segments of a corresponding Fortran program using the LINPACK programs and using the IMSL library program LEQT2F. No declarations or initializations are given for the Fortran version of the program.

```
C                       PROTRAN VERSION
      $DECLARATIONS
      MATRIX  HILB(N=20,N=20), B(N=20,NSOLS=4),X(N=20,NSOLS=4),R(20,4)
      VECTOR RNORM(4)
C
      $ASSIGN  HILB(I,J) = 1./(I+J-1) $
C                 DEFINE 3 FIXED RIGHT SIDES
      DO 10 I = 1,20
          B(I,1) = 0.0
          B(I,2) = 1.0
          B(I,3) = 1.0 + .01*SIN(100.*I)
   10 CONTINUE
      B(1,1) = 1.0
C
C             SOLVE  LINEAR SYSTEMS  OF  ORDER  N = 4,8,12,...
      DO 40 N = 4,20,4
          PRINT 15, N
   15     FORMAT('1  HILBERT MATRIX SOLUTION FOR N =' I4  /
     A           '   K = 1 FOR  B = (1,0,0,...,0)'
     B           '   K = 2 FOR  B = (1,1,1,...,1)'
     C           '   K = 3 FOR  B = .01 PERTURBATION OF K=2 CASE' /
     D           '   K = 4 FOR  X = (1,-1,1,-1,... )' /// )
C
C                  COMPUTE FOURTH B TO GIVE X = 1,-1,1,-1,...
          DO 20 I = 1,N
              $SUM HILB(I,J)*(-1.)**(J+1) ; FOR(J=1,N); IS BI4 $
   20         B(I,4) = BI4
C
C             SOLVE AND COMPUTE NORM OF THE RESIDUAL = HILB*X - B
          $LINSYS  HILB*X = B; HIGHACCURACY
          $PRINT  B,X
          $ASSIGN  R = HILB*X
                   R = R-B
                   RNORM = R'*R
                   RNORM(K) = SQRT(RNORM(K))
   40     $PRINT RNORM
      $END
```

```
                        FORTRAN VERSION
C
C                  $LINSYS USING IMSL LIBRARY
      DO 25 I = 1,N
         DO 22 K = 1,4
22          X(I,K) = B(I,K)
         DO 25 J = 1,N
25          HTEMP(I,J) = HILB(I,J)
      CALL LEQT2F(HTEMP,4,N,20,X,0,WORK,IER)
         IF( IER .NE. 0 ) PRINT 26
26          FORMAT(5X,15(3H **),'IMSL SAYS MATRIX IS SINGULAR')
C
C                  RESIDUAL IN FORTRAN
      DO 40 K = 1,4
         RNORM(K)  = 0.0
        DO 36 I = 1,N
            RIK    = 0.0
            DO 34  J = 1,N
34             RIK    =    RIK + HILB(I,J)*X(J,K)
36          RNORM(K) =   (RIK - B(I,K))**2  + RNORM(K)
40       RNORM(K)  = SQRT(RNORM(K))
      PRINT 45, RNORM
45    FORMAT(10X,'RESIDUAL FOR LEQT2F =' 4E16.5)
C
C
C                  $LINSYS USING LINPACK
      DO 55 I = 1,N
         DO 52 K = 1,4
52          Y(I,K) = B(I,K)
         DO 55 J = 1,N
55          HTEMP(I,J) = HILB(I,J)
      CALL SGECO(HTEMP,20,N,IPVT,RCOND,WORK)
         IF( 1. + RCOND .EQ. 1. ) PRINT 56
56          FORMAT(5X,15(3H **),'LINPACK SAYS MATRIX IS SINGULAR')
      DO 65 K = 1,4
65       CALL SGESL(HTEMP,20,N,IPVT,Y(1,K),0)
C
C               USE SAME CODE AS ABOVE TO COMPUTE RESIDUAL
C
```

These programs were run on a CDC 6500, which has about 14.5 decimal digits arithmetic. The LINPACK software reports that the Hilbert matrix is singular for $n = 12$; the condition number is 9.8×10^{15}. At this point the maximum residuals are 1.6×10^{-6}, 6.0×10^{-8}, 4.7×10^{-6}, and 7.8×10^{-15} for the four solutions computed. However, the maximum errors of the computed solution are of the order of 50 to 100 percent for each problem, where the "true" solution is computed by extending all the single-precision numbers to double precision by adding zeros and then solving this double-precision system. The sensitivity of this problem is illustrated by the fact that the "true" solution for the fourth right-hand side has one component of .65 even though the right side is computed to have true solution exactly equal to 1.

The IMSL library accepts the Hilbert matrix as nonsingular for both $n = 12$ and 14; it reports the $n = 16$ case as singular. The singularity test used by the IMSL software is convergence of iterative improvement; thus the solution computed is essentially the true solution of the problem actually in the machine, but this solution is so sensitive that it may well be useless. The residuals for $n = 14$ for the IMSL solution are still relatively small: less than 10^{-5} for the first three cases and 1.6×10^{-14} for the fourth.

These computations underscore the extreme ill-conditioning of the Hilbert matrix and the need to take care to double-check the validity of linear equation solutions. The lazy programmer will use SGEFA from LINPACK or fail to test IER from IMSL and have no inkling of trouble when the linear systems are singular unless the computed solutions are ridiculous. Even with $n = 18$, the solutions computed here are of the "right size"; the errors are of the order of 100 percent and do not suggest that they are wrong. Erroneous results can be obtained with much smaller Hilbert matrices using computers whose arithmetic has less precision.

The next example illustrates the use of software for a different data structure for the matrix. The differential equation problem is solved by a simple finite difference method. The coefficient matrix is tridiagonal (a band matrix of bandwidth 1).

Use of Band Matrix Software to Solve a Differential Equation — Example 6.4

The differential equation $y'' + \cos(x)y = \log(x+4)$ is solved by the scheme presented in the discussion following Equation 6.1.1. We generalize the computation slightly by discretizing with step of h instead of fixing the points .2 apart. The approximating difference equation at the point x_k is then

$$\frac{y(x_{k-1}) - 2y(x_k) + y(x_{k+1})}{h^2} + \cos(x_k)y(x_k) = \log(x_k+4) \qquad \textbf{Equation 6.4.1}$$

In the program the values x_k and $y(x_k)$ are denoted by X(K) and Y(K), respectively. The solution computed is shown in Figure 6.8.

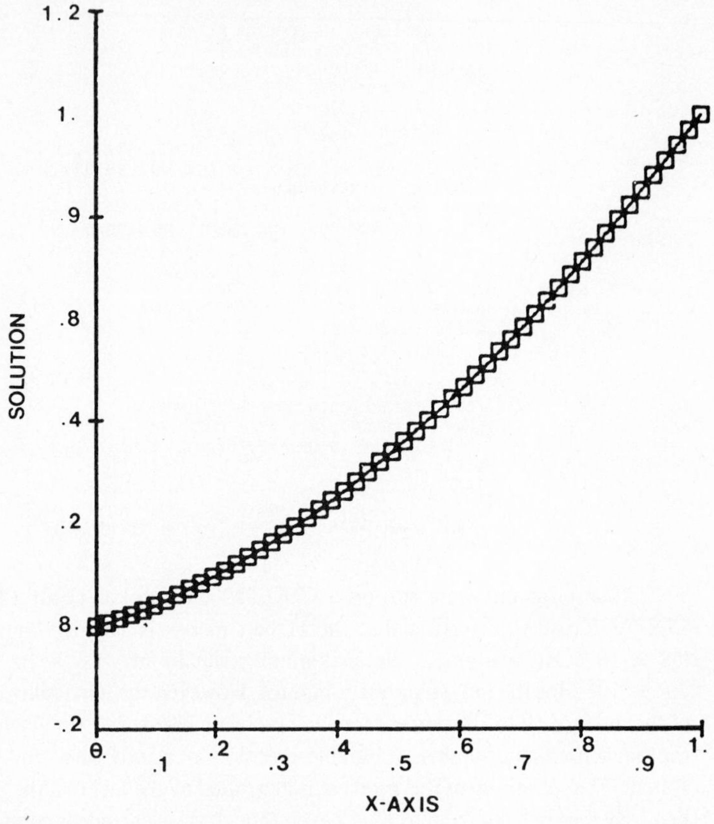

Figure 6.8 Differential equation solution. Equation 6.4.1 is solved by band matrix software using 40 discretization points.

We first give a complete program in PROTRAN and then give a program in Fortran which shows how the LINPACK software and the IMSL library software are used to solve the same problem. The major difference between LINPACK and IMSL is that IMSL has the band matrix represented by a tall and thin array (50 rows, 3 columns) and LINPACK uses a short and wide array (4 rows, 50 columns). The set-up effort, storage used, and complexity of the calls on the software are about the same for both LINPACK and IMSL.

```
      $DECLARATIONS
      BAND MATRIX DE(N= 50,1,1)
      VECTOR X(N=50), Y(N=50) $
C
C                          SET UP PROBLEM TO BE SOLVED
      N = 20
      H = 1./(N+1)
      $ASSIGN  X(I) = I*H
C                          DEFINE MATRIX FOR DISCRETE APPROXIMATION
      $ASSIGN  DE(I,J) =  1. - (IABS(I-J)-1)*(3. - H**2*COS(X(I))
C                      INITIALIZE SOLUTION Y TO BE THE RIGHT SIDE
      $ASSIGN  Y(I) = H**2 * ALOG(X(I)+4.) $
C                      ADD BOUNDARY CONDITION TERM AT X=1. TO
C                      THE LAST RIGHT SIDE
      Y(N) = Y(N) - 1.0
C                      SOLVE THE LINEAR SYSTEM AND PLOT RESULT
      $LINSYS  DE*Y = Y ; NOSAVE
      $PLOT Y ; VS X;  SYMBOL = 'Y' ; XRANGE = (0.,1.)
         TITLE = 'SOLUTION OF DIFFERENTIAL EQUATION - EXAMPLE 6.4'
      $END
```

FORTRAN VERSION

```
      REAL X(50)
              DECLARATIONS FOR IMSL LEQT1B
      REAL DE(50,3), Y(50), WORK(100)
C                    DECLARATIONS FOR LINPACK SGBCO AND SGBSL
      REAL DEL(4,50), YL(50),Z(50)
      INTEGER IPVT(50)
C
C             DECLARATIONS AND SET-UP FOR IMSL PLOT ROUTINE USPLO
      REAL RANGE(4)
      DATA RANGE/4*0.0/
      RANGE(2) = 1.0
C
C                    DISCRETIZE THE INTERVAL (0,1)
      N = 20
      H = 1./(N+1)
      DO 5 I = 1,N
    5    X(I) = I*H
C
C                    SET-UP AND SOLUTION BY IMSL LEQT1B
      DO 10  I = 1,N
          DE(I,1) = DE(I,3) = 1.0
          DE(I,2) = -2. + H**2*COS(X(I))
          Y(I)    =  H**2*ALOG(X(I)+4.)
   10 CONTINUE
      Y(N) = Y(N)-1.0
      CALL LEQT1B(DE,N,1,1,50,Y,1,50,0,WORK,IER)
      IF ( IER .NE. 0 )  PRINT 16
   16     FORMAT(//,25(3H **)/20X'LEQT1B SAYS MATRIX IS SINGULAR'//)
C
C               PLOT SOLUTION WITH IMSL LIBRARY ROUTINE
      CALL USPLO(X,Y,1,N,1,1,
     A           47HSOLUTION OF DIFFERENTIAL EQUATION - EXAMPLE 6.4, 47,
     B           1HX, 1, 1HY, 1, RANGE, 1HY, 1, IER)
C
C                     SET-UP AND SOLUTION BY LINPACK SGBCO AND SGBSL
      DO 110 I = 1,N
          DEL(4,I) = DEL(2,I) = 1.0
          DEL(3,I) = -2. + H**2*COS(X(I))
          YL(I)    = H**2*ALOG(X(I)+4.)
  110 CONTINUE
      YL(N) = YL(N) - 1.0
      CALL SGBCO(DEL,4,N,1,1,IPVT,COND,Z)
      IF(  1.+ COND .EQ. 1. )  PRINT 116
  116     FORMAT(//,25(3H **)/20X'LINPACK SAYS MATRIX IS SINGULAR'//)
      CALL SGBSL(DEL,4,N,1,1,IPVT,YL,0)
C
C                PLOT SOLUTION WITH IMSL LIBRARY ROUTINE
      CALL USPLO(X,Y,1,N,1,1,
     A           47HSOLUTION OF DIFFERENTIAL EQUATION - EXAMPLE 6.4, 47,
     B           1HX, 1, 1HY, 1, RANGE, 1HY, 1, IER)
      STOP
      END
```

PROBLEMS 6.4

6.4.1 What are the objectives of an algorithm for solving linear equations?

6.4.2 What are the objectives of a library software routine for solving linear equations?

6.4.3 Give the calling statement (in Fortran with symbolic arguments) of a good library routine for solving $\mathbf{A}\mathbf{x} = \mathbf{b}$. Explicitly state the objectives of your design. Describe an application where your design has a weakness compared with some alternative.

6.4.4 Briefly state the strengths and weaknesses of teaching people (a) how to solve problems or algorithms for solving problems and (b) how to use software to solve problems.

6.4.5 Discuss the conflicts between the library software objectives of efficiency and ease of modification.

6.4.6 Give three specific instances where maintenance would be needed for a library program due to external factors. Explain each situation briefly.

6.4.7 There are four approaches to handling errors in deeply embedded library programs:

(A) Abort the computation and print a good explanation.

(B) Abort the library program (but not the job) and return a flag indicating that an error has occurred.

(C) Fix the error as best you can and print a message explaining what happened.

(D) Fix the error as best you can and return a flag indicating that an error has occurred.

Discuss the strengths and weaknesses of each of the alternatives. Consider the context of a user with a high-level problem-oriented language for statistics where, somehow, a linear equation has been generated to be solved which (a) is singular, (b) has coefficient matrix identically 0 and right side 1, and (c) has order $n = -2$.

6.4.8 Locate a linear equation solver in your local library and test it for robustness in the presence of illegal and nonsense arguments. Examples of input to try are:

(A) Matrix order is 1, 0, -1 or a real number.

(B) Matrix argument is, in fact, a simple variable.

(C) Too few arguments are given.

(D) Matrix is declared INTEGER in main program.

(E) Matrix is identically zero.

(F) Right side vector has errors like those in (A), (B), and (D).

(G) There are various incompatibilities in declared dimensions.

(H) Various arguments are declared logical and set to .TRUE.

6.4.9 Repeat Problem 6.4.8 for the IMSL routines LEQT1F or LEQT1B.

6.4.10 Repeat Problem 6.4.8 for the LINPACK routines SGEFA or SGECO plus SGESL, or for SGBFA or SGBCO plus SGBSL.

6.4.11 The linear systems in Example 6.1 and Problem 6.2.7 are singular but consistent.

(A) Describe a method for computing their solutions using standard library software.

(B) Apply the method of part A to each system to show that it works.

(C) Explain why this method does not apply to solving all singular or nearly singular systems. In particular, consider the problems in Examples 6.2 and 6.3.

(D) Experiment with standard library software (e.g., IMSL routine LEQT1F or LINPACK routines SGECO plus SGESL) to see how it performs for this linear system.

6.4.12 Write a Fortran subroutine which does exactly what the IMSL program LEQT1F does but which uses the LINPACK programs to carry out the calculation. The arguments must be identical for LEQT1F and the new subroutine. Run the two programs on test cases and give sufficient output (nicely labeled) to illustrate that they accept the same input and produce the same output, modulo round-off errors.

6.4.13 Repeat Problem 6.4.12 for the IMSL program LEQT1B. Note that the band matrix data structure must be changed before the problem is passed on to the LINPACK programs. Give explicit details on this change and estimate its computational cost relative to the overall solution cost.

6.4.14 Repeat Problem 6.4.13 for the IMSL program LEQ1S for symmetric matrices.

6.4.15 Translate the simple PROTRAN program for the 4 by 4 system in Section 6.4.C into a Fortran program using the LINPACK software. Discuss and compare the effort required to do the translation and to write each program from scratch.

6.4.16 Repeat Problem 6.4.15 using IMSL library software.

6.4.17 Examine the Fortran code produced by the PROTRAN system for the example of Problem 6.4.15 and compare it with the Fortran code for Problem 6.4.16. Discuss why the PROTRAN-generated program is so much longer and what benefits are provided by the extra code.

6.4.18 Consider the longer PROTRAN program involving 4 matrices of different storage formats in Section 6.4.C. Translate this program into Fortran using the LINPACK software. Discuss and compare the effort required to do the translation and to write each program from scratch.

6.4.19 Repeat Problem 6.4.18 using IMSL library software.

6.4.20 Repeat Problem 6.4.17 for the example of Problem 6.4.18 and the Fortran code of Problem 6.4.19.

6.4.21 Run the PROTRAN program of Example 6.3 on the local computer system and determine at what size the Hilbert matrix becomes effectively singular on this system.

6.4.22 Complete the Fortran segments of Example 6.3 into a complete program and run it. Determine at what size the Hilbert matrix becomes effectively singular on the local computer system.

6.4.23 Solve the two point boundary value problem

$$(1+x^2)\, y'' - 4xy' - 6y = 2 - 12x^2 + 30x^4 \qquad y(0) = 0,\ y(2) = -60$$

using the method of Example 6.4. Use a value of h which gives .1 maximum error in the solution. **Hint:** The exact solution is $x^2 - x^6$.

6.4.24 Let h vary in Problem 6.4.23 and determine the order of the error as h decreases.

6.4.25 Repeat Problem 6.4.23 for the differential equation

$$y'' - y' = -x^2 - \cos x \qquad y(0) = -0.5,\ y(\pi) = -12.21464609$$

Hint: The exact solution is $-(x^3/3 + x^2 + 2x + .5\sin x + .5\cos x)$.

6.4.26 Let h vary in Problem 6.4.25 and determine the order of the error as h decreases.

6.4.27 For a given value of N consider the N^2 by N^2 matrix A with elements all zero except [with $h = 1/(N+1)$]

$$a_{ii} = 4 + h^2 \qquad a_{i,i+1} = a_{i,i-1} = a_{i,i+N} = a_{i,i-N} = -1$$

(A) Use library software for band matrices to solve $A\mathbf{u} = \mathbf{b}$ where $b_i = 4h^2$ for each i. Solve the system for N = 3 and 5.

(B) This system provides an approximate solution of the partial differential equation for u(x, y):

$$\frac{\partial^2 u}{\partial x^2} + \frac{\partial^2 u}{\partial y^2} - u = 4$$

with u = 0 on all sides of the region $0 \le x, y \le 1$. The value u_i for $i = (N^2+1)/2$ is an estimate of the solution at x = y = .5. Vary h and attempt to estimate the true value of the solution at x = y = .5 accurate to 1 percent.

(C) If the error for u(.5, .5) decreases as $0(h^2)$, determine the amount of work to obtain d correct decimal digits of u(.5, .5) as a function of N.

6.4.28 Repeat Problem 6.4.27 using software for symmetric positive definite matrices.

CASE STUDY: DESIGN OF THE INTERFACE FOR A LINEAR EQUATIONS SOLVER — 6.5

We consider in some detail the design of a library program to solve systems of linear equations. Even in this relatively simple and very standard problem we see some of the compromises that must be made in software design.

Design of a Fortran Interface — 6.5.A

We want to solve $A\mathbf{x} = \mathbf{b}$, and so we might hope to have the Fortran subroutine call:

```
CALL SOLVE(A,X,B)
```

This cannot work because the number N of equations is missing, and so we might hope for:

```
CALL SOLVE(A,X,B,N)
```

Some of the shortcomings of this design are as follows:

1. The user is not warned if A is singular or if the subroutine SOLVE fails.
2. If you have two systems of equations $A\mathbf{x}_1 = \mathbf{b}_1$ and $A\mathbf{x}_2 = \mathbf{b}_2$ with the same matrix, then A is factored twice.
3. The computation of A^{-1} is not efficient.
4. The dimensions of the Fortran arrays A, X, and B are not given. This forces them either to be fixed in advance (for example, A is 50 by 50) or to be N; both of these choices are unsatisfactory. This shortcoming is due to the Fortran language.
5. The solution process requires workspace, and so either A must be destroyed or a large, fixed amount of workspace must be declared inside the program SOLVE. This shortcoming is also due to the Fortran language.

So, while this is a simple design of the user interface, it lacks flexibility, power, and safety features, and it has Fortran language problems.

The following two designs have fewer shortcomings:

Linear Equation Solver — Design 1

```
C         NO WORKSPACE, A IS DESTROYED
      CALL SOLVE(A,X,B,N,I,J,K,L,M,M1)
      ----
      SUBROUTINE SOLVE(A,X,B,N,I,J,K,L,M,M1)
      DIMENSION A(I,J) X(I,K), B(I,K)
      ----
C     I=NUMBER OF ROWS DECLARED IN DIMENSIONS OF A,X,B
C     J=NUMBER OF COLUMNS DECLARED IN DIMENSIONS OF A
C     K=NUMBER OF COLUMNS DECLARED IN DIMENSIONS OF X,B
C     L=NUMBER OF RIGHT SIDES
C     M=SWITCH TO COMPUTE A^-1
C     M1=FLAG FOR SINGULARITY OF A
```

Linear Equation Solver — Design 2

```
C     WORKSPACE W PROVIDED, A IS NOT DESTROYED
      CALL SOLVE(A,X,B,N,I,J,K,L,M,M1,W)
      ----
      SUBROUTINE SOLVE(A,X,B,N,I,J,K,L,M,M1,W)
      DIMENSION A(I,J), X(I,K), B(I,K), W(I,J)
```

Now we have flexibility, but we also have users who will look at this argument list and say: "Good grief, I'll never figure out all this mess! All I want is to solve my little 5 by 5 system. I'll write my own program."

The situation can be improved somewhat by using better mnemonics for the names.

Design 1 — With Better Variable Names and Square Matrix A

```
SUBROUTINE SOLVE(A,X,B,NEQS,KDIMA,KDIMB,NSOLS,INVERS,ISING)
DIMENSION A(KDIMA,KDIMA), X(KDIMA,KDIMB), B(KDIMA,KDIMB)
```

Note that we forced A to be square with this change. The two arguments KDIMA and KDIMB are artifacts of Fortran, while the others are really needed by the problem. Keep in mind that in Fortran (and most other languages) the matrix A is not passed to a subroutine as some sort of object or collection of numbers. Only its address (location in memory) is passed, and a subroutine like SOLVE uses A where it is stored in the calling program and SOLVE itself does not have memory allocated for the matrix.

One might decide to avoid the INVERS switch and require the user to program something like

```
B=IDENTITY MATRIX
CALL SOLVE(A,X,B,NEQS,KDIMA,KDIMB,NEQS,ISING)
IF( ISING .EQ. 0) GO TO ERROR MESSAGE
```

For the user who wants the original simple routine we can include in the library

```
      SUBROUTINE LINSYS (A,X,B,NEQS)
      REAL A(NEQS,NEQS), X(NEQS), B(NEQS)
      CALL SOLVE(A,X,B,NEQS,NEQS,NEQS,1,ISING)
      IF (ISING .EQ. 0) PRINT 10
   10 FORMAT( 20X,20(1H*), 19HMATRIX IS SINGULAR)
      RETURN
      END
```

Thus, we see that even in this standard problem there are nontrivial design questions — and we have ignored the question of how to let the user tell the program SOLVE that A is symmetric, a band matrix, etc.

Storage Allocation and Variable Dimensions 6.5.B

Many people using matrix software become confused by the difference between the size of A in the linear equations problem $A\mathbf{x} = \mathbf{b}$ and the size of A as a Fortran array. We first note that a library program cannot assume these two sizes are the same. The routine LINSYS given above is, in fact, not very useful because of the need for flexibility in the number of equations. We illustrate this by two skeleton Fortran programs which are typical of common applications:

```
C                    FIRST PROGRAM
      REAL A(50,50), R(50), B(50)
    5 READ 10, NEQS, ((A(I,J), I=1,NEQS), J=1,NEQS)
   10 FORMAT( I10/(8F10.5))
      IF( NEQS .LE. 0) STOP
C           DO SOME THINGS HERE
      CALL SOLVE(A,X,B,NEQS,50,1,1,ISING)
      IF( ISING .EQ. 0) PRINT 20
C           DO MORE THINGS, THEN DO ANOTHER CASE
      GO TO 5
      END

C                    SECOND PROGRAM
      REAL A(50,50), X(50,10), B(50,10)
C           GENERATE FIRST PROBLEM, 5 BY 5
      CALL SOLVE(A,X,B,5,50,50,1,1,ISING)
C           GENERATE LAST PROBLEM, 10 RIGHT SIDES AND 50 BY 50
      CALL SOLVE(A,X,B,50,50,50,10,1,ISING)
      STOP
      END
```

Fortran has very limited capabilities to handle arrays of different sizes, and the most obvious and common approach is to choose a size of A for SOLVE which is always big enough, say 100 by 100. With this design, the library subroutine instructions say A must be declared 100 by 100, and SOLVE looks like this:

```
SUBROUTINE SOLVE(A,X,B,NEQS,ISING)
REAL A(100,100), X(100), B(100)
```

This approach is grossly wasteful of memory for the person who has four equations and four unknowns. The person who has 102 equations must either write a new program or get the library program and modify it.

The variable-dimension facility of Fortran used earlier overcomes both of these difficulties at the price of including the sizes of the array in the calling sequence. While using variable dimensions is clearly the choice for a library routine, we can hope that someday Fortran — or whatever our standard language is — will eliminate this redundant and confusing feature.

The PROTRAN Interface for Ax = b 6.5.C

The PROTRAN system allows the simple program

```
$ DECLARATIONS
  REAL MATRIX A(3,3)
  REAL VECTOR X(3),B(3)
$ ASSIGN A = (1.0,  0.0)
 +           (0.0, -2.0)
         B = (1.0,  1.0)
$ LINSYS A*X = B
$ PRINT X
$ END
```

for the solution of $A\mathbf{x} = \mathbf{b}$. This is close to the natural way to say "Solve $A\mathbf{x} = \mathbf{b}$." The special character $ and keyword LINSYS are used to provide a short, easy-to-recognize form of the statement.

The primary source of simplicity in PROTRAN is that vectors and matrices are more than arrays of numbers. Within the PROTRAN system the declared dimension, storage format, element data type, and range variables are always available for each matrix and vector. One can imagine them attached to the arrays of numbers, although this is not done explicitly. Thus, in the above program, the PROTRAN system checks the information for A, X, and B for consistency and then selects the appropriate IMSL library program. There is no need to explicitly state this information.

A second source of simplicity is that the PROTRAN system automatically obtains workspace for use while solving $A\mathbf{x} = \mathbf{b}$ and then gives it up when finished.

Finally, the "arguments" (the phrases following the problem statement) to a PROTRAN statement are optional (except those essential for defining the problem); they may appear in any order and use an English-like keyword for identification — and easy remembering. Consider the statement

```
$LINSYS A*X=B; HIGHACCURACY; EQUATIONS=4, NOSAVE
```

The number of equations would be the row range of B, but that is overridden by stating there are 4 equations. The first phrase, HIGHACCURACY, asks that high accuracy be obtained by using iterative improvement. The final keyword NOSAVE states that A and B need not be saved; they can be used for workspace and thus save space for programs involving very large matrices (the HIGHACCURACY phrase requires more than minimal storage, and so no saving actually occurs when it is used with the NOSAVE phrase).

The PROTRAN system does extensive checking, as illustrated by the Fortran code generated for the above program.

```
REAL        A     (3,3)
REAL        X     (3)
REAL        B     (3)
INTEGER IRNGV7(    4)
INTEGER     IAAAV7,IAABV7,IAACV7,IAADV7,IAAEV7,IAAFV7,IAAGV7,IAAHV7
INTEGER     IAAIV7,IAAJV7,IAAKV7,IAALV7,IAAMV7,IAANV7,IAAOV7,IAAPV7
INTEGER     IAAQV7,IAARV7,IAASV7,IAATV7,IAAUV7,IAAVV7
REAL*8      IMSLSD( 2500),DXXXV7,DYYYV7
INTEGER     IMSLSI( 5000),IXXXV7,IYYYV7
REAL        IMSLSR( 5000),RXXXV7,RYYYV7
COMPLEX     IMSLSC( 2500),CXXXV7,CYYYV7
LOGICAL     IMSLSL( 5000),LXXXV7,LYYYV7
COMPLEX*16 IMSLSZ( 1250),ZXXXV7,ZYYYV7
COMMON/IMSLWS/IMSLSI
```

```
      EQUIVALENCE (IMSLSI,IMSLSR,IMSLSD,IMSLSC,IMSLSL,IMSLSZ)
      DATA IWRKV7 / 5000/
C                                    CHECK LIBRARY PRECISION
      CALL IMSLLC(1,IER)
C$    DECLARATIONS
C$    REAL MATRIX A(3,3)
      IRNGV7(   1)=3
      IRNGV7(   2)=3
C$    REAL VECTOR X(3),B(3)
      IRNGV7(   3)=3
      IRNGV7(   4)=3
C$    ASSIGN  A = (1.0,  0.0)
C$   +            (0.0, -2.0)
      A     (   1,   1)=1.0
      A     (   1,   2)=0.0
      A     (   2,   1)=0.0
      A     (   2,   2)=-2.0
      IRNGV7(1)  =     2
      IRNGV7(2)  =     2
C$          B = (1.0, 1.0)
      B     (    1)=1.0
      B     (    2)=1.0
      IRNGV7(4)  =     2
C$    LINSYS  A*X=B
C                                    TURN OFF MESSAGES FROM LIBRARY
C                                    ROUTINES
      CALL IMSLU1 (0,IAAAV7)
C                                    INITIALIZE GLOBAL ERROR PARAMETER
      IER = 0
C                                    INITIALIZE WORKSPACE ALLOCATION
C                                    COUNTER
      IAABV7 = 0
C                                    INITIALIZE ADDITIONAL WORKSPACE
C                                    ALLOCATION COUNTER
      IAACV7 = 0
C                                    NUMBER OF EQUATIONS IS IRNGV7(4)
      IAADV7 = IRNGV7(4)
C                                    NUMBER OF RHS IS 1
      IAAEV7 = 1
C                                    CHECK PROBLEM CONSISTENCY
      IAAFV7 = 3
      IAAGV7 = IRNGV7(2)
      CALL IMSLL1 (IAADV7,IAADV7,6HLINSYS,7,6HA      ,3,IAAFV7,IRNGV7(1),
     *IAAGV7,IAAHV7)
      IF (IAAHV7.NE.0) IER = IAAHV7
      CALL IMSLL1 (IAADV7,IAAEV7,6HLINSYS,7,6HX      ,3,1,IAADV7,IAAEV7,I
     *AAHV7)
      IF (IAAHV7.NE.0) IER = IAAHV7
      CALL IMSLL1 (IAADV7,IAAEV7,6HLINSYS,7,6HB      ,3,1,IRNGV7(4),1,IAA
     *HV7)
      IF (IAAHV7.NE.0) IER = IAAHV7
      IF (IER.NE.0) GO TO 30001
      IAAIV7 = 3
      IAAJV7 = 3
      IAAKV7 = 3
      IAALV7 = IAADV7
C                                    ALLOCATE WORK VECTOR WK
      CALL IMSLWK (1,IAALV7,IMSLSI,IWRKV7,IAAMV7,IAABV7,IAACV7,6HLINSYS,
     *7,IER)
      IF (IER.NE.0) GO TO 30001
C                                     ALLOCATE STORAGE FOR COPY OF A
      CALL IMSLWK (1,IAADV7*IAADV7,IMSLSI,IWRKV7,IAANV7,IAABV7,IAACV7,6H
     *LINSYS,7,IER)
      IF (IER.NE.0) GO TO 30001
      IF (IAACV7.GT.0) GO TO 30002
C                                     COPY B TO X
      CALL IMSLCS (IAADV7,IAAEV7,B,IAAJV7,X,IAAKV7)
      IAAOV7 = 0
C                                     COPY A TO WORK STORAGE
      CALL IMSLCS(IAADV7,IAADV7,A,IAAIV7,IMSLSR(IAANV7),IAADV7)
      CALL IMSLL3 (IMSLSR(IAANV7),IAAEV7,IAADV7,IAADV7,X,IAAKV7,IAAOV7,I
     *MSLSR(IAAMV7),IER)
      IF (IER.EQ.0) GO TO 30003
C                                    HANDLE FATAL NUMERICAL ERRORS
      IF (IER.EQ.130) IER=131
      IF (IER.EQ.129) CALL IMSLMS (3,1,IER,6HLINSYS,7,36 ,36 HMATRIX A I
     *S ALGORITHMICALLY SINGULAR)
      IF (IER.EQ.131) CALL IMSLMS (3,1,IER,6HLINSYS,7,73 ,73 HMATRIX A I
     *S TOO ILL-CONDITIONED FOR ITERATIVE IMPROVEMENT TO BE EFFECTIVE)
      IF (IER.NE.129.AND.IER.NE.131)CALL IMSLMS (3,1,IER,6HLINSYS,7,30 ,
     *30 HPROTRAN - UNKNOWN ERROR NUMBER)
C                                    SET RANGE OF X TO ZERO
      IRNGV7(3) = 0
      GO TO 30001
C                                    NO ERRORS, SET RANGE OF X
30003 IRNGV7(3) = IAADV7
      GO TO 30004
C                                    LINSYS PROCEDURE EXIT
30002 CONTINUE
```

```
C                                              WORKSPACE LIMIT EXCEEDED
        CALL IMSLSA (6HLINSYS,7,IWRKV7+IAACV7,IER)
30001 CONTINUE
        CALL IMSLFA (IER,6HLINSYS,7)
30004 CONTINUE
C                                              RELEASE WORKSPACE
        CALL IMSLRL(IAABV7,IAABV7,IMSLSI,IWRKV7,6HLINSYS,7,IER)
30005 CONTINUE
C                                              RESTORE LIBRARY ROUTINE MESSAGE LEVEL
C
        CALL IMSLU1 (IAAAV7,IAAPV7)
C$      PRINT X
        IER = 0
        IAAQV7 = 0
C                                              GET OUTPUT UNIT NO.
        CALL IMSLU2(1,IAARV7,IAASV7)
        IAATV7 = 2
C                                              CHECK SIZE
        IAAUV7 = 1
        IAAVV7 = 1
        CALL IMSLL1(IRNGV7(3),IAAVV7,6HPRINT ,8,6HX      ,3,IAAUV7,IRNGV7(3
      *),IAAVV7,IER)
        IF(IER.NE.0) GO TO 30006
C                                              PRINT REAL VECTOR X
        CALL IMSLVR(1HX,1,X,IRNGV7(3),1,IAATV7)
        GO TO 30007
30008 CALL IMSLSA (6HPRINT ,8,IWRKV7+IAAQV7,IER)
30006 CONTINUE
30009 CALL IMSLFA (IER,6HPRINT ,8)
30007 CONTINUE
C$      END
        STOP
        END
```

PROBLEMS 6.5

6.5.1 Locate an example in your local library that has a lengthy calling sequence and define a "front-end" routine that handles a simpler class of problems by setting some default values and then calling the library program.

6.5.2 Choose two library subroutine write-ups from your local computing center and make a critique of them. Points to consider include:

(A) Are all the variables defined clearly and given good names?

(B) Does the program require arguments whose values are obscure?

(C) Is an example given?

(D) Is a reference to the algorithm source given?

(E) Are there common situations where the user must modify the program before using it?

(F) Does the program waste storage for a small problem?

(G) Can a source code be obtained easily? If so, is it well documented?

(H) Does the input have to be in an unnatural form?

ANALYSIS OF THE LINEAR EQUATIONS PROBLEM 6.6

A number of mathematical conditions are given in Chapter 1 for the solvability of $A\mathbf{x} = \mathbf{b}$. It is intuitively clear that Gauss eliminaton produces the solution $\mathbf{x}$ provided a solution exists. We need to show that the matrix factorization always exists, and as with all numerical methods, we need to analyze errors and accuracy. Gauss elimination is unlike most numerical methods in that there are no truncation or mathematical model errors. If the arithmetic were exact, one would obtain exact answers at the completion of the algorithm. Round-off error effects can be serious, and several ways to estimate them are examined.

Matrix Factorizations 6.6.A

The principal task here is to establish that the factorization in Gauss elimination always exists. We have
Theorem 6.2 *Let* A *be a square matrix. Then there are matrices* U *(upper triangular),* M *(lower triangular and nonsingular), and* P *(a permutation matrix) so that*

$$U = MPA$$

Let L *be the inverse of* M*; then we also have* LU = PA *with* L *lower triangular.*

This theorem applies to solving $A\mathbf{x} = \mathbf{b}$ as follows. If we have computed U, M, and P, then we multiply both sides by MP to obtain

$$MPA\mathbf{x} = MP\mathbf{b}$$

which is equivalent to

$$Ux = MP\mathbf{b}$$

These equations can be solved by *back substitution* if a solution exists. Note that computing $MP\mathbf{b}$ is exactly forward substitution. The permutation matrix P represents the pivoting made in Gauss elimination.

Gauss elimination works whether or not A is nonsingular; the more usual form of the matrix factorization result is as follows. Define the *principal submatrices* of A as the k by k matrices $\{a_{ij}\}$, $i, j = 1, 2, \ldots, k$, where $k = 1, 2, \ldots, n$.

Theorem 6.3 *If the principal submatrices of* A *are all nonsingular, then one may choose* P *as the identity in Theorem 6.1, and we obtain*

$$LU = A$$

With the normalization $\ell_{ij} = 1$, *this factorization of* A *is unique.*

Proof of Theorem 6.2: The proof is by induction on k, the number of columns of A. Visualize the matrix at an intermediate step partitioned as shown in Figure 6.9. Thus, $A_{k-1} = M_{k-1}P_{k-1}A$ is the induction assumption, and we now proceed to show that $k-1$ can be increased to k.

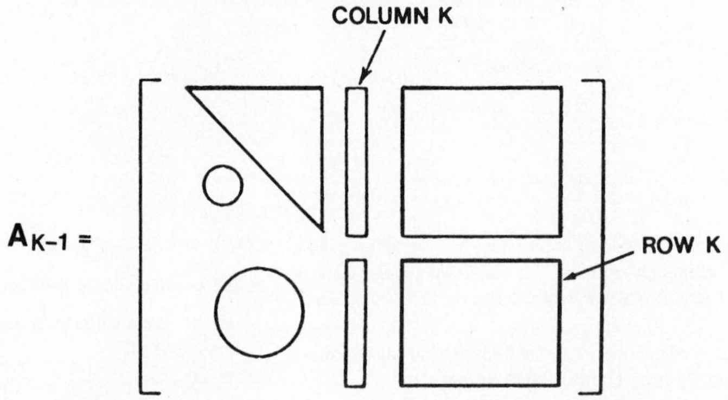

Figure 6.9 **Diagram for proof of Theorem 6.2.** The matrix A_{k-1} at the kth step of the induction argument.

There are two cases (we denote the elements of A_{k-1} by a_{ij} to simplify the notation):

Case 1: Suppose $a_{ik} = 0$ for all $i \geq k$. Then we are done with the induction step.

Case 2: Suppose $a_{ik} \neq 0$ for some $j \geq k$. Apply a permutation matrix P'_k which interchanges the k and j rows. Thus, we may now assume that $a_{kk} \neq 0$. Compute the elements in rows $k+1$ to n by the formula

$$a_{\ell m} = a_{\ell m} - \frac{a_{\ell k}}{a_{kk}} a_{km} \qquad \ell = k+1, \ldots, n \qquad m = k, \ldots n$$

It is clear that this makes $a_{\ell k} = 0$ for $\ell > k$. This formula carries out multiplying row k by the multipliers $-a_{\ell k}/a_{kk} = m_\ell$, and adding that to row ℓ. Thus its effect is the same as multiplying by the matrix

$$M'_k = \begin{pmatrix} I_{k-1} & 0 \\ 0 & M''_k \end{pmatrix} \qquad M''_k = \begin{pmatrix} 1 & & & & 0 \\ m_{k+1} & 1 & & & \\ m_{k+2} & 0 & 1 & & \\ \cdot & \cdot & \cdot & \cdot & \\ \cdot & \cdot & \cdot & \cdot & \\ \cdot & \cdot & \cdot & \cdot & \\ m_n & 0 & 0 & \ldots & 1 \end{pmatrix}$$

where I_{k-1} is a $(k-1)$-order identity matrix. M'_k is not singular, since it is lower triangular with 1s on the diagonal. Note the following forms of the two matrices here:

$$M_{k-1} = \begin{pmatrix} L_{k-2} & 0 \\ B & I_{n-k+1} \end{pmatrix} \qquad P'_k = \begin{pmatrix} I_{k-1} & 0 \\ 0 & Q \end{pmatrix}$$

where L_{k-2} is a lower triangular matrix of order $k-2$ and Q is a permutation matrix of order $n-k+1$. One can check that $P'_k M_{k-1} P'_k$ is lower triangular (the effect is to apply Q to B), and thus we have

$$P'_k M_{k-1} = P'_k M_{k-1} P'_k P'_k M^*_{k-1} P'_k$$

where M^*_{k-1} is lower triangular. Since $A_k = M'_k P'_k A_{k-1}$, we have

$$\begin{aligned} A_k &= M'_k P'_k M_{k-1} P_{k-1} A = M'_k M^*_{k-1} P'_k P_{k-1} A \\ &= M_k P_k A \end{aligned}$$

This is of the required form where $P_k = P'_k P_{k-1}$. The induction hypothesis is verified for $k = 1$ by the same reasoning and the proof is complete.

Proof of Theorem 6.3: We first need to show that the nonsingularity of the principal submatrices implies that no row interchanges are required. This argument is also by induction on k. Clearly $a_{11} \neq 0$ by this hypothesis, and so P_1 is not needed.

Recall that a triangular matrix is singular if and only if one of its diagonal elements is zero. Thus the upper triangular submatrix in A_{k-1} is nonsingular (by the induction hypothesis on the principal submatrices) and no row interchanges are required. If $a_{kk} = 0$, then the k by k principal submatrix is singular, which contradicts the hypothesis of the theorem. Thus $a_{kk} \neq 0$ and the induction proceeds with no row interchanges.

The construction in the proof of Theorem 6.2 produces a uniquely determined factorization except for the possible different choices of rows to interchange. Furthermore, M has 1s on the diagonal and thus so does its inverse L, that is, $\ell_{ii} = 1$ for all i. Since no permutations occur in Theorem 6.3, the factorization obtained is unique and the proof is complete.

When A is symmetric positive-definite, the Cholesky method produces a symmetric factorization. Note that the factorization normally does not have 1s on the diagonal of either factor.

Theorem 6.4 *Let* A *be symmetric positive-definite. Then there is a unique matrix L so that*

$$A = LL^T$$

Proof: The proof follows the idea used in the 2 by 2 example earlier. We use induction on the size of A and assume we can factor the $(m-1)$ by $(m-1)$ submatrix A into LL^T. Then let A' and L' be m by m matrices in the form

$$A' = \begin{pmatrix} A & \mathbf{y} \\ \mathbf{y}^T & a_{mm} \end{pmatrix} \qquad L' = \begin{pmatrix} L & 0 \\ \mathbf{w}^T & \ell_{mm} \end{pmatrix}$$

where **y** and **w** are $(m-1)$ vectors. For $A' = L'L'^T$, we require that

$$\begin{aligned} A &= LL^T & \mathbf{y} &= L\mathbf{w} \\ \mathbf{y}^T &= \mathbf{w}^T L^T & a_{mm} &= \ell_{mm}^2 + \mathbf{w}^T\mathbf{w} \end{aligned}$$

By hypothesis we can find L so that $A = LL^T$, and the equation $\mathbf{y} = L\mathbf{w}$ allows us to solve for the $m-1$ components of **w**. Thus we have

$$\ell_{mm} = \sqrt{a_{mm} - \mathbf{w}^T\mathbf{w}}$$

and we show that the quantity in the square root is positive by imitating the argument for the 2 by 2 case. We take $\mathbf{x} = (A^{-1}\mathbf{y}, -1)^T$ and compute that (with $\mathbf{z} = A^{-1}\mathbf{y}$ for convenience)

$$\begin{aligned} \mathbf{x}^T A' \mathbf{x} &= \mathbf{z}^T A \mathbf{z} - 2\mathbf{z}^T\mathbf{y} + a_{mm} \\ &= -\mathbf{z}^T\mathbf{y} + a_{mm} = a_{mm} - \mathbf{y}^T A^{-1} \mathbf{y} \\ &= a_{mm} - \mathbf{y}^T (LL^T)^{-1} \mathbf{y} = a_{mm} - (L^{-1}\mathbf{y})^T (L^{-1}\mathbf{y}) \\ &= a_{mm} - \mathbf{w}^T\mathbf{w} \end{aligned}$$

Since $\mathbf{x}^T A' \mathbf{x} > 0$, we have $a_{mm} - \mathbf{w}^T\mathbf{w} > 0$, and the induction step is complete.

The matrix L' is unique because there is a unique value for ℓ_{mm} which, in turn, gives a unique vector **w**, and L is unique by the induction hypothesis. This completes the proof.

Three Condition Numbers *6.6.B

The condition number of a matrix was originally introduced as a means to make an a priori (advance) estimate of how large errors can be in solving $A\mathbf{x} = \mathbf{b}$. The original condition number idea is not very reliable, but improvements have come from using the condition number as an a posteriori (after the fact) estimate; that is, we wait until we have "solved" the problem before trying to assess the correctness of the solution. Various kinds of information which were developed while solving $A\mathbf{x} = \mathbf{b}$ are useful in this assessment.

We derive three different ways to estimate the effect on the solution of errors in the original problem. The situation is as follows: We have an original problem $A\mathbf{x} = \mathbf{b}$ and a perturbed problem $A\overline{\mathbf{x}} = \mathbf{b} + \mathbf{r}$ where $\mathbf{r}$ represents the perturbation in both the right side and A. That is, if A is perturbed to $A + \delta A$, then we simply move $\delta A\mathbf{x}$ to the right side and incorporate it into $\mathbf{r}$. This is technically not quite correct since δA is multiplied by $\mathbf{x}$ and we only know $\overline{\mathbf{x}}$, but keep in mind that we are now just making rough estimates. The objective is to estimate $\delta\mathbf{x} = \mathbf{x} - \overline{\mathbf{x}}$ in terms of $\mathbf{r}$ and the problem data and, more precisely, to estimate how the uncertainty $\mathbf{r}$ in $\mathbf{b}$ is transmitted to $\delta\mathbf{x}$. In practice, $\mathbf{r}$ is the residual of the computed solution $\overline{\mathbf{x}}$.

We first define the **natural condition number**. We have

$$A\mathbf{x} = \mathbf{b} \qquad A\overline{\mathbf{x}} = \mathbf{b} + \mathbf{r}$$

By subtraction,

$$A(\overline{\mathbf{x}} - \mathbf{x}) = \mathbf{r}$$

or

$$\overline{\mathbf{x}} - \mathbf{x} = \delta\mathbf{x} = A^{-1}\mathbf{r}$$

We take the norm of each side to obtain

$$||\delta\mathbf{x}|| = ||A^{-1}\mathbf{r}|| \le ||A^{-1}||\ ||\mathbf{r}||$$

and we see as no surprise that the size of A^{-1} estimates how much the uncertainty represented by $\mathbf{r}$ may be magnified. It is more meaningful to use relative errors, and we have from the above analysis that

$$\frac{||\delta\mathbf{x}||}{||\mathbf{x}||} \le \frac{||A^{-1}||\ ||\mathbf{r}||}{||\mathbf{x}||\ ||\mathbf{b}||} \times ||\mathbf{b}|| = \frac{||A^{-1}||\ ||\mathbf{b}||}{||\mathbf{x}||} \times \frac{||\mathbf{r}||}{||\mathbf{b}||} \qquad \textbf{Equation 6.6.1}$$

which gives the natural condition number $||A^{-1}||\ ||\mathbf{b}||/||\mathbf{x}||$.

The analysis in this section is valid for any combination of compatible vector and matrix norms. For concreteness (and in solving the problems), *the reader may assume that the infinity and row-sum norms are used,* that is,

$$||\text{vector}|| = \max |\text{component}|$$
$$||\text{matrix}|| = \max_{\text{row}} \Sigma\ |\text{elements in a row}|$$

One can eliminate the dependence on $\mathbf{x}$ to obtain the **standard condition number** as follows. We have

$$A\mathbf{x} = \mathbf{b}$$

which implies that

$$||\mathbf{b}|| = ||A\mathbf{x}|| \le ||A||\ ||\mathbf{x}||$$

or

$$\frac{1}{||\mathbf{x}||} \le \frac{||A||}{||\mathbf{b}||}$$

If we substitute this into the previous estimate of $||\delta\mathbf{x}||/||\mathbf{x}||$, we get

$$\frac{||\delta\mathbf{x}||}{||\mathbf{x}||} \leq \frac{||A^{-1}||\ ||\mathbf{b}||}{||\mathbf{x}||} \times \frac{||\mathbf{r}||}{||\mathbf{b}||} \leq \frac{||A^{-1}||\ ||\mathbf{b}||\ ||A||}{|\mathbf{b}||} \times \frac{||\mathbf{r}||}{||\mathbf{b}||}$$ **Equation 6.6.2**

$$= ||A^{-1}||\ ||A|| \times \frac{||\mathbf{r}||}{||\mathbf{b}||}$$

which defines the standard condition number $||A^{-1}||\ ||A||$.

Note that both these condition numbers are only estimates of how much the uncertainty in **b** may be magnified. They almost always overestimate the magnification, sometimes by a tremendous amount, but in special cases they give the magnification factor exactly.

The **Aird-Lynch estimates** are more precise and take a little longer to derive. They give both upper and lower bounds on the error magnification. Let C be an approximate inverse of A (C will be a by-product of the Gauss elimination process in practice), and we have

$$C\mathbf{r} = C(A\overline{\mathbf{x}} - \mathbf{b}) = CA(\overline{\mathbf{x}} - \mathbf{x})$$

or

$$||\overline{\mathbf{x}} - \mathbf{x}|| = ||(CA)^{-1}C\mathbf{r}|| \leq ||(CA)^{-1}||\ ||C\mathbf{r}||$$

We use the matrix inequality (see Problem 6.6.33)

$$||B^{-1}|| \leq \frac{1}{1 - ||B - I||} \quad \text{if } ||B - I|| < 1$$

to obtain (with $B = CA$)

$$||\delta\mathbf{x}|| \leq \frac{||C\mathbf{r}||}{1 - ||CA - I||}$$

or, setting $T = ||CA - I||$,

$$\frac{||\delta\mathbf{x}||}{||\mathbf{x}||} \leq \frac{||C\mathbf{r}||}{||\mathbf{x}||(1 - T)}$$ **Equation 6.6.3**

In practice T is usually a small number because C is taken to be a reasonably good approximation to A^{-1}. It is crucial that $||C\mathbf{r}||$ not be replaced by $||C||\ ||\mathbf{r}||$, for reasons of both accuracy and computation effort. We leave it as an exercise for the reader to derive the similar estimate

$$\frac{||C\mathbf{r}||}{||\mathbf{x}||(1 + T)} \leq \frac{||\delta\mathbf{x}||}{||\mathbf{x}||}$$

Note that this last estimate provides a *lower bound on the error* in the approximate solution $\overline{\mathbf{x}}$ in terms of the residual **r**.

The difficulty with each of these error estimates is that they involve A^{-1}. There are a few times where $||A^{-1}||$ can be found without finding A^{-1} (one can look up the norms for Hilbert matrices), but these are so rare that we ignore them. We specifically consider the following common situation: The system $A\mathbf{x} = \mathbf{b}$ has been solved by Gauss elimination; we have an approximate solution $\overline{\mathbf{x}}$, its residual **r**, and the factors M and U so that $MA = U$. We now want to estimate the error $\delta\mathbf{x}$ by these three methods. We assume A is n by n in this discussion.

For the natural and standard condition numbers, the only difficulty is with $||A^{-1}||$. We have three alternatives:

1. *Compute* A^{-1} *and its norm.* This requires about $n^3 + 2n^2$ extra operations and approximately quadruples the work of solving $A\mathbf{x} = \mathbf{b}$.

2. *Estimate* $||A^{-1}||$ *roughly*. Note that, if $\mathbf{w} = A^{-1}\mathbf{y}$, then $||\mathbf{w}|| \leq ||A^{-1}||\ ||\mathbf{y}||$, and so $||A^{-1}|| \geq ||\mathbf{w}||/||\mathbf{y}||$. We can choose k vectors y_i, i = 1, 2, . . . , k and solve $A\mathbf{w}_i = \mathbf{y}_i$ and take

$$||A^{-1}|| \sim \max_i ||\mathbf{w}_i||/||\mathbf{y}_i||$$

If k is small, this requires about kn^2 operations, which is small compared with the work invested in solving $A\mathbf{x} = \mathbf{b}$. There is a heuristic argument which says that if $\mathbf{y}$ is picked at random, then the expected value of $||\mathbf{w}||/||\mathbf{y}||$ is about $||A^{-1}||/2$. Thus, it seems fairly safe to use a small value of k.

We can get the crude estimate $||A^{-1}|| \geq ||\overline{\mathbf{x}}||/||\mathbf{b}||$ practically free; it is not useful for estimates with the natural condition number, as it gives 1 as the value.

3. *Use the LINPACK estimate of* $||A^{-1}||$. The previous idea is refined with a special vector $\mathbf{v} = \mathbf{y}$ with components ± 1 chosen to improve the reliability of the estimate. The computational effort is about the same as the previous one with k = 3.

The matrix C for the Aird-Lynch estimate is $U^{-1}M$ of the factorization. To compute $\mathbf{y} = C\mathbf{r}$, one solves $A\mathbf{y} = \mathbf{r}$ using the assumption that C is an approximate inverse of A. This requires n^2 operations. There are various ways to estimate $T = ||CA - I||$:

1. *Compute* CA-I *and its norm*. This is done as suggested in Problem 6.6.31. The extra work is about n^3 operations and approximately quadruples the work of solving $A\mathbf{x} = \mathbf{b}$.

2. *Estimate* $||CA-I||$ *roughly*. This can be done using random vectors, and the work is proportional to n^2.

3. *Take* T = 1/2. This is crude, cheap, and easy to program; it is risky as A might be very nearly singular. If A is nearly singular, then $||C\mathbf{r}||$ is large and the inaccuracy of the solution is probably already known.

In summary, there is a tradeoff in reliability with work for each of these three methods. Further, the amount of work for each alternative is comparable for a given level of crudeness in the calculation of the estimates.

Sensitivity Analysis 6.6.C

The idea behind sensitivity analysis is very simple and quite general: resolve the problem with slightly different data to see how sensitive the solution is to changes in the data. For programs to solve $A\mathbf{x} = \mathbf{b}$, there are two natural ways to proceed:

1. **Perturb the right side.** Here one computes $\overline{\mathbf{x}}$ in trying to solve $A\mathbf{x} = \mathbf{b}$, and then one chooses $\mathbf{r}_i$ and solves

$$A\mathbf{y}_i = \mathbf{b} + \mathbf{r}_i \qquad i = 1, 2, \ldots, k$$

Then

$$\max_i ||\overline{\mathbf{x}} - \mathbf{y}_i||$$

estimates the sensitivity of the computed solution $\overline{\mathbf{x}}$ to the perturbations $\mathbf{r}_i$. The $\mathbf{r}_i$ should be chosen small compared to $\mathbf{b}$ — of the order of round-off errors if one is concerned about them — or the size of the original data uncertainties if they are present.

This analysis is not expensive for a few perturbations because the additional solutions are computed with the factorization of A found for the first solution.

2. **Perturb A and b.** One chooses E_i and $\mathbf{r}_i$, small compared to A and $\mathbf{b}$, respectively, and solves

$$(A + E_i)\mathbf{y}_i = \mathbf{b} + \mathbf{r}_i$$

Again,

$$\max_i ||\bar{\mathbf{x}} - \mathbf{y}_i||$$

estimates the sensitivity of $\bar{\mathbf{x}}$. This way is more expensive since no use can be made of the previous solution effort. Also note that solving for $\bar{\mathbf{z}}_i$ with a perturbed right side as

$$A\bar{\mathbf{z}}_i = \mathbf{b} + \mathbf{r}_i - E_i\mathbf{y}_i$$

gives the same result, and thus this way can be viewed as a particular way to perturb **b**. Of course, $\mathbf{y}_i$ is not known in advance, and so the full perturbations give one more confidence in the results.

There is a very easy way to perform an analysis of sensitivity to round-off errors. One simply runs the same problem with another compiler. Different compilers are almost certain to produce code which does the arithmetic in a different order, and hence they produce different round-off errors.

Iterative Improvement **6.6.D

Iterative improvement is a method to "improve" a solution already computed. Suppose $\bar{\mathbf{x}}$ has been computed in solving $A\mathbf{x} = \mathbf{b}$, and let $\mathbf{r} = \mathbf{b} - A\bar{\mathbf{x}}$ be the residual. Then we have

$$A\mathbf{x} = \mathbf{b} \quad A\bar{\mathbf{x}} = \mathbf{b} - \mathbf{r}$$

and so, with $\delta\mathbf{x} = \mathbf{x} - \bar{\mathbf{x}}$,

$$A(\mathbf{x} - \bar{\mathbf{x}}) = A\delta\mathbf{x} = \mathbf{r}$$

and we can solve for the correction $\delta\mathbf{x} = \mathbf{x} - \bar{\mathbf{x}}$. It is easy to solve for $\delta\mathbf{x}$ since A is already factored; let **y** denote the computed value we obtain for $\delta\mathbf{x}$. The idea is that the matrix A is such that one only gets, say, three digits of the solutions correct. So $\bar{\mathbf{x}} + \mathbf{y}$ will have six correct digits: three from the original solution, and three more from the correction. But this reasoning is erroneous, and such a calculation gives no improvement at all. $\bar{\mathbf{x}} + \mathbf{y}$ is usually no more accurate than $\bar{\mathbf{x}}$. To see why this is so, we analyze a particular case where we assume the following:

1. All numbers in A, **x**, and **b** are about 1.0.

2. We use 8-decimal-digit arithmetic.

3. Five digits are lost in solving $A\mathbf{x} = \mathbf{b}$, and $\bar{\mathbf{x}}$ has three correct digits.

We examine the digits in the computed numbers and let *x* denote a correct digit and *z* denote a garbage digit. The form of the numbers after computing $\bar{\mathbf{x}}$ and **r** is

A, **b** numbers:	.xxx xxxxx
$\bar{\mathbf{x}}$ numbers:	.xxx zzzzz
r numbers:	.000 xxxxx zzz

Thus, the first five digits of **r** are the correct values of the residual for the incorrect digits of $\bar{\mathbf{x}}$, but the last three digits of **r** are garbage digits generated by the arithmetic. These last three digits cannot contain information because the corresponding digits of $\bar{\mathbf{x}}$ are missing. When we compute **y**, we lose five digits; that is, the uncertainty in the **y** digits is moved five places to the left so that the **y** numbers have the following form: .000 zzzzz zzz. They are all garbage digits, and thus we gain nothing by adding **y** to **x**.

While adding **y** gives no improvement in the accuracy, the ratio $||\mathbf{y}||/||\bar{\mathbf{x}}||$ is a rather reliable estimate of the error in **x**. This ratio is called the **indicated relative error** and is inexpensive to compute. One just solves the system with another right side; the work is about n^2 to compute **r** and n^2 to solve the second system.

This approach can be made to improve the accuracy if the residual **r** is computed more accurately. We redo the above example except that 10-digit arithmetic is used to evaluate **r** instead of the 8-digit arithmetic used elsewhere. The form of the numbers is then

A, **b**	numbers:	.xxx xxxxx
$\bar{x}$	numbers:	.xxx zzzzz
r	numbers:	.000 xxxxx xxzzz
y	numbers:	.000 xxzzz zzz
$\bar{x}$ + **y**	numbers:	.xxx xxzzz

We can interpret the use of 10 digits as changing the A, b numbers to .xxx xxxxx 00 and $\bar{x}$ numbers to .xxx zzzzz 00 before calculating **r**. The 10-digit **r** numbers would be rounded (or truncated) to 8 digits before going ahead to solve for **y**.

In practice, higher precision almost always means double precision. A second fact is that, if the correction **y** does not change $\bar{x}$ (that is, if **y** is comparable to round-off in $\bar{x}$), then $\bar{x}$ is the "right" answer. Note, however, that the final residual (computed in single precision) actually may be larger than the first one. Gauss elimination is very good at achieving a small residual error even if it does not produce a very accurate solution.

Iterative Improvement of the Solution of Ax = b

Algorithm 6.6.1

1. Factor A to obtain M and U so that MA = U.
2. Solve for **x** from **y** = M**b**, U**x** = **y**
3. For k = 1, 2, . . . , maxk, do the following:
   3.1 Compute **r** = **b** − A**x** in double precision.
   3.2 Solve for **y** from **v** = M**r**, U**y** = **v**.
   3.3 If ||**y**||/||**x**|| is satisfactory, go to END.
   3.4 **x** = **x** + **y**.
   If the loop is exited here, there is no convergence and the algorithm has failed.
4. Print "Iterative Improvement Failure, last solution estimate = **x**."
5. END

The usual test for ||**y**||/||**x**|| to be satisfactory is that it be the size of round-off. Thus we could test

$$\frac{||\mathbf{y}||}{||\mathbf{x}||} \leq 10^{-t}$$

for a t-digit arithmetic calculation. A machine-independent form of this test is

$$||\mathbf{x}|| + ||\mathbf{y}|| = ||\mathbf{x}||$$

The Composite Error Estimate **6.6.E

We now make another study of the linear equations problem and identify three distinct linear systems:

Original problem: A**x** = **b**
Machine problem: A(I + P)**x**′ = (I + D)**b**
Solved problem: A(I + P)$\bar{\mathbf{x}}$ = (I + D)**b** + **r**

The original problem is the "real-world" problem, the one we actually want to solve in exact arithmetic. The machine problem is the linear system that actually exists inside the computer; there are perturbations P and D (a diagonal matrix) from the original problem. These perturbations might come from reading the numbers a_{ij} and b_i into the computer, or they might come from inherent or experimental uncertainty in these numbers. These latter uncertainties are very large compared with machine round-off errors for many real problems. The solved problem is a further perturbation because of the inadequacies in the machine arithmetic or algorithm for solving the machine problem. The residual vector **r** represents the total effect of these inadequacies.

We wish to estimate $\bar{\mathbf{x}} - \mathbf{x}$, and we have

$$\mathbf{x} = A^{-1}\mathbf{b}$$
$$\mathbf{x}' = (I + P)^{-1}A^{-1}(I + D)\mathbf{b}$$
$$\bar{\mathbf{x}} = (I + P)^{-1}A^{-1}(I + D)\mathbf{b} + (I + P)^{-1}A^{-1}\mathbf{r}$$

As usual, we assume that P, D, and **r** are relatively small. We can thus use the estimate

$$(I + P)^{-1} \sim I - P$$

and obtain

$$\begin{aligned}\bar{\mathbf{x}} &= A^{-1}\mathbf{b} - PA^{-1}\mathbf{b} + A^{-1}D\mathbf{b} + A^{-1}\mathbf{r} - PA^{-1}D\mathbf{b} - PA^{-1}\mathbf{r}\\ &\sim A^{-1}\mathbf{b} - PA^{-1}\mathbf{b} + A^{-1}D\mathbf{b} + A^{-1}\mathbf{r}\end{aligned}$$

Subtracting $\mathbf{x} = A^{-1}\mathbf{b}$ from both sides gives

$$\begin{aligned}\bar{\mathbf{x}} - \mathbf{x} &\sim -PA^{-1}\mathbf{b} + A^{-1}D\mathbf{b} + A^{-1}\mathbf{r}\\ &= -P\mathbf{x} + A^{-1}D\mathbf{b} + A^{-1}\mathbf{r}\end{aligned}$$

and

$$\frac{||\bar{\mathbf{x}} - \mathbf{x}||}{||\mathbf{x}||} \le \frac{||P\mathbf{x}||}{||\mathbf{x}||} + \frac{||A^{-1}D\mathbf{b}||}{||\mathbf{x}||} + \frac{||A^{-1}\mathbf{r}||}{||\mathbf{x}||} \qquad \textbf{Equation 6.6.4}$$

$$\le ||P|| + \frac{||A^{-1}D\mathbf{b}||}{||\mathbf{x}||} + \frac{||A^{-1}\mathbf{r}||}{||\mathbf{x}||}$$

This **composite error estimator** is an extension of the Aird-Lynch condition estimate $||C\mathbf{r}||/||\mathbf{x}||$; two terms have been added to include the effect $||P||$ of perturbing the matrix and $||A^{-1}D\mathbf{b}||/||\mathbf{x}||$ of perturbing the right side.

It is feasible to compute the composite error estimator. The norm of P is a datum item; one either knows the uncertainty in A or assumes p_{ij} is about machine round-off error. One can estimate $||A^{-1}D\mathbf{b}||$ and $||A^{-1}\mathbf{r}||$ rather efficiently, as discussed earlier, without computing A^{-1}.

It is important to note that the composite error estimator is based on the assumption that A is perturbed to $A(I+P)$ with $||P||$ known. One usually estimates $||P||$ from assumption like $|p_{ij}| \le$ EPSA. This is *not the same* as a perturbation of A to A + E where $e_{ij} = \alpha a_{ij}$ and α is a random number with $|\alpha| \le$ EPSA. We see that $P = A^{-1}E$, and thus $||P||$ can be much larger than $||E||$ if A is ill-conditioned. This effect can be observed in practice, and the composite error estimator is not a reliable error estimator for EPSA perturbations in individual elements of A. If such perturbations are present, one should use a **modified composite estimator:**

$$\frac{||\mathbf{x} - \bar{\mathbf{x}}||}{||\mathbf{x}||} \le \frac{||A^{-1}E\mathbf{x}||}{||\mathbf{x}||} + \frac{||A^{-1}D\mathbf{b}||}{||\mathbf{x}||} + \frac{||A^{-1}\mathbf{r}||}{||\mathbf{x}||} \qquad \textbf{Equation 6.6.5}$$

This estimator is more expensive to compute since $||A^{-1}E\mathbf{x}||$ must now be estimated. However, since E is a random matrix, one may estimate $||A^{-1}E\mathbf{x}||$ by solving $A\mathbf{z} = \mathbf{e}$ for several random vectors. This is not completely reliable, but it has a high probability of giving an upper bound on the error.

Comparison of Error Estimators **6.6.F

Several examples are presented with the error estimation methods applied. All computations are carried out on a CDC 6500 machine with about 14.5 decimal digits in the arithmetic.

The 10 by 10 Hilbert Matrix — Example 6.5

The problem $\mathbf{Hx} = \mathbf{b}$ has already been considered in Example 6.2; recall that $h_{ij} = 1/(i+j-1)$, and we take $\mathbf{b} = (1, 0, 0, \ldots, 0)$. The norms for this system are $\|H\| = 2.93$ and $\|H^{-1}\| = 1.21 \times 10^{13}$. The system is solved with the LINPACK programs SGEFA and SGESL to obtain the computed solution

$$\bar{\mathbf{x}} = (100.005711648351, -495.057320082578, \ldots, -924185.572651327)^T$$

This solution has residual norm $\|\mathbf{r}\| = 5.12 \times 10^{-9}$, absolute error $\|\mathbf{x} - \bar{\mathbf{x}}\| = 9.61 \times 10^6$, and relative error $\|\mathbf{x} - \bar{\mathbf{x}}\|/\|\mathbf{x}\| = 2.77 \times 10^{-4}$. The exact values of the first two components of $\bar{\mathbf{x}}$ are 100 and -495.

The three condition numbers, the indicated relative error, and the composite error estimator were computed with the following results. The quantity *digits off* is defined by

$$\log_{10}\left[\frac{\text{estimated relative error}}{\text{actual relative error}}\right]$$

Error Estimation Method	Error Estimate	Digits Off
Actual error	2.77×10^{-4}	—
Standard condition number	1.82×10^5	8.82
Natural condition number	6.43×10^{-3}	1.37
Aird-Lynch estimate	2.69×10^{-4}	-0.01
Indicated relative error	3.03×10^{-3}	1.04
Composite estimate	5.38×10^{-4}	0.29

The 4 by 4 Wilkinson Matrix — Example 6.6

The following matrix is deceptively simple since it is already in lower triangular form. However, it poses severe computational problems.

$$A = \begin{pmatrix} 0.9143 \times 10^{-4} & 0 & 0 & 0 \\ 0.8762 & 0.7156 \times 10^{-4} & 0 & 0 \\ 0.7943 & 0.8143 & 0.9504 \times 10^{-4} & 0 \\ 0.8017 & 0.6123 & 0.7165 & 0.7123 \times 10^{-4} \end{pmatrix}$$

The right side is

$$\mathbf{b} = (0.00009143, 0.87627156, 1.60869504, 2.13057123)^T$$

This makes the true solution of $\mathbf{Ax} = \mathbf{b}$ the vector $(1, 1, 1, 1)^T$. However, a double-precision computation yields

$$\bar{\mathbf{x}} = (1.0, .999999999979416, 1.00000017635355, .998226242846176)^T$$

This difference here is between the machine problem and the real-world problem; just reading A and **b** into the computer in single precision perturbs the solution this much. We have $\|A\| = 2.13$, $\|A^{-1}\| = 1.15 \times 10^{16}$, $\|\mathbf{r}\| = 1.46 \times 10^{-14}$, $\|\mathbf{x} - \bar{\mathbf{x}}\| = .00177$, and $\|\mathbf{x} - \bar{\mathbf{x}}\|/\|\mathbf{x}\| = .00177$. The results of applying the five error estimation methods are given below.

Error Estimation Method	Error Estimate	Digits Off
Actual error	1.77×10^{-3}	—
Standard condition number	1.68×10^2	4.98
Natural condition number	1.68×10^2	4.98
Aird-Lynch estimate	1.78×10^{-7}	-4.00
Indicated relative error	5.04×10^{-7}	-3.55
Composite estimate	8.72×10^{-3}	0.69

The gross underestimate made by the Aird-Lynch estimate is due to the fact that it only considers the accuracy of solving the machine problem. Similarly, the indicated relative error also grossly underestimates the error. In some Fortran environments the residual for this linear system is exactly zero, which gives an indicated relative error of zero regardless of the actual error. The composite error estimator corrects the estimate in this very unusual situation.

A Well-Behaved Example — Example 6.7

The previous two examples are extremely ill-conditioned. The 14 by 14 matrix

$$\begin{pmatrix} A & B \\ C & A \end{pmatrix}$$

where $b_{ij} = a_{8-1,j}$ and

$$A = \begin{pmatrix} 5 & 4 & 7 & 5 & 6 & 7 & 5 \\ 4 & 12 & 8 & 7 & 8 & 8 & 6 \\ 7 & 8 & 10 & 9 & 8 & 7 & 7 \\ 5 & 7 & 9 & 11 & 9 & 7 & 5 \\ 6 & 8 & 8 & 9 & 10 & 8 & 9 \\ 7 & 8 & 7 & 7 & 8 & 10 & 10 \\ 5 & 6 & 7 & 5 & 9 & 10 & 10 \end{pmatrix} \qquad C = \begin{pmatrix} \frac{1}{8} & \frac{1}{9} & \frac{1}{10} & \frac{1}{11} & \frac{1}{12} & \frac{1}{13} & 5 \\ \frac{1}{9} & \frac{1}{10} & \frac{1}{11} & \frac{1}{12} & \frac{1}{13} & 6 & \frac{1}{15} \\ \frac{1}{10} & \frac{1}{11} & \frac{1}{12} & \frac{1}{13} & 7 & \frac{1}{15} & \frac{1}{16} \\ 0 & 0 & 0 & 5 & 0 & 0 & 0 \\ 0 & 0 & 6 & 0 & 0 & 0 & 0 \\ 0 & 7 & 0 & 0 & 0 & 0 & 0 \\ 6 & 0 & 0 & 0 & 0 & 0 & 0 \end{pmatrix}$$

is more ordinary. It has $||A|| = 100$ and $||A^{-1}|| = 13.98$. The right side is chosen so that the true solution is $(1, 1, \ldots 1)^T$. The LINPACK solution has $||\mathbf{r}|| = 2.27 \times 10^{-12}$ and $||\mathbf{x}-\bar{\mathbf{x}}||/||\mathbf{x}|| = 1.45 \times 10^{-12}$.

The results of applying the five error estimation methods are given below.

Error Estimation Method	Error Estimate	Digits Off
Actual error	1.45×10^{-12}	—
Standard condition number	3.18×10^{-11}	1.34
Natural condition number	3.18×10^{-11}	1.34
Aird-Lynch estimate	1.26×10^{-12}	−0.06
Indicated relative error	1.32×10^{-12}	−0.04
Composite estimate	5.26×10^{-12}	0.56

A summary of the performance of four error estimators is given in Table 6.2. The performance observed for Examples 6.5, 6.6, and 6.7 is typical. The conclusion suggested by these performance experiments is that reliable error estimates are difficult to obtain for ill-conditioned systems, but the a posteriori approach of the Aird-Lynch and composite estimators are the best. One can find special ill-conditioned systems to make any of the estimators look bad.

Summary of the Performance of Error Estimators — Table 6.2

The ill-conditioned collection consists of 52 linear systems of moderate to extreme ill-conditioning. The random collections consist of 20 linear systems randomly generated of orders 10 and 25; such systems are very likely to be well-conditioned.

	DIGITS-OFF FOR								
	ILL-CONDITIONED			RANDOM 10 BY 10			RANDOM 25 BY 25		
	Max	Aver.	Min	Max	Aver.	Min	Max	Aver.	Min
Standard	28.5	14.6	3.1	3.4	2.6	1.6	4.4	3.4	2.6
Natural	16.3	7.2	0.8	1.7	1.1	0.5	2.0	1.5	1.1
Aird-Lynch	0.0	−0.3	−4.0	0.1	−0.1	−0.5	0.0	−0.0	−0.3
Composite	12.7	1.2	−0.2	1.1	0.7	0.2	1.0	0.7	0.5

Sensitivity Analysis for Three Linear Systems — Example 6.8

We perturb each of the three preceding problems by 10^{-7} in **b** or in A and b and compute the change in $\bar{\mathbf{x}}$. This change should be about 10^7 times the actually observed error. The results are shown in Table 6.3.

Sensitivity Analysis for Three Linear Systems — Table 6.3

As the number of perturbations is increased, the maximum observed change is taken as the error estimate.

	Number of Perturbations	ESTIMATED ERROR FOR Example 6.4 Hilbert 10 by 10 Matrix	Example 6.5 Wilkinson's 4 by 4 Matrix	Example 6.6 Well-Behaved Matrix
Perturb **b** by 10^{-7}	1	2.7×10^3	1.0×10^5	4.7×10^{-5}
	2	2.7×10^3	1.0×10^5	4.7×10^{-5}
	3	2.7×10^3	1.8×10^5	4.7×10^{-5}
	5	2.7×10^3	1.8×10^5	4.7×10^{-5}
	10	2.7×10^3	1.8×10^5	4.7×10^{-5}
Perturb **b** and A by 10^{-7}	1	4.6×10^3	5.4×10^4	1.3×10^{-5}
	2	3.0×10^4	7.6×10^4	1.3×10^{-5}
	3	3.0×10^4	7.6×10^4	3.1×10^{-5}
	5	3.0×10^4	1.5×10^5	3.1×10^{-5}
	10	3.3×10^4	1.5×10^5	3.4×10^{-5}
Actual error $\times 10^7$		2.8×10^3	1.8×10^4	1.4×10^{-5}

Iterative Improvement for Three Linear Systems — Example 6.9

The three linear systems of Example 6.7 were solved by a library program which does iterative improvement. Table 6.4 shows the results before and after the iterative improvement. An important point is that while the error (of the machine problem) decreases, the residual does not change much.

Iterative Improvement for Three Linear Systems — Table 6.4

These calculations were performed by a Purdue University library routine LINEQ1 modified to give the error and residual before the iterative improvement.

	Example 6.4 Hilbert 10 by 10 Matrix	Example 6.5 Wilkinson's 4 by 4 Matrix	Example 6.6 Well-Behaved Matrix
Original error norm	9.96×10^1	4.74×10^{-7}	4.90×10^{-13}
Final error norm	5.96×10^{-8}	7.10×10^{-15}	7.10×10^{-15}
Original residual norm	3.07×10^{-9}	7.22×10^{-15}	3.91×10^{-13}
Final residual norm	1.67×10^{-9}	5.40×10^{-15}	3.26×10^{-13}
Number of iterations	3	2	2

PROBLEMS 6.6

6.6.1 Perform an operation count for the Cholesky method as implemented in the proof of Theorem 6.3. Show that the work is about half that required for Gauss elimination.

6.6.2 Modify Gauss elimination for $\mathbf{Ax} = \mathbf{b}$ to take advantage of the fact that A is symmetric. Show that the work of the elimination can be cut in half.

6.6.3 Consider Theorem 6.1 and explain:

(A) Its connection with ordinary Gauss elimination

(B) Where pivoting enters

(C) Why it is useful in solving $\mathbf{Ax} = \mathbf{b}$

6.6.4 Assume A is a symmetric positive-definite matrix (that is, $\mathbf{x}^T\mathbf{Ax} > 0$ for all $\mathbf{x} \neq 0$). Show that

(A) A^{-1} is positive-definite

(B) A can be written as LL^T where L is a lower triangular matrix with positive diagonal elements

(C) Gauss elimination without pivoting cannot fail for A.

Hint: Use Problem 6.2.33.

6.6.5 The magnification factor for the growth of round-off error can be shown to be small for certain special matrices. Establish the indicated limit for the following cases:

(A) Tridiagonal magnification factor ≤ 2

(B) A^T is diagonally dominant — magnification factor ≤ 2

(C) Positive-definite — magnification factor ≤ 2.

6.6.6 For each of the linear systems

(i) $3x + 7y = 1$, $.04x + 8y = 24$ (ii) $x + y = 401$, $.01x - 2y = 2$ (iii) $7.5x + 10.5y = 18$, $7x + 10y = 17$

do the following:

(A) Compute the standard and natural condition numbers.

(B) Solve the systems using 3-decimal-digit arithmetic and estimate the accuracy of the computed solution using the natural and standard condition numbers.

(C) Compute the Aird-Lynch error estimate for the solution obtained in B.

(D) Interchange the two equations in each problem and repeat part B without using pivoting.

(E) Compare the error estimates with the actual error.

6.6.7 Consider the linear system with a parameter θ:

$$\begin{aligned} x \cot\theta + y \csc\theta &= b_1 \\ -x \csc\theta - y \cot\theta &= b_2 \end{aligned}$$

(A) Compute the standard condition number of this matrix.

(B) Show that the eigenvalues of the matrix are of size 1.

(C) What values of the parameter θ should cause difficulty for this system? What corresponding values of b_1 and b_2 should make the calculation particularly ill-conditioned? Give a set of specific values for θ, b_1, and b_2.

6.6.8 Various kinds of errors or uncertainty can arise in solving $A\mathbf{x} = \mathbf{b}$, and we have developed a variety of schemes (both backward and forward) to estimate the effect of these uncertainties.

(A) List three such schemes or error estimates developed in this book.

(B) Describe, in two or three sentences, their objectives or use.

(C) Describe, in two or three sentences, their strong and weak points.

(D) Apply the items of part A to the specific problem

$$A\mathbf{x} = \begin{pmatrix} 0.932 & 0.443 \\ 1.237 & 0.587 \end{pmatrix} \quad \mathbf{x} = \begin{pmatrix} 0.699 \\ 3.242 \end{pmatrix}$$

using six-digit computations. **Hint:** In some cases, one or more of the following numbers may be useful to express the results:

$$\begin{aligned} ||A|| \sim 2 \quad ||A^{-1}|| &\sim 2400 \\ {}^{x}\text{True} &= (1131.083869, -2378.038749)^T \\ {}^{x}\text{Computed} &= (1148.01, -2413.66)^T \\ \text{Residual} &= (.006, -.028)^T \end{aligned}$$

6.6.9 Consider the following problem for $A\mathbf{x} = \mathbf{b}$ using 6-decimal-digit arithmetic:

$$\begin{pmatrix} .932165 & .443126 & .417632 \\ .712345 & .915312 & .887652 \\ .632165 & .514217 & .493909 \end{pmatrix} \quad \mathbf{x} = \begin{pmatrix} .876132 \\ .815327 \\ .012345 \end{pmatrix}$$

We have $||A^{-1}||_\infty \sim 1.4E+5$, and the computed solution

$$\bar{\mathbf{x}} = (.495702E+3, -.236728E+5, .240135E+5)^T$$

has residual

$$\mathbf{r} = (.02721797, .07109741, .01931627)^T$$

Carry out the following error analysis of this problem:

(A) Estimate $||\mathbf{x} - \bar{\mathbf{x}}||/||\mathbf{x}||$ by the standard condition number.

(B) Estimate $||\mathbf{x} - \bar{\mathbf{x}}||/||\mathbf{x}||$ by the natural condition number.

(C) Estimate $||\mathbf{x} - \bar{\mathbf{x}}||/||\mathbf{x}||$ by the Aird-Lynch estimate.

(D) Estimate $||\mathbf{x} - \bar{\mathbf{x}}||/||\mathbf{x}||$ by sensitivity analysis.

(E) Compare the errors and estimates of parts A through D with the true error.

6.6.10 In an attempt to solve $A\mathbf{x} = \mathbf{b}$, there was an error $\delta\mathbf{b}$ in $\mathbf{b}$ so that a solution $\mathbf{y}$ to $A\mathbf{y} = (\mathbf{b} + \delta\mathbf{b})$ was actually found. Find an estimate of $||\mathbf{x} - \mathbf{y}||$ in terms of the size of $\delta\mathbf{b}$.

6.6.11 Consider

$$A = \begin{pmatrix} 6 & 13 & -17 \\ 13 & 29 & -38 \\ -17 & -38 & 50 \end{pmatrix} \qquad A^{-1} = \begin{pmatrix} 6 & -4 & -1 \\ -4 & 11 & 7 \\ -1 & 7 & 5 \end{pmatrix}$$

(A) What is the standard condition number of A?

(B) Suppose we attempt to solve $A\mathbf{x} = \mathbf{b}$ and obtain $\bar{\mathbf{x}}$ so that $||\mathbf{b} - A\bar{\mathbf{x}}|| \le 0.01$. How small an upper bound can be given for the absolute error $||\mathbf{x} - \bar{\mathbf{x}}||$?

(C) With the same situation as part B with $||\mathbf{b}|| = 4$, how small an upper bound can be given for the relative error $||\mathbf{x} - \bar{\mathbf{x}}||/||\mathbf{x}||$?

6.6.12 Consider the following linear systems with computed solution $\bar{\mathbf{x}}$ and true solution $\mathbf{x}$. Apply each of the error estimating procedures to estimate the error in $\bar{\mathbf{x}}$: standard condition number, natural condition number, Aird-Lynch estimate, and sensitivity analysis.

(A) $$\begin{pmatrix} 21 & 40 & 82 \\ -11 & 16 & -12 \\ 63.6 & 36 & 177 \end{pmatrix} \quad \mathbf{x} = \begin{pmatrix} 63 \\ -39 \\ 204.6 \end{pmatrix}$$

$$\bar{\mathbf{x}} = (.997, -.998, 1.0025)^T$$
$$\mathbf{x} = (1, -1, 1)^T$$

(B) $$\begin{pmatrix} 1.23 & -4.21 & 6.23 & 1.84 \\ -11.42 & 3.00 & 7.21 & -4.28 \\ 6.31 & 3.16 & 7.32 & -8.29 \\ 2.92 & -3.47 & 2.19 & 2.43 \end{pmatrix} \quad \mathbf{x} = \begin{pmatrix} 3.425 \\ -5.675 \\ 14.115 \\ 2.800 \end{pmatrix}$$

$$\bar{\mathbf{x}} = (1.002, -.002, .5, -.501)^T$$
$$\mathbf{x} = (1, 0, .5, -.5)^T$$

(C) $$\begin{pmatrix} 1043 & -3268 & 629 & -4092 \\ 4211 & -2091 & 1782 & 7604 \\ 3667 & -3828 & 1688 & 2255 \\ 2573 & -3404 & 1234 & 16 \end{pmatrix} \quad \mathbf{x} = \begin{pmatrix} -31203.96 \\ 46691.33 \\ 9410.77 \\ -4601.66 \end{pmatrix}$$

$$\bar{\mathbf{x}} = (1.05, 2.00, -.415, 6.20)^T$$
$$\mathbf{x} = (1.06, 2.03, -.42, 6.21)^T$$

6.6.13 Apply iterative improvement to the linear systems of Problem 6.6.12. Use a hand-held calculator with (at least) 8 digits to compute the "higher-precision" residuals. Otherwise, use the number of digits in the arithmetic that is used in the right side. Show the details of your work.

6.6.14 For a 100 by 100 linear system, state in percentage terms an estimate of the minimum amount of extra computations required for iterative improvement to "verify" that the solution to $A\mathbf{x} - \mathbf{b}$ is correct. Assume that a double-precision operation takes three times as long as the corresponding single-precision operation.

6.6.15 Solve the following system using four digit arithmetic and Algorithm 6.2.1 [the true solution is (2, 3)]:

$$\begin{aligned} 7x_1 + 6.990x_2 &= 34.97 \\ 4x_1 + 4x_2 &= 20.00 \end{aligned}$$

Save the factorization of the coefficient matrix and carry out iterative improvement until it converges. It should take four iterations.

6.6.16 Write a Fortran subprogram that computes the three condition numbers roughly by the methods of Section 6.6.B. Apply these to compute the error estimate based on the round-off expected in your local computer. Use this program to compare the three condition numbers for several ill-conditioned linear systems. **Hint:** Construct problems with known solutions by choosing the solution and substituting it in to find the corresponding right side.

6.6.17 How large can the order of a Hilbert matrix H_n be before all significance is lost in solving $H_n\mathbf{x} = \mathbf{b}$ with your local computer and linear equation solver? Make a plot (called a performance profile) of n versus actual accuracy.

6.6.18 Compute the standard condition number of H_n and make a performance profile (using the results of Problem 6.6.17) of standard condition number versus actual accuracy.

6.6.19 Repeat Problem 6.6.18 with the natural condition number.

6.6.20 Repeat Problem 6.6.18 with the Aird-Lynch estimate, assume the residual **r** is a random vector with size equal to round-off.

6.6.21 Study the effectiveness of sensitivity analysis by making a plot of (estimated error)/(true error) versus number of perturbations of the right side. Use H_6 as the test matrix with $\mathbf{b} = (1, 1, 1, 1, 1, 1)^T$ and perturbations of 10^{-6}.

6.6.22 Repeat Problem 6.6.21 by perturbing both the right side and the matrix.

6.6.23 Suppose that $|e_{ij}| \le |a_{ij}|$ for all i and j and that $||\mathbf{x}||_\infty \le 1$. Show that

$$\max_E ||E\mathbf{x}||$$

occurs for $|e_{ij}| = |a_{ij}|$. **Hint:** Note that the components of Ex are linear functions of each of the variables e_{ij}.

6.6.24 Consider the vector $\mathbf{b} = (2.5, 1.5, 0.05)^T$ and the matrix

$$A = \begin{pmatrix} 2 & 0 & 1 \\ 0 & 1 & 1 \\ 0 & 0 & 0.1 \end{pmatrix}$$

Let **x** be the solution of $A\mathbf{x} = \mathbf{b}$ and E a matrix with $|e_{ij}| \le |a_{ij}|\text{EPSA}$. Show that $||E\mathbf{x}|| \le 2.5$ EPSA. (**Hint:** Use Problem 6.6.23.) Compute both sides of the inequality

$$||A^{-1}E\mathbf{x}|| \le ||A^{-1}||\ ||A||\ ||\mathbf{x}||\text{EPSA}$$

and show that it fails to be sharp by a factor of over 18. That is, no matter how E might be chosen, the right side is at least 18 times larger than the left side.

6.6.25 Consider A, **x**, and **b** of Problem 6.6.24, and change the assumption on E to be $||E|| \le ||A||\text{EPSA}$. Show that then there is always a matrix E so that

$$||A^{-1}E\mathbf{x}|| = ||A^{-1}||\ ||A||\ ||\mathbf{x}||\text{EPSA}$$

Hint: The result is true for any A and **x**. Find a vector **y** with $||\mathbf{y}|| = 1$ so that $||A^{-1}\mathbf{y}|| = ||A^{-1}||$ and then a rotation matrix R with $||R|| = 1$ so that $R\mathbf{x} = ||\mathbf{x}||\mathbf{y}$. Construct E from R.

6.6.26 Design and carry out a small computational experiment to test the suggestion that the condition of a relative perturbation in the matrix is 1. Specifically, take two matrices (one ill-conditioned and one well-conditioned) of order 6, and apply perturbations I+P to these where $||P||$ is small compared to 1 but large compared to the round-off of the computer used. Compute

$$\frac{||\mathbf{x} - \bar{\mathbf{x}}||}{||\mathbf{x}||}$$

and compare it with $||P||$. Repeat for several choices of P.

6.6.27 Take A to be the N by N Hilbert matrix where N is chosen to obtain about 1 digit of accuracy in solving $A\mathbf{x} = \mathbf{b}$ on the computer used. Take EPSA equal to 10 times the round-off on the machine and perturb A by both $A(I+P)$ with $|p_{ij}| \le \text{EPSA}$ and $A+E$ with $|e_{ij}| \le \text{EPSA}$. Take $\mathbf{b} = (1, 1, \ldots, 1)^T$ and solve $A\mathbf{x} = \mathbf{b}$ with and without these perturbations.

(A) Compare the changes in the computed solutions produced by the two different perturbations.

(B) Compare the changes in the computed solution with the error estimates obtained from the corresponding composite estimators.

6.6.28 Do Problem 6.6.24 with the assumption on E changed to

$$\begin{aligned} |e_{ij}| &\le \max_{i,j} |a_{ij}| \times \text{EPSA} && \text{if } |a_{ij}| > 0 \\ &= 0 && \text{if } |a_{ij}| = 0 \end{aligned}$$

Show that the factor is 2.75.

6.6.29 Do Problem 6.6.24 with the assumption on E changed to

$$\begin{aligned} |e_{ij}| &\le ||A|| \times \text{EPSA} && \text{if } |a_{ij}| > 0 \\ &= 0 && \text{if } |a_{ij}| = 0 \end{aligned}$$

Show that the factor is 1.8333.

6.6.30 Consider Wilkinson's 4 by 4 matrix in octal. The matrix of Example 6.5 is changed to, in *octal numbers*,

$$\begin{pmatrix} .3\times 8^{-4} & 0 & 0 & 0 \\ .700 & .2\times 8^{-4} & 0 & 0 \\ .027 & .641 & .3\times 8^{-4} & 0 \\ .632 & .471 & .557 & .2\times 8^{-4} \end{pmatrix}$$

which is, in decimal,

$$\begin{pmatrix} .91552734375\times 10^{-4} & 0 & 0 & 0 \\ .875 & .6103515625\times 10^{-4} & 0 & 0 \\ .974921875 & .814453125 & .91552734375\times 10^{-4} & 0 \\ .80078125 & .611328125 & .716796875 & .6103515625\times 10^{-4} \end{pmatrix}$$

The right side for exact solution $(1, 1, 1, 1)^T$ is

$$\mathbf{b} = (.000091552734375, .87506103515625, 1.789466552734375, 2.21896728515625)^T$$

(A) Repeat the computation of Example 6.5 with this linear system.

(B) Discuss the effect of using this matrix and right side compared with the one in Example 6.5.

(C) Print the matrix and right side of Example 6.5 out of your computer to obtain the machine problem that is solved internally. How much does it differ from the original problem?

6.6.31 To compute $||CA-I||$ for the Aird-Lynch estimate, let $S = CA-I = U^{-1}MA-I$, where $U^{-1}A$ is the factorization of C (approximate A^{-1}). Then $US = MA-U$, MA is very close to U, and the columns $\mathbf{s}_i$ of S can be calculated by solving n systems of equations

$$U\mathbf{s}_i = \mathbf{d}_i\ i = 1, 2, \ldots, n$$

where $\mathbf{d}_i$ is the ith column of $D = MA - U$. Estimate the work to do this, considering the following steps individually: (A) form MA, (B) subtract U, (C) solve the n linear systems, and (D) compute the max norm of S. Show that the total work is $O(n^3)$.

6.6.32 Let λ_i and λ_n be the smallest and largest (in absolute value) eigenvalues of the n by n matrix A.

(A) Show that $||\lambda_n/\lambda_i|| \le ||A||\ ||A^{-1}||$.

(B) The eigenvalues for the matrix A in Problem 6.6.11 are .05888, .2007, and 84.74. How well does the eigenvalue ratio estimate the standard condition number of A using $||A||_\infty||A^{-1}||_\infty$?

(C) Show that $|\lambda_n/\lambda_1| = 1$ for an orthogonal matrix.

(D) Give an example of a matrix with all eigenvalues of absolute value 1 and yet where the condition number is large.

6.6.33 (A) For any matrix P with $||P|| < 1$ show that

$$||(I - P)^{-1}|| \le \frac{1}{1 - ||P||}$$

(B) Apply part A to show that

$$||\bar{x} - x|| \le \frac{||Cr||}{1 - ||CA - I||}$$

if C is a good enough approximate inverse of A so that $||CA - I|| < 1$. The vector **r** is the residual in $A\mathbf{x} - A\bar{\mathbf{x}}$.

(C) Suppose that A is factored into LU, $\bar{\mathbf{x}}$ is computed by Gauss elimination, and the factors are saved. Then what is the approximate inverse C that should be used in B? How would you compute $||Cr||$ efficiently? How would you compute $||CA - I||$ efficiently?

EIGENSYSTEM PROBLEMS AND SOFTWARE 6.7

Eigensystem Problems 6.7.A

Recall from Chapter 1 that an **eigenvector x** of the matrix A satisfies, with $\mathbf{x} \neq 0$,

$$A\mathbf{x} = \lambda\mathbf{x} \qquad \textbf{Equation 6.7.1}$$

The value λ in 6.7.1 is the **eigenvalue** associated with **x**. Normally, an n by n matrix A has n eigenvectors and associated eigenvalues. The principal characteristic of eigenvectors is that if they are taken as basis vectors for the coordinate system, then A is represented as a diagonal matrix. That is, the linear function represented by A has the simplest possible form, and almost all analysis and computations are very easy. Unfortunately, finding these eigenvectors is usually more work than directly solving the problem at hand. Equation 6.7.1 is often rewritten as $(A - \lambda I)\mathbf{x} = 0$, and then the eigenvalues are the values that make $A - \lambda I$ singular. This may be expressed as $\det(A - \lambda i) = 0$, which is frequently used to define eigenvalues. This, unfortunately, suggests the bad idea that one compute eigenvalues by solving this equation.

The **generalized eigenvalue/eigenvector problem** is, given A and B, to find λ and **x** so that

$$A\mathbf{x} = \lambda B\mathbf{x} \qquad \textbf{Equation 6.7.2}$$

We refer to both 6.7.1 and 6.7.2 as **eigensystem problems**.

The theory of eigensystems is delicate and complex, and no attempt is made to present it here. A wide variety of methods is known for attempting to solve eigensystem problems. All the simple ones are unreliable, as are many of the complicated ones. It was not until the mid-1960s that a numerically stable, reasonably efficient method, the **QR algorithm**, was discovered for solving eigensystem problems. This method is fairly simple to write down, but it is difficult to see why it should work and even more difficult to analyze mathematically. A number of polyalgorithms have been developed based on this approach — or variations of it.

No attempt is made to present the details of any of these polyalgorithms. They generally involve the following phases: the first is to transform the matrix A to a simple form (tridiagonal is best, if possible). The second phase is to iterate for the eigenvalues with methods similar to those used for finding polynomial roots. The third and simplest is to solve the linear system 6.7.1 for the components of **x** once λ is known. Transforming the matrix A is more difficult here than for solving $A\mathbf{x} = \mathbf{b}$ because the transformation must leave the eigenvalues of A unchanged. This requires more complicated methods than used in Gauss elimination.

The relationship of the second phase with finding roots of polynomials is suggested by examining the polynomial

$$p(x) = x^n - a_n x^{n-1} - \dots - a_2 x - a_1$$

and its **companion matrix**

$$P = \begin{pmatrix} 0 & 1 & 0 & 0 & \dots & 0 \\ 0 & 0 & 1 & 0 & \dots & 0 \\ 0 & 0 & 0 & 1 & \dots & 0 \\ \vdots & & & & & \vdots \\ a_1 & a_2 & a_3 & a_4 & \dots & a_n \end{pmatrix}$$

It is to be shown in Problem 6.7.1 that the zeros of p(x) are the eigenvalues of P. Thus, if A were transformed into this special form, then one could read off the polynomial coefficients and apply a polynomial root finder. It turns out to be better to transform to a more general form such as **Hessenberg form** ($a_{ij} = 0$ for $i < j-1$ or $a_{ij} = 0$ for $i > j+1$) or tridiagonal form ($a_{ij} = 0$ for $|i-j| > 1$).

ACM Algorithms and EISPACK 6.7.B

There are 18 ACM Algorithms for eigensystem problems. The early algorithms (numbers 85, 104, 122, 183, 253, 254, 270, 297, 343, 384, 405, and 464) have either been superceded or substantially incorporated into EISPACK or the IMSL library. There are three recent ACM Algorithms (numbers 496, 535, and 538) for cases of the generalized eigensystem problem 6.7.2; a version of Algorithm 496 for complex matrices and a real version of it are in the IMSL library. Algorithm 506 is an improvement of one of the basic modules (HQR3) of EISPACK, and Algorithm 530 takes advantage of skew-symmetry in the matrix A (that is, $a_{ij} = -a_{ij}$). Finally, Algorithm 517 estimates the condition number of the eigenvalues of a matrix; this type of facility is not present in EISPACK or the IMSL library.

EISPACK is a collection of 52 Fortran programs for solving eigensystem problems. This is a "systematized collection" in the sense that the basic procedures needed in eigensystem computations have been identified and implemented as separate modules. One can then use these building blocks to construct all kinds of methods for particular cases (e.g., real or complex elements, symmetric or general or tridiagonal matrices, etc.), but still a certain level of expertise is needed to construct methods. The EISPACK guide presents 22 "basic paths" of recommended ways to combine modules to solve 22 common eigensystem problems.

There are four driver programs for the most common cases:

RG — Eigenvalues and, optionally, eigenvectors of a real general matrix

RS — Version of RG for symmetric matrices

CG — Eigenvalues and, optionally, eigenvectors of a complex general matrix

CH — Version of CG for Hermitian matrices

The calling sequences for RG and RS are

```
CALL RG( KDIMA,N,A,EIGVR,EIGVI,MATZ,EIGVEC,IWORK,RWORK,IER )
CALL RS( KDIMA,N,A,EIGVR,MATZ,EIGVEC,RWORK1,RWORK2,IER )
```

where the arguments are:

A	Matrix.
KDIMA	Declared row dimension of A (and EIGVEC if used).
N	Order of A.
EIGVR,EIGVI	Real and imaginary parts of the eigenvalues of A. Vectors of length N. EIGVI ≡ 0 for symmetric matrices.
MATZ	Switch to request eigenvectors be computed. = 0 (no eigenvectors).
EIGVEC	Matrix containing the eigenvectors. If the jth eigenvalue is real, then so is its eigenvector, and that is in the jth column of EIGVEC. If the jth eigenvalue is complex, then the real and complex parts of its eigenvector are in columns j and j+1. In the second case the (j+1)th eigenvalue is the complex conjugate of the jth, and its eigenvector is also the complex conjugate of the jth and hence not explicitly given in the matrix EIGVEC.
IWORK,RWORK,RWORK1,RWORK2	Workspace vectors of length N or more.

IER Error flag.
= 0 (no error).
= K < N (index of eigenvalue where method failed).
= K > N (indicates N >KDIMA).

There is a driver program for IBM machines called EISPAC which allows the eigensystem problem to be described in terms of keywords, and it selects the combination of EISPACK programs to solve the problem.

The basic reference for EISPACK is *Matrix Eigensystem Routines — EISPACK Guide* by B. T. Smith, J. M. Boyle, J. J. Dongarra, B. S. Garbow, U. Ikebe, V. C. Klema, and C. B. Moler, Springer-Verlag Lecture Notes in Computer Science 6, Second Edition, New York, 1976. This software package is available for a nominal charge from either (1) National Energy Software Center, Argonne National Laboratory, Argonne, Illinois 60439 or (2) IMSL, Inc., NBC Building, Sixth Floor, 7500 Bellaire Blvd., Houston, Texas 77036.

IMSL Software 6.7.C

The IMSL library has 8 driver programs for the more common eigensystem problems that are built from a set of 25 basic programs. The organization and selection of these 25 programs are similar in spirit and design to EISPACK. The first four drivers correspond exactly to RG, RS, CG, and CH of EISPACK, the fifth is for band symmetric matrices, and the last three are for the generalized eigensystem problems. These programs are:

EIGRF — Real
EIGRS — Real Symmetric
EIGCC — Complex
EIGCH — Complex Hermitian
EIGBS — Band symmetric
EIGZF — Real, generalized
EIGZC — Complex, generalized
EIGZS — Real symmetric, generalized

The programs EIGZF and EIGZC are versions of ACM Algorithm 496.

The use of these programs is illustrated by the calling sequences for EIGRF and EIGRS, which are

```
CALL EIGRF( A,N,KDIMA,IJOB,EIGVAL,EIGVEC,KDIME,WORK,IER )
CALL EIGRS( A,N,KJOB,EIGVAL,EIGVEC,KDIME,WORK,IER )
```

where the arguments are:

A Matrix.

N Order of A.

KDIMA Declared row dimension of A.

EIGVAL Vector of eigenvalues of length N, complex for RF and real for RS.

IJOB Switch to request eigenvectors.
= 0 (eigenvalues only).
= 1 (eigenvalues and vectors).
= 2 (eigenvalues, vectors, and "performance" index).
= 3 ("performance" index).

KJOB Switch to specify storage mode and request eigenvectors. IJOB = MOD (KJOB,10) is the switch defined above. If IJOB = KJOB, then A is in symmetric storage mode; otherwise, A is symmetric but in full storage mode with declared row dimension N (that is, it must have N = KDIMA).

EIGVEC Matrix of eigenvectors with jth eigenvector in column j, complex for RF and real for RS. EIGVEC is used as a 1-dimensional real vector by EIGRF which may require EIGVEC to be equivalenced to a real vector of length $2N^2$.

KDIME Declared row dimension of EIGVEC.

WORK Workspace, length = N for IJOB = 0, = N or 2N for IJOB = 1, = N (N + 2) or N + N (N + 1)/2 for IJOB = 2.

IER Error flag.

The PROTRAN eigensystem statement is of the following form.

```
$EIGSYS A*X = VALUE*X; NOVECTORS
```

This form computes the eigenvalues and places them in the vector VALUE. The other options are illustrated below.

```
$EIGSYS A*X = VALUE*X
$EIGSYS A*EIGVEC = LAMBDA*EIGVEC; ORDER=N+1; SYMMETRIC
$EIGSYS A*X = VAL*X; NOSAVE; HERMITIAN
```

Unless NOVECTORS is given, the eigenvectors are computed and then the variable X must be declared a matrix of appropriate size and type; otherwise the variable for the vectors is an unused dummy.

The following example illustrates the use of IMSL software to solve eigensystem problems.

Eigensystem Computations — Example 6.10

The following PROTRAN program computes the eigenvalues of two real matrices A and P and the eigenvalues and vectors of a complex matrix Z. Note that the eigenvalues of A and P are complex so that complex vectors must be used. The matrix P is the companion matrix of the polynomial

$$P(x) = x^6 - 8x^5 + 7.3x^4 + 8.6x^3 - 12x^2 + 84x - 16.8$$

and the DO 10 loop places these coefficients (in reverse order) in the bottom row of P after P is initialized to be zero.

```
      $DECLARATIONS
      REAL MATRIX   A(6,6),P(6,6)
      COMPLEX MATRIX Z(4,4),EIGVZ(4,4)
      COMPLEX VECTOR  EIGA(6),EIGB(6),EIGZ(4),PROOTS(6)
      VECTOR  POLY(7)
C                DEFINE PROBLEMS
      $ASSIGN A = (-41., 55.,  4.,  3.,  2., 51.)
     +            (- 2., 10., 55.,  4.,  3.,  2.)
     +            (- 3.,  0., 10., 55.,  4.,  3.)
     +            (-55.,  0.,  0.,  0., 10., 55.)
     +            (-51., 55.,  4.,  3.,  2., 61.)
      $ASSIGN Z = (  (1.,2.), (2.,1.), (.5,.2), (.7,1.8) )
     +            (  (0.,1.), (3.,2.), (5.,0.), (.3,-.3) )
     +            (  (1.,2.), (0.,.4), (4.,1.), (.9,-4.) )
     +            ( (.2, .8), (1.,4.), (.9,.8), (.8,3.6) )
      $ASSIGN P(I,J) = 0.0
      $ASSIGN POLY = ( 1., -8., 7.3, 8.6, -12., 84., -16.8 ) $
C
C                MAKE P THE COMPANION OF POLY
      DO 10 I = 1,6
         P(6,I) = - POLY(8-I)
         IF( I .GT. 1 ) P(I-1,I) = 1.0
   10 CONTINUE
C             COMPUTE EIGENVALUES OF A,Z,P + EIGENVECTORS OF Z
      $EIGSYS A*V = EIGA*V; NOVECTORS
      $EIGSYS Z*EIGVZ = EIGZ*EIGVZ
      $EIGSYS P*V = EIGP*V; NOVECTORS
      $PRINT EIGA, EIGZ, EIGVZ, EIGP
C
C          CHECK EIGENVALUES OF P WITH ROOTS OF POLYNOMIAL
      $POLYNOMIAL POLY ; ROOTS = PROOTS
      $PRINT PROOTS
      $END
```

The same computation is repeated below in Fortran using the IMSL library. The output is also given, primarily to show the eigenvalues of A. The true eigenvalues are all 10, but the computed eigenvalues differ by about 2 percent. These computations were done with a CDC 6500 using more than 14-decimal-digit arithmetic. The matrix A is very ill-conditioned with respect to its eigenvalues. This example illustrates the fact that conditioning is defined with respect to a particular computation. The matrix A is not particularly ill-conditioned for solving A**x** = **b**, but it is for the eigenvalue problem A**x** = λ**x**.

```
C         EIGENSYSTEM COMPUTATIONS WITH IMSL LIBRARY SOFTWARE
      REAL A(6,6), P(6,6), POLY(7), WORK(10)
      COMPLEX Z(4,4), EIGVZ(4,4), EIGA(6), EIGZ(4), EIGP(6), PROOTS(6)
C              INITIALIZE COMPUTATION WITH DATA STATEMENTS
      DATA ((A(I,J),J=1,6),I=1,6) /
     A             -41., 55.,  4.,  3.,  2., 51.,
     B             - 2., 10., 55.,  4.,  3.,  2.,
     C             - 3.,  0., 10., 55.,  4.,  3.,
     D             - 4.,  0.,  0., 10., 55.,  4.,
     E             -55.,  0.,  0.,  0., 10., 55.,
     F             -51., 55.,  4.,  3.,  2., 61./
      DATA ((Z(I,J),J=1,4),I=1,4) /
     A              (1.,2.), (2.,1.), (.5,.2), (.7,1.8),
     B              (0.,1.), (3.,2.), (5.,0.), (.3,-.3),
     C              (1.,2.), (0.,.4), (4.,1.), (.9,-4.),
     D              (.2,.8), (1.,4.), (.9,.8), (.8,3.6) /
      DATA P / 36*0.0 /
      DATA     POLY /   1., -8., 7.3, 8.6, -12., 84., -16.8 /
C
C
C                   MAKE P THE COMPANION MATRIX OF POLY
      DO 10 I = 1,6
          P(6,1) = - POLY(8-I)
          IF( I .GT. 1 ) P(I-1) = 1.0
   10 CONTINUE
C                     REAL MATRIX A - EIGRF
C         ALL EIGENVALUES ARE 10, ILL-CONDITIONED EIGENVALUE PROBLEM
      CALL EIGRF(A,6,6,0,EIGA,DUMMY,1,WORK,IER)
      PRINT 20, EIGA
   20     FORMAT(//8X,'EIGENVALUES = '   /(3(3X,2F13.8)))
C
C                   COMPLEX - EIGCC
      CALL EIGCC( Z,4,4,1,EIGZ,EIGVZ,4,WORK,IER)
      PRINT 20, EIGZ
      PRINT 30, EIGVZ
   30     FORMAT(8X,'EIGENVECTORS = '/ ( 4(F14.7,F11.7)))
C
C                    REAL MATRIX P - EIGRF
      CALL EIGRF( P,6,6,0,EIGP,DUMMY,1,WORK,IER)
      PRINT 20, EIGP
C
C                   POLYNOMIAL ROOTS
C          CHECK EIGENVALUES OF P WITH ROOTS OF POLYNOMIAL POLY
      CALL ZRPOLY( POLY,6, PROOTS,IER)
      PRINT 40, PROOTS
   40     FORMAT(///8X,'POLYNOMIAL ROOTS ='/ (3(3X,2F13.8)))
      STOP
      END
```

```
     EIGENVALUES =
10.24712530           0     10.12355433    .21401974     10.12355433   -.21401974
 9.87643227   .21399650      9.87643227  -.21399650      9.75290149            0


     EIGENVALUES =
 7.29783603  2.49029143       .55030543  -1.48360821      1.03428113   2.04938863
 -.08242259  5.54392814


     EIGENVECTORS =
  .2110210   .2608015     .9523085  -.0763384     .8245542  -.0485157     .1632472   .7311678
  .6427176  -.1890234    -.0820943 -1.7900898   -1.3319313   .7597720     .3436453  1.1089127
 -.2062490   .4042096    -.0008159  -.1555545     .0690910   .0989909     .0850173   .1417866
  .0148069  -.3539776     .2263356  -.0673360    -.1579783   .2374960     .2824957  -.3595432


     EIGENVALUES =
 6.72364498           0      2.50185253            0     -1.79017234            0
  .17983654  1.63983124       .17983654  -1.63983124       .20500174            0


     POLYNOMIAL ROOTS =
  .20500174           0     -1.79017234            0       .17983654   1.63983124
  .17983654 -1.63983124      2.50185253            0      6.72364498            0
```

PROBLEMS 6.7

6.7.1 Show that the roots of the polynomial p(x) are the eigenvalues of the companion matrix P of p(x). **Hint:** If $P\mathbf{x} = r\mathbf{x}$, then $P^k\mathbf{x} = r^k\mathbf{x}$. Show directly from the form of P that

$$P^n\mathbf{x} = \sum_{i=0}^{n-1} a_i P^i \mathbf{x}$$

for any vector $\mathbf{x}$. Hence for an eigenvector we have $P^n\mathbf{x} - \Sigma a_i P^i \mathbf{x} = (r^n - \Sigma a_i r^i)\mathbf{x} = p(r)\mathbf{x} = 0$, and since $\mathbf{x} \neq 0$, we have $p(r) = 0$.

REFERENCES

James R. Bunch and Donald J. Rose (eds.), *Sparse Matrix Computations,* Academic Press, Inc., New York (1976).

B. S. Garbow et al., *Matrix Eigensystems Routines — EISPACK Guide,* Lecture Notes in Computer Science No. 51, Springer-Verlag, New York (1976).

L. A. Hageman and D. M. Young, *Applied Iterative Methods,* Academic Press, Inc., New York (1981).

John R. Rice, *Matrix Computations and Mathematical Software,* McGraw-Hill Book Company, New York (1981).

G. W. Stewart, *Introduction to Matrix Computations,* Academic Press, Inc., New York (1973).

7

DIFFERENTIATION AND INTEGRATION

Derivatives and integrals are the basic tools of calculus and appear in many mathematical models. This chapter presents the methods, software, and analysis to handle them in numerical computation. It is uncommon for the calculation of a derivative or integral to be the primary objective of a numerical computation, but they appear frequently as subproblems, and the derivation of methods for more complex problems often involves evaluating them. For example, after one has solved a differential equation for the pressure in a gas, one often needs to numerically integrate the pressure to obtain the total force exerted by the gas. Or, after one has processed radar data to obtain the trajectory of a satellite, one might need to numerically differentiate the position coordinates to obtain velocity estimates.

Derivatives and integrals are also very useful as topics for teaching about numerical computation and analysis. They are easily understood, one can present intuitive or pictorial motivations, the algebra is usually not too messy, and yet their calculation is not trivial.

METHODS FOR ESTIMATING DERIVATIVES 7.1

Derivatives have been studied in earlier chapters; Example 4.3 gives a detailed development of the 3-point formula for derivatives:

$$f'(x_0) \sim \frac{2x_0 - (x_2+x_3)}{(x_1-x_2)(x_1-x_3)} f(x_1) + \frac{2x_0-(x_1+x_3)}{(x_2-x_1)(x_2-x_3)} f(x_2) + \frac{2x_0 - (x_1+x_2)}{(x_3-x_1)(x_3-x_2)} f(x_3) \qquad \textbf{Equation 7.1.1}$$

and Equation 4.5.11 shows the error in this formula to be $O(h^2)$ where $h = \max(x_i - x_0)$. A more precise error estimate $h^2||f'''||/6$ is given in Example 5.9 as an application of Theorem 5.7 (here $x_0 = x_2, x_1-x_2 = x_2-x_3 = -h$). Furthermore, the divided differences of Chapter 5 give a systematic approach to computing derivative estimates based on polynomial models. So, the thing left to do is to develop some interesting examples from this material and to look more carefully for superaccurate formulas (one is mentioned already in Example 5.9).

Finite Differences 7.1.A

The formulas for estimating derivatives using polynomial models are called **finite difference formulas.** The four "variables" in these formulas are: (1) the polynomial degree, (2) the point where the derivative is estimated, (3) the order of the derivative (first, second, . . .), and (4) function values to use in these formulas. One sees there is a tremendous number of possibilities here, and so one uses divided difference techniques except for special, simple cases. These special simple cases are: (1) low-order polynomial degree, (2) estimate derivative at the left, right, or middle point used for function values, (3) low-order derivative, and (4) equally spaced points for function values. Thus, we consider estimating the mth derivative ($m = 1, 2$, or 3) using an nth-degree polynomial model ($n = m, m+1$) with the function values. . ., $f(-2h)$, $f(-h)$, $f(0)$, $f(h)$, $f(2h)$,. . . . The **central differences** correspond to estimates at 0; the common formulas are

$$f'(0) \sim \frac{f(h) - f(-h)}{2h} \qquad \textbf{Equation 7.1.2}$$

$$f''(0) \sim \frac{f(h) - 2f(0) + f(-h)}{h^2} \qquad \textbf{Equation 7.1.3}$$

$$f'''(0) \sim \frac{f(2h) - 2f(h) + 2f(-h) - f(-2h)}{2h^3} \qquad \textbf{Equation 7.1.4}$$

These formulas can be used for $x \neq 0$ simply by shifting the origin so that $0 \rightarrow x$, $h \rightarrow x+h$, and so on. The simplest **backward differences** are

$$f'(0) \sim \frac{f(h) - f(0)}{h} \qquad \textbf{Equation 7.1.5}$$

$$f'(0) \sim \frac{-3f(0) + 4f(h) - f(2h)}{2h} \qquad \textbf{Equation 7.1.6}$$

$$f'(0) \sim \frac{-11f(0) + 18f(h) - 9f(2h) + 2f(3h)}{6h} \qquad \textbf{Equation 7.1.7}$$

$$f''(0) \sim \frac{f(0) - 2f(h) + f(2h)}{h^2} \qquad \textbf{Equation 7.1.8}$$

There are similar **forward difference** formulas. Equation 7.1.5 uses linear polynomials as the model, while Equation 7.1.7 uses cubics.

The central differences are symmetric, and thus there is a good chance of obtaining superaccurate formulas. The kth derivative of x^n is zero at $x = 0$ for $n > 0$ if $k \neq n$, and so a symmetric formula (like 7.1.3) is exact for *all* odd-degree polynomials, and an antisymmetric formula (like 7.1.2 and 7.1.4) is exact for *all* even-degree polynomials. Thus, the **central differences formulas are superaccurate;** each is exact for one higher power of x than one expects from counting the number of coefficients available.

It is simple to derive finite difference formulas; it is less simple to know how to choose h. If f(x) is a tabulated function, one has little choice. There are formulas which simultaneously smooth and estimate derivatives mentioned in Chapter 11 which one might consider. If f(x) is known everywhere, then there is the danger of choosing h too large and having large errors because of an inadequate model. Or one can choose h too small (see Figure 3.2) and have large errors because of round-off (see the discussion at the end of Section 7.3).

Other Models for Discrete Data 7.1.B

Finite differences or divided differences are sometimes unsatisfactory for tabulated data because one cannot make h small enough. An alternative is to use a smooth, mathematical model on a larger piece of the data set, then differentiate that. Using higher-degree polynomials is usually not satisfactory because they are prone to oscillate too much. Splines are better models, and the simplest approach is to:

1. Interpolate the data by a spline
2. Differentiate the spline

This is usually satisfactory if the data is smooth, i.e., not contaminated by random errors. If random errors are present, then smoothing must be applied before estimating the derivative.

PROBLEMS 7.1

7.1.1 Verify that Equation 7.1.4 is exact for polynomials of degree 4 or less.

7.1.2 Derive a fourth-derivative central difference formula using fourth-degree polynomials as models. **Hint:** Use symmetry to make formulas exact for all odd-degree polynomials.

7.1.3 Carry out experiments to verify that the order of the formulas is as given below:

(A) 7.1.2 is $O(h^2)$

(B) 7.1.3 is $O(h^2)$

(C) 7.1.4 is $O(h^2)$

(D) 7.1.5 is $O(h)$

(E) 7.1.6 is $O(h^2)$

(F) 7.1.7 is $O(h^3)$

(G) 7.1.8 is $O(h)$

7.1.4 Explain why the central and backward difference formulas 7.1.3 and 7.1.8 are the same. Explain why their orders of accuracy are different.

7.1.5 Equations 7.1.3 and 7.1.6 both give $O(h^2)$ estimates of the first derivative. Carry out an experiment to see if one is actually more accurate than the other; test them for a variety of values of h to estimate $f'(0)$, $f'(1)$, and $f'(10)$ for the functions e^x, $\sin(2x)$, x^4, and $1/(1+x^2)$.

SOFTWARE FOR DIFFERENTIATION 7.2

Difference formulas are so simple that there are no packaged subprograms for simple finite differences. The only ACM algorithm for differentiation is 79, which generates central difference formulas like 7.1.2 to 7.1.4. This is convenient if one needs an 8- or 12-point formula (note that the accuracy of Algorithm 79 becomes delicate as the order of the derivative increases). The PROTRAN system allows one to differentiate an expression or a set of Fortran statements as follows:

```
$DERIVATIVE  EXP(X*SIN(X**2)-COS(X**3)); D(X) ; IS EPRIME ; AT XONE
$DERIVATIVE F(X) ; D(X) ; IS FSECOND ; AT PTS50
                         ORDER = 2 ; ERRTARGET = 0.0001
$DERIVATIVE FCOMPLX ; D(T) ; IS FPRIME ;  AT TPTS ; DEFINE
     ====
     Z = SQRT(T**T+1.)
     Y = COS( Z + A/Z)
     SUM = 0.0
     DO 50    I = 1,8
        SUM = SUM + (T+1.)*Y**(I+1)/Z**(I+T)
50 CONTINUE
   FCOMPLX = T*SUM**2
   ====
```

The expression (or function name) is given; D(X) indicates that differentiate is with respect to X (or the variable named). This PROTRAN statement uses the IMSL library routine DRVTE which estimates first, second, or third derivatives. PROTRAN only allows first or second (indicated by setting ORDER = 2).

The IMSL routine DRVTE has the form

```
FUNCTION DRVTE(F, NORDER, X, HSTART, ERRTAR, IER)
```

where F = name of function in form FUNCTION F(one argument)

NORDER = order of derivative, 1 to 3 allowed

X = point where derivative is estimated

HSTART = initial step size for finite difference method

ERRTAR = relative error target for the estimate

For tabulated data (XPTS(I), DATA(I), I = 1, 2, . . .), PROTRAN provides

```
$DERIVA, DATA; VS XPTS; IS DXDATA ; ORDER = 2
                    AT EQUIX
```

This PROTRAN statement evaluates the second derivative at the points in the vector EQUIX instead of at the XPTS values. The IMSL library routine ICSCCU is used to create a cubic spline interpolant of the data, and then the spline's derivatives are found using DCSEVU. These values are returned as components of vectors.

PROBLEMS 7.2

7.2.1 Consider the data in Problem 5.2.3(E). Estimate the first and second derivatives of the function at t = 10, 20, and 80 using finite differences. Interpolate the data by a cubic spline and use its derivatives to estimate the same values. **Hint:** Use the IMSL library routines ICSCCU and DCSEVU for the second part.

7.2.2 Consider the data in Problem 5.2.3(F). Estimate the first, second, and third derivatives of the function at t = 272 and 350 using divided differences. Interpolate the data by a cubic spline and use its derivative to estimate the same values. See the hint for Problem 7.2.1.

7.2.3 Repeat Problem 7.2.2 for the data in Problem 5.2.3(C) and use x = 1.0. Compare the results with the true values.

7.2.4 Randomly perturb the data in Problem 7.2.3 by 10 percent, .1 percent, and .001 percent, and repeat the calculation. Give the conclusions you draw about the effect of noise (random errors) on the estimation of derivatives.

7.2.5 Write a Fortran program that carries out the computation for the PROTRAN-like statement

```
DIFFERENTIATE DATA (X,Y), AT Z, ORDER=1 TO K
```

Here X and Y are given vectors of known length, K is given, and the program is to estimate all the derivatives of order 1 through K. The method to be used is:

1. Locate Z in the table of X-values (assume this table is ordered).
2. Generate a divided difference table of (X, Y), centered on Z as much as possible.
3. Generate the Newton interpolation polynomials of degree K and evaluate their derivatives at Z.
4. Print the results in a nice format.

7.2.6 Verify that the following are central difference approximations to the indicated derivatives; determine the degree of the polynomial model for each.

(A) $f^{(4)}(0) \sim \dfrac{f(-2h) - 4f(-h) + 6f(0) - 4f(h) + f(2h)}{h^4}$

(B) $f^{(5)}(0) \sim$

$$\frac{-f(-3h) + 4f(-2h) - 5f(-h) + 5f(h) - 4f(2h) + f(3h)}{2h^5}$$

(C) $f''(0) \sim \dfrac{-5f(-2h) + 80f(h) - 150f(0) + 80f(h) - 5f(2h)}{60h^2}$

(D) $f'(0) \sim \dfrac{2f(-2h) - 16f(-h) + 16f(h) - 2f(2h)}{24h}$

7.2.7 Finite difference formulas may be used to **check tables for errors.** The idea is that a small error in a table will have a large effect on the differences (derivatives of the tabulated function). The following is a list of values of a certain smooth function for x = 0, .1, .2, . . ., 1.0. There is an error in one value between .2 and .8. Use central difference formulas for f'', f''', and $f^{(4)}$ to locate the error. Which is the most effective? Explain how using more than one formula helps in locating the error.

.5403023, .4964681, .4489817, .3976572, .3424281, .2828565, .2191444, .1511473, .078896, .00224841, −.0778461

Hint: Use the formula in Problem 7.2.6 for the fourth derivative estimate.

7.2.8 Divided differences are also effective to check tables for errors. One computes the table of divided differences and checks for large differences appearing suddenly. This approach does not need equally spaced points like the approach in Problem 7.2.7. The following table has two "bad" values in it. Write a Fortran program to compute its divided difference table and locate the two bad values.

x	f(x)	x	f(x)	x	f(x)
0	0	3.2	.192979	6.0	.152051
.3	.112378	3.7	.183838	6.4	.147922
.5	.156421	4.0	.178751	6.7	.145027
.8	.194499	4.1	.177124	7.1	.141409
1.0	.207910	4.4	.172450	7.3	.139698
1.7	.218553	4.9	.165309	7.7	.136442
1.9	.216612	5.1	.162664	8.1	.133401
2.0	.215969	5.4	.158903	8.3	.131952
2.3	.210323	5.6	.155524	8.5	.130549
2.9	.198777	5.9	.153136	8.9	.127870

Hint: The error should propagate a triangle of large differences that point to the bad values.

7.2.9 The following two functions are the same:

```
FA(X) = 1.+2.*X+(X-9.)**5
FB(X) = -59048.+32807.*X-7290.*X**2+810.*X**3-
45.*X**4+X**5
```

Apply central difference formulas 7.1.2 and 7.1.3 to them to compute estimates of the first and second derivatives at x = 9.1. Use values 1, .01, .0001, and .000001 for h. Compare the estimates with the true values. State conclusions about the effect on differences of numerical instability in evaluating a function.

7.2.10 Determine the coefficients c_i of the difference formula of the form

$$f'(a) \sim c_1 f(a-h) + c_2 f(a) + c_3 f(a+2h)$$

which is exact for quadratic polynomials.

ERROR ANALYSIS FOR DIFFERENTIATION 7.3

Let D_C^k, D_B^k, and D_F^k denote, respectively, the finite difference operators:

$D_C^k f(x)$ = central difference approximation to kth derivative with $k+1$ points
$D_B^k f(x)$, $D_F^k f(x)$ = backward and forward difference approximation to kth derivative with $k+2$ points

We see that

$$||D_C^k||,\ ||D_B^k||,\ ||D_F^k|| = \frac{\text{constant}}{h^k}$$ **Equation 7.3.1**

where the constant depends on k and the type of difference approximation. The order of the error of these difference approximations is found from Theorems 5.6 and 5.7.

Theorem 7.1 *Let $f(x)$ have $k+2$ continuous derivatives. The approximation $D_C^k f(x)$ to $f^{(k)}(x)$ is superaccurate (exact for polynomials of degree $k+1$) and the error is*

$$C||f^{(k+2)}||h^2 = O(h^2)$$

where C is a constant independent of h.

Proof: The central difference formula is exact for polynomials of degree k by construction. Since the points of the formula are symmetrically placed about x_0, it easily follows that the formula is symmetric [coefficients of $f(x_0+ih)$ and $f(x_0-ih)$ are the same] if k is even and anti-symmetric [coefficients of $f(x_0+ih)$ and $f(x_0-ih)$ have opposite signs and the same absolute values] if k is odd. But for k even

$$D_C^k(x-x_0)^{k+1} = 0$$

by the symmetry. The kth derivative of $(x-x_0)^{k+1}$ is also zero at $x = x_0$, and so the formula is exact for polynomials of degree $k+1$. A similar argument holds for k odd.

Consider the error operator $L(f) = D_C^k f(x) - f^{(k)}(x)$. The norm of L is $Ch^{-k} + ||f^{(k)}||$. Note that the norm of $f^{(k)}(x)$ is just a fixed number here since f and x are fixed; only h is changing. From Theorem 5.6 (the change of interval only changes the constant) we have that $E_{k+1}(f) \le h^{k+2}||f^{(k+2)}||/(k+2)!$ and the application of Theorem 5.7 gives

$$||L(f)|| \le (Ch^{-k} + ||f^{(k)}||)(h^{k+2}||f^{(k+2)}||/(k+2)!)$$

This is equivalent to the conclusion stated and concludes the proof.

Theorem 7.2 *Let $f(x)$ have $k+1$ continuous derivatives. The approximations $D_B^k f(x)$ and $D_F^k f(x)$ to $f^{(k)}(x)$ have errors*

$$C||f^{(k+1)}||h = O(h)$$

where C is a constant independent of h.

Proof: The error operator $L = D_B^k f(x) - f^{(k)}(x)$ has norm $Ch^{-k} + ||f^{(k)}||$. The approximation is exact for polynomials of degree k and $||E_k(f)|| \le h^{k+1}||f^{(k+1)}||/(k+1)!$ from Theorem 5.6. The application of Theorem 5.7 gives

$$||L(f)|| \le (Ch^{-k} + ||f^{(k)}||)(h^{k+1}||f^{(k+1)}||/(k+1)!)$$

This is equivalent to the conclusion stated and concludes the proof.

Optimal h for Difference Formulas — Example 7.1

Figure 3.2 shows how the truncation error of the difference formulas interacts with the round-off error to limit the accuracy possible with such formulas. This leads us to consider the optimal h for difference formulas. To analyze this, let ϵ be the round-off, say one ulp; then the round-off error is about ϵ times the norm of the difference formula. On the other hand, the truncation error of the difference formulas is given in Theorems 7.1 and 7.2. A value of h is said to be optimal when these two errors are equal. The round-off error is constant $\times \epsilon/h^k$, where the constant is the sum of the coefficients in the difference formulas. From Theorem 7.1 we have the truncation error for central differences; the optimal value for h must satisfy

$$\frac{\text{constant} \times \epsilon}{h^k} = \text{constant } ||f^{(k+2)}||h^2 \qquad \textbf{Equation 7.3.2}$$

This condition is optimal in the sense that the error bounds are equal; a slightly different value of h might give the best result for a particular f(x).

Examination of the proof of Theorem 7.1 shows that the constant on the right of 7.3.2 is just the one on the left divided by (k + 2)!. Let h_c denote the optimal value of h for central differences and solve 7.3.2 to obtain

$$h_c = \sqrt[k+2]{\frac{\epsilon(k+2)!}{||f^{(k+2)}||}} \qquad \textbf{Equation 7.3.3}$$

One needs $||f^{(k+2)}||$ to compute h_c accurately, but for a rule of thumb one can make the reasonable assumption that $||f^{(k+2)}||$ is about (k + 2)!. This gives $h_c = \sqrt[k+2]{\epsilon}$. A similar argument for backward and forward differences gives the optimal h values to be $h_B = h_F = \sqrt[k+1]{\epsilon}$.

The following is a short table of the optimal h's along with the error in the derivatives for k = 1 and 2.

	CENTRAL DIFFERENCES				BACKWARD DIFFERENCES			
	FIRST DERIVATIVE		SECOND DERIVATIVE		FIRST DERIVATIVE		SECOND DERIVATIVE	
	$h_c = \sqrt[3]{\epsilon}$	Error = $\epsilon^{2/3}$	$h_c = \sqrt[4]{\epsilon}$	Error = $\epsilon^{1/2}$	$h_B = \sqrt{\epsilon}$	Error = $\epsilon^{1/2}$	$h_B = \sqrt[3]{\epsilon}$	Error = $\epsilon^{1/3}$
$\epsilon = 10^{-7}$	.005	2×10^{-5}	.018	.0003	.0003	.0003	.005	.005
$\epsilon = 10^{-10}$	.0005	2×10^{-7}	.003	10^{-5}	10^{-5}	10^{-5}	.0005	.0005
$\epsilon = 10^{-15}$	10^{-5}	10^{-10}	.0002	3×10^{-8}	3×10^{-8}	3×10^{-8}	10^{-5}	10^{-5}

PROBLEMS 7.3

7.3.1 Let E(h) denote the error in 7.1.4. Give a bound on E(h) in terms of h and derivatives of f(x). State the usual assumptions on f(x) so that E(h) goes to zero as h goes to zero. Show that

$$\lim_{h\to 0} E(h) = 0$$

if $f'''(x)$ is continuous at x = 0 even if $f^{(4)}(0)$ does not exist.

7.3.2 Investigate the sensitivity of the optimal h formula 7.3.3 for central differences. Select ϵ for the computer used and apply formulas 7.1.2, 7.1.3, and 7.1.4 for $h = h_{opt} \times f$ where f = 1.25, .8, 2, .5, 10, .1, 100, .01. Use as test cases the functions e^x at x = 1.1, $(\sin x - x)/x^3 = -1/6 + x^2/5! - x^4/7! \ldots$ at x = .02 and $x^2 - 2.2x + 2.21$ at x = 1.1. State and justify conclusions on how important it is to use an optimal h value.

7.3.3 The backward difference formula 7.1.6 has the same order of error as the central difference formula 7.1.2. Experimentally compare their actual accuracies by taking four functions, four x values, and four h values, and comparing the accuracy of the two formulas for each combination. Give the least accurate a score of 2 and the most accurate a score of 1 and compute the average rank for each formula. If they are equally accurate, the average ranks should be 1.5. Present a discussion of the conclusions reached from an analysis of this experiment.

7.3.4 Determine the accuracy of the 3-point differentiation formula 7.1.1.

7.3.5 Derive the 3-point formula for second derivatives for a general point set, that is, analogous to formula 7.1.1. Use $x_2 - x_1 = h$ and $x_3 - x_2 = \alpha h$ in the formula. Determine its accuracy.

7.3.6 Repeat Problem 7.3.3 with second derivative formulas of order $O(h^2)$, **Hint:** Equation 7.1.3 is $O(h^2)$, and the divided difference table on 0, h, 2h, and 3h gives a cubic interpolant to f. Differentiate twice and evaluate at zero.

THE ESTIMATION OF INTEGRALS 7.4

The estimation of the integral $\int_a^b f(x)dx$ is more complex than the estimates of derivatives even though integration is much "better behaved" than differentiation. We start with some of the many formulas of the classical type from the method of analytic substitution. Then, in the next section, we discuss the recent adaptive methods which provide great flexibility for handling difficult problems while remaining efficient for easy problems.

Basic Rules 7.4.A

The basic integration rules use one polynomial to model f(x) in the interval [a, b] for the estimate of $\int_a^b f(x)dx$. The simplest cases are shown in Figure 7.1. The shaded areas are used as the estimate of the area under the curve. The interval [a, b] is divided into equal parts, the integral f(x) is interpolated at the division points, and the resulting polynomial is integrated to estimate the intergral. Set $x_i = a + ih, i = 0, 1, 2, \ldots, n$ where $h = (b - a)/n$. The rules are of two types: the **closed formulas** use all the points x_i, and the **open formulas** use all but the endpoints. Both kinds of formulas are called **Newton-Cotes formulas;** they are of the form

$$\int_a^b f(x)dx \sim dh \sum_{i=0}^{n} w_i f(x_i) \qquad \text{closed}$$

$$\sim dh \sum_{i=1}^{n-1} w_i f(x_i) \qquad \text{open}$$

Equation 7.4.1

In practice, the constant d may be multiplied into the w_i. The algebra to obtain the estimate in terms of f(x) values becomes tedious as the degree of the model increases. Table 7.1 gives the values for the formulas for models of degree 0 through 6.

Newton Cotes Integration Rules, Equation 7.4.1 **Table 7.1**

m = polynomial degree in the model for f(x)
d = coefficient of h in Equation 7.4.1
Note that the formulas are symmetric about the middle

CLOSED FORMULAS, $h = (b - a)/m$ AND $x_i = a + ih, i = 0, 1, \ldots, m, n = m$

m	d	w_0	w_1	w_2	w_3	w_4	w_5	w_6
0	1	1						
1	1/2	1	1					
2	1/3	1	4	1				
3	3/8	1	3	3	1			
4	2/45	7	32	12	32	7		
5	5/288	19	75	50	50	75	19	
6	1/140	41	216	27	272	27	216	41

OPEN FORMULAS, $h = (b - a)/(m+2)$ AND $x_i = a + ih, i = 1, 2, \ldots, m+1, n = m+2$

m	d	w_1	w_2	w_3	w_4	w_5	w_6	w_7
0	1	1						
1	3/2	1	1					
2	4/3	2	−1	2				
3	5/24	11	1	1	11			
4	6/20	11	−14	26	−14	11		
5	7/1440	611	−453	562	562	−453	611	
6	8/945	460	−954	2196	−2459	2196	−954	460

Composite Rules 7.4.B

The integral of an interpolating polynomial is rarely good enough to estimate $\int_a^b f(x)dx$ accurately. The standard solution to this difficulty is to break the integral into pieces and apply a basic rule to each

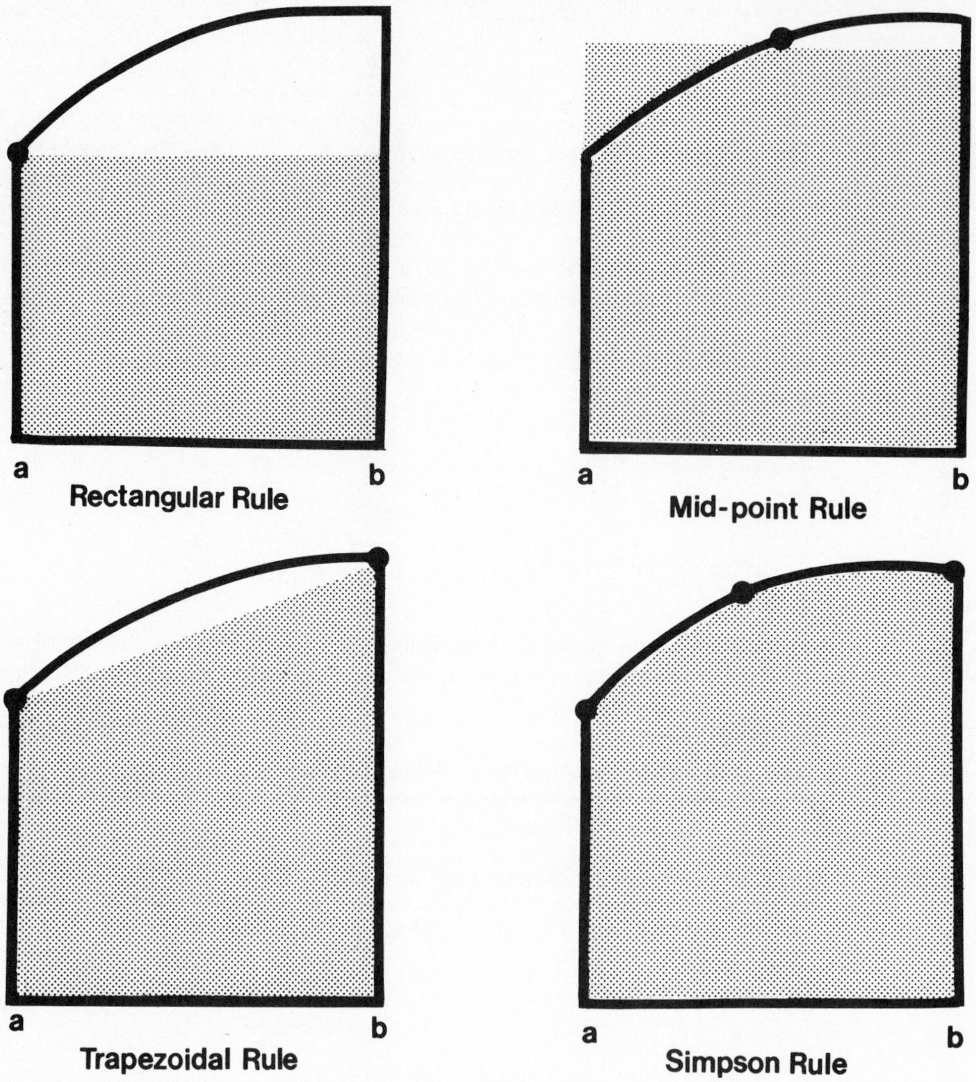

Figure 7.1 **Basic rules for numerical integration.** The rectangular and midpoint rules use a zero-degree polynomial model (top). The trapezoidal rule and Simpson rule (bottom) are the standard ways to use first- and second-degree polynomial models.

piece. If the interval [a, b] is broken into equal parts, then the resulting rules are called **composite rules.** The simpler rules (trapezoidal, Simpson, etc.) combine to form simple composite rules.

The method is illustrated for $\int_a^b f(x)dx$ using Simpson's rule and four pieces for the interval [0, 1]. We have, with $h = .25/2 = .125$,

$$\int_0^1 f(x)dx = \int_0^{.25} f(x)dx + \int_{.25}^{.5} f(x)dx + \int_{.5}^{.75} f(x)dx + \int_{.25}^{1} f(x)dx \qquad \textbf{Equation 7.4.2}$$

$$\sim \quad h/3[f(0)+4f(.125)+f(.25)] + h/3[f(.25)+4f(.375)+f(.5)]$$
$$+ \; h/3[f(.5)+4f(.625)+f(.75)] + h/3[f(.75)+4f(.875)+f(0)]$$
$$= \quad h/3[f(0)+4f(.125)+2f(.25)+4f(.375)+2f(.5)+4f(.625)+2f(.75)+4f(.875)+f(1)]$$

Note how the **Simpson rule** estimate may be computed efficiently for 2N intervals by adding terms before doing the multiplication.

Algorithm 7.4.1

```
H = (B-A)/(2*N)
$SUM F(A+I*H) ; FOR( I=1,2N-1,2) ; IS SUM1
$SUM F(A+I*H) ; FOR( I=2,2N-2,2) ; IS SUM2  $
SIMPR = H*( F(A) + F(B) + 4.*SUM1 + 2.*SUM2)/3.
```

The composite rules use a piecewise polynomial model for $f(x)$, one that is c^{-1} (no continuity at the break points) if an open Newton-Cotes formula is used, or one that is C^0 if a closed formula is used.

There are some basic rules where superaccuracy is obtained when the composite rule is constructed. The **corrected trapezoidal rule,** with $h = (b-a)$,

$$\int_a^b f(x)dx \sim h/2[f(a)+f(b)] + \frac{h^2}{12}[f'(a)-f'(b)]$$ **Equation 7.4.2.A**

is to be derived in Problem 4.5.8. It is exact for cubic polynomials. When this rule is used for a composite rule, the derivative terms at each break point cancel. The result is, with $h = (b-a)/k$, the **composite corrected trapezoidal rule** (sometimes called the *trapezoidal rule with endpoint corrections*)

$$\int_a^b f(x)dx \sim T(f) + \frac{h^2}{12}[f'(a)-f'(b)]$$ **Equation 7.4.3**

where T(f) is the composite trapezoidal rule

$$T(f) = h[f(a)+2\sum_{i=1}^{k-1} f(a+ih)+f(b)]/2$$ **Equation 7.4.4**

The formula 7.4.3 is exact for Hermite cubics even though it is a minor modification of the trapezoidal rule which is only exact for broken lines.

We made an **intuitive error analysis** for composite rules as follows: The rule is exact for polynomials of degree n, and so $f(x)$ is modeled by $p_n(x)$ which interpolates $f(x)$ at $n+1$ points. Then the error in one part of the integral is about

$$\int_{x_i}^{x_i+h} (f(x)-p_n(x))dx$$

The function $f(x)-p_n(x)$ has $n+1$ zeros in $[x_i, x_i+h]$, and so its maximum value is $O(h^{n+1})$. To motivate this statement, visualize that $f(x)-p_n(x)$ is, on a short interval, a polynomial $q(x)$ of degree $n+1$. Then $q(x) = a(x-z_1)(x-z_2)\ldots(x-z_{n+1})$ where each factor is less than h in size. The integral of $f(x)-p_n(x) \sim q(x)$ over a length h is then $hO(h^{n+1}) = O(h^{n+2})$ which is the error in one part of the integral. There are k such parts and $k = (b-a)/h$, and so the total error should be about $kO(h^{n+2}) = O(h^{n+1})$. This result is established (with exact assumptions stated) more precisely in Section 7.7.

Piecewise Polynomial Methods 7.4.C

The composite rules already use piecewise polynomial models of $f(x)$ for estimating integrals. They are usually only continuous models — though Equation 7.4.3 is exact for Hermite cubics by virtue of being superaccurate. If more smoothness is desired, then the usual practice is not to derive explicit formulas, but rather to explicitly interpolate f(x) by a spline (for example) and then integrate this interpolant exactly. In the theory of *optimal quadrature* (quadrature is a classical word for approximate integration) it is shown that the best possible (in a certain technical sense) estimates of integrals are obtained by integrating spline interpolants. This theory is beyond the scope of this text, and in most cases, the increased accuracy obtained is not large.

Integration Rules with Weight Functions **7.4.D

It is easy to obtain integration formulas which automatically incorporate a factor (a **weight function**) in the integral. They are of the form

$$\int_a^b f(x)w(x)dx \sim \sum_{i=0}^{n} w_i f(x_i) \qquad \textbf{Equation 7.4.5}$$

Weight functions arise naturally in applications, and some of them cause the ordinary integration formulas to be very inaccurate. Special formulas like those developed here can provide high accuracy even if the integrand has a troublesome factor (weight function).

An instance of these formulas occurs in Problem 4.5.1 where the following is to be established:

$$\int_0^h \sqrt{x}\, f(x)dx \sim \frac{h}{15}[4f(0)+6f(h)] \qquad \textbf{Equation 7.4.6}$$

Equation 7.4.6 is analogous to the trapezoidal rule in that the same points and model are used.

Polynomial models are not effective for functions like $\sqrt{x}$ near $x = 0$ even if the interval is made very small. In [0, h], the error of any polynomial approximation to $\sqrt{x}$ is $O(\sqrt{h})$, and integration rules based on such models perform very poorly. The advantage of this approach is that a difficulty in the integral (such as $\sqrt{x}$ or even $1/\sqrt{x}$) can be handled analytically, and the numerical method only has to handle the deviation from the model. One can interpret this approach as using a 2-part model for the integrand, one [the weight function $w(x)$] of which is handled analytically and exactly while the other is handled by the method of analytic substitution.

There are many interesting choices of $w(x)$ to consider; $w(x) = \sqrt{x}$, $1/\sqrt{x}$, e^x, e^{-x}, cos (kx), and sin(kx) often occur in applications. This approach also allows one to estimate infinite integrals such as

$$\int_0^\infty e^{-x}f(x)dx \qquad \int_0^\infty \frac{f(x)}{1+x^8}dx \qquad \int_{-\infty}^{\infty} e^{-x^2}f(x)dx$$

For example, one determines a value A so that $\int_A^\infty e^{-x}f(x)dx$ is rather small; this integral is less than e^{-A} times the maximum of $f(x)$ for $x = A$ to ∞. Even if $f(x)$ grows to infinity (for example, $f(x) = x$ or x^2), this integral usually decreases rapidly as A increases. Then one applies a rule of the form 7.4.5 to estimate this part of the integral, for example,

$$\int_A^\infty e^{-x}f(x)dx \sim w_0 f(A) + w_1 f(A+1) + w_2 f(A+4) + w_3 f(A+8)$$

The integral $\int_0^A e^{-x}f(x)dx$ is normally estimated with a standard rule that does not use the weight function e^{-x}. A special integration rule with $w(x) = e^{-x}$ could also be developed and used.

The emphasis so far has been on obtaining formulas analytically by hand. It may have occurred to some that one also can obtain them numerically during a computation. One sets up the linear equations to be solved for the w_i and then solves them with a linear equation solver just before the formula is to be used. This is particularly appropriate for formulas involving weight functions because they are usually not available in reference books, and solving even a system of four equations by hand is quite error-prone and tedious.

Gauss Rules for Superaccuracy **7.4.E

Gauss integration formulas select the integration abscissas x_i so that the formulas are superaccurate. We illustrate this by the example

$$\int_{-1}^{1} f(x) \sim w_1 f(x_1) + w_2 f(x_2) \qquad \textbf{Equation 7.4.7}$$

We are well-practiced in finding the coefficients w_1 and w_2 to make this rule exact for linear polynomials. This can be done for any pair of x_1 and x_2. Equation 7.4.7 has four variables w_1, w_2, x_1, and x_2, and a natural question is: *Can these variables be found so that 7.4.7 is exact for cubic polynomials?* There are four nonlinear equations to be solved when one chooses the basis functions 1, x, x^2, and x^3 to model f(x):

$$\begin{aligned}
2 &= w_1 + w_2 && \text{for } f(x) = 1\\
0 &= w_1x_1 + w_2x_2 && \text{for } f(x) = x\\
2/3 &= w_1x_1^2 + w_2x_2^2 && \text{for } f(x) = x^2\\
0 &= w_1x_1^3 + w_2x_2^3 && \text{for } f(x) = x^3
\end{aligned}$$

These equations have four unknowns, and so there is hope that a solution exists. There is a solution $w_1 = w_2 = 1$ and

$$x_1 = -.57735027 \qquad x_2 = .57735027$$

There is a general technique for solving this problem developed in Chapter 11 which involves **orthogonal polynomials**. At this point, we simply list in Table 7.2 the weights and abscissas for the Gauss formulas for low-degree polynomials.

To use these formulas on the general interval, [a, b], one makes the change of variable $x = [t-(a+b)/2]/h$ where $h = (b-a)/2$ to bring $\int_a^b f(t)dt$ to the form $\int_{-1}^1 f(x)dx$. The effect on the formula is illustrated for a 3-point formula; we set $c = (a+b)/2$ and obtain

$$\int_a^b f(t)dt \sim h[5f(c-.77460h)/9 + 8f(c)/9 + 5f(c+.77460h)/9] \qquad \textbf{Equation 7.4.8}$$

Superaccurate Gauss formulas also can be found for any weight functions w(x) as long as they are positive. Two examples of such formulas are

$$\int_0^1 \sqrt{1-x}\, f(x)dx \sim .3891106685f(.1788380869) + .2775559982f(.7100508021) \qquad \textbf{Equation 7.4.9}$$

$$\int_0^1 \frac{f(x)}{\sqrt{x}} dx \sim 1.30429031f(.258444253) + .6957096902f(.88441289) \qquad \textbf{Equation 7.4.10}$$

Both these formulas are exact for f(x), a cubic polynomial.

The obvious advantage of these superaccurate formulas is that they reduce by half the number of evaluations of f(x) for a given model of the integrand. They can be used as **composite Gauss formulas** in the same way as the Newton-Cotes formulas are used. Again, about half the integrand evaluations are saved.

Note that Gauss formulas provide a very efficient way to **integrate polynomials**. While the integration can be done analytically using elementary techniques, it is often much simpler in a program to use an appropriate Gauss formula (for example, a 3-point formula for quartics and quintics). Furthermore, the amount of arithmetic done is small, perhaps less than using symbolic formulas. Consider, for example, integrating a cubic spline given the knots and coefficients. It is easier to use a 2-point Gauss formula between each pair of knots than to derive and evaluate general formulas for the integrals.

PROBLEMS 7.4

7.4.1 The **composite 3/8's rule** is formed from the closed Newton-Cotes rule with m = 3 in Table 7.1.

(A) Give the rule explicitly similar to Equation 7.4.4

(B) Construct a program segment similar to Algorithm 7.4.1 which efficiently evaluates this rule.

7.4.2 The **composite midpoint rule** is formed from the open Newton-Cotes rule with m = 0 in Table 7.1

(A) Give the rule explicitly similar to Equation 7.4.4

(B) The midpoint rule is superaccurate and is comparable to the trapezoidable rule, yet it requires only one instead of two function evaluations. Count the number of function evaluations for both the composite midpoint and trapezoidal rules in terms of the number k of divisions of the interval [a, b] of integral. Discuss the relative efficiency [in terms of f(x) evaluations] of these two rules as k becomes large.

Abscissas and Coefficients for Gauss Formulas **Table 7.2**

The formula is for $\int_{-1}^{1} f(x)dx \sim \sum_{i=1}^{k} w_i f(x_i)$, the abscissas are the x_i, and the coefficients are the w_i. The formula with k points is exact for polynomials of degree $2k-1$. The abscissas and coefficients are symmetric, and so only the ones for positive x_i are given.

Abscissas		Coefficients
	k=2	
0.57735 02691 89626		1.00000 00000 00000
	k=3	
0.00000 00000 00000		0.88888 88888 88889
0.77459 66692 41483		0.55555 55555 55556
	k=4	
0.33998 10435 84856		0.65214 51548 62546
0.86113 63115 94053		0.34785 48451 37454
	k=5	
0.00000 00000 00000		0.56888 88888 88889
0.53846 93101 05683		0.47862 86704 99366
0.90617 97459 38664		0.23692 68850 56189
	k=6	
0.23861 91860 83197		0.46791 39345 72691
0.66120 93864 66265		0.36076 15730 48139
0.93246 95142 03152		0.17132 44923 79170
	k=7	
0.00000 00000 00000		0.41795 91836 73469
0.40584 51513 77397		0.38183 00505 05119
0.74153 11855 99394		0.27970 53914 89277
0.94910 79123 42759		0.12948 49661 68870
	k=8	
0.18343 46424 95650		0.36268 37833 78362
0.52553 24099 16329		0.31370 66458 77887
0.79666 64774 13627		0.22238 10344 53374
0.96028 98564 97536		0.10122 85362 90376
	k=9	
0.00000 00000 00000		0.33023 93550 01260
0.32425 34234 03809		0.31234 70770 40003
0.61337 14327 00590		0.26061 06964 02935
0.83603 11073 26636		0.18064 81606 94857
0.96816 02395 07626		0.08127 43883 61574
	k=10	
0.14887 43389 81631		0.29552 42247 14753
0.43339 53941 29247		0.26926 67193 09996
0.67940 95682 99024		0.21908 63625 15982
0.86506 33666 88985		0.14945 13491 50581
0.97390 65285 17172		0.06667 13443 08688
	k=12	
0.12523 34085 11469		0.24914 70458 13403
0.36783 14989 98180		0.23349 25365 38355
0.58731 79542 86617		0.20316 74267 23066
0.76990 26741 94305		0.16007 83285 43346
0.90411 72563 70475		0.10693 93259 95318
0.98156 06342 46719		0.04717 53363 86512

7.4.3 The composite corrected trapezoidal rule, Equation 7.4.3, is attractive, but the necessity for the values of $f'(a)$ and $f'(b)$ can be awkward at times. Derive a **modified composite corrected trapezoidal rule** by estimating $f'(a)$ and $f'(b)$ by finite difference formulas that are exact for cubic polynomials. Give the resulting formula explicitly. **Hint:** Use Equation 7.1.7.

7.4.4 Discuss the relative advantages and disadvantages of the composite Simpson rule and the rule in Problem 7.4.3.

7.4.5 Verify that the rule in Equation 7.4.6 is exact for linear polynomials.

7.4.6 Derive an integration formula of the form

$$\int_0^h f(\sqrt{x})dx \sim w_1f(0) + w_2f(h/2) + w_3f(h)$$

which is exact for quadratic polynomials. Apply the formula to estimate $\int_0^{.1} \log(2+\sqrt{x})dx$. **Hint:** The formula to be obtained is not Simpson's rule.

7.4.7 Derive an integration formula of the form

$$\int_0^h f(\sqrt{x})dx \sim w_1f(0) + w_2f'(0) + w_3f(h)$$

which is exact for quadratic polynomials. Apply the formula to estimate $\int_0^{.1} \log(2+\sqrt{x})dx$.

7.4.8 Derive an integration formula of the form

$$\int_0^h \sqrt{x}\, f(x)dx \sim w_1f(h/4) + w_2f(h/2) + w_3f(3h/4)$$

which is exact for quadratic polynomials. Apply the formula to estimate $\int_0^{.1} \sqrt{x}\cos(1+x)dx$.

7.4.9 Consider the integration formula

$$\int_0^\pi \cos(kx)f(x)dx \sim w_1^kf(0) + w_2^kf(\pi/2) + w_3^kf(\pi)$$

which is exact for quadratic polynomials. The coefficients w_i^k depend on k.

(A) Give a set of equations that determine the coefficients w_i^k.

(B) Solve these equations for $k = 10$.

(C) Apply the formula with $k = 10$ for $f(x) = e^{x/2}$ and $\cos(4x)$.

(D) Apply the formula for $f(x) = e^{x(.5+\delta)}$, $\cos((4+\delta)x)$ for small values of δ. Discuss the sensitivity of such formulas to small changes in $f(x)$ by comparing the results with those of part (C).

7.4.10 Let t be in the interval $[-1, 1]$ and set $t = \cos(\theta)$ for θ in $[0, 2\pi]$. Assume that $f(t)$ is tabulated at equally spaced points $t_i = -1+ih$, $i = 0, 1, 2,\ldots, k$ where $h = 2/k$. The problem is to estimate

$$\int_0^{2\pi} f(\theta)d\theta$$

(A) Approach this problem by making a change of variable in the integral and applying Simpson's rule for the interval $[-1, 1]$. Carry this out with $f(\theta) = \theta e^\theta$ and $k = 8$.

(B) Approach this problem by defining a special integration rule to accomplish the change of variable. Present the rule appropriate for this problem with $k = 8$. Derive a system of equations to solve for the coefficients of this formula. You need not solve it for actual coefficient values.

(C) Approach this problem by interpolating the integrand at the known points by a Newton interpolating polynomial. Make a divided difference table to find this polynomial, then integrate it numerically (to obtain the exact value) by using an appropriate Gauss formula from Table 7.2. Carry this out with $f(\theta) = \theta e^\theta$ and $k = 8$, and compare the result with that of part (A).

(D) Show that the methods in (C) and (B) should result in the same answer. Discuss the work of using each of these methods in an actual computation (say for $4 \le k \le 10$). Which is the most efficient to use? (Define the measure of efficiency carefully). Which requires the least programming effort?

7.4.11 Consider Problem 7.4.10 where $f(\theta)$ is tabulated at equally spaced points $\theta_i = ih$, $i = 0, 1,\ldots, k$ where $h = 2\pi/k$ and one is to estimate

$$\int_{-1}^1 f(t)dt$$

(A) Repeat part (A) of Problem 7.4.10, applying Simpson's rule to $[0, 2\pi]$.

(B) Repeat part (B) of Problem 7.4.10.

7.4.12 Consider the integral $\int_0^2 \sqrt{x}\, f(x)dx$. Define a composite rule by subdividing $[0, 2]$ into k parts and using a Gauss formula with a $\sqrt{x}$ weight on the first subdivision and an ordinary Gauss formula for the remainder. Give this formula explicitly and apply it to $\int_0^2 \sqrt{x}\sin(4xe^{-4x})dx$ using 5 subdivisions. **Hint:** Make a change of variable in Equation 7.4.9 for use in the first subdivision and use Equation 7.4.7 (also modified by a change of interval) for the others.

7.4.13 **Chebyshev integration** formulas have all the coefficients $w_i = 1$. Determine the polynomial degree for which the following Chebyshev formulas are exact:

(A) $$\int_{-1}^1 f(x) = \frac{2}{3}[f(-.7071067812)+f(0)+f(.7071067812)]$$

(B) $$\int_{-1}^1 f(x) = \frac{1}{2}[f(-.7946544723)+f(-.1875924741) + f(.1875924741)+f(.7946544723)]$$

7.4.14 **Laguerre integration** formulas are of the form

$$\int_0^\infty e^{-x}f(x)dx \sim \sum_{i=1}^k w_if(x_i)$$

and are exact for $f(x)$, a polynomial of degree $2k-1$. Verify that the following coefficients and abscissas are correct.

(A) $k = 2$, $x_i = .58578644, 3.4142136$, $w_i = .85355339, .14644661$

(B) $k = 3$, $x_i = .4157745568, 2.2942803603, 6.2899450829$
$w_i = .7110930099, .2785177336, .0103892565$

ADAPTIVE QUADRATURE **7.5

We use the notation

$$If = \int_a^b f(x)dx, \quad Q_kf = \sum_{i=1}^k w_if(x_i) \qquad \textbf{Equation 7.5.1}$$

Thus, $Q_k f$ is a quadrature rule (numerical integration formula) to estimate If, the integral. So far in this chapter we have picked a formula and just applied it to f(x), hoping to obtain enough accuracy. An **adaptive quadrature algorithm** chooses the w_i and x_i dynamically during the computation to adapt to the particular behavior of f(x).

One can say that traditional numerical integration is analogous to playing football and adaptive quadrature is analogous to playing basketball. In football, one examines the situation, studies the opponent, and then chooses a play (integration rule) to use. If the play works, fine; if it doesn't, then one chooses another play. In basketball, there is continuous interaction with the opponent as one changes the play (integration rule) dynamically to adapt to the opponents' behavior.

In the background of numerical integration there is a required accuracy in the estimate of If; we call it TOL, for tolerance. One wants to say something like

```
$INTEGRAL F(X); FOR(X=0.5,3.6) ; IS ANSWER ; ERRTARGET = TOL
```

and not be asked to set a step size h or a number of points k or some other vaguely known parameters. Adaptive quadrature algorithms directly attack this problem.

Good adaptive quadrature algorithms are fairly complicated, and it is both an art and a science to create them. A mathematical analysis of them is even more difficult. We study a simple algorithm here using the basic trapezoidal rule. It is not competitive for general use, but it is simple enough to understand and illustrate the features of adaptive algorithms. It is not only a model for realistic adaptive quadrature, it is also a model for adaptive algorithms for other problems of numerical computation.

The situation in the algorithm is illustrated in Figure 7.2, where [a, b] is subdivided into four parts. For simplicity, we assume that f(x) is concave on [a, b]; this is not an essential assumption. The idea is to divide the subinterval which has the largest error bound, i.e., the largest triangle above the trapezoids. The error bounds (areas of the shaded triangles in Figure 7.2) can be computed by standard trigonometric formulas; the situation for subdividing a triangle is illustrated in Figure 7.3. The formulas needed from trigonometry are

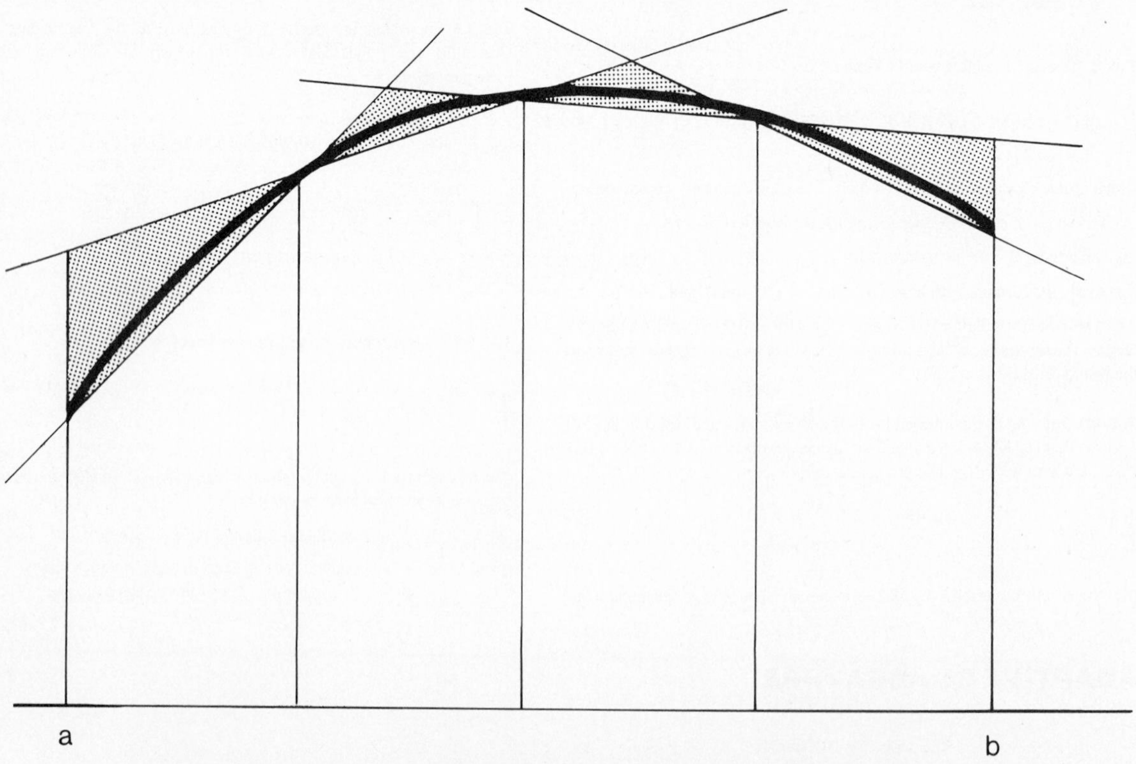

Figure 7.2 Geometry of the adaptive quadrature algorithm. The curve f(x) must lie in the shaded triangles and their areas give an upper bound on the error in the trapezoidal rule estimate.

$$d^2 = (f_R - f_L)^2 + (x_R - x_L)^2$$ **Equation 7.5.2**

$$h = \frac{d}{\cot\alpha_L + \cot\alpha_R}$$

$$\text{Error bound} = \frac{1}{2}\,dh = \text{area of shaded triangle}$$

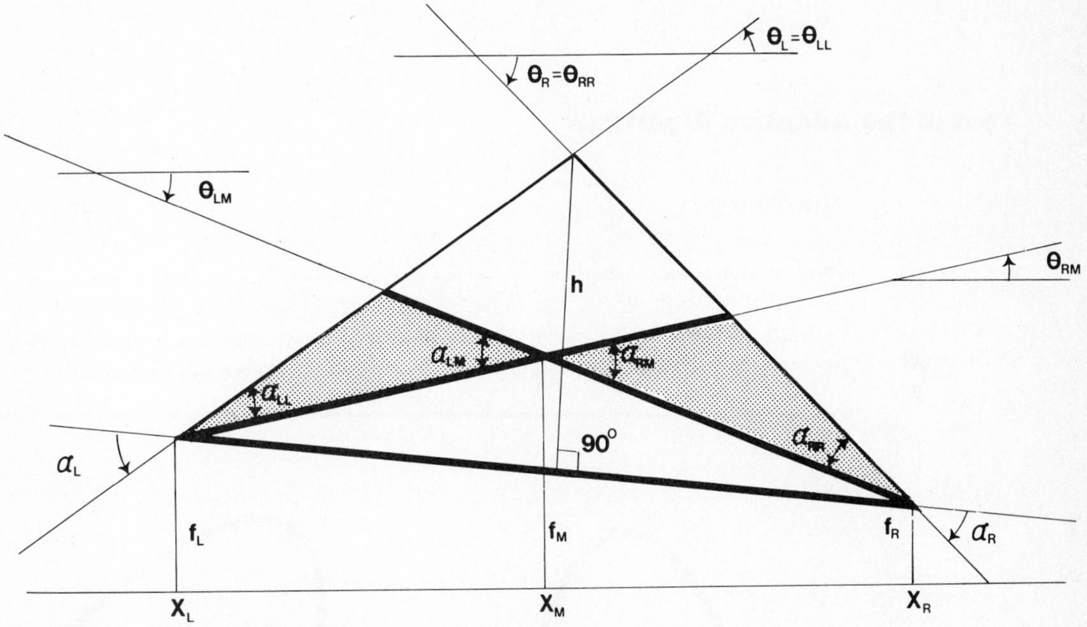

Figure 7.3 **Subdivision of a triangle.** Quantities are shown for computing the areas of a triangle and its subdivision. The slopes of lines (triangle sides) are denoted by θ, and interior angles of triangles by α. The quantities defined in this figure are used in the program of Problem 7.5.1.

When the triangle is subdivided by the point (x_M, f_M), the formulas in the subprogram in the hint for Problem 7.5.1 give the quantities for the new situation. These formulas are messy, but note that the adaptive algorithm is easily carried out by hand with a ruler and graph paper.

The adaptive strategy described above may be restated as follows:

Strategy 1: Order the intervals in a list according to the area of the error-bound triangles. The next interval to subdivide is the one at the head of the list.

An "interval" in this list consists of a pair of endpoints x_L and x_R plus other quantities retained so that they need not be recomputed every time. Examples of these other quantities are f_L, f_R, the triangle area, the trapezoid area, and the cotangents used.

This first strategy is very effective in reducing the integration error rapidly. It has two disadvantages: (1) it takes some work to keep the list organized so that one can locate the interval with the largest error-bound triangle, and (2) the list gets *very long* if high accuracy is needed.

We may discard an interval when its error bound BOUND becomes very small, specifically, if

$$\text{BOUND} \le \text{TOL}\,\frac{x_R - x_L}{B - A}$$ **Equation 7.5.3**

then the interval may be discarded. Note that when all the intervals are discarded one has

$$\text{Total error} \le \sum_{\text{intervals}} \text{BOUND} \le \sum_{\text{intervals}} \text{TOL}\,\frac{x_R - x_L}{B - A} = \frac{\text{TOL}}{B - A} \sum_{\text{intervals}} x_R - x_L = \text{TOL}$$

Discarding intervals helps with Strategy 1, and it is essential for the following:

Strategy 2: Place the integrals in a stack (with leftmost on top). The next interval to subdivide is the one on top of the stack. Discard those intervals that satisfy 7.5.3, and put the others back on top of the stack. The algorithm stops when the stack is empty.

It is easy to see that the stack of intervals cannot become too big. The shortest interval is always on top, and each interval is twice as long as the one on top of it (except that the top two may be of the same length). If there are 50 intervals in the stack, then the shortest one is $2^{-50} \sim 10^{-15}$ times the length of B-A. In most computers this means that $x_L = x_R$ because of the discreteness of the numbers. One can just automatically discard such a short interval [with a warning message that something is strange about f(x)].

Other strategies for organizing the collection of intervals or deciding when to discard them are described in Problems 7.5.2, 7.5.4, and 7.5.5.

Test of the Adaptive Algorithm — Example 7.2

The function

$$f(x) = x^{\alpha}(1.2-x)(1-e^{\beta(x-1)})$$

is convex for all α, β, and x in [0, 1]. The parameters α and β allow one to make it very smooth (say, $\alpha = 2, \beta = .2$) or very difficult to integrate (say $\alpha = 0.1, \beta = 20$). These two cases are plotted in Figure 7.4.

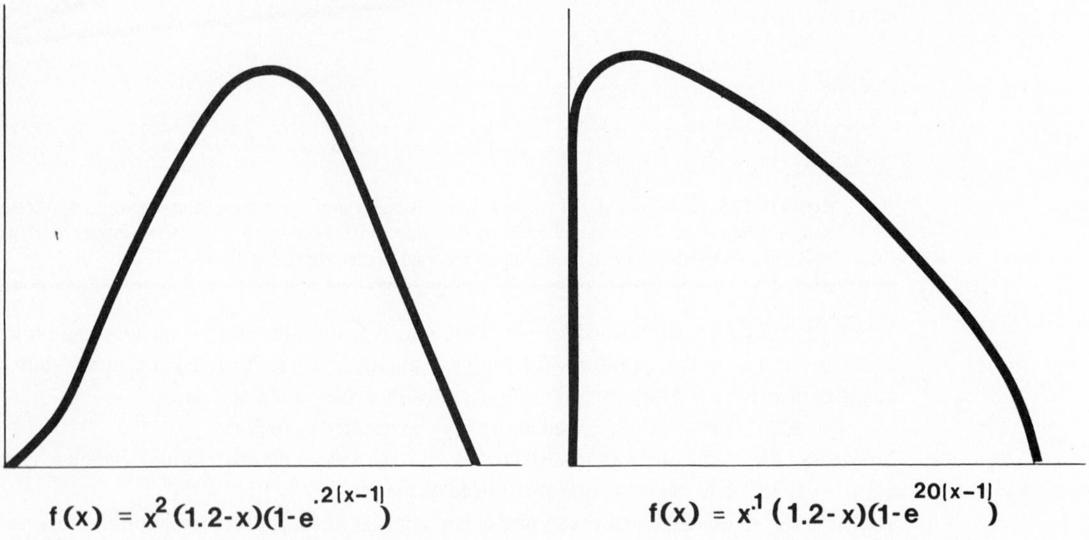

Figure 7.4 **Test functions for integration.** The left one is smooth and well-behaved; the right one is difficult to integrate.

These two cases of f(x) have been integrated with the trapezoidal rule, Simpson's rule, the adaptive quadrature algorithm with Strategy 1, and a "realistic" adaptive quadrature algorith, CADRE (in the IMSL library as DCADRE). Table 7.3 gives the number of f(x) evaluations required to achieve various tolerances.

The values given for DCADRE are the number of function evaluations for it to be satisfied that the accuracy request TOL is met. The actual errors are much smaller; 33 evaluations give 2×10^{-8} error for the smooth case and 1.4×10^{-5} error for the difficult case. The results in this table are plotted in Figure 7.5. We conclude three things from this example: (1) adaptive methods can be quite effective in handling difficult problems, (2) adaptive methods give better results for smooth problems, though not by a dramatic margin, and (3) an adaptive algorithm might require more function evaluations to achieve low-accuracy results. The reason for the third item is that a good adaptive algorithm is rather cautious about accepting a result as correct; it usually does some extra evaluations to check its preliminary conclusions.

Comparison of Integration Methods **Table 7.3**

Smooth Case, $\alpha = 2, \beta = .2$, If = .0095499658

Method	TOL = 10^{-6}	10^{-7}	10^{-8}
Trapezoidal rule	68	180	580
Simpson's rule	13	26	66
Adaptive algorithm	22	64	208
DCADRE*	33	33	41

Difficult Case, $\alpha = .1, \beta = 20$, If = .602297

Method	TOL = .01	.005	.001	.0005	.0001
Trapezoidal rule	36	67	285	510	2080
Simpson's rule	23	43	184	340	1470
Adaptive algorithm	14	19	43	60	133
DCADRE*	33	33	33	33	33

*DCADRE's actual error is much smaller than TOL.

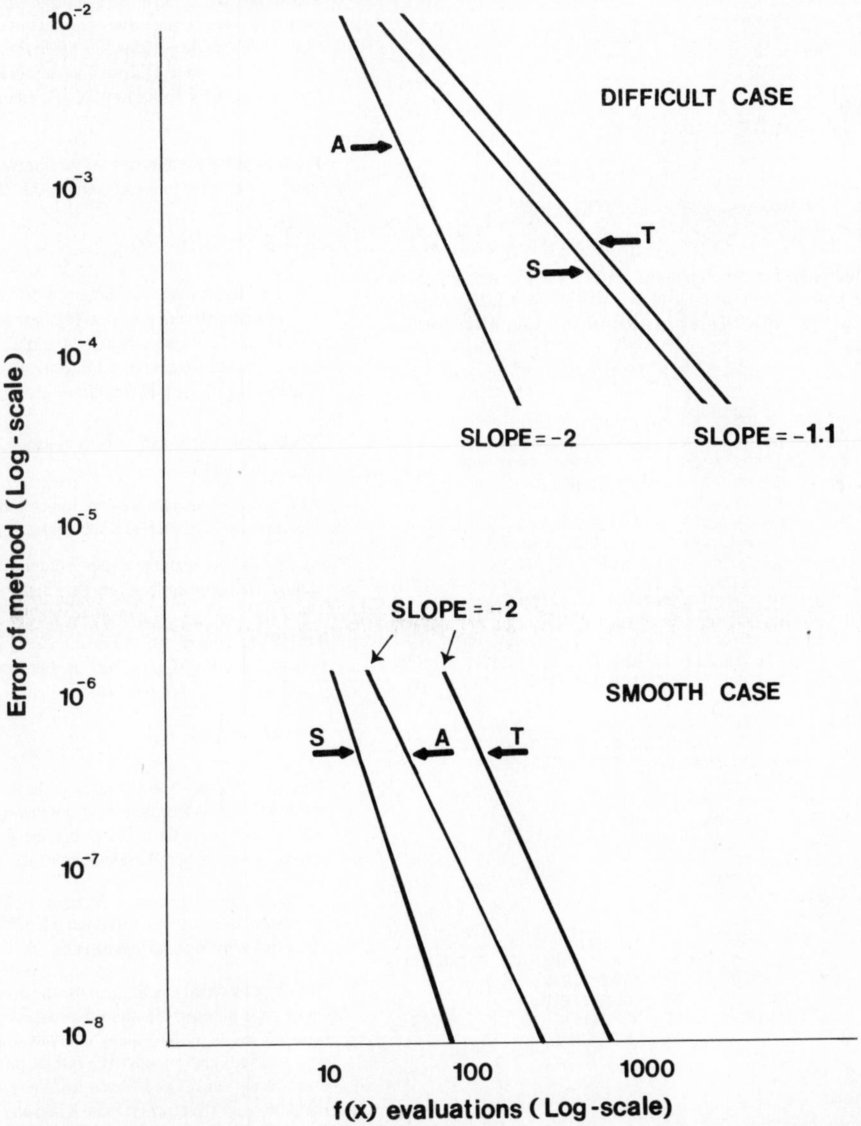

Figure 7.5 **Rates of convergence for integration methods test.** The data points are plotted for the methods: A = adaptive quadrature, T = trapezoidal rule, S = Simpson's rule. The slopes of the lines indicate the approximate rates of convergence.

PROBLEMS

7.5.1 Implement the adaptive quadrature algorithm described in this section using Strategy 1, the ordered list. Record the number of function evaluations and the length of the final list for each integral.

(A) $\int_0^1 e^x dx$, TOL $= 10^{-4}$

(B) $\int_0^1 \sin(x^2) dx$, TOL $= 10^{-4}$

(C) $\int_0^1 \log(x+10^{-5}) dx$, TOL $= 10^{-4}$

(D) $\int_0^1 \text{ABS}(x-.4) dx$, TOL $= 10^{-3}$

(E) $\int_0^1 \sqrt{x}\, dx$, TOL $= 10^{-3}$

(F) $\int_0^{15} e^{-x} dx$, TOL $= 10^{-5}$

(G) $\int_0^3 \text{sign}(\sin(\pi x)) dx$, TOL $= 10^{-2}$

(H) $\int_{-1}^1 \sin(e^x + \cos x)/(1+(1+x)\log(1+x)) dx$, TOL $= 10^{-4}$

Hint: The following Fortran subroutine carries out the subdivision of a triangle; use it along with an interval list with arrays XR(200), XL(200), FL(200), FR(200), BOUND(200), AREA(200), COTANL(200), and COTANR(200).

```
      SUBROUTINE SUBDIV(XL,XR,FL,FR,CL,CR)
C     THIS SUBROUTINE SUBDIVIDES A TRIANGLE IN THE
C ADAPTIVE QUADRATURE ALGORITHM .  THE INPUT IS
C     XL,XR  =  INTERVAL OF THE TRIANGLE
C     FL,FR  =  F(XL), F(XR)
C     CL,CR  =  COTANGENTS OF ANGLES THETA-L, THETA-R
C                   LEFT AND RIGHT TOP SIDES OF TRIANGLE
C THE OUTPUT IS THROUGH COMMON BLOCK  / OUTPUT/
C  XLL,XLM = LEFT INTERVAL, FLL = F(XLL), FLM = F(XLM)
C  COTLL  = COTANGENT OF TOP LEFT  SIDE OF LEFT TRIANGLE
C  COTLM  = COTANGENT OF TOP RIGHT SIDE OF LEFT TRIANGLE
C  BOUNDL = ERROR BOUND FROM NEW TRIANGLE ON THE LEFT
C  AREAL  = AREA IN TRAPEZOID UNDER LEFT HALF
C THE SAME OUTPUT FOR RIGHT TRIANGLE WITH R REPLACING L
C
      COMMON / OUTPUT /
     A          XLL,XLM,FLL,FLM,COTLL,COTLM,BOUNDL,AREAL,
     B          XRM,XRR,FRM,FRR,COTRM,COTRR,BOUNDR,AREAR
      DX   =   .5*(XR-XL)
      XLL = XL
      XLM = XRM =  XR-DX
      XRR = XR
      FLL = FL
      FLM = FRM = F(XLM)
      FRR = FR
      DFL = FLM - FLL
      DFR = FRR - FRM
C                  PROTECTION FROM INFINITE COTANGENTS
      IF( DFR .EQ. 0.0 )  DFR = DX*1.E-25
      IF( DFL .EQ. 0.0 )  DFL = DX*1.E-25
C        COTANGENTS OF BASES OF TRIANGLES WITH X-AXIS
      COTLL = CL
      COTLM = DX/DFR
      COTRM = DX/DFL
      COTRR = DR
C       TRIG FORMULA USED IS
C       COT(A-B) = (COT A * COT B + 1)/(COT B - COT A)
C       CLL     = COTANGENT OF ALPHA-LL
C                 LEFT  BASE ANGLE OF TRIANGLE
C       CLM     = COTANGENT OF ALPHA-LM
C                 RIGHT BASE ANGLE OF TRIANGLE
      CLL = ABS((COTRM*CL + 1.)/(COTRM - CL))
      CLM = ABS((COTRM*COTLM + 1.)/(COTRM - COTLM)
      CRR = ABS((COTLM*CR + 1.)/(COTLM - CR))
      DL  = DX*DX + DFL*DFL
      DR  = DX*DX + DFR*DFR
      BOUNDL = .5*DL/(CLL+CLM)
      BOUNDR = .5*DR/(CLM+CRR)
      AREAL  = .5*DX/(FLL+FLM)
      AREAR  = .5*DX*(FRM+FRR)
      RETURN
      END
```

7.5.2 Modify the algorithm to use the strategy **ordered list plus discards** by using Equation 7.5.3 to discard intervals during the computation. Repeat the calculation of parts (A) through (H) of Problem 7.5.1 and report the change in the length of the final list.

7.5.3 Have the implementation in Problem 7.5.1 print out the final list and show how the distribution of integration points adapts to the trouble spots of parts (C) through (G).

7.5.4 Modify the adaptive algorithm to use a **queue data structure** for the intervals. The strategy is this: *The next interval to subdivide is the one to the right of the one just subdivided. When the point B is reached, start over again at the left endpoint a.* Discard intervals using 7.5.3. Repeat the integrations of Problem 7.5.1 for this algorithm and compare the amounts of computation required.

7.5.5ture for the intervals. As the intervals are generated, they are placed in "buckets" with the intervals going in the Ith bucket if their bounds satisfy

$$10^{-I} \leq \text{BOUND} < 10^{-I+1}$$

(Different levels might be chosen to define the buckets.) The strategy used with this data structure is this: *The next interval to be subdivided is chosen from the first nonempty bucket.* Any means can be used to choose intervals from a bucket. Repeat the integrations of Problem 7.5.1, using discards (Equation 7.5.3), for this algorithm and compare the amounts of computation.

7.5.6 Examine the data structures used by the algorithms in Problems 7.5.1, 7.5.3, 7.5.4, and 7.5.5.

(A) Discuss the amount of work to place the two new intervals into the data structure when an interval is subdivided.

(B) Discuss the amount of memory used by each data structure when the accuracy requirement becomes very high.

7.5.7 The discard rule in Equation 7.5.3 is called a **proportional error rule** because the error TOL is distributed proportionally over the interval [A, B]. There is also the **fixed error rule**

$$\text{BOUND} \leq \text{TOL}$$

This rule obviously does not result in the final error less than TOL; the error is about TOL times the number of intervals generated. Experience and theory both suggest that the fixed error rule gives better adaption for difficult functions than the proportional error rule.

(A) Modify the algorithm in Problem 7.5.2 to use the fixed error rule. Apply the algorithm to parts (A) through (H) of Problem 7.5.1. Examine how large the actual error is compared to TOL.

(B) Give a modified algorithm to use the fixed error rule and still have the final result have an error less than the requested accuracy TOL. **Hint:** Make an estimate, say K, of how many intervals would be used if the integrand were well-behaved, and initially use TOL/K for the discarding test. Identify the intervals as "active" and "discarded." When all the active intervals are gone, check to see if the error estimate is actually less than TOL. If so, stop. If not, increase K and start again on the previously discarded intervals.

(C) Discuss the difficulties that might occur in using the method in the hint for part (B) if the integrand is very badly misbehaved and K has to be increased many times.

SOFTWARE FOR INTEGRATION 7.6

There are many, many angles to exploit in developing methods for numerical integration: different polynomial degrees, different placements of points, superaccurate Gauss formulas, weight functions, infinite intervals, adaptive schemes, and so forth. This variety of things, and all the possible combinations, has led to many methods over the past two centuries. There were probably 50 methods known in classical times, before 1950, when computers made numerical integration a practical reality for the working scientist. And many more have been developed since; there are 34 ACM algorithms for numerical integration. This is not because numerical integration is the most important problem; it is because there are so many things that can be done, often in a fairly short, neat program.

ACM Algorithms and IMSL Software 7.6.A

The ACM Algorithms are divided into six categories as follows: the algorithm numbers are listed for each category.

1. *Basic* [60, 84, 351] Applies one basic rule or a composite of one basic rule; a complete specification of the model is given as input. Romberg integration with good round-off control is #351 (see Problem 7.6.1).

2. *Automatic* [279, 424] A sequence of basic rules is used to attempt to achieve a specified accuracy TOL; the input is f(x), a, b, and TOL. Such software usually increases the polynomial degree or number of subdivisions in a composite rule. The method does not depend on f(x) except in terminating for accuracy TOL. Algorithm 424 is suggested as a good example of this class.

3. *Adaptive* [103, 145, 182, 198, 257, 303, 379, 400, 468] These use methods such as described in Section 7.5. Algorithms 379 and 468 are good examples of this class.

4. *Formula Generating* [125, 280, 281, 331, 417, 453] This is software to compute the coefficients and abscissas for various kinds of integration formulas. These can be very difficult to write and are useful programs. Algorithm 331 is for superaccurate Gauss formulas with a wide variety of weight functions.

5. *Multiple Integrals* [32, 146, 233, 436, 437, 438, 439, 440] Multiple integration is more difficult than one might guess because the number of function evaluations grows very rapidly with the number of independent variables. All these algorithms are based on simple extensions of one variable methods.

6. *Special* [1, 98, 353, 418, 427] Software for special problems or integrals; for example, 418 and 427 apply to $\int f(x)\cos(kx)dx$ and $\int f(x)\sin(kx)dx$.

These algorithms are just part of the software and algorithms for numerical integration. One of the responsibilities of a mathematical software library is to select out of this mass a few programs that are best suited for general use. The IMSL library has the program DCADRE, which is an adaptive algorithm. It uses different-order polynomial models on each interval and attempts to identify the common kinds of singularities. Its calling sequence is

```
FUNCTION DCADRE(F,A,B,AERR,RERR,ERROR,IER)
```

where F,A,B = the function name and interval of integration

AERR = target absolute error in the computed result

RERR = target relative error in the computed result

ERROR = DCADRE's estimate of the actual absolute error

The goal of DCADRE is to have, using the notation of 7.5.1,

$$|\text{If-DCADRE}| \le \max(\text{AERR},\text{RERR*If}) \quad \textbf{Equation 7.6.1}$$

The IMSL library has an adaptive program DBLIN for two-dimensional integrals based on DCADRE. It also has DMLIN which uses a Gauss rule for integration over hyper-rectangles in any dimension.

The IMSL library also provides a facility for integrating tabulated functions (none of the ACM algorithms do this). Most people use the trapezoidal rule for tabulated data; it is not very accurate, but is adequate for the low accuracy usually associated with such data. If the data are known to be smooth and higher accuracy is needed in the integration, then a piecewise cubic interpolant can be computed using ICSCCU, ICSICU, ICSPLN, or IQHSCU (see Section 5.3) and integrated with DCSQDU.

The PROTRAN system provides access to the IMSL programs. Typical PROTRAN statements for the function F(X) are

```
$INTEGRAL  F(X); FOR( X= A,B ); ERRTARGET= .001; ABSOLUTE; IS ANS1
$INTEGR    F(X)*COS(X+T); FOR(X= A,B+T); ERRTAR = .0008; IS AT4
$INTEGRAL  F(X)/(X4+F(X)) ; FOR(X = 1,5*A-B) ; IS INTF4
$INTEGRAL  F    ; FOR(X = A(ISELCT),B(ISELCT)) ; IS ANSI ; DEFINE
  ====
             IF( ISELCT.EQ.1)  F = SQRT(X)
             IF( ISELCT.EQ.2)  F = 1./(1.+0.1*X**2)
             IF( ISELCT.EQ.3)  F = SIN(10.*PI*X)/X
  ====
```

For tabulated data X(I), DATA(I) one can use

```
$INTEGRAL  DATA ; VS X ; IS ANSDAT
$INTEGRAL  DATA ; VS X ; ON(-1,3.*A); IS ANS5
```

to obtain the result from integrating a spline interpolant. The second PROTRAN statement restricts the integration to those points of X in the interval $[-1, 3A]$.

Performance Evaluation of Four Integration Methods — 7.6.B

Before we discuss how to select a method or software for a particular application, we demonstrate how to make a performance evaluation of integration methods. The study uses three test functions, but the program is set up so that a large number of functions can be used with little additional effort. The example also shows how easy it is to program a method like the composite 3-point Gauss formula.

Performance Evaluation of Numerical Integrators — Example 7.3

Four methods — trapezoidal rule, Simpson's rule, composite 3-point Gauss, and DCADRE — are compared for three functions. One function, e^x on [0, 1], represents the really nice, smooth, and well-behaved integrands. Another, $\sqrt{|x-.2345|}$ on [0, 1], represents the really troublesome integrands; it has a bad singularity at an interior point. If the exact location of the singularity is known, it usually pays to break the integral into two parts at the location of the singularity. The third function, $1+x^2+1/(1+100x^2)$ on $[-1, 2]$, represents the middle ground, integrands which are smooth but which also have a "bump" or some other atypical behavior.

The experimental setup is straightforward. Three test functions and four integration methods have been picked; every method is applied to each function for a range of method parameters. The parameter of

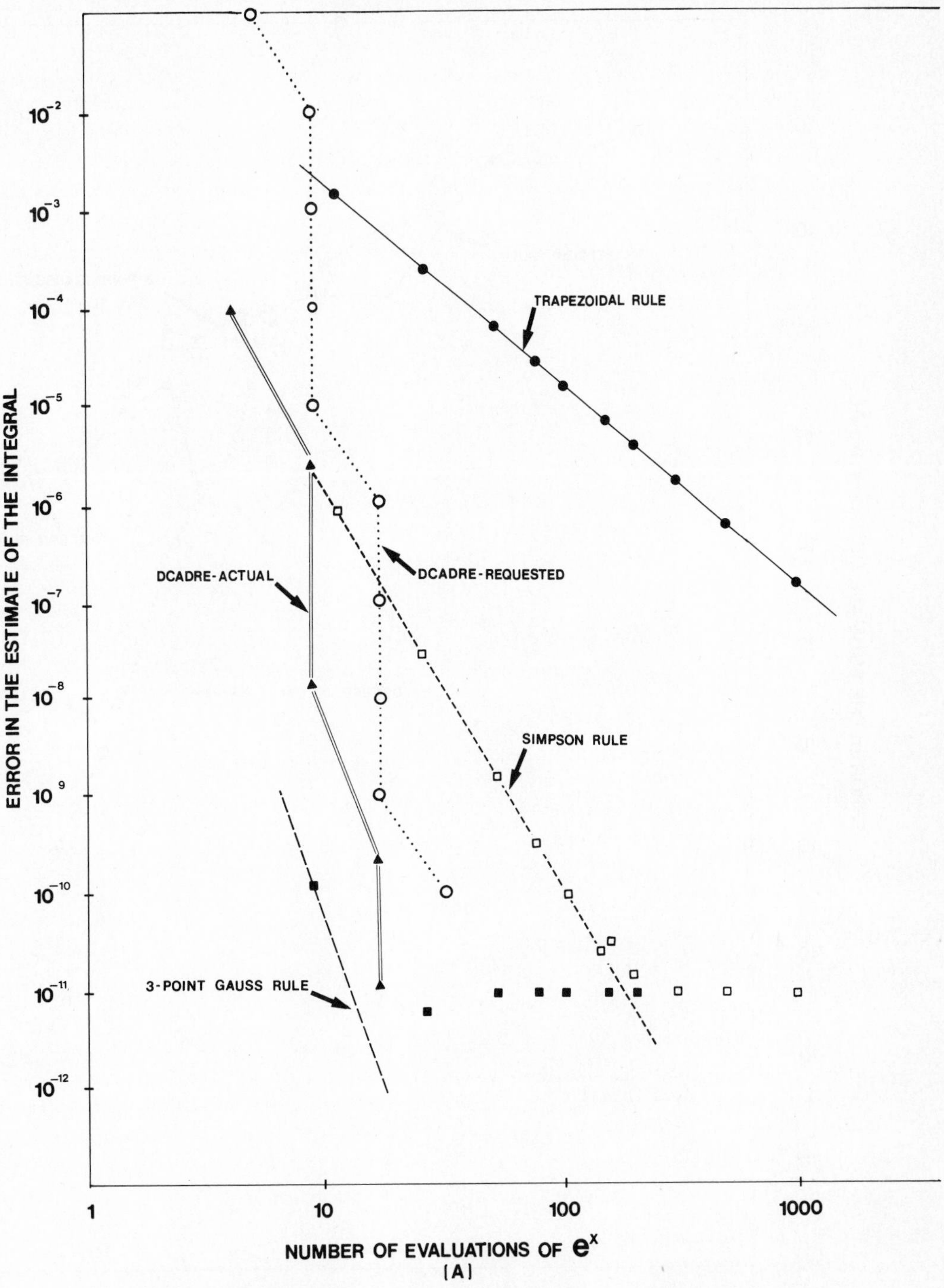

Figure 7.6 Performance of four methods on three integrands. The methods are trapezoidal rule, Simpson's rule, 3-point Gauss, and DCADRE. The integrands are (A) easy, (B) singular, and (C) presenting some difficulty. The absolute error and number of function evaluations are plotted on a log-log scale; the sizes of the integrals are 1.7, 0.5, and 6.3, respectively.

the first three methods is the number N of subintervals of [a, b]: values of N = 10, 25, 50, 75, 100, 150, 200, 300, 500, and 1000 are used. The parameter of DCADRE is the error target. The absolute error AERR is set very small so that the relative error RERR is the governing parameter; values of RERR = 10^{-1}, $10^{-2}, \ldots, 10^{-9}$ are used.

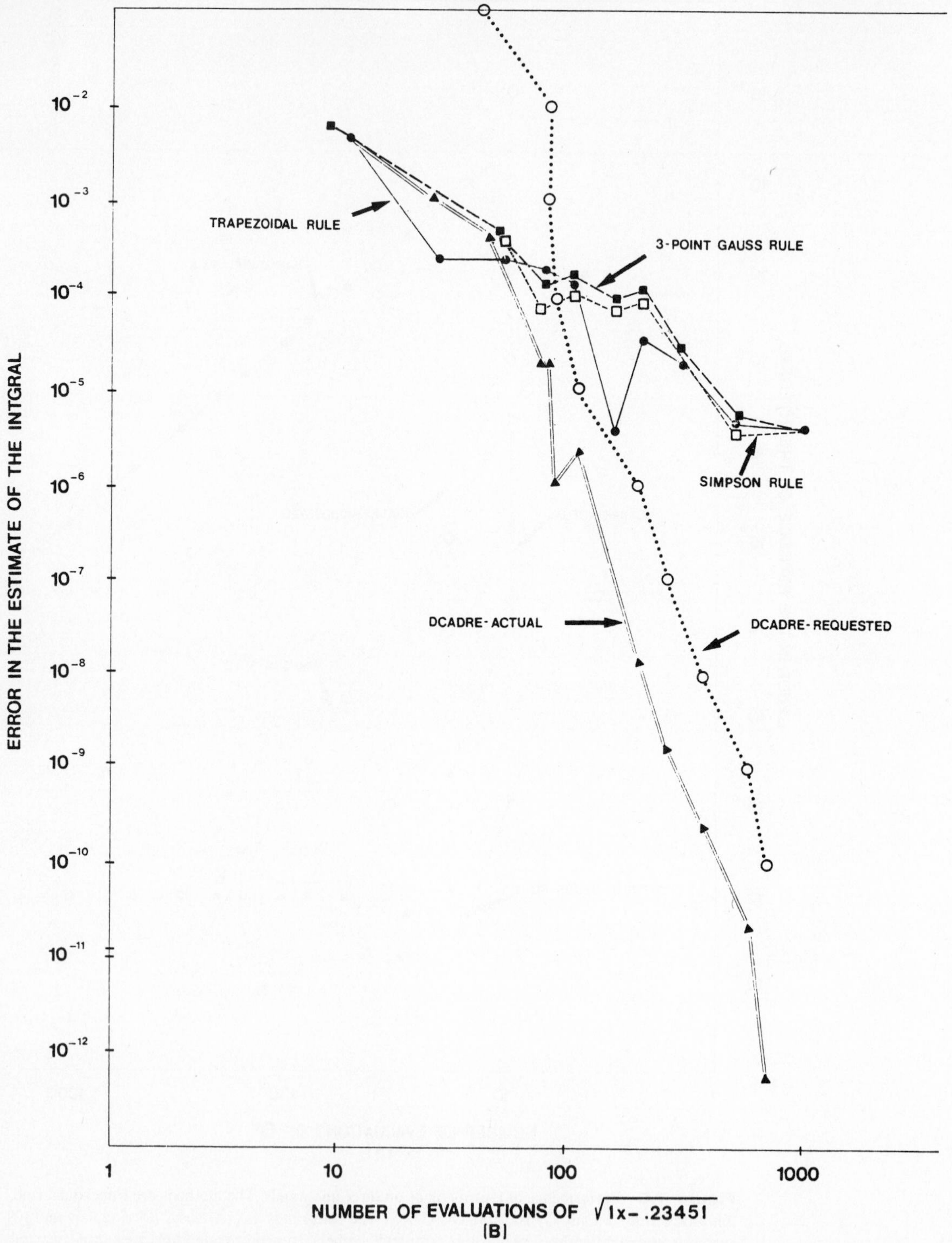

Figure 7.6 (continued)

The analysis of the experimental data is completely intuitive; one just looks at the plots of error versus number of function evaluations, shown in Figure 7.6, and reaches one's own conclusions. A more ambitious performance evaluation would apply statistical methods to the data. These four methods are so dissimilar that it is easy to draw conclusions with confidence.

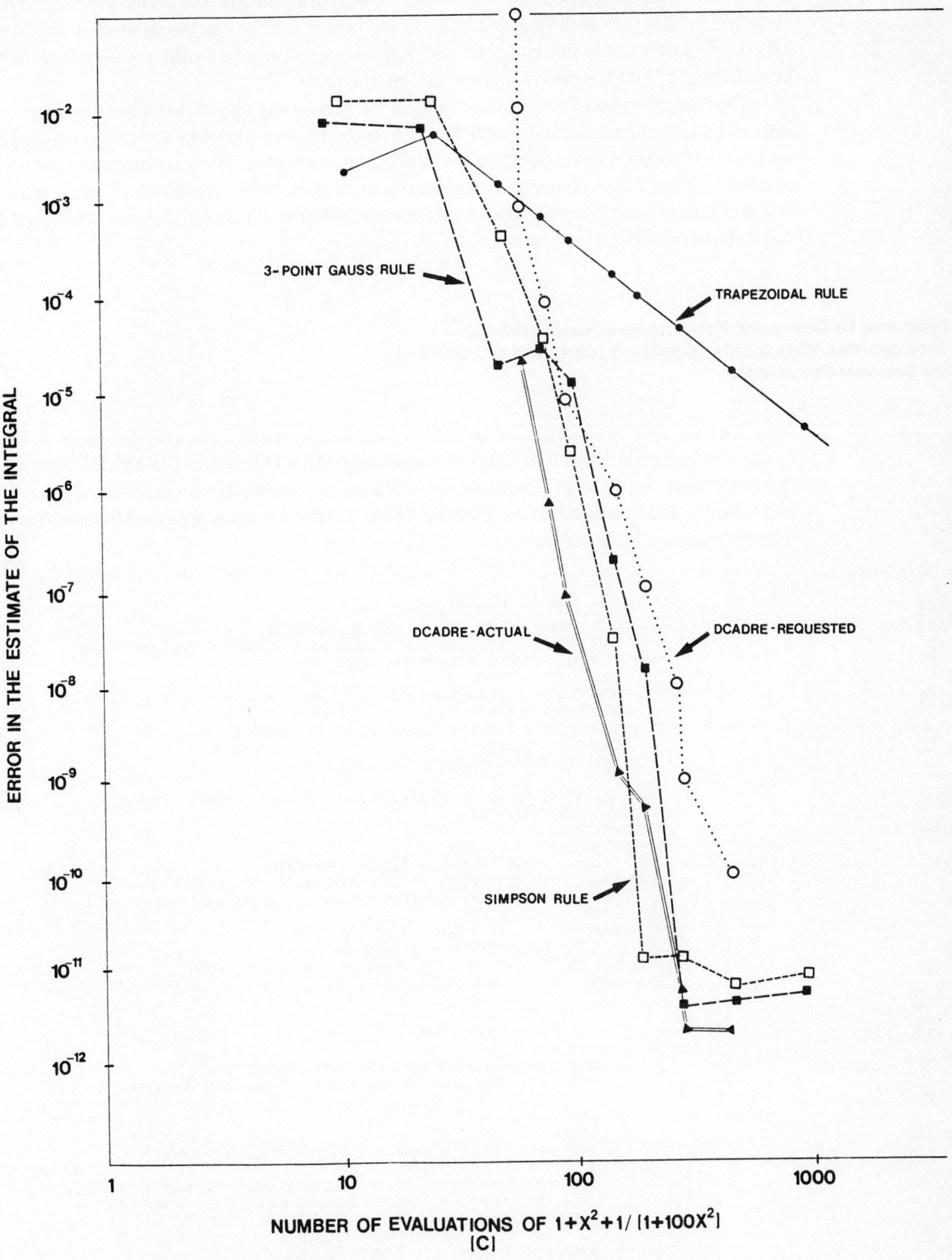

Figure 7.6 (continued)

The first integrand e^x is very easy. The sixth-degree polynomial model of 3-point Gauss applies well, and so it achieves the full 11 places of accuracy very quickly. DCADRE takes only a few more evaluations to do the same. Simpson's rule takes 10 times the number of f(x) evaluations to achieve the full 11 places, and the trapezoidal rule has a long way to go even after 1000 f(x) evaluations. All the methods achieve modest (3 to 4 digits) accuracy quickly.

The second integrand $\sqrt{|x-.2345|}$ is difficult, and none of the polynomial models are very good. There is very little difference between the three nonadaptive methods. The irregularities in the behavior of the error are due to how the points happen to fall near $x = .2345$ as the number of intervals changes. DCADRE does adapt to this integrand, and full accuracy is achieved with a reasonable number of $f(x)$ evaluations. DCADRE is clearly superior for this example.

The third intergrand $1+x^2+1/(1+100x^2)$ is mathematically smooth, but it has a bump at $x = 0$ in the interval $[-1, 2]$ of integration. DCADRE senses this bump even when low accuracy is requested and does quite a few function evaluations before it is satisfied with its answer. The other methods must wait until the number of intervals (and function evaluations) is quite large before properly integrating the bump. The 3-point Gauss method eventually converges faster than Simpson's rule, but this does not happen before the full 11 places of accuracy are obtained.

Program to Compare Four Integration Methods — Trapezoidal, Simpson's, 3-point Gauss, and DCADRE— for Several Functions

Note how the program is organized to change functions by merely changing the index JFUNK of the function subprogram F(X). The index is communicated to F(X) via a COMMON block so that the functions always appear as F(X), without any additional arguments. The counter of function evaluations is also passed to and from F(X) via this COMMON block. The program is organized to report the results in a uniform summary for each function.

```
C              EXAMPLE 7.3 - EVALUATION OF INTEGRATION SOFTWARE
C          FOUR METHODS ARE COMPARED FOR SEVERAL FUNCTIONS. THE FUNCTIONS
C      ARE SWITCHED THROUGH THE COMMON BLOCK / SELECT /
C
C          METHOD 1 - TRAPEZOIDAL RULE           H = (B-A)/N
C          METHOD 2 - SIMPSON RULE               H = (B-A)/N
C          METHOD 3 - 3 POINT GAUSS RULE         H = 3*(B-A)/N
C          METHOD 4 - DCADRE                     H NOT DEFINED
C      THE PROBLEM IS TO INTEGRATE F(X) FROM A TO B
C
      REAL ANSWER(4),ERROR(4),LOGERR(4),TRUE(3),AAA(3),BBB(3),AERR(10)
      INTEGER KOUNTF(4),N(10)
      EXTERNAL F
      COMMON / SELECT / JFUNK,KOUNT
C                   TRUE INTEGRAL VALUES, INTERVALS
      DATA TRUE / 1.71828182845, .5222099422093, 6.29919656054        /
C         F(X)=    EXP(X)    , SQRT(ABS(X-.2345)), 1+X*X+1/(1+100*X*X)
C           ON     0,1               0,1                -1,2
      DATA AAA / 0.,0.,-1./, BBB / 1.,1., 2. /
C              SET PARAMETERS FOR EXPERIMENT
      DATA N / 10, 25, 50, 75, 100, 150, 200, 300, 500, 1000  /
      DATA AERR /.1,.01,.001,.1E-3,.1E-4,.1E-5,.1E-6,.1E-7,.1E-8,.1E-9/
C
C
C              LOOP OVER FUNCTIONS
      DO  1000 JFUNK = 1,3
          PRINT 20, JFUNK,AAA(JFUNK),BBB(JFUNK),TRUE(JFUNK)
   20     FORMAT('1      FUNCTION 'I3' ON ' 2F5.2 ' HAS TRUE INTEGRAL ='
     A          F15.12 )
          A = AAA(JFUNK)
          B = BBB(JFUNK)
C             LOOP OVER THE N OR ACCURACY PARAMETER OF THE METHODS
      DO  700 L = 1,10
C             THE NUMBER OF INTERVALS IS CHOSEN SO THAT THE NUMBER OF
C             F(X) EVALUATIONS IS ABOUT THE SAME FOR THE 1ST 3 METHODS
C             RESULTS ARE ACCUMMULATED IN THE ARRAYS
C                  ANSWER  ERROR  LOGERR  KOUNTF
C             AND PRINTED AFTER ALL 4 METHODS ARE DONE
      NPART = N(L)
      H  =(B-A)/NPART
      PRINT 30, NPART,H
   30 FORMAT(//10X'EVALUATION USING N =' I4 ' INTERVALS, H =' F10.7)
C                       TRAPEZOIDAL RULE
C                  FORM TRAPEZOID SUMS FROM EQUATION 7.4.4
      KOUNT  = 0
      SUMF = 0.
      X  = A
      DO 100 K = 2,NPART
          X = X + H
          SUMF = SUMF + F(X)
```

```
  100 CONTINUE
      ANSWER(1) = H*( F(A) +2.*SUMF + F(B))/2.
      KOUNTF(1) = KOUNT
C
C                     SIMPSON RULE
C              USE ALGORITHM 7.4.1 FOR  SIMPSONS RULE
      KOUNT  = 0
      SUM1 = SUM2 = 0.
      NSIMP = NPART
C           IF NPART IS NOT EVEN USE NPART-1
      IF( MOD(NPART,2) .EQ. 1 ) NSIMP = NPART-1
      HS = (B-A)/NSIMP
      H2 = 2.*HS
      X = A + HS
      DO 200 K = 1,NSIMP-1,2
         SUM1 = SUM1 + F(X)
         X = X + H2
  200 CONTINUE
      X = A + H2
      DO 210 K = 2,NSIMP-2,2
         SUM2 = SUM2 +F(X)
         X = X + H2
  210 CONTINUE
      ANSWER(2) = HS*( F(A)+F(B)+4.*SUM1+ 2.*SUM2)/3.
      KOUNTF(2) = KOUNT
C
C             COMPOSITE 3-POINT GAUSS RULE
C             USE 3 TIMES BIGGER INTERVAL
      NPARTG = NPART/3
      HG = (B-A)/NPARTG
      H77=  .774596669241*HG/2.
      KOUNT  = 0
      SUML = SUMM = SUMR = 0.
      X = A + HG/2.
      DO 300 K = 1,NPARTG
         SUML = SUML + F(X-H77)
         SUMM = SUMM + F(X)
         SUMR = SUMR + F(X+H77)
         X = X +HG
  300 CONTINUE
      ANSWER(3) = HG*( 5.*(SUML+SUMR) + 8.*SUMM)/18.
      KOUNTF(3) = KOUNT
C
C       USE ABSOLUTE ERROR CRITERION FOR DCADRE
C     KOUNT = 0
      ANSWER(4) = DCADRE(F,A,B,AERR(L),1.E-12,ERREST,IER)
      KOUNTF(4) = KOUNT
      PRINT 401, AERR(L),ERREST
  401   FORMAT(5X,'CADRE TARGET ERROR =' E15.4,4X,'ERROR EST =',E15.4)
      DO 500 J = 1,4
         ERROR(J) = TRUE(JFUNK) - ANSWER(J)
         LOGERR(J) = ALOG10(ABS(ERROR(J)))
  500 CONTINUE
      PRINT 601, (J, ANSWER(J),ERROR(J),LOGERR(J),KOUNTF(J), J=1,4)
  601   FORMAT(2X,'METHOD',8X,'ANSWER',10X,'ERROR',5X'LOG ERROR'
     A       ,4X,'KOUNTF'/  (I6,2X,2F16.12,F9.3,I10  ))
  700 CONTINUE
C            END LOOP OVER FUNCTIONS AT 1000, OVER N AT 700
 1000 CONTINUE
      STOP
      END
      FUNCTION F(X)
      COMMON / SELECT/ JFUNK,KOUNT
      KOUNT = KOUNT + 1
      IF (JFUNK .EQ. 1 ) F = EXP(X)
      IF( JFUNK .EQ. 2 ) F = SQRT(ABS(X-.2345))
      IF( JFUNK .EQ. 3 ) F = 1.+X*X + 1./(1.+100.*X*X)
      RETURN
      END
```

Selection of Methods for Numerical Integration — 7.6.C

The selection of a method for numerical integration depends, of course, on the problem. We identify six basic types of problems and discuss appropriate methods for each. The first four are for a function which can be evaluated anywhere.

1. *Rough accuracy requirement:* One just wants a rough estimate of the size of an integral and does not expect any real trouble in the problem. A simple composite basic rule is adequate; just use Simpson's rule with 25 points or so. If there is some concern about the accuracy being good enough, one might use an automatic method based on a basic rule, but an adaptive method should be as efficient and even more reliable.

2. *One-shot integration:* Only one or two integrals are to be evaluated. A reliable adaptive method, such as DCADRE, should be used. The few extra $f(x)$ evaluations are the "insurance premiums" that one pays for reliability. If the problem has truly exceptional difficulties, then the adaptive method might fail, but this would be reported back by the error flag IER and the problem could be studied further.

3. *Difficult problem:* High accuracy requirements or unusual behavior causes real difficulty. One must be ingenious, experiment with various methods, and probably break the integral into two parts. Gauss-type formulas are usually helpful to give superaccuracy, especially for handling weight functions. One should experiment with analytic substitutions (changes of variable) in the integrand to isolate the troublesome behavior. One uses an adaptive method where the strategy is human-directed, not automatic.

4. *Sets of similar integrals:* One has a large number of similar integrals to evaluate and must pay attention to efficiency. This usually means writing a special program for the particular set of integrals. Gauss formulas should be considered to give extra accuracy at low cost; breaks or singularities in the integrands should be identified and handled by special formulas. An adaptive algorithm should be able to handle a jump in the first derivative (e.g., as in $|x-.2345|$), but it takes it a lot of time to satisfy itself that it has the correct result. One should consider applying an adaptive algorithm (for one case), examining the steps it takes, and then doing something similar without any adaptation for the rest of the integrals.

5. *Tabulated data:* The trapezoidal rule is adequate if only rough accuracy is required. If the data are equally spaced, then the composite Newton-Cotes formulas can be used for better accuracy. There can be a problem when applying a composite formula to a table with 41 points in it because 41 is prime. The best thing for higher accuracy is to compute a spline interpolant (or, perhaps, a cubic Hermite interpolant) and integrate that with the IMSL routine DCSQDU. Do not use DCADRE on the spline interpolant as it might sense the discontinuities at the knots and work much too hard.

6. *Multiple integrals:* One must recognize that multiple integrals are expensive to evaluate. If $g(w, x, y, z)$ is similar to an easy $f(x)$ which requires 25 points in Simpson's rule to integrate, then $g(w, x, y, z)$ requires about $25^4 \sim 400{,}000$ points. A hundred points in a 1-dimensional integral corresponds to a hundred million points in a 4-dimensional integral.

The starting point for multiple integrals is illustrated in the two-dimensional example

$$If = \int_a^b \int_{c(x)}^{d(x)} f(x, y)\, dydx \qquad \textbf{Equation 7.6.2}$$

One applies an algorithm, say DCADRE, successively as follows. Let

$$G2(x) = \int_{c(x)}^{d(x)} f(x, y)\, dy$$

Then

$$If = \int_a^b G2(x)dx$$

is calculated as any other integral. The function $G2(x)$ looks something like

```
FUNCTION G2(X)
EXTERNAL G1
COMMON/GTOF/XPASS
XPASS=X
G2=DCADRE(G1,C(X),D(X),.0001,.0001,ERROR, IER)
```

```
RETURN
END
FUNCTION G1(Y)
COMMON/GTOF/XPASS
G1=F(XPASS,Y)
RETURN
END
```

or, in PROTRAN,

```
FUNCTION G2(X)
$INTEGRAL  F(X,Y);  FOR( Y = C(X),D(X)); ERRTAR = .0001; IS G2
$END
```

This discussion of multiple integrals makes the problem appear simpler than it is. For example, $G2(x)$ might have singularities from the shape of the domain (expecially at $x = a$ or b) even if $F(x, y)$ is smooth. The error tolerance for the inner integral must be chosen high enough so that the outer integral is accurate and, with adaptive methods, so that $G2(x)$ is smooth.

Reverse Communication 7.6.D

The last topic of this section illustrates a software technique that is very useful in numerical computations. A common situation is to want to integrate a function that depends on an independent variable *and* other parameters. Library programs (for example, DCADRE) often assume that f(x) has the Fortran form

```
FUNCTION F(X)
```

So how does one integrate F(X,PRESS,PAR3,K5)? The most reasonable scheme in Fortran is to create a dummy function, say F1, which is F with the values of the parameters PRESS, PAR3, and K5 passed through COMMON. For example, define

```
FUNCTION F1(X)
COMMON/PASSP/PRESS,PAR3,K5
F1=F(X,PRESS,PAR3,K5)
RETURN
END
```

and then use CALL DCADRE(F1,. . .) to integrate F. This scheme is a bit messy even for this simple example; it can be much worse in real problems where F is calculated from a complete mathematical model of a bridge or airplane. The software technique of **reverse communication** eliminates this difficulty at the expense of making the library program a little more complicated. This complication is not great; it adds little to the execution time and, of course, the library program user does not care if the library program is more complicated.

Reverse communication is used in the PROTRAN system to allow integration with the following statements.

```
        $INTEGRAL  F(X,PRESS,PAR3,K5) ; FOR( PAR3 = P1,P2); ERRTAR = .005
        $INTEGRAL  T*EXP(-T*PI) - COS(N*T) ; FOR( T = 0,1.5); IS ANSF
        $INTEGRAL, SER;  ON( X = 0.,8.); DEFINE
            =====
C                FORTRAN DEFINITION OF INTEGRAND SER(X) GIVEN EXPLICITLY
C                PROTRAN $SUM CANNOT BE USED IN THIS CODE SEGMENT
            KZ = Z/PI
            Z2 = Z - PI*KZ
            X  = COS(Z2)
            SER = 0.0
            DO 20 K = -2,30
   20           SER = SER + X**(K/2)/((A*SIN(X)+X**(2*K))*(B+X/K)))
            IF( X .LT. 1.E-10 ) SER = 1./A
            ====
```

The programs containing these statements get the values of X, PRESS, K5, N, PI, A, and B in the normal fashion.

Reverse Communication for Simpson's Rule

Example 7.4

Reverse communication uses one simple idea: *Whenever the method needs a function evaluated, it returns to the calling program to do it.* For concreteness, consider an ordinary Simpson's rule program which starts as

```
SUBROUTINE SIMP(F,A,B,N)
```

to obtain an estimate for the integral of f(x) on [a, b] using n function evaluations. Here F is the name of a Fortran function subprogram and declared EXTERNAL in the calling program.

A reverse Simpson's rule program might start as

```
SUBROUTINE SIMPRV(F,X,A,B,N,KASE)
```

Now F is an ordinary variable, the value of f(x) at X. The switch KASE has 3 values:

KASE = 0	initialize the computation
KASE = 1	give the value F of f(x) at x = X
KASE = 2	calculation finished

A complete program for SIMPRV is given below and starts as

```
SUBROUTINE SIMPRV(F,X,A,B,N,ANSWER,KASE)
```

Most calls on SIMPRV do not produce an answer. The simple way to use a reverse communication program is as follows (for a = 1, b = 2, and n = 50):

```
      KASE = 0
      CALL SIMPRV(F,X,1.,2.,50,ANSWER,KASE)
   10 CONTINUE
C     COMPUTE F(X) VALUE HERE
      CALL SIMPRV(F,X,1.,2.,50,ANSWER KASE)
      IF( KASE .NE. 2 )  GO TO 10
```

Note that the first initializing call *cannot* be made as

```
CALL SIMPRV(F,X,1.,2.,50,ANSWER,0)
```

because SIMPRV changes KASE, the last argument. A better alternative which incorporates protection against an infinite loop is

```
      KASE = 0
      DO 10 K=1,KLIMIT
         CALL SIMPRV(F,X,1.,2.,50,ANSWER,KASE)
         IF( KASE .EQ. 2 )  GO TO 20
C        COMPUTER F(X) VALUE HERE
   10 CONTINUE
C     PRINT ERROR MESSAGE, PROGRAM EXCEEDED LIMIT
   20 CONTINUE
```

Protection against an infinite loop is not very likely to be needed for Simpson's rule, but it is advisable for many other methods. If the program SIMPRV is known to be reliable, then KLIMIT can be very large (for example, 1000000 or $100+n^2$. If available, a WHILE statement could be used also.

```
      KASE = 0
      DO 10 WHILE( KASE .NE. 2 )
            CALL SIMPRV(F,X,1.,2.,50,ANSWER,KASE)
C           COMPUTE F(X) VALUE HERE
   10 CONTINUE
```

The subprogram given below for SIMPRV shows the amount of extra complexity introduced; a RETURN occurs at each point where f(x) is evaluated. There is also an internal switch (JUMP in the program) to keep track of where the value is needed, and finally, there is a mechanism (a COMPUTED GO TO or CASE statement) to get back to the right point on the next call.

Subprogram for Simpson's Rule with Reverse Communication Along with a Driver for Two Examples

```
C          DRIVER TO TEST SIMPRV FOR EXP(X) AND 1/SQRT(X)
      KASE = 0
      CALL SIMPRV(F,X,0.,1.,20,ANSWER, KASE)
   10 F = EXP(X)
      CALL SIMPRV(F,X,0.,1.,20,ANSWER, KASE)
      IF( KASE .EQ.1 )       GO TO 10
          PRINT 15, ANSWER
   15     FORMAT(//5X,'ANSWER =' F15.10)
      KASE = 0
      CALL SIMPRV(F,X,1.,10.,20,ANSWER,KASE)
   20 F = 1./SQRT(X)
      CALL SIMPRV(F,X,1.,10.,20,ANSWER,KASE)
      IF( KASE .EQ. 1 )      GO TO 20
          PRINT 15, ANSWER
      STOP
      END

      SUBROUTINE  SIMPRV(F,X,A,B,N,ANSWER,KASE)
C
C               EXAMPLE 7.4
C
C      REVERSE COMMUNICATION FOR SIMPSON RULE
C          KASE = 0  FIRST CALL
C               = 1  INTERMEDIATE CALLS
C               = 2  COMPUTATION FINISHED
C          JUMP = SWITCH TO GO TO THE CORRECT LOCATION
C                 THERE ARE 4 PLACES WHERE F VALUES ARE NEEDED
C
C         SAVE ANS, H, H2, SUM1 AND SUM2 FOR FORTRAN 77
      IF( KASE .GT. 0)                        GO TO 5
                     INITIAL ENTRY FOR INITIALIZATION
          KASE = 1
          X    = A
          H    = (B-A)/(N-1)
C                  USE N+1 POINTS IF N IS EVEN
          IF( MOD(N,2) .EQ. 0 )  H = (B-A)/N
          JUMP = 1
          RETURN
C              SWITCH TO GO TO RIGHT PLACE
    5 GO TO(10,20,30,40),JUMP
C                    GET F(A), GO TO 20 NEXT TIME
   10 ANS  = F
      JUMP = 2
      X    = B
      SUM1 = 0.
      RETURN
C                    GET F(B), GO TO 30 NEXT TIME
   20 ANS  = ANS + F
      JUMP = 3
      H2   = 2.*H
      SUM1 = 0.
      X    = A + H
      RETURN
C                    SUM OVER A+H, A+3H, A+5H, ... B-H
C                    GET F AT ODD POINTS
   30 SUM1 = SUM1 + F
      X    = X + H2
      IF( X .LT. B )      RETURN
C                    PREPARE TO SUM OVER EVEN POINTS AT 40
      X    = A + H2
      JUMP = 4
      SUM2 = 0.0
      RETURN
C                    SUM OVER A+2H, A+4H, A+6H,... B-2H
C                    GET F AT EVEN POINTS
   40 X    =  X + H2
      IF( X .LT. B-H )   RETURN
      ANSWER = H*( ANS + 4.*SUM1 + 2.*SUM2 )/3.
      KASE = 2
      RETURN
      END
```

PROBLEMS 7.6

7.6.1 Romberg integration is based on the trapezoidal rule plus Richardson extrapolation. Take the interval [a, b] and let $T_{0,k}$ denote the result of applying the trapezoidal rule, 7.4.4, with 2^k intervals. A triangular table of the form

$$\begin{array}{llll} T_{00} & & & \\ T_{01} & T_{10} & & \\ T_{02} & T_{11} & T_{20} & \\ T_{03} & T_{12} & T_{21} & T_{30} \end{array}$$

is formed by Richardson extrapolation from the formula

$$T_{m,k} = (4^m T_{m-1,k+1} - T_{m-1,k})/(4^m - 1)$$

See Problem 4.5.12 for a justification of this extrapolation formula. Each $T_{m,k}$ is an estimate of the integral which is exact for piecewise polynomials of degree $2m+2$ on the subintervals of length $(b-a)/2^k$ (starting at a).

(A) Write a Fortran program

```
SUBROUTINE ROMB(F,A,B,N,T)
REAL T(N,4)
```

which computes the Romberg table for $\int_A^B F(x)dx$ up to N rows (with a maximum of 4 columns).

(B) Apply ROMB to polynomials to verify the claim about its exactness for piecewise polynomials.

(C) Enter it into the competition with the four methods in Example 7.3. Take T_{m0} or $T_{5,k-5}$ as the estimate of the integrals. Write a program for the performance evaluation similar to that of Example 7.3 and state conclusions about ROMB's performance relative to the other methods.

7.6.2 Observe experimentally that the results in the second column of the Romberg table of Problem 7.6.1 are identical with the results of Simpson's rule. Prove that this should be so from the definition of $T_{1,k}$.

7.6.3 Write a Fortran subprogram

```
FUNCTION SIMP(F,A,B,N)
```

which applies Simpson's rule to F(x) on [A, B].

(A) Check that the program is correct by recomputing the results of Example 7.3.

(B) Apply the program to the functions

$$f_1(x) = 1 + 2x + (x-9)^5$$
$$f_2(x) = -59048 + 32807x - 7290x^2 + 810x^3 - 45x^4 + x^5$$

to estimate, using N = 1, 11, 101, 1001:

$$\int_{8.9}^{9.1} f(x)dx$$

Discuss how the round-off error in $f_2(x)$ affects the integration. Compare the sensitivity of integration and differentiation to round-off by comparing this result with that of Problem 7.2.9.

7.6.4 Repeat Problem 7.6.3 for

```
FUNCTION GAUSS3(F,A,B,N)
```

which applies the composite 3-point Gauss rule to F(x) on [A, B].

7.6.5 Evaluate the sensitivity of integration methods to round-off error as follows. Take six functions whose integrals on [−1, 1] are known exactly: $1 + x$, $x^4 + x^2 + 1$, $\sin x$, $\sin(20x)$, $1/(1+40x^2)$, and $x^2\,\mathrm{sign}(x)$. During their evaluations for the integration, perturb the value by multiplying by 1 + EPS where EPS is a random number uniformly distributed in the interval [−.01, +.01]. Compare the calculated integrals to the true (unperturbed) values and compute a condition number for integration. Apply this to the following methods [made into composite rules for (A), (D), and (E)].

(A) Simpson's rule

(B) DCADRE

(C) Romberg (Problem 7.6.1)

(D) Newton-Cotes open rule for n = 6

(E) 3-point Gauss rule

Discuss how the condition number changes with an increasing number of intervals. **Hint:** For a small number of intervals do the perturbation several times to average out the randomness.

7.6.6 Write a program to compare integration by the trapezoidal rule, Simpson's rule, and composite 2-point Gauss rule. Have it print out

```
FOR H = X.XXX
TRAPEZOIDAL RULE  GIVES  X.XXXXXXXX, ERROR = X.XXEXX
SIMPSON RULE      GIVES  X.XXXXXXXX, ERROR = X.XXEXX
2-PT. GAUSS       GIVES  X.XXXXXXXX, ERROR = X.XXEXX
```

Choose H so that the trapezoidal rule gives about 2 correct digits, and apply this program to the following functions.

(A) $\int_0^2 e^{3x}dx$

(B) $\int_{-1}^1 \sqrt{x}\, dx$

(C) $\int_{-.5}^3 \frac{1+x^2}{1+10x^6}dx$

(D) $\int_0^2 e^{-x}/(.2+4x^4)dx$

(E) $\int_0^1 \cos(e^{-x}+\log(1+x^2))dx$

(F) $\int_{10}^{12} (x-10)(x-11)(x-12)e^{(x-11)/(x+11)}dx$

Hint: Use DCADRE to find correct values to 6 digits.

7.6.7 Develop **Simpson's rule for 2 dimensions**. Note that there is more than one way to do this; the generalization must retain the essential features of Simpson's rule.

(A) Describe for this rule

1. The generalization of an interval
2. The distribution of abscissas in the generalized interval
3. The essential features of Simpson's rule retained

(B) Give the equations or relations that must be satisfied by the coefficents of this rule.

(C) Describe the extension of this rule as a composite rule for integration over a rectangle.

7.6.8 Consider the integral

$$\int_a^b \sqrt{x-a}\; f(x)dx$$

(A) Describe a rule that estimates this integral using k subdivisions with Equation 7.4.9 (appropriately modified) used in the interval (a, a+H) and a 2-point Gauss rule in the remaining intervals.

(B) Describe the model for which this rule gives exact results.

(C) Implement this rule as the program

```
REAL FUNCTION INTR(F,A,B,K)
```

and apply it to $f(x) = e^x$ on [1, 2] so as to obtain 4 digits of accuracy. **Hint:** To debug the program, use the model obtained in part (B) as f(x).

7.6.9 Find an approximation to the function f(x) which satisfies the **integral equation**

$$f(x) + \int_0^1 f(t)\cos(x-t)dt = \tan(1+x^2)$$

Hint: Replace the integral by an integration formula, say composite 2-point Gauss. Examine this approximate equation and obtain a system of linear equations for the values of f(x) at the abscissas used in the integration formula. Solve this system of linear equations.

7.6.10 Outline a plan to evaluate each of the following integrals:

(A) $\int_{.01}^{\infty} \frac{1+\sin x}{x^2} dx$

(B) $\int_0^{\infty} e^{-x} \left[x^2 + \frac{\cos(x)}{\sqrt{|(x-1)(x-2)(x-3)|}} \right] dx$

(C) $\int_{-1}^{5} \log(|\sin(x)|)\, dx$

(D) $\int_0^3 x \sin\left(\frac{1}{x}\right) \sqrt{|1-x|}\, dx$

7.6.11 Write a program to compare the accuracy of the **corrected trapezoidal rule** (Equation 7.4.3) and the **modified corrected trapezoidal rule** (Problem 7.4.3). Implement both methods and apply them to the functions e^x, sin x, x^6-x^4, $1/(1+x^2)$, and xe^{-x} on [0, 1]. Use several values k for the number of subintervals (say k = 3, 7, 15, 25, and 50). Discuss the difference in the accuracy of these two formulas. **Hint:** From Problem 7.4.3 one has the following formula:

$$\int_a^{a+h} f(x)dx + \frac{h^2}{12} f'(a) \sim \frac{h}{2}[f(a)+f(a+h)]$$

$$+ \frac{h}{24}\left[-11f(a) + 18f\left(a+\frac{h}{3}\right) - 9f\left(a+\frac{2h}{3}\right) + f(a+h)\right]$$

7.6.12 Consider the integral

$$A = \int_0^1 x^{\alpha} f(x)dx$$

If α is close to zero, this is a difficult integral.

(A) Make the change of variable $y = x^{\gamma}$ in this integral and show the new integral.

(B) For α small, choose the value of γ that reduces the difficulty of the integral.

(C) Consider the integral in Example 7.2 (with $\alpha = .1$) and use DCADRE on the original integrand and on the integrand after the change of variable. Discuss the effect of this change of variable.

(D) Study the behavior of the error in part (C) as α varies from .05 to 1.0. Prepare plots that illustrate the effectiveness of the two approaches.

7.6.13 Consider the tabulated data with k+1 points and h = 1/k:

$$x_i = \frac{(1+ih)^2-1}{3} \qquad i = 0, 1, 2, \ldots, k$$

$$y_i = f(x_i)$$

Compare the accuracy obtained by using three integration methods: (i) composite trapezoid rule, (ii) integration of the Hermite cubics interpolant, and (iii) integration of the cubic spline interpolant. Use the following choices for f(x):

(A) e^x

(B) $x^3 - x^2$

(C) sin(2x)

(D) $3/[1+50(x-.2)^4]$

Hint: Use IMSL routines IQHSCU and ICSCCU to do the interpolation, then use DCSQDU to perform the integration.

7.6.14 Explain why the first call on SIMPRV to initialize it cannot be made as

```
CALL SIMPRV(F,X,1.,2.,50,ANSWER,0)
```

Run the program of Example 7.4 this way and verify the existence of a problem.

ERROR ANALYSIS FOR INTEGRATION 7.7

We use I to denote the linear functional of integration and Q to denote a numerical integration (quadrature) formula (see Equation 7.5.1); subscripts may be used at times, as in

$$I_{[a,b]}f = \int_a^b f(x)dx \qquad \textbf{Equation 7.7.1}$$

It is a simple exercise to show that

$$||I_{[a,b]}|| = (b-a) \qquad \textbf{Equation 7.7.2}$$

Note that the linear change of variable $t = (x-a)/(b-a)$ takes 7.7.1 into

$$If = (b-a)\int_0^1 f(t)dt \qquad \textbf{Equation 7.7.3}$$

Thus we can restrict our attention to integration on [0, 1] and transfer results to other intervals just by multiplying by the interval length. I and Q without any subscript refer to the interval [0, 1] of integration. The **error functional** is

$$\lambda f = Qf - If \qquad \textbf{Equation 7.7.4}$$

Theorem 7.3 *Let $f(x)$ have $n+1$ continuous derivatives in $[a, b]$ and $Q_{[a,b]}$ be exact for polynomials of degree n. Then the error λf in the integration formula is bounded by*

$$|\lambda f| \le ((b-a) + ||Q_{[a,b]}||)||E_n(f)||$$

$$\le [(1+||Q||)||f^{(n+1)}||h^{n+2}/(n+1)! = O(h^{n+2})$$

where $h = (b-a)$ and $E_n(f)$ in the polynomial interpolation error 5.5.10.
Proof: We have from Theorem 5.7 that

$$|\lambda f| = |Qf\text{-}If| \le ||\lambda||\ ||E_n(f)||$$

and applying Theorem 5.6 we obtain

$$|\lambda f| \le ||\lambda||f^{(n+1)}||h^{n+1}/(n+1)!$$

Now λ on [a, b] is h times λ on [0, 1], and so

$$||\lambda|| \le ||I_{[a,b]}|| + ||Q_{[a,b]}|| = h(1+||Q||)$$

which establishes the theorem.
Theorem 7.4 *Let $f(x)$ have $n+1$ continuous derivatives in $[a, b]$ and let $Q_{[a,b]}$ be exact for piecewise polynomials of degree n with $k+1$ equally spaced break points in $[a, b]$. Set $h = (b-a)/k$, and then the error λf in the integration formula is bounded by*

$$|\lambda f| \le (1+||Q||)||f^{(n+1)}||(b-a)h^{n+1}/(n+1)! = O(h^{n+1})$$

Proof: The error on [a, b] is less than the sum of errors on each subinterval of [a, b]. Apply Theorem 7.3 to each subinterval to obtain

$$|\lambda f| \le k(1+||Q||)||f^{(n+1)}||h^{n+2}/(n+1)!$$

Since $kh = b - a$, the conclusion of the theorem follows.

A numerical integration formula Q is said to be a **positive formula** if all its coefficients are positive. The following are **positive integration formulas.**

Closed Newton-Cotes, n = 1 to 8

Open Newton-Cotes, n = 0 and 1

Superaccurate Gauss, all n (see Problem 11.8.14)

Romberg (not discussed here — see Problem 7.6.1)

An important fact about these formulas is this: *The norm of any positive integration formula $Q_{[a,b]}$ is $(b-a)$.* Thus, $||Q|| = 1$, and $1 + ||Q||$ can be replaced by 2 in Theorems 7.3 and 7.4. To see this, note that $f(x) = 1$ gives $Q_{[a,b]}\,f = (b-a)$ (we assume the integration formula at least integrates constants exactly). On the other hand, if $||f|| \le 1$,

$$|Q_{[a,b]}f| \le ||f||\ \Sigma\ |\text{coefficients}| \le \Sigma \text{ coefficients} = (b-a)$$

and so $||Q_{[a,b]}|| \le (b-a)$.

The error estimates of Theorems 7.3 and 7.4 are adequate for most purposes; the fact that $||f^{(n+1)}||$ is rarely known with more than rough accuracy (if that) means that accurate estimates of the bound are not obtainable. There are times when one wants to compare two methods both with $||f^{(n+1)}||$ in their error bounds, and then more precise error bounds are useful. Exact, but not easy-to-evaluate, error formulas are given by the next theorem.

Theorem 7.5 *Let $f(x)$ have $n+1$ continuous derivatives in $[0, 1]$ and let Q be exact for polynomials of degree n. Then the error λf of the integration is given by*

$$(A)\quad \lambda f = \frac{1}{n!}\int_0^1 f^{(n+1)}(t)\left[\int_0^1 (x-t)_+^n dx - Q[(x-t)_+^n]\right]dt$$

$$(B)\quad \lambda f = \int_0^1 f[x_0,\ldots,x_n,x]\sum_{i=0}^{n}(x-x_i)dx \le \frac{f^{(n+1)}(\xi)}{(n+1)!}\int_0^1 \sum_{i=0}^{n}|x-x_i|dx$$

where the x_i are the abscissas of Q.

Proof: For part (A) we start with Taylor's series with integral remainder

$$f(x) = \sum_{i=0}^{n} f^{(i)}(0)\frac{x^i}{i!} + \frac{1}{n!}\int_0^1 (x-t)_+^n f^{(n+1)}(t)dt$$

Apply $I-Q$ to this expansion, and all the terms in the sum disappear because Q is exact for polynomials of degree n or less. Conclusion (A) is just $I-Q$ applied to the remainder terms with a small rearrangement.

For part (B) we start with Newton's interpolating polynomial $p_n(x)$, of degree n, that is,

$$f(x) = p_n(x) + f[x_0, x_1, \ldots x_n, x]\prod_{i=0}^{n}(x-x_i)$$

Again apply $I-Q$ to this formula, and the first expression for λf immediately results. The bound on λf then follows from taking the absolute value of the product in the integral and applying the mean value theorem for integrals. This concludes the proof.

For particular formulas Q one knows the abscissas x_i and one can often obtain more precise results by explicitly analyzing the terms in Theorem 7.5, especially if n is small.

Stopping An Automatic Integration Algorithm — Example 7.5

An automatic integration algorithm has an accuracy target TOL and is supposed to stop when the actual error is less than TOL. First consider a strategy of subdividing $[a, b]$ into $2, 4, 8, \ldots, 2^k$ subintervals and comparing the results for each k. If the basic rule used is exact for polynomials of degree n, then we have

$$Q_k f = If + \lambda_k f = If + O(h_k^{n+1})$$

where the subscript k refer the case with 2^k subintervals, $h_k = (b-a)/2^k$. We have

$$Q_k f - Q_{k+1} f = O(h_k^{n+1}) - O(h_{k+1}^{n+1}) = \frac{2^{n+1}-1}{2^{n+1}} O(h_k^{n+1}) \qquad \textbf{Equation 7.7.4}$$

The $O(h_k^{n+1})$ on the right of 7.7.4 is the error $\lambda_k f$ in $Q_k f$, and so we have

$$\lambda_k f \sim \frac{2^{n+1}}{2^{n+1}-1}(Q_k - Q_{k+1})f \qquad \textbf{Equation 7.7.5}$$

This is computable from $Q_k f$ and $Q_{k+1} f$, and we can terminate the subdividing whenever the estimate in 7.7.5 is less than TOL. For usual values of n, $2^{n+1}/(2^{n+1}-1)$ is nearly 1.

Note that we have an error estimate only for Q_k even though we have computed the presumably more accurate Q_{k+1}. One would take Q_{k+1} as the estimate of If; this normally provides a safety factor in the stopping decision. One expects $\lambda_{k+1} \sim \lambda_k/2^{n+1}$, and so an "aggressively designed" algorithm could decide to stop when $\lambda_k f$ from 7.7.5 is less than 2^{n+1} TOL. This latter choice is based on indirect evidence of the error λ_{k+1} and is much less reliable. It is typically the case in numerical computations that computing a good error estimate for an approximate solution takes about as much work as computing the approximate solution itself. This is the case in using 7.7.5; see Problem 7.7.9 for a refined version of this approach.

The error estimate 7.7.5 involves two estimates of If of the same order; $||f^{(n+1)}||$ appears in both, and hence one really does not need to know its value. Another approach to automatic numerical integration is to compute estimates of different orders using the same abscissas. For example, Simpson's rule with two intervals is

$$Q_2f = \frac{h}{3}[f(x)+4f(a+h)+2f(a+2h)+4f(a+3h)+f(a+4h)]$$

and the 5-point Newton-Cotes rule with one interval [using the same f(x) values] is

$$Q'_1f = \frac{8h}{90}[7f(a)+32f(a+h)+2f(a+2h)+32f(a+3h)+7f(a+4h)]$$

We have

$$Q_2f = If - \lambda_2 f \quad = If + O(h^5)$$
$$Q'_1f = If - \lambda'_1 f \quad = If + O(h^7)$$

and

$$(Q_2 - Q'_1)f = \lambda_2 f - \lambda'_1 f = O(h^5) - O(h^7)$$ **Equation 7.7.6**

These terms are incomparable, even with h known, because one involves $||f^{(4)}||$ and the other $||f^{(6)}||$. On the other hand, for small h, one expects the $O(h^7)$ term to be much smaller than $O(h^5)$, and so one might decide that adequate accuracy is obtained when $|Q_2f - Q'_1f| \leq TOL$. Using formulas of different orders is more risky than using formulas of the same order; the big advantage in this example is that no further f(x) evaluations are required.

PROBLEMS 7.7

7.7.1 Consider the integral

$$S = \int_0^1 \sin(e^x)dx$$

Suppose one applies a 9-point Gauss formula and a 9-point (composite) Simpson formula to estimate S.

(A) Which method should give the more accurate result? Justify the answer.

(B) Define accuracy for the response to part (A).

(C) Give an example of an f(x) where you expect the opposite selection for part (A), and justify the answer.

7.7.2 Consider an **automatic 2-point Gauss** composite integration method based on dividing each subinterval until the accuracy requirement is met.

(A) Give a precise definition of this method (say in flowchart or very high level language form).

(B) Give the stopping rule used.

(C) Compare the number of f(x) evaluations this method takes with that of an automatic Simpson's rule method. Explain why the advantage of superaccuracy in the Gauss formula is mostly lost.

7.7.3 Give the order of convergence of composite m-point closed Newton-Cotes integration as a function of m and $h = (b-a)/k$.

7.7.4 Obtain an exact expression for the error in the trapezoidal rule on [0, h). Compare it with the result obtained from Theorem 7.3. **Hint:** Use Theorem 7.5.

7.7.5 Obtain an exact expression for the error in the corrected trapezoidal rule (Equation 7.4.2). Compare it with the result obtained from Theorem 7.3. **Hint:** Use Theorem 7.5.

7.7.6 Give the order of convergence of a composite 3-point Gauss formula. Use the program of Problem 7.6.4 to verify in practice that this rate of convergence is actually obtained. Use smooth integrands for the experiment such as those in Problem 7.6.6(A),(C), and (D).

7.7.7 Develop an **automatic trapezoid rule** method where the stopping rule uses the composite midpoint rule to obtain a second estimate of the integral. Thus, on [x, x+h] one has the trapezoidal rule estimate using f(x) and f(x+h) and the midpoint rule estimate using f(x+h/2).

(A) Give a precise statement of the test for stopping the method.

(B) Give a precise definition of the method (in a flowchart or very high level language).

(C) Compare this approach with the more normal one of comparing the value on [x, x+h] with the two trapezoid sums on [x, x+h/2] and [x+h/2, x+h]. In particular, compare the difficulty of obtaining the stopping rule and the amount of computation each method is expected to take.

7.7.8 Repeat Problem 7.7.7 using Simpson's rule on each [x, x+h] as a second estimate instead of the midpoint rule.

7.7.9 With the notation of Example 7.5, consider the hypothesis H that (K is an unknown constant)

$$Q_k f = If + Kh_k^{n+1} + O(h^n{}_k{}^{+2})$$

If H is true, then

$$Q_{k+1}f = If + Kh_{k+1}^{n+1} + O(h_{k+1}^{n+2})$$

and set

$$E_k = (Q_k - Q_{k+1})f$$
$$R_k = E_k/E_{k+1}$$

(A) Show that, if H is true,

$$E_k = Kh_k^{n+1}(1 - 2^{-(n+1)})$$
$$R_k = 2^{n+1} + O(h)$$

(B) To test the hypothesis H, one can compute R_k, R_{k+1}, and R_{k+2} and if they are *all* close to 2^{n+1}, then one concludes that H is true, E_k is accurate, and the stopping test is reliable. This is the method used in DCADRE.

REFERENCES

Philip J. Davis and Philip Rabinowitz, *Methods of Numerical Integration,* Academic Press, Inc., New York (1975).

J. N. Lyness and J. J. Kaganove, "Comments on the Nature of Automatic Quadrature Routines," ACM Trans. Math. Software, **2** (1976), pp. 65–81.

A. H. Stroud, *Approximate Calculation of Multiple Integrals,* Prentice-Hall, Inc., Englewood Cliffs, N.J. (1971).

8
NONLINEAR EQUATIONS

The nonlinear equations problem is to solve equations like the following:

$$2x^2 - 4x + 1.5 = 0 \qquad \text{solve for } x$$
$$te^{3t} - t^2 = 1 \qquad \text{solve for } t$$
$$\left.\begin{aligned} a^2b + 2ab^2 - ab &= 3 \\ ab^2 - 2a^2b + 4ab &= -1 \end{aligned}\right\} \qquad \text{solve for a and b}$$

Equation 8.1.1

Such equations are denoted by $f(x) = 0$ for one equation in one unknown and $\mathbf{f}(\mathbf{x}) = 0$ for a system of equations. In the latter case we have a *vector function* $\mathbf{f}$ *of a vector* $\mathbf{x}$. Thus in Equation 8.1.1, $\mathbf{x} = (a, b)$ (that is, $x_1 = a$, $x_2 = b$) and $\mathbf{f} = (f_1, f_2)$ where

$$f_1(\mathbf{x}) = f_1(a, b) = a^2b + 2ab^2 - ab - 3$$
$$f_2(\mathbf{x}) = f_2(a, b) = ab^2 - 2a^2b + 4ab + 1$$

FORMULATING PROBLEMS AS F(X) = 0 *8.1

The purpose of this chapter is to present methods and software to solve the general nonlinear equations problem. There is also a section on the special case of polynomial equations. First, though, we show how a wide variety of problems can be brought into the standard form $f(x) = 0$ and thus can be attacked by nonlinear equation methods. The fact that so many problems can be brought into this form underscores the difficulty of this problem; if solving nonlinear equations were easy, then solving most other problems would be easy.

The key to putting problems into the form $f(x) = 0$ or $\mathbf{f}(\mathbf{x}) = 0$ is to realize that, if there are conditions to be satisfied and if they can be calculated, then a subprogram can be written whose output is the amounts by which the conditions fail to be satisfied. This subprogram defines the function $\mathbf{f}$, and we want to find input $\mathbf{x}$ so that its output $\mathbf{f}(\mathbf{x})$ is zero. It is not necessary to be able to write the function $\mathbf{f}$ as a standard mathematical function; any Fortran code will do.

How Much Life Insurance Should One Have — Example 8.1

Suppose you are married, you are the sole support of your family of four (children ages 5 and 10), and you realize that you need to have life insurance. You ask, "How much insurance do I need?" You might start by deciding how much support you want to give your family if you die. You decide that you want to:

1. Provide \$500 per month until the oldest child is 18
2. Provide \$800 per month for the next 4 years
3. Provide \$400 per month for the next year
4. Provide \$600 per month for the next 4 years
5. Provide \$150 per month for the next 15 years
6. Leave a sum of \$20,000 at this time

This decision is based on the assumption that your spouse will go to work if you die, but your insurance will supplement the family income substantially.

You might assume that your life insurance proceeds are invested at 8 percent interest, paid quarterly on the smallest balance during the preceding quarter, and the above amounts are withdrawn monthly. The problem is to determine the amount of money (life insurance) that provides the income listed above.

A program is written that simulates all the transactions in the income projection. This can be done on a quarterly basis; each 3 months there are 3 monthly withdrawals and interest is added once. Let LEFT(INS) be the function that gives the amount left from the insurance after 32 years of payments and after subtracting \$20,000. It appears as follows:

```
      REAL FUNCTION LEFT(INS)
      REAL INS, INTRST, INTQ
C         BAL = BALANCE OF MONEY, INTQ = QUARTERLY INTEREST RATE
      BAL = INS
      INTRST = .08
      INTQ = INTRST/4.
C                        FIRST PERIOD - 8 YEARS AT $500/MONTH
      WITHDR = 500
      DO 10 I = 1,4*8
   10     BAL = (BAL- 3.*WITHDR)*(1. + INTQ)
C                        SECOND PERIOD - 4 YEARS AT $800/MONTH
      WITHDR = 800
      DO 20 I = 1,4*4
C             .......... CODE OMITTED FOR MIDDLE OF CALCULATION
      WITHDR = 150
      DO 50 I = 1,4*15
   50     BAL = (BAL- 3.*WITHDR)*(1. +INTQ)
      LEFT = BAL - 20000.
      RETURN
      END
```

The problem is now to solve LEFT(INS) = 0 for INS. Such a function subprogram can be used directly with many of the methods and programs discussed in this chapter.

A Differential Equation Model of Gas Lubrication — Example 8.2

Air can be a lubricant if the parts are moving very fast and the gap between them is very small. This occurs with magnetic read heads on tape and disk drives; a simple model is shown in the diagram. The fast-moving disk "drags" the air into the gap; it is "squeezed" as the gap narrows, and a pressure is built up which keep the head and disk separated, preventing physical contact and damage. The pressure $p(t)$ inside the gap is modeled with the differential equation

$$d\left(p(t)h^3(t)\,\frac{dp(t)}{dt}\right)/dt = -kd(p(t)h(t))/dt$$

with the conditions that $p(0) = p(1) =$ atmospheric pressure $= p_0$. The physical constant k depends on the properties of air, the velocity of the disk, etc. With $p' = dp(t)/dt$, we can rewrite this equation as

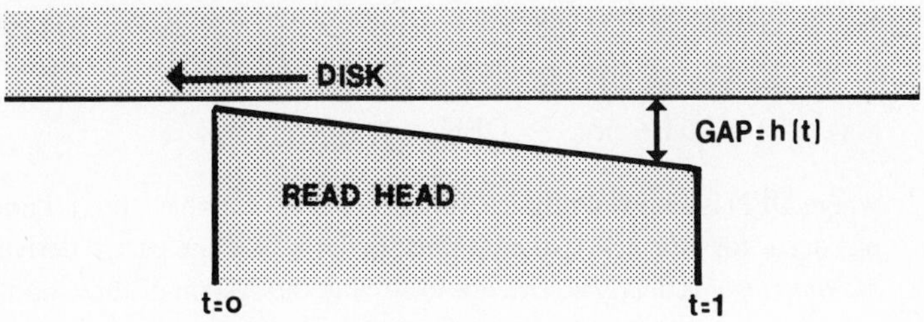

$$p'' = \left[\frac{(p')^2}{p} + \frac{3h'h^2p'}{p} + \frac{k(p'h+ph')}{(ph^3)} \right] \quad p(0) = p_0,\ p(1) = p_0$$ **Equation 8.1.2**

There are many library routines that can be applied to solve the initial value problem

$$u'' = f(t, u, u') \qquad u(0) = u_1,\ u'(0) = u_2$$

There are far fewer that apply to the two-point boundary value problem, 8.1.2. Let us symbolically denote the library program result for 8.1.2 by ODESOLVER(t, u_2); the result at point t depends on the value u_2 assumed for p' at $t = 0$. We need to solve the nonlinear equation

$$\text{ODESOLVER}(1, u_2) = p_0$$

for u_2. This is a nonlinear equation where the function involves the library program, and hence it is not easily written as a mathematical formula. However, it can be evaluated for any u_2, and that is all that is really required in order to apply nonlinear equation solving methods and software.

The effectiveness of this approach depends on the differential equation; it works well for some and is numerically unstable for others. This particular example is stable if one chooses $p'(0)$ as the unknown; it is unstable if one chooses $p'(1)$ as the unknown. This is called the **shooting method.**

Gauss Quadrature Formulas — Example 8.3

Recall the integration formula 7.4.9

$$If = \int_0^1 \sqrt{1-x}\ g(x)dx \sim w_1 g(x_1) + w_2 g(x_2) = Qf$$

which is exact for cubic polynomials. This means that the weights w_i and abscissas x_i must satisfy the four equations

$$I(x^j) = Q(x^j) \qquad j = 0, 1, 2, 3$$

The right-side linear functionals $Q(x^j)$ can be calculated analytically; call these constants c_i, $i = 1$ to 4. Rename w_1 and w_2 as x_3 and x_4 so that $\mathbf{x} = (x_1, x_2, w_1, w_2)$ and the conditions for the Gauss integration formulas are

$$f_i(\mathbf{x}) = x_3(x_1)^{i-1} + x_4(x_2)^{i-1} - c_i = 0 \qquad i = 1, 2, 3, 4$$ **Equation 8.1.3**

These equations are of the form $f_i(\mathbf{x}) = 0$, $i = 1, 2, 3, 4$, where $f_i(\mathbf{x})$ is the expression on the left side of 8.1.3. These are four equations with four unknowns in the form $\mathbf{f}(\mathbf{x}) = 0$.

The system 8.1.3 is difficult to solve; see Example 8.8 for a related system. This example and the previous one illustrate that it is often much easier to formulate a problem as a system of equations than to solve the system. There is no reliable way to tell in advance whether a system will be easy or hard to solve.

The Optimization Equations — Example 8.4

There is a close relation between methods for solving nonlinear equations and for optimization. The reason is that optimization problems can be reformulated as nonlinear equations using the general technique of setting first derivatives equal to zero. For a simple example, suppose we have a function g(x, y, z) to be maximized for $y \geq 0$, $z \geq 0$, and x arbitrary. The function g might appear as

$$g(x, y, z) = x(1+z)e^{-y} - DEN(z, x)\,(y-1)^2 - x^2 z \qquad \textbf{Equation 8.1.4}$$

where DEN is a known physical function of two variables. If it is known somehow that the maximum does not occur for y or z = 0, then it must occur where the partial derivatives of g are all equal to zero. Thus, *maximizing g* is nearly equivalent to solving the system of three nonlinear equations

$$\frac{\partial g}{\partial x} = (1+z)e^{-y} - \frac{\partial DEN}{\partial x}(y-1)^2 - 2xz = 0 \qquad \textbf{Equation 8.1.5}$$

$$\frac{\partial g}{\partial y} = -x(1+z)e^{-y} - 2(y-1)DEN(z, x) = 0$$

$$\frac{\partial g}{\partial z} = xe^{-y} - \frac{\partial DEN}{\partial z}(y-1)^2 - x^2 = 0$$

Note that if the maximum occurs for y = 0, then one can use the two equations with partial derivatives with respect to x and z. If g(x, y, z) has minima or inflection points, they also satisfy 8.1.5.

PROBLEMS 8.1

8.1.1 The points on a smooth curve where it is highest or lowest have the special property that they occur either at the ends of the curve or where the slope (derivative) is zero.

(A) Discuss how one uses this fact to find the maxima and minima of curves by solving a nonlinear equation.

(B) Give an example to show the slope might be zero without a maximum or minimum, and discuss how this affects an algorithm to locate maxima and minima by solving nonlinear equations.

(C) Discuss how to apply this approach for tabulated data. **Hint:** Model the data by an interpolant.

8.1.2 A sum of money is to be deposited in a bank which will grow to \$20,000 in 11 years. The bank pays 6 percent interest the first year, 7 percent the second year, and 8 percent thereafter. The interest is computed and added to the principal once a year.

(A) Formulate this problem as a nonlinear equation problem. Write the Fortran function subprogram to be used as f(x). Find the sum.

(B) Modify the program for a bank which pays an extra .1 percent for each \$1,000 above \$2,000 (with a limit 1 percent extra interest). Find the sum.

(C) Suppose the interest is taxable at the rate of 22 percent. Modify the program of part (B) to include this effect so that the \$20,000 final sum is after taxes. The tax is paid at the end of the year on the interest earned for that year.

8.1.3 Write a function subprogram F(X) for calculating **mortgage payments.** Given the interest rate I per year, the principal (amount borrowed) P, and the number N of years to pay, the subprogram is to return the balance at the end for a given monthly payment X. Assume payments and interest are paid monthly. **Hint:** The parameters I, P, and N are not to appear in the argument list of F(X); put them in a COMMON block.

8.1.4 Write the Fortran function subprogram F(T) needed to solve

$$\int_0^T \sin(x + \sqrt{T^2+x})\,dx = .25$$

for T using a nonlinear equation solver.

8.1.5 Give the system of nonlinear equations to be solved in order to find a minimum of the function

$$e^{x^2+y^2+z^3+w^2} + e^{x-y}\cos(zw) - xy/(1+x^2+w^2)$$

8.1.6 Give the system of nonlinear equations to be solved to minimize

$$\int_0^2 (f(x) - ae^{bx} - c)^2\,dx$$

as a function of a, b, and c.

METHODS FOR ONE NONLINEAR EQUATION 8.2

Most methods for systems of nonlinear equations are extensions of methods for one equation, and so it is important to systematically survey most of the possibilities in the simpler case of one equation. A few of the one-equation methods do not readily extend to systems of equations.

Seven Basic Iteration Methods 8.2.A

A method for solving f(x) = 0 has at least two parts: an iteration and a convergence test. The iteration generates estimates $x_1, x_2, \ldots, x_k, \ldots$ of the solution, and the test says when to stop iterating. The basic parameters of an iteration for solving f(x) = 0 are

The model for f(x), usually a low-degree polynomial

and

The general assumption about the behavior of f(x)

The second item indicates the fact that many iterations work only under certain conditions. These conditions might be rather mild [for example, $f'(x) \neq 0$ at the solution] or rather restrictive [$|f'(x)| < 1$ near the solution]. A catalog of the basic iteration methods is given in Table 8.1 along with the parameters, and several of the methods are illustrated in Figure 8.1.

We briefly show how these iteration methods use their assumptions and model to converge toward the solution x^*. The **bisection method** or *half-interval* method proceeds as follows (see Figure 8.1).

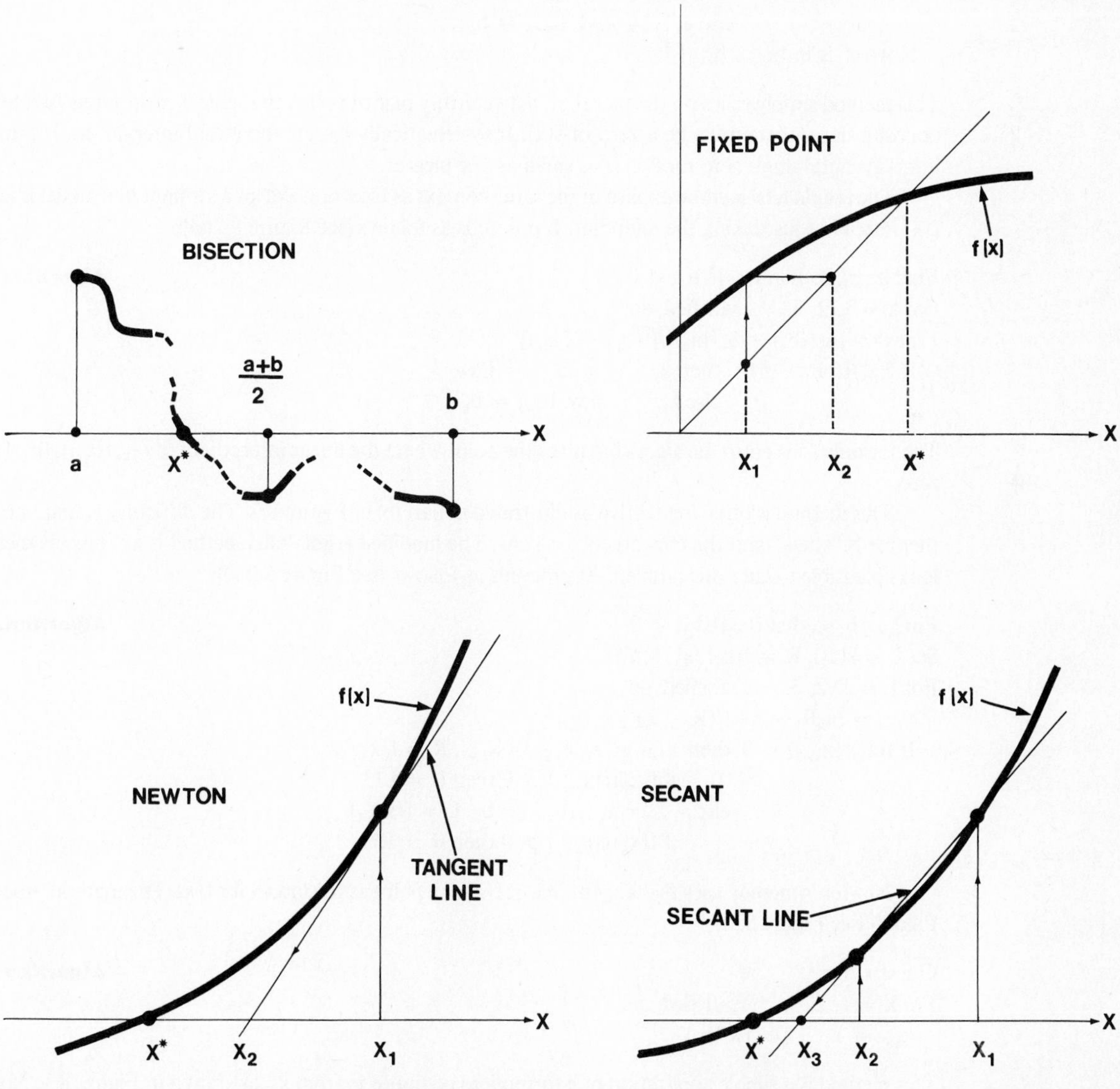

Figure 8.1 Basic iteration methods for nonlinear equations. The heavy line is f(x), and the construction generates a new, better estimate of x^* from the given information.

Properties of Seven Basic Iteration Methods for Solving Nonlinear Equations **Table 8.1**

The solution of $f(x) = 0$ is x^*. OK means continuous and well behaved near x^*.

Name	Model for f(x)	Assumption for f(x)
Bisection	None	Continuity and known sign change
Regula Falsi	Linear	Continuity and known sign change
Newton	Linear	$f'(x^*) \neq 0$, $f''(x)$ OK, good guess at x^*
Secant	Linear	$f'(x^*) \neq 0$, $f''(x)$ OK, good guess at x^*
Fixed point	$f(x) \equiv x$	$\|1+f'(x)\| < 1$, $f'(x)$ smooth, x^* bracketed
Muller	Quadratic	$f'''(x)$ OK
High-order Newton	nth-degree polynomial	$f'(x^*) \neq 0$, $f^{(n+1)}(x)$ OK

Algorithm 8.2.1

Find a_1, b_1 so that $f(a_1)f(b_1) < 0$
For $k = 1, 2, 3, \ldots$, satisfied, do:
  $mid = (a_k + b_k)/2$
  If $f(a_k)f(mid) \leq 0$ then $a_{k+1} = a_k$, $b_{k+1} = mid$
    else $a_{k+1} = mid$, $b_{k+1} = b_k$
  Now x^* is in $[a_{k+1}, b_{k+1}]$

This method simply relies on the fact that, between any pair of points that give a continuous function $f(x)$ opposite signs, there must be a zero of $f(x)$. It systematically bisects the initial interval $[a_1, b_1]$ until the interval containing a zero for $f(x)$ is as small as one pleases.

The **regula falsi method** applies in the same context as bisection except a straight line model is used for $f(x)$ instead of just taking the midpoint. It proceeds as follows [see Figure 8.2(a)]:

Algorithm 8.2.2

Find a_1, b_1, so that $f(a_1)f(b_1) < 0$
For $k = 1, 2, 3, \ldots$, satisfied, do:
  $new = [a_k f(b_k) - b_k f(a_k)]/[f(b_k) - f(a_k)]$
  If $f(a_k)f(new) \leq 0$ then $a_{k+1} = a_k$, $b_{k+1} = new$
    else $a_{k+1} = new$, $b_{k+1} = b_k$

The formula for *new* in the algorithm gives the point where the linear interpolant of $(a_k, f(a_k))$, $(b_k, f(b_k))$ is zero.

This method is often ineffective as illustrated in part (b) of Figure 8.2. The difficulty is that one end of the line is "stuck" and the convergence is slow. The **modified regula falsi method** is an improvement that looks plausible to cure this problem. It proceeds as follows [see Figure 8.2(c)]:

Algorithm 8.2.3

Find a_1, b_1 so that $f(a_1)f(b_1) < 0$
Set $L = f(a_1)$, $R = f(b_1)$, $x_1 = a_1$
For $k = 1, 2, 3, \ldots$, satisfied, do:
  $x_{k+1} = (a_k R - b_k L)/(R - L)$
  If $f(a_k)f(x_{k+1}) < 0$ then $a_{k+1} = a_k$, $b_{k+1} = x_{k+1}$, $R = f(x_{k+1})$
      if $f(x_k)f(x_{k+1}) > 0$ then $L = L/2$
    else $a_{k+1} = x_{k+1}$, $b_{k+1} = b_k$, $L = f(x_{k+1})$
      if $f(x_k)f(x_{k+1}) > 0$ then $R = R/2$

Newton's method uses the tangent line of $f(x)$ at a point as the model for $f(x)$. The method proceeds as follows (see Figure 8.1):

Algorithm 8.2.4

Guess x_1 for x^*
For $k = 1, 2, 3, \ldots$, satisfied, do:
  $x_{k+1} = x_k - f(x_k)/f'(x_k)$

This method is a simple application of a formula to compute x_2 from x_1, as shown in Figure 8.1. Note that the method breaks down if $f'(x_k) = 0$ at some point; if $f'(x^*) = 0$, it is plausible (and true) that this method does not work well.

The **secant method** is a variation of Newton's method that avoids computing the derivative of $f(x)$. It uses a linear model based on the two most recent values of $f(x)$. The method is as follows (see Figure 8.1):

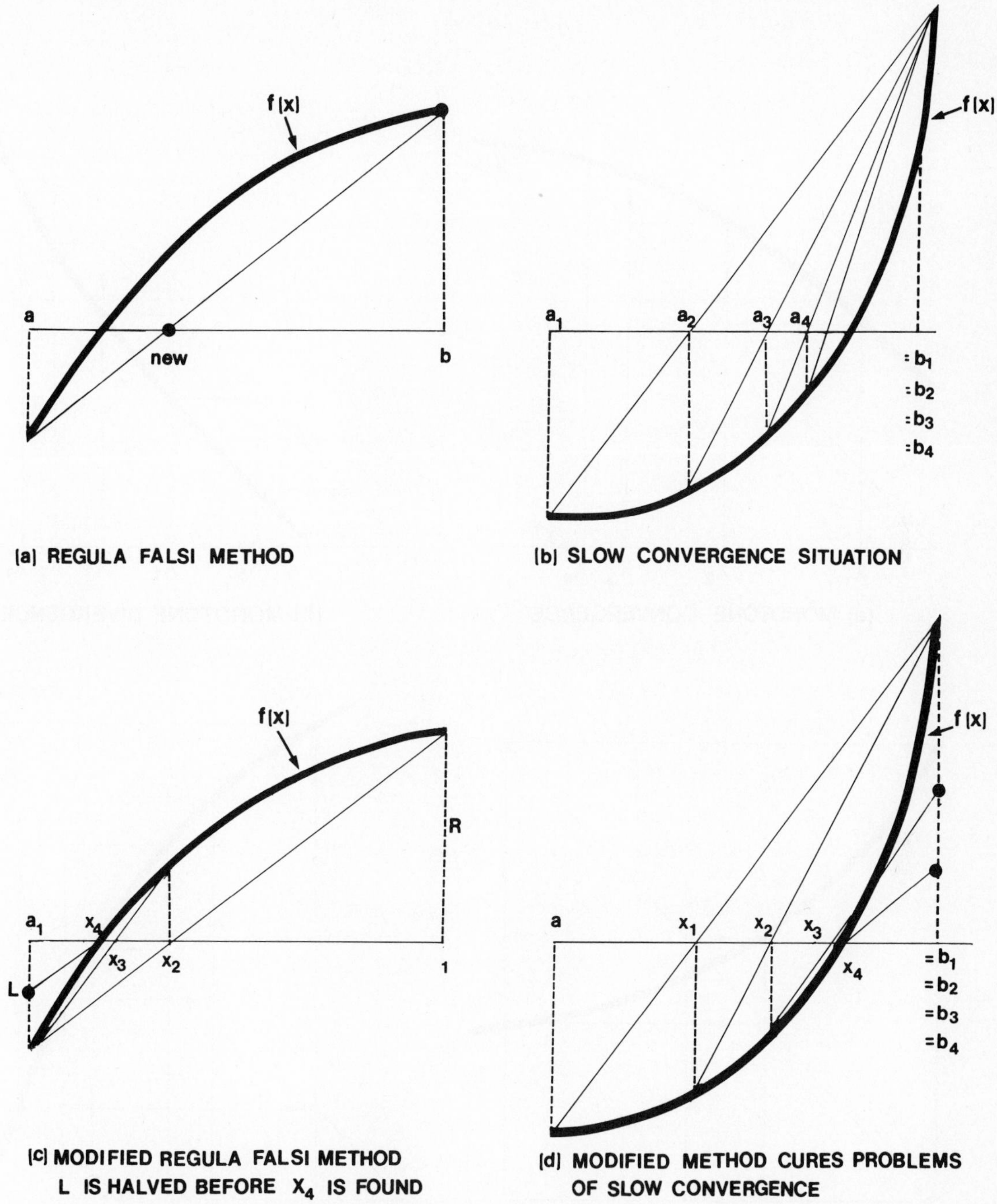

Figure 8.2 **Regula falsi and modified regula falsi methods.** (a) and (c) illustrate the two methods. (b) is a situation where regula falsi works poorly, and (d) shows how the modification cures the problem.

Algorithm 8.2.5

Guess x_1, x_2 for x^*
For $k = 2, 3, 4, \ldots$, satisfied, do
$x_{k+1} = [x_{k-1}f(x_k) - x_k f(x_{k-1})]/[f(x_k) - f(x_{k-1})]$

The formula for x_{k+1} is found by noting that the triangles $x_3, x_1, f(x_1)$, and $x_3, x_2, f(x_2)$ in Figure 8.1 are similar. One may also obtain Algorithm 8.2.5 by substituting $[f(x_k) - f(x_{k-1})]/(x_k - x_{k-1})$ for $f'(x_k)$ in Algorithm 8.2.4 to obtain the equivalent iteration

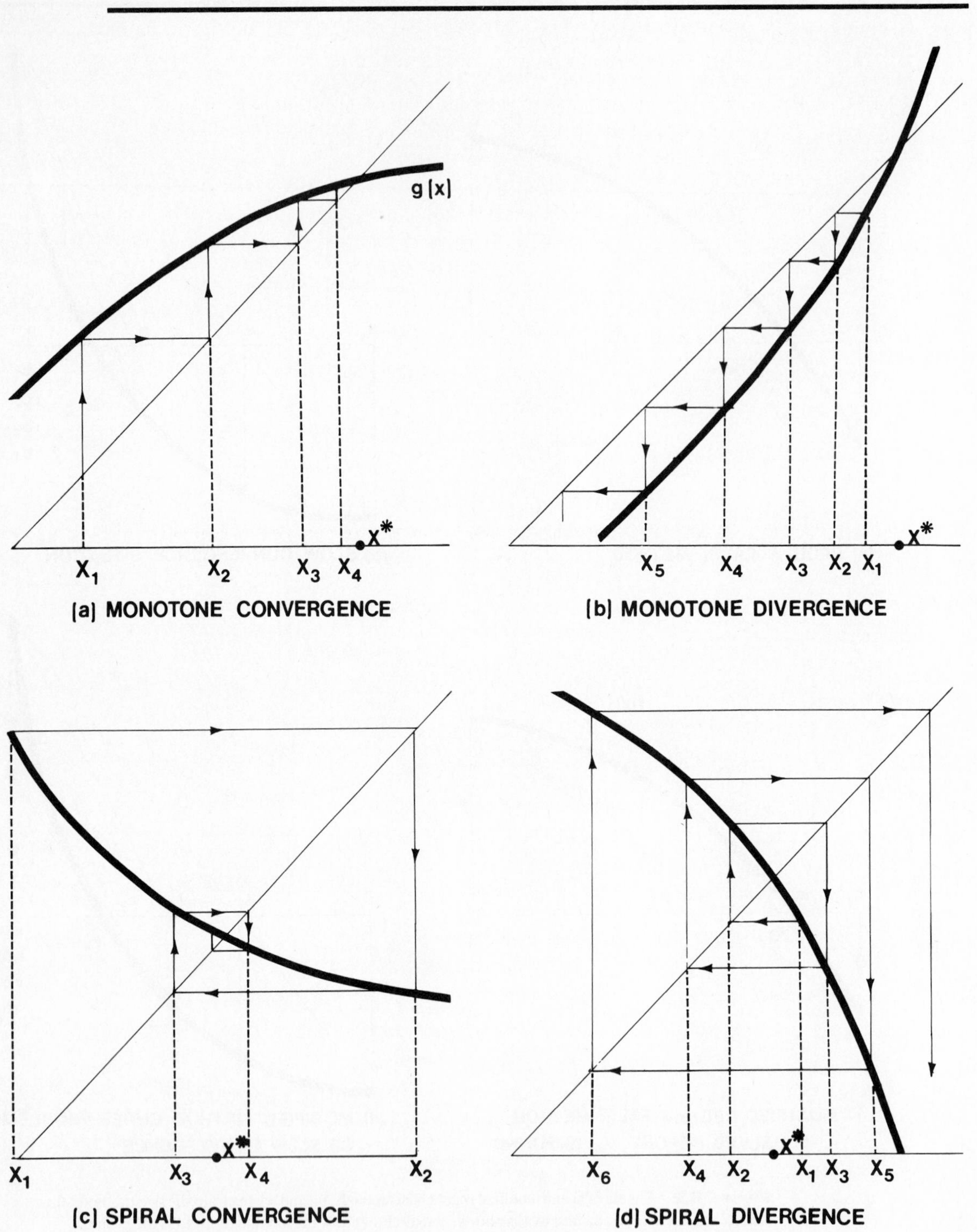

Figure 8.3 **Fixed point iteration behaviors.** The four basic patterns of behavior for fixed point iterations are shown; the heavy line is $g(x) = x + f(x)$.

$$x_{k+1} = x_k - \frac{f(x_k)(x_k - x_{k-1})}{f(x_k) - f(x_{k-1})}$$

The **fixed point method** is the simplest of all; reformulate $f(x) = 0$ as $x + f(x) = x$ and set $g(x) = x + f(x)$, and we have

Algorithm 8.2.6

Guess x_1 for x^*
For k = 1, 2, 3, . . ., satisfied, do:
$$x_{k+1} = g(x_k) = x_k + f(x_k)$$

See Figure 8.3 for various patterns of behavior in the iteration of the fixed point method.

Muller's method is the extension of the secant method to use a quadratic polynomial model; one interpolates the last three points by a quadratic and uses one of its roots as the next estimate of x^*. Here we see one problem with higher-degree polynomial models; they give more than one new estimate, and for degree higher than two, it is not easy to obtain these estimates. Muller's method chooses the root of the quadratic closest to the previous estimate; its definition is illustrated in Figure 8.4. The algorithm is as follows:

Algorithm 8.2.7

Guess x_1, x_2, x_3 for x^*
Form the divided difference table for f(x) at these points
For k = 3, 4, 5, . . ., satisfied, do:
$$s = f[x_k, x_{k-1}] + (x_k - x_{k-1})\, f[x_k, x_{k-1}, x_{k-2}]$$
$$x_{k+1} = x_k - \frac{2f(x_k)}{s + \text{sign}(s)\sqrt{s^2 - 4f(x_k)f[x_k, x_{k-1}, x_{k-2}]}}$$
Update divided difference table

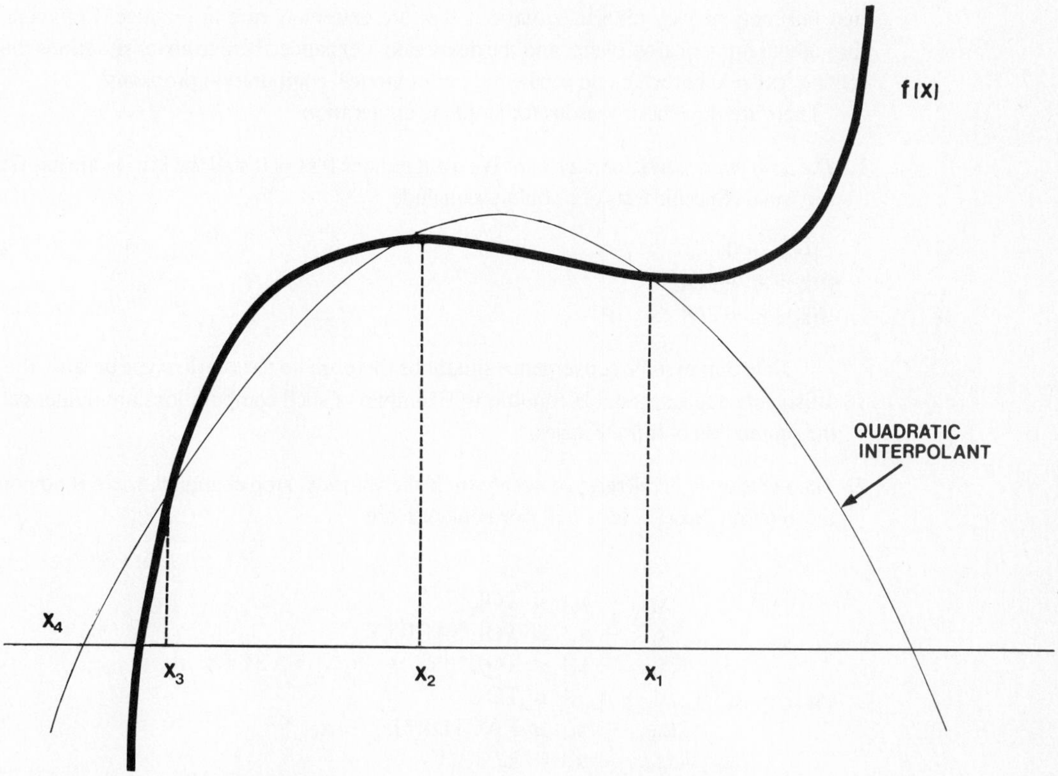

Figure 8.4 **Muller's method.** The root x_4 of the quadratic interpolant is chosen as the next estimate because it is closer to x_3.

The variable s in Algorithm 8.2.7 is the slope of the quadratic interpolant at x_k. A modified form of the formula for the roots of a quadratic polynomial is used to minimize the effects of round-off errors.

An important feature of Muller's method is that it might produce complex numbers. If one knows the zeros of f(x) are real, then one suppresses any complex numbers appearing from the square-root term. This makes the implementation messier. On the other hand, sometimes one wants to find complex zeros, and then Muller's method is attractive. One can start with real calculations, and if necessary, this algorithm goes off into the complex numbers in search of a solution.

The final iteration method we discuss is the **high-order Newton method.** It is mostly of theoretical interest, but it serves to show how the mechanism for building iterations can be extended to higher-degree polynomial models of f(x). It also shows the problems that arise with these methods. The iteration uses the nth-degree polynomial approximation to f(x) obtained from the Taylor's series at $x = x_1$.

$$f(x) \sim p_n(x) = f(x_1) + f'(x_1)(x-x_1) + f''(x_1)(x-x_1)^2/2 + \ldots + f^{(n)}(x_1)(x-x_1)^n/n!$$

The algorithm is

Algorithm 8.2.8

Guess x_1 for x^*
For $k = 1, 2, 3, \ldots$, satisfied, do:
  Compute $p_n(x)$ from Taylor's series
  Solve $p_n(x) = 0$ for roots $r_1, r_2, \ldots, r_n$
  Choose root r_i closest to x_k and set $x_{k+1} = r_i$

Convergence Tests 8.2.B

Example 3.1 shows that it is not possible to have a guaranteed convergence test, yet we must stop the iterations. Iterations for nonlinear equations usually converge fast, and the convergence test is only occasionally a troublesome part of the method. Yet one does not *ever* want to be fooled about having solved a problem, and so it is important to make the convergence test as reliable as possible. **A reliable test** is one that fails only in very unusual situations that are extremely rare in practice. Convergence tests appear throughout numerical software, and the discussion is expanded here to cover situations that rarely occur in solving $f(x) = 0$ but which do occur in other numerical computation problems.

There are three basic reasons for stopping an iteration:

1. *The problem is solved, or nearly so.* We want to have $f(x) = 0$, and the kth iterate has $f(x_k) = 0$ or $|f(x_k)|$ very small. Specific tests one could use include

Equation 8.2.1

$$f(x_k) = 0$$
$$|f(x_k)| \le \text{FTOL}$$
$$|f(x_k)| \le \text{FTOL} \times ||f||$$

Note that in some convergence situations there are no tests of this type because the answer does not satisfy any explicit, testable conditions. Examples of such computations are numerical integration and the summation of infinite series.

2. *The iteration has coverged, or nearly so.* If the values x_k stop changing, there is no point in continuing the iteration. Specific tests that one could use are

Equation 8.2.2

$$x_{k+1} = x_k$$
$$|x_{k+1} - x_k| \le \text{TOL}$$
$$|x_{k+1} - x_k| \le \text{TOL/SAFETY}$$
$$|x_{k+1} - x_k| \le \text{TOL}*(|x_k| + |x_{k+1}|)/\text{SAFETY}$$
$$|x_{k+1} - x_k| + |x_k - x_{k-1}| \le \text{TOL}$$
$$|x_{k+1} - x_k| \le \text{FACTOR}*|x_k - x_{k-1}|$$
$$x_k + (x_{k+1} - x_k) = x_k$$

The first test is simple and unsafe; exact equality between x_k and x_{k+1} is unlikely in the presence of round-off. The next five tests allow for round-off and provide for various kinds of safety factors and tolerances. There is no universal way to relate these tolerances and factors with the error $|x^* - x_k|$. The final test is supposed to be interpreted as "the most recent change is less than an ulp when added to x_k"; it is too stringent for general use.

3. *The iteration has gone on too long or the results are unreasonable.* Every iteration should have a fixed limit unless one knows that it converges in all cases. There are usually bounds on the solution so that some values for $f(x_k)$ or x_k are ridiculous and mean that the iteration has gone astray. Tests that one could use include

$$\begin{aligned} k &\ge \text{KLIMIT} \\ |f(x_k)| &\ge \text{FHUGE} \\ |x_k| &\ge \text{XHUGE} \\ |a - x_k| + |x_k - b| &\ge |b - a| \qquad (x_k \text{ not in } [a, b]) \end{aligned}$$

Equation 8.2.3

It is not always easy to choose specific values for KLIMIT, FHUGE, etc.; these values may depend on the machine parameters as well as the problem at hand.

None of these tests is completely satisfactory alone. Example 8.5 presents a number of troublesome iterations, and one of them provides an example to disprove the effectiveness of any one of the tests in 8.2.1 or 8.2.2. The moral of Example 8.5 is that a practical convergence test should use several of the above tests; a result is accepted only when it passes more than one independent test for convergence.

Troublesome Iterations for Convergence Tests

Example 8.5

A list of problems is given which cause trouble for some or all of the convergence tests given in 8.2.1 and 8.2.2. The first several problems involve solving $f(x) = 0$; a few others are given at the end.

1. Solve $1/(1+x^2) = 0$ using Newton's method or secant method. The iterates quickly give $f(x_k)$ very small to pass the tests in 8.2.1. Similar results are obtained with e^{-x}, e^{-x^2}, and $1/(1+x^5)$.

2. Solve $1/(x-.1) = 0$ using bisection, regula falsi, or modified regula falsi. Start with the interval $[-1, 1]$ or $[0, 1]$; the iterates converge to $x = .1$ and any of the tests 8.2.2 are passed. Similar results are obtained with $\text{SIGN}(x-.1)$, $\cot(x-.1)$, and $1/(x-.1)^3$.

3. Solve $e^{-1/x^2} = 0$ using Newton's, secant, or Muller's method. The iterates quickly give $f(x_k)$ very small, and the changes in the iterates are also small so that tests from both 8.2.1 and 8.2.2 are passed with x not very close to zero. Similar difficulty occurs with $x^{10} = 0$, but it is not as severe.

4. Solve $e^{-x^2}(x^2-17x+71) = 0$ using Newton's, secant, or Muller's method. The values of $f(x_k)$ become very small in the general neighborhood [6, 10] of the solutions.

5. Solve $f(x) = \sqrt{|1-e^{-x}|/\log(1/|x+4|)} = 0$ using Newton's, secant, or Muller's method. The function is very steep at $x = 0$ and incredibly steep at $x = -4$. This makes the iterates close together while some distance above the x axis; the values of $f(x_k)$ are not very small even when x_k is very close to the roots. For example, $f(-3.999) = 5.606$, $f(-3.9999999) = 3.672$.

6. Solve $f(t) = \int_{-1}^{t} 1/(.01 + \sqrt[5]{|x|})\, dx - 1.5 = 0$ using Newton's, secant, or Muller's method. If the initial guess or an intermediate iterate is very close to 0, then the slope of $f(x)$ is comparatively large and the iteration seems to converge there. An automatic or adaptive integration method may converge before sensing the spike on the integrand at $x = 0$ and hence produce an incorrect result.

7. Consider the iteration $x_{k+1} = (x_k - 2.11)*(1. + 1/k^{1.5}) + 2.11$. The convergence is slow, and so the tests 8.2.2 are prematurely passed.

8. Consider solving for the zero of $p(x)$ shown in Figure 3.5. The extreme round-off errors make Newton's, secant, and Muller's methods produce random results once the iterates get close to the zero. The tests in 8.2.2 are unlikely to be passed at any time. Similar results occur with any function which is very ill-conditioned, for example those in Problem 3.3.6

9. The **summation of an infinite series** is an iteration when

$$\sum_{k=1}^{\infty} \text{term}_k$$

is rewritten as

$$\begin{aligned} s_1 &= 0 \\ s_{k+1} &= s_k + \text{term}_k \end{aligned}$$

The Taylor's series for sin(x) has

$\text{term}_k = 0$ for k even
$\text{term}_k = x^k/k!$ for k odd

Several of the tests in 8.2.2 fail for this example because two successive iterates are identical. The ber(x) function (the real part of the Bessel function of the first kind with argument xi $\sqrt{i}$ where $i = \sqrt{-1}$ is the imaginary unit) has

$\text{term}_k = (x/2)^k/(k/2)!)^2$ for $k = 0, 4, 8, \ldots$
$\text{term}_k = 0$ otherwise

Summation of its infinite series gives four consecutive iterates which are identical.

10. The components of the iterates of some methods for solving a linear system often behave like

$$x_{k+1} = r[\sin(k\theta)/\sin((k+1)\theta)\ (x_k - x^*)] + x^*$$

It is not uncommon to have r = .99. . . or even .9999. . . with θ about .05 to .1. The value of $(x_{k+1} - x_k)$ changes very slowly once $(x_k - x^*)$ is .001 or so, and the tests 8.2.2 tend to terminate the iteration prematurely. Especially note that when r happens to be about $\sin((k+1)\theta)/\sin(k\theta)$, then $x_{k+1} \sim x_k - x^* + x^* = x_k$ and the iteration seems to have converged. This event happens when $k\theta$ is nearly an odd multiple of $\pi/2$, which occurs a few times every 20 or 30 iterations if $\theta = .05$ to .1.

The problems given in Example 8.5 show that one should use a composite convergence test for a general iteration method; only in special cases is it safe to rely on one test. The following Fortran code illustrates a rather elaborate convergence test for an iteration.

Fortran Code with Reliable Convergence Test for an Iteration

Algorithm 8.2.9

```
C              CONVERGENCE TEST
C
      LOGICAL TEST1,TEST2,TEST3,TEST4,TEST5,TEST6,TEST7
      DATA SAFETY,FACTOR,XLOW , XHIGH, FHUGE,KOUNT7,KLIMIT /
     A     5.0  , 500. , 0.0 , 1.E6 , 1.E6 ,  0   ,  12    /
C
C              LIMIT ITERATIONS TO KLIMIT
      DO 100 K = 1,KLIMIT
C         ITERATION FORMULAS GO HERE, THEY COMPUTE
C         XK1 = NEW K+1 ITERATE          FK1  = F(XK1)
C         XK  = OLD K   ITERATE          FK   = F(XK)
C         XKM1= PRECEDING K-1 ITERATE     FKM1 = F(XKM1)
C         XNORM = ESTIMATE OF GLOBAL X-SIZE
C         FNORM = ESTIMATE OF GLOBAL F-SIZE
C
C              PRELIMINARY SCREEN FOR CONVERGENCE
          TEST1 = ABS(FK1) .LT. FTOL*FNORM
          TEST2 = ABS(XK1-XK) .LT. XTOL*XNORM/SAFETY
          IF( TEST1 .OR. TEST2 )         GO TO 50
              IF( K .LT. 10 )                         GO TO 100
C
C              IF THE ITERATION IS COMPLETELY LOST AFTER 10 ITERATIONS
C              GO TO 99 AND MAKE A NEW GUESS AT ANSWER, OTHERWISE CONTINUE
             TEST3 = ABS(FK1) .GT. FHUGE  .OR.
     A               ABS(XK1-XLOW)+ABS(XK1-XHIGH) .GT. XHIGH-XLOW
             IF( TEST3 )       GO TO 99
                               GO TO 100
C
C              SOMETHING IS HAPPENING, CHECK FURTHER
   50     TEST4 = ABS(XK-XKM1) .LT. XTOL*XNORM/SAFETY*2.
C              NORMAL CONVERGENCE TEST
          IF( TEST1 .AND. TEST2 .AND. TEST4 )               GO TO 200
C
C                NORMAL CONVERGENCE DID NOT HAPPEN
C                EVALUATE ALTERNATIVE TESTS OF CONVERGENCE
            TEST5 =  FK1 .EQ. 0.0
C                IS F(XK1) EXACTLY ZERO
            IF(  TEST5 )                                    GO TO 200
```

```
            TEST6 = ABS(FB1)+ABS(FK) .LT. FTOL*FNORM*FACTOR
C                IS F(XK1) PRETTY SMALL WITH XK1 CONVERGED
            IF( TEST6 .AND. TEST2 .AND. TEST4 )              GO TO 200
C                IS F(XK1) SMALL ENOUGH WITH XK1 NEARLY CONVERGED
C                AND THIS HAS HAPPENED THREE TIMES
            TEST7 = ABS(XK1-XK)+ABS(XK-XKM1) .LT. XTOL*XNORM*FACTOR
            IF( TEST7 ) KOUNT7 = KOUNT7 + 1
            IF( TEST7 .AND. KOUNT7 .GE. 3 )                  GO TO 200
C                DID NOT PASS ANY CONVERGENCE TEST AT ALL
                                                        GO TO 100
   99   CONTINUE
C               SET XK1 = NEW GUESS AT ANSWER FOR PREVIOUS ITERATION
C               RESET ALL TESTS TO FALSE TEST1 =...= TEST7= .FALSE.
C               SET KOUNT7 = 0
  100 CONTINUE
C               ITERATION FAILED, NO CONVERGENCE FOR KLIMIT TIMES
C               DO SOMETHING
C
  200 CONTINUE
C               ITERATION CONVERGED, PRINT RESULTS
      STOP
      END
```

The principal point of this code is to show that a reliable convergence test takes many more lines of Fortran than most iteration formulas. The above code is primarily written to be easy to understand, and so some improvements in efficiency are possible. For example, the constant XTOL/SAFETY*2. in TEST4 should be computed outside the iteration loop. It is not unheard of to have 100 lines of code to check for the convergence of a general iteration when extremely high reliability is needed.

Other points of note in this code are (1) the values of FNORM and XNORM can be estimated during the iteration, for example, as the average of every tenth value (with limits to ignore values when the iteration becomes "lost"); (2) the "weak" convergence test TEST7 is accepted only after being passed three times; (3) it is important to structure an elaborate set of tests so as to minimize the overhead; (4) it is important to structure an elaborate set of tests and to provide ample comments so that the logic can be understood at some future time.

Initial Guesses for Iteration Methods *8.2.C

All the iteration methods require some kind of starting information about the solution of $f(x) = 0$. The bisection, regula falsi, and modified regula falsi are called **global methods** because this information need not

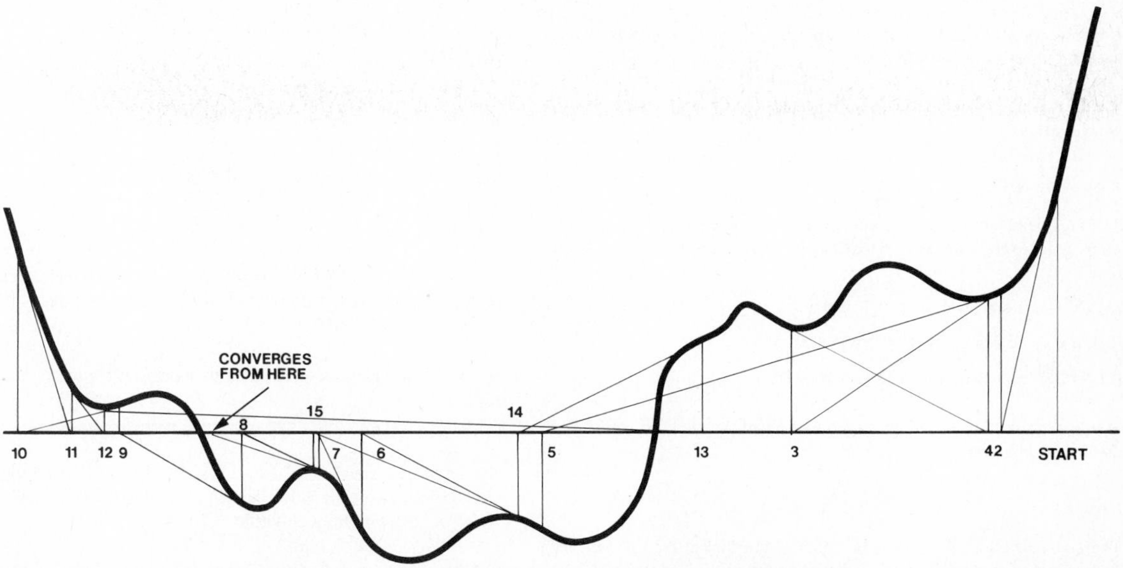

Figure 8.5 **Newton's method as a random search scheme.** The iterates wander for some time before they hit the neighborhood of the root where convergence takes place.

be accurate at all. Once the initial assumption is satisfied, these methods converge to a solution. The remaining methods are called **local methods** because their models and assumptions apply only near the solutions. The initial guesses for these methods must be close enough to the solution for the underlying model of the method to be realistic, otherwise anything can happen. It is not difficult to construct examples where the initial guesses for Newton's secant, or Muller's method must be extremely accurate for convergence to occur.

The principal source of initial guesses is "outside" information about the problem being solved. If the solution x represents the weight of a wheel on a car, then it is clear that x should be between 10 and 100 pounds and 30 might be a good guess. If such information is missing, then one must make a choice at random and hope the iteration converges with a poor initial guess. The convergence test program includes a provision for choosing new guesses if needed. Various schemes are used to do this; we do not discuss them here.

Figure 8.5 shows the "path" that Newton's method takes when applied to a complicated function. The solutions of $f(x) = 0$ are difficult to locate and require rather good initial guesses for the method to converge. This figure illustrates how Newton's method serves as a "random searching scheme" when it is far from the solution. If $f(x)$ gets large for $|x|$ large, then the Newton iterates are always "reflected" back to the region where $f(x)$ is smaller. The secant and Muller methods have a similar behavior.

PROBLEMS 8.2

8.2.1 Write a Fortran subprogram to implement the bisection method which starts as

```
FUNCTION BISECT( F,A,B,EPS )
```

Here F is the function name, [A, B] is the interval containing a zero, and EPS is the accuracy required in the zero. The value of BISECT is the zero found. Apply the subprogram to compute zeros of the following functions:

(A) $\sin(x-.2345) + .5$

(B) $xe^{-x} - .2$

(C) $\log(1+x^2) - \dfrac{1}{x+1}$

(D) $\cos(x) - \sqrt{|x|}$

(E) $x^4 - 4x^2 + 2x - 13$

(F) $x - (8x^3 - 12x^2)\log|10.5 - x| - 6$

Choose a value of EPS between 10^{-2} and 10^{-5}; print the results out neatly with full explanations of what they are.

8.2.2 Write a Fortran subprogram to implement the regula falsi method which starts as

```
FUNCTION RF( F,A,B,EPS )
```

The arguments are the same as for BISECT in Problem 8.2.1. Apply the subprogram to compute zeros of the functions A through F of Problem 8.2.1 or of

(A) $x^{10} - .01$ (start with $A = 0, B = 1$)

(B) $\tan x - .05$ (start with $A = 0, B = 1.55$)

(C) $10e^{-10x} - 1/10$ (start with $A = 0, B = 2$)

8.2.3 Write a Fortran subprogram to implement the modified regula falsi method which starts as

```
REAL FUNCTION MODRF( F,A,B,EPS )
```

The arguments are the same as for BISECT in Problem 8.2.1. Apply the subprogram to compute zeros of the functions A through F of Problem 8.2.1 or A through C of Problem 8.2.2.

8.2.4 Write the programs of Problems 8.2.2 and 8.2.3. Insert a counter in the $F(x)$ functions which is printed at the end to tell how many times F was evaluated. Use these two programs to compare the effectiveness of the modification to the regula falsi method.

8.2.5 Write a Fortran subprogram to implement Newton's method which starts as

```
REAL FUNCTION NEWTON( F,FP,GUESS,EPS )
```

Here F is the function name and FP the name of its derivative, GUESS is an initial estimate of the zero, and EPS is the accuracy desired. The value of the function is the zero found. Use the fourth convergence test of Equation 8.2.2. Apply the subprogram to compute zeros of the functions A through F of Problem 8.2.1, A through C of Problem 8.2.2, or

(A) x^2 (guess $x = 1$)

(B) x^{10} (guess $x = 1$ or 2)

(C) $x^3 - 3x + 3x^2 - 1$ (guess $x = 0$ or 20)

(D) $\sqrt{|x - .1|}$ (guess $x = 0$ or 2)

(E) $(x^2 + 1/x)e^{(x + \sin x)}\cos(x \log(1 + x^2)) - .1$ (guess $x = .01, -8$, or 12)

(F) $x^6 - 6x^5 + 15x^4 - 20x^3 + 15x^2 - 6x + 1$ (guess $x = 2$ or 20)

(G) $|\sin x - .2|$ (guess $x = .1$ or 1.57)

(H) $\sqrt[5]{(x - .2)(x - .3)^2}$ (guess $x = 0$ or $.25$)

Choose a value of EPS between 10^{-4} and 5 ulps for the machine used, and print the results neatly with full explanations. **Hint:** The main difficulty with (E) is to get FP correct.

8.2.6 Write a Fortran subprogram to implement the secant method which starts

```
FUNCTION SECANT( F,GUESS1,GUESS2,EPS )
```

The arguments are those of Newton in Problem 8.2.5, with GUESS1 and GUESS2 the two guesses for the zero. Apply the subprogram to compute zeros of functions from Problems 8.2.1, 8.2.2, and 8.2.5.

8.2.7 Compare the efforts in finding a zero of the function (E) of Problem 8.2.5 using Newton's method and the secant method. Consider the effort to prepare and debug the program (not counting writing NEWTON or SECANT), the execution time (or number of function evaluations), and the accuracy obtained. Let EPS vary from10^{-2} down to 10 ulps.

8.2.8 Write a Fortran subprogram to implement the fixed point method which starts

```
FUNCTION FIXPT( F,GUESS,EPS )
```

where the arguments are those of NEWTON of Problem 8.2.5. Use the third convergence test of Equation 8.2.2 with SAFETY = 5. Apply the subprogram to find zeros of the functions

(A) $x^2 - x$ with GUESS = .1, .4, −.2, −.8, −1.5, 1.5

(B) $\sin x - .25$ with GUESS = .2

(C) $\cos x - .25$ with GUESS = 1.3, 10.75, −4.1, 732.7

(D) $x - e^x$ with GUESS = 0, .75, 20

(E) $x + \sin(x) - x^3/3$ with GUESS = .25

Use EPS from 10^{-2} to 10^{-4}, and print the results neatly with a full explanation of what they are.

8.2.9 The problem "solve $x^2 - x - 2 = 0$" can be reformulated in several ways for fixed point iteration, including

$$x = x^2 - 2$$

$$x = \sqrt{x + 2}$$

$$x = 1 + 2/x$$

$$x = x - \frac{x^2 - x - 2}{4}$$

(A) Determine from the assumption on f(x) in Table 8.1 which of these formulations gives a convergent fixed point iteration for the zero $x = 2$. Repeat this for the zero $x = -1$. Verify the conclusions by making a few iterations on each formulation for each of the two zeros, starting at $x = 1.7$ and $-.7$. **Hint**: It is easy to do fixed point iteration on a hand calculator with memory.

Reformulate the following equations so that fixed point iteration converges:

(B) $x^3 - x + 1 = 0$

(C) $e^x - \sin x = 0$

(D) $\log(1 + x) - x^2 = 0$ for both zeros

(E) $e^x - 3x^3 = 0$ for both zeros

8.2.10 Write a Fortran subprogram to implement Muller's method starting with

```
REAL FUNCTION MULLER( F,GUESS1,GUESS2,GUESS3,EPS )
```

Here the three initial guesses at the zero are GUESS1, GUESS2, and GUESS3; F is the function name and EPS is the accuracy requirement. Do not use complex arithmetic; instead simply set the square-root term to zero in Algorithm 8.2.7 if it should be imaginary. Apply the subprogram to find zeros of the function in Problems 8.2.1, 8.2.2, and 8.2.5.

8.2.11 Consider the expression

log(e + log(e + log(e + log(e + . . .))))

(A) What does this mean in terms of limits?

(B) Relate this expression to a fixed point iteration and use this to compute its value.

8.2.12 The difficulties with the high-order Newton method, Algorithm 8.2.8, are somewhat alleviated by using **inverse interpolation** or **inverse iteration.** The method is based on using the inverse function g(y) of f(x), that is, $y = f(x)$ and $x = g(y) = g(f(x))$. The method is stated as follows:

Guess x_1, for x^*
For k = 1, 2, 3, . . ., satisfied, do:
  Compute $g_n(y)$ = first n+1 terms of the Taylor's series for g(y)
  $x_{k+1} = g_n(0)$

(A) Explain why $g_n(0)$ is a suitable value for the next iterate. **Hint:** Draw some pictures with n = 2 to examine the behavior of this method.

(B) Discuss how one can compute the Taylor's series for g(y) if one knows the derivatives of f(x).

(C) Give an explicit formula for the iteration when n = 2 in terms of derivatives of f(x) and not g(y).

8.2.13 Write a Fortran subprogram to implement the second-degree or quadratic inverse interpolation method of Problem 8.2.12. It starts as

```
FUNCTION QUADIN( F,FP,FPP,GUESS,EPS )
```

where F, FP, and FPP are the names of F(x) and its two derivatives, GUESS is an estimate of the solution, and EPS is a accuracy requirement. Apply the subprogram to compute zeros of the functions in Problems 8.2.1, 8.2.2., and 8.2.3.

8.2.14 The **discrete inverse interpolation** method is to replace the Taylor's series $g_n(y)$ of the algorithm in Problem 8.2.12 by the interpolant $p_n(y)$ at the previous n iteration points.

(A) Give a precise algorithmic definition of this method, use a divided difference table to generate $p_n(y)$, and update it as in Algorithm 8.2.7.

(B) Write a Fortran subprogram to implement the second-degree discrete inverse interpolation method or inverse Muller method which starts as

```
REAL FUNCTION INVMUL( F,GUESS1,GUESS2,GUESS3,EPS )
```

The arguments are those of MULLER in Problem 8.2.10. Apply the subprogram to find zeros of some of the functions in Problems 8.2.1, 8.2.2, and 8.2.5.

8.2.15 Compare Muller's method and the inverse Muller method on the basis of (a) the complexity of the methods and resulting computer programs and (b) the computational efficiency of the methods. For criterion (b) choose several functions and find their zeros with both MULLER (Problem 8.2.10) and INVMUL (Problem 8.2.14). Examine the accuracy obtained, the number of function evaluations used, and computer time used. Give a complete discussion of the advantages and disadvantages of each.

8.2.16 Give a discussion of the strengths and weaknesses of the various convergence tests in Equation 8.2.1. For each of these tests give an example of a function where the test would be unreliable or ineffective.

8.2.17 Discuss the strengths and weaknesses of the seven convergence tests in Equation 8.2.2. In particular:

(A) Give an example where the second or third tests are unsatisfactory because x^* is large. Explain why they are unsatisfactory.

(B) Give an example where the fourth test is unsatisfactory because x^* is very small. Explain why it is unsatisfactory.

(C) Give a simple test that combines tests 3 and 4 which is effective for both examples in parts (A) and (B).

(D) The last test is sometimes called the negligible change convergence test because it is passed when the change in x_k is less than an ulp. Discuss the advantages of this test and the danger in relying upon it alone.

(E) Give an example of an iteration which passes all the tests in Equation 8.2.2 before the iterates are close to the solution.

8.2.18 Give a specific method to estimate FNORM and XNORM during an iteration for use in Algorithm 8.2.9. Explain why you think it is reliable and effective.

8.2.19 If f(x) is badly contaminated with round-off, an iteration often converges to a small neighborhood of the solution and then "wanders around." Develop a Fortran code for a **round-off error convergence test** to detect this situation. Take care that it does not signal convergence prematurely. Insert the convergence test in a subprogram for solving $f(x) = 0$ (for example, those of Problems 8.2.5, 8.2.6, 8.2.8, or 8.2.10) and run some experiments to show that the test is effective. **Hint:** Create equations for the experiment by adding 2E−6 *(GGUBFS(123470D0)−0.5) to equations from the above problems. GGUBFS is the IMSL routine for random numbers; see Figure 2.1.

8.2.20 Prepare a graphical illustration of how the secant method behaves for the function in Figure 8.5 **Hint:** This can be done by hand, or one can use a cubic spline interpolant of data from the graph in Figure 8.5 and then run SECANT of Problem 8.2.6 on it.

8.2.21 The **discrete Newton's method** replaces the derivative in Algorithm 8.2.4 by

$$\frac{f(x_k+h) - f(x_k)}{h}$$

(A) Discuss how one would choose h for this method, and propose a reasonable method to make h depend on the problem and the tolerance XTOL requested for the zero. **Hint:** See Examples 6.3.1 and 6.7.1.

(B) Compare the amount of effort for this method with the regular Newton method both from the computational point of view and from the user's point of view.

(C) Discuss the relationship between this method and the secant method.

SPECIAL SITUATIONS AND POLYALGORITHMS **8.3

There are some special situations that must be handled in order to obtain a reliable program for solving $f(x) = 0$. Two of these are discussed here, and then we discuss how the various methods and techniques are put together in a combination to create a **polyalgorithm** for solving $f(x) = 0$.

Multiple Roots 8.3.A

The Newton and secant methods do not apply in theory if $f'(x^*) = 0$, and they perform poorly on $f(x) = x^{10}$. So do the other methods. A **multiple root** or **multiple zero** of $f(x)$ occurs at x^* when

$$f(x^*) = f'(x^*) = \ldots = f^{(p-1)}(x^*) = 0 \qquad f^{(p)}(x^*) \neq 0$$

Equation 8.3.1

and p is the **multiplicity** of the zero. In other words, $f(x) = (x-x^*)^p\phi(x)$ where $\phi(x) \neq 0$ near x^*.

The easiest tactic to handle multiple roots is to note that $g(x) = f(x)/f'(x)$ always has simple roots. We have $g(x) = (x-x^*)\phi(x)/[p\phi(x)+(x-x^*)\phi'(x)]$ so that

$$g'(x) = 1 - \frac{f(x)f''(x)}{(f'(x))^2}$$

and a calculation shows that $g'(x^*)$ is about $1/p$. Thus, a switch from solving $f(x) = 0$ to solving $g(x) = 0$ is in order if $f(x)$ is suspected of having a multiple root.

Another approach is to devise special methods for multiple roots. This is easily done for Newton's method as follows. If $f(x) \sim \text{constant}^*(x-x^*)^p$, then

$$\frac{f(x)}{f'(x)} = \frac{(x-x^*)}{p}$$

or

$$x^* = x - p\frac{f(x)}{f'(x)}$$

The iteration

$$x_{k+1} = x_k - p\frac{f(x_k)}{f'(x_k)}$$

Equation 8.3.2

is **Newton's method for multiple roots.** Similarly, a factor of p can be introduced in the secant method to handle multiple roots; see Example 8.6.

The next questions are: How does one know the iteration is near a multiple root? How does one know the multiplicity p? The first clue of a multiple root is abnormal convergence; $f(x)$ becomes very small while $|x_{k+1}-x_k|$ is still relatively large. Further, $|x_{k+1}-x_k|$ does not go to zero as fast as the theory developed in Section 8.7 suggests. A set of convergence tests can check for this phenomenon (highly reliable software must have such a check) and detect multiple zeros.

If a multiple zero is suspected and one wants to use a method such as 8.3.2 which requires the value of p, then an estimate of p can be made. One models f(x) by $a(x-x^*)^p$ and obtains, somehow, a reasonably good estimate of x^*. For example, suppose one has iterated with 8.3.2 with an incorrect value of p and achieved a fair estimate of x^* but only after an excessive number of iterations. Now choose two values x_1 and x_2 of x somewhat distant from the estimate of x^*, and one has

$$f(x_1) \sim a(x_1-x^*)^p$$
$$f(x_2) \sim a(x_2-x^*)^p$$

One solves these two equations to obtain

$$p \sim \frac{\log(f(x_1)/f(x_2))}{\log((x_1-x^*)/(x_2-x^*))} \qquad \textbf{Equation 8.3.3}$$

One can now use this corrected value of p, iterate some more, and if needed, obtain a better value of p once one is closer to x^*.

Effect of Multiple Roots — Example 8.6

The effect of modifying Newton's method for multiple roots is illustrated in this example. A similar modification to the secant method is made as follows:

$$x_{k+1} = x_k - \frac{pf(x_k)(x_k - x_{k-1})}{(f(x_k) - f(x_{k-1}))}$$

where p is an estimate of the multipicity of the zero. These methods are applied to four functions: one with multiplicity 4.5, two with triple roots, and one with a fractional order zero (i.e., the multiplicity p is less than 1 rather than the more usual small integer).

The results are shown in Table 8.2; the iterations are terminated when the change $|x_{k+1}-x_k|$ or the value of f(x) is less than 10^{-6}. The initial guesses for the zeros of the four functions are 6.0, 1.0, 0.6, and 8.45, respectively. An obvious conclusion from Table 8.2 is that the accuracy in the zero is much less than the tolerance used in stopping the iteration; the reason is that f(x) is very small in a wide region about the true zero. It is also obvious that the use of the factor p in the iteration dramatically improves the convergence rate.

More specialized observations about these results are:

1. The secant method diverges for the first function with p = 4.5 because the initial guess is far enough away that the multiplicity of the zero is not relevant.

2. The multiplicity of the zero does not need to be known very accurately in order to gain the benefit of faster convergence.

3. Newton's method does not work well for the third function because the derivative is so erratic. The derivative is estimated with a central difference formula. An examination of the iterates shows that they rapidly converge to a neighborhood of the zero, then wander aimlessly. Eventually, by chance, an iterate is close enough to the zero to pass the convergence test.

4. The modification for multiple zeros is also effective for the fractional order zero of the fourth example.

Performance of Newton and Secant Methods for Multiple Roots **Table 8.2**

P = order of the zero used in the iteration
FCOUNT = count of the f(x) evaluations [Newton's method also counts f′(x) evaluations]
FVALUE = value of f(x) at the end of the iteration
DIGITS = number of correct decimal digits in the final estimate

$f(x) = |x - 9|^{4.5}/(1 + \sin^2(x))$

	Secant Method			Newton Method		
	P=1	P=4.5	P=4.05	P=1	P=4.5	P=4.05
FCOUNT	25		7	17	4	4
FVALUE	$9*10^{-7}$		$1*10^{-9}$	$8*10^{-7}$	$4*10^{-11}$	$3*10^{-10}$
DIGITS	1.3	Diverged	2.0	1.3	2.3	2.0

$f(x) = (81 - y(108 - y(54 - y(12 - y))))*\text{sign}(y - 3)/(1 + x^2),\ y = x + 1.11111$

	Secant Method			Newton Method		
	P=1	P=3.0	P=3.3	P=1	P=3.0	P=3.3
FCOUNT	18	5	5	13	3	3
FVALUE	$8*10^{-7}$	$2*10^{-10}$	$6*10^{-10}$	$4*10^{-7}$	$8*10^{-11}$	$3*10^{-7}$
DIGITS	1.4	2.4	2.1	1.4	2.3	1.5

$f(x) = (x - 1.23)^3 + 2*10^{-8}*\text{Random}(x)$ Random(x) uniform on $(-1, 1)$

	Secant Method			Newton Method		
	P=1	P=3.0	P=3.3	P=1	P=3.0	P=3.3
FCOUNT	17	5	5	51	46	46
FVALUE	$6*10^{-7}$	$2*10^{-7}$	$2*10^{-8}$	$1*10^{-6}$	$2*10^{-8}$	$5*10^{-9}$
DIGITS	2.1	2.3	2.6	2.0	2.6	2.8

$f(x) = |x - 8.4317|^{0.4}/(1 + x^2)$

	Secant Method			Newton Method		
	P=1	P=0.4	P=0.36	P=1	P=0.4	P=0.36
FCOUNT		52	36		3	6
FVALUE		$2*10^{-4}$	$3*10^{-5}$		$3*10^{-5}$	$1*10^{-5}$
DIGITS	Diverged	4.5	6.7	Diverged	6.7	7.6

Deflation 8.3.B

One can attempt to find several different zeros of f(x) by starting a method at several different places. Experience shows this is not very satisfactory because some zeros are found more than once while others are missed. If f(x) is a polynomial $p_n(x)$, then once x^* is found, we can compute the polynomial $q_{n-1}(x) = p_n(x)/(x - x^*)$ and the search for zeros applied to $q_{n-1}(x)$. This process is called **deflation** and is used for polynomials. For a general f(x) this division is not exact, but one can imitate it by setting

$$g_k(x) = \frac{f(x)}{\prod_{i=1}^{k} (x - x_i^*)}$$

when k roots x_i^*, i = 1, 2, . . . , k, have been determined. There is a problem with this deflation when k gets large because the size of $g_k(x)$ might differ dramatically from the size of f(x). If k = 10 and the x_i^* are between 10 and 20, then $g_k(x)$ is about 10^{-11} or 10^{-12} times f(x). Thus, a better deflation method is to take the new function to be

$$g_k(x) = f(x) \prod_{i=1}^{k} \frac{1 + |x - x_i^*|}{(x - x_i^*)}$$ **Equation 8.3.4**

If x_i^* is a multiple root, then $x - x_i^*$ in 8.3.4 is replaced by $(x - x_i^*)^p$. If the multiplicity is not estimated correctly for x_i^*, then this zero may still be found more than once. When p is not an integrer, the deflation process usually introduces a difficult singularity in $g_k(x)$. If both p and x_i^* are slightly inaccurate, which is to be expected, then $g_k(x)$ has an infinite singularity right next to a zero.

Polyalgorithms for Nonlinear Equations 8.3.C

If one has an equation to solve quickly, one may use a basic method and personally examine the iterates to see that everything goes well. This is appropriate for a one-shot problem. A better approach is to use a library routine. A good one should solve easy problems in a few iterations, but not as few as a simple basic method because it must be more cautious. It also solves most difficult problems and reports to the user its failure for truly difficult (or misstated) problems. Remember that it is not difficult to foil a nonlinear equation solver. The function

$$f(x) = \begin{cases} 1 + x^2 & \text{if } x \text{ is not in } [a, b] \\ c(x-d)^2 - 1 & \text{if } x \epsilon [a, b] \end{cases}$$

$$d = \frac{a - kb}{1 - k}, \quad c = \frac{a^2 + 2}{(a-d)^2}, \quad k = \sqrt{a^2 + 2/b^2 + 2}$$

has two zeros in [a, b] and is continuous. If one chooses $a = 1037$ and $b = 1038$, most library programs will fail to find the zeros of $f(x)$ because it is $1 + x^2$ except on a small interval. If one program does find them, then a different choice of a and b can make this program fail also as no program can check all the intervals where the zero might be "hidden."

A single choice of the basic methods will not produce the high reliability that a library routine needs. It must use a combination of them in a framework to achieve confidence that most difficulties and special situations are handled properly. Such a program is called a **polyalgorithm,** and it combines several basic algorithms. The components of a polyalgorithm for nonlinear equations are:

1. *Initial guess and interval searching.*
2. *Basic iterations.*
3. *Convergence testing.*
4. *Information gathering.* Here, for example, one generates estimates of $||f||$ or maintains a list of, say, the five points that are "closest" to being zeros.
5. *Special situations testing and associated methods.*

We do not elaborate on this concept here except to say that the design of a good polyalgorithm (library routine) requires considerable art and skill. There are many conflicting objectives and trade-offs involved; the 6 lines of Fortran for Newton's method can easily become 600 lines or more.

An example, in outline form, of a polyalgorithm is given to illustrate the concept. It combines a global method, bisection, with a local method, Newton's, in an attempt to achieve a good combination of efficiency and reliability. One is to find a zero of $f(x)$ in the interval [a, b]; we take $a = 0$ and $b = 1$ to simplify the exposition.

1. The bisection method is used on [0, 1]; the points generated are 1/2, 1/4, 3/4, 1/8, 3/8, 5/8, 7/8, 1/16,. . .
2. The basic iteration is Newton's method. It is started at each bisection point and runs for 6 iterations. Up to 6 more iterations are made if convergence seems likely.
3. The iteration is stopped if one of the following three tests is passed (recall $a = 0$ and $b = 1$):

   (A) $|x_{k+1} - x_k| \le XTOL$

   and

$|f(x_{k+1})| \le$ FNORM/1000.

(B) $|x_{k+1} - x_k| \le 0.000001$

and

$|f(x_{k+1}) \le$ FTOL*NORM

(C) More than 1000 f(x) evaluations are made.

4. (A) FNORM is estimated by the average of the f(x) values at the bisection points.

   (B) A list of up to three "promising" points is maintained from the termination points of the Newton iterations.

   (C) The bisection checked for sign changes. Once one is detected, [0, 1] is replaced by the smaller interval bracketing the zero. The convergence criterion is not changed though.

5. After each 2^{m-1} search points, m = 5, 6, 7, . . . , the list of "promising" points is used as starting points for another 12 Newton iterations.

PROBLEMS 8.3

8.3.1 Devise a **round-off level convergence test** along the following lines:

1. Compute the "spread" of the most recent 3 and 6 iterates, e.g., for 3 we have the spread $|x_{k-1} - x_{k-2}| + |x_{k-2} - x_{k-3}|$. If the spreads for 3 and 6 are comparable to $|x_{k+1} - x_k|$, then we have a candidate for convergence.

2. Accept convergence only if 10 iterations have been made and $f(x_{k+1})$ is reasonably small.

(A) Present a precise definition of this convergence test in Fortran.

(B) Apply this test with Newton's method to some functions with lots of round-off and discuss its effectiveness. **Hint:** Use f(x) = formula + C* (random number) where C is adjusted to give different levels of round-off effects.

8.3.2 For functions with difficult zeros, it is sometimes useful to use a **final zero improvement** algorithm which assumes very little about f(x). For example, one takes the final iterates x_{k+1} and x_k from a method and then sets $r = x_{k+1}$, step $= 3*|x_{k+1} - x_k|$ to initialize the following: Check f(x) at r ± step; if either value is smaller than f(r), move there [change r to the place where f(x) is smaller]. If neither value is smaller, then set step = step/2 and repeat. Terminate when step has been divided 10 times or is less than 2 ulps.

(A) Present a precise definition of this algorithm in Fortran.

(B) Apply the algorithm to functions with round-off effects. **Hint:** See the hint in Problem 8.3.1; also see Figure 3.5 and Problem 3.3.6.

8.3.3 Apply the Newton or secant method to one of the following functions with the convergence test $|x_{k+1} - x_k| \le$ XTOL. Use XTOL = 10^{-3} or so. Take the last iterate and apply the final zero improvement algorithm of Problem 8.3.2. Compare the accuracy obtained by Newton's method with XTOL and with the final result.

(A) $(x - 1.11)^2$

(B) $(x - 1.11)^8$

(C) $e^x - 1 + x^2/2$

(D) The polynomial of Figure 3.5

(E) $\sin((x-\pi)^3)$

(F) $1 - x/(x - (\sin x^3)/6 + x^5/120)$

8.3.4 Study the sensitivity of estimating the multiplicity p of a root by Equation 8.3.3. Take $(x-1)^p$ for several values of p and several choices of the x_k close to 1.0. Perturb the values x_k and/or $f(x_k) = (x_k - 1)^p$ by small amounts, then estimate p. Present the results of the study as a short report which clearly presents the problem studied, the technique used, and the conclusions made.

POLYNOMIAL EQUATIONS 8.4

If the function f(x) is a polynomial p(x), then one can exploit this fact to improve upon the general methods and to devise special methods.

Application of General Methods 8.4.A

Those general methods that only use function values can make use of nested multiplication, Algorithm 4.1.1, and little else from the special fact that f(x) is a polynomial. Newton's method uses both p(x) and p′(x). Recall that Algorithm 4.1.1 puts p(x) in the form

$$p(x) = d_0 + (x - z)q(x)$$

where, obviously, $d_0 = p(z)$. The coefficients of $q(x)$ are $d_1,\ldots,d_n$ generated by Algorithm 4.1.1 because all the centers c_i are zero. Differentiate this with respect to x to obtain

$$p'(x) = (x-z)q'(x) + q(x)$$

andn Newton's method, we need to evaluate the polynomial $q(x)$ whose coefficients d_i are generated while evaluating $p(x)$. These two evaluations can be made simultaneously and inserted directly into **Newton's method for polynomials** as follows for $p(x) = a_0 + a_1x + \ldots + a_nx^n$:

Algorithm 8.4.1

For $k = 1, 2, \ldots$, satisfied, do:
  $z = x_k$, $d_n = a_n$, $c_n = a_n$
  For $i = n-1, \ldots, 1$, do:
    $d_i = a_i + za_{i+1}$
    $c_i = d_i + zd_{i+1}$
  $d_0 = a_0 + za_1$
  $x_{k+1} = x_k - d_0/c_1$

Higher-order Newton methods are also more feasible for polynomials — either those of Algorithm 8.2.8 [with the n there smaller than the degree of $p(x)$] or those in the inverse interpolation form of Problem 8.2.12. In either case, Algorithm 8.4.1 can be extended to compute the higher derivatives needed within the loop on i.

Muller's method is not changed for polynomials, but it has a special attraction because it can find complex roots. Thus, Algorithm 8.2.7 is coded using complex arithmetic, and one can compute complex roots. This feature is the special appeal of Muller's method; the inverse Muller method of Problem 8.2.14 has about the same effectiveness as Muller's method for real arithmetic and is simpler; see Problem 8.2.15.

Special Methods for Polynomials — 8.4.B

There are numerous special methods for polynomial roots, and some are quite effective. One of the oldest is the **Bernoulli method;** it is also the starting point for the best method for polynomial roots. We illustrate the Bernoulli method for quadratic polynomials to simplify the notation; it is not difficult to extend the method to higher–degree polynomials. With $p(x) = a_0 + a_1x + a_2x^2$ consider the *difference equation*:

$$a_2u_{k+2} + a_1u_{k+1} + a_0u_k = 0 \qquad \textbf{Equation 8.4.1}$$

If we know u_1 and u_2, then the solution u_k, $k = 1, 2, \ldots, \infty$ of 8.4.1 can be computed by repeated substitution into

$$u_{k+2} = -\frac{a_1u_{k+1} + a_0u_k}{a_2}$$

However, the general solution of this simple difference equation can be written down immediately as

$$u_k = \alpha r_1^k + \beta r_2^k \qquad \textbf{Equation 8.4.2}$$

where r_1 and r_2 are the roots of $p(x)$. To see this, just substitute $u_k = \alpha r_1^k$ into 8.4.1 to obtain

$$\alpha a_2r_1^{k+2} + \alpha a_1r_1^{k+1} + \alpha a_0r_1^k = \alpha r_1^k(a_2r_1^2+a_1r_1+a_0) = \alpha r_1^k p(r_1) = 0$$

The initial values u_1 and u_2 for 8.4.1 just determine the constants α and β of 8.4.2.

Equation 8.4.2 shows how to get u_k from the polynomial roots, but we want to reverse the process and get the roots from the u_k (which can be computed directly). Consider

$$\frac{u_{k+1}}{u_k} = \frac{\alpha r_1^{k+1} + \beta r_2^{k+1}}{\alpha r_1^k + \beta r_2^k} = \frac{r_1(1 + (\beta/\alpha)(r_2/r_1)^{k+1})}{1 + (\beta/\alpha)(r_2/r_1)^k} \qquad \textbf{Equation 8.4.3}$$

If we *assume* that $|r_1| > |r_2|$, then we see from 8.4.3 that

$$\frac{u_{k+1}}{u_k} = r_1 + O((r_2/r_1)^k)$$

and the root r_1 can be estimated just by taking ratios of successive values of u_k. We must have $\alpha \neq 0$; otherwise any α and β will do, and so any choice of u_1 and u_2 will do. Even if an unlucky choice of u_1 and u_2 leads to $\alpha = 0$, round-off error will quickly introduce a perturbation to make $\alpha \neq 0$ (but the convergence is delayed considerably).

If the assumption $|r_1| > |r_2|$ does not hold, then either $r_2 = -r_1$ or r_1 and r_2 are a complex conjugate pair. In either case, formulas exist to estimate the roots from the u_k; if $r_2 = -r_1$, then $u_{k+2}/u_k = r_1^2$. See Problem 8.4.5 for the complex conjugate pair case.

The general form of the **Bernoulli algorithm** for a polynomial of degree n is

Algorithm 8.4.2

Choose $u_1, u_2, \ldots, u_n$
For $k = n+1, \ldots,$ satisfied, do:

$$u_k = -\left(\sum_{i=0}^{n-1} a_{n-i}u_{k-n+i}\right)/a_n$$

Test u_k/u_{k-1} convergence
If not converging, then
Test u_k/u_{k-2} convergence
If not converging, then
Test complex pair convergence
If not converging, then
. . .

For higher-degree polynomials there are more cases one can test, but usually other things are done.

In summary the Bernoulli method uses a good idea, but it has some troublesome special cases. Consider $x^{20} - 1 = 0$, which has 20 roots *all of the same size.* This method has evolved over the years into the **Jenkins-Traub method;** this is a reliable, highly efficient method for polynomial roots. It is a "3-stage" polyalgorithm and too complicated to describe here, but it is available in library software form from the ACM Algorithms or the IMSL library.

Deflation and Purification *8.4.C

One often wants all the roots of a polynomial p(x), and once one root r is found, one can divide p(x) by x − r to get a new, lower-degree polynomial q(x). If r is exact, then q(x) is exact modulo round-off effects in the division. An important fact about polynomials is that *the deflation should use the smallest (in magnitude) roots first.* This means that the root-finding method should find the smallest roots first; just the opposite of what the Bernoulli method does, for example.

A second important fact is that once a root of the deflated polynomial is found, then it should be used as an initial guess for one or two iterations (say by Newton's method) on the original p(x). This process is called **purification** or refinement of the root.

PROBLEMS 8.4

8.4.1 Write a Fortran subprogram that implements Newton's method plus deflation and purification for polynomial roots and which starts out

```
SUBROUTINE PNEWT( A,NDEGRE,ROOTS,IFLAG )
REAL A(NDEGRE), ROOTS(NDEGRE)
```

Set IFLAG equal to the total number of Newton iterations used and IFLAG = −1 signals that failure occurred. Apply the program to compute the roots of the following polynomials (they have all real roots):

(A) $x^4 - 13x^3 + 35x^2 - 40x + 24$

(B) $x^6 - 32x^5 + 370x^4 - 1849x^3 + 3864x^2 - 3976x + 2112$

(C) $x^7 - 32x^6 + 375x^5 - 1905x^4 + 4131x^3 - 4556x^2 + 2706x - 317$

(D) $64x^6 - 80x^4 + 24x^2 - 1$

(E) $x^6 - 36x^5 + 450x^4 - 2400x^3 + 5400x^2 - 4320x + 720$

(F) $256x^8 - 3584x^6 + 13440x^4 - 13440x^2 + 1680$

(G) $128x^7 - 3x^6 - 1300x^5 + 4x^4 + 3300x^3 + 2x^2 - 1700x + 3$

8.4.2 Apply Newton's method with deflation (but without purification) to the following polynomials using the initial guesses specified in both ascending and descending order. Compare the accuracy of the results obtained.

(A) Problem 8.4.1, part (C). Guesses = 0, 1, 2, 3, 4, 8, 12.

(B) Problem 8.4.1, part (E). Guesses = 0, 1, 3, 6, 10, 16.

(C) Problem 8.4.1, part (G). Guesses = 0, .8, −.8, 3, −3, −6.5, 6.5.

8.4.3 Take the program MULLER of Problem 8.2.10 and change it to use complex arithmetic. Then add polynomial deflation, purification, and an initial guess scheme to produce a program that starts

```
SUBROUTINE PMULL( A,NDEGRE,ROOTS,IFLAG )
```

with the same arguments as PNEWT in Problem 8.4.2. Apply the program to compute the roots of the following:

(A) $x^6 - 1$

(B) $x^4 + 13x^3 + 35x^2 + 40x + 24$

(C) $1 + x^2$

(D) $x^5 - 11x^4 + 9x^3 + 30x^2 - 56x + 48$

(E) $x^4 + x^3 + 4x^2 + 2x + 4$

(F) $x^6 + x^5 + 2x^4 - 4x^2 - 4x - 8$

8.4.4 Redo Problem 8.4.2 with purification added to the algorithm. Discuss the improvement obtained; compare the results for large roots versus those for small roots.

8.4.5 Consider Bernoulli's method when the two roots largest in absolute value form a complex conjugate pair. With polar coordinates $z = re^{i\theta}$ show that

$$r^2 \sim \left(\frac{u_k u_{k+2} - u_{k+1}^2}{u_{k-1}u_{k+1} - u_k^2} \right)$$

and

$$\cos\theta \sim \left(\frac{r u_{k-1} + u_{k+1}/r}{2u_k} \right)$$

Hint: Show that the root t approximately satisfies $t^2 + pt + q = 0$ where $q = r^2$ (as above) and $p \sim (u_{k-1}u_{k+2} - u_k u_{k+1})/(u_{k-1}u_{k+1} - u_k^2)$.

SYSTEMS OF NONLINEAR EQUATIONS 8.5

Eight methods are presented for solving one nonlinear equation. Three of these, bisection, regula falsi, and modified regula falsi, cannot be extended to systems of nonlinear equations because patterns of sign changes do not "pin down" the zeros of several functions of several variables. Fixed point iteration extends with no change at all; one has

$$\mathbf{x}_{k+1} = \mathbf{f}(\mathbf{x}_k) + \mathbf{x}_k = \mathbf{g}(\mathbf{x}_k)$$

just as before. Muller's method and high-order Newton methods extend in principle, but their work increases rapidly with the number of equations, and they are rarely used.

The principal methods for systems of equations are based on linear models such as Newton's method or the secant method. A linear model of $\mathbf{f}(\mathbf{x})$ is of the form

$$\mathbf{f}(\mathbf{x}) \sim \mathbf{a}_0 + J^*(\mathbf{x} - \mathbf{x}_0) \qquad \textbf{Equation 8.5.1}$$

where J is a matrix. Usually $\mathbf{a}_0 = \mathbf{f}(\mathbf{x}_0)$, and 8.5.1 is then the first two terms of the Taylor's series of $\mathbf{f}(\mathbf{x})$ if the model J uses the first derivatives. We want to have $\mathbf{f}(\mathbf{x}) = 0$, and so set the model in 8.5.1 equal to zero and solve for $\mathbf{x}$ to obtain

$$\mathbf{x} = \mathbf{x}_0 - J^{-1}\mathbf{f}(\mathbf{x}_0) \qquad \textbf{Equation 8.5.2}$$

An iteration is formed from 8.5.2 in the obvious way. Note that we now have to solve an n by n system of linear equations *at each iteration.* One does *not* compute J^{-1}; one solves $\mathbf{a}_0 + J(\mathbf{x} - \mathbf{x}_0) = 0$ for $\mathbf{x}$.

Newton's method for systems of equations uses the linear model based on the "tangent planes." Visualize that $\mathbf{f}(\mathbf{x}) = 0$ is n equations

$$f_i(\mathbf{x}) = 0 \qquad i = 1, 2, \ldots, n$$

and $y = f_i(\mathbf{x})$ defines a surface. At $\mathbf{x}_0$ the tangent plane to this surface is

$$f_i(\mathbf{x}_0) + \sum_{j=1}^{n} \frac{\partial f_i}{\partial x_j}(x_j - x_{0,j}) \qquad \textbf{Equation 8.5.3}$$

The matrix J is the **Jacobian** matrix

$$J = \begin{pmatrix} \frac{\partial f_1}{\partial x_1} & \frac{\partial f_1}{\partial x_2} & \cdots & \frac{\partial f_1}{\partial x_n} \\ \frac{\partial f_2}{\partial x_1} & \frac{\partial f_2}{\partial x_2} & \cdots & \frac{\partial f_2}{\partial x_n} \\ \cdots & \cdots & \cdots & \cdots \\ \frac{\partial f_n}{\partial x_1} & \frac{\partial f_n}{\partial x_2} & \cdots & \frac{\partial f_n}{\partial x_n} \end{pmatrix}$$

The secant method for systems of equations is obtained by a direct extension of the idea for one equation. However, it is not so easy to present it in formulas, and so we describe it in words. At the kth step of the iteration we have saved $\mathbf{x}_k, \mathbf{x}_{k-1}, \ldots, \mathbf{x}_{k-n}$. For each function $f_i(\mathbf{x})$, we determine the plane that interpolates $f_i(\mathbf{x})$ at $f_i(\mathbf{x}_{k-j})$ for $j = 0, 1, 2, \ldots, n$. Thus n planes are computed to model the n components of $\mathbf{f}(\mathbf{x})$; each plane requires the solution of $n+1$ linear equations in $n+1$ unknowns. One then solves the n by n linear system obtained by setting these linear functions equal to zero simultaneously, that is, one locates where the planes intersect at zero simultaneously. The solution of this system is the next iterate $\mathbf{x}_{k+1}$.

Both of these methods require solving n linear equations as the last step of each iteration. This is a significant amount of work, but it is inherent in using a linear model. Both methods have an additional major computational problem. Newton's method requires that n^2 derivatives be evaluated *at every step.* If $\mathbf{f}(\mathbf{x})$ is complicated, this might be much more work than all the rest of the method. Worse yet, it may be *very* difficult to actually carry out the differentiations. For a system of 20 equations, which is not very large, the Jacobian has 400 entries; one can become very frustrated in trying to get all the derivatives correct. For this reason, one often sees the **discrete Newton method** used where the derivatives are approximated by the simple difference formula

$$\frac{\partial f_i}{\partial x_j} \sim \frac{f_i(x_1, x_2, \ldots, x_j+h, \ldots, x_n) - f_i(x_1, x_2, \ldots, x_j, \ldots, x_n)}{h}$$

This doubles the number of function evaluations per iteration and has the nontrivial problem of how to choose h properly.

The added computational problem for the secant method is that it requires the linear interpolant (plane) to be computed *for each f_i at each step.* If this is done straight-forwardly, then one solves n systems (one for each f_i) of $n+1$ linear equations; this can be a tremendous amount of computation. There are ways to reduce this work by exploiting the fact that each linear system is almost the same as the corresponding linear system at the previous iteration; only one of the interpolation points has changed.

A number of tactics have been invented to reduce the work in these methods. An easy example is to note that the Jacobian in Newton's method need not be evaluated at each iteration. One can compute a Jacobian and use it for, say, 5 iterations before recomputing it. Large systems of nonlinear equations frequently have some kind of special structure which can be (or even must be) exploited. For example, the Jacobian is frequently a sparse matrix, perhaps a band matrix. Exploiting the special structure of the Jacobian can dramatically reduce the effort in solving a system of nonlinear equations.

The most successful tactic to reduce the work in these methods has been to roughly estimate the derivatives during the iteration. The resulting methods are called **quasi-Newton methods.** The techniques to estimate the derivatives and keep improving the estimates during the iteration are rather complicated to derive but reasonably cheap to use. There are many variations within this class of methods; the ones used in practice are polyalgorithms involving many techniques to improve the efficiency and reliability of the basic quasi-Newton methods.

Solving systems of nonlinear equations is perhaps the most difficult problem in all of numerical computation. It is not unheard of for even 5 equations to be very difficult to solve; one can "hide" a solution in 5-dimensional space rather easily. To illustrate the dimension effect, visualize a rather smooth function of one variable which requires about 10 or 12 points to represent reasonably well. Now visualize n functions of n variables of the same complexity. If $n = 10$, then $10 \times 10^n = 10^{11} = 100$ billion points are needed to represent these functions with equivalent accuracy. If $n = 100$, then more points are needed than there are atoms in the universe. Another way to visualize the difficulty is as follows. Suppose one knows the solution is in a cube. Next visualize the sphere that just fits inside the cube. The volume of the cube is d^n and that of the sphere is $c\pi r^n$, where $r = d/2$ and c is more or less constant. As n becomes large we see that the volume of the sphere inside the cube becomes a negligible portion of the total volume. Now suppose that one discovers that the solution is not in the sphere. Then it must be in one of the corners of the cube. They are all the same, they are equally likely to contain the solution, and *there are 2^n of them.* For $n = 10$, there are 1,000 corners, and for $n = 100$, there are 10^{30} corners. Where does one look next? In spite of these formidable difficulties, there are

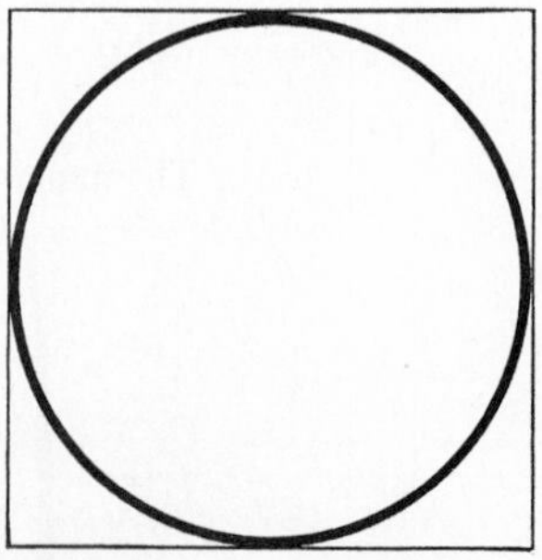

problems with hundreds or thousands of equations that need to be solved. Clearly, one must have very nice equations and exploit all the special properties in order to solve them.

There are many ways that a system of nonlinear equations can be difficult. One of the most common of these is in the scaling. This is something that one can usually do something about and sometimes dramatically improve the efficiency of solving the system. Suppose there are 10 variables, some vary between 10,000 and 10,000,000, and still others vary between 10^{-4} and 10^{-2}. This is just asking for trouble. A general nonlinear equation solver has no idea of these differences; it might choose a step of .5 which, figuratively, jumps across the universe for some variables and does not move at all for others. It is worthwhile to expend considerable effort in scaling a difficult problem so that the variables and function values vary over approximately the same range of values.

PROBLEMS 8.5

8.5.1 Derive the Jacobian matrix for each system of equations:

(A) $-2x^2 + 3xy + 4\sin y = 6$
$3x^2 - 2xy^2 + 3\cos x = -4$

(B) $xe^{(x+y)} = 3$
$ye^{(x-y)} = 4$

(C) $\sin(xy+1)/(1+x+y) = 1$
$\tan(xy+2)/(1-x+y) = 2$

8.5.2 Consider the system of equations in Problem 8.5.1, part (A). Given the 3 points $(x, y) = (0, 0), (0, 1)$ and $(1, 0)$, explicitly show the system of linear equations that determines the interpolating of the secant method for each equation in the system. **Hint:** A plane in three variables $(x, y, z = f(x, y))$ is usually represented as $ax + by + c = 0$.

8.5.3 Continue the analysis of Problem 8.5.2 and show the linear system of equations to be solved for the next iterate of the secant method. Solve the system and obtain the next iterate.

8.5.4 Suppose the nonlinear system $\mathbf{f}(\mathbf{x}) = 0$ is sparse in the sense that $f_i(\mathbf{x})$ only involves x_{i-2}, x_{i-1}, x_i, x_{i+1}, and x_{i+2}. Describe the nature of the Jacobian matrix for this system of equations.

8.5.5 Consider the system of equations in Problem 8.5.1, part (C). Given the point $(x, y) = (.5, .5)$ and taking $h = 10^{-3}$, compute the Jacobian matrix for the discrete Newton method at this point. Carry out the method and find the next iterate.

8.5.6 A system of equations might be such that the ith equation depends most heavily on the ith variable. This suggests for Newton's method that the full Jacobian be computed every k iterations while the diagonal elements $\partial f_i(\mathbf{x})/\partial x_i$ are evaluated at every iteration. Discuss and compare the amount of work for this new method as a function of k and the size n of the nonlinear system.

SOFTWARE FOR NONLINEAR EQUATIONS 8.6

The software for nonlinear equations is divided into five categories:

Simple implementation of basic algorithms

Software for a single nonlinear equation

Software for systems of nonlinear equations

Polynomial zero finders

Special procedures

It is straightforward to implement one of the basic methods along with a simple convergence test. However, even for simple methods, there are good and bad implementations. One rarely obtains a program with high efficiency and insensitivity to round-off, overflow, and underflow just by translating the standard formulas into Fortran. This is seen with the simplest case of all: the formula for roots of a quadratic equation (see Example 3.3). A common weakness of "first attempts" at nonlinear equation solvers is excess evaluations of f(x); one should never have more than one evaluation at the same point. In Algorithms 8.2.1 to 8.2.7 there are only two cases where the formulas given do not use extra f(x) evaluations.

ACM Algorithms 2, 4, 15, 25, and 26 fall in the simple category, as do IMSL library routines ZFALSE, the regula falsi method, and ZREAL1, Muller's method (this is essentially ACM Algorithm 25). The IMSL library routine ZREAL2 is almost in this category; it uses the discrete Newton method but has the capability to find several zeros on one call. The PROTRAN system provides access to the IMSL library programs through statements like

```
$NONLIN  F2(X)= 0.;  SOLUTION = ZTWO ; IN( 0., 5.5 )
                      ERRTAR = .0005 ; DEFINE
            ====
            F2 = X*(X+4.*EXP(X))*EXP(-X-X*X) - 0.7382252822
            ====
```

There are two simple software items for complex roots: ACM Algorithm 365, which does a complex variable analog of the "walk downhill" method of Problem 8.3.2, and the IMSL routine ZANLYT, a complex variable version of Muller's method.

More elaborate software for one equation includes ACM Algorithm 196, which implements Muller's method for real or complex roots; note the corrections and improvements given with its certification. The IMSL library routine ZBRENT is a polyalgorithm that combines regula falsi and the secant method. Since it is based on regula falsi, it requires an interval where a sign change occurs in f(x). The calling sequence for ZBRENT is

```
CALL ZBRENT( F,FTOL,NXTOL,A,B,MAXFN,IER )
```

where F = name of function subprogram F(X), declared EXTERNAL

FTOL = first convergence test; a zero is accepted if $|F(X)| \leq$ FTOL

NXTOL = second convergence test; iterate x_{k+1} is accepted as a zero if $-\log|x_{k+1} - x_k| \geq$ NXTOL (x_{k+1} and x_k agree to NXTOL decimal digits)

A,B = interval so $F(A)*F(B) < 0$

MAXFN = limit on number of f(x) evaluations

Note that convergence is accepted when *either* the first test *or* the second test is passed. This routine is used in PROTRAN wherever an interval is given in the problem-solving statement, e.g.,

```
$NONLINEAR , F3(ZTHREE) = 0.;  IN(2.2,1.+B) ; SOLUTION=F3Z
     DEFINE
     ====
     F3 = COS(ZTHREE) -1./(1.+ZTHREE**3)
     ====
```

The PROTRAN system uses reverse communication to allow more complicated equations to be solved. This is illustrated in the following examples:

```
$NONLINEAR GUNK(XBAR) = 0.; SOLUTION = XG ; ERRTAR = H/10.
    IN(A,B*X)  ;  DEFINE
    ====
    GUNK = HUNK(XBAR,A+3.*B,Y,XBAR/(X+Y))-7.2
    ====
$NONLIN  ZUNK(Z) = 0.;  SOLUTION = ZROOT; ERRTAR = .000002
         IN(3.4,3.5)  ;  DEFINE
    ====
 Z1   = ARRAY(3,K)/(ARRAY(4,2)**2 + Z**2)
 Z2   = SQRT( Z**2 + Z1**2)
 ZUNK = COS(Z)/(1.+Z2**2) - SIN(Z)/(ARRAY(1,K)*Z1+1.)
    ====
```

Both these functions depend on several variables besides the one being varied to solve the problem (A,B,X,Y, and HUNK for the first one, ARRAY and K for the second one). Reverse communication allows them to use whatever values these other variables have at this point in the program without creating new subprograms with variable values communicated through COMMON.

Evaluation of Software for One Nonlinear Equation — Example 8.7

Eight programs are applied to 10 equations to sample the performance of software for solving a single nonlinear equation. The programs are:

BISECT = Algorithm 8.2.1 for the bisection method

MODRF = Algorithm 8.2.3 for the modified regula falsi method

ZREAL2 = IMSL discrete Newton method, Problem 8.2.21

SECANT = Algorithm 8.2.5 for the secant method

ZREAL1 = IMSL Muller's method, Algorithm 8.2.7

FIXPT = Algorithm 8.2.6 for fixed point iteration

ZBRENT = IMSL library, Brent's polyalgorithm

QQBASC = Purdue University library, Rice's polyalgorithm

Four of the programs were written just for this example and thus represent "basic" implementations. The convergence criterion used is to accept a root if:

1. The change in the root estimate is less than XTOL

or

2. The value of the function is less than FTOL

The program QQBASC applies additional criteria before accepting a root.

The equations and results of the test are given in Table 8.3. The first two equations are very easy, and all programs except FIXPT perform well. The third equation has a large root which might cause a problem for some methods; only MODRF experienced difficulty because of this.

Test of Software For One Nonlinear Equation **Table 8.3**

Eight methods are used for each of 10 equations f(x) = 0. The termination condition = TERM, count of f(x) evaluations = FCOUNT, number of correct decimal digits = DIGITS, and value of f(x) = FVALUE are given. An asterisk is used for DIGITS if no root exists, but the program finds one anyway. All runs have FTOL = XTOL = 10^{-6}.

$f(x) = x - \cos(x)$, root = 0.739085133

Program	TERM	FCOUNT	DIGITS	FVALUE	REMARKS
BISECT	Normal	22	5.9	$-2*10^{-6}$	
MODRF	Normal	8	9.8	$-3*10^{-10}$	
ZREAL2	Normal	5	9.8	$3*10^{-10}$	
SECANT	Normal	4	6.8	$2*10^{-7}$	
ZREAL1	Normal	5	9.6	$-4*10^{-10}$	
FIXPT	Normal	26	6.2	$-9*10^{-7}$	
ZBRENT	Normal	7	10.8	$1*10^{-12}$	
QQBASC	Normal	15	10.8	$1*10^{-12}$	

$f(x) = e^{x+1.00202} - e$, root = −0.00202

Program	TERM	FCOUNT	DIGITS	FVALUE	REMARKS
BISECT	Normal	22	6.4	$-1*10^{-7}$	
MODRF	Normal	8	11.2	$-2*10^{-11}$	
ZREAL2	Normal	7	7.0	$2*10^{-7}$	
SECANT	Normal	6	7.0	$3*10^{-7}$	
ZREAL1	Normal	6	8.2	$2*10^{-8}$	
FIXPT	Limit	101			Only small change from guess
ZBRENT	Normal	7	8.6	$7*10^{-9}$	
QQBASC	Normal	17	11.6	$8*10^{-12}$	

Test of Software For One Nonlinear Equation *(Cont.)*

$f(x) = \cos(0.001x)$, root = 1570.79632679

Program	TERM	FCOUNT	DIGITS	FVALUE	REMARKS
BISECT	Normal	32	6.1	$-9*10^{-10}$	
MODRF	Normal	6	3.6	$-2*10^{-7}$	
ZREAL2	Normal	7	8.5	$1*10^{-12}$	
SECANT	Normal	6	9.3	$4*10^{-12}$	
ZREAL1	Normal	7	8.5	$8*10^{-12}$	
FIXPT	Limit	101			
ZBRENT	Normal	6	7.6	$-2*10^{-11}$	
QQBASC	Normal	17	8.3	$-2*10^{-15}$	

$f(x) = x^{20} - 1$, root = 1.0

Program	TERM	FCOUNT	DIGITS	FVALUE	REMARKS
BISECT	Normal	22	5.7	$-4*10^{-5}$	
MODRF	Normal	34	6.7	$4*10^{-6}$	
ZREAL2	Limit	200			
SECANT	Normal	4	0.1	−1.00	Accidental convergence; wrong value
ZREAL1	Normal	30	8.9	$2*10^{-8}$	
FIXPT	Diverging	4			Fourth iterate is 10^{38}
ZBRENT	Normal	6	9.8	$3*10^{-9}$	
QQBASC	Normal	13	∞	0	Exact solution obtained

$f(x) = \tan(x) - 30$, root = 1.5374753309

Program	TERM	FCOUNT	DIGITS	FVALUE	REMARKS
BISECT	Normal	20	7.0	$-1*10^{-4}$	
MODRF	Normal	27	7.8	$2*10^{-5}$	
ZREAL2	Limit	200			
SECANT	Normal	8	8.9	$1*10^{-6}$	
ZREAL1	Limit	99			
FIXPT	Limit	101			
ZBRENT	Normal	12	10.5	$2*10^{-8}$	
QQBASC	Normal	48	7.9	$1*10^{-5}$	

$f(x) = (y-4)(y+2)(y+41)$ where $y = 10^8(x - 1.01*10^{-9})$, root = 0.0000000410

Program	TERM	FCOUNT	DIGITS	FVALUE	REMARKS
BISECT	Normal	15	6.0	$2*10^6$	
MODRF	Normal	36	8.1	$3*10^2$	
ZREAL2	Normal	50	6.8	$2*10^4$	
SECANT	Normal	28	5.7	$1*10^7$	
ZREAL1	Normal	25	19.1	$-2*10^{-9}$	
FIXPT	Diverging	2			Third iterate is 10^{25}
ZBRENT	Normal	3	8.0	$3*10^2$	
QQBASC	Normal	411	7.2	$-7*10^1$	Root identified as multiple root, order = 3.00

$f(x) = 1/(1 + |x|^3)$, no roots

Program	TERM	FCOUNT	DIGITS	FVALUE	REMARKS
BISECT	N/A	2			No sign change in f(x)
MODRF	N/A	2			No sign change in f(x)
ZREAL2	Normal	31	*	$9*10^{-7}$	FTOL criterion gives false root
SECANT	Normal	24	*	$6*10^{-7}$	FTOL criterion gives false root
ZREAL1	Normal	25	*	$6*10^{-7}$	FTOL criterion gives false root
FIXPT	Limit	101			
ZBRENT	N/A	2			No sign change in f(x)
QQBASC	Normal	318			Reports that no roots were found

Test of Software For One Nonlinear Equation *(Cont.)*

$f(x) = (x^2 - 2.2x + 1.21)*\text{sign}(x - 1.1)$, root $= 1.1$

Program	TERM	FCOUNT	DIGITS	FVALUE	REMARKS
BISECT	Normal	23	6.0	$-1*10^{-12}$	
MODRF	Normal	12	3.0	$-9*10^{-7}$	
ZREAL2	Normal	19	3.1	$6*10^{-7}$	
SECANT	Normal	15	3.2	$5*10^{-7}$	
ZREAL1	Normal	4	13.7	$7*10^{-15}$	Muller's method uses quadratic model
FIXPT	Limit	101			Converging slowly, DIGITS = 2.0
ZBRENT	Normal	26	3.2	$-4*10^{-7}$	
QQBASC	Normal	85	7.1	$7*10^{-15}$	Order of root estimate = 2.00

$f(x) = |x - 9.1|^{4.5}$, root $= 9.1$

Program	TERM	FCOUNT	DIGITS	FVALUE	REMARKS
BISECT	N/A	2			No sign change in f(x)
MODRF	N/A	2			No sign change in f(x)
ZREAL2	Normal	35	1.4	$7*10^{-7}$	FTOL criterion gives early convergence
SECANT	Normal	26	1.4	$8*10^{-7}$	FTOL criterion gives early convergence
ZREAL1	Normal	11	1.3	$1*10^{-6}$	FTOL criterion gives early convergence
FIXPT	Diverging	3			Fourth iterate is 10^{44}
ZBRENT	N/A	2			No sign change in f(x)
QQBASC	Normal	49	6.1	$6*10^{-28}$	Order of root estimate = 4.51

$f(x) = |x - 8.4317|^{0.4}$, root $= 8.4317$

Program	TERM	FCOUNT	DIGITS	FVALUE	REMARKS
BISECT	N/A	2			No sign change in f(x)
MODRF	N/A	2			No sign change in f(x)
ZREAL2	Limit	200			
SECANT	Limit	102			
ZREAL1	Limit	99			
FIXPT	Limit	101			
ZBRENT	N/A	2			No sign change in f(x)
QQBASC	Normal	139	7.7	$9*10^{-4}$	Order of root estimate = 0.40

The fourth equation $x^{20} - 1 = 0$ looks easy; the zero $x = 1.0$ is simple, but this is not an easy equation. It is extremely flat for $|x| \leq .5$ and rises very rapidly for $|x| > 1.0$, for example, $f(2)$ is over a million. The initial guess used was $x = 1.5$, and the SECANT program experienced false convergence because the change in x was so small. The Newton method did not experience false convergence, but the changes in x are so small that after 100 iterations the program is not close to the zero.

The equation $\tan(x) - 30 = 0$ requires a good guess (1.5 was used for the zero 1.5374753309). The three methods using the sign change at the root do not, of course, require this good guess. Only two of the four "noninterval" methods converged from the starting point $x = 1.5$. This would normally be considered a good guess, but this equation is more difficult than normal.

The next equation is badly scaled; the XTOL criterion allows poor relative accuracy for the zeros $4.101*10^{-8}$, $-1.899*10^{-8}$, and $-40.899*10^{-8}$. In fact, within the tolerance of 10^{-6}, this equation has a multiple root of order 3 in this region. The program QQBASC detects this and returns with a triple root. The program ZREAL2 using Muller's method obtains exceptionally accurate results.

The equation $1/(1 + |x|^3) = 0$ has no roots, but the FTOL criterion used by ZREAL1, ZREAL2, and SECANT gives a false root for large x. QQBASC is able to identify asymptotes to zero at $\pm\infty$ and hence can report that it found no roots.

The next equation is almost quadratic and has a double root. The double root leads to low accuracy for those programs that use the simple FTOL convergence criterion. The $f(x)$ in this equation is exactly the model that ZREAL2 uses for $f(x)$, and so ZREAL2 converges immediately.

The last two functions have roots which only QQBASC is designed to handle. Roots of high multiplicity give low accuracy and/or slow convergence for programs unprepared for multiple roots. The fractional order root of $|x - 8.4317|^{0.4} = 0$ is too difficult for most programs even with the good initial guess of 8.45.

The last two functions have roots which only QQBASC is designed to handle. Roots of high multiplicity give low accuracy and/or slow convergence for programs unprepared for multiple roots. The fractional order root of $|x - 8.4317|^{0.4} = 0$ is too difficult for most programs even with the good initial guess of 8.45.

There are some general patterns from this experiment which are true in general:

1. FIXPT works only for a small percentage of the equations.
2. BISECT is slow for easy problems but completely reliable and good for hard ones (if it applies).
3. The polyalgorithm QQBASC is more reliable and versatile; the price one pays for this is that it uses a fair number of function evaluations in checking its results.
4. ZREAL1 (an implementation of Muller's method) is more effective than other simple methods for double roots.

Software for systems of nonlinear equations tends to be more sophisticated than for one equation because of the higher level of difficulty of the problem. One needs to do various things to maintain some efficiency when the number of variables grows. From one point of view, the methods are less sophisticated because one cannot afford to carry out schemes like bisection, high-order methods, and exhaustive searches.

There are five ACM algorithms for nonlinear systems; 314, 315, 316, 378, and 554. All use as basic method Newton's method (315), discrete Newton's (315, 316, 378, and 554), or the secant method (314). The most interesting of these is the latest, which is known as BRENTM. It is a method of Brent, but different from the Brent method for one nonlinear equation implemented in the IMSL routine ZBRENT. Until 1982 the IMSL library had a routine ZSYSTEM which was an updated Fortran version of Algorithm 316. It has since been replaced by more effective routines.

The IMSL library has two programs for systems of nonlinear equations, ZSCNT and ZSPOW. Systems of nonlinear equations are so difficult to solve that it is worthwhile to have more than one program to try on a difficult system. ZSPOW is a version of the program HVBR01 from the MINPACK package (MINPACK is a collection of programs for minimization and optimization, important topics not discussed in this book). It implements M. J. D. Powell's hybrid algorithm which is a quasi-Newton method. MINPACK was developed at Argonne National Laboratory and is available from IMSL. The calls for these routines are

```
CALL ZSCNT( F,NXTOL,NEQNS,KLIMIT,PARAM,ZEROS,FSIZE,WORK,IER )
CALL ZSPOW( F,NXTOL,NEQNS,KLIMIT,PARAM,ZEROS,FSIZE,WORK,IER )
```

where F and NXTOL are as for ZBRENT. The other arguments are:

NEQNS	=	number of equations
ZEROS	=	solution vector of length NEQNS
KLIMIT	=	limit on the iterations
WORK	=	workspace array, size 3*NEQNS + (NEQNS + 2)(NEQNS − 1)/2
PARAM	=	parameter vector for F(X); see comments below
FSIZE	=	sum of squares of the final components of F

The parameter vector PARAM is a partial solution to the problem of passing information to a function which is input to a library routine. The calling sequence of F must be

```
FUNCTION F( X,VALUES,N,PARAM )
REAL X(N), VALUES(N)
```

All the component values of f(x) are placed in the array VALUES on each call to F. The argument PARAM can be either a vector of values of parameters or the name of a subprogram which supplies information to F. This argument must be included even if F has no parameters. This approach is a reasonable alternative to passing all information through COMMON; it also places a considerable burden on the user, especially compared to using reverse communication (see Example 7.4).

A rather strenuous test was made in 1980 of eight of the "best available" nonlinear system solvers [see K. Hiebert, ACM Trans. Math. Software, 7 (1982), 5-20]. The test included ZSYSTM (Fortran version of Algorithm 316) and BRENTM (Algorithm 554). It concluded that all eight programs were close in overall effectiveness. There were variations in the kinds of problems that caused difficulty for the various programs. The problem test set had 171 systems of nonlinear equations; each of the eight programs found correct solutions for 90 to 100 of these problems. This result attests to the difficulty of solving nonlinear systems of equations and to the difficulty of the testing made.

The PROTRAN system gives access to ZSCNT through statements like

```
$NONLIN BESS(X)= 0.; GUESS = BGUESS; ERRTARGET = 1.E-8
        SOLUTION = XBESS ; DEFINE
====
C           TRUE = 2, 1.5, 2.5
    BESS(1) = XB(1) - XB(2)*XB(3) +1.25
    BESS(2) = (XB(2)-XB(1))**2 -4. + XB(2)*XB(3)
    BESS(3) = SIN(XB(2)*XB(1)-XB(3)) - 0.4794255386
         ====
```

or in a complete program like

```
$DECLARATIONS
  VECTOR F11(NVAR=20), Z11(NVAR=20), Z0(NVAR=20), VALUES(NVAR=20), Z(NVAR=20)
$ASSIGN Z0(J) = J*.04
        A  = 6.825*COS(3.14159265/7.)
$NONLIN F11(Z)= 0. ; SOLUTION = Z11 ; EQUATIONS = 11
      ERRTARGET = 0.00001; GUESS = Z0; DEFINE
   ====
   CALL F(Z,VALUES,11)
   DO 10 I  = 1,11
10    F11(I)= VALUES(I) - A*SIN(Z(I))
   ====
$PRINT A,Z0,Z11
$END
```

Here Z, Z11, Z0, and F11 are all vectors of appropriate length.

Using Nonlinear Equation Solvers to Find Gauss Integration Formulas

Example 8.8

Recall from Section 7.4.E and Example 8.3 that determining Gauss quadrature formulas can be formulated as a nonlinear equation problem:

$$I(x^j) = Q(x^j) \qquad j = 0, 1, 2, \ldots, 2n-1$$

Equation 8.6.1

We consider the particular case where, for $p > 0$,

$$I(f) = \int_0^1 x^p f(x)dx$$

Then $I(x^j) = 1/(j+p)$ and, for weights a_i and abscissas x_i,

$$Q(x^j) = \sum_{i=1}^{n} a_i (x_i)^j$$

Rename the variables so that $t_i = a_i$ and $t_{n+i} = x_i$ for $i = 1, 2, \ldots, n$. We attempt to compute the coefficients of the Gauss formula with the following PROTRAN program to solve 8.6.1.

```
      $DECLARATIONS
      VECTOR  IXJ(N=10),T(M=20),TGAUSS(M=20) $
C                      CHOOSE P AND NUMBER N OF GAUSS POINTS
      P =  0.5
      DO 100  N = 2,4
         M = 2*N
C              COMPUTE TRUE INTEGRAL VALUES IXJ
         $ASSIGN, IXJ(J) = 1./(J+P) $
C              COMPUTE GUESSES FOR T USING AD HOC FORMULAS
         A = .2*P/2**(N-1)
         B = .3*N**(.4/P-1.)/(1.+P)
         DO  10  J = 1,N
 10         T(J) = B - (A-B)*4.*((J-1.)/N - .5)**2
         F =  5./(1+P)
         XR= 1. - .5/F**K
         XL= .3/F**K
         DX= (XR-XL)/(K-1)
         DO 20 J = N+1,2*N
 20         T(J) = XL + (J-N-1)*DX
C                         SOLVE GAUSS POINT EQUATIONS
         $NONLIN, GP(T) = 0.; GUESS = T ; ERRTAR = 1.E-7
                  SOLUTION = TGAUSS  ;   DEFINE
              ====
              DO 30 J = 1,2*N
                 SUM = -IXJ(J)
                 DO 25 K = 1,N
 25                 SUM= SUM + T(K)*ABS(T(K+N))**(J-1)
 30              GP(J) = SUM
              ====
         $PRINT, TGAUSS $
 100  CONTINUE
      $END
```

This approach to finding Gauss integration formulas is deceptive and works only for small n (say n = 2 or 3). There are two reasons for this. The first is encountered already for n = 2; one needs to have a good initial guess for the solution. In preparing this example, the Gauss formulas for p = .5, 1.0, 1.5, and 3.3 were computed for 2, 3, and 4 points. About 60 to 80 computer runs were made trying out various initial guesses before all the 12 formulas were found. The only reliable way to find initial guesses is to solve the problem for n = 2 and use this answer to guess for n = 3; when this case is solved, prepare a plot of the pattern of the answers to guess for n = 4, etc.

The second reason is that the system 8.6.1 becomes very poorly conditioned as n increases. So, even if good guesses for the solution are available, before n gets very large the computations are ruined by round-off effects in the presence of this ill-conditioning. If one really wants to obtain many Gauss formulas, one should use tables of them or ACM Algorithm 331.

The solutions for p = .5 are listed below.

	Weights a_i	Abscissa x_i
n = 2	.277556	.289949
	.389110	.821162
n = 3	.125783	.164710
	.307602	.549869
	.233282	.900805
n = 4	.065681	.105140
	.196096	.376225
	.252527	.698948
	.152362	.937334

Devising methods for finding roots of polynomials has been a popular activity for over 200 years. The result is a lot of methods with totally different approaches. Many of these methods form the basis for good software; others perform poorly in both speed and reliability. The ACM Collected Algorithms contains 10 polynomial root finders (Algorithms 3, 30, 59, 105, 256, 283, 340, 419, 493) plus 5 specialized polynomial algorithms; 75 and 78 are for integer coefficients, 174 and 429 compute bounds on roots, and 329 uses the classical formulas for polynomials of degree 4 or less. The best of these are 419 and 493, implementing the Jenkins-Traub method for complex and real roots, respectively. This method is implemented in the IMSL library by ZCPOLY and ZRPOLY, which are used as follows:

```
CALL ZCPOLY( A,NDEGRE,Z,IER )
```

where A = vector of complex coefficients in *decreasing* powers of x
NDEGRE = polynomial degree
Z = vector of NDEGRE complex roots

The use of ZRPOLY is the same except A is a real vector. The IMSL library also contains ZPOLR which implements LaGuerre's method (LaGuerre's method is not described in this text); it has the same arguments as ZRPOLY.

The IMSL programs ZCPOLY and ZRPOLY are accessed in the PROTRAN system by statements like

```
$POLYNOMIAL, PCOEFS ; ROOTS = PROOTS
$POLYNOM      A ;    DEGREE = 12 ,   ROOTS = X
$ ASSIGN  COEFI  = ( 1, 0, 10, 0, 8 )
$POLYNO       COEFI ;   ROOTS = Z
```

The polynomial coefficients are given in *ascending order* so that the last statement computes the roots of $1+10x^2+8x^4 = 0$.

PROBLEMS 8.6

8.6.1 The following Fortran functions are examples of "strange" functions used to test the **robustness** of a nonlinear equation solver. A program is robust if it performs satisfactorily for very difficult or even improperly defined equations. Satisfactory performance means that the program does not abort, go into an infinite loop, print a million lines of messages, or take some similarly disagreeable action.

(A) Select one of the nonlinear equation solvers from Problems 8.2.3 (modified regula falsi), 8.2.6 (secant), 8.2.10 (Muller's), or 8.2.13 (quadratic inverse interpolation), apply it to these functions, and discuss how robust it is.

(B) Apply a library nonlinear equation solver and discuss how robust it is.

(C) Compare the robustness of the library program with the simple implementation of a basic method.

1. ```
   Y = X - 1312.11
   If( ABS(Y) .GT. 1.E+6) Y = SIGN(1.E+6,Y)
   F = ALOG10( 1.+Y**2)*(Y+16.)*SQRT(ABS(Y-8.))
   ```
2. ```
   F = 1.+X**4
   IF( ABS(X) .GT. 1.E+8) F = 1.222E+9 - ABS(X)
   ```
3. ```
   Y = AMIN1( X,88. )
   F = EXP(-Y)*(1.+.5*SIN(Y))
   ```
4. ```
   X = AMIN1(X,88.)
   F = EXP(-X)*(1.+.5*SIN(X))
   ```
5. ```
   F = 0
   ```
6. ```
   X = X+1
   F = 0.000001
   ```
7. ```
   F = (X-.12E+5)*(X+.21E+8)*.1E-9
   ```
8. ```
   F = SIN( 3.1415976/SQRT( ABS(X)))*X
   ```
9. ```
   F = (X+1.)*(X+5.)*(X-37.)*(X-103.)
   IF( ABS(F) .LT. 1.E-5*ABS(X)) F = 13.
   ```
10. ```
    X = 1.11
    F = 1.E+4
    ```

8.6.2 Apply library nonlinear equation solvers to the functions in Problems 8.2.1, 8.2.2, 8.2.3, and 8.2.5. Discuss the efficiency and effectiveness of this software compared with the basic methods implemented for the problems of Section 8.2.

8.6.3 The following function f(x) has a positive root x near zero which is the rate of return on an investment model for development of a forest. Set $y = 1 + x$; then

$$f(x) = \frac{20}{y^{15}} + \frac{36}{y^{25}} + \frac{40}{y^{33}} + \frac{475}{y^{40}} - \frac{1.12(y^{40}-1)}{(xy^{40})} - \frac{6}{y^4} - \frac{3}{y^8} - 4.5$$

(A) Make a rough plot of this function for $-1 \le x \le 1$, then determine an initial guess so that a library nonlinear equation solver converges to the desired zero. **Hint:** Use the IMSL library routine USPLO.

(B) This equation $f(x) = 0$ can be transformed into a polynomial equation by clearing all the demoninators. Discuss the strengths and weaknesses of this approach to solving $f(x) = 0$.

8.6.4 Evaluate the robustness of the convergence test for a library nonlinear equation solver by applying it to functions such as given in Example 8.5. Discuss the strengths and weaknesses of the convergence test as revealed by this evaluation. Specifically, use the functions

$$\frac{1}{(1+x^5)} \qquad e^{-x} \qquad \frac{1}{(1.1-x)^3} \qquad (x-1.1)^{10} \qquad e^{-\frac{1}{x^2}}$$

$$\sqrt{|1-e^{-x}|/|\log|x+4||} \qquad (x+1)(x-2) + \frac{\text{random}(x)}{10000}$$

$$e^{-x^2}(x^2-17x+71)$$

8.6.5 Evaluate the robustness of a library nonlinear equation solver as the tolerances for accuracy are very small. Take FTOL, XTOL = 5 ulps, 2 ulps, 1 ulps, 1/2 ulps, and 1/5 ulps, and apply the program to find the zeros of the following simple functions.

$$(x-1)(x-2)(x-3)(x-4) \qquad \cos\left(\frac{x}{100}\right) \qquad (x^2+1)\sin(x)$$

$$\frac{(x+1)}{(x^2+2)} \qquad e^x(x-1)^2 \qquad \frac{\sin(x)-x}{2} \qquad 21+x(17+x(x-5))$$

$$\cos(x)-xe^x \qquad \tan(x)-\cos(x)-.4 \qquad x-e^x \qquad x(x-3)-4(\sin(x))^2$$

8.6.6 Apply the evaluation procedure of Example 8.7 to one of the simple implementations of a basic method in Problems 8.2.2 (regula falsi), 8.2.3 (modified regula falsi), 8.2.5 (Newton), 8.2.6 (secant), 8.2.8 (fixed point), 8.2.10 (Muller's), or 8.2.13 (quadratic inverse interpolation). Discuss how this program compares with the programs evaluated in Example 8.7.

8.6.7 Use library software to solve the following systems of equations. Give the number of **f(x)** evaluations required and have output that clearly explains the problem input (tolerances, guesses, etc.) and the results obtained.

(A) $3x + 4y + e^{(z+w)} = 1.007$
$6x - 4y + e^{(3z+w)} = 11$
$x^4 - 4y^2 + 6z - 8w = 20$
$x^2 + 2y^3 + z - w = 4$

(B) $-2x^2 - 3xy + 4\sin y = -6$
$3x^2 - 2xy^2 + 3\cos x = 8$

(C) $x^2 + y^2 = 4$
$x^2 - y^2 = 1.5$

(D) $y - 4 = .001x$
$xy = 51000$

(E) $x_i + \sum_{j=1}^{4} x_j - 5 = 0, i = 1, 2, 3$

$x_1x_2x_3x_4 - 1 = 0$

Find the zero different from $x_i = 1$, all i.

(F) $x + 10y = -9 \qquad \sqrt{5}\,(z-w) = 2\sqrt{5}$

$(y-2z)^2 = 9 \qquad \sqrt{10}\,(x-w)^2 = 2\sqrt{10}$

(G) $$\frac{\sin(xy+\pi/6) + \sqrt{x^2y^2+1}}{\cos(x-y)} = -2.8$$

$$\frac{xe^{xy+\pi/6} - \sin(x-y)}{\sqrt{x^2y^2+1}} = 1.66$$

Hint: Initial guesses for these are A(−1, 1, 2, −1), B(2, −1), C(1.7, 1), D(10, 5000), E(.95, .95, .95, .8), F(.9, −.9, 1.25, −1.25), and G(20, .0).

8.6.8 The following nonlinear system arises from a model of the combustion of propane in air. The variable TOT is the sum of the 10 variables X_i, and R is a physical parameter = 4.056734. It is a difficult problem, sensitive to the choice of initial guesses because programs obtain negative values which make negative arguments for square roots.

$X_1 + X_4 - 3 = 0$
$2X_1 + X_2 + X_4 + X_7 + X_8 + X_9 + 2X_{10} - R = 10$
$2X_2 + 2X_5 + X_6 + X_7 - 8 = 0$
$2X_3 + X_5 - 4R = 0$
$X_1X_5 - 1.93*10^{-1}\, X_2X_4 = 0$
$X_6(X_2)^{1/2} - 2.597*10^{-3}*(X_2X_4*TOT)^{1/2} = 0$
$X_7(X_4)^{1/2} - 3.448*10^{-3}*(X_1X_4*TOT)^{1/2} = 0$
$X_8\, X_4 - 1.799*10^{-5}*X_2*TOT = 0$
$X_9\, X_4 - 2.155*10^{-4}*X_1*(X_3*TOT)^{1/2} = 0$
$X_{10}(X_4)^2 - 3.846*10^{-5}*(X_4)_2*TOT = 0$

(A) Run this problem using a library nonlinear equation solver.

(B) Replace X_1 through X_4 by squares (that is, $X_{1,\,NEW}^{\;2} = X_{1,OLD}$) to force these variables to be positive and rerun the problem. Discuss the change in performance of the nonlinear equation solver.

(C) Put absolute values inside the square roots and rerun the problem. Discuss the change in the performance of the nonlinear equation solver.

(D) Rewrite the equations to eliminate the square roots. Rewrite an equation of the form $a\sqrt{x} - b\sqrt{y} = 0$ as $a^2x - b^2y = 0$ (that is, multiply through by $a\sqrt{x} + b\sqrt{y}$). Rerun the problem and discuss the change in the performance of the equation solver.

8.6.9 Consider system A of Problem 8.6.7. Partition this system into 2 by 2 blocks of linear and nonlinear equations. Describe an iterative method based on solving the linear blocks by Guass elimination and substituting values into the nonlinear parts. This is a **block Jacobi method**. Write a program to implement this method and test its effectiveness. **Hint:** Solve for x and y from the first pair of equations, and for z and w from the second pair of equations.

8.6.10 Consider the system

$-2x^2 + 3xy + 4\sin y = 6$
$3x^2 - 2xy^2 + 3\cos x = -4$

Assume the tentative solution $x_0 = .829\ldots$ and $y_0 = 2.046\ldots$ has been obtained. Apply **backward error analysis** to estimate how satisfactory this solution is. **Hint:** Substitute the x_0, y_0 values in the equations, then perturb various coefficients in the equations to satisfy the equations exactly. The size of the perturbations required indicates how satisfactory the solutions are.

8.6.11 Test the effect of scaling on nonlinear system solvers by rescaling some of Problems 8.6.7 or 8.6.8 so that they are badly scaled, and then apply the program again. Discuss the effect of scaling as it becomes worse and worse. **Hint:** Given a program F that computes f(x, y), one can obtain the badly scaled version g(x, y) using

```
FUNCTION G(X,Y)
DATA SCALEX, SCALEY/1005., .0000105/
G = F(X*SCALEX, Y*SCALEY)
RETURN
END
```

8.6.12 Apply library polynomial root finders to compute the roots of the polynomials with real coefficients given in Problems 8.4.1, 8.4.3, or the following.

(A) $X^{20} - 1$

(B) $64X^{14} - 80X^{12} + 88X^{10} - 81X^8 - 104X^6 + 159X^4 - 48X^2 + 2$

(C) $X^{10} + 10X^9 + 45X^8 + 120X^7 + 210X^6 + 252X^5 + 211X^4 + 120X^3 + 45X^2 + 10X + 1$

(D) $X^{20} - X^{19} + 2X^{18} - 3X^{17} - 5X^{15} + X^{14} + 12X^{12} - 3X^{11} + X^{10} - 2X^9 + 7X^7 + 3X^2 + 4X - 8$

(E) $X^{20} + 10^3X^{19} + 10^5X^{18} + 10^7X^{17} + 10^8X^{16} + 10^{10}X^{15} + 10^{11}X^{14} + 10^{12}X^{13} + 10^{13}X^{12} + 10^{14}X^{11} + 10^{16}X^{10} + 10^{17}X^9 + 10^{17}X^8 + 10^{18}X^7 + 10^{19}X^6 + 10^{19}X^4 + 10^{20}X^3 + 10^{20}X^2 + 10^{19}X + 10^{19}$

(F) $X^{20} - X^{19} + 2^{-1}X^{18} - 2^{-4}X^{17} + 2^{-8}X^{16} - 2^{-13}X^{15} + 2^{-19}X^{14} - 2^{-26}X^{13} + 2^{-34}X^{12} - 2^{-43}X^{11} + 2^{-53}X^{10} - 2^{-64}X^9 + 2^{-76}X^8 - 2^{-89}X^7 + 2^{-103}X^6 - 2^{-118}X^5 + 2^{-134}X^4 - 2^{-151}X^3 + 2^{-169}X^2 - 2^{-189}X + 2^{-209}$

(G) $524288X^{20} - 2621440X^{18} + 5570560X^{16} - 6553600X^{14} + 4659200X^{12} - 2050048X^{10} + 549120X^8 - 84480X^6 + 6600X^4 - 200X^2 + 1$ (Chebyshev polynomial)

(H) $1250162561X^{16} + 385455882X^{15} + 845947696X^{14} + 240775148X^{13} + 247926664X^{12} + 64249356X^{11} + 4108752X^{10} + 9490840X^9 + 4178260X^8 + 837860X^7 + 267232X^6 + 44184X^5 + 10416X^4 + 1288X^3 + 224X^2 + 16X + 2$

(I) $.2X^{16} + .3X^{15} + 2.5X^{14} + 3.8X^{13} + 12.8X^{12} + 16.6X^{11} + 34.5X^{10} + 37.9X^9 + 52.4X^8 + 46.8X^7 + 44.4X^6 + 30.4X^5 + 19X^4 + 9X^3 + 3.3X^2 + .8X + .1$

8.6.13 Use library software to solve the following equations:

(A) $$\int_0^x \sin(t + \sqrt{x^2+1}\,)\, dt = .2$$

(B) $$\int_{-x}^{x} (t^3 - x)^2 \log\frac{1+t^2}{1+x^2}\, dt = 12$$

(C) $$\int_1^x \int_1^s \frac{\sqrt{1+(t-s)^2/(t^2+s^2)}}{1+(t-s)^2+(t-x)^2+(s-x)^2}\, dtds = 1$$

8.6.14 Set $a = 17.6504$, $b = d^2(te^{-t})/dt^2$ for $t = x$, $c = 14(a^2 - 2b)$, and $d = d(t^2e^{-\sqrt{t}})/dt*d(\log(1+t))/dt$ for $t = y$. Solve for x and y so that

$ax + by = x^2 - y^2 + .5$
$cx + dy = x^2 + y^2 - .5$

8.6.15 The function

$$COST(x) = \int_0^1 \frac{x^2 + tx^4 + \sin(\pi+t+x)}{(1+x+t)^2 + \sqrt{1 + 2tx^2}}\, dt$$

is to be minimized by setting its derivative to zero and solving the resulting nonlinear equation. Apply the modified regula falsi, bisection, or ZBRENT (from the IMSL library) to compute the minimizing value of x accurate to 5 digits. **Hint:** Note that COST(x) is positive for x large and $COST(0) < 0$. Use a finite difference approximation to the derivative and library software for the integral.

8.6.16 Carry out the following **evaluation of nonlinear equation methods.**

1. Write the programs in Problems 8.2.1 (bisection), 8.2.5 (Newton), 8.2.6 (secant), and 8.2.8 (fixed point).

2. Choose a library nonlinear equation solver.

3. Apply each of these programs to obtain one zero correct to five digits for the following three equations:

$$\cos(x) - xe^x = 0 \qquad 0 \le x \le \pi/2$$

$$\frac{\tan(x)}{1+x^2} - 42 = 0 \qquad 0 \le x \le \pi/2$$

$$(x-2)^3 - 3(x-2)^2\sin^2 x[1+\cot^2 x] + 3(x-2)(1-\cos^2 x)\left[\frac{1-\tan^2 x}{\cos(2x)\tan(x)}\right] = 1$$

Prepare a report that discusses

(A) The comparative difficulty of writing the four programs.

(B) The comparative difficulty in using the five programs to solve the problems.

(C) The computational efficiency of each program for these problems. Give a precise definition of your measure of efficiency.

The report is to be a complete, self-contained document describing the evaluation, how it was carried out, the data obtained, and the conclusions drawn (with supporting arguments).

ANALYSIS OF METHODS FOR NONLINEAR EQUATIONS — 8.7

Bisection, Regula Falsi — 8.7.A

The three methods based on bracketing the zero x^* of $f(x)$ are bisection, regula falsi, and modified regula falsi. The **rate of convergence for bisection** is easily established and stated as

Theorem 8.1 *Assume $f(x)$ is continuous in $[a, b]$ with $f(a)f(b) < 0$. Set $e_k = (b_k - a_k) \sim x^* - x_k$ in the bisection method Algorithm 8.2.1 with $x_k = \frac{1}{2}(a_k + b_k)$. We have*

$$e_{k+1} = \frac{1}{2} e_k = \frac{1}{2}(b-a)2^{-k-1}$$

Proof: The length of interval $[a_k, b_k]$ generated by the bisection method is halved at each iteration. It always contains a zero x^* of $f(x)$ so that the distance from its midpoint $\frac{1}{2}(a_k+b_k)$ to x^* is at most

$$\frac{1}{2}(b_k - a_k) = \frac{1}{2}(b-a)2^{-k}.$$

The rate of convergence for regula falsi is given below in a general result about methods based on linear models of $f(x)$. The length of the interval $[a_k, b_k]$ bracketing the solution does not always go to zero, however. Assume $f'(x^*) >$ so that a_k moves and b_k is fixed at b and set $e_k = x^* - a_k$; then we have

$$e_{k+1} = e_k(x^* - b)f''(\xi_k)/f'(\xi_k) \qquad \textbf{Equation 8.7.1}$$

for some $a_k \le \xi_k \le b$. This may be faster or slower than bisection, depending on the shape of $f(x)$. The modified regula falsi method is harder to analyze and is a little erratic in its convergence. However, it is a rapidly convergent method, competitive with the Newton and secant methods in this respect. See Problems 8.7.1 and 8.8.2.

Fixed Point Iteration and Δ^2-Acceleration — 8.7.B

We next analyze the **convergence rate of fixed point iteration** and show that its rate of convergence is similar in nature to that of the bisection method. The first part of the theorem precisely states the conditions required for fixed point iteration to apply.

Theorem 8.2 *Assume $g(x) = x + f(x)$ satisfies:*

1. *$[a, b]$ is mapped into $[a, b]$ by $g(x)$, that is, $x \in [a, b]$ implies $g(x) \in [a, b]$.*

2. $g'(x)$ is continuous and $|g'(x)| \leq K < 1$ *for* $x \epsilon [a, b]$.

Then we have
(i) $g(x) = x$ *has exactly one root* x^* *in* [a, b],
(ii) *The fixed point iteration* $x_{k+1} = g(x_k)$ *converges to* x^* *and, with* $e_k = x_k - x^*$,

$$|e_{k+1}| \leq K\,|e_k| \quad or \quad |e_{k+1}| \leq K^{k+1} e_0$$

(iii) *If* $g'(x)$ *is continuous near* x^*, *then*

$$|e_k| = O(|g'(x^*)|^k)$$

Proof: To prove part (i), assume $g(a) > a$ and $g(b) < b$ (otherwise a or b is the root). Recall $g(x) = x + f(x)$, and so $f(a) > 0$ and $f(b) < 0$; thus, $f(x)$ has a zero between a and b because it is continuous. If $f(x)$ has two zeros x_1 and x_2 and $f(x_3) \neq 0$ between x_1 and x_2, then the slope of $f(x)$ from x_1 to x_2 or from x_2 to x_3 is positive. This implies that $g'(x) = 1 + f'(x)$ is greater than 1 at some point in the interval x_1 to x_2 by the mean value theorem for derivatives. This would contradict assumption 2, and so only one zero can exist between a and b.

To prove part (ii), we have by the mean value theorem for derivatives that

$$e_k = x_k - x^* = g(x_{k-1}) - g(x^*) = g'(\xi_k)e_{k-1}$$

By assumption 2 we have $|g'(\xi_k)| \leq K$, and so conclusion (ii) follows immediately since $K < 1$ and K^{k+1} converges to zero.

To prove part (iii), note that as x_k converges to x^*, assumptions 1 and 2 are satisfied by smaller and smaller intervals containing x_k and x^*. By continuity of $g'(x)$, the value of K in assumption 2 converges to $g'(x^*)$. This concludes the proof.

Let $\lambda = g'(x^*)$; then Theorem 8.2 states that

$$x^* = x_k + c\lambda^k + o(\lambda^k) \qquad \textbf{Equation 8.7.2}$$

Recall that $o(-)$ means something negligible compared with the argument. If we neglect the $o(\lambda^k)$ term in 8.7.2, we can solve for x^* from three successive instances of 8.7.2.

$$x_k = x^* - c\lambda^k$$
$$x_{k-1} = x^* - c\lambda^{k-1}$$
$$x_{k-2} = x^* - c\lambda^{k-2}$$

Subtracting the first equation from the second and the second from the third eliminates x^*. Divide the two results to obtain

$$\lambda = \frac{x_k - x_{k-1}}{x_{k-1} - x_{k-2}}$$

Once λ is known, we solve the first two equations for $c\lambda^k$ as

$$c\lambda^k = (x_k - x_{k-1})/(\lambda - 1)$$

so that

$$x^* = x_k + \frac{x_k - x_{k-1}}{(\lambda - 1)} = x_k + \frac{(x_k - x_{k-1})^2}{(x_k - x_{k-1}) - (x_{k-1} - x_{k-2})} \qquad \textbf{Equation 8.7.3}$$

This formula is known as **Aitken's Δ^2-extrapolation;** the Δ refers to $x_k - x_{k-1}$ being the difference Δx_k. Of course, Equation 8.7.3 does not give x^* exactly because of the $o(\lambda^k)$ term neglected in 8.7.2. However, it gives a very worthwhile improvement as shown by the example below.

Before giving an example of the effect of Aitken extrapolation, we describe a method which repeatedly uses it. The idea is simple; if the extrapolation works, then we should use it at every opportunity. This means doing two fixed point iterations, extrapolating, doing two more fixed point iterations, etc. This is **Steffensen's method,** which is given by

Algorithm 8.7.1

Guess x_1 for x^*
For k = 1, 2,. . ., satisfied, do:
  $s_1 = g(x_k)$, $s_2 = g(s_1)$
  $d = s_2 - s_1$, $\lambda = (s_1 - x_k)/d$
  $x_{k+1} = s_2 + d/(\lambda - 1)$

This method looks somewhat different when expressed directly in terms of f(x) by the iteration formula

$$x_{k+1} = x_k - \frac{f^2(x_k)}{f(x_k + f(x_k)) - f(x_k)}$$

Equation 8.7.4

Convergence Rate of Fixed Point Iteration and Δ^2-Acceleration

Example 8.9

We choose the functions $f_1(x) = \sqrt{1+\sin(x)} - x$ and $f_2(x) = 2(1-x^2)/3 - x$ so that the fixed point iterations are

$$x_{k+1} = \sqrt{1+\sin(x_k)}\,, \quad x_{k+1} = 2(1-x_k^2)/3$$

Table 8.4 shows the number of digits in the errors of the fixed point iterations, the Δ^2-acceleration of the iteration, and Steffensen's method for these two iterations.

Errors in Fixed Point Iteration for Two Cases: Fast and Slow Convergence **Table 8.4**

*indicates that 15 or more digits are correct.

	$x = \sqrt{1+\sin(x)}$ Fast Convergence Digits of error in				$x = 2(1-x^2)/3$ Slow Convergence Digits of error in		
k	Fixed Point	Δ^2 Accel.	Steff.	k	Fixed Point	Δ^2 Accel.	Steff.
1	−0.15	−0.15	−0.15	1	0.30	0.30	0.30
2	0.39	−0.15	0.39	2	0.78	0.30	0.78
3	1.28	0.84	1.28	3	0.89	1.42	0.89
4	2.46	2.36	0.84	4	1.12	2.07	1.42
5	3.70	4.46	2.34	5	1.27	2.40	1.61
6	4.94	6.88	3.59	6	1.47	2.79	1.77
7	6.19	9.37	3.91	7	1.63	3.13	3.42
8	7.43	11.86	5.16	8	1.82	3.50	3.59
9	8.68	*	6.40	9	1.99	3.84	3.77
10	9.92		9.81	10	2.17	4.20	7.41
11	11.17		*	11	2.34	4.55	7.59
12	12.42			12	2.52	4.90	7.76
13	13.67			13	2.69	5.26	14.44
14	*			14	2.87	5.61	*
				15	3.05	5.96	
				20	3.93	7.72	
				30	5.69	11.24	
				40	7.45	*	
				50	9.21		

We see in Table 8.4 that even if the iteration is converging fast, the acceleration improves the convergence rate substantially. If the iteration is converging slowly, the acceleration still makes a substantial improvement. Note that the Steffensen iteration proceeds with a jump in accuracy after every third iterate. The definition used in Algorithm 8.7.1 has entries 3, 6, 9,. . . as the Steffensen iterates, and the others are intermediate results.

Analysis of Methods with a Linear Model 8.7.C

A method with a **linear model** takes two points a_k and b_k, interpolates $f(x)$ by a straight line there, then uses the zero of this model as the next iterate. The formula for this is

$$x_{k+1} = a_k - f(a_k)/f[a_k,b_k] \qquad \textbf{Equation 8.7.5}$$

The error of 8.7.5 is $e_{k+1} = x^* - x_{k+1}$.

Theorem 8.3. *The error of an iterate from a linear model is*

$$e_{k+1} = \frac{f[a_k, b_k, x^*]}{f[a_k, b_k]}(x^* - a_k)(x^* - b_k)$$

Proof: To simplify the notation, set $a = a_k$ and $b = b_k$ and let $p(x)$ be the linear model. We have

$$p(x) = f(a) + f[a, b](x - a) \qquad \textbf{Equation 8.7.6}$$

$$f(x) = f(a) + f[a, b](x - a) + f[a, b, x](x - a)(x - b) \qquad \textbf{Equation 8.7.7}$$

Now $p(x_{k+1}) = 0$ because x_{k+1} is defined this way and $f(x^*) = 0$. So, substitute $x = x_{k+1}$ in 8.7.6 and $x = x^*$ in 8.7.7, and subtract to obtain

$$0 = f[a, b](x^* - x_{k+1}) + f[a, b, x^*](x^* - a)(x^* - b)$$

This is just the result of the theorem and concludes the proof.

Theorem 8.3 provides the following error estimates and rates of convergence.

Corollary: *Let $f(x)$ have two continuous derivatives near x^* with $f'(x^*) \neq 0$. Then for a_k, b_k sufficiently close to x^* and ξ_1, ξ_2 points near x^* depending on k, we have*

1. Newton's Method:

$$e_{k+1} = \left[\frac{-\frac{1}{2}f''(\xi_1)}{f'(\xi_2)}\right] e_k^2$$

2. Secant Method:

$$e_{k+1} = \left[\frac{-\frac{1}{2}f''(\xi_1)}{f'(\xi_2)}\right] e_k e_{k-1}$$

3. Regula Falsi:

Case 1: $f'(x^*) > 0$, *and so* b_k *is constant, say b. Then:*

$$e_{k+1} = \left[\frac{-\frac{1}{2}f''(\xi_1)}{f'(\xi_2)(x^* - b)}\right] e_k$$

Case 2: $f'(x^*) < 0$, *and so* a_k *is constant, say a. Then:*

$$e_{k+1} = \left[\frac{-\frac{1}{2}f''(\xi_1)}{f'(\xi_2)(x^* - a)}\right] e_k$$

Proof: For Newton's method $a_k = b_k = x_k$. If x_k is sufficiently close to x^*, then $|f'(x_k)| > 0$ and we may apply Theorem 5.2 to replace the divided differences by derivatives at mean value points ξ_1 and ξ_2.

For the secant method $a_k = x_k$ and $b_k = x_{k-1}$, and the same reasoning applies as for Newton's method.

For regula falsi, Case 1, the left endpoint a_k changes every iteration and b_k stays fixed at $x = b$. The same reasoning applies as for Newton's method provided b is close enough to x^* for the assumptions on $f(x)$ to hold. This concludes the proof.

The rate of convergence of regula falsi is a familiar type: the error is decreased by a constant factor at each iteration. It is not difficult to find functions $f(x)$ where this factor

$$\frac{\frac{1}{2}\, f''(\xi_1)}{f'(\xi_2)(x^* - b)}$$

is always larger than 1/2. For example, use $f(x) = x^2 - 3/2 + 1/2$ with $a_0 = 3/4$ and $b = 2$. Thus, regula falsi might converge slower than bisection; in any case, it does not give an interval $[a_k, b_k]$ bracketing x^* that goes to zero.

The rates of convergence of the Newton and secant methods are different from anything seen so far. They are not measured by referring to a fixed function of k, but rather by relating the current error to the previous one. For Newton's method the error is *squared* at each iteration, and the error in the secant method is the product of the two previous errors. Both of these rates of convergence are superfast; once the iterates are close enough to the solution for Theorem 8.3 and its corollary to apply, one obtains full machine accuracy in 2 or 3 more iterations. The speed of this convergence is illustrated in the following example.

Newton and Secant Methods for Square Roots and Reciprocals

Example 8.10

One can compute $\sqrt{a}$ by solving $x^2 - a = 0$ and $1/a$ by solving $1/x - a = 0$. In the very early days of computing, division and square roots were done this way; the only "hardware" operations were addition, subtraction, and multiplication. We no longer think much about these operations, we just press the $\sqrt{x}$ or 1/x button on our calculator or write SQRT(X) or 1./X in Fortran. Yet inside the calculator is a "microprogram" to compute such quantities using the more basic arithmetic capabilities of the calculator. The microcode programmer can do things not possible in high-level languages (e.g., directly examine the exponent of a number), and so there are tricks the programmer can use in getting good initial guesses. The best method known for computing square roots is to make a good guess and then apply Newton's method. The same approach is feasible for implementing division, though it is not as fast as a special hardware division unit.

To compute the **square root** function by solving $x^2 - a = 0$ for $\sqrt{a}$, one applies Newton's method to obtain (after some simplification) the iteration

$$x_{k+1} = \frac{x_k^2 + a}{2x_k}$$

Equation 8.7.8

Similarly, the secant method simplifies to

$$x_{k+1} = \frac{x_k x_{k-1} + a}{x_k + x_{k-1}}$$

Equation 8.7.9

To implement **division** by solving $1/x - a = 0$ for $1/a$, one applies Newton's method to obtain (after simplification) the iteration

$$x_{k+1} = x_k(2 - x_k a)$$

Equation 8.7.10

The secant method simplifies to

$$x_{k+1} = x_k + x_{k-1} - a x_k x_{k-1}$$

Equation 8.7.11

Convergence of Newton and Secant Methods for Square Roots and Reciprocals **Table 8.5**

The number of correct digits is given; an asterisk indicates 28 or more decimal digits are correct, and two asterisks indicate machine overflow. All the square root iterations start with $x_1 = 1.0$, and the initial guesses for the reciprocals are given.

SQUARE ROOT ITERATION

	$a = 1.5$		$a = 150$		$a = 1.5*10^8$		$a = 5*10^{-4}$	
k	Newton	Secant	Newton	Secant	Newton	Secant	Newton	Secant
1	1.69	1.96	−0.71	−0.69	−3.79	−3.77	−1.89	−1.86
2	3.68	2.96	−0.34	0.12	−3.49	0.00	−1.54	−1.68
3	7.66	5.23	0.13	0.22	−3.19	0.00	−1.22	−1.45
4	15.63	8.49	0.80	0.16	−2.88	−3.17	−0.90	−1.24
5	*	14.02	1.97	0.70	−2.58	0.00	−0.54	−1.01
6		22.80	4.25	1.26	−2.28	0.00	−0.13	−0.78
7		*	8.80	2.21	−1.98	−2.54	0.41	−0.53
8			17.90	3.76	−1.67	0.00	1.26	−0.25
9			*	6.27	−1.36	0.00	2.84	0.07
10				10.33	−1.04	−1.91	5.99	0.49
11				16.80	−0.70	0.00	12.28	1.06
12				27.53	−0.32	−0.01	24.86	1.93
13				*	0.15	−1.26	*	3.32
14					0.83	0.04		5.55
15					2.02	0.06		9.17
16					4.35	−0.56		15.02
17					9.00	0.18		24.49
18					18.29	0.43		*
19					*	1.02		
20						1.81		
21						3.11		
22						5.22		
23						8.64		
24						14.16		
25						23.10		
26						*		

RECIPROCAL ITERATION

	$a = 1.5$, $x_0 = 1.0$		$a = 15{,}000$, $x_0 = 1.0$		$a = 15{,}000$, $x_0 = .001$		$a = .00005$, $x_0 = 1.0$		$a = .00005$, $x_0 = 10{,}000$	
k	Newton	Secant	Newton	Secant	Newton	Secant	Newton	Secant	Newton	Secant
1	0.60	0.30	−8.4	−4.2	0.60	0.30	0.00	0.00	0.60	0.30
2	1.20	0.49	−16.7	−8.4	1.20	0.49	0.00	0.00	1.21	0.65
3	2.41	0.79	−33.4	−12.6	2.41	0.79	0.00	0.00	2.41	0.95
4	4.82	1.28	−66.8	−21.0	4.82	1.28	0.00	0.00	4.82	1.60
5	9.63	2.07	−124.0	−33.5	9.63	2.07	0.00	0.00	9.63	2.55
6	19.27	3.34	−267.0	−54.5	19.27	3.34	0.00	0.00	19.27	4.14
7	*	5.41	**	−88.0	*	5.41	0.00	0.00	*	6.69
8		8.75		−143.0		8.75	0.01	0.00		10.83
9		14.16		−231.0		14.16	0.01	0.00		17.52
10		22.92		**		22.92	0.02	0.00		*
11		*				*	0.04	0.00		
12							0.09	0.01		
13							0.18	0.01		
14							0.36	0.02		
15							0.71	0.04		
20							22.77	0.25		
21							*	0.40		
25								0.40		
29								2.74		
30								18.76		

Table 8.5 shows the application of these iterations and illustrates their fast convergence. In the square root iteration we see the very rapid convergence *once the iteration gets close.* When the initial guess is far away, both methods are slowly locating the solution. Note that Newton's method for $a = 1.5 \times 10^8$ gains .3 digits of accuracy at each of the first 10 iterations. This is linear convergence just like bisection with a factor of .5 improvement at each step. When a fair estimate of the solution is obtained, then Newton's method obtains 28 digits correct in about five more iterations.

The secant method for square roots behaves much differently in the initial search stage; the iterates keep jumping back and forth between numbers too large and too small. Overall, the secant method takes several more iterations. For this special case the amount of computation for the two methods is the same. In the crucial range of improving from 1 to 8 digits of accuracy, we see that the secant method takes one or two more iterations.

The results for the reciprocal illustrate the necessity of a good guess for the Newton and secant methods. If one simply starts at $x = 1$, then these methods diverge when a is large (the solution is small). One can see from a plot that the iterations cross over to negative x values and then run off to minus infinity. If a guess is made simply on the basis of the exponent of a, then the convergence is fast and has a predictable number of iterations. Such a first guess would be feasible in the machine language of a hand-held calculator, and the predictability of the iteration makes this a feasible method for implementing division.

Analysis of Methods with a Quadratic Model **8.7.D

A method with a quadratic model takes three points a_k, b_k, and c_k, interpolates f(x) by a quadratic polynomial, and uses a zero of this model as the next iterate. The model is

$$p(x) = f(a_k) + f[a_k, b_k]\,(x - a_k) + f[a_k, b_k, c_k]\,(x - a_k)\,(x - b_k) \qquad \textbf{Equation 8.7.12}$$

and x_{k+1} is one of the two zeros of p(x). For an inverse interpolation method (see Problems 8.2.12 and 8.2.14) let $g(y) = f^{-1}(x)$, $\alpha_k = f(a_k)$, $\beta_k = f(b_k)$, and $\gamma_k = f(c_k)$. Then the model is

$$q(y) = g(\alpha_k) + g[\alpha_k, \beta_k]\,(y - \alpha_k) + g[\alpha_k, \beta_k, \gamma_k]\,(y - \alpha_k)\,(y - \beta_k) \qquad \textbf{Equation 8.7.13}$$

The next iterate x_{k+1} is q(0); note that α in this model corresponds to $f(a_k)$ in the model 8.7.12.

Theorem 8.4. *Assume that $f'''(x)$ is continuous. The error $x^* - x_{k+1}$ from a quadratic model 8.7.12 is*

$$e_{k+1} = -\frac{f[a_k, b_k, c_k, x^*]\,(x^* - a_k)\,(x^* - b_k)\,(x^* - c_k)}{f[a_k, b_k] + f[a_k, b_k, c_k]\,(2\xi - a_k - b_k)}$$

where ξ is between x^* and x_{k+1}. Assume $g'''(y)$ is continuous. The error from a quadratic model 8.7.13 with inverse interpolation is

$$e_{k+1} = g[\alpha_k, \beta_k, \gamma_k, 0]\alpha_k\beta_k\gamma_k$$

where $g(y) = f^{-1}(x)$, $\alpha_k = f(a_k)$, $\beta_k = f(b_k)$, and $\gamma_k = f(c_k)$.

Proof: Set $a = a_k$, $b = b_k$, and $c = c_k$ for simpler notation, and we have

$$f(x) = f(a) + f[a, b]\,(x - a) + f[a, b, c]\,(x - a)\,(x - b) + f[a, b, c, x]\,(x - a)\,(x - b)\,(x - c)$$

Thus we have

$$0 = f(x^*) = p(x^*) + f[a, b, c, x^*]\,(x^* - a)\,(x^* - b)\,(x^* - c) \qquad \textbf{Equation 8.7.14}$$

The mean value theorem for derivatives gives

$$p(x^*) = p(x_{k+1}) + p'(\xi)\,(x^* - x_{k+1}) \qquad \textbf{Equation 8.7.15}$$

Now $p(x_{k+1}) = 0$, and we compute from 8.7.12 that

$$p'(\xi) = f[a, b] + f[a, b, c]\,(2\xi - a - b)$$

and so we can combine Equations 8.7.14 and 8.7.15 to obtain

$$x^* - x_{k+1} = \frac{p(x^*)}{p'(\xi)} = -\frac{f[a, b, c, x^*]\,(x^*-a)\,(x^*-b)\,(x^*-c)}{f[a, b] + f(a, b, c)\,(2\xi - a - b)}$$

This establishes the first part of the theorem.

Set $\alpha = \alpha_k$, $\beta = \beta_k$, and $\gamma = \gamma_k$, and we have

$$\begin{aligned} g(y) &= g(\alpha) + g[\alpha, \beta]\,(y-\alpha) + g[\alpha, \beta, \gamma]\,(y-\alpha)\,(y-\beta) + g[\alpha, \beta, \gamma, y]\,(y-\alpha)\,(y-\beta)\,(y-\gamma) \\ &= q(y) + g[\alpha, \beta, \gamma, y]\,(y-\alpha)\,(y-\beta)\,(y-\gamma) \end{aligned}$$

Set $y = 0$ in this equation to obtain

$$x^* = g(0) = q(0) - g[\alpha, \beta, \gamma, 0]\alpha\beta\gamma = x_{k+1} - g[\alpha, \beta, \gamma, 0]\alpha\beta\gamma$$

This establishes the second part of the theorem and finishes the proof.

Corollary: *Let $f(x)$ have three continuous derivatives near x^* with $f'(x^*) \neq 0$. Then for a_k, b_k, and c_k sufficiently close to x^* and points ξ_1, ξ_2, and ξ sufficiently close to x^*, we have*

1. Muller's Method:

$$e_{k+1} \sim \frac{f'''(\xi_1)}{6f'(\xi_2)}\, e_k e_{k-1} e_{k-2}$$

2. Newton's Method (Third Order):

$$e_{k+1} \sim \frac{f'''(\xi_1)}{6f'(\xi_2)}\, e_k^3$$

3. Quadratic Inverse Interpolation:

$$e_{k+1} \sim g'''(\eta)\,[f'(x^*)]^3\, e_k e_{k-1} e_{k-2}$$

where $\eta = f(\xi)$.

Proof: For Newton's method we have $a = b = c = x_k$. If x_k is sufficiently close to x^*, then $|f'(x_k)| > 0$ and Theorem 5.2 is applied to replace the divided differences by derivatives at mean value points ξ_1 and ξ_2. We have $f''(x)$ bounded near x^* and $(2\xi - 2x_k)$ going to zero, and so the term $f[a_k, b_k, c_k]\,(2\xi - a_k - b_k)$ can be neglected.

For Muller's method we have $a = x_k$, $b = x_{k-1}$, and $c = x_{k-2}$, and the same reasoning applies as in Newton's method.

For inverse interpolation we have $\alpha = f(x_k)$, $\beta = f(x_{k-1})$, and $\gamma = f(x_{k-2})$. By the mean value theorem for derivatives we have

$$\alpha = f(x_k) = f(x^*) + f'(\xi_1)\,(x_k - x^*) = -f'(\xi_1)e_k \sim -f'(x^*)e_k$$

and similar expressions for β and γ. Once the a_k, b_k, and c_k are sufficiently close to x^*, we have $|f'(x)| > 0$, and so the inverse interpolation method is well defined [that is, $g(y)$ exists]. One may express the derivatives of $g(y)$ in terms of $f(x)$ by differentiating the relation $g(f(x)) = x$ three times to obtain

$$\begin{aligned} g'f' &= 1 \\ g''(f')^2 + g'f'' &= 0 \\ g'''(f')^3) + 3g''f'f'' + g'f'' &= 0 \end{aligned}$$

One may use these equations to obtain

$$g'''(f')^3 = -3\left(\frac{f''}{f'}\right)^2 - \frac{f'''}{f'}$$

This is hardly enlightening, but it does show that g''' is continuous if $f' \neq 0$ and $f(x)$ has three continuous derivatives. One applies Theorem 5.2 to the divided difference of $g(y)$, and the last relation of the corollary is established.

The convergence rates for methods based on quadratic models are even more spectacular than those of linear models, *provided one is close enough to the solution.* Thus, with Newton's third-order method, if e_k is 10^{-3}, then one expects e_{k+1} to be 10^{-9}, e_{k+2} to be 10^{-27}, and e_{k+3} to be 10^{-81}. Such rapid rates of convergence are rarely important in practice because one already has satisfactory results before this rapid convergence gets far.

Remarks on Methods Not Analyzed **8.7.E

All the basic iterative methods for one equation have been analyzed in this book except modified regula falsi; its analysis is too complicated. The methods for special situations (e.g., multiple roots) are not analyzed so as to save space. Some further results (both theoretical and experimental) on rates of convergence are given in Problems 8.7.1, 8.7.4, 8.7.6, 8.7.13, 8.7.15, and 8.7.16.

No analysis is given of polynomial root finders because the simple methods are not very interesting; there are always some situations where they are very slow. The reliable methods are polyalgorithms of some complexity, and hence their analysis is quite difficult. The Jenkins-Traub software finds *all* the zeros of a polynomial of degree n with a computational effort proportional to n^2. The proportionality constant depends on the accuracy desired, but not heavily, as the last stage converges very fast. That the effort is proportional to n^2 is expected from theoretical analysis and can be verified by computational experiments; see Problem 8.7.17.

The analysis of basic methods for nonlinear systems (fixed point, Newton, and secant) requires more elaborate mathematical machinery, but the reasoning is essentially the same as for one equation, as are the conclusions. Specifically, **convergence of the fixed point iteration for systems** is the same as in Theorem 8.2 except that K becomes a bound on all the first directional derivatives at x^*. The **convergence of Newton and secant methods** for systems is the same as in the Corollary of Theorem 8.3. The expression $|f''/f'|$ is replaced by norms of matrices of second and first partial derivatives.

PROBLEMS 8.7

8.7.1 Use the program of Problem 8.2.3 to study the convergence rate of **modified regula falsi.** Apply it to examples from Problems 8.2.1 and 8.2.2 and obtain experimental data to support the conjecture that it converges at least as fast as $e_{k+1} = e_k^{1.4}$.

8.7.2 Consider fixed point iteration for $g(x) = x - x^3$. Give a complete analysis of the convergence or lack of it for this problem.

8.7.3 Consider fixed point iteration for $g(x) = 9\log_{10}(1+x)$. Give a complete analysis of the convergence of this iteration for $x_1 > -1$. That is, for each starting greater than -1, prove divergence or convergence and, if there is convergence, find the resulting solution of $x = g(x)$.

8.7.4 Write a Fortran program to implement Steffensen's method that starts as

```
FUNCTION STEFF( F,GUESS,EPS )
```

with the same arguments as NEWTON in Problem 8.2.5. Apply this program to verify experimentally that the convergence rate of Steffensen iteration is the same as for Newton's method in the Corollary of Theorem 8.3.

8.7.5 Show how to interpret Steffensen's method as a discrete Newton method. Explicitly show the approximation to $f'(x)$ that this method uses.

8.7.6 Carry out an experimental **performance evaluation of the Aitken's Δ^2-acceleration** of fixed point iteration. Apply the acceleration to several problems and discuss:

(A) The expected improvement in the error of the accelerated result.

(B) Whether one should hope that the factor of improvement steadily increases as the accuracy required increases.

8.7.7 Carry out both an experimental and theoretical **round-off analysis of Δ^2-acceleration.** For the experimental study use a few functions $g(x)$ of the form nice(x) + c*random(x) where c is a small constant, say 10^{-5}, and random(x) is between ± 1. Repeat the analysis for the effect on round-off of rewriting the method in the form

$$x_{k+1} = \frac{x_k x_{k-2} - x_{k-1}^2}{x_k - 2x_{k-1} + x_{k-2}}$$

8.7.8 Consider the equation $x^2 + e^x = g(x) = x$. Define a modified, **two-stage fixed point iteration method** as follows:

$$x_{k+1/2} = \sqrt{g(x_k) - e^{x_k}}$$
$$x_{k+1} = \log[g(x_{k+1/2}) - x_{k+1/2}^2]$$

(A) Show that, in general, if $g(0) > 1$ and $0 \le g'(x)/g(x) \le K < 1$ for all x, then this problem has exactly one solution.

(B) Prove that the two-stage fixed point iteration converges. **Hint:** The proof of convergence is not easy.

(C) Apply the same idea to the function $g(x) = x^2 e^{1+x}$ to define another two-stage fixed point iteration.

8.7.9 (A) Prove the following theorem about the secant method.
Theorem Suppose $f(x^*) = 0$ and there is an interval $[x^* - a, x^* + a]$ in which $f'(x)$ is continuous and not zero, and x^* is the only zero of $f(x)$. Then there

exists a second interval $[x^*-b, x^*+b]$ with $b > 0$ so that the **secant method** converges to x^* given any two initial points in $[x^*-b, x^*+b]$.

(B) Give an example of a function $f(x)$ with zero x^* for which no interval $[x^*-a, x^*+a]$ exists as in this theorem, but yet for which the secant method converges. That is, the interval $[x^*-b, x^*+b]$ does exist.

(C) Give an example of a function $f(x)$ with $f(x^*) = 0$, $f'(x^*)$ exists, and the interval $[x^*-b, x^*+b]$ does not exist.

8.7.10 Give an example of a function $f(x)$ where the secant method converges but the error e_k does not behave as in the Corollary of Theorem 8.3. Instead the error behaves like K^k for $K < 1$. Explain the discrepancy between this example and the Corollary.

8.7.11 Derive a Newton iteration similar to 8.7.8 to compute the nth root of a. Assume that the value of a is in the form $m*b^e$ in scientific notation, with b the base of the computer arithmetic. Suppose m and e can be accessed directly and present a good, but easily computable, scheme to obtain an initial guess for $\sqrt[n]{a}$ using this facility. Write a program to implement this method and estimate the speed of this method of computing roots in terms of the number of arithmetic operations required. Assume that 8 digits of accuracy are required.

8.7.12 Carry out an experimental study of the effects of round-off in the algorithms of Example 8.10 for $\sqrt{x}$ and $1/x$. Estimate the maximum accuracy of each of these four iteration methods in terms of ulps for the computer used.

8.7.13 Suppose $f(x)$ and $f'(x)$ are known, but $f''(x)$ is unavailable for use in solving $f(x) = 0$.

(A) Derive the iteration for a method with a quadratic model that interpolates f and f' at x_k and f at x_{k-1}.

(B) Apply Theorem 8.4 to obtain the rate of convergence of this method.

8.7.14 The efficiency of the method in Problem 8.7.13, part (A), can be improved by alternating between using f' at x_k and at x_{k-1}. That is, f' is evaluated only at every other iteration point.

(A) Derive the pair of iteration formulas for this two-stage method.

(B) Apply Theorem 8.4 to obtain the average rate of convergence of this method. **Hint:** Different rates occur at the odd and even iterates.

8.7.15 Extend the analysis and convergence results of Section 8.7.D to **cubic models for f(x).** Specifically:

(A) State and prove for cubic models the analog of Theorem 8.4.

(B) Define Newton's method of order 4; state and prove the rate of convergence result for this method.

8.7.16 (A) Show that Newton's method applied to find a root x^* of multiplicity p has the rate of convergence

$$e_k = O\left(\left(\frac{p-1}{p}\right)^k\right)$$

(B) Show that **Newton's method for multiple roots,** Equation 8.3.2, has the same rate of convergence as the ordinary Newton's method does for simple roots.

8.7.17 Carry out an experimental study of the efficiency of library polynomial root finders (e.g., ZRPOLY, ZCPOLY, and ZPOLR from the IMSL Library). **Hint:** Generate polynomials at random of various degrees and attempt to show that the execution time is proportional to the degree squared. The random polynomials should be from the following four classes (the first two classes give polynomials with almost all "easy" roots):

1. Coefficients uniformly distributed.
2. Roots uniformly distributed.
3. k roots uniformly distributed in $|z| \le 1$ and $n-k$ uniformly distributed in $|z| \le R$. Increasing R and k makes it more difficult to compute the roots.
4. Choose the coefficients $a_i = m_i{*}b^{e_i}$ (b = computer base) with the m_i chosen at random in [1/b, 1] and the exponents e_i chosen at random in [−R, R] with R relatively large.

SELECTION OF METHODS FOR NONLINEAR EQUATIONS **8.8

Order and Efficiency of Methods 8.8.A

There are two aspects to the efficiency of a method; (1) the number of iterations it takes to converge, and (2) the amount of work per iteration. To illustrate that counting the number of iterations is not sufficient for measuring efficiency, consider method X, which is supposed to be a good method. Then define method SUPERX as follows: One iteration of method SUPERX is two iterations of method X. Now method SUPERX converges in half the number of iterations of method X, but one can hardly believe that it is any better.

In order to compare the rates of convergence of different methods, we introduce the **order of a method.** Let e_k be the error of the kth iterate; then the order of the method is the number p so that

$$\lim_{k\to\infty} \frac{e_{k+1}}{(e_k)^p} = \text{constant } K > 0 \qquad \textbf{Equation 8.8.1}$$

It is easy to see that the orders of bisection and regula falsi are 1. We have $e_k = O(K^k)$ for both of them and

$$\frac{e_{k+1}}{e_k} = K$$

Likewise, it is easy to see from the Corollary of Theorem 8.3 that the order of Newton's method is 2 because

$$\lim_{k\to\infty} \frac{e_{k+1}}{e_k^2} = \frac{1}{2}\,\frac{f''(x^*)}{f'(x^*)}$$

The special cases with $f'(x^*) = 0$ or $f''(x^*) = 0$ give different orders for Newton's method.

The order p can be interpreted as the factor of gain in the number of correct digits at each iteration. Thus, if $e_k = 10^{-r}$, then

$$e_{k+1} \sim K(e_k)^p = K(10^{-r})^p = K\ 10^{-pr}$$

A **first-order method** has $p = 1$ (such methods are said to have **linear convergence**) and has no gain in the number of correct digits through multiplying the exponent in the error. A **second-order method** with $p = 2$, for example, Newton's method, approximately doubles the number of correct digits at each iteration. The size of K may vary this up or down some, but the order p is the dominant influencing factor.

The order of some methods is not obvious, for example, the secant method has, for some constant C,

$$e_{k+1} = C\ e_k e_{k-1}$$ **Equation 8.8.2**

To estimate the order, let $d_k = \log e_k$ so that 8.8.2 becomes

$$d_{k+1} = \log C + d_k + d_{k-1}$$

or

$$d_{k+1} - d_k - d_{k-1} = \log C$$ **Equation 8.8.3**

This is a simple difference equation, and the analysis of Bernoulli's method in Section 8.4.B shows that the solution of 8.8.3 includes $\alpha r_1^{\ k} + \beta r_2^{\ k}$ where the r_i are the roots $(1 \pm \sqrt{5}\,)/2$ of

$$x^2 - x - 1 = 0$$

So

$$e_k = 10\alpha^{r^k}$$

with $r = (1 \pm \sqrt{5}\,)/2$ satisfies 8.8.2 and

$$\frac{e_{k+1}}{(e_k)^p} = 10^{\alpha r^{k+1} - \alpha r^k p}$$

It is clear that $p = r$ makes this ratio 1 and the order p must be positive, and so $p = (1 + \sqrt{5}\,)/2 = 1.618034\ldots$ is the order of the secant method.

There is a general method for obtaining the order of methods based on polynomial interpolation. Let

$$\mathbf{a} = (a_1, a_2, \ldots, a_n)$$

be the points used at the kth iteration. The polynomial interpolant $p(x)$ to $f(x)$ or $q(y)$ to $g(y) = f^{-1}(x)$ is formed at these points, and x_{k+1} is obtained as $p(x_{k+1}) = 0$ or $x_{k+1} = q(0)$. Let $\mathbf{b} = (b_1, b_2, \ldots, b_n)$ be the points used for the next iteration, and we define a matrix T which symbolically represents how **b** is obtained from **a**. The elements of T are

$$t_{ij} = \begin{cases} 1 & \text{if } a_j \text{ is used to determine } b_i \text{ by polynomial interpolation} \\ 0 & \text{if } a_j \text{ is not used to determine } b_i \text{ by polynomial interpolation} \end{cases}$$

For Newton's method we have

$$T = \begin{pmatrix} 1 & 1 \\ 1 & 1 \end{pmatrix}$$

because $a_1 = a_2$, $b_1 = b_2$, and b_1 and b_2 are both obtained by interpolation at $a_1 = a_2$. For the secant method we have

$$T = \begin{pmatrix} 1 & 1 \\ 1 & 0 \end{pmatrix}$$

because b_1 is obtained by interpolating at a_1 and a_2, and b_2 is obtained from $b_2 = a_1$, which is interpolation by a constant at one point.

A more unusual method is one which involves three points a_1, a_2, a_3, and b_1 is obtained by the secant method applied to a_2 and a_3; b_2 is obtained by the secant method applied to a_1 and a_3, and b_3 is obtained by the secant method applied at a_1 and a_2. The matrix T which represents this method is

$$T = \begin{pmatrix} 0 & 1 & 1 \\ 1 & 0 & 1 \\ 1 & 1 & 0 \end{pmatrix}$$

This method might seem to be just a curiosity, but consider a parallel computer where all three secant method calculations are made simultaneously. This parallel method would obviously execute faster than the basic secant method.

The next theorem shows how the order of convergence for this class of methods can be computed simply from the matrix representation of the method. Recall the definition of the *spectral radius* of T as the largest of the absolute values of the eigenvalue of T.

Theorem 8.5 *Let $f(x)$ have $n+1$ continuous derivatives near x^* with $f'(x^*) \neq 0$. Assume the spectral radius ρ of the matrix T is greater than* 1. *Then, for* **a** *sufficiently close to x^*, the iteration represented by T converges to x^* and the order of convergence is ρ.*

Further, if a method is the composition of two methods with representations T_1 and T_2, then $T = T_1 T_2$ represents the composite method.

This theorem is not proved here because the proof is quite complicated. Note that *the theorem does not say* that all the a_i converge to x^* with order ρ; it only says that some of them do. Indeed, consider the method defined with a_1, a_2, a_3 which uses Newton's method on a_1 and a_2 and keeps a_3 fixed at $x = 16.5$. It is represented by

$$T = \begin{pmatrix} 1 & 1 & 0 \\ 1 & 1 & 0 \\ 0 & 0 & 1 \end{pmatrix}$$

The maximum eigenvalue of T is 2, but it is obvious that 16.5 does not converge to x^*.

We now turn to the amount of work per iteration; this naturally divides into two parts: function evaluations and arithmetic "overhead." The overhead is usually quite low compared with evaluating functions, and so we can define the efficiency of a method in terms of the amount of accuracy gained per function evaluation. To motivate the definition, suppose the order of method 1 is p and the number of function evaluations per iteration is 3. Suppose the order of method 2 is q and the number of function evaluations per iteration is 1. Then three iterations of method 2 are as much work as one iteration of method 1. Now consider the order q that method 2 must have so that N iterations of it give the same error as one iteration of method 1. Let e_k and d_k denote the errors of methods 1 and 2, respectively, and, for simplicity, assume the constants K in the definition of order are 1 for both methods. Assume that both methods start the kth iteration at the same point so that $d_k = e_k$. Then we have, roughly,

$$\begin{aligned} e_{k+1} &= (e_k)^p \\ d_{k+1} &= (e_k)^q \\ d_{k+2} &= (d_{k+1})^q = ((e_k)^q)^q = e_k^{q^2} \\ d_{k+3} &= (d_{k+2})^q = (((e_k)^q)^q)^q = e_k^{q^3} \end{aligned}$$

Thus, if $e_{k+1} = d_{k+3}$, we have $p = q^3$ or $q = \sqrt[3]{p}$. In general, we define the **efficiency** of a method as $\sqrt[N]{p}$, where p is its order and it uses N function evaluations per iteration.

Table 8.6 gives a summary of the convergence and efficiency properties of methods discussed in this chapter. The **overhead** entry is the total number of arithmetic operations per iteration; a square root is counted as 8 operations.

Convergence and Efficiency Properties of Methods for 1 Nonlinear Equation **Table 8.6**

Method	Order	Efficiency	Overhead
Bisection	1	1	3
Regula falsi	1	1	6
Fixed point	1	1	0
Newton	2	$\sqrt{2} = 1.414$	2
Secant	$\frac{1+\sqrt{5}}{2} = 1.618$	1.618	5
Muller	1.839	1.839	20
Third-order Newton	3	$\sqrt[3]{3} = 1.442$	16
Quadratic inverse interpolation	1.839	1.839	8

Selection of Methods 8.8.B

After all this development and analysis of methods, one might examine Table 8.6 and pick the method with the highest efficiency, say quadratic inverse interpolation since it has a lower overhead than Muller's method. However, there is much more to making a good program for solving nonlinear equations than the efficiency of the basic method. One must also have a reliable convergence test and give attention to special

Summary of Properties of Several Implementations of the Same Task in Solving Nonlinear Equations **Table 8.7**

There is great variation among these runs in the initial guesses, the convergence tests, etc. Each programmer believed the assigned task was done. The number of function evaluations to achieve convergence given excludes cases of no convergence.

		Number of f(x) evaluations		
Equation	Method	Min	Max	Median
1	Regula falsi	3	25	9
	Secant	4	39	6
	Newton	3	32	6
2	Regula falsi	2	18	3
	Secant	2	11	3
	Newton	2	15	6
3	Regula falsi	2	45	8
	Secant	2	40	6
	Newton	2	82	6
4	Regula falsi	3	23	10
	Secant	4	10	6
	Newton	3	74	8
5	Regula falsi	2	15	4
	Secant	2	57	5
	Newton	4	337	8

	Length of subroutine in executable statements		
Subroutine	Min	Max	Median
Regula falsi	17	55	22
Secant	11	40	16
Newton	7	34	15

problems like multiple roots, round-off, overflow, and so forth. One hopes to find all these things done well in a library program, and in fact, it is a better strategy to select a program from a good library than to code up one of these methods.

Perhaps the single most important factor in a program for nonlinear equations is how well the method is implemented by the programmer. We illustrate this with data gathered from the following assignment to a class of students in engineering and science:

(A) Implement the regula falsi, Newton, and secant methods as in Problems 8.2.2, 8.2.5, and 8.2.6, except no specific convergence test is given.

(B) Apply them to the five equation:

1. $e^x = 4x$

2. $\tan x = 100x$

3. $\sin(x^2+1) = x^3$

4. $\cos(x)\log^2(x^2+3x+2)-\log^2(x+1) = \log(x+1)\,[\log(x+1)+2\log(x+2)]$

5. $(1+x)e^{-x^2+3x\cos x} = (1+x^4)\,(1+x^4)\sin x$

The students handed in the programs and results; some information about these programs is tabulated in Table 8.7.

The data in Table 8.7 show the wide variations in performance due to different implementations for the same task. This wide variation is not unusual; it has been observed in all areas of programming. Thus, it is all the more important to have a source of programs (a library) where one can have reasonable confidence in the implementations.

PROBLEMS 8.8

8.8.1 Develop a formula to estimate the order of an iterative method. Incorporate the formula into a program and apply it to several examples using bisection, secant, and Newton iterations; discuss the accuracy of the estimate. **Hint:** Take four successive iterates, x_k, x_{k+1}, x_{k+2}, and x_{k+3}; assume $x_{k+3} = x^*$ so that e_k, e_{k+1}, and e_{k+2} are known. Then solve for the order p from the relation $e_{k+i} = K(e_{k+i-1})^p$, $i = 1, 2$. It might pay to use double precision in the calculations in order to obtain enough accuracy to measure the order. Alternatively, take a problem with a known solution, choose 2 initial guesses with known error, compute the next iterates for each, and then solve for p as before.

8.8.2 Apply the formula of Problem 8.8.1 to estimate the order of the modified regula falsi method. Then compute its efficiency and overhead.

8.8.3 Apply the formula of Problem 8.8.1 to estimate the order of Steffensen's method. Then compute its efficiency and overhead.

8.8.4 Find the order of the composite method in Problem 8.7.14 by finding the matrix T that represents the two iterations and then computing the maximum eigenvalue of their product. Then compute the efficiency and overhead of this method.

8.8.5 Consider the composite method obtained by repeating the following two steps:

$$x_{k+1/2} = x_k - \frac{f(x_k)}{f'(x_k)}$$

$$x_{k+1} = x_{k+1/2} - \frac{f(x_{k+1/2})}{f'(x_k)}$$

Find the matrix T that represents this method, compute its maximum eigenvalue, and then give the efficiency and overhead of the method. **Hint:** Consider the method in three stages:

$$(x_k, x_k) \to (x_{k+1/2}, x_k) \to (x_{k+1}, x_{k+1/2}) \to (x_{k+1}, x_{k+1})$$

8.8.6 The **simultaneous n-degree method** for parallel computers is to take $n+1$ points $(a_1, a_2, \ldots a_{n+1})$ and have the next set of points $(b_1, \ldots, b_{n+1})$ obtained with b_i computed from interpolating at the a_j for $j \neq i$.

(A) Give the matrix T that represents this method. Show that the order of the method is $n-1$. Give the efficiency of this method for $n = 1$ to 10.

(B) Give the order and efficiency of Newton's method of higher order for $n = 1$ to 10.

(C) Discuss the advantages of the simultaneous n-degree method over Newton's method on a parallel computer. Assume the parallel computer can compute the b_i and the a_i simultaneously.

8.8.7 Consider the algorithm to compute π given in Problem 3.2.9. Apply the formula of Problem 8.8.1 to show that this algorithm converges with order 2.

REFERENCES

A. S. Householder, *The Numerical Treatment of a Single Nonlinear Equation,* McGraw-Hill, New York (1970).

W. C. Rheinboldt, *Methods for Solving Systems of Equations,* CBMS Series in Applied Mathematics No. 14, SIAM Publications, Philadelphia (1974).

Philip Rabinowitz (ed.), *Numerical Methods for Nonlinear Algebraic Equations,* Gordon and Breach, London (1970).

9

ORDINARY DIFFERENTIAL EQUATIONS

INTRODUCTION 9.1

The most important mathematical model for physical phenomena is the differential equation. Motion of objects, fluid, and heat flow, bending and cracking of materials, vibrations, chemical reactions, and nuclear reactions are all modeled by differential equations. If a differential equation has one independent variable, then it is an **ordinary differential equation.** Examples of such equations are

$$\frac{dy}{dx} = x + y$$

$$y' = x^2 + y^2$$

$$y'' + \cos(x)\, y' - 3y = \sin(2x)$$

The notation $y' = dy/dx$, etc., is used. If the differential equation involves more than one independent variable, then it is a **partial differential equation;** their solution is discussed in Chapter 10. One would expect a complete model of many physical situations to involve four independent variables; three space variables plus time. Unfortunately, most such problems are too big to be solved, and so differential equations are often simplified or idealized models.

Differential and Difference Equations 9.1.A

A differential equation problem needs more than a differential equation. To solve $y''' = 0$ is not a well-formulated problem since $y(x) = x^2 + 2$, $y(x) = 3x^2 - 2x + 4$, and $y(x) = 1 - 5x$ all satisfy this equation. Generally, an equation of **order m** (that is, the highest derivative appearing is the mth) requires m additional conditions in order to have a unique solution. In principle, these conditions can be of any type, for example:

$$y(3.6) = 6.3$$

$$y'(2) = 2.2$$

$$y(2) + 3y'(2) = 6$$

$$y(3)y(2) - y^2(1) = 4$$

$$\int_0^1 \cos(x)y(x)dx = 0$$

y(x) goes to zero as x goes to infinity

Most theory applies only to linear boundary conditions (all but the fourth example above are linear), and so we restrict our attention to conditions involving linear combinations of values and derivatives since most methods are developed for this case. If all the conditions occur at one point, then we have an **initial value problem,** for example:

$$y''' + (x+1)y'' + \cos(x)y' - (x^2-1)y = x^2 + y^2\sin(x+y) \qquad \textbf{Equation 9.1.1}$$
$$y(0) = 1.1,\ y'(0) = 2.2,\ y''(0)\ 3.3$$

The problem in 9.1.1 is nonlinear because the right side has the $y^2\sin(x+y)$ term in it. If the differential equation is linear in y(x) and its derivatives, then it is a **linear differential equation.** Equation 9.1.1 would be linear if the $y^2\sin(x+y)$ term on the right were removed.

There is a two-stage process which greatly simplifies the development, use, and analysis of methods for initial value problems:

1. Reduce the differential equation to a system of first-order equations.

2. Claim that the theory and methods for systems of first-order equations are the same as for one first-order equation.

The first stage can always be carried out. The claim of the second stage is almost true; it is close enough that we proceed on the basis of its truth. This means that the differential equation we study is simply

$$y' = f(x,y) \qquad y(x_0) = y_0 \qquad \textbf{Equation 9.1.2}$$

A few remarks on the difficulties with systems are made in Section 9.5; there are also special methods for second-order equations, but they are not discussed here.

The method for **reduction of a differential equation to a first-order system** is as follows. Let m be the order. First introduce new variables for each derivative up to the $(m-1)$th. Next substitute all of these in the original differential equation with the $y^{(m)}$ being replaced by the first derivative of the $(m-1)$th variable. Finally, write the differential equation for the kth variable being the first derivative of the $(k-1)$th variable. Applying this method to Equation 9.1.1, we have the original variable y and new variables $z = y'$ and $w = y''$. The system is then

$$\begin{aligned} w' + (x+1)w + \cos(x)z - (x^2-1)y &= x^2 + y^2\sin(x+y) \\ y' &= z \\ z' &= w \end{aligned}$$

which is rewritten in the standard form

$$\begin{aligned} w' &= x^2 + y^2\sin(x+y) - (x+1)w - \cos(x)z + (x^2-1)y \qquad \textbf{Equation 9.1.3} \\ y' &= z \\ z' &= w \\ y(0) &= 1.1,\ z(0) = 2.2,\ w(0) = 3.3 \end{aligned}$$

This method also reduces systems of higher-order differential equations to a (larger) system of first-order equations.

Difference equations arise naturally in the study of numerical methods for differential equations when one replaces derivatives by differences. One chooses a step size value h and substitutes central differences for derivatives of y(x) to obtain, for example, in 9.1.1:

$$\frac{y(x-2h) - 3y(x-h) + 3y(x+h) - y(x+2h)}{h^3} + (x+1)\frac{y(x-h) - 2y(x) + y(x+h)}{h^2}$$
$$+ \cos(x)\frac{y(x+h) - y(x-h)}{2h} - (x^2-1)y(x) = x^2 + y^2(x)\sin(x+y(x))$$

To make this equation useful, one has to choose a finite set of x values and do it in such a way that the terms in one equation appear in the other equations. The natural thing is to choose x values separated by h; then the equations at $x = x_0$, x_0+h, and x_0-h all involve common values of y. The remainder of the discussion uses the **model problem** $y'=f(x, y)$ in 9.1.2. Thus we only consider different difference approximations to the first derivative. These are all of the form

$$y' \sim \frac{a_{2k+1}y(x-kh) + a_{2k}y(x-(k-1)h) + \ldots + a_1y(x+kh)}{\text{constant}*h} \qquad \textbf{Equation 9.1.4}$$

To simplify the notation, suppose our initial value x_0 is zero; set $x_i = ih$ and $y(x_i) = y_i$. Then 9.1.4 is substituted into 9.1.2, and after multiplying through by the denominator of 9.1.4, we obtain at the point x_n

$$a_{2k+1}y_{n-k} + a_{2k}y_{n-k+1} + \ldots + a_1y_{n+k} = \text{constant}*h*f(x_n, y_n)$$

This equation looks better if we reorder the indexes and start counting the y indexes at the end rather than in the middle. Further, the constant*h factor on the right side can be absorbed into f, making a new f which we still call f. The **linear mth-order difference equation is**

$$a_{m+1}y_{n+m} + a_my_{n+m-1} + \ldots + a_2y_{n+1} + a_1y_n = f_n \qquad n = 1, 2,\ldots \qquad \textbf{Equation 9.1.5}$$

Of course, if f depends on the y's (as it does for a nonlinear difference equation), then f_n has many arguments.

The theory of difference equations is very similar to that of differential equations. We state a few basic facts here.

1. An mth-order linear difference equation has m solutions.

2. The solutions are normally specified by conditions of the form $y_\alpha = c_\alpha$ for m different values of α. If the α's are 1, 2,. . ., m, then these are initial conditions for the difference equations. Note that for initial conditions one can solve 9.1.5 for y_{n+m} as

   $$y_{m+n} = (f_n - a_my_{n+m-1} - \ldots - a_1y_n)/a_{m+1}$$

   and then set $n = 1$ to compute y_{m+1} from the known initial conditions. This is repeated to directly compute all the y_n.

3. The solutions of 9.1.5 for $f_n = 0$ (the **homogeneous difference equation**) are

   $$y_n = c_1r_1^n + c_2r_2^n + \ldots + c_mr_m^n \qquad \textbf{Equation 9.1.6}$$

   where the r_i are the simple roots of the **characteristic polynomial**

   $$p(x) = a_{m+1}x^m + \ldots + a_2x + a_1$$

   If p(x) has multiple roots, then 9.1.6 has a slightly different form; we do not consider this special case here.

4. The **general solution** of 9.1.5 for initial conditions is the sum of the homogeneous solution 9.1.6 and the particular solution obtained by direct use of 9.1.5 with $y_1 = y_2 = \ldots = y_m = 0$.

A natural idea for numerical methods for differential equations is to replace the derivatives by differences and then solve the resulting difference equations. In order to be efficient, we must use accurate difference approximations. This means that a first-order differential equation is replaced by a second-, third-, fourth-, or higher-order difference equation. A problem immediately arises: the differential equation has one solution, while a fourth-order difference equation has four solutions. We must be careful to get the "right" solution of the difference equation. This is not always easy or even possible; many methods that look good on the surface are, in fact, useless because one normally does not get the "right" solution.

This difficulty permeates the study of numerical methods for differential equations and greatly complicates the theory and practice of solving differential equations. It is closely related to stability problems, and if the difference equation has an unstable solution, then one will compute it, even though one does not want it since it does not correspond to the solution of the differential equation.

Stability of Differential and Difference Equations

9.1.B

Recall Example 3.6 which involves the difference equation

$$X_{n+2} = -(13/6)X_{n+1} + (5/2)X_n \qquad X_1 = 30,\ X_2 = 25 \qquad \textbf{Equation 9.1.7}$$

This difference equation is unstable, and its general solution is

$$c_1(5/6)^n + c_2(-3)^n$$

and the initial conditions give $c_1 = 36$ and $c_2 = 0$. As Example 3.6 shows, the second unstable solution enters the calculations because of round-off effects, and soon the "right" solution $36(5/6)^n$ is buried by the unstable solution.

A similar example of an unstable differential equation is

$$y' = 4y - 5e^{-x} \qquad y(0) = 1 \qquad \textbf{Equation 9.1.8}$$

where the general solution is

$$e^{-x} + c_2e^{4x}$$

and the initial condition gives $c_2 = 0$. Solving 9.1.8 numerically is very delicate; as one "follows" the true solution, any perturbation at all puts one on a neighboring solution; see Figure 9.1. The curves plotted in Figure 9.1 are called **trajectories**; there is one for each initial condition at $x = 0$. These neighboring trajectories rapidly depart from the true solution; the numerical methods discussed here are generally unable to solve problems like 9.1.8.

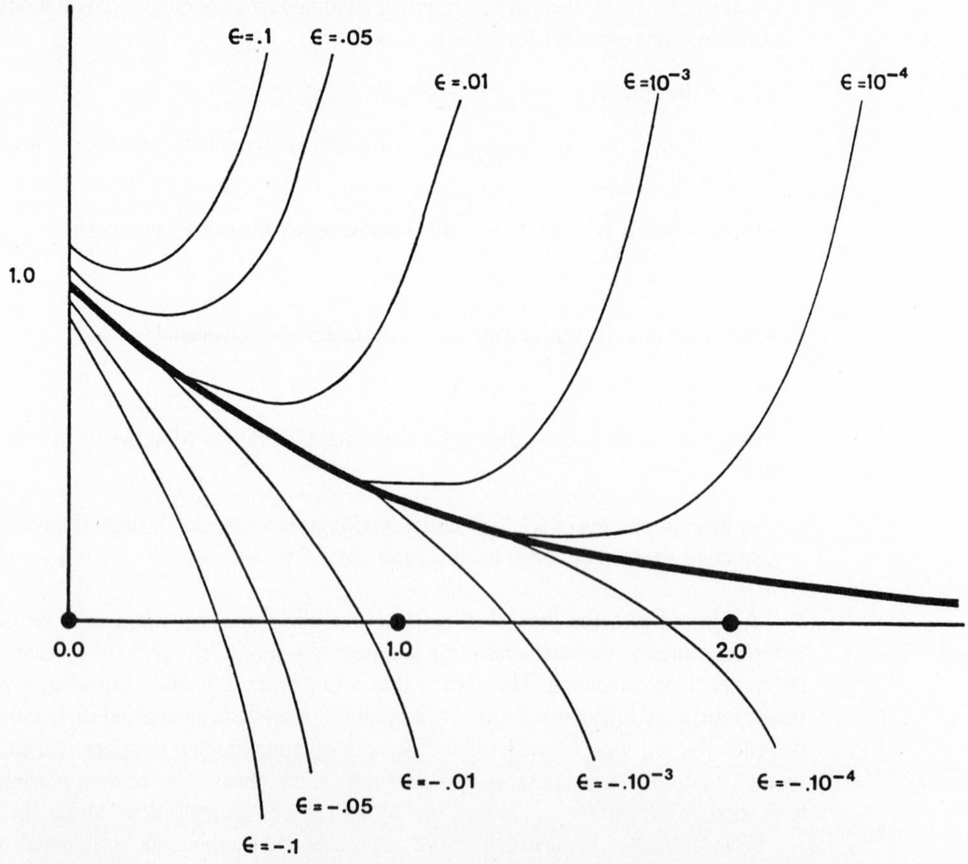

Figure 9.1 **Trajectories of solutions of an unstable differential equation.** The true solution (heavy curve) is surrounded by curves which rapidly diverge from it; their initial conditions are $1 \pm \epsilon$ at $x = 0$.

As a third example of stability problems, consider the differential equation

$$y' = -.5y + \frac{4/x - 1}{2x^2} = f(x, y) \qquad \textbf{Equation 9.1.9}$$

which has the general solution

$$y = ce^{-x/2} - \frac{1}{x^2}$$

We take the initial condition y(1) at x = 1 and find that $c = [y(1)+1]\sqrt{e}$. This is a well-behaved, stable differential equation which we might attempt to solve using a high-accuracy central difference formula to approximate y′. If we use points 1, 1+h, 1+2h,. . . and replace y′ by a 5-point central difference formula, we obtain, after a little manipulation,

$$y(x+4h) = y(x) - 8y(x+h) - 12f(x+2h,\ y(x+2h)) + 8y(x+3h) \qquad \textbf{Equation 9.1.10}$$

Suppose we know somehow not only y(1) but also y(1+h), y(1+2h), and y(1+3h) for the case $y(1) = \sqrt{e} - 1 = .6487212707$. Then equation 9.1.10 can be solved for successive values for larger x's. For h = .1 the first six steps produce:

Step	1	2	3	4	5	6
x	1.4	1.5	1.6	1.7	1.8	1.9
Computed	.839	.832	.772	.350	−2.91	−28.7
True	.840	.840	.831	.816	.797	.774
Correct digits	3.08	2.14	1.23	.33	−.57	−1.47

The accuracy dissipates rapidly. The number of correct digits for decreasing h to .01 and .001 are given for 6, 20, and 40 steps.

Step	h = .01 Correct Digits	h = .001 Correct Digits
1	7.60	12.59
6	3.05	8.03
20	−9.50	−4.52
40	−27.43	−22.45

The important fact is that the loss in accuracy depends just on the number of steps; 4.55 decimal digits of accuracy are lost in five steps (1 to 6) for each value of h. Similarly, 35.04 decimal digits are lost in 39 steps for both h = .01 and h = .001. A comparison of results for a fixed value of x shows a dramatic loss of accuracy as h decreases. For x = 1.05, h = .01 gives 6.65 correct digits after 2 steps; h = .001 gives −28.72 correct digits after 40 steps. We have here an example of a stable differential equation and an unstable numerical method.

The characteristic polynomial for 9.1.10 is

$$x^4 - 8x^3 + 8x - 1$$

which has roots 1.0, −1.0, 0.12702, and 7.87298. Note that $\log_{10} 7.87298 = .896$ and that the computation 9.1.10 loses almost exactly .896 digits per step ($5\times.896 = 4.48$, $39\times.896 = 34.94$). This suggests the fact (established later) that if the characteristic polynomial has roots larger than 1 (with positive logarithm), then the difference equation is unstable.

The examples of instability shown here all "blowup." This is a nice feature in numerical computations because the presence of an instability is signaled by ridiculously large results. This is typical (but not necessary) for one equation, though it is not typical for systems of equations that can have various kinds of oscillations which might grow rapidly or might just stay within some reasonable bounds. For a physical analogy, visualize a pendulum (with a solid arm) that is balanced exactly at the top of its swing. If it is disturbed, it starts to fall and looks for a moment like it will drop forever. But it just swings around and, if there is no friction, it swings forever. The physical instability only grows to a certain size and then the solution oscillates.

Nonlinear equations can go through different kinds of behavior, passing from very stable to nearly unstable and back again. There is no simple way to predict what will happen. Thus, it is often essential in solving differential equations that one have some information about the physical system being modeled. One needs to be able to judge the qualitative behavior of the solution, to know whether a special method for nearly unstable equations should be used, and so forth. When one is dealing with difficult differential equations, the numerical methods themselves may show various kinds of instabilities. These are qualitatively the same as instabilities in differential equations, and a familiarity of the theory of differential equations is important in understanding and interpreting the results.

PROBLEMS 9.1

9.1.1 Rewrite the following equations or systems of equations as a system of first-order ordinary differential equations.

(A) $y^{(4)} + \cos(x)y''' + e^{-x}y'' - (x^2+1)y' + xy = 2x\sin(xy)$
$y(0) = 0,\ y'(0) = 1,\ y''(0) = 2,\ y'''(0) = 3$

(B) $y^{(4)}/x + y'''/x^2 + y'' - [x/(1+x^2)]y' + x^2y = 1$
$y(1) = 1.\ y'(1) = 2,\ y(10) = 0,\ y'(10) = 0$

(C) $y''' + (xy'')^2/(1+y')^2 + \log(1+y) = 0$
$y(0) = y(1) = 0,\ y''(0) = 1$

(D) $y'' + xyzy' - e^{-x}z' + (x+z)xy = e^{-(x+y+z)}$
$z'' - (x+y)zz' + \cos(x^2+z^2)y' - (x+y)z = (x+y)/z$
$y(0) = 0,\ z(0) = 0,\ y'(0) = 1,\ z'(0) = 1$

(E) $w'' + xy' + e^{wx}z = 3 + (1+x)^w$
$y'' - z'y' + x/(1+z) = w^3 + 1$
$w' + y^2xz' = \cos(yx+2)$
$y(0) = 1,\ y'(0) = 2,\ w(0) = 0,\ w'(0) = 2,\ z(0) = 4$

9.1.2 Determine the stability of the following difference equations by considering the homogeneous solutions of the equations; do not consider the behavior of the particular solution.

(A) $y_{n+3} - y_{n+2} - .5y_{n+1} + .5y_n = n/(n+1)$
$y_1 = 1,\ y_2 = y_3 = 0$

(B) $y_{n+4} - 1.5y_{n+1} + .5y_n = 1/(1+n^2)$
$y_1 = 0,\ y_2 = 1,\ y_3 = 2,\ y_4 = 0$

(C) $y_{n+3} + 2y_{n+2} - 2y_{n+1} - y_n = 1$
$y_1 = 10,\ y_2 = y_3 = 0$

(D) $y_{n+3} - 2y_{n+2} - 2y_{n+1} + y_n = e^{n+1}$
$y_1 = .5,\ y_2 = 0,\ y_3 = .5$

(E) $y_{n+5} - 2y_{n+4} + 3y_{n+3} + 3y_{n+2} - 2y_{n+1} + y_n = n/(1+y_n)^2$
$y_1 = y_3 = y_4 = y_5 = 0,\ y_2 = 1$

Hint: The general solution is the sum of the particular solution (which must be explicitly computed) and the homogeneous solution (which can be found with a polynomial root-finding program).

9.1.3 Write a program for the difference equations of Problem 9.1.2 and confirm the results about stability by computing the first 30 terms in the solution.

9.1.4 Write a program for Equation 9.1.7 and compare its results with those of Example 3.6.

9.1.5 Replace y' in Equation 9.1.8 by $[y(x+h)-y(x)]/h$ and obtain a difference equation to approximate 9.1.8. Choose several values of h and attempt to compute $y(2) = .13533528$ accurately. Do the results get better or worse as h gets smaller?

9.1.6 Repeat Problem 9.1.5 using the central difference approximation $[y(x+h)-y(x-h)]/2h$ to approximate $y'(x)$. For the calculation use e^{-h} for y_{-1}. Is the difference equation stable? Compare the effectiveness of this method with the one in Problem 9.1.5.

9.1.7 Change the initial conditions of Equation 9.1.8 to $y(0) = 2$. Give the true solution $y(x)$. Repeat Problem 9.1.5 for this new differential equation problem.

9.1.8 Repeat Problem 9.1.5 for Equation 9.1.9.

9.1.9 Repeat Problem 9.1.6 for Equation 9.1.9 using $y(1-h)$ for y_{-1}.

BASIC METHODS FOR INITIAL VALUE PROBLEMS 9.2

There are three distinct classes of methods for ordinary differential equations. The first class consists of simple methods that are reasonably easy to understand and analyze. These methods are not recommended for anything but educational purposes. The second consists of direct extensions of the first class to obtain more accuracy and efficiency. The derivation and analysis of the second class is usually much more tedious, but not much more difficult than the first class. This second class is the starting point for the third class, which combines integration formulas of the second class with error control, starting procedures, printing control, etc., to produce a reliable, robust, and efficient method. This section presents the more important methods of the first and second classes; the third class is discussed under the topic of software. The details of deriving the second class of methods are omitted or are posed as problems for the students; the results are just stated.

The **initial value problem** considered in this section is

$$y' = f(x, y) \qquad y(0) = y_0 \qquad \textbf{Equation 9.2.1}$$

The initial point is taken to be $x = 0$ for simplicity in notation; all the discussion applies to other initial points with obvious changes.

One Step: Euler's Method 9.2.A

The simplest and one of the oldest methods is to replace y' in 9.2.1 by $[y(x+h)-y(x)]/h$ to obtain estimates of $y(x)$ at the points $x = h, 2h, 3h, \ldots$ The resulting integration formula is **Euler's method:**

$$y((k+1)h) = y(kh) + hf(kh, y(kh)) \qquad \textbf{Equation 9.2.2}$$

This and later formulas are simplified by setting $y_k \sim y(kh)$, $x_k = kh$, and $f_k = f(x_k, y_k)$; 9.2.2 then appears as

$$y_{k+1} = y_k + hf_k \qquad \textbf{Equation 9.2.3}$$

A graphical interpretation of this method is shown in Figure 9.2. At each step Euler's method follows the tangent line of the curve or trajectory passing through the current point. The output of a calculation is a tabulated set of points (x_k, y_k) where y_k is an estimate of $y(x_k)$. From Figure 9.2 we see that there are two kinds of error in this method. The first is the *error per step* or **local error**

$$T_k y = y_{k+1} - z(x_{k+1}) \qquad \textbf{Equation 9.2.4}$$

where $z(x)$ is the true solution of the differential equation

$$z' = f(x, z) \qquad z(x_k) = y_k$$

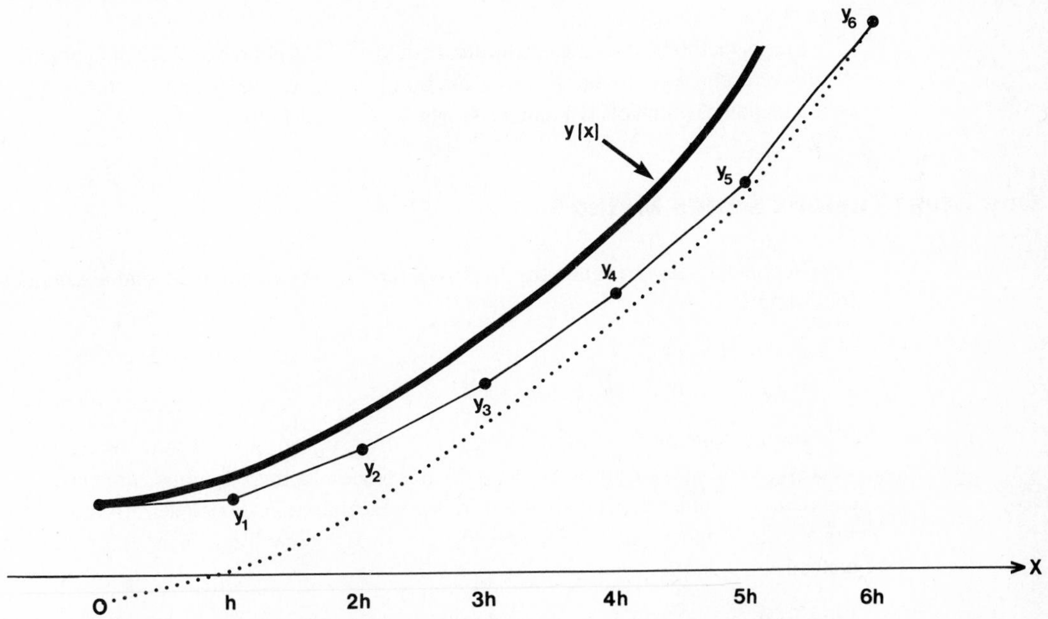

Figure 9.2 **Euler's method.** At the kth step the method follows the tangent line of the trajectory passing through (x_k, y_k). The trajectory for $k = 6$ is shown as the dotted curve.

That is, $z(x)$ defines the trajectory through (x_k, y_k); the trajectories for the points (x_0, y_0) and (x_6, y_6) are shown in Figure 9.2. The local error order is easy to obtain for most methods, and it is easy to see that $T_k y = O(h^2)$. We have by Taylor's theorem that

$$\begin{aligned} z(x_{k+1}) &= z(x_k) + z'(x_k)\,(x_{k+1}-x_k) + z''(x_k)\,(x_{k+1}-x_k)^2/2 + \ldots \\ &= y_k + f(x_k,y_k)h + O(h^2) \\ &= y_{k+1} + O(h^2) \end{aligned}$$

The local error is almost exactly the same as the **truncation error.** The difference is that the truncation error is defined as

$$|y(x_{k+1}) - (y(x_k) + h\, f(x_k, y_k))|$$

That is, the true global solution y(x) of the differential equation is used rather than z(x), the true solution with initial values x_k, y_k. These two errors are frequently confused, and in many instances, they are of the same order so that the confusion does not mislead one.

The second and more interesting error is the *global error* or **discretization error**

$$e(x) = |y(x) - y_k| \qquad \textbf{Equation 9.2.5}$$

where $k = x/h$. It is much more difficult, both in theory and in practice, to obtain reasonable estimates of the discretization error. The best one can hope for is that $e_k = O(h)$, because there are $k = O(1/h)$ errors of order $O(h^2)$ made in computing y_k. Of course, it all depends on how y(x) behaves and how closely the neighboring trajectories follow y(x). Oscillation in y(x) can make the errors cancel one another, and instability in the differential equation can make the discretization error grow rapidly with x even though the truncation error is going to zero at each step.

Round-off error is also a significant effect for Euler's method. If a round-off error of, say, 2 ulps is made at each step, then the cumulative effect at x should be about 2k ulps = 2x/h ulps. So the total error, round-off plus discretization, should behave approximately like $c_1h + c_2/h$ where c_2 has the machine round-off as one factor. If we assume that $c_1 = 2$ and $c_2 = 2$ ulps for simplicity, then these two error components are equal when $h = \sqrt{\text{ulp}}$. In a short word length calculation such as IBM with single precision (see Table 3.1), this suggests that $h = \sqrt{6*10^{-8}} \sim 2*10^{-4}$ is the smallest h for practical use; on a CDC machine in single precision $h = \sqrt{4*10^{-15}} \sim 6*10^{-8}$ is the smallest h. These estimates are for the ideal situation where f(x, y) is simple; in practice round-off error can become the limiting factor for accuracy in Euler's method for even larger h.

Euler's method is a simple, low-order method which is not recommended in practice. The significance of the problem with round-off error discussed above is due to the method's low accuracy; simple accumulation of round-off is a much less significant problem for better methods.

One Step: Taylor's Series Method 9.2.B

It is, in principle, easy to obtain the Taylor's series for y(x) from the differential Equation 9.2.1. We have, for example,

$$\begin{aligned} y'' &= f' = f_x + f_y y' = f_x + f_y f \\ y''' &= f_{xx} + 2f_{xy}f + f_{yy}f^2 + f_x f_y + f_y^2 f \end{aligned} \qquad \textbf{Equation 9.2.6}$$

We use the notation $f_x = \partial f(x, y)/\partial x$, $f_y = \partial f(x, y)/\partial y$, etc. All these derivatives can be evaluated wherever x and y(x) are given. To carry out this process further is routine but tedious by hand. There exist computer programs which differentiate arbitrary Fortran expressions (even arbitrary Fortran FUNCTION subprograms), and so one can consider obtaining a high-order Taylor's series for y(x). The **Taylor's series method** is:

Algorithm 9.2.1

For k = 0, 1, 2, . . . , do:
- $p_n(x)$ = Taylor's series polynomial of y(x) at (x_k, y_k) of degree n
- $y_{k+1} = p_n(x_k+h)$

Consider the differential equation $y' = x^2+y^2$ and n=3 in the Taylor's series method. We see that

$$\begin{aligned} p_3(x) &= y(x_k) + y'(x_k)(x-x_k) + y''(x_k)(x-x_k)^2/2 + y'''(x-x_k)^3/6 \\ &= y_k + (x_k^2+y_k^2)(x-x_k) + 2[x_k+y_k(x_k^2+y_k^2)](x-x_k)^2/2 \\ &\quad + 2\{(x_k^2+y_k^2)^2 + 2y_k[x_k+y_k(x_k^2+y_k^2)]\}(x-x_k)^3/6 \end{aligned}$$

Then $y_{k+1} = p_3(x_k+h)$ is given, in Fortran, by

```
XY2    = X(K)**2 + Y(K)**2
XYXY2  = X(K) + Y(K)*XY2
Y(K+1) = Y(K) + H*(XY2+H*(XYXY2+H*(XY2+Y(K)*XYXY2)/3.))
```

The local error in this case is the next term [the $(x-x_k)^4$ term] of the Taylor's series. In general, the local error of a Taylor's series method of degree n is $O(h^{n+1})$.

This method is not the basis of any widely used software. It is mentioned here because it illustrates the potential use of symbolic mathematical software in numerical computations. Some experiments with the method indicates that it performs well for problems with smooth solutions. Note that the Taylor's series method with degree 1 is just Euler's method.

One Step: Runge-Kutta Methods 9.2.C

An intuitive explanation of these methods is as follows:

1. Make a tentative step from x with the Euler method.
2. Evaluate y′ at this point and use this information to adjust the slope to be used at x.
3. Use the adjusted slope to make a second tentative step.
4. Evaluate y′ at this point and use this information to further adjust the slope to be used at x.
5. Repeat the tentative steps as often as desired.
6. Combine all the estimates to make the actual step to $x+h$.

There are many degrees of freedom within this framework: the number of tentative steps or stages, how long to make them (one does not have to step to $x+h$ each time), and how to combine them to make better estimates. The result is that there are whole families of Runge-Kutta methods and many particular ones that have been widely studied and used.

A key decision is how to determine the adjustments; Runge-Kutta methods use a polynomial model for $y(x)$. This is used by adopting the criterion that the Taylor's series for the actual estimate y_{k+1} must agree, as much as possible, with the Taylor's series of the true solution through (x_k, y_k). The Taylor's series method is a special degenerate case of the Runge-Kutta method where all the tentative steps are of length zero.

This method is expressed by **Runge-Kutta formulas** as follows (for the cases of 2 and 3 stages):

Equation 9.2.7

$$\begin{aligned}
s_1 &= hf(x_k, y_k)\\
s_2 &= hf(x_k+\alpha_2 h,\ y_k+\beta_2 s_1)\\
s_3 &= hf(x_k+\alpha_3 h,\ y_k+\beta_{31}s_1+\beta_{32}s_2)\\
y_{k+1} &= y_k + a_1 s_1 + a_2 s_2 \qquad \text{(two stages)}\\
y_{k+1} &= y_k + a_1 s_1 + a_2 s_2 + a_3 s_3 \qquad \text{(three stages)}
\end{aligned}$$

The two-stage formula has four parameters: α_2, β_2, a_1, and a_2. The three-stage formula has eight parameters: α_2, α_3, β_2, β_{31}, β_{32}, a_1, a_2, and a_3.

We show how the four parameters in a two-stage formula are determined by matching coefficients in the Taylor's series for $y(x_{k+1})$. We have for $y(x)$ at $x = x_{k+1}$

Equation 9.2.8

$$\begin{aligned}
y(x_{k+1}) &= y(x_k) + hy'(x_k) + \frac{h^2}{2}y''(x_k) + \frac{h^3}{6}y'''(x_k) + \dots\\
&= y(x_k) + hf(x_k, y_k) + \frac{h^2}{2}(f_x+ff_y) + \frac{h^3}{6}(f_{xx}+2ff_{xy}+f_{yy}f^2+f_xf_y+f_y^2f) + O(h^4)
\end{aligned}$$

The formulas and notation of 9.2.6 for derivatives of $y(x)$ are used here. To expand the expression for y_{k+1} in 9.2.7 we need to expand s_1 and s_2 in Taylor's series about the point (x_k, y_k). Since s_1 is already of this form, we need only use

Equation 9.2.9

$$\begin{aligned}
s_2 &= hf(x_k+\alpha_2 h,\ y_k+\beta_2 s_1)\\
&= hf(x_k, y_k) + \alpha_2 h^2 f_x + \beta_2 s_1 hf_y + \frac{(\alpha_2 h)^2}{2}hf_{xx} + \alpha_2 h\beta_2 s_1 hf_{xy} + \frac{(\beta_2 s_1)^2}{2}hf_{yy} + O(h^4)
\end{aligned}$$

We substitute 9.2.9 with $s_1 = hf$ into $y_{k+1} = y_k + a_1 s_1 + a_2 s_2$ and compare coefficients of powers of h with 9.2.8. We show the coefficients of these powers for $y(x_{k+1})$ and y_{k+1} in the following tabular form:

	$y(x_{k+1})$	y_{k+1}
h^0	y_k	y_k
h^1	f	$(a_1+a_2)f$
h^2	$\frac{1}{2}(f_x+ff_y)$	$a_2(\alpha_2 f_x+\beta_2 ff_y)$
h^3	$\frac{1}{6}(f_{xx}+2ff_{xy}+f_{yy}f^2+f_x f_y+f_y^2 f)$	$a_2\left(\frac{1}{2}\alpha_2^2 f_{xx}+\alpha_2\beta_2 ff_{xy}+\frac{1}{2}\beta_2^2 f^2 f_{yy}\right)$

The coefficients of h^0 automatically agree, and to make those of h and h^2 agree, we need to satisfy

$$a_1 + a_2 = 1 \quad \text{for } f$$ **Equation 9.2.10**

$$a_2\alpha_2 = \frac{1}{2} \quad \text{for } f_x$$

$$a_2\beta_2 = \frac{1}{2} \quad \text{for } ff_y$$

This is a system of three equations in four unknowns, and it has infinitely many solutions; one of the simplest is $a_1 = a_2 = \frac{1}{2}$, $\alpha_2 = \beta_2 = 1$. To make the coefficients of h^3 agree we need to satisfy the equations

$$a_2\alpha_2^2 = \frac{1}{3} \quad \text{for } f_{xx}$$

$$a_2\alpha_2\beta_2 = \frac{1}{3} \quad \text{for } ff_{xy}$$

$$a_2\beta_2^2 = \frac{1}{3} \quad \text{for } f_{yy}f^2$$

$$0 = \frac{1}{6} \quad \text{for } f_x f_y$$

$$0 = \frac{1}{6} \quad \text{for } f_y^2 f$$

This is obviously impossible to do for all functions f.

The **order** of a Runge-Kutta method is the exponent of the highest power of h for which the Taylor's series of $y(x_{k+1})$ and y_{k+1} agree; it is also the degree of the polynomial model used for $y(x)$. The local error of a kth-order Runge-Kutta method is $O(h^{k+1})$.

Comparison of Simple Methods for Initial Value Problems

Example 9.1

We consider Euler's method, second-order Taylor's series, and a second-order Runge-Kutta method (the one with two stages and $a_1 = a_2 = \frac{1}{2}$, $\beta_2 = \alpha_2 = 1$) and apply them to three differential equations. The first is a simple, well-behaved problem:

$$y' = [1 - xy - (xy)^2]/x^2 \qquad y(1) = -1$$ **Equation 9.2.11**

whose true solution is $y(x) = -1/x$. The second is an unstable equation, similar to the one used in Figure 9.1, but not quite so unstable:

$$y' = 3y - 4e^{-x} \qquad y(0) = 1$$ **Equation 9.2.12**

whose true solution is e^{-x} and whose general solution is $e^{-x} + c_2e^{3x}$. Thus, errors in the computation activate the e^{3x} term which soon masks the true solution. The third is a model of a smooth problem with a shock or impulse term — $ce^{-100(x-2.2)^2}$, that is, a term which is large for a short time to make a unit addition to y'. The problem is

$$y' = y^2 - ce^{-100(x-2.2)^2} \qquad y(1) = 1$$ **Equation 9.2.13**

where $c = 20/\sqrt{\pi} = 11.28379167$ makes the total integral of the impulse term equal to 1. The solution without the impulse term is $y(x) = -1/x$, the same as for the first equation of this example.

The numbers of correct digits for these three methods applied to these three problems are given in Table 9.1.

Errors in Three Simple Methods Applied to Three Simple Differential Equations **Table 9.1**

Entries are $-\log_{10}(\text{error})$ = number of correct digits after integrating 3 units (to x = 4, 3, and 4, respectively).

	h	Method		
		Euler	Taylor	Runge-Kutta
Problem 9.2.11	.1	.96	1.27	2.03
(easy)	.04	1.31	1.62	2.81
	.01	1.89	2.19	4.00
	.004	2.28	2.58	4.80
Problem 9.2.12	.1	−1.51	−2.77	−1.12
(unstable)	.04	−1.39	−2.25	−0.40
	.01	−.95	−1.53	0.80
	.004	0.58	−1.10	1.57
Problem 9.2.13	.1	1.77	1.55	2.69
(impulse term)	.04	2.22	1.98	3.75
	.01	2.83	2.60	5.02
	.004	3.24	3.00	5.82

The most important information in Table 9.1 is the behavior of the error as h decreases. As h decreases by 10 from .04 to .004, the Euler method gains .97 and 1.02 digits for the two problems where it is working. The observed error is $O(h)$ since decreasing h by a factor of 10 decreases the error by a factor of 10 (a one-digit gain in accuracy). This agrees very well with the rule of thumb that a local error of $O(h^2)$ gives a global error of $O(h)$. Similarly, the Taylor method gains .96 and 1.02 digits for these same cases as h goes from .04 to .004. The Runge-Kutta method has a local truncation error $O(h^3)$, and so we expect global error of $O(h^2)$. As h goes from .04 to .004, we see that this method gains 1.99 and 2.07 digits for two of the equations, just as expected. Even for the unstable Problem 9.2.12, the error is decreasing approximately as expected.

There is no round-off visible in these calculations; they are made with 14-decimal-digit arithmetic. In particular, the large errors in the unstable problem are due to "changing trajectories" at each step and not to round-off.

The solution to Equation 9.2.13 is shown in Figure 9.3. It has a very sharp wave front because of the impulse term, and thus it would seem to be a difficult problem to solve. It is not nearly as difficult as it appears because the impulse term is a function of x alone. This means that trajectories of the impulse part are exactly parallel, and truncation or round-off errors are not magnified at all by the "action" of the differential equation. If the impulse depended on y, say it was

$$11e^{-100(x-2.2)^2(y-1)^2} \qquad \text{or} \qquad \frac{121e^{-100(x-2.2)^2}}{1 + 11(y-.7)^2}$$

then the errors in $y(x)$ could change the impulse which would then affect the solution more strongly.

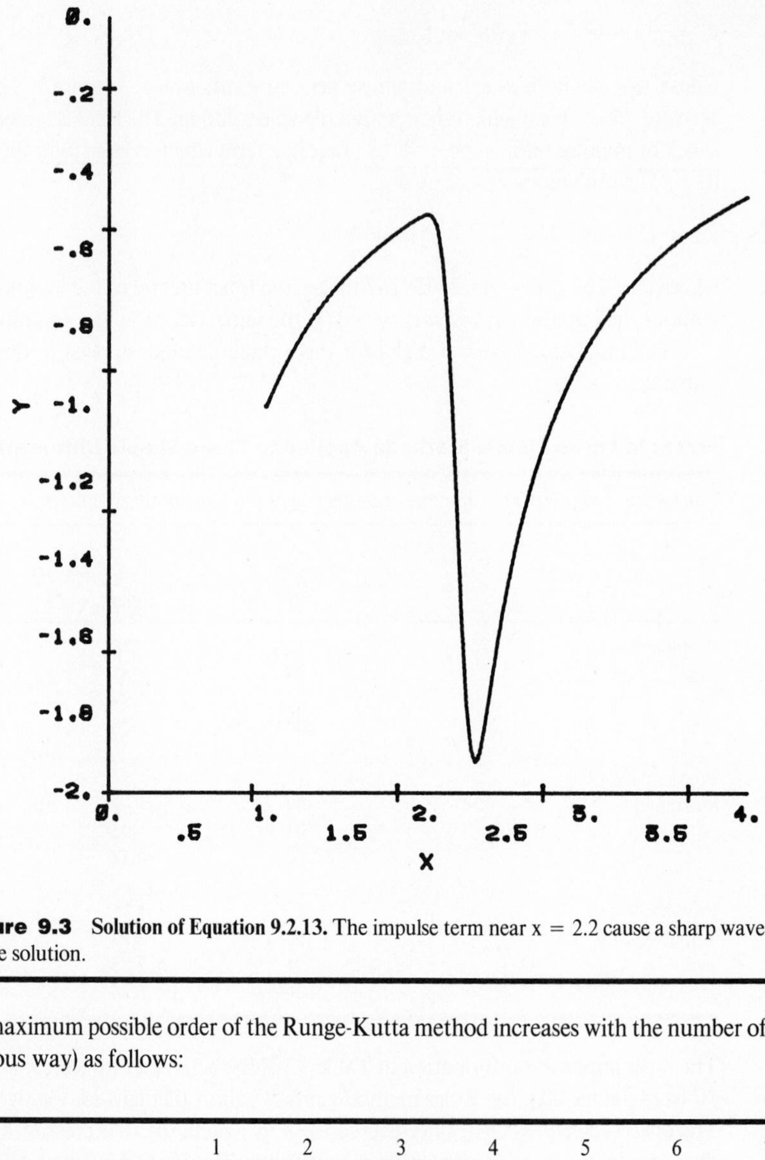

Figure 9.3 Solution of Equation 9.2.13. The impulse term near $x = 2.2$ cause a sharp wave front in the solution.

The maximum possible order of the Runge-Kutta method increases with the number of stages (but not in an obvious way) as follows:

Stages	1	2	3	4	5	6	7	8
Maximum order	1	2	3	4	4	5	6	6

The complexity of the equations to determine the parameters of Runge-Kutta formulas grows rapidly with the number of stages. The systems for third and fourth orders are given in Problems 9.2.6 and 9.2.7. Several specific Runge-Kutta formulas are given in Problems 9.2.8 through 9.2.11.

Among the simpler third-and fourth-order formulas are the following:

Equation 9.2.14

$$s_1 = hf(x_k, y_k)$$

$$s_2 = hf\left(x_k + \frac{1}{2}h, y_k + \frac{1}{2}s_1\right)$$

$$s_3 = hf(x_k + h, y_k - s_1 + 2s_2)$$

$$y_{k+1} = y_k + \frac{1}{6}(s_1 + 4s_2 + s_3) \qquad \text{(third-order Runge-Kutta)}$$

Equation 9.2.15

$$s_1 = hf(x_k, y_k)$$

$$s_2 = hf\left(x_k + \frac{1}{2}h,\ y_k + \frac{1}{2}s_1\right)$$

$$s_3 = hf\left(x_k + \frac{1}{2}h,\ y_k + \frac{1}{2}s_2\right)$$

$$s_4 = hf(x_k + h,\ y_k + s_3)$$

$$y_{k+1} = y_k + \frac{1}{6}(s_1 + 2s_2 + 2s_3 + s_4) \qquad \text{(fourth-order Runge-Kutta)}$$

It is to be shown in Problem 9.2.12 that both these Runge-Kutta formulas are extensions of Simpson's rule in the sense that if $f(x, y)$ does not depend on y, then

$$y_{k+1} \sim y_k + \int_{x_k}^{x_{k+1}} f(x)dx$$

with the integral estimated by Simpson's rule.

An important class of formulas are the **Runge-Kutta-Fehlberg,** or RKF, formulas. These formulas are determined so that the slopes s_i can be combined in two different ways: one to give an estimate y_{k+1} of order h^m and another to give an estimate z_{k+1} of order h^{m+1}. The point is that $z_{k+1} - y_{k+1}$ is a good estimate of the error in y_{k+1}; this is used to control the computation in more sophisticated methods discussed later. The **RKF45 formulas** are

Equation 9.2.16

$$s_1 = hf(x_k, y_k)$$

$$s_2 = hf\left(x_k + \frac{1}{4}h,\ y_k + \frac{1}{4}s_1\right)$$

$$s_3 = hf\left(x_k + \frac{3}{8}h,\ y_k + \frac{3}{32}s_1 + \frac{9}{32}s_2\right)$$

$$s_4 = hf\left(x_k + \frac{12}{13}h,\ y_k + \frac{1932}{2197}s_1 - \frac{7200}{2197}s_2 + \frac{7296}{2197}s_3\right)$$

$$s_5 = hf\left(x_k + h,\ y_k + \frac{439}{216}s_1 - 8s_2 + \frac{3680}{513}s_3 - \frac{845}{4104}s_4\right)$$

$$s_6 = hf\left(x_k + \frac{1}{2}h,\ y_k - \frac{8}{27}s_1 + 2s_2 - \frac{3544}{2565}s_3 + \frac{1859}{4104}s_4 - \frac{11}{40}s_5\right)$$

$$y_{k+1} = y_k + \frac{25}{216}s_1 + \frac{1408}{2565}s_3 + \frac{2197}{4104}s_4 - \frac{1}{5}s_5$$

$$z_{k+1} = y_k + \frac{16}{135}s_1 + \frac{6656}{12825}s_3 + \frac{28561}{56430}s_4 - \frac{9}{50}s_5 + \frac{2}{55}s_6$$

Here z_{k+1} is a fifth-order formula using six stages (the minimum possible) and y_{k+1} is a fourth-order formula using five stages. The fact that y_{k+1} uses one more stage than necessary to achieve fourth-order accuracy does not hurt, because one is going to evaluate $f(x, y)$ six times for the z_{k+1} formula anyway.

Multistep Methods 9.2.D

The previous methods are called one-step methods because they go from x_k to $x_k + h$ without any additional information. The multistep methods use information from $x_k, x_{k-1}, x_{k-2}, \ldots$ to compute y_{k+1} at $x_k + h$. The general form of a **multistep formula** is

$$y_{k+1} = \sum_{i=0}^{p} a_i y_{k-i} + h \sum_{i=-1}^{p} b_i y'_{k-i} \qquad \textbf{Equation 9.2.17}$$

which has $p+1$ steps. The values y_{k-i} and $y'_{k-i} = f(x_k - ih, y_{k-i})$ are saved as the method progresses for use in later steps. Note that there is a problem with getting these methods started; for small k ($k<p$) there are not enough previously computed vaues for 9.2.17.

If b_{-1} is not zero, then 9.2.17 has y_{k+1} on the left and y'_{k+1} on the right. Since $y'_{k+1} = f(x_{k+1}, y_{k+1})$, this means that a nonlinear equation must be solved (at each time step) to obtain y_{k+1}. A multistep formula with $b_{-1} \neq 0$ is called an **implicit formula**; otherwise it is an **explicit formula.** The use of implicit formulas is discussed further in the next section.

The method of undetermined coefficients is easily applied to determine parameters a_i and b_i for a particular method. To simplify the derivation, we note that we may take $x_k = 0$ (this just shifts the origin of the x coordinates) and we may take $h = 1$ (this just scales the x coordinates by a constant). If we use polynomials to model $y(x)$ and substitute $y(x) = x^j$ for $j = 0, 1, \ldots, m$, we obtain the following equations [note $y_{k+1} = y(1) = 1$, $x_{k-1} = -1$, etc.]:

$$1 = \sum_{i=0}^{p} a_i \qquad \textbf{Equation 9.2.18}$$

$$1 = \sum_{i=0}^{p} -ia_i + \sum_{i=-1}^{p} b_i$$

$$1 = \sum_{i=0}^{p} (-i)^j a_i + \sum_{i=-1}^{p} j(-i)^{j-1} b_i, \qquad j = 2, 3, \ldots, m$$

The system 9.2.18 has $m+1$ equations in $2p+3$ variables. One might expect to take $m = 2p+2$, but *all multistep methods with $m > p+3$ (m even) or $m > p+2$ (m odd) are unstable.*

A multistep method is **consistent** if the first two equations of the system 9.2.18 are satisfied. If 9.2.18 is satisfied, then one expects the local error $y_{k+1} - y(x_k+h)$ to be order h^{m+1} and the global discretization error to be order h^m. Consistency implies $m \geq 1$, and we see that if the method is not consistent, then the discretization error does not go to zero with h and the method is useless.

Since only about half the parameters in a multistep method can be used to increase the accuracy, the rest can be used for any other purpose. Examples of such purposes are efficiency (make many of the a_i and b_i zero), simple numbers for the a_i and b_i (this was very important before computers were available, and it is still nice when using hand-held calculators), and obtaining an explicit formula (note that if $b_{-1} \neq 0$, then y_{k+1} appears on *both* sides of 9.2.17 and a nonlinear equation must be solved to obtain its value). We make no attempt to explore all these possibilities; they are beyond the scope of this book. Instead, we examine a special class of multistep methods that form the basis for much of the good software for differential equations.

The Adams methods are based on the formula

$$y(x_{k+1}) = y_k + \int_{x_k}^{x_{k+1}} y'(x)dx = y_k + \int_{x_k}^{x_{k+1}} f(x, y(x))dx$$

One models $f(x, y)$ by a polynomial $p(x)$ which interpolates $y'(x)$ at various points. Then the **Adams formulas** are obtained from

$$y_{k+1} = y_k + \int_{x_k}^{x_{k+1}} p(x)dx \qquad \textbf{Equation 9.2.19}$$

This derivation is an example of the method of analytic substitution. As usual, the final formula obtained does not involve $p(x)$ explicitly and expresses y_{k+1} as y_k plus a linear combination of the y'_{k-i}. The particular formulas obtained depend on the interpolation points chosen. There are two standard choices: the **Adams-Bashforth method** of order $p+1$ uses interpolation of $y'(x)$ at $x_k, x_{k-1}, \ldots, x_{k-p}$, and the **Adams-Moulton method** of order $p+1$ uses interpolation of $y'(x)$ at $x_{k+1}, x_k, x_{k-1}, \ldots, x_{k-p+1}$. The first few instances of these formulas are tabulated in Table 9.2.

Adams Formulas **Table 9.2**

ADAMS-BASHFORTH (EXPLICIT) FORMULAS WITH ORDER 1 TO 6

Order	
1	$y_{k+1} = y_k + hy'_{k+1}$ (Euler's method)
2	$y_{k+1} = y_k + \frac{h}{2}(3y'_k - y'_{k-1})$
3	$y_{k+1} = y_k + \frac{h}{12}(23y'_k - 16y'_{k-1} + 5y'_{k-2})$
4	$y_{k+1} = y_k + \frac{h}{24}(55y'_k - 59y'_{k-1} + 37y'_{k-2} - 9y'_{k-3})$
5	$y_{k+1} = y_k + \frac{h}{720}(1901y'_k - 2774y'_{k-1} + 2616y'_{k-2} - 1274y'_{k-3} + 251y'_{k-4})$
6	$y_{k+1} = y_k + \frac{h}{1440}(4227y'_k - 7673y'_{k-1} + 9482y'_{k-2} - 6798y'_{k-3} + 2627y'_{k-4} - 425y'_{k-5})$

ADAMS-MOULTON (IMPLICIT) FORMULAS WITH ORDER 1 TO 6

Order	
1	$y_{k+1} = y_k + hy'_k$
2	$y_{k+1} = y_k + \frac{h}{2}(y'_{k+1} + y'_k)$
3	$y_{k+1} = y_k + \frac{h}{12}(5y'_{k+1} + 8y'_k - y'_{k-1})$
4	$y_{k+1} = y_k + \frac{h}{24}(9y'_{k+1} + 19y'_k - 5y'_{k-1} + y'_{k-2})$
5	$y_{k+1} = y_k + \frac{h}{720}(251y'_{k+1} + 646y'_k - 264y'_{k-1} + 106y'_{k-2} - 19y'_{k-3})$
6	$y_{k+1} = y_k + \frac{h}{1440}(475y'_{k+1} + 1427y'_k - 798y'_{k-1} + 482y'_{k-2} - 173y'_{k-3} + 27y'_{k-4})$

The **order** of an Adams formula is the degree of the polynomial model used. The local error of a kth-order formula is $O(h^{k+1})$ since x^{k+1} is the next polynomial power not used in the model. For the Adams-Bashford and Adams-Moulton methods, the order is also the number of y' terms used to compute y_{k+1}.

Predictor-Corrector Methods **9.2.E**

The multistep methods which use y'_{k+1} (that is, which have $b_{-1} \neq 0$ in 9.2.17) are more stable than those that do not. Good stability is very important for these methods, but it comes at the price of requiring the solution of a nonlinear equation at each step. Solving this equation is not as difficult as one might guess because one can use an explicit multistep formula to obtain a very good estimate of y_{k+1}. The technique is illustrated in a simple case.

The Adams-Moulton formula of order 2 is also known as the **trapezoidal method**; it uses the formula

$$y_{k+1} = y_k + \frac{h}{2}[f(x_{k+1}, y_{k+1}) + f(x_k, y_k)]$$ **Equation 9.2.20**

This is a nonlinear equation to be solved for y_{k+1}; if h is small enough, then simple fixed point iteration converges for its solution. An intuitive argument for the convergence follows; see Theorem 9.3 for a complete proof. Set $y_{k+1} = y$ for simplicity and combine all known values in 9.2.20 into the constant c; 9.2.20 is then of the form

$$y = \frac{h}{2} f(y) + c$$

For fixed point iteration, the convergence factor is $\partial(\frac{1}{2} hf(y))/\partial y \sim hM/2$ where M is f_y. As h gets small, hM/2 becomes less than 1. A good guess g_{k+1} for the solution of 9.2.20 is available from Euler's method:

$$g_{k+1} = y_k + hf(x_k, y_k) \qquad \textbf{Equation 9.2.21}$$

The local error of g_{k+1} is $O(h^2)$, and each fixed point iteration adds another factor of h (provided M is not huge). The combined method can be rewritten as

$$y_{(k+1)}^{(0)} = y_k + hf(x_k, y_k) \qquad \textbf{Equation 9.2.22}$$

$$y_{k+1}^{(j)} = y_k + \frac{h}{2} [f(x_k, y_k) + f(x_{k+1}, y_{k+1}^{(j-1)})] \qquad j = 1, 2, \ldots$$

The first formula of such a pair is the **predictor formula** and the second is the **corrector formula.** In practice, only one or two fixed point iterations with the corrector formula are required to obtain full accuracy. Note that $j = 1$ gives a two-stage Runge-Kutta formula.

An important fringe benefit of the predictor-corrector methods is that they produce a reasonable estimate of the local error in the step. Both the predictor and corrector formulas give an estimate of y_{k+1}; their difference is an estimate of the error. In the above example the predictor error is $O(h^2)$ and the corrector error is $O(h^3)$; it is common to use pairs of formulas of the same order to obtain good error estimates which are used to control the computation in practical methods. Three common predictor pairs are given in Problems 9.2.16 to 9.2.18; others can be obtained by combining explicit and implicit Adams formulas.

PROBLEMS 9.2

9.2.1 Apply the analysis of Section 9.1.B to determine whether Euler's method is stable.

9.2.2 Apply Euler's method to the following differential equations with h = .02 and .01 and compare the value of y(1) with the computed value. Does the error behave as expected when h is halved?

(A) $(x^2+1)y' + xy = 0$, $y(0) = 1$, $y(x) = 1/(1+x^2)$

(B) $y' = 2xy$, $y(0) = 1$, $y(x) = e^{x^2}$

(C) $y' \tan x - y = 1$, $y(\pi/6) = -0.5$, $y(x) = \sin x - 1$

(D) $\sqrt{1+x^2}\, y' + xy = 0$, $y(0) = 1$, $y(x) = e^{-\sqrt{1+x^2}}$

(E) $xy' - (x+y) = 0$, $y(1/e) = 0$, $y(x) = x + x\ln(x)$

(F) $xy' - x = \sqrt{x^2-y^2}$, $y(1/e) = -.8414709848$, $y(x) = x + \sin(\ln(x))$

(G) $xy' + y = 2\sqrt{xy}$, $y(.5) = 2.5$, $y(x) = (1+x)^2/x$

(H) $y^2(y-(1+x)y') + (1+x)^3 = 0$, $y(0) = 3$, $y(x) = (x+1)^3\sqrt{27+\ln(1+x)}$

9.2.3 Study the round-off effects in Problem 9.2.2 by adding a random number of size 10^{-4} to the right side of the equation. Solve the differential equation 20 times, using different random numbers each time. Use h = .05. Plot the values obtained and describe the dispersion that round-off makes about the unperturbed solution.

9.2.4 Apply the Taylor's series method of degree 2 to Problems 9.2.2 B, E, and G.

9.2.5 Apply the second-order Runge-Kutta method with $a_1 = a_2 = \frac{1}{2}$ and $\alpha_2 = \beta_2 = 1$ to Problem 9.2.2 and to:

(A) $xy' - y = \ln(1/x)$, $y(.5) = 1.5 - \ln 2$, $y(x) = 1 + x + \ln x$

(B) $x^2y' + y(1-x)(1+2x)/(1+x) = 2(1+x)^2$, $y(0.5) = 21.1253762225$, $y(x) = (1+x)^2(2+e^{1/x})$

(C) $3y^2y' - xy^3 = -12e^{3x^2/2}\sin(x)\cos^4(x/2)$, $y(0) = 2$, $y(x) = (1+\cos x)e^{x^2/2}$

(D) $(1-x^2)y' + xy = x(1-x^2)\sqrt{y}$, $y(0) = 0$, $y(x) = (x^2-1+\sqrt[4]{1-x^2})^2/9$

9.2.6 Show that the parameters of a third-order Runge-Kutta method must satisfy the system of equations

$$a_1 + a_2 + a_3 = 1 \qquad a_3\alpha_2\beta_{32} = \frac{1}{6}$$

$$a_2\alpha_2 + a_3\alpha_3 = \frac{1}{2} \qquad \alpha_2 = \beta_{21}$$

$$a_2\alpha_2^2 + a_3\alpha_3^2 = \frac{1}{3} \qquad \alpha_3 = \beta_{31} + \beta_{32}$$

9.2.7 Show that the parameters of a fourth-order Runge-Kutta method must satisfy the system of equations

$$a_1 + a_2 + a_3 + a_4 = 1 \qquad a_3\alpha_2\beta_{32} + a_4(\alpha_2\beta_{42}+\alpha_3\beta_{43}) = \frac{1}{6}$$

$$\alpha_2 a_2 + \alpha_3 a_3 + \alpha_4 a_4 = \frac{1}{2} \qquad a_3\alpha_2^2\beta_{32} + a_4(\alpha_2^2\beta_{42}+\alpha_3^2\beta_{43}) = \frac{1}{12}$$

$$\alpha_2^2 a_2 + \alpha_3^2 a_3 + \alpha_4^2 a_4 = \frac{1}{3} \qquad \begin{aligned} &a_3\alpha_2\alpha_3\beta_{32} \\ &+ a_4\alpha_4(\alpha_2\beta_{42}+\alpha_3\beta_{43}) = \frac{1}{8}\end{aligned}$$

$$\alpha_2^3 a_2 + \alpha_3^3 a_3 + \alpha_4^3 a_4 = \frac{1}{4} \qquad a_4\alpha_2\beta_{32}\beta_{43} = \frac{1}{24}$$

9.2.8 Show that the following is a third-order Runge-Kutta method by applying it to one of the differential equations in Problem 9.2.2 and observing the behavior of the error as h becomes small.

$$s_1 = hf(x_k, y_k)$$

$$s_2 = hf\left(x_k + \frac{1}{2}h,\ y_k + \frac{1}{2}s_1\right)$$

$$s_3 = hf\left(x_k + \frac{3}{4}h,\ y_k + \frac{3}{4}s_2\right)$$

$$y_{k+1} = y_k + \frac{1}{9}(2s_1+3s_2+4s_3)$$

9.2.9 Repeat Problem 9.2.8 for

$$s_1 = hf(x_k, y_k)$$

$$s_2 = hf\left(x + \frac{1}{2}h,\ y_k + \frac{1}{2}s_1\right)$$

$$s_3 = hf\left(x + \frac{1}{2}h,\ y_k + \frac{1}{4}s_1 + \frac{1}{4}s_2\right)$$

$$s_4 = hf(x+h,\ y_k - s_2 + 2s_3)$$

$$y_{k+1} = y_k + \frac{1}{6}(s_1+4s_3+s_4)$$

9.2.10 Repeat Problem 9.2.8 to show the following is a fourth-order method:

$$\begin{aligned}
s_1 &= hf(x_k, y_k)\\
s_2 &= hf(x_k+.4h,\ y_k+.4s_1)\\
s_3 &= hf(x_k+.45573725h,\ y_k+.29697761s_1+.15875964s_2)\\
s_4 &= hf(x_k+h,\ y_k+.21810040s_1-3.05096516s_2\\
&\qquad +3.83286476s_3)\\
y_{k+1} &= y_k + .17476028s_2 - .55148066s_2\\
&\qquad + 1.20553560s_3 + .17118478s_4
\end{aligned}$$

9.2.11 Repeat Problem 9.2.8 to show the following is a fifth-order method:

$$s_1 = hf(x_k, y_k)$$

$$s_2 = hf\left(x_k + \frac{1}{2}h,\ y_k + \frac{1}{2}s_1\right)$$

$$s_3 = hf\left(x_k + \frac{1}{2}h,\ y_k + \frac{1}{4}s_1 + \frac{1}{4}s_2\right)$$

$$s_4 = hf(x_k+h,\ y_k - s_2 + 2s_3)$$

$$s_5 = hf\left(x_k + \frac{2}{3}h,\ y_k + \frac{7}{27}s_1 + \frac{10}{27}s_2 + \frac{1}{27}s_4\right)$$

$$s_6 = hf\left(x_k + \frac{1}{5}h,\ y_k + \frac{28}{625}s_1 - \frac{1}{5}s_2 + \frac{456}{625}s_3 + \frac{54}{625}s_4 - \frac{378}{625}s_5\right)$$

$$y_{k+1} = y_k + \frac{1}{24}s_1 + \frac{5}{48}s_4 + \frac{27}{50}s_5 + \frac{125}{336}s_6$$

Note that the third-order estimate of Problem 9.2.9 is easily obtained in the course of calculating y_{k+1}. Discuss how this would be useful in practice.

9.2.12 Show that the Runge-Kutta formulas in Equations 9.2.14 and 9.2.15 and Problem 9.2.9 are extensions of Simpson's rule in the sense that if f(x, y) does not depend on y, then y_{k+1} is computed from

$$y_k + \int_{x_k}^{x_{k+1}} f(x)dx$$

with the integral estimated by Simpson's rule.

9.2.13 Carry out the calculations of one step of the Runge-Kutta method of Equation 9.2.15 for the following equations. Use a hand calculator and h = .2.

(A) $y' = 2 - 3xy \qquad y(0) = 0$

(B) $y' = (1+x+y^2) \qquad y(0) = 1$

(C) $y' = x+2y \qquad y(0) = 1$

9.2.14 Consider multistep methods exact for quadratics that use information at x_k, x_{k-1}. Assume that $b_{-1} = 0$ and write down the equations that the parameters must satisfy. How many degrees of freedom are there in the set of parameters that satisfy these equations? Give an example method that is simple.

9.2.15 Consider the equation

$$y(x_{k+1}) = y(x_{k-p}) + \int_{x_{k-p}}^{x_{k+1}} f(x, y(x))dx$$

Explain how to derive a class of methods from this equation by applying numerical integration to the integral.

(A) Show that using closed Newton Cotes integration rules (Table 7.1) leads to implicit methods. Give the specific integration method of this class with local truncation error in the differential equation of order h^4.

(B) Show that using open Newton Cotes integration rules (Table 7.1) leads to explicit methods. Give the specific integration method of this class with local error in the differential equation of order h^4.

9.2.16 Show that the predictor-corrector formulas (**Milne's method**)

$$y_{k+1}^{(0)} = y_k + \frac{4h}{3}(2y'_k - y'_{k-1} + 2y'_{k-2})$$

$$y_{k+1}^{(j)} = y_{k-1} + \frac{h}{3}(y'^{(j-1)}_{k+1} + 4y'_k + y'_{k-1})$$

have local error $O(h^4)$. Experimentally establish that one iteration of the corrector is sufficient in most cases. **Hint:** Take several choices for f(x, y) and for x; then apply the predictor-corrector procedure for h = .1, .01, and .001 until it converges. Compare the accuracy obtained in the first iteration with that of the final iteration y^*_{k+1}; use the value $|y_{k+1}^{(0)} - y^*_{k+1}|$ to estimate the difference between $y(x_{k+1})$ and y^*_{k+1}. A simple computer program with loops can do this experiment; use exact values for the y_{k-j}, y'_{k-j} for $j \geq 0$.

9.2.17 Show that the following predictor-corrector formulas **(Hamming's method)** have local error $O(h^5)$:

$$y_{k+1}^{(0)} = y_{k-3} + \frac{4h}{3}(2f_k - f_{k-1} + 2f_{k-2})$$

$$y_{k+1}^{(1)} = y_{k+1}^{(0)} + \frac{112}{121}(y_k - y_k^{(0)})$$

$$y_{k+1}^{(j)} = \frac{1}{8}(9y_k - y_{k-2}) + \frac{3h}{8}(y'^{(j-1)}_{k+1} + 2y'_k - y'_{k-1}) \qquad j = 2, 3, \ldots$$

The middle formula is a **modifier** which improves the value of the initial guess for the corrector.

(A) Carry out the experiment of Problem 9.2.16 without using the modifier in this method.

(B) Repeat the experiment using the modifier and discuss the improvement it makes. Note that using the modifier requires the predictor-corrector to be applied for y_k as well as for y_{k+1}.

9.2.18 Show that the following predictor-corrector pair (the **midpoint** rule plus the **trapezoid rule**) has local error $O(h^3)$.

$$y_{k+1}^{(0)} = y_{k-1} + 2hy'_k$$

$$y_{k+1}^{(j)} = y_k + \frac{h}{2}[y'^{(j-1)}_{k+1} + y'_k] \qquad j = 1, 2, \ldots$$

Repeat the experiment of Problem 9.2.16 to estimate the number of corrector iterations needed.

9.2.19 Repeat the experiment of Example 9.1 to obtain a **comparison of third-order methods.** Replace Euler's method by the third-order Adams-Bashforth method and use the third-order Taylor's series method and the third-order Runge-Kutta method of Equation 9.2.14. Use exact values of the solution to start the Adams-Bashforth method. Note that $-1/x$ approximates the true solution of 9.2.13 near $x = 1$ with very high accuracy. Discuss the effectiveness of these methods.

9.2.20 Repeat Problem 9.2.19 replacing the explicit Adams-Bashforth method with a predictor-corrector pair of third-order Adams methods.

POLYALGORITHMS FOR DIFFERENTIAL EQUATIONS — 9.3

Creating an efficient, reliable program for solving ordinary differential equations requires much more than just choosing one of the better formulas from the previous section and "coding it up." A good program needs several components integrated together carefully as a polyalgorithm.

The main components of a differential equation program are listed below.

1. *Initialization:* Determination of initial step size and starting multistep methods.
2. *Step size control:* Determination of the step size so as to control the local error, changing step size for multistep methods.
3. *Order of method control:* Selection and change of the order of the particular method to be used from a family of methods.
4. *Output:* Calculation of solution values at a specified set of points rather than wherever the program happens to compute values.
5. *Global error control:* Estimation of the cumulative effect of the local errors and control of the computation so as to keep the global error within some specified tolerance.
6. *Checking:* Each program is based on a model for the problems it is to solve; a good program performs various checks to see if the input and problem are consistent with this model.

One of the principal accomplishments of the 1970s in numerical computation was the development of reliable and efficient programs for solving differential equations. We do not have the space to discuss these components thoroughly or to analyze how they are put together; we briefly discuss the principal features of these software components.

Initialization — 9.3.A

The one-step methods have no computational difficulty with the first step except choosing its size. The next topic is step size control, and much of that is applicable here. However, step size control methods usually involve comparing current "results" (for example, local error estimates) with previous ones. Since there are no previous results for the first step, more care must be taken. The danger is that once too large a step is chosen, a large initial error is created which ruins the accuracy of the whole computation. Thus, most strategies are very conservative and start with a step size somewhat smaller than believed to be actually required. If it is too small (and thereby wastes effort by computing a solution more accurately than needed), then the step size control method should increase it quickly.

Many differential equations programs ask the user to supply an initial step size. Most users, even experienced ones, usually have no idea what the best step size should be, and thus a program that depends entirely on the user for this crucial information is not reliable. Some programs allow the user to "suggest" an initial step size, but they only use this as a starting point for their own determination. This approach is quite reasonable; when one is solving a batch of similar differential equations, a good initial step size can be determined for the first few and then the remaining runs can start with this value.

The **multistep methods** have the additional difficulty that they must have previous values at each step. The most common approach is to use a one-step method (usually Runge-Kutta) for the first few steps and then switch to the multistep method. A second approach is to have a family of multistep methods of different orders which includes a one-step method (normally the Euler method). The calculation is started with one step of a one-step method, then switches to use a two-step method for one step. The number of steps in the method is increased by one each step until the desired number is reached. Once the calculation gets started, the general scheme for controlling step size and method order selection is used.

The basic tactic in determining the step size is to make the step twice (or perhaps more) with different methods and then to compare the results. If these independently computed results agree sufficiently well, then the step size is accepted. This tactic is discussed in the next section.

Step Size Control 9.3.B

The problem is to estimate the *local error.* Most programs, even the very best, only attempt to keep this error within a specified tolerance. See Section 9.3.E for a discussion of controlling the global or overall error. In most numerical computations one cannot accurately estimate the error without solving the problem twice or more accurately than desired. For example, we may compute y_{k+1} from formula #1 which has local error $O(h^4)$ and z_{k+1} from formula #2 which has local error $O(h^5)$. Unless h is completely off, z_{k+1} is a much better estimate of $y(x_{k+1})$ than y_{k+1} is. Thus, $|y_{k+1} - z_{k+1}|$ is a reasonable estimate of the error in y_{k+1}. *This gives no information about the error in* z_{k+1} (we do expect it to be smaller). A program may choose to use $|y_{k+1} - z_{k+1}|$ as the basic quantity to control the error and still use z_{k+1} for its calculations. The idea is that even though the error in z_{k+1} is not known, it is known to be smaller than the error in y_{k+1}.

The Runge-Kutta-Fehlberg, or RKF, methods (Equation 9.2.16) are specifically designed to provide error estimates efficiently; all the quantities needed for computing y_{k+1} are also needed for z_{k+1}. Problem 9.2.11 gives a Runge-Kutta method of order five which also produces an estimate of order three. The elementary predictor-corrector pair 9.2.22 (trapezoidal plus Euler methods) has a similar property. The local error in the predictor $y_{k+1}^{(0)}$ is $O(h)$ and in the corrector y_{k+1} is $O(h^2)$, so that their difference is a good estimate of the error in $y_{(k+1)}^{(0)}$. In practice, one does not use such a low-order predictor-corrector pair very often.

The local error estimate is compared with a requested tolerance; most sophisticated programs use two tolerances:

TOLABS = absolute value tolerance
TOLREL = relative error tolerance

If $y(x)$ is the true solution, then the user may hope that the global (discretization) error satisfies

$$|y_{k+1} - y(x_{k+1})| \le \text{TOLABS} + \text{TOLREL}*|y(x_{k+1})| \qquad \textbf{Equation 9.3.1}$$

However, most programs attempt to control the local **error per step:**

$$|y_{k+1} - z(x_{k+1})| \le \text{TOLABS} + \text{TOLREL}*|z(x_{k+1})| \qquad \textbf{Equation 9.3.2}$$

where $z(x_{k+1})$ is the true solution for the initial conditions at (x_k, y_k) and not $y(x_{k+1})$. This is a **local error control.**

An approach to gain partial global error control as in 9.3.1 is to spread the user request over the interval [A, B] of integration. Set H = B − A and then replace TOLABS and TOLREL in 9.3.2 by TOLABS*h/H and TOLREL*h/H. This is called the **error per unit step** criterion, and it does correspond better to most user's idea of error. Even so, this does not provide true global error control because of the "spreading of solutions" that can occur as one moves from trajectory to trajectory during the computation.

An alternative approach to estimating the local error is to use formulas of the same order whose error coefficients are known. We have not paid much attention to the exact form of the local error terms because they involve unknown quantities and hence are not very useful, by themselves, for estimating errors. However, used in pairs they can be useful, and it is then necessary to obtain exact expressions for these error terms. For example, **the local errors in Milne's method** (see Problem 9.2.16) are $-14h^5y^{(5)}(\xi_1)/45$ and $h^5y^{(5)}(\xi_2)/90$ for the predictor and corrector, respectively (here $y^{(5)}$ is the fifth derivative; ξ_1 and ξ_2 are unknown mean value points). The values of the fifth derivatives are unknown, but it is reasonable to assume they are about the same; call the value K. Then the difference between the predicted value $y_{k+1}^{(0)}$ and corrected value y_{k+1} is

$$|y_{k+1}^{(0)} - y_{k+1}| = \frac{1}{90}h^5K + \frac{14}{45}h^5K$$

This implies that

$$h^5K = \frac{90}{29}|y_{k+1}^{(0)} - y_{k+1}| \qquad \textbf{Equation 9.3.3}$$

and the local error in y_{k+1} is estimated by

$$\frac{1}{90}h^5K = |y_{k+1}^{(0)} - y_{k+1}|/29 \qquad \textbf{Equation 9.3.4}$$

This value should be used with some caution to prevent the assumption about the fifth derivative from causing trouble. A very conservative approach would be to take the error estimate as $|y_{k+1}^{(0)} - y_{k+1}|/3$, adding a factor of 10 in the error estimate to compensate for uncertainties. On the other hand, a program might use 9.3.4 and introduce its caution elsewhere. For example, if asked to keep the local error less than 10^{-3}, it might internally use $10^{-3}/4$ as the error tolerance.

The error terms for the Adams-Bashford and Adams-Moulton methods are listed in Table 9.3.

Local Error Terms for Adams Methods **Table 9.3**

The derivatives of the solution y(x) are evaluated at an unknown mean value point.

Order	Adams-Bashford	Adams-Moulton
1	$\frac{1}{2}h^2y''$	$-\frac{1}{2}h^2y''$
2	$\frac{5}{12}h^3y'''$	$-\frac{1}{12}h^3y'''$
3	$\frac{3}{8}h^4y^{(4)}$	$-\frac{1}{24}h^4y^{(4)}$
4	$\frac{251}{720}h^5y^{(5)}$	$-\frac{19}{720}h^5y^{(5)}$
5	$\frac{95}{288}h^6y^{(6)}$	$-\frac{3}{160}h^6y^{(6)}$

Suppose now that one has a reliable method to estimate the local error at a given step. If the error is much smaller than desired, then h should be increased; if the error is too large, then h should be decreased. One might calculate an estimate of how much to change h; if the local error is $O(h^5)$, then doubling or halving h changes the error by a factor of about 32. This approach is reasonable for a one-step method such as a fourth-order Runge-Kutta formula. If the error seems too small (or large) by a factor of 10, then h can be changed by a factor of $1.58 = \sqrt[5]{10}$. This causes no problems in the calculation and keeps accuracy and efficiency somewhat balanced.

The situation is different for a multistep method. The axis in Figure 9.4 shows the x_i points during the solution of a differential equation. Suppose a three-step method (using 3 previous values to obtain y_{k+1}) is used and the step h at x_k needs to be changed. If h is changed arbitrarily, then the situation is the same as at the initial point. If h is doubled, then all the information is at hand (if it has been saved) for the new larger step size. If h is halved, then some of the required values are available. The missing intermediate values can be obtained by polynomial interpolation; the degree of the polynomial must be the same order as the method in order to preserve the accuracy. In Figure 9.4 one interpolates at x_k, $x_k - h$, $x_k - 2h$, and $x_k - 3h$ to obtain a cubic polynomial to evaluate at $x_k - h/2$. Then the values at x_k, $x_k - h/2$, and $x_k - h$ can be used to continue the computation.

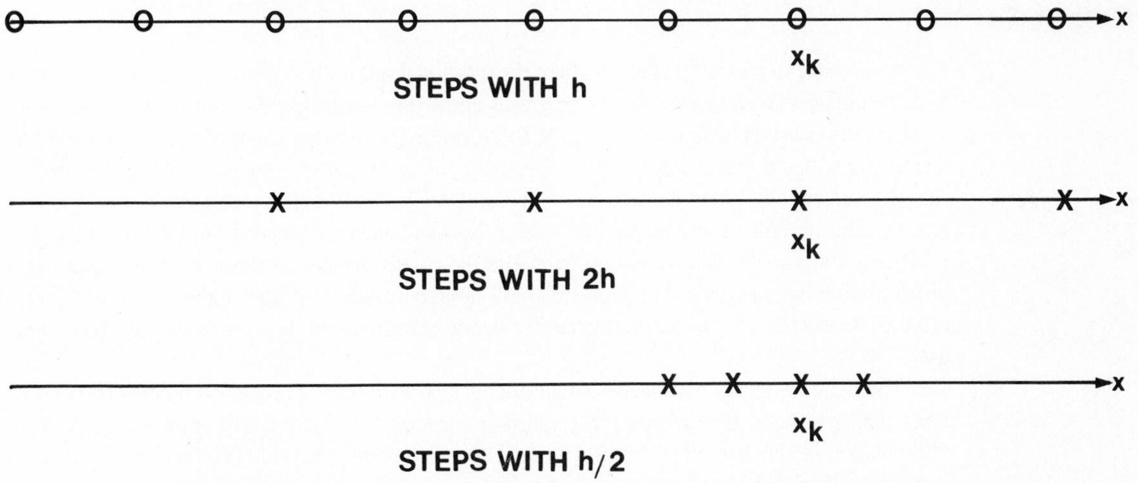

Figure 9.4 **Step size change in multistep methods.** The step size can be doubled or halved without much difficulty.

Some multistep programs actually allow unequally spaced steps. The advantage of a constant h is that the formulas are known in advance. If one is willing to derive them as needed, then arbitrary steps can be made just like for a one-step method. Deriving the formulas as needed essentially means making explicit interpolation of the past values and integrating the resulting polynomials. This causes some increase in the overhead of a method; this can be reduced by having the program biased toward using equal steps, thus gaining efficiency when things are going routinely and still retaining flexibility when changes in the step are necessary.

Most programs use additional rules to avoid changing the step size too much or too often. Typical are rules like:

Do not increase h by more than a factor of 2.

Do not increase h more than once every 5 *steps.*

Order of Method Control 9.3.C

The use of a whole range of Adams methods is not too difficult because there are formulas to generate all these methods. One does not have to store large tables of coefficients. The advantage of a higher-order formula is that, for the smooth parts of y(x), one can take very large steps within given error specifications. Using a range of methods also allows one to avoid special methods for initializing the computation.

The basic idea of a variable order method is to make a projection of the local error at each time step using the current order and using one more and one less in order. One then uses the choice that gives the smaller error. An essential feature of this approach is that there are ways to compute the three error estimates with little more work than is required for one alone. These methods are too complex to present in detail here, but they have been found efficient and reliable in practice. Note that there is an interaction between changing step size and changing order. One might really want to know, for example, if it is better to increase the order and the step size simultaneously. The better software includes tests for this interaction. The interaction between changing step size and order is not simple, and changes must be made "slowly" in order to avoid introducing instabilities into the calculation. For smooth problems and relatively high accuracy requirements, it has been observed that the order of the method will go up to 10 or 12 if the program allows that.

Most physical models are not very accurate, and so only low accuracy is required for solving differential equations involving them. However, the calculations for motion of satellites, the moon, etc., may be made with 10 or 12 decimal digits of accuracy required. These problems are relatively infrequent, but their computational requirements are very high compared with "run-of-the-mill" problems, and they receive a lot of attention.

Output Control 9.3.D

It is not possible to predict the points where the solution is naturally computed by a complex polyalgorithm to solve differential equations. Many programs allow the user to specify a set of points where computed values of $y(x)$ are to be given. This is useful, for example, if one wants a plot of the solution and one is using a plotting routine that requires evenly spaced data points. Or perhaps the accuracy requirement is high so that the numerical solution consists of many hundreds or thousands of data points; yet a good plot might require values at only a hundred points. Given a thousand unequally spaced data points, it takes some effort to obtain 100 equally spaced points from the data with accurate values. It seems plausible that the differential equation solver can produce these desired values as it goes more efficiently than one can produce them after the calculation; even if it is not more efficient, it is a worthwhile convenience to the user.

There are two basic approaches to producing solution values at specified points. The first is to force these points to be in the set where the solution is computed anyway. The second is to perform a local interpolation of the computed solution as each specified point is passed. The first approach is feasible for one-step methods; one just takes a shorter step as each specified point is about to be passed. The only danger is that this might cause an extraordinarily small step which later creates problems for the automatic step size selection. The program writer has to be sure that this does not happen. The second approach is more natural for software using multistep methods, as it must contain interpolation formulas in order to change step size.

It is a mistake to think that there is no difficulty in implementing either of these two approaches. The process of obtaining output is intertwined with the rest of the polyalgorithm control, and there are examples of programs where simply asking for output at a modest number of points can dramatically increase the computing effort. The following experiment on this effect was reported in 1976 by L. Shampine, H. Watts, and S. Davenport (see the reference at end of this chapter). The differential equations for a three-body problem (for example, the motion of a system of three bodies such as the earth, the moon, and the sun) were solved with specified accuracy of 10^{-8}. Runs were made for five well-known programs which requested output at 1, 10, 100, 1,000, and 10,000 equally spaced points. The number of evaluations of $f(x, y)$ in the equation $y' = f(x, y)$ is a rough measure of the work each program performs. The effect of the output requests on this number is given in Table 9.4.

We see from Table 9.4 that only EXTRAP is significantly affected for a moderate number of output points. All the programs become affected when output is requested at many more points than the method naturally requires to solve the differential equation. It should be noted that programs for solving differential equations often can be used in one of two different modes: one can use them to take one step or to integrate over an interval (short or long). Some programs allow the user to select which mode is used, and this choice affects the way output requests affect the computations. One can usually find a way to use a step-oriented program so that the impact of output requests is minimal. All the programs in Table 9.4 were used in the "integrate over an interval" mode.

Table 9.4 also shows that there can be substantial differences among programs in the work required to solve a differential equation. All the programs in Table 9.4 are considered to be of high efficiency for the type of method implemented. Perhaps the most significant point is that the fourth-order method is much less efficient on this problem because of the high accuracy requirement and smoothness of the solution.

Effect of Output Requests on the Work of Solving Differential Equations **Table 9.4**

Some of the five programs are discussed further in the next section. They are:
DE = multistep Adams method, variable order, and variable step
DVDQ = multistep Adams method, variable order, and variable step
RKF45 = fifth-order Runge-Kutta-Fehlberg
RKF4 = fourth-order Runge-Kutta-Fehlberg
EXTRAP = one-step extrapolation method (see DREBS in Section 9.5.B)
K = number of equally spaced output points specified
Table entries are the number of times f(x, y) is evaluated in the solution

	K = 1	10	100	1,000	10,000
DE	1,146	1,146	1,146	1,164	2,610
DVDQ	1,581	1,577	1,580	1,916	7,298
RKF45	2,372	2,379	2,565	7,204	60,335
RKF4	10,119	10,134	10,377	18,246	110,736
EXTRAP	3,768	4,121	6,687	36,555	Failed

Global Error Control 9.3.E

There are no programs available which truly control the global error. To appreciate the difficulty, visualize a differential equation $y' = f(x, y)$ which has two special points x_1 and x_2. At x_1 the differential equation becomes somewhat unstable and the trajectories rapidly separate for awhile. At x_2 the opposite occurs and the trajectories all come together and stay that way for awhile. Now consider a numerical integration which has the global error under control, and it arrives at the point x_1. The computed solution is not exactly on the true solution trajectory, so that a large error starts to occur after x_1 just because the trajectories separate. This would occur even if the differential equation were solved exactly after x_1 is reached. The only way to maintain the global error requirement is to go back to the initial point and restart the computation with better accuracy.

A practical program would not restart itself every time it found a global error too large, because that might mean dozens of reintegrations over part of the interval. It would instead go to the end of the integration interval and then estimate the accuracy required along the way before restarting the calculation. With luck, one or two iterations of this procedure would produce the desired global accuracy.

The behavior at x_2 has just the opposite effect; one discovers that the accuracy is suddenly much better than required. One would hardly redo a calculation just to get worse answers, but, philosophically, getting too much accuracy is just as bad as getting too little.

This analysis explains why there are no widely available programs that control the global error; people have not wanted to bother constructing programs that iteratively resolve the problem, and some people believe it is unwise to have a calculation with such a large uncertainty in the potential computing cost. However, there is no essential difficulty in creating a program that controls global error *provided one can estimate it reliably.*

This brings us to the central question: **How do you estimate the global error?** We first note that the idea of control of error per unit step presented in Section 9.3.B does not actually control the global error even though it is a valid attempt to govern the local error on a global basis. The basic approach to estimating the global error in solving differential equations is the same as in other numerical methods; one solves the problem more than once and then compares the results. Knowledge of the error terms can be used to make quantitative estimates just as they were made in Equation 9.3.3 for the local error. Unfortunately, the uncertainty is much greater in global error estimation because the mean value points in the error terms can be anywhere in a large interval, thus making it much less likely that terms like $y^{(4)}(\xi_1)$ and $y^{(4)}(\xi_2)$ are nearly the same.

The simplest approach is to solve the equation twice with the same program using different error tolerances. The pitfall here is that changing the tolerances may have an unpredictable effect — even no effect at all — on the computation. Examine Figure 7.6, where the work of the numerical integration of a function by DCADRE is shown. In each of the three cases there is an instance where cutting the accuracy request by a factor of 100 makes no difference in the calculation. Similar situations have been observed in solving differential equations. Thus, caution must be used in this approach, and one must convince oneself that changes in the requested accuracy tolerances are affecting the computation in a smooth, predictable way.

A better approach is to have a program that is specifically designed to obtain global error estimates. This can be done best by having the equation solved in parallel by two methods. This approach is still relatively new, but the indications are that global error estimation can be done much more reliably this way than by reusing an ordinary program. This approach is implemented in the program GERK (ACM Algorithm 504).

Checking 9.3.F

There are various kinds of checking that a program should do. These checks are worthwhile even for a program with limited use (one can waste a lot of time in discovering that a trivial input error has occurred), and they are essential for software which is expected to have extensive use. The first kind of checking is for obvious blunders in the input, for example:

Is the requested accuracy positive?

Is the length of the interval of integration zero?

Is the number of equations positive?

Are the dimensions of arrays passed compatible with the number of equations specified?

Programs for solving ordinary differential equations tend to have lengthy argument lists, and the program should do as much checking as possible for blunders such as those above.

The second kind of checking is for reasonableness of the problem presented. These checks may well be machine-, environment-, or user-dependent, for example:

Is the relative accuracy request compatible with the precision of the computer?

Is the initial step significant? An initial step of 10^{-10} at $x = 1.0$ is erroneous on a short word length (32-bit) machine because $1.0 + 10^{-7} = 1.0$ on such a machine.

Is the amount of output requested reasonable? A library program may well force a user who wants a million values of output to do something special.

The third kind of checking relates to the model of the differential equation the program has. The discussion so far in this chapter has assumed a well-behaved problem; a program designed to handle only this class of problems should make various checks during the calculation about the validity of the model. Examples of such checks are:

Has the step size decreased suddenly to almost nothing? This could occur at a singularity or from an error in defining $f(x, y)$.

Is reasonable progress being made toward solving the problem? If 10,000 steps have been made and less than 1 percent of the integration interval has been covered, then it is very likely that something is wrong.

Has the calculation become unstable?

Have certain numbers or matrices become zero or singular? A relative error request is impossible for a solution that becomes zero at some point in the interval of integration. Some methods for systems of differential equations require solving a system of linear equations; its coefficient matrix must be nonsingular.

These examples illustrate the kinds and extent of checks that can be expected in good-quality software. In writing such software, one should assume that the user is not completely sure of how the code works or the exact definition of the input arguments. Even the author of a program can be in this position six months or a year after the code is finished. All the checking done will be greatly appreciated by users. It costs very little in programming effort or execution time compared with the benefits obtained.

PROBLEMS 9.3

9.3.1 Consider the predictor-corrector method of Problem 9.3.16, Milne's method.

(A) What is the appropriate order of a Runge-Kutta method to initialize this method?

(B) Assume the correct initial step size is known. Outline an algorithm to initialize this method; give specific formulas and details.

9.3.2 Repeat Problem 9.3.1 for Hamming's method, Problem 9.2.17.

9.3.3 Repeat Problem 9.3.1 for the method in Problem 9.2.18.

9.3.4 Discuss the suitability of the Taylor's series method to initialize a predictor-corrector calculation. Assume that one is writing a general-purpose library routine for differential equations. Specifically,

(A) Describe any additional user input that might be needed.

(B) Outline the specific algorithm (assume that 3 previous points are needed for the predictor-corrector method).

(C) List the advantages and disadvantages that the Taylor's series method has compared to a Runge-Kutta method for doing this initialization.

9.3.5 Give a specific algorithm to determine the initial step size for a second-order Runge-Kutta method. Assume that a guess H1 of the step size h is given and that the algorithm corrects it so that the local error of the first step is no more than TOLABS. **Hint:** Select a specific second-order Runge-Kutta formula from 9.2.10, then use a different one for comparison to estimate the error of the first step.

9.3.6 Apply the algorithm in Problem 9.3.5 to the specific cases

(A) $y' = x + y$, $y(0) = 1$, $H1 = 0.1$, and $TOLABS = 10^{-6}$

(B) $y' = y^2$, $y(0) = 1$, $H1 = 0.01$, and $TOLABS = 10^{-6}$

(C) $y' = -y + xy$, $y(0) = 1$, $H1 = 10^{-4}$, and $TOLABS = 10^{-4}$

9.3.7 (A) Write a program that implements Milne's method (see Problem 9.2.16) that uses Equation 9.3.3 to control the step size so that 9.3.2 is satisfied.

(B) Consider the equation $y' = -y$ with $y(0) = 1$ and run the program for the following values in 9.3.2: (TOLABS, TOLREL) = (.05, .05), (.01, .01), (.0001, .0001). Record how many steps are needed to reach $x = 2.0$ and compare the error in the computed solutions with the true solution $y(x) = e^{-x}$ (stop at the first point beyond 2.0).

(C) Estimate the order p of the error $= O(h^p)$ at $x = 2.0$ as h goes to zero.

(D) Combine the error per step criterion in 9.3.2 with the count of the number of steps to estimate the error at $x = 2.0$. Discuss how this error compares with the observed error.

9.3.8 Repeat Problem 9.3.7 for the differential equations

(A) $y' = y$, $y(0) = 1$

(B) $y' = \cos(\pi x)$, $y(0) = 0$

(C) $y' = \dfrac{-y}{x+1}$, $y(0) = 1$

Hint: The true solutions to these equations are e^x, $\sin(x)/\pi$, and $1/(1+x)$, respectively.

9.3.9 Derive a local error estimation formula analogous to 9.3.4 for the Adams predictor-corrector method of order 2. **Hint:** Use Table 9.3 for error terms.

9.3.10 Derive a local error estimation formula for the predictor-corrector method of Equation 9.2.22. **Hint:** Use the corrector value as the "true" solution to estimate the error in the predicted value.

SYSTEMS OF DIFFERENTIAL EQUATIONS 9.4

The simplicity of extending methods of systems of equations is illustrated by Euler's method. For one equation $y' = f(x, y)$ it is (see 9.3.2)

$$y_{k+1} = y_k + hf_k$$

The vector equation

$$\mathbf{y}' = \mathbf{f}(x, \mathbf{y}) \qquad \textbf{Equation 9.4.1}$$

means

$$y'_i = f_i(x; y_1, y_2, \ldots, y_n) \qquad i = 1, 2, \ldots, n$$

Euler's method in vector form for 9.4.1 is

$$\mathbf{y}_{k+1} = \mathbf{y}_k + h\mathbf{f}_k \qquad \textbf{Equation 9.4.2}$$

If we let $y_{i,k}$ denote the estimate of $y_i(x)$ at x_k, then 9.4.2 in component form appears as

$$y_{i,k+1} = y_{i,k} + hf_i(x_k; y_{1,k}, y_{2,k}, \ldots, y_{n,k})$$

A similar extension occurs for Runge-Kutta and predictor-corrector formulas. The two forms of the simple Runge-Kutta method 9.2.7 are

$$s_1 = hf(x_k, y_k)$$
$$s_2 = hf(x_k+h, y_k+s_1) \quad \text{for one equation}$$
$$y_{k+1} = y_k + \frac{1}{2}(s_1+s_2)$$

Equation 9.4.3

$$\mathbf{s}_1 = \mathbf{h}\mathbf{f}(x_k, \mathbf{y}_k)$$
$$\mathbf{s}_2 = \mathbf{h}\mathbf{f}(x_k+h, \mathbf{y}_k+\mathbf{s}_1) \quad \text{for a system of equations}$$
$$\mathbf{y}_{k+1} = \mathbf{y}_k + \frac{1}{2}(\mathbf{s}_1+\mathbf{s}_2)$$

The simple predictor-corrector method 9.2.22 in both forms is

Equation 9.4.4

$$y_{k+1}^{(0)} = y_k + hf(x_k, y_k)$$
$$y_{k+1}^{(j)} = y_k + \frac{h}{2}[f(x_k, y_k) + f(x_{k+1}, y_{k+1}^{(j-1)})] \quad j = 1, 2, \ldots$$
$$\mathbf{y}_{k+1}^{(0)} = \mathbf{y}_k + \mathbf{h}\mathbf{f}(x_k, \mathbf{y}_k)$$
$$\mathbf{y}_{k+1}^{(j)} = \mathbf{y}_k + \frac{h}{2}[\mathbf{f}(x_k, \mathbf{y}_k) + \mathbf{f}(x_{k+1}, \mathbf{y}_{k+1}^{(j-1)})] \quad j = 1, 2, \ldots$$

The Taylor's series method has a similar extension once one interprets f_x, f_{xx}, etc., to expand all the derivatives of $f(x, y)$ with respect to the subscripted variables. The number of terms grows like n^{p+1} for a pth-order Taylor's series method and a system of n equations. Since $n = 10$ or 100 is not uncommon, this limits the application of this method for systems.

We see that extending the basic formulas to systems of equations essentially means replacing certain scalar items by vectors. What then are the new difficulties with systems of equations? The most obvious is that the amount of calculation to make a step increases sharply with n. If one is evaluating n functions of n variables with $\mathbf{f}(x, \mathbf{y})$, the work might be expected to be n^2 times as much as a single function of a single variable. Similarly, there is an $O(n^2)$ increase in the storage requirements for most methods.

A more important difficulty is the possibility that there are completely different behaviors among the equations and solutions of the system. A frequent class of such systems are **stiff** problems; these are also discussed in Section 9.5.D. If all the equations and solutions behave more or less the same, then it is true that about the only difference between 1 equation and 100 equations is the amount of computation. We give two examples in which disparate behaviors (stiff problems) arise:

1. *Moon rocket.* The variables of position vary relatively slowly with time over a great interval: 0 to 400,000 kilometers. The variables of angular motion about the center of gravity (rotations and oscillations) vary rapidly over a small interval. A step size appropriate for the position calculation gives no accuracy for the rotations; a step size to accurately compute the oscillation leads to a gigantic waste of computation for the position. A tolerance of 1 might be very good for the position error; it is useless for the angles of rotation.

2. *Refinery control.* Refinery operation involves high-speed chemical reactions and slow variations of temperatures and pressures as huge volumes of fluids are heated and moved. The time constant might be a hundredth of a second for one chemical reaction and five minutes for another. It might take hours to raise the temperature in a cracking tower by 10 degrees. There are dozens of chemicals involved and several large pieces of equipment and interconnections, so that a system of dozens or hundreds of differential equations is to be expected with extremely widely varying behaviors among the solutions.

When a system gets large and complicated, it is common to break it down into groups of equations with "similar" behaviors. These groups are then solved by standard software, and the interconnections between groups are analyzed and handled on an individual basis. Fortunately, the interconnections tend to be small in number for most applications. This approach is especially important when some of the equations tend to be unstable or otherwise difficult and thus require special methods as well as carefully controlled step sizes, etc.

Another aspect that arises which we have not yet considered is that the simple fixed point iteration method for solving the corrector equations does not work in more difficult problems. Then the Newton or secant method is usually used. This means that a linear system of n equations must be solved several times for each integration step. This can become very expensive as n increases and the number of steps becomes large.

SOFTWARE FOR DIFFERENTIAL EQUATIONS 9.5

Differential equation software is inherently more complicated than most software discussed in this book. This is because the differential equation problem is itself complicated. We have limited the discussion to well-behaved cases of the initial value problem, and even so, many topics and methods have been brought up. The generally available software is divided into three groups: The ACM Algorithms, the IMSL library, and other widely used programs. There is overlap in these groups; some basic programs have been modified, improved, and polished over the years so that somewhat similar versions exist (usually with different names), and it is difficult to say which is the best or who is primarily responsible.

The ACM Algorithms and Other Programs 9.5.A

There are only nine ACM Algorithms for differential equations, a remarkably low number considering the importance of this problem. One of these, Algorithm 9, is a simple recording of Runge-Kutta formulas; two others, Algorithms 194 and 461, are for specialized problems; and a fourth, Algorithm 497, is for **functional differential equations**, that is, problems of the form

$$y'(x) = f(x, y, y(L(x, y)))$$

where $L(x, y)$ is a linear functional. Examples for the functional are: $\int_0^x y(t)g(t)dt$, $x/2$, and $x-1$. We do not discuss these problems further. Algorithm 218 is Runge-Kutta program in Algol with step- size control. Improved Runge-Kutta programs have appeared since this one.

Algorithm 407, DIFSUB, is the first ACM algorithm that is a useful, production-oriented program for differential equations. It has several descendents, the best known of which are GEAR (named for the creator of DIFSUB) and EPISODE, discussed below.

Algorithm 504, GERK, is the first realistic attempt to estimate the global error reliably during the solution of a differential equation (see the discussion of Section 9.3.E). This program is quite reliable, efficient, and suitable for general use; the cost for obtaining the global error estimate is a 20 to 50 percent increase in execution time. This is a very reasonable cost, especially when compared with the common and less reliable technique of making a second run with a different accuracy request. GERK uses a Runge-Kutta-Fehlberg method similar to that used in RKF45 discussed below.

Algorithm 534, STINT, is a complicated variable-order, variable-step, multistep method designed for **stiff problems**. A stiff differential equation has rapidly decaying solutions; they are quite important in applications and difficult to solve.

There are four other programs besides those in the IMSL library that are widely used for well-behaved, general initial value problems. They are briefly described in alphabetical order:

DE/STEP These are two versions of the same program, a variable-step, variable-order Adams method. They are portable and very well documented in the book *Computer Solution of Ordinary Differential Equations: The Initial Value Problem* by L. F. Shampine and M. K. Gordon, W. H. Freeman and Company, San Francisco (1975). The programs are also available from the National Energy Software Center, Argonne National Laboratory, Argonne, Illinois 60439 for a nominal handling charge.

DEPAC This package includes three methods: Runge-Kutta (DERKF — a descendant of RKF45 described later); variable-step, variable-order Adams (DEABM — a descendent of DIFSUB, ACM Algorithm 407); and backward differentiation formulas (DEBDF — method not discussed in this book) for stiff problems. The user interface is carefully designed and oriented toward reasonably sophisticated users with relatively difficult problems. The programs are thoroughly tested, portable, and self-documented. The design philosophy is presented in *DEPAC — Design of a User-Oriented Package of ODE Solvers* by L. F. Shampine and H. A. Watts, Sandia Laboratories Report No. DAND 79-2374 (1980). The programs are available from National Energy Software Center, Argonne National Laboratory, Argonne, Illinois 60439 for a nominal handling charge.

EPISODE This is also a variable-step, variable-order Adams method. It is descended from Algorithm 407, DIFSUB. It has two distinct methods, one for nonstiff equations and one for stiff equations. The program is described in detail in the journal article *A Polyalgorithm for the Numerical Solution of Ordinary Differential Equations* by G. D. Byrne and A. Hindmarsh, ACM Trans. Math. Software, 1 (1975), pp. 71-96. See also the article *A Comparison of Two ODE Codes: GEAR and EPISODE,* Computers and Chemical Engineering, 1 (1977), pp. 133-147. The program is available from the National Energy Software Center, Argonne National Laboratory, Argonne, Illinois 60439 for a nominal charge.

RKF45 This is a Runge-Kutta-Fehlberg method using orders 4 and 5. The program was developed by L. F. Shampine and H. Watts and is described in detail in Chapter 6 of the book *Computer Methods for Mathematical Computations* by G. Forsythe, M. Malcolm, and C. Moler, Prentice-Hall, Inc., Englewood Cliffs, N.J. (1977).

IMSL Software for Initial Value Problems 9.5.B

The IMSL library has three programs for initial value problems in differential equations:

DVERK A Runge-Kutta method of orders 5 and 6; the program is adapted from one of T. Hull, W. Enright, and K. Jackson based on formulas developed by T. Verner. It is probably the best choice when accuracy requirements are moderate, say 10^{-4} relative error or less.

DGEAR A variable-step, variable-order Adams method. This is an adaption of the program GEAR by A. Hindmarsh which, in turn, is a descendant of Algorithm 407, DIFSUB. It is also related to EPISODE mentioned earlier. It has the capability of handling stiff differential equations (see Section 9.5.D); it is the best choice for these problems or problems with moderate accuracy requirements and with $f(x, y)$ expensive to evaluate.

DREBS An extrapolation method based on the program DESUB by N. Clark and P. Fox which, in turn, is descended from the Bulirsch-Stoer Algol procedure DESUB. The program EXTRAP shown in Table 9.3 is closely related to DREBS. The method used in this program is not presented in this book.

To illustrate the complexity of typical differential equation software, we discuss these three IMSL programs for a system of n differential equations:

$$\mathbf{y}' = \mathbf{f}(x, \mathbf{y}) \qquad \mathbf{y}(A) = \mathbf{v}$$ **Equation 9.5.1**

The subroutine calls used are

```
CALL DVERK( N,F,XSTART,Y,XEND,TOL,KONTRL,CONTRL,NROWW,WORK,IER )
CALL DGEAR( N,F,SUBJAC,XSTART,H,Y,XEND,TOL,ISTIFF,KONTRL,MODE,IWORK,WORK,IER )
CALL DREBS( F,Y,XSTART,N,MAXORD,KONTRL,MODE,H,HMIN,TOL,ERRORS,YSIZE,WORK,IER )
```

The arguments are

Y,F,N = solution vector, right-side function, and n.
XSTART,XEND = first and last x values for this call.
TOL = tolerance for local error.
KONTRL,CONTRL = program control switches and variables with different meanings and choices for different programs. CONTRL is a vector of 24 switches and constants.
MODE = switch to indicate mode of operation, e.g., first call on program, not first call but TOL has been reset, etc.
WORK,IWORK = workspace arrays or vectors.
NROWW = first dimension of WORK.
H,HMIN = initial step size, step size at end of last call, and lower limit on step size.
SUBJAC = name of subroutine to compute the Jacobian matrix; its form is

```
CALL SUBJAC( N,X,Y,JACOB )
```

with JACOB(i, j) = $\partial f_i/\partial y_j$. KONTRL may signal that a dummy subroutine is provided and the Jacobian elements are estimated numerically.

ISTIFF	=	switch to indicate stiff differential equation.
MAXORD	=	maximum order of rational function extrapolation.
ERRORS,YSIZE	=	estimates of local errors and solution size.

It obviously takes some study to make sense out of these arguments and to relate them to the differential equation. Complete descriptions of the arguments take 6, 7, and 3 pages, respectively, for these three programs.

An important fact is that none of these subroutines is designed to solve 9.4.2 with just one call. One writes a fairly complicated piece of code, which steps along from A to B (the last x value) and records values of y, checking for trouble (perhaps changing control switches). A realistic example of the use of DVERK is given in Example 9.2.

The Predator-Prey Problem: Coyotes versus Rabbits

Example 9.2

A simple model of the interaction of the rabbit and coyote population is constructed as follows. Let r(t) and c(t) denote the densities (number per square mile) of rabbits and coyotes. Let p_r and p_c be the natural growth rates of the two populations; that is, p_r assumes no coyotes are eating rabbits and p_c assumes there are infinitely many rabbits to be eaten. Let m (or EATRAB in the program) be the number of rabbits a coyote would like to eat a year; set s(t) = r(t)/(m*c(t)) and define lunch(t) = number of rabbits a coyote actually eats a year and starve(t) = proportion of coyotes that starve each year from the lack of rabbits. We model the population interaction by taking

$$\begin{aligned} \text{lunch}(t) &= m*\min(1, r(t)/\alpha) \\ \text{starve}(t) &= e^{-\beta s(t)} \end{aligned}$$

Equation 9.5.2

The parameters α and β allow one to adjust the model and experiment with it. The role of α is that once the density of rabbits falls below α, then the coyotes start to give up on hunting rabbits and the number they would eat per year decreases. The role of β is illustrated by the fact that when s(t) = 1 (there are just enough rabbits to feed the coyotes for one year), we have starve(t) = $e^{-\beta}$ so that the choice starve(t) = 2 percent when s(t) = 1 gives $\beta = -\ln(.02) = 1.7$.

The differential equations which model the population interaction are then

$$\begin{aligned} r' &= p_r*r - \text{lunch}(t)*c \\ c' &= p_c*c - \text{starve}(t)*c \end{aligned}$$

Equation 9.5.3

with initial conditions $r(0) = r_0$, $c(0) = c_0$.

To use DVERK we have N = 2, Y(1, t) = r(t), Y(2, t) = c(t), and

```
SUBROUTINE F(N,X,Y,YPRIME)
REAL Y(N),YPRIME(N),LUNCH
COMMON / MODEL / PR,PC,EATRAB,BETA,ALPHA
S = Y(1)/(EATRAB*Y(2))
LUNCH = AMIN1(EATRAB,Y(1)*EATRAB/ALPHA)
YPRIME(1) = PR*Y(1) - LUNCH*Y(2)
YPRIME(2) = PC*Y(2) - EXP(-S*BETA)*Y(2)
RETURN
END
```

The other eight arguments of DVERK determine how the computation is controlled. We choose the simplest possible control which gives us values every 6 months for 100 years. The resulting actions are then:

1. Choose local error parameter TOL = 10^{-3} to give enough accuracy for plotting.

2. Choose KONTRL = 1, causing all default options to be selected and allowing us to ignore the vector CONTRL.

3. Define WORK, an array of size at least N by 9, to be 2 by 9, and set NROWW = 2.

4. Loop from t = 0 to t = 100 in steps of .5 and print values every other step (INC = 2). This determines the values of TSTART and TEND for each call on DVERK inside the loop. DVERK sets TSTART = TEND when it returns.

A complete Fortran program is given below showing the simplest case. Note that there are many statements for the output and its labeling and for the plotting.

```
C          USE OF DVERK IN ITS SIMPLEST FORM TO SOLVE THE PREDATOR-
C      PREY  PROBLEM  FOR COYOTES AND RABBITS.  THE DIFFERENTIAL
C      EQUATIONS ARE
C          RPRIME = PR*R - LUNCH*C                 R(0) = RO
C          CPRIME = PC*C - STARVE*C                C(0) = CO
C      WHERE LUNCH AND STARVE ARE MODELS OF THE INTERACTION. THESE
C      ARE SEEN IN DETAIL IN THE CODE FOR THE SUBROUTINE F.
C
C          R,C    = DENSITIES OF RABBITS AND COYOTES   = Y(1), Y(2)
C          PR,PC = NATURAL POPULATION GROWTH RATES FOR R AND C
C          RO,CO = INITIAL CONDITIONS FOR R AND C
C          EATRAB= NUMBER OF RABBITS A COYOTE EATS PER YEAR
C          ALPHA = DENSITY WHERE COYOTES START TO GIVE UP HUNTING RABBITS
C          BETA   = STARVATION RATE FACTOR FOR COYOTES
       REAL Y(2),WORK(2,9),CONTRL(24)
       EXTERNAL F
       COMMON / MODEL / PR,PC,EATRAB,BETA,ALPHA
       DATA  ALPHA,BETA,PR,PC,EATRAB,RO,CO/ 30.,3.4,.2,.2,100.,12.,.005/
C           DECLARATIONS AND INITIALIZATION FOR PLOT
       REAL TP(404),PLOT(404,2),RANGE(4)
       DATA RANGE / 4*0.0 /
C                      SELECT AND SET COMPUTATION PARAMETERS
       N      = 2
       YEARS  = 110.
       INC    = 2
       TOL    = 1.E-3
       NROWW  = 2
       KONTRL = 1
C                      INITIALIZE COMPUTATION
       Y(1)   = RO
       Y(2)   = CO
       TSTART = 0.0
       TSTEP  = 0.5
       TEND   = TSTEP
       NSTEP  = YEARS/TSTEP + 1.0
C              INITIALIZE PLOT VALUES
       KP = 1
       TP(1)      = TSTART
       PLOT(1,1) = RO/100.
       PLOT(1,2) = CO
C                       PRINT PROBLEM IDENTIFICATION
       WRITE(6,2) PR,PC,BETA ,EATRAB,RO,CO,TOL,YEARS,TSTEP
     2     FORMAT('1     COYOTES AND RABBIT PROBLEM - EXAMPLE 9.2' /
     A           10X'MODEL PARAMETERS PR,PC,BETA ,EATRAB   ' 4F10.5  //
     B           10X,'INITIAL CONDITIONS = ' 20X,2F10.5 //
     C           10X,'COMPUTATION PARAMETERS TOL,YEARS,TSTEP =' 3F10.5)
C                       HEADING FOR INTERMEDIATE OUTPUT
       WRITE(6,5)
     5     FORMAT(//5X,'T',10X,'RABBITS',7X,'COYOTES',5X,'F EVALS')
C
C                     INTEGRATION LOOP
       DO 100 K = 1,NSTEP
       CALL DVERK(N,F,TSTART,Y,TEND,TOL,KONTRL,CONTRL,NROWW,WORK,IER)
C                       CHECK FOR TROUBLE
           IF( IER .NE. 0 ) WRITE(6,10) IER,TSTART,(CONTRL(I),I=10,24)
   10          FORMAT(10X,20(3H* *),' TROUBLE WITH IER =',I4,' AT ',F7.3/
     A                10X,'INTERNAL CONTROL VARIABLES ARE'/ 2(8E15.5/))
C                       INTERMEDIATE OUTPUT
          IF( MOD(K,INC) .EQ. 0 ) WRITE(6,20) TEND,Y(1),Y(2),CONTRL(24)
   20         FORMAT( F10.3, 2F14.6, F6.0 )
C             GATHER INFORMATION FOR PLOT
              KP = KP + 1
              PLOT(KP,1) = Y(1)/100
              PLOT(KP,2) = Y(2)
              TP(KP)      = TEND
           TEND = TSTART + TSTEP
  100 CONTINUE
C
C              END PARAMETER STUDY LOOP, PLOT WITH IMSL ROUTINE
         CALL USPLO(TP,PLOT,404,KP,2,1,
     A            27H COYOTES AND RABBIT PROBLEM,27,6H YEARS,6,
     B            20H COYOTES,RABBITS/100,20,
     C            RANGE,1HC,1,1HR,1,IER)
      END
      SUBROUTINE F(N,X,Y,YPRIME)
      REAL Y(N),YPRIME(N),LUNCH
      COMMON / MODEL / PR,PC,EATRAB,BETA,ALPHA
      R = Y(1)/(EATRAB*Y(2))
      LUNCH = EATRAB*AMIN1(1.,Y(1)/ALPHA)
      YPRIME(1) = PR*Y(1) - LUNCH*Y(2)
      YPRIME(2) = PC*Y(2) - EXP(-R*BETA )*Y(2)
      RETURN
      END
```

A number of solutions are shown in Figure 9.5. In every case there is an initial transient followed by a steady state, the "balance of nature" in the two populations. It takes about 100 years for this balance to occur if the initial populations are quite far from the steady-state levels. The plots in Figure 9.5 show r(t)/100 so that the two curves can be seen together. The model parameters and initial conditions for Figure 9.5 are listed below:

Case	α	β	p_r	p_c	m	r_0	c_0
(A)	30	3.4	.2	.2	110	12	.4
(B)	30	2.0	.2	.2	50	50	.2
(C)	30	3.4	.2	.2	100	12	.005
(D)	30	3.4	.26	.2	110	120	3.0
(E)	30	1.0	.2	.2	110	12	3.0
(F)	30	2.0	.2	.2	100	300	1.0

The PROTRAN system has an ordinary differential equation problem-solving statement $DIFEQU. The simplest case of its use for a single equation is

```
$DIFEQU Y' = F(X,Y); ON( 0,2.5); INITIAL = 6.2
     DEFINE
     ====
     F = X*Y - 3.4
     ====
```

which solves the differential equation $y' = xy - 3.4$ with $y(0) = 6.2$ the default output of a printed table of y(x) at 100 points is given. To solve a system of equations requires the solution to be declared a vector as in the following example:

```
$DECLARATIONS
 VECTOR Y(4), YSTART(4) , F(4)
 MATRIX TABLEY(50,4)
$ASSIGN YSTART = ( 0,-1.0,1.0,3.1415926 )
$DIFEQU Y' = F(T,Y); ON( 1.0,10.0 ); INITIAL = YSTART
        ERRTARGET = .0001; NOUTPUT = 91; SOLUTION = TABLEY
        DEFINE
        ====
F(1) = Y(1)-T*Y(2)+SIN(T*Y(3))
F(2) = Y(2)*Y(3)-COS(T*Y(1)-Y(4))
F(3) = EXP(-Y(3)*T)*T*Y(4)
F(4) = COS(Y(1)*Y(4)*T)-SIN(Y(2)*Y(3)*T)
        ====
$PRINT TABLEY
$END
```

The computed solution Y is evaluated at 91 equally spaced points and the values placed in the table TABLEY. If TABLEY is *not* declared as a matrix, then a Fortran function is created so that TABLEY(T, J) returns the values of the Jth solution at the point T.

There are two other optional phrases for DIFEQU: one is EQUATIONS = integer, which changes the number of equations from its default value of the range of Y; the other is ABSOLUTE, which changes the accuracy control from relative error in each component of the solution to absolute error.

For comparison purposes we give the PROTRAN program that corresponds to Example 9.2. It is much simpler. This simplicity is gained at the expense of losing flexibility. If one has a difficult differential equation to solve, then one usually must do special things at various places. This can be done by using DVERK directly (see Example 9.4 for a case of this), but not with the PROTRAN system. On the other hand, the PROTRAN facility is *much* easier to use to solve easy or moderately difficult problems.

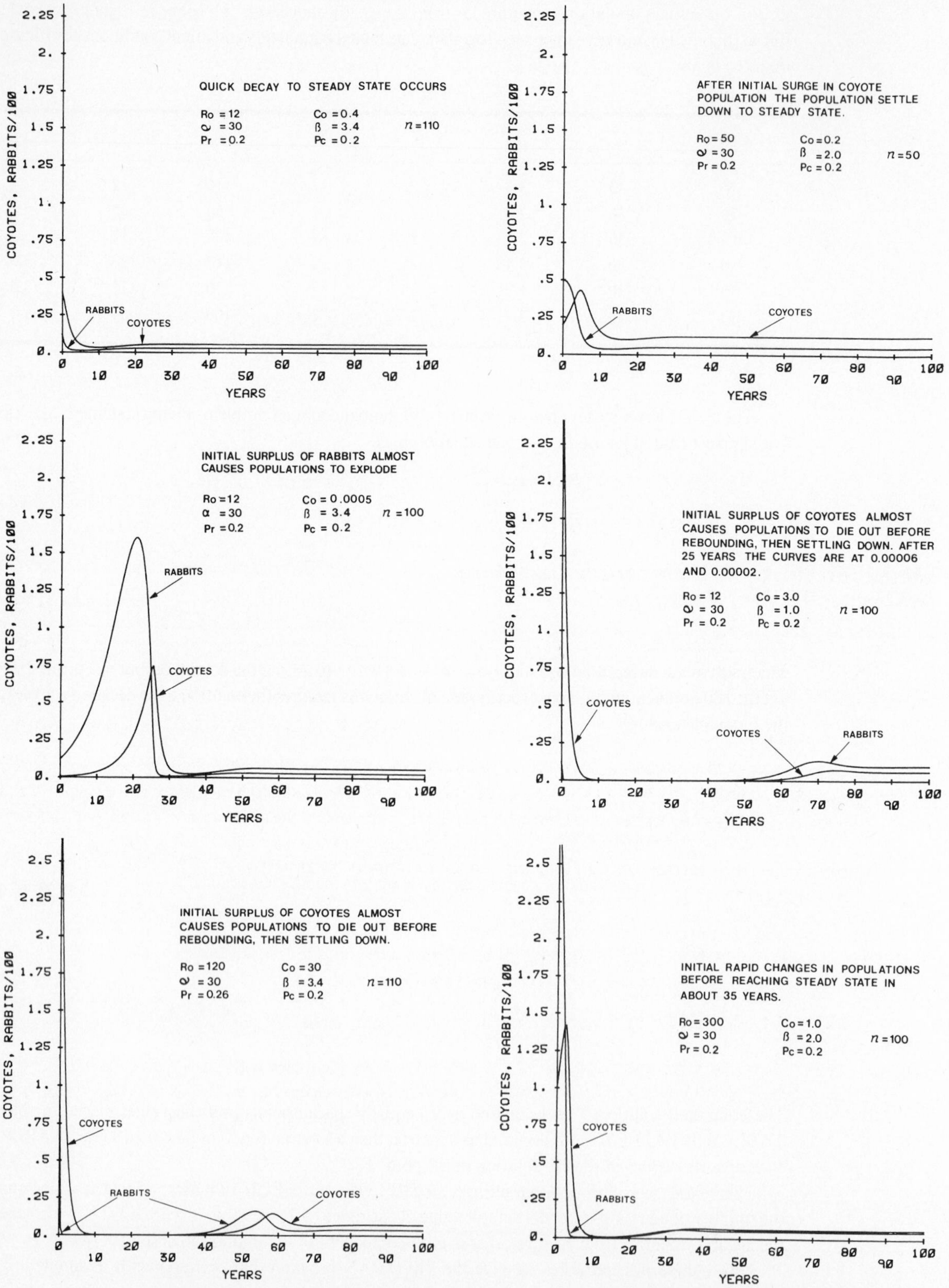

Figure 9.5 **Populations of coyotes and rabbits.** The interaction is shown for several cases. See the text for the parameters and initial conditions for these cases.

The Coyotes versus Rabbits Program in Protran

Example 9.3

To economize on space, the following program omits the comments to define the problem.

```
C                    EXAMPLE 9.3
C             COYOTES AND RABBITS DIFFERENTIAL EQUATION
C                    PROTRAN SOLUTION
      REAL LUNCH
      $DECLARATIONS
      VECTOR Y(2),YSTART(2); F(2)$
C                    MODEL PARAMETERS
      ALPHA  =  30.
      BETA   =   3.4
      EATRAB = 100.
      PR     =    0.2
      PC     =    0.2
      $ASSIGN YSTART  =   (12.,0.005)
C                    SOLVE DIFFERENTIAL EQUATION
      $DIFEQU  Y' = F(T,Y); INITIAL = YSTART; ON(0., 100.)
               ERRTARGET = .001;  SOLUTION = POP  ;  DEFINE
                ====
          S     = Y(1)/(EATRAB*Y(2))
          LUNCH = EATRAB*AMIN1(1.,Y(1)/ALPHA)
          F(1)  = PR*Y(1) - LUNCH*Y(2)
          F(2)  = PC*Y(2) - EXP(-S*BETA)*Y(2)
                ====
      $PLOT POP(T,1)/100.,POP(T,2) ; FOR(T=0.,100) ; SYMBOL = 'R','C'
          TITLE = ' RABBITS/100 AND COYOTES '
          XLABEL= ' YEARS'    ; YLABEL = 'POPULATION DENSITIES'
      $END
```

More Complicated Differential Equation Software Control Features

Example 9.4

A complete guide to using DVERK is quite long and cannot be covered here even in a concise form. However, we examine some of the additional features to illustrate what is usually found in similar software. These features are, of course, needed to handle more difficult problems which occur fairly frequently.

We introduce difficulties in the problem of Example 9.3 by attempting to model events such as:

1. *Rabbit migration:* The value of r suddenly jumps by M at time C. A neighboring valley is flooded by a new dam to cause the sudden influx of rabbits in the area being studied. Mathematically, this jump in r is modeled by a *delta* or *impulse* function on the right side of the differential equation. Such a function is hard to model numerically; the simplest approach is to add a term m(t) defined by

   $$m(t) = K \quad \text{for } C \le t \le C + d$$
   $$m(t) = 0 \quad \text{otherwise}$$
   Equation 9.5.4

   where $K*d = M$. In the present case $d = 1$ corresponds to 1 year of influx.

2. *Coyote migration:* The flood in the neighboring valley could also cause a sudden influx of coyotes. The numerical difficulties are the same as for an influx of rabbits. A sudden exodus causes similar problems.

3. *Coyotes get smarter:* Suppose a technology change (coyotes with traps?) or an education program (coyotes hunting in packs) suddenly makes the coyotes more efficient. We change the previous model at time C so that LUNCH is doubled and ALPHA is halved. The new formula for lunch(t) is then

   $$\text{lunch}(t) = m*\min(1, r(t)/\alpha) \qquad A \le t \le C$$
   $$\text{lunch}(t) = 2m*\min(1, 2r(t)/\alpha) \qquad C \le t \le B$$
   Equation 9.5.5

   This discontinuity in the right side must be handled to obtain accurate numerical results.

4. *Jump in natural population rates:* The parameters p_r and p_c of the two populations could have jumps due to events like: (A) birth control programs are instituted, (B) a medical center is opened which reduces death rates, or (C) the local animal king stops drafting young coyotes and sending them off to war. Such changes can be modeled by simply changing the parameters at time C or, more plausibly in many cases, an exponential transition can be used. For example, PR becomes a function of t as follows:

$$PR(t) = PR \qquad A \le t \le C$$
$$PR(t) = PRNEW + e^{-d(t-C)}(PR - RENEW) \qquad C \le t \le B$$

Equation 9.5.6

The parameter d governs how fast the transition is made; values of d = 50, 4, and .8 model transition times of 1 month, 1 year, and 5 years, respectively, in the present problem.

5. *New food source for coyotes:* The number m (or EATRAB) of rabbits that a coyote eats per year becomes a function of time. Perhaps a government program is instituted to feed coyotes, and they gradually lose interest in chasing rabbits. At the time this program is instituted, one would replace the constant m by a function which decays to the new level MNU. The value of MNU might be zero or, perhaps, the coyotes may set aside the week of September 18 as the time to maintain old traditions and go out and chase rabbits for a week. This gives a value of 3 to MNU. The rate of transition can be modeled exponentially as in the preceding case, or a slower transition can be assumed using the model

$$m = 100 \qquad A \le t \le C$$

Equation 9.5.7

$$m = \frac{100}{1 + (t - C)^d} \qquad C \le t \le B$$

This model has half the change made in the first year and 85 percent (with d = 1), 96 percent (with d = 2), or 99 percent (with d = 3) made by the fifth year.

It is clear that there are many ways the model can be perturbed in ways which cause numerical difficulties. We have tacitly assumed that the time C of the perturbation is known, but in many cases it is not; for example, who can predict when a flood will occur? We now examine some of the control facilities of DVERK which may help handle difficulties such as these:

KONTRL	If different from 1, then the CONTRL vector is used.
CONTRL(1)	Selection of one of five different measures of error. Important if the y(t) goes through zero or has widely differing values — either at different times or in different components. CONTRL(2) is a constant for one of these choices.
CONTRL(3)	Sets minimum step size to force program over a problem area. The default minimum step size is about 10 ulps, which is very small on some machines.
CONTRL(4)	Initial step size.
CONTRL(5),CONTRL(6)	Adjust program for scale of the problem. Crucial when [A, B] or y(t) have values far from 1.0.
CONTRL(7)	Limit on number of f(t, y) evaluations; prevents infinite loops. KONTRL is set to −1 if limit is exceeded.
CONTRL(8)	If not zero, then calculation is interrupted just after the first guess of the next step size is made. A following call with KONTRL = 4 resumes the calculation.
CONTRL(9)	If not zero, then calculation is interrupted at the end of a trial step calculation but before the step is made. The value of KONTRL indicates whether the trial step is to be made; changing KONTRL on the next call can change the decision.
CONTRL(10 to 24)	Contains information about the numerical model currently used by DVERK, e.g., step sizes, scale, error estimates, solution sizes, number of f(t, y) evaluations, etc.

A little study of these facilities shows that one can obtain a large measure of control of the calculation. One can make side calculations and check things at every step if one wants and override the automatic decisions of the polyalgorithm. To make full use of these facilities requires considerable study and experimentation, but this is much easier, is more reliable, and takes less time than writing a program from scratch.

We extend the program of Example 9.2 with the following objectives:

1. To detect the time of the perturbation and then to increase the frequency of output and increase the accuracy requirement.

2. To force the integration through the discontinuity.

3. To stop the integration 10 years after the perturbation.

To detect the perturbation we examine

CONTRL(14) = H (the step size should decrease substantially)
CONTRL(22-23) = number of successful and failed trial steps (the number of steps should increase substantially)
CONTRL(24) = number of $f(t, y)$ evaluations (this number should increase substantially)

In order to obtain a basis for comparison, a run is made without the perturbation, and these values of the CONTRL vector are printed at each timestep; they do not change for the unperturbed problem.

To force the integration through the discontinuity, we set CONTRL(3) = .0001 = the minimum step size and use CONTRL(9) to force acceptance if KONTRL is returned with value −1, which indicates the requested tolerance was not satisfied.

We choose the most difficult change in the model, a rabbit migration modeled by adding the term 9.5.4 to the differential equation. Even though we include data to start the perturbation at 28.65 years, we pretend that we do not know this time as would be the case in a more realistic situation. The function F is changed by adding the statements

```
C             PARAMETERS FOR MIGRATION OF 20 RABBITS/MILE
      REAL MIGRAT
      DATA  C, RATE, D / 28.65, 20, 1.0 /
      IF( ABS(T-C)+ABS(T-C-D) .GT. D ) THEN
            MIGRAT = 0.0
         ELSE
            MIGRAT = RATE
      END IF
```

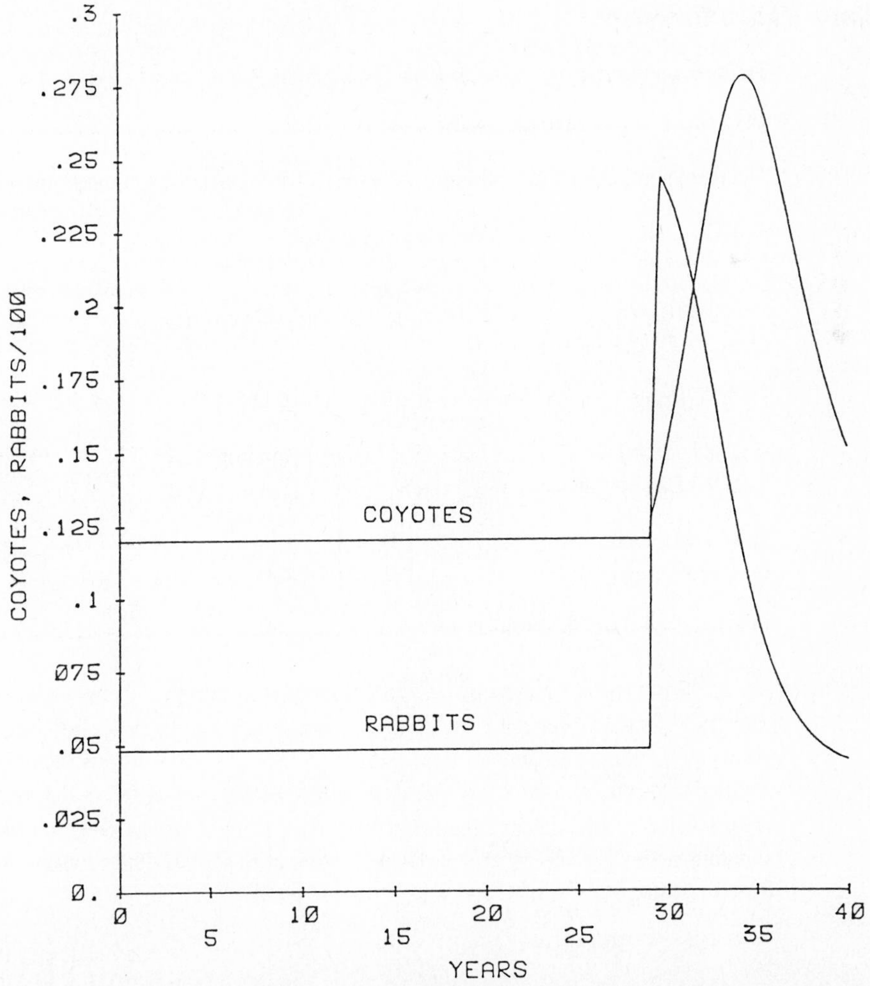

Figure 9.6 **Effect of a rabbit migration on the populations of rabbits and coyotes.** A migration of 20 rabbits per square mile occurs in a one-year period starting at time = 28.65.

The term MIGRAT is then added to the right side of the differential equation for rabbits:

```
YPRIME(1) = PR*Y(1) - LUNCH*Y(2) + MIGRAT
```

The effect of this migration is shown in Figure 9.6 for the model with parameters $\alpha = 30$, $p = 3$, $p_r = p_c = 0.2$, $m = 40$, and the initial condition $r_0 = 4.83$, $c_0 = 0.12$. The influx of 20 rabbits per square mile in one year makes a dramatic increase in the rabbit population. This new food supply initiates an equally sharp increase in the coyote population. When the rabbit migration stops, the rabbit population immediately starts falling while the coyote population continues to increase for about six years. The two populations will return to the steady state following a pattern much like that of Figure 9.5(B).

The program DVERK handles the discontinuity in $f(t, y)$ well. With a requested accuracy of .001, 68 function evaluations are required to integrate from 28.5 to 29.0 compared to the "normal" 8. The H value used is reduced from .5 to .1208. The location of the perturbation is easily recognized. The second perturbation (when the migration stops) is not recognized because DVERK has now adjusted its computation parameters to handle such sharp changes. If the requested accuracy is increased to 10^{-6}, then the integration is forced by the CONTRL(9) and KONTRL switches at the second perturbation. However, there appears to be no significant loss of accuracy at this point.

We conclude that DVERK gives one a great deal of flexibility in handling special problems (for example, the spacing of output is changed as soon as the perturbation was sensed). The price one pays is the time for the study and experimenting necessary to learn how to use all these control features.

IMSL Software for Two-Point Boundary Value Problems **9.5.C

The **two-point boundary value problem** for a system of n differential equations is stated as follows:

$$\mathbf{y}'(x) = \mathbf{f}(x, \mathbf{y}) \qquad \mathbf{M}(\mathbf{y}(A), \mathbf{y}(B)) = \mathbf{v} \qquad \textbf{Equation 9.5.8}$$

The **two-point boundary condition** involves an n by 2 matrix M so that a typical boundary condition

$$4y_4(A) - 1.62y_4(B) = \pi$$

corresponds to $m_{41} = 4$, $m_{42} = -1.62$, and $v_4 = \pi$.

Two simple approaches for solving boundary value problems are given in Examples 6.4 and 8.2. In Example 6.4 the linear problem

$$y'' + \cos(x)y = \log(x+4) \qquad y(0) = 0,\ y(1) = 1$$

is solved using finite differences and a band linear equation solver. This problem may be put in the standard form 9.5.8 by setting $y_1(x) = y'(x)$ and $y_2(x) = y(x)$ to obtain

$$\begin{aligned} y_1' &= \log(x+y_2) - \cos(x)y_2 \\ y_2' &= y_1 \end{aligned} \qquad \begin{pmatrix} 0 & 1 \\ 0 & 1 \end{pmatrix} \begin{pmatrix} y_1(0) & y_1(1) \\ y_2(0) & y_2(1) \end{pmatrix} = \begin{pmatrix} 0 \\ 1 \end{pmatrix}$$

In Example 8.2 the nonlinear problem

$$p'' = \frac{(p')^2}{p} + \frac{3h'h^2p'}{p} + \frac{k(p'h+ph')}{ph^3}$$

$$p(0) = p(1) = p_0$$

is formulated as a nonlinear equation problem (p_0, h, and k are known). This is a simple instance of the **shooting method,** which we do not discuss further in this book. This problem may be put in the standard form by setting $y_1(t) = p'(t)$ and $y_2(t) = p(t)$ to obtain

$$y_1' = \frac{y_1^2}{y_2} + \frac{3h'h^2y_1}{y_2} + \frac{k(y_1h+y_2h')}{y_2h^3} \qquad \begin{pmatrix} 0 & 1 \\ 0 & 1 \end{pmatrix} \begin{pmatrix} y_1(0) & y_1(1) \\ y_2(0) & y_2(1) \end{pmatrix} = \begin{pmatrix} p_0 \\ p_0 \end{pmatrix}$$

$$y_2' = y_1$$

The shooting method essentially introduces $y_1(0)$ as an unknown variable and then adjusts it to satisfy the condition $y_2(1) = p_0$.

The simple methods illustrated by these examples are useful at times, but they are quite restricted in applications. The IMSL library has two routines for two-point boundary value problems:

DTPTB = use of DVERK and the multiple shooting method (not discussed in this book)
DVCPR = use of variable-order, variable-step-size finite differences and deferred corrections (not discussed in this book)

These programs have 15 and 19 arguments, respectively, and thus are somewhat complicated to use. However, neither has the complex control provided by DVERK, and it is much easier to learn these arguments than it is to write a program from scratch to solve a two-point boundary value problem.

Software for Stiff Problems **9.5.D

There are several technical definitions of **stiff** for a system of differential equations; each is an attempt to mathematically describe a fairly common class of difficult problems. Two sources of stiff systems are described at the end of Section 9.4. An intuitive description of stiffness is that the system has some solutions that change very rapidly compared with other solutions, or some solutions change very rapidly sometimes and slowly at other times. Physical situations that have a transient behavior and a very stable steady state are often stiff. The coyote and rabbit problem (see Figure 9.5) has such transients, but it is not difficult enough to be considered stiff. If such a stable physical situation is perturbed, then it "springs back" to the stable situation very quickly. Or a change might define a new and different steady state; for example, a piece of electrical machinery is switched on and the electrical system moves rapidly to a new steady state.

However stiff differential systems are defined, mathematically or intuitively, one has little difficulty recognizing one when one tries to solve it by the usual methods. The problem seems to be unstable (even though the computed solutions might not appear very unusual), and the usual numerical methods require a *very large* number of steps to achieve even modest accuracy. The first time a really stiff problem is encountered, one often thinks that there is a bug in the program and that it could not possibly require such small steps to integrate the system.

One of the major advances in numerical analysis and mathematical software is the development of programs which can solve stiff systems efficiently. Before the 1970s, one was usually reduced to either using a lot of computer time with very small steps or performing complex mathematical manipulations to remove, or at least reduce, the stiffness. The IMSL program DGEAR is one such program; the argument ISTIFF allows a user to select the special methods to handle stiff problems. If DGEAR is used on a stiff problem without this switch set, then it usually returns a value for the error flag IER, indicating that the problem is probably stiff. The programs DEBDF from DEPAC, STINT (ACM Algorithm 534), and EPISODE are other examples of high-quality software for stiff problems.

Solving stiff differential systems is analogous to solving large systems of nonlinear equations in that it pays to have several good programs available to try. No one program or method is uniformly best, or even close to best, so one might want to experiment with several programs if one has a large computation involving a stiff problem. For further discussion of the performance of software for stiff problems, see the following references (and references therein): C. Addison, *Summary of the Illinois-Toronto olympiODE Test Results,* SIGNUM Newsletter, **16** (December 1981), pp. 19–21; S. Thompson, *A Comparison of Available Software for the Numerical Solution of Stiff Ordinary Differential Equations,* Report No. NPGD-TM-368, Babcock and Wilcox (June 1977), 194 pages; and P. Gaffney, *A Survey of Fortran Subroutines Suitable for Solving Stiff Oscillatory Ordinary Differential Equations,* ORNL/CSD/TM-134, Oak Ridge National Laboratory, 1982.

PROBLEMS 9.5

9.5.1 Solve the differential equations of Problem 9.2.2 using a library differential equation solver. Compare the number of evaluations of the right side used with the number of evaluations necessary for Euler's method to achieve the same accuracy. **Hint:** The right side is in a subroutine; put a counter in it and print the value of the counter after the integration is done.

9.5.2 Repeat the round-off effects study of Problem 9.2.3 using a library differential equation solver.

9.5.3 Solve the differential equations of Problem 9.2.5 using a library differential equation solver. Compare the number of evaluations of the right side used with the number used for a second-order Runge-Kutta method to achieve the same accuracy. See the hint of Problem 9.5.1

9.5.4 Solve the differential equations of Problem 9.2.5 with the fourth-order Runge-Kutta method of Problem 9.2.10. Use a step size of .01. Resolve these problems with a library differential equation solver to achieve the same accuracy. Compare the number of evaluations of the right side for both programs. See the hint of Problem 9.5.1.

9.5.5 Problems 9.5.1 to 9.5.4 use the number of evaluations of the right side to estimate the work done by a differential equation solver. There is also "overhead" in the methods which can significantly affect the time to solve the problems.

(A) Obtain execution times for the methods and discuss the correlation between execution times and the number of function evaluations.

(B) To make a more thorough study, solve the two differential equations $y' = y$ and $y' = f(x, y)$ where $f(x, y)$ is computed by the Fortran

```
   DO 10 K = 1, KTEST
10    F = EXP(SIN(X)+COS(EXP(X))*ALGO10(1+EXP(SIN(X*X)))
   F = Y
```

The equation $y' = y$ has essentially zero effort in evaluating the right side, and so almost all the execution time is overhead. By choosing KTEST large, one can make the right-side evaluations very expensive, and hence this dominates the calculation cost. Apply the library routine to these two problems to obtain a formula to estimate the execution time of solving a differential equation of the form $a_0 + a_1*K + a_2*K*WR$, where a_0, a_1, and a_2 are to be determined, K is the number of right-side evaluations, and WR is the time to evaluate the right side once. Make computer runs to verify the accuracy of this formula to model the calculation time. **Hint:** Most computer systems have a library program to give reasonably accurate times for executing parts of a program; the use of such a timing program simplifies the estimation of the coefficients a_0, a_1, and a_2.

9.5.6 Extend the study of "overhead" in a linear differential equation solver in Problem 9.5.5. Obtain a formula to model the computation time of the form $a_0 + a_1*K + a_2*K*N + a_3*N + a_4*K*WR$, where N is the number of equations and WR is the total time to evaluate *all* the right sides. Repeat the accuracy test of the formula as in Problem 9.5.5.

9.5.7 Solve the differential equations of Problem 9.1.1, parts (A), (D), and (E), using a library differential equation solver. Carry out the integration to $x = 1.0$. Attempt to achieve an accuracy of 10^{-3} at $x = 1$ and verify the accuracy by obtaining a more accurate solution.

9.5.8 Measure the cost of verifying the accuracy of solving the problems of Problem 9.5.7. What is the cost of the verification as a percentage of the cost to solve the problem in the first place? Discuss whether this cost is reasonable. **Hint:** You can measure the cost either by actual computer time (or dollars and cents) used or by the number of right-side evaluations.

9.5.9 Consider the following **two-point boundary value problem:**

$$r' = s \qquad r(0) = 0$$
$$s' = t \qquad s(0) = 0 \qquad s(10) = 1$$
$$t' = -\frac{1}{2} rs$$

Solve this problem by combining a differential equation solver with a nonlinear equation solver. Replace the condition $s(10) = 1$ by the initial condition $t(0) = z$. Solve the initial value problem that results and obtain a value of $s(x)$ at $x = 10$. Call this value $f(z)$ since it depends on z. The nonlinear equation to be solved is $f(z) = 1$.

Write a program that uses library software to carry out this method of solution. Reasonable initial guesses for z are .5 and .3.

9.5.10 Solve the two-point boundary value problem in Problem 9.5.9 using the IMSL library program DTPTB or a similar library program.

9.5.11 Solve the differential equations in Problem 9.1.1, parts (B) and (C), using the method of Problem 9.5.9. Explicitly display the nonlinear equations to be solved and discuss the choice of library equation solver made.

9.5.12 Solve the differential equations in Problem 9.1.1, parts (B) and (C), using the IMSL library program DTPTB or a similar library program.

9.5.13 The technique of **partial double precision** is to use double precision for the final addition in $y_{k+1} = y_k + h*\text{something}$. Since h is small, the term $\delta y = h*\text{something}$ has leading zeros compared to y_k and has additional accuracy in its last significant digits. Double precision at the last step preserves some of this accuracy.

(A) Apply this technique to the equation

$$y' = \frac{1}{x^2} - \frac{y}{x} - y^2 \qquad y(1) = -1$$

using the Adams-Bashford formula of order 4. Use two values of h, .1 and .001, and compare the results as computed without partial double precision. Discuss the effect of partial double precision on the accuracy at $x = 3.0$. **Hint:** The true solution is $y(x) = -1/x$. Print out values of $y(x)$ and the error for x in steps of .1. For $h = .001$ the truncation error is negligible on most computers so that all the error is due to round-off.

(B) If your computer uses more than 10 decimal digits in the arithmetic, simulate the effect of round-off by multiplying δy by $(1+10^{-10}*\text{random})$ before doing the double precision addition.

9.5.14 Repeat Problem 9.5.13 for the fourth-order Runge-Kutta formula 9.2.15.

9.5.15 The model of coyote and rabbit populations in Example 9.2 does not always lead to a balance. Change the parameters of the model for the cases graphed in Figure 9.5 so that

(A) The populations "blow up," that is, both populations increase exponentially.

(B) The populations "die out," that is, both populations decrease steadily.

9.5.16 Use the PROTRAN system to solve one of the differential equations given in Problem 9.2.2, parts (A), (B), (C), (D), (E), (F), (G), or (H).

9.5.17 Use the PROTRAN system to solve the following systems of differential equations. Table and plot the solution obtained.

(A) $y' = xy + \cos(t) - 0.5\sin(2t) \qquad y(0) = 0 \qquad 0 \le t \le 6$
$x' = x^2 + y^2 - (1+\sin(t)) \qquad x(0) = 1$

Hint: True solution is $y(t) = \sin(t)$, $x(t) = \cos(t)$.

(B) $p' = -2xpq \qquad p(1) = .1353352832 \qquad 1 \le x \le 4$
$q' = -1/(xpe^{2x}) \qquad q(1) = 1$

Hint: True solution is $p(x) = xe^{-2x}$, $q(x) = 1/x$.

(C) $x'' = -x/r^3 \qquad x(0) = .4 \quad y(0) = 0 \qquad 0 \le t \le 2$
$y'' = -y/r^3 \qquad x'(0) = 0 \quad y'(0) = 2$
$r' = (xx' + yy')/r \qquad r(0) = .4$

(D) $y'' - 3y' + 2 = 0 \qquad y(0) = 1,\ y'(0) = 0 \qquad 0 \le x \le 5$

(E) $w' = 0.1(1-y^2)w - y \qquad y(0) = 1,\ w(0) = 0 \qquad 0 \le t \le 4$
$y' = w$

9.5.18 Repeat Problem 9.5.17 using the IMSL program DVERK.

9.5.19 Use the PROTRAN system to solve the differential equation of Example 9.4, including the rabbit migration term. Vary the amount of accuracy required and discuss how effective this system is in automatically handing a step function in the differential equation.

9.5.20 Equation 9.2.13 for Example 9.1 presents a smooth model for the rabbit migration of Example 9.4.

(A) Reformulate the differential equation of Example 9.4 using $ae^{-b(t-C)^2}$ instead of a step function to model rabbit migration. Choose the values of the parameters a and b for a migration of 20 rabbits per square mile over a time span of one year.

(B) Repeat Problem 9.5.19 using this model.

(C) Repeat the calculation of Example 9.4 using this model and compare the population behaviors with those shown in Figure 9.6.

9.5.21 Five other perturbations of the rabbit and coyote populations are presented in Example 9.4. For each of these, derive the differential equations, solve them, plot and table the solutions, and discuss the general effect of these perturbations on the populations. The perturbations are:

(A) *Coyote migration;* assume 1 coyote per mile migrates over a period of 6 months. Use the basic model of Figure 9.6.

(B) *Coyotes get smarter;* use Equation 9.5.5 to model the change in one of the basic models of Figure 9.5. Have the perturbation start in year 13.

(C) *Change in rabbit birthrate or death rate;* use Equation 9.5.6 with $C = 25$ and $d = 0.8$ to model the effect in the basic model of Figure 9.6.

(D) *Change in coyote birthrate or death rate;* repeat part (C) except that $PC(t)$ is changed, not $PR(t)$.

(E) *New food source for coyotes;* use Equation 9.5.7 with $C = 47$ and $d = 2$ to model the change. Use one of the basic models of Figure 9.5.

ANALYSIS OF METHODS FOR DIFFERENTIAL EQUATIONS 9.6

The analysis of numerical methods for solving differential equations is difficult. This section presents a survey of facts about the methods with only two of the most basic results completely proved. The first section of this chapter emphasized the importance of stability for differential equation problems, and we see here that stability is closely related to the theory of numerical methods for differential equations. The discussion is divided into two parts: one-step methods and multistep methods.

One-Step Methods 9.6.A

Recall that there are two kinds of errors in numerical methods for differential equations: the local error and the global error or discretization error. The **local error** is the error made in a single step, the difference between the computed value y_{k+1} and the solution $z(x_{k+1})$ of the differential equation *with the condition that* $z(x_k) = y_k$. Let t_k denote this error, and we have

$$t_{k+1} = z(x_{k+1}) - y_{k+1}$$

Let $y^*(x)$ denote the true solution to the differential equation, and then the **global error** or **discretization error** e_{k+1} is given by

$$e_{k+1} = y^*(x_{k+1}) - y_{k+1}$$

The situation here can be summarized as follows. It is feasible to estimate t_{k+1} both in theory and in practice; for some methods it is not hard at all. The fact that all the local errors t_k are small does not guarantee that the global error e_k is small. It is difficult to estimate e_k both in theory and in practice. The quantity of real interest is e_k, not t_k.

Euler's method is simple enough that we can give a convergence proof using a simple assumption about the equation. As usual, the differential equation is

$$y' = f(x, y) \qquad y(0) = y_0 \qquad \textbf{Equation 9.6.1}$$

and the assumptions on this equation are

$$|f_y(x, y)| \le K < \infty$$
$$|y''| \le L < \infty \text{ and } y'' \text{ is continuous} \qquad \textbf{Equation 9.6.2}$$

which hold over the interval of integration and for any solution of $y' = f(x, y)$ with initial conditions close to y_0. In other words, 9.6.2 holds for all the trajectories close to the true solution $y^*(x)$ of 9.6.1. We restate Euler's method:

$$y_{k+1} = y_k + hf(x_k, y_k)$$
$$x_{k+1} = x_k + h \qquad \textbf{Equation 9.6.3}$$

and note that the step size h is constant throughout the integration. We have:

Theorem 9.1 *Assume that 9.6.2 holds for Equation 9.6.1. Then the global error of Euler's method 9.6.3 satisfies*

$$|e_k| \le \frac{hL}{2K}(e^{x_k K} - 1)$$

If h decreases and k is chosen so that $x_k = kh = x$, then we have

$$|y^*(x) - y_k| = O(h)$$

Proof: Apply Taylor's theorem to $y^*(x)$ to obtain

$$y^*(x_{k+1}) = y^*(x_k) + y^{*\prime}(x_k) + \frac{h^2}{2} y^{*\prime\prime}(\xi_k)$$

We subtract 9.6.3 from this equation to obtain

$$e_{k+1} = e_k + [y^{*\prime}(x_k) - y'_k] + \frac{h^2}{2} y^{*\prime\prime}(\xi_k)$$

$$= e_k + h[f(x_k, y^*(x_k)) - f(x_k, y_k)] + \frac{h^2}{2} y^{*\prime\prime}(\xi_k)$$

We apply the mean value theorem to $f(x, y)$ as a function of y to obtain

$$e_{k+1} = e_k + hf_y(x_k, \eta_k)\,(y^*(x_k) - y_k) + \frac{h^2}{2} y^{*\prime\prime}(\xi_k)$$

$$= e_k(1 + hf_y(x_k, \eta_k)) + \frac{h^2}{2} y^{*\prime\prime}(\xi_k)$$

Now take absolute values and apply the assumption 9.6.2 to obtain

$$|e_{k+1}| \le |e_k|(1 + hK) + \frac{h^2}{2} L$$ **Equation 9.6.4**

Equation 9.6.4 is related to the simple difference equation

$$z_{k+1} = (1 + hK)z_k + \frac{h^2}{2} L \qquad z_0 = 0$$

which has the particular solution $hL/(2K)$ and general solution $c(1 + hK)^k$. The initial condition $z_0 = 0$ gives the complete solution

$$z_k = \frac{hL}{2K}[(1 + hK)^k - 1]$$

We now establish the fact that $z_k \ge |e_k|$ for all k by induction on k. For $k = 0$ we have $z_k = e_k = 0$, and so the fact is established for $k = 0$. For $k > 0$ we note that $(1 + hK) > 1$ and $\frac{h^2}{2} L > 0$ so that if $z_k \ge |e_k|$, then $z_{k+1} \ge |e_{k+1}|$ follows immediately. We have thus established that

$$|e_k| \le \frac{hL}{2K}[(1 + hK)^k - 1]$$

The final step of the proof is to note that $e^x \ge 1 + x$ for all x. Hence $1 + hK \ge e^{hK}$ and

$$(1 + hK)^k \le e^{khK} = e^{x_k K}$$

This establishes the first part of the theorem; the second part follows since x_k is assumed to have a fixed value and there is a factor of h in the bound for $|e_k|$. This concludes the proof.

The following theorem is a direct extension of Theorem 9.1 to general Runge-Kutta methods. The assumption and method of proof are similar.

Theorem 9.2 *Assume that for all values of y that*

$$|f_y(x, y)| \le K < \infty$$

that f(x, y) has p continuous derivatives, and that the local error t_k of the Runge-Kutta method is $O(h^{p+1})$. Then, for $x_k = kh$ fixed as h goes to zero,

$$|y^*(x_k) - y_k| = O(h^p)$$

The analogy with Theorem 9.1 is that $y'' \le L$ corresponds to $t_k = O(h^{p+1})$ for the Runge-Kutta method; we have $p = 1$ in Theorem 9.1. The assumption on f_y is stronger here in that it must hold for all y; with more care one can weaken the assumption some at the expense of more complexity.

It is important to note that Runge-Kutta methods work for many equations where Theorem 9.2 does not apply. This theorem only gives a condition that is sufficient for convergence; it is not necessary. For example, consider the equations

$$\begin{aligned} y' &= y^2 & y(1) &= -1 \\ y' &= e^y & y(1) &= 1 \\ y' &= 3y + g(x) & y(1) &= 1 \end{aligned}$$

The first has $f_y = 2y$, which is not bounded, and so Theorem 9.2 does not apply. The solution of this equation is $y = -1/x$, and the Runge-Kutta methods work very well for it. The second equation is extremely unstable, and one would not expect good numerical results. We have $f_y = e^y$, and so Theorem 9.2 again does not apply, but the Runge-Kutta methods do not converge. For the third equation, $f_y = 3$, and so Theorem 9.2 applies and Runge-Kutta methods converge. However, convergence only means that good results are obtained for h sufficiently small. If g(x) is misbehaved (see Example 9.4), then h may need to be quite small before accurate results are obtained.

Multistep Methods 9.6.B

We first establish the convergence of the fixed point iteration for the corrector formulas; see Equation 9.2.22 for an example. In general, the iteration for the corrector formula is

$$y_{k+1}^{(j+1)} = chf(x_{k+1}, y_{k+1}^{(j)}) + d \qquad j = 0, 1, 2, \ldots \qquad \textbf{Equation 9.6.5}$$

where c and d do not depend on j and h is the step size of the integration.

Theorem 9.3 *Assume f(x, y) and $f_y(x, y)$ are continuous. Then the corrector iteration 9.6.5 converges provided h is small enough that, for all y closer to y_{k+1} than $y_{k+1}^{(0)}$, we have*

$$|f_y|\, h \le 1/c$$

Proof: The convergence of fixed point iteration is governed by the size of

$$\frac{\partial}{\partial y}(chf(x, y) + d) = chf_y(x, y)$$

See Theorem 8.2. If this quantity is less than 1.0 for all y, then the iteration converges. Thus, it is only necessary that the condition stated in the theorem hold for the initial guess $y_{k+1}^{(0)}$ and y between it and y_{k+1}. This concludes the proof.

Theorem 9.3 actually implies more than the convergence of the corrector iteration; it says that the convergence is very fast as h decreases. The step size h is chosen by other criteria, and experience with the common methods shows that h is small enough so that only 1 or 2 iterations are needed to obtain accuracy comparable with the truncation error. The exact number of required iterations depends on the method, but note that $y_{k+1}^{(0)}$ can be made to be a very accurate first guess by choosing an accurate predictor formula. That, coupled with the fast convergence, makes it plausible that only one corrector iteration is needed for many methods. The restriction on h in Theorem 9.3 is so severe for stiff differential equations that fixed point iteration usually cannot be used.

The convergence of multistep methods is closely related to the stability of the difference equation used. This, in turn, is determined by the behavior of the solution of the homogeneous difference equation or, equivalently, by the roots of the characteristic polynomial. Note that for a predictor-corrector method it is the corrector that matters; the predictor is just a way to obtain a good initial guess to solve the corrector equation for y_{k+1}. We now claim that we need only consider the simple differential equation $y' = \lambda y$, $y(0) = 1$ which has the solution $y = e^{\lambda x}$. That is to say, methods converge for the differential equations in general if and only if they converge for this simple equation. The intuitive justification of this is as follows. Solving $y' = f(x, y)$ is a stepwise process; one solves it on one interval then passes on to the next interval and repeats the solution process. The intervals here are not integration steps, just small intervals independent of the method. In order for a method to converge, it must converge on each of these intervals, and conversely, if it converges on each small interval, then it converges everywhere. Consider one such small interval [a, b] and expand $f(x, y)$ in a Taylor's series so that the differential equation is

$$y' = f(x, y) = f(x, y(a)) + f_y(x, y(a))\,(y(x) - y(a)) + \ldots$$

Set $z(x) = y(x) - y(a)$ and $\lambda = f_y(x, y(a))$ so that the differential equation for $z(x)$ is

$$z' = \lambda z + f(x, y(a)) + O(z^2)$$

The simple term $f(x, y(a))$ does not affect stability, and so we can ignore it. If the interval [a, b] is short, then $z(x)$ is small [since $z(a) = 0$] and the $O(z^2)$ term has negligible effect.

We gather together the relevant formulas; the **multistep formula** is 9.2.17:

$$y_{k+1} = \sum_{i=0}^{p} a_i y_{k-i} + \sum_{i=-1}^{p} b_i y'_{k-i} \qquad \textbf{Equation 9.6.6}$$

The associated **difference equation** for a particular step size h is

$$y_{k+1} = \sum_{i=0}^{p} a_i y_{k-i} + h\lambda \sum_{i=-1}^{p} b_i y_{k-i} \qquad \textbf{Equation 9.6.7}$$

whose **characteristic polynomial** is

$$q(t) = (1 - h\lambda b_{-1})\, t^{p+1} - \sum_{i=0}^{p} (a_i + h\lambda b_i) t^{p-i} \qquad \textbf{Equation 9.6.8}$$

and its **roots** are denoted by r_i, $i = 1, 2, \ldots, p+1$. The solution of the difference equation is $c_1 r_1{}^k + c_2 r_2{}^k + \ldots + c_{p+1} r_{p+1}^k$. Note that these roots depend on λh as well as the formula 9.6.6.

A numerical method is **convergent** if $|y(x) - y_k| = e(x)$ (the global error) goes to zero as h goes to zero with $kh = x$ fixed. The key questions are: Is a method convergent? If so, how fast does the global error $e(x)$ go to zero? If the method is convergent, then it is not so difficult to show that the error goes to zero at a rate easily estimated from the local error t_k, the number of steps, and the rate at which trajectories are spreading. In the simplest case $t_k = O(h^m)$ for some m, the number of steps is $O(h^{-1})$ and the spreading of the trajectories is bounded by some constant so that $e(x) = O(h^{m-1})$. Thus, we concentrate on the convergence question.

A multistep method is **stable** if it satisfies the ordinary definition of stability for a numerical method. That is, the error in the final computed value is proportional to the sum of the local errors made in the steps during the calculation. See the discussion in Section 3.3.C. The constant of proportionality is the condition number, and one hopes this is not too large, but for differential equation methods, stability merely means that the condition number is not infinite. Note that for a fixed value of x, the number of calculations to compute $y(x)$ goes to infinity as h goes to zero, so that having a finite condition number is already achieving quite a bit.

The question about convergence and stability can be answered in terms of the roots of the characteristic polynomial. First, we assume that the method is consistent (see Equation 9.2.18) which means the local error is $O(h^2)$ or better so that the global error has a chance of being $O(h)$. The first equation of 9.2.18 for consistency is

$$1 - \sum_{i=0}^{p} a_i = 0$$

which means that one of the roots of $q(t) = 0$ is 1 for $h = 0$. This is the principal root, and we number the r_i so that $r_1 = 1$. If $\lambda h > 0$, then there might not be a root exactly equal to 1, but nevertheless, we call the principal root that one, $r_1(\lambda h)$, that converges to 1 as h goes to zero.

We now introduce some technical definitions. The **root condition** is

$$\begin{aligned} |r_i| &\le 1 \quad \text{all } i \\ |r_j| &= 1 \quad \text{implies that } q'(r_j) \ne 0 \end{aligned}$$ **Equation 9.6.9**

The **strong root condition** is

$$|r_i| < 1 \quad \text{all } i > 1$$ **Equation 9.6.10**

The multistep method is **relatively stable** if

$$|r_i| \le |r_1| \quad \text{all } i > 1$$ **Equation 9.6.11**

These definitions apply for $h > 0$ as well, in which case r_i may be replaced by $r_i(\lambda h)$ to show the dependence on λ and h. The principal root r_1 corresponds to the true solution of the differential equation. The root condition says that none of the "extraneous" solutions of the difference equation grow to dominate the true solution. The strong root condition implies that all "extraneous" solutions of the difference equation decay to zero. Relative stability means that "extraneous" solutions do not grow to dominate the principal root (which might grow slightly faster than the solution of the differential equation).

The convergence and stability theory for multistep methods is summarized in Theorem 9.4 and illustrated in Figure 9.7.

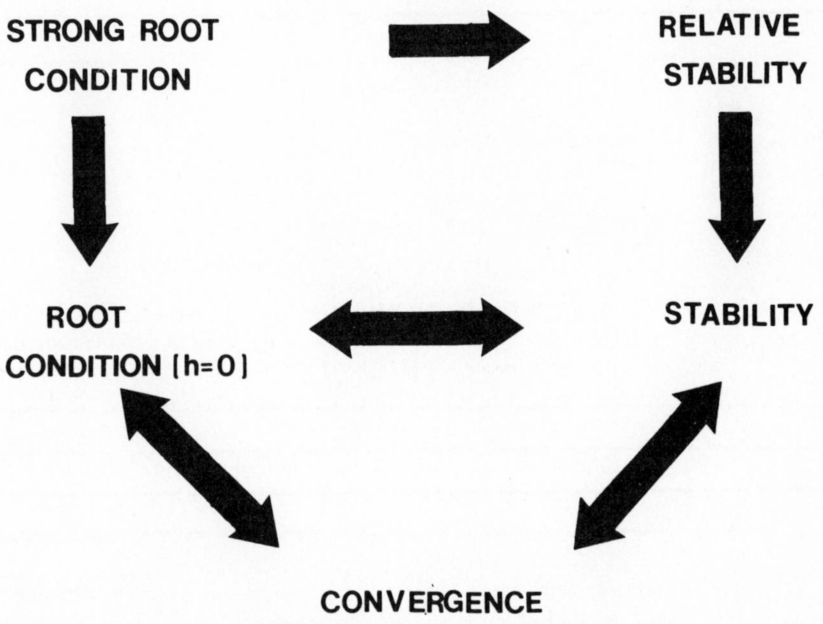

Figure 9.7 Convergence and stability theory diagram for multistep methods. The arrows indicate directions of implications; the three items at the bottom are all equivalent.

Theorem 9.4 *The following conditions are equivalent for a consistent multistep method:*

1. *The method is convergent*

2. *The method is stable*

3. *The root condition is satisfied*

Further, the strong root condition implies the root condition and relative stability; relative stability implies stability.

The significance of Theorem 9.4 is that root conditions are relatively easy to check; one just applies a polynomial root finder to the polynomials 9.6.8. Some applications of Theorem 9.4 are given in the following example.

Applications of the Theory of Convergence and Stability to Multistep Methods

Example 9.5

The simplest methods are Euler's method and the trapezoidal method (Equation 9.2.20) which have characteristic polynomials

$$t - (1+\lambda h) \qquad \left(1 - \frac{\lambda h}{2}\right)t - \left(1 + \frac{\lambda h}{2}\right)$$

both of which have principal roots $r_0(\lambda h) = 1 + \lambda h + O(h^2)$. Thus the root condition is satisfied for $h = O$.

The Adams methods all have the same characteristic polynomial $t^{p-1} - t^p$ with one root 1 and the rest 0. See Table 9.1.

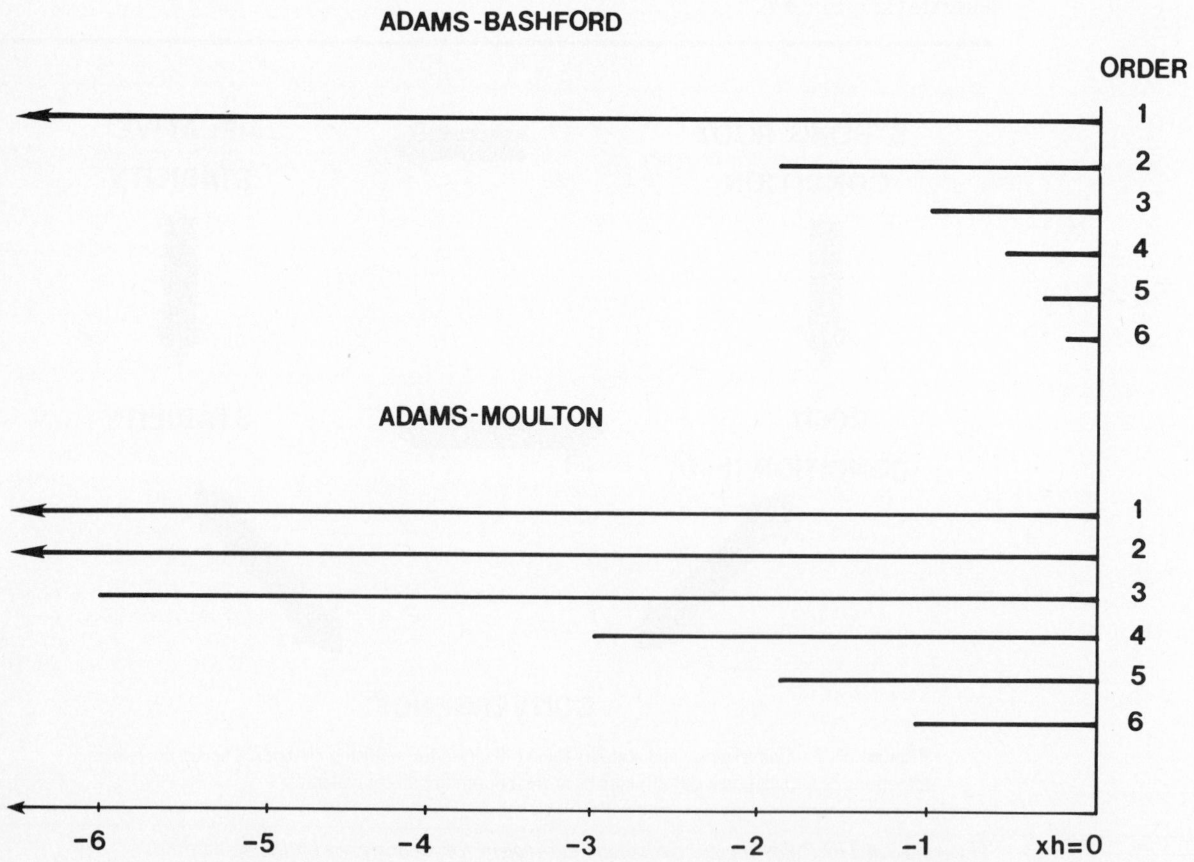

Figure 9.8 **Regions of absolute stability for Adams methods.** The step size h for $y' = \lambda y$ must be chosen so that λh lies on the heavy lines in order to guarantee that all extraneous solutions decay to zero at x = infinity.

Three more complicated methods are the **midpoint method** (Problem 9.2.18) with

$$q(t) = t^2 - 2\lambda ht - 1$$

Milne's method (Problem 9.2.16) with

$$q(t) = \left(1 - \frac{\lambda h}{3}\right)t^2 - \frac{4\lambda h}{3}t - \left(1 + \frac{\lambda h}{3}\right)$$

and **Hamming's method** (Problem 9.2.17) with

$$q(t) = \left(1 - \frac{3\lambda h}{8}\right)t^3 - \left(\frac{9}{8} + \frac{3\lambda h}{4}\right)t^2 - \frac{3\lambda h}{8}t + \frac{1}{8}$$

The roots of these polynomials with $h = 0$ are, respectively, $(1, -1)$, $(1, -1)$, and $(1, 1/16+.348i, 1/16-.348i)$. All three of these methods satisfy the root condition, but two of them just barely do; the midpoint and Milne methods do not satisfy the strong root condition. Such methods are called **weakly stable** and generally are not desirable for practical use.

Theorem 9.4 applies in the limit as h goes to zero; in actual calculations one has h positive, and the characteristic roots (and hence stability) depend on λh. For any of these methods (except one-step methods) one can ruin stability by taking λh too large (either positively, negatively, or as a complex number). Interest is thus focused on methods which allow λh to be as large as possible and still maintain stability. Traditionally, yet another kind of stability has been used for comparing methods for $h > 0$. A method is said to be **absolutely stable** if

$$|r_i(\lambda h)| < 1 \qquad \text{all } i \qquad \textbf{Equation 9.6.12}$$

This is a stronger condition than the previous; if a method is absolutely stable, then all solutions of the difference equation converge to zero as x goes to infinity. The root for Euler's method is $1+\lambda h$, and so this method is absolutely stable only for $\lambda \le 0$, although it is stable (but inefficient) for $\lambda \ge 0$. Figure 9.8 shows the ranges of λh (for λ real) where the Adams methods are absolutely stable. One sees that the Adams-Moulton methods have a considerably larger range of λh values with absolute stability than do the Adams-Bashford methods.

PROBLEMS 9.6

9.6.1 Show that Euler's method fails for the equation $y' = \sqrt{y}$ with $y(0) = 0$. The true solution is $y(x) = x^2/4$. Explain why this happens and why it does not contradict Theorem 9.1.

9.6.2 Give the particular method that one obtains from applying Simpson's rule in Problem 9.2.15. Show that this method is stable but not relatively stable (and hence weakly stable).

9.6.3 Show that all methods derived as in Problem 9.2.15 do not satisfy the strong root condition. Find an example with $p = 1$ which is relatively stable.

9.6.4 Consider the integration formula

$$y_{k+1} = 4y_k - 3y_{k-1} - 2hy'_{k-1}$$

(A) Determine the order of its local error

(B) Show that it is unstable

(C) Apply it to the differential equation $y' = y$ to show how fast the instability contaminates the computation

9.6.5 Verify experimentally that the global error for Euler's method is $O(h)$ as stated in Theorem 9.1 for the equations below. Carefully describe the experiment to be made and how the order of the error is estimated.

(A) $y' = -2y$ $\quad y(0) = 1$

(B) $y' = .5y$ $\quad y(0) = 1$

(C) $y' = y^2$ $\quad y(2) = -2$

(D) $y' = s\sqrt{y/x} - y/x$ $\quad y(.5) = 2.5$

Hint: $y(x) = (1+x)^2/x$

(E) $y' = (1+y)/\tan x$ $\quad y(\pi/6) = -0.5$

Hint: $y(x) = \sin(x) - 1$

9.6.6 Repeat the calculations of Problem 9.6.5 and compare the error with the formula given in Theorem 9.1.

9.6.7 Verify experimentally that the global error for the third-order Runge-Kutta method 9.2.14 is $O(h^3)$ as stated in Theorem 9.2. Carefully describe the experiment to be made and how the order of the error is estimated. Use the equations of Problem 9.6.5.

9.6.8 Consider the differential equation $y' = y^2$ with $y(1) = y_0$. Experimentally explore the stability of the solution of this equation as a function of y_0. Use a library routine to solve the equation. Discuss how this relates to the argument that the behavior of every equation can be modeled by an equation of the form $y' = \lambda y$.

9.6.9 Experimentally explore the potential difficulty with the weakly stable midpoint method (Problem 9.2.18). Consider the equation $y' = \lambda y$, $y(0) = 1$ with various values of λ. Carefully describe the experiment and its goals and how it is carried out. Give a complete discussion of the results. **Hint:** If the computer used has a very long word length, you may simulate a larger round-off error by using the formula in the form

$$y_{k+1} = y_{k-1} + (2hy'_k) * (1+10^{-8}\text{ random})$$

9.6.10 Repeat Problem 9.6.9 with Milne's method.

9.6.11 How large can the step size h be and still maintain a stable calculation for the following problems to be solved by a second-order Adams-Bashford method and a second-order Adams-Moulton method? Justify the answer.

(A) $y' = 6y$	$y(1) = 2$
(B) $y' = (1+x+y)^2$	$y(0) = 1$
(C) $y' = (\ln(1/x)+y)/x$	$y(.5) = 1.0$
(D) $y' = 10 + 5y(1+2x)/(1+x)^2$	$y(.5) = 14.2$
(E) $y' = -1.2y$	$y(0) = 1$

Hint: Use the conditions given in Figure 9.8.

9.6.12 The limits obtained in Problem 9.6.11 analytically are probably more strict than required in practice. Carry out a computational experiment with larger values of h than obtained in Problem 9.6.11 and approximately determine the values of h where the methods become seriously unstable.

9.6.13 Repeat Problems 9.6.11 and 9.6.12 for third-order Adams methods.

9.6.14 Repeat Problems 9.6.11 and 9.6.12 for fourth-order Adams methods.

REFERENCES

C. W. Gear, *Numerical Initial Value Problems in Ordinary Differential Equations,* Prentice-Hall, Inc., Englewood Cliffs, N.J. (1971).

L. Lapidus and W. E. Schiesser, *Numerical Methods for Differential Equations,* Academic Press, Inc., New York (1976).

L. Shampine and C. W. Gear, *A User's View of Solving Stiff Ordinary Differential Equations,* SIAM Review, **21** (1979), pp 1-17.

L. F. Shampine and M. K. Gordon, *Computer Solution of Ordinary Differential Equations: The Initial Value Problem,* W. H. Freeman and Company, San Francisco (1975).

L. F. Shampine, H. A. Watts, and S. M. Davenport, *Solving Nonstiff Ordinary Differential Equations — The State of the Art,* SIAM Review, **18** (1976), pp. 376–411.

*10 PARTIAL DIFFERENTIAL EQUATIONS

Partial differential equations are the basic tool for modeling physical phenomena. The amount of computer power spent in solving them is probably larger than any other single "class" of problems. The mathematical theory of partial differential equations is quite difficult; the theory and analysis of numerical methods for partial differential equations are the most difficult and extensive in numerical computation. In short, partial differential equations are too important to ignore and too difficult to cover adequately in an introductory text like this one.

The goal of this chapter is to give an introduction to the basic methods for solving partial differential equations; the reader is to keep in mind that, for a particular large-scale problem, the better methods are perhaps not even mentioned here. Fortunately, not all partial differential equations are difficult to solve, and the simpler methods presented here are useful (if not optimal) for a substantial number of applications. Some of the software available is also widely applicable even though the really difficult problems almost always require programs tailored for them.

PARTIAL DIFFERENTIAL EQUATIONS AS PHYSICAL MODELS 10.1

We denote partial derivatives by subscripts as follows:

$$\frac{\partial u}{\partial x} = u_x, \qquad \frac{\partial u}{\partial y} = u_y, \qquad \frac{\partial^2 u}{\partial y^2} = u_{yy}, \qquad \frac{\partial^2 u}{\partial x \partial y} = u_{xy}$$

Throughout this chapter we reserve t, x, y, and z as independent variables; think of t as time and x, y, z as coordinates in three dimensions. Examples of partial differential equations follow.

$$u_{xx} + u_{yy} = 6xy\, e^{x+y} \qquad \textbf{Equation 10.1.1}$$

$$u_t = 3\sin(x+t) + u_{xx} + (1+x^2)u_{yy} \qquad \textbf{Equation 10.1.2}$$

$$u_x + \rho(x, y)u_y = \gamma(x, y) \qquad \textbf{Equation 10.1.3}$$

$$u_{xx} + u_{yy} + u_{zz} + [100 + \sin(x+y+z) - \cos(2x-3y+z)]u = u_t + [\sin(24t)+1][x(1-x) + y(3-y) + z^2-1] \qquad \textbf{Equation 10.1.4}$$

$$u_t = e^u + 3u_{xx} + u_{yy} - \frac{1}{1+.5\sin(x)}(u_x)^2$$ **Equation 10.1.5**

These examples show the wide variety of partial differential equations; there are standard ways to classify them. The **order** is the highest number of derivatives that appears (all of the above are second order except 10.1.3, which is first order). The **dimension** is the number of "space" variables (x, y, or z); thus 10.1.2 has two dimensions plus time. An equation is **linear** if the solution u and its derivatives appear linearly; only 10.1.5 above is nonlinear. For simplicity we discuss equations with two dimensions or one dimension plus time; keep in mind that the "real" world has three dimensions plus time.

Partial differential equations are like ordinary differential equations in that boundary conditions or initial values are needed to completely determine the solution. We illustrate the variety of possibilities with three physical problems modeled by partial differential equations.

Heat Flow in a Rectangular Plate — Example 10.1

Consider a rectangular plate that is heated. Let u(x, y) denote the temperature at the point (x, y), and then the classical model for steady-state heat flow in the plate is the **Poisson equation**

$$u_{xx} + u_{yy} = f(x, y)$$ **Equation 10.1.6**

where f(x, y) is the heat source or forcing term. The f(x, y) term models the gain in heat from a source (say a flame) or the loss in heat from a sink (say a refrigerator unit). The temperature distribution also depends on what happens at the edge of the plate. The conditions at the edge of the plate are the **boundary conditions.** Figure 10.1 shows the diagram of a simple physical plate whose temperature distribution is modeled by **Laplace's equation:**

$$u_{xx} + u_{yy} = 0$$ **Equation 10.1.7**

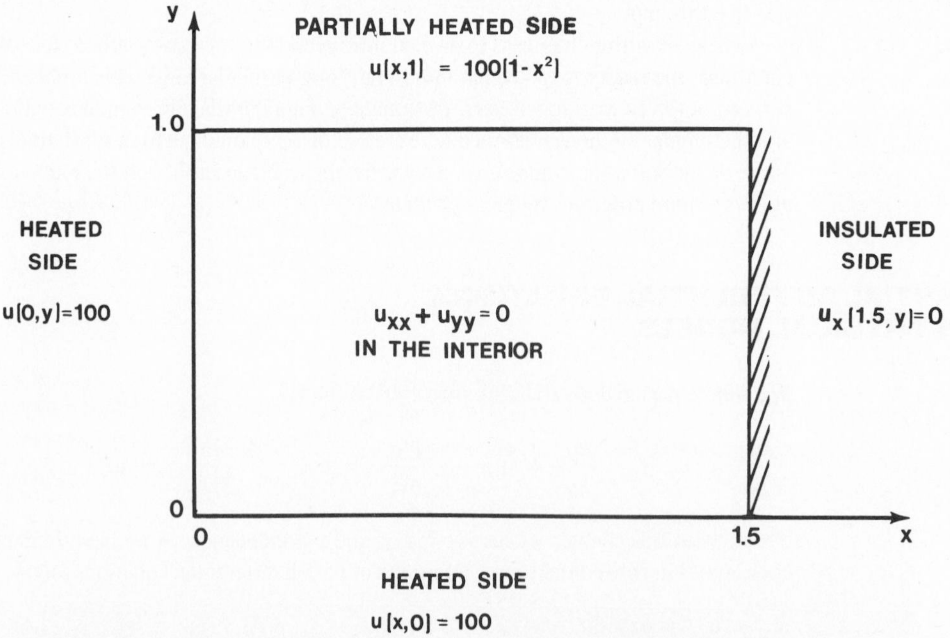

Figure 10.1 **Laplace's equation model for a heated plate.** The boundary conditions plus the partial differential equation determine the temperature distribution throughout the plate.

One can interpret the problem in Figure 10.1 as that of a plate with two sides in boiling water (heat is put into the plate along these sides), one side perfectly insulated (no heat flow means the derivative is zero on this side), and the fourth side has the temperature maintained in a variable way [there is some cooling mechanism and the function $u(x, 1) = 1 - x^2$ is probably measured rather than set by the cooling mechanism].

The Poisson equation 10.1.6 is also the classical mathematical model for the shape of a membrane. The $f(x, y)$ term models the external forces on the membrane, and $u(x, y)$ is the displacement of the membrane due to the forces.

Suppose now that a plate is placed into the situation of Figure 10.1. The temperature in the plate at the start is room temperature. Thus the temperature must change to reflect the new situation; the equation that models this process is the **heat equation**

$$u_t = u_{xx} + u_{yy} \qquad \textbf{Equation 10.1.8}$$

The problem solution is $u(x, y, t)$ which now also depends on time t, and there is an **initial condition**

$$u(x, y, 0) = 20$$

in addition to the boundary conditions shown in Figure 10.1. This initial condition models an initial room temperature of 20 degrees. The domain of x, y, and t for this equation is similar to that of Example 10.3. The initial condition 20 can be replaced by any function of x and y that represents the initial temperature distribution in the plate; for example,

$$u(x, y, 0) = 100[(1-y) + y(1-x^2)]$$

is an initial condition that satisfies three of the boundary conditions in Figure 10.1. Similarly, the conditions on the edge of the plate might depend on the time t. The condition at the top of the plate in Figure 10.1 might be $100(1-x^2)/(1+t^2)$ to model a heating mechanism that gradually decays as time increases.

The solution of 10.1.8 decays to the solution of 10.1.7, which is called the **steady-state solution** of 10.1.8. Steady state means there is no dependence on time t, and so $u_t = 0$.

Water Flow Past a Sphere — Example 10.2

Consider a sphere placed in a steady flow of water and held fixed in place. A cross section along the direction of the flow is shown in Figure 10.2. The flow is independent of the angle perpendicular to the direction of the flow, and so we have a two-dimensional mathematical model for a three-dimensional physical problem. The velocity of the fluid is the gradient of the potential $u(x, y)$; that is, the velocity vector at the point x_0, y_0 is $(u_x(x_0, y_0), u_y(x_0, y_0))$. The standard mathematical model for the velocity potential function $u(x, y)$ is again Laplace's equation 10.1.7 which is to hold outside the sphere. This problem is *axially symmetric.* The model is usually expressed in polar coordinates (as seen in Figure 10.2) so that the surface of the sphere has a simple description. **Laplace's equation in polar coordinates** is

$$(r^2 u_r)_r + \frac{1}{\sin\phi}(\sin\phi\, u_\phi)_\phi = 0 \qquad \textbf{Equation 10.1.9}$$

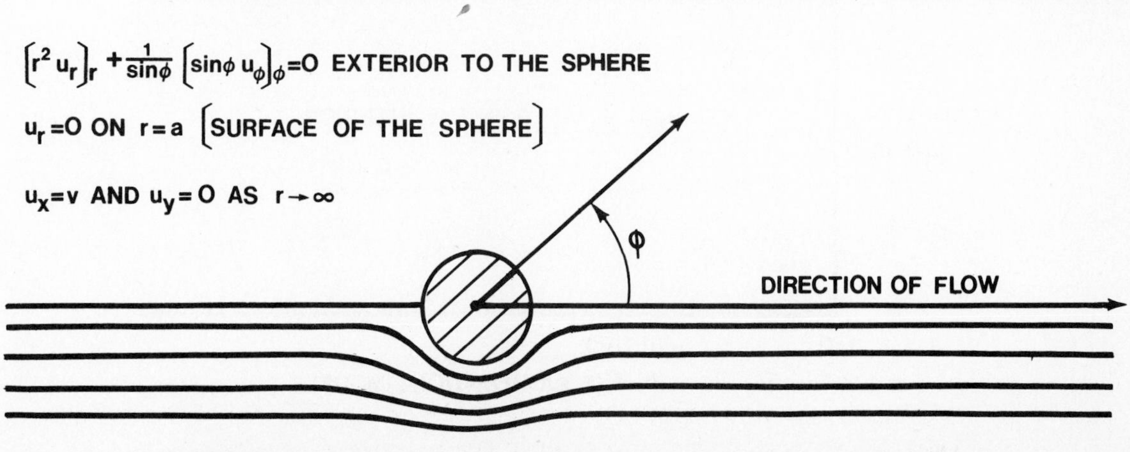

Figure 10.2 **Model for a sphere in a uniform flow of water.** The bottom half has some flow lines sketched in; the top half shows the polar coordinate system and the mathematical problem.

The boundary conditions are (1) there is no flow into or out of the sphere, $u_r = 0$ on the surface $r = a$, and (2) the flow at infinity in all directions is the uniform flow with velocity v, and so $u_x = v$ and $u_y = 0$ at r = infinity. The last conditions are expressed in polar coordinates as

$$u_r \cos\theta + u_\theta (\sin\theta)/r = v$$

$$u_r \sin\theta + u_\theta (\cos\theta)/r = 0$$

Vibrating String

Example 10.3

Consider a string that is tied to a wall at the left end, stretched tightly, and being oscillated vertically at the right end. The shape of the string depends on several factors; a typical shape is shown in Figure 10.3. Let u be the vertical displacement of the string from the rest position; $u = u(x, t)$ depends on x, the distance from the wall, and t, time. The partial differential equation model for the motion of the string is

$$(Tu_x)_x = f_0(x, t)$$

Equation 10.1.10

where $f_0(x, t)$ is a time-dependent forcing term and $T = T(x)$ is the tension in the string. We assume that the motion of the string is not very large (it stays close to horizontal). One force on the string is inertia, and with the above assumption on the motion, inertia is modeled by ρu_{tt} where $\rho(x)$ is the density of the string. Let $f_1(x, y)$ be any other forces on the string, and the model 10.1.10 becomes

$$(Tu_x)_x - \rho u_{tt} = f_1(x, t)$$

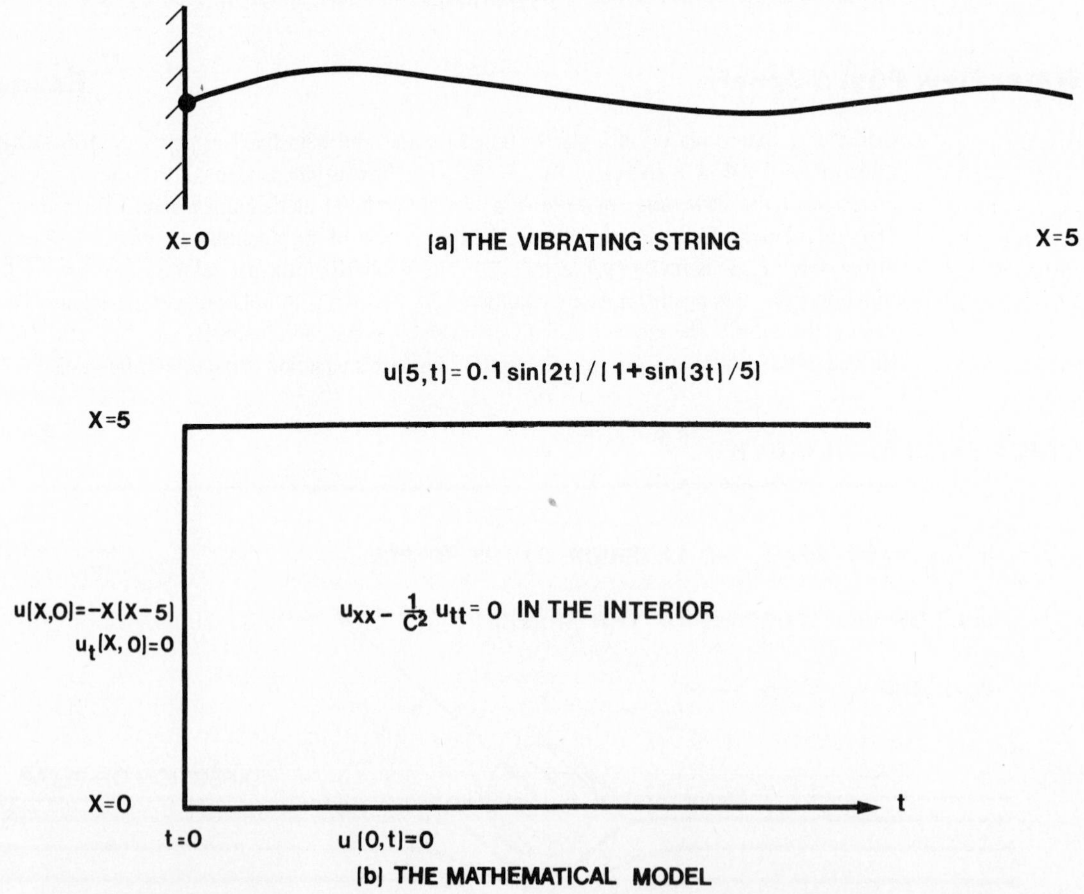

Figure 10.3 A vibrating string and its mathematical model, the wave equation. Initial conditions are given at time 0, and boundary conditions are given for x = 0, 5, and for all time.

We may further simplify the model by assuming $T(x)$ and $\rho(x)$ are constant to obtain the **wave equation**

$$u_{tt} - c^2 u_{xx} = f(x, t)$$ **Equation 10.1.11**

where $c^2 = T/\rho$ and $f(x, y) = f_1(x, y)/\rho$. Sample boundary conditions for this model are shown in Figure 10.3. The string is initially sagging a little and at rest, which gives initial conditions $u(x, 0) = -x(x-5)/100$ and $u_t(x, 0) = 0$. Then the right end is oscillated with $u(5, t) = .1 \sin(2t)/[1+.2\sin(3t)]$, and the forcing term $f(x, y)$ is zero.

These three examples show two quite different types of partial differential equations. Equations 10.1.8 and 10.1.11 are **initial value problems** or time-dependent problems where the solution is known at an initial time and then propagates through space in time. One characteristic of these problems is that the domain is open (goes to infinity) somewhere, for example, in time. This type splits into two subtypes, the **hyperbolic** problems which have both u_{xx} and u_{tt} terms (as in the wave equation) and the **parabolic** problems which have u_{xx} and u_t terms, but no u_{tt} term (as in the heat equation). The other type of problem is the **boundary value problem** (the Poisson problem) where the domain is entirely surrounded by boundary values. In Example 10.2 the boundary at infinity "surrounds" the domain and a condition at infinity is given. These problems are called **elliptic.** The natures of these three types of problems are quite different, and this is reflected in the numerical methods. Methods for initial value problems start with the initial conditions and follow the propagation of the solution, while methods for boundary value problems must solve for the entire solution simultaneously.

Another major difference in the nature of these equations is that elliptic and parabolic equations have a very strong **smoothing effect** while hyperbolic equations do not. If the boundary conditions or forcing function $f(x, y)$ have a sharp corner or jump (a singularity), the solution u of an elliptic or parabolic equation will be very smooth even at a small distance from the singularity. A singularity in a hyperbolic problem is preserved (even multiplied) and propagated to large distances from its source. This difference can be observed in common physical situations. Consider a room that has a hot stove and three windows that are very cold. There are very large changes in temperature right next to the stove and windows, but the room temperature changes rather slowly as one walks around. The room temperature is modeled by an elliptic or parabolic equation. Next consider throwing a stone in a pond at rest. The stone creates a singularity where it enters the waters, and this propagates all across the pond's surface in the form of waves. The constant c in the wave equation is the speed at which these waves travel. These waves decay slowly, and when they meet obstacles, there are new reflecting waves created. If it were not for small dissipation effects (not modeled by the wave equation), the waves would travel undiminished over the pond's surface forever.

There are many problems where this classification does not apply (for example, fourth derivatives might be involved), but these are the most important problems, and we restrict our attention to them.

DISCRETIZATION METHODS 10.2

The first step in solving a partial differential equation is to *discretize* it; the differential equations must be replaced by an approximating, finite system of algebraic equations. A large body of numerical analysis is devoted to analyzing the error due to discretizations. This analysis is not presented here, but we do give the order of the discretization errors for most of the methods discussed. Three basic discretization methods or approaches are considered here: **finite differences** (one replaces the domain by a finite point set and replaces derivatives by differences), **finite elements** (one replaces the solution u by a finite linear combination of known functions), and the **method of lines** (one replaces the two-dimensional domain by a system of lines to change the partial differential equation into a system of ordinary differential equations — this system is then solved by whatever method one wants to use). Some variations of these basic ideas are also discussed along with the sometimes difficult problem of discretizing the boundary conditions.

Finite Differences 10.2.A

The finite differences method is the most straightforward and easiest to understand. We first discuss the case of boundary value problems or elliptic problems. The method is exactly analogous to methods in ordinary differential equations. One replaces the domain by a rectangular **mesh** or **grid** of points as shown in Figure 10.4. Assume we have the partial differential equation and boundary conditions

$$u_{xx} + (1+x^2)u_x + u_{yy} = 6xy\, e^{x+y} \qquad \textbf{Equation 10.2.1}$$
$$u(x, 0) = 1 \qquad u = y \text{ for } x = 1.5 - y/2$$
$$u(0, y) = 1 - y \qquad u = 0 \text{ for } (x-.5)^2 + (y-.5)^2 = 1/\sqrt{2}$$

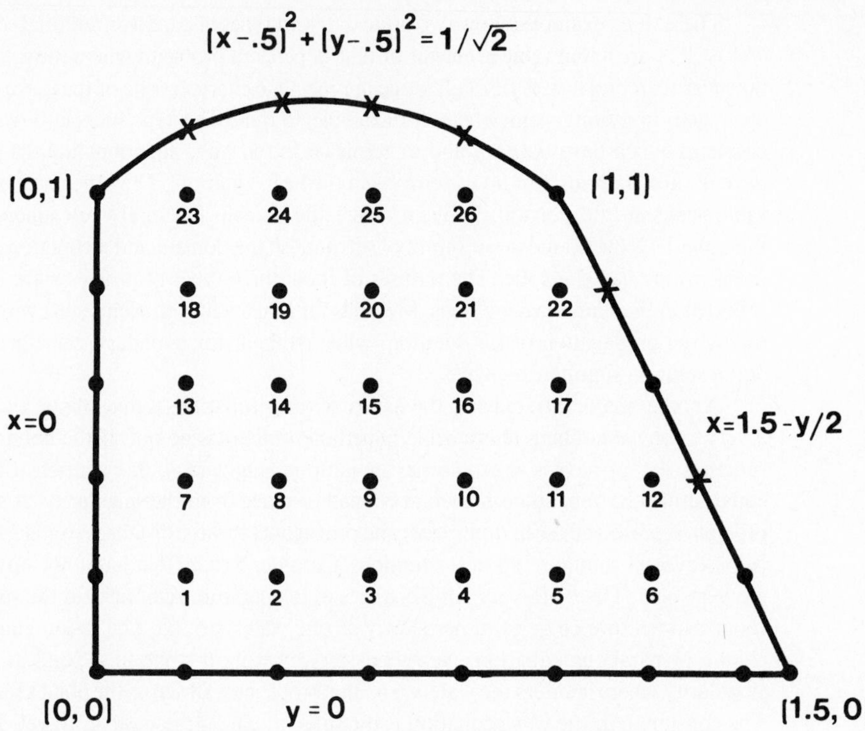

Figure 10.4 Discretization of a domain by a rectangular grid of points.

We number the discretization points in the domain as shown in Figure 10.4 and create a difference equation at each grid point. This produces 26 equations in 26 unknowns U_i for i = 1 to 26. The value U_i is an approximate value for the solution u at the ith point. We use the simplest difference formulas and two of the equations in the system are (with h = .2)

Point 8: (x = .4, y = .4)

$$\frac{U_7 - 2U_8 + U_9}{h^2} + 1.16\,\frac{U_9 - U_7}{2h} + \frac{U_{14} - 2U_8 + U_2}{h^2} = 2.1365193 \qquad \textbf{Equation 10.2.2}$$

Point 13: (x = .2, y = .6)

$$\frac{-2U_{13} + U_{14}}{h^2} + 1.04\,\frac{U_{14}}{2h} + \frac{U_{18} - 2U_{13} + U_7}{h^2} \qquad \textbf{Equation 10.2.3}$$

$$= 1.6023895 - \frac{.4}{h^2} + \frac{1.04(.4)}{2h} = -7.356105$$

Equation 10.2.2 is the typical case out in the middle of the domain; the equation involves the central point and its four immediate neighbors. Equation 10.2.3 is an easy case near the boundary; the same difference approximation is used, the value u(0, .6) = .4 is substituted from the left boundary, and these known terms are moved to the right side.

Trouble occurs next to the boundary on the top and right (at points 12 and 22–26) where the x's are shown in Figure 10.4. One must use special difference formulas for nonequally spaced points. The technique for obtaining such formulas is given in Chapter 7 (see Problem 7.3.5 and also Example 4.3). The solution of Problem 7.3.5 is

$$y''(x) \sim \frac{\alpha y(x-h) - 2(1+\alpha)y(x) + y(x+\alpha h)}{\alpha(1+\alpha)h^2}$$

If we use this difference approximation plus the result of Example 4.3 at the points 22 and 26, we obtain *Point 22:* ($x=1.0$, $y=.8$ gives $\alpha=.5$)

$$\frac{.5U_{21}-3U_{22}}{.75h^2} + \frac{2(-U_{21}-3U_{22})}{3h} + \frac{(-2U_{22}+U_{17})}{h^2} \qquad \textbf{Equation 10.2.4}$$

$$= 29.0383078 - \frac{.2}{.75h^2} - \frac{2(.8)}{3h} = +\ 19.704974$$

Point 26: ($x=.8$, $y=1.1380492$ gives $\alpha=.1380492$)

$$\frac{U_{25}-2U_{26}}{h^2} + \frac{1.64(-U_{25})}{2h} + \frac{\alpha U_{21}-2(1+\alpha)U_{26}}{\alpha(1+\alpha)h^2} \qquad \textbf{Equation 10.2.5}$$

$$= 29.0383078 - \frac{1.64(0)}{2h} - \frac{0}{\alpha(1+\alpha)h^2} = 29.0383078$$

Similar difference approximations are made at points 12, 23, 24, and 25.

Finite difference approximations are often presented in terms of **stencils.** A stencil shows the pattern of connection in the difference equation, and the entries in the stencil are the coefficients at the grid points. The stencil for the interior points of this problem is the **5-point star stencil:**

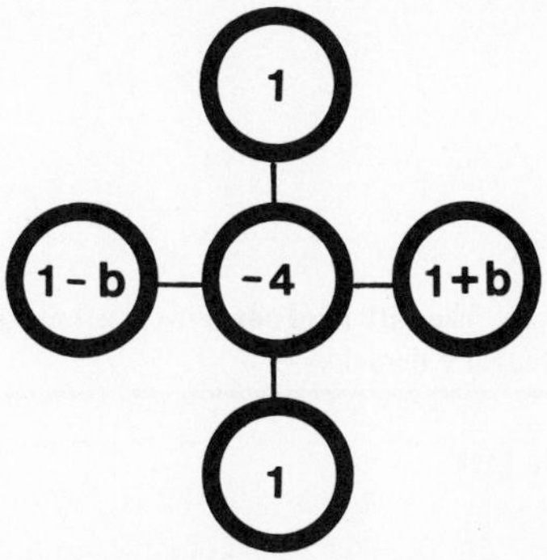

where $b = h(1+x^2)/2$ and we have multiplied the equations through by h^2 to simplify the stencil.

These difference equations are assembled into one algebraic system, and the pattern of nonzero elements is shown in Figure 10.5. These equations are solved to produce values of the U_i which approximate the solution $u(x, y)$ at the grid points. Compare this with Figure 6.5, which shows the matrix that arises from a square domain.

It is easy to see how a nonrectangular domain makes discretizing the equation more complicated and tedious to carry out. However, it has a much more drastic effect by lowering the accuracy of the solution computed. Recall from Chapter 7 (Theorem 7.1) that the central difference approximations are superaccurate; this shows up in the accuracy for the finite difference method. This is explicitly stated as follows:

Fact: *Assume that the elliptic partial differential equation and its solution are smooth enough. Then the error in the finite difference method is $O(h^2)$ if the grid is uniformly spaced of size h (including the boundary). If the grid is not uniformly spaced, then the error is $O(h)$.*

Thus there is a strong motivation to make the domains rectangles (one can also have 45-degree lines and keep a uniform grid). It is not necessary that the grid spacing be the same in the x and y variables. If h is used for the x direction and k for the y directions, then the errors in the finite difference solutions are $O(h^2+k^2)$ for a uniform grid and $O(h+k)$ otherwise.

We use the term **finite difference method** to mean the simple use of low-order finite differences as illustrated above. There are many other ways that finite differences can be used, and some of them give much more accurate methods than the simple one described here; they are also more complicated to describe and analyze.

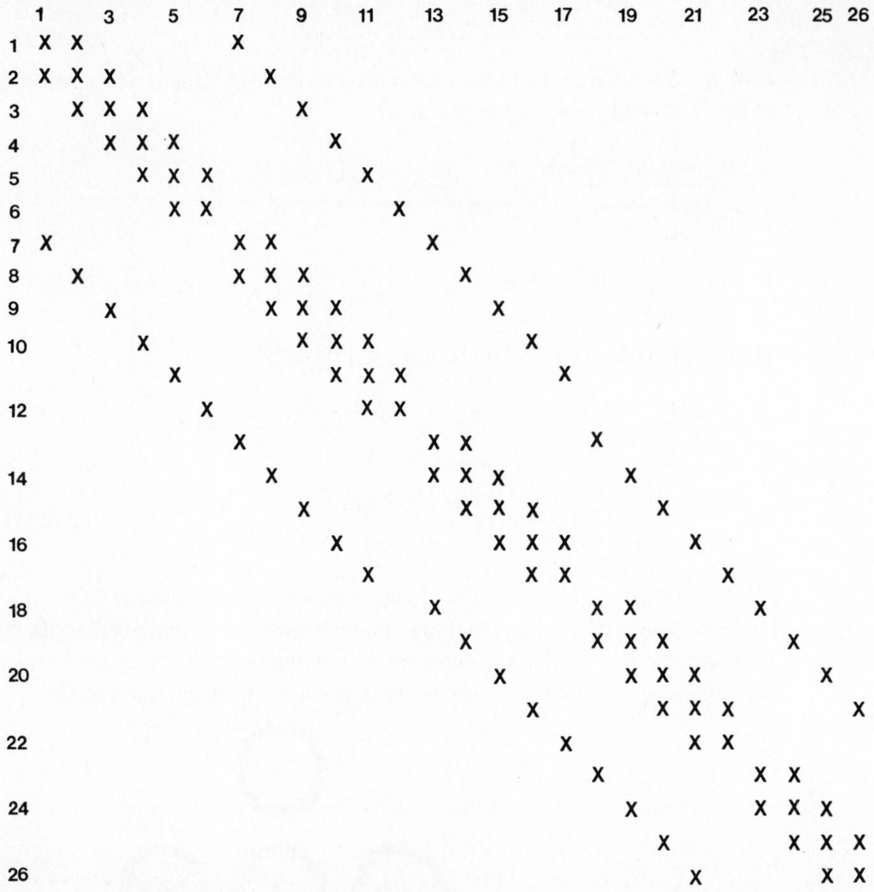

Figure 10.5 The pattern of nonzeros in a finite difference matrix for a partial differential equation on a non-rectangular domain.

Finite Difference Method for an Elliptic Problem

Example 10.4

We consider the partial differential equation

$$(1+x^2/2)u_{xx} + u_{yy} = 2 \sin y$$

on the triangular region with vertices (1, 0), (0, 1), and (1, 0). The true solution is $u(x, y) = x^2 \sin y$, and the boundary conditions are the values of the true solution. This problem is used to compare several methods for discretizing elliptic problems.

We introduce a uniform discretization grid of points with $x_i = ih$ and $y_j = jh$ where $h = 1/n$. In this case we are fortunate that all the boundary grid points fall exactly on the grid with spacing h. All the equations are of the simple form of 10.2.2 or 10.2.3. It is easy to see that there are $(n-1) + (n-2) + \ldots + 3+2+1 = n(n-1)/2$ interior grid points and unknowns. The pattern of zeros in the matrix is similar to that of Figure 10.5. The number of grid points decreases by 1 as one moves from jh to $(j+1)h$, and so the lengths of the "blocks" in the matrix decrease by one going from the upper left to the lower right.

We now consider finite differences for **initial value problems.** The general approach is the same as before, but the situation requires one to use different finite difference approximations. The physical and computational situations are illustrated in Figure 10.6. For hyperbolic problems there is a **domain of dependence** for each point (x, t); the value of u(x, t) depends just on the information inside the shaded area in Figure 10.6. The angle at the point (x, t) in the domain of dependence depends on the speed at which information is propagated in the physical problem (this is the constant c in the wave equation 10.1.10).

The domain of dependence for parabolic problems is theoretically everything from earlier times (this domain spreads out so that its boundary is parallel to the x axis); in fact the strength of the dependence decays so rapidly that real computations do not need to include everything.

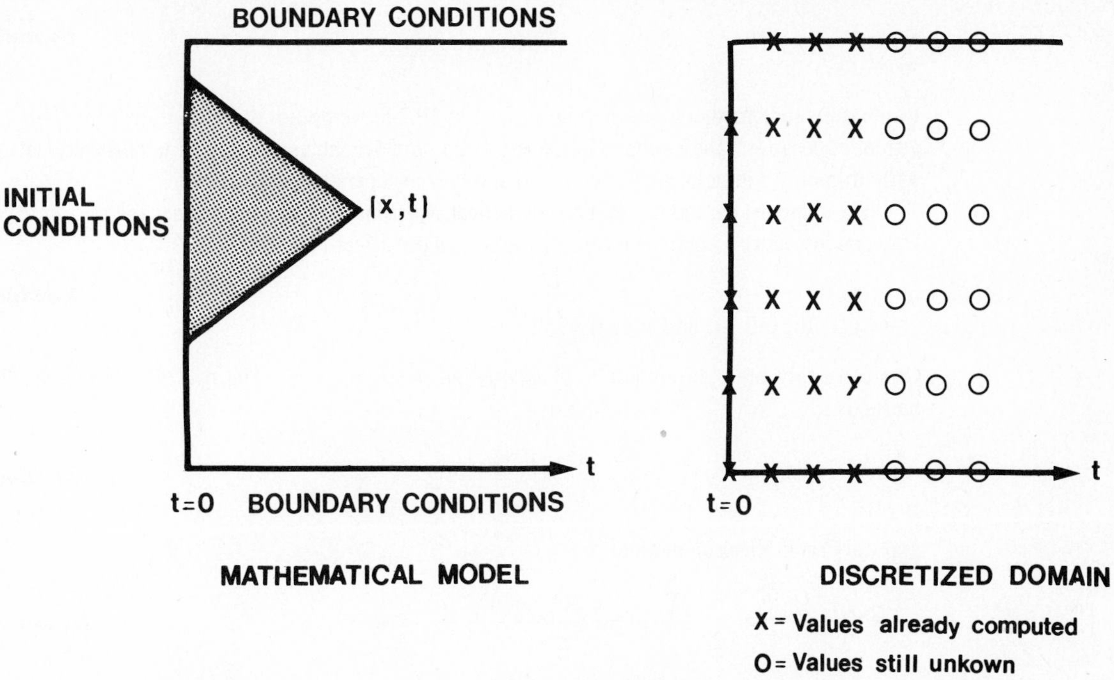

Figure 10.6 **Discretization for initial value partial differential equations.** The physical domain shows the domain of dependence for the solution at the point (x, t). In the discretized domain the computational problem is to advance the solution one time step and be consistent with the physical problem.

A numerical method for a hyperbolic problem must reflect the physical domain of dependence. For more complicated problems, this domain is not a simple triangle; it can be curved and depend on many things, and it becomes very difficult to handle properly. Ignoring these complications, consider then the discretized domain in Figure 10.6. Assume that the finite difference solution is computed at the x points; then we need to advance the solution to the next time line, to the o points. If we use the 5-point star stencil with center points on the last line of known values, we can solve the equations individually for the values at the next line in time. This method works for hyperbolic problems provided the ratio of the space discretization h and the time step k is such that the computational domain of dependence covers the physical domain of dependence.

Consider the simple wave equation problem

$$u_{tt} - c^2u_{xx} = 0 \qquad \textbf{Equation 10.2.6}$$

$u(x, 0)$ given, $u(0, t)$ and $u(1, t)$ given

Let the approximate solution to $u(x, t)$ at $x = ih$, $t = jk$ be denoted by U_{ij}. Then the 5-point star equations to advance the solutions of 10.2.6 one time step [from $t = jk$ to $t = (j+1)k$] are

$$U_{i,j+1} = 2U_{ij} - U_{i,j-1} + \frac{k^2c^2}{h^2}(U_{i+1,j} - 2U_{ij} + U_{i-1,j}) \qquad \textbf{Equation 10.2.7}$$

for $i = 1$ to $n-1$. We assume $h = 1/n$.

Fact: *Assume the hyperbolic partial differential equation and its solution are smooth enough. If $c^2k^2 \leq h^2$ so that the domain of dependence of the computed solution contains that of the true solution, then the error of the finite difference solution is $O(h^2+k^2)$.*

The condition $c^2k^2 \leq h^2$ is the **stability** condition for this method.

For many hyperbolic problems it is advantageous to replace a second-order equation like 10.2.6 by a system of first-order equations. We can introduce two new variables.

$$v = u_t$$
$$w = cu_x$$

into the wave equation 10.2.6 and obtain the pair of first-order partial differential equations

$$v_t = cw_x \qquad w_t = cv_x$$ **Equation 10.2.8**

Finite difference methods can then be applied to 10.2.8; we do not carry that out here. This approach is attractive because it allows one to follow the domains of dependence more easily. This is crucial in problems with unsmooth solutions such as with shock waves in supersonic flow.

The standard parabolic equation is the **heat equation** (10.1.8); we consider the one-dimensional case here and introduce a coefficient of u_{xx} (which does not affect the method):

$$u_t = au_{xx}$$ **Equation 10.2.9**

$$u(x, 0),\ u(0, t),\ \text{and } u(1, t) \text{ given}$$

One can apply finite differences to this equation in several ways. The two best known are the **explicit** method:

$$\frac{U_{i,j+1} - U_{i,j}}{k} = a\frac{U_{i+1,j} - 2U_{i,j} + U_{i-1,j}}{h^2}$$ **Equation 10.2.10**

and the **Crank-Nicolson** method:

$$\frac{U_{i,j+1} - U_{ij}}{k} = \frac{a}{2}\,\frac{U_{i+1,j} - 2U_{i,j} + U_{i-1,j}}{h^2} + \frac{a}{2}\,\frac{U_{i+1,j+1} - 2U_{ij+1} + U_{i-1,j+1}}{h^2}$$ **Equation 10.2.11**

The explicit method is similar in spirit to equation 10.2.8 for hyperbolic problems, while the Crank-Nicolson method has two distinct features. First, it is an approximation to the heat equation at the point $(ih, (j+1/2)k)$ even though no approximate value is computed there. Note that the t derivative approximation is superaccurate for this point [has error $O(k^2)$] and that the x derivative approximations at $t = jk$ and $t = (j+1)k$ are averaged to obtain an $O(h^2)$ approximation at this point. Second, the Crank-Nicolson stencil is an **implicit** method. That is, the unknowns on the time line $t = (j+1)k$ are related in a system of linear equations (with tridiagonal matrix), and this system must be solved at each time step.

There is a whole catalog of finite difference approximations to the heat equation (see Problem 10.2.16). The principal properties of these are summarized in the following:

Fact: *Assume the solution of the heat equation is smooth enough. The explicit method 10.2.10 gives an error in the finite difference solutions of order $O(k+h^2)$ and requires that $ak/h^2 < .5$ for stability. The implicit method 10.2.11 gives an error of order $O(k^2+h^2)$ and is always stable.*

The explicit method 10.2.10 requires $ak/h^2 < .5$ because the domain of dependence for a parabolic equation spreads very wide in both directions; the implicit methods essentially give a domain of dependence that covers all previous time.

To summarize this section, we have that finite difference methods are widely applicable, and simple, low-order approximations [i.e., the error is $O(h)$ or $O(h^2)$] can be obtained for most partial differential equations. The low order of the approximations may force one to take k and h very small to obtain reasonable accuracy, and this, in turn, may force one into very large computations. This matter is discussed in Section 10.3.C. For problems like numerical integrations, ordinary differential equations, etc., we have seen that higher-order methods are better, and this is also the case for partial differential equations. On the other hand, it is more difficult to develop and analyze higher-order methods for partial differential equations. A few comments on the difficulties are given in the next section. Furthermore, higher-order methods give more complicated formulas to program. While this is clearly a secondary disadvantage, it is sometimes used to justify using the simple methods.

Finite Element Methods 10.2.B

The finite difference method obtains a finite system of equations from a partial differential equation by discretizing the domain; values of the approximate solution are found only at a finite set of points. The finite element method obtains a finite system of equations by discretizing the solution space; the approximate solution obtained is a finite combination of known (and selected) functions. The principle of the finite element method is the standard one for numerical methods to solve general equations.

Let $Lu = f$ be a linear equation whose solution is a function, say $u(x, y)$. The steps in the method are:

1. Select some known basis functions to approximate $u(x, y)$, say

$$u(x, y) \sim \sum_{i=1}^{n} a_i b_i(x, y) = U(x, y, \mathbf{a})$$

The $b_i(x, y)$ are the **basis functions**; they play the same role as basis vectors in vector spaces.

2. Substitute $U(x, y, \mathbf{a})$ into L with the coefficients **a** to be determined to approximately solve the equation $Lu = f$.

3. Since step 2 is generally impossible to do exactly (one has only n unknowns available to satisfy an equation which holds for all values of x and y in some domain), select n conditions to approximate solving the equation $Lu = f$ and determine the coefficients a_i to satisfy this finite system of equations.

The method outlined above is more general than the finite element method. The **finite element method** requires, in addition, that the basis functions be **finite elements**, that is, functions which are zero except on a small part of the domain under consideration. The term finite elements comes from contrast with *infinitesimal elements* used in the standard derivations of differential equations for physical models using calculus techniques. The piecewise polynomials and B-splines are typical examples of finite element basis functions; the most commonly used basis elements are piecewise linear (even though they are rarely the most efficient).

The basis functions correspond to cutting up the domain into pieces and defining functions which are zero on all but one or a few of the pieces. Figure 10.7 shows two simple regions cut up into pieces using triangles and rectangles. A simple finite element basis function for a triangle is

$$\begin{aligned} b_i(x, y) &= a_i + b_i x + c_i y \qquad \text{in the triangle} \\ &= 0 \qquad \text{outside the triangle} \end{aligned}$$

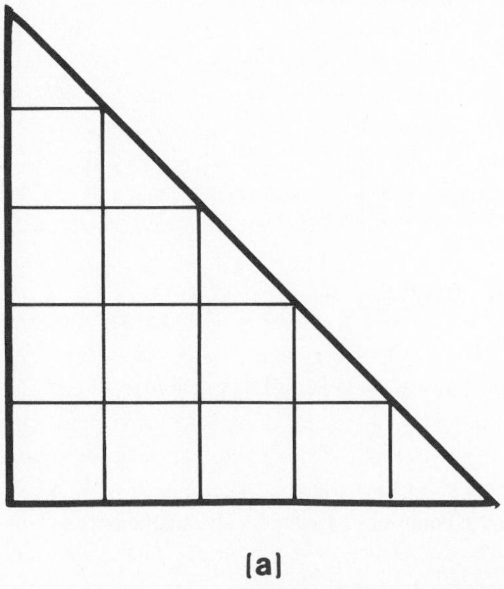

Figure 10.7 Partitions of two domains for the finite element method.

This is a C^{-1} piecewise polynomial of degree 1; that is, it is not even continuous. However, a continuous function to approximate $u(x, y)$ can be obtained by forcing the basis functions to match up at the vertices of the triangles. An approximate solution made up from this basis is a surface with triangular flat faces. To approximate $u(x, y)$ on the irregular domain in Figure 10.7(b), one uses 35 basis functions (one for each triangle) but has only 28 unknowns (the values at each of the vertices). For the rectangular partition in Figure 10.7(a) a pyramid function can be defined on a set of four rectangles by taking its value to be 1 at the center, zero along the edges, and linear everywhere else. This function is the product of the B-splines in x and y of degree 1 (see Figure 4.5). To approximate u(x, y) on the triangular domain in Figure 10.7(a), one would choose 21 of these pyramid functions: one for each of the vertices of the squares, including the boundary. A smoother, higher-degree element on four rectangles is obtained from the product of C^1-cubics or Hermite cubics in x and y. Consider the four squares defined by $x = x_{k-1}, x_k$, and x_{k+1} and $y = y_{j-1}, y_j$, and y_{j+1}. Then there are two Hermite cubic basis functions in x, $h_k(x)$ and $h_k^1(x)$ for $x_{k-1} \le x \le x_{k+1}$, and two in y, $g_j(y)$ and $g_j^1(y)$ for $y_{j-1} \le y \le y_{j+1}$ (see Problem 4.4.1 for explicit formulas). Take all four possible products

$$h_k(x)g_j(y),\ h_k(x)g_j^1(y),\ h_k^1(x)g_j(y),\ h_k^1(x)g_j^1(y) \qquad \textbf{Equation 10.2.12}$$

and then one has a basis for the C^1-cubics in two variables for the rectangular pieces. These functions are the **bicubic Hermite** basis functions. In the case of the triangular region in Figure 10.7(a) one obtains 84 basis elements: four for each of the vertices of the squares.

The **finite element conditions** to be satisfied normally involve some linear functionals. The most obvious choice is to make $LU(x, y, \mathbf{a}) = 0$ at n selected (x, y) points; this is called **collocation** and corresponds to interpolation as a way to obtain one function to approximate another. The system of equations to be solved is

$$LU(x_j, y_j, \mathbf{a}) = \sum_{i=1}^{n} a_i Lb_i(x_j, y_j) = f(x_j, y_j) \qquad \textbf{Equation 10.2.13}$$

where the points (x_j, y_j), $j = 1, 2, \ldots, n$ are the **collocation points**. If these points use the zeros of orthogonal polynomials, this method is sometimes called **orthogonal collocation**.

Another obvious choice of conditions is to make

$$E(\mathbf{a}) = \iint [LU(x, y, \mathbf{a}) - f(x, y)]^2\, dxdy = \text{minimum} \qquad \textbf{Equation 10.2.14}$$

This choice gives the **least squares method** and produces a system of n equations by applying the calculus method for minimization: set the derivatives of $E(\mathbf{a})$ equal to zero. We have

$$LU(x, y, \mathbf{a}) = \sum_{i=1}^{n} a_i Lb_i(x, y)$$

so that one obtains

$$\begin{aligned}
\frac{\partial E(\mathbf{a})}{\partial a_j} &= \iint \frac{\partial}{\partial a_j} \left[\sum_{i=1}^{n} a_i Lb_i(x, y) - f(x, y) \right]^2 dxdy \\
&= 2\iint (LU - f(x, y))Lb_j(x, y)dxdy \\
&= 2 \sum_{i=1}^{n} a_i \iint Lb_i(x, y)Lb_j(x, y)dxdy - \iint f(x, y)Lb_j(x, y)dxdy \\
&= 0
\end{aligned}$$

This gives the following linear system of equations to solve for the coefficients a_i:

$$\sum_{i=1}^{n} a_i \iint Lb_i(x, y)Lb_j(x\ y)dxdy = \iint f(x, y)Lb_j(x\ y)dxdy \quad \text{for } j = 1, 2, \ldots, n \qquad \textbf{Equation 10.2.15}$$

The conditions for collocation in 10.2.13 use the linear functionals $\lambda_j(g) = g(x_j, y_j)$ of point evaluation at step 3 of the general method, while the conditions 10.2.15 for least squares use the linear functionals

$$\lambda_j(g) = \iint g(x, y)Lb_j(x, y)dxdy$$

In each case the equation $Lu=f$ is approximately satisfied by setting $\lambda_j(LU) = \lambda_j(f)$.

A third common choice of finite element conditions gives the **Galerkin method**; it uses the linear functionals

$$\lambda_j(g) = \iint g(x, y)b_j(x, y)dxdy$$

and so the approximate system of equations $\lambda_j(LU) = \lambda_j(f)$ to be solved is

$$\sum_{i=1}^{n} a_i \iint (Lb_i(x, y))b_j(x, y)dxdy = \iint f(x, y)b_j(x, y)dxdy \qquad \textbf{Equation 10.2.16}$$

There are physical motivations of the Galerkin method which make it natural to use in many applications; we do not present these here.

The Galerkin equations may be simplified when the equation is **self-adjoint** and has **homogeneous boundary conditions.** That is, the problem is

$$Lu = (p(x, y)u_x)_x + (q(x, y)h_y)_y + r(x, y)u = f(x, y)$$
$$u = 0 \qquad \text{on the boundary}$$

in which case one can integrate 10.2.16 by parts (apply Green's theorem) to obtain

$$\sum_{i=1}^{n} a_i \iint (pU_{ix}U_{jx} + qU_{iy}U_{jy} + rU_i U_j)dxdy = \iint fU_j dxdy$$

This latter form of the Galerkin equations is the one usually used in practice. It gives a symmetric, positive definite system of equations for the a_i.

So far we have ignored the boundary conditions of the partial differential equation. There are two approaches to use; the first is to choose the basis functions to satisfy *exactly* the boundary conditions. This is great if one can manage it, but it is often very difficult to achieve. The second approach is not to take all the equations for the a_i from $LU = f$, but to take some from the boundary conditions. This is explained most easily for collocation; one has m collocation points for the differential equations and $k = (n-m)$ for the boundary conditions [assume the values of $u(x, y)$ are given as $g(x, y)$ on the boundary]. Then the full set of collocation equations is

$$\sum_{i=1}^{n} a_i Lb_i(x_j, y_j) = f(x_j, y_j) \qquad j = 1, 2, \ldots, m \qquad \textbf{Equation 10.2.17}$$

$$\sum_{i=1}^{n} a_i b_i(x_j, y_j) = g(x_j, y_j) \qquad j = m+1, m+2, \ldots, n$$

To include boundary conditions with the least squares method one minimizes

$$\iint [LU(x, y, \mathbf{a}) - f(x, y)]^2 dxdy + w \int [U(x, y, \mathbf{a}) - g(x, y)]^2 ds \qquad \textbf{Equation 10.2.18}$$

where the second integral is along the boundary, s is arc length, and w is a factor to be chosen. The system of equations resulting from setting derivatives equal to zero is

$$\sum_{i=1}^{n} a_i \left(\iint Lb_i Lb_j dxdy + w \int b_i b_j ds\right) \qquad \textbf{Equation 10.2.19}$$

$$= \iint f(x, y)Lb_j dxdy + w \int b_j g ds \qquad j = 1, 2, \ldots, n$$

Unfortunately, there is often no analysis that gives a good value for w, so that it is selected on the basis of intuition or trial and error. Most applications of the Galerkin method force the boundary conditions to be satisfied exactly by the basis functions and, in fact, frequently assume that the boundary condition is $u(x, y) = 0$ everywhere. There are some techniques to transform equations to give boundary conditions of this type (see Problems 10.2.25 and 10.2.26), but they are not completely general, and this limits the applicability of the Galerkin method.

Collocation Method for an Elliptic Problem — Example 10.5

We again consider the partial differential equation

$$(1+x^2/2)u_{xx} + u_{yy} = 2 \sin y$$

on the triangular region with vertices (0, 0), (0, 1), and (1, 0). The true solution is $u(x, y) = x^2 \sin y$, and the boundary conditions are the values of the true solution. The domain is partitioned as in Figure 10.7(a), and we choose the bicubic Hermite basis functions of Equation 10.2.12. There are 84 of these basis functions, too many for us to write down all the equations in the system to approximate $u(x, y)$. An appropriate set of 84 collocation points is shown in Figure 10.8(a). Figure 10.8(b) shows a second set of 104 collocation points if more basis elements are used along the hypotenuse of the triangle.

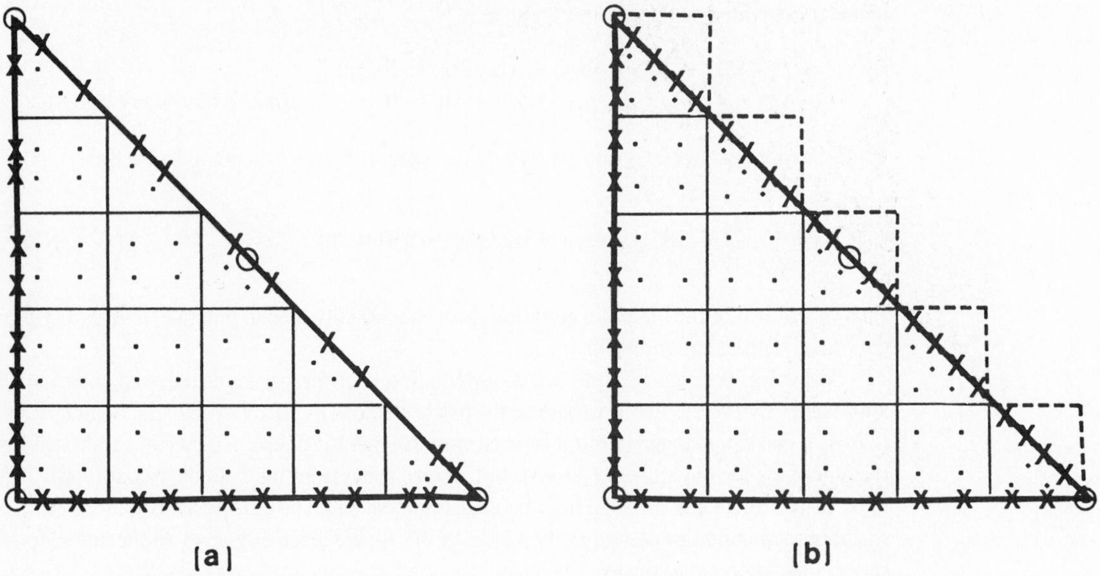

Figure 10.8 **Possible placement of collocation points.** (a) There are 50 interior collocation points (dots) for the partial differential equation, 30 "side" points (x's) for the boundary conditions, and 4 "corner" points (circles) for the boundary conditions. (b) Another set of 104 collocation points when basis elements corresponding to the dotted squares are added.

The collocation equations corresponding to 10.2.17 are rewritten to reflect the special construction of the basis elements. We associate them with the 21 vertices (s_k, t_m) (we include those on the boundary) where

$$s_k = .2(k-1) \qquad t_m = .2(m-1) \qquad 2 \le k+m \le 6$$

and the 84 unknowns a_i are renamed a_{km}, b_{km}, c_{km}, and d_{km} so that the approximation to $u(x, y)$ is

$$U(x, y, \mathbf{a}) = \sum_{2\le k+m\le 6} a_{km}h_k(x)g_m(y) + b_{km}h_k(x)g_m^1(y) + c_{km}h_k^1(x)g_m(y) + d_{km}h_k^1(x)g_m^1(y) \qquad \textbf{Equation 10.2.20}$$

The purpose of this numbering and renaming is to make it easy to follow the geometric pattern of the partition of the domain. If the partition of the domain is refined, the same scheme is still valid. Note that no simple systematic organization of the unknowns is possible with a triangulation such as shown in Figure 10.7(b). The collocation equations are then, for the 50 interior points (x_i, y_j),

$$\sum_{2\le k+m\le 6} a_{km}L(h_k(x_i)g_m(y_j)) + \ldots + d_{km}L(h_k^1(x_i)g_m^1(y_j)) = 2 \sin (y_j) \qquad \textbf{Equation 10.2.21}$$

and, for 34 boundary points (x_i, y_j),

$$\sum_{2\le k+m\le 6} a_{km}h_k(x_i)g_m(y_j) + \ldots + d_{km}h_k{}^{1}(x_i)g_m^1(y_j) = x_i^2 \sin(y_j)$$ **Equation 10.2.22**

The terms $L(h_k(x)g_m(y))$ are explicitly calculated from

$$L(h_k(x)g_m(y)) = (1+x^2/2)h_k''(x)g_m(y) + h_k(x)g_m''(y)$$

and the formulas of Problem 4.4.1 are used, for example,

$$h_k(x) = -\frac{2(x-s_{k-1})^3}{.008} + \frac{3(x-s_{k-1})^2}{.04} \qquad s_{k-1} \le x \le s_k$$

$$= -\frac{2(s_{k+1}-x)^3}{.008} + \frac{3(s_{k+1}-x)^2}{.04} \qquad s_k \le x \le s_{k+1}$$

$$h_k''(x) = -\frac{12(x-s_{k-1})}{.008} + 150 \qquad s_{k-1} \le x \le s_k$$

$$= -\frac{12(s_{k+1}-x)}{.008} + 150 \qquad s_k \le x \le s_{k+1}$$

All these little formulas would be incorporated into function subprograms of an actual program to solve this problem.

Note that **most terms in any collocation equation are zero**. This is an important consequence of the finite element method's use of basis functions which are zero except on a small domain. The Hermite cubic basis functions are zero everywhere except on a 2 by 2 block of squares. There are four nonzero basis functions for each 2 by 2 block; see 10.2.12. Thus those that are not zero on any particular square are those associated with the square's four corners (the corners are centers of 2 by 2 blocks). Specifically, at any interior collocation point there are only four sets of basis functions that are not zero there: one set for each vertex of the square containing the collocation point. See Figure 10.9, where the pattern of overlapping is shown for the domains where basis functions are not zero. Thus, no matter how many basis functions there are, there are no more than 16 nonzero terms in any particular equation from 10.2.21. There are less (only 12) nonzero terms for the collocation points in the interior of the triangles along the hypotenuse of the domain.

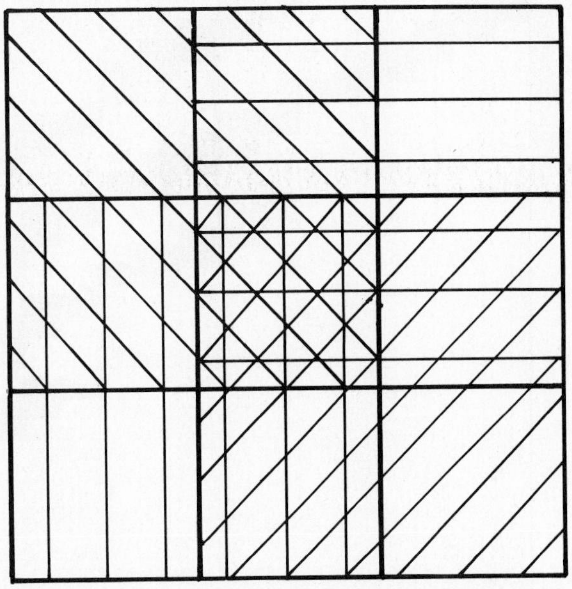

Figure 10.9 Overlapping of domains where $h_k(x)g_m(y)$ is not zero. Any collocation point in the center square has exactly 16 basis functions (4 for each corner of the center square) which are not zero at that point. The four hashings indicate the four 2 by 2 blocks where sets of Hermite cubic basis functions are nonzero.

For the boundary condition collocation points, there are 3 sets (12 functions) not zero along the hypotenuse and 2 sets (8 functions) not zero along the other two sides. Finally, there is only 1 set (4 functions) not zero at the collocation points at the three vertices of the triangle.

So far in solving this example we have:

1. Partitioned the domain of the problem
2. Chosen piecewise cubic basis functions (bicubic Hermites)
3. Chosen 84 collocation points in the domain
4. Organized the basis functions and unknowns in a manner that reflects the geometry of the problem
5. Shown how to write down the collocation equations explicitly

There are two more steps in this example:

6. Organize the collocation points in a manner that reflects the geometry of the problem
7. Assemble the equations into a linear algebraic system and solve it

In principle, any method can be used to organize (or number) the unknowns and equations (collocation points). In practice, it makes a big difference how this is done. The resulting linear system is sparse; the 84 by

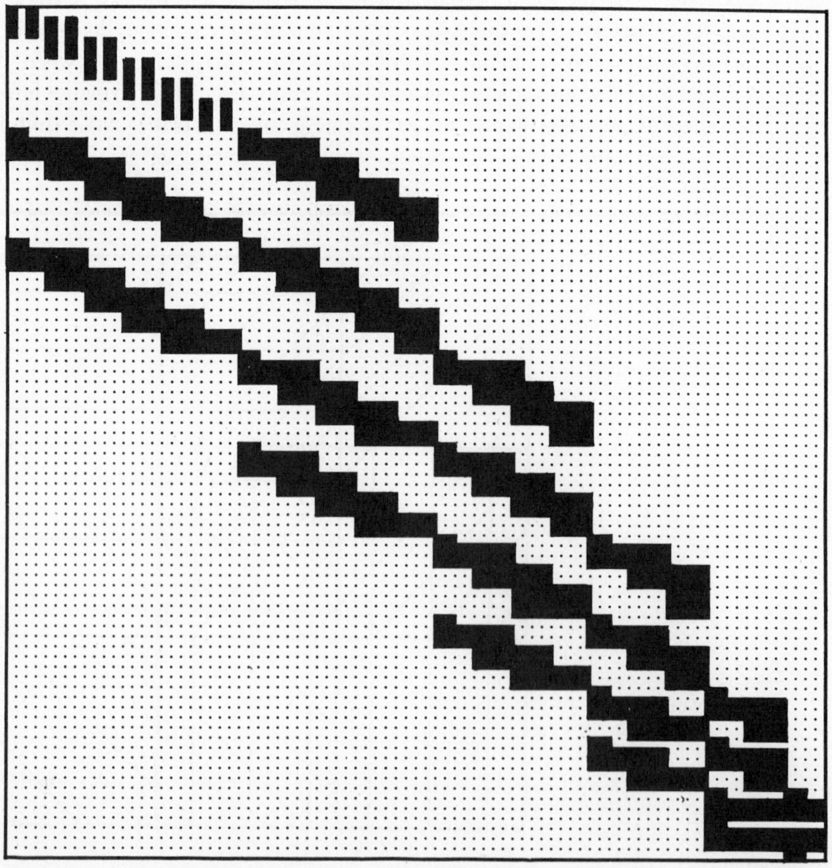

Figure 10.10 Pattern of nonzero elements in the collocation equations. This pattern is obtained from a simple, systematic ordering of the 84 unknowns and equations.

84 matrix has at most 84 × 16 nonzero elements (in fact it has far fewer than that). If the numbering is done to obtain a band matrix, then a lot of computation can be saved by using a band matrix solver. Other sparse matrix solvers might be even more efficient, but *in all cases* the efficiency depends heavily on the pattern of nonzeros in the coefficient matrix. A simple and reasonable ordering of the unknowns is to use

a_{11}, b_{11}, c_{11}, d_{11}, a_{21}, b_{21}, . . .

and to order the collocation points (equations) starting at the lower left and proceeding across and then up. The pattern of nonzero elements obtained is shown in Figure 10.10. This pattern is rather complicated though somewhat banded in form. The complication results partly from the triangular shape of the domain and partly from the fact that this ordering of the collocation points is not the best. Figures 10.11 and 10.12 show the patterns from two better orderings. The first is to always group the four collocation points in a square together. Thus the points on the lower edge of the triangle are numbered first, then the lower two parallel interior rows are numbered (left to right) together rather than one at a time. This reduces the number of "diagonals" in the matrix somewhat. The second pattern in Figure 10.12 results from ordering the collocation points "around" the corners of the squares rather than in rows.

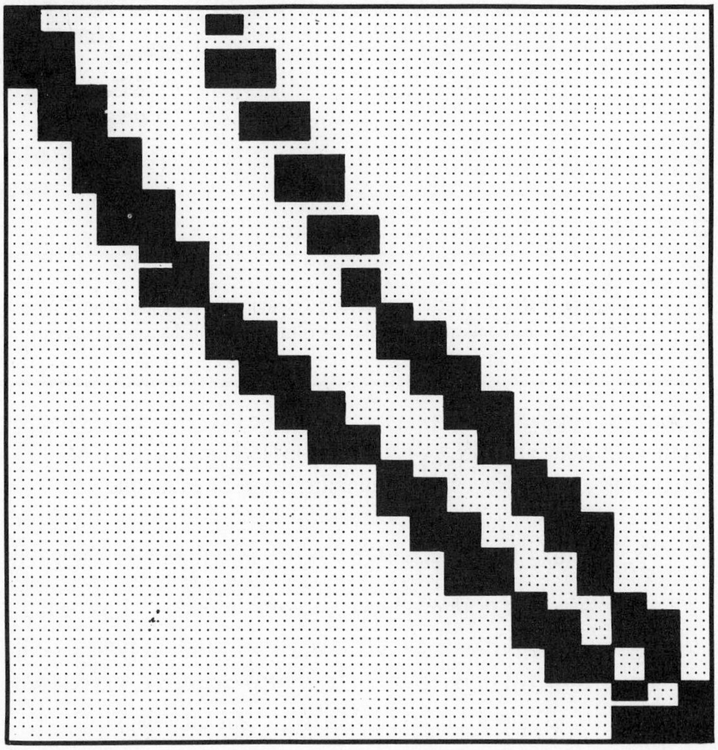

Figure 10.11 **Pattern of nonzero elements in the collocation equations.** This pattern results from ordering the unknowns and equations in 4 by 4 blocks for each element. The ordering goes vertically first.

The Least Squares Method for an Elliptic Problem — Example 10.6

We consider the same partial differential equation

$$(1+x^2/2)u_{xx} + u_{yy} = 2\sin y$$

as in Examples 10.4 and 10.5 and use the same basis functions for the finite element method. We carry out the differentiation of the least squares method to minimize 10.2.18 and obtain the system

$$\Sigma\, a_i[\iint Lb_iLb_j + w\int b_ib_j] = \iint fLb_j + w\int gb_j \qquad j = 1, 2, \ldots, n \qquad \textbf{Equation 10.2.23}$$

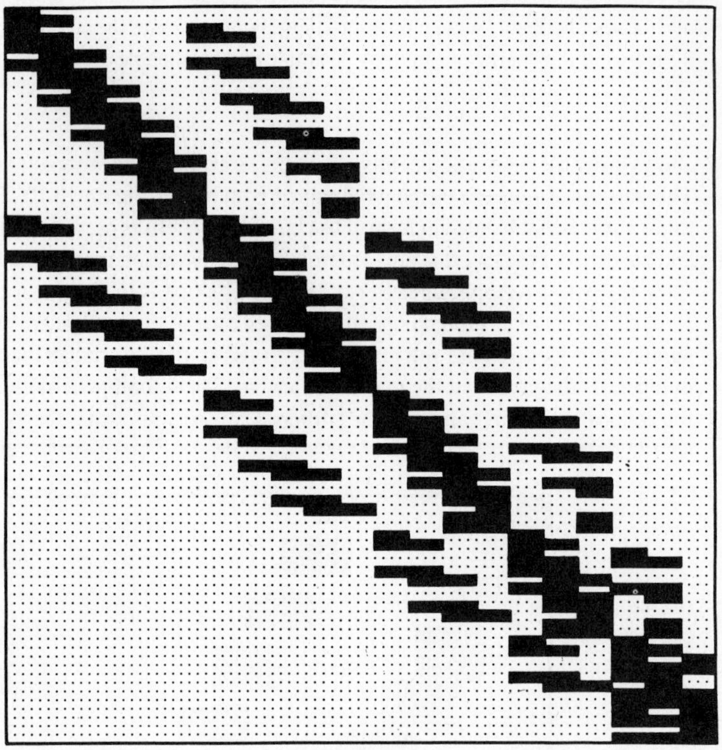

Figure 10.12 **Pattern of nonzero elements in the collocation equations.** This pattern results from ordering the equations and unknowns in 4 by 4 blocks associated with each grid point. The ordering goes horizontally first.

One must now substitute $f(x, y) = 2 \sin y$ and $g(x, y) = x^2 \sin y$ on the hypotenuse and $g(x, y) = 0$ on the other two sides, and $b_i(x, y) =$ the bicubic Hermite functions. As in Example 10.5, we reorganize the basis functions and unknowns to obtain a first set of 21 equations

Equation 10.2.24

$$\begin{aligned}
\sum_{2 \le k+m \le 7} \quad & a_{km}[\textstyle\iint L(h_k(x)g_m(y))L(h_i(x)g_j(y)) + w\int h_k(x)g_m(y)h_i(x)g_j(y)] \\
&+ b_{km}[\textstyle\iint L(h_k(x)g^1_m(y))L(h_i(x)g_j(y) + w\int h_k(x)g^1_m(y)h_i(x)g_j(y)] \\
&+ c_{km}[\textstyle\iint L(h^1_k(x)g_m(y))L(h_i(x)g_j(y)) + w\int h^1_k(x)g_m(y)h_i(x)g_j(y)] \\
&+ d_{km}[\textstyle\iint L(h^1_k(x)g^1_m(y))L(h_i(x)g_j(y)) + w\int h^1_k(x)g^1_m(y)h_i(x)g_j(y)] \\
&= \textstyle\iint 2 \sin y \; L(h_i(x)g_j(y)) + w\int (x^2 \sin y)h_i(x)g_j(y) \qquad 2 \le i+j \le 6
\end{aligned}$$

There are 63 other equations, 21 each when replacing $h_i(x)g_j(y)$ by $h_i(x)g^1_j(y)$, $h^1_i(x)g_j(y)$, and $h^1_i(x)g^1_j(y)$, respectively.

Problem 4.4.1 gives explicit formulas for the h and g functions which can be substituted into the integrals. All the integrals in the coefficient matrix (left side of 10.2.24 and similar equations) can be integrated exactly as the integrands are all piecewise polynomials. All the integrals on the right side in this example can also be integrated exactly, but this is an unusual happening. Note that *the linear system of equations is symmetric.*

A crucial question is this: *How many integrals are there and how do we evaluate them?* Since there are 84 basis functions, there might be $84^2 = 7056$ integrals to evaluate! First we note that a lot of the integrals are automatically zero because one or the other of the basis functions in the products is identically zero. The overlap of the basis functions is shown in Figure 10.9. There are nine 2 by 2 squares that overlap a particular 2 by 2 square (one for each corner in the 2 by 2 squares). Since there are four basis functions for each 2 by 2 square, there are a total of 36 basis functions [such as $h_k(x)g_m(y)$] which overlap a given one [such as $h_i(x)g_j(y)$]. Thus there are at most 36 integrals to be evaluated in any of the equations; there are fewer for equations near the boundaries. This reduces the maximum number of integrals to be evaluated

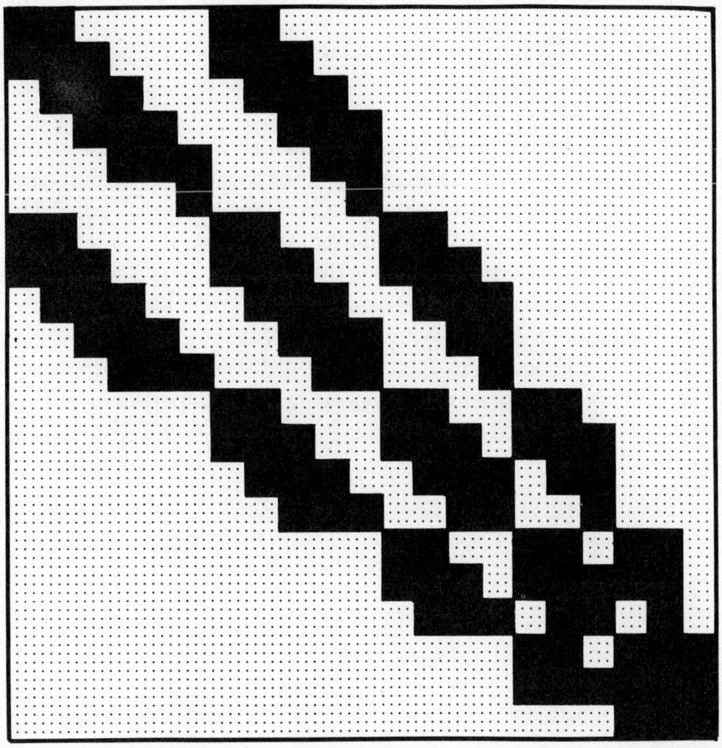

Figure 10.13 **Patterns of nonzero elements in the least squares equations.** The Hermite cubic approximate solution on the triangle has 84 coefficients determined by solving a linear system of this form.

from 7056 to less than 3024. This would still be a formidable number of integrals. The actual pattern of nonzero elements in the matrix is shown in Figure 10.13, and there are 508 such elements (and 508 integrals to evaluate).

There are three reasonable alternatives for evaluating these integrals.

1. *Derive formulas by hand.* There are really not 508 *different* integrals because of the repetitious pattern of the partition of the triangle. It is tedious, but not hopeless, to sit down and discover all the possible combinations and derive the formulas for them. About 100 different integration formulas are needed for this entire system.

2. *Derive formulas with a symbolic mathematics system.* There are several symbolic mathematics computer systems which can do all the integrations for this problem. One writes a program to generate the integrands and then asks that the integral be given. These formulas can then be used in the computer program to set up and solve the system for the partial differential equation.

3. *Use numerical integration with a* 3 *by* 3 *Gauss formula.* Recall that an n-point Gauss formula is superaccurate; it produces the exact result for polynomials of degree $2n-1$ or less. The integrands in this particular problem are all polynomials of degree 6 or less in x and y (Lb_i produces polynomials of the form $ax^3y^3 + bx^3y$ or lower degree). Thus a 4 by 4 Gauss formula in each square produces exact results for the polynomials in x and y. There is an analysis that shows that the 3 by 3 Gauss formula gives sufficient numerical integration accuracy (at least in the limit as the size of the rectangles decreases) for the overall accuracy in the approximate solution to the partial differential equation. After all, there is no point in doing a lot of work to get these integrals extremely accurate when one is going to obtain only rough accuracy for $u(x, y)$.

There is a relationship between the least squares method and collocation: if the integrals are estimated with a 2 by 2 Gauss formula, then the least squares equations are just the collocation equations using these Gauss points as collocation points.

The Galerkin Method for an Elliptic Problem — Example 10.7

We first consider the same partial differential equation and basis functions as in previous examples. In order to use the Galerkin method, we need to have the basis functions exactly satisfy the boundary conditions. Along two sides of the triangle we have $u(x, y) = 0$ as the boundary condition, and this can be satisfied exactly by discarding all the basis functions $h_k(x)$ or $g_m(y)$ associated with corner points of the form $(0, y)$ or $(x, 0)$. This eliminates 23 basis functions [the only one left for the point $(0, 0)$ is $h_1^1(x)g_1^1(y)$]. Note that this could have also been done for the collocation and least squares methods to substantially reduce the number of unknowns for this particular problem.

The boundary conditions along the hypotenuse pose a severe problem; it is clearly impossible to make the piece-wise cubic polynomials equal $x^2 \sin y$ along this line. We first put the problem into a standard form by making *all* the boundary conditions equal zero by subtracting a function $b(x, y)$ from $u(x, y)$. For this problem we choose $b(x, y) = x^3y(\sin y)/(1-x-y+xy)$ which satisfies *all* the boundary conditions simultaneously. Such a function can easily be found for rectangles and triangles (see Problems 10.2.25 and 10.2.26), but it might not be possible to obtain one for other shapes of the domain. Now set

$$v(x, y) = u(x, y) - b(x, y) = u(x, y) - \frac{x^3y(\sin y)}{1-x-y+xy} \qquad \textbf{Equation 10.2.25}$$

and note that

$$v_{xx} = u_{xx} - b_{xx}, \qquad v_{yy} = u_{yy} - b_{yy}$$

The new function $v(x, y)$ satisfies the partial differential equation

$$\begin{aligned}(1+x^2/2)v_{xx} + v_{yy} &= 2 \sin y - (1+x^2/2)b_{xx} - b_{yy} \\ v(x, y) &= 0 \text{ on all boundaries}\end{aligned} \qquad \textbf{Equation 10.2.26}$$

where b_{xx} and b_{yy} are known functions.

For this new problem we can again satisfy the boundary conditions on two sides of the triangle by discarding the 23 basis functions. To satisfy the boundary conditions along the hypotenuse, we must *modify* the basis functions to make them zero along this line. This can be done by inducing special basis functions; it is not possible to have cubic polynomial pieces satisfy this extra condition and still join up smoothly with each other. However, along the hypotenuse one can use the basis functions

$$\begin{array}{ll} h_i(x)g_m(x)(x+y-1) & h_i^1(x)g_m(h)(x+y-1) \\ h_i(x)g_m^1(y)(x+y-1) & h_i^1(x)g_m^1(y)(x+y-1) \end{array}$$

to satisfy the boundary conditions and still join up continuously (but, with these basis functions, not with continuous derivatives) with all the other basis functions. Note that this modification changes the whole method; it is not easy to say whether one achieves more or less accuracy.

The equations for the coefficients of the Galerkin approximation to $v(x, y)$ are then 8 sets of equations. The first set consists of the 3 equations

$$\sum_{\substack{2\le k+m\le 5 \\ k,\, m\ne 1}} a_{km}\iint L(h_k(x)g_m(y))\; h_i(x)g_j(y) \qquad \textbf{Equation 10.2.27}$$

$$+ \sum_{\substack{2\le k+m\le 5 \\ k=2,5 \text{ and } m=1,5}} b_{km}\iint L(h_k(x)g_m^1(y))\; h_i(x)g_j(y)$$

$$+ \sum_{\substack{2\le k+m\le 5 \\ k=1,5 \text{ and } m=2,5}} c_{km}\iint L(h_k^1(x)g_m(y))\; h_i(x)g_j(y)$$

$$+ \sum_{2\le k+m\le 5} d_{km}\iint L(h_k^1(x)g_m^1(y))\; h_i(x)g_j(y)$$

$$+ \sum_{\substack{k+m=6,7 \\ k,m \neq 1}} a_{km} \iint L(h_k(x)g_m(y)(x+y-1))\ h_i(x)g_j(y)$$

$$+ \sum_{\substack{k+m=6,7 \\ k \neq 1}} b_{km} \iint L(h_k(x)g_m^1(y)(x+y-1))\ h_i(x)g_j(y)$$

$$+ \sum_{\substack{k+m=6,7 \\ m \neq 1}} c_{km} \iint L(h_k^1(x)g_m(y)(x+y-1))\ h_i(x)g_j(y)$$

$$+ \sum_{k+m=6,7} d_{km} \iint L(h_k^1(x)g_m^1(y)(x+y-1))\ h_i(x)g_j(y)$$

$$= \iint (2 \sin y - (1+x^2/2)b_{xx} - b_{yy})\ h_i(x)g_j(y) \qquad \text{for } 4 \le i+j \le 5 \text{ and } i, j \neq 1$$

The $h_i(x)g_j(y)$ of 10.2.27 are replaced in the other 7 sets by

$h_i^1(x)g_j(y)$	6 equations with $i=2, 4$; $j=1, 3$, and $i+j \le 5$
$h_i(x)g_j^1(y)$	6 equations with $i=1, 3$; $j=2, 4$, and $i+j \le 5$
$h_i^1(x)g_h^1(y)$	10 equations with $i, j=1, 4$, and $i+j \le 5$
$h_i(x)g_j(y)(x+y-1)$	7 equations with $i+j=6, 7$, and $i, j \neq 1$
$h_i^1(x)g_j(y)(x+y-1)$	9 equations with $i+j=6, 7$, and $j \neq 1$
$h_i(x)g_j^1(y)(x+y-1)$	9 equations with $i+j=6, 7$, and $i \neq 1$
$h_i^1(x)g_j^1(y)(x+y-1)$	11 equations with $i+j=6, 7$

The pattern of nonzero elements in the coefficient matrix is the same as the least squares method; see Example 10.6 and Figure 10.13. The problem of computing the integrals that appear in the coefficient matrix is similar to that of the least squares method. Things are slightly more complicated here because the special elements near the hypotenuse have integration formulas different from the rest.

Comparison of Methods for Elliptic Problems **10.2.C

Examples 10.4, 10.5, 10.6, and 10.7 show the ordinary finite difference, collocation, least squares, and Galerkin methods applied to the same problem. The effort of deriving the equations, computing the coefficients, and solving the linear equations increases steadily through these examples. If one has a rectangular domain, then all the finite element methods become simpler and it is more efficient to set up the equations while the finite difference method remains essentially unchanged. There are special fast methods to solve the equations for both approaches provided the partial differential equation is simple and a regular mesh is used. If one has a more complicated domain, then the finite difference method is affected the most; it becomes substantially more complicated and less accurate. The collocation and least squares methods become more complicated because of handling unusual boundary shapes, but otherwise they are relatively unaffected. The Galerkin method becomes much more difficult because of the necessity to satisfy exactly the boundary conditions.

The principal advantage of the finite element methods is that they are more accurate, usually much more accurate. Thus if one requires .5 percent accuracy, one might need to solve a system of 250 to 400 algebraic equations with the ordinary finite difference method and only 50 to 100 with a finite element method as described here. Note that the most common versions of finite element methods use piecewise linear instead of piecewise cubic basis elements and that they have no accuracy advantage over ordinary finite differences.

The second advantage of finite element methods is the one that brought them into widespread use; they are more flexible in handling general shapes of the domain. This is not obvious from the examples given here, but it is so. A common way to use those methods is with triangular pieces instead of rectangular. In many cases triangles provide a much better way to cut up a domain, and other shapes are used in some application areas.

To illustrate the differences in accuracy of the methods, we choose a simple problem on a rectangular domain, namely,

$$4u_{xx} + u_{yy} - 10u = 4(5x^2 - 5x + 4)[1 - \cos(2\pi y)] - (2\pi)^2\cos(2\pi y)$$
$$u(x, y) = 0 \text{ for } x, y = 0 \text{ and } 1$$
Equation 10.2.28

The exact solution of 10.2.28 is $2(x^2 - x)[\cos(2\pi y) - 1]$.

Equation 10.2.28 has been solved using finite differences, collocation with Hermite bicubics, and Galerkin with Hermite bicubics. The results are given in Table 10.1. The differences in the accuracy obtained are already large even for coarse grids. With 225 unknowns the finite difference method achieves an accuracy of $3*10^{-3}$, while the finite element methods achieve similar accuracy with 64 or 100 unknowns. The difference in the number of unknowns of the two finite element methods is due to different methods of handling the homogeneous boundary conditions and not to any intrinsic difference in the methods. Similarly, the Galerkin method with 196 unknowns is 10 times more accurate than the finite difference method with 225 unknowns. The finite difference method with 961 unknowns does not achieve as much accuracy as the finite element methods on a 7 by 7 mesh, and yet it uses 4 to 7 times as much computer time.

Errors and Work for Solving the Elliptic Equation 10.2.28 **Table 10.1**

The computer times given are in seconds on a VAX computer with floating point accelerator. The equations are solved with a band matrix solver (Gauss elimination). The integrals in the Galerkin method are approximated with a 3 by 3 Gauss quadrature formula. Different implementations of the methods and different computers can affect these experimental results substantially, but the trend seen here is typical.

Finite Differences				
Grid	5×5	9×9	17×17	33×33
No. of equations	9	49	225	961
Set-up time	.05	.05	.27	.93
Solution time	.05	.12	1.60	20.48
Total time	.13	.17	1.88	21.45
Maximum error	$5*10^{-2}$	$1*10^{-2}$	$3*10^{-3}$	$8*10^{-4}$
Collocation with Hermite Bicubics				
Grid	3×3	5×5	7×7	11×11
No. of equations	16	64	144	400
Set-up time	.07	.12	.20	.47
Solution time	.08	.70	2.75	15.48
Total time	.17	.83	2.97	15.97
Maximum error	$3*10^{-2}$	$3*10^{-3}$	$6*10^{-4}$	$8*10^{-5}$
Galerkin with Hermite Bicubics				
Grid	3×3	5×5	7×7	11×11
No. of equations	36	100	196	484
Set-up time	.28	.70	1.50	4.05
Solution time	.27	1.22	3.72	18.93
Total time	.57	1.93	5.25	23.02
Maximum error	$1*10^{-2}$	$2*10^{-3}$	$5*10^{-4}$	$9*10^{-5}$

These solutions were obtained using the ELLPACK system discussed in Section 10.4.B. In that context, the solution methods are (in terms of the software modules used):

```
5 POINT STAR          →  AS IS               →  LINPACK BAND
HERMITE COLLOCATION   →  HERMITE COLLORDER   →  BAND GE
SPLINE GALERKIN       →  AS IS               →  LINPACK SPD BAND
```

For a given number of unknowns the finite element methods require more computation. It is more work to set up the algebraic equations, especially for the Galerkin method, and more work to solve them because the matrix is more complicated. Compare the patterns of Figure 10.5 for finite differences with those of Figures 10.10, 10.11, 10.12, and 10.13 for finite element methods. For most problems the gain in accuracy of the $O(h^4)$ finite element methods more than offsets the increased work of solving the system of equation. One exception is for "small" problems with 50 or 100 unknowns to provide rough accuracy in the solution.

Formulation of Methods in Terms of Linear Functionals **10.2.D

The collocation, least squares, and Galerkin methods are expressed in terms of linear functionals in Section 10.2.B. This formulation is made systematically here and allows us to define concisely several methods not otherwise discussed in this book. Furthermore, this abstract approach is most useful for seeing the relationship between various methods, and it provides a framework in which to define yet other methods.

Let R denote the domain of the partial differential equation $Lu=f$ where L is the differential operator. Let $Mu=g$ be the boundary condition equation on the boundary ∂R of R. Let $\mathbf{x} = (x, y)$ denote the independent variable. Then the problem is stated abstractly as

$$LU = f \qquad \mathbf{x} \text{ in } R \qquad \text{Equation 10.2.29}$$

$$Mu = g \qquad \mathbf{x} \text{ in } \partial R \qquad \text{Equation 10.2.30}$$

The methods considered here have three steps:

1. Choose basis functions $b_i(\mathbf{x})$, $i = 1, 2, \ldots, k$ to approximate $u(\mathbf{x})$.
2. Choose linear functionals λ_j, $j = 1, 2, \ldots, k$.
3. Approximate the solution $u(\mathbf{x})$ as

$$u(\mathbf{x}) \sim U(\mathbf{x}) = \sum_{i=1}^{k} a_i b_i(\mathbf{x}) \qquad \text{Equation 10.2.31}$$

with the coefficients a_i determined by the conditions

$$\lambda_j[L(U(\mathbf{x})) - f(\mathbf{x})] = 0 \qquad j = 1, 2, \ldots, m \qquad \text{Equation 10.2.32}$$

$$\lambda_j[M(U(\mathbf{x})) - g(\mathbf{x})] = 0 \qquad j = m+1, \ldots, k \qquad \text{Equation 10.2.33}$$

We introduce notation for special linear functionals as follows:

Point evaluation (at x_0): $\delta_{x_0}(f) = f(x_0)$

Derivative evaluation (at x_0): $\delta^{(k)}_{x_0}(f) = f^{(k)}(x_0)$

Definite integration (along C): $I_C(f) = \int_C f(x)dx$

Inner product [on C with $a(x)$]: $\mathbf{a}^T\mathbf{f}_C = \int_C f(x)a(x)dx$

The formulation of several methods in these terms is given starting with the three finite element methods already discussed.

Collocation: λ_j = point evaluations functionals, m for the domain R, and $k-m$ for ∂R.

Least Squares: The linear functionals combine two inner products as follows:

$$\lambda_j(f) = L(\mathbf{b}_j)^T\mathbf{f}_R + w\,\mathbf{b}_j^T\mathbf{f}_{\partial R}$$

The equation 10.2.32 is then a restatement of equations 10.2.19; recall that w is a parameter to weigh the boundary conditions with the partial differential equation. One often sees this method stated without boundary conditions to simplify the discussion.

Galerkin: Assume the basis functions $b_i(\mathbf{s})$ satisfy $Mb_i = g$ exactly for all i; then the linear functionals are

$$\lambda_j(f) = \mathbf{b}_j^T\mathbf{f}_R$$

These linear functionals make 10.2.32 become 10.2.16.

Fourier Series: The basis functions are trigonometric, and the domain R is the unit square $0 \le x, y \le 1$. The problem is $u_{xx} + u_{yy} = 0$ with $Mu = u$. For concreteness choose $b_i(\mathbf{x}) = \sin(kx)\sinh(jy)$ (there are other combinations of trigonometric and hyperbolic functions where this method is applicable). Then there are no linear functionals for 10.2.32 as $Lb_i = 0$ for all i; the linear functionals for the boundary conditions are $\lambda_j(f) = [\sin(kx)\sinh(jy)]^T \mathbf{f}_{\partial R}$.

Taylor's Series: The basis functions are polynomials $b_i(\mathbf{x}) = x^k y^j$. The domain R contains the origin $\mathbf{0} = (0, 0)$ and

$$\lambda_j(f) = \delta_{\mathbf{0}}^{(j-1)}(f) \qquad j = 1, 2, \ldots, m$$

The boundary conditions are satisfied independently, usually by choosing collocation, that is,

$$\lambda_j(f) = \delta_{\mathbf{x}_j}(f) \qquad j = m+1, \ldots, k$$

where $\mathbf{x}_j$ is on ∂R. This method is rarely seen for partial differential equations, but its analog is commonly stated for ordinary differential equations (see Section 9.2.B).

Collocation for Equation, Least Squares for Boundary Conditions: This is a combined method where

$$\lambda_j(f) = \delta_{\mathbf{x}_j}(f) \qquad j = 1, 2, \ldots, m$$

as in collocation. Rather than collocate on the boundary, we set

$$\lambda_j(f) = \mathbf{b}_\ell^T \mathbf{f} \qquad j = m+1, \ldots, k$$

where ℓ runs over a selection of the basis functions. In principle, the choice of basis to use for the boundary conditions is arbitrary; in practice, such as for finite element methods, there are natural choices to make.

The last example illustrates that there are nonstandard methods which can be constructed rather easily. More complex combinations are feasible, and they might define very effective methods whose properties are as yet unexplored.

The Method of Lines 10.2.E

The **method of lines** applies to initial value (time-dependent) problems, and it reduces a partial differential equation to a system of ordinary differential equations. The resulting system of ordinary differential equations is then solved using the sophisticated software discussed in Section 9.4. This approach has proved very effective in many instances, especially in reducing the amount of programming and analysis required to solve the partial differential equation. The time to execute the resulting program is usually more than for a specifically developed and optimized program for the problem, but this is to be expected.

The method is most directly applicable to a problem of the form

$$u_t = F(\mathbf{x}, u, u_x, u_{xx})$$
$$u(\mathbf{x}, 0) \text{ given, } u(\mathbf{x} \text{ boundary}, t) \text{ given}$$

Here $\mathbf{x}$ stands for the space variables, for example, (x, y) in a problem with two space variables plus time. Explicit examples of this form are

Equation 10.2.34

$$u_t = u_{xx} + \cos(x)u_x + [\sin 2x - \cos(t+x)]u$$
$$u(x, 0) = x(1-x) \qquad u(0, t) = 0 \qquad u(1, t) = \sin(t)$$

Equation 10.2.35

$$u_t = u_{xx} + (1+y^2)u_{yy} + [\sin(t+xy)]u_y - (1+xyt)u$$
$$u(x, y, 0) = 1 \quad u(x, 0, t) = u(x, 2, t) = 1$$

$$u(0, y, t) = 1 - \frac{4y(y-1)t}{1+t} \qquad u(2, y, t) = 1 + \frac{\sqrt{t}\,\sin(\pi y)}{1+\sqrt{t}\,/2}$$

The idea is to make a *partial discretization,* to discretize the space variables x (and y) and leave the time variable t alone. In 10.2.34 we replace the x domain [0, 1] by a discrete set of points $x_i = ih$ for $i = 0, 1, 2, \ldots, n$, where $h = 1/(n+1)$. Along each of the lines (x_i, t) for $t \geq 0$ we have a function $U_i(t)$ of a single variable. See Figure 10.14 for the case $h = 1/4$.

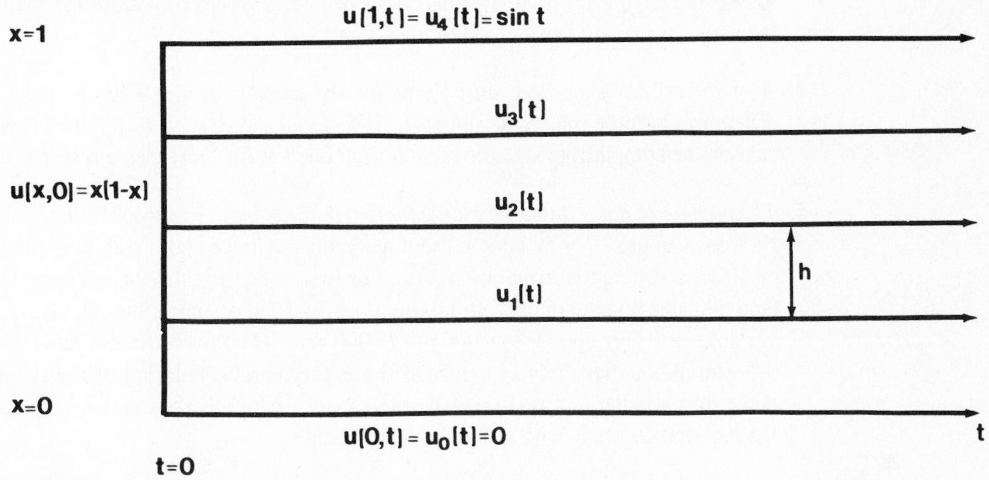

Figure 10.14 **The method of lines with a partial discretization.** The space variable x is discretized into 5 points producing 5 lines and associated functions of t. Two of these are boundary lines where the functions are given.

Suppose a simple finite difference approximation is used for u_{xx} and u_x; one obtains

$$U_1' = \frac{U_0 - 2U_1 + U_2}{h^2} + \cos(.25)\,\frac{U_2 - U_0}{2h} + [\sin(.5) - \cos(t+.25)]U_1 \qquad \textbf{Equation 10.2.36}$$

$$U_2' = \frac{U_1 - 2U_2 + U_3}{h^2} + \cos(.5)\,\frac{U_3 - U_1}{2h} + [\sin(1.) - \cos(t+.5)]U_2$$

$$U_3' = \frac{U_2 - 2U_3 + U_4}{h^2} + \cos(.75)\,\frac{U_4 - U_2}{2h} + [\sin(1.5) - \cos(t+.75)]U_3$$

$$U_1(0) = 0.1875 \qquad U_2(0) = 0.25 \qquad U_3(0) = 0.1875$$

This is a system of three differential equations for the three functions $U_1(t)$, $U_2(t)$, and $U_3(t)$; $U_0(t)$ and $U_4(t)$ are known from the boundary conditions. A real problem would, of course, have more lines than are used here for illustration. Note that the right sides of the differential equations are very similar, and we can use the general formula

$$U_i' = \frac{U_{i-1} - 2U_i + U_{i+1}}{h^2} + \cos(x_i)\,\frac{U_{i+1} - U_i}{2h} + [\sin(2x_i) - \cos(t+x_i)]U_i$$

for any number of lines.

Several observations about this method are given.

1. *One must balance the errors.* The error is due to the discretization of the space variable ($O(h^2)$ in the example) and the solution of the system of ordinary differential equations. Thus the error requested in solving the differential equations should approximately equal that in discretizing the space variable.

2. *The problem can be nonlinear in the space derivatives.* Since the ordinary differential equation methods apply equally well to nonlinear problems, there is no need for linearity on the right side of 10.2.36. The method applies to an equation like

$$u_t = (u^2+t)u_{xx} + (u_x)^2 - \sin(u+tx)$$

3. *The right side is "banded."* The ith equation in the example only involves $U_i(t)$, $U_{i+1}(t)$, and $U_{i-1}(t)$. In this linear problem the matrix (which was not defined explicitly) of coefficients of U_j on the right side is tridiagonal. Even if the system is nonlinear, there is a special banded structure to the problem which can be exploited. Some differential equation software has special provisions for "banded" right sides just to facilitate its use with the method of lines.

4. *Any discretization method can be used for the space variables.* The method is illustrated with finite differences because that is the simplest. However, it can be used with finite element discretizations just as well; the complications are no greater than one has for finite element methods for elliptic problems.

5. *The number of lines can be very large for two or three space variables.* If there is only one space variable, then one can use 20 or 50 lines without worrying too much about computer time (provided one is using an efficient differential equation solver). For two space variables this corresponds to 400 to 2,500 lines (and the same number of differential equations) and a very substantial calculation. If one has three space variables, this corresponds to 8,000 to 125,000 lines. This latter case is so large that it is unlikely that the differential equations can be solved without very careful tailoring of the program and using a very powerful computer. It pays in such cases to analyze carefully the space discretizations in order to obtain the required accuracy with as few lines as possible.

6. *The system of ordinary differential equations is frequently stiff.* See Section 9.6.D for a very brief discussion of stiffness. This means that the software used for solving the system of ordinary differential equations often must use the special techniques for stiff problems. Some of the stiff differential equations software is especially developed for the method of lines; see the discussion of Algorithm 540 in Section 10.4.A.

PROBLEMS 10.2

10.2.1 Obtain the $O(h^4)$ finite difference discretization for Laplace's equation based on a 5-point approximation to u_{xx} plus a 5-point approximation to u_{yy}. Discuss the difficulty of using this approximation near the boundary.

10.2.2 Extend the discretization of Problem 10.2.1 to the equation $(1+x^2)u_{xx} + u_{yy} + xu_x - yu_y + (x^2+y^2)u = \sin(xy)$. Explicitly display the stencil for x, y grid spacings of h and k.

10.2.3 (A) Establish that the **9-point star** for the Poisson problem

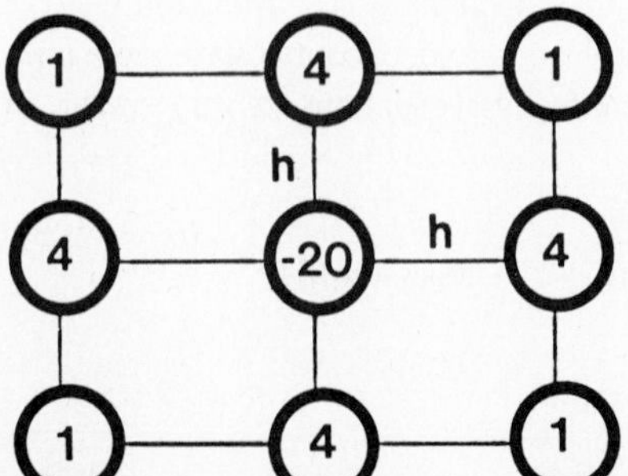

has truncation error $O(h^2)$. **Hint:** Expand u(x, y) in a Taylor's series in x and y about the center point.

(B) Experimentally verify that the error is $O(h^2)$ by applying the method to the problem $u_{xx} + u_{yy} = 2e^{x+y}$ which has the true solution e^{x+y}.

(C) Compare the difficulty of satisfying the boundary conditions for this stencil with that of Problem 10.2.1.

10.2.4 Let S_9 represent the 9-point star stencil of Problem 10.2.3 and let S_5 represent the standard 5-point star stencil. The Poisson problem $u_{xx} + u_{yy} = f(x, y)$ can be approximated by

$$\frac{S_9u}{6h^2} = f + \frac{h^2}{12} S_5f$$

(A) Write out the equations for this method applied on a rectangle with an n by n grid. Compare the work of setting up and solving these equations with the work for those of Problem 10.2.3.

(B) Show that this method has truncation error $O(h^4)$. **Hint:** Expand u(x, y) in a Taylor's series to show that $S_9u = u_{xx} + u_{yy} + \frac{h^2}{12}(u_{xxxx} + 2u_{xxyy} + u_{yyyy}) + O(h^4)$. Then note that $f_{xx} + f_{yy} = u_{xxxx} + 2u_{xxyy} + u_{yyyy}$.

(C) Experimentally verify that the error is $O(h^4)$ using the partial differential equation of Problem 10.2.3(B).

10.2.5 Consider a grid near a curved boundary as illustrated by

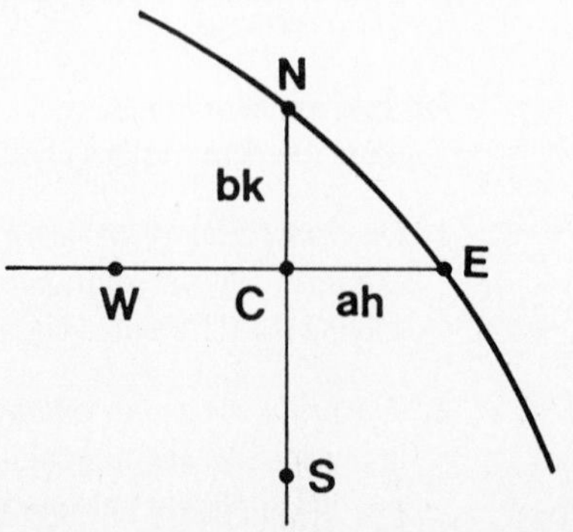

The spacing from the center point C to the north and east points, N and E, is bk and ah with $0 < a, b < 1$. If values U_E and U_N are given at N and E, then show that one can discretize a partial differential equation at C by

$$u_x = \left[\frac{1}{a(1+a)}U_E - \frac{1-a}{a}U_C - \frac{a}{(1+a)}U_W\right]/h + O(h^2)$$

$$u_{xx} = \left[\frac{1}{a(1+a)}U_E - \frac{1}{a}U_C + \frac{a}{1+a}U_W\right]/(2h^2) + O(h)$$

Give the corresponding formulas for u_y and u_{yy}. Combine these to give the discretization stencil for the equation in Problem 10.2.2.

10.2.6 Apply the 5-point star to solve the following elliptic problems in the unit square $0 \le x, y \le 1$. Use $h = .1$ and solve the linear equations with a library band matrix solver, for example, IMSL's LEQT1B. The function f used below is to be obtained from the true solution given. The boundary conditions are the values of the true solution.

(A) $(e^{xy}u_x)_x + (e^{-xy}u_y)_y - u/(1+x+y) = f$
$u = 0.75e^{xy}\sin(\pi x)\sin(\pi y)$

(B) $u_{xx} + u_{yy} = 6xy\, e^{x+y}(xy+x+y-3)$
$u = 3e^{x+y}(x-x^2)(y-y^2)$

(C) $u_{xx} + u_{yy} - 100u = -49.5 \cosh y/\cosh 1$
$u = .5\ (\cosh 10x/\cosh 10 + \cosh y/\cosh 1)$

(D) $u_{xx} + u_{yy} = -1$
$u = .295776 - (x^2+y^2)/4 - 14476(x^4-6x^2y^2+y^4)/319424$
$+ 429(x^8-28x^2y^2+70x^4y^4-28x^2y^6+y^8)/319424$

10.2.7 Consider the **biharmonic equation** $u_{xxxx} + 2u_{xxyy} + u_{yyyy} = f$. Show that the following stencil has truncation error $O(h^2)$ for a grid with equal spacing h in both directions.

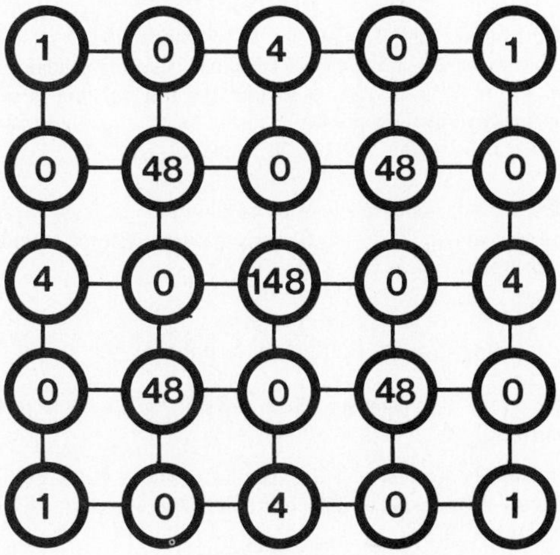

Hint: In the terminology of Problem 10.2.4, this stencil is $S_5(S_5)$ and the biharmonic equation is the Laplacian of the Laplacian.

10.2.8 An $O(h^6)$ **high-order difference** discretization can be obtained for the Poisson problem by using the 9-point star stencil of Problem 10.2.3 and replacing f(x, y) by an average value computed from the grid and half-grid points. This replacement value is obtained from the following stencil *applied to f/360* where the spacing is h/2.

(A) Discuss the additional work required to solve the Poisson problem with this discretization compared with that of Problem 10.2.3. Show that the right side f(x, y) is evaluated only about twice as often as with the $O(h^2)$ 5-point stencil.

(B) Repeat the calculation of Problem 10.2.1, part (B), and compare the accuracies obtained.

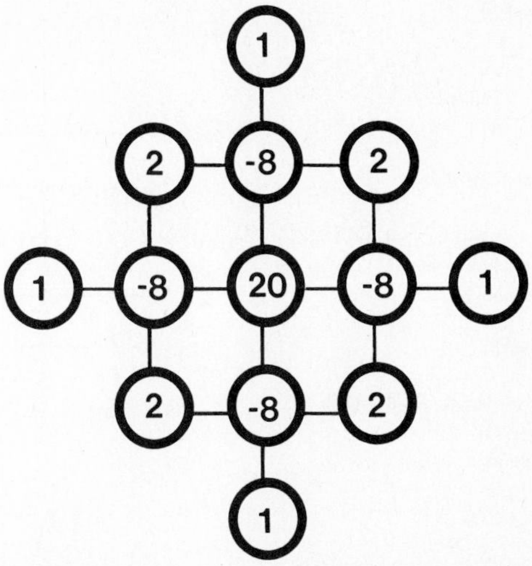

10.2.9 Consider an elliptic problem on the **L-shaped region** defined by the unit square $0 \le x, y \le 1$ with the lower-left square $0 \le x, y \le 0.5$ removed. Generate the pattern of nonzeros in the coefficient matrix of the linear system for the 5-point star discretization using $h = k = 0.2$. Discuss how the pattern behaves as h and k decrease.

10.2.10 Consider solving an elliptic problem on a rectangle with a finite element method using Hermite bicubics as basis functions. Generate the pattern of nonzeros in the coefficient matrix of the linear system for the following discretizations:

(A) Collocation

(B) Least squares

(C) Galerkin

Discuss the differences and similarities in computing the entries of these matrices.

10.2.11 Repeat Problem 10.2.10 using the basis functions $b_i(x)c_j(y)$ where the $b_i(x)$ and $c_j(y)$ are **quadratic B-splines.**

10.2.12 An elliptic problem has **homogeneous boundary conditions** if $u = 0$ on all the boundaries. Show how one can satisfy homogeneous boundary conditions on a rectangle automatically for a finite element method using Hermite bicubics as basis functions. Discuss the improvement in efficiency that results. **Hint:** Almost all the basis functions in 10.2.12 are zero on the boundary. Drop those that are not.

10.2.13 An elliptic problem has **periodic boundary conditions** on the unit square $0 \le x, y \le 1$ if the conditions are $u(0, y) = u(1, y)$ and $u_x(0, y) = u_x(1, y)$.

(A) Show how these boundary conditions can be incorporated into a 5-point star discretization.

(B) Generate the pattern of nonzeros in the coefficient matrix of the linear system using $h = k = .2$. Discuss how the pattern behaves as h and k decrease.

10.2.14 Repeat Problem 10.2.13 for collocation using Hermite bicubic basis functions.

10.2.15 Consider the least squares method for an elliptic problem on a rectangular grid using Hermite bicubics. Assume that the integrals involved in this method are estimated by using a 2 by 2 Gauss formula. That is, the four points (x_1, y_1), (x_1, y_2), (x_2, y_1), and (x_2, y_2) are used in each grid where x_1 and x_2 are the Gauss points for the x side of a grid square and y_1 and y_2 are the Gauss points for the y side. Show that with this integration method **the least squares and collocation methods are identical.**

10.2.16 The following are **finite difference discretizations** of the heat equation $u_t = cu_{xx}$. The spacing in x is h and in t is k; the abbreviation $(\delta^2 U)_{i,j}$ is used for $U_{i+1,j} - 2U_{i,j} + U_{i-1,j}$ where U_{ij} is the approximate value for $u(ih, jk)$. Show how these discretizations are obtained and establish that the truncation errors are as stated.

(1) *Explicit:*

$U_{i,j+1} = U_{i,j} + (ck/h^2)(\delta U^2)_{i,j}$
Error $= O(k+h^2)$
Stable if $ck/h^2 \leq .5$

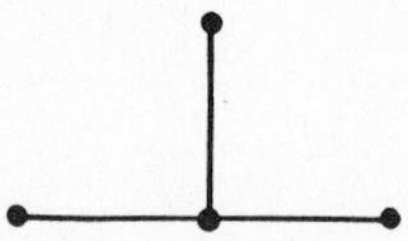

(2) *Crank-Nicolson:*

$U_{i,j+1} = U_{ij} + (ck/h^2)[(\delta^2 U)_{ij} + (\delta^2 U_{i,j+1})]/2$
Error $= O(k^2+h^2)$
Always stable

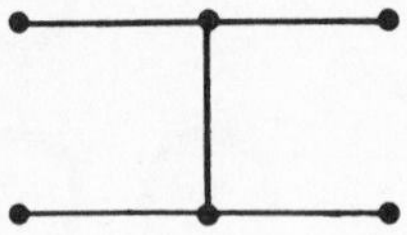

(3) *Implicit:*

$U_{i,j+1} = U_{ij} + (ck/h^2)(\delta^2 U)_{i,j+1}$
Error $= O(k+h^2)$
Always stable

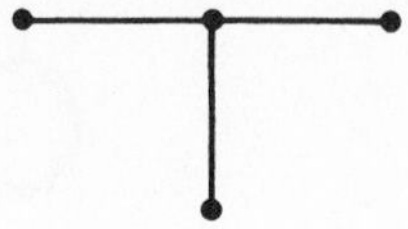

(4) *Leap-Frog:*

$U_{i,j+1} = U_{i,j-1} + (ck/h^2)(\delta^2 U)_{i,j}$
Error $= O(k^2+h^2)$
Always unstable

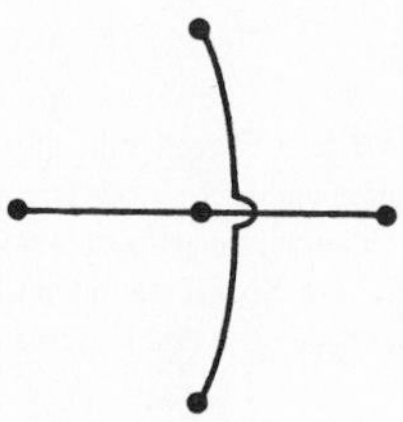

(5) *DuFort-Frankel:*

$U_{i,j+1} = U_{i,j-1} + (2ck/h^2)*$
$[U_{i+1,j} - U_{i,j+1} - U_{i,j-1} + U_{i-1,j}]$
Error $= O(k+h^2+k/h)$
Always stable

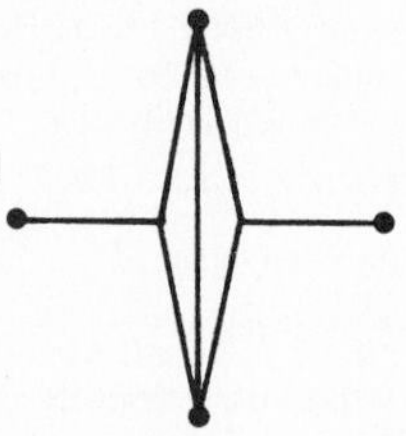

(6) *Three-level:*

$(1+a)(U_{i,j+1} - U_{ij}) - a(U_{ij} - U_{i,j-1})$
$= (ck/h^2)(\delta^2 U)_{i,j+1}$
Error $= O(k+h^2)$
$= O(k^2+h^2)$ if $a = 1/2$
Always stable with $a > 0$

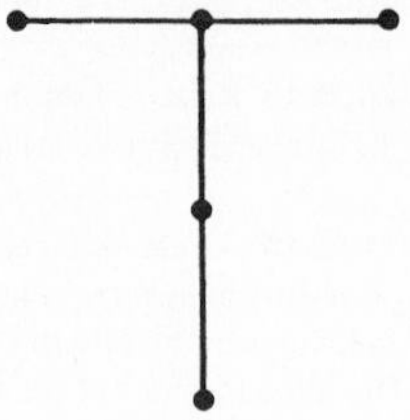

(7) *Special three-level:*

$a = .5 - h^2/(12ck)$ in (6)
Error $= O(k^2) = O(h^4)$
Always stable

(A) Show how these discretizations are derived from difference formulas.

(B) Identify which of the above discretizations are implicit. Discuss how the solution for $U_{i,j+1}$ can be carried out using a subprogram for solving tridiagonal systems of equations.

(C) Apply discretizations 1 and 4 to the heat equation with initial conditions chosen to make the true solution $u(x,t) = e^{t-x}$ on the domain $1 \leq x \leq 2$ and $t > 0$. Carry out computations that show the instability.

(D) Use a Taylor's series analysis to verify that the truncation errors of these discretizations are as stated.

10.2.17 The **Burger equation** is

$$u_t + uu_x = cu_{xx}$$

(A) Find the explicit discretization of this equation analogous to (1) in Problem 10.2.16. Experimentally show that it is unstable.

(B) Find an implicit discretization analogous to (3) of Problem 10.2.16.

(C) Perform an experiment of the discretization of part (B) to test its stability. **Hint:** In the uu_x term evaluate the u factor at time jk so that a simple tridiagonal system is solved for each time step.

(D) Find a three-level discretization analogous to (6) of Problem 10.2.16. Perform an experiment to test its stability. Compare its accuracy with the discretization of part (B). **Hint:** Evaluate u of uu_x at the middle point. Generate two lines of initial data from the function $e^{c(t-x)}$.

10.2.18 Apply the discretization of Problem 10.2.16 to the following **parabolic problems.** Choose h and k so as to obtain 2 digits' accuracy for $0 \leq t \leq 2$.

(A) $2u_t = -(4x+2)e^{x+t} + u + u_{xx}$ $\quad -1 \leq x \leq +1, t \geq 0$
$u(x,0) = (x^2-1)e^x$ $\quad u(-1,t) = u(1,t) = 0$
$u(x,t) = (x^2-1)e^{x+t}$

(B) $u_t = (\sin t \cos t)\, u_x - u^2(\sin 2t)u_{xx}$ $\quad 0 \leq x \leq 1, t \geq 0$
$u(x,0) = \sqrt{x}$ $\quad u(0,t) = \sin t$ $\quad u(1,t) = \sqrt{1-\cos 2t}$
$u(x,t) = \sqrt{x+\sin 2t}$

(C) $u_t = u_x - 4tu_{xx}/(1+t^2)$ $\quad 0 \leq x \leq 1, t \geq 0$
$u(x,0) = \sin(x)$ $\quad u(0,t) = \sin t/(1+t^2)$,
$u(1,t) = \sin(1+t)/(1+t^2)$
$u(x,t) = \sin(x+t)/(1+t^2)$

(D) $u_t = u_{xx}$ $\quad 0 \leq x \leq 1, t \geq 1$
$u(x,1) = e^{-x^2/4}$ $\quad u(0,t) = 1/\sqrt{t}$ $\quad u(1,t) = 1/(\sqrt{t}\, e^{1/(4t)})$
$u(x,t) = e^{-x^2/(4t)}/\sqrt{t}$

Hint: For three-level formulas assume that initial values are given on two lines, $t = 0$ and $t = k$.

10.2.19 Consider the **wave equation** in the form of two simultaneous first-order equations 10.2.8.

(A) Find a simple discretization of this system using simple differences to approximate the derivatives.

(B) Carry out an experiment to show this discretization is unstable. Choose the initial conditions and boundary conditions on the domain $0 \leq x \leq 1$, $t \leq 0$ for the true solution $u(x,t) = \sin(x+t)$.

10.2.20 Consider the 5-point star discretization 10.2.7 of the wave equation. Assume $c = 1$ and choose initial and boundary conditions on the domain $-1 \leq x \leq 1$, $t \geq 0$ so that the true solution is $\sin(x-t)$. Experimentally verify the condition $c^2k^2 \leq h^2$ for convergence by solving the discretized equations 10.2.7 for $k = 2h$, h, and $h/2$.

10.2.21 Show that any functions of the form $f(x-ct)$ or $g(x+ct)$ satisfy the wave equation $u_{tt} - c^2u_{xx} = 0$. Apply this to describe the solution to the **hyperbolic problem**

$u_{tt} - u_{xx} = 0$ $\quad t \geq 0, -\infty \leq x \leq \infty$
$u(x,0) = 1$ for $-1 \leq x \leq 1$, $u(x,0) = 0$ for $|x| > 1$

10.2.22 Apply the 5-point star discretization to the hyperbolic problem in Problem 10.2.21 with $h = k = .2$.

(A) Carry out the solution with 10.2.7 until $t = 3$ for $-4 \leq x \leq 4$. Discuss the accuracy of the solution obtained. **Hint:** The boundary values along $x = \pm 4$ are $u = 0$.

(B) Repeat the computation of part (A) with $h = k = .08$ and discuss the accuracy obtained.

10.2.23 Apply the 5-point star discretization 10.2.7 to the following **hyperbolic problems.** Choose h and k so as to obtain 2 digits of accuracy for $0 \leq t \leq 2$. Assume initial values from the true solution are given for the first two t lines.

(A) $4u_{tt} - u_{xx} = 0$ $\quad 0 \leq x \leq 1, t \geq 0$
$u(x,0) = \sin(2x)$ $\quad u(0,t) = \sin t$ $\quad u(1,t) = \sin(2+t)$
$u(x,t) = \sin(2x+t)$

(B) $16u_{tt} - u_{xx} = 0$ $\quad 0 \leq x \leq 1, t \geq 0$
$u(x,0) = 2e^{2x}\sin x \cos x$
$u(0,t) = \sqrt{e^{-t}(1-\cos t)/2}$ $\quad u(1,t) = e^2\sin(2-t/2)/e^{t/2}$
$u(x,t) = e^{2x-t/2}\sin(2x-t/2)$

(C) $u_{tt} - u_{xx} - u = 2e^x e^t \sin x \qquad 0 \le x \le \pi,\ t \ge 0$

$u(x, 0) = e^x \sin x \qquad u(0, t) = u(\pi, t) = 0$

$u(x, t) = e^{x+t}\sin(x)$

(D) $t^2 u_{tt} - x^2 u_{xx} = 0 \qquad 1 \le x \le 2,\ t \ge 1$

$u(x, 1) = 1/(1+x) \qquad u(1, t) = 1/(1+t) \qquad u(2, t) = 1/(1+2t)$

$u(x, t) = 1/(1+xt)$

(E) $x^2 u_{xx} - t^2 u_{tt} - \dfrac{xu}{2} u_x - x^2 t^2 u^3 = 0 \qquad 0 \le x \le 1,\ t \ge 1$

$u(x, 1) = 1/(1+x) \qquad u(0, t) = 1 \qquad u(1, t) = 1/(1+t)$

$u(x, t) = 1/(1+xt)$

10.2.24 Study **round-off effects** in the solution of initial value problems by carrying out the time step and then perturbing the result obtained by c*random(x) where random(x) is a random variable uniformly distributed on $[-1, 1]$. Choose c relatively large (say 10^{-2} or 10^{-3}) so that the effects are obvious in a short computation. **Hint:** Use the IMSL library program GGUBFS to obtain the random numbers.

(A) Repeat the computations of Problem 10.2.18 for **parabolic problems** with these effects added and compare the results obtained. Specifically discuss how fast the round-off effects accumulate as the computation progresses.

(B) Repeat the computations of Problem 10.2.23 for **hyperbolic problems** with these effects added and compare the results obtained. Specifically discuss how fast the round-off effects accumulate as the computation progresses.

10.2.25 Consider the unit square $0 \le x, y \le 1$ with functions of one variable given on the four sides: $f(0, y)$, $f(1, y)$, $f(x, 0)$, and $f(x, 1)$. The **blending function** interpolant of these four functions is

$$\begin{aligned} f(x, y) = {} & (1-x)f(0, y) + xf(1, y) + (1-y)f(x, 0) + yf(x, 1) \\ & - (1-x)(1-y)f(0, 0) - y(1-x)f(0, 1) \\ & - x(1-y)f(1, 0) - xyf(1, 1) \end{aligned}$$

(A) Show that if the four boundary functions are continuous along the boundaries, then $f(x, y)$ is a continuous function of two variables which assumes these boundary values.

(B) Extend this interpolation formula to the rectangle with corners (x_1, y_1), (x_2, y_2), (x_3, y_3), and (x_4, y_4).

(C) Apply the formula of part (B) to extend the definitions of the following four functions of one variable to a continuous function of two variables defined on the domain $-1 \le x \le 2$, $.5 \le y \le 1.5$:

$y = .5,\ -1 \le x \le 2$	$g_1(x) = 1$
$y = 1.5,\ -1 \le x \le 2$	$g_2(x) = 14(2/(8+x) - 1/(1+x^2))/3$
$x = -1,\ .5 \le y \le 1.5$	$g_3(y) = \cos((y-.5)\pi)$
$x = 2,\ .5 \le y \le 1.5$	$g_4(y) = (1.5-y)e^{y-.5}$

10.2.26 Show how the blending function interpolation formula of Problem 10.2.25 can be used to **homogenize the boundary conditions** of an elliptic problem. Consider a general linear partial differential equation for $u(x, y)$, $Au_{xx} + Cu_{yy} + Du_x + Eu_y + F_u = G$ with boundary conditions as follows:

$x = a,\ u(a, y) = u_1(y) \qquad x = b,\ u(b, y) = u_2(y)$

$y = c,\ u(x, c) = u_3(x) \qquad y = d,\ u(x, d) = u_4(x)$

Obtain a new **elliptic problem** with solution $v(x, y) = u(x, y) + f(x, y)$ where $f(x, y)$ is known and has a different (but easily obtained) differential equation and homogeneous boundary conditions: $v(x, y) = 0$ on all four sides of the rectangular domain. **Hint:** The function $f(x, y)$ is closely related to the blending function interpolant of the boundary condition functions u_1, u_2, u_3, and u_4.

10.2.27 Consider the unit triangle with vertices (0, 0), (0, 1), and (1, 1). One blending function for this domain is given by the formula

$$f(x, y) = \frac{x-y}{x} f(x, 0) + \frac{x-y}{1-y} f(1, y) + \frac{y(1-x)}{x(1-y)} f(x, x) - (x-y)\, f(1, 0)$$

(A) Show that if the three boundary functions $f(x, 0)$, $f(1, y)$, and $f(x, x)$ are continuous along the three sides of the triangle, then $f(x, y)$ is a continuous function (except at $x = y = 0$ and $x = y = 1$, where it is undefined) which assumes the boundary values.

(B) Extend this interpolation formula to the triangle with vertices (x_1, y_1), (x_2, y_2), and (x_3, y_3).

(C) Show how this blending function can be used to homogenize the boundary conditions of an elliptic problem on a triangle. **Hint:** See Problem 10.2.26.

10.2.28 A second approach to blending on a triangle goes as follows when given three functions u_1, u_2, and u_3 along the three sides.
Step 1: Determine a linear function $L(x, y)$ which assumes the values of the u_i at the three corners.
Step 2: Subtract $L(x, y)$ from each u_i so that we have functions v_i on the three sides which are zero at the vertices.
Step 3: Write $g(x, y)$ as the sum of three functions $g_1(x, y)$, $g_2(x, y)$, and $g_3(x, y)$ with the following properties: $g_i(x, y) = v_i$ on side i of the triangle, and $g_i(x, y) = 0$ on the other two sides of the triangle.
Step 4: Set $f(x, y) = g(x, y) + L(x, y)$ to obtain a blending function which interpolates the original boundary functions.

Assume the triangle has vertices (x_1, y_1), (x_2, y_2), and (x_3, y_3). Let $u_i(x, y)$ be the boundary function between (x_i, y_i) and (x_{i+1}, y_{i+1}) (with $x_4 = x_1$ and $y_4 = y_1$) and let their values at the vertices be z_1, z_2, and z_3.

(A) Show how $L(x, y)$ can be computed by solving a system of three linear equations in three unknowns. Give this system.

(B) Consider the first side of the triangle and let it be defined by $ax + by = c$. Let the parameter t vary along this side with $t = 0$ at (x_1, y_1) and $t = 1$ at (x_2, y_2). Then $v_i(0) = v_i(1) = 0$ in terms of this parameter. Let the other two sides have equations $p_1 x + r_1 y = s_1$ and $p_2 x + r_2 y = s_2$. Given a point (x_0, y_0) in the interior of the triangle, define $g_1(x, y)$ by

$$g_1(x_0, y_0) = \left(\frac{ax_0 + by_0}{c}\right) v_1(t_0)$$

where t_0 is computed as the parameter t of the point on the first side which lies on the line $p_0 x + r_0 y = s_0$ through (x_0, y_0) and (x_3, y_3). Display formulas for computing $g_1(x_0, y_0)$; that is, find a, b, c, p_1, r_1, s_1, and p_2, r_2, s_2 which are constants independent of x_0 and y_0 and then compute t_0 in terms of x_0 and y_0 and their constants. **Hint:** If $(x_3, y_3) = (0, 0)$ and sides 2 and 3 are defined by $y - r_1 x = 0$ and $y - r_2 x = 0$, then the computations may be made as follows:

Precompute a, b, c, and $d = x_2 - x_1 \neq 0$

Find line through (x_0, y_0): $s_0 = y_0/x_0$

Find x coordinate in this line and first side: $x^* = c/(a + bs_0)$

Find t parameter from $t = (x - x_1)/(x_2 - x_1)$: $t_0 = (x^* - x_1)/d$

(C) Write a Fortran function subprogram which carries out this blending function interpolation. It should start as

```
FUNCTION TBLEND(X,Y,U1,U2,U3,XV,YV)
REAL XV(3),YV(3)
```

where U1, U2, and U3 are the three functions, the evaluation is at X,Y, and the vertices have coordinates in XV and YV.

(D) Write a more efficient and more general Fortran function subprogram which has the precomputed values available through a Fortran COMMON block. It should start as

```
FUNCTION TBLEND(X,Y)
REAL L
COMMON/TINFO/XV(47,3),YV(47,3),A(47,3),B(47,3),C(47,3),L(47,3)
```

for a case with 47 triangles. Such a program would be useful when a complicated domain is broken up into triangular pieces and one blends known values along the edges of the triangles to obtain values in the interiors. The XV,YV arrays give the vertices of the triangles, the A,B,C arrays define the equations for the sides of the triangles, and the L array has the linear interpolation coefficients from the first step of the construction. The boundary functions U1, U2, and U3 have arguments (X,Y,I) where I refers to the triangle numbers. This subprogram must determine which triangle contains the point X,Y — a nontrivial calculation.

SOLUTION OF THE SYSTEM OF ALGEBRAIC EQUATIONS **10.3

Once a partial differential equation has been discretized, the next step is to solve the resulting system of algebraic equations. The methods subdivide into various categories as shown in Figure 10.15. Only a summary discussion is given of these methods; a thorough discussion requires a lengthy book in itself. Many methods are named but not decribed here; the book of Birkoff and Lynch (see references) gives more information on these methods.

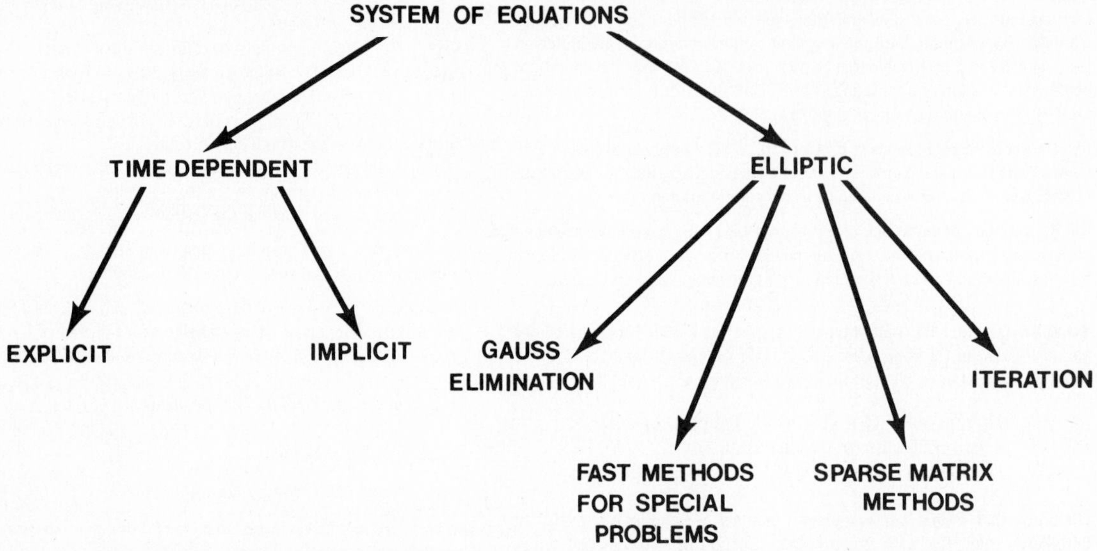

Figure 10.15 Subdivision into categories of the methods for solving the algebraic equations obtained from the discretization of a partial differential equation.

Equations from Time-Dependent Problems 10.3.A

An **explicit method** is one where the values at the next time step are given explicitly in terms of (known) values at the current time step or earlier time steps. Solving the resulting algebraic equations is straightforward; one just applies the explicit formulas. No special techniques are needed in this case, but there is one real problem: *the explicit formulas might be unstable.* The instability is exactly the same kind as arises in solving an ordinary differential equation and can quickly ruin a calculation. Recall from the discussion of explicit discretizations of the heat equation (such as 10.2.10) that one must have $k(=$ time step$) < ch^2$ for some constant c. So as h becomes small, the time step becomes *very small* and the computation becomes very costly.

An **implicit method** is one where the values at the next time step are connected together in a system of simultaneous equations. The advantage of such methods is that they can be stable even when large time steps are made. The price is paid in that there is much more calculation for each time step. Equation 10.1.11 is an example of an implicit method. The problem of solving the simultaneous equations of an implicit method are the same as for solving the equations for an elliptic problem except that one has an additional advantage. One has a very good estimate of the solution of the equations from the solution of the equations just solved. This provides a large advantage for some methods; for example, an iterative method does not have to iterate as much because the error in the solution does not need to be reduced much.

Equations from Elliptic Problems 10.3.B

Gauss elimination is attractive for solving the simultaneous equations from elliptic problems or implicit methods for time-dependent problems because it is a standard, well-understood method. Its disadvantage is that it might require too much computer time, computer memory, or both. It is almost always used in some special form to improve its efficiency; the most obvious case is **band Gauss elimination,** where the fact that the coefficients form a band matrix is used. There are simple variations on this such as **profile Gauss elimination,** where the method "follows" the profile of the lower edge of the band of nonzero elements. This simple, direct approach is the best for small or moderately sized problems with several hundred unknowns. The organizational overhead of "better" methods (except the fast methods) is usually too high for them to actually be more efficient for problems of this size. For larger problems with a few thousand unknowns or more, simple Gauss methods become very inefficient in many cases.

A useful variation of Gauss elimination when the size of the matrix exceeds the available main memory is the **frontal method.** It transforms the matrix into upper triangular form using a fixed-size submatrix in main memory. Essentially one eliminates within a block as one goes along in the Gauss elimination; as rows are finished, they are written in auxiliary memory and new, later rows brought into main memory. The name frontal comes from the idea of picking a starting point or element in the domain and doing the elimination on the equations from there. Then the elimination is made for neighboring points or elements, and a subdomain is created where the elimination has been made. This creates a *front* or boundary between the subregion where elimination has been done and where it remains to be done. This front gradually moves across the entire domain until the equations are solved. The calculations can be arranged so that the entire, large coefficient matrix is never formed explicitly; all one has to do is to keep track of the front and all the variables and equations associated with it. Only these equations need be in the main memory of the computer. This approach is particularly attractive when one has an irregular domain or irregular elements and it is not so easy to number the equations and unknowns nicely. The frontal method may require some more computation and bookkeeping, but its saving in storage usually more than compensates for that.

The "better" methods for large problems are the iteration methods and the sparse matrix methods. We do not give any further details of **iteration methods** beyond the discussion of Section 6.3. Their principal attraction is that they conserve on memory. If there are N unknowns or variables in the equations, these methods usually require only, say, 2N to 4N words of computer storage to solve the problem, in contrast to the $N\sqrt{N}$ or more required by Gauss elimination. When N is 2000, this is the difference between, say, 6000 and 90,000 words of storage required. In addition, the methods often run faster provided various parameters of the iteration methods are chosen well. Their disadvantage is that one must choose the method parameters well, and this may require considerable analysis and computation. However, the ITPACK software, for example, chooses these parameters automatically for a wide class of problems. Some of the ITPACK software is contained in the ELLPACK system discussed in Section 10.4.B. For some finite element systems none of the usual iteration methods even converge.

A **sparse matrix method** is a version of Gauss elimination (or possibly some other method) which uses special techniques to exploit the sparsity of the matrix. These methods also use special data structures for the matrix. A simple example is to store the three numbers i, j, a_{ij} for every nonzero element a_{ij} in the matrix A. This makes it more difficult to identify a row or column of the matrix A, but it can dramatically reduce the computer memory used. The analysis and description of these methods is beyond the scope of this book. Anyone solving really large systems of sparse equations, especially those arising from partial differential equations, should review the sparse matrix methods to see if they are beneficial.

The **fast methods** add another dimension to the choices available to solve the equations. These methods exploit some special property of the algebraic equations (which means the partial differential equation has a special form) in order to solve the system with extraordinary efficiency. The best known of these methods is the **FFT method**, or Fast Fourier Transform method. It applies to Poisson problems partial differential equations of the types

$$u_{xx} + u_{yy} = g(x, y) \qquad \text{domain} = \text{rectangle} \qquad \textbf{Equation 10.3.1}$$
$$u_{xx} + u_{yy} + u_{zz} = g(x, y, z) \qquad \text{domain} = \text{box}$$

and some extensions. The key requirement is that the partial differential equation *must be separable* so that the classical analytical method of separation of variables could be used if one desired to do so.

To illustrate the gain in efficiency, consider the problems in 10.3.1 using finite differences with n points for each variable. This gives n^2 or n^3 unknowns, depending on the dimension, and ordinary band matrix Gauss elimination requires about $2n^3$ or $2n^5$ words of memory for two or three dimensions and about n^4 or n^7 arithmetic operations. By contrast, the FFT method can solve the same system of equations with n^2 or n^3 words of memory and $5n^2 \log n$ or $7n^3 \log n$ arithmetic operations. The dramatic difference between these two approaches is seen in Table 10.2.

Comparison of Gauss and FFT for Solving Poisson Problems **Table 10.2**

n is the number of discretization points in each variable. This comparison is based on simple arithmetic operation counts, using only the highest powers in n in the counts. Actual software might give considerably different comparisons.

	Two Dimensions				Three Dimensions			
	Gauss		FFT		Gauss		FFT	
n	Memory	Arith.	Memory	Arith.	Memory	Arith.	Memory	Arith.
10	$2*10^3$	$1*10^4$	$1*10^2$	$2*10^3$	$2*10^5$	$1*10^7$	$1*10^3$	$2*10^4$
20	$2*10^4$	$8*10^4$	$4*10^2$	$1*10^4$	$6*10^6$	$1*10^9$	$8*10^3$	$2*10^5$
50	$2*10^5$	$6*10^6$	$3*10^3$	$1*10^5$	$6*10^8$	$8*10^{11}$	$1*10^5$	$5*10^6$
100	$2*10^6$	$1*10^8$	$1*10^4$	$3*10^5$	$2*10^{10}$	$1*10^{14}$	$1*10^6$	$5*10^7$

The FFT method itself depends on the partial differential equation having solutions related to trigonometric functions (sines and cosines) and defined on rectangles or boxes. There are two other fast methods, **cyclic reduction** and **tensor products**, which apply to more problems. These methods also require that the partial differential equations be separable so that the classical analytical method of separation of variables could be applied. The cyclic reduction method is more complicated than tensor products; it is also faster.

Computational Effort for Elliptic Problems 10.3.C

Table 10.2 is an attempt to compare methods based on estimates obtained from examining the mathematical algorithms. Such estimates are informative in that they show general trends. In Table 10.2 it is obvious that the FFT solution becomes much more efficient when n, the number of discretization points per variable, becomes large. These estimates are not especially reliable estimates of the amount of computational effort for actual programs; there are many aspects of computing that are not evident from the mathematical algorithms. For example, the Fortran statement

```
X = A(I,J,3) + SIN(Y)*B(IPIVOT(I),IPIVOT(I)-J)
```

appears to have one add, one multiply, one subtraction, and one function evaluation. However, there may be arithmetic needed to obtain the value A(I,J,3), and there are surely several machine operations needed (besides the subtraction) in obtaining the value B(IPIVOT(I),IPIVOT(I) − J). Further, the time of the machine operations needed to go to the SIN function and return the value might exceed the time of the arithmetic to compute the function value. One may expect these aspects to introduce factors of 2, 5, .5, or .2 into a comparison of the computations needed for actual programs. Recall that different people implementing exactly the same method might create programs that differ in execution time by factors as large as 2, 4, or more. As long as one understands the approximate nature of these estimates, one can obtain useful information from them.

We present two **model elliptic problems** to use in estimating computational effort. Each model problem has a two-dimensional and three-dimensional version. The first is the Poisson problem on a rectangle 10.3.1 used in Table 10.2. We assume that the right side g is smooth and so is the solution u. The second model problem is a general linear elliptic problem in two or three dimensions:

$$au_{xx} + cu_{yy} + du_x + eu_x + fu = g$$ **Equation 10.3.2**

u(x, y) given on the boundary of the domain

$$au_{xx} + bu_{yy} + cu_{zz} + du_x + eu_y + fu_z + hu = g$$

u(x, y, z) given in the boundary of the domain

The coefficients a, b, c, etc., are smooth functions of x, y or x, y, z with no special properties; the right side g and solution u are also assumed to be smooth. The domain is not rectangular, but not very complicated either. It has 3 to 5 sides, some of which are simple, smooth curves. In summary, this model problem is completely general but well behaved in all respects otherwise.

A study of the computational effort to solve these problems has been made which traces the progress in developing better methods over the period 1945–1978. See *Algorithmic Progress in Solving Partial Differential Equations* by J. R. Rice in SIGNUM Newsletter, **11** (December 1976). The striking conclusion is reached that, for the general three-dimensional elliptic problem 10.3.2, **the progress made through better methods from 1945 to 1978 exceeds the progress made through faster computers.** The factor of improvement through better methods is estimated to be 12 billion, while the speed improvement from a desk calculator to a typical large 1975 computer is only 300 million. These estimates have considerable uncertainty, but the study shows conclusively that developing better methods has been as effective as developing bigger computers as far as solving problems for an important class of physical applications.

The methods in the study for the first model problem are listed in Table 10.3 with the multiplication counts and error estimates given in terms of n. Some of the methods mentioned are not discussed in this book; this reflects the fact that this brief survey cannot discuss all the more complicated methods. Most of these methods are discussed in several of the references at the end of this chapter.

Multiplication Counts and Error Estimates of Methods for the Poisson Problem **Table 10.3**

n is the number of discretization points in each variable. Logarithms are with base 2. The 5- and 9-point stars in two dimensions correspond to 7- and 27-point stars in three dimensions.

Method	Year	Two Dimensions	Three Dimensions	Error
5-point star plus				$O(1/n^2)$
Cramer's rule	1945	4^{n^2}	5^{n^3}	
Gauss elimination	1945	n^4	n^7	
Gauss-Seidel iteration	1945	$2n^4 \log n$	$12n^5 \log n$	
SOR iteration	1954	$6n^3 \log n$	$8n^4 \log n$	
ADI iteration	1955	$18n^2 \log^2 n$	$27n^3 \log^2 n$	
9-point star plus				$O(1/n^6)$
SOR iteration	1956	$6n^3 \log n$	$20n^4 \log n$	
Tensor product	1964	$2n^3$	$2n^4$	
ADI iteration	1965	$77n^2 \log n$	$120n^3 \log n$	
5-point star plus FFT	1965	$5n^2 \log n$	$7n^2 \log n$	$O(1/n^2)$
9-point star plus ADI iteration + smooth guess	1968	$33n^2 \log^2 n$	$50n^3 \log n$	$O(1/n^6)$
5-point star plus cyclic reduction	1970	$5n^2 \log n$	$8n^3 \log n$	$O(1/n^2)$
9-point star plus FFT	1978	$7n^2 \log n$	$10n^3 \log n$	$O(1/n^6)$

There are two big effects seen in Table 10.3. First, the 9-point star provides much higher accuracy at little extra computational cost. The more effective 9-point star methods manipulate the right side also; see Problem 10.2.4 for a simple example of this approach. Second, there has been a dramatic decrease in the amount of computation from the best method of 1945 (Gauss elimination with n^4 multiplications) to the best recent methods ($5n^2 \log n$ multiplications).

The data in Table 10.3 are put into concrete form in Table 10.4, where it is assumed that the solution u of the Poisson problem is of size 1 and one wants to compute it to .1 percent accuracy. This accuracy requirement gives $n = 30$ (or 32 for the FFT methods) for the 5-point star and $n = 8$ for the 9-point star. A deliberately conservative value of n is used for the sixth-order method; $n = 3$ is actually predicted by the $O(1/n^6)$ error estimate. Table 10.4 gives estimated execution time on a computer that does 1 million operations per second (typical of larger machines of the late 1970s). It is assumed that each multiplication generates a total of 10 operations in the computation. While this method of translating multiplications into computer time is crude, it has been found useful to provide ballpark estimates. In any case, it is not likely to be heavily biased against any of the methods considered here. Table 10.4 also gives estimates of the storage required to solve three-dimensional Poisson problems.

Computer Time and Storage Estimates for .1 Percent Accuracy in the Poisson Problem **Table 10.4**

The 5-point star discretization is used unless otherwise noted. The values n = 30 (or 32 for FFT) and n = 8 are used in Table 10.3 to produce an accuracy estimated to be .1 percent. The asterisk * indicates cases which have not been done widely in practice; the double asterisk ** indicates cases where there is considerable conjecture included in the estimate.

		Two Dimensions	Three Dimensions	
Year	Method	Time	Time	Storage
1945	Cramer's rule	* 10^{530} years	* $10^{18,900}$ years	—
	Gauss-Seidel iteration	97 sec	1.2 hours	190,000
	Gauss elimination (band)	8 sec	2.5 days	25,000,000
1954	SOR iteration	2 sec	85 sec	190,000
1955	ADI iteration	.35 sec	** 16 sec	190,000
1956	SOR for 9-point star	* .06 sec	* 1.6 sec	15,000
1964	Tensor product, 9-point star	.01 sec	* .08 sec	1,500
1965	ADI for 9-point star	* .04 sec	** .48 sec	1,000
	FFT for 5-point star	.15 sec	6 sec	32,000
1968	ADI, 9-point star, smooth guess	* .017 sec	** .2 sec	1,000
1970	Cyclic reduction	.23 sec	** 11 sec	27,000
1978	FFT for 9-point star	.004 sec	** .05 sec	500

Table 10.4 shows that better methods since 1945 have increased the efficiency of solving the two-dimensional Poisson problem by a factor of 2000 and the efficiency for three-dimensional Poisson problems has increased by a factor of about 85,000. There have been equally dramatic decreases in the amount of computer memory required.

Note that Table 10.4 assumes that the same computer is used throughout. The electronic computers available in 1945 performed more like 1,000 operations per second, and some of the current computers can do 10 to 25 million operations per second when solving the Poisson problem. Thus the combination of better methods and faster computers has increased the efficiency of solving this problem by factors of perhaps 4 million and 170 million for two and three dimensions.

Table 10.5 gives multiplication counts for the second model problem 10.3.2 for both two and three dimensions. This is a completely general problem, and so no fast methods are applicable and higher-order

Multiplication and Error Estimates of Methods for a General Elliptic Problem **Table 10.5**

n is the number of discretization points in each variable. Logarithms are with base 2. The estimates in this table are much less reliable than those of Table 10.3.

Method	Year	Two Dimensions	Three Dimensions	Error
1. 5-point star and band Gauss elimination	1945	$3n^4$	$5n^7$	$O(1/n)$
2. 5-point star and Gauss-Seidel iteration	1955	$12n^4 \log n$	$60n^5 \log n$	$O(1/n)$
3. 5-point star with better boundary approximations and Gauss elimination	1960	$6n^4$	$8n^7$	$O(1/n^2)$
4. Finite elements with piecewise linear elements and Gauss elimination	1960	$6n^4$	$8n^7$	$O(1/n^2)$
5. Iteration for 3 above	1965	$20n^{3.75} \log n$	$60n^{4.75} \log n$	$O(1/n^2)$
6. Galerkin with Hermite cubics and Gauss elimination	1970	$1600n^2 + 250n^4$	$50000n^3 + 16000n^7$	$O(1/n^4)$
7. Collocation with Hermite cubics and Gauss elimination	1975	$300n^2 + 250n^4$	$4000n^3 + 16000n^7$	$O(1/n^4)$
8. Higher-order differences and Gauss elimination	1978	$500n^2 + 3n^4$	$1500n^3 + 5n^7$	$O(1/n^3)$
9. Higher-order differences and iteration	198x	$500n^2 + 20n^{3.5} \log n$	$1500n^3 + 60n^{4.5} \log n$	$O(1/n^4)$

methods are much more complex to obtain even though the problem and its solutions are very well behaved. This second model problem is much less well defined than the first, and hence there is *much less reliability* in these estimates. The unreliability is further compounded because of the lack of extensive experience with these problems, especially for three dimensions, and so the values in Tables 10.5 and 10.6 should be considered as indicative of the situations rather than as firm values.

Rough Estimates of Time and Storage to Obtain .1 percent Accuracy for a General Elliptic Problem **Table 10.6**

The number n of discretization points (or elements) is taken to be 800, 30, 15, and 12 to achieve .1 percent accuracy for methods of order $1/n$, $1/n^2$, $1/n^3$, and $1/n^4$, respectively.

		Two Dimensions	Three Dimensions	
Year	Method	Time	Time	Storage
1945	5-point star and band Gauss elimination	140 days	300 million yrs.	800 million
1955	5-point star and Gauss-Seidel iteration	4.4 years	190 centuries	5 million
1960	5-point star with better boundary approximation or Finite element with linear elements and Gauss elimination	50 seconds	23 days	50 million
1965	Iteration for 1960 5-point star method	200 seconds	55 hours	300,000
1970	Galerkin with Hermite cubics and Gauss elimination	50 seconds	70 days	170,000
1975	Collocation with Hermite cubics and Gauss elimination	50 seconds	70 days	170,000
1978	Higher-order differences and Gauss elimination	3 seconds	55 hours	750,000
198x	Higher-order differences and iteration	4 seconds	200 seconds	50,000

The increase in speed for solving the second model problem is roughly 4 million in two dimensions and 50 billion in three dimensions. The estimates of the study mentioned above have been reworked some here; the difference between 50 billion obtained here and 12 billion obtained originally for the speed-up factor is well within the range of uncertainty of these estimates. Better methods that look "just around the corner" hold out hope for another factor of 1,000 in increased speed along with a reduction by a factor of 5 to 10 in the memory required.

SOFTWARE FOR PARTIAL DIFFERENTIAL EQUATIONS 10.4

Software for partial differential equations tends to be rather large. It is not easy to make it portable, and the demands of efficiency have often led to complexities in the use of the software. There are good surveys of this software in the papers "Survey of Software for Partial Differential Equations" by M. Machura and R. S. Sweet and "Sources and Development of Mathematical Software for Elliptic Boundary Value Problems" by R. F. Boisvert and R. A. Sweet (see references at end of chapter). We do not summarize these surveys here; rather, we concentrate on some software that is widely available. This software consists of the ACM Algorithms, one IMSL routine, and three software packages or systems for partial differential equations.

ACM Algorithms and an IMSL Routine for Partial Differential Equations

10.4.A

Algorithm 392: This first algorithm is for a system of two hyperbolic equations and is a rather direct implementation of a standard difference method. The equations are of the form

$$a_1u_x + a_2u_y + a_3v_x + a_4v_y = H_1$$
$$b_1u_x + b_2u_y + b_3v_x + b_4v_y = H_2$$

where the a_i, b_i, and H_i are functions of x, y, u, and v.

Algorithm 494: PDEONE. This algorithm implements the method of lines for initial value problems with time and one space variable of the form

$$\begin{aligned} u_t &= \mathbf{f}(t, x, \mathbf{u}, \mathbf{u}_x, (D(\mathbf{u})\mathbf{u}_x)_x) \\ &\alpha\mathbf{u} + \beta\mathbf{u}_x = \gamma \qquad \text{at } x = a, b \\ &\mathbf{u}(0, x) \text{ given} \end{aligned}$$

Equation 10.4.1

The domain is $t \geq 0$ and $a \leq x \leq b$; for $x = a$ and $x = b$ there are separate functions α, β, and γ which depend on t.

This algorithm is remarkable in how much power it provides in a relatively short code (155 lines). One must provide an ordinary differential equation solver plus Fortran subprograms to define the functions **f**, α, β, λ, **u**(0, t) and the matrix of functions D. The x variable is discretized by finite differences.

Algorithm 540: PDECOL. This is a package of 19 routines (over 3,000 lines of Fortran) for the **initial value problem** with time and one space variable of the form

$$\begin{aligned} \mathbf{u}_t &= f(t, x, \mathbf{u}, \mathbf{u}_x, \mathbf{u}_{xx}) \\ &\mathbf{b}(\mathbf{u}, \mathbf{u}_x) = \mathbf{z}(t) \qquad \text{at } x = a, b \\ &\mathbf{u}(0, x) \text{ given} \end{aligned}$$

Equation 10.4.2

The domain is $t \geq 0$ and $a \leq x \leq b$. The method is based on collocation in x by piecewise polynomials (using the B-spline programs from PPPACK). The polynomial degree may be chosen between 3 and 20, the smoothness between 1 continuous derivative, and the polynomial degree less one. These equations are coupled with a differential equation solver STIFIB (included in the package) which is a version of GEARIB which, in turn, is related to DIFSUB, DGEAR, and EPISODE. As for Algorithm 494 by the same authors, the user writes a few Fortran subprograms for the various functions that appear in the problem.

Algorithm 541: FISHPAK. This is a set of programs with simple-to-use interfaces for solving **Helmholtz problems:**

$$u_{xx} + u_{yy} + au = f$$

There are separate programs for rectangular, polar, cylindrical, and spherical coordinates. The Helmholtz equation changes form in the nonrectangular coordinates, but the same type of methods can be applied. There are also programs for the interior of a sphere and the equation

$$a(x)u_{xx} + b(x)u_x + c(x)u + u_{yy} = f(x, y)$$

In all cases *the domain must be separable* as fast methods (cyclic reduction and FFT) are used. The discretization used is the 5-point star. This package consists of 4,700 lines of Fortran including complete documentation. A new version, FISHPAK 3.1, is substantially expanded in capability and is available from the National Center for Atmospheric Research.

Algorithm 543: FFT9. This algorithm is based on the fast Fourier transform (FFT) method applied to a 9-point star discretization of

$$\begin{aligned} &au_{xx} + bu_{yy} + cu = f(x, y) \\ &\quad u \text{ given on the rectangular boundary} \end{aligned}$$

where a, b, and c are constants. The discretization is of high order, $0(h^4)$ in general and $O(h^6)$ in the Poisson case ($a = b = 1, c = 0$). This algorithm is used by a single subroutine call and consists of about 1,300 lines of Fortran.

Algorithm 553: M3RK. This algorithm is a specialized ordinary differential equation solver for the system

$$\mathbf{y}' = \mathbf{f}(\mathbf{y}) \qquad \mathbf{y}(0) \text{ given}$$ **Equation 10.4.3**

where it is assumed that the system arises from discretizing **parabolic equations** such as

$$u_t = f(x, t, u, u_x, u_{xx})$$ **Equation 10.4.4**

Systems of parabolic equations and several space variables are handled as well. Users must discretize 10.4.4 themselves to obtain the ordinary differential equations 10.4.3. For a single space variable, Algorithm 540 can be used for the discretization. The system 10.4.3 is solved with a third-order Runge-Kutta method.

Algorithm 565: PDETWO/PSETM/GEARB. This is a complete set of programs for solving **initial value problems** with **two space variables.** The partial differential equation is of the form

$$\begin{aligned} &\mathbf{u}_t = \mathbf{f}(t, x, y, \mathbf{u}, \mathbf{u}_x, \mathbf{u}_y, (\mathbf{H}\mathbf{u}_x)_x, (\mathbf{V}\mathbf{u}_y)_y) \\ &\quad \mathbf{A}\mathbf{u} + \mathbf{B}\mathbf{u}_y = \mathbf{C} \qquad \text{for } a_1 \le x \le b_1 \text{ and } y = a_2 \text{ or } b_2 \\ &\quad \mathbf{D}\mathbf{u} + \mathbf{E}\mathbf{u}_x = \mathbf{F} \qquad \text{for } a_2 \le y \le b_2 \text{ and } x = a_1 \text{ or } b_1 \\ &\quad \mathbf{u}(0, x, y) = \mathbf{g}(x, y) \end{aligned}$$

The functions A, B, C, D, E, and F may depend on t, x, y, and u, while H and V may depend on t,x and y. The method of lines is used with the 5-point star discretization of x and y and then using GEARB (see Chapter 9) to solve the resulting system of ordinary differential equations. The algorithm includes a version of GEARB plus complete documentation.

Algorithm 572: HELM3D. This program solves the Helmholtz equation

$$\begin{aligned} u_{xx} + u_{yy} + u_{zz} - cu &= f(x, y, z) \\ u &= g(x, y, z) \qquad \text{on domain boundary} \end{aligned}$$

on a general domain in three dimensions; c is a constant. The equation is discretized by second-order finite differences, and the resulting system is solved by the **capacitance matrix method.** This method uses a fast method such as FFT (called CUBE here) for the Helmholtz problem on a cube containing the region. The functions f and g are extended to the containing cube, and the fast method is applied to the resulting problem. A conjugate gradient iteration is used to "adjust" the extensions so that the solution of the problem on the containing cube converges to that of the original problem.

The IMSL library has a program DPDES which implements the method of lines using a modified version of DGEAR to solve the resulting system of ordinary differential equations. This program solves the *initial value problem* with one space variable of the form

$$\begin{aligned} &\mathbf{u}_t = f(x, t, \mathbf{u}, \mathbf{u}_x, \mathbf{u}_{xx}) \\ &\mathbf{u}(t_0, x) = \mathbf{g}(x) \\ &\mathbf{a}^T\mathbf{u} + \mathbf{b}^T\mathbf{u}_x = \mathbf{c}(t) \qquad \text{for } x = x_1 \\ &\mathbf{d}^T\mathbf{u} + \mathbf{e}^T\mathbf{u}_x = \mathbf{f}(t) \qquad \text{for } x = x_2 \end{aligned}$$

This problem has a general second-order operator in the space variable and linear boundary conditions; the coefficients **a**, **b**, **d**, and **e** are constant vectors. The space variable is discretized with collocation by Hermite cubics at Gauss points; thus the lines are not equally spaced. The special version of DGEAR used takes advantage of the bandedness of both the discretized **f** and the Jacobian of the system of differential equations.

The call to DPDES is

```
CALL DPDES (NPDES,F,BNDRY,T,H,TEND,XBREAK,U,IDIMU,NX,TOL,KONTRL,WORK,IER)
```

where NPDES = number of partial differential equations.

F = subroutine to evaluate u_t from the right side:

```
SUBROUTINE F(NPDES,X,T,U,UX,UXX,UT)
REAL X,T,U(NPDES),UX(NPDES),UXX(NPDES),UT(NPDES)
```

BNDRY = subroutine to evaluate boundary conditions:

```
SUBROUTINE BNDRY(NPDES,X,T,A,B,C)
REAL X,T,A(NPDES),B(NPDES),C(NPDES)
```

Only X = x_1 or X = x_2 are valid and A = **a** or **d**, B = **b** or **e** depending on whether X = x_1 or X = x_2; similarly C = **c**(t) or **f**(t) as X = x_1 or X = x_2.

T = independent variable.

H,TEND = step size to start this call and T for stopping.

XBREAK,NX = X(I) = Ith break point of Hermite cubics, $1 \le I \le NX$.

U = U (K, 1, I) = u_k(XBREAK(I))

U(K, 2, I) = $u_{k,x}$(XBREAK(I))

TOL,KONTRL = relative tolerance request and KONTROL switch.

WORK = workspace array of length NX*NPDES*(30*NPDES + 36) + 5*NPDES + 2*NX

Note that DPDES operates in a mode similar to routines in Section 9.5.B; one writes a program that steps along from t_0 rather than solving the whole problem with one library routine call.

Other Software for Partial Differential Equations 10.4.B

There are two different approaches to the user interface for partial differential equations software. One is to use mathematical terminology and equations, the other is to use application-area terminology. In the latter case the software is aimed at a particular application (for example, structural engineering, fluid dynamics, transistor analysis) and the documentation, etc., uses words like stress, strain, fluid velocity, and potential field. There is a lot of the application-oriented software, but it is not feasible to summarize it here.

We briefly describe three systems which are more or less mathematical in their approach. Note that these and similar systems are quite expensive to develop and can involve many thousands of lines of programming. In a few instances (such as ACM Algorithms 540, 541, and 565) one can obtain these systems practically free, but normally one should expect to pay a substantial sum to obtain one of them even if its development has been heavily subsidized. The total development cost of these systems can easily reach \$50 per Fortran statement since they often involve a variety of nonroutine difficulties in the mathematics, numerical methods, computer resource analysis, language processing, and computer system interfaces.

The ELLPACK System. This system solves elliptic problems in two dimensions with general domains and in three dimensions with rectangular domains. The goal of this system is to provide a means to compare and evaluate different methods for solving elliptic problems. As a result, the system contains over 30 numerical method modules. ELLPACK has a special, high-level language as illustrated below for a simple case

```
EQUATION.   UXX + COS(X+Y)*UYY - 6.2*UY = SIN(X-Y)
BOUNDARY.             U = 1.                        ON X = 0.
                      U = COS(X)                    ON Y = 0.
                      U = 1. -X                     ON Y = 1.
   U = COS(2.)*COS(1.570796*Y) - SIN(1.57096*Y)     ON X = 2.
GRID.   10 XPOINTS $ 5 YPOINTS
DISCRETIZATION.      5 POINT STAR
INDEXING.            AS IS
SOLUTION.            LINPACK BAND
OUTPUT.              PLOT(U) $ TABLE(U)
SOLUTION.            SOR
OUTPUT.              TABLE(U)
OPTIONS.             TIME $ MEMORY
END.
```

This program defines the elliptic problem, gives a rectangular discretization grid, and specifies that the 5-point star discretization is to be used and the resulting equations solved by Gauss elimination for band matrices and by SOR iteration. The execution times are requested so that they can be compared. See Figure 2.3 for another example.

While the main purpose of ELLPACK is to compare methods, it also provides an easy-to-use tool to solve easy or moderately difficult elliptic problems. If one is faced with a truly large-scale computation, ELLPACK provides a means to experiment with various methods on simpler cases before a commitment is made to a particular method.

Methods can be added to or deleted from the ELLPACK system with ease, and so there is no fixed set. In mid-1982 the following modules were available (many of the module names given are meaningless to those without a broad familiarity with methods for partial differential equations; space limitations preclude providing reasonably detailed descriptions of each module):

Discretization:	5 POINT STAR	7 POINT STAR 3D
	HERMITE COLLOCATION	COLLOCATION
	HODIE HELMHOLTZ	HODIE ACF
	SPLINE GALERKIN	
Indexing:	AS IS	RED-BLACK
	MINIMUM DEGREE	REVERSE CUTHILL MCKEE
	NESTED DISSECTION	HERMITE COLLORDER
Solution:	LINPACK BAND	LINPACK SPD BAND
	BAND GE	BAND GE NO PIVOTING
	SPARSE GE PIVOTING	SPARSE
	SPARSE FAST	SPARSE SYMMETRIC
	SOR	ENVELOPE
	JACOBI SI	JACOBI CG
	SYMMETRIC SOR SI	SYMMETRIC SOR CG
	REDUCED SYSTEM SI	REDUCED SYSTEM CG
Complete Problem Solution:	FFT 9 POINT	P2CO TRIANGLES
	DYAKANOV CG	DYAKANOV CG 4
	MARCHING ALGORITHM	FISHPAK HELMHOLTZ
	HODIE 27 POINT 3D	CAPACITANCE MATRIX
	M00 MULTIGRID	

There are also blending function capabilities (see Problems 10.2.25 and 10.2.26) and several useful procedures to analyze the numerical methods. The ELLPACK system contains well over 50,000 lines of Fortran; its basic documentation is the book *Elliptic Problem Solving with ELLPACK* by J. R. Rice and R. F. Boisvert. This system is available from

Professor John R. Rice
Math Science 428
Purdue University
West Lafayette, Indiana 47907 Phone: (317) 494-6007

The price is about $1,000 ($200 to educational institutions) including complete documentation.

TWODEPEP. This is a system for general two-dimensional elliptic, parabolic, and eigenvalue problems. It solves systems of equations of the form

$$c_i \frac{\partial u^i}{\partial t} = \frac{\partial A_i}{\partial x} + \frac{\partial B_i}{\partial y} + f_i \qquad i = 1, 2, \ldots, N$$

where the c_i are functions of x, y, t, $u^1, u^2, \ldots, u^N$, and the A_i, B_i, and f_i are functions of x, y, t, $u^1, \ldots, u^N$, $u^1_x, \ldots, u^N_x, u^1_y, \ldots, u^N_y$. Boundary conditions are of the form

$$\begin{aligned} u^i &= F_i(x, y, t) && \text{on part 1 of the boundary} \\ A_i \cdot n_x + B_i \cdot n_y &= G_i(x, y, t, u^1, \ldots, u^N) && \text{on part 2 of the boundary} \end{aligned}$$

where (n_x, n_y) is the outward normal of the boundary. Initial conditions are specified for the time-dependent problem.

TWODEPEP also solves the elliptic problem where the c_i are all zero, and the eigenvalue problem

$$0 = \frac{\partial A_i}{\partial x} + \frac{\partial B_i}{\partial y} + f_i \ \lambda P_i u^i$$

where P_i is a function of x and y and the eigenvalue λ is to be determined.

TWODEPEP has a preprocessor which simplifies the input, a graphical output package, the ability to automatically refine and grade the triangular mesh, and an "out of core" option which makes the solution of large problems possible while increasing costs only moderately. The Galerkin finite elements available are triangles with quadratic, cubic, or quartic basis functions, with one edge curved when adjacent to a curved boundary, according to the isoparametric method. For the parabolic (time-dependent) problem, either the implicit or Crank-Nicolson scheme may be used to discretize time. Optionally, a Richardson extrapolation may be done to double the order of convergence of the time discretization.

Nonlinear algebraic equations are solved by Newton's method. The linear system which must be solved to do a Newton iteration is solved directly by Gauss elimination. If the matrix is too large to keep in core, the frontal method is used to efficiently organize its storage out of core.

The user specifies an initial triangulation with only enough triangles to define the region and supplies a function D3EST(x, y) which guides the refinement of this triangulation. D3EST should be largest where the final triangulation is to be most dense. Optimal order convergence is possible even for singular problems if this function is chosen properly.

TWODEPEP is exceptionally efficient with respect to core usage. A special node renumbering algorithm further reduces the bandwidth obtained from the Cuthill McKee algorithm, and the frontal method is used to organize the out-of-core storage of the stiffness matrix when it becomes large. On a typical problem, this frontal method implementation increases cost by less than 50 percent while reducing the core storage required from 2nb to b^2 (n = number of unknowns, b = half bandwidth), or half that for symmetric problems.

The simple user input format of TWODEPEP is illustrated for a problem in solid elasticity:

```
(1) 2 12 12 30 2
(2) ****
    ****  STRESSES IN A BLOCK WITH A SEMICIRCULAR NOTCH
    ****
(3) OXX             11.E6* (0.8*UX+0.2*VY)/0.72
    OYY             11.E6* (0.2*UX+0.8*VY)/0.72
    OXY             11.E6* (UY+VX)/2.4
    OYX             11.E6* (UY+VX)/2.4
(4) NX                 8
    NY                 8
(5) D3EST           (X**2+Y**2)**(-1)
(6) ARC=  1
    X               SIN(3.14159*S)
    Y               -COS(3.14159*S)
(7) ARC=  4
    GB1                1.0
(8) VXY             0.,-4., 4.,-4., 2.,-2., 0.,-1., 1.,0., 4.,0.,
    VXY             0.,1., 2.,2., 0.,4., 4.,4., 0.707106,-0.707106,
    VXY                0.707106,0.707106
    IABC            1,2,3, 2,6,3, 6,5,3, 5,11,3, 11,4,3, 4,1,3,
    IABC            5,6,8, 6,10,8, 10,9,8, 9,7,8, 7,12,8, 12,5,8
    I               -1,2,0,1,1,5,0,2,3,4,1,1
(9) SYMMETRY          1
    END.
```

Notes

(1) Integers on the first line define the number of triangles desired in the final triangulation (30) and related information.

(2) Lines beginning with **** are comments.

(3) The stresses (OXX, OXY=OYX,OYY) are defined in terms of the strains (ϵ_x=UX, ϵ_y=VY, ϵ_{xy}=UY+VX). (U, V) is the displacement vector. Plane stress conditions are assumed.

(4) The solution is to be output on an 8 by 8 grid covering the region.

(5) The final triangulation will be graded so that it is most dense where D3EST (x, y) is largest, in this case near the notch.

(6) The parametric equations for arc number 1 (the semicircle) are given here. The other arcs default to straight lines.

(7) A unit horizontal force is applied along arc number 4, just above the notch.

(8) The arrays defining the initial triangulation are given here.

(9) The problem is symmetric, and this is to be taken advantage of during the solution process.

Many functions and variables are defaulted in this problem. For example, the body force vector (F1, F2), the boundary force vector (GB1, GB2) on the rest of the free boundary, and the displacements (FB1, FB2) on the fixed boundary (the base) default to zero.

TWODEPEP is a product of IMSL, Inc., 7500 Bellaire Blvd., Houston, Texas 77036. It costs about $1,500 per year, which includes documentation and consulting support.

DSS (Differential Systems Simulator). This system provides for the integration of initial value problems in ordinary or partial differential equations with the method of lines. Subroutines are provided to obtain finite difference discretizations for 1 or 2 space variables in "piecewise regular" domains. Facilities are also provided for systems of first-order hyperbolic equations.

The general form of the equation is

$$\mathbf{u}_t = \mathbf{f}(\mathbf{x}, t, \mathbf{u}, \mathbf{u}_x, \mathbf{u}_{xx}, \mathbf{u}_{xxx}, \ldots)$$
$$\mathbf{g}(\mathbf{x}, t, \mathbf{u}, \mathbf{u}_x, \mathbf{u}_{xx}, \ldots) = 0 \qquad \text{for } \mathbf{x} \text{ on the boundary}$$
$$\mathbf{u}(\mathbf{x}, 0) = \mathrm{h}(\mathbf{x})$$

where **x** is a vector of one, two, or three dimensions, t is time, and the functions **f**, **g**, **h** are specified. The basic method of DSS is the method of lines; one may choose from over a dozen programs for ordinary differential equation systems. Various finite difference discretizations (3, 5, 7, 9, or 11 points plus specialized) may be selected. The system is Fortran-based and runs on a wide variety of computer systems.

A problem for DSS is specified by providing two Fortran subprograms, INITIAL for initial conditions and DERV for the equation definition. Choices among the methods available are selected by calling particular subroutines from the program DERV. The following example shows the setup to solve the system:

$$u_t = u_{xx} + [16xt - 2t - 16(v-1)](u-1) + 10e^4x$$
$$v_t = v_{xx} + u_x + 4u - 4 + x^2 - 2t - 10e^4t$$

with initial conditions $u(x, 0) = v(x, 0) = 1$ and boundary conditions

$$u(0, t) = v(0, t) = 1 \qquad u_t(0, t) = v_t(0, t) = 0$$
$$u_x(1, t) = 3 - 3u(1, t) \qquad v_x(1, t) = e^4(u(1, t) - 1)/5$$

Twenty lines are used, and the parameter NORUN can be set to use a 3-point or 5-point difference formula for the spatial derivatives. Other subprograms not shown control input/output.

This system is available from

Professor W. E. Schiesser
Whitaker No. 5
Lehigh University
Bethlehem, Pennsylvania 18015 Phone: (215) 861-4264

The price is about $1,000 including complete documentation.

```
      SUBROUTINE INITIAL
C...
      COMMON/T/T,NFIN,NORUN
     1      /Y/  U(21),  V(21)
     2      /F/ UT(21), VT(21)
     3     /SD/ UX(21),UXX(21), VX(21),VXX(21)
     4      /X/  X(21)
     5      /P/       N,           E4
C...  SET THE NUMBER OF SPATIAL INTERVALS AND THEIR LENGTH
      N=20
      DX=1./FLOAT(N)
C...
C...  COMPUTE THE VALUES OF X ALONG THE SPATIAL GRID
      N=N+1
      DO 1 I=1,N
      X(I)=DX*FLOAT(I-1)
1     CONTINUE
C...
C...  SET THE INITIAL CONDITIONS, EQUATIONS (7) AND (8)
      DO 2 I=1,N
      U(I)=1.
      V(I)=1.
2     CONTINUE
C...
C...  SET THE CONSTANT E**4 USED IN ONE OF THE BOUNDARY CONDITIONS
      E4=EXP(1.)**4
      RETURN
      END

      SUBROUTINE DERV
      COMMON/T/T,NFIN,NORUN
     1      /Y/  U(21),  V(21)
     2      /F/ UT(21), VT(21)
     3     /SD/ UX(21),UXX(21), VX(21), VXX(21)
     4      /X/  X(21)
     5      /P/       N,     F4
C...
C...  APPLY THE LEFT BOUNDARY CONDITIONS AS CONSTRAINTS, EQUATIONS (3) AND (4)
       U(1)=1.
      UT(1)=0.
       V(1)=1.
      VT(1)=0.
C...
C...  COMPUTE THE FIRST-ORDER SPATIAL DERIVATIVES
      XL=X(1)
      XU=X(N)
C...
C...     THREE-POINT CENTERED DIFFERENCES
      IF(NORUN.EQ.1)CALL DSS002(XL,XU,N,U,UX)
      IF(NORUN.EQ.1)CALL DSS002(XL,XU,N,V,VX)
C...
C...     FIVE-POINT CENTERED DIFFERENCES
      IF(NORUN.EQ.2)CALL DSS004(XL,XU,N,U,UX)
      IF(NORUN.EQ.2)CALL DSS004(XL,XU,N,V,VX)
C...
C...  APPLY THE RIGHT BOUNDARY CONDITIONS AS CONSTRAINTS, EQUATIONS (5) AND (6)
      UX(N)=3.-3.*U(N)
      VX(N)=E4*(U(N)-1.)/5.
C...
C...  COMPUTE THE SECOND-ORDER SPATIAL DERIVATIVES
C...
C...     THREE-POINT CENTERED DIFFERENCES
      IF(NORUN.EQ.1)CALL DSS002(XL,XU,N,VX,VXX)
C...
C...     FIVE-POINT CENTERED DIFFERENCES
      IF(NORUN.EQ.2)CALL DSS004(XL,XU,N,VX,VXX)
C...
C...  NOTE THAT ARRAY VX IS USED AS TEMPORARY STORAGE IN THE CALCULATION
C...  OF THE TERM ((V-1)*U ) WHICH IS FINALLY STORED IN ARRAY UXX
C...                     X X
C...
      DO 1 I=1,N
      VX(I)=(V(I)-1.)*UX(I)
1     CONTINUE
      IF(NORUN.EQ.1)CALL DSS002(XL,XU,N,VX,UXX)
      IF(NORUN.EQ.2)CALL DSS004(XL,XU,N,VX,UXX)
C...
C...  ASSEMBLE THE PDES, EQUATIONS (1) AND (2)
      DO 3 I=2,N
      EX=EXP(-4.*X(I))
      UT(I)=UXX(I)+(16.*X(I)*T-2.*T-16.*(V(I)-1.))*(U(I)-1.)+10.*X(I)*EX
      VT(I)=VXX(I)+UX(I)+4.*U(I)-4.+X(I)**2-2.*T-10.*T*EX
3     CONTINUE
      RETURN
      END
```

REFERENCES

W. F. Ames, *Numerical Methods for Partial Differential Equations,* Academic Press, Inc., New York (1977).

G. Birkhoff and R. E. Lynch, *Numerical Solution of Elliptic Problems,* SIAM Publications (1983).

R. F. Boisvert and R. A. Sweet, "Sources and Development of Mathematical Software for Elliptic Boundary Value Problems," in *Sources and Development of Mathematical Software* (W. Cowell, ed.), Prentice-Hall, Inc., Englewood Cliffs, N. J. (1982).

A. George and J. W. Lin, *Computer Solution of Large Sparse Positive Definite Systems,* Prentice-Hall, Inc., Englewood Cliffs, N. J. (1981).

J. Gladwell and R. Wait, *A survey of Numerical Methods for Partial Differential Equations,* Oxford University Press (1979).

Marek Machura and Roland Sweet, "Survey of Software for Partial Differential Equations," ACM Trans. Math. Software, **6** (1980), pp. 461-488.

J. R. Rice and R. F. Boisvert, *Elliptic Problem Solving with ELLPACK,* Springer-Verlag, (1983).

P. Roache, *Computational Fluid Dynamics,* Hermosa Publishers, Albuquerque (1972).

V. Vemuri and W. J. Karplus, *Digital Computer Treatment of Partial Differential Equations,* Prentice-Hall, Inc., Englewood Cliffs, N.J. (1981).

R. Vichnevetsky, *Computer Methods for Partial Differential Equations, Vol. 1: Elliptic Equations and the Finite Element Method* (1981) and *Vol. 2: Initial Value Problems* (1982), Prentice-Hall, Inc., Englewood Cliffs, N.J.

*11 APPROXIMATION OF FUNCTIONS AND DATA

Interpolation is a way to represent or approximate functions or data by a function of a particular type. Thus, in cubic polynomial interpolation, one chooses four points, makes the cubic interpolate at them, and then hopes that the resulting cubic is a good approximation. This approach is often unsatisfactory because the "right" interpolation points are hard to identify. Frequently, one wants to have the cubic which is "as close to the function or data as possible," i.e., which approximates well. This chapter is concerned with computing approximations of various types and with various measures of the error.

APPROXIMATION PROBLEMS 11.1

Three Classes of Approximation Problems 11.1.A

There are three rather distinct ways in which approximation problems arise, and each uses different methods.

1. *Approximation of Mathematical Functions.* One has an exact function which must be approximated by other functions. The typical example is sin (x) or e^x, which must be approximated by a polynomial because a computer can only do arithmetic. These approximations are used, for example, in the Fortran compiler's library to evaluate expressions like EXP(3.2*X)*(1.+SIN(X-ALPHA)) in a Fortran program.

   These approximation problems have the following characteristics:

   (A) Very **high accuracy** is usually needed (6 to 30 or more digits are to be correct).

   (B) There is **no uncertainty** in the function being approximated.

   (C) There may be a lot of **specialized knowledge** that can be exploited. For example, all Fortran library routines for sin (x) use the facts

   $$\sin(x+k\pi) = (-1)^k \sin(x)$$
   $$\sin(x+\pi/2) = \cos(x)$$

   to simplify the problem by reducing the interval over which the approximation is needed.

Section 11.7 discusses some of the sources for more information about this class of problems. A systematic presentation of this material is too lengthy to include here, although the methods and software discussed are applicable to many of these problems.

2. *The Representation and Compactification of Data.* One has a large set of measured data and needs a simpler and more convenient approximation. An example of this is where one has measured 192 values of atmospheric pressure as a function of altitude and wants to replace this table by a mathematical formula to be used in calculations. Another example is where one has millions of data points giving the positions of the planets and moons for the next century and wants a much more compact form of this information.

These approximation problems have the following characteristics:

(A) **Moderate accuracy** is needed (2 to 5 digits are to be correct).

(B) There is **little uncertainty** in the data.

(C) There might be **some specialized information** that can be used in selecting a model for the data, but often there is not. For example, one knows that pressure decreases roughly exponentially with altitude, and so one could model the pressure by $e^{-bx}p_6(x)$, where x is altitude and b plus the coefficients of the sixth-degree polynomial $p_6(x)$ are to be determined.

(D) The **data is discrete** and additional values cannot be obtained easily.

3. *Smoothing and Analysis of Data.* One has a set of data with a substantial uncertainty in some or all of the values. The uncertainty is usually due to inaccuracies in either the measuring devices or the techniques used to obtain the data. These uncertainties may be as large as 50 to 100 percent; they are typically a few parts in a hundred or a thousand. There are sometimes **wild points** in the data because of some unusual event that affects just one data value. For example, a value might be miscopied, an earthquake might have jiggled the meter, a bolt of lightning might have garbled the radio transmission, or lab samples might have been switched.

These approximation problems have the following characteristics:

(A) **Low accuracy** is needed (.5 to 3 digits are to be correct).

(B) There is **substantial uncertainty** in the data. The nature of the uncertainty is somewhat random, but the exact nature of the randomness is unknown.

(C) There is probably **little specialized information** about the model for the behavior underlying the data.

(D) The **data is discrete** and additional values cannot be obtained easily.

Most of the material in this chapter is directly applicable to this third class of problems. We do not discuss the statistical aspects of these problems which are important for much of data analysis.

The L_1, Least-Squares, and Chebyshev Norms 11.1.B

Approximations are made with respect to some measure of "goodness" or "closeness"; in the case of data or functions these are *norms.* For concreteness, assume that we want to approximate the function f(x) on the interval [a, b] by something of the form F(**a**, x). Here **a** denotes the parameters or coefficients of the approximation and F might be polynomials, splines, or something else. Most of the approximations discussed in this chapter are linear with

$$F(\mathbf{a}, x) = \sum_{i=1}^{n} a_i b_i(x)$$

The basis functions $b_i(x)$ are the model of the function being approximated. The distance between f(x) and F(a, x) is the norm $||f - F(\mathbf{a})||$. In Chapter 5, we used the **Chebyshev** (or **max** or $\mathbf{L}_\infty$) norm:

$$||f - F(\mathbf{a})||_\infty = \max_{a \le x \le b} |f(x) - F(\mathbf{a}, x)| \qquad \textbf{Equation 11.1.1}$$

We use the subscript infinity here to distinguish this function norm from others defined below. The **best Chebyshev approximation** is $F(\mathbf{a}^*, x)$, where $\mathbf{a}^*$ minimizes 11.1.1.

Distance measured in the Chebyshev norm is easy to understand and natural to use. It is not as widely used as it might be for two reasons: (1) it is not easy to minimize 11.1.1 to obtain best Chebyshev approximations, and (2) this norm is unsuitable when uncertainty is present in the data because it often magnifies the effect of a single uncertainty or random error. The first drawback is not as important now as it once was. In the 1950s efficient methods were not available to compute Chebyshev approximations; now some reliable, efficient software is widely available to do this. Nevertheless, the Chebyshev norm is still primarily used for the first class of approximation problems, approximating the standard mathematical functions.

Once one has trouble minimizing the maximum error 11.1.1, the next thought is to try to minimize the average error. For this, one uses the $\mathbf{L_1}$ (or **least deviation**) norm

$$||f - F(\mathbf{a})||_1 = \int_a^b |f(x) - F(\mathbf{a}, x)|dx \qquad \textbf{Equation 11.1.2}$$

This measure of distance is fairly natural and intuitive; it is even more difficult to use and analyze than the Chebyshev norm. There is some reliable software now available to compute best L_1 approximations, and so it is practical to use this norm. Its main attraction is in data analysis and smoothing; the L_1 norm is remarkably insensitive to random errors, wild points, and other uncertainties.

The most widely used measure of distance is the $\mathbf{L_2}$ (or **least-squares**) norm

$$||f - F(\mathbf{a})||_2 = \sqrt{\int_a^b [f(x) - F(\mathbf{a}, x)]^2 dx} \qquad \textbf{Equation 11.1.3}$$

It is not intuitively clear what it means to minimize 11.1.3, but it is easy to compute and analyze best least-squares approximations. This simplicity of use has led to its adoption for many problems where L_1 or L_∞ norms are more natural. In many instances this adoption is well justified because the benefits obtained from using the other norms do not offset the extra complications in obtaining them.

For the approximation of discrete data there are direct analogs of these norms. Suppose the given data is (x_i, d_i), $i = 1, 2, \ldots, k$. Then the difference $d_i - F(\mathbf{a}, x_i)$ just defines a vector, and we can use the vector norms. These are:

$$||\mathbf{d} - F(\mathbf{a}, \mathbf{x})||_\infty = \max_{1 \le i \le k} |d_i - F(\mathbf{a}, x_i)| \qquad \textbf{Equation 11.1.4}$$

$$||\mathbf{d} - F(\mathbf{a}, \mathbf{x})||_1 = \sum_{i=1}^{k} |d_i - F(\mathbf{a}, x_i)|$$

$$||\mathbf{d} - F(\mathbf{a}, \mathbf{x})||_2 = \sqrt{\sum_{i=1}^{k} (d_i - F(\mathbf{a}, x_i))^2}$$

In some cases where the x_i are highly nonuniform, the L_1 and least-squares norms of 11.1.4 should be modified to reflect this nonuniformity. One can replace the integrals of 11.1.2 and 11.1.3 by trapezoidal rule summations to obtain the **weighted vector norms**

$$||\mathbf{d} - F(\mathbf{a}, \mathbf{x})||_1 = \sum_{i=1}^{k} w_i|d_i - F(\mathbf{a}, x_i)| \qquad \textbf{Equation 11.1.5}$$

$$||\mathbf{d} - F(\mathbf{a}, \mathbf{x})||_2 = \sqrt{\sum_{i=1}^{k} w_i(d_i - F(\mathbf{a}, x_i))^2}$$

$$w_i = \frac{x_{i+1} - x_{i-1}}{2} \qquad \text{for } 2 \le i \le k$$

$$w_1 = \frac{x_2 - x_1}{2} \qquad w_k = \frac{x_k - x_{k-1}}{2}$$

Weights can be introduced into norms for other reasons. For example, one might want the accuracy to be better for one part of the data than another. These weights do not affect the methods or theory of approximation (provided they are positive), and we omit them in most of the presentations in this chapter. For similar purposes, positive **weight functions** can be introduced into the norms for functions to obtain the **weighted norms**

$$||f||_\infty = \max_{a \le x \le b} w(x)|f(x)| \qquad \textbf{Equation 11.1.6}$$

$$||f||_1 = \int_a^b w(x)|f(x)|dx$$

$$||f||_2 = \sqrt{\int_a^b w(x)f^2(x)dx}$$

Again, these weight functions do not affect the methods or theory very much, and we omit them in most of the discussion.

The Three Norms Applied to Multiple Observations of the Same Value — Example 11.1

The simplest case of approximation is when one has multiple observations of the same value. Consider, for example, measuring the family income x of the "average" college student. One can simply survey a small class and obtain data d_i, i = 1 to 9, such as

8,500, 14,600, 22,900, 16,500, 31,200, 20,000, 18,600, 24,000, 17,500

Each of these numbers is an "estimate" of x. We can approximate this data by a constant a_1, and a short analysis shows that

(A) Chebyshev approximation produces the **midrange**, which is $(\max|d_i| + \min|d_i|)/2 = 19{,}850$.

(B) Least-squares approximation produces the **average,** which is

$$\frac{1}{9}\sum_{i=1}^{9} d_i = 19{,}311$$

(C) L_1 approximation produces the **median**, which is a value so that the number of data values above and below it are the same. The median of the above data is 17,500.

The average is always somewhere between the midrange and the median.

Suppose that a new student, Johnny Moneybags, enrolls, and his family income is $62,425,000. This is a wild point for this data set, and the new values of the approximations are as follows:

Midrange = 31,216,750
Average = 6,259,880
Median = 17,500 to 18,600

The median is no longer uniquely defined; any value between 17,500 and 18,600 satisfies the definition. Note how the wild point has dramatically affected the midrange and average and yet the median has barely changed. The change in the median would be the same if Johnny Moneybags's family made $62,000 a year instead of $62,000,000.

The Three Norms Applied to Three Functions — Example 11.2

Figure 11.1 shows three functions $f_1(x) = 1$, $f_2(x) = 1 + .5\sin(6\pi x)$, and $f_3(x) = 1 + ae^{-a^2x}$ for a = 100 [the value of $f_3(0)$ is 101, which is way off the plot]. The three norms of these three functions on [0, 1] are tabulated below:

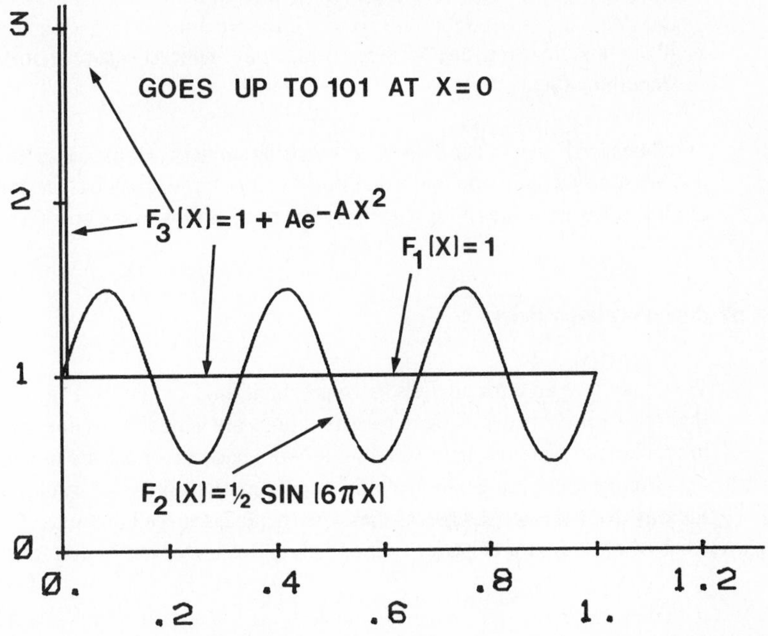

Figure 11.1 **Three functions with widely different Chebyshev norms and nearly identical L_1 norms.** $F_3(x)$ has $A = 100$ here; increasing A increases the L_∞ norm without changing the L_1 norm much.

	Chebyshev Norm	Least-Squares Norm	L_1 Norm
$f_1(x)$	1.0	1.0	1
$f_2(x)$	1.5	1.125	1
$f_3(x)$	101.0	1.52	1.01

We see that a large perturbation over a small interval strongly affects the Chebyshev norm and affects the least-squares norm to a lesser extent. The L_1 norm is insensitive to the oscillations of the types shown in Figure 11.1; it just measures the area under the curves.

Choice of Norm and Model 11.1.C

The most important step in an approximation problem is to choose a good model for the function or data. This topic has already been considered at length in earlier chapters (especially Chapter 4). We only add the observation that if there is some specialized information available about the behavior of the function or data, it pays to incorporate this into the model. Once an inappropriate model is chosen, no amount of skill and effort in analysis or computations will produce a good approximation. Such specialized models include things like

$e^{-ax}*\text{polynomial} \qquad \frac{a}{x} + \text{polynomial}$

$e^{-ax}*\text{spline} \qquad e^{-ax}*\text{Hermite cubic}$

If the extra parameter a enters nonlinearly, one estimates it somehow and then determines the remaining linear parameters by the methods presented here.

The choice of norm is less crucial but still important. The obvious tradeoff is between the ease of computing least-squares approximations against the stability of L_1 approximations in the presence of random errors and the fact that minimizing the maximum error (i.e., using the Chebyshev norm) is what one usually wants to do. There are two facts to consider in making the choice of norm:

1. It is likely, but not assured, that the maximum error of the best least-squares approximation is less than twice that of the best Chebyshev approximation.

2. If the random errors are "well-behaved," then the least-squares norm is as effective as the L_1 norm at smoothing them out.

"Well-behaved" means nearly normally distributed in the statistical sense. This is a common situation, but it is not nearly as common in the real world as it is in the textbooks on statistics. Fortunately, the existence of good software makes it feasible to try the three norms to see how they behave in a particular instance.

The Error of Approximation   11.1.D

We do not give an error analysis for approximation. For general $F(\mathbf{a}, x)$ one can say little beyond the fact that the error decreases as more basis functions are added. Thus one cannot have the problems seen with interpolation where the error *increases* as more basis functions are used in the model.

For the special case of polynomial approximations there are results that relate the properties of $f(x)$ to the way that the error behaves as the degree n increases; see Equation 5.5.11. The norm used in 5.5.11 is the Chebyshev; the error behavior is essentially the same for the L_1 and least-squares norms.

LEAST SQUARES AND REGRESSION   11.2

The primary motivation for least-squares approximation is its adequacy for a wide variety of situations. Its great strength is that this approximation problem can be solved by the direct application of matrix computation methods and software. We outline how this is done in this section. However, one should keep in mind that the least-squares criterion for best approximation is inappropriate for a certain proportion of applications that arise, and one must be prepared to use one of the other two norms. One can sometimes introduce a weight function into the least-squares norm and still use it effectively. The choice of weight functions is more of an art than a science and is not discussed further here. Arguments for using the least-squares norm based on the *principle of least squares* and the assumption of *normally distributed random errors* are suspect because one rarely knows much about the distribution of errors in a real problem. If the random errors present are significant, then it is safer to use L_1 approximation.

Formulation of Least-Squares Problems   11.2.A

We describe three somewhat different examples of problems that lead to a least-squares problem where the same numerical methods are applicable.

Overdetermined Systems of Linear Equations   Example 11.3

Suppose one has N linear equations but only $M < N$ variables. There are more conditions (equations) to be satisfied than degrees of freedom (variables), and it is unlikely that they can all be satisfied. Pictorially, the linear system appears as follows:

$$\left[\begin{array}{c} \text{Matrix} \\ A \end{array}\right] \left[\begin{array}{c} \mathbf{x} \end{array}\right] = \left[\begin{array}{c} \mathbf{b} \end{array}\right] N$$

$$\underleftrightarrow{} M$$

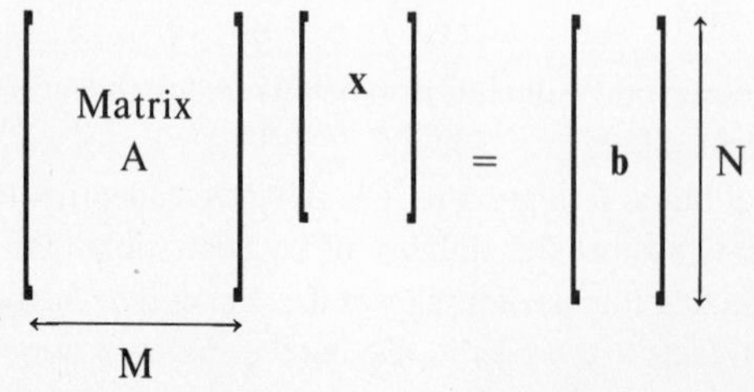

Since the equations cannot be satisfied exactly, we may attempt to satisfy them as best we can — that is, make the size of the **residual vector r** = **b** − A**x** with components

$$r_j = b_j - \sum_{i=1}^{M} a_{ji}x_i \qquad j = 1, 2, \ldots, N$$

as small as possible. The least-squares criterion is the use of the least-squares norm for the size of **r**; that is, minimize

$$\sqrt{\sum_{j=1}^{N} r_j^2} = ||\mathbf{r}||_2 \qquad \textbf{Equation 11.2.1}$$

Approximation of the Elementary Functions — Example 11.4

Consider writing a Fortran compiler and implementing the standard functions SIN(T), TAN(T), etc. Obviously, the implementation must use ordinary arithmetic operations, which means, for example, that we may want to have

sin(t) ~ polynomial of degree M − 1 in t

We can introduce the error or residual function r(t) as

$$r(t) = \sin(t) - \sum_{i=1}^{M} x_i t^{i-1} \qquad \text{for } t \epsilon [0, \pi/2]$$

We cannot make r(t) zero everywhere, and so we attempt to make it as small as possible in the sense that

$$\sqrt{\int_0^{\pi/2} r(t)^2 dt} = \text{minimum} \qquad \textbf{Equation 11.2.2}$$

The least-squares problem is then to choose the polynomial coefficients x_i to accomplish this. It might be awkward (or impossible) to evaluate the integrals in 11.2.2 when sin (t) is replaced by arctan (t) or a Bessel function, and so one might choose the coefficients x_i instead to have

$$\sqrt{\sum_{j=1}^{101} r(t_j)^2} = \text{minimum}$$

where the t_j are equally spaced in the interval [0, $\pi/2$].

Actual Fortran compilers use approximations with the Chebyshev norm to make max $|r(t)|$ = minimum.

Regression and Mathematical Modeling — Example 11.5

Consider the study of a phenomenon which involves one independent variable and one dependent variable. Examples of this are weight of cows as a function of age, repair costs of cars as a function of mileage, or lifetime income as a function of education obtained. In each case we know or believe or hope that there are several different factors that influence this relationship. Let t be the independent variable and let $f_i(t)$ express how these factors may vary (i.e., the amount of corn or hay fed the cows as a function of time; the amount of maintenance or farm use of cars as a function of mileage; the type of training or geographical location as a function of years of education). Finally, let d(t) be the dependent variable and set up the linear mathematical model

$$d(t) = \sum_{i=1}^{M} x_i f_i(t)$$

Theoretically, there should be values of the coefficients x_i which make this model exact. We would normally use the notation $d(x) \sim F(\mathbf{a}, x) = \Sigma a_i b_i(x)$, but to make the notation similar to that of linear systems of equations we have replaced x by t: the coefficients a_i by x_i and the basis functions $b_i(x)$ by $f_i(t)$.

Suppose now that we make a large number of measurements (take observations) and obtain values d_j for t values t_j, $j = 1, 2, \ldots, N$. If $N = M$, we just solve the linear system

$$d_j = d_j(t_j) = \sum_{i=1}^{M} x_i f_i(t_j) \qquad j = 1, 2, \ldots, N = M$$

for the unknown coefficients x_i. However, life is usually not so simple, and if we take N larger than M, we find that the coefficients x_i cannot be chosen to make the model exact for all observations. The discrepancy might be due to errors in the observations, incompleteness of the model, or inherent randomness in the phenomenon (or a combination of all three factors).

In order to get the "best" model possible, we decide to make the residual

$$r_j = d_j - \sum_{i=1}^{M} x_i f_i(t_j) \qquad j = 1, 2, \ldots, N$$

as small as possible. If we choose the least-square criterion, then we want

$$\sqrt{\sum_{j=1}^{N} r_j^2} = \text{minimum} \qquad \textbf{Equation 11.2.3}$$

Determining the coefficients x_i of the model to satisfy 11.2.3 is called **regression** in statistics.

In each of these three examples we minimize the square root of the sums of squares. It is easy to see that one can minimize the square root of something by minimizing the thing itself. In each case the least-squares problem can be formulated as minimizing

$$E(x_1, x_2, \ldots, x_M) = \left\|\mathbf{b} - \sum_{i=1}^{M} x_i \mathbf{a}_i\right\|_2^2 \qquad \textbf{Equation 11.2.4}$$

The $\mathbf{b}$ and $\mathbf{a}_i$ may be vectors or functions; in the three examples above we have for 11.2.1

$$\mathbf{b} = (b_1, b_2, \ldots, b_N)^T$$
$$\mathbf{a}_i = (a_{i1}, a_{i2}, \ldots, a_{iN})^T$$

for 11.2.2

$$\mathbf{b} = b(t)$$
$$\mathbf{a}_i = t^{i-1}$$

and for 11.2.3

$$\mathbf{b} = (d_1, d_2, \ldots, d_N)^T$$
$$\mathbf{a}_i = (f_i(t_1), f_i(t_2), \ldots, f_i(t_N))^T$$

The discrete problems in Examples 11.3 and 11.5 give vectors and sums; the continuous problem in Example 11.4 gives functions and integrals. This correspondence exists throughout least squares, and the techniques, methods, and analysis correspond exactly by a straightforward interchange of integrals and sums, etc. We make the presentation here using sums and vectors.

The Normal Equations 11.2.B

We apply the calculus to minimize 11.2.4 and set the derivatives of E with respect to the x_i equal to zero. Differentiation with respect to each x_k produces M equations as follows:

$$0 = \frac{\partial E}{\partial x_k} = \frac{\partial \Sigma(b_j - \Sigma x_i a_{ij})^2}{\partial x_k} = 2\Sigma(b_j - \Sigma x_i a_{ij}) a_{kj}$$

This is rewritten, for $k = 1, 2, \ldots, M$, as

$$\sum_{j=1}^{N} b_j a_{kj} = \sum_{j=1}^{N} \sum_{i=1}^{M} x_i a_{ij} a_{kj} = \sum_{i=1}^{M} x_i \sum_{j=1}^{N} a_{ij} a_{kj}$$ **Equation 11.2.5**

This is now M linear equations in the M unknowns x_i and may be expressed in matrix terms as

$$A^T A\mathbf{x} = A^T \mathbf{b}$$

These are the **normal equations.**

We can roughly estimate the work to form and solve the normal equations as follows. Only the highest-order terms are given in the operation counts used to estimate the work. To compute one entry of $A^T A$ requires N operations (one operation = one add + one multiply), and $M^2/2$ of them must be found ($A^T A$ is symmetric, and so only half of the elements need be computed). Since the normal equations are symmetric, one can apply the Cholesky method to solve them, which requires the order of $M^3/6$ operations. Thus the total work, for M and N large, is $M^2N/2 + M^3/6$.

We are about to discuss two other ways to do the least-squares problem. The normal equations approach is so simple that, unless there was something wrong with it, we would not consider another approach. The basic problem is that common model choices lead to ill-conditioned matrices $A^T A$. The conditioning might be so bad that the solutions are random numbers unrelated to the original problem; see Example 11.6. Of course, this does not always happen; it just happens often enough to make the approach unreliable. Note that the condition number of $A^T A$ is the condition number of A *squared.*

A secondary, but still important, weakness of this approach is that it is so simple that many users never see the real source of trouble: nearly linearly dependent basis vectors (columns of A) in the model. For example, a model for school children's athletic or physical characteristics might contain as variables:

Age, weight, height, and strength

These are obviously highly correlated and thus nearly linearly dependent. A model for a car's fuel economy might contain as variables:

Weight, speed, engine horsepower, engine displacement,
wind resistance, rolling friction, and tire information

Again, there are high correlations between some of these factors (e.g., speed, wind resistance, rolling friction) and thus nearly linearly dependent columns in the A matrix.

Finally, there is the not uncommon and potentially disastrous approach exemplified by the attitude:

I really don't know which variables affect the thing I'm interested in; so I'll throw in everything I can imagine and let the computer sort them out.

It does not always work out as hoped; one might get garbage or find that small random variations in the data in fact determine which variables are selected as important.

Polynomial Regression and the Hilbert Matrix — Example 11.6

Suppose we have 101 data values (observations) for equally spaced t's between 0 and 1:

$$(t_j, d_j),\ j = 1 \text{ to } 101 \text{ and } t_j = (j-1)/100$$

We believe the data varies with t as a polynomial in t of degree k; that is, we model $d(t)$ by $p_k(t)$ so that we believe

$$d_j = d(t_j) \sim p_k(t_j) = \sum_{i=1}^{k+1} x_i (t_j)^{i-1}$$

This produces the least-squares problem 11.2.4 with

$$\mathbf{a}_i = (t_1^{i-1}, t_2^{i-1}, \ldots, t_{101}^{i-1})^T$$

so that in the normal equations 11.2.5 we find the i, j element of A^TA to be

$$\sum_{j=1}^{N} a_{ij}a_{kj} = \sum_{j=1}^{101} t_j^{i-1}t_j^{k-1} = \sum_{j=1}^{101} t_j^{i+k-2}$$

This latter sum can be roughly approximated by $100 \int_0^1 t^{i+k-2}dt \sim 100/(i+k-1)$. Thus the equations for the best polynomial coefficients x_i are close to

$$x_1 + \frac{1}{2} x_2 + \frac{1}{3} x_3 + \ldots + \frac{1}{k+1} x_{k+1} = (\Sigma d_j)/100$$

$$\frac{1}{2} x_2 + \frac{1}{3} x_2 + \frac{1}{4} x_3 + \ldots + \frac{1}{k+2} x_{k+2} = (\Sigma t_j d_j)/100$$

$$\vdots \qquad\qquad\qquad \vdots$$

$$\frac{1}{k+1} x_{k+1} + \ldots \qquad + \frac{1}{2k+1} x_{2k+1} = (\Sigma t_j^k d_j)/100$$

The coefficient matrix of these normal equations is nearly the **Hilbert matrix** $H_k = \{h_{ij} = 1/(i+j-1)\}$. This matrix is seen in Example 6.5 to be very badly conditioned. For the Hilbert matrix of order 10 (ninth-degree polynomials) the process of solving this system can (and sometimes does) magnify the uncertainty in the data d_i by a factor larger than $3*10^{12}$. Even if this computation is made with 10-digit arithmetic, one should not expect any accuracy in the polynomial coefficients x_i just because of the round-off errors. Furthermore, the accuracy of the data is rarely so good that one can allow for such a large magnification in the uncertainty. As Example 6.5 shows, the uncertainty in the data is not magnified by as much as the standard condition number, but it is still magnified by 10^5 or 10^6. This latter magnification is inherent in this problem and cannot be alleviated by replacing the normal equations by another method of computation.

Gram-Schmidt Orthogonalization 11.2.C

If we have vectors $\mathbf{a}_i$, i = 1, 2,. . ., M, which are orthogonal (these are the columns of A), then the least-squares problem is trivial to solve. To see this, note that A^TA is diagonal since the rows of A^T are just the columns of A and the only nonzero dot products are the $\mathbf{a}_k^T\mathbf{a}_k$ on the diagonal of A^TA. Thus we can give an explicit solution for the best coefficients in this case as

$$x_i = \frac{\mathbf{b}^T\mathbf{a}_i}{\mathbf{a}_i^T\mathbf{a}_i} \qquad \textbf{Equation 11.2.6}$$

Thus we can attempt to make the columns of A orthogonal instead of forming and solving the normal equations. The classical method to do this is **Gram-Schmidt orthogonalization.** Explicitly the problem is this: Given vectors $\mathbf{a}_1, \mathbf{a}_2, \ldots, \mathbf{a}_M$, find an equivalent set $\mathbf{v}_1, \mathbf{v}_2, \ldots, \mathbf{v}_M$ which are orthonormal. Making the $\mathbf{v}_i$ have length 1 simplifies the computation and later use of the vectors. The idea is quite simple. We take $\mathbf{a}_1$ and divide by its Euclidean length $||\mathbf{a}_1|| = (\mathbf{a}_1^T\mathbf{a}_1)^{1/2}$ to get $\mathbf{v}_1$. We now subtract off the component of $\mathbf{a}_2$ in the directon of $\mathbf{v}_1$, and the remainder is orthogonal to $\mathbf{v}_1$. See the diagram in Figure 11.2. This remaining vector is now normalized by dividing by its length, which gives $\mathbf{v}_2$. In algebraic terms we have

$$\mathbf{v}_1 = \frac{\mathbf{a}_1}{||\mathbf{a}_1||}$$

$$\mathbf{v}_2 = \frac{\mathbf{a}_2 - (\mathbf{a}_2^T\mathbf{v}_1)\mathbf{v}_1}{||\mathbf{a}_2 - (\mathbf{a}_2^T\mathbf{v}_1)\mathbf{v}_1||}$$

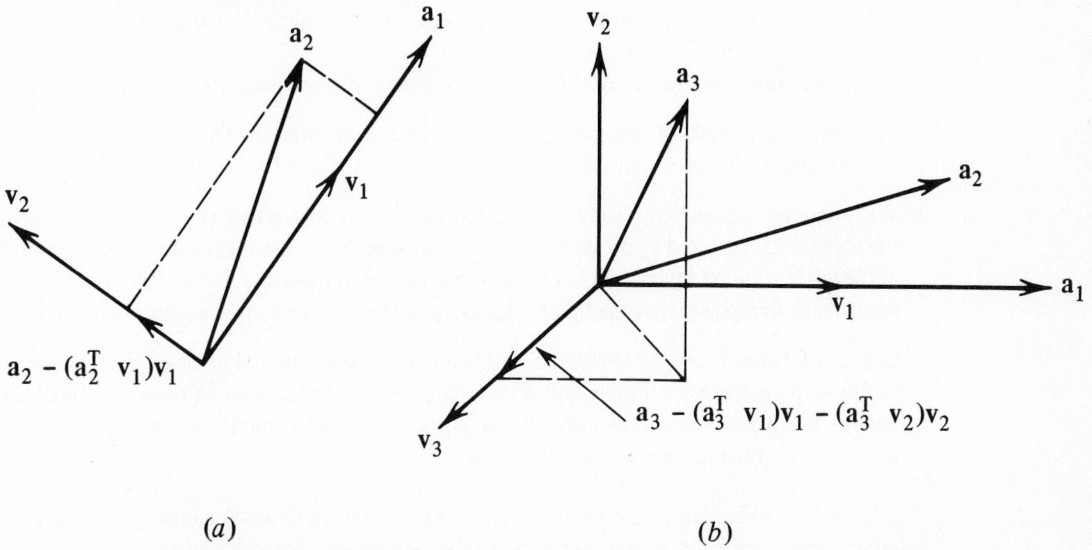

Figure 11.2 The geometric visualization of the Gram-Schmidt process for (a) two vectors and (b) three vectors.

The process is continued by subtracting off the components of $\mathbf{a}_3$ in the directions $\mathbf{v}_1$ and $\mathbf{v}_2$ and obtaining the remainder. This is normalized to obtain $\mathbf{v}_3$ (see Figure 11.2). In algebraic terms we have

$$\mathbf{v}'_3 = \mathbf{a}_3 - (\mathbf{a}_3^T\mathbf{v}_1)\mathbf{v}_1 - (\mathbf{a}_3^T\mathbf{v}_2)\mathbf{v}_2$$
$$\mathbf{v}_3 = \mathbf{v}'_3/||\mathbf{v}'_3||$$

It is evident now that the general step is

$$\mathbf{v}'_k = \mathbf{a}_k - \sum_{j=1}^{k-1} (\mathbf{a}_k^T\mathbf{v}_j)\mathbf{v}_j$$

$$\mathbf{v}_k = \mathbf{v}'_k/||\mathbf{v}'_k||$$

Gram-Schmidt Orthogonalization **Algorithm 11.2.1**

For k = 1 to M do

$$\mathbf{v}'_k = \mathbf{a}_k - \sum_{j=1}^{k-1} (\mathbf{a}_k^T\mathbf{v}_j)\mathbf{v}_j$$

$$\mathbf{v}_k = \mathbf{v}'_k/||\mathbf{v}'_k||$$

end of k-loop

It is easy to check that $\mathbf{v}_j^T\mathbf{v}_k = 0$ for $j = 1, 2, \ldots, k-1$ so that the vectors generated are orthogonal. If the vectors $\mathbf{a}_i$ and $\mathbf{v}_k$ are the columns of the matrices A and V, then 11.2.1 produces a relationship A = VT where T is an upper triangular matrix with kth column proportional to $(\mathbf{a}_k^T\mathbf{v}_1, \mathbf{a}_k^T\mathbf{v}_2, \ldots, \mathbf{a}_k^T\mathbf{v}_{k-1}, 1, 0, \ldots, 0)^T$. The original least-squares problem is to find $\mathbf{x}$ so that $A\mathbf{x} \sim \mathbf{b}$, and after Gram-Schmidt we can easily solve $V\mathbf{y} \sim \mathbf{b}$.

The coefficients y_i of the orthogonal vectors $\mathbf{v}_k$ are simply $\mathbf{v}_i^T\mathbf{b}$. To calculate the x_i (if desired), one may use back substitution on the triangular system relating the $\mathbf{a}_k$ and $\mathbf{v}_k$, that is, $\mathbf{y} = T\mathbf{x}$; see Problem 11.6.5. This approach is sometimes numerically unstable if the vectors $\mathbf{a}_k$ are nearly linearly dependent; in this case one can often formulate the computation so that the $\mathbf{a}_k$ are never used once the $\mathbf{v}_k$ are obtained and thus the x_i are not needed.

We estimate the amount of work for Gram-Schmidt as follows: There are $M^2/2$ terms of the form $(\mathbf{a}_k^T \mathbf{v}_j)\mathbf{v}_j$ to process. Each one requires N operations (recall that an operation is an add plus a multiply) for the dot product and N operations for the vector subtraction. The work to actually compute the x_i is M dot products of N vectors or MN operations, which is small compared with the orthogonalization work. The total is thus M^2N. If N is about the same size as M, then this is about 50 percent more work than using the normal equations. If N is very large compared to M, a not unusual case, then Gram-Schmidt is about twice as much work as using the normal operations.

There are three advantages to using this method over the normal equations approach:

1. The condition number of the problem is not squared in the process. This helps for a certain (relatively small) number of cases.

2. When one gets garbage instead of the solution, one knows where and why it arises. Let us assume that the $\mathbf{a}_i$ are all about 1 in size (if they are not, it is a good practice to make them so.) Then if one of the $\mathbf{v}'_k$ is of the order of round-off error in size, all information about it is lost. One can test for this happening and report back to the user that the first k vectors are linearly dependent to within round-off error.

3. One can introduce another tolerance (an estimate of observational error or model uncertainty) and simply skip vectors $\mathbf{v}'_k$ whose length is less than this tolerance. One can report to the user that these vectors (columns of A) have been dropped from the model (matrix A) because they are linearly dependent on the previously processed vectors.

There is a modern version of Gram-Schmidt called **modified Gram-Schmidt orthogonalization,** which is simply a rearrangement of the order of doing the calculation. The formulas for it are:

Modified Gram-Schmidt Orthogonalization **Algorithm 11.2.2**

For $k = 1$ to M do

$\mathbf{a}_k = \mathbf{a}_k / \|\mathbf{a}_k\|$

$\mathbf{a}_j = \mathbf{a}_j - (\mathbf{a}_j^T \mathbf{a}_k)\mathbf{a}_k \qquad \text{for } j = k+1, k+2, \ldots, M$

end of k-loop

This method's advantages over the classical Gram-Schmidt are:

1. It requires less storage. Note that the formulas do not use a different name for the new vectors $\mathbf{v}_i$ — they are computed and placed in the same storage as the original vectors.

2. It is easier to program.

3. It is a numerically stable method; that is, the answers are as accurate as one can reasonably expect from any computational method.

4. One can use a "pivoting" strategy — namely, choose the largest remaining vector as the one to be processed next. This is useful in a small number of cases, and examples can be constructed where this pivoting is as valuable as pivoting is in Gauss elimination.

Orthogonal Matrix Factorization 11.2.D

Instead of doing Gauss elimination, suppose we find an orthogonal matrix Q (recall $Q^TQ = I$) and an upper triangular matrix R so that

$$QA = R$$

Then to solve $A\mathbf{x} = \mathbf{b}$ we multiply by Q on both sides to obtain

$$QA\mathbf{x} = Q\mathbf{b} = R\mathbf{x}$$

and thus $\mathbf{x}$ may be obtained by back substitution on the vector $Q\mathbf{b}$. Note that the fact that $Q^T = Q^{-1}$ does not play an essential role in this even though we do have $A = Q^TR$ as a factorization of A.

The Gram-Schmidt orthogonalization provides an orthogonal matrix factorization. With the notation introduced in the discussion of Algorithm 11.2.1 (Gram-Schmidt) we have A = VT where the column vectors of V are orthonormal, that is, V is an orthogonal matrix. Thus $V^TA = T$, V^T plays the role of Q, and T plays the role of R in the present notation.

The attraction of orthogonal factorization lies with the fact that multiplying A or **b** by Q does not change the size of anything, i.e., does not magnify any round-off errors or uncertainties associated with the matrix A or vector **b**. It is a process with condition number 1, the best we could hope for. To show this, we see that $||Q\mathbf{x}||_2 = ||\mathbf{x}||_2$ for any vector **x** from the analysis

$$||Q\mathbf{x}||_2^2 = (Q\mathbf{x})^TQ\mathbf{x} = \mathbf{x}^TQ^TQ\mathbf{x} = \mathbf{x}^T\mathbf{x} = ||\mathbf{x}||_2^2$$

since $Q^TQ = I$. Recall the discussion of pivoting in Gauss elimination as a means to control error magnification; such a process is not needed here.

Consider reflecting vectors with respect to some plane, as in Figure 11.3. The idea here is to choose the plane so that $\mathbf{a} = (a_1, a_2, \ldots, a_N)^T$ is reflected onto the first coordinate axis, that is, $H\mathbf{a} = (-\sigma, 0, 0, \ldots, 0)^T$ where H represents the reflection. This linear transformation is then applied to $\mathbf{a}_1$, the first column of the matrix A.

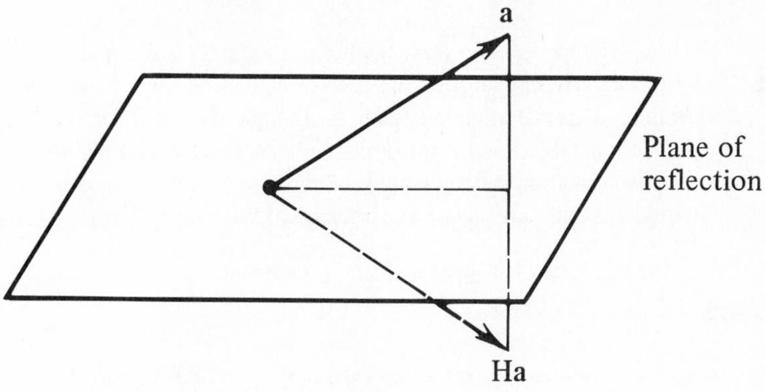

Figure 11.3 **An elementary reflection.** The vector a is reflected with respect to the plane by the elementary reflection matrix H.

The matrix H, which represents this **elementary reflection (Householder transformation),** is easily found as follows. Let $\mathbf{e}_1 = (1, 0, 0, \ldots, 0)^T$ = first coordinate vector or first column of the identity matrix, $\sigma = \pm 1$, and then set

Equation 11.2.7

$$\mathbf{u} = \mathbf{a}_1 + \sigma\mathbf{e}_1$$

$$c = \frac{1}{2}||\mathbf{u}||^2$$

$$H = I - \frac{\mathbf{u}\mathbf{u}^T}{c}$$

Note that $\mathbf{u}\mathbf{u}^T$ is full matrix, whereas $\mathbf{u}^T\mathbf{u}$ is just one number. We leave it to the reader to verify that H is an orthogonal matrix ($H^TH = I$) and $H\mathbf{a}_1 = -\sigma\mathbf{e}_1$.

The matrix H is constructed so that HA has its first column of the same form as the first column of A by Gauss elimination. One must apply H to the other columns of A also and then, as in Gauss elimination, one applies the same scheme to the (N − 1) by (N − 1) matrix left. Note that one never explicitly forms the matrix H; ones computes HA as follows (the columns of A are overwritten to this algorithm):

Algorithm 11.2.3

$$\mathbf{u} = \mathbf{a}_1 + \sigma\mathbf{e}_1$$

$$c = \frac{1}{2}||\mathbf{u}||^2$$

$$\mathbf{a}_1 = -\sigma\mathbf{e}_1$$

For j = 2, 3, . . ., N do
  $d_j = \mathbf{u}^T\mathbf{a}_j/c$
  $\mathbf{a}_j = \mathbf{a}_j - d_j\mathbf{u}$
end of j-loop

A careful implementation of these Householder transformations is included in the least-squares software of Lawson-Hanson discussed later.

An estimate of the work for the orthogonal factorization method yields about $M^2N - M^3/3$ operations (one add + one multiply). If N is about the same size as M, then this is about the same work as using the normal equations. If N is large compared to M, then orthogonal factorization involves about the same work as Gram-Schmidt and twice the work of using the normal equations.

This method's advantages are:

1. It is a numerically stable method; that is, the answers are as accurate as one can reasonably expect from any computational method.

2. One may apply the **singular value analysis** (a topic not discussed here) to the matrix R to obtain detailed insight into the linear dependencies that might exist in the original problem.

After having seen three methods to solve the least-squares problem, one may ask: Which is the best? Reliable, efficient software has been created using each of these three methods. Whatever "tricks" exist to handle a special situation (such as multiple data sets for the same model) for one method, there are corresponding tricks for the other methods. Lawson and Hanson, whose software is discussed later, have carried out an extensive analysis of all three methods in a wide variety of hard, practical problems. They conclude that, on balance, the orthogonal factorization method is the best.

PROBLEMS 11.2

11.2.1 Give a definition of the *residual* of a least-squares solution of $A\mathbf{x} = \mathbf{b}$. Show that the residual is orthogonal to the columns of A.

11.2.2 Let $\mathbf{b} = (.01, 0, 1)^T$, $\mathbf{c} = (.0101, 0, 1)^T$, and

$$A = \begin{pmatrix} 1 & 0 \\ 0 & 1 \\ 0 & 0 \end{pmatrix}$$

(A) Compute the least-squares solutions $\mathbf{x}$ and $\bar{\mathbf{x}}$ to $A\mathbf{x} = \mathbf{b}$, $A\bar{\mathbf{x}} = \mathbf{c}$.

(B) What is the relative difference in size between **b** and **c**? Between **x** and $\bar{\mathbf{x}}$? Explain how these differences can be so far apart.

(C) Give an example of **b** and **c** where the relative difference in **x** and $\bar{\mathbf{x}}$ is 10^5 times that of **b** and **c**.

11.2.3 Consider

$$A = \begin{pmatrix} 1.000 & 1.050 \\ 1.000 & 1.000 \\ 1.000 & 1.000 \end{pmatrix} \qquad A + E = \begin{pmatrix} 1.000 & 1.051 \\ 1.000 & 1.001 \\ 1.000 & 1.000 \end{pmatrix}$$

$$\mathbf{b} = (2.050, 2.000, 2.000)^T \qquad \mathbf{c} = (2.050, 1.500, 2.500)^T$$

(A) Show that $(1.000, 1.000)^T$ is the least-squares solution to both $A\mathbf{x} = \mathbf{b}$ and $A\mathbf{x} = \mathbf{c}$.

(B) Show that the least-squares solutions $\mathbf{x}_E$ and $\bar{\mathbf{x}}_E$ to $(A + E)\mathbf{x} = \mathbf{b}$ and $(A + E)\bar{\mathbf{x}} = \mathbf{c}$ are $\mathbf{x}_E = (1.0097, 0.9898)^T$ and $\bar{\mathbf{x}}_E = (1.3088, 0.6958)^T$.

(C) Compute relative differences in size between A and A + E, between **x** and $\mathbf{x}_E$, and between $\bar{\mathbf{x}}$ = and $\bar{\mathbf{x}}_E$.

(D) It is technically complicated to explain "why" such large variations in these differences can occur. However, what lesson should be drawn from this example?

11.2.4 Consider

$$A = \begin{pmatrix} 1.000 & 1.000 \\ 1.000 & 1.040 \\ 1.000 & 1.000 \end{pmatrix} \qquad A + E = \begin{pmatrix} 1.000 & 1.0001 \\ 1.000 & 1.041 \\ 1.000 & 1.000 \end{pmatrix}$$

$$\mathbf{b} = (2.000, 2.040, 2.000)^T \qquad \mathbf{c} = (1.5000, 2.040, 2.500)^T$$

(A) Show that $(1.000, 1.000)^T$ is the least-squares solution to both $A\mathbf{x} = \mathbf{b}$ and $A\mathbf{x} = \mathbf{c}$.

(B) Compute the least-squares solutions $\mathbf{x}_E$ and $\bar{\mathbf{x}}_E$ to $(A + E)\mathbf{x}_E = \mathbf{b}$ and $(A + E)\bar{\mathbf{x}}_E = \mathbf{c}$.

(C) Compute the relative differences in size between A and A + E, between **x** and $\mathbf{x}_E$, and between $\bar{\mathbf{x}}$ and $\bar{\mathbf{x}}_E$. Compare the size of these differences and give a discussion about the sensitivity of the least-squares solution to perturbations in the matrix A.

11.2.5 Consider **nonlinear least-squares approximation** to a function f(t) on the interval [0, 1] by $F(\mathbf{a}, t) = a_1 e^{a_2 t}$.

(A) Derive the normal equations for the coefficients of the best approximation. Use the continuous form of the norm (i.e., use integrals).

(B) Repeat part (A) with the approximation made on the discrete set $t_i = (i-1)/k$ for i = 1 to k+1.

11.2.6 Repeat Problem 11.2.5 for approximations by $F(\mathbf{a}, t) = a_1 e^{a_2 t} + a_3$.

11.2.7 Consider least-squares approximation to f(t) by

$$F(\mathbf{a}, t) = \sum_{i=1}^{N} a_i b_i(t)$$

on the interval [a, b].

(A) Display the normal equations for this approximation.

(B) Suppose that the basis $b_i(t)$ are **orthogonal functions**, that is,

$$\int_a^b b_i(t)b_j(t)dt = 0 \quad \text{if } i \neq j$$
$$= 1 \quad \text{if } i = j$$

Show that the error of the best least-squares approximation $F(\mathbf{a}^*, t)$ is

$$\sqrt{\int_a^b f(t)^2 dt - \sum_{i=1}^{N} (a_i^*)^2}$$

11.2.8 Consider least-squares approximation to $f(x)$ for x in $[0, \pi]$ by

$$F(\mathbf{a}, x) = a_1 + \sum_{i=2}^{n} a_i \cos((i-1)x)$$

Derive the normal equations for this problem, making use of the properties of the functions $\cos(ix)$. **Hint:** Examine the values of

$$\int_0^\pi \cos(ix)\cos(jx)dx.$$

11.2.9 Consider **least-squares broken line approximations** as follows. A set $T = \{0 = t_0 < t_1 < \ldots < t_k < t_{k+1} = 1\}$ of breakpoints is given. The broken line (first-degree spline) function is represented in terms of the truncated powers (see Equation 4.3.2) as follows:

$$s(x) = a_1 + a_2 x + \sum_{i=1}^{k} b_i(x - t_i)_+$$

Assume a set of data (x_i, d_i), $i = 1, 2, \ldots, M$, is given. Derive the normal equations for the best least-squares coefficients of the broken line to fit this data set. Simplify these equations using the properties of the functions $(x - t_i)_+$.

11.2.10 Use the normal equations derived in Problem 11.2.9 to obtain broken line least-squares approximations to the following data on the point set $x_i = (i-1)/50$ for $i = 1, 2, \ldots, 51$.

(A) $d_i = \cos(\pi x_i)$, $t_j = j/10$ for $j = 0$ to 10

(B) $d_i = x_i(1 - x_i)$, $t_j = j/10$ for $j = 0$ to 10

(C) $d_i = \sqrt{x_i}\,\sqrt[3]{1 - x_i}$, $t_j = j/20$ for $j = 0$ to 20

(D) $d_i = \sqrt{x_i}\,\sqrt[3]{1 - x_i}$, $t_j = .5[1 - \cos(j\pi/20)]$ for $j = 0$ to 21

11.2.11 Repeat Problem 11.2.9 using the B-spline representation of the broken line (see Equation 4.3.3 and Figure 4.6)

$$s(x) = \sum_{i=1}^{k+2} a_i B_{i-1}(x)$$

11.2.12 Repeat Problem 11.2.10 using the normal equations derived in Problem 11.2.11.

11.2.13 Compare the amount of work to compute the broken line approximation using the representations of Problems 11.2.9 and 11.2.11. Express the work (approximately) in terms of k, the number of break points, and M, the number of data points, when both k and M are large.

11.2.14 Consider least-squares approximations by **polynomials in linear rationals,** that is,

$$F(\mathbf{a}, x) = \sum_{i=1}^{n} a_i \left(\frac{p + qx}{r + sx}\right)^{i-1}$$

(A) Derive the normal equations for the coefficients a_i assuming that p, q, r, and s are given and one is approximating $f(x)$ on $[0, 5]$.

(B) Suppose $p = 0$, $q = s = 4$, and $r = 1$. Replace the interval $[0, 5]$ by the discrete set $x_i = (i-1)/20$ for $i = 1, 2, \ldots, 101$ and let $f(x) = (4x + x^8)/(1 + x^2 + x^8)$. Write a program to compute the best least-squares approximations and their errors for $n = 2, 3, 4, 5$, and 6. Discuss how the error decreases as n increases.

(C) Compute ordinary polynomial approximation for part (B) and compare the errors with those of the linear rationals. **Hint:** Write the program for part (B) for general values of p, q, r, and s; then set $p = s = 0$, $q = r = 1$ for this case.

11.2.15 In Gram-Schmidt orthogonalization the vectors are normalized at each step. Describe the variant of Gram-Schmidt where the vectors are not normalized until the end of the algorithm. Explain why this variant is less efficient.

11.2.16 Give the calling sequence for a good design of a Fortran library routine for the linear least-squares problem $A\mathbf{x} = \mathbf{b}$. Explicitly state the algorithmic and software objectives of the design and which ones were weighted most heavily. Define all the variables that appear in the calling sequence. Describe an example application where this design is weak compared to some reasonable alternative (briefly describe the alternative).

11.2.17 Perform a detailed operation count for Gram-Schmidt orthogonalization of m vectors of length n. What steps correspond to back substitution in Gauss elimination?

11.2.18 Show how Gram-Schmidt orthogonalization can be used to solve $A\mathbf{x} = \mathbf{b}$ by orthogonalizing the columns of A and then using the method for orthogonal matrices.

11.2.19 In this book we have studied the following four linear algebra problems: (1) Solve $A\mathbf{x} = \mathbf{b}$; (2) compute A^{-1}; (3) find the least-squares solution to $A\mathbf{x} = \mathbf{b}$; and (4) compute det (A). Discuss in a comparative manner the following points for these problems:

(A) The difficulty of the matrix theory underlying the computation.

(B) The actual amount of computation required to solve the problems (i.e., the amount of execution time for comparable-sized matrices).

(C) The amount of preliminary analysis that one would expect to make in order to write a library subroutine to solve each of these problems for a large class of matrices A.

11.2.20 Write a Fortran subroutine to carry out Gram-Schmidt orthogonalization and apply it to solve least-squares problems. The specific examples to be used are:

(A) $\mathbf{a}_i = \left(\frac{1}{i+1}, \frac{1}{i+2}, \ldots, \frac{1}{i+n}\right)^T$ for $i = 1$ to 10 and $n = 20$

$b_j = 1$ for all j

(B) $\mathbf{a}_i = [\sin(i/n), \sin(2i/n), \sin(3i/n), \ldots, \sin(i)]^T$ for $i = 1$ to 10 and $n = 10$

$b_1 = 1$ and $b_j = 0$ for $j > 1$

(C) $\mathbf{a}_i$ = random vector of length n for $i = 1$ to N

b_j = random number

11.2.21 Repeat Problem 11.2.19 for modified Gram-Schmidt orthogonalization.

11.2.22 Compare the lengths and difficulty of writing the Fortran subroutines of Problems 11.2.20 and 11.2.21. Compare the computed values for each of the three least-squares problems.

11.2.23 Modify the subroutines of Problem 11.2.20 or 11.2.21 to include a test for linear dependency of the vectors. Make the tolerance (estimate of model uncertainty) an input variable. If the tolerance is zero, then the subroutine should reset it to the round-off level of the computer used (times a small constant, say 2 or 5). What effect does this tolerance have on least-squares problem (A) of Problem 11.2.20? Make some runs with varying tolerances and report on the effects.

11.2.24 Describe an algorithm for solving the least-squares problem using elementary reflections. The level of detail should be the same as Algorithm 6.2.1.

11.2.25 Implement the algorithm of Problem 11.2.24 as a Fortran subroutine and apply it to the least-squares problems of Problem 11.2.20.

11.2.26 Suppose the vectors $\mathbf{a}_k$ have been orthogonalized by Algorithm 11.2.1. Give an algorithm to compute the coefficients s_i from the quantities $\mathbf{b}^T v_k$. **Hint:** Save information generated in Algorithm 11.2.1 and use it.

11.2.27 Derive a **least-squares integration formula** as follows. The integral $\int_{-3h}^{3h} f(x)dx$ is estimated by: (1) making a least-squares approximation to f(x) by a quadratic polynomial on the five points $-3h$, $-2h$, 0, 2h, and 3h, and (2) integrating this quadratic polynomial and taking the result as the estimate of the integral.

(A) Show that the estimate is of the form

$$\int_{-3h}^{3h} f(x)dx = a_1 f(-3h) + a_2 f(-2h) + a_3 f(0) + a_4 f(2h) + a_5 f(3h)$$

Hint: Use the fact twice that linear methods applied to linear problems produce linear formulas.

(B) Describe a method to compute the five coefficients a_i, i = 1 to 5.

(C) Actually compute the coefficients.

(D) Take the coefficients obtained in part (C) and determine the coefficients for the integral $\int_0^h f(x)dx$ using the same scheme and the points 0, h/6, h/2, 5h/6, h.

11.2.28 Assume the normal equations are derived for the continuous case of least-squares approximation on $[0, \pi]$ by cosines (see Problem 11.2.8). Suppose the integrals involving f(x) are approximated as follows:

$$\int_0^{\pi} \cos(ix)f(x)dx \sim \sum_{j=1}^{K} b_j^{(i)} f(x_j)$$

for $1 \le i \le N$ and K = 2N. Estimate the amount of work (in terms of the number of multiplications) to solve the normal equations and to estimate the right-side integrals.

11.2.29 Suppose one is to estimate the value of the linear functional

$$\lambda(f) = \int_0^{\pi} [f(x) + f''(x)]dx$$

from the information $f(x_i)$, $i = 1, 2, \ldots, m > 9$. One proceeds as follows:

(1) Obtain a least-squares approximation to the data $(x_i, f(x_i))$ by

$$F(\mathbf{a}, x) = a_0 + \sum_{j=1}^{3} [a_j \cos(jx) + a_{j+3}\sin(jx)]$$

(2) Estimate $\lambda(f)$ by $\lambda(F(\mathbf{a}))$.

(A) Show that there are constants b_i which do not depend on the $f(x_i)$ values so that $\lambda(f)$ is estimated by

$$\lambda(f) \sim \sum_{i=1}^{m} b_i f(x_i) = \lambda(F(\mathbf{a}))$$

(B) Describe a method for computing the b_i.

11.2.30 Compare the accuracy of the normal equation computations with Gram-Schmidt and modified Gram-Schmidt.

(A) Compute least-squares approximations to f(x) = cos(x) on [0, 1] by polynomials of degree k using the normal equations and the power form of polynomials. Increase k until the computation breaks down on the computer used.

(B) Repeat part (A) using Gram-Schmidt orthogonalization.

(C) Repeat part (B) using modified Gram-Schmidt orthogonalization.

(D) Discuss the comparative effectiveness of these three methods and the limitation that machine round-off places on computing least-squares approximations.

11.2.31 Consider **local least-squares smoothing** as follows:

(1) Given (x_i, y_i), $i = 1, 2, \ldots, K+1$ data points with the x_i evenly spaced $(x_i = x_1 + (i-1)h)$, compute the least-squares polynomial approximations to the y_i by polynomials of degree $n < K$. (2) Assume K is even and evaluate the polynomial at $x_{K/2}$. (3) Take this value as the smoothed estimate of the data at $x_{K/2}$.

(A) Show that the estimate obtained has a linear formula:

$$y^*_{K/2} \sim \sum_{i=1}^{K+1} b_i y_i$$

(B) Describe a method to compute the coefficients b_i. Show that the b_i do not depend on x_1, they only depend on h, K, and n.

(C) Show how to obtain the values of the b_i for any value of h if one has the values for h = 1.

(D) Verify that the following table of coefficients is correct (for h = 1). Show that $b_{K/2-j} = b_{K/2+j}$ if K is even.

Table of $b_{K/2-j} * d_K$

	Degree n=3					Degree n=5			
K+1 points =	5	7	9	11	13	7	9	11	13
j=0	17	7	59	89	25	131	179	143	677
1	12	6	54	84	24	75	135	120	600
2	−3	3	39	69	21	−30	30	60	390
3		−2	14	44	16	5	−55	−10	110
4			−21	9	9		15	−45	−135
5				−36	0			18	−198
6					−11				110
d_K =	35	21	231	429	143	231	429	429	2431

11.2.32. Consider **least-squares estimation of derivatives.**

(A) Repeat parts (A), (B), and (C) of Problem 10.2.31 except that the derivative of the polynomial is taken at step (2) and used as the smoothed derivative estimate at $x_{K/2}$.

(B) Verify that the following table of coefficients of the coefficients b'_i is correct (for h = 1). Show that $b'_{K/2-j} = -b'_{K/2+j}$ if K is even.

Table of $b'_{K/2-j} * d'_K$

	Degree n=3				
K+1 points =	5	7	9	11	13
j=0	0	0	0	0	0
1	8	58	126	296	832
2	−1	67	193	503	1489
3		−22	142	532	1796
4			−86	294	1578
5				−300	660
6					−1133
d'_K =	12	252	1188	5148	24024

L_1 AND CHEBYSHEV APPROXIMATION **11.3

The theories behind both L_1 and Chebyshev approximation are too complex and difficult to present here. The numerical methods that have been developed from these theories are more complex and require more computation than the methods for least squares — but one could hardly hope for them to be as simple and easy as for least squares. On the other hand, these methods are reasonably efficient, and it is practical to use them in a wide variety of applications. If the problem at hand is such that least squares might not be entirely appropriate (e.g., one may really want to minimize the maximum error or the data might be contaminated significantly with errors of an unknown nature), then one should try one of the programs discussed later and see how effective these other two norms are. In this section we give a brief summary of the properties of best approximations in the L_1 and Chebyshev norms.

L_1 Approximation 11.3.A

L_1 approximation may be applied to either functions or overdetermined systems of equations. In the case of functions on [0, 1], one differentiates

$$\int_0^1 |f(x) - F(\mathbf{a}, x)|dx$$

with respect to the coefficients a_i and ignores certain technical mathematical problems [the integrand is not differentiable where $f(x) = F(\mathbf{a}, x)$]. One obtains the conditions

$$\int_0^1 \text{sign}(f(x) - F(\mathbf{a}, x))b_i(x)dx = 0 \qquad \textbf{Equation 11.3.1}$$

for $i = 1, 2, \ldots, n$; the integrand in 11.3.1 is just $b_i(x)$ times a step function with values +1 or −1. Equation 11.3.1 is not very easy to use, but it shows that the only thing that matters is the sign of the error. This may be rephrased as saying that the best approximation $F(a^*, x)$ must interpolate the function $f(x)$ at the "right" points. Some computational methods for L_1 approximation to functions thus concentrate on finding these interpolation points.

There is one simple thing to try for L_1 approximation. If $F(\mathbf{a}, x)$ is a polynomial or trigonometric polynomial, then there are known points which have a good chance of producing the best L_1 approximation. These are called **canonical points** $\{z_k\}$, and three sets of them for n basis functions $b_i(x)$ are:

$$\text{For } b_i(x) = \sin(ix), \text{ interval} = [0, \pi], \quad z_k = \frac{k\pi}{n+1} \qquad \textbf{Equation 11.3.2}$$

$$\text{For } b_i(x) = \cos(ix), \text{ interval} = [0, \pi], \quad z_k = \frac{(2k-1)\pi}{2(n+1)} \qquad \textbf{Equation 11.3.3}$$

$$\text{For } b_i(x) = x^{i-1}, \text{ interval} = [-1, 1], \quad z_k = \cos\frac{k\pi}{n+1} \qquad \textbf{Equation 11.3.4}$$

The important property of these points is this: *If $F(\mathbf{a}, x)$ interpolates $f(x)$ at the canonical points and there is no other sign change in $f(x) - F(\mathbf{a}, x)$, then $F(\mathbf{a}, x)$ is the best L_1 approximation to $f(x)$.* Thus one can interpolate $f(x)$ at these points, check the resulting error function, and, perhaps, obtain the best L_1 approximation. This approach very often works.

The canonical points for other intervals can be obtained by linearly mapping the given intervals to other intervals. The canonical points for L_1 approximation by polynomials are the Chebyshev points which previously have been seen to be good interpolation points.

If one has discrete data or an overdetermined system of linear equations, about the only simple fact that one obtains from the analog of 11.3.1 is that the best L_1 approximations must interpolate the data at n points (or exactly satisfy n of the linear equations). The best known computational methods for discrete L_1 approximation involve reformulating the problem as a special linear programming problem and then applying the **simplex method** (especially tuned for this particular problem).

Recall that the median is a special case of L_1 approximation for n = 1 and need not be uniquely determined. The possible lack of uniqueness is present in all of L_1 approximation even though it becomes very unlikely as n increases.

Chebyshev Approximation 11.3.B

Consider the problem of minimizing $|f(x) - F(\mathbf{a}, x)|$ where $\mathbf{a} = (a_1, a_2, \ldots, a_n)$ gives one n degrees of freedom. Given a trial approximation $F(\mathbf{a}^1, x)$, use the degrees of freedom to "push down" the error at the point where it is largest. After a certain amount of pushing, the error will become equally large at some other point, and pushing down at the first point no longer reduces the maximum error. As long as the maximum error is achieved at n or fewer points, we can push down the error at each of them simultaneously and reduce the maximum error. This intuitive argument is illustrated in Figure 11.4(a) and leads us to conclude that the best Chebyshev approximation must attain its maximum error in at least n+1 points. A more careful argument shows that, with a mild assumption on the basis functions $b_i(x)$, the best Chebyshev approximation is characterized by **alternation of the error n times** [see Figure 11.4 (b)]: *$F(\mathbf{a}^*, x)$ is the best Chebyshev approximation to $f(x)$ if there are $n+1$ points x_j, $x_j < x_{j+1}$, so that*

$$|f(x_j) - F(\mathbf{a}^*, x_j)| = (-1)^j d \qquad \textbf{Equation 11.3.5}$$

where

$$d = \pm \, ||f - F(\mathbf{a}^*)||_\infty$$

The condition 11.3.5 leads to efficient methods to compute $F(\mathbf{a}^*, x)$.

If one has discrete data, then condition 11.3.5 still determines the best Chebyshev approximation, and the same methods, slightly modified, can be used to compute it. If one only has an overdetermined system of linear equations, the maximum error is attained for n+1 equations, but there is no required pattern for the signs of the error. Thus it is usually somewhat more work to compute the Chebyshev solution of $A\mathbf{x} = \mathbf{b}$ with m equations than it is to compute the Chebyshev approximation to discrete data with m points.

The alternation condition 11.3.5 does not apply to some sets of basis functions: for example, approximation by x, x^2, and x^3 on the interval [0, 1] or by 1, x^2, and x^4 on the interval [−1, 1]. For these cases, more complicated conditions (and corresponding numerical methods) can be obtained.

SOFTWARE FOR APPROXIMATION 11.4

We discuss four important collections of software for approximation: the ACM Algorithms, the IMSL library, the Lawson-Hanson software, and PPPACK (for piecewise polynomials). Software and algorithms for the approximation of standard mathematical functions are not included here; see Section 11.7 for information. The LINPACK software also has relevant programs (see Table 6.1 in Section 6.4.B for QR factorization and singular-values software).

The ACM Algorithms 11.4.A

There are over 25 ACM Algorithms for approximation, many of which are substantial pieces of software. These are placed into four groups, and the more important ones in each group are briefly described.

For **least-squares approximation,** there is *Algorithm 296* for discrete polynomial approximation. It is in Algol and uses orthogonal polynomial methods discussed in Section 11.8. *Algorithm 544* computes least-squares solutions to the overdetermined linear system $A\mathbf{x} = \mathbf{b}$ along with linear equality constraints. The formulation of the problem in this form allows one to use any basis functions $b_i(x)$ in the approximation. This algorithm, for example, allows one to fit data with the value and slope of the approximation specified at particular points. It allows for weighted least squares and uses the modified Gram-Schmidt method. *Algorithms 164 and 176* are in Algol and compute surface or multivariate least-squares approximations.

Algorithms 458 and 551 for **discrete L_1 approximation** are similar in performance. *Algorithm 563* allows one to add linear constraints to the L_1 approximation problem. All these algorithms formulate the

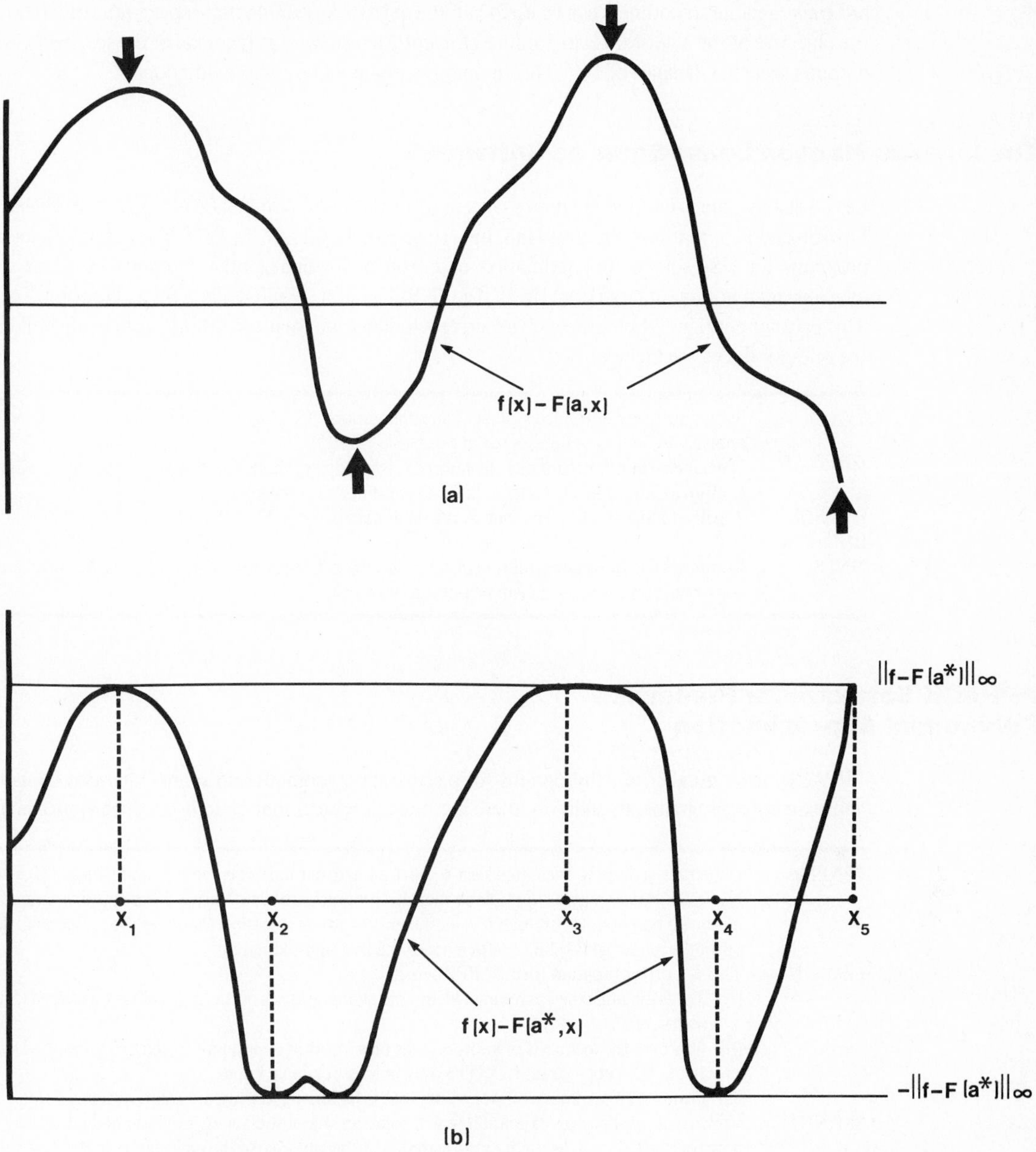

Figure 11.4 **Chebyshev approximation.** (a) The degrees of freedom in F(**a**, x) allow one to push the maximum error down at various points. (b) The best approximation is characterized by alternation n times (n = 4 here).

problem as an overdetermined system of linear equations and use some specialized form of the simplex method.

Algorithm 501 is a Fortran translation of *Algorithm 409* for **discrete Chebyshev approximation** to data. Any basis functions $b_l(x)$ can be used in the approximation provided best approximations are characterized by alternation of the error curve. *Algorithm 510* computes **piecewise linear Chebyshev approximations;** it has several modes of operation. *Algorithm 495* solves overdetermined linear systems in the Chebyshev sense; it uses a linear programming (simplex) method because the criterion of alternation is not applicable with this formulation.

Among the other algorithms, *Algorithms 276, 295, 375, and 376* are for **exponential approximation,** i.e., approximation by $a_1e^{a_2x} + a_3$ or related forms. *Algorithm 525* is a general algorithm for **piecewise polynomial approximation to functions.** It applies to functions f(x) defined on intervals and requires one to provide derivative values if smooth piecewise polynomials are computed. The polynomial degree is arbitrary, and the smoothness can be up to half the degree. Any of the three norms (and others) are allowed; the objective of the algorithm is to produce *efficiently* a piecewise polynomial of the specified kind which is within a specified distance of f(x). Thus it does not compute best approximations.

The Lawson-Hanson Least-Squares Software 11.4.B

Least-squares approximation is studied at length in the book *Solving Least Squares Problems* by C. L. Lawson and R. J. Hanson, Prentice-Hall, Inc., Englewood Cliffs, N. J., 1974. They include a set of Fortran programs for least-squares approximation based on orthogonal matrix factorization. This software is available for a nominal charge from IMSL, Inc., NBC Building, 7500 Bellaire Blvd., Houston, Texas 77036. This package contains 14 programs plus 6 drivers to illustrate their use. Many of these are building blocks; the ones for direct use include:

SVA	Solves the overdetermined system of linear equations $A\mathbf{x} = \mathbf{b}$ in the least-squares sense. A singular value analysis (a method not presented in this book) is made.
HFTI	Special program for use when the matrix A is nearly "rank deficient" (some columns are almost a linear combination of others). To be used for ill-conditioned problems.
BNDSOL BNDACC	A pair of programs for use when A is a band matrix.
NNLS	Computes a least-squares solution of $A\mathbf{x} = \mathbf{b}$ subject to the constraint that $x_i \geq 0$ for all i. General linear constraints on the solution can be put into this form.

PPPACK Software for Piecewise Polynomial Approximation 11.4.C

PPPACK has a number of subprograms for piecewise polynomials and splines that can be used to build approximation programs. In addition, there are three programs that directly produce approximations:

L2APPR	Constructs a discrete, weighted least-squares approximation of degree $N+1$ and knots $T(i), i = 1, 2, \ldots, N+k$. The knots may be multiple so that this program produces least-squares approximations by general piecewise polynomials (though it is inefficient for smoothness less than half the polynomial degree). The output is the set of B-spline coefficients of the best approximation.
L2MAIN	This is a driver program for L2APPR which (A) Reads in data to be approximated and the characteristics of the approximation desired (degree, break points, etc.). (B) Improves the locations of knots or adds new knots in an attempt to achieve a specified least-squares error. The subprogram L2KNTS only processes simple knots. (C) Prints out a summary of everything that is happening during the computation.
SMOOTH	Constructs a spline approximation which balances smoothness with goodness of fit. Let (x_i, y_i) be given data for $i = 1, 2, \ldots, M$, with δy_i an estimate of the variance of the uncertainty in the data, and let p be a smoothing parameter, $0 < p < 1$. Let s(x) be a spline of degree $2m-1$ with knots at the x_i, $i = 2$ to $N-1$. The **smoothing spline** minimizes $$p\sum_{i=1}^{M}\left(\frac{y_i - s(x_i)}{\delta y_i}\right)^2 + (1-p)\int_{x_1}^{x_M}[s^{(m)}(t)]^2dt \qquad \textbf{Equation 11.4.1}$$ SMOOTH computes the cubic ($m = 2$) smoothing spline s(x) and returns its piecewise polynomial coefficients a_{ij} for $i = 1$ to $N-1$, $j = 1, 2, 3, 4$. The values a_{i1} are the smoothed values of the data at the knots.

IMSL Software for Approximation 11.4.D

The IMSL library has programs for all the principal approximation methods. Some are in IMSL library Chapter I, "Interpolation, Approximation, and Smoothing," and some are in IMSL library Chapter R, "Regression Analysis." For **least-squares approximation** the basic program is

```
IFLSQ(BASIS,X,Y,NPTS,A,NBASIS,WORK,IER)
```

which computes the approximation to the data (x_j, y_j) by

$$F(\mathbf{a}, x) = \sum_{i=1}^{NBASIS} a_i b_i(x) \qquad \textbf{Equation 11.4.2}$$

The arguments of IFLSQ are

X,Y	=	array of (x_j, y_j) data points for $j = 1, 2, \ldots$, NPTS.
BASIS	=	name of Fortran subprogram of the form REAL FUNCTION BASIS (I,X) which computes the value of the Ith basis function $b_i(x)$ at X. Declare BASIS to be EXTERNAL where IFLSQ is used.
A,NBASIS	=	coefficients a_i of the basis for $i = 1, 2, \ldots$, NBASIS.
WORK,IER	=	work space array of length NBASIS*(NBASIS + 3) and error flag.

There are special programs for **least-squares polynomial approximations,** RLFOTH, RLFOTW, and RLFOR. The basic one is RLFOTH; RLFOTW provides for weighting the approximation, and RLFOR computes numerous associated statistical quantities automatically. RLFOTH approximates with 11.4.2 where the $b_i(x)$ are **orthogonal polynomials** (see Section 11.8); the value of $F(\mathbf{a}, x)$ can be found from RLOPDC with the output of RLFOTH and without any need for the user to know about orthogonal polynomials. The primary attraction of RLFOTH is that it avoids the ill-conditioned computation illustrated in Example 11.6.

There are two programs for **least-squares cubic spline approximation,** ICSFKU and ICSVKU. ICSFKU uses spline basis functions for $b_i(x)$ in 11.4.2, but the approximation is returned in the piecewise polynomial representation

$$F(\mathbf{a}, x) = a_{0,j} + \sum_{i=1}^{3} a_{ij}(x - t_j)^i \qquad \textbf{Equation 11.4.3}$$

for $t_j \leq x \leq t_{j+1}$ where the $t_j = 1, 2, \ldots$, NKNOTS are the knots of the spline. ICSFKU is called as follows:

```
CALL ICSFKU(X,Y,NPTS,MODE,TKNOTS,NKNOTS,AO,A,NDIMA,ERROR,WORK,IER)
```

where TKNOT	=	knots t_j, $j = 1, 2, \ldots$, NKNOTS of the cubic spline.
A0,A	=	cubic polynomial coefficients of 11.4.3; A is dimensioned REAL A(NDIMA, N3), where NDIMA is at least NKNOTS and a_{ij} = A(j, i) (note switched indices).
ERROR	=	Least-squares error of the approximation.
MODE	=	Control switch for various special cases to be used by ICSVKU. MODE = 0 is for normal use.
WORK,IER	=	Work space of size NKNOTS (for MODE = 0) and error flag.

The program ICSVKU has the same arguments except MODE is omitted. It varies the knot locations to further minimize the least-squares error and produces (at least locally) a **best nonlinear cubic spline approximation.** The resulting knots are returned in the array TKNOTS. ICSVKU treats the data as points on a curve rather than just discrete data so that the least-squares error is weighted by $(x_{i+1} - x_{i-1})/(x_{NPTS} - x_1)$ at x_i.

The program for **general discrete L_1 approximations** is RLLAV which has the form

```
RLLAV(DATMOD,NDIMD,NPTS,NBASIS,IOPT,A,ERROR,ITER,IRANK,IWORK,WORK,IER)
```

The data and model for the problem are both encoded in the array REAL DATMOD (NDIMD, N2), where NDIMD ≥ NPTS, N2 ≥ NBASIS + 5. The first NBASIS columns of DATMOD are the basis functions evaluated at the x_1, and the next column is the data, i.e., in 11.4.2.

DATMOD(j, i) = $b_i(x_j)$ $1 \le i < \text{NBASIS}$
DATMOD(j, NBASIS+1) = y_j

Note that the underlying values of x_j are not explicitly used. The last four columns of DATMOD are used as work space. Other arguments of interest are

IOPT = switch to automatically include the basis function $b_i(x) = 1$. IOPT = 0 accomplishes this; A(NBASIS+1) is the corresponding coefficient.
A,ERROR = coefficients a_1 of the best L_1 approximation and the resulting error.

The other arguments are work space, error flag, or variables about how the algorithm operated.

There are two programs for **Chebyshev approximation.** One, RLLMV, is identical in use to RLLAV (except no integer work space is required) and produces the best Chebyshev approximation. RLLMV is a version of ACM Algorithm 495. The other, IRATCU, computes **continuous rational function approximations** of the form

$$F(\mathbf{a}, x) = \frac{\sum_{i=1}^{L+1} p_i [b(x)]^{i-1}}{\sum_{j=1}^{M+1} q_j [b(x)]^{j-1}} \qquad \textbf{Equation 11.4.4}$$

where $\mathbf{a} = (p_1, p_2, \ldots, p_{L+1}, q_1, q_2, \ldots, q_{M+1})$ and $b(x)$ is a single monotonic function. Ordinary rational functions correspond to $b(x) = x$, and polynomials are obtained when $M = 0$. The argument list of IRATCU is

```
IRATCU(F,BOFX,WEIGHT,A,B,LNUMER,MDENOM,PCOEF,QCOEF,WORK,IER)
```

where F = Fortran subprogram REAL FUNCTION F(X) for f(x)
A,B = interval of approximation
BOFX = monotone function b(x) FUNCTION subprogram name
WEIGHT = weight function, reciprocal of w(x) in 11.1.6
PCOEF,QCOEF = coefficients p_1, $i = 1, 2, \ldots,$ LNUMER and q_j, $j = 1, 2, \ldots,$ MDENOM of the best Chebyshev approximation.
WORK,IER = work space of $k(k+6)$ where k = LNUMER + MDENOM + 2 and error flag.

Finally, there are three **spline data smoothing programs,** ICSSCU, ICSSCV, and ICSMOU. These programs compute least squares and cubic spline approximations to data (x_j, y_j) and produce smooth curves. ICSSCV has logic in it which attempts to terminate the smoothing process when the difference between the curve and the data is purely random variation. ICSSCU is similar except that one specifies the amount of smoothing to be done. The program ICSMOU is primarily for **wild point removal;** it replaces some data values by smoothed values in an attempt to remove wild points. It is usually quite effective if there are no more than 25 percent wild points in the otherwise smooth data.

The PROTRAN system provides for **discrete least-squares approximations** by polynomials, splines, or a general set of functions. The basic forms of the statement are

```
$APPROXIMATE Y; VS X; BY YAPPRX
$APPROXIMATE Y; VS X; AT NEWPTS; IS NEWY
```

The data (x_i, y_i) is in the vectors X and Y; the first form defines a function (YAPPRX in this example) which is the approximation, while the second form returns a vector of values (NEWY in this example) at the specified vector of points (NEWPTS).

The type of approximation is specified by the phrase USING; the default SPLINES is obtained in the examples above. The following examples illustrate the other options of the APPROXIMATE statement:

```
          $APPROXIMATE DATA; VS XPTS; BY PFIT
                  USING POLYNOMIALS; COEFFICIENTS = POLYA
          $APPROXIMATE DATA; VS XPTS; NPOINTS = NPTS-3
                  AT ZPTS; IS NUVALU; NOUTPUT = 2*NPTS+1
                  USING SPLINES; ERROR = DATAER
          $APPROXIMATE DATA; VS XPTS; BY EXPFIT
                  USING EXPMOD(K,X), K,X; NBASIS = 4
                  COEFFICIENTS = EXPCOE
C             THE FOLLOWING FORTRAN FUNCTION APPEARS LATER
C             FOR USE WITH THE ABOVE $APPROXIMATE STATEMENT
C                   FUNCTION EXPMOD (K,X)
C                   EXPMOD = EXP(K*X/10.)
C                   RETURN
C                   END
          $APPROXIMATE DATA; VS XPTS
                  AT X100; IS Y100; NOUTPUT = 100
                  USING COSINE(PI*NCYCLE,ALPHA-BETA),NCYCLE,ALPHA; NBASIS = 6
C             THE FOLLOWING FORTRAN FUNCTION APPEARS LATER
C             FOR USE WITH THE ABOVE $APPROXIMATE STATEMENT
C                   FUNCTION COSINE(CYC,DIFF)
C                   .... CODE TO COMPUTE VALUE OF COSINE
C                   RETURN
C                   END
```

Note that the BY phrase cannot be used with specified basis functions if the expression depends on any parameter besides the independent variable and the basis function index. The use of PI and BETA in the last example precludes the use of a BY phrase. The PROTRAN $APPROXIMATE statement accesses the IMSL library routines IFLSQ, ICCSCU, or ICCSCV.

The use of the IMSL software is illustrated in the case studies of the next two sections. Problems based on the software in this section are given at the end of Section 11.6 after the two case studies.

CASE STUDY: THE REPRESENTATION OF DATA **11.5

The main objective of this case study is to show the ability of various models to represent data. Secondary objectives are to illustrate the use of software for approximation and to compare interpolation with approximation.

We choose three sets of data:

Data Set 1: $y(x) = 4x\sin(x^2/4-1)e^{-1.55x}$, $0 \le x \le 6.5$, $-.75 \le y \le .25$. This is very well-behaved mathematical data and easy to model with simple forms of various kinds. The curve is discretized by taking 26 points $x_i = (i-1)*.08$ in [0.0, 2.0], 30 points $x_{26+i} = 2.0 + i*0.1$ in [2.1, 5.0], and 20 points $x_{56+i} = 5.0 + i*.075$ in [5.075, 6.5].

Data Set 2: **Example 5.8 data,** $10.0 \le x \le 14.0$, $.42 \le y \le 4.64$. This data set has already been seen to be difficult to model by polynomials.

Data Set 3: **Titanium data, Problem 5.4.11**, $575 \le x \le 624$, $.6 \le y \le 2.2$. This is a difficult data set to model and has a moderate amount of uncertainty in it.

These three sets of data are shown in Figure 11.5.

Seven models are considered for these data sets. Some of these models are obviously unsuited for some of the data, and so we do not discuss all possible combinations. As we list the models, we discuss which programs are used and how the particular model is implemented by library software.

Least-squares approximations are used for all models except model 7 because these are the easiest to obtain. In this type of application the measure of approximation is not a critical factor. We use Chebyshev approximations for model 7 because that is the only software available for this model.

Model 1: Polynomials of degree 0, 1, 2, ... This model is handled directly by the PROTRAN $APPROXIMATE statement.

Model 2: Special polynomial forms for each data set. We construct polynomial-type models of a special form for each data set. In each case, a particular form was selected and tested. For data sets 2 and 3, this initial form was unsatisfactory and two improvements were considered for each data set. For data set 1, we use $e^{-1.5x}$ times a polynomial so as to incorporate the exponential decay of the data into the model in an approximate way. This is accomplished using the basis function

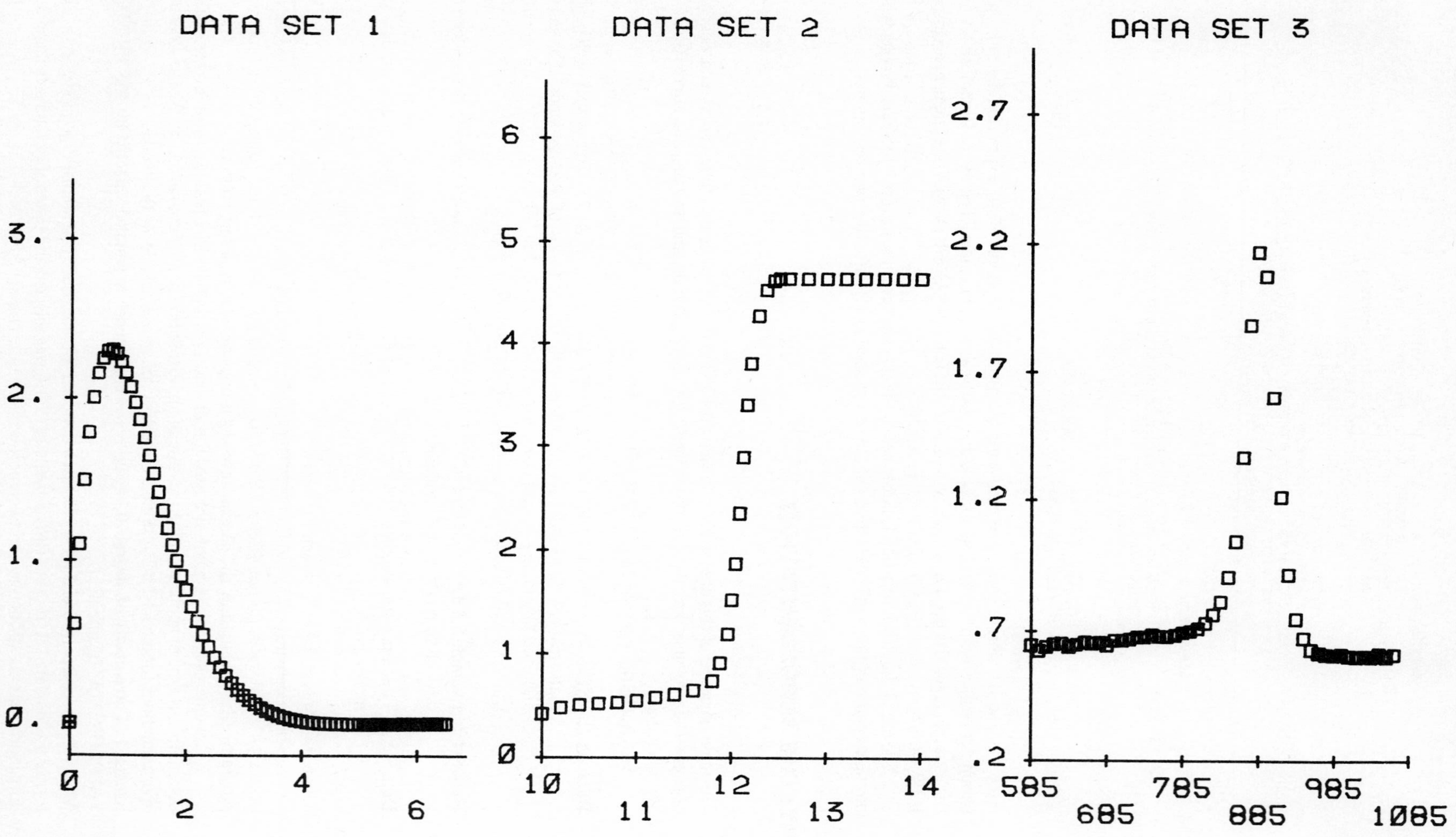

Figure 11.5 **The three data sets of the case study.** The uncertainty in each data set is moderate or less and the primary objective is to obtain a good mathematical model of the curves.

```
FUNCTION EXPOL(K,X)
POLY = 1.0
IF(K.GT.1) POLY = X**(K-1)
EXPOL = EXP(-1.5*X)*POLY
RETURN
END
```

along with the PROTRAN $APPROXIMATE statement with user-supplied basis functions:

```
$APPROXIMATE DATA ; VS XPTS1 ; BY POLY1 ; USING EXPOL(K,X),K,X
          NBASIS = N
```

For data set 2, we first try to model the shape by a polynomial in arctangents using the basis function

```
FUNCTION  ATANPO(K,X)
ATANPO = 1.0
IF(K.LE.1)  RETURN
ATANPO = ATAN((8.*X-98.)/(K-1))**(K-1)
RETURN
END
```

plus the $APPROXIMATE statement as above replacing EXPOL by ATANPO.

For data set 3, we start with the function $1/[1+.006*(x-898)^2]$ which has a bump something like the data. We first try to model the data by polynomials in this function plus straight lines by using the basis function

```
      FUNCTION RATPOL(K,X)
      IF( K .EQ. 1 ) RATPOL = 1.0
      IF( K .EQ. 2 ) RATPOL = X
      IF( K .EQ. 3 ) RATPOL = 1./(1.+.006*(X-892.)**2)
      IF( K .EQ. 3 ) RETURN
C           BASIS FOR DATA3 MODEL, TRY 1
      RATPOL = 1./(1. + .006*((X-892.)/(K-2.))**2)**(K-3)
      RETURN
      END
```

and use the $APPROXIMATE statement as before.

The initial models for data sets 2 and 3 do not represent the data well, and so a second try was made replacing the formula in ATANPO by the three lines

```
C          BASIS FOR DATA2 MODEL, TRY 2
      ATANPO = ATAN((10.*X-121.)/(K-1))
      IF( K .EQ. 2 )   RETURN
      ATANPO = (X-12.1)**(K-2)*ATAN((10.*X-121.)/(K-1))
```

This gives a basis of 1 plus polynomials times $\tan^{-1}[(10x-121)/(K-1)]$. The second try for data set 3 replaces last line of RATPOL by

```
C          BASIS FOR DATA3 MODEL, TRY 2
      IF( MOD(K,2) .EQ. 1 )  THEN
          RATPOL = (X-892.)**(K-3)/(1. + .006*((X-892.)/(K-2.))**2)**(K-3)
        ELSE
          RATPOL = (X-892.)**(K/2)
      ENDIF
```

These special polynomial models give improved representations, but another effort was made. The third try for data set 2 replaces the above three lines by

```
C          BASIS FOR DATA2 MODEL, TRY 3
      ATANPO = ATAN(10.*X-121.)
      IF( K .EQ. 2 )      RETURN
      ATANPO = (X-12.25)**(K-2)*ATANPO
```

The third try for data set 3 replaces the above combination arctangent and polynomial basis by a simpler polynomial times an arctangent weight function. The five lines of code in the second try are replaced by

```
C          BASIS FOR DATA3 MODEL, TRY 3
      RATPOL = (X-892.)**(K-3)/(1. + .006*((X-892.)/(K-2.))**2)
```

Model 3: Cubic splines with equally spaced knots. The IMSL library program ICSFKU is used. The PROTRAN statement $APPROXIMATE with USING SPLINES does not necessarily provide equally spaced knots.

Model 4: Cubic splines with knots concentrated where the data vary most. The program ICSFKU is used here also. The actual sets of knots selected are listed below:

NKNOTS	Interior knots for data set 1
5	1.0, 3.0, 5.0
7	0.7, 1.5, 3.0, 4.5, 5.5
10	0.5, 1.0, 1.6, 2.5, 3.5, 4.5, 5.3, 6.0
NKNOTS	**Interior knots for data set 2**
5	11.95, 12.15, 12.4
7	11.8, 12.0, 12.1, 12.25, 12.5
10	11.4, 11.85, 11.98, 12.06, 12.14, 12.26, 12.36, 12.6
NKNOTS	**Interior knots for data set 3**
5	850, 900, 940
7	830, 880, 900, 920, 960
10	800, 845, 875, 890, 905, 935, 955, 1000

These interior knots are embedded in a set which includes the endpoints of the interval plus one artificial knot outside each end of the interval. The first set of knots is thus defined by

```
$ASSIGN XKNTS11 = (XPTS1(1)-1.0, XPTS1(1), 1.0, 3.0, 5.0, XPTS1(76), XPTS1(76)+1.0)
```

Model 5: Hermite cubics with equally spaced break points. This model is implemented with the PROTRAN $APPROXIMATE statement with user-supplied basis functions. Thus we create a function HCUBIC(K,X) which implements the Hermite cubic functions given in Problem 4.4.1 and Figure 5.5.

Function Subprogram for Hermite Cubic Basis

```
        FUNCTION HCUBIC(K,X)
C          HERMITE CUBIC BASIS FUNCTIONS
C     T CONTAINS INTERIOR KNOTS PLUS TWO ENDPOINTS PLUS TWO DUMMY POINTS
C     OUTSIDE THE INVERVAL. THE BASIS FUNCTIONS ARE ORDERED WITH 2 PER
C     KNOT STARTING WITH THE LEFT END POINT OF THE INTERVAL.
        COMMON / HINFO / T(12),NKNOTS
        IKNOT = (K+3)/2
        IF( MOD(K,2) .EQ. 1 ) THEN
C                    K IS ODD, USE H(T) = FUNCTION VALUE BASIS
               HCUBIC = HERMC(T,NKNOTS,X,IKNOT)
            ELSE
C                    K IS EVEN, USE H1(T) = DERIVATIVE VALUE BASIS
               HCUBIC = HERMC1(T,NKNOTS,X,IKNOT)
        ENDIF
        RETURN
        END
```

Function Subprograms for Hermite Cubics

```
      FUNCTION HERMC(T,NKNOTS,X,I)
      REAL T(NKNOTS)
      IF( X .LT. T(I+1) .AND. X .GT. T(I-1) )  GO TO 20
C            X IS NOT IN THE KNOT INTERVAL, SET HERMC = 0
      HERMC = 0.0
      RETURN
   20 IF( X .GT. T(I) )       THEN
C            X IS IN RIGHT INTERVAL T(I) TO T(I+1)
```

```
             DT = T(I+1)-T(I)
             DX = T(I+1) - X
         ELSE
C            X IS IN LEFT INTERVAL T(I-1) TO T(I)
             DT = T(I)-T(I+1)
             DX = X - T(I)
       ENDIF
       HERMC = (3. - 2.*DX/DT)*DX**2/DT**2
       RETURN
       END

       FUNCTION HERMC1(T,NKNOTS,X,I)
       REAL T(NKNOTS)
       IF( X .LT. T(I+1) .AND. X .GT. T(I-1) )  GO TO 20
C            X IS NOT IN THE KNOT INTERVAL, SET HERMC1 = 0
       HERMC1 = 0.0
       RETURN
    20 DX = X - T(I)
       IF( X .GT. T(I) )       THEN
C            X IS IN RIGHT INTERVAL T(I) TO T(I+1)
             DT2 = (T(I)-T(I+1))**2
             DX2 = (X - T(I+1))**2
         ELSE
C           X IS IN LEFT INTERVAL T(I-1) TO T(I)
            DT2 = (T(I)-T(I-1))**2
            DX2 = (X - T(I-1))**2
       ENDIF
       HERMC1 = DX2*DX/DT2
       RETURN
       END
```

Model 6: Hermite cubics with break points concentrated where the data most varies. The knots of model 4 are used as break points. Otherwise, this model is implemented just like model 5.

Model 7: Rational functions. This model is obtained using the IMSL library program IRATCU. Since IRATCU requires a continuous function, we obtain it by interpolating the data using splines. This is accomplished by the PROTRAN statement.

```
$INTERPOLATE DATA; VS XPTS; BY SPLINE; USING SPLINES
```

The Fortran function SPLINE produced from this statement is then approximated by rational functions using IRATCU. Various values of the degree L of the numerator and M of the denominator are used.

The results of this case study are primarily visual; one examines the representations obtained and judges how effective they are. For some cases, the difference between the data and the representation is too small to be seen by the eye on a normal plot; for such cases, one plots the difference between the data and the representation. This difference, the **error curve,** is a very valuable tool in judging the quality of an approximation or representation of data.

Figures 11.6 through 11.10 show the results for the **polynomial representations,** models 1 and 2. Data set 1 is from a well-behaved mathematical function, and polynomials do very well once the degree gets large enough to handle the basic shape of the curve. The errors in the representation decrease exponentially as the degree is raised further. The polynomial representations do not do well for data sets 2 and 3. The oscillations seen in Figure 11.7 (top) and Figure 11.9 (top) continue as the degree is increased and the error decreases slowly. As the polynomial degree approaches the number of data points (30 for data set 2), large oscillations appear between the data points, and polynomials never give nice smooth curves to represent these data. The maximum errors of these polynomial representations are:

Degree	Data 1	Data 2	Data 3	Parameters
6	.20	.82	.87	7
8	.0088	.64	.73	9
11	.0012	.53	.52	12

Figures 11.7 and 11.9 (bottom) show the first attempt using a **special polynomial representation** of model 2. These are clearly substantial improvements over the ordinary polynomials of model 1, but still are not very satisfactory. Figures 11.8 and 11.10 show the second and third special polynomial representations for data sets 2 and 3, respectively. The second and third representations of data set 2 are rather good, but those of data set 3 are still not very good. There are both undue oscillations and large errors in the representations of data set 3. The maximum errors of the special polynomial representations of model 2 are

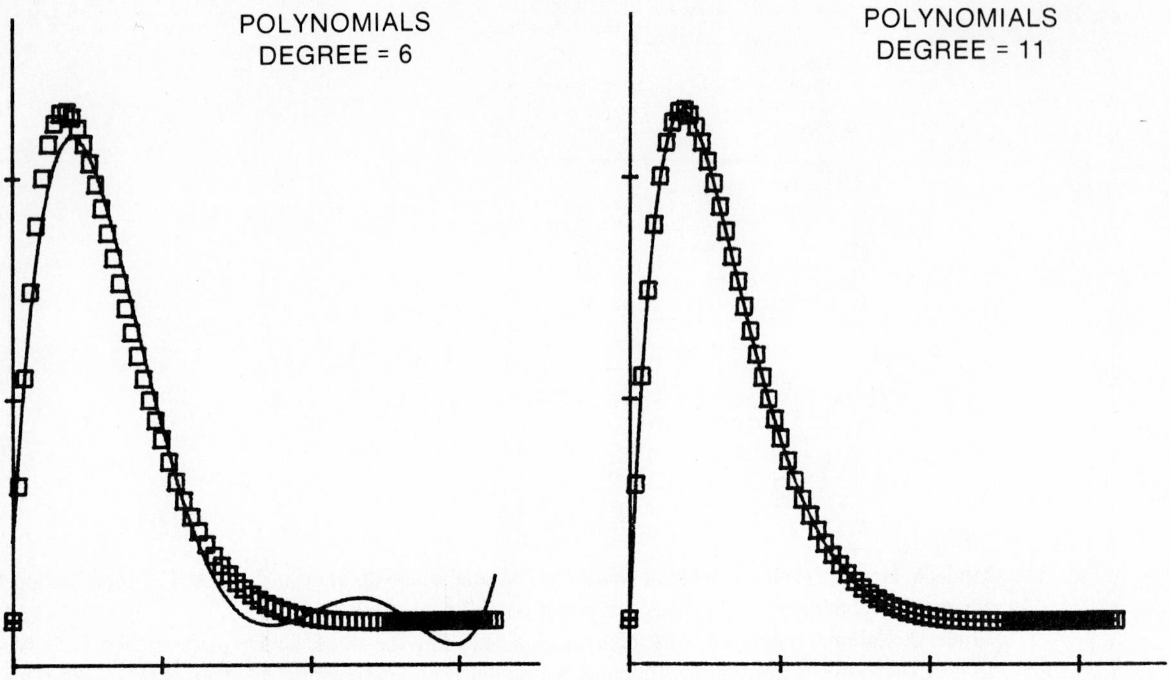

Figure 11.6 **Polynomial representation of data set 1.** Polynomial degrees of 6 (left) and 11 (right) are used; the resulting maximum errors are .2 and .0012.

FIRST TRY

Degree	Data 1	Data 2	Data 3	Parameters
3	.16	.61	.54	4
5	.0032	.39	.23	6
6	.00064	.39	.23	7
8	.000015	.27	.22	9
11	.0000000041	.18	.22	12

SECOND TRY

Degree	Data 2	Data 3	Parameters
6	.088	.51	7
8	.076	.35	9
11	.070	.26	12

THIRD TRY

Degree	Data 2	Data 3	Parameters
6	.087	.20	7
8	.076	.15	9
11	.073	.11	12

Note that in each case the most satisfactory special polynomial representation is a polynomial times an appropriate weight function.

Spline representations are shown in Figure 11.11 and 11.12. The degrees of freedom in these representations are the same as for polynomials shown in Figure 11.7 (top). Plots for data set 1 are not shown, as the data and representations appear identical with the scale used here. Splines provide a better

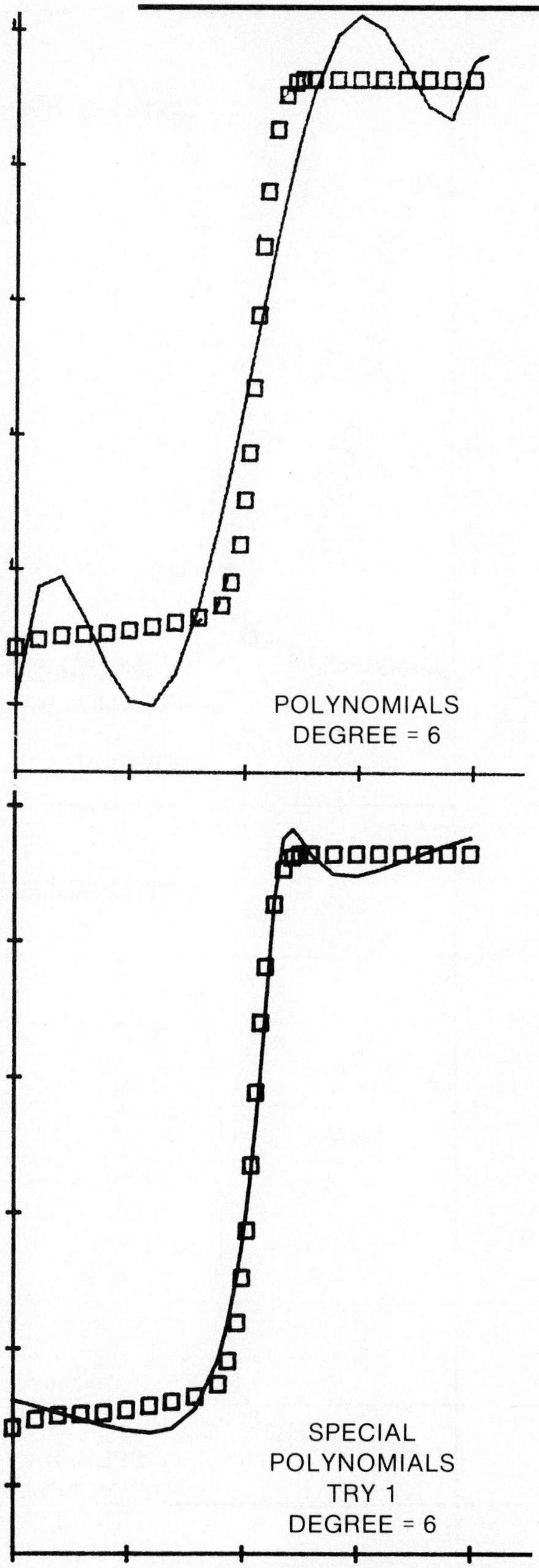

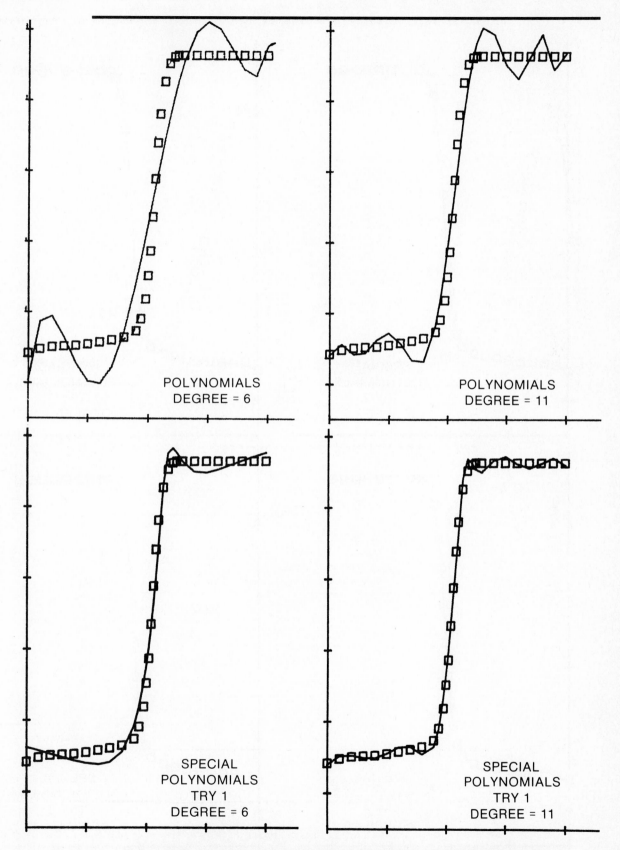

Figure 11.7 **Polynomial and special polynomial representations of data set 2.** The top figures show polynomial representations of degrees 6 and 11; the bottom show the representations of model 2 for degrees 6 and 11.

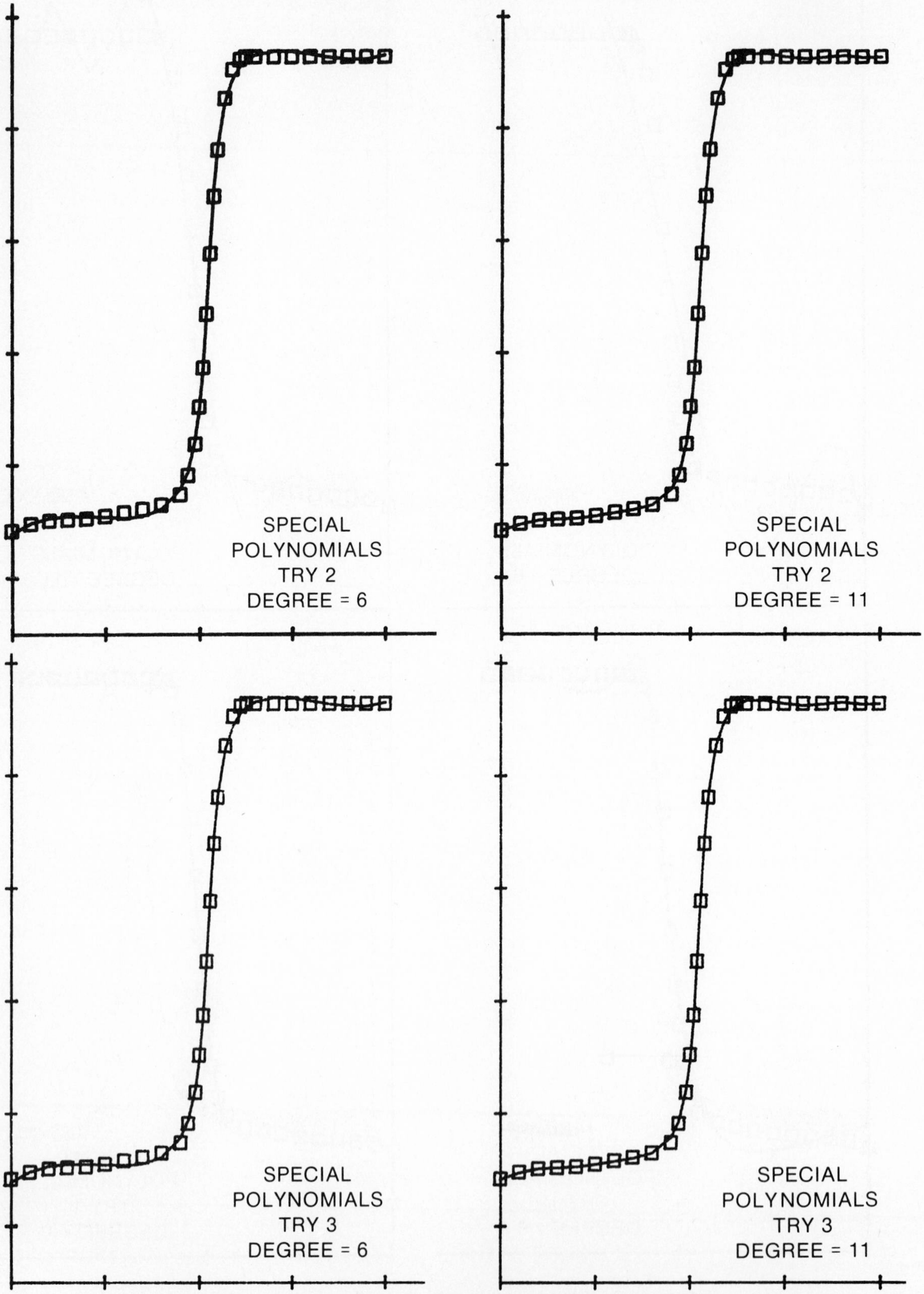

Figure 11.8 **Two more special polynomial representations of data set 2.** The second and third tries of model 2 are shown.

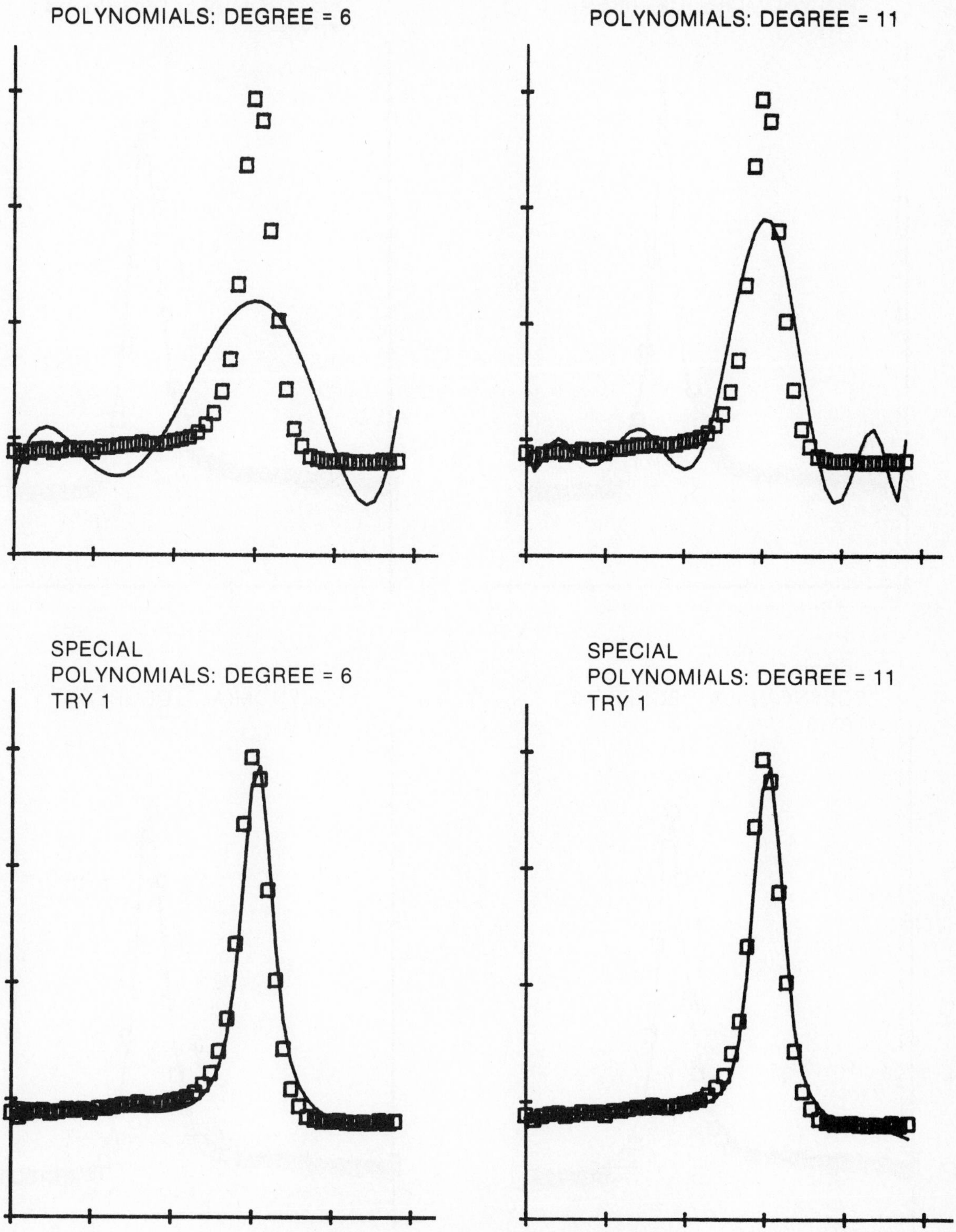

Figure 11.9 **Polynomial and special polynomial representation of data set 3.** The polynomial representations (top) of degrees 6 and 11 do poorly; the special polynomial representations (bottom) are much better.

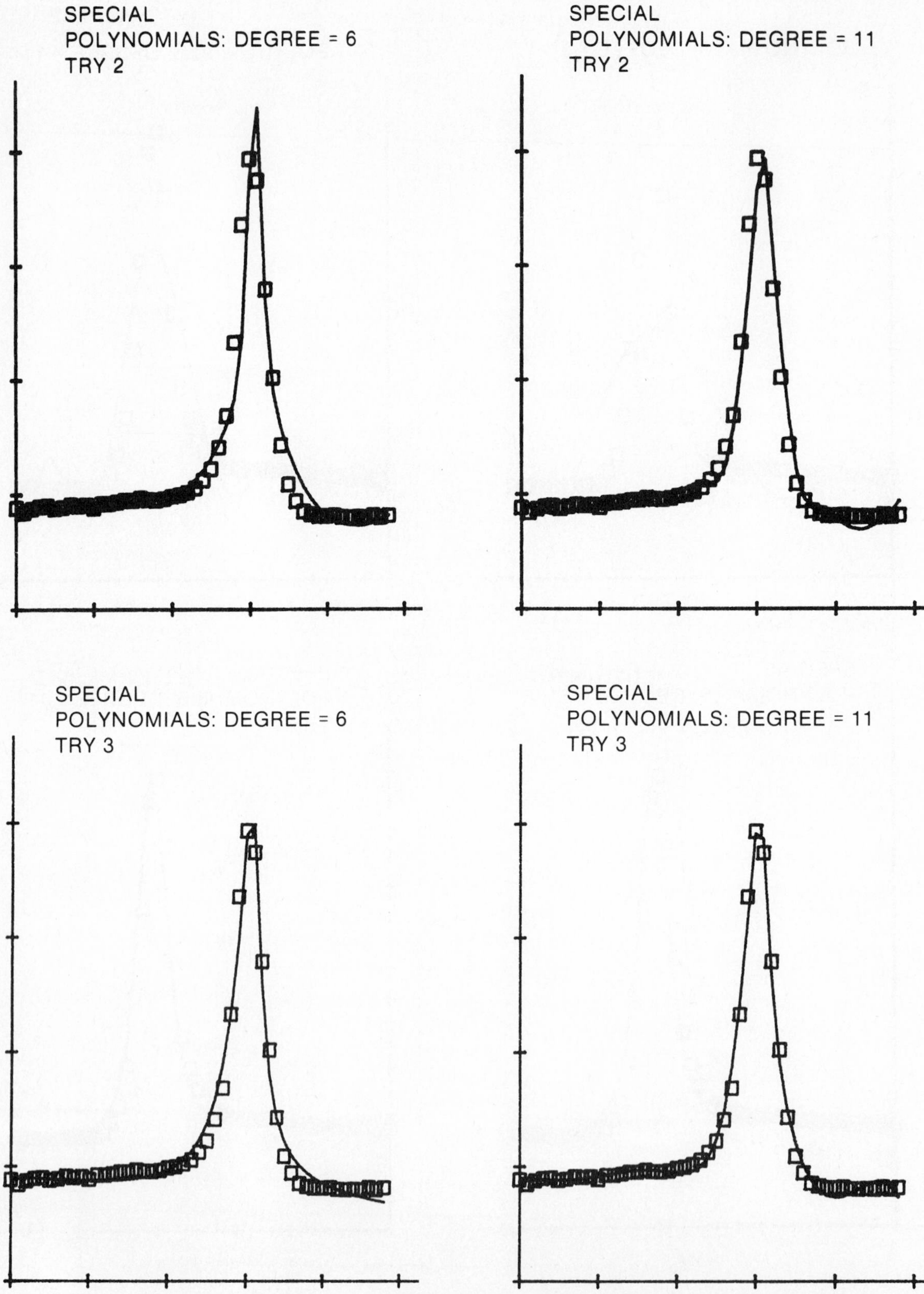

Figure 11.10 **Two more special polynomial representations of data set 3.** The second and third tries of model 2 are shown; they improve only slightly on the first try.

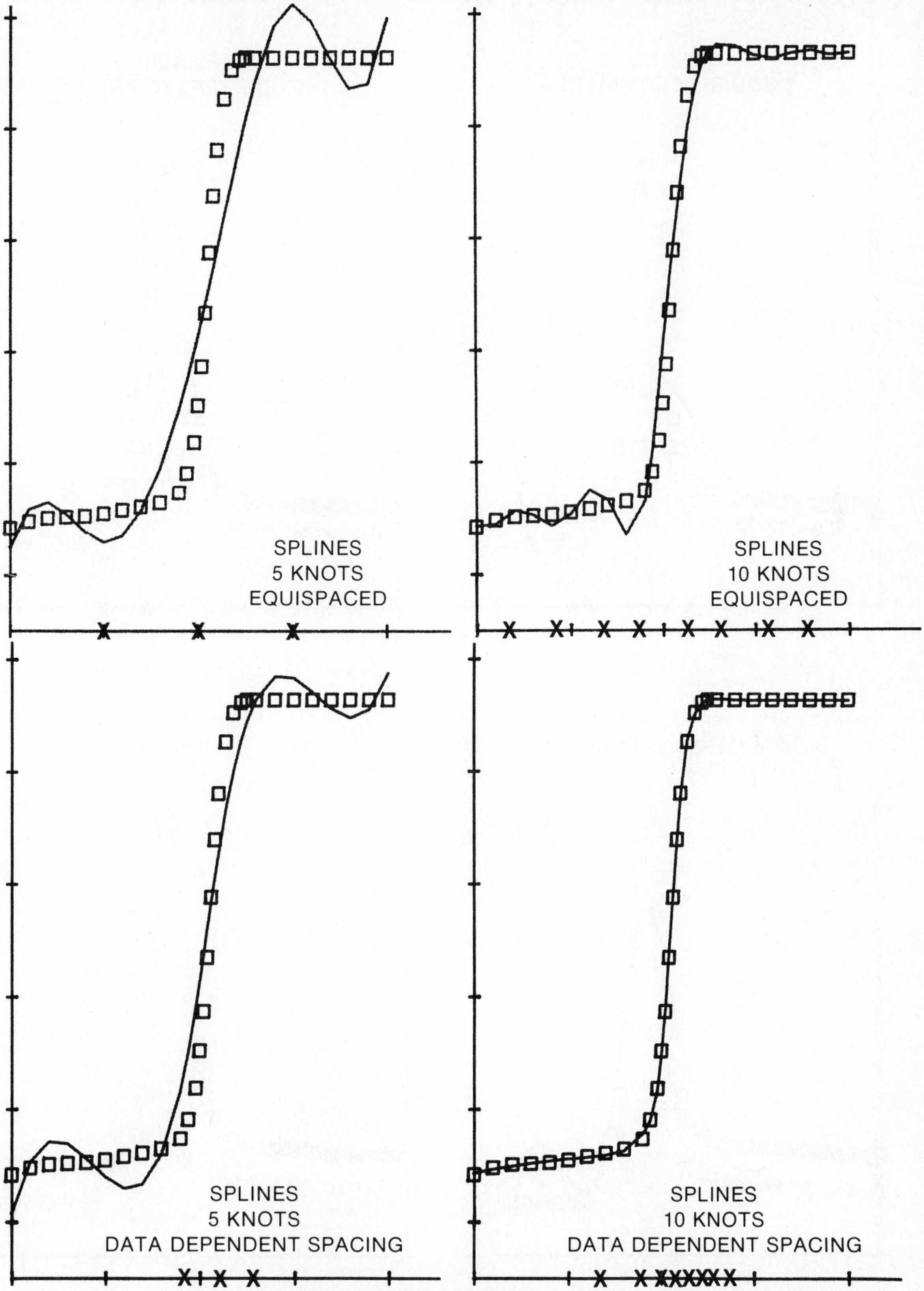

Figure 11.11 **Spline representations of data set 2.** The top figures show representations with equispaced knots located at the x's. The bottom figures show representations with data-dependent knots.

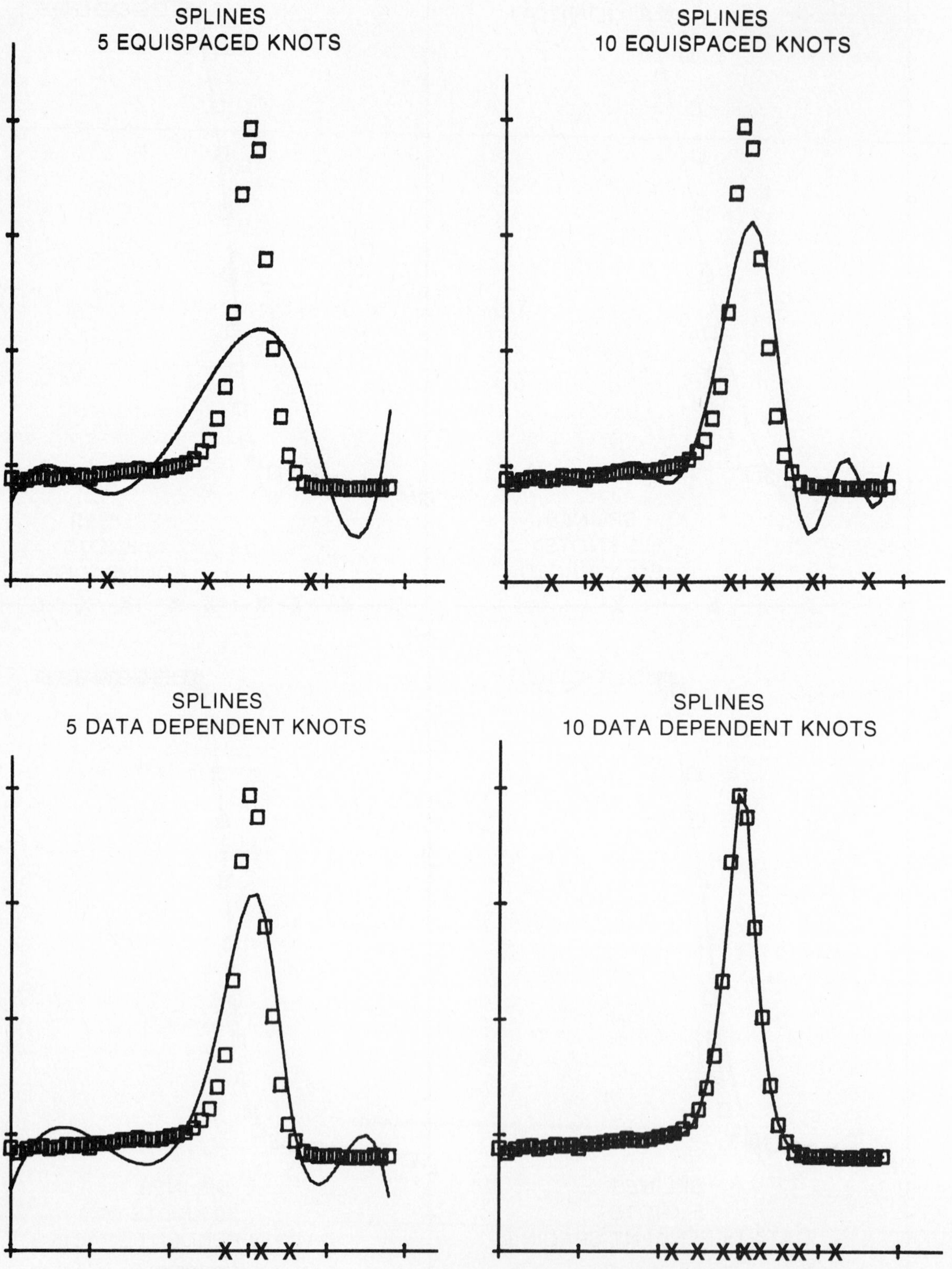

Figure 11.12 Spline representations of data set 3. The top figures show representations with equispaced knots located at the x's. The bottom figures show the dramatic improvement obtained by using data-dependent knots.

representation of the mathematically well-behaved data set 1 for a small number of parameters, but polynomials become more accurate as the number of parameters increases.

Splines with **equispaced knots** represent the other two data sets better than ordinary polynomials (compare the top curves of Figures 11.7 and 11.9 with those of Figures 11.11 and 11.12). However, the special polynomial forms provide superior representations (compare the bottom curves of Figures 11.8 and 11.10 with the top curves of Figure 11.11 and 11.12). The maximum errors of the representations by splines with equispaced knots are:

Knots	Data 1	Data 2	Data 3	Parameters
5	.12	1.03	.89	7
7	.019	.80	.58	9
10	.0073	.30	.46	12

Splines with **data-dependent knots** provide a dramatic improvement in the representations of data sets 2 and 3, as seen in the bottom curves of Figures 11.11 and 11.12. The splines with 10 data-dependent knots appear as nice smooth curves that pass through the given data points. Data set 3 is, in fact, contaminated by noticeable measurement errors, and the spline representation smooths these out very nicely. These examples show the power obtained by allowing the knots to vary in spline approximation. No attempt was made here to choose the *best* knots; the knots were chosen merely by examining the data. If *optimal* or *best* knots are found, then it is known that data set 3 can be accurately represented using only 6 knots. The maximum errors of the representations by splines with data-dependent knots are:

Knots	Data 1	Data 2	Data 3	Parameters
5	.094	.59	.44	7
7	.015	.072	.30	9
10	.0034	.053	.10	12

Representations by **Hermite cubics** are shown in Figures 11.13 and 11.14. Plots for data set 1 are not shown, as the data and representations appear identical with the scale used here. These representations have about twice as many degrees of freedom as the corresponding polynomial or spline representations, and thus one would expect them to provide better fits. They do provide better representations, as seen by comparing Figures 11.13 and 11.14 with Figures 11.11 and 11.12.

Hermite cubics with **equispaced break points** provide better representations than splines, but there is still evidence of oscillation even with 10 break points. These representations are about as accurate as the special polynomials but, perhaps because of the higher number of parameters, they tend to oscillate more. The maximum errors of the representations by Hermite cubics with equispaced break points are:

Break points	Data 1	Data 2	Data 3	Parameters
5	.061	.43	.61	10
7	.017	.26	.14	14
10	.0046	.14	.076	20

As with splines, **data-dependent break points** provide a dramatic improvement over equispaced break points. The same data-dependent points are used as knots for the splines and break points for the Hermite cubics. The representations with 10 break points appear as nice smooth curves passing through the given data points. If the location of the break points were optimized, one would expect to obtain equally nice curves with somewhat fewer break points. The maximum errors of the representations by Hermite cubics with data-dependent break points are:

Break points	Data 1	Data 2	Data 3	Parameters
5	.036	.12	.049	10
7	.0068	.034	.077	14
10	.0018	.016	.0091	20

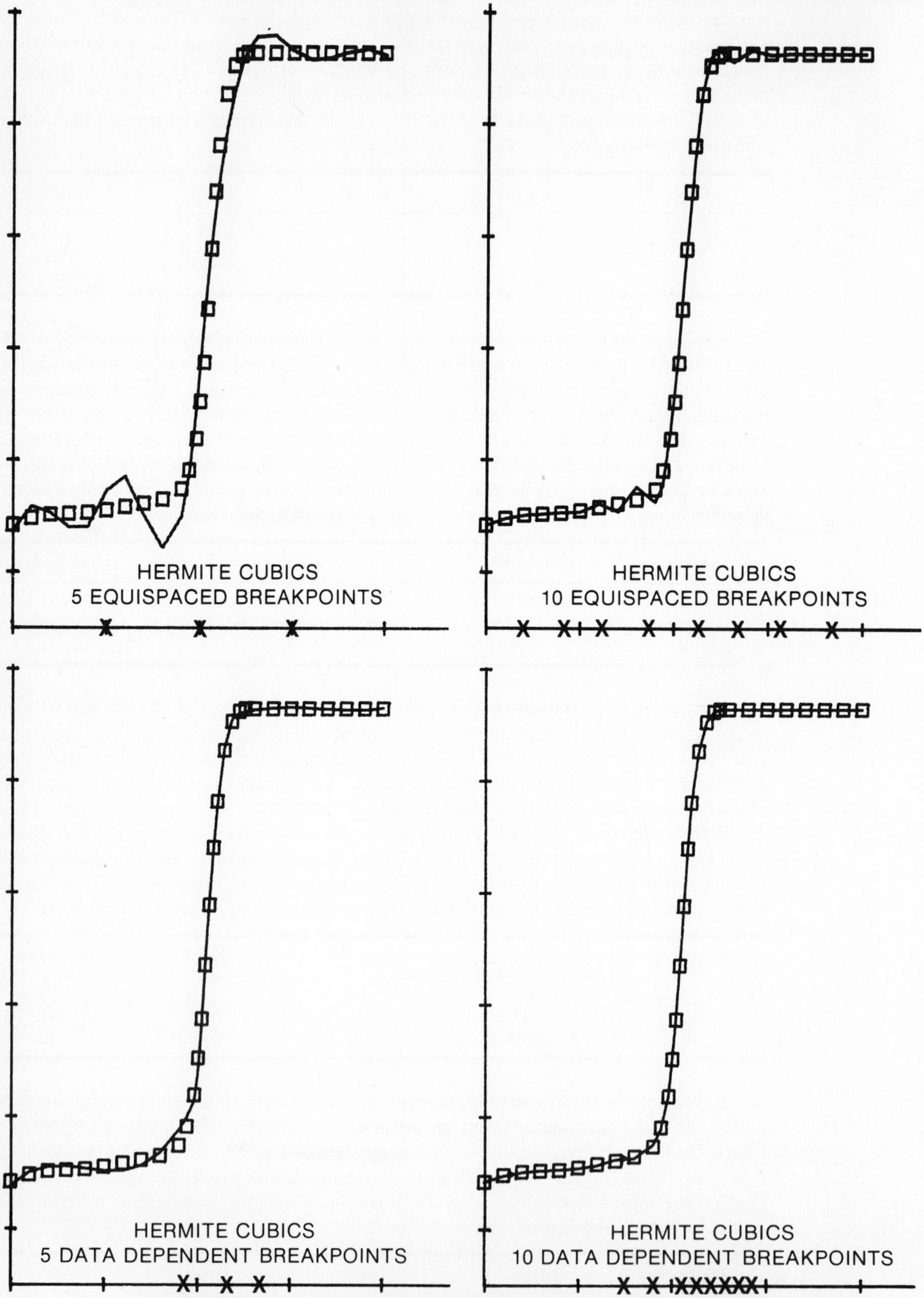

Figure 11.13 **Hermite cubic representations of data set 2.** The top figures show representation with equispaced break points located at the x's. The bottom figures show representations with data-dependent break points.

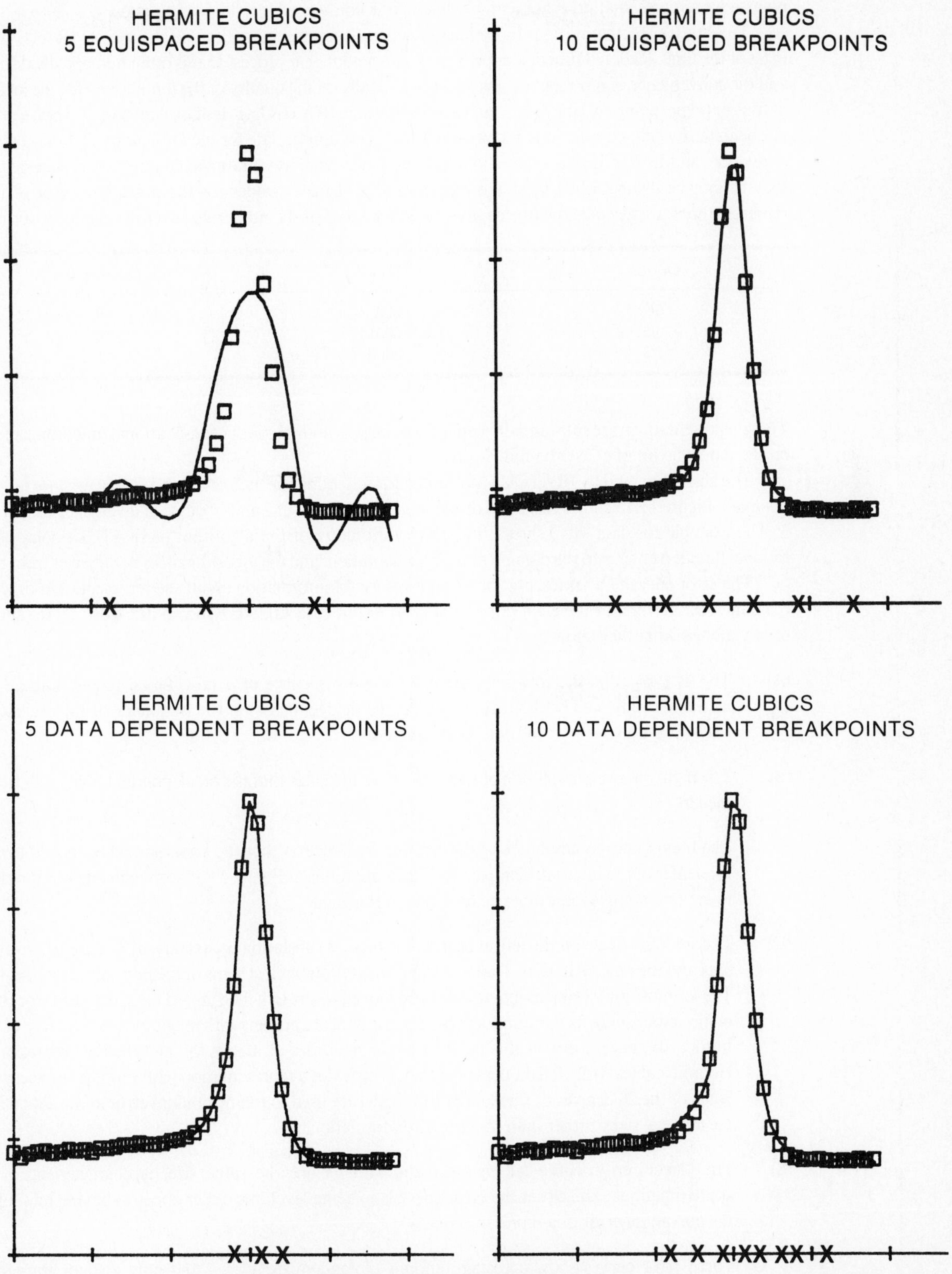

Figure 11.14 Hermite cubic representations of data set 3. The top figures show representations with equispaced break points located at the x's. The bottom figures show the dramatic improvement obtained by using data-dependent break points.

Note that the error for data set 3 actually increased from 5 to 7 break points. This suggests that the location of the 7 interior break points can be improved considerably. Note also that 3 properly chosen interior break points give a representation that is comparable with 8 equispaced interior break points.

The study of representations by **rational functions** is not a success because the routine IRATCU fails most of the time. Rational function approximation is a nonlinear process that is often numerically difficult, and the convergence of most algorithms depends critically on the quality of the initial guess for the location of the extreme points of the error curve. The routine IRATCU is designed to handle very smooth, mathematically defined functions and uses an initial guess appropriate for such functions. Data set 1 is such a function, and IRATCU converges about half the time; the representations obtained are so accurate that they cannot be distinguished from the data in a plot. Typical values for the maximum error of these representations are listed below (the degrees listed are those of the numerator over the denominator).

Degrees	Data 1	Parameters
6/2	.00052	9
6/3	.00014	10
7/3	.000057	11

These representations are substantially better than the polynomial ones because rational functions can take on the flat behavior of e^{-x} without difficulty.

The algorithm used by IRATCU is not suited for functions like data sets 2 and 3; convergence is rarely obtained. Figure 11.15 shows two cases of convergence for data set 2 and one case of divergence for data set 3. The example for data set 3 shows the primary difficulty of the algorithm of IRATCU; poles of the rational function enter into the domain of the representation, and the algorithm does not recover from this.

The error curve of a representation often gives useful information about the representation or about the data itself. Several of the error curves obtained in this case study are shown in Figure 11.16, and we briefly discuss what they show.

(A) This is typical of the roly-poly nature of the error curve of a polynomial representation of a mathematically well-behaved function. As the degree increases, the frequency of the oscillations tends to get higher near the ends of the interval.

(B) The highly uneven amplitude of the error curve indicates that the break points should be shifted to the left.

(C) The highly uneven amplitude of the error curve indicates that the knots should be moved toward the center of the interval. Compare the representations in Figure 11.11 (top right and bottom right) to see the improvement that occurs if this shift is made.

(D) The smooth wiggle on the left indicates that there is substantial systematic difference between the data and the representation. That is, the representation has lost some of the information of the data. The leftmost interior break point should be moved to the left. The jagged nature of the error curve in the center suggests that random errors in the data are present with magnitude of the order of .12. In fact, the uncertainty in this data is only of the order of .03 or .04, and the representation by Hermite cubics with 10 data-dependent knots provides a representation with this level of accuracy. Some of the 20 degrees of freedom of this model are used to follow random error in the data where the curve is steep rather than to represent information.

(E) The "level" error curve (all maxima and minima are the same size) is characteristic of L_∞ approximations. The closer the error curve is to being level, the closer one is to having minimized the maximum error of a representation.

(F, G) These error curves show a certain amount of random oscillation and only a small amount of systematic oscillation. This suggests that both of these representations contain almost all of the information content of the data, and further increases in the degrees of freedom only allow the representations to follow random errors that contaminate the data. It is known from other analysis that the uncertainty of some of the data points on the hump is about .03 to .04. Thus, the

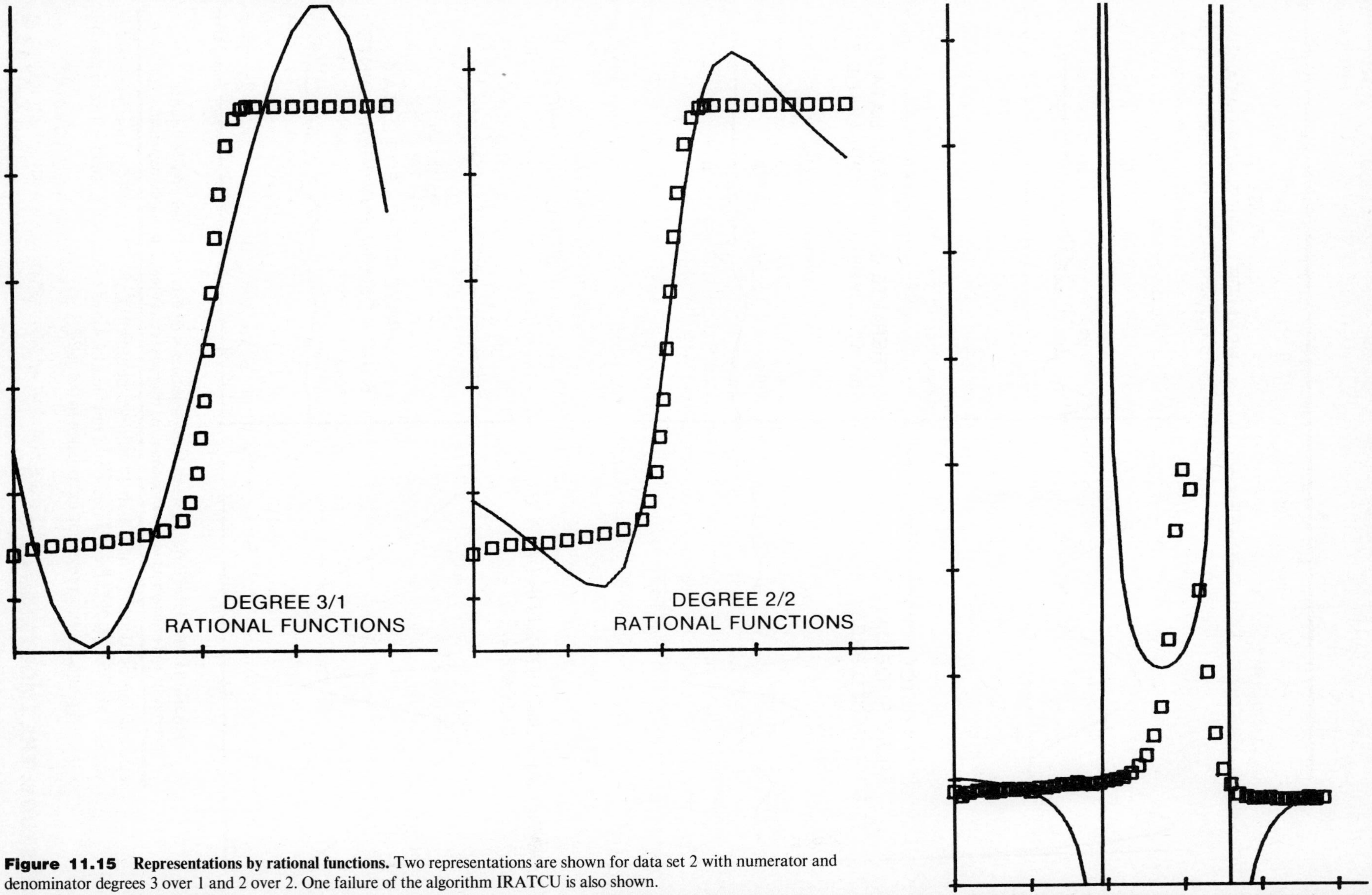

Figure 11.15 Representations by rational functions. Two representations are shown for data set 2 with numerator and denominator degrees 3 over 1 and 2 over 2. One failure of the algorithm IRATCU is also shown.

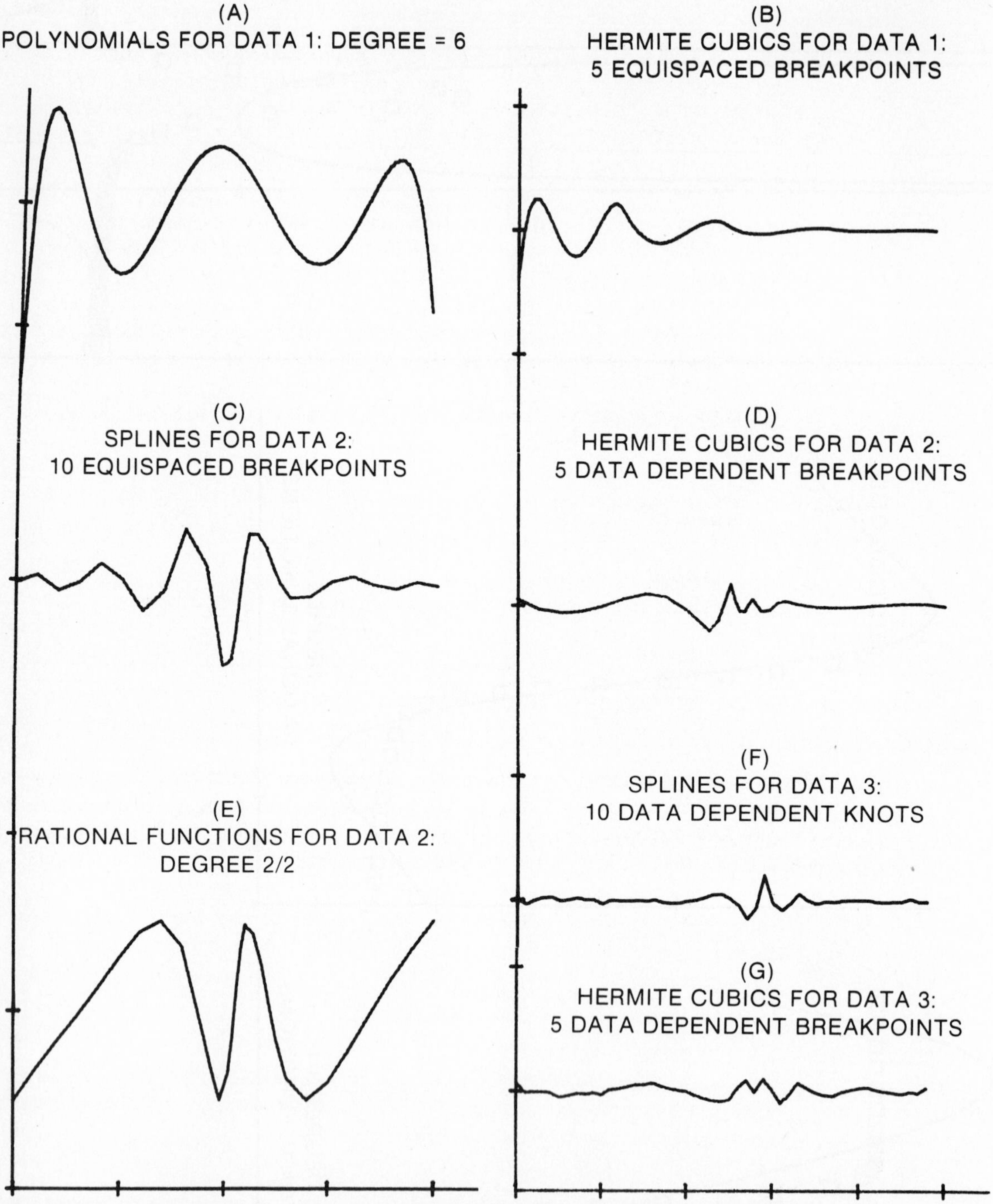

Figure 11.16 **Error curves for selected representations of the data sets.** Examination of the error curve often gives important information about the representation or the nature of the data itself.

representation by Hermite cubics with 10 data-dependent break points provides a false indication of accuracy. Many of the 20 degrees of freedom of this model are used to follow the random error in the data at the hump rather than representing information in the data.

CASE STUDY: THE SMOOTHING OF DATA **11.6

The main objective of this case study is to show the ability of various programs to smooth data contaminated with random errors. We model the situation as follows: The data (x_i, y_i) are given and y_i

should be $f(x_i)$ where $f(x)$ is a smooth (but probably unknown) function. The actual data is then

$$y_i = f(x_i) + e_i \qquad \textbf{Equation 11.6.1}$$

where e_i is a random error or uncertainty in the data. The process of **smoothing** is to approximate the data (x_i, y_i) and attempt to retrieve the information $f(x_i)$ and suppress the uncertainty e_i.

It is essential in smoothing that the approximation be made with $F(\mathbf{a}, x)$ which models $f(x)$ well; otherwise, much of the error in the approximation is due to $||f(x)-F(\mathbf{a}, x)||$ being large, and the random uncertainties are not smoothed. One can, and often does, use a **local model** for $f(x)$; that is, the approximate or smoothed value for y_i is based on $y_{i-k}, \ldots, y_{i-1}, y_i, y_{i+1}, \ldots, y_{i+k}$ for some small value of k. With this approach, one needs only to have a good local model of $f(x)$ (which is usually a low-degree polynomial). If a good **global model** for $f(x)$ is known, then using it for global smoothing (that is, approximating all the data at once) normally provides results superior to local smoothing.

For this case study, we choose $f(x) = 1 + \sin(2x+1)/(1+x^2)$ so that polynomials model $f(x)$ rather well and splines model it very well. The data is artificially created by choosing 41 points $x_i = (i-1)*.075$ and then adding random errors to $f(x_i)$ to obtain y_i values. We consider several types of random errors as follows (we number the data sets starting at 4 to avoid confusion with the previous case study).

Data Set 4: Uniformly distributed random errors. We choose random errors between $\pm$ .25 (about 12 percent maximum error) and generate the data by

```
$RANDOM; ARRAY UNIFM; UNIFORM (-.25,.25)
$ASSIGN DATA4(I) = F(XPTS(I)) + UNIFM(I)
```

Data Set 5: Normally distributed random errors. We choose random errors with mean 0 and standard deviation .12. This gives a level of error roughly comparable to that of data set 4. This data set is generated by

```
$RANDOM; ARRAY NORMAL; NORMAL(0.0,0.12)
$ASSIGN DATA5(I) = F(XPTS(I)) + NORMAL(I)
```

Data Set 6: Widely varying errors. The errors in data sets 4 and 5 are rather similar in size; we obtain a much wider variation (typical of some real-world situations) by transforming the uniform distribution. Let e be a uniform random variable in $[-1, +1]$; then $e_t = (1-|e|)^3/e$ is in $[-\infty, +\infty]$ and the probability of a value e_t greater than b is about $1/(3eb)$. This data set is generated by

```
$RANDOM; ARRAY UNIFM; UNIFORM(-1.0,1.0)
$ASSIGN DATA6(I) = F(XPTS(I)) + .12*(1-ABS(UNIFM(I)))**3/UNIFM(I)
```

Data Set 7: No errors except 3 wild points. We take $f(x)$ and change 3 values to correspond to "blunders" in measuring the experimental data.

```
$ASSIGN DATA7(I) = F(XPTS(I)) $
 DATA7(6) = -1.73
 DATA7(28) = 4.019
 DATA7(35) = 7.9795
```

Since the numbers obtained by random number generators may vary from place to place, we tabulate the data actually used with

$$f(x) = 1 + \sin(2x+1)/(1+x^2)$$

for $0 \le x \le 2.0$.

The following smoothing methods are applied to these data sets:

Smoothing 1: Least squares with polynomials. We use the PROTRAN $APPROXIMATE statement:

```
$APPROXIMATE DATA4; VS XPTS; USING POLYNOMIALS
            BY POLY; NBASIS = NDEGRE+1
```

DATA 4						
Point						
1	2.07458	1.78801	2.07548	1.97954	2.08945	1.63480
7	2.03053	1.74630	1.79267	1.42920	1.14101	1.32438
13	1.17944	0.93214	0.87631	0.80062	0.69002	0.79622
19	0.73527	0.60637	0.80011	0.95631	0.64858	0.95624
25	0.62853	0.55175	0.90018	1.00167	0.60299	1.05339
31	0.87300	0.99931	1.01089	1.11733	0.95633	1.15222
37	1.09389	0.86498	1.04563	1.11432	1.15554	

DATA 5						
Point						
1	2.09515	1.94785	1.83083	1.95798	1.73243	1.75251
7	1.60373	1.68300	1.60707	1.51219	1.31365	1.18910
13	1.03146	1.04792	0.93769	0.91373	0.73682	0.80826
19	1.00345	0.84188	0.72821	0.86364	0.86234	0.85700
25	0.79855	0.85057	0.81876	0.95008	1.07824	1.08758
31	0.80249	1.00298	0.67181	1.01412	0.95017	1.04864
37	1.21784	0.90520	1.01076	1.17494	1.00784	

DATA 6						
Point						
1	1.89664	−1.76941	1.94221	3.69694	2.35251	1.90543
7	1.73288	1.69572	1.59439	1.48457	1.28077	1.28149
13	1.17735	1.11698	−1.55335	0.95225	0.89538	0.84735
19	0.81142	0.81219	0.76914	0.76088	0.75853	0.75956
25	0.76784	0.45808	1.04996	0.81208	0.84253	0.87360
31	0.88356	0.98538	0.92549	0.95408	0.97491	1.64395
37	0.99630	0.99153	1.04047	1.06191	1.04289	

DATA 7						
Point						
1	1.84147	1.90766	1.94236	1.94488	1.91704	−1.73000
7	1.78694	1.69563	1.59448	1.48878	1.38302	1.28087
13	1.18508	1.09762	1.01978	0.95224	0.89527	0.84874
19	0.81228	0.78532	0.76714	0.75694	0.75388	0.75708
25	0.76564	0.77870	0.79543	4.01900	0.83670	0.85978
31	0.88362	0.90763	0.93127	0.95410	7.97950	0.99580
37	1.01406	1.03030	1.04438	1.05619	1.06570	

Smoothing 2: L_1 smoothing with polynomials. The IMSL library program RLLAV is used. The data and polynomial are packaged into the array DATMOD with 5 extra columns for work space. This array is constructed as follows (assuming DATA4 and XPTS are known):

```
      $DECLARATIONS
       MATRIX DATMOD(NXPTS = 41, NCOL = 15)
       VECTOR DATA4(41), XPTS(41) $
C              GET DATA4 AND XPTS
       NCOL = NDEGRE + 1
      $ASSIGN DATMOD(I,J) = XPTS(I)**(J-1) $
       DO 10 I = 1, NXPTS
   10      DATMOD(I, NCOL+1) = DATA4(I)
```

The smoothing is accomplished by

```
CALL RLLAV(DATMOD,41,NXPTS,NCOL,0,PCOEFS,ERROR,ITER,IRANK,IWORK,WORK,IER)
```

The arrays PCOEFS, IWORK, and WORK must be declared of length 10, 10, and 24 if degree up to 10 is used.

Smoothing 3: Least squares with smoothing cubic splines. We use the PROTAN statement

```
$APPROXIMATE DATA4; VS XTPS; USING SPLINES
          BY SPLINE; ERROR = ERREST
```

This accesses the IMSL library routines ICSSCU and ICSSCV. The phrase ERROR = ERREST may be omitted to obtain a default calculation, or ERREST may be set to an estimate of the standard deviation of the random errors present.

Smoothing 4: Wild point removal. The IMSL program ICSMOU is primarily designed to remove wild points; we apply it to all these data sets to examine its effect.

Least-squares polynomial smoothing, *smoothing 1,* is illustrated in Figure 11.17 for **data sets 4 and 5.** Polynomial models of degrees 4 and 8 are used; neither do well at extracting the curve for f(x) from this data. This should not be a surprise; the contamination of errors is high, and it is unrealistic to hope that accurate information about f(x) is obtained with only 41 data points. Note that increasing the polynomial degree does not improve the results obtained; the extra degrees of freedom in the 8th-degree polynomial are partially used to follow some of the "accidental" trends in the data created by the random errors. If better definition of f(x) is required, then the right thing to do is to obtain more data points.

The random errors in data sets 4 and 5 are uniformly and normally distributed, respectively. Statistical theory (not discussed in this text) suggests that least-squares smoothing should do as well as one can expect. **Data sets 6 and 7** have errors of a different nature; there are a few large errors and many (in DATA6) or no (in DATA7) small ones. Statistical theory suggests that least squares does not do well for smoothing such data, and the results presented in Figure 11.18 confirm this. The fourth-degree model for data set 6 is badly distorted by the large errors at the left end and is not similar to those obtained from data sets 4 and 5. The eighth-degree model obtained for data set 6 shows little resemblance to the underlying curve f(x). The models for f(x) obtained from data set 7 are clearly widely distorted by the three wild points present.

L_1 polynomial smoothing, *smoothing 2,* uses the same models as above but a different norm for measuring the error in the approximation. These polynomials minimize the average error rather than the sum of the squares of the errors. Figure 11.19 shows the results for **data sets 4 and 5** with polynomial degrees 4 and 8. The results for degree 4 differ little from those in Figure 11.17. The results for degree 8 are quite similar to those obtained by least-squares smoothing. Note that the polynomial models of degree n exactly interpolate the data at $n+1$ data points. This is characteristic of L_1 approximations.

The results for **data sets 6 and 7** are shown in Figure 11.20, and they are *much superior* to the least-squares results. For both data sets, the *outliers* or *wild points* are essentially ignored by the L_1 approximation, and the model is determined primarily by the "main trend" of the data. This behavior is characteristic of L_1 approximations and illustrates the superior robustness of L_1 smoothing. If the errors are more or less all the same (as the uniform or normal errors are in data sets 4 and 5), then L_1 does about as well as least squares. If the errors are erratic or the data might be contaminated by wild (or nearly wild) points, then L_1 smoothing is much better.

The above examples suggest that high-degree polynomial models are not very satisfactory for smoothing. The natural oscillatory nature of polynomials makes it too easy for them to follow various random errors. Spline models might do better, and *smoothing 3* provides **least-squares cubic spline smoothing.** This software does not allow one to control the spline in any direct way; it has a knot at each data point and chooses the spline coefficients based on its analysis of the data. If one provides a value ERREST of the standard deviation of the errors, then this information is incorporated into its analysis. Figure 11.21 shows the results of smoothing these from data sets using the default of providing no estimate of the size of the errors present. The results for **data set 4** and **data set 5** are reasonably smooth curves, similar in nature to the underlying f(x) except for extraneous, but small, oscillations. The results are substantially better than using polynomials and least squares (see Figure 11.17) or L_1 (see Figure 11.19). The results for **data set 6** are better than using least squares and polynomials (see Figure 11.18), but not as good as L_1 and polynomials (see Figure 11.20). The smoothing spline for **data set 7** is a constant; it is very smooth, but provides little information about the underlying f(x).

Figure 11.22 shows the results of providing an estimate ERREST = 0.1 of the standard deviation of the errors in the data. This value is approximately correct for data sets 4 and 5; it is not accurate for data sets 6 and 7 whose errors have larger standard deviations, and the standard deviation means little for such data in any event. The changes in the smoothings obtained are dramatic except for **data set 5** where essentially the same result is obtained. The default value for ERREST in $APPROXIMATE; USING SPLINES uses a different IMSL library routine than when ERREST is assigned a value; the underlying algorithms used by the two routines are completely different. **Data set 4** is now smoothed much less and has far too many wiggles. If ERREST is increased to .2, then a curve similar to, but better than, the fourth-degree polynomial models is obtained for both data sets 4 and 5. If ERREST is increased to .3, then the smoothed model is a straight line for these data sets.

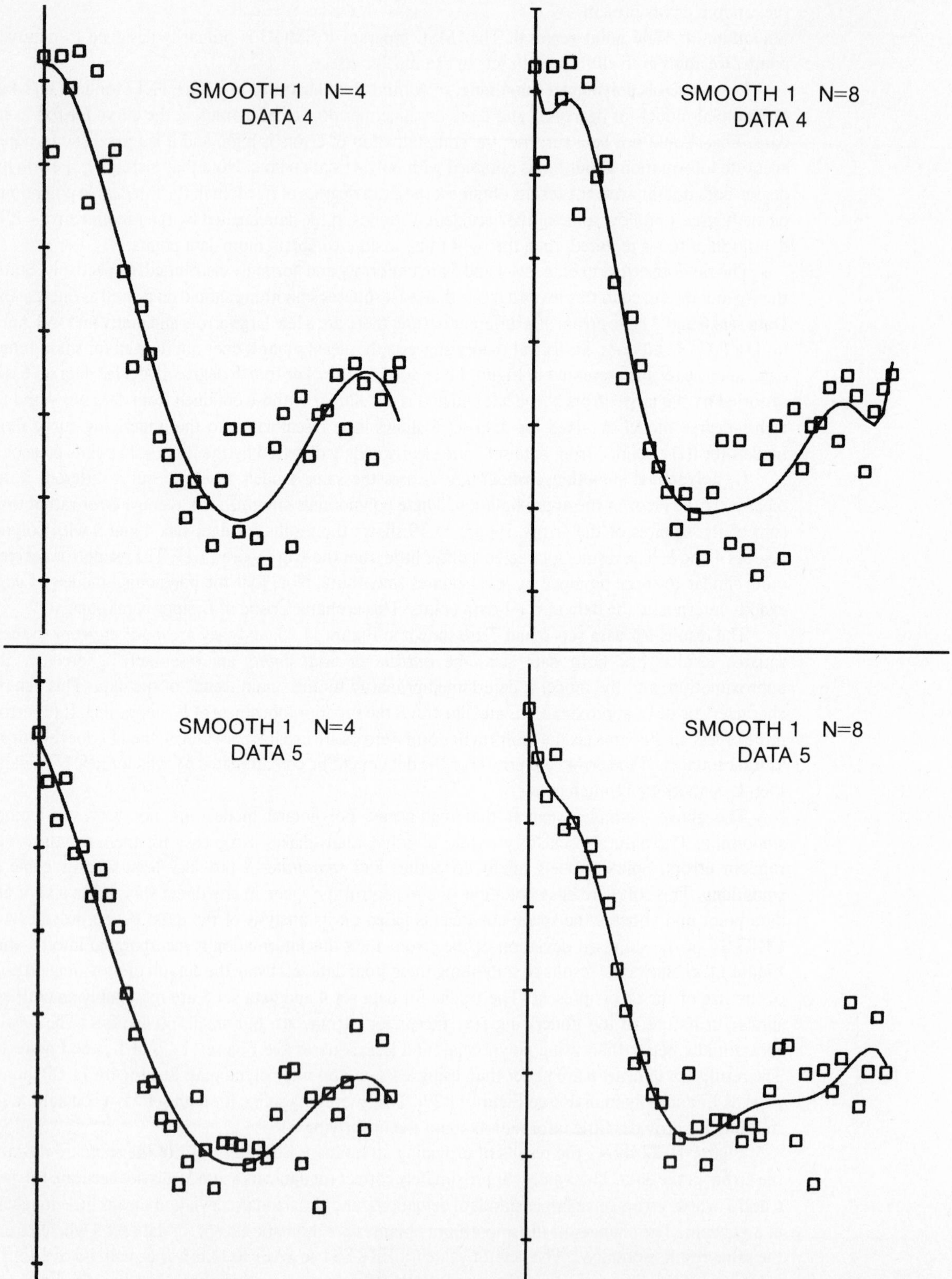

Figure 11.17 **Least-squares polynomial smoothing of data sets 4 and 5.** Smoothing with polynomial models of degree 4 (left) and 8 (right) are shown as solid lines.

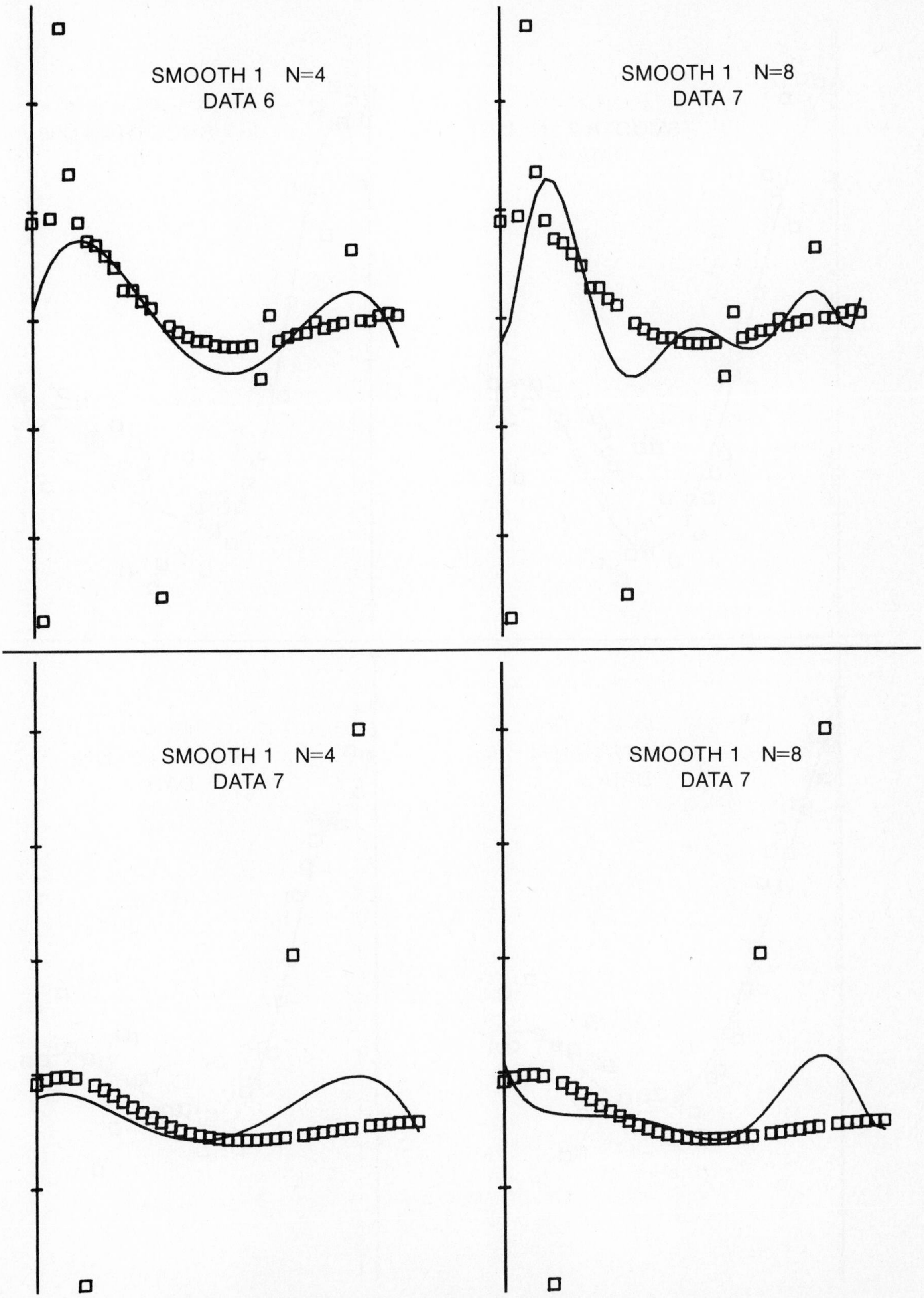

Figure 11.18 **Least-squares polynomial smoothing of data sets 6 and 7.** Smoothing with polynomial models of degree 4 (left) and 8 (right) are shown as solid lines.

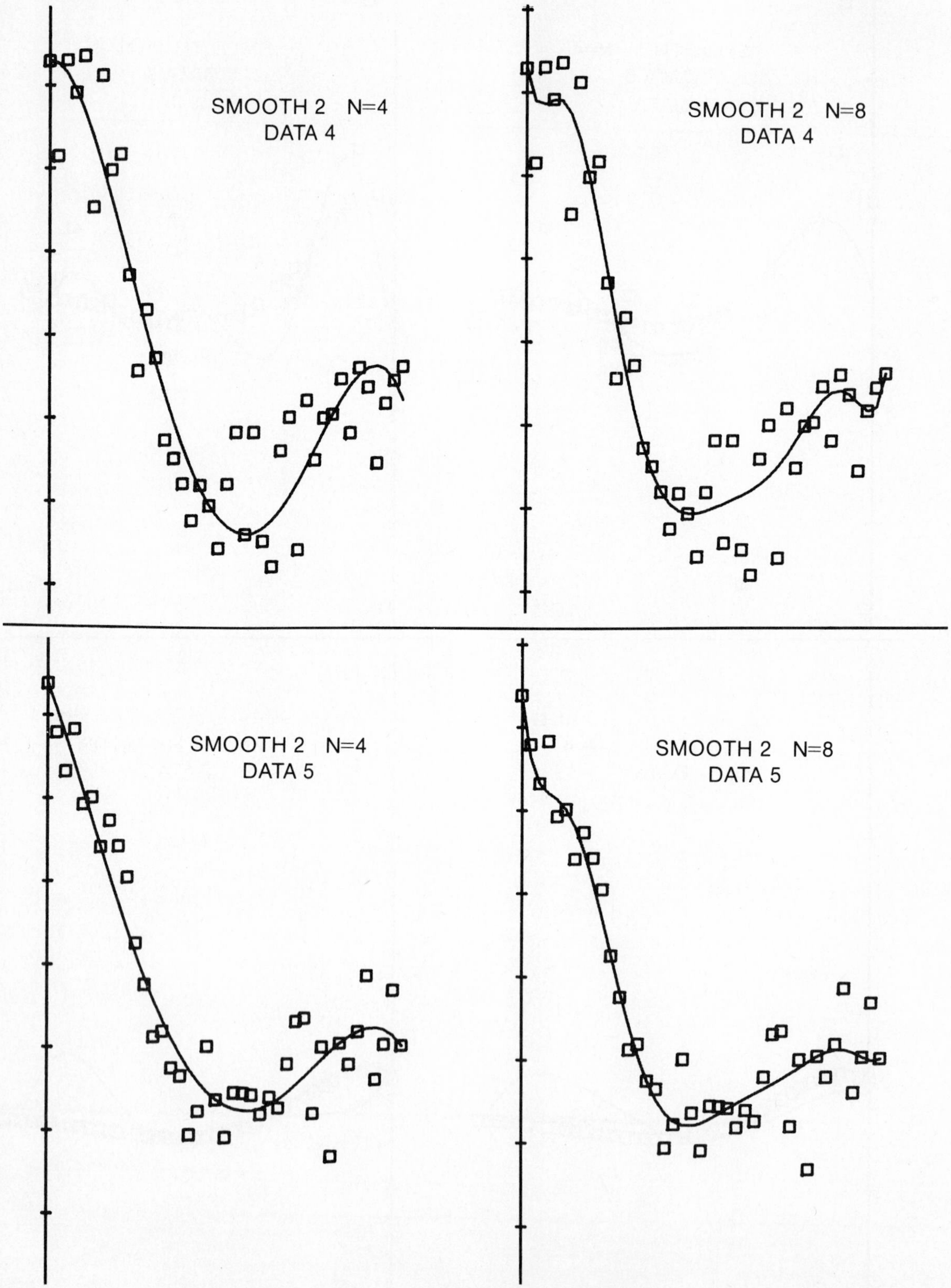

Figure 11.19 **L_1 polynomial smoothing of data sets 4 and 5.** Smoothing with polynomial models of degree 4 (left) and 8 (right) are shown. The polynomials are shown as solid lines.

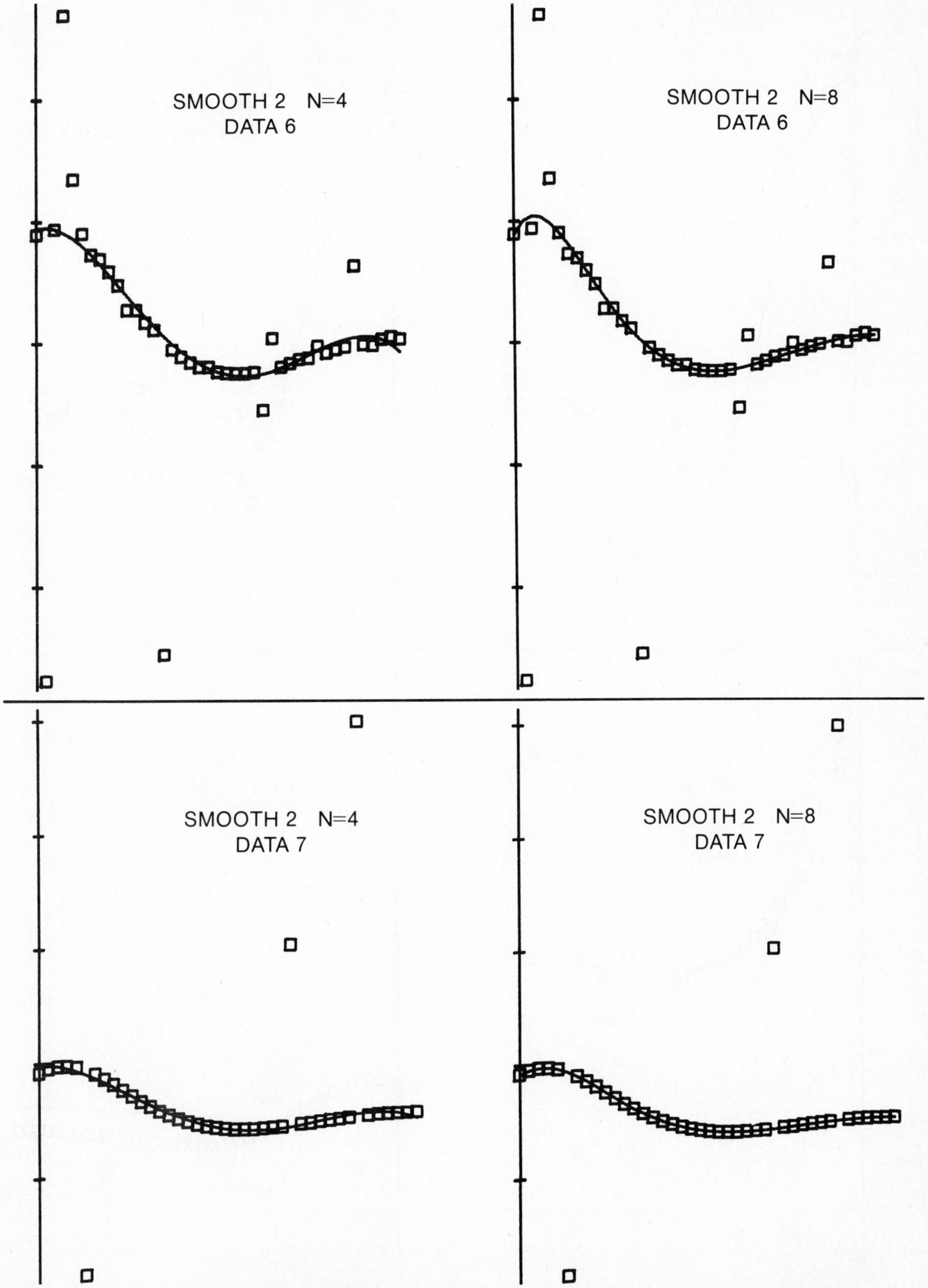

Figure 11.20 **L_1 polynomial smoothing of data sets 6 and 7.** Smoothing with polynomial models of degree 4 (left) and 8 (right) are shown. The results are much better than least-squares smoothing. The polynomials are shown as solid lines.

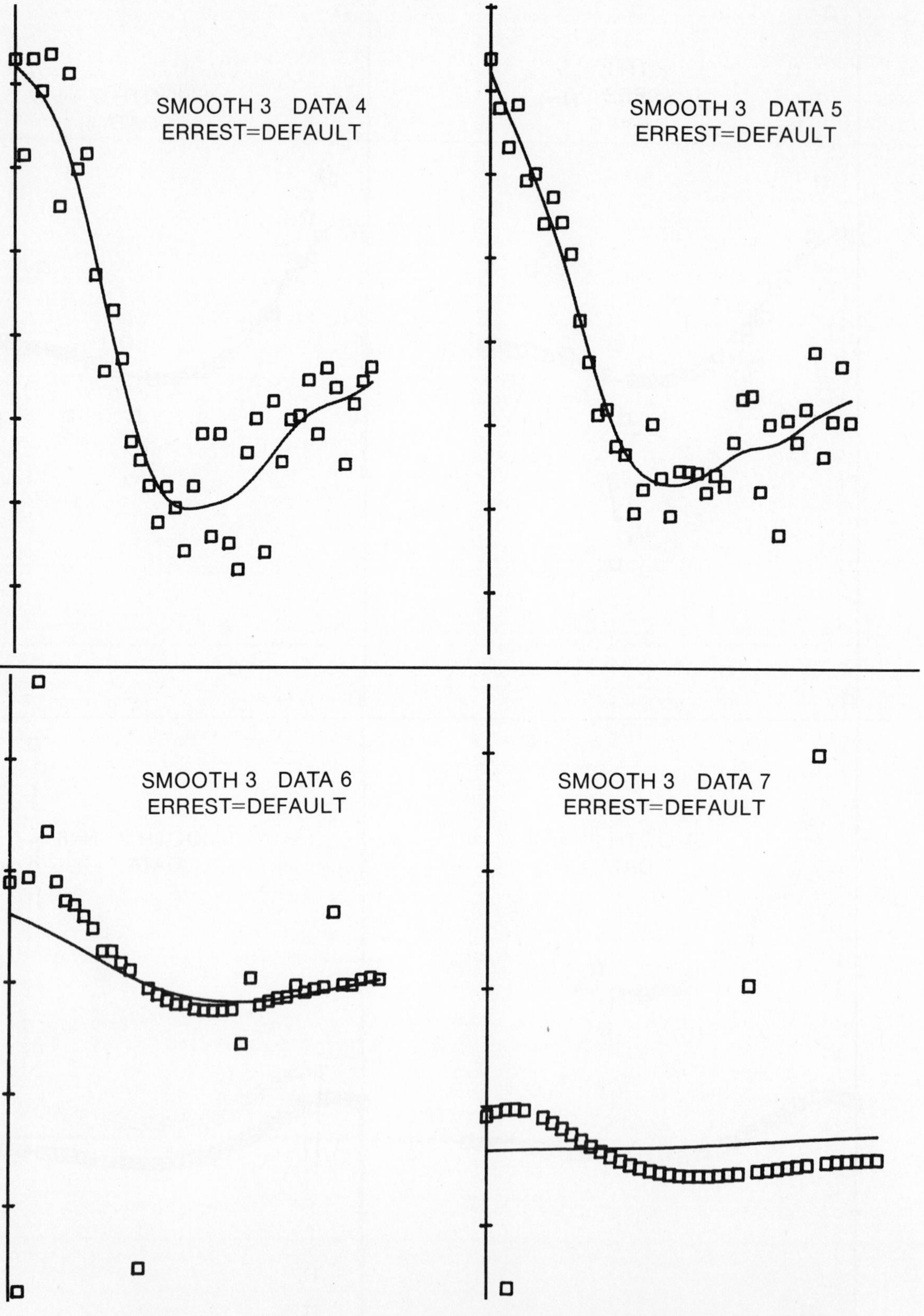

Figure 11.21 **Cubic spline, least-squares smoothing of the four data sets.** There is reasonable smoothing for data sets 4 and 5, while data set 7 is smoothed too much. The default of giving no estimate of the size of the errors is used. The cubic splines are shown as solid lines.

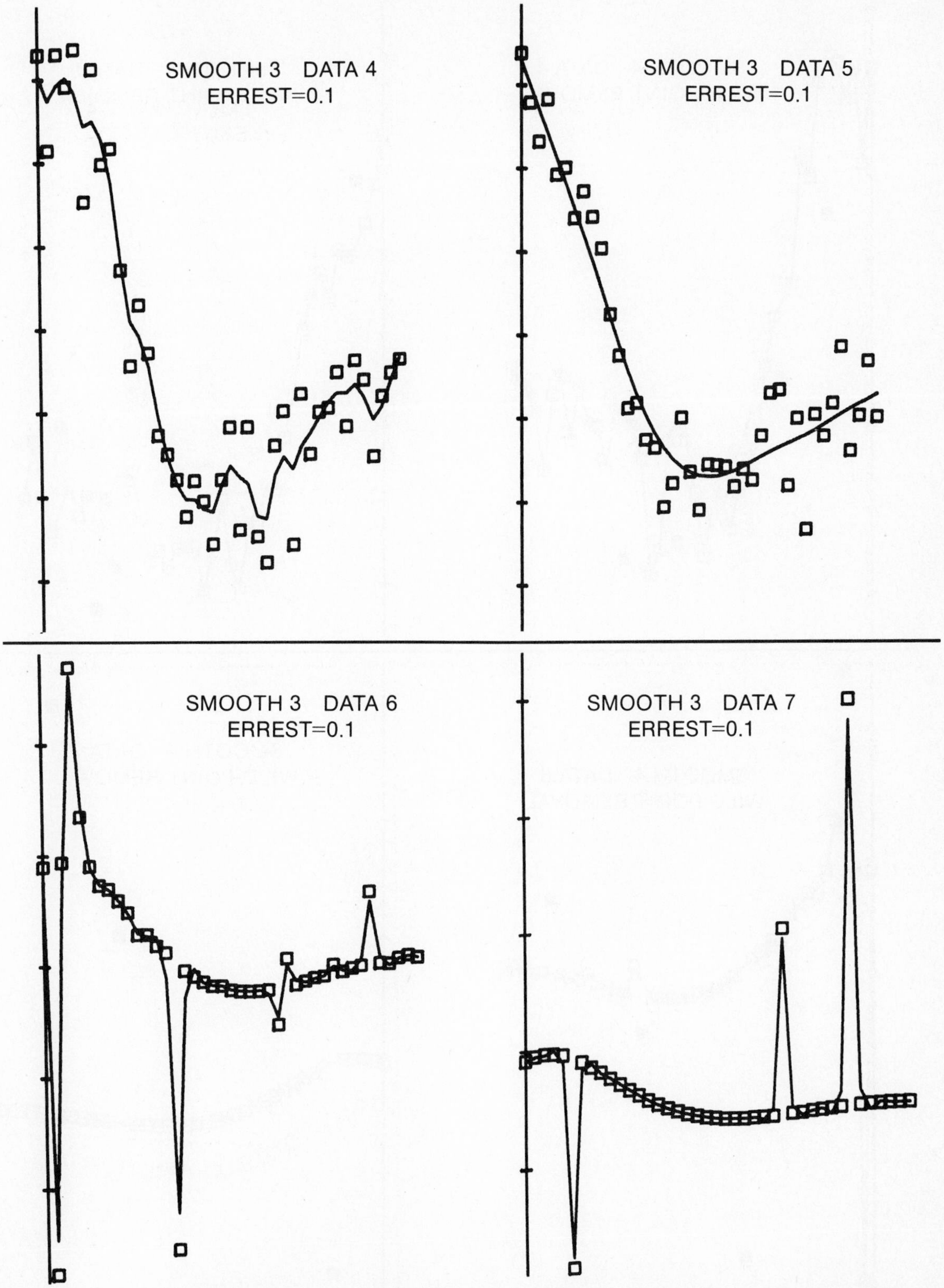

Figure 11.22 **Cubic spline, least-squares smoothing of the four data sets.** The error is estimated to have standard deviation .1. There is almost no smoothing for data sets 6 and 7. The cubic splines are shown as solid lines.

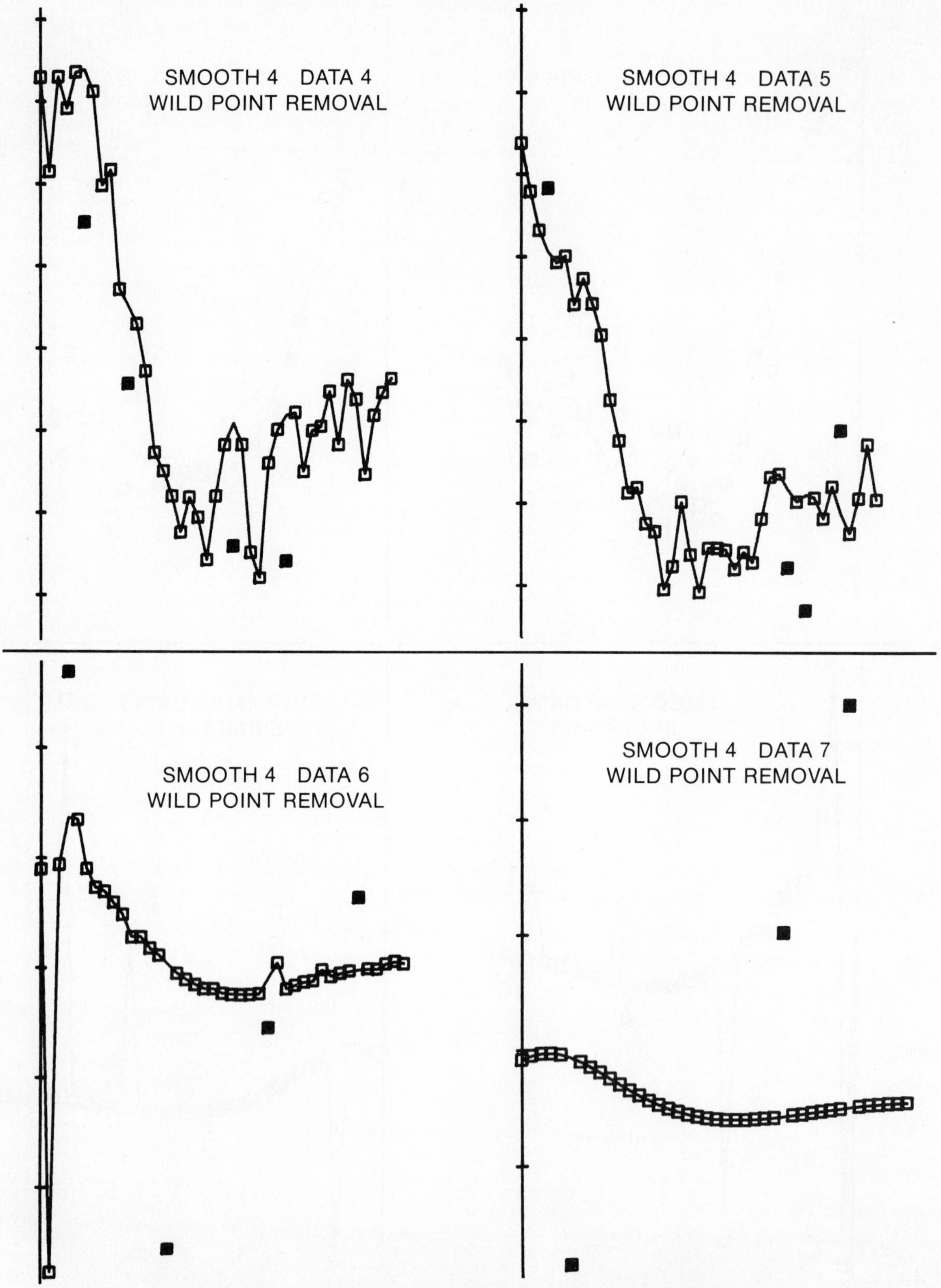

Figure 11.23 Wild point removal applied to the four data sets. The results are quite good for data sets 6 and 7 and perhaps helpful for data sets 4 and 5. The smoothed data is shown as the solid line; the points deleted as wild points are shown solid.

Providing the estimates ERREST = 0.1 gives smoothing splines which nearly interpolate **data sets 6 and 7** and provide essentially no smoothing. Increasing ERREST to .2 or .3 does not change the results much.

The final smoothing method, using the IMSL routine ICSMOU, is not intended to produce a smooth curve; its objective is to detect and replace a few **wild points** in the data and to leave the rest of the data alone. The results of applying this program to the four data sets are shown in Figure 11.23. Four iterations of wild point removal were requested, which suggests to ICSMOU that as many as four wild points are present. This method is very effective for data sets 6 and 7. ICSMOU does not remove wild points right at the ends of a data set, which explains why the wild point at the left end of data set 6 is not removed. The wild point removal has some beneficial effect for data sets 4 and 5, although it is hard to say which points are wild.

PROBLEMS 11.4 to 11.6

11.6.1 Write a Fortran subprogram that has the same input as the IMSL program IFLSQ. Use the normal equations method to solve the least-squares problem and use a library linear equation solver to solve the normal equations. Prepare two test problems to show how the program works.

11.6.2 Compare the program of Problem 11.6.1 with IFLSQ for the following basis function:

(A) $f_i(x) = x^{i-1}$

(B) $f_i(x) = \sin(ix)$

(C) $f_i(x) = [x/(1+5x^2)]^i$

(D) $f_i(x) = B(x-i)$ where $B(x) = 0$ for $|x| > 1$, $B(0) = 1$, and $B(x)$ is piecewise linear on $[-1, 1]$.

(E) $f_i = 1/(1 + x^{i-1})$

(F) $f_i(x) = e^{-(i-1)x}$

Compare the performance of the two programs on the basis of speed and accuracy. **Hint:** To compare accuracy, use the basis of part (A) or (F) and see how many basis functions the programs can handle before they fail.

11.6.3 Repeat Problem 11.6.1 using the modified Gram-Schmidt method to solve the least-squares problem. **Hint:** See Problem 11.6.5.

11.6.4 Repeat Problem 11.6.2 for the program of Problem 11.6.3.

11.6.5 Consider the **modified Gram-Schmidt** method and let x_i be the coefficients in the original basis and the y_i be the coefficients in the orthogonal vector basis.

(A) Develop an algorithm to compute the x_i from the y_i. **Hint:** Save all the dot products $\mathbf{a}_j^T \mathbf{a}_k$ of Algorithm 11.2.2 and do back substitution in a triangular system with these values as elements.

(B) Implement the algorithm of part (A) as a Fortran program. Explain how it is used in conjunction with the program of Problem 11.6.3 and prepare an example to illustrate its use.

(C) This algorithm might be numerically unstable. Devise a numerical experiment to test the stability of the program in part (B). Use at least 12 sets of vectors $\mathbf{a}_k$ of length 10, half of which are generated at random and half of which are generated to be nearly linearly dependent. Use the results to discuss the level of numerical instability that should be expected from this algorithm.

11.6.6 Prepare a subprogram that provides a **basis for spline approximations.** Let T(i) be the knots and use the truncated power representation for the splines.

(A) Use linear splines and evaluate the behavior of this basis for the data in Example 4.2. Use various values of h to test the numerical stability of the basis.

(B) Repeat part (A) for quadratic splines. Construct data analogous to that of Example 4.2 to test the numerical stability.

(C) Repeat part (A) for cubic splines. Construct data analogous to that of Example 4.2 and use it along with data from the function sin (10x) for $0 \le x \le 6$ to test the numerical stability.

11.6.7 Repeat Problem 11.6.6 using the B-spline basis for linear and quadratic splines. **Hint:** Use the function BVALUE from PPPACK or the formulas of Problems 4.3.6 and 4.3.7.

11.6.8 Compare the program of Problem 11.6.6, part (C), with the IMSL program ICSFKU. Make the performance comparison on the basis of speed and accuracy.

11.6.9 Make a **robustness test** of the library software available for least-squares approximation. Construct one set of examples that are mathematically unusual or illegal. e.g., fewer data points than basis functions, repeated basis functions, repeated x values with different y values, x points in random order, x and y values *very* large or *very* small. Construct another set that have Fortran errors or are incorrectly defined, e.g., negative number of data points or basis functions, program arguments of the wrong type, arrays declared with dimensions too small for the problem, arrays having the wrong number of dimensions, etc. Prepare a summary report that lists all the weaknesses found and give an overall evaluation of the robustness of the programs tested.

11.6.10 Consider the following table of values of the freezing point of **alcohol-water solutions** as a function of the percentage of alcohol by volume.

Alcohol in Solution, %	Freezing Point, °C	Alcohol in Solution, %	Freezing Point, °C
3.13	−1.0	27.0	−12.2
6.00	−2.0	29.5	−14.0
8.47	−3.0	32.4	−16.0
14.0	−5.0	36.1	−18.9
17.0	−6.1	40.5	−23.6
20.2	−7.5	46.3	−28.7
21.5	−8.7	53.8	−33.9
23.1	−9.4	63.6	−41.0
24.8	−10.6	78.2	−51.3

(A) Find a suitable mathematical representation of these data.

(B) Use the model of part (A) to prepare a plot of the physical relationship and a table of values for 0, 5, 10, . . ., 80 percent alcohol.

11.6.11 Consider the following table of values of the specific gravity of **phosphoric acid** as a function of the percent H_3PO_4.

H_3PO_4, %	Specific Gravity	H_3PO_4, %	Specific Gravity
0	1.0000	35	1.216
1	1.0038	40	1.254
2	1.0092	45	1.293
4	1.0200	50	1.335
6	1.0309	55	1.379
8	1.0420	60	1.426
10	1.0532	65	1.475
12	1.0647	70	1.526
14	1.0764	75	1.579
16	1.0884	80	1.633
18	1.1008	85	1.689
20	1.1134	90	1.746
22	1.1263	92	1.770
24	1.1395	94	1.794
26	1.1529	96	1.819
28	1.1665	98	1.844
30	1.1805	100	1.870

(A) Find a suitable mathematical representation of these data.

(B) Use the model of part (A) to prepare a plot of the physical relationship and a table of values for 0, 5, 10,. . ., 100 percent H_3PO_4.

11.6.12 Consider the following table of values for the solubility of **carbon monoxide** in water as a function of temperature.

Temperature of CO,°C	Solubility	Temperature CO,°C	Solubility
0	.03537	20	.02319
1	.03455	21	.02281
2	.03375	22	.02244
3	.03297	23	.02208
4	.03222	24	.02174
5	.03149	25	.02142
6	.03078	26	.02110
7	.03009	27	.02080
8	.02942	28	.02051
9	.02878	29	.02024
10	.02816	30	.01998
11	.02757	35	.01877
12	.02701	40	.01775
13	.02646	45	.01690
14	.02593	50	.01615
15	.02543	60	.01488
16	.02494	70	.01440
17	.02448	80	.01430
18	.02402	90	.01420
19	.02360	100	.01410

(A) Find a suitable mathematical representation of these data.

(B) Use the representation to prepare a plot of the physical relationship and a table of values for 0, 5, 10,. . ., 100 degrees centigrade.

11.6.13 Consider the following table of values of the viscosity of 40 percent aqueous **ethyl alcohol** solutions as a function of temperature.

Temperature of C_2H_5OH, °C	Viscosity	Temperature of C_2H_5OH, °C	Viscosity
0	7.14	45	1.289
5	5.59	50	1.132
10	4.39	55	.998
15	3.53	60	.893
20	2.91	65	.802
25	2.35	70	.727
30	2.02	75	.663
35	1.72	80	.601
40	1.482		

(A) Find a suitable mathematical representation of these data.

(B) Use the representation to prepare a plot of the physical relationship and a table of values for 0, 2, 4, 6,. . . . , 50 degrees centrigrade.

11.6.14 Consider the following table of values of the vapor pressure of **carbon tetrachloride** as a function of temperature.

Temperature of CCl_4, °C	Pressure	Temperature CCl_4, °C	Pressure
−69.7	.145	30	143.0
−65.3	.224	35	176.2
−59.6	.384	40	215.8
−56.8	.504	45	262.5
−54.8	.595	50	317.1
−50.1	.925	55	379.3
−40	2.208	60	450.8
−30	4.745	65	530.9
−20	9.708	70	622.3
−10	18.47	76.75	760
0	32.95	80	843
+10	55.97	90	1122
20	90.99	100	1463
25	114.5		

(A) Find a suitable mathematical representation of these data.

(B) Use the representation to prepare a plot of the physical relationship and a table of values for −50, −40, −30, . . . , 100 degrees centigrade.

11.6.15 Consider the following table of values of the mass of **water vapor** in saturated air as a function of temperature.

Temperature of Air, °C	Mass	Temperature of Air, °C	Mass	Temperature of Air, °C	Mass
−31.1	.302	10.0	9.401	50.0	83.05
−30.0	.341	11.1	10.08	51.1	87.44
−28.9	.378	12.2	10.81	52.2	92.06
−27.8	.421	13.3	11.59	53.3	96.87
−26.7	.469	14.4	12.40	54.4	101.8
−25.6	.524	15.6	13.27	55.6	107.1
−24.4	.584	16.7	14.19	56.7	112.5
−23.3	.648	17.8	15.17	57.8	118.2
−22.2	.719	18.9	16.20	58.9	124.1
−21.1	.796	20.0	17.30	60.0	130.2
−20.0	.883	21.1	18.45	61.1	136.7
−18.9	.977	22.2	19.69	62.2	143.4
−17.8	1.229	23.3	20.98	63.3	150.3
−16.7	1.318	24.4	22.34	64.4	157.5
−15.6	1.439	25.6	23.78	65.6	165.1

(Continued)

Temperature of Air, °C	Mass	Temperature of Air, °C	Mass	Temperature of Air, °C	Mass
−14.4	1.574	26.7	25.31	66.7	172.9
−13.3	1.698	27.8	26.91	67.8	181.1
−12.2	1.860	28.9	28.60	68.9	189.5
−11.1	2.046	30.0	30.39	70.0	198.2
−10.0	2.231	31.1	32.27	71.1	207.3
−8.9	2.439	32.2	34.23	72.2	216.8
−7.8	2.668	33.3	36.29	73.3	226.5
−6.7	2.938	34.4	38.49	74.4	236.7
−5.6	3.224	35.6	40.78	75.6	247.2
−4.4	3.517	36.7	43.21	76.7	258.1
−3.3	3.824	37.8	45.74	77.8	269.5
−2.2	4.147	38.9	48.40	78.9	281.2
−1.1	4.488	40.0	51.21	80.0	293.4
0.0	4.849	41.1	54.12	81.1	305.9
1.1	5.234	42.2	57.16	82.2	319.0
2.2	5.643	43.3	60.39	83.3	332.4
3.3	6.080	44.4	63.75	84.4	346.3
4.4	6.547	45.6	67.28	85.6	360.8
5.6	7.048	46.7	70.94	86.7	375.7
6.7	7.581	47.8	74.83	87.8	391.2
7.8	8.149	48.9	78.86	88.9	407.1
8.9	8.755			90.0	423.5
				91.1	440.5
				92.2	458.0
				93.3	476.2

(A) Find a suitable mathematical representation of these data.

(B) Use the representation to prepare a plot of the physical relationship and a table of values for −30, −25, −20, . . . , 95 degrees centigrade.

11.6.16 Consider the following table of data from a **girl's profile.**

x	Nancy	x	Nancy	x	Nancy	x	Nancy
1.50	.845	4.70	1.760	7.30	1.750	11.80	1.525
1.60	.855	4.74	1.775	7.40	1.700	11.90	1.600
1.70	.870	4.76	1.785	7.50	1.635	12.00	1.665
1.80	.895	4.80	1.815	7.60	1.550	12.20	1.805
1.90	.915	4.85	1.840	7.70	1.465	12.40	1.935
2.00	.975	4.90	1.850	7.80	1.360	12.60	2.045
2.10	1.060	4.95	1.860	7.90	1.295	12.80	2.165
2.20	1.170	5.00	1.870	8.00	1.215	13.00	2.295
2.30	1.260	5.05	1.870	8.05	1.190	13.40	2.520
2.40	1.345	5.10	1.865	8.10	1.170	13.80	2.745
2.50	1.425	5.15	1.860	8.15	1.155	14.20	2.970
2.60	1.535	5.20	1.855	8.20	1.150	14.60	3.240
2.70	1.600	5.25	1.845	8.25	1.145	15.00	3.510
2.80	1.700	5.30	1.835	8.30	1.135	15.40	3.765
2.90	1.770	5.35	1.830	8.40	1.125	15.80	4.050
3.00	1.815	5.40	1.825	8.50	1.110	16.00	4.210
3.10	1.845	5.45	1.825	8.60	1.105	16.10	4.310
3.20	1.850	5.50	1.830	8.70	1.100	16.20	4.405
3.30	1.840	5.55	1.840	8.80	1.100	16.30	4.475
3.40	1.810	5.60	1.860	8.90	1.100	16.40	4.545
3.50	1.765	5.70	1.900	9.00	1.100	16.50	4.600
3.60	1.735	5.80	1.945	9.20	1.100	16.60	4.640
3.65	1.710	5.90	1.985	9.40	1.100	16.70	4.665
3.70	1.685	6.00	2.010	9.60	1.105	16.80	4.695
3.75	1.665	6.10	2.045	9.80	1.115	16.90	4.710
3.80	1.660	6.20	2.065	10.00	1.125	17.00	4.735
3.85	1.655	6.30	2.090	10.20	1.150	17.10	4.750

(Continued)

x	Nancy	x	Nancy	x	Nancy	x	Nancy
3.90	1.655	6.35	2.095	10.40	1.165	17.20	4.755
3.95	1.660	6.40	2.100	10.60	1.185	17.30	4.760
4.00	1.670	6.45	2.095	10.80	1.205	17.40	4.760
4.10	1.700	6.50	2.090	11.00	1.235	17.60	4.765
4.20	1.745	6.60	2.080	11.10	1.255	17.80	4.760
4.30	1.760	6.70	2.065	11.20	1.270	18.00	4.750
4.35	1.765	6.80	2.040	11.30	1.290	18.20	4.745
4.40	1.765	6.90	1.980	11.40	1.310	18.40	4.740
4.50	1.770	7.00	1.920	11.50	1.335	18.60	4.745
4.60	1.760	7.10	1.870	11.60	1.385	18.80	4.745
4.65	1.755	7.20	1.810	11.70	1.450	19.00	4.760

(A) Find a mathematical representation of the data which is accurate to about 1 percent.

(B) The data given is distorted by a rotation and change of scale from the original girl's profile. Find the rotation and change of scale in the y value that produces a realistic profile and show how the representation of part (A) can be used to produce a realistic plot of the data.

11.6.17 Consider the following mathematical functions which are given with (a) a formula, (b) an interval to use, and (c) a special basis to use as a model. For each of these functions obtain least-squares approximations by polynomials, by cubic splines, and by the special basis. Compare the effectiveness of each model in terms of the number of coefficients required to obtain a 1 percent error in the approximation and the visual similarity with the function of a model with 8 percent error in the approximation.

(A) $|x - .50505|$ on $[0, 1]$, special basis $f_i(x) = |x - .5|^{(i-1)}$

(B) $\sin(2\pi x + 3.1)$ on $[0, 4]$, special basis $f_i(x) = \cos(2\pi i x)$

(C) $1/(1 + 25x^6)$ on $[-4, 4]$, special basis $f_i(x) = 1/(1 + ix^2)^{(i-1)}$

(D) $|\sin(5x - 0.1)|$ on $[-1, 3]$, special basis $f_i(x) =$ linear B-splines

(E) $1/(1 + 40x^8)$ on $[.5, 10]$, special basis $f_i(x) = x^{i-3}$

(F) $\sqrt{|x - .0001| + .000001}$ on $[0, 1]$, special basis $f_i(x) = x^{(i-1)/2}$

(G) $\sin(2x^2 + 2)$ on $[0, 5]$, special basis $f_i(x) = \sin(ix)$

Hint: Discretize the functions by choosing about 50 to 200 points in the interval. Be sure to include any "special" points in the data sets, for example, $x = .50505$ for the first one.

11.6.18 Data are specified below which are to be artificially contaminated with uniformly distributed random errors as indicated. Compute L_1 and least-squares approximations to the resulting data and compare their effectiveness in **smoothing uniform errors.** Use the model specified with the data and estimate the loss of information due to the presence of these random errors.

(A) Alcohol-water solution (Problem 11.6.10), error range ± 2.0; use model from part (A) of Problem 11.6.10.

(B) Phosphoric acid (Problem 11.6.11), error range ± 0.2; use model from part (A) of Problem 11.6.11.

(C) Carbon tetrachloride (Problem 11.6.14), error range ± 4; use model of part (A) of Problem 11.6.14.

(D) Same as part (C) except error range is ± 4 percent relative.

Hint: Carry out the computations using software as in the case study of Section 11.6. If the model originally obtained for the data cannot be used with the programs RLLAV (which is unlikely), then obtain another good model.

11.6.19 Repeat Problem 11.6.18 with normally distributed errors instead of uniform errors. Let the errors have mean zero and variance equal to the range specified in Problem 11.6.18.

11.6.20 Repeat Problem 11.6.18 with errors e computed as $10^{-5}/u^4$ where u is a random variable uniformly distributed in $[-1, +1]$. Multiply each error e by the range given in the problem.

11.6.21 Apply the IMSL program ICSMOU to the data of Problem 11.6.20 and discuss its effectiveness in removing large errors (wild points) from the data.

APPROXIMATION OF MATHEMATICAL FUNCTIONS **11.7

There is a very large number of standard mathematical functions used in scientific computing which must be approximated by polynomials, piecewise polynomials, or rational functions in order to be evaluated. These range from sine, cosine, and logarithm through hyperbolic functions, the Gamma function to specialized functions like the parabolic cylinder functions, the Fermi-Dirac functions, the hypergeometric functions, etc. We do not discuss this topic in detail here because the really good approximations depend on exploiting the special properties of the functions. This means that one should consider each of these functions in considerable depth and review their mathematical behavior in detail.

The practicing scientist hopes, of course, that the software library has programs for these functions. There are just over 100 ACM Algorithms for such functions, and the index to the Collected Algorithms of the ACM references at least another 100 algorithms that have appeared in other journals. The IMSL library has 49 programs in Chapter M for mathematical functions. There is also FUNPACK mentioned in Section 2.3.C, a high-quality set of machine language programs tuned for the major scientific computers.

We briefly describe five books that are sources for the background theory and techniques for approximating and evaluating mathematical functions. Some of these books also contain extensive sets of coefficients of approximations for specific functions.

Handbook of Mathematical Functions with Formulas, Graphs, and Mathematical Tables, National Bureau of Standards, Applied Mathematics Series 55 U.S. Government Printing Office, Washington, D.C. (1964), 1,043 pages. This standard reference work prepared by 28 authors contains a massive amount of information. Over 200,000 copies have been printed, and it is the starting point for information about the standard mathematical functions.

Mathematical Functions and Their Approximations, by Yudell L. Luke, Academic Press, New York (1975), 568 pages. This work can be viewed as an updated supplement of the previous book for a large group of the mathematical functions: Gamma, Binomial, elementary, hypergeometric, Bessel, and many related functions. Tables of coefficients of many approximations are given. The mathematical level of the text is advanced.

Computer Approximations, by J. F. Hart, E. W. Cheney, C. L. Lawson, H. J. Maehly, C. K. Mesztenyi, J. R. Rice, H. C. Thacher, and C. Witzgall, John Wiley, New York (1968), reprinted and corrected, Robert E. Krieger Pub. Co., Huntington, New York (1978), 343 pages. This book has four chapters on the general techniques and background for designing mathematical function routines; these are at a moderate mathematical level. There are then two chapters which discuss in considerable detail the following functions: square root, cube root, exponential, hyperbolic, logarithmic, trigonometric, inverse trigonometric, Gamma, error, Bessel, and complete elliptic integrals. These are followed by 150 pages of tables of coefficients of Chebyshev approximations by polynomials and rational functions. These approximations give accuracies from low up to about 25 digits.

Computer Evaluation of Mathematical Functions, by C. T. Fike, Prentice-Hall, Inc., Englewood Cliffs, N.J. (1968), 227 pages. This is a text that covers somewhat the same material as the first four chapters of *Computer Approximations* in a more leisurely way. The mathematics is at the level of a college senior. Very few actual approximations are given.

Software Manual for the Elementary Functions, by William J. Cody and William Waite, Prentice-Hall, Inc., Englewood Cliffs, N.J. (1980), 269 pages. This book presents a detailed analysis of preparing, testing, and verifying software for the following functions (in Fortran notation): SQRT, ALOG, ALOG10, EXP, **(power), SIN, COS, TAN, COT, ASIN, ACOS, ATAN, ATAN2, SINH, COSH, and TANH. An elaborate set of software has been developed to verify the implementations of these functions; this software is available for a nominal fee from IMSL, Inc., NBC Building, 7500 Bellaire Blvd., Houston, Texas 77036, or National Energy Software Center, Argonne National Laboratory, 9700 Cass Ave., Argonne, Illinois 60439.

ORTHOGONAL POLYNOMIALS **11.8

Recall the discussion from Section 11.2 where we consider approximating sin (t) by polynomials. Replace sin (t) by g(t) and the powers t^{i-1} by basis functions $f_i(t)$, and the least-squares problem becomes

$$\int_a^b r(t)^2 dt = \int_a^b [y(t) - F(\mathbf{a}, t)]^2 dt = \text{minimum}$$

We apply the calculus as in 11.2 to obtain the **normal equations**

$$\frac{\partial}{\partial a_k} \int_a^b [g(t) - F(\mathbf{a}, t)]^2 dt = 2\int_a^b [g(t) - F(\mathbf{a}, t)] f_k(t) dt = 0$$

or, exactly analogous to Equation 11.2.5,

$$\int_a^b F(\mathbf{a}, t) f_k(t) dt = \sum_{i=1}^{m} a_i \int_a^b f_i(t) f_k(t) dt = \int_a^b g(t) f_k(t) \qquad k = 1, 2, \ldots, n$$

Equation 11.8.1

The functions $f_i(t)$ are said to be **orthogonal functions** on [a, b] if

$$\int_a^b f_i(t) f_k(t) dt = 0 \qquad \text{if } i \neq k$$

Equation 11.8.2

or, with a positive weight function w(t),

$$\int_a^b f_i(t) f_k(t) w(t) dt = 0 \qquad \text{if } i \neq k$$

If the integral of $f_i(t)^2 w(t)$ is 1, then the functions are called **orthonormal.** The advantage of orthogonal functions is that the coefficient matrix in 11.8.1 is then diagonal, and the least-squares problem is trivially solved; if the $f_i(x)$ are orthonormal, the best coefficients are

$$a_k = \int_a^b g(t) f_k(t) w(t) dt$$

Equation 11.8.3

Recall that the objective of Gram-Schmidt orthogonalization is to produce orthogonal vectors so that the normal equations can be solved by Equation 11.2.6 which is analogous to 11.8.3.

We introduce the notation

$$\mathbf{g}^T\mathbf{f} = \int_a^b g(t) f(t) w(t) dt$$

Equation 11.8.4

because this integral plays a role here just like the dot product for vectors. If we interpret 11.8.4 as the dot product of the functions g(t) and f(t), then the development of least-squares approximation for functions exactly parallels that for vectors. Simple examples of orthogonal functions are sines and cosines; we have

$$\int_0^\pi \sin(it)\sin(kt) dt = 0 \qquad \text{if } i \neq k$$

$$\int_0^\pi \cos(it)\cos(kt) dt = 0 \qquad \text{if } i \neq k$$

We note that all the material in this section can be carried through with the integral replaced by a sum on a fixed set of points.

We limit our attention now to a **sequence of orthogonal polynomials** $p_0(t), p_1(t), \ldots, p_k(t), \ldots$ where $p_k(t)$ is of exact degree k and $\mathbf{p}_i^T\mathbf{p}_k = 0$ for $i \neq k$. It is easy to see that 1, t, and $3t^2 - 1$ are orthogonal on [−1, +1], for example,

$$\int_{-1}^{1} 1*(3t^2-1)dt = t^3 - t|_{-1}^{1} = 0$$

Some basic properties of orthogonal polynomials are given by Theorem 11.1.

Theorem 11.1 *Let $p_k(t)$ be a sequence of orthogonal polynomials on [a, b] and let $q(t)$ be an arbitrary polynomial of degree m. Then we have*

(A) *$q(t)$ may be uniquely represented with the $p_k(t)$ as basis functions by*

$$q(t) = b_0p_0(t) + b_1p_1(t) + \ldots + b_mp_m(t) \qquad \textbf{Equation 11.8.5}$$

(B) *$q(t)$ is orthogonal to all $p_k(t)$ with $k > m$, that is, $\mathbf{q}^T\mathbf{p}_k = 0$*

(C) *$p_k(t)$ has k simple zeros in the interval [a, b]*

(D) *There are coefficients A_k, B_k, and C_k so that*

$$p_{k+1}(t) = (A_kt-B_k)p_k(t) - C_kp_{k-1}(t) \qquad \textbf{Equation 11.8.6}$$

Proof: For part (A), let c and d be the coefficients of t^m in $q(t)$ and $p_m(t)$. Then $r(t) = q(t) - (c/d)\,p_m(t)$ is a polynomial of degree $m-1$. One can use an induction argument to show that if $r(t)$ is represented by $p_i(t)$ with $i \le m-1$, then $q(t)$ is represented by 11.8.5 with coefficient $b_m = c/d$.

For part (B), compute $\mathbf{q}^T\mathbf{p}_k$ from 11.8.5 and note that $b_i\mathbf{p}_i^T\mathbf{p}_k = 0$ for all the i since i is less than k.

For part (C), assume that $p_k(t)$ changes sign at $z_1, z_2, \ldots, z_j$ in [a, b]. Consider the polynomial of degree j

$$r(t) = (t-z_1)(t-z_2)\ldots(t-z_j)$$

and note that $r(t)*p_k(t)$ is positive throughout the interval [a, b] and thus $\mathbf{r}^T\mathbf{p}_k \neq 0$. Therefore, $j \ge k$ because $p_k(t)$ is orthogonal to all polynomials of degree less than j. On the other hand, $p_k(t)$ cannot have more than k zeros (and hence sign changes) anywhere because it is a polynomial of degree k, that is, $j \le k$. We conclude $j = k$.

For part (D) we make a direct construction. Define $p_{-1}(t) = 0$ and set $S_k = \mathbf{p}_k{}^T\mathbf{p}_k$, α_k = coefficient of t^k in $p_k(t)$,

$$A_k = \alpha_{k+1}/\alpha_k \qquad \textbf{Equation 11.8.7}$$

$$B_k = \frac{A_k}{S_k}\int_a^b tp_k{}^2(t)w(t)dt$$

$$C_k = \frac{A_k}{S_{k-1}}\int_a^b tp_k(t)p_{k-1}(t)w(t)dt \qquad \text{for } k \ge 1$$

The definition of A_k makes the coefficient of t^{k+1} correct. We now show that the polynomial $p_{k+1}(t)$ defined by 11.8.6 is orthogonal to $p_j(t)$ for all $j < k$. We multiply 11.8.6 by $w(t)p_k(t)$ and integrate from a to b to obtain

$$\mathbf{p}_{k+1}{}^T\mathbf{p}_k = A_k\int_a^b tp_k{}^2(t)w(t)dt - B_k\mathbf{p}_k{}^T\mathbf{p}_k - C_k\mathbf{p}_k{}^T\mathbf{p}_{k-1}$$

The last term is zero by orthogonality, and the first two cancel by the definition of B_k. Multiply 11.8.6 by $w(t)p_{k-1}(t)$ and integrate from a to b to obtain

$$\mathbf{p}_{k+1}{}^T\mathbf{p}_{k-1} = A_k\int_a^b tp_k(t)p_{k-1}(t)w(t)dt - B_k\mathbf{p}_k{}^T\mathbf{p}_{k-1} - C_k\mathbf{p}_{k-1}{}^T\mathbf{p}_{k-1}$$

The middle term is zero by orthogonality, and the other two cancel by the definition of C_k. If one multiplies 11.8.6 by $w(t)p_j(t)$ for $j < k-1$ and integrates from a to b, one sees that each of the resulting terms is zero. This concludes the proof.

Equation 11.8.6 of Theorem 11.1 is called the **three-term recurrence** and has two important applications. First, suppose the coefficients A_k, B_k, C_k are known. Then given a value for t, one can evaluate

$p_i(t)$ from 11.8.6. Less obvious, but equally important, is that these coefficients can be used to evaluate a combination of orthogonal polynomials. Suppose

$$q(t) = a_0p_0(t) + a_1p_1(t) + \ldots + a_np_n(t)$$

then to evaluate $q(x)$ we have **nested multiplication for orthogonal polynomials.** Given the three-term recurrence coefficients A_i, B_i, and C_i, a value x, and the polynomial $q(t) = a_0p_0(t) + a_1p_1(t) + \ldots + a_np_n(t)$, then the value of $q(x)$ is computed by

Nested Multiplication for Orthogonal Polynomials

Algorithm 11.8.1

$b_n = a_n$
$b_{n-1} = a_{n-1} + b_n(A_{n-1}x - b_{n-1})$
For $i = n-1, n-2, \ldots, 0$ do
  $b_i = a_i + b_{i+1}(A_ix - B_i) - b_{i+2}C_{i+1}$
Then $q(x) = b_0$

This algorithm is very similar to Algorithm 4.1.1 for the Newton form of polynomials. It requires about 3n additions and multiplications to evaluate $q(x)$ compared to 2n additions and n multiplications for the Newton form. See Problem 11.8.12 for a hint on how to establish this algorithm. This algorithm is especially efficient for the Chebyshev polynomials (see Problem 11.8.2) which have $A_0 = 1$, $A_i = 2$ for $i > 0$, $B_i = 0$, and $C_i = 1$ so that the algorithm only requires 2n additions and n multiplications.

The second use of the three-term recurrence is to define and construct the orthogonal polynomials for a given interval [a, b] and weight function $w(x)$. The coefficients A_i, B_i, and C_i can be computed by the formulas of Equation 11.8.7. Once $p_k(t)$ is known, then the coefficients are computed and $p_{k+1}(t)$ is constructed. This approach is particularly easy when the integration in the orthogonality is replaced by summation, and it is widely used in software for least-squares polynomial approximation.

Several standard systems of orthogonal polynomials are given in Problems 11.8.1 to 11.8.4 and 11.8.11.

The next result shows how the Gauss quadrature rules of Chapter 7 are related to orthogonal polynomials. Recall that a Gauss rule is

$$\int_a^b f(t)w(t)dt \sim \sum_{i=0}^{n} w_if(t_i) \qquad \textbf{Equation 11.8.8}$$

where the w_i and t_i are chosen to make this formula exact for polynomials of degree $2n-1$. We have

Theorem 11.2 *The abscissas t_i of the Gauss rule 11.8.8 are the zeros of the orthogonal polynomial $p_{n+1}(t)$ for the interval [a, b] and the weight function $w(t)$.*

Proof: Suppose $f(t)$ in 11.8.8 is the polynomial $q(t)$ of degree $m \leq 2n-1$. Whatever the t_i are, we know that there are w_i which make 11.8.8 exact for polynomials of degree n or less; we assume those w_i are chosen. Now assume $m > n$, as the rule is exact for $m \leq n$ just by the choice of the weights w_i. Write $q(t) = r(t) + s(t)\,(t-t_0)\,(t-t_1)\,\ldots\,(t-t_n)$ where $r(t)$ is a polynomial of degree $n-1$ and $s(t)$ is a polynomial of degree $m-n$. We have then

$$\int_a^b q(t)w(t)dt = \int_a^b r(t)w(t)dt + \int_a^b s(t) \prod_{i=0}^{n} (t-t_i)w(t)dt$$

$$\sum_{i=0}^{n} w_iq(t_i) = \sum_{i=0}^{n} w_ir(t_i) + \sum_{i=0}^{n} w_is(t_i)*0 = \sum_{i=0}^{n} w_ir(t_i)$$

The sum of the $w_ir(t_i)$ equals the integral $r(t)w(t)$ by the choice of the weights w_i. We see that $(t-t_0)(t-t_1)\ldots(t-t_n) = cp_n(t)$. Thus the integral with $s(t)$ is

$$c\int_a^b s(t)p_n(t)w(t)dt$$

and it is zero because of the orthogonality $\mathbf{s}^T\mathbf{p}_n = 0$ [part (B) of Theorem 11.1] as the degree of s(t) is $m-n \le n-1$. This concludes the proof.

PROBLEMS 11.8

11.8.1 The **Legendre polynomials** $P_k(t)$ are orthogonal on $[-1, 1]$ with $w(t) = 1$ and normalized by $P_k(1) = 1$. Establish the following facts about this system of orthogonal polynomials. The square bracket in the sum denotes the integer part.

(A) $\mathbf{P}_k{}^T\mathbf{P}_k = 2/(2k+1)$

(B) $A_k = (2k+1)/(k+1)$, $B_k = 0$, $C_k = k/(k+1)$

(C) $2^kP_k(t) = \sum_{j=0}^{[k/2]} (-1)^j \binom{k}{j}\binom{2k-2j}{k} t^{2k-2j}$

$P_0(t) = 1$ $\quad P_1(t) = t$
$P_2(t) = (3t^2-1)/2$ $\quad P_3(t) = (5t^3-3t)/2$
$P_4(t) = (35t^4-30t^2+3)/8$ $\quad P_5(t) = (63t^5-70t^3+15t)/8$

11.8.2 The **Chebyshev polynomials** $T_k(t)$ are orthogonal on $[-1, 1]$ with $w(t) = 1/\sqrt{1-t^2}$ and normalized by $T_k(1) = 1$. Establish the following facts about them:

(A) $\mathbf{T}_k{}^T\mathbf{T}_k = \pi/2$ (for $k > 0$) or π (for $k = 0$)

(B) $A_k = 2$ (for $k > 0$) or 1 (for $k = 0$), $B_k = 0$, $C_k = 1$

(C) $T_k(t) = \frac{k}{2}\sum_{j=0}^{[k/2]} \frac{(-1)^j(k-j-1)!(2t)^{k-2j}}{j!(k-2j)!}$

$T_0(t) = 1$ $\quad T_1(t) = t$
$T_2(t) = 2t^2-1$ $\quad T_3(t) = 4t^3-3t$
$T_4(t) = 8t^4-8t+1$ $\quad T_5(t) = 16t^5-20t^3+5t$

11.8.3 The **Laguerre polynomials** $L_k^\alpha(t)$ are orthogonal on $[0, \infty]$ with $w(t) = t^\alpha e^{-t}$ and normalized by (A) below. Establish the following facts about them [$\Gamma(t)$ denotes the Gamma function].

(A) $\mathbf{L}_k^{\alpha T}\mathbf{L}_k^\alpha = \Gamma(\alpha+k+1)/k!$

(B) $A_k = -1/(k+1)$, $B_k = (2k+\alpha+1)$, $C_k = (k+\alpha)/(k+1)$

(C) $L_k^\alpha(t) = \sum_{j=0}^{k} \binom{k+\alpha}{k-j}\frac{(-t)^j}{j!}$

$L_0^0(t) = 1$ $\quad L_1^0(t) = (-t+1)$
$L_2^0(t) = (t^2-4t+2)/2$ $\quad L_3^0(t) = (-t^3+9t^2-18t+6)/6$
$L_4^0(t) = (t^4-16t^3+72t^2-96t+24)/24$

11.8.4 The **Hermite polynomials** $H_k(t)$ are orthogonal on $[-\infty, \infty]$ with $w(t) = e^{-t^2}$ and normalized by (A) below. Establish the following facts about them:

(A) $\mathbf{H}_k{}^T\mathbf{H}_k = \sqrt{\pi}\, 2^k k!$

(B) $A_k = 2$, $B_k = 0$, $C_k = 2k$

(C) $H_k(t) = k!\sum_{j=0}^{[k/2]} \frac{(-1)^j(2t)^{k-2j}}{j!(k-2j)!}$

$H_0(t) = 1$ $\quad H_1(t) = 2t$
$H_2(t) = 4t^2-2$ $\quad H_3(t) = 8t^3-12t$
$H_4(t) = 16t^4-48t^2+12$ $\quad H_5(t) = 32t^5-160t^3+120t$

11.8.5 Write the following polynomials in terms of Legendre polynomials:

(A) $x^3 - x^2 + x - 1$

(B) $3x^4 - 4x^3 + 5x^2 + 6x - 1$

(C) $4x^5 - 5x^4 - 3x^2 + 7x + 7$

(D) $6x^6 - 4x^4 + 3x^3 - x^2 + x - 12$

11.8.6 Repeat Problem 11.8.5 for Chebyshev polynomials.

11.8.7 Repeat Problem 11.8.5 for Laguerre polynomials.

11.8.8 Repeat Problem 11.8.8 for Hermite polynomials.

11.8.9 Establish the nested multiplication algorithm for orthogonal polynomials. **Hint:** In the sum $b_ip_i(t)$, substitute for $p_m(t)$ by the three-term recurrence relation and proceed by induction, reducing the degree one each time.

11.8.10 Evaluate the following polynomials using nested multiplication (see Algorithm 11.8.1) for orthogonal polynomials.

(A) $3T_4(x) - 4T_2(x) + 6.1T_1(x) + T_0(x)$ for $x = 0.5$

(B) $7P_7(x) - P_6(x) + 5P_4(x) - 12P_2(x) + P_1(x) + 12P_0(x)$ for $x = 0.8$

(C) $H_5(x) - 6H_4(x) + 2H_3(x) - H_2(x) + H_1(x) + 10H_0(x)$ for $x = -2$

(D) $L_5^1(x) - 10L_4^1(x) - 8L_3^1(x) + 2L_2^1(x) - L_1^1(x)$ for $x = 6$

(E) $T_{10}(x) - T_8(x) + 6T_6(x) + 4T_4(x) - T_1(x)$ for $x = 0.1$

11.8.11 The **discrete Chebyshev polynomials** $t_{k,N}(x)$ are orthogonal by summation on the point set $-N, -N+1, \ldots, 0, \ldots, N\text{-}1, N$ with $w(x) = 1$. Verify that they are given explicitly by

$$t_{k,N}(j) = \sum_{i=0}^{k} (-1)^{i+N} \frac{(N+i)!(k+j)!(2N-i)!}{(i!)^2(N-1)!(k+j-i)!(2k)!}$$

11.8.12 Let $x_i = i\pi/N$ for $i = -N+1$ to N. Verify that the **trigonometric polynomials** (sines and cosines) of order N or less are orthogonal by summation over the x_i with $w(x) = 1$.

11.8.13 Let r(t) be the error (residual) of the best least-squares approximation to f(t) by orthogonal polynomials $p_i(t)$. Show that $\mathbf{r}^T\mathbf{p}_i = 0$ for all i.

11.8.14 Establish that **Gauss quadrature formulas are positive,** that is, if

$$Q_f = \sum_{i=1}^{n} w_i f(x_i)$$

is a Gauss quadrature formula, then $w_i > 0$. **Hint:** Let $\ell_j(x)$ be the Lagrange basis polynomial for the jth point among the n abscissa x_i and show that w_j is the integral of $\ell_j^2(x)$.

REFERENCES

M. Abramowitz and I. A. Stegun (eds.), *Handbook of Mathematical Functions,* National Bureau of Standards, Appl. Math. Ser. No. 55, U.S. Government Printing Office (1964).

John M. Chambers, *Computational Methods for Data Analysis,* John Wiley, New York (1977).

W. J. Cody and W. Waite, *Software Manual for the Elementary Functions,* Prentice-Hall, Inc., Englewood Cliffs, N.J. (1981). The programs in this book are available from IMSL.

Walter Gautschi, "Computational Methods in Special Functions," in *Theory and Applications of Special Functions* (R. Askey, ed.) Academic Press, New York (1975), pp. 1–98.

J. F. Hart et al., *Computer Approximations,* John Wiley, New York (1968); reprinted by Robert E. Krieger Pub. Co., Huntington, New York (1978).

Charles L. Lawson and Richard J. Hanson, *Solving Least Squares Problems,* Prentice-Hall, Inc., Englewood Cliffs, N.J. (1978).

L. L. Schumaker, "Fitting Surfaces to Scattered Data," in *Approximation Theory III* (Lorentz et al., eds.) Academic Press, New York (1976), pp. 203–268.

*12 SOFTWARE PRACTICE, COSTS, AND ENGINEERING

Programming and software development are activities which many people enter gradually, without any conscious decision to do so. The programs are just adjuncts to another activity. For example, one might be studying the chemical reactions inside a blast furnace for a steel mill. This study evolves into a model for a typical blast furnace, and the model is implemented as a computer program. The capabilities of the program are enhanced to handle a variety of features of real blast furnaces. The model is so successful that it becomes the basis for a computer program to do real-time simulations and production control of blast furnaces. The person who started out writing a 100-line Fortran program for some little problem becomes in charge of a project that includes a program with 20,000 to 50,000 lines of code.

If no conscious decision is made to become heavily involved in computing and programming, it is likely that no systematic thought or study is given to programming as a separate activity. The purpose of this chapter is to provide a brief overview of software practice and engineering. This field is still very young and very dynamic; new ideas are constantly being put forward and then attacked as useless — or worse. In spite of this, there are a number of well-identified facts and principles which everyone with a substantial involvement in software (either direct or indirect) should know; some of these are presented here.

Perhaps the most important thing is to realize that programming is a high-level intellectual activity. There are large differences in the productivity of programmers, there are many skills to be learned, and a certain special talent is required. Some people believe they have learned to program once they have made a few small programs work. One should compare this with learning to play golf. It only takes a few hours to explain the rules of golf and to illustrate the basic techniques of the golf swing. Novices are then able to play golf in the sense that they are eventually able to get the ball in each of the holes. It is a great mistake for them to think that they are real golfers just because they have been around the course a few times.

SOFTWARE TYPES AND LIFE CYCLES 12.1

We classify software in three ways: by size, by lifetime, and by number of users. The sizes for software are:

Small. The code is within the complete grasp of a single person; one can become familiar with all its details. Small programs are usually a few hundred lines of code, but many programmers can grasp a program of more than 5,000 lines of code (over 100 pages).

Medium. The code is within the complete grasp of a small group of people, and each of them can be familiar with all its main functions and much of its detail. Such software may range from a few thousands lines to perhaps as many as 50,000 lines.

Large No one person is familiar with all the functions of the software; for any given person involved with it, there are large segments that have never been seen, whose operation has never been considered, by that person. Such software may range from perhaps 20,000 lines to several hundred thousand, even millions, of lines.

In this text, we are primarily concerned with small programs, but one must realize that large software is made from small and medium software. One of the difficulties in constructing large software systems is that some software engineering techniques do not scale up from small to large software as one expects.

Many programs have a short lifetime. They are written, debugged, and run just a few times before being discarded. We call such software **one-shot** or **disposable programs. Permanent programs** have a longer lifetime; they may be **production programs** which are used many times without change. Or they may be **modeling programs** which are frequently changed and used over a long period of time. For example, the program might model automobile tires in many ways and be a basic tool in the design of tires and equipment to make tires. Each time a new design is explored, the modeling program is changed. The key factor is that production and modeling programs are used by people unfamiliar with much of the detail. Much of the medium software and most of the large software are both production and modeling software. The payroll program for a company is used every week or month, and it is also changed from time to time as the tax laws, the company's benefit programs, and the accounting procedures change.

If only a few people use a program, then one might decide that many user conveniences and facilities are not necessary. When a problem arises, it might be feasible to contact the originator or the "current expert" for guidance. If many people use a program, then not all of them will have access to an expert and one must plan for the program to be used by someone with no knowledge of how it works and with only the written documentation as a guide. In some cases, there will be people who want to make changes in the program who have no contact with experts. Thus, programs with many users should have certain qualities which are unnecessary or optional for programs with a few users.

A student usually is involved only with small, one-shot, single-user programs during his or her education. A large portion of the "real-world" programming is for large, permanent software with many users. The life cycle of the student program is fairly simple: a little thought is given to how the program is to work, the code is written, a crash effort is made to debut it (the assignment due date is generally very close to when the effort starts), a run is made, and the program is submitted for grading and then discarded.

The life cycle of larger software is more complicated. Figure 12.1 gives a pie-chart breakdown of the total activity for large software systems. The first pie chart includes maintenance over the entire life cycle of the system, while the other three charts exclude maintenance. The principal stages of a large software project are as follows:

Specification. The general functional requirements of the system are analyzed and transformed into a concrete set of specifications for the software. The input and output are defined precisely.

Design. The overall structure of the system is developed with specific choices of formats, files, data representations, etc. Algorithms are identified for implementation. The detail at this stage can go down to flowcharts for each program planned for the system.

Coding. The first code is written for the programs, and preliminary debugging is done. This is usually the least troublesome of the activities.

Testing. The obvious program errors are removed in the coding stage, and the programs are now tested to see if they perform according to the specifications and design.

Integration. The various programs are put together to build the whole system, and it is tested for performance and correctness.

Documentation. This activity is actually part of each of the others. At each stage one must have reports that describe the specifications, design, and implementation of the software. Some of the documentation is for the team that is building the software, some is for programmers who will maintain it later, and some is for its users.

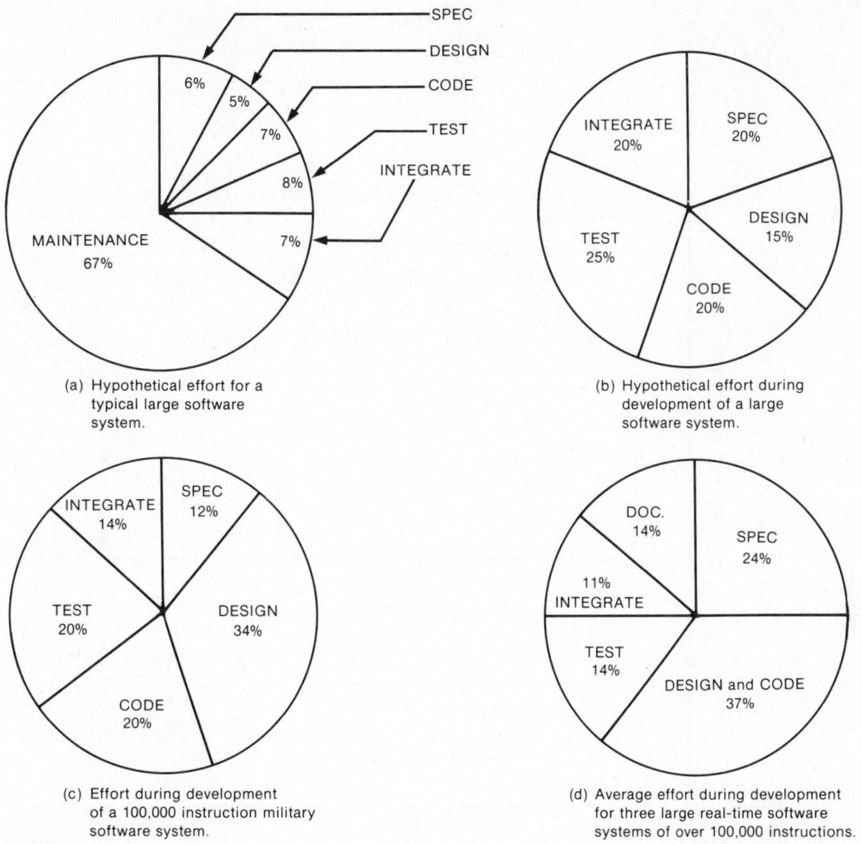

Figure 12.1 **Effort required on various activities of large-scale software development.** Chart (a) includes all costs of a software system. Charts (b), (c), and (d) exclude maintenance costs. The efforts are measured in dollars spent.

Maintenance. This involves changing the software as the requirements evolve and as errors in the design and implementation are found.

It seems incredible that 67 percent of the cost for a software system is in maintenance, but this percentage is realistic for a large, long-lived system. For example, the maintenance cost of the system in pie chart (c) of Figure 12.1 reached 40 percent after 5 years and was estimated at that time to eventually reach 60 percent. It is not uncommon for some parts of a large system to be rewritten three or four times.

The level of activity on a large software project follows a rather standard pattern, as illustrated in Figure 12.2. The level of activity for a small, one-shot program may be a fairly constant effort; students are working on their assignment full-time in the few hours they have allotted to it. However, even huge software systems must be specified by a fairly small group of people, and the design is made by a larger but still relatively small group. Once the design is fairly detailed, then one can put a large number of people to work on writing and debugging the programs. Activity peaks at about the time the software system is released for use. The first release typically does not have some facilities that are planned. Other requirements are often discovered when the system becomes operational (before release), and the team of programmers is busy implementing software to meet these requirements for the second (or third or fourth . . .) release. About this time, one usually discovers other things that the system can "almost" do or that it could do "better." Changes of this type are called "enhancements," and they become the principal activity for a time after the first release. Activity begins to taper off after a spat of enhancements and modifications are made to correct errors, to improve efficiency, and to generally perfect the system. After a few years the system is in a nearly steady state, though maintenance is still required to accommodate changes in requirements, computing equipment, and such things. The maintenance phase is a lower level of activity, but it stretches over so many years that its cost usually exceeds the total of all other costs.

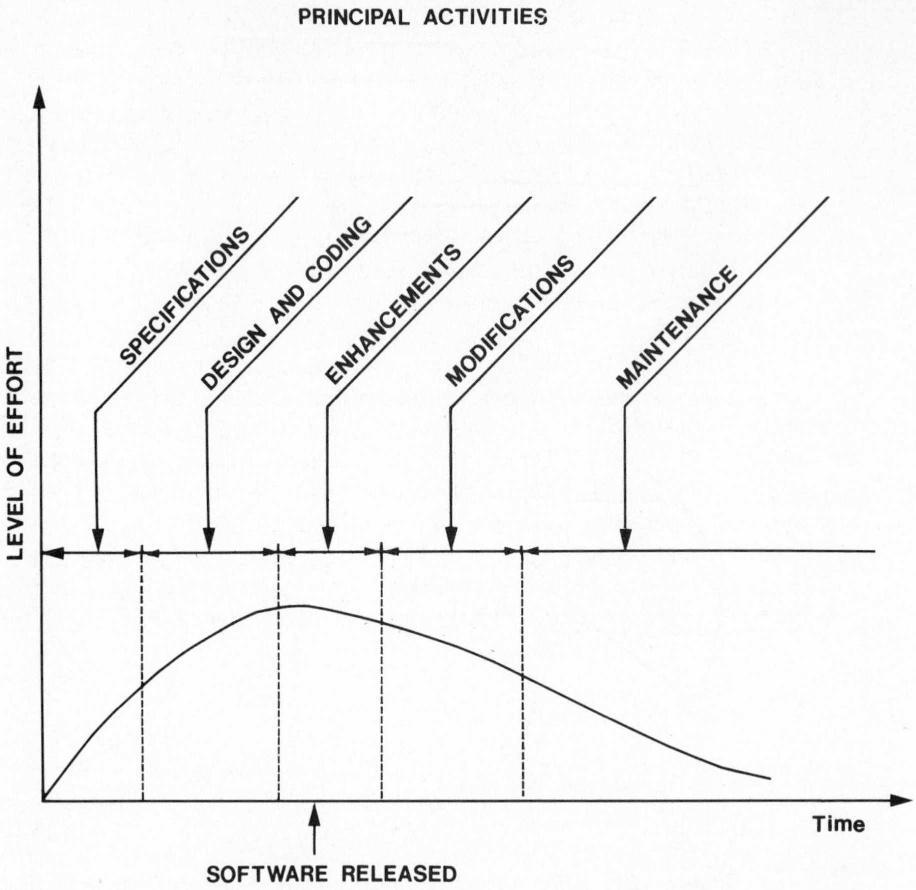

Figure 12.2 **Level of activity on a typical large software project.** The principal activities are indicated at various stages of the project; they extend over much longer times than just when they are the principal activity. There is also a small management activity which extends over the entire life of the project.

The life cycle portrayed above is typical, but every real project seems to have some special features that cause some variation from the norm. The shape of the activity curve in Figure 12.2 can be changed by putting more or fewer people on the project. One of the difficult tasks in large software development is to put the right number of people to work on a project. If there are too many, they get in each other's way, develop unneeded "bells and whistles" for the system, and generally waste money. If there are too few, the system does not get finished in time. The most critical point seems to be the start of the project; there are many stories of projects which had too many programmers too soon and the result was long delays. This phenomenon is illustrated by the saying: *Ten programmers can do it in a year, one hundred programmers in two years.* How much truth there is in this saying is not known, but it is widely suspected to reflect reality.

PROGRAMMING ENVIRONMENT AND PRACTICE 12.2

We now consider the situation of a single programmer working on a small program (say less than 5,000 lines of code). The programmer works in a certain environment using certain programming methods and tools to help write and debug the program. In this section we survey the facilities and practices the programmer should use.

The fundamental context of programming is an input-output device (terminal or cards and printer) and a language processor (a Fortran compiler). Many people have nothing more to work with, but there are many useful tools and practices available, at least for some people.

The Design of Small Programs 12.2.A

We have already noted in Chapter 1 the importance of **clarity in programming.** The use of meaningful variable names, ample comments, simple logic structures, and nice program layouts are all ways to give clarity to a program. Various rules of structured programming aid in achieving clarity, but they cannot achieve it alone. There is no substitute for thoughtful consideration of the algorithm and a logical development of its implementation. The fact that there are many different ways to achieve clarity does not excuse one from not achieving it.

The important role of clarity in programming is seen from the definition of a small program; it must be such that the programmer's mind can completely grasp it. It is crucial to both the original programmer and any later readers that they are able to understand the program. Writing clear programs is a skill much like writing clear English; some are naturally talented for it, most manage it only with practice, and some never manage it.

If a program is longer than a page or two, one should be systematic in developing its structure. There are two common methods to consider: **top-down** and **bottom-up** design. In top-down design, one starts with the overall objective of the program and refines it by finding subtasks that are combined to achieve the objective. This approach is also called **stepwise refinement,** and the structure of the program is developed as illustrated in Figure 12.3. The main program is divided into three parts, A, B, and C, which might become the three principal subprograms of the final program. Each of these parts is processed in the same way; for example, part B is subdivided into parts BA, BB, BC, and BD. This process is continued until a level of detail is reached at the bottom where relatively short programs are possible for each part.

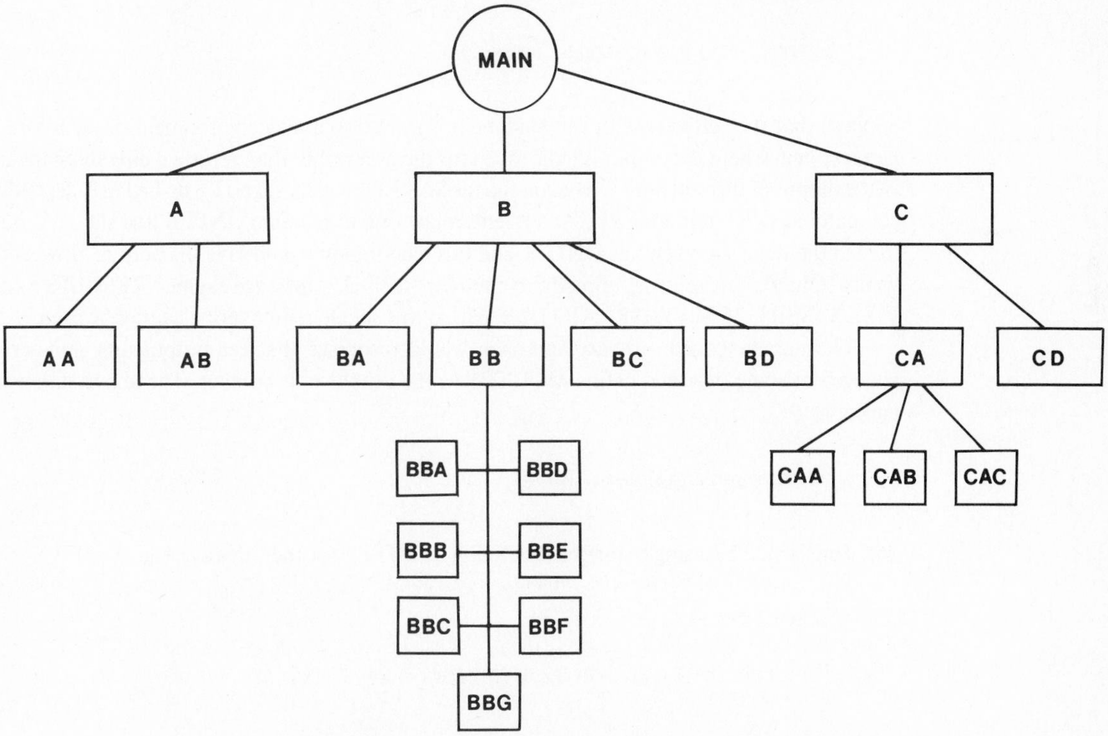

Figure 12.3 **Structure obtained in a top-down design of a program.** The main task is divided into three parts. These are then subdivided into two, four, and two parts at the second level. Two subdivisions at the third level are also shown: BB is divided into seven parts and CA into three parts.

Bottom-up design consists of reversing the order of the structuring. One identifies all the basic subprograms, procedures, and functions at the bottom and then combines them into larger and larger functional units (software modules) until one reaches the top where the overall objective of the program is met.

Top-down design is more widely used, and many feel it to be more natural. However, top-down design does require one to have some idea about what is practical at the bottom. There have been real instances of designs which finally ended up with a subprogram at the bottom which was impossible to produce. This has occurred after considerable effort had been invested in the project; the usual result in this case is to revise the objectives of the project to eliminate the need for the impossible program. It is better to recognize early that one has an impossible subprogram; the worst case is when the subprogram is not impossible, just very difficult and time-consuming to construct, with long delays in the project resulting. The design of small programs is usually made with a combination of these two approaches; one has a good idea of the bottom-level capabilities available, and one directs the top-down design toward them. This combination approach is also frequently used by the original design team for a large software project.

The structured, systematic approach to program design naturally leads to modularity in software. Software modules are programs that have a well-identified function. The modules should be natural for a logical subdivision of the program, and **modular programming** can help greatly to give clarity to the software. A companion to the modular software idea is the approach of **isolating functionality** and **parameterizing software.** In this approach one identifies certain functions and features of the software and isolates them in a single module. One also identifies particular variables or parameters of the project and gives them a specific, unique name that is used throughout the software. This approach makes it much easier to make changes in the software and greatly reduces the costs of enhancements, modifications, and maintenance. This approach is illustrated by the following examples.

Parameterization of Software — Example 12.1

1. **Parameterizing Output Devices.** A typical output statement is

```
WRITE(6,1016) XBAR, MAXERR, NTERMS
```

Suppose that the software with this statement is moved to a new environment or incorporated into a larger system where the output is to be saved for the user rather than returned directly to the user. That is, the output of this software is to go on the file SAVEIT, which is UNIT 8 or TAPE 8 (depending on the computer system's terminology). All systems allow one to redefine UNIT 6 (the standard output unit used in the write statement) as UNIT 8, and this redefinition would save the output. However, one still wants some output returned directly to the user (such as a message saying "RESULTS SAVED ON FILE SAVEIT, 26 MAY 1981 AT 11:24:36"), so this simple renumbering cannot be used.

The parameterized software approach would recognize that the output unit number might be changed at some time and define MOUTPT as the output unit number. The above statement would appear as

```
WRITE(MOUTPT,1016) XBAR, MAXERR,NTERMS
```

and there would be a single statement defining MOUTPT for the software, e.g.,

```
DATA MOUTPT /6/
```

or

```
MOUTPT = 6
```

The value of MOUTPT would be communicated to subprograms by placing MOUTPT in a labeled COMMON statement. Later one can change where all the output goes by changing just one line.

2. **Machine Parameters.** In many computations one includes certain constants of the computer and Fortran system. See Table 3.1 for machine parameters related to arithmetic. To parameterize the software, one introduces a variable, say RMACH, for round-off of the machine. The various constants (for a 9-decimal-digit machine) listed in the following table can be replaced by the simple expressions as listed.

Unparameterized	Parameterized
1.E-9	RMACH
1.E-7	100.*RMACH
8	– IFIX(ALOG10(RMACH)) – 1
.00003	SQRT(RMACH)

When the software is moved to a new computer, one needs merely to replace

```
DATA RMACH /1.E-9/
```

by, say,

```
DATA RMACH /1.E-14/
```

and the round-off level dependencies are all adjusted. With the unparameterized alternative, one has to examine all the constants in the software and determine if they are related to the machine round-off. Some of them can be difficult to identify; for example, it might be hard to see that .01 in the software is the programmer's approximation to 2.*RMACH**0.25.

3. **Parameterizing Data Representations.** Programs that manipulate data or data structures often benefit from parameterization. Consider a satellite navigational system that involves four satellites. The calculations involve the positions of the four satellites and time, quantities that might by represented by the variables

X(I,J,K), T(K)   I = 1 to 3
J = 1 to 4
K = 1 to KDATA

where X(I,J,K) is the Ith coordinate of the Jth satellite at time T(K). The software would have statements of the following kinds in it:

```
      SUBROUTINE MASAGE(X,T,KDATA)
      REAL X(3,4,KDATA),T(KDATA)
      REAL XTEMP(3,200),T(200)
C     ...   MORE FORTRAN
      READ(5,109)(X(I,J,NOW),I=1,3),J=1.4),T(NOW)
C     ...   MORE FORTRAN
      DO 200 NOW=1,50
          N4 = 4*(NOW-1)
          DO 200 J=1,4
              X(I,J,NOW) = XTEMP(I,N4+J)
C     ...   MORE FORTRAN
     $SUM .25*ABS(X(1,J,NOW)-X(1,J,NOW-1));FOR(J=1,4);IS DIFF1
C     ...   MORE PROTRAN
     $END
```

Suppose now that after a few years a new, more accurate system is to be developed using 8 satellites instead of 4. The algorithms and data processing used in the old software are all applicable provided one changes the 4 to 8 in appropriate places. To make this modification, one needs to examine all of the code and identify where the assumption of 4 satellites is used. If one had realized that the software might be used with a different number of satellites, or that other changes would be made, one could ease the modification with code of following form:

```
      SUBROUTINE MASAGE(X,T,KDATA)
      PARAMETER(NSATEL=4, NTEMP=200)
      REAL X(3,NSATEL,KDATA), T(KDATA)
      REAL XTEMP(3,NTEMP), T(NTEMP)
      COMMON/PARAMS/MINPUT, MOUTPT, RMACH, ...
C     ...    MORE FORTRAN
      READ(MINPUT,109) ((X(I,J,NOW),I=1,3),J=1,NSATEL),T(NOW)
C     ...    MORE FORTRAN
      DO 200 NOW=1, NTEMP/NSATEL
          N4 = NSATEL*(NOW-1)
          DO 200 J=1, NSATEL
              X(I,J,NOW) = XTEMP(I,N4+J)
C    ...     MORE FORTRAN
     $SUM ABS(X(1,J,NOW)-X(1,J,NOW-1))/NSATEL;FOR(J=1,NSATEL);IS DIFF1
C    ...     MORE PROTRAN
     $END
```

The PARAMETER statement used here is part of Fortran 77; in older Fortran one could make assignments NSATEL=4 and NTEMP=200, which would parameterize the executable statements but not the declarations. The dimension changes would have to be made individually in the older Fortran. Again, changing one line of code updates this subroutine to accommodate the new data representation. Furthermore, even if NSATEL and NTEMP are never changed, the parameterized program is easier to understand.

Isolation of Functionality — Example 12.2

1. **Isolating the Tax Formulas.** Consider the payroll and accounting software for a typical company. Someplace in the program there are formulas to compute the taxes on the pay. There are several kinds of taxes, and the tax information goes to various places (employee paychecks, periodic reports to the federal and state governments, checks to the government, records of the company, etc.). The tax laws change frequently but irregularly. There should be one and only one module in the software system that contains formulas and rules for taxes. When the tax laws change, one can modify this module to reflect the change with some confidence that all the tax records and payments of the company remain correct (they will be, at least, consistent).

   In a top-down software design, this module would be further subdivided into modules for federal income tax, state income tax, social security tax, state disability tax, unemployment tax, and so forth. Note how this logical structure adds clarity as well as decreases the costs of maintenance.

2. **Hiding the Printed Output Device Characteristics.** The output of software is often affected by changes in the computing environment. Not only might unit numbers in Fortran READ and WRITE statements require changes, but the format of the output might need overhauling as one changes from line printer to large-screen terminal to small-screen terminal to acoustic to microfiche forms of output. Consider a program with the statement

```
      WRITE(6,606) MODE, LOCATE
  606 FORMAT(//5H ****,20X,37H CONDITION PURPLE OCCURRED DURING MODE, I2
     A       ,44H SEARCH OPERATION OF GALACTIC SPACE QUADRANT, I6, //)
```

   which prints two pairs of blank lines and one message of 114 characters between them. This is fine for a line printer, but if the software environment is changed so that the output is displayed on a screen with 60 characters per line, this message is either truncated or broken at an odd place. One might then change the FORMAT statement to be

```
  606 FORMAT(/11H ATTENTION/26H CONDITION PURPLE FOR MODE, I2,
     A        19H SEARCH OF QUADRANT, I6)
```

   This now fits well on a screen with 60 characters per line.

   Suppose, as sometimes happens, the software contains hundreds of messages. It is a major project to identify all message FORMAT statements and rephrase them to fit on the 60-character line. And then, when the software is moved to a hand-held computer with a 48-character-per-line screen, all the messages must be changed again. An alternative is to have one subroutine which writes messages; it takes any string of characters and prints it with logical break points (such as between words) at the ends of lines. One can even adjust the margins on both sides to make them straight if one wants. The statement above would then be replaced by something like

```
      MESSGE(606,1) = MODE
      MESSGE(606,2) = LOCATE
      CALL PRINTL(606)
```

   where PRINTL has access to all messages, knows to insert the integer values of MODE and LOCATE into message 606, and then prints the required lines. It is not easy to write the program PRINTL (it is not that difficult either), but once it is done, one can change the output device and only affect this one program. If PRINTL is properly parameterized, just one statement in it need be changed to accommodate devices with different numbers of characters per line.

Software Tools 12.2.B

The essential tools for programming are the language processor (Fortran compiler, PROTRAN preprocessor) and the diagnostics that it supplies. Many programmers only use these tools (and possibly a text editor), but there are a number of other tools which can be very useful in developing and debugging programs. We list the principal ones with a brief description of their function. Many of these are widely distributed or easily obtained, so programmers should inquire about them at their local computing centers. Some of the better compilers incorporate some of these facilities.

1. **Static Analyzers.** Static analyzers are tools that examine the code and generate useful information and make various checks. The compiler itself does static analysis in checking that each statement is legal. Other types of checking that static analysis tools provide are:

   A. **Data Flow Analysis.** Are there variables which are used before a value has been assigned to them? Are there variables which are never used? Do the arguments of a subprogram agree in number, type, dimension, etc., with arguments used in a call to the program?

   B. **Control Flow Analysis.** Are there code segments that can never be reached? Are there statement labels that are never used? A **cross-reference table** gives information about the usage of all variables, labels, etc., in a program and is a useful aid for both data flow and control flow analysis.

   C. **Eccentric Statements.** Some statements or combinations of them are legal but not very logical. The following code contains a number of strange Fortran constructions which are likely to be errors and which some tools identify as suspicious:

```
    X = X + 0.0
    Y = Y*1.0
    GO TO 6
  6 N = 3
    N = 5
 10 IF(X.EQ.XNEW(X,N)) GO TO 10
    IF(X.NE.Y) GO TO 15
 15 Y = Y*0.0
    DO 20 ILOOP = 1,1
 20 CONTINUE
```

   One can concoct examples where each of these strange constructions are desired (especially for Fortran programs written automatically by preprocessors), but having them flagged is a valuable aid in most program development.

2. **Dynamic Analyzers.** Dynamic analyzers monitor the execution of the program to collect useful information and perform various checks. Some of the types of checking and data collected are listed here; probe inserters and test data generators discussed below are special kinds of dynamic analyzers.

   A. **Execution Performance.** Statistics are collected which show where the program spends its time. This may be in the form of time in statements (giving a **performance profile**), the number of times each labeled statement is executed, or the number of calls on each subprogram. It is well-established that programmers have difficulty in predicting which parts of a complex program use the most time.

   B. **Subscript Checking.** The indexes for all dimensioned arrays are checked to see if the actual values fall within the range specified by the declarations. Subscript-out-of-range errors can produce strange results that are very difficult to diagnose.

   C. **Snapshots.** The tool produces a snapshot of the state of the computation at various times. The values of all variables are recorded, and the current control status is described (one is at line 83 in DO-Loop 200 with 16 loops of subprogram SUB3 called by subprogram CALLER at line 29, which is called in the main program at line 32). Snapshots are particularly valuable for programs that fail unexpectedly; many such tools allow the snapshot to be taken at the exact point of failure.

3. **Probe Insertion.** There are tools which insert special code to trace and analyze the execution of a program. These probes are of two types:

   A. **Tracing.** Tracing a variable XTRACE means that each time XTRACE is assigned a new value, that value is printed along with the location where the assignment is made. One can also trace FUNCTION and SUBROUTINE calls and common block references as well as variables. One can trace whole arrays or individual elements of an array. Caution must sometimes be used to avoid obtaining hundreds of pages of output.

   B. **Assertion testing.** Subscript checking is checking the assertion that *the array index is within the declared limits.* Assertions of general types can be stated and automatically inserted by tools. An example insertion is $x^2 + y^2 \leq 1$; the tool would insert a test of this assertion each time x or y is changed and print a message any time it is not true. Other typical assertions are:
   (i) INDEX1 + INDEX2 ≤ IMAX
   (ii) WGHT4 ≥ 0.0
   (iii) $SUM COEF(I); FOR (I=1,NTERMS); IS SUMCOE $
   ABS (SUMCOE − 1.0) ≤ 10.*RMACH

4. **Test Data Generation.** Testing a program requires that it be run with data that exercise the functionality of the program. Simple criteria for adequate testing include (a) executing every statement in the program, (b) taking every possible branch from each IF statement, and (c) executing every path in the program. It is reasonable to expect the testing of a program to execute every statement at least once; executing every path through the programs might be unreasonably difficult to achieve. Some programs with loops have infinitely many paths.

   Testing usually starts with the programmer selecting data which represent the various "normal" uses of the program plus data which represent "extreme" cases (vectors of length 1, weights of 0, very long vectors, very large weights, etc.). These data usually fail to exercise everything that needs to be tested, and it can be very difficult to devise new data to exercise the remainder. Test generation tools are intended to provide these data automatically. This is a difficult task which, in some cases, involves unsolved problems or impractical computations. These tools are very helpful but not foolproof.

5. **Formatters.** These tools make the program layout more attractive and readable without changing the functionality of the code. Typical actions in Fortran are:

   Indent DO-Loops and IF-THEN-ELSE statements

   Terminate each DO-Loop with its own CONTINUE statement

   Replace statement labels with regularly increasing labels

   Replace FORMAT labels with a systematic set

   Move FORMATs to the end of a program

   Adjust spacing in lists and expressions

   Align variables in long declaration statements

   Putting a program into a nice, standard format has a surprisingly beneficial effect on clarity, especially once one becomes accustomed to a particular standard.

6. **Structurers.** These tools reorganize the logical control of a program into a standard structured form in order to increase its clarity. The principal tasks are to identify IF-THEN-ELSE and CASE constructions, rearrange the code in the most appropriate way, and insert comments which identify the structure. The following is a "before" and "after" example of what one can expect from a structuring tool.

An Unstructured Segment of Fortran

```
      IF(K.EQ.1) GO TO 212
      IF(K.EQ.2) GO TO 18
      GO TO 106
  212 X(1) = 5.
      Y(K) = K+2.5
```

```
 32 IF(K*J.LE.4) GO TO 184
 30 L4 = K*J-K+1
    X(L4) = Y(L4) = 1.0
210 IF(K-J.GE.7) GO TO 265
    GO TO 184
 18 X(K) = 6.
    Y(K) = K-1.5
    GO TO 32
106 IF(K.NE.3) GO TO 10
    X(K) = Y(K) = 0.0
    GO TO 23
265 IF(K.GE.J+7) GO TO 10
    X(K-J+1) = 0.0
    Y(K-J) = 1.0
    GO TO 10
184 IF(K*J.LE.4) GO TO 23
180 L = K*J-2*K
    X(L) = Y(L) = 0.0
 23 IF(K-J.GE.7) X(K-J+1) = 1.0
    IF(K*J.LE.4) GO TO 30
    GO TO 265
 10 IF(K-J.GE.7) Y(K-J+1) = 0.0
```

An Equivalent Segment that Has Been Structured

```
C       CASE STATEMENT
      IF(K.EQ.1) THEN
              X(1) = 5.0
              Y(K) = K+2
        ELSE IF(K.EQ.2) THEN
              X(K) = 6.
              Y(K) = K-1
        ELSE IF(K.EQ.3) THEN
              X(K) = 0.0
              Y(K) = 0.0
      END IF
C       END CASE STATEMENT
C      IF-THEN-ELSE STATEMENT
      IF(K*J.LE.4) THEN
               L4 = K*J-K+1
              X(L4) = 1.0
              Y(L4) = 1.0
        ELSE
                L = K*J-2*K
              X(L) = 0.0
              Y(L) = 0.0
      END IF
C      IF-THEN-ELSE STATEMENT
      IF(K-J.GE.7) THEN
              X(K-J+1) = 1.0
              Y(K-J+1) = 0.0
        ELSE
              X(K-J+1) = 0.0
              Y(K-J+1) = 1.0
      END IF
```

7. **Dialect Translators.** Fortran varies in detail on different systems, and one must usually make a number of small changes when software is moved from one environment to another. The same changes are required when one has a new computer system installed. Most of these changes are routine, but it is usually tedious (and error-prone) to make them all. There are tools designed to help with this task by identifying the idiosyncrasies and making the required changes. One valuable tool is a **precision transformer**, to change from single precision to double precision or vice versa. This is much more difficult to do automatically and reliably than one would expect. These tools also have some mechanisms to change all the machine and system characteristics *provided* the original program is properly written with these changes in mind. These characteristics which change from single to double precision include, for example,

Round-off level	Characters per word
Overflow threshold	Largest integer
Underflow threshold	Exponent range

8. **Language Verifiers and Code Auditors.** One of the most direct and practical ways to avoid later complications with programs is to write them within language standards. This usually means sacrificing the use of some nice language features (available locally), and so it is not attractive in the short run, but it can have big payoffs in the long run. Many Fortran compilers have a switch which makes them accept only standard Fortran, and this is valuable for those who wish to use standard Fortran.

   There are now two standard Fortrans, Fortran 66 and Fortran 77. Fortran 66 is what most people know as Fortran; full language processors for Fortran 77 became widely available only in 1982, and for many more years some installations will not have Fortran 77 available. So there is some motivation to continue using the Fortran 66 standard for certain software, but that motivation decreases each year. Fortran 77 removes most of the idiosyncrasies of Fortran 66 and adds several very useful facilities (IF-THEN-ELSE, character data types, file handling), and so it is much more attractive for most applications.

   In addition to tools that check language standards, some large programming operations have tools which check (and perhaps enforce) other standards. These tools include **code auditors** which check requirements like:

   A. Comments within executable code start in column 36.

   B. No subprogram has more than 100 executable statements.

   C. The arithmetic IF [for example, IF(X-415.) 20,35,108] is not used.

   D. There are no GO TO statements that jump to preceding statements in the program.

   The **PFORT verifier** is a combination of language verifier and code auditor. It verifies that programs are written in "portable Fortran"; that is, no constructions are used which are known to be handled differently on different major computer systems. Unfortunately, there are a number of Fortran 66 standard items which have been implemented in several different ways by major computer manufacturers (partly because the standard itself was unclear or not precise enough). Examples of such items are NAMELIST, EQUIVALENCE, ENTRY, and several more complicated FORMAT descriptors. The PFORT tool also checks for a few items which are not covered by the Fortran 66 standard and which are known to cause trouble when programs are moved. An example of this is the number of characters packed in a word: CDC computers allow 10 characters per word (use of A10 format), many others allow 6 characters (use of A6 format), IBM only allows 4 characters, and some minicomputers only pack 2 characters per word. PFORT flags any use of more than one character per word as dangerous.

SOFTWARE QUALITY AND COSTS 12.3

Software Quality 12.3.A

Software has a number of different qualities or properties that are somewhat independent. Figure 12.4 identifies the more important qualities and shows how the general value of software depends on them. The importance of these qualities depends on the use of the program. A one-shot, small program might need only to be accurate and device-efficient. Software of more permanent value which is widely used needs to have all these qualities be good. In this section we define the qualities of software and briefly discuss the conflicts that arise in constructing high-quality software. No attempt is made to discuss how to achieve high quality, but we do discuss the high cost of good-quality software, which shows that it is not achieved easily.

The definitions of the qualities in Figure 12.4 are given in alphabetical order.

Accurate. The output is correct or sufficiently precise for the intended use.

Clear Code. The software is well-written, well-structured, and understandable.

Complete. Everything needed for the software is included; the user need only supply the information required to define the computation.

Consistent. The software is written with a uniform style and level of commenting. Internal data structures are of consistent design, and similar approaches are used in similar

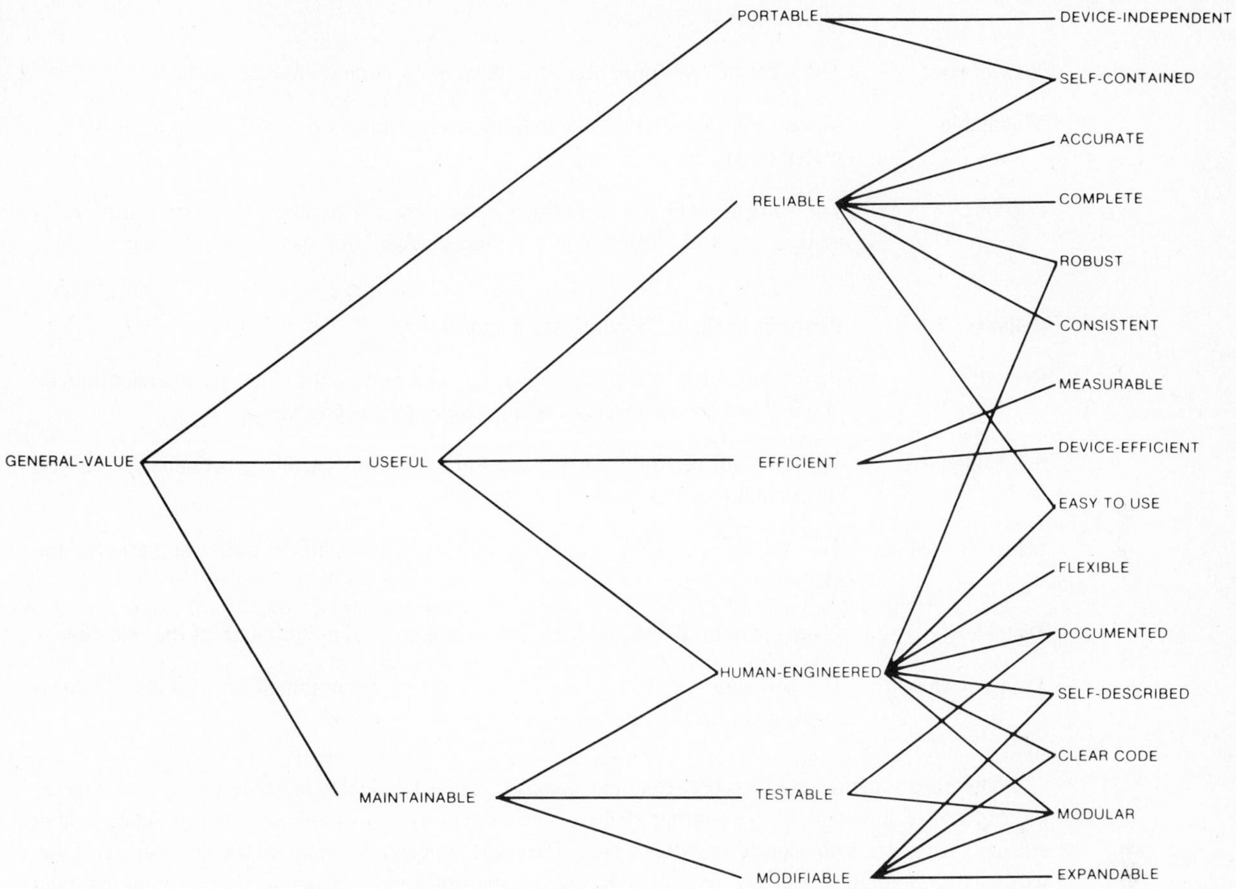

Figure 12.4 **Software quality dependencies.** The various general qualities of software depend on a number of specific, somewhat independent basic qualities.

situations. The input and output use consistent formats, terminology, and specifications.

Device-Efficient. The computation uses a nearly minimal (or at least reasonable) amount of computer time, memory, and other resources.

Device-Independent. The software avoids dependence on particular features of the computing environment as much as possible. Those items that depend on the hardware or system software in an essential way are clearly identified and easily located or changed.

Documentation. Reports and user guides, which explain how to use the software, define its intended use, define input and output, give error messages, etc. Different reports describe the methods, data structures, algorithms, and organization of the software.

Easy to Use. The input required is natural for the computation, and the output is clearly identified, understandable, and complete.

Efficient. Computing resources are not wasted.

Expandable. New features and functions can be added. Increased computer capacity can be accommodated to make larger or more difficult computations.

Flexible. The input and problem do not have to be in a rigid form for the software. Closely related problems can be solved with small, natural changes in the input.

Human-Engineered. Use of the software does not waste the time and energy of the users or give them unnecessary frustrations.

Measurable. The software's performance (time, memory, accuracy, etc.) can be measured.

Modifiable. Modest changes can be made in the software's function or methods in a natural way with modest effort.

Portable. The software will run in another computing environment (different hardware or system) as is or with minor, routine changes (for example, changing machine constants).

Reliable. Performs intended functions satisfactorily.

Robust: Performance degrades gracefully as the usage moves away from the intended domain of use. There are no surprises or nitpicking causes of failure.

Self-Contained. The software performs all the necessary functions itself, e.g., initializes variables, checks inputs, issues diagnostics, etc.

Self-Described. The software contains complete information about its use, assumptions, and methods.

Testable. There are natural tests to check the correctness and performance of the software.

Transportable. The software will run in another computing environment with modest changes requiring much less effort than rewriting the programs.

There are numerous conflicts between these qualities; raising the quality in one respect is often done at the expense of lower quality in another respect. The most obvious example of this is efficiency: **high efficiency conflicts with almost everything else.** The most efficient program is totally tailored to the particular computation and the particular hardware and software facilities used. However, extreme efficiency (in use of computing resources) usually does not give high efficiency in the overall problem-solving process. Note that if one is allowed to sacrifice accuracy, then the software could just return 1.738 as the result, independent of the input data or computation to be made. This can be extremely efficient! To always return 1.738 is, of course, silly, but it shows that no one quality is likely to completely dominate the evaluation of software. Compromises and tradeoffs are always necessary.

Ease of use also has several important conflicts with other qualities. Better flexbility means more complexity, and the user wants something simple. Flexibility usually manifests itself through option switches and more argument for various parameters. The user might have to assign values to some of these parameters even when they are irrelevant to the computation. More parameters also means more documentation, which, in turn, makes it harder to learn how to use the software. A useful tactic to help solve this conflict is to have a program with maximum flexibility (and many arguments) and then to have some simpler interface programs which merely set various arguments to default values and perform other services for the user.

Ease of use can conflict with portability when some particularly nice local facility is available. For example, NAMELIST input for Fortran is very nice in some situations but dangerous for portability reasons.

Program documentation conflicts with ease of use; one quickly learns that subroutine write-ups are misleading, confusing, and generally inscrutable. This is sometimes true even when great effort has been spent to make them clear, complete, and easy to understand. Error after error after error is made because the user misses various fine points about a program's use. Some people would rather spend four days writing their own program than spend half a day figuring out how to use someone else's program.

It is not completely clear why documentation is hard to understand. Perhaps it is because write-ups have such a high density of (perhaps unfamiliar) information that people cannot absorb it. The reader gets the general idea and then jumps to (usually wrong) conclusions about the details. The process of getting all the details correct often involves several tries and considerable frustration. Care should be taken in documentation to word things, choose names, etc., so as to increase the probabilities of the reader's jumping to the right conclusions. Perhaps if there were documentation standards, then everyone would become familiar with the standard format and information and understand program write-ups better and more quickly.

Software Costs **12.3.B**

There is universal agreement that software costs are high. The beginner's or student's experience with programming is not a reasonable guide to the effort (and hence cost) it takes to develop good-quality, usable software. A student often expects to spend an afternoon at a terminal to produce a program of 50 to 100 lines for a homework assignment. At this rate, the student could expect to produce perhaps 2,000 to 4,000 lines of code in a month. This is almost 10 times as much as programmers actually produce in practice.

There is much less agreement on what **software costs** actually are or how they should be measured. One study [see L. H. Putnam, *Software Costs Estimating and Life-Cycle Control,* IEEE Catalog EHO 165-1 (1980), pp. 29–31] covered over 400 military software projects which ranged from 1 month to 8 years in length, involved from 2 to 200 people at a time, and produced from 50 to 1 million lines of code. **Programmer productivity** is usually measured in **lines of code per man-month** (one programmer working one month), which we abbreviate *lines per month.* The number of lines is obtained by averaging over the entire life cycle of the project, from initial design to final delivery. The results of this study show a wide variation: productivity ranged from 5 to 5,000 lines per month. The average productivity was 200 lines per month, and two-thirds of the projects had productivity between 75 and 550 lines per month.

In another study [see C. E. Watson and C. P. Felix, "A Method of Programming Measurement and Estimation," *IBM Systems J.,* **16** (1977)] 60 software projects were analyzed, involving 28 languages and 66 computer systems, and produced from 4,000 to 500,000 lines of code. The median productivity was 275 lines per month, with 25 percent of the projects achieving less than 150 lines per month and 25 percent achieving more than 440 lines per month. More specific information is that the IMSL library development had a productivity of about 160 lines per month, the EISPACK routines about 55 lines per month, and the NAG library about 260 lines per month.

In terms of 1980 dollars, this means that **software costs** are expected to be about $20 to $25 per line with $12 to $32 being in the normal range. In extreme cases, costs have reached $1,000 per line. These costs include everything involved in the software production: programmer's salary, computer time, writing and duplicating user guides, secretarial support, heat, etc. There are wide variations on how these things are measured, but equating one man-month to $5,000 is a reasonable approach.

As an example of how large such costs can be, the Safeguard missile project involved about 2.2 million lines of code generated with a productivity of about 35 lines per month. That means over $300 million was spent on the software for this project. The yearly software cost for all of the Department of Defense is estimated to be in the range of $10 to $15 billion.

Since software costs vary so much, there is great interest in knowing what affects these costs and how they can be controlled. In this area there are a lot of strongly held opinions supported by very few facts. Table 12.1 lists 15 **properties that affect programming.** The study of Watson and Felix, mentioned above, attempted to assess the effect of these properties on software productivity. Values for these properties were obtained for the 60 software projects studied, and Table 12.1 gives the productivity averages for the usual or normal situations and the extremes in each direction. The productivity for the normal situations is given in the "Average" column; note that these are rather closely clustered about the value of 275 lines per month, obtained as the overall average productivity for all 60 projects. The "Variation" column then gives the **difference in productivity** between the extremes defined in the rightmost column. For example, the productivity for more-than-normal complexity in the user interface was 124 lines per month, and 500 lines per month for less-than-normal complexity. The difference, 376 lines per month, is given in the "Variation" column.

The factors that influence programming productivity can be grouped from Table 12.1 as follows:

Most significant: User interface
Experience and skill of programmmers

Very significant: Constraints on storage

Significant: Programming methods used
Complexity of project
Amount of documentation

Less significant: Logical complexity of code
Numerical versus nonnumerical
Constraints on timing

Properties That Influence Programming Productivity **Table 12.1**

The productivity for the normal or average situation is given in the "Average" column. The difference in productivity between extremes is given in the "Variation" column, and the definition of the extremes is given in the right column. The extreme giving the lowest productivity is always given second.

Property of Programming Task or Method	PRODUCTIVITY IN LINES OF CODE PER MAN-MONTH		
	Average	Variation	Variation Is Between
Complexity of user interface	295	376	Below and above normal
User involvement in requirements definition	267	286	No and much involvement
Experience and qualifications of programmers	257	278	High and low qualifications
Experience with same- or larger-sized application	221	264	Minimal and extensive experience
Experience with language used	225	263	Extensive and minimal experience
Percent of programmers involved in software specifications	242	238	> 50% and < 25% involvement
Constraints on storage use	277	198	Minimal and severe constraints
Use of structured programming	—	132	< 66% and > 33% use
Overall code complexity	—	129	Below and above average
Pages of documentation per 1,000 lines of code	252	125	< 32 and > 88 pages
Use of top-down programming design	237	125	> 66% and < 33% use
Inspections of the program design and code	300	119	> 66% and < 33% inspection
Complexity of program logic	299	80	Below and above average
Percent of program non-math and formatting	311	79	> 66% and < 33% non-math
Constraints on timing	317	76	Minimal and severe constraints

The reliability of these data is questioned by some people. For example, constraints on timing (e.g., for interactive systems or real time control) was found to be the least important factor of all, including 14 other factors not reported upon here. Some experts feel that constraints on timing decrease productivity by a factor of 5, making the variation for this property larger than any observed in this study. As the field of software engineering matures, uncertainties like this will be greatly reduced.

It is discouraging that **software productivity is increasing rather slowly.** There was a large jump in productivity in the early 1960s when higher-level languages (Fortran, Algol, Cobol, etc.) were introduced. It is not that the number of lines per month increased, but the number of lines needed for most tasks decreased dramatically. The common programming languages of the early 1980s [Fortran, Cobol, Pascal, Ada(?)] are close to having the same power as the languages of 20 years ago. That is, a particular task takes about as many lines of code now as it did in the early 1960s. The better compilers, supporting software tools and interactive terminals, have increased software productivity by perhaps a factor of 2 or 3; that compares to increases in hardware capacity (speed and memory) of several orders of magnitude over the same period. Furthermore, the cost of hardware has decreased substantially while the cost of programmers has increased

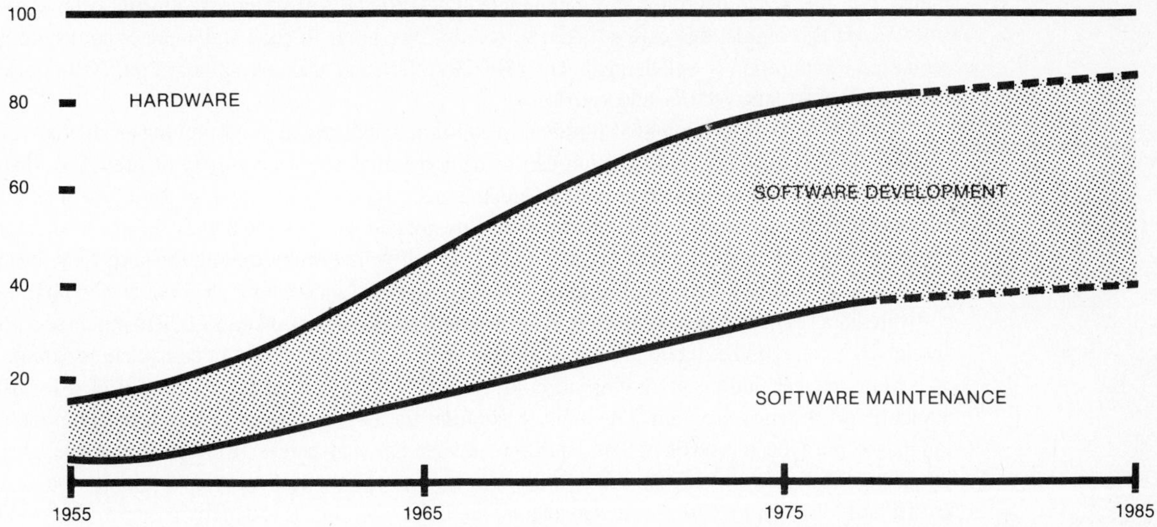

Figure 12.5 Trends in the components of the cost of computing. The estimated percentage of software maintenance is lower here than suggested by Figure 12.1 because one-shot programs are included here.

substantially. The net result has been a dramatic shift of the cost of computing from hardware to software. Figure 12.5 sketches an estimate of the trend in the proportions of these costs over time.

SOFTWARE PARTS AND VERY HIGH LEVEL LANGUAGES ** 12.4

Most **current software is handcrafted and custom-made.** Therein lies much of the reason for the high cost of software; every project is seen to have some special circumstances that require all its software to be specially developed. Many really large projects even find it "necessary" to develop a new, special programming language for the project. Currently the Department of Defense has over 500 different programming languages in use. It's as though when one wants a new table, one decides that it should be 127 centimeters long by 66 centimeters wide with five legs 73 centimeters high and built with screws 3.637 centimeters long having 3.25 threads per centimeter. One goes out and has all these parts custom-made to build the table. One can even claim that it is wasteful to order a table from a catalog with a 54-by-30-inch top that is 30 inches high because it is bigger than needed. Never mind that it costs $133 instead of $3,331 for the custom-made one.

This book adopts the principle that it is much better to use someone else's program rather than to write one's own tailor-made program. It does not matter in most applications that the standard program might take 37 percent more time to execute or that it might take the programmer half a day to learn how to use it. In fact, high-quality library programs which are robust and do a lot of error checking are likely to run faster than quickly developed specially tailored programs.

The goal in scientific (and other) computing is to do programming with **software parts** which are widely available from catalogs. A software parts technology for software development is to be established, just as there are standard parts technology for building electronic circuits, bridges, and plumbing systems. A software part is much like a library routine: it does a well-identified, standard computational task. Ideally, a software part has three pieces: (1) a front interface or *prologue* that checks the input data for consistency and which makes any special changes of data representations, (2) an algorithm or method that actually carries out the task, and (3) a back interface or *epilogue* that puts the result into a standard form and labels it properly. Such parts can be organized into catalogs and used interchangeably.

Most library routines, including those from the IMSL library and the other packages mentioned in this text, do not completely qualify as a software parts for two reasons. First, they do not thoroughly check the input data. For example, the LINPACK routines for solving $\mathbf{Ax}=\mathbf{b}$ do not check that the number N of linear equations is positive. The IMSL routines check this, but they do not check that the sizes of the A matrix and the **x** and **b** vectors are compatible. The PROTRAN system statements behave more like software parts; considerable care is taken to see that the input to each statement is consistent and the requested computation is well-defined. The PROTRAN system also uses standard representations within the domain of scalars, vectors, and matrices.

A **software parts technology** will provide a substantial increase in programming productivity. Factors of 5 or 10 in productivity improvement can be demonstrated in a wide variety of situations. If software parts and library collections can provide so much benefit, then why are there so few of them and why are they so little used? The answers to these questions are not completely known; they seem to lie in the areas of programmer psychology, the way organizations view software purchases, and the surprising difficulty in creating good-quality software collections. A number of well-funded, long-term projects to establish large software libraries have failed completely. Many organizations cannot spend $1,000 to purchase a program, though they can spend $20,000 in salaries and associated costs to produce an equivalent program.

Many people find programming an enjoyable activity, and it takes the fun out of it to just use a standard, off-the-shelf program. The main reason that the Department of Defense has 500 programming languages must be the challenge and pride of ownership that comes from inventing one's very own language. More down-to-earth reasons that programmers do not use libraries are the associated frustrations: it is hard to find what is available, there are often many too many programs to consider (the Purdue University Computing Center provides well over 100 library programs to solve linear equations), subroutine write-ups are hard to understand, and too many programmers have been burned by inferior programs.

There is an approach to software parts use that has proved very successful. That is to imbed the program in a very high level language specifically tailored for a certain class of problems. A **high-level language** is something like Fortran, Pascal, or Cobol; it is high only when compared to low-level languages like assembly or machine language. These are also known as **algorithmic languages**, reflecting the fact that they are intended to be used to specify algorithms in a reasonable, step-by-step way. A **very high level language** involves much larger steps, ones where it is not obvious what is happening. For example, they might include statements like *integrate this function, sort this list of numbers, plot these functions.* Frequently, these languages merely provide a means to state a problem and then request that it be solved. For this reason, these languages are also called **problem-oriented languages, problem-solving systems, problem-statement languages.** For example, they include statements like: *solve this linear system of equations, find the roots of this polynomial, compute the resistance of this circuit, find the resonant frequencies of this bridge.*

PROTRAN is an example of a problem-statement language that is merged into Fortran. It uses the IMSL library routines as software parts to implement problem-solving statements. SPSS (see Section 2.3.D) is an example of several very widely used statistical systems. The users of these systems do not write programs in the usual sense, but they do gain access to a number of Fortran programs (software parts?) to solve certain statistical problems. The ELLPACK language (see Figure 2.3) is another example of a problem-solving system. It has a rather fixed format for describing an elliptic partial differential equation and then requesting that it be solved. Such languages are being introduced throughout science and engineering. They provide powerful scientific tools and, incidentally, dramatically increase programming productivity by practically eliminating programming. One study has estimated that it takes 500 times less effort to solve a linear elliptic partial differential equation using ELLPACK than to write the equivalent Fortran program.

There is a serious problem in making a specialized very high level language widely available. It must run on most common computer systems, which means that the language translator and software parts must work on many different systems. Yet the specialized nature of the language means that the demand for its use might be so low that it does not pay to produce ordinary language translators for all these computers. A compiler for a simple language can easily cost $100,000 (that is just enough for 5,000 lines of code), and so to make compilers available on the 10 most widely available computer systems means that an investment of $1 million is required. Some areas, such as statistics, have a huge community of users where it does pay to make such a large investment, but this is not the case for many others.

An interesting approach is to have the language processor translate into a widely available standard language instead of into machine language. This means that only one language processor needs to be written to make the language available everywhere the standard language is available. The approach is discussed in more detail in the following example.

Fortran Preprocessors for Very High Level Languages

Example 12.3

The idea is to have a preprocessor read the very high level language input, analyze it, and then write a Fortran program that defines arrays, initializes variables, calls library routines, etc., to carry out the computation. This Fortran program is then compiled and loaded along with the language library (the software parts) and finally executed to carry out the desired computation. This organization is illustrated in Figure 12.6. The PROTRAN system is an example of this approach and it is implemented by a Fortran preprocessor.

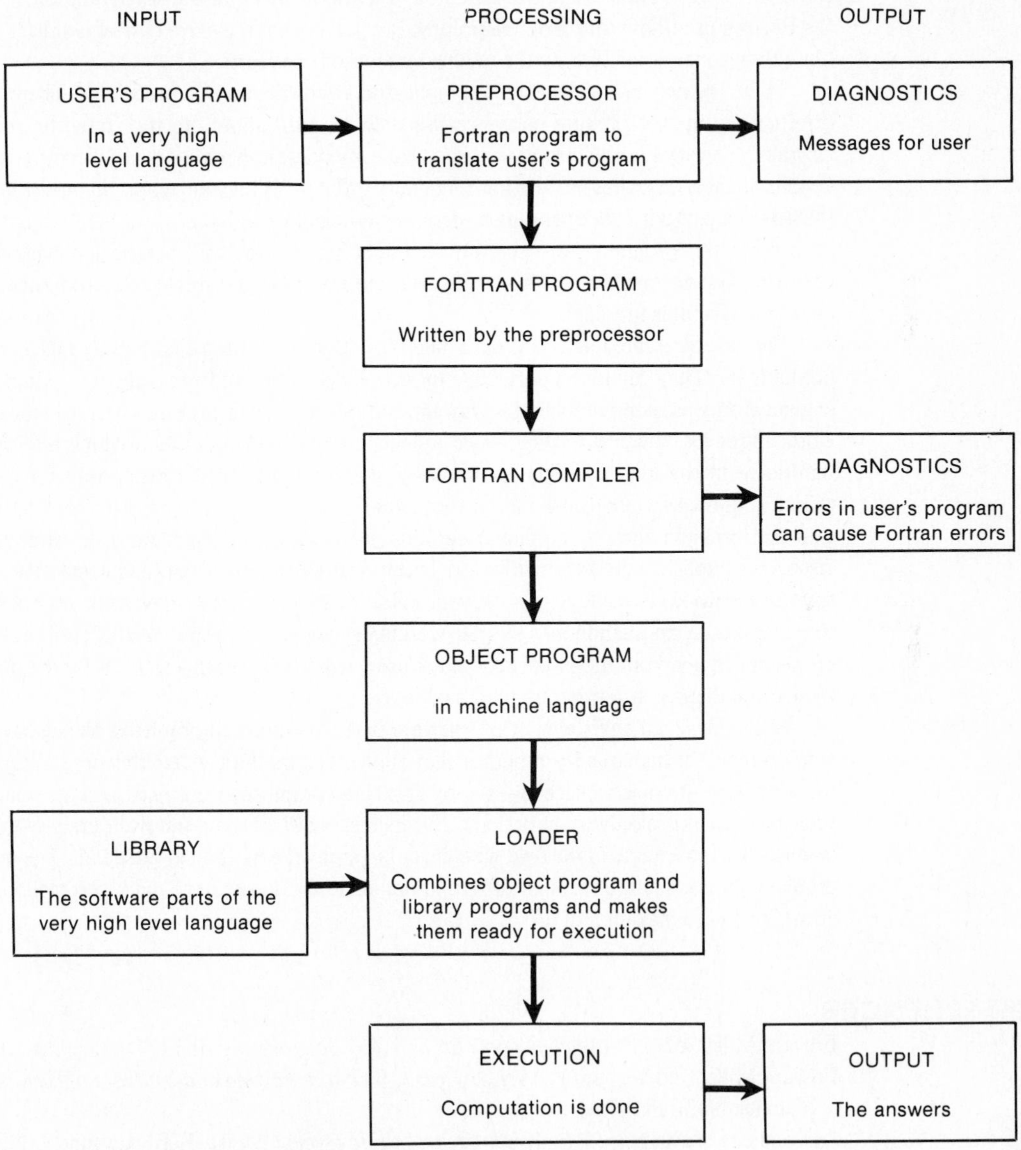

Figure 12.6 Organization of a Fortran preprocessor run. The middle boxes show the steps in processing the user's program. The input is on the left and the output on the right.

There are **two main advantages** to this approach: (1) the preprocessor is written in Fortran, and this can be done so that it runs, with little or no modification, on almost any computer which has Fortran; (2) the library of software parts is written and used as ordinary Fortran subroutines. If care is taken in writing the library programs, they can also be moved easily to any computer which has Fortran. In summary, this approach provides a very inexpensive way to make a language and its supporting software widely available.

There are also, of course, disadvantages. The most important is the added difficulties when errors occur. An error in the user's program or data might show up when the Fortran program is compiled or at execution time. In either case, the Fortran diagnostics and system error messages are harder to connect to the user's program. The severity of this problem can be reduced by making the preprocessor more sophisticated in its checking of the user's program.

A more obvious, but actually less serious, disadvantage is that there is more than one language translation required. A language processor written in machine language could translate the user's program into machine language much faster than a Fortran preprocessor can translate it to Fortran. One reason for this is the inefficiency of READ and WRITE in most Fortran systems. It is not uncommon for a Fortran preprocessor to take longer to write the translated program in an 80A1 format than it takes the Fortran compiler to read it, analyze it, translate it, and write the machine language program (which is longer than the Fortran program written by the preprocessor). Even so, the extra cost of language processing is much more than compensated for by the reduced programming effort.

There are two other less serious complications with Fortran preprocessors. There usually is some loss of efficiency in the software parts because they are not tailored to the actual machine used. Whoever "installs" the very high level language must have a modest understanding of the local computer's operating system. In most cases the installation is not very difficult. While one might regret the loss of efficiency and the involvement with the operating system, the efficiency can be regained by an effort much smaller than developing the program from scratch. A direct translation to machine language would involve the operating system much more than a Fortran preprocessor and might need some rewriting when a new operating system is installed.

We have presented software parts and very high level languages as ways to increase programming productivity. They can be very effective for this; indeed one can foresee the time when most scientists and engineers only use computers in this way and actually do very little programming in the current sense of the word. However, there is another aspect of this approach of computing which may well be much more significant in the long run. This approach provides a dramatically faster way for the **dissemination of technical know-how.** Consider the current situation when a new and better method is found to solve a standard problem such as nonlinear systems of equations or calculating the strength of bridges. The discoverer publishes the new method in a technical journal, it is read, and soon after it is included in a survey of methods in the field or an advanced book. As the method becomes better known, it is included in some textbooks and handbooks so that working scientists can use it. It can easily take 10 years for this know-how to get from the discoverer to the user. And the user still has to study the method, learn how it works, and then write a program to carry it out.

In the idealized environment of software parts for standard problems, the discoverer or a colleague would prepare a high-quality program that applies the method. After this program has been tested and found reliable, it could replace an existing library program (software part) and the scientist would receive the benefit of this discovery in perhaps 2 years instead of 10. And not everybody would have to learn its details; only the experts in the field would want to study the method in full detail. The net result would be a dramatic increase in the speed of disseminating technical know-how and a corresponding decrease in the effort for one to make use of it.

REFERENCES

Edward Miller (ed.), *Automated Tools for Software Engineering,* IEEE Catalog No. EHO 150-3 (1979).

Edward Miller and William E. Howden (eds.), *Software Testing and Validation Techniques,* IEEE Catalog No. EHO 138-8 (1978).

Lawrence H. Putnam (ed.), *Software Cost and Life-Cycle Control,* IEEE Catalog No. EHO 165-1 (1980).

Marvin V. Zelkowitz, Alan C. Shaw, and John D. Gannon, *Principles of Software Engineering and Design,* Prentice-Hall, Englewood Cliffs, N.J. (1979).

*13 SOFTWARE PERFORMANCE EVALUATION

A number of software qualities were discussed in Chapter 12; we now consider the practical question of how to measure them. Qualities which are easy to understand and measure are speed and accuracy. Reliability and ease of use are equally important but more difficult to measure. Less obvious, but still very important, are qualities like portability (ease of moving the software to another computer system) and maintenance (ease of making minor fixes or enhancements) This chapter focuses on evaluating just three qualities: efficiency (speed, memory use, etc.), reliability (and robustness), and portability. The next chapter is devoted to evaluating accuracy.

It is essential to recognize that software performance evaluation is primarily an experimental science and that performance studies must use proper scientific methods. These methods include:

1. *Developing a controlled and well-designed experimental framework.*

2. *Using precisely defined measures of performance.*

3. *Using explicitly stated criteria of evaluation.*

4. *Providing complete information about the performance data.*

5. *Applying systematic or statistical methods to analyze the data.*

These methods are fundamental in any experimental science, but software performance evaluation is still very young, and few standard approaches have been adopted. The result is that a large amount of past software performance evaluation is of questionable or no value (see the paper by Crowder, Dembo and Mulvey in the references). For example, a 1979 study of 50 papers to evaluate algorithms and software for a certain class of problems concluded that none of them used consistently good experimental techniques. One paper contains the statement:

> *Since the methods were coded for different machines in different languages by different programmers, there is little point in giving a detailed assessment of the results, particularly since so many of the problems were degenerate. However, the results show that...*

Such an experiment cannot show anything, but it is often hard to evaluate the conclusions because the data which lead to them are not given. Further, many authors are not so candid in admitting that there are serious flaws in the design of their evaluation.

Space limitations preclude giving a systematic presentation of an abstract framework and principles of experimental design for software evaluation. However, there are a few questions that one should ask even when making an informal or quick evaluation. If the answers to the following questions are uncertain, then one should have considerable doubt about the reliability of the conclusions reached:

1. *Is the amount of data (evidence) large enough that the results are not just concidence?* Three or four data points are almost never sufficient to give confidence in results; usually dozens and sometimes hundreds of data points are needed to reduce the effects of random variations to an acceptable level.

2. *Does the data really cover the problem domain of the software?* The data must adequately represent the set of problems for which the software is intended. The reliability of linear equation solvers cannot be adequately evaluated just by using random matrices. The efficiency of adaptive quadrature programs cannot be evaluated adequately just by using simple, smooth mathematical functions.

3. *Have extraneous sources of variation been controlled or ruled out?* Program A can appear to be faster than program B because a particular Fortran compiler does a poor job on a crucial part of program B. The quirks and idiosyncrasies of computer hardware or systems can change the relative speed or memory use of two programs by 30 to 50 percent or more. Doing low accuracy or small problems on a computer with lots of digits can fail to show up numerical instabilities. If the evaluation involves people (such as for ease of use or maintenance), then the variations due to different people can be many times larger than the variations being evaluated.

4. *Can the results be reproduced?* Would another person with the same software, same computing environment, and same general strategy arrive at the same data and same conclusions?

5. *Are there plausible explanations for the observed variations?* Experimental results do not have to have theoretical explanations, but they help give confidence in the results.

PROGRAM EFFICIENCY 13.1

Program efficiency refers to the use of computer resources by the program. The principal resources are **time, memory**, and **input-output** (I/O). Time is usually measured in seconds of use of a central processor or arithmetic unit. Most computer systems provide a utility program to "read the clock." Thus in Fortran one has something like

```
CALL SECOND(TSTART)
...
CALL SECOND(TEND)
TIME = TEND-TSTART
```

so that TIME is the number of seconds used to execute the code between the two calls on SECOND. Keep in mind that reading the clock also takes time, and so very short calculations usually cannot be timed accurately this way.

To time a short calculation, say computing log(20), one runs the following pair of programs:

```
      CALL SECOND(TSTART)
      DO 10 I = 1, 20000
10      A = ALOG10(20.)
      CALL SECOND(TEND)
      TIME = (TEND-TSTART)/20000
```

```
      CALL SECOND(TSTART)
      DO 10 I = 1, 20000
10      A = 20.0
      CALL SECOND(TEND)
      TIME = (TEND-TSTART)/20000
```

The difference in the two values of TIME is the time to compute log(20) 20,000 times. Note that some optimizing Fortran compilers can defeat this approach by removing the statement to compute A from the loop since it does not depend on I. In this case one can use A = ALOG10 (20. + B*I) and A = 20. + B*I where B is set to 0 elsewhere.

Memory used may be **main memory** in the computer or **auxiliary memory** such as disk files. For most programs one is usually interested in the amount of main memory used. This amount is known by the computer system and available from it. Some systems automatically print this information with each job, while others might require a special request. For Fortran programs, a request (such as MAP or LOAD) to the system link editor usually produces a table of the memory used by each program. Even so, it is often less convenient to obtain precise information for memory than for time.

An alternative for shorter programs is to add up (by inspecting the actual code) the locations in arrays and then add 10 times the number of statements to account for the machine language program and simple variables. While this is less precise, it is adequate for many situations and the only alternative in those systems which fail to provide memory use data.

Input-output use is of three general types: (1) information exchanged with the outside world (lines read, pages printed, etc.), (2) information exchanged with auxiliary memory (access to saved files, libraries, etc.), and (3) exchanges between main memory and auxiliary memory during execution as the job (or parts of it) is moved in and out by the system. The first type of I/O is easy to measure. The second is harder to measure but infrequently of great consequence. The third type of I/O is due either to time-sharing (multiprocessing) or to having a job that cannot fit in main memory. The I/O of time-sharing is usually considered part of the sytem work and not of the program itself. Even though one is not "charged" for this I/O, it is often one of the reasons for slow response in time-shared systems. The I/O for jobs that do not fit into main memory can be hard to measure. The person who wrote the program probably knows how to measure it since he or she controlled the I/O. Another user may have to rely on general system information which does not distinguish between various types of I/O. Virtual memory systems have the operating system in control of I/O during job execution, and the amount of I/O used is usually hard to obtain and can vary greatly between different runs of the same program.

Once one measures the resources used, one then must relate it to the software and its input. In the simplest case, a program just does one thing [for example, evaluate TAN (12.6)], and there is no need to do more than measure its performance. Most software accepts a range of problems as input, and **performance evaluation** is to relate the performance to the problem or, more precisely, to certain features of the problem input. A simple model of the situation is illustrated in Figure 13.1. The **problem space** is the set of all inputs to the program; this set is logically divided into two parts. The first part is the intended inputs, problems for which the program is designed. The second part is the possible but unintended inputs. Thus, a program may be designed to integrate only smooth functions, and any performance evaluation must distinguish between smooth functions and others.

The **problem features** are characteristics or properties of problems. To be useful, they must be measurable and well correlated with peformance. For example, the size N of a linear system is a feature easy to measure and strongly correlated with the time and memory which a Gauss elimination program takes to solve the system. The condition number of the matrix is not correlated with time and memory, but it is strongly correlated with the accuracy obtained. The condition number is not so easily measured, but it is an important feature because accuracy is so important.

Software is normally designed in terms of problem features and not an explicit set of problems. Thus a differential equation solver might be designed for small systems (up to 20 equations) of initial value problems that are well behaved and where moderate accuracy (1 to 3 decimal digits) is needed. The words *small, 20, initial value, well behaved, moderate,* and *1 to 3 decimal digits* are all features of the problem space for this particular program. It is usually necessary to think in terms of features because the problem space is too large for one to consider all or most of the individual problems.

Real software often is intended for a broad spectrum of problems with many different features, and one wants to evaluate several aspects of performance. There is usually interplay and tradeoffs between the various program properties. One method may run fast but give poor accuracy, while another may run fast, give acceptable accuracy, and use enormous amounts of memory. Note that *several performance criteria are always relevant to performance evaluation.* If one thinks only speed is important, then one is logically led to the program:

```
      PRINT 10
   10 FORMAT(5X,10(2H**),' THE ANSWER IS 1.7296')
      STOP
      END
```

Not only is this extremely fast, but it uses almost no memory or I/O. It is also highly reliable and robust, broadly applicable, easy to use, easily maintained, and very portable. It is only lacking in accuracy.

Evaluating complex software with a large problem space is a substantial undertaking. Comparing several programs with a large problem space is even more difficult. One rarely finds that a single program is

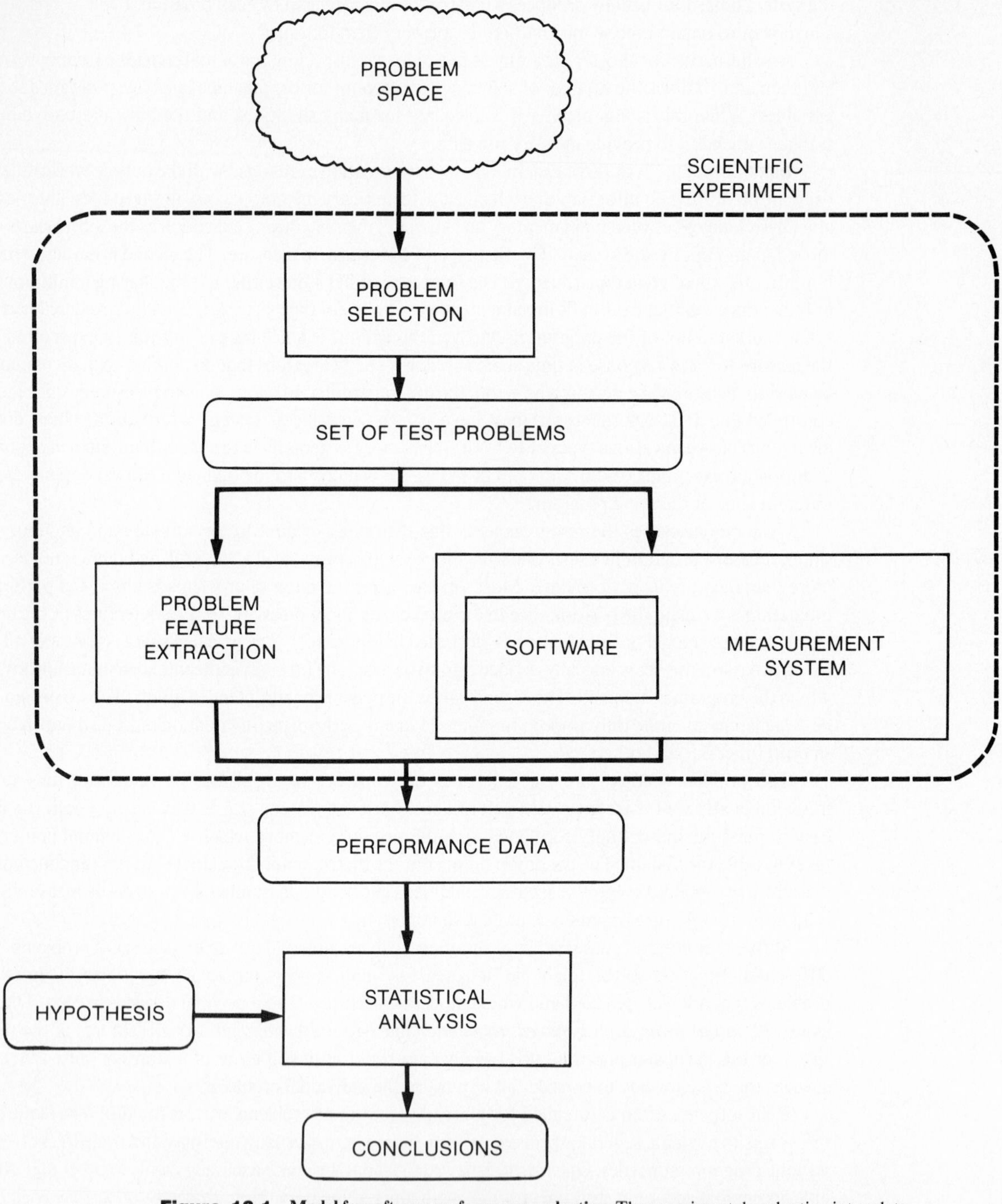

Figure 13.1 Model for software performance evaluation. The experimental evaluation is to relate the performance data to the problem features or to the problems themselves. The problem features are characteristics like size, type, complexity, dimension, etc.

best for all the problems and all the criteria of performance. Indeed, the interplay between several features, several programs, and several performance criteria can become so complex that it is hard to understand the interrelationships even after long study.

A useful tool for performance evaluation is the **performance profile.** This is a graph of one performance measure versus one problem feature. For N linear equations, one might have performance profiles of time versus N, memory versus N, accuracy versus condition number, or memory versus sparsity. Figures 13.2 and 13.3 show four performance profiles, two simple ones for linear equations and two more complex ones for numerical integration software.

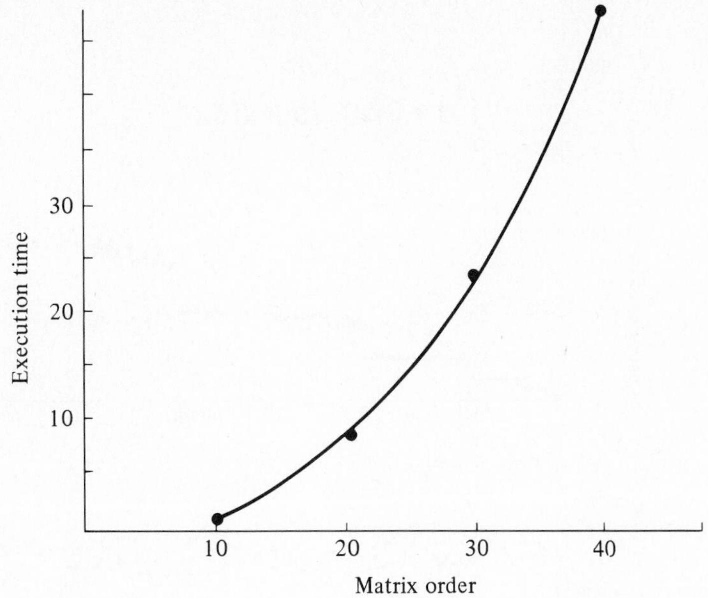

(a)

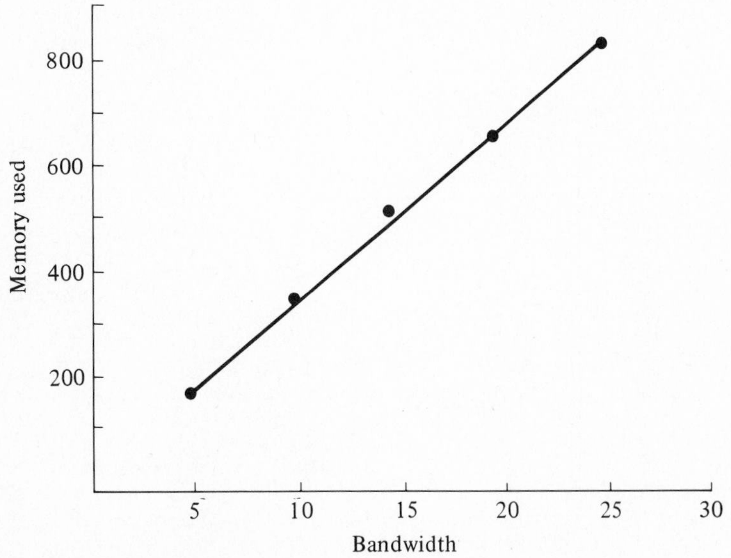

(b)

Figure 13.2 **Two performance profiles for software to solve Ax = b.** (a) Execution time versus matrix order for a standard Gauss elimination program. (b) Memory versus bandwidth for a band matrix routine and 25 by 25 matrices.

The computer hardware and system software (especially the Fortran compiler) can have a substantial effect on performance. It is obvious that a faster machine will (or, at least, should) execute all programs faster. But the execution time of program A might be reduced by 72 percent, while program B's time is only reduced by 65 percent. One should expect the relative performance in speed to change by about 25 to 35 percent when one changes computing environments. In other words, the fact that program A runs 20 percent faster than program B might well be due to the computing environment and not reflect any inherent speed advantage of program A. Much larger variations due to the computing environment are possible; differences of 500 percent have been observed in exceptional circumstances. The following example shows 90 percent differences and, more significantly, shows one cannot write Fortran code that operates "best" in several computing environments.

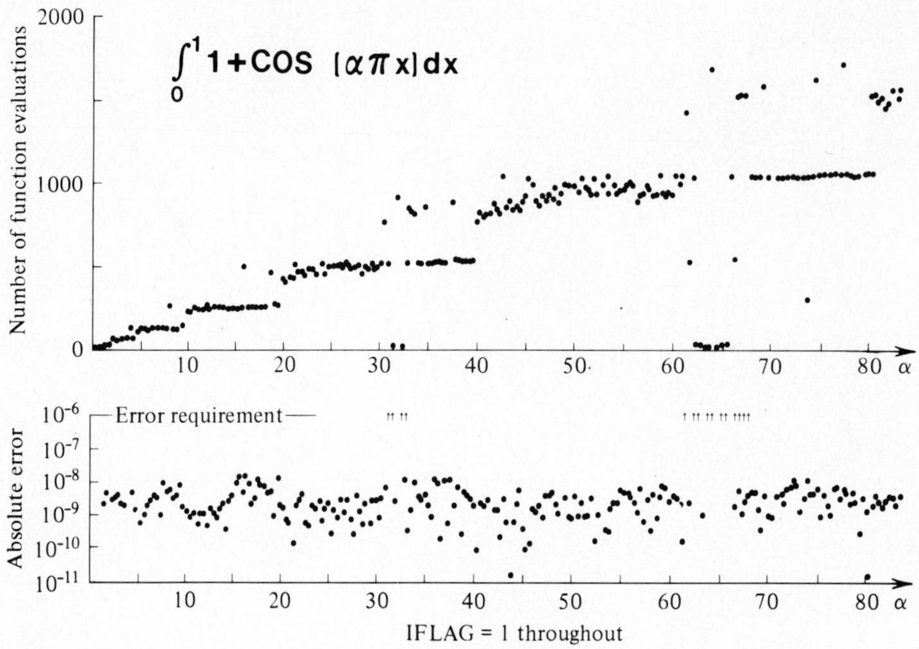

(a)

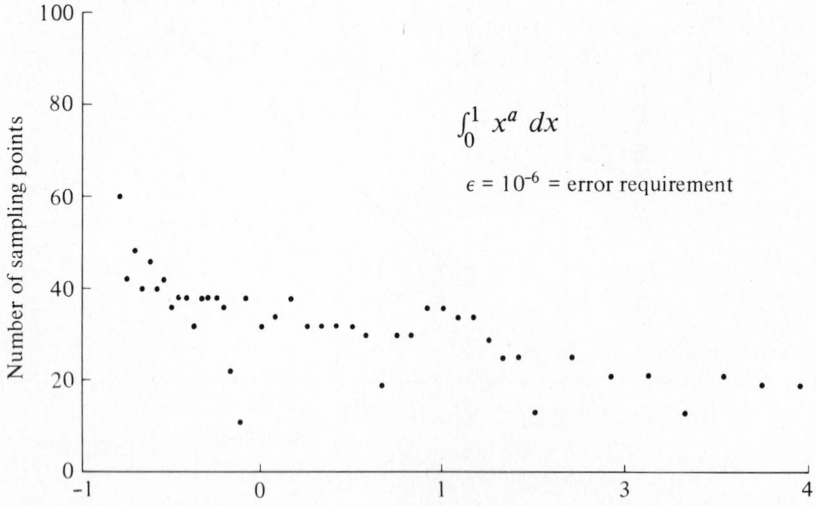

(b)

Figure 13.3 **Two performance profiles for numerical integration software.** (a) DCADRE applied to $\int_0^1 [\cos(\alpha\pi x) + 1]\,dx$. This profile shows the work increasing as the oscillation increases, but in an unexpected way. The large errors near $\alpha = 32$ and 64 are due to an interaction between the algorithm and α. (b) DQUAD applied to $\int_0^1 x^\alpha dx$. This profile shows that the work is unaffected by the singularity strength; it decreases slowly as α increases.

Computing Environment Effects on Software for Solving Ax = b

Example 13.1

This example is based on the study *The Influence of the Compiler on the Cost of Mathematical Software — In Particular on the Cost of Triangular Factorization,* by B. Parlett and Y. Wang, ACM Trans. Math. Software **1** (1975), pp. 35–46. Five different environments are considered, involving two different computers:

CDC 6400 with RUN, FUN, and FTN compilers

IBM 360/50 with G and H compilers

The inner loop of the Crout version of Gauss eliminations is

$$a_{ij} \leftarrow a_{ij} - \sum_{k} a_{ik} * a_{kj}$$

This mathematical formula is implemented by three different sets of Fortran code:

Code 1 — Maximum Use of Indexes

```
      DO 1 K = 1,M
1         A(I,J) = A(I,J) - A(I,K)*A(K,J)
```

Code 2 — Remove Fixed Index Term from Loop

```
      SUM = A(I,J)
      DO 2 K = 1,M
2         SUM = SUM - A(I,K)*A(K,J)
      A(I,J)  = SUM
```

Code 3 — Case 2 with a Temporary Variable T Added

```
      SUM = A(I,J)
      DO 3 K = 1,M
            T = A(I,K)*A(K,J)
3           SUM = SUM - T
      A(I,J)    = SUM
```

Programs for solving linear equations were written which were identical except for this segment of code. These three programs were timed for linear systems of order 25, 50, and 75 on each computer with each compiler. Table 13.1 presents the results for the 75 by 75 case; the others were similar. The fastest code gets a score of 100 and the slower ones are proportionally higher. Note that the time is based on the entire linear equation solving time, not just the time for the inner loop. Of course, the inner loop accounts for the bulk (probably over 98 percent) of the time for the whole program.

Execution Time Comparisons for Three Ways to Do the Inner Loop of the Crout Algorithm **Table 13.1**

Times are normalized in each column so that the fastest is 100.

	IBM 360/50		CDC 6400		
	G compiler	H compiler	RUN compiler	FUN compiler	FTN compiler
CODE 1:	149	117	115	119	100
CODE 2:	100	100	100	100	104
CODE 3:	102	105	190	190	107

We see that Code 3, which is unnatural, is never best. However, the penalty for this "minor" variation varies from 2 to 90 percent. Code 1 directly expresses the desired calculation. Our hope for "optimizing" compilers (as all of these are to some extent) is that they can produce the best code for a particular calculation — at least if it is a two-line DO loop. Only the FTN compiler achieves this, and all the others produce code which is substantially less efficient, with a 15 to 49 percent loss in efficiency.

Not only do these examples show that there is no one best way to code a calculation, they also show that seemingly trivial differences in code can produce very large differences in execution time.

The data in this study allow us to examine the value of different levels of optimization in compilers. The same data that give Table 13.1 are normalized so that the fastest time for each code on each computer is 100; the results are shown in Table 13.2. There we see that the IBM H compiler produces object code which is three to four times faster than that produced by the G compiler. Similarly, the CDC FTN compiler produces code that is 40 to 150 percent faster than the RUN or FUN compilers (which are quite similar). One may interpret this by saying that, even though small code changes can produce large differences in efficiency, the choice of compiler can produce much larger differences yet.

Execution Time Comparisons of Compilers for Three Programs on Two Machines Table 13.2

Times are normalized so that the fastest execution time for a program and machine is 100.

	IBM 360/50		CDC 6400		
	G compiler	H compiler	RUN compiler	FUN compiler	FTN compiler
CODE 1:	395	100	165	170	100
CODE 2:	311	100	139	137	100
CODE 3:	304	100	257	255	100

SOFTWARE RELIABILITY AND ROBUSTNESS 13.2

Recall from Chapter 12 that **software reliability** measures how well the software performs its intended functions. **Software robustness** measures how the performance degrades as usage moves away from the intended domain of use. Robust software should have no surprises (even when misused) or nitpicking causes of failure.

Reliability is defined in terms of elementary probability. A program has **reliability of use** x if the number of successes in its use divided by the total number of uses is x. This definition is not very convenient because it depends on knowing how the program is to be used, and reliability of use can and does change as the usage of the program changes. A program has **problem reliability** x if the number of problems for which it succeeds divided by the total number of problems is x. This definition uses an implicit assumption that all input problems are equally likely in use of the program. A program has **code reliability** x if the number of correct statements in the program divided by the total number of statments is x. Reliability of use is the most relevant definition of reliability even though it is the most difficult to measure. Code reliability is widely analyzed but is of less interest because there is no theoretical or experimentally observed correlation between code reliability and reliability of use. A program with just 1 error in 10,000 statements can fail every time, while there are examples of software with dozens of known errors which are used daily in hundreds of jobs with no failures.

Reliability of use can be measured by monitoring the software's performance as it is used. There are various drawbacks to this approach; one wants to know beforehand whether the software for controlling a missile, airplane, or space shuttle is reliable or not. Systematic testing and analysis can be used to estimate problem reliability. Testing consists of executing the program on a large sample of problems chosen in some way from the problem space. Note that it is sometimes very difficult to choose problems uniformly and at random as one needs to do: for example, for software that integrates functions or differential equations. If one has valid information about the probabilities of problems appearing in actual use, one can even use testing to estimate reliability of use.

The weakness of testing using random problem choices is illustrated in solving linear systems. If one chooses matrices A with random elements a_{ij}, one is very unlikely to obtain an ill-conditioned matrix. A test involving thousands of random matrices might fail to reveal that a program for solving $\mathbf{Ax} = \mathbf{b}$ is numerically unstable for ill-conditioned matrices. Yet this program has low reliability of use because ill-conditioned matrices arise frequently in practice.

Robustness does not have an easy mathematical definition, but it is easier to test a program for robustness. The usual approach is to assign someone to attack, assault, misuse, and abuse the program. The person is told what the program is supposed to do and what its input is, and then proceeds to push the program to and past its limits in various ways. Problem 6.4.8 illustrates one type of misuse (incorrect or illegal arguments) to be tried. While this is an ad hoc approach, it can be effective, especially if the person doing the testing has had experience with similar software.

Suppose that one has measured the reliability and robustness of a program and found it unsatisfactory. What does one do to improve things? Reliability is usually a property of the details of the Fortran program and its underlying methods and algorithms. There are few general principles to apply to increase reliability, and the ones that exist can usually be summarized as "analyze, check, and test the program more carefully." The application of various software tools can reveal some kinds of programming errors. However, in the end someone has to dig into the program and find out what makes it unreliable. Some algorithms and methods are inherently unreliable, and software that uses them must either be discarded or be used with great caution.

Robustness is also a property of the program and its underlying methods. There is a general approach that can be used systematically to enhance robustness. A program is designed with some model of the problems and methods in mind; unfortunately, this model is rarely written down, and many programmers are not even aware they have one. The program writer should mentally formulate this model clearly, and while writing the program, repeatedly ask "What happens with this code if the problem is bad or the method does not work as I expect?" If the answer is poor behavior, gross errors, etc., then the program writer should insert code that either (1) checks the problem and method to see if they are all right or (2) provides insurance against bad problems and behaviors. Examples of the first kind of code are to check:

That polynomial degrees are not negative

That arguments to square roots are not negative

That the number of differential equations agrees with the number of right sides

That the function for integration is actually smooth

That the terms being summed from an infinite series are getting small

If something does not check as it should, then the program can print a diagnostic, set an error flag, or take some other appropriate action. Examples of the second kind of code are:

Limit all iterations to some maximum number

Adjust the arguments of all mathematical functions (SQRT, SIN, COS, ALOG, EXP, . . .) to legal values

Force all real variables that should have integer values to be integers; the following code does this:

```
I = X + .1*SIGN(X)
X = I
```

Reorder lists that should be ordered but are not

In some of these cases, one would also issue a warning of some kind.

The beginning of every program should have code to check the assumptions the program makes about the input. An equation solver should check that the number of equations is positive. An integration program should check that the limits of integration are in the right order (if that fact is used by the program). An interpolation program should check that the abscissa are in increasing order if that is assumed. One should check that the convergence tests and error targets are positive and realistic (i.e., one should not permit a request for 12 digits of accuracy when using a 10-digit machine).

SOFTWARE PORTABILITY 13.3

Software portability refers to the properties of software when it is moved to another computing environment. Portability also comes into play when new hardware or systems are installed in a computing center. One of the great attractions when higher-level languages like Fortran and Algol were introduced was *machine independence*: the program could express the computation independently of the computer used to do it. Fortran and Algol have not been as machine-independent as originally hoped, but they are incomparably more portable than assembly and machine language.

The obvious obstacle to machine independence and portability is the precision or word length of the machine. A Fortran program to compute π to 10 digits can be in single precision on CDC machines but must be in double precision on IBM machines. A Fortran program can operate with EXP (144.2) on some machines and not on others. Features such as these are called **hardware dependencies,** and they might cause a Fortran program to be nonportable. One important use of Table 3.1 (Floating Point Characteristics of Computers) is to help determine program portability.

Once one realizes that hardware dependencies are unavoidable, one can take steps to minimize this effect. Several useful techniques have been developed, but all rely on one important assumption: **The programmer realizes that the code is hardware dependent.** Once a hardware dependency is recognized, one should take two steps:

1. *Insert comments in the code explaining the hardware dependency.*
2. *Define variables (usually one is all that is needed) that determine this dependency, set their values once, and use them consistently.*

To further alert one to the hardware dependencies, there should be a block of comments at the start of the program which lists them all.

The use of a variable to define hardware dependencies makes it much easier to change the variable for a new machine. There are complex Fortran codes where it is almost as much work to move the codes as to rewrite them for a new machine. An example of how this can occur follows.

How Hardware Dependencies Can Make a Program Unchangeable Example 13.2

Consider a program that needs a lot of memory, and so it is decided that various tables of data are to be packed. In a 48-bit machine, one can pack four 3-decimal-digit integers per word. One uses the formula

```
NPACK = N1 + 1028*(N2 + 1028*(N3 + 1028*N4))
```

to put N1, N2, N3, and N4 into NPACK. Recall that $1028 = 2^{10}$, and so the largest NPACK can be is $(1028)^2 * 999$ or about 2^{40}, which fits in 48 bits. The numbers can be retrieved using the MOD function and integer division: for example,

```
N3 = MOD(NPACK/1056784,1028)
```

where $1056784 = 1028^2$.

Suppose the programmers decided to use 34,000 words of memory for tables and divided it up into 16,500 packed with four 3-digit numbers, 8,500 packed with four 2-character variables, 4,000 with six 2-digit numbers, and 5,000 with two 7-digit numbers. These tables are then used in dozens of routines, and they are further subdivided among subtables. In the end the code has hundreds of different, somewhat odd numbers derived from the initial assumptions of 48 bits and 34,000 words divided into four parts.

A new computer is installed which has 32 bits per word, and it is decided that the program should handle larger problems. This means these tables must be completely reworked along with *all* the code that refers to them. This requires that the logic be understood at each place where the code uses one of the numbers derived from the initial assumptions. It can be very time-consuming and boring to dig into this program, to identify each of these places, and to make the appropriate changes. Some programs with this type of dependency exist without a single comment or line of documentation explaining the assumptions.

If the programmers had introduced variables as follows:

```
C
C     NTABLE = 34000 = SIZE OF PACKED TABLES
C            = NTAB3 + NTAB2C + NTAB2 + NTAB7
C     NTAB3  = 16500 = SIZE OF TABLES OF 3 DIGITS
C     NTAB2C = 8500  = SIZE OF TABLES OF 2 CHARACTERS
C     NTAB2  = 4000  = SIZE OF TABLES OF 2 DIGITS
C     NTAB7  = 5000  = SIZE OF TABLES OF 7 DIGITS
```

and then introduced utility functions like this:

```
C     PACK3(N1,N2,N3,N4) = INTEGER FUNCTION TO PACK FOUR 3-DIGIT
C                          NUMBERS IN A 48 BIT WORD
C     UNPAK3(N,I) = INTEGER FUNCTION TO UNPACK THE I-TH
C                   3-DIGIT NUMBER FROM A 48 BIT WORD
```

the task of moving this code to a new machine might be accomplished in one-hundredth the time required for the unplanned, undocumented code.

Note that some hardware dependencies can also affect maintenance and enhancement. In the above example, one would meet almost the same difficulties when attempting to fix an error in the program or to enhance its capabilities.

Hardware dependencies can be handled even more cleanly by using functions to provide information about the hardware. Some libraries have such functions which are provided with the correct values when the library is installed. If the code is moved to a new environment, then all one has to do is be sure that these library programs are provided. One can anticipate in the future that these functions will become a standard part of Fortran (and similar languages) just as SIN(X) is now.

A Set of Fortran Functions for Machine Arithmetic Characteristics — Example 13.3

The following set of functions has been proposed for inclusion in Fortran to provide information about the underlying hardware. A set similar to this can be expected for various languages and comprehensive numerical software libraries.

RADIX(X)	=	base or radix of the number system
PRECISION(X)	=	number of digits in the number system
HUGE(X)	=	largest number in the system
TINY(X)	=	smallest positive number in the system
EPSILON(X)	=	number "almost" negligible compared to 1.0
MINEXP(X)	=	minimum exponent of number system
MAXEXP(X)	=	maximum exponent of number system

The argument x only plays a role in determining the type of arithmetic (this is an instance of generic function types in Fortran 77). The first three functions are defined for integers, and the rest for both single and double precision. Thus HUGE(1) = HUGE(13) = largest integer in the Fortran system, while TINY(1.0) and TINY(1.0 D0) are the smallest positive single and double precision numbers, respectively.

A related set of functions has been proposed to directly manipulate floating point numbers. The more interesting of these are

EXPONENT(X)	=	exponent of X in the number system
FRACTION(X)	=	mantissa or fractional part of X in the number system
SCALE(X,E)	=	multiply X by b^E where b is the number system base; this is done without round-off by an exponent add

The use of these functions is illustrated by code to terminate a simple iteration. This code uses two simple tests: (1) assume convergence when the difference in iterates is less than 20 times round-off; (2) assume divergence when the difference is larger than one-tenth the square root of the largest machine number. The Fortran code might appear as follows:

```
C
C                 SET HARDWARE DEPENDENT CONSTANTS
      CONVRG   =  20.*EPSILON(1.0)
      DIVRG    =  0.1*SQRT(HUGE(1.0))
      LIMIT    =  5*PRECISION(1.0)
      DO 10 I  =  1, LIMIT
C                 COMPUTE ITERATES XOLD, XNEW
C                 THEN TEST FOR CONVERGENCE/DIVERGENCE
         DIFF      =  ABS((XOLD-XNEW)/XNEW)
         IF(DIFF .LE. CONVRG)       GO TO 20
         IF(DIFF .GT. DIVRG)        GO TO 99
   10 CONTINUE
```

There are two technical definitions relevant to portability. Software is **portable** if it runs correctly on different systems with no changes at all. Software is **transportable** if it can be made to run on different systems with a few straightforward changes. The general use of the word "portable" corresponds to the technical definition of transportable and not portable. We see that most numerical software can only hope to be transportable, as hardware dependencies must be handled by changes in the code. Much more numerical software could be portable if Fortran provided information about the hardware characteristics.

Once hardware dependencies are properly handled, one would hope that using standard Fortran would be enough to provide portability. Alas, such is not the case. There are hundreds of Fortran dialects, and while many of the differences are enhancements (e.g., adding nonstandard features), a significant portion are restrictions. In fact, the Fortran standard is confusing at places and gives the compiler writer choices at other places. The net result is that **one cannot rely on standard Fortran working the same (or at all) in all Fortran systems.**

A complete analysis of the dialects and differences would take 50 or 100 pages; we give a few of the more "unreliable" Fortran statements or constructions.

1. *Ordering of the declaration statements.* There is no ordering of the declaration statements that is legal on all major Fortran systems. It is common to require that DATA statements follow all other declarations.

2. *Mixing types in COMMON blocks.* Some hardware has special ways to store numbers that can ruin the alignment of variables in COMMON if integers, reals, double precision, logical, and complex are mixed. It is especially risky to mix "2 storage word" variables (such as double precision or complex) or "half storage word" variables (such as logical or short integer) with other types.

3. *EQUIVALENCE.* This should be avoided. The Fortran standard does not require it to work the way most people believe it works, and different compilers implement it differently.

4. *Complicated formats.* Different Fortrans may interpret (or even reject) formats that conform to the standard. This usually happens with complicated formats involving nested parentheses and multiple specifications.

5. *Constant lengths.* Some compilers fail if a constant is too long. Thus if one sets π to a 15-digit value to be sure to get a good value on all machines (at least in single precision), one gets a fatal error on some systems.

6. *A-Format, character storage.* The number of characters that can be stored per word is a hardware dependency, just as the precision of numbers. However, some Fortran systems allow even fewer than the hardware could support. Almost all allow 4 characters per word (A4 format) and CDC allows 10 (A10 format). The only truly portable assumption is 1 character per word (A1 format).

7. *Saving values between subprogram calls.* Fortran does not require values to be saved or remembered between calls on subprograms. The number of Fortran systems that "forget" values is increasing.

There are many nice enhancements of Fortran which are not standard but which are tempting to use. The situation is further confused because there are now two standard Fortrans: **Fortran 66** and **Fortran 77**. Fortran 66 is the Fortran adopted by the American National Standards Institute (ANSI) in 1966, and Fortran 77 was adopted in 1977. Another standard Fortran can be expected to become available in the late 1980s. Most Fortran systems are currently in between these two; they have removed the silly restrictions of Fortran 66 [such as allowing A(2*I+1) but not A(1+I*2) or not allowing DO 10 I = K+1, 2*K] and added some of the nice, new features of Fortran 77 (such as IF-THEN-ELSE). The problem is that one does not know what one can count on, and so for several more years those who want to write portable programs must make the pessimistic assumptions that only Fortran 66 is available and then use only part of that. Fortunately, only a few rarely used features of Fortran 66 will disappear when Fortran 77 becomes universally available.

PFORT is an important tool for producing portable Fortran software. It was developed by studying a large number of Fortran systems and identifying those features which work the same in all the systems. PFORT checks Fortran code to see if any statements are present which are known to cause portability problems. A program that passes the PFORT checks is very unlikely to encounter portability problems. PFORT was developed at Bell Telephone Laboratories and is in the public domain; it is widely available in computing centers (see references).

In addition to the general portability problems noted above, there is a large number of compiler idiosyncrasies in Fortran systems. These aberrations were not designed to be there, but a combination of events made them happen anyway. One example is that the statement

```
IF(X .NE. 0.0) Y = 1./X
```

allows a division by 0 on one Fortran system. There are numbers (fortunately rarely encountered) which look like 0 to the division unit but which are not 0, and hence X .NE. 0.0 is .TRUE. In this Fortran system the statement

```
IF(1.0*X .NE. 0.0) Y = 1./X
```

does avoid division by 0. In another Fortran system this statement produces a diagnostic because one is multiplying by 1.0.

A second example occurs in a program that needs ultra-precise control of round-off and uses

```
X = (X+0.5) + 0.5
```

to control the bias in round-off. One Fortran compiler replaces this by X = X+1.0 (which has no effect on round-off) in spite of the violation of the rules about parenthesis in arithmetic. Fortran allows this interpretation. To make the calculation proceed as desired, it is necessary to use the statement X = X+0.5 followed several statements later by X = X+0.5.

Finally, we point out that ad hoc constants can cause considerable concern in maintaining and transporting software. An **ad hoc constant** is a constant in a program that has no obvious source and has been determined by the programmer as a value that makes the program work. Values for ad hoc constants are usually determined by a combination of guesswork and experimentation. There is nothing wrong with their use *provided they are properly identified.* The difficulty arises when someone else is trying to understand the program and thinks the value of the constant should be derivable from scientific formulas, machine parameters, or some such thing. In fact, many constants that are believed to be ad hoc by the original programmer have turned out to be derived from other quantities once one has a better understanding of the methods used.

In summary, there are five **principles for portable software:**

1. *Document everything well, and identify variables and constants used.*

2. *Isolate machine and system dependencies by comments and by introducing variables for them.*

3. *Use a portable subset of Fortran such as specified by PFORT. At least use a Fortran compiler that checks for standard Fortran.*

4. *Identify ad hoc constants and constructions, and explain the intuitive ideas behind them.*

5. *Run the program on at least three completely different computer systems.*

REPORTING COMPUTATIONAL EXPERIMENTS 13.4

The performance evaluation of software is part of experimental science. The analysis of algorithms and related techniques can give a good indication of what to expect from many programs, but actual measurements must be taken to be certain of the performance. For example, the execution time of a program using Gauss elimination should increase like N^3 for solving N equations. However, it makes a big difference whether it is $0.05N^3$ or $500N^3$. For small N (say $N \leq 6$), the execution time is almost surely better represented by $a + bN + cN^2$ (with appropriate coefficients a, b, and c), and there is always the chance that a programming error has completely changed the expected behavior.

There are certain standard procedures that have been adopted in the experimental sciences in order to achieve confidence in the validity of experimentally based conclusions. At the highest level these procedures are required to *be systematic, organized, and objective, consider all relevant influences, and report exactly what was done and what the results were.* Each experimental science develops its own techniques, and the material in this chapter has been an exposition of some of these techniques for numerical software. In addition, there are the general techniques of the design of experiments from the statistical point of view. While these statistical procedures are not discussed in this book, they are an essential part of many software performance evaluations.

Table 13.3 presents a checklist for reporting computational experiments. Some of these items are not needed for all experiments, and conversely, some experiments need other items. Nevertheless, this checklist is a good guide as to the amount and kind of information that is required to instill confidence in the conclusions drawn from experiments with software.

Checklist for Reporting Computational Evaluations **Table 13.3**

	Algorithm information
Required:	Complete description of algorithm plus the class of problems it is supposed to handle
Nice:	Information on computational complexity, convergence rates, error estimates, work per step, etc.
	Computer program and computational environment
Required:	Programming language and compiler
	Computer, operating system, and options used
	Input formats, tolerances, and other program "settings"
	Special techniques or tactics used
Nice:	Information on the availability of the programs, user's manual, etc.
	Experimental design and results
Required:	A clear statement of the experimental objectives
	Documentation of procedures used, preprocessing of problems, or postprocessing of data
	Description of data to be obtained, including units of measurement and accuracy
	Problem population considered and sampling method used
Nice:	Use of standard problems, preprocessing, units of measurements, etc.
	Availability of problems, programs, and procedures for others to use
	Reporting the results
Required:	Complete description of the experimental design and procedures
	Justification of experimental design and performance measures used
	How measurements were made with detailed breakdowns (if appropriate)
	Failures that occurred, with explanation, if possible
	Program parameters used (for example, tolerances, initial states, options, switches)
Nice:	Effects of varying components of the experiment such as termination criteria, tolerances, or measurement techniques
	Conclusions stated
Required:	Clear distinction between objective results and speculation
	Description of hypotheses and assumptions made
Nice:	Directions for future study or algorithm improvement
	Identification of special problems classes where interesting things were observed

REFERENCES

P. J. Brown (ed.), *Software Portability,* Cambridge University Press, London (1977).

Wayne Cowell (ed.) *Portability of Numerical Software,* Lecture Notes in Computer Science 57, Springer-Verlag, New York (1977), 539 pages.

Harlan Crowder, Ron S. Dembo, and John M. Mulvey, *On Reporting Computational Experiments with Mathematical Software,* ACM Trans. Math. Software, **5** (1979), pp. 193-203.

Lloyd D. Fosdick (ed.), *Performance Evaluation of Numerical Software,* North-Holland, Amsterdam (1979), 335 pages.

M. A. Hennell and L. M. Delves (eds.), *Production and Assessment of Numerical Software,* Academic Press, New York (1980)

B. G. Ryder, *The PFORT Verifier,* Software Practice and Experience, **4** (1974), pp. 359-378.

**14 THE VALIDATION OF NUMERICAL COMPUTATIONS

The question considered in this chapter is simple, but fundamental: *How do you know the answers from a numerical computation are correct?* One can never know with absolute certainty; there is always the possibility that the underlying physical theories are wrong, that the real-world data used are wrong, or that the computer hardware malfunctions. One can, however, reduce the uncertainty substantially by using a variety of techniques discussed here. Keep in mind that it is normally expensive to validate the results of a numerical computation. Just to make one reasonable error estimate normally doubles the computational cost. The analysis and checking of a computation for the presence of all types of errors and uncertainties can easily increase the cost by an order of magnitude. There are applications where extreme measures are required (nuclear power plant design, air traffic control, manned space flight systems, etc.); in each instance the programmer or user of numerical software should make a conscious decision about the amount of effort to be put into validating the software and its results. Experience shows that time and time again this aspect of computation is slighted. A programmer is so excited when a program finally runs correctly a couple of times that he or she pronounces it finished, completely checked out, and certified. In fact, the program might be such that it gives correct results only about half the time.

Three principal sources of uncertainty are identified in Figure 3.1. We rename them slightly here as follows:

Model Uncertainty: The underlying physical theories and data might be incorrect, or the mathematical model might not accurately reflect reality. The physical problem might be inherently ill-conditioned or the mathematical model formulated so as to yield unstable computations.

Numerical Uncertainty: The arithmetic inaccuracies (round-off) might contaminate the answers, the algorithm might be numerically unstable, or the methods might be terminated prematurely (before convergence to correct results occurs).

Software Uncertainty: The program might have blunders in it; the numerical methods, algorithms, or library software might be inappropriate or inaccurate; or the execution might be incorrect due to errors in compilers, data lost or changed by the system, using the wrong program, or similar events.

There is no single technique to measure the size of all these uncertainties; we discuss each source of uncertainty separately. The technique of sensitivity analysis is probably the most generally applicable technique and, fortunately, is often one of the easiest to use.

VALIDATION OF MODELS IN NUMERICAL COMPUTATION 14.1

The key idea in validating models is **consistency:** the model must be consistent with experimental observations and with expected behavior. If the program models the bending of pipes, there is *no substitute* for actually bending some pipes in a controlled and measured situation and then comparing the results with the program's. The behavior expected for a model of pipe bending includes: (1) if no force is applied, then the pipe does not bend at all; (2) the amount of bending increases as the amount of force increases until eventually the pipe breaks or collapses; (3) as the thickness of a pipe's walls increases, the amount it bends decreases. A thorough check of the model used in a program will include a battery of tests for expected behavior in limiting or special cases.

The development and validation of models (either physical or mathematical) are not the topics of this book, and so we do not discuss them in detail. Instead we cite an example of the kind of thing that can go wrong to underscore the prime importance of this aspect of numerical computation. There is an immense set of computer programs used to certify and analyze the designs of nuclear power plants. One aspect of this analysis is predicting what would happen if a melt-down occurs, that is, if the reactor core gets out of control, heats up, and eventually melts. One safety device in these power plants is a huge tank of water that is to be pumped into the core if it gets too hot. The model of this process includes things like the temperature of the core, the capacity of the pumps and pipes, the amount of water, and so forth. After some years of using this program, it was decided to build a test apparatus to see how well this water cooling system works. After all, there is no actual experimental data for a power plant melt-down since one has never occurred. Gas was used to heat a fake metal core, and when the core was hot enough, the pumps were started. To everyone's great surprise, almost no water went into the core, and almost no cooling took place. The reason was that the first water into the core turned to steam which built up enough pressure to overpower the pumps and keep the rest of the water from entering. No one had thought about the water turning to steam, and so this phenomenon was not included in the mathematical model or in the design of this cooling system.

It has been seriously proposed to build a real nuclear power plant and then deliberately let it melt down just to obtain experimental data to use in validating the programs that model such plants. Even though the cost would be huge (perhaps $500 million), it was felt that it would be worth it in order to have more confidence in the computer models. The main obstacle to this proposal is not the cost but a location where people are willing to let a deliberate nuclear power plant accident occur.

Consistency with experimental observations is obviously the best way to check a model's validity, but there are many instances where direct observations are impossible. For example, the position of Neptune in 1989 cannot be observed for some time, the flight characteristics of a new jet liner cannot be measured before it is built, and the earthquake damage to a particular skyscraper cannot (one hopes) be measured directly. If a program is to model such things, one attempts to compare the program's predictions with the closest known experimental data (it is easy to see if a program can correctly predict the 1979 position of Neptune; it is not so easy to assess the correctness of earthquake damage for a new skyscraper design by comparing data from previous earthquakes). An alternative approach is to check the consistency of the program's results with other models. These models might be simpler ones that apply only to special situations, or they might be equally complex ones that are independently obtained.

For truly critical programs, it is reasonable to give the assignment to two or three different groups. These groups are kept separated to avoid the interchange of bad ideas, and then, when each group is finished, the models are compared. If they all agree, then one has much greater confidence that they are correct. If they disagree (which frequently happens in the first comparison), then the source of the difference is tracked down and a further analysis made of which program's model is correct at this point.

SENSITIVITY ANALYSIS AND ERROR ESTIMATION 14.2

Sensitivity analysis for matrix computations is introduced in Section 6.6.C, and its use is illustrated in Example 6.8. The principle behind sensitivity analysis is this: *Change the computation slightly and see how* much the solution changes. The changes might be made in the numerical data (this is the case for matrix computations), in the round-off made (e.g., change from single to double precision), in the methods used (e.g., use the IMSL differential equation solver DGEAR instead of DVERK), or in the model (e.g., add the terms for the gravitational attraction of the moon to see if they affect the satellite's orbit). The object is to find how changes in any part of the computation affect the solution; if these small problem changes produce acceptably small solution changes, then one's confidence in the correctness of the computation is increased.

The number of changes for use in sensitivity analysis is limited only by ingenuity. In most programs there are things to perturb that are appropriate only for this specific program. We give a list of types of changes or perturbations that are more generally applicable:

1. **Numerical Data:** The data can be perturbed at random by a certain percentage (say 1 percent or .01 percent) that approximates the likely uncertainty in the actual data. Sensitivity analysis shows that the computation in Example 5.1 is numerically unstable; the instability there is due to the nature of the physical problem and not to the numerical method. If there are only a few data items in the problem, one may decide to perturb each individually to access the importance of each source of uncertainty. A powerful tool for detecting numerical instability is ACM Algorithm 532, "Software for Round-off Analysis." This software takes a Fortran-like program and analyzes it to find input data which makes the computation as numerically unstable as it can. Algorithm 532 is primarily applicable to matrix computations.

2. **Round-Off:** If one changes from single to double precision, then the digits of the two solutions which agree are probably correct (as far as round-off is concerned). Changing from a short word length machine (such as IBM or DEC) to a long word length machine (such as CDC or CRAY) has a similar effect. See Table 3.1 for relevant information for common computers. A simple but effective technique is to change Fortran compilers; each compiler will translate the Fortran into machine language in a different way, thereby giving different round-off errors in the results. The differences observed can be attributed to round-off effects. ACM Algorithm 532 mentioned above may be viewed as a tool that attempts to maximize round-off error effects in matrix computations.

3. **Methods Used:** One can try very different methods (such as finite differences and finite elements for partial differential equations) or very similar methods (such as open and closed fourth-order Newton-Cotes integration formulas). Drastic changes in methods in a large program might be, of course, very expensive. If the program is well designed, then the various methods used are isolated into separate modules unless they are very simple. Modularity makes it much easier to assess the effect of changing methods. This is particularly easy when library software is being used; one can simply replace one library routine by another (perhaps even from a different library). Even if the same general method is used, one can change the method parameters (e.g., step size for a differential equation solver or the number of points for a least-squares fit or integration routine). See Example 7.2 for a study of the effects on accuracy resulting from changing method parameters.

4. **Model:** Modifications in the model are sometimes easy to make and sometimes very difficult. The interesting changes quite often make the whole solution process more difficult, thereby resulting in a lot of programming effort as well as computing costs. For example, if one adds the gravitational attraction of the moon to a model for a satellite orbit, one has to be able to compute the relative position of the moon at all times. It is "known" how to do this, but it is still a lot of work to actually obtain the formulas and data to determine the moon's position and to put them into the program correctly. Another, more realistic example occurs in fluid or gas dynamics with a model that assumes the fluid has no viscosity or is at constant temperature. Such simplifications in the model can produce very inaccurate results in various physical environments. But adding viscosity to the model may well change a linear partial differential equation to a nonlinear one. This change would then cause one to completely change the numerical methods used and could result in a major rewrite of the computer program. An advantage of higher-level languages like PROTRAN is that only a few lines have to be changed in order to change the method. Similarly, changing a model to allow temperature to vary results in adding another partial differential equation to be solved. The numerical methods will probably also change, and there will be the additional effort to obtain data for the boundary conditions and physical constants of the fluids and gases. Thus we see that sensitivity analysis for the model can be a major project; sometimes this analysis is necessary if one really wants a high level of confidence in the correctness of the result.

One approach to sensitivity analysis is to parameterize the model in some way. For example, one might model the temperature t(x, y) of a gas at the point x, y by

$$t(x, y) = a_0 + a_1 p(x, y) + a_2 p^2(x, y) \qquad \textbf{Equation 14.1.1}$$

where p(x, y) is the pressure. One can then vary a_1 and a_2 to get some idea of the effect of nonconstant temperature [we assume that p(x, y) is being computed somewhat independently of t(x, y)]. This is only partially satisfactory, because even though it uses a nonconstant temperature dependence, it does not use the complete mathematical model of temperature behavior which involves a separate partial differential equation.

It is particularly tempting to use parameterized models when one is unsure of the proper mathematical model. One can then try to adjust the parameters to fit some existing data. This is especially useful when there is no obvious or standard analytical or theoretical guidance for choosing some parts of the model. One may choose a simple relationship (such as 14.1.1, relating temperature to pressure) with a few parameters and then fit the model to actual data. This process is **calibration** of the model. It is often successful and, if it works, can substantially simplify the model. If good values for a_0, a_1, and a_2 in 14.1.1 can be found, then one can avoid introducing another partial differential equation into the model.

Callibration must be used with caution if a large number of parameters are introduced into the model. If one has enough parameters, one can probably choose values for them to make the model fit all the existing data fairly well. The agreement between the data and the model is then due to the large number of parameters and not to the correctness of the model. In other words, the model can fit the existing data and yet produce incorrect results for any new data.

A realistic example of this effect occurs in stock market speculations where people have developed elaborate computer programs which faithfully "predict" the stock over a period of, say, the last 15 years. These people then believe (or, at least, try to convince others) that they have a faithful model of the stock market for the future. What they have is a model with many, many parameters (perhaps hundreds) which can be adjusted to fit any 15 years of stock market behavior. Unfortunately, the correct parameters for the next year (or even the next month) will not be known until the year is past.

Sensitivity analysis is a very general and useful tool for validating numerical computations, but it has its limitations. The most serious one is that complex models (these are the most important ones, of course) may have dozens or even hundreds of data items and parameters. If there are just 20 independent items to change, then to examine the effect of changes of 0 and ± 5 percent in each item requires $3^{20} = 3.5$ billion additional computer runs of the model. One may assume (hope?) that there is no interaction between changes in the items and thereby reduce the number of computations to $2 \times 20 = 40$, but one is frequently unable to justify this assumption. A complete sensitivity analysis for 100 items requires $3^{100} = 10^{47}$ computations, which is clearly impossible to carry out.

An alternative to sensitivity is **error analysis**, where a mathematical analysis is made of the effect of changes (or uncertainties) throughout an entire computation. If the error analysis is successful, then one can say with certainty: *"If the changes in these data items are less than x percent, then the changes in the answers are less than y percent."* There can be several error analyses for the same computation as in the case of matrix computations (see Section 6.6 and especially Examples 6.5, 6.6, 6.7, and 6.9). The importance of the error analysis approach is seen from the fact that perhaps 20 percent of this text is devoted to the topic.

There are two principal weaknesses to the error analysis approach: (1) *one might be unable to do the required mathematical analysis,* and (2) *the errors might be so grossly overestimated that the estimates are useless.* It is a fact of life that error analysis is mathematically difficult; in some instances, it is essentially impossible. People are simply unable to carry through the mathematics for an error analysis of many complicated computations. The difficulty of the mathematical analysis leads one to make simplifying assumptions during the analysis. This makes the estimates less accurate even though they are still correct in the sense that the errors must be less than estimated. Just how bad these estimates can be is seen in Example 6.5, where the actual error of $2.77*10^{-4}$ in the solution of a linear system of equations is estimated by one analysis to be $1.82*10^5$, an overestimate by a factor of 650,000,000.

In conclusion, neither sensitivity analysis nor error analysis gives an automatic, reliable way to validate numerical computations. Each is a good tool for many problems to provide reasonable confidence in the correctness of the results. For a very high level of confidence or a very complex problem, one must be prepared to spend a great deal of effort in a special study to validate the computations.

SOFTWARE ERRORS 14.3

A software error occurs when the program does something other than the programmer intended. Examples of obvious software errors are the following:

1. A program to sort numbers returns 1, 2, 4, 3, 5 for the input 5, 1, 2, 4, 3.

2. A program contains the code segments:

```
C            PRINT THE COMPONENT XFORCE IN THE X-DIRECTION
      WRITE(6,10) YFORCE
   10 FORMAT(10X, 'XFORCE=', F15.6)
C            ......
C        PROCESS ALL BUT THE FIRST OF THE NITEMS
      DO 10 ITEM = 1, NITEMS
C            ......
C        PLOT THE DATA AND THE LEAST SQUARES FIT
      CALL USPLO(DATA,POINTS,101,51,3,2,34,
     +     31HPLOT DATA AND LEAST SQUARES FIT,
     +     4HDATA,4,17HLEAST SQUARES FIT, 17,
     +     WORKSP,XYRANG,51,ICHAR,IER
```

3. A statistical analysis program prints

```
THE SUM OF SQUARES OF THE ERRORS IS -.0000045
```

There are, in fact, four errors in the Fortran call to USPLO, not all of which are obvious.

While there are many errors which can be identified without question as software errors, there are frequent situations where it is debatable whether something is a software error or even whether an error exists at all. These situations arise when it is not clear what the programmer intended to do. At first thought, one would think this could happen only if the programmer has left and has not documented the program well. This situation does arise, but, more commonly, this uncertainty arises in programs that use heuristics. A **heuristic** is a piece of an algorithm which is not based on any exact mathematical or physical analysis but which is something the programmer's intuition says is the right (or, at least, a good) thing to do. The majority of numerical computations involve heuristics. For example, almost any test for convergence is a heuristic because we know that one cannot test convergence reliably except in very special situations. The convergence tests in numerical computations are thus almost always heuristics. For an example from another context, consider a program to play chess. The play strategy used in the program is all heuristics, and so it is difficult to say whether any of the choices are "errors." Indeed, one can believe that a programmer can make an error when one is faced with a choice of three moves and selects a move not intended by the programmer, yet obtains a program that plays a stronger game of chess than if the programmer had not made the "error."

We conclude that there is not a clear distinction between software errors and variations in the methods or models used in the program. In fact, many programmers have realized that they have made a poor choice of heuristic at a point in a program only after they have seen the program perform poorly in some situation.

It is not as important to detect *all* the software errors (or other errors) in programs as one might think. For example, the statistics program that sometimes produces a negative sum of squares of statistical errors when the true error is zero is not likely to mislead anyone. In fact, several widely used statistical programs in the 1960s and 1970s would do this, and this "error" was frequently the only clue that many naive users had that their underlying model was completely unsatisfactory. The current statistical programs are usually more careful in the short cuts they use to compute this sum of squares, and the result might be more, rather than less, incorrect conclusions being made by naive users. The really good statistical software detects that the computation is ill-conditioned and reports this to the user so that the user will not accept the results even if the sum of squares is computed correctly.

The fact is that the usefulness, reliability, or robustness of a program does not depend strongly on the number of errors in the program. These three measures of value are related to the frequency with which the program fails in actual use. Thus, errors in a part of a program that is rarely, if ever, used does not affect the quality of the program much or at all. Many robust numerical computation programs have sophisticated "error recovery" mechanisms. That is, when the computation does not seem to be going "right" (a heuristic test is applied), the current subcomputation is abandoned and another tact used. Thus, it may be that "incorrect" garbage rather than "correct" garbage is being computed, but it makes no difference if the error recovery mechanism is reliable. Further, many robust programs have "safety net" code which is prefaced by comments like:

```
C
C     I DO NOT BELIEVE IT IS POSSIBLE FOR THE PROGRAM
C     TO REACH THIS POINT, BUT IF IT DOES WE ISSUE A
C     WARNING, COMPUTE NEW INITIAL POINTS AT RANDOM AND
C     RESTART THE ITERATION
  999 CONTINUE
```

The code following these comments might, in fact, be impossible to reach, but since the programmer could not prove that, provisions are made for the unlikely eventuality. For further discussion of this topic, see Section 13.2

We summarize the preceding discussion by saying that **software performance is much more important than software correctness.** Even so, no one wants to have software errors, especially since it is hard to predict in advance what effect an error might have on performance.

There are two principal approaches to the detection of software errors: **testing** and **analysis.** Software testing is a kind of performance evaluation where the only quality being tested is correctness (or accuracy). Software analysis (more commonly called **software verification** or **program proving**) is analysis aimed at establishing the correctness of a program.

Chapter 13 is devoted to software performance evaluation, and many of the techniques presented there are directly applicable to testing for correctness. The principal one is to have a set of problems (input data) with known solutions that covers the problem domain of the software. One then runs the program on all these problems to see if correct results are obtained. Some tools are mentioned in Section 12.2.B to aid software correctness testing. They are oriented toward generating input that thoroughly exercises the program. The difficulties such tools face are seen by considering the situation mentioned above where the programmer cannot see how to execute a part of the program. If the programmer cannot imagine input to exercise this code segment, then it is unlikely that test data generater will find such input.

Program proving is based on the following assumptions:

1. There is a formal (mathematical) statement of what the program is to do. This means that there are complete formulas or mathematical specifications of the output to be produced as a function of the input.

2. There are mechanisms to verify analytically the correctness of statements as the formal input assumptions are "processed" or "transformed" by the program. The end result is that the input assumptions are transformed (analytically and exactly) to properties of the output which include the requirements on the program.

An example of formal specifications for a program to sort positive integers is:

Input: NITEMS *with* $1 \le \text{NITEMS} \le 1000$
N_i *with* $1 \le i \le \text{NITEMS}$
$0 \le N_i \le 10^{10}$

Output: M_j *with* $1 \le j \le \text{NITEMS}$
We have
(a) $M_j \le M_{j+1}$ *for all* $j \le \text{NITEMS} - 1$
(b) *The set M_j is a rearrangement of the set N_i*

There are two reasons that program proving might not be applicable: (1) Assumption 1 does not hold for the program; (2) Assumption 2 does not hold. Assumption 1 fails whenever the program contains heuristic segments. One can, in fact, mathematically define most heuristic code segments in such a way that the code itself is the formal mathematical specification of what the code is to do. This automatically makes such code segments correct, but that is not very useful information. Assumption 1 also usually fails whenever one is unable to give a precise, concise, and realistic mathematical description of the problem domain intended for a program. There is, for example, no way to formally specify the set of differential equations which the IMSL subroutine DVERK is supposed to solve.

Assumption 2 usually fails because the processing and transformations required are too complex and/or are too much work. There are elaborate analytical programs to do this processing automatically for some classes of programs, but they may require years (if not centuries) of computer time when applied to typical applications programs. There is further difficulty in that some of the processes and effects presented in numerical computation cannot be handled by these programs (e.g., round-off uncertainty or mathematical function properties).

Thus we conclude that it is not likely that much numerical software will be proved correct for some years. However, this technique can still be very useful in that one can reasonably hope to automatically prove various **partial correctness** results about numerical software. That is, one proves that certain facts are true about a program's behavior or output even if these do not imply that the program is completely correct. A simple, but very important, example of this is the possibility of proving this: *All the array indices in this program are within the declared ranges.* If this can be done reliably and automatically, it would add considerably to the reliability of the software while relieving the programmer of spending time, effort, and lines of code in checking array indices. Such a tool would be valuable even if it did not always succeed; a statement that all indices proved to be in range except in subroutine MIXUP would be very useful.

REFERENCES

William C. Hetzel (ed.), *Program Test Methods,* Prentice-Hall, Inc.., Englewood Cliffs, N.J. (1973).

Edward Miller and William E. Howden (eds.), *Software Testing and Validation Techniques,* IEEE Catalog No. EHO 138-8. (1978).

**15 PROTRAN

HOW PROTRAN WORKS 15.1

PROTRAN is an extension of Fortran which provides easy access to the problem-solving abilities of the IMSL library plus a number of other conveniences. It works using two passes or phases in processing a program. The first pass reads the PROTRAN statements and replaces them by appropriate Fortran statements; one PROTRAN statement might become a hundred Fortran statements. The second pass compiles this Fortran program in the usual way; the result is then executed to do the computations. This approach to language translation uses a **Fortran preprocessor.** See Example 12.3 for further discussion of Fortran preprocessors.

Figure 15.1 shows the general organization of the translation and execution of a PROTRAN program. Normally the programmer does not look at the Fortran program generated. If there are Fortran errors, the offending lines and error messages are printed, which is usually sufficient for correcting the errors. Note that PROTRAN might issue diagnostic messages at execution or run time; these diagnostics are extensions of the simple Fortran run time diagnostics such as for square roots of negative numbers.

Two of the important services provided by PROTRAN are problem setup checking and workspace allocation. By **problem setup checking** we mean that the input to every IMSL library routine is exhaustively checked to see if the problem setup is, at least, legal. For example, in solving AX = B, the current size (row range and column range) of B determines the size of the linear system solved. So X must have as many rows and columns as B, and A must have as many rows as B and as many columns as B has rows. All these numbers are also checked to be positive. If these checks are satisfied, then the linear system is, as least, set up correctly. Experience has shown that problem setup is a significant source of errors in numerical computation which are often difficult to locate. This checking feature of PROTRAN greatly increases the reliability of numerical computations.

Workspace allocation refers to providing the temporary storage locations that numerical methods need. Fortran requires that this storage be created by a programmer and passed down to any library routine used. This process is tedious (mysterious to many users of library routines) and error prone. PROTRAN automatically takes care of providing this storage for its problem-solving statements. If the PROTRAN system does not have enough storage available for temporary workspace use, it issues a diagnostic at run time and states how much is needed. This can then be supplied using the OPTION statement. It is not practical for the preprocessor to compute the maximum amount of workspace that will be needed.

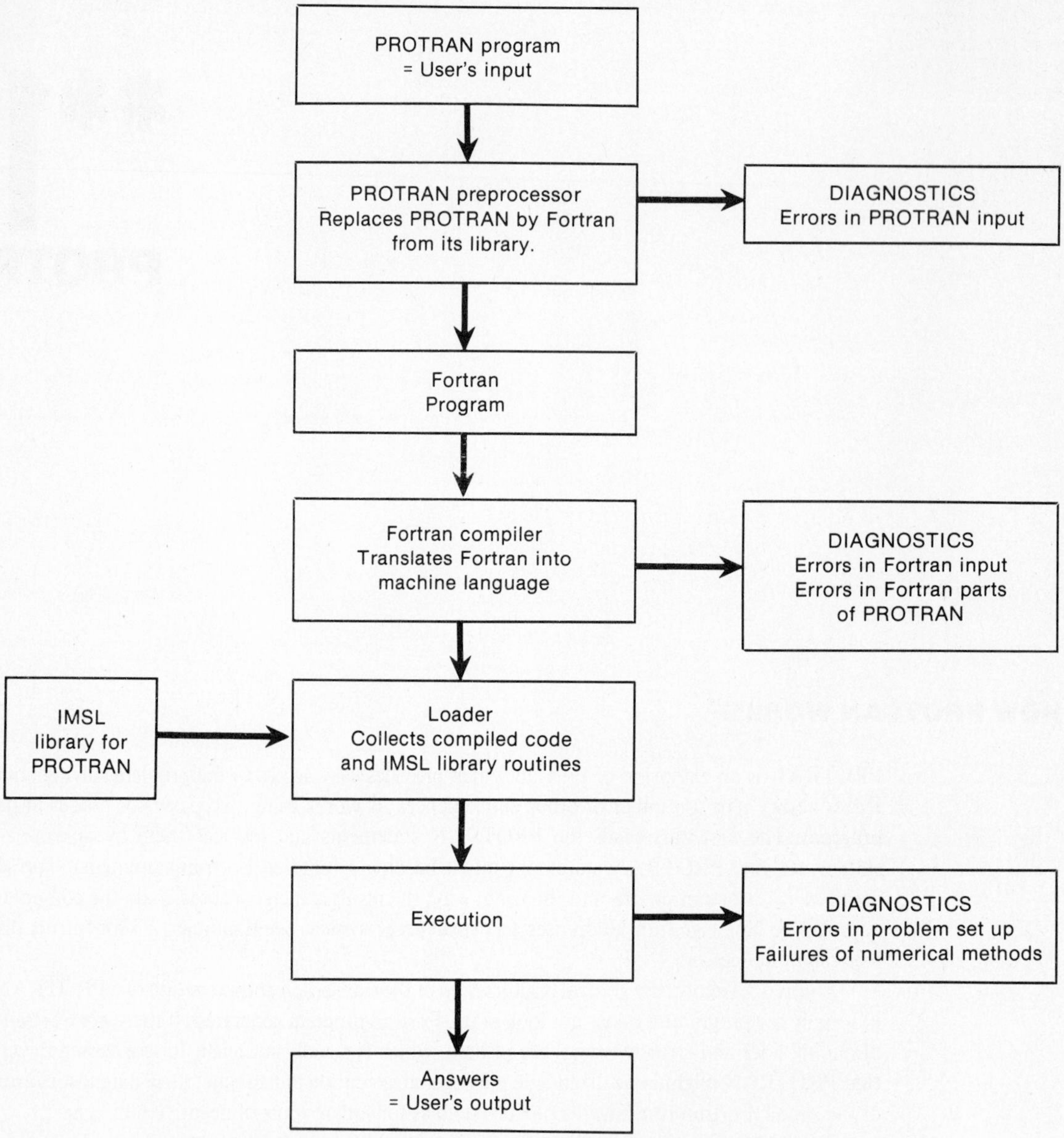

Figure 15.1 **Organization for running a PROTRAN program.** The PROTRAN preprocessor creates a Fortran program to do the computations. The PROTRAN library provides pieces of Fortran code, and the IMSL library provides software for solving numerical problems. The loader might also get compiled code from other libraries in the system.

A PROTRAN program can have PROTRAN and Fortran statements intermixed; the preprocessor translates the PROTRAN into Fortran to create a complete Fortran program. There are three simple rules which must be followed in order to avoid conflicts between names in the user's Fortran variables and the Fortran that PROTRAN generates during the translation.

Rule 1: **Do not use a Fortran name of 6 characters ending with V7.** The default characters V and 7 can be changed in an OPTION statement.

Rule 2: **Do not use a label between 30000 and 31000.** The default initial label 30000 can be changed in an OPTION statement.

Rule 3: **Do not use the name of any PROTRAN library program.** These are 6-character names beginning with IMSL. The regular IMSL library routines have been renamed and modified for use in the PROTRAN system.

The PROTRAN statements start with a $ followed by a keyword which identifies the statement. The keyword is followed by some problem information which varies from statement to statement, for example,

```
$LINSYS A*X=B
$SUM X(I)**2+SQRT(Y(I))
$PRINT A,X
```

The form of the problem information is tailored to the particular problem or task, but all additional information is given in a uniform manner using keyword phrases. Sometimes certain of these phrases are required, as in the case of $SUM where one must specify the variable of summation and its range. The **keyword phrases** consist of a keyword followed by a list of 0, 1, 2, etc., arguments. The punctuation of the list (that is, choice of special characters used) varies from phrase to phrase to make it most natural. The phrases are separated by a semicolon or end-of-line. The above sample statements are given with keyword phrases in the following table with the special characters used for punctuation indicated.

	Number of Arguments	Punctuation Used
`$LINSYS A*X=B; NOSAVE`	0	none
`EQUATIONS=6`	1	=
`$SUM X(I)**2+SQRT(Y(I)); IS SUMXY`	1	blank
`FOR(I = 1,101,2)`	4	( ) = ,
`$PRINT A,X; PAGEWD=129`	1	=

The PROTRAN statements are terminated by (1) start of another PROTRAN statement, (2) a $ as last character, or (3) $FORTRAN.

PROTRAN VARIABLES: SCALARS, VECTORS, AND MATRICES 15.2

PROTRAN introduces three new variable types: *scalars, vectors,* and *matrices.* **Scalars** are like simple Fortran variables; **vectors** and **matrices** are like one- and two-dimensional Fortran arrays. Consider the following simple PROTRAN program:

```
COLUMN789
      $DECLARATIONS
       REAL MATRIX A(5,5)
       REAL VECTOR R(N=5), X(N=5), RESID(N=5)
       REAL SCALAR MAXERR
      $ASSIGN A = ( 3.1, 4.2, 5.3)
     +            (-1.0, 0.0, 5.3)
     +            (-5.3, 1.0, 3.5)
           R(I) = 1./(1.+I)
              N = 3
      $LINSYS A*X = R
      $PRINT A, X, R, N
      $ASSIGN RESID = A*X
              RESID = RESID-R
      $NORM RESID; IS MAXERR
      $PRINT MAXERR ; FORMAT = EMAXP
      $END
```

It uses one matrix, three vectors, and one scalar. One can also use these variables as ordinary Fortran arrays in Fortran statements. The variable N is not declared to be a scalar, but could be declared INTEGER SCALAR N. The important fact is that PROTRAN includes the arithmetic of matrices, vectors, scalars, and other vector-matrix statements (such as $NORM). Thus R is set in the first ASSIGN statement by the PROTRAN equivalent of the mathematical definition

$$r_i = \frac{1}{1+i}$$